# JOEL WHITBURN'S
# TOP
# R&B
## Singles 1942-1988

Compiled from **Billboard's** *Rhythm & Blues* charts, 1942-1988

Record Research Inc.
P.O. Box 200
Menomonee Falls, Wisconsin 53051

ISBN 0-89820-068-7

Published independently by Record Research Inc.
P.O. Box 200, Menomonee Falls, Wisconsin  53051

The author wishes to extend a special note of thanks to:

Betty Grendysa for her enthusiastic tabulation and affirmation of the chart data;

Peter Grendysa for his dedication and energy in gathering and confirming the biographical information;

Robert Pruter for his assistance in contributing to the biographical notes;

Kim Whitburn for coordinating and editing this expansive revision;

And, to Bill Hathaway, Kim Gaarder, Brent Olynick and Joanne Wagner for their help in seeing this work to its fruition.

# CONTENTS

# AUTHOR'S NOTE

New Orleans jazz, Chicago blues, Memphis gospel, Southwestern boogie, the Philly sound, Detroit soul, West Coast funk and New York City street-corner harmonies. That musical locomotive known as Rhythm & Blues steams across America, planting its seeds of soul.

The odyssey of this book begins with *Billboard's* first Rhythm & Blues chart, the *Harlem Hit Parade* of October 24, 1942. It ends, more than 13,000 titles later, with the *Hot Black Singles* chart of July 2, 1988. Along the way, the music has engulfed the nation and spawned a legacy.

The hits between these covers spell out the rich heritage of R&B. From the rural blues to the urban rhythms, there flows an interracial appeal as the genre pulsates through the American popular culture. With the many hues of its broad spectrum, Rhythm & Blues continues to be a vibrant and thriving sector of the music industry. A study of this research will reveal the extent to which R&B has indelibly influenced Western popular tradition. And, perhaps manifest an even deeper appreciation for this art form.

In the following introductory pages, musicologist Pete Grendysa traces the history of R&B from the turn of the century to the early days of rock 'n' roll. The five decades of hits, researched within this book, will take you on the rest of the Rhythm & Blues journey.

JOEL WHITBURN

# BLACK MUSIC — *An Introduction*

The history of black music on records in America is as long as that of recorded sound. On October 29, 1902, a quartet of black singers from Dinwiddie County, Virginia traveled north to record at the Camden, New Jersey studios of the Victor Talking Machine Company. The six tracks they laid down on the 29th and 31st of October were released as six single-sided discs in December, on Victor's Monarch label. The songs included five spirituals and one secular number, "Down At The Old Camp Ground". With these recordings, the Dinwiddie Quartet earned the distinction of being the first black singers on record.

Then, as now, the white public bought the vast majority of phonograph records, and in the first two decades of the 20th Century, the public fancy was much taken by white performers in blackface, with such stellar show business names as Sophie Tucker and Al Jolson adding black songs to their repertoire. During this period, recordings by black artists were confined to traditional and religious songs, usually done by quartets and larger groups from the great black schools — Tuskegee, Fisk, Utica Institute, and Hampton Institute. More important to popular music, some blacks were finding their way into vaudeville troupes, touring the world and singing secular songs.

By the time of the First World War, blacks in America had achieved the modest level of affluence that permitted them to buy phonographs and records in large numbers. The recording industry was largely indifferent to this growing market, and continued to produce records for the white market. If black bought them, too, then so much the better. The lively black press decried this attitude and began demanding black music by black artists.

The first black singer to bring this message home in a way that could not be ignored was Mamie Smith. In 1920, a black composer, Perry Bradford, convinced Okeh to let Mamie Smith record one of his songs, rather than Sophie Tucker as had been planned. Smith had already been turned away by Victor earlier that year. Thus, "You Can't Keep A Good Man Down", released in July, 1920, was more than just another blackface rendition.

Sales of that record were much higher than expected, due in part to vigorous publicity in the black newspapers, urging the community to support one of their own. In August, Okeh brought Smith back into the studio, and her next release, "Crazy Blues", was heavily promoted by the label in black markets. It sold well enough to be called a hit, and the doors were finally opened to black popular music.

The sudden emergence of the black artist on record would be considered a revolution even by today's standards. Virtually every record company had at least one black artist on their roster. Most labels, however, carefully reflected the segregation of the time by issuing special "Race" series, and the embryonic hot jazz bands and swing combos that arose during this period were likewise kept apart from the mainstream of popular music. In 1921, the year total record sales in America first reached one hundred million, the first black-owned and black-operated record company was started with the intention of recording the broad spectrum of black music, rather than just "the blues". Black Swan survived only until March, 1924, when it was absorbed by Paramount, a much larger company with a successful "Race" series of its own.

Some of the most popular black artists of the early days are today remembered only by scholars and collectors: Lucille Hegamin, Esther Bigeou, the Norfolk Jazz Quartet, Daisy Martin. Others attained lasting fame: Alberta Hunter, Kid Ory, Bessie Smith, Ethel Waters, Louis Armstrong, Tampa Red. A rich variety of musical styles were represented, from hot jazz, blues, quartets, choral groups, and vaudeville troupers, to concert singers, preachers, and big bands. Record companies scoured the backwoods and regional music centers such as New Orleans, Chicago, and Kansas City to find black musical talent.

The cold hand of the Depression took hold on the recording industry almost immediately. Records became a luxury item, and disposable income had vanished. From one hundred million sales in 1927, the annual total dropped to a previously unthinkable six million in 1932. All recording artists suffered, but the black suffered most of all. Despite a black population of over fourteen million, pressings of some "race" records were reduced to mere hundreds of copies.

A very few fortunate black artists made their way into the new "free" medium of radio, among them the Mills Brothers, Three Keys, Southernaires, and Golden Gate Quartet. Radio exposure helped spur record sales, as did the emergence of new and cheaper labels such as Decca, Bluebird, and the American Record Company's remarkable stable of labels: Romeo, Challenger, Banner, Melotone, and Perfect, sold through various department stores and dime store chains. It was through releases on these labels that black artists were able to survive the Depression.

The 1940's and the Second World War brought a return of prosperity for the economy in general and black artists in particular. The Swing Era brought Duke Ellington, Count Basie, Fletcher Henderson, Jimmie Lunceford, and many other excellent black bands to prominence. Just as the industry was enjoying its first one hundred million sales year since the 1920's, wartime conditions dealt several blows. First was the rationing of shellac, an essential ingredient in the compounding of 78rpm platters and available only from the Far East. The number of new releases had to be cut, and purchasers of the new records were asked to trade in an old one in exchange — to be ground up and recycled.

Then, in July, 1942, the American Federation of Musicians declared a ban on all recording for its members, and nearly all musicians and some vocalists belonged to the union. In response, the record companies shut down their operations for nearly two years, until the strike was settled. Finally, the ever-widening net of Selective Service, the dreaded Draft, was decimating the rosters of the big bands.

Both the musician's recording ban and the Draft played important roles in the development of modern rhythm and blues. The strike encouraged the formation of new independent record companies, who quickly made their peace with the union and were able to record new songs with new artists, while the major labels could only stand idle. The center of activity for independent labels was Los Angeles, but new companies began appearing in Chicago and New York.

The death of the big bands, caused in part by the Draft and also by wartime fuel rationing and travel restrictions, brought about the popularity of smaller units. The music made by self-contained vocal/instrumental combos such as the King Cole Trio and Louis Jordan's Tympany Five was truly black, but had great appeal to white audiences, too, and both Cole and Jordan were closely copied by many other black acts in the 1940's.

It was in this atmosphere of turmoil and rapid change that *Billboard* began chronicling the sales of black records with *Harlem Hit Parade*. The *Harlem Hit Parade* based its rankings on sales reported by a few major record stores in large Eastern cities. As its scope was widened to cover other areas of the country, the chart was retitled "Race Records" (A bit after the fact, as most record companies had quietly discontinued using that term after the war.)

Finally, on June 25, 1949, the chart was renamed "Rhythm & Blues", reflecting a term that had come into general use about four years before. "Rhythm & Blues" became an all-encompassing generic term covering all forms of black popular music, and it was used by *Billboard* for twenty years, until it was succeeded by "Soul". R&B included down home blues, big city jump bands, vocal groups, jazz, urban shouters, and torchy night club singers. Into this stew was thrown everything that appealed to black record buyers — witness the early rock 'n' roll records by Elvis Presley, Carl Perkins, and Jimmy Clanton.

And it was rhythm and blues that provided the foundation for rock 'n' roll in the early 1950's. Beginning in 1950, large numbers of mostly-teenaged white buyers began seeking out R&B records. The vibrant earthy appeal of the music, singers, and lyrics was in stark contrast to the pop music of the time, still firmly rooted in Tin Pan Alley traditions. Swing music was only a shadow of its former glory, and the steady diet of crooners and slick bands was seen as something belonging to an older generation. The omnipresent generation gap has always been manifested primarily in music and dress, and the times were ripe for a change in both.

The excitement of the first years of rock 'n' roll are fondly recalled by many and the subject of scholarly research by others. Suffice to say that the birth of rock music, based on R&B and country, was not an easy one. The first rock 'n' roll records were little more than uptempo rhythm and blues, but as the popularity of this music spread and more white artists starting making the music, a new name was needed.

The *Billboard* R&B charts of the late 1950's and early 1960's reflect this change, and include a large number of artists who, in retrospect, would not be included in any list of pure R&B artists today. Eventually, rock 'n' roll became the mainstream of popular music and rhythm and blues continued its evolution as an easily recognizable genre. Just as public pressure had brought about the change from "race" to "rhythm & blues", the latter term gave way to "Soul" in 1969. The soul "style" had appeared in the late 1950's with the infusion of large doses of gospel fervor into the R&B mixture. In 1982, "Soul" was changed to, simply, "Black".

The music and artists represented between these covers encompass such a wide range of styles and sounds that perhaps no single term or simple definition is possible. In total, however, they represent the greatest single contribution of America to the popular culture of the world. The influence of rhythm and blues on all other forms of popular music cannot be overstated, and it continues today in the same capacity of leadership and innovation in music.

Peter Grendysa

## HARLEM HIT PARADE

| DATE | POSITIONS | CHART TITLE |
|------|-----------|-------------|
| 10/24/42 | 10 | Harlem Hit Parade |
| 2/1/45 final chart | | |

## JUKE BOX — Race / R&B

| | | |
|------|------|------|
| 2/8/45 | 2-15 | Most-Played Juke Box Race Records |
| 6/25/49 | 5-15 | Most-Played Juke Box Rhythm & Blues Records |
| 11/15/52 | 8-10 | Most Played in Juke Boxes |
| 6/30/56 | 9-10 | Most Played R&B in Juke Boxes |
| 6/17/57 final chart | | |

## BEST SELLERS — Race / R&B

| | | |
|------|------|------|
| 5/22/48 | 10-15 | Best Selling Retail Race Records |
| 6/25/49 | 5-15 | Best Selling Retail Rhythm & Blues Records |
| 11/15/52 | 9-10 | National Best Sellers |
| 2/20/54 | 9-15 | Best Sellers in Stores |
| 6/30/56 | 14-15 | R&B Best Sellers in Stores |
| 2/3/58 | 20 | R&B Best Sellers in Stores |
| 10/13/58 final chart | | |

## JOCKEYS — R&B

| | | |
|------|------|------|
| 1/22/55 | 14-15 | Most Played by Jockeys |
| 6/30/56 | 13-15 | Most Played R&B by Jockeys |
| 10/13/58 final chart | | |

## HOT R&B / SOUL / BLACK

| | | |
|------|------|------|
| 10/20/58 | 30 | Hot R&B Sides |
| 11/3/62 | 30 | Hot R&B Singles |
| **NO R&B CHART 11/30/63 until 1/23/65** | | |
| 1/30/65 | 40 | Hot Rhythm & Blues Singles |
| 6/5/65 | 40 | Top Selling Rhythm & Blues Singles |
| 4/9/66 | 40 | Top Selling R&B Singles |
| 8/6/66 | 50 | Top Selling R&B Singles |
| 1/13/68 | 50 | Best Selling R&B Singles |
| 4/6/68 | 50 | Best Selling Rhythm & Blues Singles |
| 8/23/69 | 50 | Best Selling Soul Singles |
| 6/30/73 | 60 | Best Selling Soul Singles |
| 7/14/73 | 100 | Hot Soul Singles |
| 6/26/82 | 100 | Black Singles |
| 10/20/84 | 100 | Hot Black Singles |

## OCTOBER 24, 1942 — JULY 2, 1988

The research for this book begins with *Billboard Magazine's* first Rhythm & Blues chart, the *Harlem Hit Parade*, published on October 24, 1942. It ends, 46 years later, with the July 2, 1988 *Hot Black Singles* chart. See the *Billboard Rhythm & Blues Chart History* on the preceding page for a synopsis of the chart changes.

## JUKE BOX / BEST SELLERS / JOCKEYS CHARTS

In early 1945, the *Harlem Hit Parade* evolved into the R&B *Juke Box* chart. In 1948, a second R&B chart was introduced, the *Best Sellers*. The third R&B category, the *Jockeys* chart, began its run in 1955. During these years in which *Billboard* published multiple R&B charts, 1948 to 1958, many records hit on more than one of these charts. The chart data shown for the records that made multiple charts is as follows:

> Date Charted = the earliest of the dates charted
> Peak Position = the highest ranking achieved on any of
> the charts
> Weeks at #1 or #2
> and Weeks Charted = the chart on which it achieved its
> highest totals

A chart-by-chart breakdown of the highest position a record attained on any of the multiple charts is listed below the title. Remember that prior to 1948, there was only one chart on which R&B records could have charted, the *Harlem Hit Parade*, later known as the *Juke Box* chart.

## ALL-ENCOMPASSING CHART

With the end of the multiple charts, *Billboard* introduced an all-encompassing *Hot R&B* chart on October 20, 1958. After several years, the content of this Top 30 Rhythm & Blues chart was top-heavy with pop artists and pop titles, so it was discontinued on November 30, 1963. Please note that some records debuted or were still climbing the November 23, 1963 chart, the last chart before the recess.

## UNPUBLISHED CHARTS 1963 — 1965

*Billboard* did not publish a Rhythm & Blues chart from November 30, 1963 to January 23, 1965. During this 14-month period, many R&B artists continued to turn out hits. By cross-checking other Rhythm & Blues rankings of that time, we determined which R&B titles that charted on *Billboard's Hot 100* pop chart would have also appeared on a *Billboard* R&B chart. These titles are included in this book and designated with the word **HOT** in the pop position column. All of their data listed is taken directly from *Billboard's Hot 100* pop chart.

R&B records that hit the *Billboard* pop chart from September to November of 1963 and, in all likelihood, would have made *Billboard's* R&B chart, after 11/23/63, are also included with their pop chart data.

## HOT RHYTHM & BLUES/SOUL/BLACK CHARTS, 1965 — PRESENT

On January 30, 1965, *Billboard* resumed their R&B chart, with the Top 40 *Hot Rhythm & Blues Singles* chart. Keep in mind that the popularity of some titles was waning by this time. Therefore, they were dropping in position with their first appearance on the January 30, 1965 R&B chart. Their peak positions and total weeks charted may be less than what they could have achieved had there been a *Billboard* chart when these records were first released.

Other than changes in name (Soul/Black) or expansion in size (40 to 100), there have been no other major revisions in the *Hot R&B* chart since then.

## DUETS

Songs by duos are listed under both artists. For example, a song by Brian Holland and Lamont Dozier is listed under both Holland and Dozier. The precise duo name is shown in bold type below the song title.

Noted recording duos (with seven or more duets) are listed alone, appearing below the first artist shown. For example, all of the Marvin Gaye and Tammi Terrell duets appear below Marvin Gaye's solo listing. None of their duets are listed with Marvin Gaye's or Tammi Terrell's solo hits.

## CHART DATES

A record's Debut Date is *Billboard's* actual issue date from the chart it first appeared on. It is not taken from the "week ending" dates as shown on the various charts when they were originally published. The issue and week ending dates were different until January 13, 1962, when *Billboard* began using one date system for both the issue and the charts inside.

## ACCURACY FACTOR

Approximately 85% of the titles within this book were checked for accuracy of title, artist name, and label and number against the records within our library. Discrepancies between the published *Billboard* title, artist name, record label and number, and the actual records were corrected when possible. Please let us know of any corrections to title, artist, or label listing of the remaining 15% of the records. Suggestions for improvement are always welcome.

## BIOGRAPHICAL NOTES

Biographical information was gathered from a wide variety of published materials, private correspondence, and personal interviews, with factual conflicts resolved by all available means.

The artist section lists each artist's charted hits in chronological order. A sequential number is shown in front of each song title to indicate that artist's number of charted hits. All Top 10 hits are highlighted in dark type.

## EXPLANATION OF COLUMNAR HEADINGS:

**DEBUT DATE:** Date record first charted

**PEAK POS:** Record's highest charted position (highlighted in bold type)

**WKS CHR:** Total weeks charted

**POP POS:** Peak position achieved on *Billboard*'s early pop charts, *Hot 100* chart or *Bubbling Under the Hot 100* chart.

**LABEL & NUMBER:** Original record label and number

## OTHER DATA AND SYMBOLS

(★★**49**★★)   Number indicates the artist's ranking among the All-Time Top 200 R&B artists

( ¹ )   A superior number next to a record that peaked at No.1 or No.2 indicates the total weeks the record held that position

( + )   Indicates record peaked in the year after it first charted

( ● )   RIAA certified gold record (million seller)

( ▲ )   RIAA certified platinum record (two million seller)

The Record Industry Association of America began certifying gold records in 1958 and platinum records in 1976. Prior to these dates, there are most certainly some hits that would have qualified for these certifications. Also, some record labels have never requested RIAA certification for their hits.

( *HOT* )   The word *HOT* in the pop position column indicates an R&B hit during *Billboard*'s R&B chart recess, 11/30/63 through 1/23/65. All chart data was taken directly from *Billboard's Hot 100* chart. (See *Researching The Charts* for further explanation.)

Letter(s) in brackets after titles indicate:

[ I ]   Instrumental recording
[ N ]   Novelty recording
[ C ]   Comedy recording
[ S ]   Spoken word recording
[ F ]   Foreign language recording
[ X ]   Christmas recording
[ R ]   Reissue of a previously charted single

( / )   This symbol is shown when dividing a two-sided hit. Complete chart data is shown for each side except in cases where both sides of a record were shown as a single listing on the charts. For the "B" side of these records, only the weeks it charted as a "tag along" are listed.

See *Billboard Rhythm & Blues Chart History* for an explanation of chart names listed under records from 1948-1958.

# THE ARTIST SECTION

Lists, alphabetically by artist name, every record that made **Billboard's** R&B charts from 10/24/42 through 7/2/88.

| DEBUT DATE | PEAK POS | WKS CHR | ARTIST — Record Title | POP POS | Label & Number |
|---|---|---|---|---|---|

# A

### AALON
Guitarist/vocalist/songwriter Aalon Butler. Formed own band in 1975. Discovered by Eric Burdon. Band's drummer, Ronnie Hammond, joined War in 1979.

| DEBUT DATE | PEAK POS | WKS CHR | ARTIST — Record Title | POP POS | Label & Number |
|---|---|---|---|---|---|
| 8/20/77 | **44** | 14 | 1  Cream City ................................................. | | Arista 0249 |

### ABACO DREAM
New York City R&B/rock group: leader Paul Douglas, Dennis Williams, David Williams, Frank Maio and Mike Sassano.

| 9/13/69 | **25** | 8 | 1  Life And Death In G & A.............................. *written by Sylvester "Sly Stone" Stewart* | *74* | A&M 1081 |
|---|---|---|---|---|---|

### GREGORY ABBOTT
New York City singer/songwriter. At age 8, member of St. Patrick's Cathedral Choir. Majored in Psychology at Boston University and Stanford; taught English at Berkeley.

| 8/16/86 | **1** [2] | 27 | 1  **Shake You Down**........................................... | *1* | Columbia 06191 |
|---|---|---|---|---|---|
| 2/21/87 | **5** | 15 | 2  **I Got The Feelin' (It's Over)** ........................ | *56* | Columbia 06632 |
| 5/07/88 | **5** | 16 | 3  **I'll Prove It To You** .................................... | | Columbia 07774 |

### PAULA ABDUL
Los Angeles singer/choreographer. In 1987, named "Choreographer of the Year" by MTV. Choreographed Janet Jackson videos and "The Tracy Ullman Show".

| 5/21/88 | **8** | 16 | 1  **Knocked Out** .............................................. | *41* | Virgin 99329 |
|---|---|---|---|---|---|

### COLONEL ABRAMS
Born in Detroit, raised in New York City. Singer/songwriter. Worked with the band 94 East, when Prince was their guitarist. Colonel Abrams is his real name.

| 4/28/84 | **73** | 5 | 1  Leave The Message Behind The Door ............... | | Streetwise 1123 |
|---|---|---|---|---|---|
| 8/17/85 | **20** | 14 | 2  Trapped..................................................... | | MCA 52638 |
| 1/18/86 | **78** | 5 | 3  The Truth .................................................. | | MCA 52728 |
| 3/01/86 | **7** | 15 | 4  **I'm Not Gonna Let** ..................................... | | MCA 52773 |
| 6/28/86 | **68** | 8 | 5  Over And Over............................................ | | MCA 52847 |
| 7/18/87 | **6** | 16 | 6  **How Soon We Forget** ................................. | | MCA 53121 |
| 11/28/87+ | **54** | 12 | 7  Nameless.................................................. | | MCA 53208 |

### THE ACCENTS
Vocal group consisting of lead Robert Draper, Jr., with Robert Armstrong, Billy R. Hood, James L. Jackson, Arvid Garrett, and Israel L. Goudeau, Jr. Garrett had been in the Three Sharps & A Flat.

| 1/26/59 | **16** | 6 | 1  Wiggle, Wiggle .......................................... | *51* | Brunswick 55100 |
|---|---|---|---|---|---|

### ACE SPECTRUM
New York City group consisting of Henry "Red" Zant, Aubrey "Troy" Johnson, Elliot Isaac and Rudy Gay.

| 8/17/74 | **20** | 14 | 1  Don't Send Nobody Else ................................ | *57* | Atlantic 3012 |
|---|---|---|---|---|---|

### BUDDY ACE
Singer from Jasper, Texas. First recorded for Peacock in 1955.

| 8/20/66 | **25** | 7 | 1  Nothing In The World Can Hurt Me (Except You) . | | Duke 397 |
|---|---|---|---|---|---|
| 2/11/67 | **33** | 6 | 2  Hold On (To This Old Fool) ............................. | | Duke 414 |

### JOHNNY ACE
Vocalist/pianist/organist/composer, born John Marshall Alexander, Jr. on 6/9/29 in Memphis. Worked with B.B. King band, then formed The Beale Streeters with Bobby Bland and Earl Forrest before going solo. Shot and killed himself backstage at the City Auditorium in Houston on 12/24/54.

**JOHNNY ACE with THE BEALE STREETERS:**

| 8/09/52 | **1** [9] | 20 | 1  **My Song** ................................................... *Best Seller #1 / Juke Box #2* | | Duke 102 |
|---|---|---|---|---|---|
| 1/31/53 | **3** | 10 | 2  **Cross My Heart** ......................................... *Juke Box #3 / Best Seller #4* | | Duke 107 |
| 7/04/53 | **1** [5] | 14 | 3  **The Clock** ............................................... *Best Seller #1(5) / Juke Box #1(4)* | | Duke 112 |

**JOHNNY ACE:**

| 12/26/53+ | **2** [1] | 19 | 4  **Saving My Love For You** ............................. *Juke Box #2 / Best Seller #3* | | Duke 118 |
|---|---|---|---|---|---|
| 6/19/54 | **6** | 2 | 5  **Please Forgive Me** ...................................... *Juke Box #6 / Best Seller #10* | | Duke 128 |
| 10/23/54 | **9** | 3 | 6  **Never Let Me Go** ....................................... *Juke Box #9* | | Duke 132 |

| DEBUT DATE | PEAK POS | WKS CHR | ARTIST — Record Title | POP POS | Label & Number |
|---|---|---|---|---|---|
| | | | **JOHNNY ACE — Continued** | | |
| 1/22/55 | **1** 10 | 19 | 7 Pledging My Love ........................................ | *17* | Duke 136 |
| | | | Jockey #1(10) / Best Seller #1(9) / Juke Box #1(9) 5 & 7: with the Johnny Otis Orchestra | | |
| 8/06/55 | **7** | 5 | 8 **Anymore** ................................................ | | Duke 144 |
| | | | Jockey #7 / Juke Box #8 / Best Seller #9 6 & 8: with the Johnny Board Orchestra | | |
| | | | **BARBARA ACKLIN** | | |
| | | | Singer/songwriter, born on 2/28/44 in Chicago. Cousin to Monk Higgins, who produced her first sessions for Special Agent in 1966 (as Barbara Allen). Back-up vocalist at Chess Records in the mid-60s. | | |
| 3/23/68 | **30** | 7 | 1 Show Me The Way To Go ............................ | | Brunswick 55366 |
| | | | GENE CHANDLER & BARBARA ACKLIN | | |
| 7/06/68 | **3** | 15 | 2 **Love Makes A Woman** .............................. | *15* | Brunswick 55379 |
| 10/26/68 | **16** | 11 | 3 From The Teacher To The Preacher ............... | *57* | Brunswick 55387 |
| | | | GENE CHANDLER & BARBARA ACKLIN | | |
| 12/07/68+ | **23** | 8 | 4 Just Ain't No Love .................................... | *67* | Brunswick 55388 |
| 2/22/69 | **33** | 6 | 5 Am I The Same Girl ................................... | *79* | Brunswick 55399 |
| | | | exact same recording as Young-Holt Unlimited's "Soulful Strut", except piano part is replaced by Barbara's voice | | |
| 11/08/69 | **30** | 4 | 6 After You .............................................. | | Brunswick 55421 |
| 10/10/70 | **28** | 5 | 7 I Did It ................................................. | *121* | Brunswick 55440 |
| 12/25/71+ | **44** | 3 | 8 Lady Lady Lady ....................................... | | Brunswick 55465 |
| 12/02/72 | **49** | 2 | 9 I Call It Trouble ...................................... | | Brunswick 55486 |
| 6/15/74 | **14** | 14 | 10 Raindrops ............................................. | | Capitol 3892 |
| 2/22/75 | **73** | 7 | 11 Special Loving ....................................... | | Capitol 4013 |
| 6/14/75 | **98** | 3 | 12 Give Me Some Of Your Sweet Love .................. | | Capitol 4061 |
| | | | **ACT I** | | |
| 2/24/73 | **22** | 8 | 1 Friends Or Lovers .................................... | *101* | Spring 132 |
| 7/14/73 | **90** | 3 | 2 Takes Two Of Us ...................................... | | Spring 137 |
| | | | **THE AD LIBS** | | |
| | | | 4-man, 1-woman group from Newark. Originally called the Creators. Consisted of Mary Ann Thomas (lead singer), Hugh Harris, Danny Austin, Norman Donegan and Dave Watt. First recorded for T-Kay in 1962. | | |
| 1/30/65 | **6** | 10 | 1 **The Boy From New York City** ..................... | *8* | Blue Cat 102 |
| 3/15/69 | **34** | 6 | 2 Giving Up .............................................. | | Share 104 |
| | | | **BOBBY ADAMS** | | |
| 6/27/70 | **49** | 2 | 1 Love Ain't Nothing But A Business.................. | | Hometown 101 |
| | | | **FAYE ADAMS** | | |
| | | | Real name: Faye Tuell. Vocalist from Newark, New Jersey. With two older sisters in gospel trio, the Tuell Sisters, from age five. Married Tommy Scruggs in 1942. Joined Joe Morris Blues Cavalcade in late 1952. Recorded with Morris on Atlantic as "Fay Scruggs". | | |
| 8/22/53 | **1** 10 | 21 | 1 **Shake A Hand** ...................................... | *22* | Herald 416 |
| | | | Juke Box #1(10) / Best Seller #1(9) | | |
| 12/12/53+ | **1** 1 | 15 | 2 **I'll Be True** .......................................... | | Herald 419 |
| | | | Best Seller #1 / Juke Box #2 above 2: with the Joe Morris Orchestra | | |
| 8/21/54 | **1** 5 | 18 | 3 **Hurts Me To My Heart** ............................ | | Herald 434 |
| | | | Best Seller #1(5) / Juke Box #1(5) | | |
| 6/03/57 | **13** | 2 | 4 Keeper Of My Heart .................................. | | Imperial 5443 |
| | | | Jockey #13 | | |
| | | | **GAYLE ADAMS** | | |
| | | | From Washington, DC. Worked as comedienne; tried race car driving before turning to singing. Produced by Willie Lester and Rodney Brown. | | |
| 7/19/80 | **75** | 5 | 1 Stretch' In Out.......................................... | | Prelude 8012 |
| 11/21/81+ | **24** | 14 | 2 Love Fever.............................................. | | Prelude 8040 |
| | | | **JOHNNY ADAMS** | | |
| | | | Born Lathan John Adams on 1/5/32 in New Orleans. Nicknamed "The Tan Canary". With gospel groups The Soul Revivers and Bessie Griffin & The Soul Consolators. First recorded on the Ric label in 1959. | | |
| 6/30/62 | **27** | 5 | 1 A Losing Battle......................................... | | Ric 986 |
| 12/07/68+ | **34** | 6 | 2 Release Me ............................................. | *82* | SSS Int'l. 750 |
| 6/21/69 | **8** | 12 | 3 **Reconsider Me** ...................................... | *28* | SSS Int'l. 770 |
| 10/25/69 | **45** | 3 | 4 I Can't Be All Bad .................................... | *89* | SSS Int'l. 780 |

| DEBUT DATE | PEAK POS | WKS CHR | ARTIST — Record Title | POP POS | Label & Number |
|---|---|---|---|---|---|
| | | | **JOHNNY ADAMS — Continued** | | |
| 8/29/70 | **41** | 5 | 5 I Won't Cry ............................................. | | SSS Int'l. 809 |
| | | | *originally released on Ric 961* | | |
| 5/20/78 | **75** | 8 | 6 After All The Good Is Gone ........................... | | Ariola 7701 |
| | | | **MARIE ADAMS** | | |
| | | | From Lyndon, Texas. Sang in gospel groups. Recorded with Bill Harvey for Peacock in 1952. Worked with Pluma Davis and Johnny Otis into the 60s. | | |
| 6/28/52 | **3** | 7 | 1 **I'm Gonna Play The Honky Tonks** ................ | | Peacock 1583 |
| | | | *Juke Box #3 / Best Seller #7* | | |
| | | | *with Bill Harvey's Band* | | |
| | | | **ADC BAND** | | |
| | | | 8-man, 1-woman band led by Kaiya Matthews and Michael Judkins. | | |
| 10/21/78 | **6** | 17 | 1 **Long Stroke** .......................................... *101* | | Cotillion 44243 |
| 2/17/79 | **72** | 7 | 2 Fire Up ................................................. | | Cotillion 44246 |
| 9/01/79 | **69** | 7 | 3 Talk That Stuff ....................................... | | Cotillion 45003 |
| 5/10/80 | **75** | 5 | 4 In The Moonlight ..................................... | | Cotillion 45014 |
| 7/12/80 | **67** | 6 | 5 Hangin' Out ............................................ | | Cotillion 45019 |
| 2/27/82 | **46** | 10 | 6 Roll With The Punches ............................... | | Cotillion 47001 |
| | | | **CANNONBALL ADDERLEY** | | |
| | | | Born Julian Edwin Adderley on 9/15/28 in Tampa. Nickname derived from "Cannibal" - in tribute to his love for food. Alto saxophonist/leader of jazz combo featuring brother Nat Adderley (cornet) and Joe Zawinul (piano). Own combo with Nat from 1955. First recorded for EmArcy in 1955. With Miles Davis band in the late 50s. Died of a stroke on 8/8/75 in Gary, Indiana. | | |
| 5/15/61 | **21** | 1 | 1 African Waltz ............................... [I] *41* | | Riverside 45457 |
| | | | **CANNONBALL ADDERLEY SEXTET** | | |
| 1/07/67 | **2**² | 16 | 2 **Mercy, Mercy, Mercy** ..................... [I] *11* | | Capitol 5798 |
| 4/29/67 | **46** | 4 | 3 Why? (Am I Treated So Bad) ............... [I] *73* | | Capitol 5877 |
| 1/10/70 | **29** | 10 | 4 Country Preacher ........................... [I] *86* | | Capitol 2698 |
| | | | **CANNONBALL ADDERLEY QUINTET** | | |
| | | | **AFRIQUE** | | |
| | | | American disco group featuring David T. Walker (guitar) and Chuck Rainey (bass). | | |
| 6/23/73 | **33** | 6 | 1 Soul Makossa ............................... [I] *47* | | Mainstream 5542 |
| | | | **AFRO CUBAN BAND** | | |
| 9/16/78 | **84** | 7 | 1 Rhythm Of Life .................................... | | Arista 0355 |
| | | | **AFTERBACH** | | |
| | | | Six-piece group from Sacramento, led by Michael and Robert Brooken, brothers who studied classical music. First known as Little Robert & The Fondells. | | |
| 7/25/81 | **38** | 11 | 1 It's You ............................................... | | ARC 02222 |
| | | | **THE AFTERNOON DELIGHTS** | | |
| | | | Female studio quartet from Boston. | | |
| 8/15/81 | **23** | 11 | 1 General Hospi-Tale ......................... [N] *33* | | MCA 51148 |
| | | | *parody of TV's "General Hospital"* | | |
| | | | **JEWEL AKENS** | | |
| | | | Vocalist/producer, born in Texas in 1940. | | |
| 3/13/65 | **21** | 5 | 1 The Birds And The Bees ...................... *3* | | Era 3141 |
| | | | **AL B. SURE!** | | |
| | | | Singer born in Boston, raised in Mt. Vernon, New York. | | |
| 3/12/88 | **1**³ | 18 | 1 **Nite And Day** .............................. *7* | | Warner 28192 |
| 6/11/88 | **1**² | 19 | 2 **Off On Your Own (Girl)** .................. *49* | | Warner 27870 |
| | | | **GERALD ALBRIGHT** | | |
| | | | Prominent session musician (saxophone/bass) born and raised in Los Angeles. Attended Locke High School with Patrice Rushen and Ndugu. | | |
| 11/21/87+ | **12** | 15 | 1 **So Amazing** ............................... [I] | | Atlantic 89163 |
| 3/19/88 | **59** | 9 | 2 New Girl On The Block ......................... | | Atlantic 89117 |
| | | | **RENEE ALDRICH** | | |
| 10/10/87 | **75** | 8 | 1 Just Begun To Love You ......................... | | Jam Pack. 2010 |
| | | | **ALEEM featuring LEROY BURGESS** | | |
| | | | New York-based trio formed in 1980, consisting of twin brothers Taharqa and Tunde-Ra Aleem with Leroy Burgess III. Burgess was lead singer of Black Ivory. | | |
| 9/08/84 | **83** | 6 | 1 Release Yourself .......................... | | NIA 1241 |
| | | | *shown as:* **THE ALEEMS** | | |

| DEBUT DATE | PEAK POS | WKS CHR | ARTIST — Record Title | POP POS | Label & Number |
|---|---|---|---|---|---|
| | | | **ALEEM featuring LEROY BURGESS — Continued** | | |
| 3/08/86 | **23** | 13 | 2 Love's On Fire ................................................ | | Atlantic 89439 |
| 6/21/86 | **62** | 7 | 3 Fine Young Tender ........................................ | | Atlantic 89401 |
| 9/12/87 | **51** | 11 | 4 Love Shock .................................................... | | Atlantic 89206 |
| | | | **ARTHUR ALEXANDER** | | |
| | | | Born on 5/10/40 in Florence, Alabama. Teamed with Rick Hall in studio work at Muscle Shoals. First recorded for Judd in 1960. | | |
| 10/27/62 | **10** | 7 | 1 **Anna (Go To Him)** ...................................... | *68* | Dot 16387 |
| 5/29/76 | **92** | 4 | 2 Sharing The Night Together ........................... | | Buddah 522 |
| | | | **DAVID ALEXANDER** | | |
| 8/22/87 | **75** | 6 | 1 Ms. X ............................................................ | | Sound Town 0019 |
| | | | **GOLDIE ALEXANDER** | | |
| | | | Canadian male vocalist. | | |
| 5/01/82 | **68** | 6 | 1 Show You My Love ....................................... | | Arista 0681 |
| | | | **HANK ALEXANDER - see JIMMY JOHNSON** | | |
| | | | **MARGIE ALEXANDER** | | |
| | | | Born Marjorie Lucille Alexander on 10/11/48 in Carrollton, Georgia. With Gospel Crusaders Of Los Angeles in the mid-60s. Returned to Atlantic in 1968. Worked Club 400 from 1968-71. Joined the Clarence Carter band in 1971. | | |
| 8/31/74 | **50** | 8 | 1 Keep On Searching ....................................... | | Fut. Stars 1005 |
| 1/08/77 | **92** | 3 | 2 Worth A Whippin' ......................................... | | Chi-Sound 17606 |
| 8/27/77 | **68** | 8 | 3 Gotta Get A Hold On Me ............................... | | Chi-Sound 1033 |
| | | | **ALFIE - see ALFIE SILAS** | | |
| | | | **ALFONZO** | | |
| | | | Full name: Alfonzo Jones. | | |
| 7/10/82 | **22** | 16 | 1 Girl, You Are The One.................................... | | Joe-Wes 81003 |
| 11/20/82 | **34** | 11 | 2 Change The World........................................... | | Larc 81011 |
| 1/22/83 | **48** | 8 | 3 Your Booty Makes Me Moody........................... | | Larc 81016 |
| | | | **ALISHA** | | |
| | | | Dance/disco teenager from Brooklyn, New York. | | |
| 4/14/84 | **84** | 4 | 1 All Night Passion ......................................... | *103* | Vanguard 35244 |
| 12/14/85 | **75** | 11 | 2 Baby Talk..................................................... | *68* | Vanguard 35262 |
| | | | **ALL POINTS BULLETIN BAND** | | |
| 1/31/76 | **47** | 14 | 1 Sexy Ways-Pretty Legs.................................... | | Little C. 10102 |
| 4/14/79 | **98** | 2 | 2 Get Up And Get Down .................................... | | Little C. 10109 |
| | | | **ANNISTEEN ALLEN** | | |
| | | | Born Ernestine Allen on 11/11/20 in Champaign, Illinois; raised in Toledo. With Don Albert in 1939 and Lucky Millinder from 1946-51. Also see Lucky Millinder. | | |
| 3/07/53 | **8** | 2 | 1 **Baby I'm Doin' It** ...................................... | | King 4608 |
| | | | Best Seller #8 answer song to The "5" Royales' "Baby Don't Do It"; featuring Big John Greer on tenor sax | | |
| | | | **DONNA ALLEN** | | |
| | | | Born in Key West; raised in Tampa. Former Tampa Bay Buccaneers' cheerleader. | | |
| 11/15/86+ | **5** | 22 | 1 **Serious**..................................................... | *21* | 21 Records 99497 |
| 5/23/87 | **14** | 13 | 2 Satisfied ...................................................... | | 21 Records 99459 |
| 9/26/87 | **55** | 10 | 3 Sweet Somebody ......................................... , | | 21 Records 99418 |
| | | | **JONELLE ALLEN** | | |
| | | | Singer/actress from New York City. Made TV debut at age 4. Attended the Professional Children's School. In the Broadway shows "Two Gentlemen Of Verona", "Hair" and "George M.". Appeared in many films. | | |
| 4/22/78 | **89** | 6 | 1 Baby I Just Wanna Love You ........................... | | Alex. 007 |
| | | | **R. JUSTICE ALLEN** | | |
| 11/01/86 | **91** | 4 | 1 Crackin' Up................................................... | | Catawba 0940 |
| | | | **THE RANCE ALLEN GROUP** | | |
| | | | Detroit group: brothers Rance, Tom, Steve and Esau Allen with cousins Judy, Linda and Annie Mendez. | | |
| 5/05/73 | **31** | 7 | 1 I Got To Be Myself ....................................... | | Gospel Tr. 1208 |
| 1/04/75 | **61** | 9 | 2 Ain't No Need Of Crying ............................... | | Truth 3210 |

| DEBUT DATE | PEAK POS | WKS CHR | ARTIST — Record Title | POP POS | Label & Number |
|---|---|---|---|---|---|
| | | | **THE RANCE ALLEN GROUP — Continued** | | |
| 4/02/77 | 100 | 1 | 3 Truth Is Marching On............................. | | Capitol 4394 |
| | | | shown only as: **RANCE ALLEN** | | |
| 2/17/79 | 24 | 19 | 4 I Belong To You ................................... | | Stax 3217 |
| 8/25/79 | 41 | 9 | 5 Smile ................................................ | | Stax 3221 |
| | | | **RICKY ALLEN** | | |
| | | | Born on 1/6/35 in Nashville. Moved to Chicago in 1958. | | |
| 8/31/63 | 20 | 4 | 1 Cut You A-Loose .................................. | 126 | Age 29118 |
| | | | **VEE ALLEN** | | |
| | | | Sister of Al Perkins. | | |
| 2/03/73 | 26 | 10 | 1 Can I................................................ | 107 | Lion 140 |
| | | | **THE ALLEY CATS** | | |
| | | | Group from Los Angeles, formed as the Valiants. Consisted of Billy Storm (lead), Chester Pipkin, Ed Wallis and Bryce Caulfield. First recorded for Keen in 1957. Recorded as the Untouchables for Madison in 1960. Later known as Africa; recorded with The Checkmates, Ltd. | | |
| 2/09/63 | 21 | 2 | 1 Puddin N' Tain (Ask Me Again, I'll Tell You The Same) .................................... | 43 | Philles 108 |
| | | | **GENE ALLISON** | | |
| | | | Born on 8/29/34 in Nashville. Sang with the Skylarks and Fairfield Four gospel groups. First recorded for Calvert in 1956. | | |
| 12/23/57+ | 3 | 11 | 1 **You Can Make It If You Try** .......................... | 36 | Vee-Jay 256 |
| | | | Jockey #3 / Best Seller #14 with the Joe Morris Orchestra | | |
| 4/21/58 | 11 | 4 | 2 Have Faith ......................................... | 73 | Vee-Jay 273 |
| | | | Jockey #11 / Best Seller #20 with the Sonny Thompson Orchestra | | |
| 11/24/58 | 19 | 6 | 3 Everything Will Be All Right .......................... | | Vee-Jay 299 |
| | | | **ALPACA PHASE III** | | |
| 8/24/74 | 80 | 6 | 1 I Like To Party .................................... | | Atlantic 3038 |
| | | | **HERB ALPERT** | | |
| | | | Producer/composer/trumpeter/bandleader, born on 3/31/35 in Los Angeles. Played trumpet since age 8. A&R director for Keen Records, produced first Jan & Dean session, wrote "Wonderful World" hit for Sam Cooke. Formed A&M Records with Jerry Moss in 1962. Used studio musicians until early 1965, then own band. | | |
| 4/29/78 | 87 | 5 | 1 Skokiaan ..................................... [I] | | Horizon 115 |
| | | | **HERB ALPERT/HUGH MASEKELA** | | |
| 8/04/79 | 4 | 21 | 2 ● Rise ........................................ [I] | 1 | A&M 2151 |
| 11/24/79+ | 20 | 14 | 3 Rotation ..................................... [I] | 30 | A&M 2202 |
| 3/08/80 | 65 | 6 | 4 Street Life .................................. [I] | 104 | A&M 2221 |
| 6/28/80 | 44 | 8 | 5 Beyond ...................................... [I] | 50 | A&M 2246 |
| 9/13/80 | 64 | 7 | 6 Kamali ...................................... [I] | | A&M 2268 |
| 8/01/81 | 37 | 10 | 7 Magic Man ................................... [I] | 79 | A&M 2356 |
| 10/31/81 | 74 | 5 | 8 Manhattan Melody ........................... [I] | | A&M 2375 |
| 8/20/83 | 77 | 5 | 9 Garden Party................................. [I] | 81 | A&M 2562 |
| 8/11/84 | 52 | 10 | 10 Bullish ..................................... [I] | 90 | A&M 2655 |
| | | | **HERB ALPERT/TIJUANA BRASS** | | |
| 8/17/85 | 73 | 7 | 11 "8" Ball ..................................... [I] | | A&M 2757 |
| 2/14/87 | 3 | 14 | 12 **Keep Your Eye On Me**................... | 46 | A&M 2915 |
| | | | vocals by Lisa Keith & Terry Lewis | | |
| 4/25/87 | 1² | 15 | 13 **Diamonds**.................................... | 5 | A&M 2929 |
| | | | lead & background vocals by Janet Jackson & Lisa Keith | | |
| 7/18/87 | 7 | 13 | 14 **Making Love In The Rain**....................... | 35 | A&M 2949 |
| | | | vocal by Lisa Keith | | |
| | | | **ALTON & JOHNNY - see ALTON McCLAIN and/or JOHNNY BRISTOL** | | |
| | | | **BILLY ALWAYS** | | |
| | | | Mahalia Jackson's Godson. | | |
| 5/29/82 | 74 | 7 | 1 Didn't We Do It ................................... | | Waylo 114 |
| | | | **AM-FM** | | |
| | | | Group consisting of 3 former members of Vaughn Mason's Crew. | | |
| 1/09/82 | 36 | 14 | 1 You Are The One ............................... | | Dakar 4568 |

| DEBUT DATE | PEAK POS | WKS CHR | ARTIST — Record Title | POP POS | Label & Number |
|---|---|---|---|---|---|

### THE AMBASSADORS
Ex-gospel vocal group, from Philadelphia, featuring twin lead voices of Herley Johnson and Bobby Todd, with Orlando Oliphant. They later formed Creme D' Cocoa.

| 3/08/69 | **43** | 2 | 1 I Really Love You............................................ | *123* | Arctic 147 |
|---|---|---|---|---|---|

### AMBROSIA
Los Angeles-based trio: David Pack, Joe Puerta and Burleigh Drummond.

| 5/10/80 | **35** | 9 | 1 Biggest Part Of Me.......................................... | *3* | Warner 49225 |
|---|---|---|---|---|---|

### THE AMES BROTHERS
Vocal group from Malden, Massachusettes, formed in the late 40s. Family name Urick. Consisted of Ed, Gene, Joe and Vic. Own TV series in 1955.

| 5/09/60 | **30** | 1 | 1 China Doll ...................................... | *38* | RCA 7655 |
|---|---|---|---|---|---|

### ALBERT AMMONS
Born in 1907 in Chicago. Father of tenor sax star Gene Ammons. Formed boogie-woogie piano duo with Pete Johnson in New York in 1938. Temporary paralysis in both hands during the mid-40s, but recovered. Died on 12/2/49 (42).

| 2/08/47 | **5** | 1 | 1 **Swanee River Boogie**.................................. [I] with his Rhythm Kings | | Mercury 8018 |
|---|---|---|---|---|---|

### GENE AMMONS
Born Eugene Ammons on 4/14/25 in Chicago. Son of boogie-woogie pianist Albert Ammons. Nicknamed Jug. Tenor sax player with the Billy Eckstine Band, 1944-47 and Woody Herman in 1949. Formed own group in 1950. Had the first release on the Chess labe!. Died in 1974 (49).

| 9/20/47 | **3** | 1 | 1 **Red Top**...................................... [I] | | Mercury 8048 |
|---|---|---|---|---|---|
| 7/29/50 | **9** | 2 | 2 **My Foolish Heart** ............................... [I] Best Seller #9 / Juke Box #9 | | Chess 1425 |
| 3/17/51 | **10** | 1 | 3 **Jug** ......................................... [I] Juke Box #10 | | Prestige 735 |

### AMUZEMENT PARK
Former backup group for the Impressions and Tyrone Davis. Consisted of lead Paul Richmond, Darryl Ellis, Norval Hodges, Fred Entesari, Aaron Jamal, Rico McFarland & Ruben Locke, Jr. Richmond wrote "Shining Star" for the Manhattans in 1980.

| 7/17/82 | **47** | 13 | 1 Groove Your Blues Away............................... | | Our Gang 1008 |
|---|---|---|---|---|---|
| 2/26/83 | **80** | 6 | 2 Do You Still Love Me .................................... | | Our Gang 1016 |
| 9/29/84 | **62** | 6 | 3 No.................................................... **AMUZEMENT PARK BAND** | | Atlantic 89653 |

### ANACOSTIA
Group produced by Van McCoy.

| 10/21/72 | **41** | 6 | 1 On And Off (Part 1)..................................... | *90* | Columbia 45685 |
|---|---|---|---|---|---|

### CARL ANDERSON
Singer/actor. Played "Judas" in the original Broadway cast and film version of the rock opera "Jesus Christ Superstar".

| 3/17/84 | **83** | 3 | 1 Magic................................................ | | Epic 04360 |
|---|---|---|---|---|---|
| 6/01/85 | **84** | 3 | 2 Can't Stop This Feeling .................................. | | Epic 04842 |
| 8/23/86 | **54** | 9 | 3 Friends And Lovers ..................................... **GLORIA LORING & CARL ANDERSON** Gloria played Liz Curtis on TV soap opera "Days Of Our Lives" | *2* | USA Car. 06122 |

### ELTON ANDERSON
Born in Lake Charles, Louisiana in 1932. Sang and played guitar with the Sid Lawrence band. First recorded for Vin.

| 2/01/60 | **22** | 3 | 1 Secret Of Love................................. with the Sid Lawrence Combo | *88* | Mercury 71542 |
|---|---|---|---|---|---|

### JESSE ANDERSON

| 4/11/70 | **35** | 7 | 1 I Got A Problem ........................................ | *95* | Thomas 805 |
|---|---|---|---|---|---|

### ROSHELL ANDERSON
Male vocalist from New Orleans. Announcer and news anchor on radio and TV stations in Alabama, Florida, Georgia, Washington and Wisconsin; known as "Mike Anderson".

| 12/08/73+ | **77** | 6 | 1 Know What You're Doing When You Leave ........ | | Sunburst 1076 |
|---|---|---|---|---|---|
| 6/15/74 | **69** | 6 | 2 Grapevine Will Lie Sometimes ........................ | | Sunburst 529 |

### VICKI ANDERSON - see JAMES BROWN

**24**

| DEBUT DATE | PEAK POS | WKS CHR | ARTIST — Record Title | POP POS | Label & Number |
|---|---|---|---|---|---|
| | | | **ANDREWS SISTERS** Patty, Maxene and LaVerne emerged from Minneapolis to become the most popular female vocal group of the entire pre-1955 era. LaVerne died on 5/8/67 (52). | | |
| 11/13/43 | **3** | 6 | 1  Pistol Packin' Mama ....................................... <br> BING CROSBY & the ANDREWS SISTERS <br> a reported million-seller | *2* | Decca 23277 |
| 1/20/45 | **3** | 3 | 2  Rum And Coca-Cola ...................................... <br> uses calypso melody from Trinidad ("L'Anee' Pasee'", 1906); <br> a reported million-seller | *1* | Decca 18636 |
| 1/20/45 | **9** | 1 | 3  Don't Fence Me In........................................ <br> BING CROSBY & ANDREWS SISTERS <br> a reported million-seller; <br> from the film "Hollywood Canteen"; <br> above 3: with Vic Schoen & His Orchestra | *1* | Decca 23364 |
| | | | **INEZ ANDREWS** Gospel vocalist from Birmingham, Alabama. With Dorothy Love & Gospel Harmonettes in the early 50s. With the Caravans from 1956-61; formed own group, the Andrewettes. Went solo in the late 60s. | | |
| 4/21/73 | **48** | 2 | 1  Lord Don't Move The Mountains ...................... | | Song Bird 1203 |
| | | | **LEE ANDREWS & THE HEARTS** Born Arthur Lee Andrew Thompson in North Carolina; moved to Philadelphia at age 2. Formed vocal group, The Hearts, in 1953. First recorded for Rainbow in 1954. Group on Chess included Roy Calhoun, Thomas Curry, Ted Weems and Wendell Calhoun. | | |
| 8/05/57 | **11** | 5 | 1  Long Lonely Nights ....................................... <br> Jockey #11 | *45* | Chess 1665 |
| 1/06/58 | **4** | 6 | 2  Teardrops.................................................... <br> Jockey #4 / Best Seller #13 | *20* | Chess 1675 |
| | | | **RUBY ANDREWS** Born Ruby Stackhouse on 3/12/47 in Hollandale, Mississippi. In music class at Hyde Park High School with Minnie Riperton. With Vondells vocal group, recorded for Kellmac in 1965. Back-up with C.O.D.'s in 1965. Worked as dancer. First recorded as Ruby Andrews for Zodiac in 1967. | | |
| 8/26/67 | **9** | 11 | 1  Casonova (Your Playing Days Are Over) ......... <br> co-written by singer Jo Armstead | *51* | Zodiac 1004 |
| 10/05/68 | **48** | 2 | 2  The Love I Need............................................ | | Zodiac 1010 |
| 6/14/69 | **18** | 15 | 3  You Made A Believer (Out Of Me)..................... | *96* | Zodiac 1015 |
| 5/02/70 | **34** | 11 | 4  Everybody Saw You/ | *118* | |
| | | 9 | 5  Can You Get Away / | | Zodiac 1017 |
| 2/06/71 | **47** | 2 | 6  You Ole Boo Boo You ...................................... | | Zodiac 1020 |
| | | | **ANGELIC GOSPEL SINGERS** Group consisting of Margaret W. Allison (lead, piano), Lucille Shird, Ella Mae Norris and Josephine McDowell. Worked with Dixie Hummingbirds in the early 50s. | | |
| 8/20/49 | **13** | 1 | 1  Touch Me Lord Jesus...................................... <br> Best Seller #13 | | Gotham 605 |
| | | | **THE ANGELS** Female pop trio from Orange, New Jersey, formed as the Starlets with sisters Phyllis "Jiggs" & Barbara Allbut, and Linda Jansen (lead singer). Jansen was replaced by Peggy Santiglia in 1962. Disbanded in 1967. | | |
| 8/24/63 | **2[1]** | 10 | 1  My Boyfriend's Back ..................................... | *1* | Smash 1834 |
| | | | **PAUL ANKA** Born on 7/30/41 in Ottawa, Canada. Performer since age 12. Father financed first recording, "I Confess" (RPM 472), in 1956. Wrote "My Way" for Frank Sinatra, "She's A Lady" for Tom Jones. Also wrote theme for TV's "Tonight Show". Own variety show in 1973. Long-time popular entertainer in Las Vegas. | | |
| 9/09/57 | **1[2]** | 11 | 1  Diana ......................................................... <br> Best Seller #1 / Jockey #2 | *1* | ABC-Para. 9831 |
| 2/10/58 | **14** | 6 | 2  You Are My Destiny ...................................... <br> Best Seller #14 / Jockey #14 | *7* | ABC-Para. 9880 |
| 6/15/59 | **6** | 12 | 3  Lonely Boy.................................................. | *1* | ABC-Para. 10022 |
| 9/21/59 | **12** | 11 | 4  Put Your Head On My Shoulder ....................... | *2* | ABC-Para. 10040 |
| 1/18/60 | **13** | 6 | 5  It's Time To Cry ............................................ | *4* | ABC-Para. 10064 |
| 11/14/60 | **29** | 1 | 6  Summer's Gone ............................................ | *11* | ABC-Para. 10147 |
| | | | **ANNETTE** Born Annette Funicello on 10/22/42 in Utica, New York. Became a Mouseketeer in 1955. Backing group: The Afterbeats. In several teen films in the early 60s. Co-starred with Frankie Avalon in the 1987 film "Back To The Beach". | | |
| 1/11/60 | **27** | 2 | 1  First Name Initial.......................................... | *20* | Vista 349 |

| DEBUT DATE | PEAK POS | WKS CHR | ARTIST — Record Title | POP POS | Label & Number |
|---|---|---|---|---|---|
| | | | **ANTHONY & THE CAMP** Dance quartet led by producer/composer Anthony Malloy (former member of Temper). | | |
| 6/21/86 | **80** | 5 | 1  What I Like.................................................... | | Warner 28730 |
| | | | **ANTHONY & THE IMPERIALS - see LITTLE ANTHONY** | | |
| | | | **ALAN ANTHONY** | | |
| 7/24/82 | **82** | 5 | 1  Turn Back The Hands Of Time......................... | | Chalet 1227 |
| | | | **MARKUS ANTHONY** | | |
| 9/27/86 | **88** | 5 | 1  One Night Love............................................. | | R&R 940 |
| | | | **RAY ANTHONY** Born Raymond Antonini on 1/20/22 in Bentleyville, Pennsylvania. Trumpter/bandleader. | | |
| 2/23/59 | **12** | 7 | 1  Peter Gunn ................................... theme from the TV series of the same title | *8* | Capitol 4041 |
| | | | **APOLLONIA 6** Female trio formed by Prince, led by Patty (Apollonia) Kotero (co-star of film "Purple Rain"). With former Vanity 6 members Brenda Bennett and Susan Moonsie. | | |
| 9/29/84 | **14** | 14 | 1  Sex Shooter ................................................ from the film "Purple Rain" | *85* | Warner 29182 |
| | | | **AQUARIAN DREAM** Disco group formed by Norman Connors, featuring singer Connie Harvey. | | |
| 3/19/77 | **83** | 5 | 1  Phoenix....................................................... | | Buddah 560 |
| | | | **THE AQUATONES** Group formed in Valley Stream, Long Island, New York in 1957. Consisted of Lynn Nixon, Larry Vannata (lead singers); David Goddard and Eugene McCarthy. Female lead Nixon trained as an operatic soprano. | | |
| 5/19/58 | **11** | 2 | 1  You .......................................................... Jockey #11 / Best Seller #20 | *21* | Fargo 1001 |
| | | | **ARCHIBALD** Singer/guitarist, born Leon T. Gross on 9/14/12 in New Orleans. Also known as Archie Boy. Piano style influenced Fats Domino. Died of a heart attack in January of 1973. | | |
| 6/10/50 | **10** | 2 | 1  **Stack-A-Lee (Parts I & II)** ........................... Best Seller #10 recorded by others as "Stagger Lee" and "Stag-O-Lee" | | Imperial 5068 |
| | | | **JO ARMSTEAD** Singer/songwriter, born Josephine Armstead on 10/8/44 in Yazoo City, Mississippi. With The Ikettes in 1961. Recorded as Dina Johnson in 1962. Co-wrote "Let's Go Get Stoned" and "Casanova (Your Playing Days Are Over)". Own Giant label in 1967. | | |
| 5/18/68 | **28** | 8 | 1  A Stone Good Lover...................................... | *129* | Giant 704 |
| 10/12/68 | **50** | 2 | 2  I've Been Turned On ..................................... | | Giant 707 |
| 5/25/74 | **91** | 3 | 3  Stumblin' Blocks, Steppin' Stones.................... | | Truth 1214 |
| | | | **CHUCK ARMSTRONG** | | |
| 8/07/76 | **75** | 7 | 1  Give Me All Your Sweet Lovin'......................... | | R&R 15313 |
| | | | **LOUIS ARMSTRONG** Trumpeter/vocalist, born Daniel Louis Armstrong in New Orleans, on 8/4/01 (not 7/4/1900, as Armstrong claimed). Nickname: Satchmo. Resident of Colored Waif's Home in New Orleans and played cornet in the Home's band. Joined Joe "King" Oliver in Chicago in 1922. By 1929, had become the most widely-known black musician. Influenced dozens of singers and trumpet players, both black and White. Numerous appearances on radio, TV and in films. Died on 7/6/71 in New York. | | |
| 3/31/45 | **3** | 4 | 1  **I Wonder**................................................... | | Decca 18652 |
| 4/13/46 | **4** | 2 | 2  **The Frim Fram Sauce** ................................. ELLA FITZGERALD & LOUIS ARMSTRONG | | Decca 23496 |
| 11/26/49 | **14** | 1 | 3  That Lucky Old Sun ...................................... Juke Box #14 with Gordon Jenkin's Orchestra & Chorus | *19* | Decca 24752 |
| | | | **VANESSA BELL ARMSTRONG** | | |
| 11/28/87 | **80** | 9 | 1  You Bring Out The Best In Me ......................... | | Jive 1051 |
| | | | **ARNIE'S LOVE** | | |
| 3/15/86 | **74** | 6 | 1  Natural High ............................................... | | Profile 5091 |
| | | | **CALVIN ARNOLD** | | |
| 1/27/68 | **22** | 6 | 1  Funky Way ................................................. | *72* | Venture 605 |
| 8/23/75 | **79** | 6 | 2  Satisfy My Woman........................................ | | IX Chains 7009 |

| DEBUT DATE | PEAK POS | WKS CHR | ARTIST — Record Title | POP POS | Label & Number |
|---|---|---|---|---|---|
| | | | **CALVIN ARNOLD — Continued** | | |
| 1/17/76 | 79 | 5 | 3 (I'm Your) Friendly Neighborhood Freak (Part 1) . | | IX Chains 7013 |
| | | | **ARPEGGIO** | | |
| | | | Disco quartet. | | |
| 3/10/79 | 44 | 9 | 1 Love And Desire (Part I) ................................... | 70 | Polydor 14535 |
| | | | **STEVE ARRINGTON** | | |
| | | | Vocalist/drummer from Dayton, Ohio. Ex-member of Slave. | | |
| | | | STEVE ARRINGTON'S HALL OF FAME: | | |
| 9/04/82 | 68 | 10 | 1 Way Out ...................................................... | | Konglather 7491 |
| 2/19/83 | 18 | 16 | 2 Nobody Can Be You ........................................ | | Atlantic 89876 |
| 5/21/83 | 33 | 13 | 3 Weak At The Knees............................................ | | Atlantic 89831 |
| 1/21/84 | 25 | 10 | 4 Hump To The Bump .......................................... | | Atlantic 89715 |
| 3/31/84 | 85 | 3 | 5 15 Rounds .................................................... | | Atlantic 89688 |
| | | | STEVE ARRINGTON: | | |
| 3/23/85 | 17 | 15 | 6 Feel So Real ................................................. | 104 | Atlantic 89576 |
| 6/22/85 | 8 | 17 | 7 **Dancin' In The Key Of Life** ......................... | 68 | Atlantic 89535 |
| 11/16/85 | 80 | 2 | 8 Turn Up The Love ........................................... | | Atlantic 89499 |
| 4/05/86 | 42 | 10 | 9 The Jammin' National Anthem ....................... | | Atlantic 89428 |
| 6/14/86 | 28 | 14 | 10 Homeboy ...................................................... | | Atlantic 89397 |
| 9/05/87 | 33 | 12 | 11 Stone Love...................................................... | | Manhattan 50098 |
| | | | **THE ART OF NOISE** | | |
| | | | British techno-pop trio: Anne Dudley, J.J. Jeczalik and Gary Langan. | | |
| 2/18/84 | 10 | 18 | 1 **Beat Box** ...................................... [I] 101 | | Island 99782 |
| 6/09/84 | 23 | 13 | 2 Close (To The Edit) ................................ [I] 102 | | Island 99754 |
| 1/25/86 | 60 | 9 | 3 Legs .......................................................... [I] | | China 42932 |
| 2/22/86 | 90 | 2 | 4 Moments In Love.......................................... | | Island 99561 |
| | | | **TREVOR HORN, PAUL MORLEY with THE ART OF NOISE** | | |
| | | | **THE ARTISTICS** | | |
| | | | Vocal group formed at Marshall High School in Chicago in 1958. Sang at the Democratic National Convention in 1960. Back-up work for Major Lance. First recorded for Okeh in 1963, with Curt Thomas, Larry Johnson, Jessie Bolian and Aaron Floyd. Lead singer Robert Dobyne added in 1963; replaced by Marvin Smith (ex-El Dorados) in 1964. Smith left in 1967, but sang on studio recordings. Other lead singers were Tommy Green and Fred Pettis. Disbanded in 1973. | | |
| 12/25/65+ | 25 | 5 | 1 This Heart Of Mine ...................................... | 115 | Okeh 7232 |
| 11/26/66 | 9 | 16 | 2 **I'm Gonna Miss You** ................................. | 55 | Brunswick 55301 |
| 3/25/67 | 26 | 8 | 3 Girl I Need You ............................................ | 69 | Brunswick 55315 |
| 3/21/70 | 48 | 3 | 4 Just Another Heartache ................................ | | Brunswick 55431 |
| 1/30/71 | 48 | 3 | 5 Make My Life Over ....................................... | | Brunswick 55444 |
| | | | **ARTISTS UNITED AGAINST APARTHEID** | | |
| | | | Benefit group of 49 superstar artists formed in protest of the South African government - proceeds to benefit political prisoners in South Africa. | | |
| 11/16/85 | 21 | 13 | 1 Sun City ..................................................... | 38 | Manhattan 50017 |
| | | | **CLARENCE ASHE** | | |
| 6/06/64 | 99 | 1 | 1 Trouble I've Had ..................................... [S] *Hot* | | Chess 1896 |
| | | | **ASHFORD & SIMPSON**    ★★62★★ | | |
| | | | Husband and wife vocal/songwriting duo: Nickolas Ashford (b: 5/4/42, Fairfield, SC) and Valerie Simpson (b: 8/26/46, New York City). Team wrote for Chuck Jackson and Maxine Brown. Joined staff at Motown and wrote and produced for many of the label's top stars. Valerie recorded solo in 1972. | | |
| 11/24/73+ | 37 | 12 | 1 (I'd Know You) Anywhere .............................. | 88 | Warner 7745 |
| 4/06/74 | 77 | 6 | 2 Have You Ever Tried It................................. | | Warner 7781 |
| 6/22/74 | 37 | 10 | 3 Main Line .................................................... | | Warner 7811 |
| 10/19/74 | 53 | 7 | 4 Everybody's Got To Give It Up....................... | | Warner 8030 |
| 3/15/75 | 73 | 7 | 5 Bend Me ...................................................... | | Warner 8070 |
| 3/20/76 | 96 | 2 | 6 It'll Come, It'll Come, It'll Come ................... | | Warner 8179 |
| 6/19/76 | 58 | 7 | 7 Somebody Told A Lie ................................... | | Warner 8216 |
| 11/20/76+ | 52 | 14 | 8 Tried, Tested And Found True....................... | | Warner 8286 |
| 3/19/77 | 27 | 12 | 9 So So Satisfied............................................. | | Warner 8337 |
| 6/11/77 | 39 | 13 | 10 Over And Over ............................................ | | Warner 8391 |
| 9/24/77 | 15 | 17 | 11 Send It ....................................................... | | Warner 8453 |
| 1/21/78 | 10 | 17 | 12 **Don't Cost You Nothing**.............................. | 79 | Warner 8514 |

| DEBUT DATE | PEAK POS | WKS CHR | ARTIST — Record Title | POP POS | Label & Number |
|---|---|---|---|---|---|
| | | | **ASHFORD & SIMPSON — Continued** | | |
| 5/27/78 | 35 | 12 | 13 By Way Of Love's Express ............................. | | Warner 8571 |
| 8/26/78 | 2⁵ | 17 | 14 **Is Seems To Hang On** ................................... | | Warner 8651 |
| 12/02/78+ | 12 | 12 | 15 Is It Still Good To Ya ................................. | | Warner 8710 |
| 4/07/79 | 70 | 5 | 16 Flashback............................................. | | Warner 8775 |
| 7/07/79 | 2³ | 19 | 17 **Found A Cure**...................................... | 36 | Warner 8870 |
| 11/10/79 | 19 | 13 | 18 Nobody Knows ........................................ | | Warner 49099 |
| 7/12/80 | 6 | 16 | 19 **Love Don't Make It Right** ........................... | | Warner 49269 |
| 11/01/80 | 35 | 12 | 20 Happy Endings ....................................... | | Warner 49594 |
| 2/07/81 | 65 | 6 | 21 Get Out Your Handkerchief........................... | | Warner 49646 |
| 9/19/81 | 34 | 9 | 22 It Shows In The Eyes ................................ | | Warner 49805 |
| 4/17/82 | 9 | 21 | 23 **Street Corner** ....................................... | 56 | Capitol 5109 |
| 8/14/82 | 20 | 12 | 24 Love It Away ......................................... | | Capitol 5146 |
| 7/23/83 | 17 | 14 | 25 High-Rise............................................. | | Capitol 5250 |
| 11/05/83 | 45 | 11 | 26 It's Much Deeper ..................................... | | Capitol 5284 |
| 2/18/84 | 78 | 5 | 27 I'm Not That Tough .................................. | | Capitol 5310 |
| 9/29/84 | 1³ | 24 | 28 **Solid** ................................................ | 12 | Capitol 5397 |
| 1/19/85 | 4 | 16 | 29 **Outta The World**.................................... | 102 | Capitol 5435 |
| 4/20/85 | 29 | 13 | 30 Babies................................................ | 102 | Capitol 5468 |
| 8/02/86 | 4 | 17 | 31 **Count Your Blessings**.............................. | 84 | Capitol 5598 |
| | | | **TYRONE ASHLEY** | | |
| | | | Born Sammy Campbell in New Jersey. First recorded with the Del-Larks for East-West in 1958. Went solo in 1968. Formed own group, Sagittarian Fire, in the mid-70s. | | |
| 12/05/70+ | 46 | 6 | 1 Let Me Be Your Man ................................. | | Phil. L.A. 342 |
| | | | **ASPHALT JUNGLE** | | |
| 4/26/80 | 60 | 6 | 1 Freakin Time Pt. 1 ................................... | | TEC 765 |
| | | | **THE ASTORS** | | |
| | | | Vocal group formed at Melrose High School in Memphis, in 1958, as The Chips. Consisted of Curtis Johnson (lead), Eddie Stanbeck (tenor), Richard Harris (first tenor) and Sam Byrnes (baritone, bass). First recorded for Stax in 1960. Name changed to Astors in 1963. | | |
| 7/03/65 | 12 | 8 | 1 Candy ................................................. | 63 | Stax 170 |
| | | | **ATKINS** | | |
| | | | Family group from Los Angeles. | | |
| 4/24/82 | 79 | 4 | 1 Feel It, Don't Fight It ................................ | | Warner 50037 |
| | | | **THE ATLANTA DISCO BAND** | | |
| 11/01/75+ | 38 | 15 | 1 Bad Luck...................................... [I] | 94 | Ariola Am. 7611 |
| 3/27/76 | 56 | 6 | 2 Do What You Feel ..................................... | 104 | Ariola Am. 7616 |
| | | | **ATLANTA RHYTHM SECTION** | | |
| | | | Group of session musicians from Studio One, Doraville, Georgia; formed in 1971. | | |
| 4/02/77 | 93 | 4 | 1 So In To You ......................................... | 7 | Polydor 14373 |
| | | | **ATLANTIC STARR**   ★★107★★ | | |
| | | | Band formed, in 1976, in White Plains, New York, by brothers Wayne, Jonathan and David Lewis. Included: Sharon Bryant, William Sudderth, Damon Rentie, Clifford Archer, Porter Carroll and Joseph Phillips. Rentie replaced by Koran Daniels in 1980. Reorganized in 1984 with the Lewis brothers, Phillips, and vocalist Barbara Weathers. | | |
| 8/12/78 | 16 | 16 | 1 Stand Up .............................................. | | A&M 2065 |
| 12/02/78+ | 49 | 7 | 2 Keep It Comin'........................................ | | A&M 2101 |
| 5/19/79 | 46 | 9 | 3 (Let's) Rock 'N' Roll .................................. | | A&M 2135 |
| 2/28/81 | 5 | 19 | 4 **When Love Calls** ................................... | 101 | A&M 2312 |
| 6/13/81 | 16 | 14 | 5 Send For Me .......................................... | | A&M 2340 |
| 2/27/82 | 2² | 18 | 6 **Circles** .............................................. | 38 | A&M 2392 |
| 6/12/82 | 14 | 13 | 7 Love Me Down ........................................ | | A&M 2420 |
| 9/04/82 | 32 | 10 | 8 Perfect Love .......................................... | | A&M 2435 |
| 10/22/83 | 4 | 18 | 9 **Touch A Four Leaf Clover**........................... | 87 | A&M 2580 |
| 2/11/84 | 11 | 16 | 10 More, More, More ..................................... | | A&M 2619 |
| 5/26/84 | 50 | 9 | 11 Second To None ...................................... | | A&M 2638 |
| 4/06/85 | 6 | 17 | 12 **Freak-A-Ristic** ..................................... | 90 | A&M 2718 |
| 6/29/85 | 33 | 10 | 13 Cool, Calm, Collected................................. | 110 | A&M 2742 |

| DEBUT DATE | PEAK POS | WKS CHR | ARTIST — Record Title | POP POS | Label & Number |
|---|---|---|---|---|---|
| | | | **ATLANTIC STARR — Continued** | | |
| 8/24/85 | **13** | 15 | 14 Silver Shadow................................................ | | A&M 2766 |
| 11/16/85+ | **4** | 26 | 15 **Secret Lovers**............................................. | 3 | A&M 2788 |
| 3/08/86 | **4** | 21 | 16 If Your Heart Isn't In It .............................. | 57 | A&M 2822 |
| 9/27/86 | **86** | 5 | 17 Armed And Dangerous................................... | | Manhattan 50043 |
| 3/07/87 | **1** ² | 21 | 18 **Always** ...................................................... | 1 | Warner 28455 |
| 6/13/87 | **10** | 16 | 19 **One Lover At A Time** .................................. | 58 | Warner 28327 |
| 10/10/87 | **51** | 14 | 20 All In The Name Of Love .............................. | | Warner 28215 |
| 1/30/88 | **65** | 8 | 21 Thankful ..................................................... | | Warner 28100 |
| | | | **ATTITUDE** | | |
| 2/19/83 | **42** | 14 | 1 We Got The Juice........................................... | | Atlantic 89879 |
| 7/16/83 | **90** | 2 | 2 Love Me Tonight ........................................... | | Atlantic 89823 |
| | | | **ATTITUDES** | | |
| | | | Los Angeles-based quartet of top sidemen: David Foster (keyboards, composer), Danny Kortchmar (guitar), Paul Stallworth (bass) and Jim Keltner (drums). | | |
| 8/28/76 | **43** | 9 | 1 Sweet Summer Music ..................................... | 94 | Dark Horse 10011 |
| | | | **AURRA** | | |
| | | | Consisted of ex-Slave members Steve Washington and Tom Lockett, Jr. (saxophones), with Philip Fields (keyboards) and vocalists Starleana Young and Curt Jones. Young and Jones later formed the duo Deja. | | |
| 6/14/80 | **86** | 3 | 1 In The Mood (To Groove)................................ | | Dream 0355 |
| 4/18/81 | **16** | 22 | 2 Are You Single ............................................. | | Salsoul 2139 |
| 12/05/81+ | **6** | 20 | 3 **Make Up Your Mind** .................................... | 71 | Salsoul 7017 |
| 4/17/82 | **36** | 9 | 4 A Little Love ................................................ | | Salsoul 7023 |
| 7/10/82 | **64** | 8 | 5 Checking You Out ......................................... | | Salsoul 7027 |
| 12/18/82+ | **40** | 11 | 6 Such A Feeling ............................................. | | Salsoul 7043 |
| 4/30/83 | **78** | 4 | 7 Baby Love ................................................... | | Salsoul 7049 |
| | | | **PATTI AUSTIN** | | |
| | | | Born on 8/10/48 in New York City. Back-up work in New York. God-daughter of Quincy Jones. Appeared in the 1988 film "Tucker". Also see Yutaka. | | |
| 7/12/69 | **46** | 2 | 1 Family Tree ................................................. | | United Art. 50520 |
| 2/05/77 | **63** | 6 | 2 Say You Love Me .......................................... | | CTI 33 |
| 2/04/78 | **90** | 4 | 3 We're In Love .............................................. | | CTI 41 |
| 6/28/80 | **45** | 11 | 4 Body Language ............................................. | | CTI 9600 |
| 8/08/81 | **24** | 18 | 5 Do You Love Me? .......................................... | | Qwest 49754 |
| 11/28/81+ | **55** | 11 | 6 Every Home Should Have One ........................ | 62 | Qwest 49854 |
| 3/27/82+ | **9** | 38 | 7●**Baby, Come To Me** ...................................... PATTI AUSTIN with JAMES INGRAM | 1 | Qwest 50036 |
| 5/14/83 | **6** | 21 | 8 **How Do You Keep The Music Playing** ............. JAMES INGRAM & PATTI AUSTIN theme from the film "Best Friends" | 45 | Qwest 29618 |
| 7/09/83 | **92** | 3 | 9 In My Life .................................................. PATTI AUSTIN & JERRY BUTLER | | CTI 59 |
| 2/04/84 | **15** | 14 | 10 It's Gonna Be Special..................................... from the film "Two Of A Kind" | 82 | Qwest 29373 |
| 4/21/84 | **33** | 11 | 11 Rhythm Of The Street .................................. | | Qwest 29305 |
| 7/21/84 | **49** | 10 | 12 Shoot The Moon............................................ | | Qwest 29234 |
| 2/16/85 | **39** | 10 | 13 Gimme, Gimme, Gimme ................................ NARADA MICHAEL WALDEN with PATTI AUSTIN | 106 | Warner 29077 |
| 10/19/85 | **24** | 16 | 14 Honey For The Bees ...................................... | | Qwest 28935 |
| 3/08/86 | **13** | 16 | 15 The Heat Of Heat ......................................... | 55 | Qwest 28788 |
| 7/12/86 | **72** | 10 | 16 Gettin' Away With Murder .............................. | | Qwest 28659 |
| | | | **SIL AUSTIN** | | |
| | | | Born Sylvester Austin in 1929 in Donellon, Florida. Tenor saxophonist. Played with the Tiny Bradshaw Band before forming own group. | | |
| 11/17/56 | **3** | 9 | 1 **Slow Walk**................................................[I] Best Seller #3 / Juke Box #4 / Jockey #6 | 17 | Mercury 70963 |
| | | | **AVALANCHE "77"** | | |
| 5/21/77 | **98** | 1 | 1 Mister Boogie Man........................................ | | Boblo 513 |
| 7/09/77 | **98** | 2 | 2 Feel Like Being Funky ................................... | | Boblo 527 |

| DEBUT DATE | PEAK POS | WKS CHR | | ARTIST — Record Title | POP POS | Label & Number |
|---|---|---|---|---|---|---|
| | | | | **FRANKIE AVALON** | | |
| | | | | Born Francis Avallone on 9/18/39 in Philadelphia. Teen idol managed by Bob Marucci. Worked in bands in Atlantic City, NJ in 1953. Radio and TV with Paul Whiteman, mid-50s. Singer/trumpet player with Rocco & His Saints in 1957. Co-starred in many films with Annette. In films "Disc Jockey Jamboree" (1957), "Guns Of The Timberland" (1960), "The Carpetbaggers" (1962) and "Back To The Beach" (1987). | | |
| 2/03/58 | 8 | 8 | 1 | **Dede Dinah** .............................................. Jockey #8 / Best Seller #11 | 7 | Chancellor 1011 |
| 8/11/58 | 10 | 5 | 2 | **Ginger Bread** ........................................... Jockey #10 / Best Seller #14 | 9 | Chancellor 1021 |
| 3/02/59 | 10 | 11 | 3 | **Venus** ...................................................... | 1 | Chancellor 1031 |
| 7/20/59 | 26 | 2 | 4 | Bobby Sox To Stockings .............................. | 8 | Chancellor 1036 |
| 1/11/60 | 6 | 7 | 5 | **Why** ......................................................... | 1 | Chancellor 1045 |
| 2/21/76 | 97 | 3 | 6 | Venus ........................................................ disco version of Frankie's 1959 hit | 46 | De-Lite 1578 |
| | | | | **AVERAGE WHITE BAND** | | |
| | | | | Vocal/instrumental group formed in Scotland in 1972. Consisted of Alan Gorrie (vocal, bass), Hamish Stuart (vocal, guitar), Onnie McIntyre (vocal, guitar), Malcolm Duncan (saxophone), Roger Ball (keyboards, saxophone) and Robbie McIntosh (drums). McIntosh died of drug poisoning in 1974, replaced by Steve Ferrone. | | |
| 11/23/74+ | 5 | 20 | 1 ● | **Pick Up The Pieces** ................................... [I] | 1 | Atlantic 3229 |
| 4/12/75 | 7 | 17 | 2 | **Cut The Cake** ........................................... | 10 | Atlantic 3261 |
| 8/16/75 | 25 | 11 | 3 | If I Ever Lose This Heaven ........................... | 39 | Atlantic 3285 |
| 11/15/75 | 22 | 13 | 4 | School Boy Crush......................................... | 33 | Atlantic 3304 |
| 9/04/76 | 21 | 10 | 5 | Queen Of My Soul ....................................... | 40 | Atlantic 3354 |
| 11/13/76+ | 35 | 13 | 6 | A Love Of Your Own .................................... | 101 | Atlantic 3363 |
| 3/05/77 | 55 | 9 | 7 | Cloudy ...................................................... | | Atlantic 3388 |
| 6/04/77 | 21 | 14 | 8 | Get It Up ................................................... | | Atlantic 3402 |
| | | | | **BEN E. KING & AWB** | | |
| 9/10/77 | 25 | 12 | 9 | A Star In The Ghetto ................................... | | Atlantic 3427 |
| | | | | **AWB & BEN E. KING** | | |
| 5/20/78 | 33 | 9 | 10 | Your Love Is A Miracle................................. | | Atlantic 3481 |
| 3/31/79 | 32 | 13 | 11 | Walk On By................................................. 1-4, 6-7, 10-11 shown only as: **AWB** | 92 | Atlantic 3563 |
| 6/14/80 | 40 | 9 | 12 | Let's Go 'Round Again ................................. | 53 | Arista 0515 |
| 9/20/80 | 60 | 6 | 13 | For You, For Love ........................................ | 106 | Arista 0553 |
| | | | | **ROY AYERS** | | |
| | | | | Born on 9/10/40 in Los Angeles. Vibraphone player. With Herbie Mann in the early 60s. Formed own group, Ubiquity, in 1970. Also see Herbie Mann. | | |
| | | | | **ROY AYERS UBIQUITY:** | | |
| 5/01/76 | 70 | 6 | 1 | Mystic Voyage ............................................ [I] | | Polydor 14316 |
| 7/31/76 | 70 | 6 | 2 | The Golden Rod ........................................... [I] | | Polydor 14337 |
| 9/03/77 | 19 | 17 | 3 | Running Away............................................. | | Polydor 14415 |
| | | | | **ROY AYERS:** | | |
| 2/04/78 | 29 | 16 | 4 | Freaky Deaky .............................................. | | Polydor 14451 |
| 10/21/78 | 56 | 8 | 5 | Get On Up, Get On Down .............................. | | Polydor 14509 |
| 12/23/78+ | 59 | 8 | 6 | Heat Of The Beat ........................................ | | Polydor 14523 |
| | | | | **ROY AYERS/WAYNE HENDERSON** | | |
| 6/30/79 | 41 | 11 | 7 | Love Will Bring Us Back Together.................. | | Polydor 14573 |
| 11/24/79+ | 32 | 17 | 8 | Don't Stop The Feeling.................................. | | Polydor 2037 |
| 3/08/80 | 73 | 3 | 9 | What You Won't Do For Love ........................ | | Polydor 2066 |
| 11/10/84 | 35 | 13 | 10 | In The Dark ................................................ | | Columbia 04653 |
| 4/06/85 | 89 | 3 | 11 | Poo Poo La La ............................................. | | Columbia 04821 |
| 10/19/85 | 49 | 9 | 12 | Slip n' Slide ............................................... | | Columbia 05613 |
| 1/25/86 | 20 | 12 | 13 | Hot............................................................. | | Columbia 05752 |
| 5/10/86 | 62 | 7 | 14 | Programmed For Love................................... | | Columbia 05874 |

# B

| DEBUT DATE | PEAK POS | WKS CHR | | ARTIST — Record Title | POP POS | Label & Number |
|---|---|---|---|---|---|---|
| | | | | **BABYFACE** | | |
| | | | | Male vocalist/instrumentalist. Co-wrote Pebbles' "Girlfriend" and The Whispers' "Rock Steady" with L.A. Reid (of The Deele). | | |
| 4/04/87 | 42 | 11 | 1 | Lovers ....................................................... | | Solar 70004 |
| 6/27/87 | 8 | 16 | 2 | **I Love You Babe** ....................................... | | Solar 70009 |

| DEBUT DATE | PEAK POS | WKS CHR | ARTIST — Record Title | POP POS | Label & Number |
|---|---|---|---|---|---|
| | | | **BABYFACE — Continued** | | |
| 12/05/87+ | **29** | 16 | 3 Mary Mack ........................................ | | Solar 70016 |
| 4/16/88 | **65** | 9 | 4 If We Try ......................................... | | Solar 70022 |
| | | | **BAD BOYS featuring K LOVE** | | |
| 8/17/85 | **69** | 8 | 1 Bad Boys ......................................... | | Starlite 959 |
| | | | **BAD GIRLS** | | |
| 12/12/81+ | **67** | 8 | 1 Too Through ..................................... | | BC 4011 |
| | | | **WALLY BADAROU** | | |
| 3/01/86 | **33** | 12 | 1 Chief Inspector ........................... [I] | | Island 99557 |
| | | | **J.R. BAILEY** Born James Bailey. Singer, formerly with the Velvetones, Crickets and the New Yorkers. With the Cadillacs from 1956-72. Wrote "Everybody Plays The Fool" hit for Main Ingredient, "Love, Love, Love" hit for Donny Hathaway. | | |
| 12/28/68 | **49** | 1 | 1 Love Won't Wear Off................................... | | Calla 158 |
| 7/01/72 | **31** | 9 | 2 Love, Love, Love................................... | | Toy 3801 |
| 1/06/73 | **29** | 8 | 3 After Hours ....................................... | | Toy 3805 |
| 6/29/74 | **90** | 3 | 4 Everything I Want I See In You ..................... | | MAM 3639 |
| 8/16/75 | **77** | 5 | 5 The Entertainer (If They Could Only See Me Now)...................................... adaptation of "The Entertainer" by Scott Joplin | | Midland I. 10305 |
| | | | **PEARL BAILEY** Born on 3/29/18 in Newport News, Virginia. Brother Bill also an entertainer. First worked as a dancer in Philadelphia. Band vocalist from 1933-45. Appeared in several films. Married drummer Louis Bellson in 1952. Long run in Broadway musical "Hello, Dolly" in the 60s. Frequent bouts with ill health. | | |
| 1/12/46 | **4** | 1 | 1 **15 Years (And I'm Still Serving Time)**........... with Mitchell Ayres Orchestra | | Columbia 36837 |
| | | | **PHILIP BAILEY** Born on 5/8/51 in Denver. Percussionist/co-lead vocalist with Earth, Wind & Fire since 1971. | | |
| 8/06/83 | **10** | 16 | 1 **I Know**......................................... | | Columbia 03968 |
| 12/17/83+ | **43** | 10 | 2 Trapped.......................................... | | Columbia 04241 |
| 9/29/84 | **61** | 6 | 3 Photogenic Memory ............................. | | Columbia 04607 |
| 12/15/84+ | **3** | 19 | 4●**Easy Lover**.................................... **PHILIP BAILEY with PHIL COLLINS** | 2 | Columbia 04679 |
| 5/04/85 | **56** | 8 | 5 Walking On The Chinese Wall ....................... | 46 | Columbia 04826 |
| 4/19/86 | **20** | 13 | 6 State Of The Heart ............................... | | Columbia 05861 |
| | | | **ANITA BAKER** Born in Memphis on 12/20/57. Lead female vocalist of Chapter 8 from 1976-84. | | |
| 5/21/83 | **49** | 12 | 1 No More Tears/ | | |
| | | 4 | 2 Will You Be Mine ................................. | | Beverly Glen 2005 |
| 8/20/83 | **5** | 20 | 3 **Angel** ......................................... | | Beverly Glen 2010 |
| 12/24/83+ | **28** | 15 | 4 You're The Best Thing Yet ....................... | | Beverly Glen 2011 |
| 4/28/84 | **67** | 8 | 5 Feel The Need.................................... | | Beverly Glen 2013 |
| 3/22/86 | **23** | 13 | 6 Watch Your Step ................................. | | Elektra 69554 |
| 6/14/86 | **2** ² | 24 | 7 **Sweet Love**.................................... | 8 | Elektra 69557 |
| 10/18/86 | **6** | 19 | 8 **Caught Up In The Rapture**...................... | 37 | Elektra 69511 |
| 3/07/87 | **8** | 18 | 9 **Same Ole Love (365 Days A Year)**................. | 44 | Elektra 69484 |
| 7/25/87 | **5** | 20 | 10 **No One In The World**........................... | 44 | Elektra 69456 |
| 8/15/87 | **15** | 15 | 11 Ain't No Need To Worry .......................... **THE WINANS featuring ANITA BAKER** | | Qwest 28274 |
| | | | **LaVERN BAKER** ★★**102**★★ Born Delores Williams on 11/11/29 in Chicago. Recorded as "Little Miss Share Cropper" and "Bea Baker". After working with the Todd Rhodes Orchestra, 1952-53, toured Europe, solo. Returned to work for Atlantic Records and became one of the most popular female R&B singers in the early rock era. | | |
| 1/15/55 | **4** | 15 | 1 **Tweedlee Dee** ................................. Best Seller #4 / Jockey #4 / Juke Box #4 | 14 | Atlantic 1047 |
| 5/07/55 | **3** | 11 | 2 **Bop-Ting-A-Ling/** Jockey #3 / Best Seller #4 / Juke Box #10 | | |
| 5/14/55 | **9** | 4 | 3 **That's All I Need** ............................. Jockey #9 | | Atlantic 1057 |

| DEBUT DATE | PEAK POS | WKS CHR | ARTIST — Record Title | POP POS | Label & Number |
|---|---|---|---|---|---|
| | | | **LaVERN BAKER — Continued** | | |
| 10/22/55 | **2**[3] | 16 | 4 **Play It Fair** .................................. Jockey #2 / Juke Box #2 / Best Seller #3 | | Atlantic 1075 |
| 3/10/56 | **13** | 4 | 5 My Happiness Forever/ Jockey #13 | | |
| 3/24/56 | **15** | 1 | 6 Get Up Get Up .............................. Jockey #15 | | Atlantic 1087 |
| 9/29/56 | **4** | 7 | 7 **Still**/ Jockey #4 / Best Seller #7 | 97 | |
| 9/29/56 | **7** | 10 | 8 **I Can't Love You Enough** ...................... Jockey #7 / Juke Box #7 | 22 | Atlantic 1104 |
| 12/15/56+ | **1**[1] | 18 | 9 **Jim Dandy**/ Jockey #1 / Juke Box #2 / Best Seller #3 | 17 | |
| | | 2 | 10 Tra La La ..................................... 1-4 & 9-10 shown as: **LaVERN BAKER & THE GLIDERS** Best Seller flip | 94 | Atlantic 1116 |
| 5/13/57 | **7** | 6 | 11 **Jim Dandy Got Married** ...................... Jockey #7 / Best Seller #11 | 76 | Atlantic 1136 |
| 10/20/58 | **24** | 4 | 12 It's So Fine ................................... | | Atlantic 2001 |
| 12/22/58+ | **2**[5] | 19 | 13 **I Cried A Tear** ............................... | 6 | Atlantic 2007 |
| 5/04/59 | **5** | 12 | 14 **I Waited Too Long** .......................... | 33 | Atlantic 2021 |
| 8/10/59 | **12** | 10 | 15 So High So Low .............................. | 52 | Atlantic 2033 |
| 12/14/59 | **18** | 4 | 16 Tiny Tim ..................................... | 63 | Atlantic 2041 |
| 3/07/60 | **13** | 4 | 17 Shake A Hand ................................ | | Atlantic 2048 |
| 5/01/61 | **17** | 5 | 18 Saved ........................................ | 37 | Atlantic 2099 |
| 12/15/62+ | **9** | 8 | 19 **See See Rider** .............................. | 34 | Atlantic 2167 |
| 2/13/65 | **31** | 5 | 20 Fly Me To The Moon .......................... | 84 | Atlantic 2267 |
| 2/05/66 | **37** | 3 | 21 Think Twice ................................... **JACKIE WILSON & LaVERN BAKER** | 93 | Brunswick 55287 |
| | | | **THE BALLADS** Vocal group formed in Oakland in 1961. Consisted of Nathan Robertson, Jon Foster, Rico Thompson and Lesley LaPalma. | | |
| 6/29/68 | **8** | 12 | 1 **God Bless Our Love** ........................... | 65 | Venture 615 |
| | | | **HANK BALLARD & THE MIDNIGHTERS** ★★**74**★★ Vocal group from Detroit, formed in 1952 as The Royals: Henry Booth, Charles Sutton, Lawson Smith and Sonny Woods. In late 1953, Henry "Hank" Ballard (b: 11/18/36, Detroit) replaced Smith and became lead singer. Name changed to Midnighters in 1954. Had the original recording of "The Twist", written by Ballard, who is still active as a solo artist. After group disbanded in 1965, re-formed with Frank Stadford, Walter Miller and Wesley Hargrove. Worked in the James Brown Revue. | | |
| | | | **THE ROYALS:** | | |
| 8/01/53 | **6** | 9 | 1 **Get It** ...................................... Juke Box #6 / Best Seller #8 | | Federal 12133 |
| | | | **THE MIDNIGHTERS Formerly THE ROYALS:** | | |
| 4/24/54 | **1**[7] | 26 | 2 **Work With Me Annie** ......................... Best Seller #1(7) / Juke Box #1(4) pop version of tune known as "Dance With Me Henry" | 22 | Federal 12169 |
| 7/10/54 | **2**[1] | 17 | 3 **Sexy Ways** .................................. Juke Box #2 / Best Seller #3 | | Federal 12185 |
| | | | **THE MIDNIGHTERS:** | | |
| 9/04/54 | **1**[2] | 14 | 4 **Annie Had A Baby** ........................... Best Seller #1 / Juke Box #3 | 23 | Federal 12195 |
| 12/11/54 | **10** | 1 | 5 **Annie's Aunt Fannie** ......................... Best Seller #10 | | Federal 12200 |
| 6/18/55 | **14** | 1 | 6 Henry's Got Flat Feet (Can't Dance No More) ...... Best Seller #14 | | Federal 12224 |
| 8/20/55 | **10** | 1 | 7 **It's Love Baby (24 Hours A Day)** ................. Best Seller #10 / Jockey #10 | | Federal 12227 |
| | | | **HANK BALLARD & THE MIDNIGHTERS:** | | |
| 3/16/59 | **4** | 8 | 8 **Teardrops On Your Letter**/ | 87 | |
| 4/06/59 | **16** | 10 | 9 The Twist .................................... | 28 | King 5171 |
| 4/13/59 | **16** | 6 | 10 Kansas City ................................. | 72 | King 5195 |
| 3/28/60 | **21** | 7 | 11 The Coffee Grind ............................. | | King 5312 |
| 5/30/60 | **2**[2] | 21 | 12 **Finger Poppin' Time** ......................... | 7 | King 5341 |
| 7/25/60 | **6** | 13 | 13 **The Twist** ................................. [R] | 28 | King 5171 |
| 10/10/60 | **1**[3] | 15 | 14 **Let's Go, Let's Go, Let's Go** ................... | 6 | King 5400 |
| 1/16/61 | **3** | 7 | 15 **The Hoochi Coochi Coo** ...................... | 23 | King 5430 |

| DEBUT DATE | PEAK POS | WKS CHR | ARTIST — Record Title | POP POS | Label & Number |
|---|---|---|---|---|---|
| | | | **HANK BALLARD & THE MIDNIGHTERS — Continued** | | |
| 2/20/61 | **17** | 5 | 16 Let's Go Again (Where We Went Last Night)....... | 39 | King 5459 |
| 5/01/61 | **12** | 4 | 17 The Continental Walk ................................... | 33 | King 5491 |
| 6/26/61 | **10** | 10 | 18 **The Float**/ | 92 | |
| 7/24/61 | **3** | 8 | 19 **The Switch-A-Roo**..................................... | 26 | King 5510 |
| 8/21/61 | **9** | 8 | 20 **Nothing But Good** ..................................... | 49 | King 5535 |
| 11/02/68 | **15** | 9 | 21 How You Gonna Get Respect (When You Haven't Cut Your Process Yet)................................ **HANK BALLARD along with "THE DAPPS"** | | King 6196 |
| 11/25/72 | **43** | 3 | 22 From The Love Side.................................... shown only as: **HANK BALLARD** | | Polydor 14128 |
| | | | **AFRIKA BAMBAATAA & SOULSONIC FORCE** Rap/funk group led by New York club D.J. Bambaataa, with his three rappers and turntable whiz D.J. Jazzy Jay. | | |
| 6/12/82 | **4** | 17 | 1 ●**Planet Rock** ........................................ certified gold for the 12″ single | 48 | Tommy Boy 823 |
| 1/29/83 | **36** | 12 | 2 Looking For The Perfect Beat ....................... | | Tommy Boy 831 |
| 3/03/84 | **48** | 10 | 3 Renegades Of Funk................................... | | Tommy Boy 839 |
| 9/15/84 | **87** | 4 | 4 Unity ...................................... **AFRIKA BAMBAATAA & JAMES BROWN** | | Tommy Boy 847 |
| 7/05/86 | **70** | 8 | 5 Bambaataa's Theme (Assault On Precinct 13).. [I] **AFRIKA BAMBAATAA & Family** | | Tommy Boy 879 |
| | | | **BAND OF GOLD** | | |
| 11/17/84 | **62** | 5 | 1 Love Songs Are Back Again .......................... Let's Put It All Together/Betcha By Golly Wow/Side Show/ Have You Seen Her/Reunited/You Make Me Feel Brand New/ Kiss And Say Goodbye - medley | 64 | RCA 13866 |
| | | | **THE BANDWAGON** | | |
| 5/11/68 | **48** | 2 | 1 Baby Make Your Own Sweet Music .................. | | Epic 10255 |
| | | | **BANKS & HAMPTON** Vocal/songwriting duo of Homer Banks and Carl Hampton. | | |
| 4/02/77 | **80** | 4 | 1 I'm Gonna Have To Tell Her .......................... | | Warner 8344 |
| | | | **BUNNY BANKS TRIO** Trio of Clem Moorman (piano), Ernie Ransom (guitar) and Henry Padgett (bass). (No relation to the Buddy Banks Sextet.) | | |
| 1/30/43 | **1**[5] | 12 | 1 **Don't Stop Now** ......................................... vocals by Bonnie Davis & the Picadilly Pipers | | Savoy 102 |
| | | | **DARRELL BANKS** Born Darrell Eubanks in 1938 in Buffalo. Killed by a gunshot in Detroit, in March of 1970. | | |
| 7/16/66 | **2**[1] | 15 | 1 **Open The Door To Your Heart**...................... | 27 | Revilot 201 |
| 10/22/66 | **34** | 4 | 2 Somebody (Somewhere) Needs You .................. | 55 | Revilot 203 |
| | | | **RON BANKS** Born on 5/10/51 in Detroit. Former lead singer of The Dramatics. Also see The Brides Of Funkenstein. | | |
| 10/01/83 | **65** | 7 | 1 Truly Bad ............................................... | | CBS Assoc. 04142 |
| 12/03/83+ | **31** | 14 | 2 Make It Easy On Yourself .............................. | | CBS Assoc. 04242 |
| | | | **ROSE BANKS** | | |
| 5/08/76 | **50** | 9 | 1 Whole New Thing ........................................ | | Motown 1383 |
| | | | **BANZAII** | | |
| 8/23/75 | **81** | 6 | 1 Chinese Kung Fu .................................... [I] | 98 | Scepter 12407 |
| | | | **BAR-KAYS** ★★**56**★★ Vocal/instrumental combo: Jimmy King (guitar), Ronnie Caldwell (organ), James Alexander (bass), Carl Cunningham (drums), Phalon Jones (saxophone) and Ben Cauley (trumpet). Formed by Al Jackson, drummer with Booker T & The MG's. The plane crash that killed Otis Redding (10/10/67) also claimed the lives of all the Bar-Kays except Cauley and Alexander (who were not on the plane). Alexander re-formed the band. Appeared in the film "Wattstax"; much session work at Stax. Lineup since 1987: Larry Dodson (vocals), Harvey Henderson (tenor sax), and Winston Stewart (keyboards). Also see The Newcomers. | | |
| 5/27/67 | **3** | 14 | 1 **Soul Finger**/ [I] | 17 | |
| 8/12/67 | **28** | 7 | 2 Knucklehead.............................. [I] | 76 | Volt 148 |
| 10/28/67 | **36** | 5 | 3 Give Everybody Some ................................ [I] | 91 | Volt 154 |

**33**

| DEBUT DATE | PEAK POS | WKS CHR | ARTIST — Record Title | POP POS | Label & Number |
|---|---|---|---|---|---|
| | | | **BAR-KAYS — Continued** | | |
| 12/25/71+ | **10** | 10 | 4 **Son Of Shaft** | 53 | Volt 4073 |
| 8/21/76 | **5** | 23 | 5 **Shake Your Rump To The Funk** | 23 | Mercury 73833 |
| 2/05/77 | **8** | 13 | 6 **Too Hot To Stop (Pt. 1)** | 74 | Mercury 73888 |
| 5/28/77 | **29** | 12 | 7 Spellbound | | Mercury 73915 |
| 1/07/78 | **11** | 13 | 8 Let's Have Some Fun | 102 | Mercury 73971 |
| 4/08/78 | **22** | 15 | 9 Attitudes | | Mercury 73994 |
| 12/09/78+ | **9** | 17 | 10 **Holy Ghost** | | Stax 3216 |
| 12/23/78+ | **26** | 12 | 11 I'll Dance | | Mercury 74039 |
| 3/10/79 | **14** | 14 | 12 Shine/ | 102 | |
| 6/16/79 | **61** | 6 | 13 Are You Being Real | | Mercury 74048 |
| 10/20/79 | **3** | 18 | 14 **Move Your Boogie Body** | 57 | Mercury 76015 |
| 2/09/80 | **25** | 14 | 15 Today Is The Day | 60 | Mercury 76063 |
| 11/29/80+ | **7** | 17 | 16 Boogie Body Land | | Mercury 76088 |
| 3/28/81 | **42** | 9 | 17 Body Fever | | Mercury 76097 |
| 10/31/81 | **5** | 19 | 18 **Hit And Run** | 101 | Mercury 76123 |
| 3/27/82 | **27** | 10 | 19 Freaky Behavior | | Mercury 76143 |
| 10/23/82 | **9** | 21 | 20 **Do It (Let Me See You Shake)** | | Mercury 76187 |
| 3/19/83 | **13** | 15 | 21 She Talks To Me With Her Body | | Mercury 810435 |
| 3/31/84 | **2**[1] | 19 | 22 **Freakshow On The Dance Floor** | 73 | Mercury 818631 |
| | | | from the film "Breakin'" | | |
| 7/14/84 | **17** | 13 | 23 Dirty Dancer | | Mercury 880045 |
| 10/06/84 | **12** | 16 | 24 Sexomatic | | Mercury 880255 |
| 8/03/85 | **12** | 15 | 25 Your Place Or Mine | | Mercury 880966 |
| 12/07/85 | **67** | 5 | 26 Banging The Walls | | Mercury 884232 |
| 9/12/87 | **9** | 14 | 27 **Certified True** | | Mercury 888837 |
| 12/26/87+ | **56** | 9 | 28 Don't Hang Up | | Mercury 870018 |
| | | | **BARBARA & THE BROWNS** | | |
| 5/02/64 | **97** | 2 | 1 Big Party | *Hot* | Stax 150 |

**BARBARA & THE UNIQUES**
Chicago trio: Barbara Livsey, Gwen Livsey and Doris Lindsey. Barbara had been in the Duettes with Mary-Francis Hayes from 1963-65. Toured with the Five Du-Tones Revue. Uniques disbanded in 1972. In 1981, recorded as "Sas" with Doris Lindsey.

| | | | | | |
|---|---|---|---|---|---|
| 12/12/70+ | **16** | 11 | 1 There It Goes Again | 91 | Arden 3001 |

**CHRIS BARBER'S JAZZ BAND**
Trombonist/leader Barber was born on 4/17/30 in Welwyn Garden City, England. Prolific and popular dixieland-styled band formed in 1949. Lineup on hit song included Barber (trombone), Monty Sunshine (clarinet), Dick Bishop (guitar), Dick Smith (bass) and Ron Bowden (drums).

| | | | | | |
|---|---|---|---|---|---|
| 3/02/59 | **28** | 1 | 1 Petite Fleur (Little Flower) [I] | 5 | Laurie 3022 |
| | | | written in 1952 by jazz great Sidney Bechet | | |

**GATO BARBIERI**
Tenor saxophone player born Leandro Barbieri on 11/28/33 in Rosario, Argentina. Toured Europe with Jim Hall, Lalo Schifrin and Ted Curson in the 60s. With Don Cherry in the late 60s.

| | | | | | |
|---|---|---|---|---|---|
| 1/22/77 | **63** | 7 | 1 Fiesta [I] | 104 | A&M 1885 |

**BOBBY BARE**
Born on 4/7/35 in Ironton, Ohio. Country singer/songwriter/guitarist.

| | | | | | |
|---|---|---|---|---|---|
| 2/09/59 | **16** | 8 | 1 The All American Boy [N] | 2 | Fraternity 835 |
| | | | written by Bill Parsons, but Bobby Bare is the real vocalist on this song (label error listed Parsons as the artist) - upon it's release, Bare was in the Army, so Parsons toured with the hit, lip synching to the record | | |

**BLUE LU BARKER**
Born Louisa Barker on 11/13/13 in New Orleans. Married New Orleans jazz guitarist/ banjo player Danny Barker in 1930. First recorded with Erskine Butterfield as "Lu Blue" in 1938. Worked in New Orleans clubs and on cruise ships into the 70s.

| | | | | | |
|---|---|---|---|---|---|
| 12/11/48+ | **4** | 3 | 1 A Little Bird Told Me | 4 | Capitol 15308 |
| | | | Juke Box #4 | | |
| | | | with Danny Barker's Band | | |

**BEVERLY BARKLEY - see MIAMI DISCO BAND**

**TYRONE BARKLEY**

| | | | | | |
|---|---|---|---|---|---|
| 12/01/79 | **85** | 3 | 1 Man Of Value | | Midsong Int. 1016 |

| DEBUT DATE | PEAK POS | WKS CHR | ARTIST — Record Title | POP POS | Label & Number |
|---|---|---|---|---|---|
| | | | **JIMMY BARNES**<br>Singer from Newark, New Jersey. | | |
| 2/16/59 | **14** | 9 | 1 No Regrets ..................................................... | *90* | Gibraltar 101 |
| | | | **J.J. BARNES**<br>Born James Jay Barnes on 11/30/43 in Detroit. First recorded for Kable in 1960. Member of The Holidays in 1966. | | |
| 2/26/66 | **18** | 11 | 1 Real Humdinger ......................................... | *80* | Ric-Tic 110 |
| 5/20/67 | **9** | 15 | 2 **Baby Please Come Back Home** ...................... | *61* | Grooveeville 1006 |
| 11/04/67 | **44** | 3 | 3 Now That I Got You Back ........................... | | Grooveeville 1008 |
| | | | **KATHY BARNES**<br>Country singer born in Henderson, Kentucky. Sang in duo with brother Larry; later worked with Gene Autry. Went solo in 1975. Recorded soul music in 1978. | | |
| 7/15/78 | **88** | 3 | 1 I'm In Love With Love................................. | | Republic 021 |
| 12/16/78+ | **78** | 7 | 2 Off............................................................. | | Republic 032 |
| | | | **CHARLIE BARNET**<br>Saxophonist/vocalist/band leader, born Charles Daly Barnet on 10/26/13. Nicknamed Mad Mab. First led his own band at age 16 - on an ocean liner. One of the first white band leaders to feature black musicians. Married six times. | | |
| 11/07/42+ | **8** | 4 | 1 **Things Ain't What They Used To Be** ........... [I] | | Decca 18507 |
| 2/13/43 | **2**[1] | 8 | 2 **That Old Black Magic** ................................<br>vocal by Frances Wayne | | Decca 18541 |
| 5/22/43 | **4** | 2 | 3 **Washington Whirligig/** | [I] *20* | |
| 6/05/43 | **3** | 12 | 4 **Oh! Miss Jaxon**.......................................<br>vocal by Peanuts Holland | | Decca 18547 |
| | | | **THE BARONS**<br>West Coast vocal group. | | |
| 1/14/56 | **14** | 2 | 1 I Know I Was Wrong .................................<br>Jockey #14 | | Imperial 5359 |
| | | | **RICHARD BARRETT - see THE CHANTELS** | | |
| | | | **RAY BARRETTO**<br>Percussionist born in Brooklyn in 1939. With Tito Puente and Herbie Mann before forming his own group. | | |
| 5/25/63 | **17** | 3 | 1 El Watusi..............................................[F-N] | *17* | Tico 419 |
| | | | **DON BARRON - see MASTER OF CEREMONY** | | |
| | | | **KEITH BARROW**<br>Singer from Chicago. Died on 10/22/83 (29). Had own gospel group, the Soul Shakers, at age 14. Received MS in educational psychology from New York University. His mother is the vice president of the PUSH organization. | | |
| 6/03/78 | **26** | 15 | 1 You Know You Wanna Be Loved ...................... | | Columbia 10722 |
| 2/03/79 | **79** | 8 | 2 Turn Me Up (Part 1) ................................... | | Columbia 10901 |
| | | | **BARRY & THE TAMERLANES**<br>Pop trio led by Barry DeVorzon. | | |
| 11/23/63 | **23** | 1 | 1 I Wonder What She's Doing Tonight ................ | *21* | Valiant 6034 |
| | | | **CLAUDJA BARRY**<br>Dance/disco singer from Jamaica. Raised in Toronto, Canada. Appeared in the musicals "Hair" and "Catch My Soul". | | |
| 5/26/79 | **37** | 9 | 1 Boogie Woogie Dancin' Shoes .......................... | *56* | Chrysalis 2313 |
| 11/29/86 | **98** | 2 | 2 Down And Counting .................................... | | Epic 06308 |
| 3/28/87 | **33** | 11 | 3 Can't You Feel My Heart Beat...................... | | Epic 06669 |
| 7/11/87 | **60** | 8 | 4 Secret Affair .............................................. | | Epic 07198 |
| | | | **JOE BARRY**<br>Singer/guitarist born Joe Barrios in Cut Off, Louisiana. | | |
| 5/01/61 | **15** | 4 | 1 I'm A Fool To Care ..................................... | *24* | Smash 1702 |
| | | | **LEN BARRY**<br>Born Leonard Borisoff on 12/6/42 in Philadelphia. In group, The Dovells, 1957-63. | | |
| 9/25/65 | **11** | 14 | 1 1-2-3 ........................................................ | *2* | Decca 31827 |

| DEBUT DATE | PEAK POS | WKS CHR | ARTIST — Record Title | POP POS | Label & Number |
|---|---|---|---|---|---|
| | | | **DAVE BARTHOLOMEW** Trumpeter/vocalist, born on 12/24/20 in Edgard, Louisiana. Formed own band in New Orleans in 1946 and became the first to record with R&B artists Roy Brown and Fats Domino. Writer/arranger/bandleader for Fats Domino, Lloyd Price, Shirley & Lee, The Spiders, and Bobby Mitchell. Band included Lee Allen and Earl Palmer. | | |
| 2/11/50 | **14** | 1 | 1 Country Boy.................................................... Juke Box #14 | | DeLuxe 3223 |
| | | | **CHRIS BARTLEY** Singer/guitarist, born on 4/17/49 in New York City. Sang with the Soulful Inspirations and own group, the Mindbenders, in the mid-60s. | | |
| 7/22/67 | **10** | 11 | **1 The Sweetest Thing This Side Of Heaven** ....... | *32* | Vando 101 |
| | | | **GARY BARTZ** Sax player from Baltimore. Attended Juilliard School. Worked with Art Blakey, McCoy Tyner, and Miles Davis. First solo recording in 1968 for Milestone. | | |
| 9/10/77 | **95** | 3 | 1 Love Ballad................................................. [I] | | Capitol 4462 |
| 8/12/78 | **89** | 5 | 2 Shake Your Body ........................................... | | Capitol 4600 |
| 6/14/80 | **93** | 2 | 3 Music........................................................ [I] | | Arista 0514 |
| | | | **COUNT BASIE** Born William Basie on 8/21/04 in Red Bank, New Jersey. Died on 4/26/84. Pianist/organist/band leader. Learned music and piano from mother, organ from Fats Waller. With Walter Page's Blue Devils, and Bennie Moten's band. Leader of Barons Of Rhythm with Buster Smith in 1935. Nicknamed "Count" at this time. First recorded with own band in 1937 for Decca. Appeared in many films and continued touring into the 70s. Also see Illinois Jacquet. | | |
| 5/22/43 | **6** | 6 | **1 Rusty Dusty Blues** ...................................... | *18* | Columbia 36675 |
| 3/17/45 | **6** | 3 | **2 Red Bank Boogie** ...................................... [I] | | Columbia 36766 |
| 9/15/45 | **3** | 1 | **3 Jimmy's Blues**........................................... 1 & 3: vocals by Jimmy Rushing | *10* | Columbia 36831 |
| 2/15/47 | **2**¹ | 6 | **4 Open The Door, Richard!** ........................... [N] vocals by Harry Edison, Bill Johnson & Ensemble | *1* | Victor 20-2127 |
| 7/09/55 | **2**² | 20 | **5 Every Day** ................................................ Best Seller #2 / Juke Box #2 / Jockey #6 vocal by Joe Williams (also see 1952 version by Williams) | | Clef 89149 |
| 2/04/56 | **8** | 3 | **6 April In Paris** .......................................... [I] Juke Box #8 | *28* | Clef 89162 |
| 3/09/68 | **26** | 6 | 7 For Your Precious Love.................................. **JACKIE WILSON & COUNT BASIE** | *49* | Brunswick 55365 |
| 5/04/68 | **37** | 4 | **8 Chain Gang**.............................................. **JACKIE WILSON & COUNT BASIE** | *84* | Brunswick 55373 |
| | | | **FONTELLA BASS** Born on 7/3/40 in St. Louis. Vocalist/pianist/organist. Mother was a member of Clara Ward Gospel Troupe. Sang in church choirs; with Oliver Sain Band, St. Louis; with Little Milton blues show to 1964. Married to trumpet player Lester Bowie. | | |
| 2/06/65 | **5** | 15 | **1 Don't Mess Up A Good Thing**........................ **FONTELLA BASS & BOBBY McCLURE** | *33* | Checker 1097 |
| 6/19/65 | **27** | 6 | 2 You'll Miss Me (When I'm Gone) ....................... **FONTELLA BASS & BOBBY McCLURE** | *91* | Checker 1111 |
| 9/25/65 | **1**⁴ | 19 | **3 Rescue Me**............................................... | *4* | Checker 1120 |
| 1/29/66 | **13** | 7 | 4 Recovery .................................................. | *37* | Checker 1131 |
| 4/23/66 | **31** | 5 | 5 I Can't Rest/ | | |
| 5/07/66 | **33** | 2 | 6 I Surrender ............................................... | *78* | Checker 1137 |
| 9/17/66 | **34** | 7 | 7 You'll Never Ever Know................................. | | Checker 1147 |
| | | | **SHIRLEY BASSEY** Born on 1/8/37 in Cardiff, Wales. | | |
| 7/14/73 | **67** | 5 | 1 Never, Never, Never ..................................... | *48* | United Art. 211 |
| | | | **JOE BATAAN** Born Bataan Nitollano in 1942 in New York City. Afro-Filipino ancestry. First recorded in 1966. | | |
| 9/13/69 | **41** | 3 | 1 Crystal Blue Persuasion ............................... | | Uptite 0014 |
| 2/08/75 | **59** | 12 | 2 The Bottle (La Botella) ............................... [I] shown only as: **BATAAN** | *102* | Salsoul 8701 |
| | | | **BAZUKA** Instrumental studio group assembled by producer Tony Camillo. | | |
| 3/22/75 | **29** | 20 | 1 Dynomite - Part I ....................................... [I] | *10* | A&M 1666 |
| 12/06/75 | **92** | 4 | 2 Love Explosion ........................................... | | A&M 1744 |

**36**

| DEBUT DATE | PEAK POS | WKS CHR | ARTIST — Record Title | POP POS | Label & Number |
|---|---|---|---|---|---|
| | | | **THE B.B.&Q. BAND** Studio musician quartet: Kevin Robinson, Tony Bridges, Cheili Minucci and Kevin Nance. Group named for Brooklyn, Bronx, and Queens. | | |
| 7/18/81 | **8** | 18 | 1 **On The Beat** ........................................ | | Capitol 4993 |
| 12/12/81+ | **72** | 7 | 2 Time For Love ............................................. | | Capitol 5071 |
| 7/17/82 | **21** | 15 | 3 Imagination.................................. | | Capitol 5118 |
| 3/15/86 | **72** | 8 | 4 On The Shelf ............................................. | | In Your Face 1775 |
| | | | **B.B.C.S.& A.** | | |
| 5/22/82 | **82** | 3 | 1 Rock Shock..................................... | | Sam 12346 |
| | | | **THE BEACH BOYS** Group formed in Hawthorne, California in 1061. Consisted of brothers Brian (keyboards, bass), Carl (guitar), and Dennis Wilson (drums); their cousin Mike Love (lead vocals, saxophone), and Al Jardine (guitar). Known in high school as Kenny & The Cadets, Carl & The Passions, then The Pendletones. First recorded for X/Candix in 1961. Jardine was replaced by David Marks from March, 1962 to March, 1963. Brian replaced by Bruce Johnston for personal appearances since April, 1965. Dennis Wilson drowned on 12/28/83 (39). Brian active again in 1987. Also see Fat Boys. | | |
| 4/20/63 | **20** | 8 | 1 Surfin' U.S.A. ......................................... | *3* | Capitol 4932 |
| 8/31/63 | **18** | 6 | 2 Surfer Girl/ | *7* | |
| 8/24/63 | **28** | 2 | 3 Little Deuce Coupe.................................... | *15* | Capitol 5009 |
| 11/16/63 | **27** | 2 | 4 Be True To Your School ............................. | *6* | Capitol 5069 |
| | | | featuring cheerleading by The Honeys, and the march "On Wisconsin" | | |
| | | | **EDDIE BEALE SEXTET - see TONI HARPER** | | |
| | | | **WALTER BEASLEY** Contemporary jazz-R&B saxophonist/singer/songwriter born in southern California. Began playing sax professionally at age 14. Formerly a music professor at the Boston Berklee School of Music. | | |
| 12/05/87+ | **49** | 13 | 1 I'm So Happy................................... | | Polydor 887163 |
| 5/07/88 | **79** | 6 | 2 On The Edge ............................... [I] | | Polydor 887413 |
| | | | **BEASTIE BOYS** New York white rap trio formed in 1981, consisting of King Ad-Rock (Adam Horovitz - son of playwright Israel Horovitz), MCA (Adam Yauch) and Mike D (Michael Diamond). | | |
| 5/17/86 | **55** | 8 | 1 Hold It, Now Hit It ................................. | | Def Jam 05864 |
| 11/15/86 | **22** | 13 | 2 It's The New Style/ | | |
| 12/06/86+ | **34** | 13 | 3 Paul Revere ........................................ | | Def Jam 06341 |
| 4/11/87 | **83** | 5 | 4 Brass Monkey.................................... | *48* | Def Jam 07020 |
| | | | **BEATMASTER** | | |
| 7/07/84 | **79** | 6 | 1 Lipservice.................................... | | Tommy Boy 842 |
| | | | **THE BEAVERS - see JIMMY BRISCOE** | | |
| | | | **BECK FAMILY** Family group from Philadelphia, consisting of brothers Tony, Tyrone and Menelick "Mendy" and sister Joanna Beck with cousins Donnie Wilson and Nick Mundy. Worked as gospel group until 1969. Another sister, Charlotte, records in Sweden as "Sven & Lotte Hedlund". | | |
| 4/07/79 | **43** | 9 | 1 Can't Shake The Feeling.............................. | | Lejoint 34003 |
| | | | **BEE GEES** Pop trio of brothers from Manchester, England: Barry (b: 9/1/47) and twins Robin and Maurice Gibb (b: 12/22/49). First performed December of 1955. | | |
| 7/24/76 | **4** | 14 | 1● **You Should Be Dancing** ............................. | *1* | RSO 853 |
| 11/06/76 | **37** | 16 | 2● Love So Right ..................................... | *3* | RSO 859 |
| 1/29/77 | **31** | 12 | 3 Boogie Child .......................................... | *12* | RSO 867 |
| 1/21/78 | **4** | 17 | 4▲ **Stayin' Alive** ...................................... | *1* | RSO 885 |
| 3/04/78 | **8** | 14 | 5▲ **Night Fever**.................................. | *1* | RSO 889 |
| | | | above 2: from the film "Saturday Night Fever" | | |
| 12/02/78+ | **10** | 15 | 6▲ **Too Much Heaven** ............................... | *1* | RSO 913 |
| 2/17/79 | **44** | 8 | 7▲ Tragedy........................................... | *1* | RSO 918 |
| 5/05/79 | **57** | 6 | 8● Love You Inside Out .............................. | *1* | RSO 925 |
| 7/02/83 | **77** | 4 | 9 The Woman In You..................................... | *24* | RSO 813173 |

| DEBUT DATE | PEAK POS | WKS CHR | ARTIST — Record Title | POP POS | Label & Number |
|---|---|---|---|---|---|
| | | | **JIMMY BEE with ERNIE FIELDS JR. ORCH.** Vocalist from Baltimore. To Los Angeles in 1956. Back-up vocals for Specialty label. With Billy Williams Revue from 1959-63. Fields is son of trombonist/bandleader Ernie Fields. | | |
| 5/15/76 | 91 | 2 | 1 Breakin' Up Is Hard To Do .............................. | | Calla 111 |
| | | | **THE BEGINNING OF THE END** Consisted of brothers Raphael "Ray" (organ), Liroy "Roy" (guitar), Frank "Bud" Munnings (drums) and Fred Henfield (bass) - from the Bahamas. | | |
| 5/08/71 | 7 | 14 | 1 **Funky Nassau-Part I**.............................. | 15 | Alston 4595 |
| | | | **HARRY BELAFONTE** Folk singer/actor, born Harold George Belafonte, Jr. on 3/1/27 in Harlem. | | |
| 2/23/57 | 7 | 3 | 1 **Banana Boat (Day-O)**.............................. Best Seller #7 / Jockey #9 / Juke Box #9 | 5 | Victor 6771 |
| 4/06/57 | 10 | 5 | 2 **Mama Look At Bubu** .............................. Best Seller #10 | 11 | Victor 6830 |
| | | | **BELL & JAMES** Duo of Leroy Bell and Casey James. Began as songwriting team for Bell's uncle, producer Thom Bell. | | |
| 11/18/78+ | 7 | 24 | 1●**Livin' It Up (Friday Night)** ............................ | 15 | A&M 2069 |
| 5/12/79 | 54 | 8 | 2 You Never Know What You've Got.................. | 103 | A&M 2137 |
| 10/27/79 | 65 | 5 | 3 Shakedown ....................................... | | A&M 2185 |
| 12/15/79+ | 50 | 11 | 4 Only Make Believe............................... | | A&M 2204 |
| | | | **THE BELL NOTES** Quintet from Long Island, NY: Carl Bonura (sax), Ray Ceroni (guitar), Lenny Giamblavo (bass), Peter Kane (piano) and John Casey (drums). | | |
| 3/16/59 | 19 | 4 | 1 I've Had It................................... | 6 | Time 1004 |
| | | | **ARCHIE BELL & THE DRELLS**   ★★141★★ Archie was born on 9/1/44 in Henderson, Texas. Lead singer of the Drells, vocal group from Leo Smith Junior High School in Houston. First recorded for Ovid in 1967. Recorded "Tighten Up" with group consisting of Bell, Huey "Billy" Butler, Joe Cross and James Wise. Bell was in US Army at time of hit. Later recordings consisted of Bell, Wise, Lee Bell and Willie Parnell. Still active in Seaboard "beach" music scene. Also see the Philadelphia International All Stars. | | |
| 4/06/68 | 1² | 15 | 1●**Tighten Up**................................... with the TSU Tornadoes band | 1 | Atlantic 2478 |
| 8/03/68 | 5 | 10 | 2 **I Can't Stop Dancing** .......................... | 9 | Atlantic 2534 |
| 10/19/68 | 17 | 7 | 3 Do The Choo Choo/ | 44 | |
| 11/30/68 | 25 | 3 | 4 Love Will Rain On You.......................... | | Atlantic 2559 |
| 1/04/69 | 6 | 10 | 5 **There's Gonna Be A Showdown** ................... | 21 | Atlantic 2583 |
| 4/12/69 | 40 | 2 | 6 I Love My Baby............................... | 94 | Atlantic 2612 |
| 6/28/69 | 13 | 9 | 7 Girl You're Too Young ......................... | 59 | Atlantic 2644 |
| 9/20/69 | 36 | 5 | 8 My Balloon's Going Up ........................ | 87 | Atlantic 2663 |
| 1/03/70 | 46 | 3 | 9 A World Without Music ........................ | 90 | Atlantic 2693 |
| 11/28/70 | 33 | 5 | 10 Wrap It Up.................................. a pop hit for the Fabulous Thunderbirds in 1986 (POS 50) | 93 | Atlantic 2768 |
| 3/03/73 | 11 | 10 | 11 Dancing To Your Music ....................... | 61 | Glades 1707 |
| 6/23/73 | 36 | 9 | 12 Ain't Nothing For A Man In Love/ | | |
| | | 5 | 13 You Never Know What's On A Woman's Mind... | | Glades 1711 |
| 6/14/75 | 25 | 13 | 14 I Could Dance All Night....................... | | TSOP 4767 |
| 12/27/75+ | 42 | 9 | 15 The Soul City Walk .......................... | | TSOP 4774 |
| 2/28/76 | 7 | 12 | 16 **Let's Groove (Part 1)**........................ | | TSOP 4775 |
| 4/09/77 | 68 | 7 | 17 Everybody Have A Good Time .................. | | Phil. Int. 3615 |
| 9/17/77 | 63 | 14 | 18 Glad You Could Make It ...................... | | Phil. Int. 3632 |
| 1/21/78 | 56 | 6 | 19 I've Been Missing You ........................ | | Phil. Int. 3637 |
| 8/11/79 | 21 | 16 | 20 Strategy .................................... | | Phil. Int. 3710 |
| 5/09/81 | 49 | 11 | 21 Any Time Is Right ........................... shown only as: **ARCHIE BELL** | | Becket 45 |
| | | | **JERRY BELL** | | |
| 5/02/81 | 88 | 3 | 1 Love Will Make It All Right .......................... | | MCA 51077 |
| | | | **MADELINE BELL** In cast of "Black Nativity", toured England in the mid-60s; remained there. Formed group Blue Mink, 1969-73. Commercial jingle singer since then. | | |
| 3/09/68 | 32 | 8 | 1 I'm Gonna Make You Love Me ...................... | 26 | Philips 40517 |

| DEBUT DATE | PEAK POS | WKS CHR | ARTIST — Record Title | POP POS | Label & Number |
|---|---|---|---|---|---|
| | | | **RUEBEN BELL** | | |
| 10/07/72 | **38** | 7 | 1 It's Too Late ................................................. | | DeLuxe 140 |
| | | | **WILLIAM BELL** ★★**180**★★ | | |
| | | | Born William Yarborough on 7/16/39 in Memphis. Own Peachtree and Wilbe labels. With Rufus Thomas band in 1953. Formed vocal group the Del Rios with Harrison Austin (tenor), Melvin Jones (baritone) and David Brown (bass). With Phineas Newborn band in the late 50s. In US Army from 1962-66. | | |
| 7/09/66 | **27** | 8 | 1 Share What You Got ..................................... | | Stax 191 |
| 10/08/66 | **29** | 6 | 2 Never Like This Before................................. | | Stax 199 |
| 4/22/67 | **18** | 10 | 3 Everybody Loves A Winner ......................... | 95 | Stax 212 |
| 1/06/68 | **33** | 6 | 4 Everyday Will Be Like A Holiday .................... | | Stax 237 |
| 4/27/68 | **16** | 6 | 5 A Tribute To A King ................................. | 86 | Stax 248 |
| | | | tribute to Otis Redding | | |
| 9/07/68 | **17** | 11 | 6 Private Number.......................................... | 75 | Stax 0005 |
| | | | **JUDY CLAY & WILLIAM BELL** | | |
| 12/21/68+ | **10** | 13 | 7 I Forgot To Be Your Lover .......................... | 45 | Stax 0015 |
| 1/11/69 | **45** | 3 | 8 My Baby Specializes ................................. | 104 | Stax 0017 |
| | | | **WILLIAM BELL & JUDY CLAY** | | |
| 5/24/69 | **39** | 4 | 9 My Whole World Is Falling Down..................... | | Stax 0032 |
| 5/12/73 | **22** | 11 | 10 Lovin' On Borrowed Time ............................. | 101 | Stax 0157 |
| 10/06/73 | **54** | 9 | 11 I've Got To Go On Without You....................... | | Stax 0175 |
| 4/06/74 | **39** | 13 | 12 Gettin' What You Want (Losin' What You Got).... | | Stax 0198 |
| 12/11/76+ | **1**¹ | 26 | 13● Tryin' To Love Two................................... | 10 | Mercury 73839 |
| 6/11/77 | **66** | 7 | 14 Coming Back For More................................ | | Mercury 73922 |
| 11/05/77 | **30** | 15 | 15 Easy Comin' Out (Hard Goin' In)..................... | | Mercury 73961 |
| 2/26/83 | **65** | 9 | 16 Bad Time To Break Up ................................. | | Kat Family 03502 |
| 5/10/86 | **59** | 7 | 17 I Don't Want To Wake Up (Feelin' Guilty).......... | | Wilbe 202 |
| | | | **WILLIAM BELL & JANICE BULLOCK** | | |
| 8/23/86 | **65** | 8 | 18 Headline News........................................... | | Wilbe 404 |
| | | | **BELLE EPOQUE** | | |
| | | | Female disco trio from Paris, France. | | |
| 3/11/78 | **26** | 12 | 1 Miss Broadway ......................................... | 92 | Big Tree 16109 |
| | | | **REGINA BELLE** | | |
| | | | Raised in Englewood, New Jersey. Featured female vocalist with The Manhattans for over two years. | | |
| 5/09/87 | **2**³ | 17 | 1 Show Me The Way ..................................... | 68 | Columbia 07080 |
| 9/19/87 | **11** | 14 | 2 So Many Tears............................................ | | Columbia 07388 |
| 12/26/87+ | **14** | 14 | 3 Without You............................................ | 89 | Elektra 69426 |
| | | | **PEABO BRYSON & REGINA BELLE** from the film "Leonard Pt. 6" | | |
| 3/26/88 | **21** | 11 | 4 How Could You Do It To Me .......................... | | Columbia 07735 |
| | | | **THE BELMONTS - see DION** | | |
| | | | **BELOYD** | | |
| 10/15/77 | **69** | 6 | 1 Get Into Your Life ...................................... | | 20th Century 2353 |
| | | | **JESSE BELVIN** | | |
| | | | Born on 12/15/32 in San Antonio, Texas. To Los Angeles in 1939. First recorded "All That Wine Is Gone" with Big Jay McNeely in 1950. Wrote "Earth Angel" for the Penguins. A pivotal figure in the development of the R&B sound on the West Coast. Jesse and his wife were killed in an automobile accident on 2/6/60. Marvin Phillips recorded in vocal duo, Marvin & Johnny, with Emory "Johnny" Perry. Also see The Shields. | | |
| 1/24/53 | **2**² | 11 | 1 Dream Girl................................................ | | Specialty 447 |
| | | | **JESSE & MARVIN** (Phillips) Juke Box #2 / Best Seller #7 | | |
| 12/08/56 | **7** | 3 | 2 Goodnight My Love ................................... | | Modern 1005 |
| | | | Juke Box #7 / Best Seller #10 with 11-year-old Barry White (later a producer/singer) on piano | | |
| 2/02/59 | **25** | 2 | 3 Funny ..................................................... | 81 | RCA 7387 |
| 4/13/59 | **7** | 10 | 4 Guess Who ............................................... | 31 | RCA 7469 |
| | | | written by Jesse's wife, Jo Anne Belvin | | |

| DEBUT DATE | PEAK POS | WKS CHR | ARTIST — Record Title | POP POS | Label & Number |
|---|---|---|---|---|---|
| | | | **BOYD BENNETT & His Rockets** | | |
| | | | Born in Muscle Shoals, Alabama on 12/7/24. Attended high school in Tennessee and formed first band there. Later became a disc jockey in Kentucky. | | |
| 8/13/55 | **7** | 8 | 1 **Seventeen** ...................... | **5** | King 1470 |
| | | | Jockey #7 / Best Seller #8 | | |
| 10/08/55 | **13** | 2 | 2 My Boy - Flat Top.......................... | 39 | King 1494 |
| | | | Jockey #13 | | |
| | | | above 2: vocals by Big Moe | | |
| | | | **JOE BENNETT & THE SPARKLETONES** | | |
| | | | Teenage band from Spartanburg, South Carolina. Consisted of Joe Bennett (vocals, guitar), Howard Childress (guitar), Wayne Arthur (bass) and Irving Denton (drums). | | |
| 10/14/57 | **11** | 2 | 1 Black Slacks .......................... | 17 | ABC-Para. 9837 |
| | | | Jockey #11 | | |
| | | | **GEORGE BENSON** ★★95★★ | | |
| | | | Born on 3/22/43 in Pittsburgh. Played guitar from age eight. Played in Brother Jack McDuff's trio in 1964. House musician at CTI Records to early 70s. Influenced heavily by Wes Montgomery. | | |
| 7/19/75 | **98** | 3 | 1 Supership ...................... | 105 | CTI 25 |
| | | | GEORGE "BAD" BENSON | | |
| 5/29/76 | **3** | 18 | 2 **This Masquerade** .......................... | **10** | Warner 8209 |
| 10/23/76 | **55** | 7 | 3 Breezin' .......................... [I] | 63 | Warner 8268 |
| 4/16/77 | **34** | 8 | 4 Everything Must Change.......................... | 106 | Warner 8360 |
| 6/11/77 | **41** | 7 | 5 Gonna Love You More.......................... | 71 | Warner 8377 |
| 7/16/77 | **2** [2] | 21 | 6 **The Greatest Love Of All** .......................... | 24 | Arista 0251 |
| | | | from the film "The Greatest"; a #1 hit for Whitney Houston in 1986 | | |
| 3/11/78 | **2** [2] | 17 | 7 **On Broadway**.......................... | **7** | Warner 8542 |
| 7/22/78 | **39** | 9 | 8 Lady Blue .......................... | | Warner 8604 |
| 3/03/79 | **3** | 17 | 9 **Love Ballad** .......................... | 18 | Warner 8759 |
| 7/07/79 | **55** | 8 | 10 Unchained Melody .......................... | | Warner 8843 |
| 6/28/80 | **1** [3] | 21 | 11 **Give Me The Night** .......................... | **4** | Warner 49505 |
| 10/11/80 | **9** | 16 | 12 **Love X Love** .......................... | 61 | Warner 49570 |
| 12/27/80+ | **33** | 12 | 13 Turn Out The Lamplight.......................... | 109 | Warner 49637 |
| 8/22/81 | **6** | 15 | 14 **Love All The Hurt Away** .......................... | 46 | Arista 0624 |
| | | | ARETHA FRANKLIN & GEORGE BENSON | | |
| 10/31/81+ | **1** [1] | 19 | 15 **Turn Your Love Around** .......................... | **5** | Warner 49846 |
| 2/27/82 | **16** | 12 | 16 Never Give Up On A Good Thing .......................... | 52 | Warner 50005 |
| 5/21/83 | **3** | 18 | 17 **Inside Love (So Personal)** .......................... | 43 | Warner 29649 |
| 7/30/83 | **21** | 15 | 18 Lady Love Me (One More Time) .......................... | 30 | Warner 29563 |
| 12/22/84+ | **15** | 15 | 19 20/20.......................... | 48 | Warner 29120 |
| 3/23/85 | **24** | 14 | 20 I Just Wanna Hang Around You.......................... | 102 | Warner 29042 |
| 7/13/85 | **87** | 4 | 21 New Day .......................... | | Warner 28969 |
| 8/09/86 | **13** | 15 | 22 Kisses In The Moonlight .......................... | | Warner 28640 |
| 11/15/86+ | **16** | 14 | 23 Shiver .......................... | | Warner 28523 |
| | | | **JO JO BENSON - see PEGGY SCOTT** | | |
| | | | **BROOK BENTON** ★★33★★ | | |
| | | | Born Benjamin Franklin Peay on 9/19/31 in Camden, South Carolina. Singer/songwriter. In the Camden Jubilee Singers. To New York in 1948, joined Bill Langford's Langfordaires. With Jerusalem Stars in 1951. First recorded own name for Okeh in 1953. Wrote "Looking Back", "A Lover's Question", "The Stroll", "It's Just A Matter Of Time", "Endlessly", "Thank You Baby", and many other hits. Died on 4/9/88 (56) of complications from spinal meningitis. | | |
| 2/09/59 | **1** [9] | 15 | 1 **It's Just A Matter Of Time/** | **3** | |
| 2/09/59 | **23** | 3 | 2 Hurtin' Inside .......................... | 78 | Mercury 71394 |
| 5/04/59 | **3** | 12 | 3 **Endlessly/** | 12 | |
| 5/04/59 | **5** | 12 | 4 **So Close** .......................... | 38 | Mercury 71443 |
| 7/20/59 | **1** [4] | 14 | 5 **Thank You Pretty Baby**.......................... | 16 | Mercury 71478 |
| 10/19/59 | **1** [3] | 17 | 6 **So Many Ways** .......................... | **6** | Mercury 71512 |
| 1/04/60 | **12** | 2 | 7 This Time Of The Year .......................... [X] | 66 | Mercury 71554 |
| 1/25/60 | **1** [10] | 17 | 8 **Baby (You've Got What It Takes)** .......................... | **5** | Mercury 71565 |
| | | | DINAH WASHINGTON & BROOK BENTON | | |
| 4/18/60 | **15** | 4 | 9 The Ties That Bind.......................... | 37 | Mercury 71566 |
| 5/23/60 | **1** [4] | 13 | 10 **A Rockin' Good Way (To Mess Around And Fall In Love)** .......................... | **7** | Mercury 71629 |
| | | | DINAH WASHINGTON & BROOK BENTON | | |

| DEBUT DATE | PEAK POS | WKS CHR | ARTIST — Record Title | POP POS | Label & Number |
|---|---|---|---|---|---|
| | | | **BROOK BENTON — Continued** | | |
| 8/22/60 | **1** [9] | 14 | 11 **Kiddio/** | *7* | |
| 10/10/60 | **21** | 1 | 12 The Same One | *16* | Mercury 71652 |
| 11/28/60+ | **5** | 10 | 13 **Fools Rush In** | *24* | Mercury 71722 |
| 2/20/61 | **2** [1] | 13 | 14 **For My Baby/** | *28* | |
| 2/20/61 | **6** | 14 | 15 **Think Twice** | *11* | Mercury 71774 |
| 5/29/61 | **2** [4] | 12 | 16 **The Boll Weevil Song** [N] | *2* | Mercury 71820 |
| 9/11/61 | **14** | 6 | 17 Frankie And Johnny | *20* | Mercury 71859 |
| 1/06/62 | **12** | 5 | 18 Revenge | *15* | Mercury 71903 |
| 6/02/62 | **19** | 3 | 19 Hit Record | *45* | Mercury 71962 |
| 9/08/62 | **3** | 15 | 20 **Lie To Me** | *13* | Mercury 72024 |
| 12/08/62+ | **2** [1] | 13 | 21 **Hotel Happiness** | *3* | Mercury 72055 |
| 3/30/63 | **4** | 8 | 22 **I Got What I Wanted** | *28* | Mercury 72099 |
| 7/06/63 | **7** | 10 | 23 **My True Confession** | *22* | Mercury 72135 |
| 10/05/63 | **15** | 7 | 24 Two Tickets To Paradise | *32* | Mercury 72177 |
| 1/25/64 | **35** | 7 | 25 Going Going Gone | *Hot* | Mercury 72230 |
| 5/09/64 | **43** | 8 | 26 Too Late To Turn Back Now/ | *Hot* | |
| 5/16/64 | **47** | 7 | 27 Another Cup Of Coffee | *Hot* | Mercury 72266 |
| 7/18/64 | **75** | 7 | 28 A House Is Not A Home<br>from the film of the same title | *Hot* | Mercury 72303 |
| 10/03/64 | **53** | 7 | 29 Lumberjack | *Hot* | Mercury 72333 |
| 12/19/64+ | **67** | 4 | 30 Do It Right | *Hot* | Mercury 72365 |
| 12/18/65 | **26** | 5 | 31 Mother Nature, Father Time | *53* | RCA 8693 |
| 7/12/69 | **11** | 8 | 32 Nothing Can Take The Place Of You | *74* | Cotillion 44034 |
| 1/17/70 | **1** [1] | 14 | 33●**Rainy Night In Georgia** | *4* | Cotillion 44057 |
| 4/25/70 | **25** | 6 | 34 My Way | *72* | Cotillion 44072 |
| 6/13/70 | **31** | 4 | 35 Don't It Make You Want To Go Home<br>**BROOK BENTON with THE DIXIE FLYERS** | *45* | Cotillion 44078 |
| 12/26/70+ | **18** | 9 | 36 Shoes<br>**BROOK BENTON with THE DIXIE FLYERS** | *67* | Cotillion 44093 |
| 1/07/78 | **49** | 17 | 37 Makin' Love Is Good For You | | Olde World 1100 |
| | | | **CHUCK BERNARD**<br>Native of St. Louis. Career began after move to Chicago in the mid-60s. | | |
| 3/05/66 | **36** | 4 | 1 Funny Changes | | Satellite 2008 |
| | | | **ROD BERNARD**<br>Born on 8/12/40 in Opelousas, Louisiana. Singer/guitarist. On local radio since age 10. Deejay for KSLO in 1957. First recorded for Carl in 1957. Formed the Shondells with Warren Storm and Skip Stewart. | | |
| 4/13/59 | **12** | 4 | 1 This Should Go On Forever | *20* | Argo 5327 |
| | | | **CHUCK BERRY** ★★**71**★★<br>Born Charles Edward Anderson Berry on 10/18/26 in San Jose, California. Grew up in St. Louis. Muddy Waters introduced Chuck to Leonard Chess (Chess Records) in Chicago. First recording, "Maybellene", was an instant success. Appeared in the film "Rock, Rock, Rock" in 1956, and several others. Regarded by many as rock 'n roll's most influential artist. Film documentary/concert tribute to Chuck, "Hail! Hail! Rock 'N' Roll", released in 1987. | | |
| 8/06/55 | **1** [11] | 16 | 1 **Maybellene/**<br>Juke Box #1(11) / Best Seller #1(9) / Jockey #1(9) | *5* | |
| 9/10/55 | **10** | 1 | 2 Wee Wee Hours<br>Juke Box #10 / Jockey #15 | | Chess 1604 |
| 10/29/55 | **2** [1] | 11 | 3 **Thirty Days (To Come Back Home)**<br>Juke Box #2 / Jockey #6 / Best Seller #8 | | Chess 1610 |
| 2/25/56 | **8** | 5 | 4 **No Money Down**<br>Jockey #8 / Best Seller #11 | | Chess 1615 |
| 6/09/56 | **2** [1] | 7 | 5 **Roll Over Beethoven**<br>Juke Box #2 / Best Seller #7 / Jockey #8 | *29* | Chess 1626 |
| 10/06/56 | **4** | 6 | 6 **Too Much Monkey Business/**<br>Juke Box #4 / Best Seller #7 / Jockey #11 | | |
| 10/20/56 | **5** | 8 | 7 **Brown-Eyed Handsome Man**<br>Jockey #5 | | Chess 1635 |
| 4/13/57 | **1** [5] | 15 | 8 **School Day**<br>Jockey #1(5) / Best Seller #1(1) / Juke Box #1(1) | *3* | Chess 1653 |
| 7/22/57 | **12** | 1 | 9 Oh Baby Doll<br>Jockey #12 | *57* | Chess 1664 |

| DEBUT DATE | PEAK POS | WKS CHR | ARTIST — Record Title | POP POS | Label & Number |
|---|---|---|---|---|---|
| | | | **CHUCK BERRY — Continued** | | |
| 11/18/57 | 6 | 9 | 10 **Rock And Roll Music** ........................................ | 8 | Chess 1671 |
| | | | Best Seller #6 / Jockey #7 | | |
| 2/24/58 | 1³ | 11 | 11 **Sweet Little Sixteen** ................................. | 2 | Chess 1683 |
| | | | Best Seller #1(3) / Jockey #1(3) | | |
| 5/05/58 | 2² | 12 | 12 **Johnny B. Goode** ................................ | 8 | Chess 1691 |
| | | | Jockey #2 / Best Seller #5 | | |
| 9/15/58 | 9 | 8 | 13 **Carol** ................................................. | 18 | Chess 1700 |
| | | | Jockey #9 | | |
| 12/15/58 | 13 | 3 | 14 Sweet Little Rock And Roll ........................ | 47 | Chess 1709 |
| 4/13/59 | 3 | 13 | 15 **Almost Grown** ...................................... | 32 | Chess 1722 |
| 7/06/59 | 16 | 8 | 16 Back In The U.S.A. ................................... | 37 | Chess 1729 |
| 4/04/60 | 18 | 3 | 17 Too Pooped To Pop ('Casey')...................... | 42 | Chess 1747 |
| 3/07/64 | 23 | 10 | 18 Nadine (Is It You?)................................... | Hot | Chess 1883 |
| 5/23/64 | 10 | 11 | 19 **No Particular Place To Go** ...................... | Hot | Chess 1898 |
| 8/01/64 | 14 | 9 | 20 You Never Can Tell................................... | Hot | Chess 1906 |
| 10/24/64 | 54 | 6 | 21 Little Marie .......................................... | Hot | Chess 1912 |
| 12/12/64+ | 41 | 7 | 22 Promised Land ....................................... | Hot | Chess 1916 |
| 9/30/72 | 42 | 7 | 23●My Ding-A-Ling..................................... | 1 | Chess 2131 |

**HARMON BETHEA**
Vocalist from Washington, DC. Attended Washington Junior College of Music. In Progressive Four gospel group in 1948, recorded for DC in 1949. In vocal group the Cap-Tans from 1950. Formed The Maskman & The Agents.

| 12/08/73+ | 59 | 10 | 1 Talking About The Boss And I....................... | | Musicor 1483 |
|---|---|---|---|---|---|

**HAROLD BETTERS**

| 11/14/64 | 74 | 8 | 1 Do Anything You Wanna (Part I) .................. [I] Hot | Gateway 747 |
|---|---|---|---|---|

**CHARLES BEVEL**
Born on 12/7/38 in Swifton, Mississippi. Singer/songwriter. Raised in San Diego.

| 4/13/74 | 77 | 6 | 1 Sally B. White ............................................. | A&M 1501 |
|---|---|---|---|---|

**BEVERLY & DUANE**
Duo of Beverly Wheeler and Duane Williams.

| 12/23/78+ | 79 | 4 | 1 Glad I Gotcha Baby ................................... | Ariola 7728 |
|---|---|---|---|---|
| 4/21/79 | 92 | 2 | 2 Living In A World................................... | Ariola 7741 |

**FRANKIE BEVERLY - see MAZE**

**B. FATS**

| 11/22/86 | 69 | 11 | 1 Whoppit ..................................................... | Posse 1223 |
|---|---|---|---|---|

**B-H-Y**
Group consisting of Ron Baker (bass), Norman Harris (guitar) and Earl Young (drums). Harris died in 1987.

| 11/17/79 | 86 | 5 | 1 We Funk The Best.................................... | Salsoul 2106 |
|---|---|---|---|---|

**BIDDU ORCHESTRA**
Biddu is an Indian-born songwriter/producer. To England, worked as a baker. Began producing for Beacon Records in 1969.

| 10/25/75 | 80 | 3 | 1 Summer Of '42 ............................... [I] 57 | Epic 50139 |
|---|---|---|---|---|
| | | | disco version of the movie theme | |

**BIG AUDIO DYNAMITE**
Band formed by guitarist Mick Jones (co-founder of The Clash). Includes Don Letts (vocals), Greg Roberts, Dan Donovan and Leo "E-Zee Kill" Williams.

| 2/14/87 | 66 | 7 | 1 Badrock City ............................................. | Columbia 06708 |
|---|---|---|---|---|

**BIG BOPPER**
Born Jiles Perry Richardson on 10/24/30 in Sabine Pass, Texas. Disc jockey at KTRM in Beaumont, Texas. Wrote "Running Bear" for Johnny Preston. Died with Buddy Holly and Ritchie Valens in a plane crash on 2/3/59 at the age of 28.

| 9/22/58 | 3 | 15 | 1 **Chantilly Lace**....................................... [N] 6 | Mercury 71343 |
|---|---|---|---|---|
| | | | Jockey #3 / Best Seller #7 | |

**BIG MACEO**
Vocalist/pianist, born Major Merriweather on 3/31/05 in Atlanta. Prominent session musician in Chicago. Lost the use of his left hand due to a stroke in 1946, but continued to play and record until 1950. Died of a heart attack in Chicago, 2/26/53. Also see Tampa Red.

| 12/01/45 | 4 | 1 | 1 **Things Have Changed** ................................ | Bluebird 0735 |
|---|---|---|---|---|
| | | | features Tampa Red on guitar | |

| DEBUT DATE | PEAK POS | WKS CHR | ARTIST — Record Title | POP POS | Label & Number |
|---|---|---|---|---|---|
| | | | **BIG MAYBELLE**<br>Vocalist/pianist, born Mabel Louise Smith on 5/1/24 in Jackson, Tennessee. With the Sweethearts Of Rhythm (all-girl orchestra); recorded with the Christine Chatman Orchestra in 1944 (Decca). Illness forced semi-retirement in the late 60s. Died on 1/23/72 in Cleveland from a diabetic coma. | | |
| 1/03/53 | **3** | 6 | 1 **Gabbin' Blues**........................<br>Juke Box #3 / Best Seller #8 | | Okeh 6931 |
| 6/06/53 | **10** | 2 | 2 **Way Back Home**........................<br>Best Seller #10 / Juke Box #10 | | Okeh 6955 |
| 11/21/53 | **5** | 2 | 3 **My Country Man**........................<br>Juke Box #5 / Best Seller #9<br>above 3: with the Leroy Kirkland Orchestra | | Okeh 7009 |
| 6/30/56 | **11** | 5 | 4 Candy........................<br>Best Seller #11<br>with the Kelly Owens Orchestra | | Savoy 1195 |
| 11/12/66 | **27** | 5 | 5 Don't Pass Me By ........................ | | Rojac 14969 |
| 1/14/67 | **23** | 6 | 6 96 Tears........................ | *96* | Rojac 112 |
| | | | **BIG THREE TRIO**<br>Chicago combo: Leonard "Baby Doo" Caston (piano), Bernardo Dennis (guitar) and Willie Dixon (bass). Ollie Crawford replaced Dennis in Fall of 1947. Dixon later became Chicago's premier blues songwriter/producer. | | |
| 4/03/48 | **10** | 2 | 1 **You Sure Look Good To Me**........................<br>also released on Columbia 30110 | | Columbia 38093 |
| | | | **MR. ACKER BILK**<br>Clarinetist/composer, born Bernard Stanley Bilk on 1/28/29 in Somerset, England. | | |
| 5/12/62 | **7** | 10 | 1●**Stranger On The Shore** ........................ [I] | *1* | Atco 6217 |
| | | | with the Leon Young String Chorale | | |
| | | | **BILLY & BABY GAP**<br>Duo produced by Charlie Wilson (The Gap Band): Billy Young and Anthony Walker. | | |
| 10/05/85 | **75** | 5 | 1 Rock The Nation ........................ | | Total Exp. 2424 |
| | | | **BILLY & LILLIE**<br>Vocal duo of Billy Ford (b: 3/9/25, Bloomfield, New Jersey) and Lillie Bryant (b: 2/14/40, Newburg, New York). Backing group: Billy Ford & The Thunderbirds. | | |
| 1/20/58 | **6** | 8 | 1 **La Dee Dah**........................<br>Best Seller #6 / Jockey #9 | *9* | Swan 4002 |
| | | | **BIONIC BOOGIE**<br>A Gregg Diamond disco production. | | |
| 3/18/78 | **79** | 8 | 1 Risky Changes........................ | | Polydor 14450 |
| | | | **BIRDLEGS & PAULINE & Their Versatility Birds**<br>3-woman, 1-man group from Chicago. Birdlegs is Sidney Chivers, Pauline is his wife. | | |
| 6/08/63 | **18** | 6 | 1 Spring........................ | *94* | Vee-Jay 510 |
| | | | **EDWIN BIRDSONG**<br>Rapper from Los Angeles. Sang in the LA Community Choir. Attended Juilliard School. Worked with Roy Ayers as manager and writer from 1976-77. | | |
| 3/21/81 | **65** | 7 | 1 Rapper Dapper Snapper........................ | | Salsoul 2135 |
| 5/22/82 | **55** | 8 | 2 She's Wrapped Too Tight (She's A Button Buster)........................ | | Salsoul 7024 |
| | | | **LARRY BIRDSONG**| | |
| 7/21/56 | **11** | 1 | 1 Pleadin' For Love........................<br>Jockey #11<br>with Louis Brooks & His Hi-Toppers | | Excello 2076 |
| | | | **ELVIN BISHOP**<br>Born on 10/21/42 in Tulsa, Oklahoma. Lead guitarist with Paul Butterfield's Blues Band (1965-68). | | |
| 5/22/76 | **82** | 7 | 1●Fooled Around And Fell In Love ........................<br>lead vocal by Mickey Thomas (Jefferson Starship) | *3* | Capricorn 0252 |
| | | | **BITS & PIECES** | | |
| 8/08/81 | **45** | 11 | 1 Don't Stop The Music........................ | | Mango 109 |
| | | | **BIZ MARKIE**<br>Rap ham born in Harlem on 4/8/64. Real name: Marcel Hall. | | |
| 12/27/86+ | **84** | 6 | 1 Make The Music With Your Mouth........................ | | Prism 2008 |
| 6/25/88 | **80** | 5 | 2 Vapors ........................ | | Cold Chill. 27890 |

| DEBUT DATE | PEAK POS | WKS CHR | ARTIST — Record Title | POP POS | Label & Number |
|---|---|---|---|---|---|
| | | | **BLACK BLOOD**<br>Eight member band from Baton Rouge, Louisiana. Produced by Valerian E. Smith. | | |
| 6/07/75 | 63 | 6 | 1 A.I.E. (A Mwana) ..................................... [F] | | Mainstream 5567 |
| | | | **THE BLACKBYRDS**<br>Founded in 1973 by jazz studies professor Donald Byrd while teaching at Howard University, Washington, DC. | | |
| 8/03/74 | 23 | 13 | 1 Do It, Fluid ............................................. | 69 | Fantasy 729 |
| 2/01/75 | 4 | 17 | 2 **Walking In Rhythm**................................... | 6 | Fantasy 736 |
| 7/26/75 | 22 | 11 | 3 Flyin' High ............................................ | 70 | Fantasy 747 |
| 2/14/76 | 3 | 16 | 4 **Happy Music** ......................................... | 19 | Fantasy 762 |
| 7/17/76 | 37 | 10 | 5 Rock Creek Park....................................... | 93 | Fantasy 771 |
| 2/12/77 | 15 | 12 | 6 Time Is Movin'....................................... | 95 | Fantasy 787 |
| 5/28/77 | 30 | 11 | 7 Party Land............................................. | | Fantasy 794 |
| 12/17/77+ | 20 | 15 | 8 Soft And Easy ......................................... | 102 | Fantasy 809 |
| 4/01/78 | 19 | 14 | 9 Supernatural Feeling ................................. | 102 | Fantasy 819 |
| 12/27/80+ | 38 | 12 | 10 What We Have Is Right............................... | | Fantasy 904 |
| 3/28/81 | 52 | 9 | 11 Love Don't Strike Twice ............................. | | Fantasy 910 |
| | | | **THE BLACK FLAMES** | | |
| 12/12/87 | 71 | 10 | 1 Are You The Woman? ................................<br>from the film "Less Than Zero" | | Def Jam 07651 |
| | | | **BLACK HEAT**<br>Group consists of Johnell Gray (keyboards), Bradley Owens (guitar), Naamon "Chip" Jones (bass) and Raymond Green (percussion). | | |
| 12/08/73+ | 46 | 13 | 1 No Time To Burn...................................... | | Atlantic 2987 |
| | | | **BLACK ICE** | | |
| 11/26/77+ | 85 | 10 | 1 Shake Down-Pt. 1 .................................... | | HDM 503 |
| 11/21/81+ | 64 | 10 | 2 I Just Wanna Hold You .............................. | | Montage 1204 |
| | | | **BLACK IVORY**<br>New York City trio formed as the Mellow Sounds. Consisted of lead singer LeRoy Burgess III, Stuart Bascombe and Russell Patterson. Discovered by Patrick Adams, leader of the Sparks. Burgess was later in The Aleems. | | |
| 11/06/71+ | 38 | 9 | 1 Don't Turn Around...................................... | | Today 1501 |
| 4/15/72 | 32 | 6 | 2 You And I ............................................. | 111 | Today 1508 |
| 9/09/72 | 46 | 4 | 3 I'll Find A Way ....................................... | | Today 1511 |
| 1/27/73 | 37 | 7 | 4 Time Is Love .......................................... | | Today 1516 |
| 6/09/73 | 45 | 8 | 5 Spinning Around....................................... | | Today 1520 |
| 6/01/74 | 44 | 11 | 6 What Goes Around (Comes Around)................. | | Kwanza 7800 |
| 2/08/75 | 40 | 13 | 7 Will We Ever Come Together ....................... | | Buddah 443 |
| 12/22/84+ | 73 | 8 | 8 You Are My Lover ..................................... | | Panoramic 200 |
| | | | **BLACK SATIN Featuring FRED PARRIS**<br>Group consists of ex-Five Satins members Fred Parris, Richie Freeman and Jimmy Curtis, with Nate Marshall. | | |
| 8/30/75 | 49 | 10 | 1 Everybody Stand And Clap Your Hands (For The Entertainer)........................................... | | Buddah 477 |
| | | | **BLACKSMOKE** | | |
| 8/21/76 | 96 | 2 | 1 (Your Love Has Got Me) Screamin'.................... | | Choc. City 003 |
| | | | **BILL BLACK'S COMBO**<br>Bill was born on 9/17/26 in Memphis; died of a brain tumor on 10/21/65. Bass guitarist. Session work in Memphis; backed Elvis Presley (with Scotty Moore, guitar; D.J. Fontana, drums) on most of his early records. Formed own band in 1959. | | |
| 11/30/59+ | 1⁴ | 15 | 1 **Smokie - Part 2** ................................ [I] | 17 | Hi 2018 |
| 3/28/60 | 1⁴ | 17 | 2 **White Silver Sands** ................................ [I] | 9 | Hi 2021 |
| 10/10/60 | 9 | 10 | 3 **Don't Be Cruel** ..................................... [I]<br>Bill played bass on Elvis Presley's original #1 pop hit | 11 | Hi 2026 |
| 4/24/61 | 22 | 1 | 4 Hearts Of Stone ...................................... [I] | 20 | Hi 2028 |
| 10/05/63 | 47 | 6 | 5 Monkey-Shine......................................... [I] | *Hot* | Hi 2069 |
| | | | **JEANNE BLACK**<br>Born on 10/25/37 in Mount Baldy, California. Appearances on local TV show, "Hometown Jamboree". Discovered by Cliffie Stone. | | |
| 5/23/60 | 11 | 6 | 1 He'll Have To Stay...................................<br>answer song to Jim Reeves' "He'll Have To Go" | 4 | Capitol 4368 |

| DEBUT DATE | PEAK POS | WKS CHR | ARTIST — Record Title | POP POS | Label & Number |
|---|---|---|---|---|---|
| | | | **MARION BLACK** | | |
| 2/13/71 | **39** | 8 | 1 Go On Fool.................................................. | *124* | Avco Embs. 4559 |
| | | | **SHELLY BLACK** | | |
| 6/19/76 | **95** | 3 | 1 Free & Red Hot (Part 1) ................................. | | Vigor 1730 |
| | | | **J. BLACKFOOT** | | |
| | | | Born John Colbert in Greenville, Mississippi; raised in Memphis. Former lead singer with the Soul Children. | | |
| 11/26/83+ | **4** | 24 | 1 **Taxi**.................................................... | 90 | Sound Town 0004 |
| 6/02/84 | **63** | 8 | 2 I Stood On The Sidewalk and Cried................... | | Sound Town 0006 |
| 2/23/85 | **62** | 9 | 3 Don't You Feel It Like I Feel It....................... | | Sound Town 0011 |
| 7/20/85 | **77** | 5 | 4 Hiding Place............................................. | | Sound Town 0015 |
| 11/29/86+ | **33** | 15 | 5 U-Turn .................................................. | | Edge 001 |
| 4/18/87 | **78** | 8 | 6 Bad Weather ........................................... | | Edge 006 |
| 5/30/87 | **28** | 17 | 7 Tear Jerker............................................. | | Edge 007 |
| | | | **J. BLACKFOOT featuring ANN HINES** | | |
| 11/28/87 | **58** | 10 | 8 Respect Yourself........................................ | | Edge 012 |
| | | | **BLAKE & HINES** | | |
| | | | Male duo formed in Detroit: songwriter/multi-instrumentalist Cory Blake and vocalist Andra Hines. | | |
| 2/28/87 | **50** | 10 | 1 Sherry.................................................... | | Motown 1878 |
| 5/30/87 | **59** | 7 | 2 Road Dog................................................. | | Motown 1893 |
| | | | **BILLY BLAND** | | |
| | | | Born on 4/5/32 in Wilmington, North Carolina. First recorded for Old Town in 1955. | | |
| 3/28/60 | **11** | 9 | 1 Let The Little Girl Dance................................ | 7 | Old Town 1076 |
| | | | **BOBBY BLAND** ★★**11**★★ | | |
| | | | Born Robert Calvin Bland on 1/27/30 in Rosemark, Tennesse. Nicknamed "Blue". Sang in gospel group "The Miniatures" in Memphis, late 40s. Member of the Beale Streeters which included Johnny Ace, B.B. King, Rosco Gordon, Earl Forest and Willie Nix in 1949. Driver and valet for B.B. King; appeared in the Johnny Ace Revue, early 50s. First recorded in 1952, for the Modern label. Frequent tours with B.B. King into the 80s. | | |
| | | | **BOBBY "BLUE" BLAND:** | | |
| 8/19/57 | **1** $^2$ | 14 | 1 **Farther Up The Road** ................................ | 43 | Duke 170 |
| | | | Jockey #1 / Best Seller #5 | | |
| 10/06/58 | **10** | 9 | 2 **Little Boy Blue** .................................... | | Duke 196 |
| | | | Jockey #10 | | |
| 5/04/59 | **13** | 11 | 3 I'm Not Ashamed ...................................... | | Duke 303 |
| 11/02/59 | **28** | 2 | 4 Is It Real ............................................... | | Duke 310 |
| | | | **BOBBY BLAND:** | | |
| 12/21/59+ | **2** $^1$ | 18 | 5 **I'll Take Care Of You** ............................. | 89 | Duke 314 |
| 4/11/60 | **9** | 5 | 6 **Lead Me On** ......................................... | | Duke 318 |
| 10/10/60 | **9** | 18 | 7 **Cry Cry Cry** ......................................... | 71 | Duke 327 |
| 2/06/61 | **1** $^1$ | 16 | 8 **I Pity The Fool** ..................................... | 46 | Duke 332 |
| 7/24/61 | **2** $^1$ | 20 | 9 **Don't Cry No More** ................................. | 71 | Duke 340 |
| 12/04/61 | **2** $^1$ | 15 | 10 **Turn On Your Love Light** ......................... | 28 | Duke 344 |
| 3/17/62 | **9** | 13 | 11 **Ain't That Loving You** ............................ | 86 | Duke 338 |
| 4/07/62 | **12** | 8 | 12 Who Will The Next Fool Be ........................... | 76 | Duke 347 |
| 8/25/62 | **10** | 11 | 13 **Yield Not To Temptation** ......................... | 56 | Duke 352 |
| 9/29/62 | **5** | 13 | 14 **Stormy Monday Blues**.............................. | 43 | Duke 355 |
| 1/19/63 | **1** $^2$ | 12 | 15 **That's The Way Love Is/** ......................... | 33 | |
| 2/02/63 | **6** | 12 | 16 **Call On Me** ......................................... | 22 | Duke 360 |
| 8/10/63 | **28** | 2 | 17 Sometimes You Gotta Cry A Little.................... | 56 | Duke 366 |
| 12/28/63+ | **91** | 3 | 18 The Feeling Is Gone.................................... | Hot | Duke 370 |
| 3/07/64 | **20** | 9 | 19 Ain't Nothing You Can Do............................. | Hot | Duke 375 |
| 6/13/64 | **42** | 9 | 20 Share Your Love With Me ............................. | Hot | Duke 377 |
| 10/24/64 | **49** | 6 | 21 Ain't Doing Too Bad (Part 1)......................... | Hot | Duke 383 |
| 1/02/65 | **99** | 1 | 22 Black Night/ | Hot | |
| 1/09/65 | **78** | 3 | 23 Blind Man.............................................. | Hot | Duke 386 |
| 4/24/65 | **25** | 3 | 24 Ain't No Telling/ | 93 | |
| 5/01/65 | **23** | 4 | 25 Dust Got In Daddy's Eyes ............................ | 125 | Duke 390 |
| 9/18/65 | **4** | 10 | 26 **These Hands (Small But Mighty)**.................. | 63 | Duke 385 |
| 1/22/66 | **8** | 15 | 27 **I'm Too Far Gone (To Turn Around)**.............. | 62 | Duke 393 |

| DEBUT DATE | PEAK POS | WKS CHR | ARTIST — Record Title | POP POS | Label & Number |
|---|---|---|---|---|---|
| | | | **BOBBY BLAND — Continued** | | |
| 6/04/66 | **6** | 11 | 28 **Good Time Charlie** ........................................ | 75 | Duke 402 |
| 9/17/66 | **9** | 10 | 29 **Poverty** ................................................ | 65 | Duke 407 |
| 12/10/66+ | **13** | 9 | 30 Back In The Same Old Bag Again ................... | 102 | Duke 412 |
| 4/15/67 | **6** | 11 | 31 **You're All I Need** ...................................... | 88 | Duke 416 |
| 7/22/67 | **6** | 11 | 32 **That Did It** ............................................ | | Duke 421 |
| 12/02/67 | **30** | 7 | 33 A Touch Of The Blues ............................... | | Duke 426 |
| 2/24/68 | **23** | 11 | 34 Driftin' Blues ...................................... | 96 | Duke 432 |
| 6/08/68 | **16** | 9 | 35 Save Your Love For Me ........................... | | Duke 435 |
| 11/23/68+ | **12** | 11 | 36 Rockin' In The Same Old Boat ..................... | 58 | Duke 440 |
| 5/10/69 | **14** | 10 | 37 Gotta Get To Know You............................ | 91 | Duke 447 |
| 8/23/69 | **9** | 10 | 38 **Chains Of Love** ..................................... | 60 | Duke 449 |
| 1/24/70 | **10** | 10 | 39 If You've Got A Heart ............................. | 96 | Duke 458 |
| 5/30/70 | **16** | 7 | 40 If Love Ruled The World/ | | |
| | | 16 | 41 Lover With A Reputation ....................... | | Duke 460 |
| 11/21/70 | **20** | 10 | 42 Keep On Loving Me (You'll See The Change)....... | 89 | Duke 464 |
| 5/08/71 | **18** | 8 | 43 I'm Sorry................................................ | 97 | Duke 466 |
| 1/22/72 | **6** | 12 | 44 **Do What You Set Out To Do** ..................... | 64 | Duke 472 |
| 8/26/72 | **36** | 7 | 45 I'm So Tired ...................................... | | Duke 477 |
| 10/27/73+ | **5** | 16 | 46 **This Time I'm Gone For Good** .................... | 42 | Dunhill 4369 |
| 2/23/74 | **17** | 16 | 47 Goin' Down Slow .................................. | 69 | Dunhill 4379 |
| 8/03/74 | **9** | 15 | 48 **Ain't No Love In The Heart Of The City** ........ | 91 | Dunhill 15003 |
| 11/16/74+ | **3** | 15 | 49 **I Wouldn't Treat A Dog (The Way You Treated Me)** ..................................... | 88 | Dunhill 15015 |
| 6/28/75 | **21** | 13 | 50 Yolanda................................................ | 104 | ABC 12105 |
| 10/11/75 | **41** | 10 | 51 I Take It On Home .................................. | | ABC 12133 |
| 1/31/76 | **34** | 12 | 52 Today I Started Loving You Again................. | 103 | ABC 12156 |
| 5/22/76 | **12** | 15 | 53 It Ain't The Real Thing ........................... | | ABC 12189 |
| 7/31/76 | **20** | 11 | 54 Let The Good Times Roll ......................... | 101 | ABC/Impl. 31006 |
| | | | **BOBBY BLAND & B.B. KING** | | |
| 6/18/77 | **18** | 14 | 55 The Soul Of A Man ............................... | | ABC 12280 |
| 3/04/78 | **82** | 6 | 56 Sittin' On A Poor Man's Throne ................... | | ABC 12330 |
| 5/20/78 | **14** | 17 | 57 Love To See You Smile............................ | | ABC 12360 |
| 10/07/78 | **55** | 7 | 58 Come Fly With Me ................................ | | ABC 12405 |
| 11/17/79 | **71** | 10 | 59 Tit For Tat ........................................ | | MCA 41140 |
| 3/29/80 | **76** | 4 | 60 Soon As The Weather Breaks ..................... | | MCA 41197 |
| 3/14/81 | **92** | 4 | 61 You'd Be A Millionaire ........................... | | MCA 51068 |
| 8/21/82 | **40** | 11 | 62 Recess In Heaven ................................. | | MCA 52085 |
| 11/16/85 | **54** | 16 | 63 Members Only ..................................... | | Malaco 2122 |
| | | | **MARCIE BLANE** Born on 5/21/44 in Brooklyn, New York. | | |
| 12/08/62 | **14** | 5 | 1 Bobby's Girl ..................................... | 3 | Seville 120 |
| | | | **C.L. BLAST** Male vocalist. | | |
| 6/21/80 | **93** | 2 | 1 I Wanna Get Down................................. | | Cotillion 45016 |
| 10/27/84 | **81** | 4 | 2 50/50 Love ....................................... | | Park Place 104 |
| | | | **BLONDIE** New York City techno-pop sextet formed in 1975, led by vocalist Debbie Harry. | | |
| 2/21/81 | **33** | 10 | 1● Rapture....................................... | 1 | Chrysalis 2485 |
| | | | **BLOODSTONE** From Kansas City, Missouri. Formed as the Sinceres, consisted of Charles McCormick, Willis Draffen, Charles Love, Henry Williams, and Roger Durham (d: 1973). | | |
| 4/14/73 | **4** | 17 | 1● **Natural High**............................... | 10 | London 1046 |
| 9/01/73 | **7** | 15 | 2 **Never Let You Go** ............................. | 43 | London 1051 |
| 2/09/74 | **2**[1] | 19 | 3 **Outside Woman** .............................. | 34 | London 1052 |
| 7/06/74 | **22** | 13 | 4 That's Not How It Goes.......................... | 82 | London 1055 |
| 2/15/75 | **4** | 16 | 5 **My Little Lady** ............................... | 57 | London 1061 |
| 10/18/75 | **18** | 15 | 6 Give Me Your Heart ............................. | | London 1062 |
| 4/03/76 | **19** | 11 | 7 Do You Wanna Do A Thing ...................... | 101 | London 1064 |
| 7/04/76 | **58** | 9 | 8 Just Like In The Movies ......................... | | London 1067 |

| DEBUT DATE | PEAK POS | WKS CHR | ARTIST — Record Title | POP POS | Label & Number |
|---|---|---|---|---|---|
| | | | **BLOODSTONE — Continued** | | |
| 4/03/82 | 5 | 21 | 9 We Go A Long Way Back.............................. | | T-Neck 02825 |
| 8/14/82 | 18 | 13 | 10 Go On And Cry ..................................... | | T-Neck 03049 |
| 12/18/82+ | 44 | 10 | 11 My Love Grows Stronger (Part 1).................. | | T-Neck 03394 |
| 5/26/84 | 42 | 11 | 12 Instant Love........................................ | | T-Neck 04465 |
| 9/29/84 | 69 | 5 | 13 Bloodstone's Party ................................ | | T-Neck 04592 |
| | | | **BLOOD, SWEAT & TEARS** | | |
| | | | Pop/jazz group formed in 1968 by Al Kooper, who was replaced by lead singer David Clayton-Thomas in 1969. | | |
| 5/10/69 | 46 | 2 | 1 ● You've Made Me So Very Happy ...................... | *2* | Columbia 44776 |
| 8/02/69 | 45 | 2 | 2 ● Spinning Wheel.................................... | *2* | Columbia 44871 |
| | | | **THE BLOSSOMS** | | |
| | | | Female group formed at Fremont High, Los Angeles in 1954. Consisted of Fanita James, Gloria Jones, and twins Nannette & Annette Williams. First recorded for Flair in 1954. Appeared regularly on TV's "Shindig" from 1965 with Darlene (Love) Wright. Later included Jean King and Grazia Nitzsche. Love and James were members of Bob B. Soxx & The Blue Jeans. Love was later a prominent session singer; starred in the 1987 film "Lethal Weapon". Also see The Crystals. | | |
| 12/02/67 | 45 | 2 | 1 Good, Good Lovin' ................................. | *115* | Reprise 0639 |
| | | | **KURTIS BLOW** | | |
| | | | Born Kurt Walker on 8/9/59 in New York City. Began as a disco DJ. Also see The Krush Groove All Stars. | | |
| 6/14/80 | 4 | 19 | 1 ● The Breaks (Part 1) ............................... | *87* | Mercury 76075 |
| | | | certified gold for the 12″ single | | |
| 10/04/80 | 31 | 11 | 2 Throughout Your Years, Part I ...................... | | Mercury 76083 |
| 2/07/81 | 75 | 4 | 3 Hard Times ....................................... | | Mercury 76093 |
| 8/28/82 | 37 | 11 | 4 Tough ............................................ | | Mercury 76170 |
| 7/09/83 | 35 | 12 | 5 Party Time........................................ | | Mercury 812687 |
| 9/08/84 | 45 | 10 | 6 8 Million Stories.................................. | | Mercury 880170 |
| 1/05/85 | 29 | 15 | 7 Basketball ................................... [N] | *71* | Polydor 881529 |
| 9/28/85 | 74 | 6 | 8 America .......................................... | | Mercury 884079 |
| 11/09/85+ | 16 | 17 | 9 If I Ruled The World ............................. | | Mercury 884269 |
| 9/27/86 | 20 | 16 | 10 I'm Chillin'....................................... | | Mercury 888004 |
| | | | **PEGGI BLU** | | |
| | | | Won 1986 top female vocalist award on TV's "Star Search". | | |
| 4/25/87 | 91 | 3 | 1 Tender Moments ................................. | | Capitol 5676 |
| 6/27/87 | 44 | 10 | 2 All The Way With You ............................. | | Capitol 44014 |
| | | | PEGGI BLU with BERT ROBINSON | | |
| | | | **THE BLUE-BELLES - see PATTI LaBELLE & THE BLUE BELLES** | | |
| | | | **BLUE MAGIC** | | |
| | | | Philadelphia vocal group: Theodore Mills (lead), Vernon Sawyer (second tenor, baritone), Wendell Sawyer (baritone), Keith Bartons (second tenor) and Richard Pratt (bass). | | |
| 3/31/73 | 30 | 4 | 1 Spell ............................................. | | Atco 6910 |
| 8/04/73 | 36 | 11 | 2 Look Me Up........................................ | | Atco 6938 |
| 12/15/73+ | 14 | 16 | 3 Stop To Start..................................... | *74* | Atco 6949 |
| 4/20/74 | 1 [1] | 16 | 4 ● Sideshow ........................................ | *8* | Atco 6961 |
| 10/12/74 | 5 | 14 | 5 **Three Ring Circus** ............................. | *36* | Atco 7004 |
| 3/15/75 | 45 | 6 | 6 Love Has Found Its Way To Me...................... | | Atco 7014 |
| 7/26/75 | 17 | 12 | 7 Chasing Rainbows ................................ | | Atco 7031 |
| 3/13/76 | 15 | 11 | 8 Grateful.......................................... | *104* | Atco 7046 |
| 6/19/76 | 73 | 6 | 9 Freak-N-Stein .................................... | | Atco 7052 |
| 9/25/76 | 48 | 8 | 10 Teach Me (It's Something About Love) ............. | | Atco 7061 |
| 12/11/76+ | 40 | 11 | 11 Summer Snow ..................................... | | WMOT 4003 |
| 4/11/81 | 77 | 8 | 12 Land Of Make-Believe ............................ | | Capitol 4977 |
| 4/02/83 | 69 | 7 | 13 Magic # .......................................... | | Mirage 99914 |
| | | | **THE BLUE NOTES - see HAROLD MELVIN** | | |

| DEBUT DATE | PEAK POS | WKS CHR | ARTIST — Record Title | POP POS | Label & Number |
|---|---|---|---|---|---|
| | | | **BLUES WOMAN** | | |
| | | | Real name: Marion Abernathy. Later recorded under her real name for King/Federal Records, 1947-49. | | |
| 3/02/46 | 4 | 6 | 1  Voo-It! Voo-It! ................................. | | Juke Box 502 |
| | | | with the Buddy Banks Sextet | | |
| | | | **EDDIE BO** | | |
| | | | Singer/pianist/producer, born Edwin J. Bocage in New Orleans on 9/20/30. Nicknamed "Spider". Frequent session work in New Orleans. First recorded for Ace in 1954. | | |
| 7/19/69 | 13 | 11 | 1  Hook And Sling-Part I ................................. | 73 | Scram 117 |
| | | | **BOB & EARL** | | |
| | | | Bob Relf & Earl Nelson. Bobby Day sang with Earl Nelson (as Bob & Earl) in 1960, however, Day was not involved in either of Bob & Earl's charted hits. Earl Lee Nelson (wife's name was Jackie) recorded as Jackie Lee. Earl was also lead singer on the Hollywood Flames hit "Buzz-Buzz-Buzz". | | |
| 12/21/63+ | 44 | 11 | 1  Harlem Shuffle .............................. | *Hot* | Marc 104 |
| | | | produced by Barry White | | |
| 7/02/66 | 26 | 6 | 2  Baby, It's Over................................. | | Mirwood 5517 |
| | | | **BOB B. SOXX & THE BLUE JEANS** | | |
| | | | Bobby Sheen with Darlene Love and Fanita James (both formerly with The Blossoms). Love and James later replaced by Gloria Jones and Carolyn Willis. | | |
| 12/08/62+ | 7 | 9 | 1  Zip-A-Dee Doo-Dah ....................................... | 8 | Philles 107 |
| | | | **THE BOBBETTES** | | |
| | | | Female vocal quintet (ages 11-15) from New York City. Consisted of sisters Emma and Janice Pought, Laura Webb, Helen Gathers, and Reather Dixon. Originally called the Harlem Queens. | | |
| 9/02/57 | 1⁴ | 13 | 1  Mr. Lee........................................ | 6 | Atlantic 1144 |
| | | | Jockey #1 / Best Seller #2 with the Reggie Obrecht Orchestra; song inspired by group's 5th grade teacher at P.S. 109 | | |
| | | | **BOBBY JIMMY & THE CRITTERS** | | |
| | | | Los Angeles comic rap group. Bobby Jimmy is standup comedian Russ Parr. | | |
| 8/02/86 | 27 | 10 | 1  Roaches ................................. [N] | | Macola 0924 |
| | | | parody of Timex Social Club's hit "Rumors" | | |
| | | | **ANGELA BOFILL** | | |
| | | | Vocalist born in West Bronx, New York in 1954. Formed group the Puerto Rican Supremes at Hunter College High School; attended Manhattan School Of Music. Toured and recorded with Ricardo Morrero. Performed with Dizzy Gillespie and Cannonball Adderley. Lead soloist/arranger/composer/conductor for Dance Theater of Harlem. | | |
| 3/17/79 | 23 | 15 | 1  This Time I'll Be Sweeter ............... | 104 | Arista/GRP 2500 |
| 12/22/79+ | 18 | 16 | 2  What I Wouldn't Do (For The Love Of You)......... | | Arista/GRP 2503 |
| 5/03/80 | 67 | 5 | 3  Angel Of The Night .......................... | | Arista/GRP 2504 |
| 11/21/81+ | 21 | 13 | 4  Something About You .......................... | | Arista 0636 |
| 2/20/82 | 26 | 12 | 5  Holdin' Out For Love ......................... | | Arista 0662 |
| 1/29/83 | 5 | 18 | 6  **Too Tough** ........................... | | Arista 1031 |
| 5/07/83 | 12 | 20 | 7  Tonight I Give In ........................... | | Arista 1060 |
| 11/26/83+ | 20 | 16 | 8  I'm On Your Side .......................... | | Arista 9109 |
| 3/24/84 | 65 | 6 | 9  Special Delivery ......................... | | Arista 9156 |
| 11/17/84 | 59 | 9 | 10  Can't Slow Down ......................... | | Arista 9270 |
| 2/23/85 | 84 | 2 | 11  Let Me Be The One .......................... | | Arista 9312 |
| 10/26/85 | 72 | 6 | 12  Tell Me Tomorrow ......................... | | Arista 9414 |
| | | | **HAMILTON BOHANNON** | | |
| | | | Born on 3/7/42 in Newnan, Georgia. Graduated from Clark College, Atlanta; worked as a music teacher. With Stevie Wonder as drummer, 1965-67. Bandleader/arranger for Motown tours until the mid-70s. | | |
| 11/16/74 | 78 | 5 | 1  South African Man (Pt. 1).................... | | Dakar 4539 |
| 6/21/75 | 39 | 12 | 2  Foot Stompin Music ........................ | 98 | Dakar 4544 |
| 9/27/75 | 62 | 7 | 3  Disco Stomp (Part 1) ....................... | | Dakar 4549 |
| 2/28/76 | 65 | 7 | 4  Bohannon's Beat (Pt. 1) .................... | | Dakar 4551 |
| 8/13/77 | 67 | 5 | 5  Bohannon Disco Symphony........................... | | Mercury 73939 |
| 8/05/78 | 9 | 19 | 6  **Let's Start The Dance**................. | 101 | Mercury 74015 |
| 1/13/79 | 82 | 4 | 7  Me And The Gang........................ | | Mercury 74035 |
| 3/17/79 | 43 | 7 | 8  Cut Loose ...................... | | Mercury 74044 |
| 8/04/79 | 60 | 6 | 9  The Groove Machine ....................... | | Mercury 74085 |
| 4/12/80 | 54 | 7 | 10  Baby I'm For Real ........................ | | Mercury 76054 |
| | | | written by Marvin Gaye | | |

| DEBUT DATE | PEAK POS | WKS CHR | ARTIST — Record Title | POP POS | Label & Number |
|---|---|---|---|---|---|
| | | | **HAMILTON BOHANNON — Continued** | | |
| | | | BOHANNON: | | |
| 10/18/80 | **59** | 7 | 11 Throw Down The Groove (Part I) ..................... | | Phase II 5650 |
| 12/27/80+ | **76** | 4 | 12 Dance, Dance, Dance All Night ....................... | | Phase II 5651 |
| 2/14/81 | **54** | 6 | 13 Don't Be Ashame To Call My Name ................. | | Phase II 5654 |
| 6/06/81 | **91** | 2 | 14 Goin' For Another One ................................. | | Phase II 02062 |
| 9/12/81 | **41** | 11 | 15 Let's Start II Dance Again.......................... | | Phase II 02573 |
| | | | BOHANNON featuring DR. PERRI JOHNSON | | |
| 5/15/82 | **72** | 6 | 16 I've Got The Dance Fever............................ | | Phase II 02897 |
| | | | rap intro narrated by Rick Alston | | |
| 7/17/82 | **69** | 7 | 17 The Party Train (Parts I & II) ...................... | | Phase II 02998 |
| 2/12/83 | **63** | 7 | 18 Make Your Body Move................................ | | Phase II 103 |
| | | | written by Ray Parker, Jr. | | |
| 9/24/83 | **87** | 3 | 19 Wake Up................................................ | | Phase II 114 |
| | | | **BOILING POINT** | | |
| 4/01/78 | **35** | 14 | 1 Let's Get Funktified................................ | | Bullet 05 |
| | | | **MICHAEL BOLTON** | | |
| | | | Former lead singer of Blackjack in the late 1970s; from New Haven, Connecticut. | | |
| 9/12/87 | **62** | 11 | 1 That's What Love Is All About........................ | 19 | Columbia 07322 |
| 3/12/88 | **58** | 8 | 2 (Sittin' On) The Dock Of The Bay.................... | 11 | Columbia 07680 |
| | | | **BOMBERS** | | |
| 3/10/79 | **79** | 9 | 1 (Everybody) Get Dancin' ............................. | | West End 1215 |
| | | | **ANGELO BOND** | | |
| 4/12/75 | **32** | 16 | 1 Reach For The Moon (Poor People) ................... | | ABC 12077 |
| | | | **GARY U.S. BONDS** | | |
| | | | Singer/songwriter, born Gary Anderson on 6/6/39 in Jacksonville, Florida. To Norfolk, Virginia in the mid-50s. Signed to Legrand by Frank Guida. Wrote "Friend Don't Take Her", hit for Johnny Paycheck in 1972. | | |
| 10/31/60 | **5** | 14 | 1 New Orleans.................................... | 6 | Legrand 1003 |
| 5/29/61 | **3** | 12 | 2 Quarter To Three ........................... | 1 | Legrand 1008 |
| | | | Bonds wrote lyrics to instrumental track by Gene "Daddy G" Barge's "A Night With Daddy G" | | |
| 8/07/61 | **12** | 6 | 3 School Is Out........................... | 5 | Legrand 1009 |
| 1/27/62 | **5** | 11 | 4 Dear Lady Twist.......................... | 9 | Legrand 1015 |
| 8/07/82 | **82** | 4 | 5 Out Of Work .................................... | 21 | EMI America 8117 |
| | | | produced by Bruce Springsteen and Miami Steve Van Zandt | | |
| | | | **BONEY M** | | |
| | | | Vocal group created in Germany by producer/composer Frank Farian. | | |
| 2/24/79 | **75** | 4 | 1 Dancing In The Streets..................... | 103 | Sire 1036 |
| | | | **BOOGALOO** | | |
| | | | Born Kent Harris in Oklahoma City, Oklahoma in 1930. | | |
| 11/10/56 | **9** | 1 | 1 Cops And Robbers ....................... | | Crest 1030 |
| | | | Juke Box #9 | | |
| | | | **THE BOOGIE BOYS** | | |
| | | | Harlem-based rap group: William (Boogie Knight) Stroman, Joe (Romeo J.D.) Malloy and Rudy (Lil' Rahiem) Sherrif (left group in 1988). | | |
| 7/13/85 | **6** | 17 | 1 A Fly Girl ........................... | 102 | Capitol 5498 |
| 11/02/85 | **60** | 7 | 2 You Ain't Fresh ........................... | | Capitol 5522 |
| 7/05/86 | **62** | 9 | 3 Girl Talk............................. | | Capitol 5594 |
| 1/17/87 | **84** | 5 | 4 Share My World ....................... | | Capitol 5649 |
| | | | **THE BOOGIE MAN ORCHESTRA** | | |
| 11/29/75+ | **83** | 8 | 1 (Theme From) Lady, Lady, Lady (Are You Crazy For Me?)...........................[I] | | Boogie Man 226 |

| DEBUT DATE | PEAK POS | WKS CHR | ARTIST — Record Title | POP POS | Label & Number |
|---|---|---|---|---|---|
| | | | **BOOKER T. & THE MG's**　★★**188**★★ | | |
| | | | Band formed by session men from Stax Records, Memphis, in 1962. Consisted of Booker T. Jones (b: 11/12/44, Memphis), keyboards; Steve Cropper (b: 10/21/42, Ozark Mountains, MO.), guitar; Donald "Duck" Dunn (b: 11/24/41, Memphis), bass; and Al Jackson, Jr. (b: 11/27/34, Memphis; murdered in 1975), drums. MG stands for Memphis Group. Jones was in a band with classmate Maurice White of Earth, Wind & Fire. Cropper and Dunn had been in the Mar-Keys. Much session work, recordings included horns by Andrew Love, Wayne Jackson and Joe Arnold, plus Isaac Hayes, piano. Jones received music degree from Indiana University, and married Priscilla Coolidge, sister of Rita. Produced for Rita Coolidge, Earl Klugh and Bill Withers. Produced Willie Nelson's "Stardust" album. Cropper and Dunn joined the Blues Brothers. Group disbanded in 1968, and reorganized for a short time in 1973. Also see Albert King. | | |
| 8/25/62 | **1**⁴ | 15 | 1 ●**Green Onions** ............................................. [I] | *3* | Stax 127 |
| 2/22/64 | **97** | 3 | 2　Mo-Onions .................................................... [I] | *Hot* | Stax 142 |
| 8/15/64 | **95** | 2 | 3　Soul Dressing ............................................... [I] | *Hot* | Stax 153 |
| 5/22/65 | **10** | 8 | 4　**Boot-Leg** ...................................................... [I] | *58* | Stax 169 |
| 9/03/66 | **18** | 11 | 5　My Sweet Potato/ | *85* | |
| 11/19/66 | **37** | 5 | 6　　Booker-Loo ............................................. [I] | | Stax 196 |
| 4/08/67 | **6** | 15 | 7　**Hip Hug-Her** ............................................... [I] | *37* | Stax 211 |
| 8/19/67 | **10** | 10 | 8　**Groovin'** ..................................................... [I] | *21* | Stax 224 |
| 7/13/68 | **7** | 12 | 9　**Soul-Limbo** ................................................ [I] | *17* | Stax 0001 |
| 11/23/68+ | **35** | 10 | 10　Hang 'Em High ........................................... [I] | *9* | Stax 0013 |
| | | | 　　from the film of the same title | | |
| 4/05/69 | **7** | 10 | 11　**Time Is Tight** ............................................. [I] | *6* | Stax 0028 |
| | | | 　　from the soundtrack "Uptight" | | |
| 6/28/69 | **35** | 5 | 12　Mrs. Robinson ........................................... [I] | *37* | Stax 0038 |
| | | | 　　from the film "The Graduate" | | |
| 10/04/69 | **46** | 2 | 13　Slum Baby ................................................. [I] | *88* | Stax 0049 |
| 4/03/71 | **21** | 9 | 14　Melting Pot ............................................... [I] | *45* | Stax 0082 |
| 8/11/73 | **67** | 8 | 15　Sugarcane ................................................. | | Stax 0169 |
| | | | 　　　**M.G.'s** | | |
| 5/28/77 | **68** | 5 | 16　Sticky Stuff............................................... [I] | | Asylum 45392 |
| 10/24/81 | **35** | 14 | 17　I Want You .............................................. | | A&M 2374 |
| | | | 　　　**BOOKER T.** | | |
| | | | **JAMES BOOKER** | | |
| | | | Singer/pianist/organist, born on 12/17/39 in New Orleans. Also known as "Little Booker". First recorded for Imperial in 1954. With Dee Clark's band in 1960. Session work at Duke/Peacock in Houston. Died on 11/8/83 (43). | | |
| 11/21/60+ | **3** | 10 | 1　**Gonzo**...................................................... [I] | *43* | Peacock 1697 |
| | | | 　　inspired by character in film "The Pusher" | | |
| | | | **TAKA BOOM** | | |
| | | | Former member of The Undisputed Truth. Sister of Chaka Khan and Mark Stevens (of the Jamaica Boys). | | |
| 4/28/79 | **20** | 14 | 1　Night Dancin' ............................................. | *74* | Ariola 7748 |
| 8/11/79 | **70** | 4 | 2　Red Hot .................................................... | | Ariola 7761 |
| 11/23/85 | **63** | 9 | 3　Middle Of The Night ..................................... | | Mirage 99628 |
| | | | **BOONE'S JUMPIN' JACKS** | | |
| | | | Band consisting of Chester Boone, Buster Smith, George Johnson, Chauncey Graham, Lloyd Phillips, Vernon King and Shadrack Anderson. | | |
| 5/29/43 | **4** | 2 | 1　**Please Be Careful (If You Can't Be Good)** ........ | | Decca 8632 |
| | | | **PAT BOONE** | | |
| | | | Born Charles Eugene Boone on 6/1/34 in Jacksonville, Florida. Married Red Foley's daughter, Shirley, in 1954. His pop chart success during the 50s was matched only by Elvis Presley. | | |
| 9/24/55 | **14** | 2 | 1　Ain't That A Shame...................................... | *1* | Dot 15377 |
| | | | 　　Jockey #14 | | |
| 11/26/55 | **12** | 1 | 2　At My Front Door (Crazy Little Mama)............... | *7* | Dot 15422 |
| | | | 　　Best Seller #12 / Jockey #13 | | |
| 3/02/57 | **10** | 1 | 3　**Don't Forbid Me** ......................................... | *1* | Dot 15521 |
| | | | 　　Juke Box #10 | | |
| 7/22/57 | **12** | 5 | 4　Love Letters In The Sand .............................. | *1* | Dot 15570 |
| | | | 　　Best Seller #12 | | |
| | | | 　　from the film "Bernadine" | | |

| DEBUT DATE | PEAK POS | WKS CHR | ARTIST — Record Title | POP POS | Label & Number |
|---|---|---|---|---|---|
| | | | **DUKE BOOTEE**<br>Born Edward Fletcher in Elizabeth, New Jersey. Worked in the house band at Sugarhill Records. On the soundtrack for the film "Beat Street". Also see Grandmaster Flash. | | |
| 12/25/82+ | **32** | 12 | 1 Message II (Survival) ...................................<br>**MELLE MEL & DUKE BOOTEE** | | Sugar Hill 594 |
| 5/05/84 | **60** | 8 | 2 Live Wire (I Want A Girl That Sweats)............... | | Mercury 818809 |
| | | | **BOOTSY'S RUBBER BAND - see WILLIAM "BOOTSY" COLLINS** | | |
| | | | **BOOTY PEOPLE** | | |
| 5/29/76 | **55** | 7 | 1 Spirit Of '76 ................................................ | | Calla 110 |
| | | | **BEA BOOZE**<br>Born Muriel Nichols on 5/23/20 in Baltimore; died in 1975. Vocalist/guitarist. Toured with Louis Armstrong and Andy Kirk in the mid-40s. | | |
| 11/14/42+ | **1**⁴ | 22 | 1 **See See Rider Blues** ...........................<br>a #14 hit in 1925 for the song's writer, Ma Rainey | *20* | Decca 8633 |
| 5/22/43 | **6** | 1 | 2 **Please Be Careful**............................... | | Decca 8644 |
| | | | **THE BOPPERS** | | |
| 1/13/79 | **90** | 2 | 1 There She Goes Again .................................. | | Fantasy 843 |
| | | | **EARL BOSTIC**<br>Saxophonist/clarinetist/flutist, born Earl Eugene Bostic on 4/25/13 in Tulsa, Oklahoma. Formal training at Xavier University in New Orleans. With Hot Lips Page and Lionel Hampton; own band in 1944. Arranger for Artie Shaw, Paul Whiteman, Louis Prima and others. Wrote "Let Me Off Uptown", "The Major And The Minor" and "Brooklyn Boogie". Died of a heart attack on 10/28/65. | | |
| 5/15/48 | **10** | 3 | 1 **Temptation** ...................................... [I]<br>Juke Box #10 / Best Seller #13 | | Gotham 160 |
| 9/08/51 | **6** | 2 | 2 **Sleep**............................................ [I]<br>Juke Box #6 / Best Seller #9 | | King 4444 |
| 11/10/51 | **1**⁴ | 20 | 3 **Flamingo** ..................................... [I]<br>Best Seller #1 / Juke Box #6 | | King 4475 |
| | | | **SAM BOSTIC**<br>Lead singer of Circuitry. | | |
| 3/09/85 | **47** | 11 | 1 Cold Tears ..................................... | | Atlantic 89581 |
| | | | **BOTTOM & COMPANY**<br>Septet of studio musicians, includes Richard "Krush" Griffith who was the musical director for James Brown. | | |
| 5/25/74 | **96** | 2 | 1 You're My Life.................................... | | Motown 1291 |
| 10/25/75 | **93** | 3 | 2 Here For The Party.............................. | | Motown 1363 |
| | | | **BOTTOM LINE** | | |
| 10/16/76 | **85** | 7 | 1 That's The Way To Go ................................ | | Greedy 103 |
| | | | **JIMMY BOWEN with The Rhythm Orchids**<br>Born on 11/30/37 in Santa Rita, New Mexico. Formed The Rhythm Orchids at West Texas State University with Buddy Knox, Don Lanier and Dave "Dicky Doo" Alldred. Jimmy became a producer and record executive on the West Coast. Currently president of MCA Records in Nashville. | | |
| 3/30/57 | **9** | 1 | 1 **I'm Stickin' With You** ...............................<br>Jockey #9<br>originally on Triple-D label (flip: "Party Doll" by Buddy Knox) | *14* | Roulette 4001 |
| | | | **DAVID BOWIE**<br>Pop-rock singer/film and theater actor, born Robert Jones on 1/8/47 in London. Highly theatrical performer. | | |
| 9/06/75 | **21** | 12 | 1●Fame .................................................. | *1* | RCA 10320 |
| 4/16/83 | **14** | 16 | 2●Let's Dance.......................................... | *1* | EMI America 8158 |
| | | | **THE BOX TOPS**<br>Pop-rock group formed in Memphis in 1966. Led by vocalist/guitarist Alex Chilton. | | |
| 9/09/67 | **30** | 11 | 1●The Letter ........................................ | *1* | Mala 565 |
| | | | **BOY GEORGE**<br>Born George O'Dowd on 6/14/61. Former lead singer of Culture Club. | | |
| 12/19/87+ | **21** | 13 | 1 Live My Life................................................<br>from the film "Hiding Out" | *40* | Virgin 99390 |

| DEBUT DATE | PEAK POS | WKS CHR | ARTIST — Record Title | POP POS | Label & Number |
|---|---|---|---|---|---|
| | | | **EDDIE BOYD** | | |
| | | | Vocalist/guitarist/pianist/organist, born Edward Riley Boyd on 11/25/14 in Stovall, Mississippi. To Chicago in 1941, worked with Memphis Slim, John Lee "Sonny Boy" Williamson, and Muddy Waters. Session work for RCA Victor in 1947. To Paris in the late 60s; resident of Finland since 1971. | | |
| 10/04/52 | **1**[7] | 15 | 1 **Five Long Years** ............................................ | | J.O.B. 1007 |
| | | | Juke Box #1(7) / Best Seller #1(2) | | |
| 3/21/53 | **3** | 6 | 2 **24 Hours** ................................................ | | Chess 1533 |
| | | | Juke Box #3 / Best Seller #10 | | |
| 7/04/53 | **3** | 7 | 3 **Third Degree**............................................ | | Chess 1541 |
| | | | Juke Box #3 / Best Seller #7 | | |
| | | | **THE BOYS IN THE BAND** | | |
| 10/10/70 | **34** | 4 | 1 Money Music ............................................. | *103* | Spring 106 |
| | | | featuring Herman Griffin | | |
| | | | **BOYS ON THE BLOCK** | | |
| 8/29/87 | **76** | 5 | 1 Let It Be..................................................... | | Fantasy 286 |
| | | | **CALVIN BOZE** | | |
| | | | Singer/trumpeter. First recorded for Score/Aladdin in 1949. | | |
| 6/10/50 | **9** | 1 | 1 **Safronia-B**............................................... | | Aladdin 3055 |
| | | | Juke Box #9 / Best Seller #10 | | |
| | | | **JAMES BRADLEY** | | |
| | | | Born on 3/31/53 in Bay City, MI. Gospel singer in the Genetter Bradley Singers. | | |
| 4/21/79 | **72** | 5 | 1 I'm In Too Deep ........................................... | | Malaco 1056 |
| | | | **JAN BRADLEY** | | |
| | | | Born on 7/6/43 in Byhalia, Mississippi; raised in Robbins, Illinois. First recorded for Formal in 1961. Became a social worker in 1976. | | |
| 2/02/63 | **8** | 11 | 1 **Mama Didn't Lie**...................................... | *14* | Chess 1845 |
| 1/30/65 | **24** | 8 | 2 I'm Over You................................................ | *93* | Chess 1919 |
| | | | **TINY BRADSHAW** | | |
| | | | Vocalist/drummer/pianist/leader, born Myron Bradshaw in 1905 in Youngstown, Ohio. With Marion Hardy's Alabamians, the Savoy Bearcats, Mills Blue Rhythm Band, and Luis Russell before forming own band in 1934. USO tour of Japan in 1945. Died in December of 1958 (53). | | |
| 5/20/50 | **2**[1] | 21 | 1 **Well, Oh Well** ......................................... | | King 4357 |
| | | | Best Seller #2 / Juke Box #2 | | |
| 10/14/50 | **5** | 4 | 2 **I'm Going To Have Myself A Ball** .................. | | King 4397 |
| | | | Juke Box #5 / Best Seller #7 | | |
| 9/15/51 | **10** | 1 | 3 **Walking The Chalk Line**............................ | | King 4457 |
| | | | Juke Box #10 | | |
| 1/10/53 | **3** | 14 | 4 **Soft**........................................... [I] | | King 4577 |
| | | | Best Seller #3 / Juke Box #4 | | |
| 8/08/53 | **9** | 1 | 5 **Heavy Juice** ........................................ [I] | | King 4621 |
| | | | Juke Box #9 | | |
| | | | above 2: featuring Red Prysock on tenor sax | | |
| | | | **BRAINSTORM** | | |
| | | | Big band formed in Detroit in 1976. Consisted of Belita Karen "B.B." Woods (vocals), Charles Overton, Jeryl Bright, Larry H. "Leap" Sims, Gerald "Jumpin' Jerry" Kent, Trenita Womack, E. Lamont "Stro" Johnson, Willie Wooten, and Renell Gonsalves (son of famous Ellington saxman Paul Gonsalves). | | |
| 1/22/77 | **48** | 11 | 1 Wake Up And Be Somebody ........................... | *86* | Tabu 10811 |
| 5/14/77 | **14** | 17 | 2 Lovin' Is Really My Game (Pt. I) ...................... | | Tabu 10961 |
| 3/18/78 | **84** | 6 | 3 We're On Our Way Home Part 1 ...................... | | Tabu 5502 |
| 6/02/79 | **65** | 6 | 4 Hot For You ................................................. | | Tabu 5514 |
| 8/18/79 | **84** | 7 | 5 You Put A Charge In My Life........................... | | Tabu 5518 |
| | | | **BILL BRANDON** | | |
| | | | Vocalist/trumpeter/bassist/drummer, born in Huntsville, Alabama in 1944. | | |
| 4/08/72 | **33** | 7 | 1 Stop This Merry-Go-Round ............................ | | Moonsong 9001 |
| 2/25/78 | **30** | 10 | 2 We Fell In Love While Dancing ....................... | *80* | Prelude 71102 |
| | | | **BRASIL '88 - see SERGIO MENDES** | | |

| DEBUT DATE | PEAK POS | WKS CHR | ARTIST — Record Title | POP POS | Label & Number |
|---|---|---|---|---|---|
| | | | **BRASS CONSTRUCTION** | | |
| | | | 9-man, multi-ethnic band formed in Brooklyn in 1968 by Randy Muller. Included Wade Williamston, Joseph Arthur Wong, Morris Price, Wayne Parris, Jesse Ward, Mickey Grudge, Sandy Billups and Larry Payton. Vocalist Muller was in steel band, the Panharmonics, with Rafael Cameron; also produced the band Skyy. | | |
| 3/20/76 | 1¹ | 18 | 1 **Movin'** .......................................[I] | *14* | United Art. 775 |
| 8/28/76 | 24 | 10 | 2 Changin'.......................................[I] | | United Art. 837 |
| 1/08/77 | 8 | 13 | 3 **Ha Cha Cha (Funktion)** ...................[I] | *51* | United Art. 677 |
| 4/23/77 | 42 | 8 | 4 The Message (Inspiration)/ | | United Art. 957 |
| | | 3 | 5 What's On Your Mind (Expression) ................ | | United Art. 957 |
| 1/28/78 | 18 | 15 | 6 L-O-V-E-U ....................................[I] | *104* | United Art. 1120 |
| 7/15/78 | 77 | 5 | 7 Celebrate........................................ | | United Art. 1204 |
| 10/14/78 | 58 | 7 | 8 Help Yourself ................................... | | United Art. 1242 |
| 12/16/78+ | 56 | 9 | 9 Get Up .......................................[I] | | United Art. 1262 |
| 1/26/80 | 41 | 9 | 10 Right Place .................................... | | United Art. 1332 |
| 11/22/80 | 71 | 9 | 11 How Do You Do (What You Do To Me) .............. | | Liberty 1387 |
| 3/13/82 | 23 | 17 | 12 Can You See The Light......................... | | Liberty 1453 |
| 7/24/82 | 59 | 8 | 13 Attitude...................................... | | Liberty 1473 |
| 4/23/83 | 28 | 14 | 14 Walkin' The Line ............................. | | Capitol 5219 |
| 5/26/84 | 38 | 11 | 15 Never Had A Girl............................. | | Capitol 5361 |
| 8/25/84 | 53 | 9 | 16 Partyline.................................... | | Capitol 5382 |
| 8/10/85 | 76 | 6 | 17 Give And Take................................ | | Capitol 5500 |
| | | | **BRASS FEVER** | | |
| 1/22/77 | 94 | 2 | 1 Time Is Running Out..........................[I] | | ABC/Impl. 31010 |
| | | | **DHAR BRAXTON** | | |
| 7/12/86 | 61 | 8 | 1 Jump Back (Set Me Free) ...................... | | Sleeping Bag 19 |
| | | | features vocals by Chocolette | | |
| | | | **BREAK MACHINE** | | |
| | | | Trio consisting of Lindsay Blake, Lindell Blake and Cortez Jordan. | | |
| 5/05/84 | 78 | 5 | 1 Street Dance ................................. | *105* | Sire 29319 |
| | | | **BREAKFAST CLUB** | | |
| | | | New York-based dance/pop quartet. Madonna with group for a short time, early 80s. Member Steve Bray co-produced Madonna's "True Blue" album. | | |
| 5/09/87 | 64 | 8 | 1 Right On Track ............................... | *7* | MCA 52954 |
| | | | **BREAKWATER** | | |
| | | | 8-man group from Philadelphia, formed in 1971 as Black Magic: Kae Williams (lead vocals), Lincoln "Love" Gilmore, James "Gee" Jones, Vince Garnell, Gene Robinson Jr., Greg Scott, Steve Green, and John "Dutch" Braddock. | | |
| 4/14/79 | 71 | 5 | 1 Work It Out .................................. | | Arista 0404 |
| 6/21/80 | 59 | 6 | 2 Splashdown Time .............................. | | Arista 0518 |
| 8/16/80 | 79 | 5 | 3 Say You Love Me Girl ......................... | | Arista 0542 |
| | | | **THE BRECKER BROTHERS** | | |
| | | | Formed in New York City by sessionmen/brothers Randy and Michael Brecker. | | |
| 5/24/75 | 16 | 15 | 1 Sneakin' Up Behind You.......................[I] | *58* | Arista 0122 |
| 5/01/76 | 95 | 4 | 2 If You Wanna Boogie...Forget It ........................ | | Arista 0182 |
| | | | shown as: **THE BRECKER BROTHERS BAND** | | |
| | | | **BRENDA & HERB** | | |
| | | | Duo of Brenda Reid and Herb Rooney. Herb was with the Continentals, Velvets and Masters. Brenda was lead singer of the Masterettes which evolved into the Exciters. | | |
| 9/09/78 | 70 | 4 | 1 Tonight I'm Gonna Make You A Star................ | | H&L 4699 |
| | | | **BRENDA & THE BIG DUDES** | | |
| 3/22/86 | 72 | 8 | 1 Weekend Special................................ | | Capitol 5555 |
| | | | **BRENDA & THE TABULATIONS** ★★184★★ | | |
| | | | Philadelphia group formed in 1966 with Brenda Payton, Jerry Jones, Eddie Jackson and Maurice Coates. Bernard Murphy was added in 1969. Reorganized in 1970 with vocalists Brenda Payton, Pat Mercer and Deborah Martin. | | |
| 2/25/67 | 8 | 13 | 1 **Dry Your Eyes**............................... | *20* | Dionn 500 |
| 6/10/67 | 19 | 7 | 2 Who's Lovin' You/ | *66* | |
| 6/24/67 | 44 | 2 | 3 Stay Together Young Lovers ........................ | *66* | Dionn 501 |
| 9/23/67 | 41 | 2 | 4 Just Once In A Lifetime ................................ | *97* | Dionn 503 |
| 12/02/67+ | 27 | 8 | 5 When You're Gone ................................ | *58* | Dionn 504 |

| DEBUT DATE | PEAK POS | WKS CHR | ARTIST — Record Title | POP POS | Label & Number |
|---|---|---|---|---|---|
| | | | **BRENDA & THE TABULATIONS — Continued** | | |
| 4/20/68 | 45 | 2 | 6 To The One I Love | | Dionn 507 |
| 6/21/69 | 43 | 3 | 7 The Price You Have To Pay | | Dionn 512 |
| 12/20/69+ | 12 | 11 | 8 The Touch Of You | 50 | Top & Bottom 401 |
| 5/09/70 | 12 | 9 | 9 And My Heart Sang (Tra La La) | 64 | Top & Bottom 403 |
| 8/08/70 | 15 | 9 | 10 Don't Make Me Over | 77 | Top & Bottom 404 |
| 1/09/71 | 42 | 3 | 11 A Child No One Wanted | 120 | Top & Bottom 406 |
| 3/27/71 | 10 | 13 | 12 **Right On The Tip Of My Tongue** | 23 | Top & Bottom 407 |
| 8/21/71 | 14 | 9 | 13 A Part Of You | 94 | Top & Bottom 408 |
| 12/25/71+ | 34 | 6 | 14 Why Didn't I Think Of That | 107 | Top & Bottom 411 |
| 4/07/73 | 48 | 2 | 15 One Girl Too Late | | Epic 10954 |
| 10/02/76 | 61 | 9 | 16 Home To Myself | | Choc. City 004 |
| 5/07/77 | 31 | 11 | 17 (I'm A) Superstar | | Choc. City 009 |

## JACKIE BRENSTON

Born on 8/15/30 in Clarksdale, Mississippi. Died of a heart attack on 12/15/79. Vocalist/saxophonist with Ike Turner's Kings Of Rhythm.

| DEBUT DATE | PEAK POS | WKS CHR | ARTIST — Record Title | POP POS | Label & Number |
|---|---|---|---|---|---|
| 5/12/51 | 1 5 | 18 | 1 **Rocket "88"** | | Chess 1458 |

Juke Box #1(5) / Best Seller #1(3)
with His Delta Cats (Ike Turner's Kings of Rhythm);
regarded by many as the first Rock & Roll hit

## BRIAN & BRENDA

Formerly married vocal/songwriting duo of Brian Russell (b: Falkirk, Scotland) and Brenda Gordon (b: Brooklyn, NY). Both moved to Toronto at age 12. Hosts of the Canadian TV series "Music Machine". With Dr. Music, back-up group for Ray Stevens in Toronto. Back-up for "The Sonny & Cher Show" TV series. Wrote for Anne Murray, Chaka Khan, Philippe Wynne and Walter Jackson. Brenda Russell began solo career in 1979.

| DEBUT DATE | PEAK POS | WKS CHR | ARTIST — Record Title | POP POS | Label & Number |
|---|---|---|---|---|---|
| 1/14/78 | 67 | 9 | 1 That's All Right Too | | Rocket 40809 |

## BRICK

Disco-jazz group formed in Atlanta in 1972. Consisted of Jimmy Brown (vocals, sax), Ray Ransom (piano), Donald Nevins (sax), Reggie Hargis (guitar) and Eddie Irons (drums). Session work in the early 70s.

| DEBUT DATE | PEAK POS | WKS CHR | ARTIST — Record Title | POP POS | Label & Number |
|---|---|---|---|---|---|
| 1/03/76 | 82 | 7 | 1 Music Matic | | Main Street 119 |
| 10/09/76 | 1 4 | 23 | 2 **Dazz** | 3 | Bang 727 |
| 3/19/77 | 48 | 11 | 3 That's What It's All About | | Bang 732 |
| 8/27/77 | 2 3 | 21 | 4 **Dusic** | 18 | Bang 734 |
| 12/24/77+ | 7 | 15 | 5 **Ain't Gonna' Hurt Nobody** | 92 | Bang 735 |
| 4/21/79 | 34 | 11 | 6 Raise Your Hands | | Bang 4802 |
| 7/14/79 | 47 | 9 | 7 Dancin' Man | | Bang 4804 |
| 5/24/80 | 38 | 10 | 8 All The Way | 106 | Bang 4810 |
| 8/23/80 | 21 | 17 | 9 Push Push | | Bang 4813 |
| 7/25/81 | 10 | 16 | 10 **Sweat (Til You Get Wet)** | | Bang 02246 |
| 11/14/81 | 58 | 10 | 11 Wide Open | | Bang 02599 |
| 9/11/82 | 62 | 7 | 12 Free Dancer | | Bang 03157 |

## THE BRIDES OF FUNKENSTEIN

Offshoot group of George Clinton's Parliament/Funkadelic corporation. Included Lynn Mabry, Dawn Silva, Ron Banks and Larry Demps.

| DEBUT DATE | PEAK POS | WKS CHR | ARTIST — Record Title | POP POS | Label & Number |
|---|---|---|---|---|---|
| 9/30/78 | 7 | 16 | 1 **Disco To Go** | 101 | Atlantic 3498 |
| 2/24/79 | 76 | 4 | 2 Amorous | | Atlantic 3556 |
| 1/12/80 | 67 | 8 | 3 Never Buy Texas From A Cowboy (Pt. 1) | | Atlantic 3640 |

## ALICIA BRIDGES

Atlanta-based disco singer/songwriter.

| DEBUT DATE | PEAK POS | WKS CHR | ARTIST — Record Title | POP POS | Label & Number |
|---|---|---|---|---|---|
| 8/19/78 | 31 | 17 | 1 ● I Love The Nightlife (Disco 'Round) | 5 | Polydor 14483 |

## DEE DEE BRIDGEWATER

Born in Memphis; raised in Flint, Michigan. Sang professionally since age 16. Toured USSR with Illinois Jazz Band. With Thad Jones-Mel Lewis Big Band in 1970. In the Broadway show "The Wiz", as "Glinda, The Good Witch", in 1975.

| DEBUT DATE | PEAK POS | WKS CHR | ARTIST — Record Title | POP POS | Label & Number |
|---|---|---|---|---|---|
| 6/10/78 | 95 | 2 | 1 Just Family | | Elektra 45466 |
| 4/21/79 | 37 | 10 | 2 Bad For Me | | Elektra 46031 |
| 10/18/80 | 52 | 8 | 3 One In A Million (Guy) | | Elektra 47046 |

| DEBUT DATE | PEAK POS | WKS CHR | ARTIST — Record Title | POP POS | Label & Number |
|---|---|---|---|---|---|
| | | | **BRIEF ENCOUNTER**<br>North Wilkesboro, North Carolina group. Included lead singer Maurice Whittington and brothers Larry, Belmont, Monte and Gary Bailey. | | |
| 4/03/76 | 82 | 6 | 1 What About Love ............................... | | Capitol 4229 |
| 7/02/77 | 78 | 5 | 2 In A Very Special Way ...................... | | Capitol 4426 |
| | | | **BRIGHTER SIDE OF DARKNESS**<br>Group formed at Calumet High School, Chicago in 1971; featuring 12-year-old lead singer Darryl Lamont, Ralph Eskridge, Randolph Murph and Larry Washington. | | |
| 10/28/72+ | 3 | 21 | 1 ● Love Jones........................................ | 16 | 20th Century 2002 |
| 7/14/73 | 48 | 8 | 2 I Owe You Love........................................ | | 20th Century 2034 |
| | | | **CHARLES BRIMMER**<br>Born on 10/10/48 in New Orleans. | | |
| 5/17/75 | 43 | 12 | 1 God Bless Our Love ............................... | | Chelsea 3017 |
| 8/06/77 | 98 | 2 | 2 God Bless Our Love ......................... [R] | | Chelsea 3017 |
| | | | **BRINKLEY & PARKER** | | |
| 4/06/74 | 86 | 4 | 1 Don't Get Fooled By The Pander Man............... | | Darnel 111 |
| | | | **CHARLES BRINKLEY** | | |
| 1/25/75 | 81 | 5 | 1 I'll Be What You Want Me To Be ...................... | | Music Mac. 3145 |
| | | | **JIMMY BRISCOE & THE LITTLE BEAVERS**<br>Group from Baltimore. Consisted of Jimmy Briscoe (lead), Robert Makins, Stanford Stansbury (tenors), Kevin Barnes and Maurice Pully (baritones). All were 13 years old at the time of their first recording for Atlantic in 1971. | | |
| 7/28/73 | 68 | 11 | 1 Where Were You (When I Needed You) ............. | | Phi-Kappa 400 |
| 8/10/74 | 59 | 11 | 2 Ebony Princess................................ | | Phi-Kappa 600 |
| 6/14/75 | 86 | 5 | 3 I Only Feel This Way When I'm With You ......... | | Phi-Kappa 604 |
| 11/29/75 | 93 | 6 | 4 I'll Care For You ............................... | | Phi-Kappa 700 |
| 10/22/77 | 91 | 4 | 5 Invitation To The World .............................<br>shown as: **JIMMY BRISCOE & The Beavers** | | Wanderick 70001 |
| | | | **JOHNNY BRISTOL**<br>Vocalist/composer/producer from Morgantown, North Carolina. Teamed with Jackie Beaver, recorded as Johnny & Jackie for Tri-Phi, 1961. Teamed with Harvey Fuqua as Motown producers to 1973. Production work for CBS. | | |
| 7/06/74 | 2² | 17 | 1 **Hang On In There Baby**.............................. | 8 | MGM 14715 |
| 11/16/74 | 20 | 13 | 2 You And I........................................ | 48 | MGM 14762 |
| 3/29/75 | 23 | 10 | 3 Leave My World.......................................... | 104 | MGM 14792 |
| 7/26/75 | 72 | 8 | 4 Love Takes Tears....................................... | | MGM 14814 |
| 10/16/76 | 5 | 20 | 5 **Do It To My Mind**................................. | 43 | Atlantic 3360 |
| 3/26/77 | 36 | 10 | 6 You Turned Me On To Love/ | 106 | |
| 6/04/77 | 47 | 10 | 7 I Sho Like Groovin' With Ya........................ | | Atlantic 3391 |
| 4/01/78 | 27 | 14 | 8 Waiting On Love ................................ | | Atlantic 3421 |
| 2/02/80 | 73 | 3 | 9 Hang On In There Baby ...............................<br>**ALTON** (McClain) **& JOHNNY**<br>new version of #1 above | | Polydor 2050 |
| 10/04/80 | 76 | 3 | 10 My Guy/My Girl .......................................<br>**AMII STEWART & JOHNNY BRISTOL** | 63 | Handshake 5300 |
| 2/07/81 | 75 | 5 | 11 Love No Longer Has A Hold On Me .................. | | Handshake 5304 |
| | | | **TINA BRITT**<br>Tina Brittingham, singer from Florida. | | |
| 5/22/65 | 20 | 6 | 1 The Real Thing .......................................<br>also released on Lost-Nite 253 | 103 | Eastern 604 |
| 11/02/68 | 39 | 3 | 2 Who Was That ............................... | | Veep 1280 |
| | | | **BROADWAY**<br>Group led by vocalist Patti Williams. | | |
| 7/24/76 | 73 | 4 | 1 You To Me Are Everything ............................ | 86 | Granite 540 |
| 12/02/78 | 92 | 3 | 2 Kiss You All Over..........................<br>disco version of Exile's #1 pop hit | | Hilltak 7802 |
| 4/14/79 | 83 | 4 | 3 This Funk Is Made For Dancing ...................... | | Hilltak 7805 |
| | | | **BRONNER BROTHERS** | | |
| 7/07/84 | 80 | 5 | 1 I'm Not That Bad A Man To Love .................... | | Neighbor 003 |
| 10/20/84 | 66 | 9 | 2 Self Conscious............................................ | | Neighbor 005 |

**55**

| DEBUT DATE | PEAK POS | WKS CHR | ARTIST — Record Title | POP POS | Label & Number |
|---|---|---|---|---|---|
| | | | **ROBERT BROOKINS** | | |
| 12/27/86+ | 95 | 5 | 1 Our Lives.................................................... | | MCA 52949 |
| | | | **BROOKLYN DREAMS - see DONNA SUMMER** | | |
| | | | **ELLA BROOKS** | | |
| 7/25/87 | 89 | 5 | 1 It's Easy When You're On Fire......................... | | QMI 53095 |
| | | | **HADDA BROOKS** | | |
| | | | Vocalist/pianist in Los Angeles during the mid-40s. Appeared on early TV programs. The Hadda Brooks Trio consisted of Brooks (piano, vocals), Basie Day (bass) and Al Wichard (drums). On some records, Jimmy Black (alto sax) is heard. In 1947, the Hadda Brooks Quartet included: Brooks (piano), Teddy Bunn (guitar), Red Callendar (bass) and Al Wichard (drums). Recorded into the early 50s. Also see Smokey Hogg. | | |
| 5/24/47 | 4 | 3 | 1 **That's My Desire** ....................................... [I] | | Modern 147 |
| 9/25/48 | 9 | 2 | 2 **Out Of The Blue** ....................................... [I]<br>Best Seller #9 / Juke Box #12 | | Modern 600 |
| 10/16/48 | 3 | 1 | 3 **What Have I Done?** ................................. [I]<br>Juke Box #3 | | Modern 602 |
| | | | **LOUIS BROOKS & HIS HI-TOPPERS** | | |
| | | | Brooks was leader/pianist of small popular band in Nashville. Vocalist Earl Gaines was born on 8/19/35 in Decatur, Alabama. Also see Larry Birdsong. | | |
| 7/09/55 | 2² | 15 | 1 **It's Love Baby (24 Hours a Day)** ....................<br>Jockey #2 / Juke Box #2 / Best Seller #3<br>vocal by Earl Gaines | | Excello 2056 |
| | | | **MEL BROOKS** | | |
| | | | Comedic movie producer/director/actor. Married to actress Anne Bancroft. | | |
| 4/10/82 | 69 | 5 | 1 It's Good To Be The King............................ [C] | | WMOT 1396 |
| | | | **RAMONA BROOKS** | | |
| 10/01/77 | 94 | 6 | 1 Skinnydippin................................................ | | Manhattan 1052 |
| | | | **BOBBY BROOM** | | |
| | | | Formerly with jazz trumpeter Tom Browne. | | |
| 8/22/81 | 52 | 8 | 1 Saturday Night ........................................... [I] | | Arista/GRP 2516 |
| | | | **BROTHER BONES & HIS SHADOWS** | | |
| | | | "Brother Bones" (knuckle bones and whistling) with group featuring organ and Joe Darensbourg (clarinet). | | |
| 1/08/49 | 9 | 5 | 1 **Sweet Georgia Brown** ................................... | 10 | Tempo 652 |
| | | | Juke Box #9 / Best Seller #10<br>original Harlem Globetrotters theme with whistling chorus | | |
| | | | **BROTHER TO BROTHER** | | |
| | | | Group formed by Michael Burton from St. Louis. Consisted of Burton (lead vocalist), Billy Jones, Frankie Prescott and Yogi Horton. Burton was a staff writer for Stang Records; the others were studio musicians. | | |
| 7/27/74 | 9 | 16 | 1 **In The Bottle**............................................. | 46 | Turbo 039 |
| 2/28/76 | 71 | 8 | 2 Let Your Mind Be Free ................................. | | Turbo 045 |
| 8/14/76 | 30 | 11 | 3 Chance With You ........................................ | | Turbo 048 |
| | | | **BROTHERHOOD** | | |
| | | | Jazz group consisting of Tony Trevias, Les Coulter, Nathan White, Don DeLaTorre, Scottie White, Dwight White and Delbert White. | | |
| 11/20/76+ | 43 | 10 | 1 Home Is Where The Heart Is...........................<br>**BOBBY WOMACK & BROTHERHOOD** | | Columbia 10437 |
| 7/29/78 | 77 | 4 | 2 Change Of Pace ......................................... [I] | | MCA 40916 |
| | | | **BROTHERLY LOVE** | | |
| 2/26/72 | 20 | 8 | 1 Mama's Little Baby....................................... | | Music Mer. 1004 |
| | | | **BROTHERS BY CHOICE** | | |
| 9/09/78 | 79 | 7 | 1 She Puts The Ease Back Into Easy ................... | | ALA 103 |
| 2/17/79 | 51 | 12 | 2 Baby You Really Got Me Going ........................ | | ALA 104 |
| 1/26/80 | 39 | 11 | 3 Oh, Darlin................................................. | | ALA 108 |
| 7/05/80 | 87 | 6 | 4 How Much I Feel ........................................ | | ALA 110 |
| | | | **BROTHERS GUIDING LIGHT FEATURING DAVID** | | |
| 11/10/73+ | 61 | 11 | 1 Getting Together ........................................ | | Mercury 73389 |

| DEBUT DATE | PEAK POS | WKS CHR | ARTIST — Record Title | POP POS | Label & Number |
|---|---|---|---|---|---|
| | | | **THE BROTHERS JOHNSON** ★★155★★ | | |
| | | | Los Angeles duo of brothers George (b: 5/17/53) and Louis (b: 4/13/55). Played since age 7, had own band, the Johnson Three + 1, with brother Tommy and cousin Alex Weir. With Billy Preston band to 1975. Also see Quincy Jones. | | |
| 4/17/76 | 1¹ | 17 | 1 ●I'll Be Good To You | 3 | A&M 1806 |
| 8/14/76 | 4 | 14 | 2 Get The Funk Out Ma Face | 30 | A&M 1851 |
| 11/27/76+ | 26 | 10 | 3 Free And Single | 103 | A&M 1881 |
| 6/18/77 | 1¹ | 19 | 4 ●Strawberry Letter 23 | 5 | A&M 1949 |
| 10/29/77 | 20 | 12 | 5 Runnin' For Your Lovin' | 107 | A&M 1982 |
| 3/11/78 | 50 | 7 | 6 Love Is | | A&M 2015 |
| 9/30/78 | 45 | 9 | 7 Ride-O-Rocket | 104 | A&M 2086 |
| 11/18/78 | 45 | 8 | 8 Ain't We Funkin' Now | 102 | A&M 2098 |
| 2/16/80 | 1² | 18 | 9 Stomp! | 7 | A&M 2216 |
| 5/24/80 | 16 | 11 | 10 Light Up The Night | | A&M 2238 |
| 8/09/80 | 36 | 10 | 11 Treasure | 73 | A&M 2254 |
| 6/20/81 | 11 | 14 | 12 The Real Thing | 67 | A&M 2343 |
| 9/12/81 | 51 | 9 | 13 Dancin' Free | | A&M 2368 |
| 11/27/82 | 13 | 11 | 14 Welcome To The Club | | A&M 2506 |
| 3/26/83 | 75 | 5 | 15 I'm Giving You All Of My Love | | A&M 2527 |
| 7/07/84 | 12 | 15 | 16 You Keep Me Coming Back | 102 | A&M 2654 |
| 5/07/88 | 52 | 9 | 17 Kick It To The Curb | | A&M 3013 |
| | | | **BROTHERS OF SOUL** | | |
| | | | Detroit group: Fred Bridges, Robert Eaton and Richard Knight. | | |
| 4/13/68 | 32 | 5 | 1 I Guess That Don't Make Me A Loser | | Boo 1004 |
| | | | **BROWN SUGAR - see CLYDIE KING** | | |
| | | | **AL BROWN'S TUNETOPPERS** | | |
| | | | From Fairmont, West Virginia. Tunetoppers formed in 1953. | | |
| 5/02/60 | 14 | 8 | 1 The Madison | 23 | Amy 804 |
| | | | dance calls by Cookie Brown | | |
| | | | **ALEX BROWN** | | |
| | | | Female vocalist. | | |
| 4/10/76 | 65 | 7 | 1 Love Really Hurts Without You | | Roxbury 2024 |
| 5/18/85 | 66 | 6 | 2 (Come On) Shout | 76 | Mercury 880694 |
| | | | from the film "Girls Just Want To Have Fun" | | |
| | | | **BOBBY BROWN** | | |
| | | | Born on 2/5/69 in Boston. Former member of The New Edition. | | |
| 10/25/86 | 1² | 18 | 1 Girlfriend | 57 | MCA 52866 |
| 2/14/87 | 31 | 12 | 2 Girl Next Door | | MCA 53022 |
| 5/28/88 | 1² | 19 | 3 Don't Be Cruel | 8 | MCA 53327 |
| | | | **BUSTER BROWN** | | |
| | | | Vocalist/harmonica player, born on 8/15/11 in Cordele, Georgia. Died on 1/31/76. | | |
| 12/07/59+ | 1¹ | 25 | 1 Fannie Mae | 38 | Fire 1008 |
| 2/10/62 | 19 | 3 | 2 Sugar Babe | 99 | Fire 507 |
| | | | **CHARLES BROWN** ★★160★★ | | |
| | | | Vocalist/pianist, born in 1922 in Texas City, Texas. Taught at Carver High School in Baytown, Texas. To Los Angeles in 1943. Joined Johnny Moore's Three Blazers in in 1944. Formed own band in 1948. Married to Mabel Scott from 1949-51. Active in music into the 80s. Also see Mabel Scott. | | |
| | | | CHARLES BROWN TRIO: | | |
| 2/12/49 | 4 | 5 | 1 Get Yourself Another Fool | | Aladdin 3020 |
| | | | Best Seller #4 / Juke Box #6 | | |
| 3/19/49 | 9 | 2 | 2 Long Time/ | | |
| | | | Best Seller #9 / Juke Box #11 | | |
| 4/16/49 | 13 | 1 | 3 It's Nothing | | Aladdin 3021 |
| | | | Juke Box #13 | | |
| 4/23/49 | 1¹⁵ | 27 | 4 Trouble Blues | | Aladdin 3024 |
| | | | Best Seller #1(15) / Juke Box #1(11) | | |
| | | | CHARLES BROWN: | | |
| 8/20/49 | 4 | 10 | 5 In The Evening When The Sun Goes Down | | Aladdin 3030 |
| | | | Juke Box #4 / Best Seller #5 | | |
| 12/03/49 | 5 | 9 | 6 Homesick Blues | | Aladdin 3039 |
| | | | Juke Box #5 / Best Seller #6 | | |

| DEBUT DATE | PEAK POS | WKS CHR | ARTIST — Record Title | POP POS | Label & Number |
|---|---|---|---|---|---|
| | | | **CHARLES BROWN — Continued** | | |
| 12/10/49 | **15** | 1 | 7  I'll Miss You ................................................. | | Exclusive 120 |
| | | | Juke Box #15 | | |
| | | | with Johnny Moore's Three Blazers | | |
| 4/22/50 | **6** | 8 | 8  **My Baby's Gone** ........................................ | | Aladdin 3051 |
| | | | Best Seller #6 / Juke Box #10 | | |
| 2/10/51 | **1** [14] | 24 | 9  **Black Night**............................................... | | Aladdin 3076 |
| | | | Juke Box #1(14) / Best Seller #1(13) | | |
| 7/28/51 | **7** | 5 | 10  **I'll Always Be In Love With You** ................... | | Aladdin 3091 |
| | | | Juke Box #7 | | |
| 10/20/51 | **2** [1] | 9 | 11  **Seven Long Days** ..................................... | | Aladdin 3092 |
| | | | Best Seller #2 / Juke Box #5 | | |
| 3/01/52 | **7** | 3 | 12  **Hard Times**.............................................. | | Aladdin 3116 |
| | | | Best Seller #7 | | |
| 12/26/60 | **21** | 2 | 13  Please Come Home For Christmas................ [X] | 76 | King 5405 |
| | | | **CHUCK BROWN & THE SOUL SEARCHERS** | | |
| | | | Washington, DC-based 9-member group. | | |
| 12/16/78+ | **1** [4] | 21 | 1 ● Bustin' Loose, Part 1 ................................. | 34 | Source 40967 |
| 5/12/79 | **81** | 2 | 2  Game Seven ............................................. | | Source 41013 |
| 5/03/80 | **55** | 7 | 3  Sticks & Stones ....................................... | | Source 41226 |
| 7/21/84 | **26** | 13 | 4  We Need Some Money (Bout Money)................. | | T.T.E.D. 3004 |
| | | | **CLEO BROWN** | | |
| | | | Vocalist/pianist, born on 12/8/09 in Meridan, Missouri. Toured US as classical pianist while still a teenager. On Chicago radio in 1932 with Texas Guinan; own program on CBS debuted in 1935. Her version of "Pinetop's Boogie Woogie" (with Gene Krupa on drums) helped spark the boogie woogie revival craze of the late 30s. | | |
| 12/31/49 | **13** | 1 | 1  Cook That Stuff ........................................ | | Capitol 70057 |
| | | | Juke Box #13 | | |
| | | | **CLYDE BROWN** | | |
| | | | Vocalist from Cleveland, Ohio. With the Drifters vocal group in England from November, 1974. Recorded for Bell/Arista (UK), and Epic (UK). | | |
| 9/15/73 | **73** | 6 | 1  Ghetto Cowboy ......................................... | | Atlantic 2976 |
| 10/12/74 | **78** | 4 | 2  You Call Me Back........................................ | | Atlantic 2908 |
| | | | **DEE BROWN & LOLA GRANT** | | |
| 8/27/66 | **45** | 2 | 1  We Belong Together ................................... | | Shurfine 014 |
| | | | **DENNIS BROWN** | | |
| | | | Singer/songwriter, born in February of 1956 in Kingston, Jamaica. With the Falcons group (Jamaica); first recorded for Studio One in 1972. | | |
| 5/08/82 | **42** | 10 | 1  Love Has Found Its Way................................ | | A&M 2407 |
| | | | **GATEMOUTH BROWN** | | |
| | | | Born Clarence Brown, Jr. on 4/18/24 in Vinton, Louisiana. Raised in Orange, Texas. Vocalist/guitarist/violinist/drummer. Recorded for Aladdin in 1947. His brother James recorded as "Widemouth" Brown. Initially played country and and bluegrass music until the early 40s. The first artist on Don Robey's Peacock label in 1949. Returned to country music and recorded successfully with Roy Clark. | | |
| 11/12/49 | **8** | 1 | 1  **Mary Is Fine/** | | |
| | | | Juke Box #8 | | |
| | | | features Jack McVea on alto sax | | |
| 11/12/49 | **9** | 1 | 2  **My Time Is Expensive** ............................. | | Peacock 1504 |
| | | | Juke Box #9 | | |
| | | | **GLORIA D. BROWN** | | |
| 8/23/86 | **69** | 1 | 1  What Does It Take....................................... | | Krystal 916 |
| | | | **JAMES BROWN**   ★★ **1** ★★ | | |
| | | | Born on 5/3/28 in Macon, Georgia. Raised in Augusta. Formed own vocal group, the Famous Flames. Cut a demo record of own composition "Please Please Please", in November of 1955, at radio station WIBB in Macon. Signed to King/Federal Records in January, 1956 and re-recorded the song. Cameo appearances in films "The Blues Brothers" and "Rocky IV". One of the originators of "Soul" music, billed as "The Godfather Of Soul". His backing group, The JB's, featured various personnel, including: Nat Kendrick, Bootsy Collins, Maceo Parker and Fred Wesley. | | |
| 4/07/56 | **5** | 19 | 1  **Please, Please, Please**.................................. | 105 | Federal 12258 |
| | | | Jockey #5 / Best Seller #6 / Juke Box #9 | | |
| 11/10/58+ | **1** [1] | 22 | 2  **Try Me** ..................................................... | 48 | Federal 12337 |
| 4/20/59 | **20** | 2 | 3  I Want You So Bad ...................................... | | Federal 12348 |
| 2/22/60 | **15** | 11 | 4  I'll Go Crazy.............................................. | | Federal 12369 |

| DEBUT DATE | PEAK POS | WKS CHR | ARTIST — Record Title | POP POS | Label & Number |
|---|---|---|---|---|---|
| | | | **JAMES BROWN — Continued** | | |
| 5/30/60 | **7** | 14 | 5 **Think/** | *33* | |
| 5/30/60 | **14** | 8 | 6 You've Got The Power.................... | *86* | Federal 12370 |
| | | | female vocal by Bea Ford | | |
| 9/26/60 | **20** | 2 | 7 This Old Heart.................... | *79* | Federal 12378 |
| 3/13/61 | **8** | 8 | 8 **Bewildered**.................... | *40* | King 5442 |
| 5/29/61 | **4** | 12 | 9 **I Don't Mind**.................... | *47* | King 5466 |
| 8/07/61 | **2**¹ | 19 | 10 **Baby, You're Right**.................... | *49* | King 5524 |
| 9/18/61 | **17** | 10 | 11 Just You And Me, Darling.................... | | King 5547 |
| 12/18/61+ | **2**⁴ | 17 | 12 **Lost Someone**.................... | *48* | King 5573 |
| 4/21/62 | **5** | 17 | 13 **Night Train**.................... [I] | *35* | King 5614 |
| 7/28/62 | **16** | 5 | 14 Shout And Shimmy.................... | *61* | King 5657 |
| 10/06/62 | **21** | 1 | 15 Mashed Potatoes U.S.A..................... | *82* | King 5672 |
| 12/08/62 | **18** | 6 | 16 Three Hearts In A Tangle .................... | *93* | King 5701 |
| 3/02/63 | **24** | 2 | 17 Like A Baby.................... | | King 5710 |
| 5/11/63 | **6** | 12 | 18 **Prisoner Of Love**.................... | *18* | King 5739 |
| 8/10/63 | **25** | 5 | 19 These Foolish Things.................... | *55* | King 5767 |
| 10/12/63 | **77** | 5 | 20 Signed, Sealed, And Delivered .................... | *Hot* | King 5803 |
| 1/25/64 | **23** | 10 | 21 Oh Baby Don't You Weep (Part 1).................... | *Hot* | King 5842 |
| 2/15/64 | **95** | 2 | 22 Please, Please, Please .................... | *Hot* | King 5853 |
| 5/02/64 | **95** | 2 | 23 Caledonia.................... | *Hot* | Smash 1898 |
| 7/04/64 | **99** | 1 | 24 The Things That I Used To Do .................... | *Hot* | Smash 1908 |
| 8/15/64 | **24** | 10 | 25 Out Of Sight .................... | *Hot* | Smash 1919 |
| 12/26/64+ | **92** | 2 | 26 Have Mercy Baby .................... | *Hot* | King 5968 |
| 7/17/65 | **1**⁸ | 17 | 27 **Papa's Got A Brand New Bag (Part I)**.................... | *8* | King 5999 |
| 11/13/65 | **1**⁶ | 16 | 28 **I Got You (I Feel Good)** .................... | *3* | King 6015 |
| 12/25/65 | **34** | 4 | 29 Try Me .................... [I] | *63* | Smash 2008 |
| | | | instrumental version of #2 above | | |
| 3/05/66 | **38** | 2 | 30 I'll Go Crazy.................... | *73* | King 6020 |
| | | | live version of #4 above; recorded at the Apollo Theater, 10/24/62 | | |
| 3/12/66 | **6** | 10 | 31 **Ain't That A Groove (Part 1)**.................... | *42* | King 6025 |
| 5/07/66 | **1**² | 12 | 32 **It's A Man's Man's Man's World** .................... | *8* | King 6035 |
| 8/06/66 | **11** | 10 | 33 Money Won't Change You (Part 1) .................... | *53* | King 6048 |
| 10/15/66 | **4** | 13 | 34 **Don't Be A Drop-Out** .................... | *50* | King 6056 |
| 1/21/67 | **7** | 8 | 35 **Bring It Up** .................... | *29* | King 6071 |
| 3/18/67 | **21** | 6 | 36 Kansas City .................... | *55* | King 6086 |
| 5/13/67 | **5** | 11 | 37 **Let Yourself Go** .................... | *46* | King 6100 |
| 7/22/67 | **1**³ | 16 | 38 **Cold Sweat (Part 1)**.................... | *7* | King 6110 |
| 10/28/67 | **11** | 9 | 39 Get It Together (Part 1) .................... | *40* | King 6122 |
| 12/23/67+ | **4** | 11 | 40 **I Can't Stand Myself (When You Touch Me)/** | *28* | |
| 1/27/68 | **3** | 11 | 41 **There Was A Time** .................... | *36* | King 6144 |
| 3/16/68 | **47** | 2 | 42 You've Got To Change Your Mind.................... | *102* | King 6151 |
| | | | **BOBBY BYRD & JAMES BROWN** | | |
| 3/23/68 | **1**² | 12 | 43 **I Got The Feelin'** .................... | *6* | King 6155 |
| 5/25/68 | **2**¹ | 14 | 44 **Licking Stick - Licking Stick (Part 1)**.................... | *14* | King 6166 |
| 6/01/68 | **13** | 6 | 45 America Is My Home (Part 1) .................... [S] | *52* | King 6112 |
| 8/03/68 | **15** | 6 | 46 I Guess I'll Have To Cry, Cry, Cry.................... | *55* | King 6141 |
| | | | all of above on King shown as: **JAMES BROWN & The Famous Flames** | | |
| 9/14/68 | **1**⁶ | 12 | 47 **Say It Loud - I'm Black And I'm Proud (Part 1)** .................... | *10* | King 6187 |
| 11/23/68 | **9** | 10 | 48 **Goodbye My Love** .................... | *31* | King 6198 |
| 2/01/69 | **1**² | 11 | 49 **Give It Up Or Turnit A Loose** .................... | *15* | King 6213 |
| 4/05/69 | **33** | 5 | 50 Soul Pride (Part 1) .................... [I] | *117* | King 6222 |
| 4/12/69 | **3** | 10 | 51 **I Don't Want Nobody To Give Me Nothing (Open Up The Door, I'll Get It Myself)** .................... | *20* | King 6224 |
| 6/07/69 | **11** | 9 | 52 The Popcorn .................... [I] | *30* | King 6240 |
| 6/21/69 | **1**² | 15 | 53 **Mother Popcorn (You Got To Have A Mother For Me) (Part 1)**.................... | *11* | King 6245 |
| 9/06/69 | **16** | 7 | 54 Lowdown Popcorn .................... [I] | *41* | King 6250 |
| 9/13/69 | **8** | 8 | 55 **World (Part 1)** .................... | *37* | King 6258 |
| 10/25/69 | **2**² | 9 | 56 **Let A Man Come In And Do The Popcorn (Part One)**.................... | *21* | King 6255 |

| DEBUT DATE | PEAK POS | WKS CHR | ARTIST — Record Title | POP POS | Label & Number |
|---|---|---|---|---|---|
| | | | **JAMES BROWN — Continued** | | |
| 11/29/69 | 3 | 12 | 57 Ain't It Funky Now (Part 1) ...................... [I] | 24 | King 6280 |
| 12/27/69+ | 6 | 8 | 58 Let A Man Come In And Do The Popcorn (Part Two)........................................................ | 40 | King 6275 |
| 2/21/70 | 3 | 11 | 59 It's A New Day (Part 1)................................. | 32 | King 6292 |
| 3/28/70 | 20 | 5 | 60 Funky Drummer (Part 1)............................... | 51 | King 6290 |
| 5/02/70 | 2² | 11 | 61 Brother Rapp (Part 1)................................... | 32 | King 6310 |
| 7/25/70 | 2³ | 12 | 62 Get Up (I Feel Like Being Like A) Sex Machine (Part 1)...................................................... | 15 | King 6318 |
| 10/10/70 | 1² | 13 | 63 Super Bad (Part 1 & Part 2).......................... | 13 | King 6329 |
| 1/09/71 | 4 | 9 | 64 Get Up, Get Into It, Get Involved (Part 1)....... | 34 | King 6347 |
| 3/06/71 | 3 | 11 | 65 Soul Power (Part 1)..................................... | 29 | King 6368 |
| 5/15/71 | 15 | 5 | 66 I Cried..................................................... | 50 | King 6363 |
| 6/12/71 | 6 | 9 | 67 Escape-ism (Part 1).............................. [S] | 35 | People 2500 |
| 7/10/71 | 1¹ | 11 | 68 Hot Pants (She Got To Use What She Got, To Get What She Wants) (Part 1) .................... | 15 | People 2501 |
| 8/28/71 | 1² | 12 | 69 Make It Funky (Part 1)................................ | 22 | Polydor 14088 |
| 11/13/71 | 7 | 11 | 70 I'm A Greedy Man (Part I)............................ | 35 | Polydor 14100 |
| 2/12/72 | 1¹ | 10 | 71 Talking Loud And Saying Nothing (Part I) ..... | 27 | Polydor 14109 |
| 3/04/72 | 6 | 8 | 72 King Heroin .................................... [S] | 40 | Polydor 14116 |
| 5/13/72 | 4 | 9 | 73 There It Is (Part 1)................................... | 43 | Polydor 14125 |
| 7/01/72 | 7 | 10 | 74 Honky Tonk (Part 1) ............................ [I] | 44 | Polydor 14129 |
| 8/12/72 | 1⁴ | 15 | 75●Get On The Good Foot (Part 1) .................. | 18 | Polydor 14139 |
| 11/18/72+ | 3 | 13 | 76 I Got A Bag Of My Own .............................. | 44 | Polydor 14153 |
| 12/23/72+ | 17 | 10 | 77 What My Baby Needs Now Is A Little More Lovin'................................................. | 56 | Polydor 14157 |
| | | | **JAMES BROWN-LYN COLLINS** | | |
| 1/20/73 | 4 | 10 | 78 I Got Ants In My Pants (and i want to dance) (Part 1)...................................................... | 27 | Polydor 14162 |
| 3/24/73 | 13 | 6 | 79 Down And Out In New York City ................... from the film "Black Caesar" | 50 | Polydor 14168 |
| 5/12/73 | 15 | 8 | 80 Think............................................... | 77 | Polydor 14177 |
| 7/14/73 | 37 | 6 | 81 Think............................................... | 80 | Polydor 14185 |
| | | | **VICKI ANDERSON & JAMES BROWN** above 2: each different versions of #5 above | | |
| 8/25/73 | 6 | 15 | 82 Sexy, Sexy, Sexy........................................ from the film "Slaughter's Big Rip-Off" | 50 | Polydor 14194 |
| 11/10/73+ | 4 | 17 | 83 Stoned To The Bone (Part 1) ....................... | 58 | Polydor 14210 |
| 3/09/74 | 1² | 17 | 84●The Payback (Part I) ................................. | 26 | Polydor 14223 |
| 6/08/74 | 1² | 15 | 85 My Thang ................................................ | 29 | Polydor 14244 |
| 8/24/74 | 1¹ | 14 | 86 Papa Don't Take No Mess (Part I) ................. | 31 | Polydor 14255 |
| 11/02/74+ | 4 | 15 | 87 Funky President (People It's Bad)................. | 44 | Polydor 14258 |
| 2/22/75 | 19 | 9 | 88 Reality ................................................... | 80 | Polydor 14268 |
| 4/19/75 | 16 | 12 | 89 Sex Machine (Part I)................................. new version of #62 above | 61 | Polydor 14270 |
| 7/12/75 | 11 | 13 | 90 Hustle!!! (Dead On It)............................... | | Polydor 14281 |
| 10/18/75 | 28 | 9 | 91 Superbad, Superslick Part I.......................... | | Polydor 14295 |
| 11/29/75+ | 31 | 11 | 92 Hot (I Need To Be Loved, Loved, Loved, Loved)... | | Polydor 14301 |
| 3/27/76 | 70 | 4 | 93 (I Love You) For Sentimental Reasons.............. | | Polydor 14304 |
| 6/05/76 | 4 | 19 | 94 Get Up Offa That Thing............................... | 45 | Polydor 14326 |
| 10/23/76 | 47 | 8 | 95 I Refuse To Lose ...................................... | | Polydor 14354 |
| 12/11/76+ | 13 | 18 | 96 Bodyheat (Part 1) ..................................... | 88 | Polydor 14360 |
| 4/30/77 | 35 | 9 | 97 Kiss In 77 .............................................. | | Polydor 14388 |
| 7/30/77 | 20 | 15 | 98 Give Me Some Skin..................................... | | Polydor 14409 |
| | | | **JAMES BROWN & THE J.B.'s** | | |
| 12/17/77+ | 45 | 10 | 99 If You Don't Give A Dogone About It................ | | Polydor 14438 |
| 4/22/78 | 38 | 9 | 100 Eyesight ............................................... | | Polydor 14465 |
| 6/24/78 | 26 | 12 | 101 The Spank ............................................. | | Polydor 14487 |
| 12/16/78+ | 52 | 8 | 102 For Goodness Sakes, Look At Those Cakes (Part I)........................................................ | | Polydor 14522 |
| 5/26/79 | 15 | 14 | 103 It's Too Funky In Here ............................. | | Polydor 14557 |
| 9/08/79 | 63 | 6 | 104 Star Generation ..................................... | | Polydor 2005 |
| 1/26/80 | 63 | 6 | 105 Regrets .............................................. | | Polydor 2054 |

**60**

| DEBUT DATE | PEAK POS | WKS CHR | ARTIST — Record Title | POP POS | Label & Number |
|---|---|---|---|---|---|
| | | | **JAMES BROWN — Continued** | | |
| 11/15/80 | **46** | 13 | 106 Rapp Payback (Where iz Moses) ........................ | | T.K. 1039 |
| 4/04/81 | **80** | 4 | 107 Stay With Me................................................. | | T.K. 1042 |
| 5/28/83 | **73** | 9 | 108 Bring It On...Bring It On/ | | |
| | | 5 | 109 The Night Time Is The Right Time (To Be With The One That You Love) ........................ | | Augusta S. 94023 |
| 9/15/84 | **87** | 4 | 110 Unity ....................................................... | | Tommy Boy 847 |
| | | | AFRIKA BAMBAATAA & JAMES BROWN | | |
| 12/28/85+ | **10** | 17 | 111 **Living In America**............................... | *4* | Scotti Br. 05682 |
| | | | from the film "Rocky IV"; produced by Dan Hartman | | |
| 10/04/86 | **26** | 10 | 112 Gravity................................................ | 93 | Scotti Br. 06275 |
| 1/17/87 | **10** | 14 | 113 **How Do You Stop** ................................ | | Scotti Br. 06568 |
| 5/14/88 | **2**¹ | 16 | 114 **I'm Real**.......................................... | | Scotti Br. 07783 |
| | | | **JOCELYN BROWN** | | |
| | | | Born and raised in North Carolina. Backing vocalist for Luther Vandross, George Benson, John Lennon and many others. Singer with the disco groups Inner Life and Salsoul Orchestra. | | |
| 4/28/84 | **2**¹ | 22 | 1 **Somebody Else's Guy** ................................... | 75 | Vinyl Dreams 71 |
| 9/08/84 | **49** | 9 | 2 I Wish You Would ................................... | | Vinyl Dreams 72 |
| 1/25/86 | **38** | 10 | 3 Love's Gonna Get You................................... | | Warner 28889 |
| 2/28/87 | **38** | 12 | 4 Ego Maniac ................................... | | Warner 28698 |
| 7/11/87 | **72** | 6 | 5 Whatever Satisfies You ................................... | | Warner 28322 |
| 10/03/87 | **94** | 1 | 6 Caught In The Act................................... | | Warner 28220 |
| | | | **MAXINE BROWN** | | |
| | | | Born in Kingstree, South Carolina. With gospel groups Manhattans and Royaltones in New York City in the late 1950s. | | |
| 1/23/61 | **2**² | 14 | 1 **All In My Mind** ..................................... | *19* | Nomar 103 |
| 4/17/61 | **3** | 6 | 2 **Funny** ........................................... | *25* | Nomar 106 |
| 1/04/64 | **99** | 2 | 3 Coming Back To You ................................... | *Hot* | Wand 142 |
| 10/24/64+ | **24** | 13 | 4 Oh No Not My Baby ................................... | *Hot* | Wand 162 |
| 2/20/65 | **26** | 6 | 5 It's Gonna Be Alright ................................... | 56 | Wand 173 |
| 5/08/65 | **10** | 11 | 6 **Something You Got** ............................... | 55 | Wand 181 |
| 3/04/67 | **20** | 7 | 7 Hold On I'm Coming ................................... | 91 | Wand 1148 |
| 6/03/67 | **46** | 3 | 8 Daddy's Home ................................... | 91 | Wand 1155 |
| | | | above 3: **CHUCK JACKSON & MAXINE BROWN** | | |
| 9/27/69 | **15** | 9 | 9 We'll Cry Together ........................ | 73 | Commonw. 3001 |
| 4/11/70 | **44** | 3 | 10 I Can't Get Along Without You ........................ | | Commonw. 3008 |
| | | | **NAPPY BROWN** | | |
| | | | Born Napoleon Culp Brown on 10/12/29 in Charlotte, North Carolina. Sang with gospel group, the Golden Bell Quintet in the late 40s. With Selah Singers for a short time. Recorded with the Heavenly Lights for Savoy in 1954. Returned to gospel music, recording with the Bell Jubilee Singers of North Carolina and as Brother Napoleon Brown. Toured England in 1986. | | |
| 4/16/55 | **2**³ | 15 | 1 **Don't Be Angry** ................................... | 25 | Savoy 1155 |
| | | | Juke Box #2 / Best Seller #2 / Jockey #4 | | |
| 7/23/55 | **10** | 3 | 2 **Pitter Patter** ................................... | | Savoy 1162 |
| | | | Best Seller #10 / Jockey #13 above 2: with the Howard Biggs Orchestra | | |
| 10/20/58 | **8** | 12 | 3 **It Don't Hurt No More** ................................... | 89 | Savoy 1551 |
| | | | with the Teacho Wiltshire Orchestra | | |
| 12/07/59 | **22** | 2 | 4 I Cried Like A Baby ................................... | | Savoy 1575 |
| | | | recorded in 1956 with the Kelly Owens Orchestra | | |
| | | | **O'CHI BROWN** | | |
| 6/07/86 | **88** | 1 | 1 Whenever You Need Somebody ........................ | | Mercury 884572 |
| 8/30/86 | **73** | 4 | 2 100% Pure Pain ................................... | | Mercury 884886 |
| | | | **OSCAR BROWN JR.** | | |
| | | | Born in Chicago on 10/10/26. Radio actor while still a teenager. Worked as a journalist and in public relations. Hosted Jazz Scene, USA TV series, in 1962. | | |
| 3/23/74 | **27** | 14 | 1 The Lone Ranger ................................... | 69 | Atlantic 3001 |
| | | | **PETER BROWN** | | |
| | | | Vocalist/keyboardist/producer, born on 7/11/53 in Blue Island, Illinois. Attended Art Institute of Chicago. | | |
| 7/16/77 | **3** | 23 | 1 **Do You Wanna Get Funky With Me** ............... | *18* | Drive 6258 |
| 2/11/78 | **5** | 22 | 2 **Dance With Me** ........................................ | *8* | Drive 6269 |

| DEBUT DATE | PEAK POS | WKS CHR | ARTIST — Record Title | POP POS | Label & Number |
|---|---|---|---|---|---|
| | | | **PETER BROWN — Continued** | | |
| 9/02/78 | **25** | 15 | 3 You Should Do It.......................... | *54* | Drive 6272 |
| | | | above 2: background vocals by Betty Wright | | |
| 6/16/79 | **9** | 17 | 4 **Crank It Up (Funk Town) Pt. 1** ................ | *86* | Drive 6278 |
| 6/07/80 | **74** | 3 | 5 Can't Be Love-Do It To Me Anyway................. | | Drive 6286 |
| 1/08/83 | **49** | 11 | 6 Baby Gets High............................ | *104* | RCA 13413 |
| 3/31/84 | **50** | 10 | 7 They Only Come Out At Night .............. | *102* | Columbia 04381 |
| | | | **POLLY BROWN** | | |
| | | | English, lead singer of British groups Pickettywitch and Sweet Dreams. | | |
| 11/15/75 | **94** | 2 | 1 Special Delivery........................... | | Ariola Am. 7603 |
| | | | **RANDY BROWN** | | |
| | | | Vocalist/songwriter from Memphis. | | |
| 3/25/78 | **89** | 4 | 1 I'd Rather Hurt Myself (Than To Hurt You)........ | | Parachute 506 |
| 9/16/78 | **22** | 17 | 2 I Wanna Make Love To You.................. | | Parachute 517 |
| 4/07/79 | **47** | 7 | 3 You Says It All ........................... | *72* | Parachute 523 |
| 6/23/79 | **71** | 5 | 4 I Thought Of You Today ................... | | Parachute 526 |
| 3/08/80 | **16** | 16 | 5 We Ought To Be Doin' It.................. | | Choc. City 3204 |
| 4/11/81 | **31** | 13 | 6 If I Don't Love You ...................... | | Choc. City 3224 |
| | | | **ROY BROWN**   ★★**118**★★ | | |
| | | | Vocalist/pianist, born on 9/10/25 in New Orleans. Formed gospel group, the Rookie Four, at age 12. To Los Angeles as a professional boxer in 1942. Returned to singing in 1945. One of the originators of the New Orleans R&B sound. Died on 5/25/81 (55) in Los Angeles. | | |
| 6/12/48 | **13** | 1 | 1 Good Rockin' Tonight ..................... | | DeLuxe 1093 |
| | | | Best Seller #13<br>written by Brown; with Bob Ogden's Orchestra | | |
| 10/23/48 | **1**¹ | 17 | 2 **'Long About Midnight** ................... | | DeLuxe 1154 |
| | | | Best Seller #1 / Juke Box #3 | | |
| 1/01/49 | **6** | 6 | 3 **'Fore Day In The Morning/** | | |
| | | | Best Seller #6 / Juke Box #6 | | |
| 1/22/49 | **5** | 6 | 4 **Rainy Weather Blues**.................... | | DeLuxe 3198 |
| | | | Juke Box #5 / Best Seller #9 | | |
| 3/19/49 | **2**⁴ | 16 | 5 **Rockin' At Midnight** .................... | | DeLuxe 3212 |
| | | | Best Seller #2 / Juke Box #2 | | |
| 4/09/49 | **8** | 1 | 6 **Miss Fanny Brown** ..................... | | DeLuxe 3128 |
| | | | Juke Box #8 | | |
| 4/16/49 | **11** | 2 | 7 Good Rockin' Tonight ................ [R] | | DeLuxe 3093 |
| | | | Best Seller #11 | | |
| 9/17/49 | **9** | 6 | 8 **Please Don't Go**........................ | | DeLuxe 3226 |
| | | | Juke Box #9 | | |
| 11/19/49 | **3** | 12 | 9 **Boogie At Midnight**..................... | | DeLuxe 3300 |
| | | | Best Seller #3 / Juke Box #3 | | |
| 6/24/50 | **1**³ | 18 | 10 **Hard Luck Blues**........................ | | DeLuxe 3304 |
| | | | Best Seller #1 / Juke Box #3<br>with the Griffin Brothers Orchestra; a reported million-seller | | |
| 9/23/50 | **2**¹ | 11 | 11 **Love Don't Love Nobody** .............. | | DeLuxe 3306 |
| | | | Best Seller #2 / Juke Box #3 | | |
| 10/21/50 | **8** | 1 | 12 **Long About Sundown/** | | |
| | | | Best Seller #8 | | |
| 10/28/50 | **6** | 2 | 13 **Cadillac Baby**........................ | | DeLuxe 3308 |
| | | | Best Seller #6 | | |
| 8/25/51 | **8** | 1 | 14 **Big Town** ............................ | | DeLuxe 3318 |
| | | | Best Seller #8<br>with Tiny Bradshaw's Orchestra | | |
| 12/01/51+ | **6** | 5 | 15 **Bar Room Blues** ....................... | | DeLuxe 3319 |
| | | | 2-6, 8-11 & 15 shown as: **ROY BROWN & His Mighty, Mighty Men**<br>Juke Box #6 | | |
| 3/23/57 | **13** | 2 | 16 **Party Doll**............................ | *89* | Imperial 5427 |
| | | | Jockey #13 / Best Seller #14 | | |
| 5/20/57 | **5** | 7 | 17 **Let The Four Winds Blow** .............. | *29* | Imperial 5439 |
| | | | Jockey #5 | | |

| DEBUT DATE | PEAK POS | WKS CHR | ARTIST — Record Title | POP POS | Label & Number |
|---|---|---|---|---|---|
| | | | **RUTH BROWN** ★★**55**★★ | | |
| | | | Born on 1/30/28 in Portsmouth, Virginia as Ruth Weston. In late 1946, sang for one month with Lucky Millinder's band, then fired. Later heard by Duke Ellington, who alerted Herb Abramson of the then-new Atlantic Records, who signed her to a contract. Became Atlantic Records' top selling artist of the 1950s. Married for a time to Willis Jackson. In later years, had acting roles in the TV shows "Hello, Larry" and "Checking In", plus several Broadway and Las Vegas musicals. Appeared in the films "Under The Rainbow" (1981) and "Hairspray" (1988). | | |
| 9/17/49 | 4 | 10 | 1  **So Long** .............................................<br>Best Seller #4 / Juke Box #4<br>with Eddie Condon's NBC Television Orchestra | | Atlantic 879 |
| 10/28/50 | 1 11 | 25 | 2  **Teardrops From My Eyes**...........................<br>Best Seller #1(11) / Juke Box #1(7) | | Atlantic 919 |
| 3/17/51 | 3 | 4 | 3  **I'll Wait For You** ..................................<br>Best Seller #3 / Juke Box #6 | | Atlantic 930 |
| 7/21/51 | 7 | 4 | 4  **I Know**...............................................<br>Best Seller #7<br>above 3: with Budd Johnson's Orchestra | | Atlantic 941 |
| 4/12/52 | 1 7 | 16 | 5  **5-10-15 Hours** ....................................<br>Best Seller #1(7) / Juke Box #1(6)<br>a reported million-seller | | Atlantic 962 |
| 9/06/52 | 3 | 9 | 6  **Daddy Daddy** ......................................<br>Best Seller #3 / Juke Box #4 | | Atlantic 973 |
| 2/14/53 | 1 5 | 16 | 7  **(Mama) He Treats Your Daughter Mean**.........<br>Best Seller #1(5) / Juke Box #1(5)<br>featuring Taft Jordan on trumpet | 23 | Atlantic 986 |
| 6/20/53 | 3 | 10 | 8  **Wild Wild Young Men/**<br>Best Seller #3 | | |
| 7/18/53 | 7 | 2 | 9  **Mend Your Ways**...................................<br>Juke Box #7 | | Atlantic 993 |
| 8/07/54 | 1 8 | 17 | 10 **Oh What A Dream**................................<br>Juke Box #1(8) / Best Seller #1(4)<br>written especially for Ruth by Chuck Willis | | Atlantic 1036 |
| 10/30/54 | 1 1 | 12 | 11 **Mambo Baby** ......................................<br>Best Seller #1(1) Juke Box #1(1) / Jockey #6 | | Atlantic 1044 |
| 1/29/55 | 13 | 1 | 12 Bye Bye Young Men...............................<br>Jockey #13 | | Atlantic 1051 |
| 6/04/55 | 7 | 5 | 13 **I Can See Everybody's Baby/**<br>Jockey #7 / Juke Box #7 | | |
| 6/11/55 | 4 | 8 | 14 **As Long As I'm Moving** .........................<br>Best Seller #4 / Juke Box #4 / Jockey #7 | | Atlantic 1059 |
| 9/03/55 | 4 | 7 | 15 **It's Love Baby (24 Hours A Day)**.................<br>Jockey #4 / Best Seller #14 | | Atlantic 1072 |
| 12/03/55 | 8 | 3 | 16 **Love Has Joined Us Together**....................<br>**RUTH BROWN & CLYDE McPHATTER**<br>Jockey #8 | | Atlantic 1077 |
| 12/31/55+ | 3 | 7 | 17 **I Wanna Do More** ................................<br>10-14 & 17 shown as: **RUTH BROWN & HER RHYTHMAKERS**<br>Jockey #3 | | Atlantic 1082 |
| 5/26/56 | 10 | 1 | 18 **Sweet Baby Of Mine** .............................<br>Juke Box #10 | | Atlantic 1091 |
| 3/02/57 | 6 | 10 | 19 **Lucky Lips**.........................................<br>Jockey #6 / Juke Box #6 / Best Seller #12 | 25 | Atlantic 1125 |
| 10/06/58 | 7 | 4 | 20 **This Little Girl's Gone Rockin'/**<br>Jockey #7<br>sax solo by King Curtis | 24 | |
| 10/27/58 | 17 | 5 | 21 Why Me................................................ | | Atlantic 1197 |
| 7/06/59 | 23 | 2 | 22 Jack O'Diamonds .................................... | 96 | Atlantic 2026 |
| 10/19/59 | 5 | 11 | 23 **I Don't Know** ...................................... | 64 | Atlantic 2035 |
| 4/04/60 | 10 | 5 | 24 **Don't Deceive Me** ................................ | 62 | Atlantic 2052 |
| | | | **SHARON BROWN** | | |
| 4/17/82 | 51 | 12 | 1  I Specialize In Love ................................ | | Profile 5006 |
| | | | **SHAWN BROWN** | | |
| 4/20/85 | 73 | 8 | 1  Rappin' Duke ........................................ | | JWP 1460 |
| | | | **SHEREE BROWN** | | |
| | | | Los Angeles singer/songwriter/guitarist (since age 10). Songwriter for Syreeta and Patrice Rushen. | | |
| 10/10/81 | 65 | 7 | 1  You'll Be Dancing All Night......................... | | Capitol 5026 |
| 8/28/82 | 69 | 5 | 2  Happy Music ......................................... | | Capitol 5144 |

| DEBUT DATE | PEAK POS | WKS CHR | ARTIST — Record Title | POP POS | Label & Number |
|---|---|---|---|---|---|
| | | | **SHIRLEY BROWN** | | |
| | | | Born on 1/6/47 in West Memphis, Arkansas. Raised in East St. Louis. Worked with Albert King. | | |
| 9/28/74 | **1**² | 16 | 1 **Woman To Woman**........................................ | 22 | Truth 3206 |
| 5/10/75 | **32** | 13 | 2 It Ain't No Fun .............................................. | 94 | Truth 3223 |
| 2/12/77 | **14** | 15 | 3 Blessed Is The Woman (With A Man Like Mine)... | 102 | Arista 0231 |
| 6/25/77 | **50** | 10 | 4 I Need Somebody To Love Me ......................... | | Arista 0254 |
| 7/22/78 | **92** | 3 | 5 I Can't Move No Mountains ............................ | | Arista 0334 |
| 9/15/79 | **73** | 5 | 6 After A Night Like This................................ | | Stax 3222 |
| 11/29/80 | **73** | 5 | 7 You've Got To Like What You Do .................... | | 20th Century 2473 |
| 3/24/84 | **73** | 8 | 8 Leave The Bridges Standing .......................... | | Sound Town 0005 |
| 9/01/84 | **68** | 8 | 9 I Don't Play That ........................................ | | Sound Town 0007 |
| 12/22/84+ | **70** | 9 | 10 This Used To Be Your House .......................... | | Sound Town 0009 |
| 5/25/85 | **69** | 8 | 11 Boyfriend ................................................. | | Sound Town 0012 |
| | | | **VEDA BROWN** | | |
| 6/30/73 | **34** | 10 | 1 Short Stopping........................................... | | Stax 0163 |
| 3/02/74 | **87** | 6 | 2 Don't Start Loving Me (If You're Gonna Stop) ..... | | Stax 0194 |
| | | | **WINI BROWN** | | |
| | | | Vocalist based in Chicago. Married to Charles Fowlkes (baritone saxophonist with Lionel Hampton, Tiny Bradshaw, Arnett Cobb, and Count Basie). Also see Lionel Hampton. | | |
| 5/10/52 | **10** | 1 | 1 **Be Anything (But Be Mine)**......................... | | Mercury 8270 |
| | | | Best Seller #10 | | |
| | | | with Bill Doggett on organ | | |
| | | | **TOM BROWNE** | | |
| | | | Jazz trumpeter, first played classical music at the High School of Music and Art in New York City. With Weldon Ervine in 1975, Sonny Fortune and Fatback Band in 1976. | | |
| 8/02/80 | **1**⁴ | 21 | 1 **Funkin' For Jamaica (N.Y.)**......................... | | GRP 2506 |
| 1/24/81 | **4** | 18 | 2 **Thighs High (Grip Your Hips And Move)**........ | | GRP 2510 |
| 5/16/81 | **59** | 7 | 3 Let's Dance.............................................. | | GRP 2513 |
| 12/12/81+ | **23** | 12 | 4 Fungi Mama/Bebopafunkadiscolypso ................ | | GRP 2518 |
| 3/27/82 | **72** | 4 | 5 Bye Gones............................................... | | GRP 2519 |
| 10/01/83 | **11** | 18 | 6 Rockin' Radio ........................................... | | Arista 9088 |
| 1/28/84 | **63** | 6 | 7 Cruisin'................................................... | | Arista 9144 |
| 10/20/84 | **36** | 14 | 8 Secret Fantasy .......................................... | | Arista 9272 |
| | | | **BROWNMARK** | | |
| | | | Bassist/songwriter/producer from Minneapolis. Joined Prince's band, The Revolution, as bassist at age 18. Founded the band, Mazarati. | | |
| 2/06/88 | **48** | 11 | 1 Next Time................................................ | | Motown 1923 |
| | | | **THE BROWNS** | | |
| | | | Family trio: Jim Ed Brown (b: 4/1/34, Sparkman, AR) and his sisters Maxine (b: 4/27/32, Sampti, LA) and Bonnie (b: 7/31/37, Sparkman, AR). | | |
| 8/24/59 | **10** | 10 | 1 **The Three Bells**....................................... | 1 | RCA 7555 |
| 5/09/60 | **17** | 3 | 2 The Old Lamplighter.................................... | 5 | RCA 7700 |
| | | | **TYRONE BRUNSON** | | |
| | | | Vocalist/bass player from Washington, DC. Played with Osaris, Special Delivery, Destiny, and Family. | | |
| 11/13/82+ | **14** | 18 | 1 The Smurf ............................................... | | Believe 03163 |
| 3/05/83 | **25** | 14 | 2 Sticky Situation ........................................ | | Believe 03511 |
| | | | **TYRONE "TYSTICK" BRUNSON** | | |
| 7/02/83 | **70** | 5 | 3 Hot Line.................................................. | | Believe 03937 |
| | | | **TYRONE "TYSTICK" BRUNSON** | | |
| 1/28/84 | **22** | 13 | 4 Fresh..................................................... | | Believe 04330 |
| | | | **ANITA BRYANT** | | |
| | | | Born on 3/25/40 in Barnsdale, Oklahoma. As Miss Oklahoma, she was second runner-up to Miss America in 1958. | | |
| 6/13/60 | **16** | 6 | 1 Paper Roses ............................................. | 5 | Carlton 528 |
| | | | **LEON BRYANT** | | |
| | | | Vocalist/pianist, produced by John Christopher. | | |
| 5/30/81 | **81** | 3 | 1 Mighty Body (Hotsy Totsy) ........................... | | De-Lite 811 |

| DEBUT DATE | PEAK POS | WKS CHR | ARTIST — Record Title | POP POS | Label & Number |
|---|---|---|---|---|---|
| | | | **RAY BRYANT COMBO** | | |
| | | | Pianist/leader, born Raphael Bryant on 12/24/31 in Philadelphia. At Blue Note in the in the late 40s. With Billy Kretchmer from 1951-53. First recording with trio for for Epic in 1955. Also see Aretha Franklin. | | |
| 3/14/60 | 12 | 6 | 1 Little Susie, Part 4 ..................................... [I] | | Signature 12026 |
| 4/11/60 | 5 | 18 | 2 **The Madison Time - Part 1** ....................[S-I] | 30 | Columbia 41628 |
| | | | includes Bryant (piano), Harry Edison (trumpet), Urbie Green (trombone), Buddy Tate (tenor sax), Tommy Bryant (bass) and Bill English (drums); dance calls by Baltimore DJ Eddie Morrison (d: 2/28/87 [61]) | | |
| 3/27/61 | 22 | 2 | 3 Sack Of Woe ......................................... [I] | | Columbia 41940 |
| | | | **PEABO BRYSON** ★★49★★ | | |
| | | | Born Robert Peabo Bryson on 4/13/51 in Greenville, South Carolina. Singer/producer. With Al Freeman & The Upsetters in 1965. With Moses Dillard & The Tex-Town Display from 1968-73. First solo recording for Bang in 1970. Also see Michael Zager. | | |
| 1/17/76 | 25 | 13 | 1 Do It With Feeling | 94 | Bang 720 |
| | | | MICHAEL ZAGER'S MOON BAND featuring Peabo Bryson | | |
| 8/28/76 | 22 | 16 | 2 Underground Music/ | | |
| | | 10 | 3 It's Just A Matter Of Time ........................... | | Bullet 01 |
| 1/08/77 | 27 | 14 | 4 Just Another Day..................................... | | Bullet 02 |
| 6/11/77 | 23 | 12 | 5 I Can Make It Better ................................. | | Bullet 03 |
| 1/07/78 | 6 | 21 | 6 **Reaching For The Sky**.............................. | 102 | Capitol 4522 |
| | | | MICHAEL ZAGER'S MOON BAND featuring Peabo Bryson | | |
| 5/06/78 | 13 | 17 | 7 Feel The Fire ........................................ | | Capitol 4573 |
| 6/17/78 | 76 | 10 | 8 Do It With Feeling ......................... [R] | | Bang 737 |
| | | | MICHAEL ZAGER'S MOON BAND featuring Peabo Bryson | | |
| 11/25/78+ | 2² | 18 | 9 **I'm So Into You** ................................... | 109 | Capitol 4656 |
| 3/24/79 | 28 | 10 | 10 Crosswinds ........................................ | | Capitol 4694 |
| 6/30/79 | 44 | 8 | 11 She's A Woman .................................... | | Capitol 4729 |
| 11/24/79+ | 8 | 14 | 12 **Gimme Some Time** ................................ | 102 | Capitol 4804 |
| | | | NATALIE COLE & PEABO BRYSON | | |
| 2/16/80 | 16 | 11 | 13 What You Won't Do For Love ...................... | | Capitol 4826 |
| | | | NATALIE COLE & PEABO BRYSON | | |
| 3/22/80 | 12 | 14 | 14 Minute By Minute ................................. | | Capitol 4844 |
| 7/05/80 | 39 | 13 | 15 I Love The Way You Love .......................... | | Capitol 4887 |
| 12/06/80+ | 13 | 16 | 16 Make The World Stand Still ....................... | | Atlantic 3775 |
| | | | ROBERTA FLACK & PEABO BRYSON | | |
| 2/07/81 | 34 | 13 | 17 Lovers After All..................................... | 54 | Arista 0587 |
| | | | MELISSA MANCHESTER & PEABO BRYSON | | |
| 3/28/81 | 46 | 6 | 18 Love Is A Waiting Game .......................... | | Atlantic 3803 |
| | | | ROBERTA FLACK & PEABO BRYSON | | |
| 4/11/81 | 61 | 8 | 19 Turn The Hands Of Time .......................... | | Capitol 4989 |
| 10/31/81+ | 6 | 20 | 20 **Let The Feeling Flow** ............................. | 42 | Capitol 5065 |
| 4/03/82 | 36 | 9 | 21 There's No Guarantee ............................. | | Capitol 5098 |
| 9/11/82 | 22 | 13 | 22 Give Me Your Love ................................ | | Capitol 5157 |
| 12/11/82+ | 16 | 17 | 23 We Don't Have To Talk (About Love) ................ | | Capitol 5188 |
| 3/26/83 | 54 | 8 | 24 Remember When (So Much In Love) ................. | | Capitol 5210 |
| | | | PEABO BRYSON/ROBERTA FLACK: | | |
| 7/09/83 | 5 | 20 | 25 **Tonight, I Celebrate My Love**...................... | 16 | Capitol 5242 |
| 11/05/83 | 68 | 6 | 26 Maybe............................................. | | Capitol 5283 |
| 12/24/83+ | 41 | 12 | 27 You're Looking Like Love To Me.................... | 58 | Capitol 5307 |
| | | | PEABO BRYSON: | | |
| 2/11/84 | 53 | 9 | 28 D.C. Cab .......................................... | | MCA 52328 |
| | | | from the film of the same title | | |
| 5/12/84 | 6 | 20 | 29 **If Ever You're In My Arms Again**.................. | 10 | Elektra 69728 |
| 8/25/84 | 35 | 12 | 30 Slow Dancin' ...................................... | 82 | Elektra 69699 |
| 6/15/85 | 39 | 9 | 31 Take No Prisoners (In The Game Of Love).......... | 78 | Elektra 69632 |
| 8/31/85 | 36 | 9 | 32 There's Nothin' Out There ......................... | | Elektra 69612 |
| 12/21/85+ | 63 | 10 | 33 Love Always Finds A Way .......................... | | Elektra 69585 |
| 10/04/86 | 44 | 12 | 34 Good Combination................................. | | Elektra 69517 |
| 2/14/87 | 92 | 3 | 35 Catch 22.......................................... | | Elektra 69492 |
| 12/26/87+ | 14 | 14 | 36 Without You....................................... | 89 | Elektra 69426 |
| | | | PEABO BRYSON & REGINA BELLE | | |
| | | | from the film "Leonard Pt. 6" | | |

| DEBUT DATE | PEAK POS | WKS CHR | ARTIST — Record Title | POP POS | Label & Number |
|---|---|---|---|---|---|
| | | | **B.T. EXPRESS** Brooklyn group formed in 1972 as King Davis House Rockers. Later called Madison Street Express and Brooklyn Trucking Express. Consisted of Bill Risbrook and Carlos Ward (saxes, flute), Michael Jones (keyboards), Richard Thompson (guitar, vocals), Louis Risbrook (bass, organ, vocals), Dennis Rowe (percussion), Leslie Ming (drums) and Barbara Joyce Lomas (vocals). | | |
| 8/03/74 | **1**¹ | 21 | 1 ●**Do It ('Til You're Satisfied)**............... | *2* | Scepter 12395 |
| 1/25/75 | **1**¹ | 16 | 2 ●**Express** ............... [I] | *4* | Roadshow 7001 |
| 8/09/75 | **5** | 17 | 3 **Give It What You Got/** | *40* | |
| | | 12 | 4 Peace Pipe............... | *31* | Roadshow 7003 |
| 1/17/76 | **31** | 10 | 5 Close To You............... | *82* | Roadshow 7005 |
| 5/29/76 | **6** | 15 | 6 **Can't Stop Groovin' Now, Wanna Do It Some More**............... | *52* | Columbia 10346 |
| 9/11/76 | **37** | 8 | 7 Energy To Burn............... | | Columbia 10399 |
| 12/10/77+ | **12** | 20 | 8 Shout It Out............... | | Columbia 10649 |
| 4/19/80 | **24** | 12 | 9 Give Up The Funk (Let's Dance)............... | | Columbia 11249 |
| 9/06/80 | **76** | 4 | 10 Does It Feel Good............... | | Columbia 11336 |
| 12/13/80+ | **51** | 11 | 11 Stretch............... | | Columbia 11400 |
| | | | **BUCHANAN & GOODMAN** Bill Buchanan and Richard "Dickie" Goodman created the "break-in" record - segments of popular records taped and spliced into the dialogue of a radio show. | | |
| 8/11/56 | **4** | 7 | 1 **Flying Saucer (Parts 1 & 2)** ............... [N] Best Seller #4 / Jockey #7 | *3* | Luniverse 101 |
| | | | **BUCK** | | |
| 6/14/75 | **65** | 8 | 1 I Can't Quit Your Love............... | | Playboy 6039 |
| | | | **BUDDY & CLAUDIA** Duo of Ernest "Buddy" Griffin and Claudia "Swann" (Swanson). | | |
| 2/26/55 | **14** | 1 | 1 I Wanna Hug Ya, Kiss Ya, Squeeze Ya............... Jockey #1 | | Chess 1586 |
| | | | **BULL & THE MATADORS** | | |
| 8/31/68 | **9** | 13 | 1 **The Funky Judge**............... | *39* | Toddlin' Town 108 |
| | | | **JANICE BULLOCK** | | |
| 5/10/86 | **59** | 7 | 1 I Don't Want To Wake Up (Feelin' Guilty)............ WILLIAM BELL & JANICE BULLOCK | | Wilbe 202 |
| 6/06/87 | **61** | 10 | 2 Do You Really Love Me............... | | WRC 206 |
| | | | **BUMBLE BEE UNLIMITED** Seven-member, New York-based disco act. | | |
| 12/25/76+ | **81** | 5 | 1 Love Bug............... | *92* | Mercury 73864 |
| | | | **VERNON BURCH** Guitarist from Washington, DC. Worked with the Delfonics from age 13 to 15. Worked with the Stairsteps, then with the Bar-Kays for 4 years. Appeared as "Marvin Gaye" in the film "Hollywood Nights", in 1980. | | |
| 2/22/75 | **15** | 13 | 1 Changes (Messin' With My Mind)............... | *101* | United Art. 587 |
| 10/25/75 | **99** | 2 | 2 Frame Of Mind............... | | United Art. 705 |
| 8/06/77 | **95** | 4 | 3 Leaving You Is Killing Me............... | | Columbia 10564 |
| 11/11/78+ | **32** | 12 | 4 Love Is............... | | Choc. City 015 |
| 3/10/79 | **41** | 8 | 5 Brighter Days............... | | Choc. City 017 |
| 9/22/79 | **27** | 11 | 6 Never Can Find A Way (Hot Love)............... | | Choc. City 3201 |
| 12/22/79+ | **35** | 10 | 7 Get Up............... | | Choc. City 3203 |
| 10/11/80 | **54** | 9 | 8 Fun City............... | | Choc. City 3211 |
| 12/05/81+ | **18** | 15 | 9 Do It To Me............... | | Spector 00019 |
| 4/03/82 | **46** | 9 | 10 Playing Hard To Get............... | | Spector 00021 |
| | | | **LEROY BURGESS - see ALEEM** | | |
| | | | **CEELE BURKE** Steel guitarist/banjo player. Worked with Les Hite, Louis Armstrong, Fats Waller and Charlie Echols in Los Angeles during the 30s. | | |
| 8/07/43 | **4** | 19 | 1 **From Twilight 'Til Dawn**............... | | Capitol 136 |
| | | | **KENI BURKE** Born Kenneth Burke on 9/28/53 in Chicago. Former bass player in the Five Stairsteps. | | |
| 5/30/81 | **66** | 8 | 1 Let Somebody Love You............... | | RCA 12228 |

| DEBUT DATE | PEAK POS | WKS CHR | ARTIST — Record Title | POP POS | Label & Number |
|---|---|---|---|---|---|
| | | | **KENI BURKE — Continued** | | |
| 8/28/82 | **63** | 5 | 2 Risin' To The Top........................................ | | RCA 13271 |
| | | | **SOLOMON BURKE** ★★**72**★★ | | |
| | | | Born in 1936 in Philadelphia. Preached and broadcast from own church, "Solomon's Temple", in Philadelphia from 1945-55 as the "Wonder Boy Preacher". Church was founded for him by his grandmother. First recorded for Apollo in 1954. Left music to attend mortuary school, returned in 1960. Also see The Soul Clan. | | |
| 9/04/61 | **7** | 19 | 1 **Just Out Of Reach (Of My Two Open Arms)**..... | *24* | Atlantic 2114 |
| 2/24/62 | **5** | 12 | 2 **Cry To Me**............................................. | *44* | Atlantic 2131 |
| 6/09/62 | **15** | 11 | 3 I'm Hanging Up My Heart For You/ | *85* | |
| 6/16/62 | **20** | 7 | 4   Down In The Valley .................................. | *71* | Atlantic 2147 |
| 5/11/63 | **2**⁵ | 12 | 5 **If You Need Me** ......................................... | *37* | Atlantic 2185 |
| 11/02/63 | **8** | 4 | 6 **You're Good For Me** ................................... | *49* | Atlantic 2205 |
| 2/08/64 | **51** | 8 | 7 He'll Have To Go ...................................... | *Hot* | Atlantic 2218 |
| 4/18/64 | **33** | 10 | 8 Goodbye Baby (Baby Goodbye)........................ | *Hot* | Atlantic 2226 |
| 7/18/64 | **58** | 8 | 9 Everybody Needs Somebody To Love ................ | *Hot* | Atlantic 2241 |
| 10/10/64 | **92** | 3 | 10 Yes I Do ................................................ | *Hot* | Atlantic 2254 |
| 11/28/64 | **57** | 5 | 11 The Price................................................ | *Hot* | Atlantic 2259 |
| 3/06/65 | **1**³ | 13 | 12 **Got To Get You Off My Mind** ....................... | *22* | Atlantic 2276 |
| 5/29/65 | **2**³ | 15 | 13 **Tonight's The Night**.................................. | *28* | Atlantic 2288 |
| 9/11/65 | **24** | 6 | 14 Someone Is Watching. ............................... | *89* | Atlantic 2299 |
| 2/05/66 | **31** | 3 | 15 Baby Come On Home ................................ | *96* | Atlantic 2314 |
| 9/03/66 | **38** | 5 | 16 Keep Looking......................................... | *109* | Atlantic 2349 |
| 2/04/67 | **15** | 9 | 17 Keep A Light In The Window Till I Come Home... | *64* | Atlantic 2378 |
| 7/15/67 | **11** | 10 | 18 Take Me (Just As I Am) .............................. | *49* | Atlantic 2416 |
| 12/30/67 | **47** | 2 | 19 Detroit City ............................................ | *104* | Atlantic 2459 |
| 5/04/68 | **32** | 6 | 20 I Wish I Knew (How It Would Feel To Be Free) .... | *68* | Atlantic 2507 |
| 3/08/69 | **47** | 4 | 21 Up Tight Good Woman ................................ | *116* | Bell 759 |
| 5/10/69 | **15** | 6 | 22 Proud Mary. ........................................... | *45* | Bell 783 |
| 3/20/71 | **26** | 9 | 23 The Electronic Magnetism (That's Heavy, Baby).. | *96* | MGM 14221 |
| 4/01/72 | **13** | 13 | 24 Love's Street And Fool's Road........................ | *89* | MGM 14353 |
| | | | from the film "Cool Breeze" | | |
| 7/22/72 | **42** | 4 | 25 We're Almost Home ................................... | | MGM 14402 |
| 10/07/72 | **49** | 2 | 26 Get Up And Do Something For Yourself............ | | MGM 14425 |
| 7/14/73 | **97** | 2 | 27 Shambala ............................................... | | MGM 14571 |
| 6/15/74 | **14** | 10 | 28 Midnight And You .................................... | | ABC 4388 |
| 1/11/75 | **19** | 14 | 29 You And Your Baby Blues ........................... | *96* | Chess 2159 |
| 5/31/75 | **72** | 7 | 30 Let Me Wrap My Arms Around You ................. | | Chess 2172 |
| 9/23/78 | **91** | 4 | 31 Please Don't You Say Goodbye To Me .............. | | Amherst 736 |
| | | | **HAROLD BURRAGE** | | |
| | | | Born on 3/30/31 in Chicago. Died of a heart attack on 11/25/66. First recorded for Decca in 1950. | | |
| 8/21/65 | **31** | 8 | 1 Got To Find A Way ..................................... | *128* | M-Pac! 7225 |
| | | | **BURRELL** | | |
| 6/18/88 | **78** | 4 | 1 I'll Wait For You (Take Your Time) ................. | | Virgin 99357 |
| | | | **JENNY BURTON** | | |
| | | | Born on 11/18/57 in New York City. Former lead singer of C-Bank, the studio band of John Robie. | | |
| 4/16/83 | **87** | 4 | 1 One More Shot......................................... | | Next Plat. 50011 |
| | | | **C-BANK featuring Jenny Burton** | | |
| 12/17/83+ | **21** | 17 | 2 Remember What You Like ............................ | *81* | Atlantic 89748 |
| 5/05/84 | **88** | 3 | 3 Rock Steady............................................. | | Atlantic 89683 |
| 2/16/85 | **19** | 15 | 4 Bad Habits.............................................. | *101* | Atlantic 89583 |
| 11/29/86 | **68** | 9 | 5 Do You Want It Bad Enuff............................ | | Atlantic 89343 |
| | | | **BILLY BUTLER & THE CHANTERS** | | |
| | | | Singer/songwriter/guitarist, born on 6/7/45 in Chicago. Youngest brother of Jerry Butler. Formed group the Enchanters at Wells High School. First recorded for Okeh in 1963, produced by Curtis Mayfield. Group name changed to Chanters in 1964. Consisted of Butler (lead), Errol Batts (tenor) and Jesse Tillman (baritone). Group disbanded in 1966. Butler formed the group Infinity in 1969, with Phyllis Knox, Larry Wade and Errol Batts. Went solo again in 1974. (Not to be confused with guitarist of same name who worked with Bill Doggett.) | | |
| 6/12/65 | **6** | 11 | 1 **I Can't Work No Longer**................................ | *60* | Okeh 7221 |

| DEBUT DATE | PEAK POS | WKS CHR | ARTIST — Record Title | POP POS | Label & Number |
|---|---|---|---|---|---|
| | | | **BILLY BUTLER & THE CHANTERS — Continued** | | |
| 7/16/66 | **24** | 13 | 2 Right Track.................................................. | | Okeh 7245 |
| 11/29/69 | **41** | 3 | 3 Get On The Case......................................... | | Fountain 1102 |
| | | | shown only as: **INFINITY** | | |
| 5/29/71 | **38** | 6 | 4 I Don't Want To Lose You............................. | | Memphis 103 |
| | | | **BILLY BUTLER & INFINITY** | | |
| 4/14/73 | **48** | 2 | 5 Hung Up On You ........................................ | | Pride 1026 |
| | | | **BILLY BUTLER & INFINITY** | | |
| | | | **JERRY BUTLER** ★★**15**★★ | | |
| | | | Born on 12/8/39 in Sunflower, Mississippi. Older brother of Billy Butler. Sang in the Northern Jubilee Gospel Singers, with Curtis Mayfield. Later with the Quails. In 1957, Butler and Mayfield joined the Roosters with Sam Gooden and brothers Arthur & Richard Brooks. Changed name to the Impressions in 1957. Left for solo career in autumn of 1958. Teamed again with writer Mayfield for a string of hits from 1960-66. | | |
| 7/28/58 | **3** | 7 | 1 **For Your Precious Love**............................. | *11* | Abner/Fal. 1013 |
| | | | **JERRY BUTLER & THE IMPRESSIONS** Jockey #3 / Best Seller #10 | | |
| 10/20/58 | **29** | 1 | 2 Come Back My Love .................................. | | Abner/Fal. 1017 |
| | | | **THE IMPRESSIONS featuring JERRY BUTLER** | | |
| 3/02/59 | **17** | 3 | 3 Lost............................................................ | | Abner/Fal. 1024 |
| | | | with Riley Hampton's Orchestra | | |
| 5/30/60 | **25** | 4 | 4 A Lonely Soldier ...................................... | | Abner/Fal. 1035 |
| 10/24/60 | **1**⁷ | 16 | 5 **He Will Break Your Heart** ...................... | *7* | Vee-Jay 354 |
| 3/13/61 | **10** | 11 | 6 **Find Another Girl**................................... | *27* | Vee-Jay 375 |
| 7/31/61 | **8** | 9 | 7 **I'm A Telling You** .................................. | *25* | Vee-Jay 390 |
| 1/06/62 | **14** | 6 | 8 Moon River ............................................. | *11* | Vee-Jay 405 |
| | | | from the film "Breakfast At Tiffany's" | | |
| 9/01/62 | **18** | 2 | 9 Make It Easy On Yourself .......................... | *20* | Vee-Jay 451 |
| 10/27/62 | **23** | 5 | 10 You Can Run (But You Can't Hide) ............... | *63* | Vee-Jay 463 |
| 11/23/63+ | **31** | 11 | 11 Need To Belong.......................................... | *Hot* | Vee-Jay 567 |
| 4/04/64 | **56** | 6 | 12 Giving Up On Love ..................................... | *Hot* | Vee-Jay 588 |
| 6/27/64 | **95** | 2 | 13 I Don't Want To Hear Anymore/ | *Hot* | |
| 8/01/64 | **61** | 6 | 14 I Stand Accused.......................................... | *Hot* | Vee-Jay 598 |
| 9/05/64 | **5** | 13 | 15 **Let It Be Me** .......................................... | *Hot* | Vee-Jay 613 |
| | | | **BETTY EVERETT & JERRY BUTLER** | | |
| 12/05/64+ | **42** | 7 | 16 Smile ........................................................ | *Hot* | Vee-Jay 633 |
| | | | **BETTY EVERETT & JERRY BUTLER** | | |
| 3/13/65 | **33** | 5 | 17 Good Times................................................ | *64* | Vee-Jay 651 |
| 11/27/65 | **33** | 3 | 18 Just For You............................................... | | Vee-Jay 707 |
| 2/12/66 | **25** | 7 | 19 For Your Precious Love............................... | *99* | Vee-Jay 715 |
| | | | new version of his first charted record | | |
| 8/06/66 | **34** | 7 | 20 Love (Oh, How Sweet It Is) ......................... | *103* | Mercury 72592 |
| 1/28/67 | **8** | 10 | 21 **I Dig You Baby** ...................................... | *60* | Mercury 72648 |
| 10/28/67 | **23** | 7 | 22 Mr. Dream Merchant .................................. | *38* | Mercury 72721 |
| 1/20/68 | **15** | 10 | 23 Lost.......................................................... | *62* | Mercury 72764 |
| | | | not the same tune as his 1959 hit of the same title | | |
| 5/11/68 | **4** | 16 | 24 **Never Give You Up**................................. | *20* | Mercury 72798 |
| 9/21/68 | **1**¹ | 13 | 25 **Hey, Western Union Man** ....................... | *16* | Mercury 72850 |
| 12/21/68+ | **9** | 9 | 26 **Are You Happy** ...................................... | *39* | Mercury 72876 |
| 3/08/69 | **1**² | 14 | 27●**Only The Strong Survive** ....................... | *4* | Mercury 72898 |
| 6/07/69 | **3** | 12 | 28 **Moody Woman** ....................................... | *24* | Mercury 72929 |
| 8/30/69 | **4** | 12 | 29 **What's The Use Of Breaking Up** ............. | *20* | Mercury 72960 |
| 11/29/69 | **12** | 7 | 30 Don't Let Love Hang You Up ....................... | *44* | Mercury 72991 |
| 1/24/70 | **21** | 7 | 31 Got To See If I Can't Get Mommy (To Come Back Home).................................................... | *62* | Mercury 73015 |
| 3/28/70 | **15** | 6 | 32 I Could Write A Book .................................. | *46* | Mercury 73045 |
| 9/12/70 | **42** | 2 | 33 Where Are You Going ................................. | *95* | Mercury 73101 |
| | | | from the soundtrack "Joe" | | |
| 11/14/70 | **36** | 5 | 34 Special Memory .......................................... | *109* | Mercury 73131 |
| 1/09/71 | **32** | 4 | 35 You Just Can't Win (By Making The Same Mistake).................................................... | *94* | Mercury 73163 |
| | | | **GENE** (Chandler) **& JERRY** | | |
| 3/06/71 | **8** | 11 | 36 If It's Real What I Feel................................ | *69* | Mercury 73169 |
| 6/19/71 | **44** | 2 | 37 Ten And Two (Take This Woman Off The Corner) | *126* | Mercury 73195 |
| | | | **GENE & JERRY** | | |
| 7/10/71 | **38** | 4 | 38 How Did We Lose It Baby............................. | *85* | Mercury 73210 |

| DEBUT DATE | PEAK POS | WKS CHR | ARTIST — Record Title | POP POS | Label & Number |
|---|---|---|---|---|---|
| | | | **JERRY BUTLER — Continued** | | |
| 9/25/71 | 33 | 8 | 39 Walk Easy My Son.......................... | 93 | Mercury 73241 |
| 12/11/71+ | 3 | 17 | 40● Ain't Understanding Mellow .................... | 21 | Mercury 73255 |
| 5/20/72 | 20 | 8 | 41 I Only Have Eyes For You ...................... | 85 | Mercury 73290 |
| 7/29/72 | 6 | 13 | 42 (They Long To Be) Close To You ..................... | 91 | Mercury 73301 |
| | | | JERRY BUTLER featuring BRENDA LEE EAGER | | |
| 11/11/72 | 6 | 10 | 43 One Night Affair........................... | 52 | Mercury 73335 |
| 6/23/73 | 26 | 10 | 44 Can't Understand It ......................... | | Mercury 73395 |
| 10/13/73 | 64 | 7 | 45 The Love We Had Stays On My Mind................ | | Mercury 73422 |
| 12/01/73+ | 15 | 13 | 46 Power Of Love ......................... | | Mercury 73443 |
| | | | 40, 45 & 46: JERRY BUTLER & BRENDA LEE EAGER | | |
| 2/23/74 | 58 | 9 | 47 That's How Heartaches Are Made.................... | | Mercury 73459 |
| 7/13/74 | 46 | 11 | 48 Take The Time To Tell Her .......................... | | Mercury 73495 |
| 11/16/74+ | 33 | 13 | 49 Playing On You.............................. | | Mercury 73629 |
| 10/02/76 | 55 | 6 | 50 The Devil In Mrs. Jones.......................... | | Motown 1403 |
| 2/26/77 | 7 | 16 | 51 I Wanna Do It To You............................. | 51 | Motown 1414 |
| 7/30/77 | 28 | 12 | 52 Chalk It Up ............................... | | Motown 1421 |
| 10/14/78 | 14 | 17 | 53 (I'm Just Thinking About) Cooling Out ............. | | Phil. Int. 3656 |
| 3/10/79 | 86 | 2 | 54 Nothing Says I Love You Like I Love You ......... | | Phil. Int. 3673 |
| 3/22/80 | 49 | 9 | 55 The Best Love I Ever Had ....................... | | Phil. Int. 3746 |
| 8/30/80 | 75 | 4 | 56 Don't Be An Island ........................ | | Phil. Int. 3113 |
| | | | JERRY "THE ICEMAN" BUTLER featuring Debra Henry of 'Silk' | | |
| 9/11/82 | 83 | 4 | 57 No Love Without Changes........................... | | Fountain 400 |
| 7/09/83 | 92 | 3 | 58 In My Life ............................ | | CTI 59 |
| | | | PATTI AUSTIN & JERRY BUTLER | | |
| | | | **JONATHAN BUTLER** | | |
| | | | Born In Capetown, South Africa. Soul singer/guitarist/songwriter. | | |
| 9/20/86 | 58 | 9 | 1 If You're Ready (Come Go With Me) ................. | | Jive 1027 |
| | | | RUBY TURNER featuring JONATHAN BUTLER | | |
| 4/25/87 | 5 | 17 | 2 Lies................................... | 27 | Jive 1038 |
| 9/12/87 | 22 | 12 | 3 Holding On.............................. | | Jive 1063 |
| 1/16/88 | 10 | 16 | 4 Take Good Care Of Me........................ | | Jive 1083 |
| | | | **BY ALL MEANS** | | |
| | | | Los Angeles-based trio: James Vorner (vocals, piano), Lynn Roderick (vocals, actress) and composer Billy Sheppard (guitar). | | |
| 5/14/88 | 26 | 13 | 1 I Surrender To Your Love .............................. | | Island 99361 |
| | | | **DON BYAS** | | |
| | | | Born Carlos Wesley Byas on 10/21/12 in Muskogee, Oklahoma. Died on 8/24/72 in Amsterdam, Holland. Tenor saxophonist. Played alto sax with Bennie Moten, Terrence Holden and Walter Page's Blue Devils until 1933. Own band, Don Carlos & Collegiate Ramblers, at Langston College. With Lionel Hampton, Eddie Barefield, Buck Clayton, Andy Kirk, Count Basie (1941-43), and many others. Toured Europe with Don Redman's Band in September, 1946. Settled in France. | | |
| 9/25/48 | 14 | 2 | 1 London Donnie ......................... [I] | | Savoy 668 |
| | | | Best Seller #14 / Juke Box #14 | | |
| 9/25/48 | 14 | 1 | 2 September Song ......................... [I] | | Savoy 626 |
| | | | Juke Box #14 | | |
| | | | above 2: recorded in 1946 | | |
| | | | **BOBBY BYRD** | | |
| | | | Born on 8/15/34 in Toccoa, Georgia. Founder and leader of James Brown's vocal group, the Famous Flames. | | |
| 4/04/64 | 52 | 6 | 1 Baby Baby Baby ......................... | Hot | Smash 1884 |
| | | | ANNA KING-BOBBY BYRD | | |
| | | | written by Carolyn Franklin; produced by James Brown | | |
| 2/20/65 | 14 | 8 | 2 We Are In Love......................... | 120 | Smash 1964 |
| 3/16/68 | 47 | 2 | 3 You've Got To Change Your Mind.................... | 102 | King 6151 |
| | | | BOBBY BYRD & JAMES BROWN | | |
| 9/19/70 | 14 | 10 | 4 I Need Help (I Can't Do It Alone) Pt. 1 .............. | 69 | King 6323 |
| | | | with vocals by James Brown, Gigi Kinard & Roberta Dubois | | |
| 6/12/71 | 30 | 7 | 5 I Know You Got Soul ...................... | 117 | King 6378 |
| | | | recorded at the Olympia Theater, Paris, with the James Brown Band | | |
| 9/25/71 | 34 | 5 | 6 Hot Pants-I'm Coming, Coming, I'm Coming ....... | 85 | Brownstone 4203 |
| 2/12/72 | 40 | 6 | 7 Keep On Doin' What You're Doin'.................... | 88 | Brownstone 4205 |
| 7/14/73 | 82 | 3 | 8 Try It Again ........................... | | Kwanza 7703 |
| 2/01/75 | 57 | 6 | 9 Back From The Dead ...................... | | Int. Bros. 901 |

| DEBUT DATE | PEAK POS | WKS CHR | ARTIST — Record Title | POP POS | Label & Number |
|---|---|---|---|---|---|
| | | | **DONALD BYRD** | | |
| | | | Trumpeter/flugelhorn player, born on 12/9/32 in Detroit. With Air Force bands, 1951-53, and George Wallington in 1955. With Art Blakey Jazz Messengers in the mid-50s. Own bands from the 60s. Founded the Blackbyrds in 1973 while teaching jazz at Howard University in Washington, DC. | | |
| 6/30/73 | 19 | 7 | 1 Black Byrd................................................[I] | 88 | Blue Note 212 |
| 11/15/75 | 43 | 13 | 2 Change (Makes You Want To Hustle) Part 1 ....... | | Blue Note 726 |
| 4/10/76 | 61 | 8 | 3 (Fallin' Like) Dominoes................................. | | Blue Note 783 |
| 5/14/77 | 95 | 3 | 4 Dancing In The Street ................................ | | Blue Note 965 |
| 3/31/79 | 74 | 5 | 5 Loving You ............................................. | | Elektra 46019 |
| | | | **DONALD BYRD & 125TH STREET, N.Y.C.:** | | |
| 8/15/81 | 15 | 17 | 6 Love Has Come Around............................... | | Elektra 47168 |
| 1/23/82 | 77 | 3 | 7 I Love Your Love....................................... | | Elektra 47241 |
| 9/11/82 | 38 | 10 | 8 Sexy Dancer............................................ | | Elektra 69972 |
| | | | **GARY BYRD & G.B. Experience** | | |
| 7/23/83 | 69 | 8 | 1 The Crown.............................................. | | Wondirect. 4507 |
| | | | **ROY BYRD** | | |
| | | | Vocalist/pianist/guitarist/drummer, born Henry Roeland Byrd on 12/19/18 in Bogalusa, Louisiana. Street musician in New Orleans in the early 30s. Nicknamed Professor Longhair. With the Mid-Drifs from 1947-49. Formed own group, Professor Longhair & The Four Hairs, in 1949. Extremely influential piano style. Died on 1/30/80 (61). | | |
| 8/12/50 | 5 | 2 | 1 **Bald Head**.............................................. | | Mercury 8175 |
| | | | Best Seller #5 / Juke Box #10 with His Blues Jumpers | | |
| | | | **EDWARD BYRNES - see CONNIE STEVENS** | | |

# C

| DEBUT DATE | PEAK POS | WKS CHR | ARTIST — Record Title | POP POS | Label & Number |
|---|---|---|---|---|---|
| | | | **C & THE SHELLS** | | |
| | | | Group consisting of Calvin White, Andrea Bolden and Lonzine Wright. First recorded as the Sandpebbles for Calla Records, 1967-68. | | |
| 4/05/69 | 28 | 7 | 1 You Are The Circus .................................... | | Cotillion 44024 |
| 5/31/69 | 46 | 2 | 2 Good Morning Starshine ............................. | | Cotillion 44033 |
| | | | **THE CADETS** | | |
| | | | Name given to vocal group The Jacks by Modern/RPM Records, for recordings on the Modern label. The name "Jacks" was used on RPM. Formed as a spiritual group in Los Angeles in 1947. Group consisted of Willie Davis, Ted Taylor, Aaron Collins, Lloyd McCraw and Will "Dub" Jones. Davis was lead on records by the "Jacks" and Collins or Jones as the "Cadets". Group enjoyed great success with cover versions of R&B hits. Davis and Collins joined The Flares in 1961. Taylor had a successful solo career. Dub Jones joined the Coasters in early 1958 and left them in 1968. Collins' sisters, Betty and Rose, recorded for Modern/RPM as "The Teen Queens". | | |
| 7/21/56 | 4 | 8 | 1 **Stranded In The Jungle** ..........................[N] | 15 | Modern 994 |
| | | | Best Seller #4 / Jockey #4 / Juke Box #5 Prentice Moreland replaces Ted Taylor | | |
| | | | **THE CADILLACS** | | |
| | | | Vocal group formed at P.S. 139 in Harlem in 1953. Originally called the Carnations. The Cadillacs were the first R&B vocal group to extensively use choreography in their stage routines. Consisted of Earl "Speedy" Carroll (lead vocals), Charles Brooks, Robert Phillips, Papa Clark and Earl Wade. Carroll left the group in 1958 to join the Coasters. | | |
| 1/07/56 | 3 | 15 | 1 **Speedoo**............................................... | 17 | Josie 785 |
| | | | Best Seller #3 / Juke Box #4 / Jockey #5 song title is variation on Carroll's nickname | | |
| 1/05/57 | 11 | 1 | 2 Rudolph The Red-Nosed Reindeer ................[X] | | Josie 807 |
| | | | Jockey #11 above 2: with the Jesse Powell Orchestra | | |
| 2/02/59 | 20 | 3 | 3 Peek-A-Boo .............................................. | 28 | Josie 846 |
| 9/18/61 | 30 | 1 | 4 What You Bet ........................................... | | Smash 1712 |
| | | | **SHIRLEY CAESAR** | | |
| | | | Born in 1939 in Durham, North Carolina. With sisters Anne & Joyce, and cousin Esther as the Caesar Sisters in 1949. Recorded as Baby Shirley for Federal in 1951. With the Caravans gospel group from 1958, leader from 1961-67. Billed as the "First Lady Of Gospel Music". | | |
| 4/19/75 | 40 | 12 | 1 No Charge................................................ | 91 | Hob/Scep. 12402 |

| DEBUT DATE | PEAK POS | WKS CHR | ARTIST — Record Title | POP POS | Label & Number |
|---|---|---|---|---|---|
| | | | **CAESARS** | | |
| 3/25/67 | **48** | 2 | 1 Get Yourself Together .................................... | | Lanie 2001 |
| | | | **JOE CAIN & THE RED PARROT ORCHESTRA** | | |
| 2/05/83 | **69** | 10 | 1 Perez Prado-Tito Puente Latin Medley ............. <br> Oye Como Va/Cherry Pink, And Apple Blossom White/ <br> Patricia/Mambo Jambo/Mambo No. 5 | | Zoo York 03504 |
| | | | **GENERAL CAINE** | | |
| 7/24/82 | **72** | 9 | 1 Girls ......................................................... | | Tabu 02947 |
| 9/03/83 | **74** | 5 | 2 Bomb Body ................................................ | | Tabu 04062 |
| | | | **AL CAIOLA** | | |
| | | | Born on 9/7/20 in Jersey City, New Jersey. Guitarist/composer/bandleader. First <br> recorded for Savoy in 1955. Prolific studio work. | | |
| 2/20/61 | **24** | 3 | 1 The Magnificent Seven ................................ [I] <br> from the film of the same title | *35* | United Art. 261 |
| | | | **CALDERA** | | |
| | | | Group consisting of Jorge Stranz, Eduardo del Barrio (vocals), Steve Tavaglione <br> Michael Azevedo, Carlos Vega, and Dean Cortez. | | |
| 1/22/77 | **92** | 5 | 1 Out Of The Blue ........................................ | | Capitol 4371 |
| | | | **BOBBY CALDWELL** | | |
| | | | Vocalist/composer/multi-instrumentalist, born on 8/15/51 in New York City. Wrote <br> tracks for "New Mickey Mouse Club" TV show and commercials. With Johnny Winter in <br> the early 1970s. | | |
| 10/14/78+ | **6** | 23 | 1 **What You Won't Do For Love** ........................ | *9* | Clouds 11 |
| 6/02/79 | **36** | 11 | 2 Can't Say Goodbye ..................................... | *103* | Clouds 15 |
| 9/22/79 | **40** | 9 | 3 My Flame.................................................... | | Clouds 18 |
| 4/12/80 | **28** | 12 | 4 Coming Down From Love ............................. | *42* | Clouds 21 |
| 4/17/82 | **54** | 10 | 5 Jamaica ..................................................... | *105* | Polydor 2202 |
| 9/18/82 | **67** | 7 | 6 All Of My Love............................................ | *77* | Polydor 2212 |
| | | | **RUE CALDWELL** | | |
| 12/24/83+ | **77** | 6 | 1 The Party Starts When I'm With You ............... | | Critique 703 |
| | | | **CALHOON** | | |
| 10/18/75 | **92** | 3 | 1 (Do You Wanna) Dance Dance Dance ............... | | Warner/Spc. 0405 |
| | | | **TERRY CALLIER** | | |
| | | | Born in Chicago in 1951. Folksinger/harmonica player. | | |
| 8/04/79 | **78** | 3 | 1 Sign Of The Times ...................................... | | Elektra 46054 |
| | | | **CAB CALLOWAY** | | |
| | | | Born Cabell Calloway on 12/25/07 in Rochester, New York. Nicknamed "His Hi-De-Ho <br> Highness Of Jive". Vocalist/leader/alto saxophonist/drummer. Brother of bandleader <br> Blanche Calloway. Raised in Baltimore, moved to Chicago. Worked with the Missourians <br> in 1929, later renamed the Cab Calloway Orchestra. Appearances in many films, <br> including "The Blues Brothers". From the late 30s to mid-40s, his band was <br> consistently among the most popular and included Ben Webster, Chu Berry, Dizzy <br> Gillespie, and Cozy Cole. | | |
| 2/02/46 | **3** | 2 | 1 **The Honeydripper** .................................... | | Columbia 36894 |
| 9/25/48 | **13** | 1 | 2 The Calloway Boogie ................................... <br> Juke Box #13 | | Columbia 38227 |
| 10/14/78 | **91** | 2 | 3 Minnie The Moocher ................................... <br> Cab's theme based on the traditional folk song "Willy the Weeper"; <br> released on Brunswick 6074 in 1931 (POS 1) | | RCA 11364 |
| | | | **CAMEO**  ★★**53**★★ | | |
| | | | New York City soul/funk group, formed in 1974, as The New York City Players by Larry <br> "Mr. B" Blackmon (drums) and Gregory "Straps" Johnson (keyboards). Vocals by Wayne <br> Cooper and Tomi "Tee" Jenkins. Blackmon and Johnson had been in group, East Coast. <br> Members included Gary Dow, Eric Curham, Anthony Lockett and brothers Nathan & <br> Arnett Leftenant. | | |
| 1/22/77 | **33** | 18 | 1 Rigor Mortis ............................................. | *103* | Choc. City 005 |
| 6/11/77 | **70** | 7 | 2 Post Mortem.............................................. | | Choc. City 010 |
| 9/03/77 | **20** | 15 | 3 Funk Funk ................................................. | *104* | Choc. City 011 |
| 3/25/78 | **21** | 15 | 4 It's Serious ............................................... | | Choc. City 013 |
| 7/08/78 | **60** | 9 | 5 It's Over ................................................... | | Choc. City 014 |
| 12/09/78+ | **17** | 11 | 6 Insane...................................................... | | Choc. City 016 |
| 3/31/79 | **76** | 5 | 7 Give Love A Chance .................................... | | Choc. City 018 |
| 6/30/79 | **3** | 22 | 8 **I Just Want To Be**.................................... | | Choc. City 019 |

| DEBUT DATE | PEAK POS | WKS CHR | ARTIST — Record Title | POP POS | Label & Number |
|---|---|---|---|---|---|
| | | | **CAMEO — Continued** | | |
| 10/27/79+ | **10** | 20 | 9 **Sparkle** ................................................ | | Choc. City 3202 |
| 5/03/80 | **11** | 15 | 10 **We're Goin' Out Tonight** ........................... | | Choc. City 3206 |
| 7/26/80 | **8** | 14 | 11 **Shake Your Pants** .................................. | | Choc. City 3210 |
| 10/25/80 | **4** | 20 | 12 **Keep It Hot** ........................................ | | Choc. City 3219 |
| 2/21/81 | **27** | 12 | 13 Feel Me ............................................... | | Choc. City 3222 |
| 5/16/81 | **3** | 19 | 14 **Freaky Dancin'** .................................... | 102 | Choc. City 3225 |
| 8/29/81 | **25** | 11 | 15 I Like It .............................................. | | Choc. City 3227 |
| 3/20/82 | **12** | 15 | 16 Just Be Yourself ..................................... | 101 | Choc. City 3231 |
| 6/12/82 | **10** | 15 | 17 **Flirt** ............................................... | | Choc. City 3233 |
| 9/25/82 | **54** | 6 | 18 Alligator Woman ..................................... | | Choc. City 3235 |
| 4/30/83 | **14** | 11 | 19 Style ................................................. | | Atl. Art. 812054 |
| 8/20/83 | **47** | 7 | 20 Slow Movin' .......................................... | | Atl. Art. 814077 |
| 2/18/84 | **1**⁴ | 20 | 21 **She's Strange** ...................................... | 47 | Atl. Art. 818384 |
| 6/02/84 | **21** | 12 | 22 Talkin' Out The Side Of Your Neck ................. | | Atl. Art. 818870 |
| 8/18/84 | **45** | 7 | 23 Hangin' Downtown ................................... | | Atl. Art. 880169 |
| 6/08/85 | **3** | 16 | 24 **Attack Me With Your Love** ......................... | | Atl. Art. 880744 |
| 8/31/85 | **2**¹ | 16 | 25 **Single Life** ......................................... | | Atl. Art. 884010 |
| 12/28/85+ | **76** | 9 | 26 A Good-Bye ........................................... | | Atl. Art. 884270 |
| 8/16/86 | **1**³ | 24 | 27 **Word Up** ............................................ | 6 | Atl. Art. 884933 |
| 12/13/86+ | **1**² | 16 | 28 **Candy** ............................................... | 21 | Atl. Art. 888193 |
| 3/21/87 | **3** | 15 | 29 **Back And Forth** ..................................... | 50 | Atl. Art. 888385 |
| | | | **CAMERON** | | |
| | | | Born Rafael Cameron in Guyana. With Randy Muller (leader of Brass Construction) in steel band, the Panharmonics. | | |
| 7/05/80 | **16** | 18 | 1 Magic Of You (Like The Way) ...................... | | Salsoul 2124 |
| 10/11/80 | **33** | 11 | 2 Funkdown .......................................... | | Salsoul 2129 |
| 2/14/81 | **67** | 7 | 3 Feelin'. ............................................. | | Salsoul 2134 |
| | | | **RAFAEL CAMERON:** | | |
| 6/27/81 | **21** | 16 | 4 Funktown USA ...................................... | | Salsoul 2144 |
| 10/10/81 | **53** | 9 | 5 Boogie's Gonna Get Ya' ............................ | | Salsoul 2157 |
| 7/31/82 | **59** | 8 | 6 Desires. ............................................. | | Salsoul 7031 |
| 10/09/82 | **81** | 4 | 7 Shake It Down ...................................... | | Salsoul 7035 |
| | | | **G.C. CAMERON** | | |
| | | | Lead singer with the Spinners from 1968-72. | | |
| 10/30/71 | **50** | 2 | 1 Act Like A Shotgun ................................. | | Mowest 5005 |
| 7/14/73 | **76** | 2 | 2 No Matter Where .................................... | | Motown 1234 |
| 11/17/73 | **84** | 5 | 3 Let Me Down Easy ................................... | | Motown 1261 |
| 10/04/75 | **38** | 12 | 4 It's So Hard To Say Goodbye To Yesterday ........ | | Motown 1364 |
| 3/19/77 | **24** | 12 | 5 You're What's Missing In My Life ................... | | Motown 1412 |
| | | | **TONY CAMILLO - see BAZUKA** | | |
| | | | **CANDELA** | | |
| 6/05/82 | **47** | 9 | 1 Love You Madly ..................................... | | Arista 0682 |
| | | | **CANDY & THE KISSES** | | |
| | | | New York trio: sisters Candy and Suzanne Nelson, and schoolmate Jeanette Johnson. | | |
| 11/21/64+ | **51** | 10 | 1 The 81 ............................................... | Hot | Cameo 336 |
| | | | **ACE CANNON** | | |
| | | | Born on 5/5/34 in Grenada, Mississippi. Saxophonist since age 10. Worked with Bill Black's Combo and Hi Records' studio band. | | |
| 1/06/62 | **3** | 12 | 1 **Tuff** ...................................... [I] | 17 | Hi 2040 |
| | | | **FREDDY CANNON** | | |
| | | | Born Frederick Picariello on 12/4/40 in Lynn, Massachusetts. Local work with own band, Freddy Karmon & The Hurricanes. Nickname "Boom Boom" came from big bass drum sound on his records. Band arrangements by Frank Slay on all Swan recordings. Also see Danny & The Juniors. | | |
| 6/01/59 | **13** | 9 | 1 Tallahassee Lassie .................................. song written by Freddy's mother | 6 | Swan 4031 |
| 1/11/60 | **14** | 5 | 2 Way Down Yonder In New Orleans................... jazz song written in 1922 | 3 | Swan 4043 |

| DEBUT DATE | PEAK POS | WKS CHR | ARTIST — Record Title | POP POS | Label & Number |
|---|---|---|---|---|---|
| | | | **FREDDY CANNON — Continued** | | |
| 6/30/62 | **15** | 5 | 3 Palisades Park ............................................ | *3* | Swan 4106 |
| | | | written by Chuck ("Gong Show") Barris | | |
| | | | **THE CAPITOLS** | | |
| | | | Vocal group from Detroit, formed in 1962. Consisted of lead singer Sam George (murdered on 3/17/82 [39]), "Donald Norman" Storball (guitar) and "Richard Mitchell" McDougall (keyboards).. | | |
| 4/09/66 | **2**¹ | 20 | 1 **Cool Jerk** ............................................ | *7* | Karen 1524 |
| 9/03/66 | **49** | 3 | 2 I Got To Handle It ............................... | *74* | Karen 1525 |
| 12/03/66 | **26** | 6 | 3 We Got A Thing That's In The Groove ............... | *65* | Karen 1526 |
| 1/25/69 | **42** | 4 | 4 Soul Brother, Soul Sister ........................ | | Karen 1543 |
| | | | **CAPRELLS** | | |
| 1/22/77 | **87** | 6 | 1 What You Need Baby ........................ | | Ariola Am. 7649 |
| | | | **THE CAPRIS** | | |
| | | | Italian group from Queens, New York, formed in 1958. Consisted of Nick Santamaria, Vinny Narcardo, Mike Mincelli, Frank Reina and John Apostol. Disbanded in 1959; re-formed when song "There's A Moon Out Tonight" was reissued on Lost Nite and became a hit in 1961. | | |
| 2/06/61 | **11** | 5 | 1 There's A Moon Out Tonight ........................ | *3* | Old Town 1094 |
| | | | first released on Planet in 1958 | | |
| | | | **CAPTAIN & TENNILLE** | | |
| | | | The Captain: Daryl Dragon (b: 8/27/42, Los Angeles); and Toni Tennille (b: 5/8/43, Montgomery, AL). Husband and wife. Dragon is the son of notable conductor Carmen Dragon. Keyboardist with The Beach Boys, nicknamed the "Captain" by Mike Love. Duo had own TV show on ABC from 1976-77. | | |
| 2/16/80 | **58** | 6 | 1●Do That To Me One More Time ....................... | *1* | Casablanca 2215 |
| | | | **CAPTAIN SKY** | | |
| | | | Born Daryl L. Cameron on 7/10/57 in Chicago. Attended Chicago Conservatory of Music. | | |
| 12/02/78+ | **33** | 13 | 1 Wonder Worm ......................................... | | AVI 225 |
| 6/16/79 | **35** | 12 | 2 Dr. Rock .............................................. | *105* | AVI 273 |
| 11/17/79 | **52** | 9 | 3 Moon Child .......................................... | | AVI 299 |
| 9/20/80 | **51** | 9 | 4 Sir Jam A Lot........................................ | | TEC 768 |
| 11/14/81 | **72** | 5 | 5 Station Break ....................................... | | WMOT 02407 |
| 11/22/86 | **80** | 5 | 6 You Bring Me Up ................................... | | Triple 1205 |
| | | | **IRENE CARA** | | |
| | | | Vocalist/dancer/pianist, born on 3/18/59 in New York City. Professional debut at age seven. Won Obie Award for "The Me Nobody Knows" in 1970. Much TV work, including "Electric Company"; in films "Fame", "DC Cab" and "The Cotton Club". | | |
| 5/07/83 | **2**⁵ | 22 | 1●**Flashdance...What A Feeling** ....................... | *1* | Casablanca 811440 |
| | | | from the film "Flashdance" | | |
| 10/29/83 | **41** | 12 | 2 Why Me? .............................................. | *13* | Geffen 29464 |
| 12/24/83+ | **65** | 8 | 3 The Dream (Hold On To Your Dream) ............... | *37* | Geffen 29396 |
| | | | from the film "D.C. Cab" | | |
| 4/07/84 | **23** | 12 | 4 Breakdance........................................... | *8* | Geffen 29328 |
| 8/04/84 | **83** | 4 | 5 You Were Made For Me ........................... | *78* | Geffen 29257 |
| | | | **THE CARDINALS** | | |
| | | | Baltimore vocal group formed in 1946 as the Mellotones. Consisted of Ernie Warren, Meredith "Prince" Brothers, Leon "Tree Top" Hardy and Donald "Jack" Johnson. Later joined by Jack "Sam" Aydelotte as guitarist and fifth voice. | | |
| 10/06/51 | **7** | 1 | 1 **Shouldn't I Know?** ............................... | | Atlantic 938 |
| | | | Best Seller #7 | | |
| 3/15/52 | **6** | 3 | 2 **The Wheel Of Fortune** ............................ | | Atlantic 958 |
| | | | Best Seller #6 | | |
| 4/02/55 | **4** | 13 | 3 **The Door Is Still Open**............................ | | Atlantic 1054 |
| | | | Jockey #4 / Juke Box #7 / Best Seller #10 | | |
| | | | written by Chuck Willis | | |
| | | | **CARL CARLTON** ★★190★★ | | |
| | | | Born in 1952 in Detroit. Singing since age nine. First recorded for Lando in 1964. | | |
| | | | **LITTLE CARL CARLTON:** | | |
| 7/06/68 | **36** | 7 | 1 **Competition Ain't Nothin'**............................ | *75* | Back Beat 588 |
| 10/19/68 | **19** | 7 | 2 46 Drums - 1 Guitar................................. | *105* | Back Beat 598 |
| 6/07/69 | **42** | 2 | 3 Look At Mary Wonder (How I Got Over)............. | | Back Beat 603 |
| 10/25/69 | **38** | 5 | 4 Don't Walk Away ................................... | | Back Beat 610 |
| 6/20/70 | **12** | 9 | 5 Drop By My Place................................... | *78* | Back Beat 613 |

| DEBUT DATE | PEAK POS | WKS CHR | ARTIST — Record Title | POP POS | Label & Number |
|---|---|---|---|---|---|
| | | | **CARL CARLTON — Continued** | | |
| | | | CARL CARLTON: | | |
| 1/16/71 | **47** | 3 | 6 I Can Feel It/ | | |
| | | 1 | 7 You've Got So Much (To Learn About Love) ..... | | Back Beat 617 |
| 12/16/72+ | **42** | 6 | 8 I Won't Let The Chump Break Your Heart ......... | | Back Beat 627 |
| 8/11/73 | **81** | 8 | 9 You Can't Stop A Man In Love......................... | | ABC 11378 |
| 9/14/74 | **11** | 13 | 10 Everlasting Love ...................................... | 6 | Back Beat 27001 |
| 2/08/75 | **13** | 12 | 11 Smokin' Room ......................................... | 91 | ABC 12059 |
| 5/24/75 | **71** | 7 | 12 Morning, Noon And Nightime....................... | | ABC 12089 |
| 4/10/76 | **67** | 10 | 13 Ain't Gonna Tell Nobody (About You) .............. | | ABC 12166 |
| 8/30/80 | **57** | 8 | 14 This Feeling's Rated X-Tra........................... | | 20th Century 2459 |
| 6/20/81 | **2**⁸ | 26 | 15● She's A Bad Mama Jama (She's Built, She's Stacked)............................................ | 22 | 20th Century 2488 |
| 2/13/82 | **65** | 6 | 16 I Think It's Gonna Be Alright ...................... | | 20th Century 2601 |
| 8/28/82 | **17** | 17 | 17 Baby I Need Your Loving ............................ | 103 | RCA 13313 |
| 1/08/83 | **54** | 8 | 18 Swing That Sexy Thang.............................. | | RCA 13406 |
| 8/24/85 | **28** | 12 | 19 Private Property ...................................... | | Casabln. 880949 |
| 1/18/86 | **88** | 2 | 20 Slipped, Tripped (Fooled Around And Fell In Love) ............................................... | | Casabln. 884274 |
| | | | **PAULI CARMAN** | | |
| | | | Former lead singer of Champaign. | | |
| 5/10/86 | **26** | 13 | 1 Dial My Number ...................................... | | Columbia 05865 |
| 9/05/87 | **72** | 6 | 2 In The Heat Of The Night ........................... | | Columbia 07290 |
| | | | **JEAN CARNE** | | |
| | | | Born Sarah Jean Perkins in Columbus, Georgia. Attended Morris Brown College in Atlanta. Worked with Doug Carn Band, recorded for Black Jazz in 1969. Backup singer for Earth, Wind & Fire and Duke Ellington. Also see Norman Connors and Al Johnson. | | |
| 3/05/77 | **23** | 13 | 1 Free Love ............................................. | | Phil. Int. 3614 |
| 8/26/78 | **54** | 12 | 2 Don't Let It Go To Your Head ....................... | | Phil. Int. 3654 |
| 12/22/79+ | **43** | 12 | 3 My Love Don't Come Easy ........................... | | Phil. Int. 3732 |
| 9/19/81 | **35** | 12 | 4 Love Don't Love Nobody (Part 1).................... | | TSOP 02501 |
| 7/03/82 | **49** | 9 | 5 If You Don't Know Me By Now ...................... | | Motown 1620 |
| | | | all of above shown as: **JEAN CARN** | | |
| 1/08/83 | **74** | 6 | 6 Let's Stay Together ................................... | | Gordy 1652 |
| | | | **BOBBY MILITELLO featuring JEAN CARNE** | | |
| 5/24/86 | **1**² | 21 | 7 **Closer Than Close**................................. | | Omni 99531 |
| 9/20/86 | **21** | 12 | 8 Flame Of Love ........................................ | | Omni 99511 |
| 1/17/87 | **79** | 4 | 9 Everything Must Change.............................. | | Omni 99489 |
| 4/02/88 | **23** | 13 | 10 Ain't No Way ......................................... | | Atlantic 89116 |
| | | | **KIM CARNES - see JAMES INGRAM and/or KENNY ROGERS** | | |
| | | | **JAMES CARR** | | |
| | | | Born on 6/13/42 in Memphis. With Soul Stirrers gospel group, early 1960's. Managed by Phil Walden and Duane Allman. | | |
| 4/16/66 | **7** | 8 | 1 **You've Got My Mind Messed Up** ................... | 63 | Goldwax 302 |
| 7/30/66 | **21** | 6 | 2 Love Attack ........................................... | 99 | Goldwax 309 |
| 10/29/66 | **23** | 7 | 3 Pouring Water On A Drowning Man .................. | 85 | Goldwax 311 |
| 2/04/67 | **10** | 11 | 4 **The Dark End Of The Street** ........................ | 77 | Goldwax 317 |
| 7/01/67 | **30** | 4 | 5 Let It Happen ......................................... | 106 | Goldwax 323 |
| 9/23/67 | **42** | 5 | 6 I'm A Fool For You .................................... | 97 | Goldwax 328 |
| 1/20/68 | **16** | 11 | 7 A Man Needs A Woman ............................... | 63 | Goldwax 332 |
| 12/14/68+ | **39** | 7 | 8 Freedom Train......................................... | | Goldwax 338 |
| 4/12/69 | **44** | 4 | 9 To Love Somebody .................................... | | Goldwax 340 |
| | | | **JERRY CARR** | | |
| | | | Vocalist/guitarist from Detroit. | | |
| 12/12/81+ | **69** | 8 | 1 This Must Be Heaven ................................. | | Cherie 3872 |
| | | | **WYNONA CARR** | | |
| | | | Also recorded spirituals as Sister Wynona Carr. | | |
| 3/09/57 | **15** | 1 | 1 Should I Ever Love Again ............................ | | Specialty 589 |
| | | | Jockey #15 | | |
| | | | **CARRIE - see CARRIE LUCAS** | | |

| DEBUT DATE | PEAK POS | WKS CHR | ARTIST — Record Title | POP POS | Label & Number |
|---|---|---|---|---|---|
| | | | **THE CARTER BROTHERS** | | |
| | | | Trio from Garland, Alabama. Consisted of Roman (guitar), Jerry (piano) and Albert Carter (guitar). | | |
| 7/03/65 | 21 | 6 | 1 Southern Country Boy ..................................... | *133* | Jewel 745 |
| | | | **BENNY CARTER & HIS ORCHESTRA** | | |
| | | | Born Bennett Lester Carter on 8/8/07 in New York City. Alto saxophonist/leader/ trumpeter/clarinetist/pianist. "America's Amazing Man Of Music". Mainly self-taught. Played in several bands, including Duke Ellington, until 1935. To Europe until 1938. Own band to 1946. Moved to Los Angeles and did movie soundtrack work. Appeared in the film "The Snows Of Kilimanjaro" in 1952. | | |
| 2/12/44 | 2² | 6 | 1 **Hurry, Hurry!/** | 27 | |
| | | | vocal by Savannah Churchill; band includes J.J. Johnson (trombone) | | |
| 2/19/44 | 8 | 1 | 2 **Poinciana** .............................................. [I] | *11* | Capitol 144 |
| 8/19/44 | 1² | 17 | 3 **I'm Lost**....................................................... | | Capitol 165 |
| | | | vocal by Dick Gray | | |
| | | | **CLARENCE CARTER** ★★116★★ | | |
| | | | Born in 1936 in Montgomery, Alabama. Blind since age 1. Self-taught on guitar from age eleven. Teamed with vocalist/pianist Calvin Scott as Clarence & Calvin, recorded for Fairlane, early 60s. Recorded for Duke as C&C Boys. Auto accident in 1966 caused retirement of Scott, Carter then went solo. Married for a time to Candi Staton. | | |
| 1/07/67 | 35 | 6 | 1 Tell Daddy ..................................... | | Fame 1010 |
| 6/03/67 | 38 | 5 | 2 Thread The Needle ........................................ | 98 | Fame 1013 |
| 1/20/68 | 20 | 7 | 3 Looking For A Fox ........................................ | 62 | Atlantic 2461 |
| 5/25/68 | 49 | 3 | 4 Funky Fever/ | 88 | |
| 7/06/68 | 2² | 19 | 5● **Slip Away** ............................................. | *6* | Atlantic 2508 |
| 11/16/68+ | 3 | 13 | 6● **Too Weak To Fight** .................................... | *13* | Atlantic 2569 |
| 3/08/69 | 4 | 9 | 7 **Snatching It Back** ..................................... | *31* | Atlantic 2605 |
| 7/05/69 | 9 | 7 | 8 **The Feeling Is Right** ................................. | *65* | Atlantic 2642 |
| 10/04/69 | 9 | 9 | 9 **Doin' Our Thing** ...................................... | *46* | Atlantic 2660 |
| 1/31/70 | 23 | 6 | 10 Take It Off Him And Put It On Me.................... | 94 | Atlantic 2702 |
| 4/25/70 | 6 | 11 | 11 **I Can't Leave Your Love Alone** .................. | *42* | Atlantic 2726 |
| 7/25/70 | 2¹ | 13 | 12● **Patches** ............................................... | *4* | Atlantic 2748 |
| 11/21/70 | 13 | 8 | 13 It's All In Your Mind ................................. | 51 | Atlantic 2774 |
| 5/08/71 | 12 | 8 | 14 The Court Room ................................. [N] | 61 | Atlantic 2801 |
| 8/14/71 | 25 | 7 | 15 Slipped, Tripped And Fell In Love .................... | 84 | Atlantic 2818 |
| 12/11/71 | 41 | 4 | 16 Scratch My Back (And Mumble In My Ear) ......... | 101 | Atlantic 2842 |
| 12/16/72 | 46 | 4 | 17 Back In Your Arms............................... | | Fame 91006 |
| 3/17/73 | 40 | 5 | 18 Put Your Shoes On And Walk .......................... | 112 | Fame 179 |
| | | | also released on Fame 10309 | | |
| 6/16/73 | 17 | 13 | 19 Sixty Minute Man/ | 65 | |
| | | 7 | 20 Mother-In-Law ............................................. | | Fame 250 |
| 11/10/73+ | 15 | 14 | 21 I'm The Midnight Special ............................. | 101 | Fame 330 |
| 9/13/75 | 49 | 12 | 22 I Got Caught.............................................. | | ABC 12130 |
| 9/05/81 | 81 | 4 | 23 It's A Monster Thing..................................... | | Venture 145 |
| | | | **MEL CARTER** | | |
| | | | Singer/TV actor born on 4/22/43 in Cincinatti. Sang on local radio from age 4; with Lionel Hampton on stage show at age 9. Named Top Gospel Tenor in 1957. First recorded for Mercury in 1959. | | |
| 8/17/63 | 30 | 2 | 1 When A Boy Falls In Love.............................. | 44 | Derby 1003 |
| | | | **RALPH CARTER** | | |
| | | | Played Mike Evans on the TV series "Good Times". | | |
| 8/02/75 | 37 | 11 | 1 When You're Young And In Love .................... | 95 | Mercury 73695 |
| 1/10/76 | 59 | 9 | 2 Extra, Extra (Read All About It) ..................... | | Mercury 73746 |
| | | | **DELIA CARTRELL** | | |
| 12/25/71+ | 24 | 8 | 1 See What You Done Done .............................. | 101 | Right On 109 |
| | | | **THE CASCADES** | | |
| | | | Group from San Diego consisting of John Gummoe, Eddie Snyder, David Stevens, David Wilson and David Zabo. | | |
| 2/23/63 | 7 | 9 | 1 **Rhythm Of The Rain** ................................... | *3* | Valiant 6026 |
| | | | written by John Gummoe | | |

| DEBUT DATE | PEAK POS | WKS CHR | ARTIST — Record Title | POP POS | Label & Number |
|---|---|---|---|---|---|
| | | | **AL CASEY COMBO** | | |
| | | | Guitarist/pianist/bandleader/producer, originally from Phoenix. Much session work with Lee Hazlewood productions, including Sanford Clark and Duane Eddy. Not to be confused with black guitarist of the same name. Also see Ray Sharpe. | | |
| 9/01/62 | 22 | 3 | 1 Jivin' Around ............................................. [I] | | Stacy 936 |
| | | | **ALVIN CASH** | | |
| | | | Born on 2/15/39 in St. Louis. Singer/dancer. Formed song/dance troupe, The Crawlers, in 1960, with brothers Robert, Arthur and George (ages 8-10). They never sang on any of Alvin's hits. The brothers left the act to become the dance team the Little Step Brothers. Moved to Chicago in 1963. First recorded for Mar-V-Lus in 1964. Cut "Twine Time" with backing band, the Nightlighters from Louisville, who changed their name to the Registers. | | |
| | | | ALVIN CASH & THE CRAWLERS: | | |
| 1/30/65 | 4 | 12 | 1 **Twine Time** ............................................. [I] | 14 | Mar-V-Lus 6002 |
| 4/03/65 | 29 | 4 | 2 Barracuda ................................................. | 59 | Mar-V-Lus 6005 |
| | | | ALVIN CASH & THE REGISTERS: | | |
| 7/23/66 | 12 | 11 | 3 Philly Freeze ............................................ | 49 | Mar-V-Lus 6012 |
| 12/17/66+ | 42 | 8 | 4 Alvin's Boo-Ga-Loo ................................... | 74 | Mar-V-Lus 6014 |
| 11/16/68 | 13 | 8 | 5 Keep On Dancing ...................................... | 66 | Toddlin' Town 111 |
| | | | ALVIN CASH | | |
| | | | **CA$HFLOW** | | |
| | | | Atlanta funk/rap quartet. Kary Hubbert, lead singer. | | |
| 2/22/86 | 8 | 17 | 1 **Party Freak** ............................................ | | Mercury 884454 |
| 5/31/86 | 12 | 16 | 2 Mine All Mine ........................................... | | Atl. Art. 884722 |
| 9/20/86 | 64 | 8 | 3 Reach Out................................................ | | Atl. Art. 888005 |
| | | | **CASHMERE** | | |
| | | | Trio from Chicago consisting of Dwight Dukes (lead vocals, guitar), McKinley Horton (keyboards) and Daryl Burgee (drums). Dukes was formerly in Heaven And Earth. | | |
| 1/15/83 | 35 | 14 | 1 Do It Anyway You Wanna............................. | | Philly W. 2009 |
| 8/27/83 | 75 | 5 | 2 Try Your Lovin' ......................................... | | Philly W. 204 |
| 12/15/84+ | 48 | 12 | 3 Can I...................................................... | | Philly W. 99682 |
| 4/13/85 | 68 | 8 | 4 We Need Love............................................ | | Philly W. 99654 |
| | | | **RICH CASON & The Galactic Orchestra** | | |
| 9/17/83 | 46 | 9 | 1 Year 2001 Boogie ...................................... | | Larc 81029 |
| 3/31/84 | 64 | 6 | 2 Street Symphony ....................................... | | Private I 04403 |
| | | | **CASPER** | | |
| 7/12/80 | 86 | 4 | 1 Groovy Ghost Show .................................... | | AVI 311 |
| | | | **JIMMY CASTOR** | | |
| | | | Jimmy was born on 6/2/43 in New York City. Singer/songwriter/saxophonist/arranger. Attended PS169 and JHS164 with Frankie Lymon and Leslie "Uggams" Crane. Wrote and recorded "I Promise To Remember" for Wing in 1956, with vocal group, The Juniors: Al Casey, Jr. (son of jazz guitarist), Orton Graves and Johnny Williams. Castor replaced Frankie Lymon in the Teenagers, in 1957. Played sax on "Rinky Dink", hit by Dave "Baby" Cortez. Formed the Jimmy Castor Bunch in 1972, with Gerry Thomas (keyboards, trumpet), Doug Gibson (bass), Harry Jensen (guitar), Lenny Fridie, Jr. (congas) and Bobby Manigault (drums). | | |
| 12/31/66+ | 16 | 8 | 1 Hey, Leroy, Your Mama's Callin' You............. [I] | 31 | Smash 2069 |
| | | | THE JIMMY CASTOR BUNCH: | | |
| 5/20/72 | 4 | 11 | 2●Troglodyte (Cave Man)............................. [N] | 6 | RCA 1029 |
| 7/14/73 | 72 | 4 | 3 Soul Serenade ........................................... | | RCA 0953 |
| 1/11/75 | 22 | 18 | 4 The Bertha Butt Boogie (Part 1) .................. [N] | 16 | Atlantic 3232 |
| 6/28/75 | 25 | 13 | 5 Potential ................................................. | | Atlantic 3270 |
| 10/11/75 | 23 | 12 | 6 King Kong - Pt. I ..................................... [N] | 69 | Atlantic 3295 |
| 3/06/76 | 42 | 9 | 7 Supersound.............................................. | | Atlantic 3316 |
| | | | JIMMY CASTOR: | | |
| 6/19/76 | 97 | 1 | 8 Bom Bom ................................................ | | Atlantic 3331 |
| | | | featuring The Everything Man | | |
| 10/23/76 | 67 | 10 | 9 Everything Is Beautiful To Me ...................... | | Atlantic 3362 |
| 1/29/77 | 28 | 16 | 10 Space Age................................................ | 101 | Atlantic 3375 |
| 2/04/78 | 82 | 4 | 11 Maximum Stimulation................................. | | Atlantic 3455 |
| 6/30/79 | 50 | 8 | 12 Don't Do That! ......................................... | | Cotillion 44253 |
| 5/24/80 | 93 | 3 | 13 Can't Help Falling In Love With You/ | | |
| | | 3 | 14 Stay With Me (Spend The Night).................... | | Long Dist. 702 |
| 8/25/84 | 84 | 3 | 15 Amazon.................................................... | | Dream 0360 |

| DEBUT DATE | PEAK POS | WKS CHR | ARTIST — Record Title | POP POS | Label & Number |
|---|---|---|---|---|---|
| | | | **JIMMY CASTOR — Continued** | | |
| 1/05/85 | 81 | 4 | 16 It Gets To Me.................................. | | Dream 70361 |
| 4/16/88 | 29 | 11 | 17 Love Makes A Woman.......................... | | Sleep. B. 40134 |
| | | | JOYCE SIMS featuring JIMMY CASTOR | | |
| | | | **THE CASUALS - see THE ORIGINAL CASUALS** | | |
| | | | **CATCH** | | |
| 4/14/84 | 82 | 9 | 1 Get On Freak................................... | | Columbia 04462 |
| 11/24/84 | 86 | 4 | 2 Indecisive ..................................... | | Columbia 04667 |
| | | | **CATE BROS.** | | |
| | | | Duo of twins Ernie (vocals/piano) and Earl (guitar), born on 12/26/42 in Fayetteville, Arkansas. Produced by Steve Cropper. | | |
| 3/27/76 | 96 | 3 | 1 Union Man..................................... | 24 | Asylum 45294 |
| | | | **CATS 'N' JAMMERS** | | |
| | | | Combo from Chicago, also known as Cats 'N' Jammer Trio and Cats And Jammer Three. Formed in Spring of 1945 by Adam Lambert (guitar), Sylvester Hickman (bass) and Bill Samuels (piano). Heard frequently on the Dave Garroway radio show, and on own program on WBBM-Chicago. One of the first acts to record for Mercury Records. Also recorded as the Bill Samuels Trio for Miracle in 1949. Samuels moved to Minneapolis in the early 50s and died there in the early 70s. Adam Lambert went to the Four Shades of Rhythm for a time, and Sylvester Hickman remained active in Chicago combos into the 70s. | | |
| 4/06/46 | 3 | 1 | 1 I Cover The Water Front ..................... | | Mercury 2003 |
| 11/16/46 | 5 | 1 | 2 Port Wine .................................... | | Mercury 8012 |
| | | | above 2: vocals by Bill Samuels | | |
| | | | **C-BANK - see JENNY BURTON** | | |
| | | | **CELI BEE & THE BUZZY BUNCH** | | |
| | | | Puerto Rican disco band led by female vocalist Celinas. | | |
| 5/28/77 | 86 | 5 | 1 Superman...................................... | 41 | APA 17001 |
| | | | **CENTERFOLD** | | |
| | | | Minneapolis-based duo produced by Monte Moir (formely with The Time): Keni Towns and Phil Jones. | | |
| 2/20/88 | 66 | 7 | 1 Party Rebels ................................. | | Columbia 07360 |
| | | | **CENTRAL LINE** | | |
| | | | London-based group consisting of Linton Beckles (vocals, percussion), Henry Defoe (guitar), Lipson Francis (keyboards) and Camelle Hinds (bass). | | |
| 10/10/81 | 14 | 20 | 1 Walking Into Sunshine ....................... | 84 | Mercury 76126 |
| 2/05/83 | 54 | 6 | 2 You've Said Enough............................ | | Mercury 76192 |
| 3/17/84 | 49 | 8 | 3 Time For Some Fun ........................... | | Mercury 814749 |
| | | | **CERRONE** | | |
| | | | Composer/producer/drummer, born Jean-Marc Cerrone in France in 1952. | | |
| 2/26/77 | 29 | 12 | 1 Love In 'C' Minor - Pt. 1....................[I] | 36 | Cotillion 44215 |
| 1/28/78 | 72 | 6 | 2 Supernature................................... | 70 | Cotillion 44230 |
| 12/16/78+ | 60 | 8 | 3 Je Suis Music ................................ | | Cotillion 44244 |
| 7/31/82 | 85 | 4 | 4 Back Track ................................... | | Pavillion 02962 |
| 11/22/86 | 89 | 2 | 5 Oops, Oh No .................................. | | Palass 0934 |
| | | | CERRONE & LaTOYA JACKSON | | |
| | | | **CHABUKOS** | | |
| 12/29/73+ | 39 | 12 | 1 Witch Doctor Bump ........................... | | Mainstream 5546 |
| | | | **CHAD** | | |
| | | | Singer/songwriter/producer born and raised in New York City. Attended New York's Music and Art High School. Former lead singer of BB&Q Band & Flique. Session work with Mtume. | | |
| 10/03/87 | 14 | 12 | 1 Luv's Passion And You ....................... | | RCA 5293 |
| 2/06/88 | 66 | 6 | 2 Jennie ....................................... | | RCA 6848 |
| | | | **CHAIN REACTION** | | |
| | | | Group member Norris Harris was the baritone of Moment Of Truth. | | |
| 3/05/77 | 96 | 3 | 1 Never Lose Never Win ....................... | | Ariola Am. 7651 |

| DEBUT DATE | PEAK POS | WKS CHR | ARTIST — Record Title | POP POS | Label & Number |
|---|---|---|---|---|---|
| | | | **CHAIRMEN OF THE BOARD** | | |
| | | | Vocal group formed in Detroit in 1969. Consisted of General Norman Johnson, Danny Woods, Harrison Kennedy and Eddie Curtis. First recorded for Invictus in 1969. Johnson was leader of The Showmen from 1961-67; wrote "Patches", hit for Clarence Carter. Johnson went solo in 1976. | | |
| 1/24/70 | 8 | 13 | 1●Give Me Just A Little More Time | 3 | Invictus 9074 |
| 5/23/70 | 19 | 6 | 2 (You've Got Me) Dangling On A String | 38 | Invictus 9078 |
| 8/08/70 | 14 | 9 | 3 Everything's Tuesday | 38 | Invictus 9079 |
| 11/14/70 | 4 | 13 | 4 Pay To The Piper | 13 | Invictus 9081 |
| 2/20/71 | 10 | 8 | 5 Chairman Of The Board | 42 | Invictus 9086 |
| 5/08/71 | 28 | 6 | 6 Hanging On (To) A Memory | 111 | Invictus 9089 |
| 10/02/71 | 48 | 2 | 7 Try On My Love For Size | 103 | Invictus 9099 |
| 11/27/71 | 33 | 5 | 8 Men Are Getting Scarce | 104 | Invictus 9103 |
| 7/01/72 | 30 | 3 | 9 Everybody's Got A Song To Sing | | Invictus 9122 |
| 5/12/73 | 7 | 13 | 10 Finder's Keepers | 59 | Invictus 1251 |
| 3/30/74 | 52 | 8 | 11 Life And Death | | Invictus 1263 |
| 6/15/74 | 80 | 5 | 12 Everybody Party All Night | | Invictus 1268 |
| | | | **THE CHAKACHAS** | | |
| | | | Belgian sextet led by Gaston Boogaerts. | | |
| 1/08/72 | 11 | 14 | 1●Jungle Fever [I] | 8 | Polydor 15030 |
| | | | **THE CHAMBERS BROTHERS** | | |
| | | | Four Mississippi-born brothers: George (bass), Willie (guitar), Lester (harmonica), and Joe (guitar). Formed as a gospel group in Los Angeles in 1954. Drummer Brian Keenan added in 1965. Appearance at the Newport Folk Festival in 1965 marked group's transition to folk music. | | |
| 1/09/71 | 40 | 5 | 1 Funky | 106 | Columbia 45277 |
| 3/30/74 | 76 | 6 | 2 Let's Go, Let's Go, Let's Go | 106 | Avco 4632 |
| | | | lead vocal by Willie | | |
| | | | **EDDIE CHAMBLEE** | | |
| | | | Born on 2/24/20 in Atlanta. Tenor saxophonist. In service bands from 1941-46; own combo in 1946. With Sonny Thompson and the Four Blazes in the early 50s. With Lionel Hampton in 1954; Cozy Cole, 1959-60. Recorded with wife, Dinah Washington, for Mercury in 1957. | | |
| 5/14/49 | 9 | 8 | 1 Back Street [I] | | Miracle 133 |
| | | | Juke Box #9 / Best Seller #10 | | |
| | | | **CHAMPAIGN** | | |
| | | | Inter-racial sextet from Champaign, Illinois. Consisted of Rena Jones and Pauli Carman (vocals), Michael Day (guitar, keyboards), Dana Walden (keyboards), Howard Reeder (guitar), Michael Reed (bass) and Rocky Maffit (drums). | | |
| 2/07/81 | 4 | 22 | 1 How 'Bout Us | 12 | Columbia 11433 |
| 7/04/81 | 73 | 5 | 2 I'm On Fire | | Columbia 02110 |
| 2/12/83 | 2² | 25 | 3 Try Again | 23 | Columbia 03563 |
| 8/06/83 | 62 | 7 | 4 Let Your Body Rock | | Columbia 04013 |
| 9/15/84 | 10 | 14 | 5 Off And On Love | 104 | Columbia 04600 |
| 12/15/84+ | 43 | 12 | 6 This Time | | Columbia 04721 |
| | | | **THE CHAMPS** | | |
| | | | Los Angeles instrumental combo of prominent studio musicians. Fluctuating lineup featured Jim Seals, Dash Crofts and Glen Campbell. | | |
| 3/03/58 | 1⁴ | 13 | 1 Tequila [I] | 1 | Challenge 1016 |
| | | | Best Seller #1(4) / Jockey #1(4) | | |
| 6/02/58 | 10 | 1 | 2 El Rancho Rock [I] | 30 | Challenge 59007 |
| | | | Jockey #10 / Best Seller #20 | | |
| | | | **THE CHAMPS' BOYS ORCHESTRA** | | |
| 5/29/76 | 98 | 2 | 1 Tubular Bells [I] | 98 | Janus 259 |
| | | | theme from the film "The Exorcist" | | |
| | | | **GENE CHANDLER** ★★48★★ | | |
| | | | Singer/producer, born Eugene Dixon on 7/6/37 in Chicago. Formed the Gaytones at Englewood High School in 1955. Joined the Dukays in 1957. In US Army, Germany from 1957-60. Rejoined the Dukays in 1960. Consisted of Eugene Dixon (lead), Shirley Jones and James Lowe (tenors), Earl Edwards (baritone) and Ben Broyles (bass). First recorded for Nat in 1961. Changed name to "Gene Chandler" to avoid contract conflicts, then left group. Had own label, Mr. Chand, from 1969-1973. | | |
| 1/20/62 | 1⁵ | 13 | 1 Duke Of Earl | 1 | Vee-Jay 416 |
| | | | written by Chandler | | |

| DEBUT DATE | PEAK POS | WKS CHR | ARTIST — Record Title | POP POS | Label & Number |
|---|---|---|---|---|---|
| | | | **GENE CHANDLER — Continued** | | |
| 11/24/62 | **25** | 2 | 2　You Threw A Lucky Punch/<br>　　background vocals by Cal Carter & Friends | 49 | |
| 2/09/63 | **11** | 12 | 3　Rainbow ...................................... | 47 | Vee-Jay 468 |
| 8/03/63 | **17** | 9 | 4　Man's Temptation ........................... | 71 | Vee-Jay 536 |
| 5/02/64 | **92** | 2 | 5　Soul Hootenanny (Pt. I) .................... | Hot | Constell. 114 |
| 7/11/64 | **19** | 10 | 6　Just Be True ................................ | Hot | Constell. 130 |
| 9/26/64 | **39** | 9 | 7　Bless Our Love .............................. | Hot | Constell. 136 |
| 1/30/65 | **18** | 2 | 8　What Now ................................... | 40 | Constell. 141 |
| 3/27/65 | **40** | 2 | 9　You Can't Hurt Me No More.............. | 92 | Constell. 146 |
| 4/10/65 | **3** | 15 | 10　**Nothing Can Stop Me** .................. | 18 | Constell. 149 |
| 9/18/65 | **40** | 2 | 11　Good Times................................ | 92 | Constell. 160 |
| 12/04/65+ | **2** [1] | 12 | 12　**Rainbow '65 (Part I)**...................<br>　　live version of #3 above | 69 | Constell. 158 |
| 11/12/66+ | **3** | 14 | 13　**I Fooled You This Time** ................ | 45 | Checker 1155 |
| 3/11/67 | **16** | 9 | 14　Girl Don't Care ........................... | 66 | Brunswick 55312 |
| 5/13/67 | **9** | 10 | 15　**To Be A Lover** .......................... | 94 | Checker 1165 |
| 9/23/67 | **46** | 2 | 16　There Goes The Lover....................... | 98 | Brunswick 55339 |
| 3/23/68 | **30** | 7 | 17　Show Me The Way To Go ................<br>　　**GENE CHANDLER & BARBARA ACKLIN** | | Brunswick 55366 |
| 6/08/68 | **19** | 10 | 18　River Of Tears ............................ | | Checker 1199 |
| 9/14/68 | **22** | 10 | 19　There Was A Time.......................... | 82 | Brunswick 55383 |
| 10/26/68 | **16** | 11 | 20　From The Teacher To The Preacher ..................<br>　　**GENE CHANDLER & BARBARA ACKLIN** | 57 | Brunswick 55387 |
| 7/04/70 | **8** | 15 | 21●**Groovy Situation** ........................ | 12 | Mercury 73083 |
| 11/14/70 | **29** | 7 | 22　Simply Call It Love ........................ | 75 | Mercury 73121 |
| 1/09/71 | **32** | 4 | 23　You Just Can't Win (By Making The Same<br>　　　Mistake) .......................<br>　　**GENE & JERRY** (Butler) | 94 | Mercury 73163 |
| 6/05/71 | **14** | 10 | 24　You're A Lady ............................. | 116 | Mercury 73206 |
| 6/19/71 | **44** | 2 | 25　Ten And Two (Take This Woman Off The Corner)<br>　　**GENE & JERRY** | 126 | Mercury 73195 |
| 1/08/72 | **47** | 2 | 26　Yes I'm Ready (If I Don't Get To Go)................ | | Mercury 73258 |
| 4/01/78 | **51** | 12 | 27　Tomorrow I May Not Feel The Same ................ | | Chi-Sound 1168 |
| 10/28/78+ | **3** | 22 | 28　**Get Down** ............................... | 53 | Chi-Sound 2386 |
| 8/04/79 | **31** | 11 | 29　When You're #1 ........................... | 99 | Chi-Sound 2411 |
| 11/17/79 | **73** | 4 | 30　Do What Comes So Natural ............... | | 20th Century 2428 |
| 4/26/80 | **28** | 15 | 31　Does She Have A Friend? ................ | 101 | Chi-Sound 2451 |
| 10/04/80 | **73** | 3 | 32　Lay Me Gently ............................ | | 20th Century 2468 |
| 5/08/82 | **40** | 9 | 33　I'll Make The Living If You Make The Loving<br>　　　Worthwhile................................ | | Chi-Sound 1001 |
| 5/21/83 | **89** | 4 | 34　You're The One............................<br>　　**JAIME LYNN & GENE CHANDLER** | | Salsoul 7051 |
| 10/19/85 | **61** | 8 | 35　Haven't I Heard That Line Before.................... | | FastFire 7003 |
| 2/22/86 | **43** | 10 | 36　Lucy............................................. | | FastFire 7005 |
| | | | **CHANGE**<br>European/American studio group formed by Italian producer Jacques Fred Petrus. Led by Paolo Granolio (guitar) and David Romani (bass). Luther Vandross sang on several songs from group's first two albums. Later group, based in New York, included lead vocals by James Robinson and Deborah "Crab" Cooper. | | |
| 4/12/80 | **5** | 20 | 1　A Lover's Holiday ........................ | 40 | RFC 49208 |
| 8/02/80 | **23** | 12 | 2　Searching ................................ | | RFC 49512 |
| 10/25/80 | **49** | 9 | 3　The Glow Of Love........................<br>　　above 2: lead vocals by Luther Vandross | | RFC 49587 |
| 4/11/81 | **7** | 18 | 4　**Paradise** ................................ | 80 | Atlantic 3809 |
| 7/11/81 | **40** | 9 | 5　Hold Tight ................................ | 89 | Atlantic 3832 |
| 4/10/82 | **16** | 14 | 6　The Very Best In You...................... | 84 | Atlantic 4027 |
| 7/17/82 | **71** | 6 | 7　Hard Times (It's Gonna Be Alright) ................ | | Atlantic 4063 |
| 3/05/83 | **33** | 11 | 8　This Is Your Time .......................... | | Atlantic 89883 |
| 7/09/83 | **89** | 3 | 9　Don't Wait Another Night ................. | | Atlantic 89828 |
| 4/14/84 | **7** | 15 | 10　**Change Of Heart**........................ | | Atlantic 89684 |
| 7/28/84 | **61** | 7 | 11　It Burns Me Up ........................... | | Atlantic 89642 |
| 4/06/85 | **56** | 10 | 12　Let's Go Together ......................... | | Atlantic 89570 |

| DEBUT DATE | PEAK POS | WKS CHR | ARTIST — Record Title | POP POS | Label & Number |
|---|---|---|---|---|---|
| | | | **BRUCE CHANNEL**<br>Born on 11/28/40 in Jacksonville, Texas. Appeared on "Louisiana Hayride" in 1958.<br>First recorded for LeCam in 1962. | | |
| 2/24/62 | **2**¹ | 12 | 1 **Hey! Baby** ....................................... <br> harmonica player: Delbert McClinton | *1* | Smash 1731 |
| | | | **CHANSON**<br>Studio disco band. Lead vocals by James Jamerson Jr. & David Williams. | | |
| 9/23/78 | **8** | 20 | 1 **Don't Hold Back** ............................... | *21* | Ariola 7717 |
| 5/05/79 | **72** | 5 | 2 I Can Tell ........................................ | | Ariola 7743 |
| 11/17/79 | **67** | 5 | 3 Rock Don't Stop ................................ | | Ariola 7773 |
| | | | **CHANTAY'S**<br>Teenage surf/rock quintet from Santa Ana, California consisting of Bob Spickard,<br>Brian Carman, Rob Marshall, Warren Waters and Bob Welch. First recorded for Downey<br>in 1962. Disbanded in 1966. | | |
| 4/13/63 | **11** | 11 | 1 Pipeline ................................... [I] <br> originally released on Downey 104 | *4* | Dot 16440 |
| | | | **THE CHANTELS**<br>Vocal group from the Bronx. Formed in high school, with lead Arlene Smith,<br>Sonia Goring, Rene Minus, Jackie Landry and Lois Harris. Group name taken from<br>that of a rival school, St. Francis de Chantelle. Auditioned for Richard Barrett<br>who became their manager and obtained a contract with Gone/End Records. | | |
| 1/27/58 | **2**¹ | 13 | 1 **Maybe** ....................................... <br> Jockey #2 / Best Seller #5 <br> re-released on Roulette 7064 | *15* | End 1005 |
| 4/14/58 | **16** | 4 | 2 **Every Night (I Pray)** ......................... <br> Best Seller #16 | *39* | End 1015 |
| 7/14/58 | **14** | 2 | 3 I Love You So ................................... <br> Jockey #14 | *42* | End 1020 |
| 8/31/59 | **29** | 1 | 4 Summer's Love ................................. <br> **RICHARD BARRETT with THE CHANTELS** | *93* | Gone 5060 |
| 9/11/61 | **6** | 12 | 5 **Look In My Eyes** ............................. | *14* | Carlton 555 |
| | | | **THE CHANTERS**<br>Group from Queens, New York, formed in 1957. Consisted of Larry Pendergrass,<br>Fred Paige, Bud Johnson, Elliot Green, and Bobby Thompson. Johnson's father is<br>famous bandleader Budd Johnson, who arranged their sessions. Group disbanded in the<br>early 60s. Not to be confused with Billy Butler's Chanters. | | |
| 6/19/61 | **9** | 12 | 1 **No, No, No** ................................... <br> recorded in 1958; first released on DeLuxe 6177 | *41* | DeLuxe 6191 |
| | | | **THE CHANTERS - see BILLY BUTLER** | | |
| | | | **ANGELICA CHAPLIN**<br>Singer raised in southern California. Discovered by Mic Murphy (The System). | | |
| 5/23/87 | **94** | 3 | 1 Anyone Else .................................... | | Mercury 888012 |
| | | | **CHAPTER 8**<br>Detroit group originally formed in 1971 as the all-male backup band for the Detroit<br>Emeralds. Led by Michael J. Powell and David Washington, emerged in 1973 as<br>Chapter 8. Female vocalist Carolyn Crawford joined in 1975, replaced in 1976 by<br>Anita Baker. In 1984, Baker pursued a solo career, replaced by Valerie Pinkston.<br>1988 lineup: Powell (producer, guitar), Washington (bass), Pinkston (vocals),<br>Courtlen Hale (sax), Gerald Lyles (vocals) and Vernon Fails (keyboards). | | |
| 8/25/79 | **38** | 12 | 1 Ready For Your Love ........................... | | Ariola 7763 |
| 12/08/79 | **81** | 7 | 2 I Just Wanna Be Your Girl .................... | | Ariola 7777 |
| 4/26/80 | **55** | 6 | 3 Don't You Like It .............................. | | Ariola 802 |
| 12/14/85 | **89** | 5 | 4 How Can I Get Next To You .................... | | Beverly Glen 2024 |
| | | | **CHARIOTEERS**<br>Group formed at Wilberforce College, Ohio in 1930 as the Harmony Four. Immensely<br>popular on radio with Bing Crosby on the Kraft Music Hall. Consisted of Billy<br>Williams (lead), Edward Jackson, Ira Williams and Howard Daniel. Billy Williams<br>left in 1950 to form his own quartet. First recorded for Decca in 1935. | | |
| 7/16/49 | **8** | 3 | 1 A Kiss And A Rose ............................. <br> Juke Box #8 | *19* | Columbia 38438 |
| | | | **CHARLENE - see STEVIE WONDER** | | |

| DEBUT DATE | PEAK POS | WKS CHR | ARTIST — Record Title | POP POS | Label & Number |
|---|---|---|---|---|---|
| | | | **BOBBY CHARLES** Born Robert Charles Guidry in 1938 in Abbeville, Louisiana. Vocalist/composer. First recorded for Chess in 1955. Wrote "See You Later, Alligator", "Walkin' To New Orleans" and "(I Don't Know Why I Love You) But I Do". | | |
| 3/24/56 | **14** | 1 | **1** See You Later, Alligator ................................. Jockey #14 | | Chess 1609 |
| 8/18/56 | **11** | 3 | **2** Time Will Tell............................................ Jockey #11 | | Chess 1628 |
| | | | **JIMMY CHARLES** Born in 1942 in Paterson, New Jersey. Won Apollo Amateur Contest in 1958. | | |
| 9/05/60 | **8** | 10 | **1** A Million To One......................................... vocal backing by The Revelletts | 5 | Promo 1002 |
| | | | **LEE CHARLES** Full name is Lee Charles Nealy. | | |
| 4/13/68 | **41** | 3 | **1** Standing On The Outside .............................. | | Revue 11007 |
| 8/11/73 | **65** | 6 | **2** I Just Want To Be Loved .............................. | | Hot Wax 7303 |
| | | | **RAY CHARLES** ★★**3**★★ Born Ray Charles Robinson on 9/23/30 in Albany, Georgia. To Greenville, Florida while still an infant. Partially blind at age 5, completely blind at 7 (glaucoma). Studied classical piano and clarinet at State School for Deaf and Blind Children, St. Augustine, Florida, 1937-45. With local Florida bands, moved to Seattle in 1948. Formed the McSon Trio (also known as the Maxim Trio and the Maxine Trio) with G.D. McGhee (guitar) and Milton Garred (bass). First recordings were very much in the King Cole Trio style. Formed own band in 1954. Extremely popular performer with many TV and film appearances. Also see Guitar Slim. | | |
| 4/09/49 | **2**¹ | 11 | **1** Confession Blues ........................................ **MAXINE TRIO** Juke Box #2 / Best Seller #5 | | Downbeat 171 |
| 2/10/51 | **5** | 6 | **2** Baby Let Me Hold Your Hand ........................ Juke Box #5 / Best Seller #7 | | Swingtime 250 |
| 3/22/52 | **8** | 1 | **3** Kiss Me Baby ............................................ Juke Box #8 / Best Seller #10 | | Swingtime 274 |
| 4/03/54 | **5** | 9 | **4** It Should've Been Me .................................. Juke Box #5 / Best Seller #7 | | Atlantic 1021 |
| 8/21/54 | **10** | 1 | **5** Don't You Know.......................................... Best Seller #10 | | Atlantic 1037 |
| 1/22/55 | **1**¹ | 20 | **6** I've Got A Woman/ Juke Box #1 / Best Seller #2 / Jockey #4 | | |
| 1/15/55 | **4** | 15 | **7** Come Back................................................ Jockey #4 / Juke Box #8 / Best Seller #9 | | Atlantic 1050 |
| 7/02/55 | **1**¹ | 12 | **8** A Fool For You/ Jockey #1 / Best Seller #2 / Juke Box #2 | | |
| 7/09/55 | **9** | 5 | **9** This Little Girl Of Mine............................... Jockey #9 | | Atlantic 1063 |
| 10/29/55 | **8** | 5 | **10** Blackjack/ Best Seller #8 / Juke Box #8 / Jockey #10 | | |
| 11/05/55 | **5** | 4 | **11** Greenbacks.............................................. Juke Box #5 / Jockey #12 6-7, 10 & 11: recorded at a radio station in Atlanta | | Atlantic 1076 |
| 2/25/56 | **1**² | 15 | **12** Drown In My Own Tears/ Juke Box #1(2) / Jockey #1(1) / Best Seller #2 | | |
| | | 2 | **13** Mary Ann ................................................ Juke Box flip | | Atlantic 1085 |
| 6/16/56 | **5** | 8 | **14** Hallelujah I Love Her So/ Best Seller #5 / Juke Box #6 / Jockey #11 | | |
| | | 2 | **15** What Would I Do Without You....................... Best Seller flip | | Atlantic 1096 |
| 10/20/56 | **6** | 5 | **16** Lonely Avenue........................................... Jockey #6 / Juke Box #6 / Best Seller #8 | | Atlantic 1108 |
| 2/16/57 | **9** | 6 | **17** Ain't That Love.......................................... Juke Box #9 / Best Seller #11 / Jockey #12 | | Atlantic 1124 |
| 11/11/57 | **14** | 3 | **18** Swanee River Rock (Talkin' 'Bout That River) .... Best Seller #14 / Jockey #14 | 34 | Atlantic 1154 |
| 12/15/58 | **14** | 9 | **19** Rockhouse (Part 2) ..................................... [I] | 79 | Atlantic 2006 |
| 1/05/59 | **5** | 18 | **20** (Night Time Is) The Right Time ..................... | 95 | Atlantic 2010 |
| 4/27/59 | **19** | 6 | **21** That's Enough .......................................... 16, 18 & 21: vocals by The Cookies (aka: Raeletts) | | Atlantic 2022 |
| 7/13/59 | **1**¹ | 17 | **22** What'd I Say (Part I) ................................... | 6 | Atlantic 2031 |
| 11/23/59 | **11** | 5 | **23** I'm Movin' On ............................................ | 40 | Atlantic 2043 |

| DEBUT DATE | PEAK POS | WKS CHR | ARTIST — Record Title | POP POS | Label & Number |
|---|---|---|---|---|---|
| | | | **RAY CHARLES — Continued** | | |
| 2/08/60 | **17** | 7 | 24 Don't Let The Sun Catch You Cryin'................ | 95 | Atlantic 2047 |
| 5/23/60 | **16** | 3 | 25 Just For A Thrill............................... | | Atlantic 2055 |
| 6/27/60 | **2**¹ | 13 | 26 **Sticks And Stones** ......................................... | 40 | ABC-Para. 10118 |
| 8/08/60 | **13** | 8 | 27 Tell The Truth............................... | | Atlantic 2068 |
| 9/26/60 | **3** | 16 | 28 **Georgia On My Mind** .............................. | 1 | ABC-Para. 10135 |
| | | | first popularized in 1931 by Frankie Trumbauer (POS 10) | | |
| 12/12/60+ | **10** | 8 | 29 **Ruby** ................................................ | 28 | ABC-Para. 10164 |
| 2/06/61 | **10** | 7 | 30 **Them That Got** ................................ | 58 | ABC-Para. 10141 |
| 3/20/61 | **1**¹ | 12 | 31 **One Mint Julep**.............................[I] | 8 | Impulse 200 |
| 6/26/61 | **8** | 6 | 32 **I've Got News For You/** | 66 | |
| 6/26/61 | **25** | 2 | 33 I'm Gonna Move To The Outskirts Of Town...... | 84 | Impulse 202 |
| 9/18/61 | **1**⁵ | 15 | 34 **Hit The Road Jack** .............................. | 1 | ABC-Para. 10244 |
| 12/18/61+ | **1**² | 10 | 35 **Unchain My Heart/** | 9 | |
| 12/18/61+ | **10** | 11 | 36 **But On The Other Hand Baby** .................. | 72 | ABC-Para. 10266 |
| 4/14/62 | **7** | 9 | 37 **Hide 'Nor Hair/** | 20 | |
| 4/14/62 | **7** | 8 | 38 **At The Club** ................................ | 44 | ABC-Para. 10314 |
| 5/19/62 | **1**¹⁰ | 16 | 39●**I Can't Stop Loving You** ...................... | 1 | ABC-Para. 10330 |
| 8/18/62 | **5** | 9 | 40 **You Don't Know Me**.......................... | 2 | ABC-Para. 10345 |
| 12/08/62 | **1**³ | 11 | 41 **You Are My Sunshine/** | 7 | |
| 12/08/62 | **23** | 2 | 42 Your Cheating Heart............................ | 29 | ABC-Para. 10375 |
| 3/09/63 | **9** | 8 | 43 **Don't Set Me Free**.............................. | 20 | ABC-Para. 10405 |
| 5/04/63 | **7** | 8 | 44 **Take These Chains From My Heart**.............. | 8 | ABC-Para. 10435 |
| 7/06/63 | **9** | 8 | 45 **No One/** | 21 | |
| 7/06/63 | **15** | 6 | 46 Without Love (There Is Nothing) .................... | 29 | ABC-Para. 10453 |
| 9/28/63 | **3** | 9 | 47 **Busted**................................... | 4 | ABC-Para. 10481 |
| 12/07/63+ | **20** | 9 | 48 That Lucky Old Sun .............................. | Hot | ABC-Para. 10509 |
| 2/22/64 | **39** | 7 | 49 Baby, Don't You Cry ............................ | Hot | ABC-Para. 10530 |
| 2/29/64 | **38** | 7 | 50 My Heart Cries For You .......................... | Hot | ABC-Para. 10530 |
| 5/30/64 | **51** | 6 | 51 My Baby Don't Dig Me .......................... | Hot | ABC-Para. 10557 |
| 7/18/64 | **55** | 6 | 52 No One To Cry To............................... | Hot | ABC-Para. 10571 |
| 8/01/64 | **50** | 5 | 53 A Tear Fell ...................................... | Hot | ABC-Para. 10571 |
| 9/26/64 | **52** | 7 | 54 Smack Dab In The Middle ...................... | Hot | ABC-Para. 10588 |
| 1/30/65 | **14** | 2 | 55 Makin' Whoopee ................................ | 46 | ABC-Para. 10609 |
| 1/01/66 | **5** | 14 | 56 **Crying Time**................................... | 6 | ABC-Para. 10739 |
| 4/16/66 | **10** | 8 | 57 **Together Again** ................................ | 19 | ABC-Para. 10785 |
| 6/04/66 | **1**¹ | 13 | 58 **Let's Go Get Stoned** .......................... | 31 | ABC/TRC 10808 |
| | | | co-written by Jo Armstead | | |
| 9/24/66 | **22** | 7 | 59 I Chose To Sing The Blues ...................... | 32 | ABC/TRC 10840 |
| 12/24/66 | **45** | 2 | 60 I Don't Need No Doctor......................... | 72 | ABC/TRC 10865 |
| 6/10/67 | **5** | 14 | 61 **Here We Go Again** ............................ | 15 | ABC/TRC 10938 |
| 9/09/67 | **21** | 9 | 62 In The Heat Of The Night ...................... | 33 | ABC/TRC 10970 |
| | | | from the Sidney Poitier film of the same title | | |
| 11/18/67 | **9** | 10 | 63 **Yesterday** ..................................... | 25 | ABC/TRC 11009 |
| 3/02/68 | **11** | 9 | 64 That's A Lie .................................... | 64 | ABC/TRC 11045 |
| 6/15/68 | **13** | 13 | 65 Understanding/ | 46 | |
| 7/13/68 | **30** | 7 | 66 Eleanor Rigby................................... | 35 | ABC/TRC 11090 |
| 1/11/69 | **21** | 7 | 67 If It Wasn't For Bad Luck .............................. | 77 | ABC 11170 |
| | | | **RAY CHARLES & JIMMY LEWIS** | | |
| 5/24/69 | **28** | 5 | 68 Let Me Love You................................. | 94 | ABC/TRC 11213 |
| 10/04/69 | **31** | 5 | 69 We Can Make It .............................. | 101 | ABC/TRC 11239 |
| 3/14/70 | **18** | 6 | 70 Laughin & Clownin............................. | 98 | ABC/TRC 11259 |
| 10/10/70 | **19** | 9 | 71 If You Were Mine ............................... | 41 | ABC/TRC 11271 |
| 3/20/71 | **13** | 10 | 72 Don't Change On Me ........................... | 36 | ABC/TRC 11291 |
| 3/27/71 | **13** | 12 | 73 Booty Butt.............................[I] | 36 | Tangerine 1015 |
| | | | **THE RAY CHARLES ORCHESTRA** | | |
| 9/04/71 | **16** | 9 | 74 Feel So Bad.................................... | 68 | ABC/TRC 11308 |
| 7/22/72 | **25** | 6 | 75 Look What They've Done To My Song, Ma ........ | 65 | ABC/TRC 11329 |
| 12/23/72 | **47** | 3 | 76 Hey Mister ..................................... | 115 | ABC/TRC 11337 |
| 4/28/73 | **21** | 9 | 77 I Can Make It Thru The Days (But Oh Those Lonely Nights)...................................... | 81 | ABC/TRC 11351 |
| 11/10/73 | **30** | 10 | 78 Come Live With Me................................ | 82 | Crossover 973 |

| DEBUT DATE | PEAK POS | WKS CHR | ARTIST — Record Title | POP POS | Label & Number |
|---|---|---|---|---|---|
| | | | **RAY CHARLES — Continued** | | |
| 5/18/74 | **77** | 5 | 79 Louise............................................................ | | Crossover 974 |
| 8/09/75 | **22** | 10 | 80 Living For The City .......................................... | 91 | Crossover 981 |
| 4/17/76 | **98** | 2 | 81 America The Beautiful ...................................... | | Crossover 985 |
| 12/17/77+ | **35** | 12 | 82 I Can See Clearly Now .................................... | | Atlantic 3443 |
| 11/24/79 | **69** | 5 | 83 Just Because.................................................. | | Atlantic 3634 |
| | | | **SONNY CHARLES** | | |
| | | | Vocalist from Fort Wayne, Indiana. Former lead of The Checkmates, Ltd. | | |
| 5/17/69 | **8** | 12 | 1 **Black Pearl**............................................. | 13 | A&M 1053 |
| | | | **SONNY CHARLES & THE CHECKMATES, LTD.** | | |
| 10/02/82+ | **2**³ | 23 | 2 **Put It In A Magazine**...................... | 40 | Highrise 2001 |
| 1/22/83 | **53** | 6 | 3 Always On My Mind ...................................... | | Highrise 2006 |
| | | | **CHARME** | | |
| 11/10/84 | **75** | 6 | 1 Georgy Porgy.............................................. | | Atlantic 13909 |
| | | | **THE CHARMETTES** | | |
| 11/23/63 | **100** | 1 | 1 Please Don't Kiss Me Again........................... *Hot* | | Kapp 547 |
| | | | **THE CHARMS** | | |
| | | | Vocal group from Cincinnati consisting or Otis Williams, Richard Parker, Donald Peak, Joe Penn and Rolland Bradley. Group first recorded for Rockin' in 1953. Otis later moved into the field of Country music. | | |
| 10/30/54 | **1**⁹ | 19 | 1 **Hearts Of Stone**......................................... | 15 | DeLuxe 6062 |
| | | | Best Seller #1(9) / Jockey #1(2) / Juke Box #1(2) | | |
| 1/22/55 | **5** | 9 | 2 **Ling, Ting, Tong/** | 26 | |
| | | | Jockey #5 / Best Seller #6 / Juke Box #9 | | |
| 1/22/55 | **15** | 1 | 3 Bazoom (I Need Your Lovin') ........................ | | DeLuxe 6076 |
| | | | Jockey #15 | | |
| 3/05/55 | **8** | 8 | 4 **Two Hearts** .............................................. | | DeLuxe 6065 |
| | | | Jockey #8 / Best Seller #9 | | |
| | | | **OTIS WILLIAMS & HIS CHARMS:** | | |
| 1/28/56 | **14** | 1 | 5 That's Your Mistake ...................................... | 48 | DeLuxe 6091 |
| | | | Jockey #14 | | |
| 4/14/56 | **5** | 12 | 6 **Ivory Tower** .............................................. | 11 | DeLuxe 6093 |
| | | | Jockey #5 / Juke Box #8 / Best Seller #9 | | |
| 6/24/57 | **5** | 4 | 7 **United** ...................................................... | | DeLuxe 6138 |
| | | | Best Seller #5 | | |
| | | | **CHAZ** | | |
| 10/16/82 | **76** | 6 | 1 (We Want To) Rock You................................ | | Prom./MCA 32003 |
| | | | **OLIVER CHEATHAM** | | |
| | | | Singer from Detroit. | | |
| 5/21/83 | **37** | 13 | 1 Get Down Saturday Night .............................. | | MCA 52198 |
| 9/06/86 | **35** | 12 | 2 S.O.S.......................................................... | | Critique 726 |
| 2/07/87 | **87** | 5 | 3 Celebrate (Our Love) .................................... | | Critique 8527 |
| | | | **CHUBBY CHECKER**   ★★**137**★★ | | |
| | | | Born Ernest Evans on 10/3/41 in Philadelphia. Did impersonations of famous singers. First recorded for Parkway in 1959. Cover version of Hank Ballard's "The Twist" started worldwide dance craze. | | |
| 8/08/60 | **2**³ | 16 | 1 **The Twist** ................................................. | 1 | Parkway 811 |
| 11/21/60 | **15** | 6 | 2 The Hucklebuck............................................ | 14 | Parkway 813 |
| 2/06/61 | **1**² | 11 | 3 **Pony Time**................................................. | 1 | Parkway 818 |
| 7/31/61 | **26** | 2 | 4 Let's Twist Again ......................................... | 8 | Parkway 824 |
| 11/20/61 | **11** | 5 | 5 The Fly ..................................................... | 7 | Parkway 830 |
| 12/11/61+ | **4** | 15 | 6 **The Twist** ..........................................[R] | 1 | Parkway 811 |
| | | | except for Bing Crosby's "White Christmas", "The Twist" is the only song in chart history to return to the #1 position on the pop charts after an absence of one year or more | | |
| 3/24/62 | **3** | 12 | 7 **Slow Twistin'** ............................................ | 3 | Parkway 835 |
| | | | female vocal by Dee Dee Sharp | | |
| 10/13/62 | **13** | 10 | 8 Popeye (The Hitchhiker)/ | 10 | |
| 11/17/62 | **3** | 12 | 9 **Limbo Rock**.............................................. | 2 | Parkway 849 |
| 3/23/63 | **16** | 5 | 10 Let's Limbo Some More/ | 20 | |
| 4/20/63 | **15** | 3 | 11 Twenty Miles............................................. | 15 | Parkway 862 |
| 6/15/63 | **18** | 2 | 12 Birdland ................................................... | 12 | Parkway 873 |
| 12/07/63+ | **17** | 14 | 13 Hooka Tooka............................................. *Hot* | | Parkway 890 |

**83**

| DEBUT DATE | PEAK POS | WKS CHR | ARTIST — Record Title | POP POS | Label & Number |
|---|---|---|---|---|---|
| | | | **CHUBBY CHECKER — Continued** | | |
| 3/14/64 | **23** | 9 | 14 Hey, Bobba Needle ................................ | *Hot* | Parkway 907 |
| 6/06/64 | **40** | 7 | 15 Lazy Elsie Molly ................................ | *Hot* | Parkway 920 |
| 8/29/64 | **50** | 7 | 16 She Wants T' Swim ................................ | *Hot* | Parkway 922 |
| 1/02/65 | **70** | 4 | 17 Lovely, Lovely (Loverly, Loverly) ................... | *Hot* | Parkway 936 |
| 7/02/88 | **40** | 8 | 18 The Twist ................................ | 16 | Tin Pan 887571 |
| | | | THE FAT BOYS with CHUBBY CHECKER rap version of Chubby's 1960/1962 hit | | |
| | | | **THE CHECKMATES, LTD.** Integrated quintet from Fort Wayne, Indiana. Consisted of Sonny Charles (vocals), Bobby Stevens, Harvey Trees, Bill Van Buskirk and Marvin Smith. Discovered by Nancy Wilson. Recorded with The Alley Cats (a.k.a. Africa). Disbanded from 1970-74. | | |
| 5/17/69 | **8** | 12 | 1 **Black Pearl** ................................ | 13 | A&M 1053 |
| | | | SONNY CHARLES & THE CHECKMATES, LTD. | | |
| 5/15/76 | **96** | 2 | 2 All Alone By The Telephone ...................... | | Polydor 14313 |
| | | | **CHEE-CHEE & PEPPY** Duo of Keith "Chee-Chee" Bolling (b: 1957, Frankfort, PA) and Dorothy "Peppy" Moore (b: 1959, Morristown, PA). Bolling had been with the Ambassadors Of Song. Duo was formed by producer Jesse James. First recorded for Branding Iron in 1971. | | |
| 5/08/71 | **12** | 14 | 1 I Know I'm In Love ................................ | 49 | Buddah 225 |
| 10/30/71 | **46** | 3 | 2 Never Never Never ................................ | | Buddah 254 |
| | | | **CHEECH & CHONG** Comedians Richard 'Cheech' Marin (b: Watts, California) and Thomas Chong (b: Edmonton, Alberta, Canada). Starred in movies since 1980. Chong was the guitarist of Bobby Taylor's Vancouvers. | | |
| 9/15/73 | **58** | 9 | 1 Basketball Jones Featuring Tyrone Shoelaces.... ................................ [N] | 15 | Ode 66038 |
| 12/03/77 | **56** | 4 | 2 Bloat On Featuring The Bloaters ................ [C] | 41 | Ode 50471 |
| | | | **JUDY CHEEKS** Born in Miami, daughter of gospel singer and preacher, Rev. Julius Cheeks. | | |
| 9/16/78 | **53** | 9 | 1 Mellow Lovin' ................................ | 65 | Salsoul 2063 |
| | | | **CHER** Pop singer/Oscar-winning actress (for "Moonstruck"). Born Cherilyn LaPierre in El Centro, California on 5/20/46. Former backup singer for Phil Spector. From 1963 until their divorce in 1974, in successful recording duo with husband Sonny Bono. Own TV series with Bono from 1971-77. | | |
| 3/03/79 | **21** | 13 | 1 ● Take Me Home ................................ | 8 | Casablanca 965 |
| | | | **CHERI** Canadian duo originally consisting of Rosalind Milligan Hunt, daughter of Geraldine Hunt (composer of "Murphy's Law") and Lynn Cullerier. Later consisted of Rosalind Hunt and Amy Roslyn. | | |
| 3/13/82 | **5** | 17 | 1 **Murphy's Law** ................................ [N] | 39 | Venture 149 |
| 10/09/82 | **53** | 10 | 2 Give It To Me Baby ................................ | | Venture 5022 |
| 3/05/83 | **40** | 13 | 3 Working Girl ................................ | | 21 Records 107 |
| 7/16/83 | **56** | 9 | 4 Small Town Lover ................................ | | 21 Records 109 |
| | | | **CHERRELLE** Born Cheryl Norton in Los Angeles. Drummer/vocalist. Cousin of vocalist Pebbles. Moved to Detroit in 1979. Discovered by Michael Henderson. Accompanied by the Secrets: Jimmy "Jam" Harris, Terry Lewis and Monte Noir (all ex-members of Time). | | |
| 4/28/84 | **8** | 18 | 1 **I Didn't Mean To Turn You On** ...................... | 79 | Tabu 04406 |
| 8/18/84 | **37** | 11 | 2 Fragile...Handle With Care ...................... | | Tabu 04556 |
| 10/05/85 | **26** | 17 | 3 You Look Good To Me ...................... | | Tabu 05608 |
| 1/25/86 | **2**[3] | 19 | 4 **Saturday Love** ................................ | 26 | Tabu 05767 |
| | | | CHERRELLE with ALEXANDER O'NEAL | | |
| 5/24/86 | **18** | 15 | 5 Artificial Heart ................................ | | Tabu 05901 |
| 1/23/88 | **2**[2] | 14 | 6 **Never Knew Love Like This** ................... | 28 | Tabu 07646 |
| | | | ALEXANDER O'NEAL featuring CHERRELLE | | |
| | | | **AVA CHERRY** Vocalist from Chicago. Toured with David Bowie from 1974-78. | | |
| 2/09/80 | **39** | 8 | 1 Love Is Good News ................................ | 107 | RSO 1017 |
| 5/03/80 | **79** | 3 | 2 I Just Can't Shake The Feeling ...................... | | RSO 1027 |
| | | | **CHEYNE** | | |
| 6/01/85 | **62** | 9 | 1 Call Me Mr. 'Telephone' (Answering Service) ...... | 106 | MCA 52576 |

**84**

| DEBUT DATE | PEAK POS | WKS CHR | | ARTIST — Record Title | POP POS | Label & Number |
|---|---|---|---|---|---|---|

**THE CHI-LITES** ★★41★★

Chicago vocal group: Eugene Record (lead), Robert "Squirrel" Lester (tenor), Marshall Thompson (baritone) and Creadel "Red" Jones (bass). First recorded as the Hi-Lites on Daran in 1963. Name changed to Chi-Lites in 1964. Jones left in 1973, first replaced by Stanley Anderson, then Willie Kensey. Doc Roberson replaced Kensey in 1975. Record went solo in 1976, and tenors David Scott and Danny Johnson were added. Vandy Hampton replaced Johnson in 1977. Re-formed in 1980 with all four original members. Jones retired in 1983, group continued as a trio. Also see Donnell Pitman.

| DEBUT DATE | PEAK POS | WKS CHR | # | ARTIST — Record Title | POP POS | Label & Number |
|---|---|---|---|---|---|---|
| 2/08/69 | 10 | 9 | 1 | Give It Away | 88 | Brunswick 55398 |
| 7/26/69 | 15 | 6 | 2 | Let Me Be The Man My Daddy Was/ | 94 | |
| 10/18/69 | 47 | 2 | 3 | The Twelfth Of Never | 122 | Brunswick 55414 |
| 2/14/70 | 30 | 5 | 4 | 24 Hours Of Sadness | 119 | Brunswick 55426 |
| 7/04/70 | 11 | 14 | 5 | I Like Your Lovin' (Do You Like Mine) | 72 | Brunswick 55438 |
| 11/21/70+ | 8 | 12 | 6 | Are You My Woman? (Tell Me So) | 72 | Brunswick 55442 |
| 4/03/71 | 4 | 12 | 7 | (For God's Sake) Give More Power To The People | 26 | Brunswick 55450 |
| 7/17/71 | 17 | 7 | 8 | We Are Neighbors | 70 | Brunswick 55455 |
| 10/16/71 | 35 | 9 | 9 | I Want To Pay You Back (For Loving Me) | 95 | Brunswick 55458 |
| 10/23/71 | 1² | 12 | 10 | Have You Seen Her | 3 | Brunswick 55462 |
| 4/08/72 | 1² | 15 | 11 | Oh Girl | 1 | Brunswick 55471 |
| 7/22/72 | 8 | 10 | 12 | The Coldest Days Of My Life (Part 1) | 47 | Brunswick 55478 |
| 9/30/72 | 25 | 8 | 13 | A Lonely Man | 57 | Brunswick 55483 |
| 12/09/72+ | 13 | 9 | 14 | We Need Order | 61 | Brunswick 55489 |
| 2/10/73 | 3 | 11 | 15 | A Letter To Myself | 33 | Brunswick 55491 |
| 6/02/73 | 46 | 2 | 16 | My Heart Just Keeps On Breakin' | 92 | Brunswick 55496 |
| 7/21/73 | 2¹ | 16 | 17 | Stoned Out Of My Mind | 30 | Brunswick 55500 |
| 11/03/73+ | 17 | 14 | 18 | I Found Sunshine | 47 | Brunswick 55503 |
| 1/19/74 | 3 | 17 | 19 | Homely Girl | 54 | Brunswick 55505 |
| 4/27/74 | 8 | 14 | 20 | There Will Never By Any Peace (Until God Is Seated At The Conference Table) | 63 | Brunswick 55512 |
| 8/24/74 | 15 | 11 | 21 | You Got To Be The One | 83 | Brunswick 55514 |
| 12/21/74+ | 7 | 17 | 22 | Toby/ | 78 | |
| | | 17 | 23 | That's How Long | | Brunswick 55515 |
| 9/20/75 | 27 | 11 | 24 | It's Time For Love/ | 94 | |
| | | 11 | 25 | Here I Am | | Brunswick 55520 |
| 11/15/75 | 91 | 4 | 26 | Don't Burn No Bridges | | Brunswick 55522 |

**JACKIE WILSON & THE CHI-LITES**

| DEBUT DATE | PEAK POS | WKS CHR | # | ARTIST — Record Title | POP POS | Label & Number |
|---|---|---|---|---|---|---|
| 1/17/76 | 32 | 8 | 27 | The Devil Is Doing His Work | | Brunswick 55525 |
| 6/05/76 | 50 | 13 | 28 | You Don't Have To Go | | Brunswick 55528 |
| 9/25/76 | 30 | 14 | 29 | Happy Being Lonely | | Mercury 73844 |
| 3/12/77 | 95 | 3 | 30 | Vanishing Love/ | | Mercury 73886 |
| | | 2 | 31 | I Turn Away | | Mercury 73886 |
| 7/23/77 | 63 | 6 | 32 | My First Mistake | | Mercury 73934 |
| 10/29/77 | 87 | 5 | 33 | If I Had A Girl | | Mercury 73954 |
| 11/01/80 | 36 | 15 | 34 | Heavenly Body | | Chi-Sound 2472 |
| 2/14/81 | 48 | 9 | 35 | Have You Seen Her | | Chi-Sound 2481 |
| | | | | new version of #10 above | | |
| 10/24/81 | 70 | 6 | 36 | Me And You | | Chi-Sound 2503 |
| 1/23/82 | 15 | 17 | 37 | Hot On A Thing (Called Love) | | 20th Century 2600 |
| 3/19/83 | 7 | 18 | 38 | Bottom's Up | | Larc 81015 |
| 6/11/83 | 28 | 13 | 39 | Bad Motor Scooter | | Larc 81023 |
| 3/10/84 | 33 | 11 | 40 | Stop What You're Doin' | | Private I 04365 |
| 6/09/84 | 41 | 10 | 41 | Gimme Whatcha Got | | Private I 04484 |

**CHIC** ★★200★★

Disco group formed in New York City by producers Bernard Edwards, bass; and Nile Rodgers, guitar. Vocalists were Norma Jean Wright (replaced by Alfa Anderson) and Luci Martin; and Tony Thompson on drums. Wright began solo career in 1978; recorded as Norma Jean. Edwards recorded with the studio group Roundtree in 1978. Rodgers joined the Honeydrippers in 1984. Thompson joined the Power Station in 1985 and Edwards became their producer.

| DEBUT DATE | PEAK POS | WKS CHR | # | ARTIST — Record Title | POP POS | Label & Number |
|---|---|---|---|---|---|---|
| 10/29/77+ | 6 | 22 | 1 | ●Dance, Dance, Dance (Yowsah, Yowsah, Yowsah) | 6 | Atlantic 3435 |
| 4/01/78 | 12 | 17 | 2 | Everybody Dance | 38 | Atlantic 3469 |
| 10/21/78 | 1⁵ | 20 | 3 | ▲Le Freak | 1 | Atlantic 3519 |

| DEBUT DATE | PEAK POS | WKS CHR | ARTIST — Record Title | POP POS | Label & Number |
|---|---|---|---|---|---|
| | | | **CHIC — Continued** | | |
| 2/17/79 | **5** | 15 | 4 **I Want Your Love** ................................ | 7 | Atlantic 3557 |
| 6/23/79 | **1** [6] | 18 | 5 ● **Good Times** ................................ | 1 | Atlantic 3584 |
| 10/13/79 | **33** | 8 | 6 My Forbidden Lover ................................ | 43 | Atlantic 3620 |
| 12/08/79+ | **42** | 8 | 7 My Feet Keep Dancing ................................ | 101 | Atlantic 3638 |
| 7/05/80 | **8** | 14 | 8 **Rebels Are We** ................................ | 61 | Atlantic 3665 |
| 10/25/80 | **51** | 7 | 9 Real People ................................ | 79 | Atlantic 3768 |
| 12/26/81+ | **34** | 12 | 10 Stage Fright ................................ | 105 | Atlantic 3887 |
| 5/01/82 | **14** | 13 | 11 Soup For One ................................ | 80 | Mirage 4032 |
| | | | theme song from the film of the same title | | |
| 11/06/82 | **48** | 11 | 12 Hangin' ................................ | | Atlantic 89954 |
| 12/24/83+ | **57** | 9 | 13 Give Me The Lovin' ................................ | | Atlantic 89725 |
| | | | **CHICAGO** | | |
| | | | Jazz-oriented rock group formed in Chicago in 1967 as The Big Thing, later Chicago Transit Authority. To Los Angeles in the late 60s. Lead singer Peter Cetera left in 1985, replaced by Jason Scheff. | | |
| 12/01/79 | **91** | 4 | 1 Street Player ................................ | | Columbia 11124 |
| | | | **THE CHICAGO BEARS SHUFFLIN' CREW** | | |
| | | | Super Bowl XX Champs - featuring (in order): Walter Payton, Willie Gault, Mike Singletary, Jim McMahon, Otis Wilson, Steve Fuller, Mike Richardson, Richard Dent, Gary Fencik and William Perry. | | |
| 2/08/86 | **75** | 4 | 1 Superbowl Shuffle ................................ [N] | 41 | Red Label 71012 |
| | | | **CHICAGO GANGSTERS** | | |
| | | | Group from Chicago. Led by brothers Sam (keyboards, guitar, vocals), Leroy (trombone), Chris (drums) and James McCant (vocals). | | |
| 9/13/75 | **67** | 9 | 1 Blind Over You ................................ | | Gold Plate 1947 |
| 2/28/76 | **74** | 5 | 2 I Choose You ................................ | | Gold Plate 1949 |
| 1/29/77 | **97** | 2 | 3 Music For The People ................................ | | Gold Plate 1953 |
| 10/01/77 | **86** | 5 | 4 I'm An Outlaw ................................ | | Gold Plate 1954 |
| | | | **THE CHIFFONS** | | |
| | | | Vocal group from the Bronx. Formed while high school classmates; worked as back-up singers in 1960. Consisted of Judy Craig, Barbara Lee, Patricia Bennett and Sylvia Peterson. First recorded for Big Deal in 1960. Also recorded as The Four Pennies on the Rust label. | | |
| 3/02/63 | **1** [4] | 14 | 1 **He's So Fine** ................................ | 1 | Laurie 3152 |
| 6/29/63 | **6** | 7 | 2 **One Fine Day** ................................ | 5 | Laurie 3179 |
| 9/07/63 | **40** | 9 | 3 A Love So Fine ................................ | Hot | Laurie 3195 |
| 11/09/63 | **95** | 1 | 4 When The Boy's Happy (The Girl's Happy) ......... | Hot | Rust 5070 |
| | | | **THE FOUR PENNIES** | | |
| 11/16/63+ | **36** | 10 | 5 I Have A Boyfriend ................................ | Hot | Laurie 3212 |
| 8/01/64 | **81** | 3 | 6 Sailor Boy ................................ | Hot | Laurie 3262 |
| | | | **DESMOND CHILD & ROUGE** | | |
| | | | Vocal group formed in 1975. Consisted of Desmond Child, Diana Grasselli, Myriam Valle and Maria Vidal. | | |
| 2/17/79 | **95** | 2 | 1 Our Love Is Insane ................................ | 51 | Capitol 4669 |
| | | | **CHILL FACTOR** | | |
| | | | Chicago-based trio: Ruben (lead vocals), Rico (guitar) and Gregg (keyboards). | | |
| 8/29/87 | **88** | 3 | 1 Conversation ................................ | | Warner 28364 |
| 11/28/87+ | **62** | 11 | 2 Never My Love ................................ | | Warner 28159 |
| | | | **THE CHIPMUNKS - see DAVID SEVILLE** | | |
| | | | **CHOCOLATE MILK** | | |
| | | | Group from New Orleans. Consisted of Frank Richard (lead vocal), Amadee Castanell (saxophone), Joe Foxx (trumpet), Robert Dabon (keyboards), Mario Tio (guitar) and Dwight Richards (drums). | | |
| 6/07/75 | **15** | 17 | 1 Action Speaks Louder Than Words ................ | 69 | RCA 10290 |
| 3/27/76 | **79** | 8 | 2 How About Love ................................ | | RCA 10569 |
| 9/11/76 | **56** | 10 | 3 Comin' ................................ | | RCA 10758 |
| 4/08/78 | **14** | 16 | 4 Girl Callin' ................................ | | RCA 11222 |
| 4/21/79 | **39** | 14 | 5 Say Won'tcha ................................ | | RCA 11547 |
| 8/25/79 | **59** | 7 | 6 Groove City ................................ | | RCA 11689 |
| 7/05/80 | **40** | 12 | 7 Hey Lover ................................ | | RCA 12030 |
| 10/10/81 | **15** | 18 | 8 Blue Jeans ................................ | | RCA 12335 |

| DEBUT DATE | PEAK POS | WKS CHR | ARTIST — Record Title | POP POS | Label & Number |
|---|---|---|---|---|---|
| | | | **CHOCOLATE MILK — Continued** | | |
| 1/30/82 | 41 | 10 | 9 Let's Go All The Way .................................... | | RCA 13026 |
| 11/13/82+ | 39 | 12 | 10 Take It Off ........................................... | | RCA 13364 |
| 3/26/83 | 65 | 8 | 11 Who's Getting It Now .................................. | | RCA 13447 |
| | | | **CHOCOLATE SYRUP** | | |
| | | | Group consisting of Lenny Wolfe, Jimmy Holiday, L.J. Reynolds, Carl Smith and Norris Harris. Reynolds joined The Dramatics in 1973; began solo career in 1981. | | |
| 11/13/71 | 31 | 9 | 1 Let One Hurt Do ...................................... | 104 | Law-Ton 1553 |
| | | | **L.J. REYNOLDS & CHOCOLATE SYRUP** | | |
| 5/18/74 | 97 | 2 | 2 Just In The Nick Of Time............................... | | Brown Dog 9000 |
| | | | **THE CHOICE FOUR** | | |
| | | | Group from Washington, DC, formed in 1970. Consisted of lead Bobby Hamilton, Ted Maduro, Pete Marshall and Charles Blagmore. Maduro and Marshall had been in the Love Tones, Blagmore was in the Stridels. | | |
| 8/17/74 | 85 | 4 | 1 The Finger Pointers, Pt. 1 ............................. | | RCA 0315 |
| 11/02/74 | 63 | 7 | 2 You're So Right For Me ................................ | | RCA 10088 |
| 9/06/75 | 45 | 12 | 3 When You're Young And In Love .................... | 91 | RCA 10342 |
| 4/10/76 | 57 | 9 | 4 Hey, What's That Dance You're Doing.............. | 107 | RCA 10602 |
| 7/17/76 | 76 | 9 | 5 Just Let Me Hold You For A Night................... | | RCA 10714 |
| | | | **CHOICE M.C.'s featuring FRESH GORDON** | | |
| | | | Brooklyn, New York rap quintet with 19-year-old computer whiz, Fresh Gordon. | | |
| 11/02/85 | 20 | 15 | 1 Gordy's Groove (Mayberry Mix) ....................... | | Tommy Boy 871 |
| | | | mix includes theme tune from TV's "The Andy Griffith Show" | | |
| | | | **CHOPS** | | |
| 11/03/84 | 86 | 4 | 1 Your Red Hot Love ..................................... | | Atlantic 89606 |
| | | | **THE CHORDETTES** | | |
| | | | Female vocal group from Sheboygan, Wisconsin; formed in 1946. Consisted of Janet Ertel, Carol Bushman, Lynn Evans (lead - replaced Dorothy Schwartz in 1953), and Margie Needham (replaced Jinny Lockard in 1953). With Arthur Godfrey from 1949-53. Ertel married Cadence owner Archie Bleyer. | | |
| 3/17/58 | 3 | 9 | 1 **Lollipop**............................................. | 2 | Cadence 1345 |
| | | | Best Seller #3 / Jockey #4 | | |
| | | | **THE CHORDS** | | |
| | | | Group from the Bronx, formed in 1954 by members of three other vocal groups. Consisted of Carl Feaster (lead tenor), Jimmy Keyes (tenor), Floyd "Buddy" McRae (tenor), Claude Feaster (baritone), William "Ricky" Edwards (bass) and Rupert Branker (piano). Group appeared on the Colgate Comedy Hour TV show, singing "Say Hey, Willie" with Willie Mays. Also recorded as The Chordcats and The Sh-Booms. | | |
| 7/03/54 | 2² | 15 | 1 **Sh-Boom** ..................................... | 5 | Cat 104 |
| | | | Juke Box #2 / Best Seller #3 the original version of this rock classic; written by the group; "Sh-Boom" was "B" side to their cover version of Patti Page's hit "Cross Over The Bridge" | | |
| | | | **THE CHRISTIAN TABERNACLE BAPTIST CHOIR - see REV. MACEO WOODS** | | |
| | | | **JANICE CHRISTIE** | | |
| | | | Former member of Wild Sugar, the female backing vocal trio of Fatback. | | |
| 6/28/86 | 56 | 9 | 1 I'm Hungry For Your Love ............................. | | Supertronics 014 |
| 11/22/86+ | 22 | 14 | 2 Heat Stroke................................................ | | Supertronics 016 |
| | | | **LOU CHRISTIE** | | |
| | | | Born Lugee Alfredo Giovanni Sacco on 2/19/43 in Glen Willard, PA. Joined vocal group, the Classics, first recorded for Starr in 1960. Started long association with songwriter Twyla Herbert. Recorded as "Lugee & The Lions" for Robbee in 1961. | | |
| 5/04/63 | 11 | 9 | 1 Two Faces Have I ..................................... | 6 | Roulette 4481 |
| | | | **GAVIN CHRISTOPHER** | | |
| | | | Chicago-born singer/composer/producer. | | |
| 6/23/79 | 77 | 6 | 1 Feelin' The Love ...................................... | | RSO 933 |
| 4/26/86 | 25 | 17 | 2 One Step Closer To You................................. | 22 | Manhattan 50028 |
| 1/30/88 | 10 | 15 | 3 **You Are Who You Love** ............................. | | EMI-Man. 50108 |
| | | | **SHAWN CHRISTOPHER** | | |
| 12/04/82+ | 38 | 11 | 1 Too Late................................................ | | Larc 81012 |
| 8/20/83 | 44 | 10 | 2 Say It Again ............................................ | | Larc 81022 |

| DEBUT DATE | PEAK POS | WKS CHR | ARTIST — Record Title | POP POS | Label & Number |
|---|---|---|---|---|---|
| | | | **EUGENE CHURCH** | | |
| | | | Los Angeles native. Born on 1/23/38. Recorded with Jesse Belvin as The Cliques. | | |
| 12/22/58+ | **6** | 19 | **1 Pretty Girls Everywhere**.............................. | *36* | Class 235 |
| | | | EUGENE CHURCH & THE FELLOWS | | |
| | | | featuring backing vocals by Bobby Day | | |
| 8/24/59 | **14** | 4 | **2** Miami ...................................................... | *67* | Class 254 |
| 12/04/61 | **19** | 5 | 3 Mind Your Own Business................................ | | King 5545 |
| | | | **SAVANNAH CHURCHILL** | | |
| | | | Born Savannah Valentine on 8/21/20 in Colfax, Louisiana. Died of pneumonia on 4/20/74 in Brooklyn. Moved to Brooklyn in 1926. Vocalist/violinist. After her husband David Churchill died in an automobile accident in 1941, she pursued a singing career to support her two children. With Benny Carter, recorded for Capitol in 1943. Toured with Nat Cole, London Palladium with Hoagy Carmichael in 1951. Bizarre accident in 1956 at the Midwood Club in Brooklyn seriously injured her and halted her career - a drunk fell on her from the balcony, breaking her pelvis. Diagnosed as having cancer at time of death. Also see Benny Carter. | | |
| 10/27/45 | **3** | 1 | **1 Daddy Daddy** .......................................... | | Manor 1004 |
| | | | with Benny Carter's Orchestra | | |
| 3/22/47 | **1**[8] | 25 | **2 I Want To Be Loved (But Only By You)** .......... | *21* | Manor 1046 |
| | | | with the Sentimentalists | | |
| 5/01/48 | **10** | 1 | **3 Time Out For Tears** .................................. | *20* | Manor 1116 |
| | | | above 2: with Harry Carney (baritone sax) and Trummy Young (trombone) | | |
| 7/31/48 | **14** | 1 | 4 I Want To Cry............................................ | | Manor 1129 |
| | | | Juke Box #14 | | |
| | | | above 2: with The Four Tunes | | |
| | | | **CI CI** | | |
| 2/16/85 | **85** | 5 | **1** (You Got Me) Hypnotized .............................. | | Creat. F. 1500 |
| | | | **CINDY & ROY** | | |
| | | | Cindy's real name is Cynthia Biggs. | | |
| 9/22/79 | **41** | 9 | **1** While We Still Have Time ............................. | | Casablanca 2202 |
| | | | **CHUCK CISSEL** | | |
| | | | Singer/actor from Tulsa, Oklahoma. Attended the University of Oklahoma. Studied with the Joffrey Ballet in New York City. Made numerous commercials and appeared in many Broadway shows. His name rhymes with "sizzle". Marva King was a vocalist with Madagascar. | | |
| 12/08/79+ | **38** | 14 | **1** Cisselin' Hot............................................... | | Arista 0471 |
| 4/19/80 | **87** | 3 | **2** Forever ..................................................... | | Arista 0499 |
| 2/13/82 | **43** | 8 | **3** If I Had The Chance...................................... | | Arista 0650 |
| | | | CHUCK CISSEL & MARVA KING | | |
| | | | **CITISPEAK** | | |
| | | | Quartet from Baltimore, consisting of Jerome Montague, Leon Askew , Alan Mitchell, and Jeanne Harris. Name derived from street language in the film "Blade Runner". | | |
| 3/10/84 | **67** | 6 | **1** I Don't Need Your Handouts........................... | | Streetwise 106 |
| | | | **C.J. & CO.** | | |
| | | | Detroit group, assembled by Dennis Coffey, which included Cornelius Brown Jr., Curtis Durden, Joni Tolbert, Connie Durden and Charles Clark. | | |
| 6/11/77 | **2**[1] | 20 | **1 Devil's Gun** ............................................. | *36* | Westbound 55400 |
| 12/17/77 | **93** | 5 | 2 We Got Our Own Thing - Pt. 1......................... | | Westbound 55406 |
| | | | **JIMMY CLANTON** | | |
| | | | Born on 9/2/40 in Baton Rouge, Louisiana. Played in local bands, discovered by Ace Records while making a demo at Cosimo's studio in New Orleans. Recorded with famous New Orleans session men, including Huey "Piano" Smith, Earl King (guitar) and Lee Allen (tenor sax). Toured with Dick Clark's Caravan Of Stars, appeared in films and on TV. Was a disc jockey for a time in Lancaster, Pennsylvania. | | |
| 7/28/58 | **1**[1] | 17 | **1 Just A Dream**............................................ | *4* | Ace 546 |
| | | | Best Seller #1 / Jockey #2 | | |
| | | | written by Clanton | | |
| 11/10/58 | **28** | 1 | **2** A Part Of Me ............................................ | *38* | Ace 551 |
| 1/18/60 | **19** | 9 | **3** Go, Jimmy, Go............................................ | *5* | Ace 575 |
| | | | **ERIC CLAPTON** | | |
| | | | Prolific rock-blues guitarist/vocalist; born on 3/30/45 in Ripley, England. A member of The Roosters, The Yardbirds and John Mayall's Bluesbreakers. Founder of Cream and Blind Faith. | | |
| 9/07/74 | **33** | 9 | 1●I Shot The Sheriff....................................... | *1* | RSO 409 |

| DEBUT DATE | PEAK POS | WKS CHR | ARTIST — Record Title | POP POS | Label & Number |
|---|---|---|---|---|---|

### CLARK SISTERS
Gospel group from Detroit. Consisted of Karen, Jackie, Dorinda, Niecy and Elbernita "Twinkie" Clark. Mother Mattie Moss Clark is International Music Director of COGIC (Church Of God In Christ).

| | | | | | |
|---|---|---|---|---|---|
| 7/30/83 | 16 | 16 | 1 You Brought The Sunshine (Into My Life) .......... | | Elektra 69810 |

### CHRIS CLARK
Born in 1946 in Los Angeles. Worked as receptionist at Motown. TV writer since 1969. Co-wrote screenplay for the film "Lady Sings The Blues".

| | | | | | |
|---|---|---|---|---|---|
| 10/29/66 | 41 | 2 | 1 Love's Gone Bad ........................................... | *105* | V.I.P. 25038 |

### CLAUDINE CLARK
Born on 4/26/41 in Macon, Georgia. Moved to Philadelphia when very young. First recorded for Herald in 1958. Also recorded for Swan as "Joy Dawn".

| | | | | | |
|---|---|---|---|---|---|
| 7/14/62 | 3 | 17 | 1 Party Lights ................................................. | *5* | Chancellor 1113 |

### DEE CLARK
Born Delecta Clark on 11/7/38 in Blythsville, Arkansas. To Chicago in 1941. In Hambone Kids with Sammy McGrier and Ronny Strong, first recorded for Okeh in 1952. Joined vocal group the Goldentones in 1953. Group became the Kool Gents; billed as The Delegates for Vee-Jay recording in 1956. First solo recording for Falcon, 1957.

| | | | | | |
|---|---|---|---|---|---|
| 11/17/58 | 3 | 19 | 1 Nobody But You........................................... | *21* | Abner 1019 |
| 6/01/59 | 9 | 9 | 2 Just Keep It Up ........................................... | *18* | Abner 1026 |
| 9/14/59 | 2[1] | 10 | 3 Hey Little Girl.............................................. | *20* | Abner 1029 |
| 1/18/60 | 10 | 3 | 4 How About That .......................................... | *33* | Abner 1032 |
| 3/27/61 | 30 | 1 | 5 Your Friends ............................................... | *34* | Vee-Jay 372 |
| 5/22/61 | 3 | 11 | 6 Raindrops................................................... | *2* | Vee-Jay 383 |
| | | | written by Dee Clark & Phillip Upchurch | | |
| 11/10/62 | 18 | 3 | 7 I'm Going Back To School............................... | *52* | Vee-Jay 462 |
| 11/02/63 | 92 | 5 | 8 Crossfire Time.............................................. | *Hot* | Constellation 108 |

### SANFORD CLARK
Born in 1935 in Tulsa, Oklahoma. Moved to Phoenix in his teens. Enlisted in US Air Force in 1960. Recorded again in mid-60s.

| | | | | | |
|---|---|---|---|---|---|
| 9/01/56 | 5 | 2 | 1 The Fool ..................................... | *7* | Dot 15481 |
| | | | Juke Box #5 / Jockey #10 | | |
| | | | written by Naomi Ford, wife of producer Lee Hazlewood; featuring Al Casey on guitar; originally issued on MCI | | |

### STANLEY CLARKE
Born on 6/30/51 in Philadelphia. Violinist/cellist/bassist. Studied classical music music at the Philadelphia Musical Academy. With Silver and Joe Henderson. With Chick Corea in Return To Forever. Much session work, solo debut in 1974. With George Duke in Clarke/Duke Project in 1981. Also see Howard Hewett.

| | | | | | |
|---|---|---|---|---|---|
| 1/03/76 | 94 | 2 | 1 Silly Putty ..................................... | | Nemperor 002 |
| 7/29/78 | 76 | 6 | 2 Slow Dance ................................... | | Nemperor 7518 |
| 6/07/80 | 43 | 10 | 3 We Supply .................................... | | Epic 50890 |
| 4/11/81 | 6 | 19 | 4 Sweet Baby ................................... | *19* | Epic 01052 |
| | | | STANLEY CLARKE/GEORGE DUKE | | |
| 8/15/81 | 49 | 8 | 5 I Just Want To Love You ............................... | | Epic 02397 |
| 9/25/82 | 81 | 3 | 6 Straight To The Top ...................................... | | Epic 03038 |
| 10/08/83 | 37 | 13 | 7 Heroes ....................................................... | | Epic 04155 |
| | | | STANLEY CLARKE/GEORGE DUKE | | |
| 6/16/84 | 21 | 12 | 8 Heaven Sent You........................................... | | Epic 04485 |
| | | | vocal by Howard Hewett | | |
| 5/25/85 | 52 | 9 | 9 Born In The U.S.A. ..................................... | | Epic 04914 |
| | | | shown as: THE STANLEY CLARKE BAND cover version of Bruce Springsteen's hit | | |

### TONY CLARKE
Born in New York City, raised in Detroit. Trained to be a chef. Wrote hits "Pushover" and "Two Sides To Every Story". Acted in film "They Call Me Mr. Tibbs". Died in 1970.

| | | | | | |
|---|---|---|---|---|---|
| 3/14/64 | 88 | 1 | 1 (The Story Of) Woman, Love And A Man............ | *Hot* | Chess 1880 |
| 3/27/65 | 10 | 11 | 2 The Entertainer ......................................... | *31* | Chess 1924 |

### CLASSIC SULLIVANS
Chicago group formed in 1971. Consisted of family members Eddie (b: 1/31/42), Barbara and Lorraine Sullivan. Eddie recorded as Eddie Sull in 1966.

| | | | | | |
|---|---|---|---|---|---|
| 3/31/73 | 34 | 5 | 1 I Don't Want To Lose You.............................. | | Kwanza 7678 |

| DEBUT DATE | PEAK POS | WKS CHR | ARTIST — Record Title | POP POS | Label & Number |
|---|---|---|---|---|---|
| | | | **THE CLASSICS** | | |
| | | | White vocal quartet from Brooklyn, formed in 1958. Consisted of Emil Stucchio (lead), Johnny Gambale, Tony Victor and Jamie Troy. First known as the Perennials. First recorded for Dart in 1959. Recorded as back-up for Herb Lance on Promo, 1961. | | |
| 6/05/61 | **27** | 1 | 1 Life Is But A Dream, Sweetheart ...................... *109* | | Mercury 71829 |
| | | | **JUDY CLAY** | | |
| | | | Real name: Judy Guion. Vocalist from New York City. In back-up group with Cissy Houston, Dionne and Dee Dee Warwick, for Don Covay, Wilson Pickett, and many others. | | |
| 12/09/67+ | **20** | 8 | 1 Storybook Children ......................... *54* | | Atlantic 2445 |
| | | |     **BILLY VERA & JUDY CLAY** | | |
| 3/02/68 | **41** | 4 | 2 Country Girl-City Man ......................... *36* | | Atlantic 2480 |
| | | |     **BILLY VERA & JUDY CLAY**<br>    above 2: with The Sweet Inspirations | | |
| 9/07/68 | **17** | 11 | 3 Private Number......................... *75* | | Stax 0005 |
| | | |     **JUDY CLAY & WILLIAM BELL** | | |
| 1/11/69 | **45** | 3 | 4 My Baby Specializes ......................... *104* | | Stax 0017 |
| | | |     **WILLIAM BELL & JUDY CLAY** | | |
| 4/04/70 | **45** | 3 | 5 Greatest Love......................... *122* | | Atlantic 2697 |
| | | | **OTIS CLAY** | | |
| | | | Born on 2/11/42 in Waxhaw, Mississippi. To Muncie, Indiana in 1953. Sang with the Morning Glories (family gospel group), Voices Of Hope, and Christian Travelers. To Chicago in 1957, joined Golden Jubalaires, Blue Jays and Pilgrim Harmonizers. Leader of Gospel Songbirds, recorded for Nashboro in 1964. Group included Maurice Dollison ("Cash McCall"). With Sensational Nightingales from 1964-65. Own label, Echo, in 1975. | | |
| 8/05/67 | **34** | 6 | 1 That's How It Is (When You're In Love)............. *131* | | One-derful 4848 |
| 12/16/67 | **48** | 3 | 2 Lasting Love ................. | | One-derful 4850 |
| 8/24/68 | **47** | 2 | 3 She's About A Mover ......................... *97* | | Cotillion 44001 |
| 11/04/72 | **24** | 10 | 4 Trying To Live My Life Without You ................. *102* | | Hi 2226 |
| 10/06/73 | **73** | 6 | 5 If I Could Reach Out ......................... | | Hi 2252 |
| 6/18/77 | **44** | 11 | 6 All Because Of Your Love ......................... | | Kayvette 5130 |
| | | | **TOM CLAY** | | |
| | | | Disc jockey. | | |
| 8/07/71 | **32** | 4 | 1 What The World Needs Now Is Love/Abraham, Martin & John......................... [S] | 8 | Mowest 5002 |
| | | |     vocal accompaniment by The Blackberries | | |
| | | | **MERRY CLAYTON** | | |
| | | | Real name: Mary Clayton. Back-up vocalist from Los Angeles. In Raelettes with Ray Charles. Formed vocal group, Sisters Love. Duet with Bobby Darin in 1962. Did backing vocal on Rolling Stones' "Gimme Shelter". Acted in the 1987 film "Maid To Order". | | |
| 12/25/71+ | **42** | 5 | 1 After All This Time ......................... | | Ode 66018 |
| 1/13/73 | **30** | 8 | 2 Oh No, Not My Baby......................... *72* | | Ode 66030 |
| 8/03/74 | **72** | 6 | 3 Jump Back ......................... | | Ode 66048 |
| | | |     **TOM SCOTT & THE L.A. EXPRESS featuring MERRY CLAYTON** | | |
| 8/16/75 | **42** | 8 | 4 Keep Your Eye On The Sparrow......................... *45* | | Ode 66110 |
| | | |     from the TV series "Baretta" | | |
| 3/01/80 | **53** | 8 | 5 Emotion ......................... | | MCA 41195 |
| 4/11/81 | **52** | 8 | 6 One Alone......................... | | RCA 12179 |
| | | |     **MICHAEL WYCOFF featuring MERRY CLAYTON** | | |
| 5/29/82 | **71** | 7 | 7 Before The Night Is Over ......................... | | Elektra 47451 |
| | | |     **LESLIE SMITH & MERRY CLAYTON** | | |
| 4/09/88 | **79** | 5 | 8 Yes......................... *45* | | RCA 6989 |
| | | |     from the film "Dirty Dancing" | | |
| | | | **WILLIE CLAYTON** | | |
| | | | Born on 3/29/55 in Indianola, Mississippi. First recorded for Duplex in 1969. Moved to Chicago in 1971. | | |
| 3/03/84 | **78** | 5 | 1 Tell Me ......................... | | Compleat 120 |
| 7/14/84 | **84** | 5 | 2 What A Way To Put It ......................... | | Compleat 124 |
| | | | **THE CLEFTONES** | | |
| | | | Vocal group from Queens, New York, formed in 1955. Consisted of Herbie Cox (lead), Charlie James (first tenor), Berman Patterson (second tenor), William McClain (baritone) and Warren Corbin (bass). Group originally called the Silvertones. Group re-formed in 1970 for "revival" shows. Appeared at the Apollo & 9 Alan Freed shows. | | |
| 5/19/56 | **8** | 6 | 1 **Little Girl Of Mine**......................... *57* | | Gee 1011 |
| | | |     Best Seller #8 / Juke Box #8 / Jockey #15<br>    with Jimmy Wright & His Orchestra | | |

| DEBUT DATE | PEAK POS | WKS CHR | ARTIST — Record Title | POP POS | Label & Number |
|---|---|---|---|---|---|
| 5/29/61 | 10 | 3 | **THE CLEFTONES — Continued**<br>2 Heart And Soul ........................................ | 18 | Gee 1064 |
| | | | **ANGELA CLEMMONS** | | |
| 8/30/80 | 61 | 7 | 1 Out Here On My Own ..................................... | | Epic 50919 |
| 9/26/87 | 81 | 7 | 2 B.Y.O.B. (Bring Your Own Baby) ...................... | | Portrait 07368 |
| 12/19/87+ | 73 | 10 | 3 This Is Love ................................................. | | Portrait 07642 |
| | | | **JIMMY CLIFF**<br>Jamaican reggae singer/composer. Real name: James Chambers. Starred in films "The Harder They Come" (1975) and "Club Paradise" (1986). | | |
| 9/25/82 | 76 | 4 | 1 Special ....................................................... | | Columbia 03216 |
| 11/26/83 | 89 | 4 | 2 Reggae Night .............................................. | | Columbia 04141 |
| 2/18/84 | 75 | 5 | 3 We All Are One ............................................ | | Columbia 04335 |
| | | | **BUZZ CLIFFORD**<br>Born Reese Francis Clifford III on 10/8/42 in Berwyn, Illinois. | | |
| 3/13/61 | 27 | 1 | 1 Baby Sittin' Boogie ................................... [N]<br>babies voices by the producer's son and daughter | 6 | Columbia 41876 |
| | | | **LINDA CLIFFORD**<br>Vocalist from Brooklyn. Former Miss New York State. With Jericho Jazz Singers; had own trio in 1967. | | |
| 2/23/74 | 75 | 6 | 1 (It's Gonna Be) A Long Long Winter ................ | | Paramount 0269 |
| 12/24/77+ | 94 | 6 | 2 From Now On ............................................... | | Curtom 0133 |
| 5/06/78 | 3 | 16 | 3 **Runaway Love** .......................................... | 76 | Curtom 0138 |
| 8/26/78 | 68 | 7 | 4 If My Friends Could See Me Now ...................... | 54 | Curtom 0140 |
| 3/31/79 | 49 | 6 | 5 Bridge Over Troubled Water .......................... | 41 | RSO 921 |
| 5/05/79 | 15 | 12 | 6 Don't Give It Up ........................................ | | RSO 927 |
| 8/18/79 | 14 | 18 | 7 Between You Baby And Me ...........................<br>**CURTIS MAYFIELD & LINDA CLIFFORD** | | RSO 941 |
| 11/10/79 | 36 | 11 | 8 I Just Wanna Wanna ................................... | | RSO 1012 |
| 5/17/80 | 34 | 11 | 9 Love's Sweet Sensation ...............................<br>**CURTIS MAYFIELD & LINDA CLIFFORD** | | RSO 1029 |
| 8/30/80 | 40 | 9 | 10 Red Light ...............................................<br>from the film "Fame" | 41 | RSO 1041 |
| 11/01/80 | 43 | 8 | 11 Shoot Your Best Shot.................................. | | RSO 1053 |
| 12/27/80+ | 53 | 9 | 12 I Had A Talk With My Man ........................... | | Capitol 4958 |
| 9/15/84 | 76 | 6 | 13 A Night With The Boys ............................... | | Red Label 7000 |
| 11/24/84+ | 62 | 11 | 14 Sneakin' Out ............................................ | | Red Label 7002 |
| | | | **GEORGE CLINTON**<br>Born on 7/22/40 in Plainfield, Ohio. Lead singer of The Parliaments. Became leader/producer of Funkadelic and Parliament. Headed "A Parliafunkadelicament Thang", a corporation of nearly 40 musicians that recorded as Parliament and Funkadelic plus various offshoot bands: Bootsy's Rubber Band, The Brides Of Funkenstein, Horny Horns, Parlet and the P.Funk All Stars. | | |
| 10/23/82 | 19 | 13 | 1 Loopzilla .................................................. | | Capitol 5160 |
| 1/29/83 | 1 4 | 26 | 2 **Atomic Dog** .............................................. | 101 | Capitol 5201 |
| 5/28/83 | 73 | 5 | 3 Get Dressed .............................................. | | Capitol 5222 |
| 11/19/83+ | 15 | 14 | 4 Nubian Nut ............................................... | | Capitol 5296 |
| 3/03/84 | 26 | 11 | 5 Last Dance ................................................ | | Capitol 5332 |
| 6/02/84 | 72 | 4 | 6 Quickie .................................................... | | Capitol 5324 |
| 5/25/85 | 32 | 12 | 7 Double Oh-Oh ............................................ | 101 | Capitol 5473 |
| 9/14/85 | 69 | 8 | 8 Bullet Proof .............................................. | | Capitol 5504 |
| 3/29/86 | 13 | 15 | 9 Do Fries Go With That Shake ........................ | | Capitol 5558 |
| 7/05/86 | 41 | 11 | 10 Hey Good Lookin'....................................... | | Capitol 5602 |
| | | | **CLOCKWORK** | | |
| 2/25/84 | 37 | 12 | 1 I'm Your Candy Girl..................................... | | Private I 04375 |

| DEBUT DATE | PEAK POS | WKS CHR | | ARTIST — Record Title | POP POS | Label & Number |
|---|---|---|---|---|---|---|
| | | | | **THE CLOVERS** ★★69★★ | | |
| | | | | Group from Washington, DC. Formed as a trio at Washington High School in 1946. By 1949, lineup included John "Buddy" Bailey (lead), Matthew McQuater (tenor), Harold Lucas (baritone), Harold Winley (bass) and Bill Harris (guitar). First recorded for Rainbow Records in 1950, joined Atlantic six months later. Toured with the Drifters, Ruth Brown, and Joe Turner. In 1954, appeared on the first Alan Freed Show and in "Showtime At The Apollo" TV series. Bailey entered the Army in 1952, replaced by Billy Mitchell. Upon Bailey's return, Mitchell stayed in the group. A Clovers unit containing some original members is still performing. | | |
| 6/09/51 | **1**² | 21 | 1 | **Don't You Know I Love You** .......................... Best Seller #1 / Juke Box #2 | | Atlantic 934 |
| 9/29/51 | **1**⁶ | 22 | 2 | **Fool, Fool, Fool** ........................................ Best Seller #1(6) / Juke Box #1(3) | | Atlantic 944 |
| 4/19/52 | **2**¹ | 18 | 3 | **One Mint Julep/** Best Seller #2 / Juke Box #2 | | |
| 4/26/52 | **3** | 8 | 4 | **Middle Of The Night** .................................. Juke Box #3 / Best Seller #4 | | Atlantic 963 |
| 7/26/52 | **1**¹ | 14 | 5 | **Ting-A-Ling/** Best Seller #1(1) / Juke Box #1(1) | | |
| 7/26/52 | **7** | 3 | 6 | **Wonder Where My Baby's Gone** .................. Juke Box #7 | | Atlantic 969 |
| 11/08/52 | **2**¹ | 10 | 7 | **Hey, Miss Fannie/** Juke Box #2 / Best Seller #5 | | |
| 11/29/52+ | **3** | 9 | 8 | **I Played The Fool** ...................................... Best Seller #3 / Juke Box #7 | | Atlantic 977 |
| 3/14/53 | **3** | 12 | 9 | **Crawlin'** ................................................... Best Seller #3 / Juke Box #3 | | Atlantic 989 |
| 7/25/53 | **2**⁴ | 18 | 10 | **Good Lovin'** .............................................. Best Seller #2 / Juke Box #2 | | Atlantic 1000 |
| 12/05/53 | **9** | 1 | 11 | **Comin' On** ................................................ Juke Box #9 | | Atlantic 1010 |
| 3/20/54 | **2**⁵ | 21 | 12 | **Lovey Dovey/** Best Seller #2 / Juke Box #2 | | |
| 3/27/54 | **4** | 15 | 13 | **Little Mama** .............................................. Best Seller #4 / Juke Box #6 #10-13: Charlie White replaces Buddy Bailey | | Atlantic 1022 |
| 7/31/54 | **7** | 9 | 14 | **I've Got My Eyes On You/** Best Seller #7 | | |
| 8/07/54 | **6** | 7 | 15 | **Your Cash Ain't Nothin' But Trash** ............. Juke Box #6 / Best Seller #9 | | Atlantic 1035 |
| 4/09/55 | **14** | 1 | 16 | Blue Velvet .................................................. Best Seller #14 | | Atlantic 1052 |
| 9/24/55 | **10** | 2 | 17 | Nip Sip ....................................................... Jockey #10 / Best Seller #15 | | Atlantic 1073 |
| 1/28/56 | **3** | 11 | 18 | **Devil Or Angel/** Juke Box #3 / Best Seller #4 / Jockey #4 | | |
| 2/04/56 | **8** | 3 | 19 | **Hey, Doll Baby** .......................................... Jockey #8 | | Atlantic 1083 |
| 6/23/56 | **4** | 11 | 20 | **Love, Love, Love** ....................................... Jockey #4 / Juke Box #7 / Best Seller #10 | 30 | Atlantic 1094 |
| 12/07/59 | **23** | 3 | 21 | Love Potion No. 9 ......................................... #14-21: Billy Mitchell replaces Charlie White | 23 | United Art. 180 |
| | | | | **CLUB HOUSE** | | |
| 8/06/83 | **61** | 8 | 1 | Do It Again/Billie Jean.................................. | 75 | Atlantic 89795 |
| | | | | **CLUB NOUVEAU** | | |
| | | | | Sacramento-based dance/disco group formed and fronted by Jay King (producer/owner of King Jay Records). Early lineup: vocalists Valerie Watson and Samuelle Prater, with Denzil Foster and Thomas McElroy. Prater, Foster and McElroy left in 1988; replaced by David Agent and Kevin Irving. | | |
| 9/06/86 | **8** | 15 | 1 | **Jealousy** ................................................... | | Warner 28551 |
| 12/20/86+ | **4** | 14 | 2 | **Situation #9** .............................................. | | Warner 28494 |
| 2/14/87 | **2**³ | 15 | 3● | **Lean On Me** ............................................... | 1 | Warner 28430 |
| 5/02/87 | **2**² | 15 | 4 | **Why You Treat Me So Bad** .......................... | 39 | Warner 28360 |
| 1/23/88 | **42** | 11 | 5 | Heavy On My Mind ....................................... | | Tommy Boy 903 |
| 5/14/88 | **34** | 9 | 6 | It's A Cold, Cold World! ................................ | | Warner 28101 |

| DEBUT DATE | PEAK POS | WKS CHR | ARTIST — Record Title | POP POS | Label & Number |
|---|---|---|---|---|---|
| | | | **THE COASTERS** ★★179★★ | | |
| | | | Group formed in Los Angeles in late 1955 from elements of the Robins. Originally consisted of Carl Gardner (ex-Robins), lead; Leon Hughes, tenor; Billy Guy, baritone lead; Bobby Nunn (ex-Robins), bass; and Adolph Jacobs, guitar. Noted for serio-comic recordings, primarily of Leiber & Stoller songs. Will "Dub" Jones (ex-Cadets) replaced Nunn in late 1958 and is heard on "Charlie Brown" and "Along Came Jones". Earl "Speedo" Carroll (ex-Cadillacs) joined group in 1961. Bobby Nunn died of a heart attack on 11/5/86 (61). Today there are two or three "Coasters" groups still working, some of which contain one or two original members. Also see Bobby Hendricks. | | |
| 3/31/56 | 8 | 6 | 1 **Down In Mexico**/ | | |
| | | | Juke Box #8 / Best Seller #9 / Jockey #9 | | |
| | | 1 | 2 Turtle Dovin'..................................... | | Atco 6064 |
| | | | Juke Box flip | | |
| 9/08/56 | 11 | 2 | 3 **One Kiss Led To Another** ............................ | 73 | Atco 6073 |
| | | | Jockey #11 | | |
| 5/13/57 | 1¹³ | 21 | 4 **Searchin'**/ | 3 | |
| | | | Best Seller #1(13)/ Jockey #1(7) / Juke Box #1(2) | | |
| 5/06/57 | 2² | 14 | 5 **Young Blood**.................................. | 8 | Atco 6087 |
| | | | Jockey #2 | | |
| 6/09/58 | 1⁷ | 14 | 6 **Yakety Yak** ........................................... | 1 | Atco 6116 |
| | | | Best Seller #1(7) / Jockey #1(6) | | |
| 2/16/59 | 2² | 12 | 7 **Charlie Brown** .................................. [N] | 2 | Atco 6132 |
| 6/15/59 | 14 | 6 | 8 Along Came Jones ................................... [N] | 9 | Atco 6141 |
| 8/31/59 | 1⁴ | 16 | 9 **Poison Ivy**........................................ [N] | 7 | Atco 6146 |
| 12/21/59 | 29 | 1 | 10 Run Red Run/ | 36 | |
| | | | all of above: written & produced by Jerry Leiber & Mike Stoller | | |
| 1/18/60 | 17 | 6 | 11 What About Us ................................... | 47 | Atco 6153 |
| 6/27/60 | 14 | 8 | 12 Wake Me, Shake Me ................................. | 51 | Atco 6168 |
| 6/12/61 | 16 | 4 | 13 Little Egypt (Ying-Yang).......................... [N] | 23 | Atco 6192 |
| 3/28/64 | 64 | 6 | 14 T'ain't Nothin' To Me ................................. [N] | Hot | Atco 6287 |
| | | | **JOYCE COBB** | | |
| 9/27/80 | 90 | 3 | 1 How Glad I Am ...................................... | 107 | Cream 8040 |
| | | | **EDDIE COCHRAN** | | |
| | | | Pop vocalist/guitarist/film actor, born Edward Ray Cochrane on 10/3/38 in Oklahoma City, Oklahoma. Killed in a car accident in England on 4/17/60; accident also injured Gene Vincent. | | |
| 7/01/57 | 7 | 1 | 1 **Sittin' In The Balcony**.............................. | 18 | Liberty 55056 |
| | | | Jockey #7 | | |
| 9/22/58 | 11 | 7 | 2 Summertime Blues ....................................... | 8 | Liberty 55144 |
| | | | Best Seller #11 / Jockey #13 | | |
| | | | **JOE COCKER - see THE CRUSADERS** | | |
| | | | **THE C.O.D.'s** | | |
| | | | Chicago group consisting of Larry Brownlee, Robert Lewis and Carl Washington. Brownlee wrote all their songs and later became a member of the Lost Generation and Mystique; he died in 1978. | | |
| 12/18/65+ | 5 | 10 | 1 **Michael**........................................... | 41 | Kellmac 1003 |
| | | | **BILL CODAY** | | |
| | | | Vocalist from Chicago, produced by Willie Mitchell. | | |
| 2/06/71 | 14 | 12 | 1 Get Your Lie Straight................................ | 105 | Crayon 48204 |
| | | | also released on Galaxy 777 | | |
| 7/17/71 | 48 | 3 | 2 When You Find A Fool, Bump His Head............. | | Galaxy 779 |
| | | | **COFFEE** | | |
| | | | Chicago female group formed in 1973: Betty Caldwell (lead), Elaine Sims, Glenda Hester and Lenora "Dee Dee" Bryant. Caldwell left in 1979 and Hester became lead. | | |
| 4/03/82 | 77 | 5 | 1 Take Me Back................................... | | De-Lite 817 |
| 6/12/82 | 68 | 6 | 2 If This World ................................... | | De-Lite 819 |
| | | | **DENNIS COFFEY & The Detroit Guitar Band** | | |
| | | | Detroit native Coffey was a session guitarist for The Temptations, Jackson 5 and others. Also see C.J. & Co. | | |
| 10/30/71 | 9 | 15 | 1 ●Scorpio................................... [I] | 6 | Sussex 226 |
| 2/26/72 | 11 | 9 | 2 Taurus .................................... [I] | 18 | Sussex 233 |
| 6/24/72 | 43 | 2 | 3 Ride, Sally, Ride ........................... [I] | 93 | Sussex 237 |
| | | | shown only as: **DENNIS COFFEY** | | |
| 1/11/75 | 75 | 7 | 4 Getting It On '75 ................................. [I] | | Sussex 631 |
| 9/17/77 | 94 | 2 | 5 Our Love Goes On Forever ........................... | | Westbound 55402 |

| DEBUT DATE | PEAK POS | WKS CHR | ARTIST — Record Title | POP POS | Label & Number |
|---|---|---|---|---|---|
| | | | **COGNAC - see SALSOUL ORCHESTRA** | | |
| | | | **ANN COLE** | | |
| | | | Born Cynthia Coleman on 1/24/34 in Newark, New Jersey. Father, Wallace, was a member of famous spiritual group, the Coleman Brothers. Formed own group, the Colemanaires in 1949. Changed name to sing secular music. Introduced the song "Got My Mojo Working", often wrongly attributed to Muddy Waters. Confined to a wheelchair after an auto accident in the 60s. | | |
| 1/28/56 | **10** | 1 | 1 **Are You Satisfied** ...................................... Juke Box #10 with Dave McRae's Orchestra | | Baton 218 |
| 1/26/57 | **14** | 2 | 2 **In The Chapel**........................................ Best Seller #14 / Jockey #14 with the Suburbans | | Baton 232 |
| 12/15/62 | **21** | 3 | 3 **Have Fun**............................................ | | Roulette 4452 |
| | | | **COZY COLE** | | |
| | | | Born William Randolph Cole on 10/17/09 in East Orange, New Jersey. Died of cancer on 1/29/81 (71). Lead drummer for many swing bands, including Benny Carter, Willie Bryant, Cab Calloway, and Louis Armstrong. Professional debut in 1928. Recorded with Jelly Roll Morton in 1930. Appeared with Benny Goodman in the 1944 film "Make Mine Music". | | |
| 5/27/44 | **10** | 1 | 1 **Just One More Chance** .......................... [I] with the Cozy Cole All-Stars | | Keynote 1300 |
| 10/06/58 | **1** 6 | 15 | 2 **Topsy II**................................................ [I] | 3 | Love 5004 |
| | | | **NAT KING COLE** ★★**13**★★ | | |
| | | | Born Nathaniel Adams Coles on 3/17/17 in Montgomery, Alabama. Died of lung cancer on 2/15/65 in Santa Monica, CA (48). Raised in Chicago. Own band, the Royal Dukes, at age 17. First recorded in 1936 in band led by brother Eddie. Toured with "Shuffle Along" musical revue, resided in Los Angeles. Formed trio in 1939: Nat (piano), Oscar Moore (guitar - later joined brothers group, Johnny Moore's Three Blazers) and Wesley Prince (bass - replaced several years later by Johnny Miller). Long series of top-selling records led to his solo career in 1950. In the films "St. Louis Blues", "Cat Ballou" and many other film and TV appearances. Stopped performing in 1964, due to ill health. Daughter Natalie is also a recording star. | | |
| | | | **KING COLE TRIO:** | | |
| 11/21/42+ | **1** 1 | 7 | 1 **That Ain't Right** ...................................... | | Decca 8630 |
| 11/06/43 | **1** 2 | 14 | 2 **All For You**.......................................... originally released on Excelsior 103 | 18 | Capitol 139 |
| 4/15/44 | **1** 10 | 26 | 3 **Straighten Up And Fly Right/** | 9 | |
| 5/06/44 | **2** 1 | 14 | 4 **I Can't See For Lookin'** ............................ | 28 | Capitol 154 |
| 9/23/44 | **9** | 4 | 5 **I Realize Now/** | | |
| 9/30/44 | **1** 4 | 22 | 6 **Gee, Baby, Ain't I Good To You?** ................ | 15 | Capitol 169 |
| 10/21/44 | **4** | 14 | 7 **I'm Lost**............................................ | | Excelsior 105 |
| 12/02/44 | **5** | 5 | 8 **It's Only A Paper Moon** .......................... | | Capitol 20012 |
| 5/12/45 | **3** | 3 | 9 **If You Can't Smile And Say Yes** .................... | | Capitol 192 |
| 8/25/45 | **2** 2 | 5 | 10 **I'm A Shy Guy**...................................... | | Capitol 208 |
| 1/12/46 | **3** | 2 | 11 **Come To Baby, Do**................................ | | Capitol 224 |
| 6/08/46 | **3** | 11 | 12 **Get Your Kicks On Route 66**........................ | 11 | Capitol 256 |
| 11/23/46 | **3** | 6 | 13 **The Christmas Song** .......................... [X] holiday classic selected for NARAS Hall Of Fame; a reported million-seller | 3 | Capitol 311 |
| 11/30/46 | **3** | 8 | 14 **(I Love You) For Sentimental Reasons** ........... | 1 | Capitol 304 |
| 5/31/47 | **3** | 2 | 15 **Meet Me At No Special Place (And I'll Be There At No Particular Time)** ................ | | Capitol 393 |
| 1/31/48 | **9** | 4 | 16 **Those Things Money Can't Buy** .................... | 22 | Capitol 15011 |
| 2/07/48 | **8** | 2 | 17 **What'll I Do?**........................................ from the Broadway musical "Music Box Revue of 1923" | 22 | Capitol 15019 |
| 5/15/48 | **2** 1 | 12 | 18 **Nature Boy**.......................................... NAT "KING" COLE Juke Box #2 / Best Seller #3 backed by Frank DeVol's Orchestra; possibly based on the Yiddish song "Schweig Mein Hartz" (Be Calm, My Heart); a reported million-seller | 1 | Capitol 15054 |
| 10/30/48 | **12** | 2 | 19 **Lillette**............................................ Juke Box #12 | | Capitol 15224 |
| 1/01/49 | **8** | 1 | 20 **The Christmas Song** ............................ [X-R] Juke Box #8 | 24 | Capitol 15201 |
| 1/01/49 | **10** | 1 | 21 **Kee-Mo Ky-Mo (The Magic Song)**.................. Juke Box #10 | | Capitol 15240 |
| 1/22/49 | **7** | 1 | 22 **Flo And Joe** ........................................ Juke Box #7 | | Capitol 15320 |

| DEBUT DATE | PEAK POS | WKS CHR | ARTIST — Record Title | POP POS | Label & Number |
|---|---|---|---|---|---|
| | | | **NAT KING COLE — Continued** | | |
| 12/31/49 | **9** | 1 | 23 **Exactly Like You/** | | |
| | | | Best Seller #9 | | |
| 2/18/50 | **6** | 1 | 24 **My Mother Told Me** ................................ | | Capitol 70050 |
| | | | Best Seller #6 | | |
| 2/18/50 | **8** | 3 | 25 **For You, My Love**................................ | | Capitol 847 |
| | | | **NAT KING COLE TRIO with NELLIE LUTCHER** | | |
| | | | Juke Box #8 / Best Seller #12 | | |
| 4/22/50 | **7** | 5 | 26 **I Almost Lost My Mind** ........................... | *26* | Capitol 889 |
| | | | Best Seller #7 / Juke Box #10 | | |
| | | | with The Starlighters vocal group | | |
| | | | **NAT KING COLE:** | | |
| 7/08/50 | **1**⁴ | 16 | 27 **Mona Lisa** .......................................... | *1* | Capitol 1010 |
| | | | Juke Box #1 / Best Seller #3 | | |
| | | | from the film "Capt. Carey, U.S.A."; sold over 3 million copies | | |
| 3/17/51 | **8** | 1 | 28 **Jet**................................................ | *20* | Capitol 1365 |
| | | | Best Seller #8 | | |
| | | | with the Ray Charles Singers & Joe Lippman's Orchestra | | |
| 5/05/51 | **3** | 11 | 29 **Too Young** ...................................... | *1* | Capitol 1449 |
| | | | Best Seller #3 / Juke Box #4 | | |
| | | | 27 & 29: with Les Baxter's Orchestra; a reported million-seller | | |
| 2/09/52 | **5** | 4 | 30 **Walkin'**.......................................... | | Capitol 1863 |
| | | | Juke Box #5 | | |
| 2/21/53 | **10** | 1 | 31 **Pretend** .......................................... | *2* | Capitol 2346 |
| | | | Best Seller #10 | | |
| | | | with Nelson Riddle's Orchestra; a reported million-seller | | |
| 6/27/53 | **7** | 2 | 32 **Can't I?** .......................................... | *16* | Capitol 2389 |
| | | | Juke Box #7 | | |
| | | | accompanied by Billy May's Orchestra | | |
| 9/29/56 | **15** | 2 | 33 **That's All There Is To That** .................... | *16* | Capitol 3456 |
| | | | **NAT "KING" COLE & THE FOUR KNIGHTS** | | |
| | | | Best Seller #15 | | |
| | | | orchestra conducted by Nelson Riddle | | |
| 7/01/57 | **1**² | 17 | 34 **Send For Me/** | *6* | |
| | | | Jockey #1 / Best Seller #2 | | |
| 7/22/57 | **3** | 1 | 35 **My Personal Possession** ........................... | *21* | Capitol 3737 |
| | | | **NAT "KING" COLE & THE FOUR KNIGHTS** | | |
| | | | Best Seller #3 | | |
| 4/21/58 | **2**¹ | 16 | 36 **Looking Back** ................................... | *5* | Capitol 3939 |
| | | | Jockey #2 / Best Seller #3 | | |
| | | | with the Dave Cavanaugh Orchestra | | |
| 8/31/59 | **12** | 9 | 37 Midnight Flyer ................................... | *51* | Capitol 4248 |
| 3/07/60 | **15** | 5 | 38 Whatcha' Gonna Do/ [I] | *92* | |
| | | | piano solo by Nat | | |
| 4/04/60 | **27** | 2 | 39 Time And The River .......................... | *30* | Capitol 4325 |
| 8/08/60 | **12** | 4 | 40 My Love ....................................... | *47* | Capitol 4393 |
| | | | **NAT KING COLE-STAN KENTON** | | |
| 9/08/62 | **7** | 11 | 41 **Ramblin' Rose** ................................ | *2* | Capitol 4804 |
| 12/22/62+ | **15** | 4 | 42 Dear Lonely Hearts ......................... | *13* | Capitol 4870 |
| 6/22/63 | **11** | 5 | 43 Those Lazy-Hazy-Crazy Days Of Summer ......... | *6* | Capitol 4965 |
| 10/05/63 | **19** | 4 | 44 That Sunday, That Summer .................. | *12* | Capitol 5027 |
| 2/22/64 | **49** | 6 | 45 My True Carrie, Love ...................... | *Hot* | Capitol 5125 |
| 4/25/64 | **22** | 9 | 46 I Don't Want To Be Hurt Anymore/ | *Hot* | |
| 4/11/64 | **100** | 1 | 47 People.......................................... | *Hot* | Capitol 5155 |
| | | | from the Broadway musical "Funny Girl" | | |
| | | | **NATALIE COLE**   ★★**54**★★ | | |
| | | | Born on 2/6/50 in Los Angeles. Daughter of Nat "King" Cole. Professional debut at age 11. Married her producer, Marvin Yancey, Jr. | | |
| 7/26/75 | **1**² | 19 | 1 **This Will Be** ................................... | *6* | Capitol 4109 |
| 12/06/75+ | **1**¹ | 17 | 2 **Inseparable**................................... | *32* | Capitol 4193 |
| 5/01/76 | **1**¹ | 18 | 3 **Sophisticated Lady (She's A Different Lady)**... | *25* | Capitol 4259 |
| 9/04/76 | **10** | 15 | 4 **Mr. Melody**................................... | *49* | Capitol 4328 |
| 1/22/77 | **1**⁵ | 20 | 5●**I've Got Love On My Mind**................... | *5* | Capitol 4360 |
| 7/02/77 | **9** | 11 | 6 **Party Lights**................................... | *79* | Capitol 4439 |
| 11/19/77+ | **1**² | 24 | 7●**Our Love**................................... | *10* | Capitol 4509 |
| 5/06/78 | **6** | 18 | 8 **Annie Mae**................................... | | Capitol 4572 |
| 9/09/78 | **53** | 8 | 9 Lucy In The Sky With Diamonds .................... | | Capitol 4623 |
| 3/03/79 | **9** | 16 | 10 **Stand By** ................................... | *108* | Capitol 4690 |
| 6/02/79 | **34** | 10 | 11 Sorry ....................................... | *109* | Capitol 4722 |

| DEBUT DATE | PEAK POS | WKS CHR | ARTIST — Record Title | POP POS | Label & Number |
|---|---|---|---|---|---|
| | | | **NATALIE COLE — Continued** | | |
| 10/20/79 | 59 | 6 | 12 Your Lonely Heart......................................... | | Capitol 4767 |
| 11/24/79+ | 8 | 14 | 13 Gimme Some Time .................................... | 102 | Capitol 4804 |
| | | | NATALIE COLE & PEABO BRYSON | | |
| 2/16/80 | 16 | 11 | 14 What You Won't Do For Love ...................... | | Capitol 4826 |
| | | | NATALIE COLE & PEABO BRYSON | | |
| 5/31/80 | 21 | 15 | 15 Someone That I Used To Love ...................... | 21 | Capitol 4869 |
| 10/04/80 | 38 | 8 | 16 Hold On...................................................... | | Capitol 4924 |
| 7/25/81 | 35 | 10 | 17 You Were Right Girl ................................... | | Capitol 5021 |
| 10/03/81 | 34 | 10 | 18 Nothin' But A Fool ..................................... | | Capitol 5053 |
| 7/30/83 | 45 | 9 | 19 Too Much Mister ....................................... | | Epic 04000 |
| 4/27/85 | 16 | 13 | 20 Dangerous ................................................. | 57 | Modern 99648 |
| 7/27/85 | 28 | 12 | 21 A Little Bit Of Heaven................................ | 81 | Modern 99630 |
| 6/13/87 | 2¹ | 20 | 22 **Jump Start** ............................................. | 13 | Manhattan 50073 |
| 8/29/87 | 5 | 13 | 23 I Don't Think That Man Should Sleep Alone... | 68 | Geffen 28417 |
| | | | RAY PARKER JR. with NATALIE COLE | | |
| 10/03/87 | 4 | 20 | 24 **I Live For Your Love** ............................... | 13 | Manhattan 50094 |
| 12/05/87+ | 10 | 16 | 25 Over You .................................................... | 5 | Geffen 28152 |
| | | | RAY PARKER JR. with NATALIE COLE | | |
| 2/20/88 | 9 | 16 | 26 **Pink Cadillac** ........................................... | 5 | EMI-Man. 50117 |
| | | | written & recorded by Bruce Springsteen (flip of his 1984 pop hit "Dancing In The Dark") | | |
| 6/25/88 | 31 | 8 | 27 When I Fall In Love .................................. | 95 | EMI-Man. 50138 |
| | | | Natalie's father recorded this tune on his 1957 #1 pop album "Love Is The Thing" | | |
| | | | **DURELL COLEMAN** Vocalist from Roanoke, Virginia. Singing since age 12. Moved to Los Angeles in 1983. Was the 1985 winner of TV's "Star Search" (male vocalist category). | | |
| 9/07/85 | 25 | 13 | 1 Somebody Took My Love ............................. | | Island 99605 |
| 12/14/85+ | 37 | 13 | 2 Do You Love Me........................................ | | Island 99586 |
| | | | **COLLAGE** | | |
| 6/04/83 | 56 | 9 | 1 Get In Touch With Me ............................... | | Solar 69829 |
| 8/03/85 | 86 | 7 | 2 Romeo Where's Juliet? ............................... | | Constell. 52588 |
| | | | **MITTY COLLIER** Born on 6/21/41 in Birmingham, Alabama. Toured with gospel group the Hayes Ensemble. Moved to Chicago in 1959. Won Al Benson's Talent Contest at Regal Theater. First recorded for Chess in 1961. Returned to gospel singing in 1972. | | |
| 10/12/63 | 20 | 2 | 1 I'm Your Part Time Love ............................ | | Chess 1871 |
| 9/26/64 | 41 | 10 | 2 I Had A Talk With My Man.......................... | Hot | Chess 1907 |
| 1/30/65 | 29 | 4 | 3 No Faith, No Love ..................................... | 91 | Chess 1918 |
| 4/02/66 | 10 | 9 | 4 **Sharing You**.............................................. | 97 | Chess 1953 |
| | | | **COLLINS & COLLINS** Philadelphia brother-sister duo of Bill and Tonee Collins. | | |
| 6/07/80 | 68 | 6 | 1 Top Of The Stairs....................................... | | A&M 2233 |
| | | | **ALBERT COLLINS** Blues vocalist/guitarist, born on 10/3/32 in Leona, Texas. Toured with Piney Brown from 1951-54. Recorded for Ace in 1955. Worked Montreux Jazz Festival, in Switzerland, in 1975. Appeared in the 1987 film "Adventures In Babysitting". | | |
| 3/11/72 | 46 | 3 | 1 Get Your Business Straight ........................... | | Tumbleweed 1002 |
| | | | **"BOOTSY" COLLINS - see WILLIAM "BOOTSY" COLLINS** | | |
| | | | **KEANYA COLLINS** | | |
| 10/11/69 | 42 | 4 | 1 You Don't Own Me..................................... | | Itco 103 |
| | | | **LYN COLLINS** Born on 6/12/48 in Lexington, Texas. With Charles Pikes & The Scholars in the mid-60s. Joined James Brown Revue in 1969. | | |
| 7/15/72 | 9 | 17 | 1 **Think (About It)** ...................................... | 66 | People 608 |
| | | | produced by James Brown | | |
| 12/23/72+ | 17 | 10 | 2 What My Baby Needs Now Is A Little More Lovin'...................................................... | 56 | Polydor 14157 |
| | | | JAMES BROWN-LYN COLLINS | | |
| 3/17/73 | 37 | 4 | 3 Mama Feel Good ........................................ | | People 618 |
| 7/07/73 | 45 | 9 | 4 How Long Can I Keep It Up/ | | |
| 9/08/73 | 35 | 9 | 5 Take Me As I Am ....................................... | | People 623 |

| DEBUT DATE | PEAK POS | WKS CHR | ARTIST — Record Title | POP POS | Label & Number |
|---|---|---|---|---|---|
| | | | **LYN COLLINS — Continued** | | |
| 11/17/73 | **64** | 8 | 6  We Want To Parrty, Parrty, Parrty .................... | | People 630 |
| 5/18/74 | **77** | 8 | 7  Give It Up Or Turnit A Loose........................ | | People 636 |
| 8/10/74 | **53** | 9 | 8  Rock Me Again & Again & Again & Again & Again & Again .................... | | People 641 |
| 10/11/75 | **82** | 5 | 9  If You Don't Know Me By Now ........................ | | People 659 |
| | | | **PHIL COLLINS** | | |
| | | | Pop vocalist/drummer/composer, born on 1/31/51 in London. Lead singer of Genesis. | | |
| 12/15/84+ | **3** | 19 | 1 ● Easy Lover............................................ | 2 | Columbia 04679 |
| | | | **PHILIP BAILEY with PHIL COLLINS** | | |
| 4/20/85 | **80** | 2 | 2  One More Night...................................... | 1 | Atlantic 89588 |
| 5/11/85 | **8** | 14 | 3  Sussudio............................................ | 1 | Atlantic 89560 |
| | | | **RODGER COLLINS** | | |
| | | | Singer from Oakland. | | |
| 2/18/67 | **44** | 5 | 1  She's Looking Good ....................................... | 101 | Galaxy 750 |
| | | | **WILLIAM "BOOTSY" COLLINS** | | |
| | | | Born on 10/26/51 in Cincinnati. Singer/bass player. Formed own band, the Pacesetters, in 1968, with his brother Phelps "Catfish" Collins, Frankie "Kash" Waddy and Philippe Wynne. Band became James Brown's JB's from 1969-71, then the House Guests. Joined Funkadelic/Parliament aggregation in 1972. Later led Bootsy's Rubber Band including Phelps Collins, Frank Waddy, Joel "Razor Sharp" Johnson, Gary "Mudbone" Cooper and Robert "P-Nut" Johnson. Collins featured his alter-egos "Bootzilla" and "Casper" in stage shows. | | |
| 6/05/76 | **18** | 15 | 1  Stretchin' Out (In A Rubber Band).................... | | Warner 8215 |
| | | | **BOOTSY'S RUBBER BAND:** | | |
| 8/28/76 | **25** | 13 | 2  I'd Rather Be With You ............................... | | Warner 8246 |
| 12/18/76+ | **69** | 7 | 3  Psychoticbumpschool ................................ | 104 | Warner 8291 |
| 3/12/77 | **6** | 13 | 4  The Pinocchio Theory ............................... | | Warner 8328 |
| 6/25/77 | **19** | 14 | 5  Can't Stay Away .................................... | 104 | Warner 8403 |
| 2/04/78 | **1**¹ | 19 | 6  Bootzilla ........................................... | | Warner 8512 |
| 5/20/78 | **17** | 13 | 7  Hollywood Squares .................................. | | Warner 8575 |
| 5/05/79 | **13** | 14 | 8  Jam Fan (Hot)....................................... | | Warner 8818 |
| | | | **BOOTSY:** | | |
| 7/28/79 | **38** | 9 | 9  Bootsy Get Live ..................................... | | Warner 49013 |
| 11/08/80 | **25** | 14 | 10  Mug Push .......................................... | | Warner 49599 |
| | | | **WILLIAM "BOOTSY" COLLINS:** | | |
| 2/14/81 | **51** | 9 | 11  F-Encounter ....................................... | | Warner 49661 |
| 4/10/82 | **29** | 11 | 12  Take A Lickin' And Keep On Kickin' ................ | 103 | Warner 50044 |
| 7/10/82 | **78** | 4 | 13  Shine-O-Myte (Rag Popping)........................ | | Warner 29965 |
| 10/09/82 | **12** | 15 | 14  Body Slam! ........................................ | | Warner 29889 |
| | | | **BOOTSY'S RUBBER BAND** | | |
| | | | **WILLIE COLLINS** | | |
| | | | New York-based vocalist; originally from North Carolina. | | |
| 5/03/86 | **43** | 13 | 1  Let's Get Started.................................... | | Capitol 5554 |
| | | | **COLTS** | | |
| | | | Group from Bakersfield, California. Consisted of Ruben Grundy (lead), Joe Grundy, Carl Moland, and Leroy Smith. Managed by Buck Ram. | | |
| 10/29/55 | **11** | 1 | 1  Adorable ........................................... | | Vita 112 |
| | | | Best Seller #11 | | |
| | | | **TONY COMER & CROSSWINDS** | | |
| 10/20/84 | **77** | 5 | 1  Don't Give Up...................................... | | Vidcom 844 |
| | | | **COMMODORES**  ★★**43**★★ | | |
| | | | Formed in Tuskegee, Alabama in 1970. Consisted of Lionel Richie (vocals, saxophone), William King (trumpet), Thomas McClary (guitar), Milan Williams (keyboards), Ronald LaPread (bass) and Walter "Clyde" Orange (drums). First recorded for Motown in 1972. In film "Thank God It's Friday". Richie began solo work in 1981. | | |
| 5/25/74 | **7** | 15 | 1  Machine Gun ................................... [I] | 22 | Motown 1307 |
| 11/09/74+ | **12** | 15 | 2  I Feel Sanctified .................................... | 75 | Motown 1319 |
| 4/26/75 | **1**¹ | 17 | 3  Slippery When Wet .................................. | 19 | Motown 1338 |
| 9/13/75 | **13** | 15 | 4  This Is Your Life ................................... | | Motown 1361 |
| 12/20/75+ | **2**² | 20 | 5  Sweet Love........................................ | 5 | Motown 1381 |
| 9/04/76 | **1**² | 17 | 6  Just To Be Close To You............................. | 7 | Motown 1402 |
| 12/25/76+ | **9** | 14 | 7  Fancy Dancer ...................................... | 39 | Motown 1408 |

| DEBUT DATE | PEAK POS | WKS CHR | ARTIST — Record Title | POP POS | Label & Number |
|---|---|---|---|---|---|
| | | | **COMMODORES — Continued** | | |
| 5/28/77 | 1¹ | 17 | 8 Easy................................... | 4 | Motown 1418 |
| 9/03/77 | 4 | 13 | 9 Brick House ......................... | 5 | Motown 1425 |
| 12/24/77+ | 1¹ | 14 | 10 Too Hot Ta Trot .................. | 24 | Motown 1432 |
| 6/24/78 | 1² | 17 | 11 Three Times A Lady.............. | 1 | Motown 1443 |
| 9/30/78 | 21 | 11 | 12 Flying High ........................ | 38 | Motown 1452 |
| 8/18/79 | 8 | 13 | 13 Sail On ............................. | 4 | Motown 1466 |
| 10/06/79 | 1¹ | 17 | 14 Still .................................. | 1 | Motown 1474 |
| 12/22/79+ | 21 | 13 | 15 Wonderland ........................ | 25 | Motown 1479 |
| 6/28/80 | 8 | 14 | 16 Old-Fashion Love.................. | 20 | Motown 1489 |
| 9/13/80 | 27 | 11 | 17 Heroes .............................. | 54 | Motown 1495 |
| 12/20/80+ | 34 | 11 | 18 Jesus Is Love ...................... | | Motown 1502 |
| 6/27/81 | 5 | 18 | 19 Lady (You Bring Me Up).......... | 8 | Motown 1514 |
| 9/26/81 | 5 | 20 | 20 Oh No .............................. | 4 | Motown 1527 |
| 2/13/82 | 42 | 6 | 21 Why You Wanna Try Me.......... | 66 | Motown 1604 |
| | | | Lionel Richie's last song as lead singer | | |
| 11/27/82+ | 19 | 18 | 22 Painted Pictures ................. | 70 | Motown 1651 |
| 9/17/83 | 20 | 16 | 23 Only You........................... | 54 | Motown 1694 |
| 1/19/85 | 1⁴ | 22 | 24 Nightshift.......................... | 3 | Motown 1773 |
| | | | a tribute to Marvin Gaye and Jackie Wilson | | |
| 5/25/85 | 22 | 11 | 25 Animal Instinct.................... | 43 | Motown 1788 |
| 8/31/85 | 65 | 7 | 26 Janet ............................... | 87 | Motown 1802 |
| 10/04/86 | 2¹ | 20 | 27 Goin' To The Bank................ | 65 | Polydor 885358 |
| 1/24/87 | 38 | 12 | 28 Take It From Me .................. | | Polydor 885538 |
| | | | **COMMON SENSE** | | |
| 3/14/81 | 58 | 7 | 1 Voices Inside My Head ............. | | BC 4008 |
| | | | **CON FUNK SHUN**   ★★98★★ | | |
| | | | Band formed as Project Soul in Vallejo, California in 1968 by high school classmates Mike Cooper (lead vocals, guitar) and Louis McCall (drums). To Memphis in 1972, changed name to Con Funk Shun. First recorded for Fretone in the mid-70s. Session work for Stax records. Included Karl Fuller, Paul Harrell, Felton Pilate II, Danny Thomas, Cedric Martin and Peto Escovedo (son of Azteca's Pete Escovedo and brother of Sheila E.) | | |
| 1/29/77 | 66 | 8 | 1 Sho Feels Good To Me ............. | | Mercury 73883 |
| 10/29/77+ | 1² | 21 | 2 Ffun ................................. | 23 | Mercury 73959 |
| 3/25/78 | 31 | 11 | 3 Confunkshunizeya ................. | 103 | Mercury 73985 |
| 7/01/78 | 5 | 17 | 4 Shake And Dance With Me ....... | 60 | Mercury 74008 |
| 10/21/78 | 28 | 9 | 5 So Easy ............................. | | Mercury 74024 |
| 5/05/79 | 4 | 21 | 6 Chase Me ........................... | | Mercury 74059 |
| 9/01/79 | 24 | 12 | 7 (Let Me Put) Love On Your Mind.. | | Mercury 76002 |
| 1/05/80 | 60 | 6 | 8 Da Lady ............................. | | Mercury 76026 |
| 3/15/80 | 8 | 18 | 9 Got To Be Enough ................. | 101 | Mercury 76051 |
| 6/21/80 | 27 | 13 | 10 By Your Side ....................... | | Mercury 76066 |
| 10/11/80 | 87 | 4 | 11 Happy Face ........................ | | Mercury 76079 |
| 11/22/80+ | 8 | 20 | 12 Too Tight ........................... | 40 | Mercury 76089 |
| 3/28/81 | 42 | 11 | 13 Lady's Wild......................... | | Mercury 76099 |
| 12/12/81+ | 19 | 13 | 14 Bad Lady ........................... | | Mercury 76128 |
| 7/03/82 | 79 | 4 | 15 Straight From The Heart ......... | | Mercury 76159 |
| 11/13/82 | 31 | 12 | 16 Ain't Nobody, Baby ............... | | Mercury 76185 |
| 2/19/83 | 15 | 13 | 17 Ms. Got-The-Body................. | | Mercury 76198 |
| 5/28/83 | 47 | 7 | 18 You Are The One .................. | | Mercury 812117 |
| 10/29/83+ | 5 | 20 | 19 Baby, I'm Hooked (Right Into Your Love)........ | 76 | Mercury 814581 |
| 2/18/84 | 33 | 12 | 20 Don't Let Your Love Grow Cold ...... | 103 | Mercury 818369 |
| 4/06/85 | 4 | 17 | 21 Electric Lady ...................... | 102 | Mercury 880636 |
| 7/13/85 | 12 | 17 | 22 I'm Leaving Baby .................. | | Mercury 880914 |
| 11/02/85 | 47 | 10 | 23 Tell Me What (I'm Gonna Do) ...... | | Mercury 884189 |
| 5/31/86 | 8 | 16 | 24 Burnin' Love ...................... | | Mercury 884762 |
| 10/04/86 | 80 | 5 | 25 She's A Star....................... | | Mercury 884992 |
| | | | **CONCEPT** | | |
| 11/02/85 | 72 | 7 | 1 Mr. DJ............................... | | Tuckwood 105 |

| DEBUT DATE | PEAK POS | WKS CHR | ARTIST — Record Title | POP POS | Label & Number |
|---|---|---|---|---|---|
| | | | **ARTHUR CONLEY** | | |
| | | | Born on 1/4/46 in Atlanta. Discovered by Otis Redding in 1965. First recorded for NRC as Arthur & The Corvets. Also see The Soul Clan. | | |
| 3/11/67 | **2**⁵ | 15 | 1 ● **Sweet Soul Music** ........................ | 2 | Atco 6463 |
| | | | tune originally written by Sam Cooke as "Yeah Man" | | |
| 7/01/67 | **20** | 6 | 2 Shake, Rattle And Roll ................... | 31 | Atco 6494 |
| | | | above 2: produced by Otis Redding | | |
| 3/30/68 | **5** | 12 | 3 **Funky Street** ............................. | 73 | Atco 6563 |
| 6/22/68 | **17** | 6 | 4 People Sure Act Funny ................... | 58 | Atco 6588 |
| 11/09/68 | **41** | 4 | 5 Aunt Dora's Love Soul Shack .......... | 85 | Atco 6622 |
| 1/18/69 | **41** | 2 | 6 Ob-La-Di, Ob-La-Da ...................... | 51 | Atco 6640 |
| 4/25/70 | **33** | 5 | 7 God Bless ................................... | 107 | Atco 6747 |
| | | | **CONNIE** | | |
| 12/14/85+ | **41** | 17 | 1 Funky Little Beat ......................... | | Sunnyview 3028 |
| 5/17/86 | **50** | 9 | 2 Experience ................................. | | Sunnyview 3034 |
| | | | **NORMAN CONNORS** | | |
| | | | Born on 3/1/48 in Philadelphia. Jazz drummer with Archie Shepp, John Coltrane, Pharoah Sanders, and others. Own group on Buddah in 1972. Produced Michael Henderson, Jean Carn, Dee Dee Bridgewater and Phyllis Hyman. Formed the disco group Aquarian Dream. | | |
| 11/08/75 | **10** | 14 | 1 **Valentine Love** ......................... | 97 | Buddah 499 |
| | | | vocals by Michael Henderson and Jean Carn | | |
| 7/17/76 | **23** | 11 | 2 We Both Need Each Other ............... | 101 | Buddah 534 |
| 8/28/76 | **4** | 17 | 3 **You Are My Starship** ................... | 27 | Buddah 542 |
| | | | vocal by Michael Henderson | | |
| 1/15/77 | **29** | 9 | 4 Betcha By Golly Wow ..................... | 102 | Buddah 554 |
| | | | featuring Phyllis Hyman | | |
| 5/21/77 | **16** | 14 | 5 Once I've Been There ..................... | | Buddah 570 |
| | | | vocal by Prince Phillip Mitchell | | |
| 7/08/78 | **31** | 12 | 6 This Is Your Life ......................... | | Arista 0343 |
| 9/13/80 | **28** | 11 | 7 Take It To The Limit ..................... | | Arista 0548 |
| 12/06/80+ | **20** | 16 | 8 Melancholy Fire ........................... | | Arista 0581 |
| 1/23/82 | **86** | 2 | 9 She's Gone ................................. | | Arista 0632 |
| 3/05/88 | **26** | 14 | 10 I Am Your Melody ....................... | | Capitol 44110 |
| | | | NORMAN CONNORS featuring SPENCER HARRISON | | |
| | | | **JUNE CONQUEST - see DONNY HATHAWAY** | | |
| | | | **CONSUMER RAPPORT** | | |
| | | | New York studio group, featuring Frank Floyd (pit singer in Broadway show "The Wiz") | | |
| 5/03/75 | **19** | 14 | 1 Ease On Down The Road ................. | 42 | Wing & Prayer 101 |
| | | | from the Broadway musical "The Wiz" | | |
| | | | **THE CONTINENTAL 4** | | |
| | | | Group consisting of Freddie Kelly (falsetto lead), Ronnie McGregor and Larry McGregor (tenors), and Anthony Burke (baritone). | | |
| 3/13/71 | **49** | 2 | 1 I Don't Have You ......................... | | Jay Walking 009 |
| 5/29/71 | **19** | 8 | 2 Day By Day (Every Minute Of The Hour) .......... | 84 | Jay Walking 011 |
| | | | **THE CONTOURS** | | |
| | | | Group formed in Detroit; led by Dennis Edwards, who joined the Temptations in 1968. Other members included Billy Gordon, Billy Hoggs, Joe Billingslea, Sylvester Potts, Huey Davis (guitar), and Hubert Johnson (d: 7/11/81). | | |
| 8/25/62 | **1**³ | 17 | 1 Do You Love Me ........................... | 3 | Gordy 7005 |
| 1/26/63 | **21** | 4 | 2 Shake Sherry ............................... | 43 | Gordy 7012 |
| 4/04/64 | **41** | 6 | 3 Can You Do It .............................. | Hot | Gordy 7029 |
| 1/30/65 | **15** | 3 | 4 Can You Jerk Like Me/ ................... | 47 | Gordy 7037 |
| 1/30/65 | **37** | 1 | 5   That Day When She Needed Me ...... | | Gordy 7037 |
| 8/21/65 | **12** | 11 | 6 First I Look At The Purse ............... | 57 | Gordy 7044 |
| 6/18/66 | **18** | 6 | 7 Just A Little Misunderstanding ........ | 85 | Gordy 7052 |
| 4/15/67 | **35** | 7 | 8 It's So Hard Being A Loser .............. | 79 | Gordy 7059 |
| | | | **THE CONTROLLERS** | | |
| | | | Group from Fairfield, Alabama, formed in 1965 as the Epics. Became the Soul Controllers in 1970. Consisted of Reginald and Larry McArthur, Lenard Brown and Ricky Lewis. Most songs written by David Camon (keyboards). Later based in Miami. | | |
| 8/14/76 | **82** | 5 | 1 The People Want Music ................... | | Juana 3406 |

| DEBUT DATE | PEAK POS | WKS CHR | ARTIST — Record Title | POP POS | Label & Number |
|---|---|---|---|---|---|
| | | | **THE CONTROLLERS — Continued** | | |
| 10/15/77 | **8** | 19 | 2 Somebody's Gotta Win, Somebody's Gotta Lose........................ | *102* | Juana 3414 |
| 2/25/78 | **37** | 10 | 3 Heaven Is Only One Step Away...................... | | Juana 3416 |
| 12/23/78+ | **65** | 9 | 4 If Somebody Cares......................... | | Juana 3419 |
| 9/29/79 | **90** | 4 | 5 I Can't Turn The Boogie Loose .................. | | Juana 3424 |
| 2/02/80 | **43** | 9 | 6 We Don't ...................... | | Juana 3426 |
| 4/24/82 | **76** | 5 | 7 My Love Is Real ...................... | | Juana 3701 |
| 9/01/84 | **30** | 14 | 8 Crushed ...................... | | MCA 52450 |
| 2/16/85 | **85** | 3 | 9 Just For You...................... | | MCA 52511 |
| | | | with Valerie DeNece | | |
| 3/22/86 | **12** | 16 | 10 Stay...................... | | MCA 52704 |
| 7/05/86 | **34** | 12 | 11 Distant Lover ...................... | | MCA 52865 |
| 8/29/87 | **24** | 12 | 12 Sleeping Alone ...................... | | MCA 53149 |
| 2/27/88 | **69** | 7 | 13 Play Time ...................... | | MCA 53214 |
| | | | **CONVERTION** | | |
| 2/21/81 | **90** | 5 | 1 Let's Do It ...................... | | Sam 5017 |
| | | | **THE CONWAY BROTHERS** | | |
| | | | Family group from Chicago. Consisted of brothers Huston (lead vocals, bass), James (guitar), Fredrick (keyboards) and Hiawatha (drums). Formed in 1976. | | |
| 7/06/85 | **81** | 5 | 1 Turn It Up...................... | | Paula 1245 |
| 3/15/86 | **81** | 5 | 2 Raise The Roof ...................... | | PBT 302 |
| 3/28/87 | **84** | 7 | 3 I Can't Fight It...................... | | Ichiban 112 |
| | | | **SAM COOKE** ★★**34**★★ | | |
| | | | Born on 1/22/35 in Chicago. Died from a gunshot wound on 12/11/64 (29) in Los Angeles. Son of a Baptist minister, sang in choir from age 6. His nephew is singer R.B. Greaves. Sam joined gospel group, the Highway Q.C.'s. Lead singer of the Soul Stirrers from 1950-56. First recorded secular songs in 1956 as "Dale Cook" on Specialty. String of hits on Keen label led to contract with RCA. Shot by female motel manager under mysterious circumstances. Considered by many as the definitive soul singer. | | |
| 10/21/57 | **1**⁶ | 18 | 1 **You Send Me** ...................... | *1* | Keen 34013 |
| | | | Best Seller #1(6) / Jockey #1(6) | | |
| | | | written by Sam's brother, Charles "L.C." Cooke | | |
| 12/23/57+ | **1**¹ | 10 | 2 **I'll Come Running Back To You**................... | *18* | Specialty 619 |
| | | | Jockey #1 / Best Seller #7 | | |
| 2/03/58 | **17** | 1 | 3 **Desire Me**/ | *47* | |
| | | | Best Seller #17 | | |
| 2/24/58 | **15** | 1 | 4 **(I Love You) For Sentimental Reasons**............ | *17* | Keen 4002 |
| | | | Jockey #15 | | |
| 4/07/58 | **7** | 2 | 5 **You Were Made For Me**/ | *39* | |
| | | | Jockey #7 | | |
| 4/07/58 | **10** | 2 | 6 **Lonely Island** ...................... | *26* | Keen 4009 |
| | | | Jockey #10 / Best Seller #15 | | |
| 8/25/58 | **4** | 17 | 7 **Win Your Love For Me**...................... | *22* | Keen 2006 |
| 12/01/58 | **12** | 15 | 8 Love You Most Of All ...................... | *26* | Keen 2008 |
| 3/09/59 | **2**² | 14 | 9 **Everybody Likes To Cha Cha Cha**................ | *31* | Keen 2018 |
| 7/13/59 | **13** | 6 | 10 Only Sixteen ...................... | *28* | Keen 2022 |
| 11/23/59 | **25** | 1 | 11 There, I've Said It Again ...................... | *81* | Keen 2105 |
| 4/11/60 | **22** | 2 | 12 Teenage Sonata ...................... | *50* | RCA 7701 |
| 6/06/60 | **2**² | 10 | 13 **Wonderful World** ...................... | *12* | Keen 2112 |
| 8/29/60 | **2**⁴ | 13 | 14 **Chain Gang** ...................... | *2* | RCA 7783 |
| 12/19/60 | **23** | 5 | 15 Sad Mood...................... | *29* | RCA 7816 |
| 4/03/61 | **25** | 4 | 16 That's It-I Quit-I'm Movin' On ...................... | *31* | RCA 7853 |
| 6/19/61 | **20** | 6 | 17 Cupid ...................... | *17* | RCA 7883 |
| 2/17/62 | **1**³ | 15 | 18 **Twistin' The Nite Away**...................... | *9* | RCA 7983 |
| 6/23/62 | **2**⁴ | 18 | 19 **Bring It On Home To Me**/ | *13* | |
| | | | backing vocal by Lou Rawls | | |
| 6/23/62 | **4** | 11 | 20 **Having A Party** ...................... | *17* | RCA 8036 |
| 10/20/62 | **2**¹ | 12 | 21 **Nothing Can Change This Love**/ | *12* | |
| 10/13/62 | **3** | 15 | 22 **Somebody Have Mercy**...................... | *70* | RCA 8088 |
| 2/09/63 | **2**¹ | 10 | 23 **Send Me Some Lovin'** ...................... | *13* | RCA 8129 |
| 5/11/63 | **1**¹ | 10 | 24 **Another Saturday Night**...................... | *10* | RCA 8164 |
| 8/10/63 | **4** | 11 | 25 **Frankie And Johnny** ...................... | *14* | RCA 8215 |

| DEBUT DATE | PEAK POS | WKS CHR | ARTIST — Record Title | POP POS | Label & Number |
|---|---|---|---|---|---|
| | | | **SAM COOKE — Continued** | | |
| 11/02/63 | **7** | 4 | 26 Little Red Rooster ...................................... | *11* | RCA 8247 |
| 1/25/64 | **11** | 10 | 27 Good News...................................... | *Hot* | RCA 8299 |
| 6/06/64 | **11** | 10 | 28 Good Times/ | *Hot* | |
| 6/13/64 | **35** | 8 | 29 Tennessee Waltz...................................... | *Hot* | RCA 8368 |
| | | | Hugo & Luigi produced all of above RCA recordings | | |
| 10/10/64 | **93** | 3 | 30 That's Where It's At/ | *Hot* | |
| 1/30/65 | **40** | 1 | 31 Cousin Of Mine ........................................... | *31* | RCA 8426 |
| 1/30/65 | **2**³ | 12 | 32 Shake/ | *7* | |
| 1/30/65 | **9** | 11 | 33 **A Change Is Gonna Come**........................... | *31* | RCA 8486 |
| 4/17/65 | **15** | 7 | 34 It's Got The Whole World Shakin' .................... | *41* | RCA 8539 |
| 8/14/65 | **18** | 9 | 35 Sugar Dumpling ....................................... | *32* | RCA 8631 |
| | | | **SAMONA COOKE** | | |
| 7/08/78 | **91** | 3 | 1 One Night Affair........................................... | | Mercury 74004 |
| | | | **THE COOKIE CREW** | | |
| 2/20/88 | **75** | 7 | 1 Females (Get On Up) ..................................... | | TVT 4009 |
| | | | **THE COOKIES** | | |
| | | | Female trio consisting of Margie Hendrix, Ethel "Earl-Jean" McCrea and Pat Lyles. First recorded for Lamp (Aladdin) Records in 1954. Brought to Atlantic Records by A&R man Jesse Stone in 1955. After three records under their own name and backing work for Atlantic artists, this trio became The Raeletts with Ray Charles. A new Cookies trio, with varying membership, began recording in 1962 on Dimension - featured Ethel McCrea. Did back-up work for Neil Sedaka, Carole King and Little Eva. Also see Joe Turner and Chuck Willis. | | |
| 3/31/56 | **9** | 2 | 1 **In Paradise** ............................................. | | Atlantic 1084 |
| | | | Juke Box #9 / Best Seller #12 | | |
| 12/01/62+ | **6** | 10 | 2 **Chains**................................................ | *17* | Dimension 1002 |
| 3/30/63 | **3** | 10 | 3 **Don't Say Nothin' Bad (About My Baby)** ........ | *7* | Dimension 1008 |
| 11/30/63+ | **33** | 11 | 4 Girls Grow Up Faster Than Boys ..................... | *Hot* | Dimension 1020 |
| | | | **LES COOPER & The Soul Rockers** | | |
| | | | Singer/pianist/arranger/leader, born on 3/15/31 in Norfolk, Virginia. In 1952, member of the vocal group, the Empires. In 1957, group included: Johnny Barnes (lead), Bobby Dunn and William Goodman. In 1957, they recorded as the Whirlers for Whirlin' Disc, then disbanded. Cooper became manager of the Charts and the Ladders. | | |
| 12/08/62 | **12** | 7 | 1 Wiggle Wobble............................................ [I] | *22* | Everlast 5019 |
| | | | tenor sax solo by Joe Grier (former lead singer of the Charts) | | |
| | | | **MICHAEL COOPER** | | |
| | | | Singer/guitarist/songwriter/producer born and raised in Vallejo, California. Formed Project Soul while in high school in 1968. Changed group name to Con Funk Shun in 1972. Cooper went solo in 1986. | | |
| 11/07/87+ | **3** | 20 | 1 **To Prove My Love** ....................................... | | Warner 28200 |
| 4/16/88 | **24** | 12 | 2 Dinner For Two............................................ | | Warner 27934 |
| | | | **VIVIAN COPELAND** | | |
| 11/29/69 | **38** | 2 | 1 He Knows The Key (Is Always In The Mailbox).... | | D'Oro 3500 |
| | | | **CORNBREAD & BISCUITS** | | |
| | | | Comedy duo. | | |
| 10/24/60 | **25** | 3 | 1 The Big Time Spender.................................. [C] | *75* | Maske 102 |
| | | | backing music by Lea Lendon | | |
| | | | **CORNELIUS BROTHERS & SISTER ROSE** | | |
| | | | Family group from Dania, Florida. Consisted of Edward, Carter and Rose. Billie Jo was added in 1973. All 15 Cornelius children play instruments or sing. | | |
| 6/12/71 | **20** | 8 | 1●Treat Her Like A Lady .................................. | *3* | United Art. 50721 |
| 6/10/72 | **5** | 13 | 2●Too Late To Turn Back Now ......................... | *2* | United Art. 50910 |
| 9/30/72 | **28** | 7 | 3 Don't Ever Be Lonely (A Poor Little Fool Like Me)...................................................... | *23* | United Art. 50954 |
| 1/27/73 | **43** | 3 | 4 I'm Never Gonna Be Alone Anymore................ | *37* | United Art. 50996 |
| 10/20/73 | **79** | 5 | 5 I Just Can't Stop Loving You.......................... | *104* | United Art. 313 |
| 2/02/74 | **88** | 4 | 6 Big Time Lover ....................................... | | United Art. 377 |
| 12/21/74+ | **59** | 10 | 7 Since I Found My Baby............................... | | United Art. 534 |

| DEBUT DATE | PEAK POS | WKS CHR | ARTIST — Record Title | POP POS | Label & Number |
|---|---|---|---|---|---|
| | | | **CORNER BOYS** | | |
| | | | Group consisting of Victor Drayton, Jerry Akines, Johnny Bellmon and Reginald Turner. Originally called the Formations, also recorded as Silent Majority and Hot Ice. | | |
| 8/09/69 | **46** | 3 | 1 Gang War (Don't Make Sense)......................... | | Neptune 13 |
| | | | **CORONETS** | | |
| | | | Group consisting of Charles Carothers (lead), Lester Russaw (first tenor), Sam Griggs (second tenor), George Lewis (second tenor) and William Griggs (bass). Carothers was replaced by Bobby Ward in 1955. | | |
| 9/19/53 | **3** | 10 | 1 **Nadine**................................................... | | Chess 1549 |
| | | | Juke Box #3 written by disc jockey Alan Freed | | |
| | | | **THE CORSAIRS** | | |
| | | | Vocal quartet from North Carolina consisting of brothers Jay "Bird" (lead singer), James and Moses Uzzell with cousin George Wooten. First recorded for Smash in 1961. | | |
| 1/13/62 | **10** | 16 | 1 **Smoky Places**.............................................. | *12* | Tuff 1808 |
| 5/12/62 | **26** | 2 | 2 I'll Take You Home...................................... | *68* | Tuff 1818 |
| | | | **DAVE "BABY" CORTEZ** | | |
| | | | Born David Cortez Clowney on 8/13/38 in Detroit. Singer/songwriter/pianist/organist. In vocal group the Pearls from 1955-57. Frequent session work in New York. First recorded (as David Clowney) for Ember in 1956. | | |
| 4/13/59 | **5** | 13 | 1 **The Happy Organ** ..................................... [I] | *1* | Clock 1009 |
| 8/04/62 | **9** | 14 | 2 **Rinky Dink** ............................................ [I] | *10* | Chess 1829 |
| 6/16/73 | **45** | 3 | 3 Someone Has Taken Your Place...................... | | All Platinum 2343 |
| | | | **BILL COSBY** | | |
| | | | Born on 7/12/38 in Philadelphia. Top comedian of records, nightclubs, film and TV. His first 7 comedy albums were all million sellers. Played Alexander Scott on TV series "I Spy". Star of the #1 NBC-TV series "The Cosby Show". | | |
| 9/09/67 | **18** | 9 | 1 Little Ole Man (Uptight-Everything's Alright).. [N] | *4* | Warner 7072 |
| 5/01/76 | **11** | 13 | 2 Yes, Yes, Yes............................................. [C] | *46* | Capitol 4258 |
| 7/31/76 | **59** | 7 | 3 I Luv Myself Better Than I Luv Myself .......... [C] | | Capitol 4299 |
| | | | **COSMIC ECHOES - see LONNIE LISTON SMITH** | | |
| | | | **CLIFFORD COULTER** | | |
| | | | Vocalist discovered by Bill Withers. | | |
| 5/17/80 | **85** | 3 | 1 Don't Wanna See You Cry............................. | | Columbia 11202 |
| | | | **COUNTRY BOYS & CITY GIRLS FEATURING LEE MAYE** | | |
| | | | Arthur Lee Maye was born in Alabama, raised in Los Angeles. Played major league baseball with the Milwaukee Braves and Washington Senators. First recorded for RPM in 1955. | | |
| 10/16/76 | **99** | 2 | 1 Forgetting Someone..................................... | | Happy Fox 511 |
| | | | **THE COUNTS** | | |
| | | | Vocal quintet from Indianapolis. | | |
| 3/20/54 | **6** | 5 | 1 **Darling Dear** ........................................... | | Dot 1188 |
| | | | Juke Box #6 / Best Seller #9 | | |
| | | | **LOU COURTNEY** | | |
| 1/07/67 | **13** | 10 | 1 Skate Now ................................................ | *71* | Riverside 4588 |
| 4/08/67 | **17** | 10 | 2 Do The Thing ............................................ | *80* | Riverside 4589 |
| 7/15/67 | **46** | 4 | 3 You Ain't Ready ......................................... | | Riverside 4591 |
| 12/02/67 | **43** | 5 | 4 Hey Joyce................................................. | | Pop Side 4594 |
| 9/01/73 | **48** | 14 | 5 What Do You Want Me To Do .......................... | | Epic 11062 |
| 3/09/74 | **67** | 7 | 6 I Don't Need Nobody Else.............................. | | Epic 11088 |
| | | | **DON COVAY** | | |
| | | | Born in March of 1938 in Orangeburg, South Carolina. Singer/songwriter. Member of the Rainbows, recorded in 1956 for Pilgrim. Recorded as "Pretty Boy" with Little Richard's band for Atlantic in 1957. Formed group, The Goodtimers, in 1960. Wrote "Pony Time", "Chain Of Fools", "Sookie Sookie" and "See Saw". Also see The Soul Clan. | | |
| 9/05/64 | **35** | 10 | 1 Mercy, Mercy............................................. | *Hot* | Rosemart 801 |
| 12/26/64 | **97** | 2 | 2 Take This Hurt Off Me................................. | *Hot* | Rosemart 802 |
| 6/12/65 | **21** | 9 | 3 Please Do Something .................................... | | Atlantic 2286 |
| 11/06/65 | **5** | 15 | 4 **See Saw**................................................. | *44* | Atlantic 2301 |
| | | | 1, 3 & 4: **DON COVAY & THE GOODTIMERS** | | |
| 2/25/67 | **50** | 2 | 5 Shingaling '67 ........................................... | *133* | Atlantic 2375 |

| DEBUT DATE | PEAK POS | WKS CHR | ARTIST — Record Title | POP POS | Label & Number |
|---|---|---|---|---|---|
| | | | **DON COVAY — Continued** | | |
| 1/31/70 | 43 | 2 | 6 Black Women ..................... | | Atlantic 2666 |
| 6/30/73 | 6 | 13 | 7 **I Was Checkin' Out She Was Checkin' In**........ | | Mercury 73385 |
| 11/03/73 | 63 | 11 | 8 Somebody's Been Enjoying My Home ............... | | Mercury 73430 |
| 5/04/74 | 21 | 14 | 9 It's Better To Have (And Don't Need)................. | 63 | Mercury 73469 |
| 2/01/75 | 83 | 6 | 10 Rumble In The Jungle.................... | | Mercury 73648 |
| 7/19/80 | 74 | 6 | 11 Badd Boy......................... | | Newman 500 |
| | | | **THE COVER GIRLS** | | |
| | | | New York City-based black female dance trio: Louise "Angel" Sabater, Sunshine Wright and Caroline Jackson. | | |
| 2/21/87 | 34 | 14 | 1 Show Me......... ................... | 44 | Fever 1911 |
| 7/18/87 | 82 | 6 | 2 Spring Love.................... | 98 | Fever 1913 |
| 10/31/87 | 47 | 14 | 3 Because Of You ............... | 27 | Fever 1914 |
| | | | **FLOYD CRAMER** | | |
| | | | Nashville's top session pianist. Born on 10/27/33 in Shreveport, Louisiana. | | |
| 10/24/60 | 3 | 15 | 1 **Last Date** ....................... [I] | 2 | RCA 7775 |
| 4/24/61 | 16 | 5 | 2 On The Rebound ................. [I] | 4 | RCA 7840 |
| | | | **CAROLYN CRAWFORD** | | |
| | | | Won Motown recording contract at WCHB-Detroit Talent Contest in 1963. Later with Hodges, James, And Smith. Joined Chapter 8 in 1975; went solo in 1976. | | |
| 2/13/65 | 39 | 1 | 1 My Smile Is Just A Frown (Turned Upside Down) | | Motown 1064 |
| 1/06/79 | 66 | 6 | 2 Coming On Strong ........................ | | Mercury 74036 |
| | | | **RANDY CRAWFORD** | | |
| | | | Born Veronica Crawford on 2/18/52 in Macon, Georgia and raised in Cincinnati. Recorded and toured Europe with Crusaders. Most Outstanding Performance award at Tokyo Music Festival in 1980. | | |
| 7/28/79 | 17 | 16 | 1 Street Life ......................... | 36 | MCA 41054 |
| | | | CRUSADERS/RANDY CRAWFORD | | |
| 4/26/80 | 34 | 10 | 2 Same Old Story (Same Old Song) ..................... | | Warner 49222 |
| 7/05/80 | 68 | 5 | 3 Last Dance At Danceland ...................... | | Warner 49276 |
| 4/25/81 | 58 | 11 | 4 When I Lose My Way ................. | | Warner 49709 |
| 7/25/81 | 70 | 6 | 5 Secret Combination ...................... | | Warner 49767 |
| 5/29/82 | 50 | 11 | 6 One Hello................................ | 110 | Warner 29998 |
| | | | from the film "I Ought To Be In Pictures" | | |
| 9/04/82 | 68 | 5 | 7 Look Who's Lonely Now ................. | | Warner 29987 |
| 10/09/82 | 16 | 15 | 8 Your Precious Love ...................... | 102 | Warner 29893 |
| | | | AL JARREAU & RANDY CRAWFORD | | |
| 2/05/83 | 69 | 6 | 9 Imagine ............................. | 108 | Warner 29801 |
| 8/27/83 | 29 | 11 | 10 Nightline ......................... | | Warner 29530 |
| 6/28/86 | 58 | 10 | 11 Can't Stand The Pain ................. | | Warner 28664 |
| 10/25/86 | 90 | 4 | 12 Desire ............................ | | Warner 28583 |
| | | | **THE CRAWLERS - see ALVIN CASH** | | |
| | | | **PEE WEE CRAYTON** | | |
| | | | Born Connie Curtis Crayton on 12/18/14 in Rockdale, Texas. Singer/guitarist. Moved to Los Angeles in 1935. Formed own trio in 1945. First recorded for Four Star in 1947. Recorded with the Red Callender Sextet in 1954. Died of a heart attack on 6/25/85 in Los Angeles. | | |
| 10/23/48 | 1[3] | 13 | 1 **Blues After Hours**.......................... | | Modern 624 |
| | | | Juke Box #1(3) / Best Seller #1(1) | | |
| 12/25/48+ | 5 | 10 | 2 **Texas Hop**.......................... | | Modern 643 |
| | | | Best Seller #5 / Juke Box #5 | | |
| 7/16/49 | 6 | 11 | 3 **I Love You So** ...................... | | Modern 675 |
| | | | Juke Box #6 / Best Seller #7 | | |
| | | | **CREATIVE SOURCE** | | |
| | | | Vocal/dance group from Los Angeles, formed in 1972. Consisted of Don Wyatt, Celeste Rhodes, Steve Flanagan, Barbara Berryman and Barbara Lewis. Formed by Ron Townson of the Fifth Dimension. Wyatt had been in the Colts (in 1958) and the Fortunes (in 1959) and with Nat Cole's back-up group. Lewis had been in the Elgins. | | |
| 8/25/73 | 48 | 12 | 1 You Can't Hide Love ...................... | 114 | Sussex 501 |
| 1/05/74 | 88 | 6 | 2 You're Too Good To Be True ............... | 108 | Sussex 508 |
| 3/02/74 | 21 | 16 | 3 Who Is He And What Is He To You ................. | 69 | Sussex 509 |
| 2/22/75 | 62 | 7 | 4 Migration ............................ | | Sussex 632 |
| 12/20/75 | 92 | 3 | 5 Pass The Feelin' On ...................... | | Polydor 14291 |

| DEBUT DATE | PEAK POS | WKS CHR | ARTIST — Record Title | POP POS | Label & Number |
|---|---|---|---|---|---|
| | | | **CREME D' COCOA** Philadelphia quartet: Jennifer Holmes Johnson, Herley Johnson, Orlando Oliphant and Bobby Todd. The male singers had all been in the Ambassadors; Jennifer was a member of the Ebonys. | | |
| 10/14/78 | 63 | 8 | 1 Do What You Feel .......................................... | | Venture 102 |
| 4/14/79 | 38 | 12 | 2 Mr. Me, Mrs. You............................................. | | Venture 106 |
| 9/22/79 | 30 | 10 | 3 Doin' The Dog................................................. | | Venture 112 |
| 1/19/80 | 47 | 9 | 4 I Don't Ever (Wanna Love Nobody But You)........ | | Venture 118 |
| | | | **THE CRESCENDOS** Vocal quartet from Nashville. Dale Ward, lead singer. | | |
| 1/27/58 | 4 | 12 | 1 **Oh, Julie** .................................................. Best Seller #4 / Jockey #9 | 5 | Nasco 6005 |
| | | | **THE CRESTS** New York City vocal group formed in 1955. Consisted of lead singer Johnny Mastrangelo (Maestro - shown as Mastro on all Crests' hits), Harold Torres, Talmadge Gough, J.T. Carter and Patricia Van Dross. Discovered by Al Browne, first recorded for Joyce in 1957. Van Dross left group in 1958. Mastrangelo left for solo work as Johnny Maestro in 1960, replaced by James Ancrum. Maestro later formed the Brooklyn Bridge. | | |
| 1/12/59 | 4 | 11 | 1 **16 Candles** ................................................ | 2 | Coed 506 |
| 5/25/59 | 17 | 4 | 2 Six Nights A Week........................................... | 28 | Coed 509 |
| 10/05/59 | 14 | 8 | 3 The Angels Listened In ................................. | 22 | Coed 515 |
| | | | **THE CRICKETS** Pop quartet led by Buddy Holly (b: Charles Hardin Holley on 9/7/36 in Lubbock, Texas). In February of 1957, Buddy assembled his backing group, The Crickets: Jerry Allison (drums), Niki Sullivan (rhythm guitar) and Joel B. Maudlin (bass). Recorded at Norman Petty's studio in Clovis, New Mexico. Because of contract arrangements, all Brunswick records were released as The Crickets, and all Coral records were released as Buddy Holly. Holly split from The Crickets in autumn of 1958. Holly, Ritchie Valens and the Big Bopper were killed in a plane crash near Mason City, Iowa on 2/3/59. | | |
| 9/09/57 | 2¹ | 11 | 1●**That'll Be The Day** ................................... Best Seller #2 / Jockey #5 | 1 | Brunswick 55009 |
| 12/02/57+ | 2¹ | 14 | 2 **Peggy Sue** ................................................ shown only as: **BUDDY HOLLY** Best Seller #2 / Jockey #4 first known as "Cindy Lou"; renamed after Allison's girlfriend | 3 | Coral 61885 |
| 12/23/57 | 13 | 5 | 3 Oh, Boy! .................................................... Jockey #13 / Best Seller #15 | 10 | Brunswick 55035 |
| 3/17/58 | 4 | 6 | 4 **Maybe Baby** .............................................. Jockey #4 / Best Seller #8 all of above: produced by Norman Petty | 17 | Brunswick 55053 |
| | | | **CRICKETS** Group formed in the Bronx, in 1951. Consisted of Grover "Dean" Barlow (lead), Harold Johnson (tenor, guitar), Eugene Stapleton (tenor), Leon Carter (baritone), and Rodney Jackson (bass). Contracted to Joe Davis, who sold some of their material to MGM in 1953 and then recorded them for his own labels. The original group only recorded together for six months. A second Crickets group containing Barlow made a few sessions for Joe Davis in 1954. Barlow left for a solo career. Not to be confused with Buddy Holly's group of the same name. | | |
| 7/04/53 | 10 | 1 | 1 **You're Mine** ............................................... Juke Box #10 | | MGM 11428 |
| | | | **G.L. CROCKETT** Blues singer, born George L. Crockett in Carrollton, Mississippi, around 1929. Died in Chicago on 2/15/67. | | |
| 7/10/65 | 10 | 13 | 1 **It's A Man Down There**............................... | 67 | 4 Brothers 445 |
| | | | **GENERAL CROOK** Born on 2/28/45 in Mt. Byou and raised in Greenville, Mississippi. Moved to Chicago in 1963. First recorded for Capitol in 1969. Composed, arranged and produced all of his hits. | | |
| 8/22/70 | 22 | 11 | 1 Gimme Some (Part 1) ..................................... | | Down To Earth 73 |
| 12/26/70+ | 37 | 4 | 2 Do It For Me ................................................. | | Down To Earth 74 |
| 11/06/71 | 31 | 8 | 3 What Time It Is ............................................. | | Down To Earth 77 |
| 10/06/73 | 71 | 9 | 4 The Best Years Of My Life ............................. | 108 | Wand 11260 |
| 3/30/74 | 57 | 11 | 5 Tell Me What'Cha Gonna Do............................ | | Wand 11270 |
| 7/20/74 | 59 | 10 | 6 There's Fever In The Funkhouse...................... | | Wand 11276 |
| | | | **BEVERLY CROSBY** | | |
| 6/11/77 | 77 | 4 | 1 You Can Be My Lover .................................... | | Bareback 526 |

| DEBUT DATE | PEAK POS | WKS CHR | ARTIST — Record Title | POP POS | Label & Number |
|---|---|---|---|---|---|

## BING CROSBY

The most popular entertainer of the 20th century's first 50 years. Harry Lillis Crosby was born on 5/2/01 (or 04) in Tacoma, Washington. He and singing partner Al Rinker were hired in 1926 by Paul Whiteman; with Harry Barris they became the Rhythm Boys and gained an increasing following. The trio split from Whiteman in 1930, and Bing sang briefly with Gus Arnheim's band. It was his early-1931 smash with Arnheim, "I Surrender, Dear", which earned Bing a CBS radio contract, and launched an unsurpassed solo career. Over the next three decades the resonant Crosby baritone and breezy persona sold more than 300 million records and was featured in over 50 movies (won Academy Award for "Going My Way", 1944). Bing died of a heart attack on a golf course on 10/14/77.

| DEBUT DATE | PEAK POS | WKS CHR | ARTIST — Record Title | POP POS | Label & Number |
|---|---|---|---|---|---|
| 11/14/42 | 1³ | 9 | 1 White Christmas ..................... [X] <br> from the film "Holiday Inn"; <br> the biggest-selling record of all time with total sales through <br> the years of over 30 million; selected for the NARAS Hall Of Fame | 1 | Decca 18429 |
| 9/11/43 | 3 | 8 | 2 Sunday, Monday, or Always .................. <br> above 2: with the Ken Darby Singers; from the film "Dixie"; | 1 | Decca 18561 |
| 11/13/43 | 3 | 6 | 3 Pistol Packin' Mama ................... <br> BING CROSBY & the ANDREWS SISTERS | 2 | Decca 23277 |
| 1/01/44 | 8 | 1 | 4 I'll Be Home For Christmas.................. [X] <br> with John Scott Trotter's Orchestra | 3 | Decca 18570 |
| 1/01/44 | 9 | 1 | 5 White Christmas ............... [X-R] | 6 | Decca 18429 |
| 1/20/45 | 9 | 1 | 6 Don't Fence Me In................... <br> BING CROSBY & ANDREWS SISTERS <br> from the film "Hollywood Canteen"; <br> all of above: reported million-sellers | 1 | Decca 23364 |

## ANDRE CROUCH

Born on 7/1/42 in Los Angeles. With twin sister Sandra in choir of Church Of God In Christ (COGIC). Teamed with Perry Morgan in group, the Disciples. Also see Michael Jackson.

| DEBUT DATE | PEAK POS | WKS CHR | ARTIST — Record Title | POP POS | Label & Number |
|---|---|---|---|---|---|
| 1/19/80 | 69 | 11 | 1 I'll Be Thinkin' Of You ................... <br> featuring Kristle Murden | | Light 655 |

## CROWD PLEASERS

Six-piece band from Detroit.

| DEBUT DATE | PEAK POS | WKS CHR | ARTIST — Record Title | POP POS | Label & Number |
|---|---|---|---|---|---|
| 5/12/79 | 71 | 9 | 1 Freaky People, Pt. 1 ................... | | Westbound 55420 |

## CROWN HEIGHTS AFFAIR

Disco group from Bedford-Stuyvesant, New York, formed as the Neu Day Express, and led by Phil Thomas (vocals). Group also included Bert Reid (tenor sax), James Baynard (trumpet), Raymond Reid (trombone), William Anderson (guitar), Howard Young (keyboards), Muki Wilson (bass) and Raymond Rock (vocals, drums).

| DEBUT DATE | PEAK POS | WKS CHR | ARTIST — Record Title | POP POS | Label & Number |
|---|---|---|---|---|---|
| 6/08/74 | 96 | 3 | 1 Leave The Kids Alone................... | | RCA 0243 |
| 6/14/75 | 5 | 18 | 2 Dreaming A Dream ................... | 43 | De-Lite 1570 |
| 11/29/75+ | 20 | 13 | 3 Every Beat Of My Heart ................... | 83 | De-Lite 1575 |
| 4/24/76 | 17 | 15 | 4 Foxy Lady ................... [I] | 49 | De-Lite 1581 |
| 1/29/77 | 16 | 14 | 5 Dancin' ................... | 42 | De-Lite 1588 |
| 7/23/77 | 60 | 8 | 6 Do It The French Way ................... | | De-Lite 1592 |
| 9/09/78 | 41 | 11 | 7 Say A Prayer For Two ................... | | De-Lite 908 |
| 3/10/79 | 20 | 12 | 8 Dance Lady Dance ................... | | De-Lite 912 |
| 3/29/80 | 74 | 7 | 9 You Gave Me Love................... | 102 | De-Lite 803 |
| 6/21/80 | 72 | 5 | 10 Sure Shot ................... | | De-Lite 805 |
| 8/07/82 | 31 | 9 | 11 Somebody Tell Me What To Do ................... | | De-Lite 821 |

## CROWS

Harlem group, formed in the early 50s. Consisted of Bill Davis (baritone-tenor, lead), Daniel "Sonny" Norton (lead), Harold Major (tenor), Gerald Hamilton (bass) and Mark Jackson (tenor, guitar). Discovered at Apollo Amateur Night.

| DEBUT DATE | PEAK POS | WKS CHR | ARTIST — Record Title | POP POS | Label & Number |
|---|---|---|---|---|---|
| 4/10/54 | 2² | 11 | 1 Gee ................... <br> Juke Box #2 / Best Seller #6 | 14 | Rama 5 |

## ARTHUR "BIG BOY" CRUDUP

Born on 8/24/05 in Forest, Mississippi. Died of a stroke on 3/28/74 in Nassawadox, Virginia (68). Singer/guitarist. Nicknamed "Big Boy". Sang in the gospel group Harmonizing Four in the 40s. First recorded for Bluebird in 1941. Toured with Sonny Boy Williamson and Elmore James. Inactive from 1953-59. Session for Fire in 1959; supposedly arranged for by Elvis Presley, who ranked Crudup as a major influence. Toured England in 1970; toured with Bonnie Raitt in 1974.

| DEBUT DATE | PEAK POS | WKS CHR | ARTIST — Record Title | POP POS | Label & Number |
|---|---|---|---|---|---|
| 5/05/45 | 3 | 8 | 1 Rock Me, Mama ................... | | Bluebird 0725 |
| 5/12/45 | 5 | 1 | 2 Who's Been Foolin' You ................... | | Bluebird 34-0725 |
| 12/29/45 | 3 | 1 | 3 Keep Your Arms Around Me................... | | Bluebird 0738 |
| 10/05/46 | 3 | 3 | 4 So Glad You're Mine/ | | |
| 11/09/46 | 4 | 2 | 5 Ethel Mae ................... | | Victor 1949 |

| DEBUT DATE | PEAK POS | WKS CHR | ARTIST — Record Title | POP POS | Label & Number |
|---|---|---|---|---|---|
| | | | **ARTHUR "BIG BOY" CRUDUP — Continued** | | |
| 11/03/51 | 9 | 2 | 6  I'm Gonna Dig Myself A Hole........................ | | RCA 0141 |
| | | | Juke Box #9 / Best Seller #10 | | |
| | | | **THE CRUSADERS** | | |
| | | | Instrumental jazz-oriented group formed in Houston, as the Swingsters, in the early 50s. To California in the early 60s, name changed to Jazz Crusaders. Became The Crusaders in 1971. Included Joe Sample (keyboards), Wilton Felder (reeds), Nesbert "Stix" Hooper (drums) and Wayne Henderson (trombone). | | |
| 5/13/72 | 39 | 9 | 1  Put It Where You Want It ........................... [I] | 52 | Blue Thumb 208 |
| 4/21/73 | 31 | 7 | 2  Don't Let It Get You Down....................... [I] | 86 | Blue Thumb 225 |
| 4/13/74 | 70 | 7 | 3  Scratch ............................................ [I] | 81 | Blue Thumb 249 |
| 2/15/75 | 41 | 10 | 4  Stomp And Buck Dance................................ | 102 | Blue Thumb 261 |
| 11/01/75 | 84 | 5 | 5  Creole ................................................ | | Blue Thumb 267 |
| 6/05/76 | 21 | 13 | 6  Keep That Same Old Feeling ......................... | | Blue Thumb 269 |
| 10/30/76 | 92 | 2 | 7  And Then There Was The Blues...................... | | Blue Thumb 270 |
| 6/11/77 | 63 | 7 | 8  Feel It .............................................. | | Blue Thumb 272 |
| 8/13/77 | 84 | 3 | 9  Free As The Wind ................................... | | Blue Thumb 273 |
| 9/23/78 | 93 | 4 | 10  Bayou Bottoms.................................... | | Blue Thumb 278 |
| 7/28/79 | 17 | 16 | 11  Street Life ....................................... | 36 | MCA 41054 |
| | | | **CRUSADERS/RANDY CRAWFORD** | | |
| 8/16/80 | 41 | 10 | 12  Soul Shadows .................................... | | MCA 41295 |
| 10/03/81 | 67 | 6 | 13  I'm So Glad I'm Standing Here Today................ | 97 | MCA 51177 |
| | | | **CRUSADERS Guest Artist - JOE COCKER** | | |
| 3/31/84 | 27 | 12 | 14  New Moves ........................................ | | MCA 52365 |
| 6/23/84 | 57 | 6 | 15  Dead End............................................ | | MCA 52398 |
| | | | **CRYSTAL GRASS** | | |
| 5/17/75 | 73 | 6 | 1  Crystal World .................................... | 102 | Polydor 15101 |
| 9/13/75 | 92 | 4 | 2  Love To Dance This One With You ................... | | Polydor 15109 |
| | | | **THE CRYSTALS** | | |
| | | | Female vocal group from Brooklyn. Consisted of Barbara Alston, Lala Brooks, Dee Dee Kennibrew, Mary Thomas and Patricia Wright. Discovered by producer Phil Spector. | | |
| 11/27/61 | 5 | 10 | 1  There's No Other (Like My Baby) ................... | 20 | Philles 100 |
| 6/02/62 | 18 | 3 | 2  Uptown ....................................... | 13 | Philles 102 |
| 10/06/62 | 2¹ | 10 | 3  He's A Rebel ..................................... | 1 | Philles 106 |
| | | | written by Gene Pitney | | |
| 1/26/63 | 18 | 6 | 4  He's Sure The Boy I Love.......................... | 11 | Philles 109 |
| | | | above 2: featuring Darlene Love (lead) and The Blossoms | | |
| 5/11/63 | 5 | 10 | 5  Da Doo Ron Ron (When He Walked Me Home) .. | 3 | Philles 112 |
| 8/31/63 | 8 | 9 | 6  Then He Kissed Me ..................................... | 6 | Philles 115 |
| 2/01/64 | 92 | 3 | 7  Little Boy ......................................... | Hot | Philles 119 |
| 8/01/64 | 98 | 1 | 8  All Grown Up ...................................... | Hot | Philles 122 |
| | | | **THE JOE CUBA SEXTET** | | |
| | | | Raunchy Latin-rock combo. | | |
| 8/06/66 | 44 | 4 | 1  El Pito (I'll Never Go Back To Georgia) .......... [F] | 115 | Tico 470 |
| 10/15/66 | 21 | 10 | 2  'Bang' 'Bang'............................................. [F] | 63 | Tico 475 |
| 12/31/66+ | 45 | 4 | 3  Oh Yeah! ...................................... | 62 | Tico 490 |
| | | | **CUCA** | | |
| 4/09/88 | 62 | 7 | 1  Young Love............................................ | | Alpha Int. 100 |
| | | | **XAVIER CUGAT** | | |
| | | | Born on 1/1/1900 in Barcelona, Spain. Bandleader/vocalist/composer/arranger. Specialized in Latin-American music since forming own band in the late 20s. Many appearances in movies, on radio and TV. Formerly married to Abbe Lane and Charo. | | |
| 4/17/43 | 9 | 1 | 1  Brazil............................................. | 2 | Columbia 36651 |
| | | | Brazilian samba ("Aquarelo do Brasil"); from the animated film "Saludos Amigos" | | |

| DEBUT DATE | PEAK POS | WKS CHR | ARTIST — Record Title | POP POS | Label & Number |
|---|---|---|---|---|---|
| | | | **FRANK CULLEY** Tenor saxophonist, born in Salisbury, Maryland on 8/7/18; raised in Norfolk, Virginia. Nicknamed "Cole Slaw" and "Floorshow". First recorded for Lenox in 1948. Recorded with Wynonie Harris and formed own band with pianist Van "Piano Man" Walls. Much studio work for Atlantic Records in the early 50s. Recorded with Jimmy Rushing for Parrot in 1953. | | |
| 5/14/49 | 11 | 3 | 1 Cole Slaw .................................................. Juke Box #11 / Best Seller #12 "Sorghum Switch" is the original title of this 1942 tune | | Atlantic 874 |
| 12/24/49+ | 10 | 4 | 2 **After Hour Session** ................................... Best Seller #10 / Juke Box #12 | | Atlantic 888 |
| | | | **CULTURE CLUB** Formed in London, in 1981. Consisted of George "Boy George" O'Dowd (b: 6/14/61), vocals; Roy Hay, guitar, keyboards; Mikey Craig, bass; and Jon Moss, drums. Designer Sue Clowes originated distinctive costuming for the group. | | |
| 2/12/83 | 39 | 14 | 1 Do You Really Want To Hurt Me ..................... | 2 | Epic/Virgin 03368 |
| 5/07/83 | 34 | 13 | 2 Time (Clock Of The Heart)............................. | 2 | Epic/Virgin 03796 |
| 8/13/83 | 70 | 6 | 3 I'll Tumble 4 Ya .......................................... | 9 | Epic/Virgin 03912 |
| 2/25/84 | 67 | 4 | 4●Karma Chameleon........................................ | 1 | Epic/Virgin 04221 |
| 3/17/84 | 8 | 15 | 5 **Miss Me Blind** ........................................... backing vocal by Jermaine Stewart | 5 | Epic/Virgin 04388 |
| 6/09/84 | 75 | 4 | 6 It's A Miracle.............................................. | 13 | Epic/Virgin 04457 |
| 10/27/84 | 87 | 3 | 7 The War Song............................................. | 17 | Epic/Virgin 04638 |
| 12/22/84+ | 61 | 10 | 8 Mistake No. 3 ............................................. | 33 | Epic/Virgin 04727 |
| 5/10/86 | 87 | 2 | 9 Move Away ................................................. | 12 | Epic/Virgin 05847 |
| | | | **CLIFFORD CURRY** Member of the Echoes vocal group at Austin high in Knoxville, Tennessee. Recorded as the Five Pennies for Savoy in 1955. Own group, the Bingos, in 1956. Recorded as the Hollyhocks for Excello/Nasco in 1957. With the Bubba Suggs band from 1959-64. Recorded as Sweet Clifford for Excello in 1963. With the Fabulous Six, Contenders from 1964-67. Solo from 1967. | | |
| 5/20/67 | 45 | 3 | 1 She Shot A Hole In My Soul ........................... | 95 | Elf 90002 |
| | | | **LOUIS CURRY** | | |
| 6/01/68 | 27 | 4 | 1 A Toast To You ........................................... | | M-S 203 |
| | | | **MINI CURRY** Singer/songwriter from Detroit. | | |
| 6/27/87 | 34 | 11 | 1 I Think I'm Over You ................................... | | Total Exp. 2707 |
| | | | **CHANTAL CURTIS** | | |
| 8/11/79 | 86 | 5 | 1 Get Another Love.......................................... | | Keylock 7200 |
| | | | **THE CUT** | | |
| 10/11/86 | 77 | 5 | 1 Kindness For Weakness ............................... | | Supertronics 015 |
| | | | **CYBOTRON** Detroit trio. | | |
| 8/27/83 | 52 | 9 | 1 Clear ........................................................ | | Fantasy 939 |
| | | | **CYMANDE** 8-man, afro-rock band from the West Indies. | | |
| 1/27/73 | 22 | 9 | 1 The Message .............................................. | 48 | Janus 203 |
| 6/30/73 | 51 | 5 | 2 Bra .......................................................... | 102 | Janus 215 |
| | | | **THE CYMBALS - see LEE WILLIAMS** | | |
| | | | **ANDRE CYMONE** Born Andre Simon Anderson in Minneapolis. Former bass player of Prince's band, The Revolution. Went solo in 1981. | | |
| 8/21/82 | 79 | 4 | 1 Livin' In The New Wave................................. | | Columbia 03037 |
| 11/20/82 | 72 | 5 | 2 Kelly's Eyes ............................................... | 107 | Columbia 03301 |
| 9/17/83 | 37 | 11 | 3 Make Me Wanna Dance ................................. | | Columbia 04066 |
| 8/03/85 | 10 | 15 | 4 **The Dance Electric** .................................... | | Columbia 05435 |
| 12/07/85 | 63 | 9 | 5 Lipstick Lover ............................................. | | Columbia 05710 |
| 3/01/86 | 75 | 4 | 6 Satisfaction................................................. | | Columbia 05787 |
| | | | **CYRE'** Actress/songwriter/commercial jingle singer raised in the Bronx. | | |
| 4/04/87 | 60 | 8 | 1 Last Chance................................................. | | Fresh 8 |

| DEBUT DATE | PEAK POS | WKS CHR | ARTIST — Record Title | POP POS | Label & Number |
|---|---|---|---|---|---|

# D

### da'KRASH
Funk quintet formed in 1981 in East St. Louis. Discovered by Jesse Johnson (The Time). 1988 lineup: Robert Jordan (vocals), Brian Tate, Edgar Hinton, Dee Dee James and Gabriel Acevedo.

| | | | | | |
|---|---|---|---|---|---|
| 1/23/88 | 5 | 16 | 1 **Wasn't I Good To Ya?**.................................. | | Capitol 44107 |
| 6/11/88 | 80 | 4 | 2 Trapped In Phases............................................ | | Capitol 44147 |

### E.G. DAILY
Singer/actress Elizabeth Daily. In films "Pee-Wee's Big Adventure" & "Valley Girl".

| | | | | | |
|---|---|---|---|---|---|
| 5/10/86 | 71 | 8 | 1 Say It, Say It ................................................ | *70* | A&M 2825 |

### DALE & GRACE
Vocal duo of Dale Houston (of Ferriday, LA), & Grace Brossard (of Prairieville, LA).

| | | | | | |
|---|---|---|---|---|---|
| 11/02/63 | 6 | 4 | 1 **I'm Leaving It Up To You** ............................ | *1* | Montel 921 |

### DALTON & DUBARRI
Duo of Gary Dalton (bass, guitar) and Kent Dubarri (drums, percussion). First recorded for Columbia in 1973.

| | | | | | |
|---|---|---|---|---|---|
| 6/02/79 | 79 | 5 | 1 I (You) Can Dance All By My (Your) Self............. | | Hilltak 7806 |
| 9/15/79 | 76 | 5 | 2 Til The Day I Started Lovin' You...................... | | Hilltak 7902 |

### DAMARIS
New York City bilingual commercial jingle singer. Won grand prize in the 10th American Song Festival. Her name rhymes with "glamorous".

| | | | | | |
|---|---|---|---|---|---|
| 6/30/84 | 79 | 4 | 1 You Stopped Loving Me .................................. | | Columbia 04458 |

### TERRI DANCER

| | | | | | |
|---|---|---|---|---|---|
| 2/01/86 | 71 | 6 | 1 Learn From The Burn ................................... | | Reflection 001 |

### THE DANDERLIERS
Chicago group: Dallas Taylor (tenor), James Campbell (tenor), Bernard Dixon (first tenor), Walter Stephenson (baritone) and Richard Thomas (bass). Thomas was replaced by Louis Johnson after two records were released.

| | | | | | |
|---|---|---|---|---|---|
| 4/23/55 | 10 | 3 | 1 **Chop Chop Boom**...................................... | | States 147 |
| | | | Jockey #10 / Best Seller #14 | | |
| | | | with the Al Smith Orchestra; lead vocals by Dallas Taylor | | |

### DANA DANE
Anecdotal rapper and art alumnus of New York's High School of Music and Art. Rap partner is "DJ Clark Kent".

| | | | | | |
|---|---|---|---|---|---|
| 12/21/85+ | 21 | 19 | 1 Nightmares ................................................ | | Profile 5086 |
| 1/31/87 | 44 | 9 | 2 Delancey Street ........................................... | | Profile 5124 |
| 8/08/87 | 11 | 16 | 3 Cinderfella Dana Dane ................................. | | Profile 5151 |
| 11/28/87+ | 30 | 12 | 4 This Be The Def Beat .................................... | | Profile 5171 |

### THE DANLEERS
Quintet from Brooklyn consisting of Jimmy Weston (lead), Johnny Lee (first tenor), Willie Ephraim (second tenor), Nat McCune (baritone) and Roosevelt Mays (bass). Group named after their manager, Danny Webb, who wrote "One Summer Night". Name sometimes misspelled "Dandleers".

| | | | | | |
|---|---|---|---|---|---|
| 7/28/58 | 4 | 9 | 1 **One Summer Night**...................................... | *7* | Mercury 71322 |
| | | | Jockey #4 / Best Seller #11 | | |
| | | | original release on AMP-3 label by the Dandleers | | |

### DANNY & THE JUNIORS
Formed while at high school in Philadelphia in 1955 as the Juvenairs, with Danny Rapp (b: 5/10/41), lead; David White, first tenor; Frank Maffei, second tenor; and Joe Terranova, baritone. Danny Rapp committed suicide on 4/8/83 (41).

| | | | | | |
|---|---|---|---|---|---|
| 12/16/57+ | 1 [5] | 14 | 1 **At The Hop** ............................................... | *1* | ABC-Para. 9871 |
| | | | Best Seller #1 / Jockey #2 | | |
| 3/24/58 | 16 | 3 | 2 Rock And Roll Is Here To Stay ....................... | *19* | ABC-Para. 9888 |
| | | | Best Seller #16 | | |
| | | | with guest Freddy Cannon | | |

### THE DAPPS - see HANK BALLARD

### TERENCE TRENT D'ARBY
England-based singer born in New York City; raised in Florida. Last name is Darby.

| | | | | | |
|---|---|---|---|---|---|
| 9/26/87 | 19 | 12 | 1 If You Let Me Stay........................................ | *68* | Columbia 07398 |
| 1/16/88 | 1 [1] | 18 | 2 **Wishing Well** ............................................. | *1* | Columbia 07675 |
| 5/28/88 | 2 [2] | 18 | 3 **Sign Your Name** ........................................ | *4* | Columbia 07911 |

| DEBUT DATE | PEAK POS | WKS CHR | ARTIST — Record Title | POP POS | Label & Number |
|---|---|---|---|---|---|
| | | | **BOBBY DARIN** Vocalist/pianist/guitarist/drummer, born Walden Robert Cassotto on 5/14/36 in the Bronx. Died of heart failure on 12/20/73 (37) in Los Angeles. First recorded in 1956 with "The Jaybirds" (Decca). First appeared on TV, in March, 1956, on the Tommy Dorsey Show. Married to actress Sandra Dee, 1960-67. Nominated for an Oscar for his performance in the film "Captain Newman, MD". Formed own record company, Direction, in 1968. | | |
| 7/21/58 | 1 ² | 9 | 1 Splish Splash ............................... Jockey #1 / Best Seller #2 | 3 | Atco 6117 |
| 8/25/58 | 8 | 3 | 2 Early In The Morning ........................ THE RINKY-DINKS Jockey #8 / Best Seller #17 originally issued on Brunswick as by the Ding Dongs (to conceal Darin's identity who was under contract to Atco); Atco took over the master and re-issued it as The Rinky-Dinks | 24 | Atco 6121 |
| 10/13/58 | 6 | 13 | 3 Queen Of The Hop ............................ | 9 | Atco 6127 |
| 5/18/59 | 4 | 11 | 4 Dream Lover ................................. | 2 | Atco 6140 |
| 9/21/59 | 6 | 17 | 5 Mack The Knife ............................. written in 1928 as "Moritat" or "Theme From The Threepenny Opera" | 1 | Atco 6147 |
| 2/15/60 | 15 | 6 | 6 Beyond The Sea ............................. | 6 | Atco 6158 |
| 2/09/63 | 9 | 11 | 7 You're The Reason I'm Living .............. | 3 | Capitol 4897 |
| 7/06/63 | 28 | 1 | 8 18 Yellow Roses ............................ | 10 | Capitol 4970 |
| | | | **LARRY DARNELL** Vocalist/dancer, born Leo Edward Donald in 1929 in Columbus, Ohio. Died of cancer on 7/3/83 (53). With Brownskin Models revue during the mid-40s. Settled in New Orleans, working at the Dew Drop Inn. Along with Paul Gayten, Roy Brown, and Annie Laurie, was instrumental in the formation of the New Orleans style of R&B. In April of 1979, suffered severe injuries in a mugging in Akron, Ohio; in late 1980, a lung was removed due to cancer. | | |
| 11/12/49 | 1 ⁸ | 22 | 1 For You, My Love ........................... Juke Box #1(8) / Best Seller #1(6) written by Paul Gayten | | Regal 3240 |
| 11/12/49+ | 2 ¹ | 16 | 2 I'll Get Along Somehow (I & II) ........... Juke Box #2 / Best Seller #3 | | Regal 3236 |
| 2/11/50 | 8 | 2 | 3 Lost My Baby .............................. Juke Box #8 | | Regal 3240 |
| 8/05/50 | 4 | 8 | 4 I Love My Baby ............................. Best Seller #4 / Juke Box #10 | | Regal 3274 |
| 11/25/50 | 5 | 6 | 5 Oh Babe ................................... Best Seller #5 / Juke Box #5 | | Regal 3298 |
| | | | **THE DARTELLS** Oxnard, California band consisting of Dick Burns, Corky Wilkie, Rich Peil, Doug Phillips, Randy Ray and Gary Peeler. First recorded for Arlen in 1963. | | |
| 5/25/63 | 15 | 6 | 1 Hot Pastrami ............................... | 11 | Dot 16453 |
| | | | **SARAH DASH** Born on 8/18/43 in Trenton, NJ. Original member of The Blue-Belles and LaBelle. | | |
| 1/06/79 | 70 | 8 | 1 Sinner Man ................................. | 71 | Kirshner 4278 |
| 0/30/79 | 91 | 3 | 2 (Come And Take This) Candy From Your Baby ... | | Kirshner 4281 |
| | | | **BETTY DAVIS** Formerly married to Miles Davis. | | |
| 8/11/73 | 66 | 9 | 1 If I'm In Luck I Might Get Picked Up ................ | | Just Sunsh. 503 |
| 6/21/75 | 97 | 2 | 2 Shut Off The Lights ....................... | | Island 024 |
| | | | **BILLY DAVIS** Born on 6/26/39 in St. Louis. With Emeralds vocal group, recorded for Bobbin in 1959. Group later became the St. Louis Gospel Singers. Founding member of the Fifth Dimension. Married Marilyn McCoo in 1969; began recording as a duo in 1976. | | |
| 6/21/75 | 82 | 6 | 1 Three Steps From True Love ............... | | ABC 12106 |
| | | | **CARL DAVIS & THE CHI-SOUND ORCHESTRA** Studio band assembled by Carl Davis, an influential Chicago A&R man and producer. | | |
| 2/05/77 | 65 | 7 | 1 Windy City Theme ........................... | | Chi-Sound 904 |
| | | | **GEATER DAVIS** Southern singer; died in October of 1985. | | |
| 12/05/70+ | 45 | 6 | 1 Sweet Woman Love .......................... | | House Of O. 2401 |
| 7/14/73 | 64 | 7 | 2 Your Heart Is Gold ........................ | | Seventy 7 130 |

| DEBUT DATE | PEAK POS | WKS CHR | ARTIST — Record Title | POP POS | Label & Number |
|---|---|---|---|---|---|
| | | | **JOHN DAVIS & The Monster Orchestra** Singer/songwriter/producer/arranger, born on 8/31/52 in Philadelphia. Music degree at Philadelphia Music Academy. In US Naval Academy Band. Wrote score for Broadway musical "Gotta Go Disco". | | |
| 4/10/76 | 100 | 1 | 1  Night And Day ....................................... | *109* | Sam 5002 |
| 4/16/77 | 86 | 4 | 2  Up Jumped The Devil................................ | | Sam 5005 |
| | | | **MARTHA DAVIS** Vocalist/pianist born on 12/14/17 in Wichita, Kansas; raised in Chicago. "Queen Of The Ivories". Did comedy song routine with husband, Calvin Ponder as "Martha Davis & Spouse". Recorded for Jewel with a trio consisting of Ralph Williams (guitar), Calvin Ponder (bass) and Lee Young (drums). | | |
| 7/17/48 | 11 | 1 | 1  Little White Lies ................................... Juke Box #11 | | Jewel 2002 |
| 9/04/48 | 6 | 7 | 2  **Don't Burn The Candle At Both Ends** ........... Juke Box #6 | | Decca 24483 |
| 11/13/48 | 9 | 5 | 3  **Daddy-O** ........................................... Juke Box #9 above 2: featuring Louis Jordan | | Decca 24502 |
| | | | **MARY DAVIS** | | |
| 11/28/87 | 89 | 3 | 1  Steppin' Out........................................ | | Tabu 07612 |
| | | | **MIZ DAVIS** | | |
| 4/17/76 | 75 | 10 | 1  Sing A Happy Funky Song ........................... | | New 10 |
| | | | **RAINY DAVIS** Denise Lorraine Davis, born on Christmas Eve in Brooklyn. Singer/songwriter. | | |
| 4/19/86 | 24 | 19 | 1  Sweetheart ........................................ | | Supertronics 013 |
| 1/31/87 | 14 | 13 | 2  Lowdown So & So ................................... | | Columbia 06598 |
| 5/16/87 | 41 | 9 | 3  Still Waiting...................................... written by Prince | | Columbia 07072 |
| 6/18/88 | 41 | 9 | 4  Indian Giver ...................................... | | Columbia 07912 |
| | | | **RUTH DAVIS** Vocalist from Arkansas. Back-up singer for Ray Charles, Tina Turner, and Billy Preston. Recorded a string of hits in duo with Bo Kirkland, beginning in 1976. | | |
| 6/24/78 | 98 | 2 | 1  Lost In A Love Zone .................................. | | Claridge 434 |
| | | | **SAMMY DAVIS, JR.** Born on 12/8/25 in New York City. Vocalist/dancer/actor of Broadway, film and TV. With family dance act, the Will Mastin Trio, in the early 40s. | | |
| 11/30/63+ | 17 | 17 | 1  The Shelter Of Your Arms ........................... | *Hot* | Reprise 20216 |
| | | | **SKEETER DAVIS** Country singer, born Mary Penick on 12/30/31 in Dry Ridge, Kentucky. Recorded with friend Betty Davis as the Davis Sisters, until Betty was killed in a car accident on 8/2/53. Formerly married to TV's "Nashville Now" host, Ralph Emery. | | |
| 3/16/63 | 4 | 10 | 1  **The End Of The World**................................ produced by Chet Atkins | **2** | RCA 8098 |
| | | | **THE SPENCER DAVIS GROUP** White R&B-styled rock band formed in Birmingham, England in 1963: Spencer Davis, and Peter York, with brothers Steve (vocals) & Muff Winwood. Steve formed the rock group Traffic, and became successful solo pop artist. | | |
| 4/22/67 | 48 | 3 | 1  I'm A Man ........................................... | *10* | United Art. 50144 |
| | | | **TYRONE DAVIS**  ★★**30**★★ Born on 5/4/38 in Greenville, Mississippi; raised in Saginaw, Michigan. To Chicago in 1959. Worked as valet/chauffeur for Freddie King until 1962. Working local clubs when discovered by Harold Burrage. First recorded for Four Brothers, in 1965 as "Tyrone The Wonder Boy". His younger sister, Jean Davis, was a member of Facts Of Life. | | |
| 12/21/68+ | 1³ | 14 | 1 ● Can I Change My Mind ............................. | *5* | Dakar 602 |
| 3/29/69 | 5 | 9 | 2  **Is It Something You've Got** .......................... | *34* | Dakar 605 |
| 3/21/70 | 1² | 14 | 3 ● Turn Back The Hands Of Time...................... | *3* | Dakar 616 |
| 7/04/70 | 8 | 11 | 4  I'll Be Right Here ................................. | *53* | Dakar 618 |
| 10/03/70 | 12 | 9 | 5  Let Me Back In .................................... | *58* | Dakar 621 |
| 3/20/71 | 10 | 9 | 6  **Could I Forget You** ............................... | *60* | Dakar 623 |
| 7/03/71 | 18 | 8 | 7  One-Way Ticket ................................... | *75* | Dakar 624 |
| 10/30/71 | 15 | 7 | 8  You Keep Me Holding On ........................... | *94* | Dakar 626 |
| 3/04/72 | 5 | 11 | 9  **I Had It All The Time**.............................. | *61* | Dakar 4501 |
| 7/01/72 | 26 | 6 | 10  Was I Just A Fool................................. | | Dakar 4507 |

| DEBUT DATE | PEAK POS | WKS CHR | ARTIST — Record Title | POP POS | Label & Number |
|---|---|---|---|---|---|
| | | | **TYRONE DAVIS — Continued** | | |
| 10/28/72 | **28** | 9 | 11  If You Had A Change In Mind ......................... | *107* | Dakar 4513 |
| 3/31/73 | **5** | 12 | 12  **Without You In My Life** ............................. | *64* | Dakar 4519 |
| 7/14/73 | **9** | 13 | 13  **There It Is** ....................................... | *32* | Dakar 4523 |
| 10/13/73 | **19** | 11 | 14  Wrapped Up In Your Warm And Tender Love ..... | | Dakar 4526 |
| 1/12/74 | **11** | 17 | 15  I Wish It Was Me..................................... | *57* | Dakar 4529 |
| | | | all of above: produced by Willie Henderson | | |
| 5/11/74 | **11** | 14 | 16  What Goes Up (Must Come Down)..................... | *89* | Dakar 4532 |
| 8/31/74 | **27** | 13 | 17  Happiness Is Being With You......................... | | Dakar 4536 |
| 12/07/74+ | **38** | 10 | 18  I Can't Make It Without You......................... | | Dakar 4538 |
| 3/01/75 | **36** | 12 | 19  Homewreckers...................................... | | Dakar 4541 |
| 7/12/75 | **38** | 13 | 20  A Woman Needs To Be Loved ....................... | | Dakar 4545 |
| 12/06/75+ | **1** [1] | 20 | 21  **Turning Point** ..................................... | | Dakar 4550 |
| 5/08/76 | **9** | 13 | 22  **So Good (To Be Home With You)** ................. | | Dakar 4553 |
| 8/21/76 | **2** [3] | 16 | 23  **Give It Up (Turn It Loose)** ....................... | *38* | Columbia 10388 |
| 12/25/76+ | **39** | 10 | 24  Ever Lovin' Girl ................................... | | Dakar 4561 |
| 1/08/77 | **33** | 9 | 25  Close To You...................................... | | Columbia 10457 |
| 5/14/77 | **6** | 16 | 26  **This I Swear** ..................................... | *102* | Columbia 10528 |
| 10/01/77 | **32** | 16 | 27  All You Got ....................................... | | Columbia 10604 |
| 2/25/78 | **12** | 20 | 28  Get On Up (Disco)................................. | *102* | Columbia 10684 |
| 7/15/78 | **65** | 8 | 29  Can't Help But Say ............................... | | Columbia 10773 |
| 2/24/79 | **6** | 20 | 30  **In The Mood** .................................... | | Columbia 10904 |
| 7/21/79 | **72** | 6 | 31  Ain't Nothing I Can Do ............................ | | Columbia 11035 |
| 11/03/79 | **37** | 14 | 32  Be With Me ....................................... | | Columbia 11128 |
| 2/16/80 | **58** | 7 | 33  Can't You Tell It's Me ............................. | | Columbia 11199 |
| 9/13/80 | **36** | 11 | 34  How Sweet It Is (To Be Loved By You) .............. | | Columbia 11344 |
| 9/19/81 | **62** | 8 | 35  Just My Luck ..................................... | | Columbia 02269 |
| 11/20/82+ | **3** | 20 | 36  **Are You Serious** ................................. | *57* | Highrise 2005 |
| 4/23/83 | **49** | 9 | 37  A Little Bit Of Loving.............................. | | Highrise 2009 |
| 10/01/83 | **38** | 14 | 38  I Found Myself When I Lost You ................... | | Ocean Fr. 2001 |
| 1/28/84 | **33** | 12 | 39  Let Me Be Your Pacifier............................ | | Ocean Fr. 2004 |
| 9/05/87 | **84** | 5 | 40  I'm In Love Again.................................. | | Future 102 |
| 4/02/88 | **54** | 11 | 41  Do You Feel It .................................... | | Future 103 |
| | | | **DAVY D** | | |
| | | | Rap disc jockey David Reeves, Jr. from Hollis, Queens, New York. Previously recorded as Davy DMX. Former DJ for Kurtis Blow. Wrote "Action" for Orange Krush and "The Bubble Bunch" for Jimmy Spicer. | | |
| 3/10/84 | **59** | 7 | 1  One For The Treble (Fresh) ......................... | | CBS Assoc. 04355 |
| | | | shown as: **DAVY DMX** | | |
| 8/01/87 | **92** | 4 | 2  Have You Seen Davy.................................. | | Def Jam 07136 |
| | | | **CLIFF DAWSON** | | |
| | | | Vocalist from New York City. Worked as back-up singer. | | |
| 7/10/82 | **39** | 11 | 1  It's Not Me You Love................................. | | Boardwalk 147 |
| 2/19/83 | **16** | 19 | 2  Never Say I Do (If You Don't Mean It) .............. | | Boardwalk 173 |
| | | | **CLIFF DAWSON & RENEE DIGGS** (member of Starpoint) | | |
| | | | **BOBBY DAY** | | |
| | | | Born Robert Byrd on 7/1/32 in Ft. Worth, Texas. To Watts, Los Angeles in 1948. Formed the Hollywood Flames in 1950. Group also known as: The Flames, Four Flames, Hollywood Four Flames, Jets, Tangiers, and then The Satellites. Bobby recorded with all of these groups, then solo, and with the duo, Bob & Earl. Wrote "Little Bitty Pretty One" and recorded the original version. Not to be confused with Bobby Byrd, singer with James Brown's Famous Flames. Also see Eugene Church. | | |
| 9/01/58 | **1** [3] | 15 | 1  **Rock-in Robin/** | *2* | |
| | | | Jockey #1 / Best Seller #2 | | |
| | | 3 | 2  Over And Over........................................ | *41* | Class 229 |
| | | | Best Seller flip  revived by the Dave Clark Five in 1965 (POS 1-Pop) | | |
| | | | **MARGIE DAY** | | |
| | | | Born Margaret Hoeffler in Norfolk, Virginia, in 1926. Attended Virginia State College. Recorded with Four Bars + A Melody for Savoy in 1947. Joined the Griffin Brothers in 1950. With Paul "Hucklebuck" Williams in 1954. | | |
| 11/25/50 | **7** | 3 | 1  **Street-Walkin' Daddy** ................................. | | Dot 1010 |
| | | | Juke Box #7 | | |

| DEBUT DATE | PEAK POS | WKS CHR | ARTIST — Record Title | POP POS | Label & Number |
|---|---|---|---|---|---|
| | | | **MARGIE DAY — Continued** | | |
| 1/27/51 | **5** | 7 | 2 **Little Red Rooster** ............................................. | | Dot 1019 |
| | | | Best Seller #5 / Juke Box #5 | | |
| 12/29/51 | **10** | 1 | 3 **Pretty Baby** ..................................................... | | Dot 1070 |
| | | | Best Seller #10 | | |
| | | | vocals by Margie Day & Tommy Brown | | |
| | | | all of the above backed by the Griffin Brothers | | |
| | | | **MORRIS DAY** | | |
| | | | Leader of Minneapolis funk group, The Time (formerly Prince's backing band). Born in Springfield, Illinois; raised in Minneapolis. Acted in the 1984 film "Purple Rain". | | |
| 9/14/85 | **3** | 18 | 1 **The Oak Tree** ................................................... | 65 | Warner 28899 |
| 12/21/85+ | **15** | 17 | 2 Color Of Success .............................................. | | Warner 28809 |
| 4/12/86 | **34** | 11 | 3 Character, The ................................................. | | Warner 28729 |
| 1/30/88 | **1**² | 13 | 4 **Fishnet**......................................................... | 23 | Warner 28201 |
| 4/23/88 | **26** | 11 | 5 Daydreaming................................................... | | Warner 27917 |
| | | | **JOHNNY DAYE** | | |
| 12/11/65 | **40** | 2 | 1 Marry Me......................................................... | | Jomada 600 |
| | | | produced by Johnny Nash | | |
| | | | **TAYLOR DAYNE** | | |
| | | | Real name: Leslie Wonderman. Female dance singer from Long Island. | | |
| 6/18/88 | **21** | 21 | 1 I'll Always Love You ......................................... | 3 | Arista 9700 |
| | | | **BUTCH DAYO - see VAUGHAN MASON** | | |
| | | | **DAYTON** | | |
| | | | Funk/rock ensemble from Ohio, formed as Magnum by Shawn Sandridge and Chris Jones. Sandridge was a music and science teacher; worked with Junie Morrison and Sun. | | |
| 7/25/81 | **62** | 7 | 1 Cutie Pie ......................................................... | | Liberty 1414 |
| 6/19/82 | **17** | 15 | 2 Hot Fun In The Summertime ............................ | 58 | Liberty 1468 |
| 10/01/83 | **54** | 8 | 3 It Must Be Love ............................................... | | Capitol 5269 |
| 3/31/84 | **69** | 7 | 4 The Sound Of Music......................................... | | Capitol 5327 |
| 8/17/85 | **81** | 6 | 5 This Time ........................................................ | | Capitol 5487 |
| | | | **DAZZ BAND**     ★★**161**★★ | | |
| | | | Cleveland ultrafunk band, formerly Kinsman Dazz. "Dazz" means "danceable jazz". Formed by Bobby Harris (vocalist, saxophone) by merging Bell Telefunk and the house band at Cleveland's Kinsman Grill. Included Pierre DeMudd, Sennie "Skip" Martin III, Eric Fearman, Kevin Frederick, Kenny Pettus, Michael Wiley and Isaac Wiley. | | |
| | | | **KINSMAN DAZZ:** | | |
| 12/02/78+ | **46** | 12 | 1 I Might As Well Forget About Loving You .......... | 104 | 20th Century 2390 |
| 12/15/79+ | **33** | 14 | 2 Catchin' Up On Love.......................................... | | 20th Century 2345 |
| | | | **DAZZ BAND:** | | |
| 12/13/80+ | **65** | 12 | 3 Shake It Up..................................................... | | Motown 1500 |
| 3/14/81 | **51** | 9 | 4 Invitation To Love............................................ | 109 | Motown 1507 |
| 8/01/81 | **44** | 12 | 5 Knock! Knock!................................................. | | Motown 1515 |
| 3/13/82 | **1**⁵ | 26 | 6 **Let It Whip**.................................................... | 5 | Motown 1609 |
| 7/31/82 | **20** | 12 | 7 Keep It Live (On The K.I.L.)............................... | | Motown 1622 |
| 1/29/83 | **9** | 15 | 8 **On The One For Fun** ...................................... | | Motown 1659 |
| 4/30/83 | **76** | 4 | 9 Cheek To Cheek............................................... | | Motown 1676 |
| 7/02/83 | **63** | 7 | 10 Party Right Here ............................................. | | Motown 1680 |
| 11/26/83+ | **9** | 22 | 11 **Joystick**...................................................... | 61 | Motown 1701 |
| 4/21/84 | **12** | 14 | 12 Swoop (I'm Yours) .......................................... | | Motown 1725 |
| 10/13/84 | **9** | 18 | 13 **Let It All Blow**.............................................. | 84 | Motown 1760 |
| 2/02/85 | **12** | 16 | 14 Heartbeat ...................................................... | 110 | Motown 1775 |
| 8/03/85 | **21** | 12 | 15 Hot Spot........................................................ | | Motown 1800 |
| 7/12/86 | **48** | 10 | 16 L.O.V.E. M.I.A................................................. | | Geffen 28635 |
| | | | shown only as: **DAZZ** | | |
| 9/20/86 | **44** | 8 | 17 Wild And Free ................................................ | | Geffen 28658 |
| 4/09/88 | **38** | 11 | 18 Anticipation.................................................... | | RCA 7614 |
| | | | **THE DEACONS** | | |
| | | | Syl Johnson's back-up band from Chicago, featuring Syl's brother Jimmy on guitar. | | |
| 12/07/68 | **24** | 5 | 1 Sock It To Me, Part 1 ...................................[I] | 121 | Shama 100 |

| DEBUT DATE | PEAK POS | WKS CHR | ARTIST — Record Title | POP POS | Label & Number |
|---|---|---|---|---|---|
| | | | **SHELBRA DEANE** | | |
| 11/20/76 | **88** | 8 | 1 A Man's Got Too Much Dog In Him ................... | | Casino 070 |
| 3/05/77 | **50** | 12 | 2 Don't Touch Me ............................................ | | Casino 114 |
| | | | **DeBARGE** | | |
| | | | Family group from Grand Rapids, Michigan. Consisted of lead vocalist Eldra (keyboards), Mark (trumpet, saxophone), James (keyboards), Randy (bass) and Bunny DeBarge (vocals). Brothers Bobby and Tommy were in Switch. | | |
| 9/18/82 | **46** | 8 | 1 Stop! Don't Tease Me ...................................... | | Gordy 1635 |
| 12/18/82+ | **2**⁴ | 28 | 2 **I Like It**................................................. | *31* | Gordy 1645 |
| 4/23/83 | **5** | 20 | 3 **All This Love** .......................................... | *17* | Gordy 1660 |
| 10/15/83 | **1**ᵇ | 23 | 4 **Time Will Reveal**...................................... | *18* | Gordy 1705 |
| 3/03/84 | **11** | 14 | 5 Love Me In A Special Way............................... | *45* | Gordy 1723 |
| 2/23/85 | **1**¹ | 18 | 6 **Rhythm Of The Night** ............................... | *3* | Gordy 1770 |
| | | | from the Berry Gordy film "The Last Dragon" | | |
| 6/08/85 | **2**⁴ | 17 | 7 **Who's Holding Donna Now** ......................... | *6* | Gordy 1793 |
| 11/30/85+ | **29** | 14 | 8 The Heart Is Not So Smart ............................. | | Gordy 1822 |
| | | | EL DeBARGE with DeBARGE | | |
| 7/18/87 | **33** | 10 | 9 Dance All Night ............................................ | | Striped H. 7004 |
| 12/19/87+ | **73** | 12 | 10 You Babe.................................................... | | Striped H. 7007 |
| | | | **BUNNY DeBARGE** | | |
| | | | Member of the family group DeBarge. | | |
| 1/31/87 | **18** | 13 | 1 Save The Best For Me (Best Of Your Lovin') ....... | | Gordy 1869 |
| | | | **CHICO DeBARGE** | | |
| | | | DeBarge sibling, but not a member of the group DeBarge. | | |
| 9/20/86 | **7** | 20 | 1 **Talk To Me** ............................................. | *21* | Motown 1858 |
| 2/28/87 | **59** | 9 | 2 The Girl Next Door ...................................... | | Motown 1875 |
| 10/10/87 | **43** | 10 | 3 I've Been Watching You ................................. | | Motown 1909 |
| 12/26/87+ | **18** | 16 | 4 Rainy Night ................................................ | | Motown 1922 |
| 7/02/88 | **53** | 8 | 5 Kiss Serious................................................ | | Motown 1935 |
| | | | **EL DeBARGE** | | |
| | | | Eldra DeBarge (born on 6/4/61). Lead singer of family group DeBarge. | | |
| 9/14/85 | **7** | 13 | 1 **You Wear It Well** ..................................... | | Gordy 1804 |
| 11/30/85+ | **29** | 14 | 2 The Heart Is Not So Smart ............................. | | Gordy 1822 |
| | | | EL DeBARGE with DeBARGE | | |
| 5/03/86 | **1**¹ | 19 | 3 **Who's Johnny**.......................................... | *3* | Gordy 1842 |
| | | | theme from the film "Short Circuit" | | |
| 8/02/86 | **7** | 16 | 4 **Love Always**............................................ | *43* | Gordy 1857 |
| 11/01/86 | **32** | 13 | 5 Someone .................................................... | *70* | Gordy 1867 |
| | | | **DEBBIE DEB** | | |
| 7/07/84 | **43** | 10 | 1 When I Hear Music ....................................... | | Jam Pack. 3011 |
| 5/30/87 | **72** | 7 | 2 I'm Searchin'................................................ | | Jam Pack. 703 |
| | | | **DEBLANC** | | |
| | | | Singer/dancer/club deejay, born Ralph DeBlanc in 1949 in Los Angeles. Formed own group, DeBlanc, later known as Starfire. Went solo in 1975. | | |
| 2/07/76 | **70** | 6 | 1 Oh No, Not My Baby...................................... | | Arista 0161 |
| | | | **DECO** | | |
| | | | Duo of Phillip Ingram and Zane Giles, formerly in the group Switch. Phillip is the brother of James Ingram. Zane is from Charleston, West Virginia. | | |
| 11/12/83 | **77** | 4 | 1 Fresh Idea .................................................. | | Qwest 29491 |
| | | | **JAY DEE** | | |
| | | | Born Earl Nelson. Also recorded with Bobby Day as "Bob & Earl", "Earl Cosby" and "Jackie Lee". | | |
| 5/04/74 | **88** | 5 | 1 Strange Funky Games And Things ................... | | Warner 7798 |
| | | | **JOEY DEE & THE STARLITERS** | | |
| | | | Born Joseph DiNicola on 6/11/40 in Passaic, New Jersey. In September, 1960, Joey & The Starlighters became the house band at the Peppermint Lounge, New York City. After 1964, group included 3 members who later formed The Young Rascals, plus guitarist Jimi Hendrix. | | |
| 12/25/61+ | **8** | 11 | 1 **Peppermint Twist - Part I**............................ | *1* | Roulette 4401 |
| | | | inspired by New York City's Peppermint Lounge club | | |

| DEBUT DATE | PEAK POS | WKS CHR | ARTIST — Record Title | POP POS | Label & Number |
|---|---|---|---|---|---|
| | | | **THE DEELE** | | |
| | | | Group from Cincinnati. Consisted of Darnell "Dee" Bristol and Carlos "Satin" Greene (lead vocals), Stanley Burke, Kenny Edmonds, Kevin Roberson and Antonio "L.A." Reid. Reid co-wrote Pebbles' "Girlfriend" and The Whispers' "Rock Steady" with Babyface. | | |
| 11/12/83+ | 3 | 22 | 1 **Body Talk** .................................. | 77 | Solar 69785 |
| 3/10/84 | 25 | 14 | 2 Just My Luck ............................... | | Solar 69749 |
| 7/21/84 | 66 | 7 | 3 Surrender .................................. | | Solar 69712 |
| 5/11/85 | 14 | 14 | 4 Material Thangz.......................... | 101 | Solar 69644 |
| 9/07/85 | 66 | 8 | 5 Suspicious ................................. | | Solar 69615 |
| 7/25/87 | 48 | 10 | 6 Can-U-Dance .............................. | | Solar 70007 |
| 11/14/87+ | 4 | 24 | 7 **Two Occasions**.......................... | 10 | Solar 70015 |
| 5/14/88 | 10 | 15 | 8 Shoot 'Em Up Movies.................... | | Solar 70023 |
| | | | **DEEP VELVET** | | |
| 11/17/73 | 83 | 5 | 1 Hanna-Mae................................. | | Aware 034 |
| | | | **RICK DEES & HIS CAST OF IDIOTS** | | |
| | | | Born Rigdon Osmond Dees III in Memphis, in 1950. Disc Jockey working at WMPS-Memphis when he conceived idea for "Disco Duck". Currently one of America's top radio DJs. | | |
| 10/02/76 | 15 | 15 | 1▲Disco Duck (Part 1)...................... [N] | 1 | RSO 857 |
| 1/29/77 | 93 | 2 | 2 Dis-Gorilla (Part 1)...................... [N] | 56 | RSO 866 |
| | | | **SAM DEES** | | |
| | | | Singer/songwriter from Birmingham, Alabama; raised in Rochester, New York. | | |
| 7/14/73 | 58 | 8 | 1 Just Out Of Reach ....................... | | Atlantic 2937 |
| 12/22/73+ | 59 | 10 | 2 So Tied Up ................................. | | Atlantic 2991 |
| 9/21/74 | 15 | 13 | 3 Worn Out Broken Heart................. | | Atlantic 3205 |
| 2/22/75 | 76 | 4 | 4 The Show Must Go On .................. | | Atlantic 3243 |
| 2/14/76 | 84 | 7 | 5 Storybook Children ...................... | | Big Tree 16054 |
| 5/06/78 | 89 | 6 | 6 Say Yeah.................................... | | Polydor 14455 |
| | | | **DEJA** | | |
| | | | Duo of Starleana Young & Curt Jones. First known as Symphonic Express. Both were members of Slave and Aurra. | | |
| 9/05/87 | 2¹ | 15 | 1 **You And Me Tonight** .................. | 54 | Virgin 99422 |
| 1/23/88 | 17 | 13 | 2 That's Where You'll Find Me .......... | | Virgin 99375 |
| | | | **DELEGATION** | | |
| | | | England-based disco trio: Ricky Bailey, Ray Patterson and Bruce Dunbar. Dunbar is from Texas, Bailey and Patterson from Jamaica. | | |
| 1/06/79 | 6 | 19 | 1 **Oh Honey** ................................. | 45 | Shady Brook 1048 |
| 6/09/79 | 45 | 11 | 2 Someone Oughta Write A Song (About You Baby) | | Shady Brook 1047 |
| 5/10/80 | 50 | 9 | 3 Welcome To My World .................. | | Mercury 76056 |
| 8/30/80 | 66 | 6 | 4 Heartache No. 9 .......................... | | Mercury 76071 |
| 3/07/81 | 54 | 7 | 5 In Love's Time............................. | | Mercury 76094 |
| | | | **THE DELFONICS** ★★139★★ | | |
| | | | Group from Philadelphia. Formed in 1965 as the Four Gents. Consisted of William and Wilbert Hart, Ritchie Daniels, and Randy Cain. First recorded for Moon Shot, 1967. Daniels left for the service in 1968, group continued as a trio. Cain was replaced by Major Harris, formerly with the Jarmels, in 1971. Harris went solo, 1974. | | |
| 2/10/68 | 2⁴ | 15 | 1 **La - La - Means I Love You** ........... | 4 | Philly Groove 150 |
| 5/04/68 | 33 | 5 | 2 He Don't Really Love You................ | 92 | Moon Shot 6703 |
| 5/18/68 | 15 | 7 | 3 I'm Sorry .................................. | 42 | Philly Groove 151 |
| 9/07/68 | 12 | 10 | 4 Break Your Promise ..................... | 35 | Philly Groove 152 |
| 12/21/68+ | 14 | 7 | 5 Ready Or Not Here I Come (Can't Hide From Love)/ | 35 | |
| 2/08/69 | 41 | 4 | 6    Somebody Loves You................... | 72 | Philly Groove 154 |
| 7/12/69 | 48 | 3 | 7 Funny Feeling ............................. | 94 | Philly Groove 156 |
| 8/23/69 | 6 | 11 | 8 **You Got Yours And I'll Get Mine** .... | 40 | Philly Groove 157 |
| 1/17/70 | 3 | 14 | 9●**Didn't I (Blow Your Mind This Time)**.. | 10 | Philly Groove 161 |
| 6/13/70 | 8 | 9 | 10 Trying To Make A Fool Of Me ......... | 40 | Philly Groove 162 |
| | | | 1-10: produced by Thom Bell and written by Bell and William Hart | | |
| 9/19/70 | 12 | 8 | 11 When You Get Right Down To It ...... | 53 | Philly Groove 163 |
| 6/19/71 | 9 | 9 | 12 **Over And Over**/ | | |
| | | 9 | 13    Hey! Love ................................. | 52 | Philly Groove 166 |

| DEBUT DATE | PEAK POS | WKS CHR | ARTIST — Record Title | POP POS | Label & Number |
|---|---|---|---|---|---|
| | | | **THE DELFONICS — Continued** | | |
| 10/30/71 | **13** | 8 | 14 Walk Right Up To The Sun................................ | *81* | Philly Groove 169 |
| 6/03/72 | **15** | 11 | 15 Tell Me This Is A Dream .............................. | *86* | Philly Groove 172 |
| 1/27/73 | **47** | 4 | 16 Think It Over........................................ | *101* | Philly Groove 174 |
| 5/05/73 | **22** | 7 | 17 I Don't Want To Make You Wait ...................... | *91* | Philly Groove 176 |
| 9/22/73 | **88** | 3 | 18 Alfie .............................................. | | Philly Groove 177 |
| 1/05/74 | **26** | 13 | 19 I Told You So ...................................... | *101* | Philly Groove 182 |
| 6/08/74 | **60** | 8 | 20 Lying To Myself ..................................... | | Philly Groove 184 |
| | | | **THE DELL-VIKINGS** | | |
| | | | Group formed at the Air Force Serviceman's Club in Pittsburgh in 1955. Consisted of Norman Wright, Corinthian "Kripp" Johnson, Donald "Gus" Backus, David Lerchey, and Clarence E. Quick. Gus formed a second "Del Vikings" group in 1957 to record for Mercury. Johnson remained with Dot and re-formed the group with Chuck Jackson, who went on to a successful solo career. | | |
| 3/16/57 | **2**¹ | 17 | 1 **Come Go With Me**................................... | 4 | Dot 15538 |
| | | | Juke Box #2 / Best Seller #3 / Jockey #3 | | |
| | | | written by Quick; first released on FeeBee Records | | |
| 7/15/57 | **9** | 4 | 2 **Cool Shake**........................................ | *12* | Mercury 71132 |
| | | | **DEL VIKINGS** | | |
| | | | Jockey #9 | | |
| | | | with the Carl Stevens Orchestra; lead vocals by Gus Backus | | |
| 7/29/57 | **5** | 8 | 3 **Whispering Bells** .................................. | 9 | Dot 15592 |
| | | | Best Seller #5 / Jockey #5 | | |
| | | | lead vocal by Kripp Johnson | | |
| | | | **THE DELLS**   ★★35★★ | | |
| | | | Vocal group formed at Thornton Township High School in Harvey, Illinois. Consisted of Johnny Funches (lead), Marvin Junior (tenor), Verne Allison (tenor), Mickey McGill (baritone) and Chuck Barksdale (bass). First recorded as the El-Rays for Chess in 1953. Group remained intact into the 80s, with exception of Funches, who was replaced by Johnny Carter (ex-Flamingos) in 1960. Also see Barbara Lewis. | | |
| 11/10/56 | **4** | 11 | 1 **Oh What A Nite** .................................... | | Vee-Jay 204 |
| | | | Best Seller #4 / Jockey #5 / Juke Box #5 | | |
| 6/05/65 | **23** | 4 | 2 Stay In My Corner ................................... | *122* | Vee-Jay 674 |
| 11/25/67 | **22** | 9 | 3 O-O, I Love You...................................... | *61* | Cadet 5574 |
| 2/17/68 | **11** | 9 | 4 There Is............................................ | *20* | Cadet 5590 |
| 5/18/68 | **27** | 7 | 5 Wear It On Our Face ................................ | *44* | Cadet 5599 |
| 6/22/68 | **1**³ | 18 | 6 **Stay In My Corner** ................................ | *10* | Cadet 5612 |
| | | | new version of #2 above | | |
| 10/19/68 | **3** | 13 | 7 **Always Together** ................................... | *18* | Cadet 5621 |
| 1/11/69 | **15** | 8 | 8 Does Anybody Know I'm Here ........................ | *38* | Cadet 5631 |
| 3/29/69 | **20** | 8 | 9 I Can't Do Enough/ | *98* | |
| 3/22/69 | **44** | 2 | 10  Hallways Of My Mind .............................. | *92* | Cadet 5636 |
| 5/31/69 | **5** | 12 | 11 **I Can Sing A Rainbow/Love Is Blue** .............. | *22* | Cadet 5641 |
| 8/16/69 | **1**¹ | 13 | 12 **Oh, What A Night** ................................. | *10* | Cadet 5649 |
| 11/08/69 | **13** | 6 | 13 On The Dock Of The Bay ........................... | *42* | Cadet 5658 |
| 1/24/70 | **10** | 10 | 14 **Oh What A Day**.................................... | *43* | Cadet 5663 |
| 4/18/70 | **5**ˉ | 10 | 15 **Open Up My Heart/** | *51* | |
| | | 9 | 16  Nadine ........................................... | | Cadet 5667 |
| 7/18/70 | **27** | 7 | 17 Long Lonely Nights ................................ | *74* | Cadet 5672 |
| 1/09/71 | **30** | 6 | 18 The Glory Of Love ................................. | *92* | Cadet 5679 |
| 8/07/71 | **8** | 15 | 19 **The Love We Had (Stays On My Mind)** ............ | *30* | Cadet 5683 |
| 2/05/72 | **23** | 6 | 20 It's All Up To You/ | *94* | |
| | | 6 | 21  Oh, My Dear ....................................... | | Cadet 5689 |
| 11/11/72 | **35** | 8 | 22 Just As Long As We're In Love...................... | | Cadet 5694 |
| 4/14/73 | **3** | 16 | 23● Give Your Baby A Standing Ovation ............. | *34* | Cadet 5696 |
| 9/08/73 | **10** | 16 | 24 **My Pretending Days Are Over** ...................... | *51* | Cadet 5698 |
| 12/01/73+ | **8** | 16 | 25 **I Miss You**........................................ | *60* | Cadet 5700 |
| 5/11/74 | **11** | 13 | 26 I Wish It Was Me You Loved ........................ | *94* | Cadet 5702 |
| 9/14/74 | **18** | 12 | 27 Learning To Love You Was Easy (It's So Hard Trying To Get Over You) ........................ | | Cadet 5703 |
| 4/26/75 | **59** | 7 | 28 The Glory Of Love ..................... [R] | | Cadet 5707 |
| 7/12/75 | **46** | 10 | 29 Love Is Missing From Our Lives ..................... | | Cadet 5710 |
| | | | **THE DELLS/THE DRAMATICS** | | |
| 11/08/75 | **17** | 13 | 30 We Got To Get Our Thing Together.................. | *104* | Mercury 73723 |
| 2/07/76 | **58** | 8 | 31 The Power Of Love ................................. | *106* | Mercury 73759 |

| DEBUT DATE | PEAK POS | WKS CHR | ARTIST — Record Title | POP POS | Label & Number |
|---|---|---|---|---|---|
| | | | **THE DELLS — Continued** | | |
| 6/26/76 | 49 | 12 | 32 Slow Motion ................................................. | *102* | Mercury 73807 |
| 9/25/76 | 68 | 5 | 33 No Way Back ............................................... | | Mercury 73842 |
| 5/07/77 | 20 | 12 | 34 Our Love ..................................................... | | Mercury 73909 |
| 8/06/77 | 29 | 17 | 35 Betcha Never Been Loved (Like This Before) ...... | | Mercury 73901 |
| 1/21/78 | 57 | 9 | 36 Private Property ........................................... | | Mercury 73977 |
| 7/15/78 | 24 | 13 | 37 Super Woman.............................................. | *108* | ABC 12386 |
| 1/27/79 | 34 | 10 | 38 (You Bring Out) The Best In Me...................... | | ABC 12440 |
| 8/09/80 | 17 | 17 | 39 I Touched A Dream ...................................... | | 20th Century 2463 |
| 12/13/80 | 76 | 5 | 40 Passionate Breezes....................................... | | 20th Century 2475 |
| 1/28/84 | 23 | 14 | 41 You Just Can't Walk Away ............................ | *107* | Private I 04343 |
| 5/05/84 | 46 | 8 | 42 One Step Closer ........................................... | | Private I 04448 |
| 7/28/84 | 60 | 9 | 43 Love On .................................................... | | Private I 04540 |
| | | | **JIMMY DELPHS** | | |
| | | | Singer from Toledo, Ohio. | | |
| 6/01/68 | 29 | 2 | 1 Don't Sign The Paper Baby (I Want You Back) .... | 96 | Karen 1538 |
| | | | **DELTA RHYTHM BOYS** | | |
| | | | Group formed in 1934 at Langston University, Oklahoma. To Dillard University in New Orleans in 1936. Worked with Dr. Frederick Hall as "The New Orleans Quintet" and the "Frederick Hall Quintet". Appeared in Broadway musicals, revues, several films and short subjects. Most famous lineup: Carl Jones, Traverse Crawford, Kelsey Pharr and Otha Lee Gaines. Rene DeKnight was accompanist and arranger. Group disbanded after Gaines' death on 7/15/87 (73). | | |
| 1/26/46 | 3 | 2 | 1 **Just A-Sittin' And A-Rockin'**......................... | 17 | Decca 18739 |
| | | | lyrics written by Lee Gaines, adapted from a Duke Ellington tune | | |
| | | | **THE EXOTIC SOUNDS OF MARTIN DENNY** | | |
| | | | Born on 4/10/11 in New York City. Composer/arranger/pianist. Originated the "Exotic Sounds of Martin Denny" in Hawaii, featuring Julius Wechter (Baja Marimba Band) on vibes and marimba. | | |
| 5/04/59 | 11 | 11 | 1 Quiet Village .............................................. [I] | 4 | Liberty 55162 |
| | | | written by Les Baxter | | |
| | | | **DEODATO** | | |
| | | | Born Eumir Deodato Almeida on 6/21/42 in Rio de Janeiro, Brazil. Keyboardist/ composer/arranger. Kool & The Gang's producer from 1979-82. | | |
| 9/01/73 | 42 | 12 | 1 Rhapsody In Blue..................................... [I] | 41 | CTI 16 |
| | | | classic George Gershwin tune; hit for Paul Whiteman, 1924 (POS 3) | | |
| 1/08/77 | 96 | 6 | 2 Peter Gunn ............................................. [I] | 84 | MCA 40631 |
| 7/22/78 | 81 | 6 | 3 Whistle Bump ............................................. | | Warner 8606 |
| | | | shown as: **EUMIR DEODATO** | | |
| 6/26/82 | 70 | 6 | 4 Happy Hour .............................................. | 70 | Warner 29984 |
| | | | lead vocal by Kelly Barretto | | |
| | | | **DEREK B** | | |
| 3/19/88 | 82 | 6 | 1 Get Down..................................................... | | Profile 5170 |
| | | | **DEREK & CYNDI** | | |
| 9/21/74 | 70 | 5 | 1 You Bring Out The Best In Me ......................... | | Thunder 8251 |
| | | | **SUGAR PIE DeSANTO** | | |
| | | | Born Umpeylia Marsema Balinton on 10/16/35 in Brooklyn. To San Francisco while a child. Toured with Johnny Otis Revue, first recorded for Federal in 1955. Recorded with husband, guitarist Pee Wee Kingsley, for Aladdin in 1958. With James Brown Revue from 1959-60. | | |
| 9/05/60 | 4 | 9 | 1 **I Want To Know**............................................ | | Check 103 |
| | | | originally released on Veltone 103 | | |
| 4/18/64 | 48 | 5 | 2 Slip-In Mules (No High Heel Sneakers) ............... | *Hot* | Checker 1073 |
| 8/13/66 | 37 | 6 | 3 In The Basement - Part 1 ............................... | 97 | Cadet 5539 |
| | | | **ETTA JAMES & SUGAR PIE DeSANTO** | | |
| | | | **TERI DeSARIO with K.C.** | | |
| | | | Terry is a singer/songwriter from Miami. K.C. is Harry "KC" Casey, lead singer of KC & The Sunshine Band. | | |
| 2/09/80 | 20 | 13 | 1●Yes, I'm Ready............................................ | 2 | Casablanca 2227 |
| | | | **JACKIE DeSHANNON** | | |
| | | | Pop singer/prolific composer, born Sharon Myers on 8/21/44 in Hazel, Kentucky. First recorded as Sherry Lee Myers for Glenn in 1959. | | |
| 7/17/65 | 40 | 2 | 1 What The World Needs Now Is Love................. | 7 | Imperial 66110 |
| | | | written & produced by Burt Bacharach and Hal David | | |

| DEBUT DATE | PEAK POS | WKS CHR | ARTIST — Record Title | POP POS | Label & Number |
|---|---|---|---|---|---|
| | | | **TONY DESHAWN** | | |
| 4/11/87 | 92 | 4 | 1 Real Lover .................................................. | | Amazon 520 |
| | | | **DESTINATION** | | |
| 3/12/77 | 87 | 8 | 1 I've Got To Dance (To Keep From Crying) ......... | | AVI 128 |
| 11/10/79 | 68 | 6 | 2 Move On Up/Up Up Up.................................. | | Butterfly 41084 |
| | | | **DETROIT EMERALDS** | | |
| | | | Group formed in Little Rock, Arkansas by the Tilmon brothers: Abrim (d: 1982, heart attack), Ivory, Cleophus and Raymond. In 1970, group reduced to trio of: Abrim, Ivory and friend James Mitchell. 1977 group consisted of Abrim Tilmon, Paul Riser, Johnny Allen and Maurice King. "Sweet" James Epps of The Fantastic Four was a cousin of the Tilman brothers. The group's backing band, from 1971-73, later recorded as Chapter 8. | | |
| 3/02/68 | 22 | 9 | 1 Show Time ................................................ | 89 | Ric-Tic 135 |
| 1/24/70 | 32 | 9 | 2 If I Lose Your Love ..................................... | | Westbound 156 |
| 7/11/70 | 41 | 3 | 3 I Can't See Myself Doing Without You/ | | |
| | | 3 | 4 Just Now & Then ........................................ | | Westbound 161 |
| 2/20/71 | 7 | 12 | 5 Do Me Right ............................................. | 43 | Westbound 172 |
| 7/24/71 | 18 | 10 | 6 Wear This Ring (With Love)............................ | 91 | Westbound 181 |
| 1/01/72 | 5 | 13 | 7 You Want It, You Got It ............................... | 36 | Westbound 192 |
| 6/10/72 | 4 | 13 | 8 Baby Let Me Take You (In My Arms) .............. | 24 | Westbound 203 |
| 11/25/72+ | 22 | 9 | 9 Feel The Need In Me .................................... | 110 | Westbound 209 |
| 6/02/73 | 10 | 11 | 10 You're Gettin' A Little Too Smart ................. | 101 | Westbound 213 |
| 11/24/73 | 79 | 6 | 11 Lee.......................................................... | | Westbound 220 |
| 5/21/77 | 73 | 5 | 12 Feel The Need.......................................... | 90 | Westbound 55401 |
| | | | **DETROYT** | | |
| 10/13/84 | 84 | 4 | 1 Physical Lover............................................ | | Tabu 04611 |
| | | | **WILLIAM DeVAUGHN** | | |
| | | | Vocalist/songwriter/guitarist from Washington, DC. Worked for the federal government. Backed on hits by MFSB band. | | |
| 3/30/74 | 1¹ | 19 | 1●Be Thankful For What You Got .................... | 4 | Roxbury 0236 |
| 8/31/74 | 10 | 12 | 2 Blood Is Thicker Than Water ....................... | 43 | Roxbury 2001 |
| 12/21/74+ | 51 | 9 | 3 Give The Little Man A Great Big Hand ............. | | Roxbury 2205 |
| 6/14/80 | 37 | 13 | 4 Figures Can't Calculate ................................ | | TEC 767 |
| | | | **DEVONS** | | |
| 6/07/69 | 46 | 3 | 1 Someone To Treat Me ................................. | | King 6226 |
| | | | **BARRY DeVORZON - see BARRY & THE TAMERLANES** | | |
| | | | **THE DEVOTIONS** | | |
| | | | Quintet from New York City. | | |
| 10/17/70 | 49 | 3 | 1 Dawning Of Love........................................ | | Colossus 126 |
| | | | **AL DEXTER & HIS TROOPERS** | | |
| | | | Born Albert Poindexter on 5/4/05 in Jacksonville, Texas. Died on 1/28/84 (84). Vocalist/guitarist/violinist/composer. | | |
| 11/06/43 | 5 | 3 | 1 Pistol Packin' Mama .................................... | 1 | Okeh 6708 |
| | | | first country song to be featured on "Your Hit Parade"; a reported million-seller | | |
| | | | **DIABLOS** | | |
| | | | Group from Detroit: brothers Nolan (b: 1/22/34; d: 2/21/77, lead) & Jimmy "Big Jim" Strong, Willie Hunter, Quentin Eubanks and Bob "Chico" Edwards. Eubanks replaced by George Scott in 1959. Nolan & Jimmy are cousins of Barrett Strong. | | |
| 1/28/56 | 12 | 1 | 1 Way You Dog Me Around ............................. | | Fortune 518 |
| | | | Jockey #12 | | |
| | | | **GREGG DIAMOND** | | |
| | | | Writer/producer for Gloria Gaynor, George McCrae and the Andrea True Connection. | | |
| 11/25/78 | 57 | 9 | 1 Star Cruiser ............................................... | 102 | Marlin 3329 |

| DEBUT DATE | PEAK POS | WKS CHR | ARTIST — Record Title | POP POS | Label & Number |
|---|---|---|---|---|---|
| | | | **THE DIAMONDS** | | |
| | | | From Toronto, Canada: David Somerville (lead), Ted Kowalski (tenor), Phil Leavitt (baritone) and Bill Reed (bass). Attained stardom through cover versions of R&B hits. Somerville later sang folk music under the name "David Troy". Michael Douglas replaced Leavitt in early 1958. Reed and Kowalski replaced in 1959 by Evan Fisher and John Felton (killed in a plane crash, 1982). David teamed with Four Preps co-founder Bruce Belland as a duet from 1962-69. Not to be confused with black group of the same name who recorded earlier for Atlantic Records. | | |
| 7/07/56 | **14** | 1 | 1 Love, Love, Love............................................ Jockey #14 | *30* | Mercury 70889 |
| 10/13/56 | **8** | 1 | 2 **Ka-Ding-Dong** ........................................... Juke Box #8 | *35* | Mercury 70934 |
| 3/23/57 | **2**² | 16 | 3 **Little Darlin'** ........................................... Jockey #2 / Best Seller #3 / Juke Box #3 | *2* | Mercury 71060 |
| 7/22/57 | **12** | 1 | 4 Words Of Love.............................................. Jockey #12 written by Buddy Holly | *13* | Mercury 71128 |
| 9/23/57 | **12** | 2 | 5 Zip Zip..................................................... Jockey #12 | *16* | Mercury 71165 |
| 11/25/57 | **6** | 6 | 6 **Silhouettes** .............................................. Jockey #6 | *10* | Mercury 71197 |
| 1/06/58 | **5** | 10 | 7 **The Stroll**.............................................. Jockey #5 / Best Seller #7 all of above: orchestra arrangements by David Carroll | *4* | Mercury 71242 |
| | | | **MANU DIBANGO** | | |
| | | | Born in 1934 in Cameroon, Africa. Saxophonist/pianist. To Europe in 1949. First recorded in Belgium, in 1952. Played jazz until 1960, switched to African music. Returned to Africa for a time, then back to Europe. | | |
| 6/23/73 | **21** | 9 | 1 Soul Makossa ............................................. [I] | *35* | Atlantic 2971 |
| 10/13/73 | **77** | 7 | 2 Dangwa.................................................... [I] above 2: recorded in Paris | *109* | Atlantic 2983 |
| | | | **DICKY DOO & THE DON'TS** | | |
| | | | Vocal group from Philadelphia, consisting of Gerry "Jerry Grant" Granahan (lead), Harvey Davis (baritone), Ray Gangi (tenor), Al Ways (bass) and Dave "Dicky Doo" Alldred (ex-drummer of the Rhythm Orchids). | | |
| 2/24/58 | **8** | 3 | 1 **Click-Clack**.............................................. Jockey #8 / Best Seller #14 | *28* | Swan 4001 |
| | | | **BO DIDDLEY** | | |
| | | | Unique and influential R&B-rock vocalist/guitarist/violinist/trombonist/harmonica player. Born Otha Ellas Bates McDaniels on 12/30/28 in McComb, Mississippi. Adopted as an infant by his mother's cousin, Mrs. Gussie McDaniel. Moved to Chicago in 1934. | | |
| 5/07/55 | **1**² | 18 | 1 **Bo Diddley/** Juke Box #1 / Best Seller #2 / Jockey #3 | | Checker 814 |
| | | 11 | 2 I'm A Man.................................................. Best Seller flip / Juke Box flip | | |
| 7/16/55 | **11** | 4 | 3 Diddley Daddy ............................................ Best Seller #11 / Jockey #11 with the Moonglows, vocal group | | Checker 819 |
| 1/07/56 | **4** | 1 | 4 **Pretty Thing** ............................................ Juke Box #4 | | Checker 827 |
| 3/16/59 | **17** | 5 | 5 I'm Sorry ................................................ with the Carnations, vocal group | | Checker 914 |
| 8/03/59 | **14** | 5 | 6 Crackin Up ............................................... | *62* | Checker 924 |
| 9/14/59 | **3** | 15 | 7 **Say Man** .................................................. [N] | *20* | Checker 931 |
| 12/28/59 | **23** | 1 | 8 Say Man, Back Again........................................ [N] above 2: vocals by Jerome Green | *106* | Checker 936 |
| 4/18/60 | **20** | 2 | 9 Road Runner .............................................. | *75* | Checker 942 |
| 8/25/62 | **21** | 9 | 10 You Can't Judge A Book By The Cover ............. | *48* | Checker 1019 |
| 1/21/67 | **17** | 9 | 11 Ooh Baby................................................. | *88* | Checker 1158 |
| | | | **DIFOSCO** | | |
| | | | Born Difosco Ervin. Former lead singer of The Pastels; known as Big Dee Irwin. Produced the Los Angeles group Tribe. | | |
| 7/31/76 | **89** | 5 | 1 Face To Face.............................................. | | Roxbury 2027 |
| | | | **RENEE DIGGS - see CLIFF DAWSON** | | |

## VARETTA DILLARD
Born on 2/3/33 in New York. Crippled since birth. Won two amateur contests at the Apollo, signed by Savoy Records in 1951. Sang with vocal group, the Tri-Odds, during the 60s.

| | | | | | |
|---|---|---|---|---|---|
| 7/05/52 | **8** | 3 | 1 **Easy, Easy Baby** ........................... | | Savoy 847 |
| | | | Best Seller #8 / Juke Box #8 | | |
| 7/11/53 | **6** | 10 | 2 **Mercy, Mr. Percy** ........................ | | Savoy 897 |
| | | | Best Seller #6 / Juke Box #8 | | |
| 2/26/55 | **6** | 7 | 3 **Johnny Has Gone** ........................ | | Savoy 1153 |
| | | | Best Seller #6 / Jockey #8 / Juke Box #8 | | |
| | | | tribute to Johnny Ace | | |

## DIMPLES - see RICHARD "DIMPLES" FIELDS

## MARK DINNING
Born on 8/17/33 in Drury, Oklahoma. Died of a heart attack on 3/22/86 (52). Brother of the Dinning Sisters vocal trio. First recorded for MGM in 1957. Later worked with brother in Ace Dinning Duo out of Kansas City.

| | | | | | |
|---|---|---|---|---|---|
| 1/18/60 | **5** | 8 | 1 **Teen Angel** ........................... | *1* | MGM 12845 |
| | | | written by Mark's sister, Jeannie | | |

## DION
Born Dion DiMucci on 7/18/39 in the Bronx. Formed Dion & The Timberlanes in 1957, then Dion & The Belmonts in 1958. Belmonts included: Angelo D'Aleo, Freddie Milano and Carlo Mastrangelo. Group named for Belmont Ave. in the Bronx. Dion went solo in 1960. Brief reunion with the Belmonts in 1967 and 1972, periodically since then. He currently records contemporary Christian songs.

### DION & THE BELMONTS:

| | | | | | |
|---|---|---|---|---|---|
| 9/29/58 | **12** | 2 | 1 No One Knows ........................... | *19* | Laurie 3015 |
| | | | Jockey #12 / Best Seller #19 | | |
| 3/07/60 | **19** | 5 | 2 Where Or When ........................... | *3* | Laurie 3044 |
| | | | above 2: #1 hits in 1937 by Hal Kemp & His Orchestra | | |

### DION:

| | | | | | |
|---|---|---|---|---|---|
| 10/02/61 | **4** | 13 | 3 **Runaround Sue** ........................... | *1* | Laurie 3110 |
| 6/09/62 | **16** | 5 | 4 Lovers Who Wander ........................... | *3* | Laurie 3123 |
| 12/22/62 | **24** | 2 | 5 Love Came To Me ........................... | *10* | Laurie 3145 |
| 2/09/63 | **5** | 11 | 6 **Ruby Baby** ........................... | *2* | Columbia 42662 |
| 10/19/63 | **17** | 5 | 7 **Donna The Prima Donna** ........................... | *6* | Columbia 42852 |
| | | | shown as: **DION DiMUCCI** | | |

## DIONNE & FRIENDS - see DIONNE WARWICK

## DIONNE & KASHIF - see DIONNE WARWICK and/or KASHIF

## THE DIPLOMATS
Washington, DC group.

| | | | | | |
|---|---|---|---|---|---|
| 2/01/64 | **89** | 3 | 1 Here's A Heart ........................... | *Hot* | Arock 1004 |

## DIRECT CURRENT

| | | | | | |
|---|---|---|---|---|---|
| 6/02/79 | **83** | 4 | 1 Everybody Here Must Party ........................... | | T.E.C. 759 |

## DISCO FOUR

| | | | | | |
|---|---|---|---|---|---|
| 9/11/82 | **51** | 8 | 1 Whip Rap ........................... | | Profile 5010 |
| 2/05/83 | **84** | 5 | 2 We're At The Party ........................... | | Profile 5016 |

## DISCO TEX & THE SEX-O-LETTES
Disco studio group assembled by producer Bob Crewe. Featuring lead voice Sir Monti Rock III (real name: Joseph Montanez, Jr.), owner of a chain of hairdressing salons.

| | | | | | |
|---|---|---|---|---|---|
| 12/07/74+ | **32** | 16 | 1 Get Dancin' ........................... | *10* | Chelsea 3004 |
| 4/26/75 | **33** | 12 | 2 I Wanna Dance Wit' Choo (Doo Dat Dance), Part 1 ........................... | *23* | Chelsea 3015 |
| 8/14/76 | **99** | 2 | 3 Dancin' Kid ........................... | *60* | Chelsea 3045 |

## DISCO 3 - see FAT BOYS

## DIVINE SOUNDS
Brooklyn rap trio.

| | | | | | |
|---|---|---|---|---|---|
| 5/12/84 | **22** | 14 | 1 What People Do For Money ........................... | | Specific 946 |
| 10/20/84 | **63** | 8 | 2 Changes (We Go Through) ........................... | | Specific 950 |

### DIXIEAIRES

New York City group formed in 1946: Caleb "J.C." Ginyard, Jr. (d: 1978), Jimmy Smith, Joe Floyd and Johnny Hines. Ginyard was leader of the Jubalaires from 1936-46; later formed the Du Droppers. Sang in Europe with the Golden Gate Quartet from 1955-71.

| DEBUT DATE | PEAK POS | WKS CHR | ARTIST — Record Title | POP POS | Label & Number |
|---|---|---|---|---|---|
| 11/20/48 | 9 | 2 | 1 **Go Long** ............................................... <br> *Juke Box #9 / Best Seller #13* | | Gotham 163 |

### THE DIXIEBELLES

Black female trio from Memphis: Shirley Thomas, Mary Hunt, Mildred Pratcher.

| | | | | | |
|---|---|---|---|---|---|
| 9/28/63 | 9 | 13 | 1 **(Down At) Papa Joe's** ........................ | *Hot* | Sound Stage 2507 |

### THE DIXIE CUPS

Female trio from New Orleans: sisters Barbara Ann and Rosa Lee Hawkins, with Joan Marie Johnson. Discovered by singer/producer Joe Jones.

| | | | | | |
|---|---|---|---|---|---|
| 5/02/64 | 1³ | 13 | 1 **Chapel Of Love** ................................. | *Hot* | Red Bird 001 |
| 7/18/64 | 12 | 9 | 2 **People Say** ....................................... | *Hot* | Red Bird 006 |
| 10/24/64 | 39 | 6 | 3 **You Should Have Seen The Way He Looked At Me** .............................................. | *Hot* | Red Bird 012 |
| 12/19/64+ | 51 | 9 | 4 **Little Bell** ......................................... | *Hot* | Red Bird 017 |
| 4/10/65 | 20 | 4 | 5 **Iko Iko** ............................................. | *20* | Red Bird 024 |

### THE DIXIE DRIFTER

Real name: Enoch Gregory; deejay at WWRL in New York.

| | | | | | |
|---|---|---|---|---|---|
| 8/28/65 | 8 | 9 | 1 **Soul Heaven** ................................... | | Roulette 4641 |
| 5/25/74 | 98 | 2 | 2 **I Am The Black Book** ........................ | | IX Chains 7003 |

### THE DIXIE FLYERS - see JACKIE MOORE and DEE DEE WARWICK

### DIXIE HUMMINGBIRDS

Gospel group from Greenville, South Carolina. Formed in the mid-30s by James L. Davis. First recorded for Decca in 1939. Lead singer Ira Tucker added in 1939. Group based in Philadelphia from 1942. Radio work as the Jericho Boys and Swanee Quintet. Consisted of Ira Tucker and James Walker (leads), James L. Davis (baritone), Beechie Thompson (tenor), Willie Bobo (bass) and Howard Carroll (guitar). Backed Paul Simon on his #2 pop hit "Loves Me Like A Rock".

| | | | | | |
|---|---|---|---|---|---|
| 9/22/73 | 72 | 8 | 1 **Loves Me Like A Rock** ........................ | | Peacock 3198 |

### FLOYD DIXON

Born on 2/8/29 in Marshall, Texas. Vocalist/pianist. Moved to Los Angeles at age 13. Key figure in the West Coast R&B scene. Still active in music, with numerous overseas tours. Also see Eddie Williams.

| | | | | | |
|---|---|---|---|---|---|
| 3/12/49 | 10 | 1 | 1 **Dallas Blues** ................................... <br> *Juke Box #10* | | Modern 653 |
| 12/17/49 | 14 | 1 | 2 **Mississippi Blues** ............................. <br> *Juke Box #14* <br> above 2: with the Floyd Dixon Trio | | Modern 700 |
| 11/11/50 | 8 | 1 | 3 **Sad Journey Blues** ........................... <br> *Juke Box #8* <br> also released on Aladdin 3073 | | Peacock 1544 |
| 1/20/51 | 4 | 6 | 4 **Telephone Blues** ............................. <br> *Juke Box #4 / Best Seller #5* <br> with Johnny Moore's Three Blazers | | Aladdin 3075 |
| 7/26/52 | 4 | 11 | 5 **Call Operator 210** ........................... <br> *Best Seller #4 / Juke Box #5* | | Aladdin 3135 |

### WILLIE DIXON

Born on 7/1/15 in Vicksburg, Mississippi. Vocalist/guitarist/bassist/composer/producer. Golden Gloves heavyweight champion in Chicago in 1936 (as "James Dixon"). Formed the combo Five Breezes; recorded for Bluebird in 1940. Later formed the Four Jumps Of Jive (Mercury) and the Big Three Trio (Columbia). Wrote hundreds of blues songs and produced a majority of the Chicago blues records into the 70s. Also see Rosetta Howard, and the Nighthawks.

| | | | | | |
|---|---|---|---|---|---|
| 9/10/55 | 6 | 4 | 1 **Walking The Blues** ............................ <br> *Juke Box #6* | | Checker 822 |

### D.J. JAZZY JEFF & THE FRESH PRINCE

Philadelphia rap duo: disc jockey Jeff Townes with rapper Will Smith.

| | | | | | |
|---|---|---|---|---|---|
| 9/27/86 | 81 | 5 | 1 Girls Ain't Nothing But Trouble ...................... | | Word-up 001 |
| 2/14/87 | 61 | 9 | 2 The Magnificent Jazzy Jeff ........................... <br> shown as: *JAZZY JEFF & FRESH PRINCE* | | Jive 1029 |
| 5/30/87 | 65 | 8 | 3 A Touch Of Jazz ....................................... <br> shown as: *JAZZY JEFF & FRESH PRINCE* | | Jive 1042 |
| 4/16/88 | 10 | 20 | 4 **Parents Just Don't Understand** .................... | *12* | Jive 1099 |

| DEBUT DATE | PEAK POS | WKS CHR | ARTIST — Record Title | POP POS | Label & Number |
|---|---|---|---|---|---|
| | | | **DO, RAY & ME TRIO** Also known as "Do-Re-Mi Trio". Group formed in late 1946 with Al "Stomp" Russell (tenor, piano), Joel Cowan (tenor, guitar) and Joe Davis, who sang and played bass. Still active into the 70s, with Russell, Buddy Hawkins, and Al Moore. | | |
| 12/18/48+ | **2**³ | 19 | 1 **Wrapped Up In A Dream** ................................. Best Seller #2 / Juke Box #2 | | Commod. 7505 |
| | | | **CARL DOBKINS, JR.** Born in Cincinnati in 1941. Singer/guitarist. Discovered by deejay Gil Shepard. First recorded for Fraternity in 1958. Left music in the mid-60s. | | |
| 8/03/59 | **11** | 4 | 1 My Heart Is An Open Book .......................... | 3 | Decca 30803 |
| | | | **DOC SAUSAGE & His Mad Lads** Born Lucius Tyson. Vocalist/drummer. First recorded for Decca in 1940, with own band, the Five Pork Chops. | | |
| 2/04/50 | **4** | 7 | 1 **Rag Mop** ............................................. Best Seller #4 / Juke Box #4 originally a country hit by Johnnie Lee Wills | | Regal 3251 |
| | | | **JIMMY DOCKETT** | | |
| 7/28/73 | **87** | 4 | 1 Count Your Blessings (And Move On) ............... | | Flo Feel 100 |
| | | | **DR. AMERICA** | | |
| 12/11/82+ | **51** | 9 | 1 1990 ............................................... | | Elektra 69896 |
| | | | **DR. BUZZARD'S ORIGINAL "SAVANNAH" BAND** New York City Thirties-styled disco group formed by brothers Stony and "August" Darnell" Browder, with Cory Daye, lead singer. Darnell left in 1980 to form Kid Creole & The Coconuts | | |
| 10/02/76 | **92** | 3 | 1 I'll Play The Fool............................. | 80 | RCA 10762 |
| 11/13/76+ | **31** | 15 | 2 Whispering/Cherchez La Femme/Se Si Bon ........ | 27 | RCA 10827 |
| 4/16/77 | **72** | 7 | 3 Sour And Sweet/Lemon In The Honey ............... | | RCA 10923 |
| | | | **DR. HOOK** Group formed in New Jersey in 1968. Fronted by Ray Sawyer (Dr. Hook - because of eye patch) and Dennis Locorriere. | | |
| 4/12/80 | **67** | 7 | 1●Sexy Eyes .......................................... | 5 | Capitol 4831 |
| | | | **DR. JECKYLL & MR. HYDE** Rappers from Charles Evans Hughes High School, New York City: Andre "Dr. Jeckyll" Harrell and Alonzo "Mr. Hyde" Brown. Brown recorded as "Lonnie Love" in 1981. Also see Pumpkin & The Profile All-Stars. | | |
| 2/06/82 | **31** | 12 | 1 Genius Rap ........................................ | | Profile 5004 |
| 10/15/83 | **79** | 4 | 2 Gettin' Money...................................... | | Profile 7029 |
| 8/11/84 | **60** | 8 | 3 Fast Life........................................... | | Profile 5048 |
| 3/08/86 | **89** | 2 | 4 Freshest Rhymes In The World...................... | | Profile 5092 |
| | | | **DR. JOHN** Born Malcolm "Mac" Rebennack on 11/21/40 in New Orleans. Pioneer 'swamp rock' styled instrumentalist. With Leonard James & The Nighttrainers and Paul Gayten in 1955. Session work in the mid-50s. Recorded with Ronnie Baron as "Drits & Dravy". Moved to Los Angeles in the mid-60s. Character "Dr. John The Night Tripper" is based on the act originated by Lawrence "Prince Lala" Nelson. Also see Jackie Moore. | | |
| 7/21/73 | **19** | 9 | 1 Right Place Wrong Time .......................... | 9 | Atco 6914 |
| 9/15/73 | **76** | 4 | 2 Such A Night ..................................... above 2: backing vocals by Robbie Montgomery and Jessie Smith (ex-Ikettes) | 42 | Atco 6937 |
| 3/24/84 | **80** | 4 | 3 Jet Set ........................................... | | Streetwise 2219 |
| | | | **NELLA DODDS** | | |
| 11/14/64 | **74** | 3 | 1 Come See About Me............................... | Hot | Wand 167 |
| 1/09/65 | **96** | 2 | 2 Finders Keepers, Losers Weepers.................. | Hot | Wand 171 |
| | | | **BILL DOGGETT** Born on 2/16/16 in Philadelphia. Pianist/organist. Formed own band in 1938. Recorded with the Jimmy Mundy Band in 1939. Performed with the Ink Spots, Illinois Jacquet, Lucky Millinder, Louis Jordan, Ella Fitzgerald, Louis Armstrong, Coleman Hawkins, and many others. Formed own combo in 1952. Still active into the 80s. Also see Wini Brown and John Greer. | | |
| 8/18/56 | **1**¹³ | 28 | 1 **Honky Tonk (Parts 1 & 2)**........................ [I] Best Seller #1(13) / Jockey #1(5) / Juke Box #1(1) written by Doggett; with Clifford Scott on sax | 2 | King 4950 |
| 12/01/56 | **4** | 8 | 2 **Slow Walk** ....................................... [I] Best Seller #4 / Juke Box #9 / Jockey #10 | 26 | King 5000 |

| DEBUT DATE | PEAK POS | WKS CHR | ARTIST — Record Title | POP POS | Label & Number |
|---|---|---|---|---|---|
| | | | **BILL DOGGETT — Continued** | | |
| 3/02/57 | **10** | 3 | 3 **Ram-Bunk-Shush**.................................[I] | *67* | King 5020 |
| | | | Best Seller #10 / Jockey #12 | | |
| 3/03/58 | **13** | 1 | 4 Leaps And Bounds .........................[I] | | King 5101 |
| | | | Jockey #13 | | |
| 10/20/58 | **3** | 15 | 5 **Hold It** .....................................[I] | *92* | King 5149 |
| 1/05/59 | **15** | 5 | 6 Rainbow Riot ...............................[I] | | King 5159 |
| 3/23/59 | **27** | 2 | 7 Monster Party ..............................[I] | | King 5176 |
| 11/09/59 | **30** | 1 | 8 Yocky Dock (Part 1)........................[I] | | King 5256 |
| | | | **THOMAS DOLBY** | | |
| | | | Pop synthesizer whiz born Thomas Morgan Dolby Robertson, of British parentage, on 10/14/58 in Cairo, Egypt. | | |
| 5/21/83 | **49** | 9 | 1 She Blinded Me With Science ........................ | *5* | Capitol 5204 |
| | | | **FATS DOMINO**  ★★**9**★★ | | |
| | | | Born Antoine Domino on 2/26/28 in New Orleans. Classic New Orleans R&B piano-playing vocalist; heavily influenced by Fats Waller and Albert Ammons. Joined the Dave Bartholomew Band in the mid-40s. Signed to Imperial record label in 1949. Heard on many sessions cut by other R&B artists, including Lloyd Price and Joe Turner. In the films "Shake Rattle And Roll", "Jamboree", "The Big Beat" and "The Girl Can't Help It". Teamed with co-writer Dave Bartholomew on the majority of his hits. Lives in New Orleans with wife Rosemary and eight children. Frequently appears in Las Vegas. One of the most influential and popular R&B stars. | | |
| 2/18/50 | **2**¹ | 9 | 1 **The Fat Man** ..................... | | Imperial 5058 |
| | | | Juke Box #2 / Best Seller #6 | | |
| | | | a reported million-seller; his first recording | | |
| 11/18/50 | **5** | 9 | 2 **Every Night About This Time** ...................... | | Imperial 5099 |
| | | | Best Seller #5 / Juke Box #5 | | |
| 12/29/51 | **9** | 1 | 3 **Rockin' Chair**................................ | | Imperial 5145 |
| | | | Best Seller #9 | | |
| 4/26/52 | **1**¹ | 20 | 4 **Goin' Home** ........................ | *30* | Imperial 5180 |
| | | | Best Seller #1 / Juke Box #3 | | |
| | | | a reported million-seller | | |
| 10/04/52 | **10** | 1 | 5 **Poor, Poor Me**............................ | | Imperial 5197 |
| | | | Juke Box #10 | | |
| 12/13/52 | **9** | 1 | 6 **How Long**.................................. | | Imperial 5209 |
| | | | Best Seller #9 | | |
| 4/25/53 | **2**⁴ | 14 | 7 **Goin' To The River** ....................... | *24* | Imperial 5231 |
| | | | Best Seller #2 / Juke Box #3 | | |
| | | | a reported million-seller | | |
| 7/25/53 | **3** | 14 | 8 **Please Don't Leave Me**...................... | | Imperial 5240 |
| | | | Juke Box #3 / Best Seller #5 | | |
| 10/17/53 | **10** | 1 | 9 **Rose Mary**.................................. | | Imperial 5251 |
| | | | Best Seller #10 | | |
| 12/26/53+ | **6** | 11 | 10 **Something's Wrong** ......................... | | Imperial 5262 |
| | | | Best Seller #6 / Juke Box #6 | | |
| 4/10/54 | **10** | 1 | 11 **You Done Me Wrong** ...................... | | Imperial 5272 |
| | | | Best Seller #10 | | |
| 2/12/55 | **14** | 1 | 12 Thinking Of You ......................................... | | Imperial 5323 |
| | | | Jockey #14 | | |
| 3/19/55 | **7** | 7 | 13 **Don't You Know**........................... | | Imperial 5340 |
| | | | Jockey #7 / Best Seller #12 | | |
| 5/14/55 | **1**¹¹ | 26 | 14 **Ain't That A Shame**........................ | *10* | Imperial 5348 |
| | | | Best Seller #1(11) / Jockey #1(10) / Juke Box #1(8) | | |
| | | | label shows title as "Ain't It A Shame" | | |
| 9/17/55 | **1**³ | 14 | 15 **All By Myself**............................. | | Imperial 5357 |
| | | | Jockey #1 / Juke Box #2 / Best Seller #3 | | |
| 11/26/55 | **1**¹ | 12 | 16 **Poor Me/** | | |
| | | | Jockey #1 / Best Seller #3 / Juke Box #3 | | |
| 12/10/55 | **6** | 4 | 17 **I Can't Go On** ........................... | | Imperial 5369 |
| | | | Jockey #6 | | |
| 2/11/56 | **5** | 13 | 18 **Bo Weevil/** | *35* | |
| | | | Jockey #5 / Best Seller #6 / Juke Box #6 | | |
| 2/11/56 | **9** | 4 | 19 **Don't Blame It On Me**............................. | | Imperial 5375 |
| | | | Jockey #9 | | |
| 4/21/56 | **1**⁹ | 20 | 20 **I'm In Love Again/** | *3* | |
| | | | Jockey #1(9) / Juke Box #1(9) / Best Seller #1(7) | | |
| 5/05/56 | **5** | 14 | 21 **My Blue Heaven**.................................. | *21* | Imperial 5386 |
| | | | Jockey #5 | | |
| | | | originally hit #1 in 1927 for both Gene Austin and Paul Whiteman | | |

| DEBUT DATE | PEAK POS | WKS CHR | | ARTIST — Record Title | POP POS | Label & Number |
|---|---|---|---|---|---|---|
| | | | | **FATS DOMINO — Continued** | | |
| 8/04/56 | **2**¹ | 13 | 22 | **When My Dreamboat Comes Home/** <br> Juke Box #2 / Jockey #8 <br> originally a #3 hit in 1937 for Guy Lombardo | *14* | |
| 8/04/56 | **5** | 11 | 23 | **So-Long** ............................................ <br> Jockey #5 / Best Seller #6 | *44* | Imperial 5396 |
| 10/06/56 | **1**¹¹ | 23 | 24 | **Blueberry Hill/** <br> Jockey #1(11) / Best Seller #1(8) / Juke Box #1(8) <br> originally a #1 hit in 1940 for Guy Lombardo | *2* | |
| 10/27/56 | **2**² | 5 | 25 | **Honey Chile** ..................................... <br> Best Seller #2 / Jockey #5 | | Imperial 5407 |
| 12/29/56+ | **1**⁸ | 16 | 26 | **Blue Monday/** <br> Best Seller #1(8) / Juke Box #1(8) / Jockey #1(7) <br> from the film "The Girl Can't Help It" | *5* | |
| 2/02/57 | **12** | 2 | 27 | What's The Reason I'm Not Pleasing You ........ <br> Jockey #12 <br> originally a #1 hit in 1935 for Guy Lombardo | *50* | Imperial 5417 |
| 3/09/57 | **1**⁶ | 16 | 28 | **I'm Walkin'** ...................................... <br> Best Seller #1(6) / Jockey #1(5) / Juke Box #1(5) | *4* | Imperial 5428 |
| 5/13/57 | **13** | 1 | 29 | The Rooster Song.................................. <br> Jockey #13 | | Imperial EP 147 |
| 5/20/57 | **2**¹ | 11 | 30 | **Valley Of Tears/** <br> Jockey #2 / Juke Box #3 / Best Seller #4 | *6* | |
| | | 4 | 31 | It's You I Love.................................... <br> Best Seller flip / Juke Box flip | *22* | Imperial 5442 |
| 8/19/57 | **12** | 1 | 32 | What Will I Tell My Heart/ <br> Jockey #12 <br> first popularized in 1951 by Eddy Howard | *64* | |
| 9/30/57 | **14** | 3 | 33 | When I See You .................................. <br> Jockey #14 | *29* | Imperial 5454 |
| 11/04/57 | **7** | 6 | 34 | **Wait And See** ................................... <br> Jockey #7 / Best Seller #14 <br> from the film "Jamboree" | *23* | Imperial 5467 |
| 12/23/57 | **15** | 1 | 35 | The Big Beat ..................................... <br> Jockey #15 <br> from the film of the same title | *26* | Imperial 5477 |
| 3/03/58 | **10** | 4 | 36 | **Yes, My Darling**................................. <br> Jockey #10 | *55* | Imperial 5492 |
| 5/19/58 | **14** | 5 | 37 | Sick And Tired/ <br> Jockey #14 / Best Seller #15 | *22* | |
| | | 2 | 38 | No, No.......................................... <br> Best Seller flip | *55* | Imperial 5515 |
| 7/14/58 | **4** | 3 | 39 | **Little Mary** .................................... <br> Jockey #4 / Best Seller #15 | *48* | Imperial 5526 |
| 9/22/58 | **15** | 2 | 40 | Young School Girl ............................... <br> Jockey #15 | *92* | Imperial 5537 |
| 11/24/58 | **2**¹ | 15 | 41 | **Whole Lotta Loving/** | *6* | |
| 1/05/59 | **26** | 3 | 42 | Coquette........................................ <br> popularized in 1928 by Guy Lombardo - his theme song | *92* | Imperial 5553 |
| 3/09/50 | **13** | 7 | 43 | Telling Lies ..................................... | *50* | Imperial 5569 |
| 5/18/59 | **7** | 9 | 44 | **I'm Ready** ...................................... | *16* | Imperial 5585 |
| 8/10/59 | **1**¹ | 13 | 45 | **I Want To Walk You Home/** | *8* | |
| 8/10/59 | **22** | 4 | 46 | I'm Gonna Be A Wheel Some Day................... | *17* | Imperial 5606 |
| 11/16/59+ | **2**¹ | 14 | 47 | **Be My Guest/** | *8* | |
| 12/07/59 | **19** | 5 | 48 | I've Been Around ................................ | *33* | Imperial 5629 |
| 7/11/60 | **2**¹ | 11 | 49 | **Walking To New Orleans/** | *6* | |
| 8/01/60 | **28** | 3 | 50 | Don't Come Knockin'............................. | *21* | Imperial 5675 |
| 10/10/60 | **8** | 5 | 51 | **Three Nights A Week** ........................... | *15* | Imperial 5687 |
| 11/14/60 | **7** | 12 | 52 | **My Girl Josephine/** | *14* | |
| 1/09/61 | **28** | 1 | 53 | Natural Born Lover ............................. | *38* | Imperial 5704 |
| 2/20/61 | **7** | 7 | 54 | **What A Price/** | *22* | |
| 2/13/61 | **19** | 7 | 55 | Ain't That Just Like A Woman.................... | *33* | Imperial 5723 |
| 6/26/61 | **18** | 5 | 56 | It Keeps Rainin'................................. | *23* | Imperial 5753 |
| 7/31/61 | **2**¹ | 12 | 57 | **Let The Four Winds Blow** ...................... | *15* | Imperial 5764 |
| 6/16/62 | **22** | 2 | 58 | My Real Name ................................... | *59* | Imperial 5833 |
| 11/09/63 | **24** | 2 | 59 | Red Sails In The Sunset ......................... <br> Bing Crosby and Guy Lombardo both had #1 versions in 1935 | *35* | ABC-Para. 10484 |
| 1/04/64 | **63** | 5 | 60 | Who Cares ...................................... | *Hot* | ABC-Para. 10512 |

| DEBUT DATE | PEAK POS | WKS CHR | ARTIST — Record Title | POP POS | Label & Number |
|---|---|---|---|---|---|
| | | | **FATS DOMINO — Continued** | | |
| 2/29/64 | **86** | 2 | 61 Lazy Lady ............................................ | *Hot* | ABC-Para. 10531 |
| 9/19/64 | **99** | 2 | 62 Sally Was A Good Old Girl .............................. | *Hot* | ABC-Para. 10584 |
| 10/31/64 | **99** | 2 | 63 Heartbreak Hill................................. | *Hot* | ABC-Para. 10596 |
| | | | **THE DOMINOES**    ★★**167**★★ | | |
| | | | Group formed in New York in 1950, by Billy Ward and Rose Marks, a talent agent. Group originally called The Ques. Consisted of Clyde McPhatter (lead), Charlie White (tenor), Joe Lamont (baritone), Bill Brown (bass), and Billy Ward (piano). Won Talent Contest at the Apollo in 1950. On Arthur Godfrey's Talent Scouts TV Show in 1950, singing "Goodnight Irene". Signed by King/Federal in late 1950. Lead singers included, at various times, Clyde McPhatter (1950-53; first billed as "Clyde Ward", supposedly Ward's younger brother), Jackie "Sonny" Wilson (1953-57) and Eugene Mumford. Group active until the early 60s. | | |
| 2/03/51 | **6** | 10 | 1 **Do Something For Me**.............................. | | Federal 12001 |
| | | | Best Seller #6 / Juke Box #8 | | |
| 5/26/51 | **1** 14 | 30 | 2 **Sixty-Minute Man** .............................. | *17* | Federal 12022 |
| | | | Best Seller #1(14) / Juke Box #1(12) a reported million-seller | | |
| 11/24/51 | **8** | 1 | 3 **I Am With You**................................ | | Federal 12039 |
| | | | Best Seller #8 | | |
| 4/26/52 | **7** | 5 | 4 **That's What You're Doing To Me**................ | | Federal 12059 |
| | | | Best Seller #7 / Juke Box #9 | | |
| 5/24/52 | **1** 10 | 20 | 5 **Have Mercy Baby** .............................. | | Federal 12068 |
| | | | Juke Box #1(10) / Best Seller #1(7) | | |
| | | | **BILLY WARD & HIS DOMINOES:** | | |
| 11/15/52 | **8** | 9 | 6 **I'd Be Satisfied** .............................. | | Federal 12105 |
| | | | Best Seller #8 / Juke Box #8 | | |
| 1/10/53 | **3** | 7 | 7 **The Bells/** | | |
| | | | Juke Box #3 / Best Seller #6 | | |
| 3/14/53 | **4** | 2 | 8 **Pedal Pushin' Papa**.......................... | | Federal 12114 |
| | | | Juke Box #4 | | |
| 6/06/53 | **5** | 7 | 9 **These Foolish Things Remind Me Of You**........ | | Federal 12129 |
| | | | Best Seller #5 / Juke Box #5 | | |
| 9/05/53 | **8** | 3 | 10 **You Can't Keep A Good Man Down**................ | | Federal 12139 |
| | | | Juke Box #8 lead vocal by Jackie Wilson | | |
| 11/28/53 | **2** 1 | 9 | 11 **Rags To Riches**.............................. | | King 1280 |
| | | | Juke Box #2 / Best Seller #3 | | |
| 7/01/57 | **5** | 10 | 12 **Star Dust**................................. | *12* | Liberty 55071 |
| | | | Best Seller #5 / Jockey #6 lead vocal by Eugene Mumford; there have been 19 charted (pop) versions of this Hoagy Carmichael tune | | |
| | | | **THE DOOBIE BROTHERS** | | |
| | | | Rock/R&B-styled group formed in San Jose, California in 1970. Various personnel included: lead vocalists Tom Johnston and Michael McDonald, with Pat Simmons, John Hartman, Dave Shogren, Tiran Porter, Mike Hossack, Keith Knudsen, Jeff Baxter, Cornelius Bumpus, John McFee and Chet McCracken. Disbanded in 1983; re-grouped in early 1988. | | |
| 5/22/76 | **57** | 10 | 1 Takin' It To The Streets ................................. | *13* | Warner 8196 |
| 3/17/79 | **72** | 7 | 2● What A Fool Believes................................. | *1* | Warner 8725 |
| 6/09/79 | **74** | 3 | 3 Minute By Minute.............................. | *14* | Warner 8828 |
| 9/20/80 | **40** | 9 | 4 Real Love ..................................... | *5* | Warner 49503 |
| | | | **HAROLD DORMAN** | | |
| | | | Born on 12/23/31 in Drew, Mississippi. Pop-country singer/songwriter. | | |
| 4/11/60 | **7** | 7 | 1 **Mountain Of Love** ........................... | *21* | Rita 1003 |
| | | | **JIMMY DORSEY** | | |
| | | | Jimmy was born on 2/29/04 in Shenandoah, Pennsylvania. Died of cancer on 6/12/57. Great alto sax & clarinet soloist/bandleader, beginning in 1935. Recorded with brother Tommy in the Dorsey Brothers Orchestra, 1928-35 and 1953-56. | | |
| 4/03/43 | **8** | 1 | 1 **Brazil**..................................... | *14* | Decca 18460 |
| | | | vocals by Bob Eberle & Helen O'Connell; Brazilian samba - ("Aquarelo do Brasil"); featured in the film "Saludos Amigos" | | |
| 3/18/44 | **10** | 1 | 2 **When They Ask About You** ........................ | *4* | Decca 18582 |
| | | | vocal by Kitty Kallen; from the film "Stars On Parade" | | |
| 5/27/57 | **4** | 13 | 3 **So Rare** ............................. [I] | *2* | Fraternity 755 |
| | | | Jockey #4 / Best Seller #5 / Juke Box #9 featuring Jimmy on sax - recorded in New York on 11/11/56; originally a #1 hit in 1937 for Guy Lombardo | | |

| DEBUT DATE | PEAK POS | WKS CHR | ARTIST — Record Title | POP POS | Label & Number |
|---|---|---|---|---|---|
| | | | **LEE DORSEY** | | |
| | | | Born Irving Lee Dorsey on 12/24/24 in New Orleans. Moved to Portland, Oregon at age 10. Prizefighter in early 50s as "Kid Chocolate". Major hits produced by Allen Toussaint & Marshall Sehorn. Lee died of emphysema in New Orleans on 12/1/86. | | |
| 8/28/61 | 1¹ | 19 | 1 Ya Ya ......................................................... | 7 | Fury 1053 |
| 2/10/62 | 22 | 5 | 2 Do-Re-Mi................................................... | 27 | Fury 1056 |
| 6/19/65 | 7 | 13 | 3 Ride Your Pony ....................................... | 28 | Amy 927 |
| 1/15/66 | 5 | 10 | 4 Get Out Of My Life, Woman ........................ | 44 | Amy 945 |
| 8/06/66 | 5 | 11 | 5 Working In The Coal Mine ........................ | 8 | Amy 958 |
| 11/19/66 | 10 | 8 | 6 Holy Cow ................................................. | 23 | Amy 965 |
| 10/28/67 | 31 | 5 | 7 Go-Go Girl................................................. | 62 | Amy 998 |
| 6/28/69 | 33 | 5 | 8 Everything I Do Gohn Be Funky (From Now On) .. | 95 | Amy 11055 |
| 11/07/70 | 46 | 4 | 9 Yes We Can................................................. | | Polydor 14038 |
| 2/18/78 | 93 | 6 | 10 Night People................................................. | | ABC 12326 |
| | | | **THE TOMMY DORSEY ORCHESTRA** | | |
| | | | Tommy was born on 11/19/05 in Mahanoy Plane, PA; choked to death 11/26/56. Great trombonist and bandleader beginning in 1935. Tommy and brother Jimmy recorded together as the Dorsey Brothers Orchestra from 1928-35, reunited 1953-56. Hosted musical variety TV show, 1954-56. Warren Covington fronted band after Tommy's death. | | |
| 11/07/42+ | 2¹ | 13 | 1 There Are Such Things ........................... a reported million-seller | 1 | Victor 27974 |
| 1/30/43 | 2² | 13 | 2 It Started All Over Again ........................... above 2: vocals by Frank Sinatra & the Pied Pipers | 4 | Victor 1522 |
| 7/10/43 | 10 | 1 | 3 In The Blue Of The Evening ....................... vocal by Frank Sinatra; also released on Victor 27947 | 1 | Victor 1530 |
| 7/17/43 | 6 | 6 | 4 Boogie Woogie .............................. [I-R] featuring pianist Howard Smith; a #3 hit in 1938 for Tommy; originally known as "Pine Top's Boogie Woogie" by Clarence "Pine Top" Smith (POS 20 in 1929); a reported million-seller | 5 | Victor 26054 |
| 10/20/58+ | 19 | 3 | 5 Tea For Two Cha Cha ........................... [I] classic tune, originally a #1 hit for Marion Harris in 1925 | 7 | Decca 30704 |
| | | | **KENNY DOSS** | | |
| 3/22/80 | 43 | 9 | 1 Sugar......................................................... | | Bearsville 49197 |
| | | | **DOTTIE & RAY** | | |
| 2/13/65 | 35 | 3 | 1 I Love You Baby ..................................... | 126 | LeSage 701 |
| | | | **DOUBLE EXPOSURE** | | |
| | | | Quartet from Philadelphia, featuring lead singer James Williams, Joseph Harris, Leonard "Butch" Davis and Charles Whittington. | | |
| 5/22/76 | 63 | 13 | 1 Ten Percent ............................................. | 54 | Salsoul 2008 |
| 10/23/76 | 84 | 3 | 2 Everyman (Has To Carry His Own Weight)......... | | Salsoul 2013 |
| 1/29/77 | 44 | 13 | 3 My Love Is Free ....................................... | 104 | Salsoul 2012 |
| 7/28/79 | 33 | 13 | 4 I Got The Hots For Ya ............................. | | Salsoul 2091 |
| | | | **DOUG E. FRESH & THE GET FRESH CREW** | | |
| | | | Rap trio formed in 1985 by Doug E. Fresh with Barry Bee and Chill Will. | | |
| 8/31/85 | 4 | 21 | 1 The Show.................................................. | | Reality 960 |
| 7/26/86 | 19 | 13 | 2 All The Way To Heaven............................. | | Reality 969 |
| 12/20/86+ | 38 | 11 | 3 Lovin' Ev'ry Minute Of It ........................ | | Reality 971 |
| 4/25/87 | 56 | 8 | 4 Play This Only At Night............................. | | Reality 978 |
| 4/09/88 | 17 | 4 | 5 Keep Risin' To The Top ............................. | | Reality 3101 |
| | | | **CARL DOUGLAS** | | |
| | | | Born in Jamaica, West Indies. Studied engineering in the U.S. and in England. | | |
| 10/26/74+ | 1¹ | 17 | 1 ● Kung Fu Fighting....................................... | 1 | 20th Century 2140 |
| 2/15/75 | 8 | 11 | 2 Dance The Kung Fu ................................. | 48 | 20th Century 2168 |
| | | | **CAROL DOUGLAS** | | |
| | | | Born on 4/7/48 in Brooklyn, New York. Worked on commercials. Member of The Chantels vocal group in the early 70s. Went solo in 1974. | | |
| 12/07/74+ | 9 | 17 | 1 Doctor's Orders......................................... | 11 | Midland I. 10113 |

| DEBUT DATE | PEAK POS | WKS CHR | ARTIST — Record Title | POP POS | Label & Number |
|---|---|---|---|---|---|
| | | | **THE DOVELLS** | | |
| | | | Vocal group formed at Overbrook High School in Philadelphia; originally called the Brooktones. Consisted of Leonard Borisoff ("Len Barry"), Arnie Silver, Jerry Gross ("Jerry Summers"), Mike Freda ("Mike Dennis") and Jim Meeley ("Danny Brooks"). Brooks left in 1962; Barry left in late 1963. Group continued as a trio. Recorded as "The Magistrates" for MGM in 1968. | | |
| 10/02/61 | 7 | 12 | 1 **Bristol Stomp**............................................ Bristol: town near Philadelphia | 2 | Parkway 827 |
| 6/23/62 | 28 | 3 | 2 Bristol Twistin' Annie................................. | 27 | Parkway 838 |
| 6/01/63 | 10 | 9 | 3 **You Can't Sit Down** ................................ | 3 | Parkway 867 |
| | | | **AL DOWNING** | | |
| | | | Vocalist/pianist, born on 1/9/40 in Lenapah, Oklahoma. Session work with Wanda Jackson. First recorded for White Rock in 1958. Duets with Esther Phillips in 1963. | | |
| 12/28/74+ | 68 | 5 | 1 Baby Let's Talk It Over/ | | |
| 2/01/75 | 31 | 11 | 2 I'll Be Holding On..................................... | 85 | Chess 2158 |
| | | | **DON DOWNING** | | |
| 7/14/73 | 65 | 3 | 1 Lonely Days, Lonely Nights......................... | | Roadshow 7004 |
| | | | **WILL DOWNING** | | |
| | | | Singer/songwriter/producer from Brooklyn. | | |
| 2/20/88 | 48 | 10 | 1 Free....................................................... | | Island 99374 |
| 5/28/88 | 45 | 10 | 2 Sending Out An S.O.S............................... | | Island 99336 |
| | | | **GENE DOZIER & The Brotherhood** | | |
| 10/28/67 | 46 | 2 | 1 A Hunk Of Funk ............................... [I] | 121 | Minit 32026 |
| | | | **LAMONT DOZIER** | | |
| | | | Born on 6/16/41 in Detroit. Singer/songwriter/producer. Recorded as "Lamont Anthony" for Anna in 1961. With brothers Brian and Eddie Holland in highly successful songwriting and production team for Motown. Trio left Motown in 1968 and formed own Invictus/Hot Wax label. Recorded in duo with Brian Holland in 1973. | | |
| 9/09/72 | 9 | 15 | 1 **Why Can't We Be Lovers**............................ | 57 | Invictus 9125 |
| 7/21/73 | 46 | 10 | 2 Slipping Away ......................................... HOLLAND-DOZIER | | Invictus 1253 |
| 9/29/73 | 61 | 8 | 3 New Kind Of Woman.................................. HOLLAND-DOZIER | | Invictus 1254 |
| 12/08/73+ | 4 | 19 | 4 **Trying To Hold On To My Woman**................. | 15 | ABC 11407 |
| 5/11/74 | 4 | 15 | 5 **Fish Ain't Bitin'** .................................... | 26 | ABC 11438 |
| 11/30/74+ | 4 | 16 | 6 **Let Me Start Tonite** ............................... | 87 | ABC 12044 |
| 4/19/75 | 41 | 9 | 7 All Cried Out........................................... | 101 | ABC 12076 |
| 9/04/76 | 89 | 3 | 8 Can't Get Off Until The Feeling Stops.............. | | Warner 8240 |
| 2/06/82 | 61 | 7 | 9 Shout About It......................................... | | M&M 502 |
| | | | **THE DRAMATICS** ★★51★★ | | |
| | | | Detroit group first recorded for Wingate as the Dynamics in 1966. Members in 1971: Ron Banks (lead singer), William Howard, Larry Demps, Willie Ford and Elbert Wilkins. Howard and Wilkins replaced by L.J. Reynolds and Lenny Mayes in 1973. Reynolds, formerly of Chocolate Syrup, began solo career in 1981. Banks recorded solo in 1983. Drummer Carl Smalls was a member of Undisputed Truth and Sweat Band. Also see The Dells. | | |
| 6/24/67 | 43 | 2 | 1 All Because Of You..................................... | | Sport 101 |
| 7/03/71 | 3 | 15 | 2 **Whatcha See Is Whatcha Get** ...................... | 9 | Volt 4058 |
| 12/18/71+ | 16 | 11 | 3 Get Up And Get Down ................................ | 78 | Volt 4071 |
| 2/26/72 | 1⁴ | 13 | 4 **In The Rain**.......................................... | 5 | Volt 4075 |
| 8/19/72 | 18 | 10 | 5 Toast To The Fool ..................................... | 67 | Volt 4082 |
| 4/28/73 | 5 | 13 | 6 **Hey You! Get Off My Mountain** ................... | 43 | Volt 4090 |
| 9/29/73 | 12 | 15 | 7 Fell For You ............................................ | 45 | Volt 4099 |
| 2/23/74 | 49 | 10 | 8 And I Panicked ........................................ | | Volt 4105 |
| 6/08/74 | 30 | 10 | 9 Choosing Up On You/ | | |
| 7/27/74 | 25 | 14 | 10 Door To Your Heart ................................ | 62 | Cadet 5704 |
| 11/23/74 | 63 | 6 | 11 Don't Make Me No Promises/ all of above (except #5 & 8): produced by Tony Hester | | |
| 1/25/75 | 74 | 6 | 12 Tune Up ............................................... | | Cadet 5706 |
| 5/03/75 | 4 | 12 | 13 **Me And Mrs. Jones** ............................... | 47 | ABC 12090 |
| 7/12/75 | 46 | 10 | 14 Love Is Missing From Our Lives ..................... THE DELLS/THE DRAMATICS | | Cadet 5710 |
| 8/23/75 | 22 | 16 | 15 (I'm Going By) The Stars In Your Eyes.............. 10, 13 & 15: **RON BANKS & THE DRAMATICS** | 81 | ABC 12125 |

| DEBUT DATE | PEAK POS | WKS CHR | ARTIST — Record Title | POP POS | Label & Number |
|---|---|---|---|---|---|
| | | | **THE DRAMATICS — Continued** | | |
| 9/27/75 | 26 | 12 | 16 No Rebate On Love........................................ | | Mainstream 5571 |
| 12/27/75+ | 10 | 16 | 17 **You're Fooling You** .................................... | *87* | ABC 12150 |
| 6/05/76 | 49 | 6 | 18 Treat Me Like A Man ................................... | | ABC 12180 |
| 10/02/76 | 23 | 13 | 19 Finger Fever............................................... | | ABC 12220 |
| 12/18/76+ | 3 | 19 | 20 **Be My Girl** ............................................... | *53* | ABC 12235 |
| 4/09/77 | 9 | 17 | 21 **I Can't Get Over You**............................... | *101* | ABC 12258 |
| 8/20/77 | 4 | 19 | '22 **Shake It Well** .......................................... | *76* | ABC 12299 |
| 2/18/78 | 17 | 15 | 23 Ocean Of Thoughts And Dreams ..................... | *106* | ABC 12331 |
| 6/17/78 | 22 | 12 | 24 Stop Your Weeping ..................................... | | ABC 12372 |
| 9/23/78 | 56 | 7 | 25 Do What You Want To Do ............................ | | ABC 12400 |
| | | | written by Hall & Oates | | |
| 5/05/79 | 35 | 10 | 26 I Just Wanna Dance With You....................... | | MCA 41017 |
| 7/07/79 | 40 | 12 | 27 That's My Favorite Song.............................. | | MCA 41056 |
| 2/02/80 | 9 | 18 | 28 **Welcome Back Home**.................................. | | MCA 41178 |
| 6/28/80 | 79 | 3 | 29 Be With The One You Love .......................... | | MCA 41241 |
| 10/25/80 | 59 | 9 | 30 Get It ...................................................... | | MCA 51003 |
| 12/27/80+ | 26 | 15 | 31 You're The Best Thing In My Life.................... | | MCA 51041 |
| 4/10/82 | 40 | 13 | 32 Live It Up ................................................. | | Capitol 5103 |
| 8/07/82 | 62 | 8 | 33 Treat Me Right ........................................... | | Capitol 5140 |
| 5/17/86 | 61 | 9 | 34 One Love Ago............................................. | | Fantasy 967 |

### DREAMBOY

Group formed at Oak Park High School, Michigan, in 1979. Consisted of Jeff Stanton (vocals), Jeff Bass (guitar), Jimi Hunt (keyboards), Paul Stewart, Jr. (bass) and George "Dewey" Twymon (drums).

| DEBUT DATE | PEAK POS | WKS CHR | ARTIST — Record Title | POP POS | Label & Number |
|---|---|---|---|---|---|
| 1/07/84 | 17 | 17 | 1 Don't Go................................................... | | Qwest 29389 |
| 10/06/84 | 45 | 13 | 2 I Promise (I Do Love You) ............................ | *106* | Qwest 29190 |

### DREAMGIRLS - see SHERYL LEE RALPH

### EDDIE DRENNON & B.B.S. UNLIMITED

| DEBUT DATE | PEAK POS | WKS CHR | ARTIST — Record Title | POP POS | Label & Number |
|---|---|---|---|---|---|
| 12/06/75+ | 36 | 10 | 1 Let's Do The Latin Hustle.............................. | | Friends & Co 124 |

### PATTI DREW

Born on 12/29/44 in Charleston, SC. To Evanston, Illinois, 1956. Lead singer of The Drew-Vels. First recorded under own name for Quill, 1966. Left music, 1971.

| DEBUT DATE | PEAK POS | WKS CHR | ARTIST — Record Title | POP POS | Label & Number |
|---|---|---|---|---|---|
| 10/14/67 | 22 | 8 | 1 Tell Him ................................................... | *85* | Capitol 5861 |
| | | | solo version (also see Drew-Vels version); featuring bass singer, Carlton Black | | |
| 7/13/68 | 34 | 13 | 2 Workin' On A Groovy Thing ........................... | *62* | Capitol 2197 |
| 12/07/68 | 40 | 2 | 3 Hard To Handle .......................................... | *93* | Capitol 2339 |
| 6/07/69 | 38 | 5 | 4 The Love That A Woman Should Give To A Man . | *119* | Capitol 2473 |

### THE DREW-VELS

Vocal group from Evanston, Illinois. Consisted of sisters Patti, Lorraine and Erma Drew; with bass singer Carlton Black (married to Erma).

| DEBUT DATE | PEAK POS | WKS CHR | ARTIST — Record Title | POP POS | Label & Number |
|---|---|---|---|---|---|
| 2/08/64 | 90 | 2 | 1 Tell Him ................................................... | *Hot* | Capitol 5055 |
| | | | also see Patti Drew's solo version above | | |

### THE DRIFTERS ★★28★★

Vocal group formed to showcase lead singer Clyde McPhatter on Atlantic in 1953. Included Gerhart and Andrew Thrasher, Bill Pinkney and McPhatter (who went solo in 1955). Group continued with various lead singers until 1958. In 1958, manager George Treadwell disbanded the group and brought in The Five Crowns and renamed them The Drifters. The majority of The Drifters' pop hits were sung by 3 different lead singers: Ben E. King, 1959-60; Rudy Lewis, 1961-63; and Johnny Moore, 1957, and 1963-66. Rudy died of a heart attack in summer of 1964. Many personnel changes throughout career and several groups have used the name in later years.

| DEBUT DATE | PEAK POS | WKS CHR | ARTIST — Record Title | POP POS | Label & Number |
|---|---|---|---|---|---|
| | | | **CLYDE McPHATTER & THE DRIFTERS:** | | |
| 10/31/53 | 1[11] | 21 | 1 **Money Honey**........................................... | | Atlantic 1006 |
| | | | Best Seller #1(11) / Juke Box #1(1) | | |
| 3/13/54 | 2[3] | 14 | 2 **Such A Night/** | | |
| | | | Juke Box #2 / Best Seller #5 | | |
| | | | **THE DRIFTERS featuring CLYDE McPHATTER:** | | |
| 3/06/54 | 7 | 3 | 3 **Lucille**................................................... | | Atlantic 1019 |
| | | | Best Seller #7 / Juke Box #7 | | |
| 6/19/54 | 1[8] | 23 | 4 **Honey Love** ............................................. | *21* | Atlantic 1029 |
| | | | Best Seller #1(8) / Juke Box #1(8) a reported million-seller | | |

| DEBUT DATE | PEAK POS | WKS CHR | ARTIST — Record Title | POP POS | Label & Number |
|---|---|---|---|---|---|
| | | | **THE DRIFTERS — Continued** | | |
| 11/13/54 | **7** | 5 | 5 Bip Bam................................................<br>Best Seller #7 | | Atlantic 1043 |
| 12/18/54+ | **2**¹ | 4 | 6 White Christmas ...............................[X]<br>Best Seller #2 / Juke Box #6<br>vocal duet: Clyde McPhatter & Bill Pinkney (bass);<br>recorded in November, 1953 | 80 | Atlantic 1048 |
| 3/26/55 | **2**² | 15 | 7 What'Cha Gonna Do.............................<br>Jockey #2 / Best Seller #3 / Juke Box #4 | | Atlantic 1055 |
| | | | **THE DRIFTERS:** | | |
| 11/05/55 | **1**¹ | 10 | 8 Adorable/<br>Juke Box #1 / Best Seller #5 / Jockey #5 | | |
| 12/10/55 | **5** | 9 | 9 Steamboat ........................................<br>Juke Box #5 / Best Seller #6 / Jockey #6<br>Bill Pinkney, lead singer | | Atlantic 1078 |
| 12/24/55+ | **5** | 3 | 10 White Christmas ........................[X-R]<br>**THE DRIFTERS featuring CLYDE McPHATTER**<br>Jockey #5 / Best Seller #13 | | Atlantic 1048 |
| 5/12/56 | **10** | 4 | 11 Ruby Baby ........................................<br>Juke Box #10 / Best Seller #13 | | Atlantic 1089 |
| 9/08/56 | **11** | 5 | 12 I Gotta Get Myself A Woman/<br>Best Seller #11 | | |
| | | 3 | 13 Soldier Of Fortune.............................<br>Best Seller flip | | Atlantic 1101 |
| 12/29/56 | **12** | 1 | 14 White Christmas ........................[X-R]<br>**THE DRIFTERS featuring CLYDE McPHATTER**<br>Jockey #12 | | Atlantic 1048 |
| 3/09/57 | **10** | 4 | 15 Fools Fall In Love...............................<br>Jockey #10 / Juke Box #10 | 69 | Atlantic 1123 |
| 6/08/59 | **1**¹ | 19 | 16 There Goes My Baby ............................ | 2 | Atlantic 2025 |
| 10/19/59 | **5** | 14 | 17 (If You Cry) True Love, True Love/<br>Johnny Lee Williams, lead singer | 33 | |
| 11/02/59 | **2**³ | 12 | 18 Dance With Me................................... | 15 | Atlantic 2040 |
| 2/29/60 | **4** | 12 | 19 This Magic Moment............................. | 16 | Atlantic 2050 |
| 6/06/60 | **9** | 8 | 20 Lonely Winds .................................... | 54 | Atlantic 2062 |
| 10/03/60 | **1**¹ | 15 | 21 Save The Last Dance For Me................. | 1 | Atlantic 2071 |
| 1/23/61 | **6** | 6 | 22 I Count The Tears ............................<br>16, 18-22: Ben E. King, lead singer | 17 | Atlantic 2087 |
| 4/10/61 | **6** | 7 | 23 Some Kind Of Wonderful .................... | 32 | Atlantic 2096 |
| 6/26/61 | **13** | 6 | 24 Please Stay ...................................... | 14 | Atlantic 2105 |
| 10/09/61 | **10** | 10 | 25 Sweets For My Sweet ......................... | 16 | Atlantic 2117 |
| 12/01/62+ | **4** | 15 | 26 Up On The Roof ................................ | 5 | Atlantic 2162 |
| 4/20/63 | **7** | 9 | 27 On Broadway.................................... | 9 | Atlantic 2182 |
| 10/05/63 | **24** | 4 | 28 I'll Take You Home ............................ | 25 | Atlantic 2201 |
| 2/01/64 | **43** | 7 | 29 Vaya Con Dios...................................<br>23-27 & 29: Rudy Lewis, lead singer | Hot | Atlantic 2216 |
| 5/02/64 | **56** | 7 | 30 One Way Love .................................. | Hot | Atlantic 2225 |
| 6/27/64 | **4** | 14 | 31 Under The Boardwalk ......................... | Hot | Atlantic 2237 |
| 9/26/64 | **33** | 7 | 32 I've Got Sand In My Shoes .................. | Hot | Atlantic 2253 |
| 11/14/64 | **18** | 9 | 33 Saturday Night At The Movies .............. | Hot | Atlantic 2260 |
| 2/06/65 | **10** | 3 | 34 At The Club .................................... | 43 | Atlantic 2268 |
| 12/10/66 | **37** | 5 | 35 Baby What I Mean ............................ | 62 | Atlantic 2366 |
| 8/26/67 | **36** | 4 | 36 Ain't It The Truth ............................ | | Atlantic 2426 |
| 9/14/74 | **83** | 5 | 37 Kissin' In The Back Row Of The Movies............<br>8, 11-12, 15, 28, 30-37: Johnny Moore, lead singer | | Bell 600 |
| | | | **"D" TRAIN**<br>Duo from Erasmus Hall High, in Brooklyn: James "D Train" Williams (vocals) and<br>Hubert Eaves III (keyboards). Also see James (D-Train) Williams. | | |
| 12/19/81+ | **13** | 17 | 1 You're The One For Me ...................... | | Prelude 8043 |
| 5/22/82 | **15** | 16 | 2 Keep On ........................................ | | Prelude 8049 |
| 10/16/82 | **42** | 11 | 3 Walk On By .................................... | | Prelude 8057 |
| 4/23/83 | **20** | 12 | 4 Music .......................................... | | Prelude 8068 |
| 7/09/83 | **55** | 10 | 5 Keep Giving Me Love ........................ | | Prelude 584 |
| 11/26/83+ | **5** | 19 | 6 Something's On Your Mind .................. | 79 | Prelude 8080 |
| 3/24/84 | **43** | 9 | 7 You're The Reason ........................... | | Prelude 8082 |
| 6/22/85 | **59** | 8 | 8 Just Another Night (Without Your Love)............ | | Prelude 694 |

| DEBUT DATE | PEAK POS | WKS CHR | ARTIST — Record Title | POP POS | Label & Number |
|---|---|---|---|---|---|
| | | | **THE DU DROPPERS** Group formed in New York City in 1952. Consisted of Caleb "J.C." Ginyard, Jr. (lead - d: 1978), Willie Ray (tenor), Harvey Ray (baritone) and Bob Kornegay (bass). Ginyard was a veteran of the Jubalaires and Dixieaires. First recorded for Red Robin in 1952. Ginyard left to join the Golden Gate Quartet in 1955; group disbanded. | | |
| 4/18/53 | **3** | 14 | 1 **I Wanna Know** .................... Best Seller #3 / Juke Box #4 | | Victor 5229 |
| 6/27/53 | **3** | 5 | 2 **I Found Out (What You Do When You Go 'Round There)** ........................ Best Seller #3 answer song to "I Wanna Know" | | Victor 5321 |
| | | | **DORIS DUKE** Born Doris Curry in Sandersville, Georgia. With gospel groups Raspberry Singers, Evangelistic Gospel Singers, Davis Sisters, and Caravans. Back-up work in New York City from 1963. Recorded as Doris Willingham for Hy-Monty in 1967. Toured Europe as back-up singer with Nina Simone in 1968. Inactive since mid-70s. | | |
| 2/21/70 | **7** | 11 | 1 **To The Other Woman (I'm The Other Woman)** . | *50* | Canyon 28 |
| 5/23/70 | **36** | 6 | 2 Feet Start Walking .................... | *109* | Canyon 35 |
| | | | **GEORGE DUKE** Born on 1/12/46 in San Rafael, California. Singer/songwriter/keyboardist/ percussionist. Own group in San Francisco during the mid-50s. With the Don Ellis Big Band, and Jean-Luc Ponty. With Mothers Of Invention from 1971-75. Own group from 1977. With Stanley Clarke in the Clarke/Duke Project. Also see Howard Hewett. | | |
| 11/12/77+ | **2**¹ | 17 | 1 **Reach For It**.................... | *54* | Epic 50463 |
| 4/08/78 | **4** | 19 | 2 **Dukey Stick (Part One)**.................... | | Epic 50531 |
| 9/23/78 | **68** | 4 | 3 Movin' On .................... | | Epic 50593 |
| 2/03/79 | **25** | 15 | 4 Say That You Will .................... | | Epic 50660 |
| 11/10/79+ | **23** | 16 | 5 I Want You For Myself .................... | | Epic 50792 |
| 4/11/81 | **6** | 19 | 6 **Sweet Baby** .................... | *19* | Epic 01052 |
| | | | STANLEY CLARKE/GEORGE DUKE | | |
| 2/06/82 | **15** | 14 | 7 Shine On .................... | *41* | Epic 02701 |
| 6/26/82 | **83** | 3 | 8 Ride On Love .................... | | Epic 02932 |
| 4/02/83 | **59** | 9 | 9 Reach Out (Part 1) .................... | | Epic 03760 |
| 10/08/83 | **37** | 13 | 10 Heroes .................... | | Epic 04155 |
| | | | STANLEY CLARKE/GEORGE DUKE | | |
| 3/30/85 | **37** | 11 | 11 Thief In The Night .................... | | Elektra 69649 |
| 9/13/86 | **57** | 7 | 12 Broken Glass.................... | | Elektra 69524 |
| 11/22/86 | **60** | 11 | 13 Good Friend .................... | | Elektra 69504 |
| | | | **DUNCAN SISTERS** | | |
| 11/03/79 | **89** | 3 | 1 Rock Along Slowly .................... | | EarMarc 5501 |
| 2/23/80 | **94** | 2 | 2 Sadness In My Eyes .................... | | EarMarc 5503 |
| | | | **DARRYL DUNCAN** | | |
| 3/05/88 | **71** | 6 | 1 James Brown (Pt. 1).................... | | Motown 1924 |
| | | | **GENE DUNLAP** Drummer from Detroit; also plays guitar and keyboards. Worked in a music store with Earl Klugh; later played in the Earl Klugh group. Worked with Grant Green and Roy Ayers. | | |
| 3/28/81 | **72** | 5 | 1 Before You Break My Heart.................... featuring The Ridgeways (three sisters & a brother) | | Capitol 4978 |
| 5/30/81 | **94** | 4 | 2 Rock Radio .................... | | Capitol 4996 |
| 11/21/81 | **61** | 9 | 3 Something Inside My Head.................... featuring Phillippe Wynne | | Capitol 5055 |
| | | | **DUNN & BRUCE STREET** Duo of Dunn Pearson, Jr. and Bruce Gray. | | |
| 1/30/82 | **45** | 10 | 1 If You Come With Me .................... | | Devaki 4005 |
| 7/03/82 | **36** | 12 | 2 Shout For Joy .................... | | Devaki 1009 |
| 12/18/82+ | **63** | 9 | 3 I Owe It To Me .................... | | Devaki 1014 |

| DEBUT DATE | PEAK POS | WKS CHR | ARTIST — Record Title | POP POS | Label & Number |
|---|---|---|---|---|---|
| | | | **JACK DUPREE & MR. BEAR** | | |
| | | | Born William Thomas Dupree on 7/4/10 in New Orleans. Vocalist/pianist. Nickname "Champion Jack" derived from stint as professional boxer in Chicago from 1932-40. First recorded for Solo in 1942. Settled in Europe in 1960. Noted for his serio-comic patter songs. Mr. Bear is Teddy McRae. | | |
| 8/20/55 | **6** | 11 | 1 **Walking The Blues**.................................. | | King 4812 |
| | | | Jockey #6 / Juke Box #6 / Best Seller #7 | | |
| | | | Mr. Bear is not actually on this side - flip side only | | |
| | | | **ROBBIE DUPREE** | | |
| | | | Singer/songwriter, born Robert Dupuis in Brooklyn, in 1947. | | |
| 7/26/80 | **85** | 2 | 1 Steal Away .................................. | *6* | Elektra 46621 |
| | | | **ADA DYER** | | |
| | | | Backing singer for Norman Connors and member of the dance group, Warp 9. | | |
| 4/02/88 | **33** | 11 | 1 I Bet Ya, I'll Let Ya.................................. | | Motown 1905 |
| | | | **DYKE & THE BLAZERS** | | |
| | | | Band led by Arlester "Dyke" Christian (b: 1943, Brooklyn). With O'Jays backing band, the Blazers, in the mid-60s. Dyke was shot to death in 1971. | | |
| 2/11/67 | **17** | 24 | 1 **Funky Broadway - Part 1**.................................. | *65* | Orig. Sound 64 |
| 7/08/67 | **41** | 5 | 2 So Sharp .................................. | *130* | Orig. Sound 69 |
| 4/20/68 | **22** | 8 | 3 **Funky Walk - Part 1 (East)**.................................. | *67* | Orig. Sound 79 |
| 4/26/69 | **7** | 12 | 4 **We Got More Soul** .................................. | *35* | Orig. Sound 86 |
| 9/14/69 | **4** | 11 | 5 **Let A Woman Be A Woman - Let A Man Be A Man/** | *36* | |
| 4/04/70 | **20** | 7 | 6 Uhh .................................. | *118* | Orig. Sound 89 |
| 1/24/70 | **30** | 6 | 7 You Are My Sunshine .................................. | *121* | Orig. Sound 90 |
| 7/18/70 | **32** | 9 | 8 Runaway People .................................. | *119* | Orig. Sound 96 |
| | | | **DYNAMIC BREAKERS** | | |
| 1/05/85 | **83** | 5 | 1 Dynamic Total Control.................................. | | Sunnyview 3016 |
| | | | **DYNAMIC CORVETTES** | | |
| 5/10/75 | **68** | 8 | 1 Funky Music Is The Thing, Pt. 1.................... | | Abet 9459 |
| | | | **DYNAMIC SUPERIORS** | | |
| | | | Group from Washington, DC, formed in 1963. Consisted of lead Tony Washington, George Spann (tenor), George Wesley Peterbark, Jr. (tenor), Michael McCalphin (baritone) and Maurice Washington (bass). | | |
| 9/21/74 | **16** | 16 | 1 Shoe Shoe Shine .................................. | *68* | Motown 1324 |
| | | | produced by Ashford & Simpson | | |
| 3/29/75 | **13** | 14 | 2 Leave It Alone.................................. | *102* | Motown 1342 |
| 8/23/75 | **51** | 8 | 3 Nobody's Gonna Change Me .................................. | | Motown 1359 |
| 10/11/75 | **53** | 7 | 4 Deception .................................. | | Motown 1365 |
| 7/23/77 | **53** | 7 | 5 Nowhere To Run - Part 1 .................................. | | Motown 1419 |
| | | | **THE DYNAMICS** | | |
| | | | Detroit group consisting of Samuel Stevenson, Isaac "Zeke" Harris, George White and Fred "Sonny" Baker. | | |
| 11/02/63 | **44** | 10 | 1 Misery.................................. | *Hot* | Big Top 3161 |
| 3/01/69 | **17** | 11 | 2 Ice Cream Song.................................. | *59* | Cotillion 44021 |
| 11/22/69 | **47** | 2 | 3 Dum-De-Dum.................................. | | Cotillion 44045 |
| 6/09/73 | **40** | 9 | 4 What A Shame.................................. | | Black Gold 8 |
| 9/15/73 | **49** | 8 | 5 Funky Key.................................. | | Black Gold 9 |
| 3/30/74 | **92** | 2 | 6 She's For Real (Bless You) .................................. | | Black Gold 11 |
| | | | **DYNASTY** | | |
| | | | Los Angeles group consisting of Kevin Spencer and Nidra Beard (formerly with the Sylvers) and Linda Carriere (formerly with DeBlanc and Starfire). Group formed by Leon Sylvers, who joined them in 1981. | | |
| 9/29/79 | **36** | 13 | 1 I Don't Want To Be A Freak (But I Can't Help Myself).................................. | | Solar 11694 |
| 7/05/80 | **6** | 19 | 2 **I've Just Begun To Love You**.................... | *87* | Solar 12021 |
| 11/01/80 | **34** | 16 | 3 Do Me Right .................................. | *103* | Solar 12127 |
| 3/14/81 | **64** | 6 | 4 Something To Remember.................................. | | Solar 12180 |
| 7/04/81 | **26** | 16 | 5 Here I Am .................................. | | Solar 47932 |
| 11/14/81 | **31** | 12 | 6 Love In The Fast Lane .................................. | | Solar 47946 |
| 11/13/82 | **52** | 9 | 7 Strokin'.................................. | | Solar 69927 |
| 2/19/83 | **39** | 8 | 8 Check It Out.................................. | | Solar 69843 |

| DEBUT DATE | PEAK POS | WKS CHR | ARTIST — Record Title | POP POS | Label & Number |
|---|---|---|---|---|---|
| | | | **DYNASTY — Continued** | | |
| 2/27/88 | 41 | 10 | 9 Don't Waste My Time.................................... | | Solar 70019 |
| 6/11/88 | 56 | 9 | 10 Tell Me (Do U Want My Love)? ......................... | | Solar 70024 |
| | | | **THE DYNATONES** | | |
| 10/01/66 | 46 | 2 | 1 The Fife Piper.............................................. [I] | | HBR 494 |
| | | | originally released on St. Clair 117 | | |
| | | | **CLIFTON DYSON** | | |
| | | | 19 year old singer from Brooklyn. | | |
| 7/31/82 | 51 | 12 | 1 Slow Your Body Down.................................. | | Network 69993 |
| | | | **RONNIE DYSON** | | |
| | | | Born on 6/5/50 in Washington, DC; raised in Brooklyn. Lead part in the Broadway musical "Hair". In the film "Putney Swope". | | |
| 7/11/70 | 9 | 13 | 1 (If You Let Me Make Love To You Then) Why Can't I Touch You? ............................. | 8 | Columbia 45110 |
| | | | from the off-Broadway musical "Salvation" | | |
| 10/31/70 | 9 | 9 | 2 I Don't Wanna Cry ..................................... | 50 | Columbia 45240 |
| 7/03/71 | 37 | 6 | 3 When You Get Right Down To It ................... | 94 | Columbia 45387 |
| 2/17/73 | 15 | 9 | 4 One Man Band (Plays All Alone)..................... | 28 | Columbia 45776 |
| 7/07/73 | 29 | 12 | 5 Just Don't Want To Be Lonely....................... | 60 | Columbia 45867 |
| 4/27/74 | 62 | 8 | 6 We Can Make It Last Forever ....................... | | Columbia 46021 |
| 6/26/76 | 6 | 22 | 7 The More You Do It (The More I Like It Done To Me).................................................. | 62 | Columbia 10356 |
| 12/11/76+ | 75 | 7 | 8 (I Like Being) Close To You ......................... | | Columbia 10441 |
| 9/17/77 | 30 | 15 | 9 Don't Be Afraid ......................................... | | Columbia 10599 |
| 1/28/78 | 77 | 3 | 10 Ain't Nothing Wrong ................................ | | Columbia 10667 |
| 3/27/82 | 66 | 6 | 11 Bring It On Home ...................................... | | Cotillion 47005 |
| 5/08/82 | 57 | 10 | 12 Heart To Heart ......................................... | | Cotillion 40917 |
| 8/13/83 | 23 | 13 | 13 All Over Your Face .................................... | | Cotillion 99841 |

# E

| DEBUT DATE | PEAK POS | WKS CHR | ARTIST — Record Title | POP POS | Label & Number |
|---|---|---|---|---|---|
| | | | **BRENDA LEE EAGER** | | |
| | | | Lead singer of Jerry Butler's back-up group. | | |
| | | | **JERRY BUTLER & BRENDA LEE EAGER:** | | |
| 12/11/71+ | 3 | 17 | 1 ● Ain't Understanding Mellow ........................ | 21 | Mercury 73255 |
| 7/29/72 | 6 | 13 | 2 (They Long To Be) Close To You ................... | 91 | Mercury 73301 |
| | | | shown as: **JERRY BUTLER featuring BRENDA LEE EAGER** | | |
| 10/13/73 | 64 | 7 | 3 The Love We Had Stays On My Mind................. | | Mercury 73422 |
| 12/01/73+ | 15 | 13 | 4 Power Of Love ............................................ | | Mercury 73443 |
| | | | **BRENDA LEE EAGER:** | | |
| 10/11/75 | 71 | 6 | 5 Good Old Fashioned Lovin' ........................... | | Playboy 6047 |
| 10/20/84 | 72 | 6 | 6 Watch My Body Talk................................... | | Private I 04621 |
| | | | **CHARLES EARLAND** | | |
| | | | Keyboard player from Philadelphia. Played sax while in the Temple University Band. Worked with Jimmy McGriff and Lou Donaldson from 1968-70, then formed his own group. | | |
| 5/08/76 | 72 | 6 | 1 From My Heart To Yours ............................. | | Mercury 73793 |
| 2/27/82 | 65 | 7 | 2 The Only One ............................................. | | Columbia 02710 |
| 6/12/82 | 92 | 3 | 3 Animal..................................................... | | Columbia 02881 |
| | | | **THE EARLS** | | |
| | | | White vocal group formed at the Tecumseh Social Club in the Bronx in 1957. Originally called the High Hatters. Consisted of Larry Figueiredo ("Larry Chance"), lead; Bob Del Din, Eddie Harder, Larry Palumbo, and Jack Wray. First recorded for Rome in 1961. Disbanded in 1970; re-formed with Chance, Ronnie Calabrese and Tony Obert in 1975. | | |
| 1/19/63 | 29 | 2 | 1 Remember Then.......................................... | 24 | Old Town 1130 |
| | | | **EARONS** | | |
| | | | Astro-funk band from "Earon Earth", known by numbers, not names. Consisted of Earon .22 (guitar), Earon .33 (keyboards), Earon .69 (bass), Earon .18 (drums) and Earon .28 (lead vocals). | | |
| 7/02/83 | 72 | 4 | 1 Video Baby .............................................. | | Boardwalk 179 |
| 4/21/84 | 36 | 13 | 2 Land Of Hunger ........................................ | | Island 99776 |

| DEBUT DATE | PEAK POS | WKS CHR | ARTIST — Record Title | POP POS | Label & Number |
|---|---|---|---|---|---|
| 8/04/84 | 52 | 7 | **EARONS — Continued**<br>3 Beat Sixteen............................................... | | Island 99727 |

**EARTH, WIND & FIRE** ★★27★★

Los Angeles-based group formed by Chicago-bred producer/songwriter/vocalist/ percussionist/kalimba player Maurice White. In 1969, White, former session drummer for Chess Records and member of The Ramsey Lewis Trio, formed the Salty Peppers; recorded for Capitol. Maurice's brother Verdine White was the group's bassist. 18 months later, the brothers hired a new band and recorded as Earth, Wind & Fire - named for the 3 elements of Maurice's astrological sign. Co-lead singer Philip Bailey joined as lead singer in 1971. Group generally contained 8-10 members, with frequent personnel shuffling. Appeared in the films "That's the Way of the World" (1975) and "Sgt. Pepper's Lonely Hearts Club Band" (1978). Elaborate, mystical stage shows featured an array of magic acts and pyrotechnics. Group members Philip Bailey, Wade Flemons, Ronnie Laws and Maurice White had solo hits.

| DEBUT DATE | PEAK POS | WKS CHR | ARTIST — Record Title | POP POS | Label & Number |
|---|---|---|---|---|---|
| 7/10/71 | 43 | 5 | 1 Love Is Life...................................................... | 93 | Warner 7492 |
| 2/26/72 | 44 | 3 | 2 I Think About Lovin' You ................................ | | Warner 7549 |
| 7/28/73 | 25 | 11 | 3 Evil ................................................................... | 50 | Columbia 45888 |
| 11/10/73+ | 23 | 13 | 4 Keep Your Head To The Sky ........................... | 52 | Columbia 45953 |
| 3/02/74 | 4 | 17 | 5 **Mighty Mighty**........................................... | 29 | Columbia 46007 |
| 7/06/74 | 6 | 13 | 6 **Kalimba Story**........................................... | 55 | Columbia 46070 |
| 9/21/74 | 23 | 11 | 7 Devotion.......................................................... | 33 | Columbia 10026 |
| 11/30/74+ | 61 | 11 | 8 Hot Dawgit.............................................. [I]<br>RAMSEY LEWIS & EARTH, WIND & FIRE | 50 | Columbia 10056 |
| 2/08/75 | 1² | 16 | 9●**Shining Star** ........................................... | *1* | Columbia 10090 |
| 3/15/75 | 20 | 12 | 10 Sun Goddess ........................................... [I]<br>RAMSEY LEWIS & EARTH, WIND & FIRE | 44 | Columbia 10103 |
| 7/05/75 | 5 | 14 | 11 **That's The Way Of The World** ..................... | *12* | Columbia 10172 |
| 11/22/75+ | 1² | 18 | 12●**Sing A Song**............................................ | *5* | Columbia 10251 |
| 3/27/76 | 11 | 13 | 13 Can't Hide Love ............................................ | 39 | Columbia 10309 |
| 7/10/76 | 1² | 17 | 14●**Getaway**.................................................. | *12* | Columbia 10373 |
| 11/20/76+ | 4 | 16 | 15 **Saturday Nite** ........................................... | 21 | Columbia 10439 |
| 3/19/77 | 26 | 11 | 16 On Your Face ................................................. | | Columbia 10492 |
| 10/15/77 | 1⁷ | 20 | 17 **Serpentine Fire** ......................................... | *13* | Columbia 10625 |
| 2/25/78 | 12 | 13 | 18 **Fantasy** ...................................................... | 32 | Columbia 10688 |
| 7/29/78 | 1¹ | 16 | 19●**Got To Get You Into My Life** ..................... | *9* | Columbia 10796 |
| 11/18/78+ | 1¹ | 17 | 20●**September** ................................................ | *8* | ARC 10854 |
| 5/19/79 | 2⁴ | 13 | 21●**Boogie Wonderland** .................................. | *6* | ARC 10956 |
| 7/07/79 | 2² | 17 | 22●**After The Love Has Gone**<br>EARTH, WIND & FIRE with THE EMOTIONS | *2* | ARC 11033 |
| 10/13/79 | 23 | 10 | 23 In The Stone ................................................. | 58 | ARC 11093 |
| 12/22/79+ | 47 | 7 | 24 Star ................................................................ | 64 | ARC 11165 |
| 9/27/80 | 8 | 12 | 25 **Let Me Talk** ............................................... | 44 | ARC 11366 |
| 11/22/80+ | 10 | 13 | 26 **You** ............................................................ | 48 | ARC 11407 |
| 2/07/81 | 15 | 11 | 27 And Love Goes On ........................................ | 59 | ARC 11434 |
| 10/10/81 | 1⁸ | 22 | 28●**Let's Groove** ............................................. | *3* | ARC 02536 |
| 1/23/82 | 15 | 11 | 29 Wanna Be With You ...................................... | 51 | ARC 02688 |
| 1/22/83 | 4 | 17 | 30 **Fall In Love With Me**................................. | *17* | Columbia 03375 |
| 4/16/83 | 15 | 11 | 31 **Side By Side** ............................................... | 76 | Columbia 03814 |
| 7/30/83 | 57 | 8 | 32 Spread Your Love.......................................... | | Columbia 04002 |
| 11/12/83 | 10 | 14 | 33 **Magnetic**.................................................... | 57 | Columbia 04210 |
| 1/28/84 | 23 | 11 | 34 Touch ............................................................ | *103* | Columbia 04329 |
| 4/21/84 | 67 | 6 | 35 Moonwalk ...................................................... | | Columbia 04427 |
| 10/17/87 | 1¹ | 15 | 36 **System Of Survival**................................... | 60 | Columbia 07608 |
| 1/30/88 | 3 | 12 | 37 **Thinking Of You**........................................ | 67 | Columbia 07695 |
| 4/16/88 | 22 | 10 | 38 Evil Roy ........................................................ | | Columbia 07687 |

**EASTBOUND EXPRESSWAY**

| DEBUT DATE | PEAK POS | WKS CHR | ARTIST — Record Title | POP POS | Label & Number |
|---|---|---|---|---|---|
| 1/13/79 | 87 | 3 | 1 Never Let Go ................................................. | | AVI 237 |

**EAST COAST**

Group consisting of Larry Blackmon and Gregory Johnson (members of Cameo), Gary Dow, Eric Durham and Anthony Lockett, with brothers Nathan & Arnett Leftenant.

| DEBUT DATE | PEAK POS | WKS CHR | ARTIST — Record Title | POP POS | Label & Number |
|---|---|---|---|---|---|
| 2/24/79 | 64 | 10 | 1 The Rock........................................................ | | RSO 922 |
| 10/20/79 | 67 | 5 | 2 Meat The Beat ............................................... | | RSO 1002 |

| DEBUT DATE | PEAK POS | WKS CHR | ARTIST — Record Title | POP POS | Label & Number |
|---|---|---|---|---|---|
| | | | **THOMAS EAST & THE FABULOUS PLAYBOYS** | | |
| 2/08/69 | 46 | 4 | 1 I Get A Groove............................................. | | Toddlin' Town 112 |
| 12/22/73+ | 52 | 10 | 2 Funky Music, Part 1 ...................................... | | MGM 14684 |
| | | | **SHEENA EASTON** | | |
| | | | Pop singer/actress, born on 4/27/59 in Glasgow, Scotland. Also see Prince. | | |
| 1/05/85 | 3 | 16 | 1 **Sugar Walls** ............................................ | 9 | EMI America 8253 |
| | | | written & produced by Prince (as Alexander Nevermind) | | |
| | | | **EBB TIDE** | | |
| 2/01/75 | 78 | 8 | 1 Give Me Your Best Shot Baby - Part 1 .............. | | Sound Gems 100 |
| | | | **EBO** | | |
| 12/21/85+ | 37 | 18 | 1 I'd Rather Be Myself ................................... | | Domino 8908 |
| | | | **EBONEE WEBB** | | |
| | | | Octet from Memphis, produced by Allen Jones. | | |
| 6/27/81 | 35 | 12 | 1 Anybody Wanna Dance ................................ | | Capitol 5008 |
| 9/26/81 | 16 | 17 | 2 Something About You................................. | | Capitol 5044 |
| 2/20/82 | 77 | 5 | 3 Woman.................................................... | | Capitol 5089 |
| 2/05/83 | 37 | 10 | 4 Too Hot To Be Cool .................................. | | Capitol 5181 |
| | | | **EBONY RHYTHM FUNK CAMPAIGN** | | |
| | | | Chicago band produced by Carl Davis. Consisted of Lloyd Thomas (guitar), Michael Woods & George Dennie (keyboards), Lester Johnson (bass) and Dwayne Gavin (drums). Vocals by Pamela Tanner and Tony Roberts. | | |
| 3/29/75 | 68 | 9 | 1 How's Your Wife ...................................... | | Innovation 9159 |
| | | | **EBONY, IVORY & JADE** | | |
| 9/06/75 | 92 | 4 | 1 Samson..................................................... | | Columbia 10196 |
| | | | **THE EBONYS** | | |
| | | | Vocal group from Camden, New Jersey, formed in 1968. Consisted of Jenny Holmes, David Beasley, James Tuten and Clarence Vaughan. Discovered by Leon Huff. Jenny Holmes was later in Creme D'Cocoa. | | |
| 5/22/71 | 10 | 11 | 1 **You're The Reason Why**.............................. | 51 | Phil. Int. 3503 |
| 11/13/71 | 46 | 3 | 2 Determination ......................................... | | Phil. Int. 3510 |
| 5/26/73 | 14 | 13 | 3 It's Forever .............................................. | 68 | Phil. Int. 3529 |
| 3/16/74 | 34 | 13 | 4 I Believe .................................................. | | Phil. Int. 3541 |
| 8/03/74 | 69 | 5 | 5 Life In The Country .................................... | | Phil. Int. 3548 |
| 8/28/76 | 83 | 9 | 6 Making Love Ain't No Fun (Without The One You Love) Part 1 ................................... | | Buddah 537 |
| | | | **BILLY ECKSTINE**    ★★**122**★★ | | |
| | | | Born William Clarence Eckstein on 7/8/14 in Pittsburgh. Nicknamed "Mr. B". Vocalist/trumpeter/valve trombonist. With Earl Hines in 1939. Formed own band in 1943. One of the pioneers of the bop movement, his band included Dizzy Gillespie, Charlie Parker, Gene Ammons, Miles Davis and Sarah Vaughan. Solo work after 1947. Also see Earl Hines. | | |
| 9/02/44 | 3 | 6 | 1 **I Stay In The Mood For You** ........................ | | DeLuxe 2000 |
| | | | with the DeLuxe All-Stars | | |
| 10/27/45 | 3 | 1 | 2 **Last Night & Now Tonite Again/** | | |
| 10/13/45 | 4 | 1 | 3 **Lonesome Lover Blues**............................. | | National 9015 |
| 11/03/45 | 3 | 1 | 4 **A Cottage For Sale** ................................. | 8 | National 9014 |
| | | | a reported million-seller | | |
| 5/04/46 | 3 | 2 | 5 **Prisoner Of Love** ..................................... | 10 | National 9017 |
| | | | written in 1931; a reported million-seller | | |
| 9/07/46 | 3 | 1 | 6 **You Call It Madness (But I Call It Love)** ......... | 13 | National 9019 |
| 10/16/48 | 11 | 2 | 7 Everything I Have Is Yours ........................... | 30 | MGM 10259 |
| | | | Best Seller #11 with the Sonny Burke Orchestra; from the 1933 film "Dancing Lady" | | |
| 1/01/49 | 12 | 1 | 8 Blue Moon/ | 21 | |
| | | | Juke Box #12 / Best Seller #13 | | |
| 2/05/49 | 6 | 1 | 9 **Fools Rush In**............................................ | | MGM 10311 |
| | | | Juke Box #6 / Best Seller #13 | | |
| 1/22/49 | 4 | 8 | 10 **Bewildered** ............................................. | 27 | MGM 10340 |
| | | | Best Seller #4 / Juke Box #13 | | |
| 4/30/49 | 14 | 3 | 11 Caravan .................................................. | 27 | MGM 10368 |
| | | | Best Seller #14 / Juke Box #14 | | |

| DEBUT DATE | PEAK POS | WKS CHR | ARTIST — Record Title | POP POS | Label & Number |
|---|---|---|---|---|---|
| | | | **BILLY ECKSTINE — Continued** | | |
| 5/28/49 | **15** | 1 | 12 Somehow.......................................... <br> Best Seller #15 | 25 | MGM 10383 |
| 7/30/49 | **7** | 2 | 13 **Temptation/** <br> Juke Box #7 / Best Seller #9 | | |
| 10/15/49 | **12** | 1 | 14 Crying............................................. <br> Juke Box #12 <br> 8-11, 13 & 14: with Hugo Winterhalter's Orchestra | 27 | MGM 10458 |
| 3/04/50 | **6** | 4 | 15 **Sitting By The Window** ..................... <br> Best Seller #6 / Juke Box #8 <br> 10 & 15: with the Quartones | 23 | MGM 10602 |
| 4/21/51 | **4** | 12 | 16 **I Apologize**.................................... <br> Best Seller #4 / Juke Box #4 <br> with Pete Rugolo's Orchestra; a reported million-seller | **6** | MGM 10903 |
| 6/14/52 | **8** | 1 | 17 **Kiss Of Fire** ................................... <br> Juke Box #8 <br> with the Nelson Riddle Orchestra; <br> adapted from the Argentine tango "El Choclo" | 16 | MGM 11225 |
| 10/16/76 | **84** | 3 | 18 The Best Thing .............................. | | A&M 1858 |
| | | | **ECSTASY, PASSION & PAIN** <br> Group from New York City, consisting of Barbara Roy (vocals, guitar), Billy Gardner (organ), Joseph Williams, Jr. (bass), Althea "Cookie" Smith (drums) and Alan Tizer (percussion). Roy had sung with niece Brenda Gaskins, worked as guitarist with Inez & Charlie Foxx. | | |
| 2/09/74 | **17** | 14 | 1 I Wouldn't Give You Up .................... | 102 | Roulette 7151 |
| 6/15/74 | **14** | 13 | 2 Good Things Don't Last Forever ........... | 93 | Roulette 7156 |
| 9/21/74 | **19** | 10 | 3 Ask Me........................................ | 52 | Roulette 7159 |
| 3/01/75 | **14** | 12 | 4 One Beautiful Day .......................... | 48 | Roulette 7163 |
| 5/01/76 | **71** | 5 | 5 Touch And Go .............................. | 98 | Roulette 7182 |
| 2/12/77 | **99** | 2 | 6 Passion ...................................... | | Roulette 2205 |
| | | | **EDDIE & ERNIE** <br> Duo of Edgar Campbell and Ernest Johnson. First recorded for Checker in 1963. | | |
| 2/06/65 | **34** | 4 | 1 Time Waits For No One ................... | | Eastern 602 |
| | | | **EDDIE & FREDDIE** | | |
| 4/09/77 | **95** | 3 | 1 Make Like.................................... | | October 1006 |
| | | | **EDDIE - "D"** <br> Eddie Drummond - rapper. | | |
| 4/13/85 | **75** | 6 | 1 Backstabbin' ................................ <br> also released on Philly World 99662 | 103 | Philly W. 819 |
| | | | **DUANE EDDY** <br> All-time #1 rock and roll instrumentalist, originator of the "twangy" guitar sound; born on 4/26/38 in Corning, New York. Began association with producer/songwriter Lee Hazlewood in 1955. His backing band, The Rebels, featured top sessionmen: Larry Knechtel (piano), Jim Horn and Steve Douglas (saxes). Eddy appeared in several films. Married to country/pop singer Jesse Colter, 1962-68. Also see Ray Sharpe. | | |
| 7/28/58 | **8** | 8 | 1 **Rebel-'Rouser**................................[I] <br> Best Seller #8 / Jockey #10 <br> handclaps and rebel yells by The Rivingtons | 6 | Jamie 1104 |
| 9/22/58 | **17** | 2 | 2 Ramrod ....................................[I] <br> Best Seller #17 <br> recorded in 1956, originally released on Ford 500; <br> sax and vocals overdubbed in 1958 | 27 | Jamie 1109 |
| 12/15/58 | **22** | 4 | 3 Cannonball ................................[I] | 15 | Jamie 1111 |
| 7/27/59 | **17** | 5 | 4 Forty Miles Of Bad Road..................[I] | 9 | Jamie 1126 |
| 6/27/60 | **17** | 6 | 5 Because They're Young.....................[I] <br> from the film of the same title | 4 | Jamie 1156 |
| 2/23/63 | **28** | 1 | 6 Boss Guitar.................................. <br> female vocal backing by The Rebelettes (The Blossoms) | 28 | RCA 8131 |
| | | | **ALTON EDWARDS** | | |
| 5/22/82 | **75** | 5 | 1 I Just Wanna (Spend Some Time With You)........ | | Columbia 02796 |
| | | | **DEE EDWARDS** <br> Born Doris Edwards in Birmingham, Alabama. First recorded in Detroit for Tuba, 1962. | | |
| 5/12/79 | **78** | 4 | 1 Don't Sit Down .............................. | | Cotillion 44249 |
| 9/06/80 | **64** | 6 | 2 Mr. Miracle Man ............................ | | Cotillion 46003 |

| DEBUT DATE | PEAK POS | WKS CHR | ARTIST — Record Title | POP POS | Label & Number |
|---|---|---|---|---|---|
| | | | **DENNIS EDWARDS** | | |
| | | | Born on 2/3/43 in Birmingham, Alabama. Lead singer of The Contours until 1968. Lead singer of The Temptations from 1968-77, 1980-84, 1987-present. | | |
| 2/11/84 | 2² | 23 | 1 **Don't Look Any Further** | 72 | Gordy 1715 |
| | | | female vocal by Siedah Garrett | | |
| 5/26/84 | 15 | 14 | 2 (You're My) Aphrodisiac | | Gordy 1737 |
| 8/03/85 | 77 | 4 | 3 Amanda | | Gordy 1799 |
| 9/07/85 | 23 | 12 | 4 Coolin' Out | | Gordy 1805 |
| | | | **JOHN EDWARDS** | | |
| | | | Born in 1946 in St. Louis. With James & Bobby Purify in Columbus, Georgia. To Chicago, worked the Bonanza Club in 1970. Discovered by Donny Hathaway and Curtis Mayfield, Replaced Philippe Wynne in the Spinners in 1977. | | |
| 10/13/73 | 45 | 9 | 1 Stop This Merry-Go-Round | | Aware 035 |
| 3/30/74 | 54 | 10 | 2 Messing Up A Good Thing | | Aware 037 |
| 8/17/74 | 8 | 14 | 3 **Careful Man** | 109 | Aware 043 |
| 12/28/74+ | 60 | 8 | 4 Vanishing Love | | Aware 045 |
| 8/07/76 | 59 | 8 | 5 Baby, Hold On To Me | | Cotillion 44203 |
| 1/15/77 | 85 | 4 | 6 Nobody, But You | | Cotillion 44212 |
| | | | **TOMMY EDWARDS** | | |
| | | | Born on 2/17/22 in Richmond, Virginia. Died on 10/23/69 in Richmond (47). Vocalist/pianist/composer. Performing since age 9. Wrote "That Chick's Too Young To Fry" in 1946. First recorded for Top in 1949. | | |
| 11/17/51 | 10 | 1 | 1 **All Over Again** | | MGM 11035 |
| | | | Best Seller #10 | | |
| 9/15/58 | 1³ | 14 | 2 **It's All In The Game** | 1 | MGM 12688 |
| | | | Best Seller #1 / Jockey #3 written by U.S. Vice President Charles Dawes in 1912 as "Melody In A Major"; Tommy's original version charted in 1951 (POS 18-Pop) on MGM 11035 | | |
| 3/09/59 | 18 | 5 | 3 Please Mr. Sun | 11 | MGM 12757 |
| | | | Tommy's original version charted in 1952 (POS 22-Pop) on MGM 11134 | | |
| 6/22/59 | 27 | 1 | 4 My Melancholy Baby | 26 | MGM 12794 |
| | | | first charted in 1915 by Walter Van Brunt | | |
| | | | **EGYPTIAN LOVER** | | |
| | | | Los Angeles techno-funk vocalist Greg Broussard. Former disc jockey. | | |
| 9/01/84 | 67 | 8 | 1 Egypt, Egypt | | Freak Beat 00661 |
| 12/06/86+ | 50 | 10 | 2 The Lover | | Egypt. E. 00771 |
| 3/21/87 | 52 | 14 | 3 Freak-A-Holic | | Egypt. E. 00774 |
| | | | **THE 8TH DAY** | | |
| | | | Group from Detroit, assembled by producers Holland-Dozier-Holland in 1966. Consisted of former session musicians Melvin Davis (lead vocals, drums), Tony Newton (bass), Michael Anthony and Bruce Nazarian (guitars), Jerry Paul (percussion), Carole Stallings (vocals, electric violin), Anita Sherman (vibes, vocals) and Lynn Harter (vocals). First recorded for Kapp in 1967. | | |
| 5/01/71 | 3 | 14 | 1 ● **She's Not Just Another Woman** | 11 | Invictus 9087 |
| 9/11/71 | 3 | 14 | 2 **You've Got To Crawl (Before You Walk)** | 28 | Invictus 9098 |
| 1/01/72 | 27 | 8 | 3 If I Could See The Light | 79 | Invictus 9107 |
| 4/08/72 | 29 | 5 | 4 Eeny-Meeny-Miny-Mo | | Invictus 9117 |
| | | | **EL CHICANO** | | |
| | | | Mexican-American band, formed in Los Angeles as the VIP's, 1965. Included Jerry Salas (lead vocals), Mickey Lespron, Robert Espinosa, Fred Sanchez and Andre Baeza. | | |
| 4/25/70 | 20 | 9 | 1 Viva Tirado - Part I [I] | 28 | Kapp 2085 |
| | | | originally released on Gordo 703 | | |
| 9/15/73 | 98 | 2 | 2 Tell Her She's Lovely | 40 | MCA 40104 |
| | | | **EL COCO** | | |
| | | | Los Angeles-based disco sextet led by producers Laurin Rinder and Michael Lewis. | | |
| 10/09/76 | 54 | 12 | 1 Let's Get It Together [I] | 61 | AVI 115 |
| 11/19/77+ | 22 | 15 | 2 Cocomotion [I] | 44 | AVI 147 |
| 9/02/78 | 31 | 12 | 3 Dancing In Paradise [I] | 91 | AVI 203 |

| DEBUT DATE | PEAK POS | WKS CHR | ARTIST — Record Title | POP POS | Label & Number |
|---|---|---|---|---|---|
| | | | **THE EL DORADOS** Group from Englewood High School in Chicago, 1952. Named after the car, Cadillac El Dorado. Consisted of Jewel Jones, Pirkle Lee Moses, Richard Nickens, Arthur Basset, and James Maddox. | | |
| 9/24/55+ | **1**[1] | 18 | 1 **At My Front Door** .............................. Juke Box #1 / Best Seller #2 / Jockey #2 title also known as "Crazy Little Mama"; lead vocals by Pirkle Lee Moses | *17* | Vee-Jay 147 |
| 2/11/56 | **8** | 2 | 2 **I'll Be Forever Loving You** ..................... Jockey #8 | | Vee-Jay 165 |
| | | | **ELAINE & ELLEN** Vocal duo of twin sisters. | | |
| 8/30/80 | **91** | 2 | 1 Fill Me Up ..................... | | Ovation 1148 |
| | | | **DONNIE ELBERT** Born on 5/25/36 in New Orleans; raised in Buffalo, New York. Multi-instrumentalist/ vocalist. With the Vibraharps from 1955-57. Went solo in 1957. A&R director for Polygram Records, Canada, in the mid-80s. | | |
| 6/03/57 | **12** | 3 | 1 What Can I Do ..................... Best Seller #12 | *61* | DeLuxe 6125 |
| 11/07/70 | **26** | 11 | 2 Can't Get Over Losing You ..................... | *98* | Rare Bullet 101 |
| 10/16/71 | **6** | 12 | 3 **Where Did Our Love Go** ..................... | *15* | All Platinum 2330 |
| 1/15/72 | **30** | 5 | 4 Sweet Baby ..................... | *92* | All Platinum 2333 |
| 2/05/72 | **14** | 8 | 5 I Can't Help Myself (Sugar Pie, Honey Bunch) ..... | *22* | Avco 4587 |
| 4/15/72 | **30** | 4 | 6 If I Can't Have You ..................... | | All Platinum 2336 |
| 12/01/73 | **77** | 5 | 7 This Feeling Of Losing You ..................... | | All Platinum 2346 |
| 8/31/74 | **70** | 5 | 8 Love Is Strange ..................... | | All Platinum 2351 |
| 2/19/77 | **94** | 3 | 9 What Do You Do/ | | |
| | | 3 | 10 Will You Love Me Till Tomorrow ..................... | | All Platinum 2367 |
| | | | **ELBOW BONES & THE RACKETEERS** | | |
| 2/25/84 | **82** | 4 | 1 A Night In New York ..................... | | EMI America 8184 |
| | | | **THE ELECTRIC EXPRESS** | | |
| 7/17/71 | **15** | 9 | 1 It's The Real Thing - Pt. I ..................... [I] | *81* | Linco 1001 |
| | | | **THE ELECTRIC INDIAN** Instrumental group assembled from top Philadelphia studio musicians. Some members later joined MFSB. | | |
| 8/30/69 | **46** | 2 | 1 Keem-O-Sabe ..................... [I] | *16* | United Art. 50563 |
| | | | **THE ELEGANTS** White vocal group formed in Staten Island, New York in 1957: Vito Picone (lead singer), Arthur Venosa, Frank Tardogno, Carmen Romano and James Mochella. All were veterans of other groups. | | |
| 7/28/58 | **1**[4] | 17 | 1 **Little Star** ..................... Best Seller #1(4) / Jockey #1(4) | *1* | Apt 25005 |
| | | | **ELEKTRIK DRED** | | |
| 9/24/83 | **82** | 5 | 1 Butter Up ..................... | | Snd. Flor. 1001 |
| | | | **THE ELEVENTH HOUR** Studio group fronted by singer/songwriter Kenny Nolan. | | |
| 10/04/75 | **45** | 16 | 1 Hollywood Hot ..................... | *55* | 20th Century 2215 |
| | | | **THE ELGINS** Group from Detroit, consisting of Saundra Mallett Edwards, Johnny Dawson, Cleotha Miller, Robert Fleming and Norbert McClean. Originally called the Downbeats. | | |
| 2/19/66 | **4** | 13 | 1 **Darling Baby** ..................... | *72* | V.I.P. 25029 |
| 9/24/66 | **9** | 14 | 2 **Heaven Must Have Sent You** ..................... | *50* | V.I.P. 25037 |
| 8/05/67 | **35** | 4 | 3 It's Been A Long Long Time ..................... | *92* | V.I.P. 25043 |
| | | | **ELI'S SECOND COMING** Bobby Eli. | | |
| 6/19/76 | **88** | 5 | 1 Love Chant (Part I) ..................... | | Silver Blue 7302 |
| | | | **YVONNE ELLIMAN** Born on 12/29/51 in Honolulu, Hawaii. Portrayed Mary Magdalene in the rock opera "Jesus Christ, Superstar". Joined with Eric Clapton during his 1974 comeback tour. | | |
| 5/07/77 | **57** | 7 | 1 Hello Stranger ..................... | *15* | RSO 871 |

| DEBUT DATE | PEAK POS | WKS CHR | ARTIST — Record Title | POP POS | Label & Number |
|---|---|---|---|---|---|
| | | | **YVONNE ELLIMAN — Continued** | | |
| 4/01/78 | **60** | 8 | 2 ● If I Can't Have You ....................................... | *1* | RSO 884 |
| | | | from the film "Saturday Night Fever" | | |
| | | | **DUKE ELLINGTON** ★★**152**★★ | | |
| | | | Born Edward Kennedy Ellington on 4/29/1899 in Washington, D.C. Jazz music's leading bandleader/composer/arranger. Studied piano since age 7; formed first band around 1918. To New York, in 1923, at Fats Waller's suggestion. In late 1927, began 5-year association with the famous Cotton Club. His 50-minute suite, "Black, Brown, and Beige", was introduced at Carnegie Hall in 1943. Worked with noted arranger/composer Billy Strayhorn from 1939 on. Died on 5/24/74 (75). | | |
| 11/21/42 | **10** | 1 | 1 Hay-Foot, Straw Foot ..................................... | | Victor 1505 |
| 5/08/43 | **1**³ | 25 | 2 Don't Get Around Much Anymore ............... [I] | 8 | Victor 26610 |
| | | | recorded on 5/4/40 & issued as "Never No Lament" - main solos by Johnny Hodges, Cootie Williams, Lawrence Brown and Duke | | |
| 8/28/43 | **1**¹ | 16 | 3 A Slip Of The Lip/ | 19 | |
| 9/04/43 | **1**¹ | 18 | 4 Sentimental Lady ..................................... [I] | 19 | Victor 1528 |
| | | | above 2: recorded on 7/28/42 | | |
| 1/08/44 | **1**⁸ | 18 | 5 Do Nothin' Till You Hear From Me ............. [I] | 10 | Victor 1547 |
| | | | recorded on 3/15/40 & issued on Victor 26598 as "Concerto for Cootie", a showcase for Cootie Williams | | |
| 3/04/44 | **1**⁴ | 14 | 6 Main Stem .............................................. [I] | 23 | Victor 1556 |
| | | | recorded on 6/26/42; Ben Webster featured | | |
| 6/03/44 | **4** | 18 | 7 My Little Brown Book/ | | |
| | | | vocal by Herb Jeffries | | |
| 6/10/44 | **7** | 7 | 8 Someone .............................................. [I] | | Victor 1584 |
| 12/23/44 | **9** | 3 | 9 I Don't Mind............................................ | | Victor 1598 |
| | | | 1 & 9: vocals by Ivie Anderson | | |
| 1/20/45 | **4** | 8 | 10 I'm Beginning To See The Light/ | 6 | |
| | | | vocal by Joya Sherrill | | |
| 1/27/45 | **10** | 1 | 11 Don't You Know I Care............................. | | Victor 1618 |
| 3/03/45 | **4** | 3 | 12 I Ain't Got Nothin' But The Blues ................ | | Victor 1623 |
| | | | vocals by Al Hibbler and Kay Davis | | |
| 11/20/48 | **15** | 1 | 13 Don't Be So Mean To Baby......................... | | Columbia 38295 |
| | | | Best Seller #15 | | |
| | | | 11 & 13: vocals by Al Hibbler | | |
| | | | **SHIRLEY ELLIS** | | |
| | | | Born in 1941 in the Bronx. Singer/songwriter. Was in the group the Metronomes. | | |
| 11/16/63+ | **8** | 14 | 1 The Nitty Gritty ....................................... | *Hot* | Congress 202 |
| 2/22/64 | **72** | 6 | 2 (That's) What The Nitty Gritty Is ...................... | *Hot* | Congress 208 |
| 1/30/65 | **4** | 9 | 3 The Name Game........................................ | 3 | Congress 230 |
| 3/27/65 | **16** | 8 | 4 The Clapping Song (Clap Pat Clap Slap) ............ | 8 | Congress 234 |
| | | | above 2: written by Shirley's manager & husband, Lincoln Chase | | |
| 3/25/67 | **31** | 5 | 5 Soul Time .............................................. | 67 | Columbia 44021 |
| | | | **LORRAINE ELLISON** | | |
| | | | Singer/songwriter from Philadelphia. Formed gospel group, the Ellison Singers; recorded for Sharp/Savoy in 1962. Recorded with gospel group, the Golden Chords, for CBS in 1963. Went solo in 1964. Successful songwriter with Sam Cooke. | | |
| 10/16/65 | **22** | 6 | 1 I Dig You Baby........................................... | 103 | Mercury 72472 |
| 10/15/66 | **11** | 8 | 2 Stay With Me............................................. | 64 | Warner 5850 |
| 9/30/67 | **43** | 4 | 3 Heart Be Still ......................................... | 89 | Loma 2074 |
| | | | **ELUSION** | | |
| 6/06/81 | **84** | 3 | 1 All Toys Break ......................................... | | Cotillion 46009 |
| | | | **THE EMOTIONS** ★★**93**★★ | | |
| | | | Female trio from Chicago, consisting of sisters Wanda (lead), Sheila and Jeanette Hutchinson. First worked as child gospel group called the Heavenly Sunbeams. Left gospel, became The Emotions in 1968. Jeanette replaced by cousin Theresa Davis in 1970, and later by sister Pamela; returned to group in 1978. | | |
| 5/03/69 | **3** | 13 | 1 So I Can Love You ...................................... | 39 | Volt 4010 |
| 9/13/69 | **27** | 9 | 2 The Best Part Of A Love Affair ....................... | 101 | Volt 4021 |
| 1/24/70 | **40** | 7 | 3 Stealing Love/ | | |
| | | | 7 | 4 When Tomorrow Comes .............................. | | Volt 4031 |
| 10/03/70 | **29** | 7 | 5 Heart Association ..................................... | | Volt 4045 |
| 5/01/71 | **47** | 3 | 6 You Make Me Want To Love You....................... | | Volt 4054 |
| 10/16/71+ | **13** | 18 | 7 Show Me How ......................................... | 52 | Volt 4066 |
| 3/25/72 | **18** | 8 | 8 My Honey And Me ..................................... | 113 | Volt 4077 |

| DEBUT DATE | PEAK POS | WKS CHR | ARTIST — Record Title | POP POS | Label & Number |
|---|---|---|---|---|---|
| | | | **THE EMOTIONS — Continued** | | |
| 7/15/72 | **23** | 10 | 9 I Could Never Be Happy................................ | 93 | Volt 4083 |
| 1/27/73 | **37** | 4 | 10 From Toys To Boys ................................ | 112 | Volt 4088 |
| 9/01/73 | **91** | 2 | 11 Runnin' Back (And Forth)............................. | | Volt 4095 |
| 3/23/74 | **53** | 7 | 12 Put A Little Love Away ............................ | 73 | Volt 4106 |
| 9/14/74 | **82** | 6 | 13 Baby I'm Through ................................ | | Volt 4110 |
| 7/10/76 | **16** | 16 | 14 Flowers/ | 87 | |
| 10/23/76 | **13** | 19 | 15 I Don't Wanna Lose Your Love ..................... | 51 | Columbia 10347 |
| 5/28/77 | **1**⁴ | 22 | 16● **Best Of My Love** ................................ | 1 | Columbia 10544 |
| 10/08/77 | **7** | 17 | 17 **Don't Ask My Neighbors**........................... | 44 | Columbia 10622 |
| 11/12/77+ | **31** | 18 | 18 Shouting Out Love/ | | |
| 3/25/78 | **59** | 8 | 19 Baby, I'm Through ............................... | | Stax 3200 |
| 7/29/78 | **6** | 14 | 20 **Smile**............................................ | 102 | Columbia 10791 |
| 10/14/78 | **44** | 9 | 21 Whole Lot Of Shakin'.............................. | | Columbia 10828 |
| 1/27/79 | **58** | 7 | 22 Walking The Line................................. | | Columbia 10874 |
| 5/19/79 | **2**⁴ | 13 | 23● **Boogie Wonderland** ............................ | 6 | ARC 10956 |
| | | | **EARTH, WIND & FIRE with THE EMOTIONS** | | |
| 11/17/79 | **30** | 12 | 24 What's The Name Of Your Love?..................... | | ARC 11134 |
| 3/01/80 | **75** | 6 | 25 Where Is Your Love? ............................. | | ARC 11205 |
| 7/25/81 | **48** | 10 | 26 Turn It Out ..................................... | | ARC 02239 |
| 11/07/81 | **68** | 7 | 27 Now That I Know ................................ | | ARC 02535 |
| 3/10/84 | **34** | 11 | 28 You're The One................................... | | Red Label 001 |
| | | | lead vocals by Sheila | | |
| 6/02/84 | **52** | 9 | 29 You're The Best ................................. | | Red Label 002 |
| 9/15/84 | **87** | 4 | 30 Are You Through With My Heart..................... | | Red Label 003 |
| | | | **THE EMPEROR'S** | | |
| 12/17/66+ | **30** | 8 | 1 Karate ......................................... | 55 | Mala 543 |
| | | | **THE ENCHANTERS** | | |
| | | | Trio from Philadelphia, formed in 1961: Zola Pearnell, Samuel Bell and Charles Boyer. | | |
| | | | **GARNET MIMMS & THE ENCHANTERS:** | | |
| 9/07/63 | **1**³ | 12 | 1 **Cry Baby** ...................................... | 4 | United Art. 629 |
| 11/23/63+ | **26** | 9 | 2 For Your Precious Love/ | Hot | |
| 11/16/63 | **30** | 9 | 3 Baby Don't You Weep ................................ | Hot | United Art. 658 |
| 7/18/64 | **78** | 7 | 4 A Quiet Place ................................... | Hot | United Art. 715 |
| | | | **THE ENCHANTERS:** | | |
| 9/05/64 | **91** | 3 | 5 I Wanna Thank You................................. | Hot | Warner 5460 |
| | | | **ENCHANTMENT** | | |
| | | | Group from Pershing High School in Detroit. Formed in 1966 with Ed "Mickey" Clanton, Bobby Green, Davis Banks, Emanuel Johnson and Joe Thomas. Did soundtrack for the film "Deliver Us From Evil". | | |
| 7/17/76 | **67** | 6 | 1 Come On And Ride ................................ | | Desert Mn. 6403 |
| 12/11/76+ | **5** | 24 | 2 **Gloria**.......................................... | 25 | United Art. 912 |
| 5/28/77 | **3** | 22 | 3 **Sunshine** ...................................... | 45 | Roadshow 991 |
| 1/07/78 | **1**¹ | 19 | 4 **It's You That I Need** ............................ | 33 | Roadshow 1124 |
| 6/17/78 | **14** | 11 | 5 If You're Ready (Here It Comes) ..................... | | Roadshow 1212 |
| 3/17/79 | **38** | 9 | 6 Anyway You Want It............................... | 109 | Roadshow 11481 |
| 6/23/79 | **29** | 13 | 7 Where Do We Go From Here ........................ | | Roadshow 11609 |
| 2/21/81 | **47** | 8 | 8 Moment Of Weakness.............................. | | RCA 12163 |
| 9/04/82 | **45** | 10 | 9 I Know Your Hot Spot ............................. | | Columbia 03079 |
| 2/11/84 | **64** | 5 | 10 Don't Fight The Feeling ............................. | | Columbia 04332 |
| | | | **ENERGETICS** | | |
| | | | Quintet from Boston. Consisted of Melvin Franklin, Roscoe Mills, Joey Lites, Herbert Jackson and John Border. First recorded for Tip Top. | | |
| 3/31/79 | **98** | 2 | 1 Come Down To Earth ............................. | | Atlantic 3565 |
| | | | **ENERGY** | | |
| 3/09/74 | **66** | 6 | 1 Function At The Junction ............................. | | Shout 302 |

| DEBUT DATE | PEAK POS | WKS CHR | ARTIST — Record Title | POP POS | Label & Number |
|---|---|---|---|---|---|
| | | | **BARBARA JEAN ENGLISH** | | |
| | | | Born in Sumpter, South Carolina. Recorded as Barbara English & The Fashions in 1959. Group included Frankie Brunson, who with other members later formed People's Choice. English worked as secretary at Alithia Record Company in New Jersey. | | |
| 9/22/73 | 65 | 9 | 1 You Need Somebody To Love You (While You're Looking For Someone To Love) ................. | | Alithia 6053 |
| | | | **ENTERTAINERS IV** | | |
| 2/19/66 | 29 | 6 | 1 Temptation Walk (People Don't Look No More) ... | | Dore 749 |
| | | | **EON** | | |
| 8/26/78 | 72 | 5 | 1 (You're The) Biggest Joke In Town ................... | | Ariola 7707 |
| | | | **EPMD** | | |
| | | | Long Island rap duo: Erick Sermon and Parrish Smith. EPMD: Erick and Parrish Making Dollars. Parrish was a football tight end at Southern Connecticut State University. | | |
| 4/30/88 | 22 | 17 | 1 You Gots To Chill........................................... | | Fresh 80118 |
| | | | **ERAMUS HALL** | | |
| | | | 7-piece band from Detroit, originally known as 7 Below Zero. Renamed by George Clinton. Consisted of Michael Gatheright (lead vocals), Joe Anderson, Marvin Williams, Bernard Provost, James Wilkerson, William Tillery, and Billy Dorsey. | | |
| 12/08/84 | 83 | 4 | 1 I Can't Keep My Head ................................. | | Capitol 5419 |
| | | | **ERIC B. & RAKIM** | | |
| | | | Rap duo: disc jockey Eric Barrier (from Elmhurst, New York) and rapper William Griffin (from Long Island). | | |
| 10/04/86 | 48 | 10 | 1 Eric B. Is President........................................ shown as: **ERIC B. featuring RAKIM** | | Zakia 014 |
| 5/30/87 | 64 | 10 | 2 I Know You Got Soul ..................................... | | 4th & B'way 7438 |
| 10/03/87 | 38 | 12 | 3 I Ain't No Joke ............................................ | | 4th & B'way 448 |
| 3/05/88 | 65 | 8 | 4 Paid In Full ............................................... | | 4th & B'way 7456 |
| | | | **ERUPTION** | | |
| | | | Jamaican techno-funk quintet featuring male vocalist Precious Wilson. | | |
| 3/04/78 | 30 | 13 | 1 I Can't Stand The Rain................................. | 18 | Ariola 7686 |
| | | | **ESCORTS** | | |
| | | | Group formed and recorded at Rahway State Prison in New Jersey. Consisted of lead Reginald Haynes, Laurence Franklin, Robert Arrington, William Dugger, Stephen Carter, Frank Heard and Marion Murphy. | | |
| 8/04/73 | 45 | 13 | 1 Look Over Your Shoulder ............................. | | Alithia 6052 |
| 1/12/74 | 83 | 7 | 2 I'll Be Sweeter Tomorrow ............................. | | Alithia 6055 |
| 4/13/74 | 61 | 9 | 3 Disrespect Can Wreck ................................. | | Alithia 6062 |
| 7/20/74 | 58 | 9 | 4 Let's Make Love At Home Sometime................ | | Alithia 6066 |
| | | | **COKE ESCOVEDO** | | |
| | | | Percussionist from Los Angeles. Prominent session musician, worked with Cal Tjader in the 60s. Toured with Santana in 1971. Uncle of Sheila E. | | |
| 3/06/76 | 84 | 5 | 1 Make It Sweet............................................. | | Mercury 73758 |
| | | | **THE ESQUIRES** | | |
| | | | Quintet from Milwaukee, formed at North Division High School in 1957 by Gilbert Alvis (lead vocals) and Betty Moorer (left, 1965). Harvey Scales, lead singer of own group, The Seven Sounds, was an early member. Joined by Sam Pace in 1961, Shawn Taylor in 1965. Recorded back-up for Millard Edwards on Constellation in 1966. Edwards joined the group in 1967. Taylor left shortly thereafter, returned in early 1971. | | |
| 9/02/67 | 3 | 15 | 1 Get On Up................................................. | 11 | Bunky 7750 |
| 12/09/67+ | 9 | 9 | 2 And Get Away ............................................ | 22 | Bunky 7752 |
| 3/09/68 | 41 | 4 | 3 You Say ................................................... | 126 | Bunky 7753 |
| 6/08/68 | 48 | 2 | 4 Why Can't I Stop......................................... | | Bunky 7755 |
| 11/30/68 | 29 | 11 | 5 You've Got The Power................................... | 91 | Wand 1193 |
| 3/08/69 | 37 | 5 | 6 I Don't Know .............................................. | | Wand 1195 |
| 2/27/71 | 18 | 10 | 7 Girls In The City ......................................... | 120 | Lamarr 1001 |
| 9/18/76 | 62 | 9 | 8 Get Up '76 ................................................. | | Ju-Par 104 |
| | | | all of above: Gilbert Moorer, lead vocals | | |

| DEBUT DATE | PEAK POS | WKS CHR | ARTIST — Record Title | POP POS | Label & Number |
|---|---|---|---|---|---|
| | | | **ESSENCE** | | |
| | | | Male vocal group from Chicago, formed as the Turbulations in 1965. Recorded for Gueva in 1969. Named changed to Essence in 1973. Group on Epic consisted of Marzette Griffith (lead), Anthony Redmond & Bob Tabor (tenors), Fred Smith (baritone), and Marcus Alexander (bass). | | |
| 8/30/75 | 91 | 4 | 1 Sweet Fools............................................. | | Epic 50133 |
| | | | **THE ESSEX** | | |
| | | | Quintet formed by members of the US Marine Corps at Camp LeJeune, North Carolina in 1962. Consisted of Anita Humes (lead), Walter Vickers, Rodney Taylor, Billie Hill and Rudolph Johnson. | | |
| 6/29/63 | 1² | 11 | 1 **Easier Said Than Done**............................. | *1* | Roulette 4494 |
| 9/21/63 | 11 | 8 | 2 A Walkin' Miracle ..................................... | *12* | Roulette 4515 |
| 11/16/63 | 56 | 5 | 3 She's Got Everything ................................. | *Hot* | Roulette 4530 |
| | | | **GLORIA ESTEFAN - see MIAMI SOUND MACHINE** | | |
| | | | **ET - see EDDIE TOWNS** | | |
| | | | **ETHICS** | | |
| | | | Group from Philadelphia, led by Ronald "Tyson" Presson. Later recorded as the Love Committee. | | |
| 6/07/69 | 32 | 6 | 1 Farewell ................................................. | | Vent 1006 |
| 10/18/69 | 43 | 2 | 2 Tell Me.................................................. | | Vent 1007 |
| | | | **ETTA & HARVEY - see ETTA JAMES** | | |
| | | | **E.U.** | | |
| | | | E.U.: Experience Unlimited. 8-member male group from Washington, D.C. Also see Salt-N-Pepa. | | |
| 2/27/88 | 1¹ | 18 | 1 Da'Butt ................................................. | *35* | EMI-Man. 50115 |
| | | | from the film "School Daze" | | |
| | | | **EURYTHMICS - see ARETHA FRANKLIN** | | |
| | | | **LINDA EVANS** | | |
| | | | Born in Los Angeles, sang with girl groups the Charms and Quotations in the late 60s. First solo recording for Wattsound in 1973. Toured with Billy Paul. Did back-up session work, recorded "I Can Tell" with Chanson. | | |
| 3/24/79 | 70 | 4 | 1 Don't You Need............................................ | | Ariola 7739 |
| | | | **MARGIE EVANS** | | |
| | | | Born Marjorie Ann Johnson on 7/17/40 in Shreveport, Louisiana. To Los Angeles in 1958. With Billy Ward from 1958-64, Ron Marshall Orchestra, 1964-69. With Johnny Otis for US and Far East tours, 1969-72. | | |
| 6/30/73 | 55 | 4 | 1 Good Feeling ........................................... | | United Art. 246 |
| 7/09/77 | 47 | 8 | 2 Good Thing Queen - Part 1 ........................... | | ICA 002 |
| | | | **WARREN EVANS** | | |
| | | | Vocalist formerly with the Buddy Johnson Orchestra. | | |
| 2/17/45 | 6 | 2 | 1 **I Wonder**..................................................... | | National 9003 |
| | | | **EVASIONS** | | |
| 7/25/81 | 20 | 15 | 1 Wikka Wrap ............................................ | | Sam 5020 |
| | | | **BETTY EVERETT** | | |
| | | | Born on 11/23/39 in Greenwood, Mississippi. Vocalist/pianist. Performed in gospel choirs. To Chicago in the late 50s. First recorded for Cobra in 1958. Toured England in the mid-60s. | | |
| 11/23/63+ | 51 | 10 | 1 You're No Good........................................ | *Hot* | Vee-Jay 566 |
| | | | #1 pop hit for Linda Ronstadt in 1975 | | |
| 2/29/64 | 6 | 13 | 2 **The Shoop Shoop Song (It's In His Kiss)**......... | *Hot* | Vee-Jay 585 |
| 6/27/64 | 66 | 5 | 3 I Can't Hear You ...................................... | *Hot* | Vee-Jay 599 |
| 9/05/64 | 5 | 13 | 4 **Let It Be Me** ......................................... | *Hot* | Vee-Jay 613 |
| | | | BETTY EVERETT & JERRY BUTLER | | |
| 11/28/64+ | 65 | 6 | 5 Getting Mighty Crowded ............................. | *Hot* | Vee-Jay 628 |
| 12/05/64+ | 42 | 7 | 6 Smile .................................................... | *Hot* | Vee-Jay 633 |
| | | | BETTY EVERETT & JERRY BUTLER | | |
| 1/11/69 | 2¹ | 13 | 7 **There'll Come A Time**............................... | *26* | Uni 55100 |
| 4/26/69 | 29 | 6 | 8 I Can't Say No To You................................. | *78* | Uni 55122 |
| 11/29/69 | 17 | 7 | 9 It's Been A Long Time................................. | *96* | Uni 55174 |
| 5/16/70 | 46 | 5 | 10 Unlucky Girl ......................................... | | Uni 55219 |
| 12/12/70+ | 22 | 8 | 11 I Got To Tell Somebody ............................. | *96* | Fantasy 652 |

| DEBUT DATE | PEAK POS | WKS CHR | ARTIST — Record Title | POP POS | Label & Number |
|---|---|---|---|---|---|
| | | | **BETTY EVERETT — Continued** | | |
| 4/17/71 | **32** | 6 | 12 Ain't Nothing Gonna Change Me | *113* | Fantasy 658 |
| 7/14/73 | **79** | 4 | 13 Danger | | Fantasy 696 |
| 1/05/74 | **38** | 14 | 14 Sweet Dan | | Fantasy 714 |
| 9/23/78 | **78** | 3 | 15 True Love (You Took My Heart) | | United Art. 1200 |
| | | | **THE EVERLY BROTHERS** | | |
| | | | Donald (real name: Isaac Donald) was born on 2/1/37 in Brownie, Kentucky; Philip on 1/19/39 in Chicago. Vocal duo/guitarists/songwriters. Parents were Folk and Country singers. Don (beginning at age 8) and Phil (age 6) sang with parents through high school. Invited to Nashville by Chet Atkins and first recorded there for Columbia in 1955. Signed to Archie Bleyer's Cadence Records in 1957. Duo split up in July of 1973, and reunited in September of 1983. | | |
| 6/10/57 | **5** | 12 | 1 **Bye Bye Love** <br> Best Seller #5 / Jockey #5 | *2* | Cadence 1315 |
| 9/30/57 | **1**¹ | 14 | 2 **Wake Up Little Susie** <br> Jockey #1 / Best Seller #2 | *1* | Cadence 1337 |
| 4/28/58 | **1**⁵ | 15 | 3 **All I Have To Do Is Dream** <br> Best Seller #1(5) / Jockey #1(3) | *1* | Cadence 1348 |
| 8/18/58 | **2**³ | 12 | 4 **Bird Dog/** <br> Jockey #2 / Best Seller #3 | *1* | |
| 9/01/58 | **2**¹ | 3 | 5 **Devoted To You** <br> Jockey #2 <br> all of above: written by Boudleaux & Felice Bryant | *10* | Cadence 1350 |
| 10/05/59 | **22** | 5 | 6 ('Til) I Kissed You | *4* | Cadence 1369 |
| 5/09/60 | **1**¹ | 10 | 7 **Cathy's Clown** | *1* | Warner 5151 |
| 10/17/60 | **16** | 5 | 8 So Sad (To Watch Good Love Go Bad) | *7* | Warner 5163 |
| 3/20/61 | **25** | 2 | 9 Ebony Eyes | *8* | Warner 5199 |
| | | | **THE EXCITERS** | | |
| | | | Quartet from Jamaica, New York, consisting of Herb Rooney with wife Brenda Reid, Carol Johnson and Lillian Walker. Johnson and Walker replaced by Ronnie Pace and Skip McPhee in the late 70s. Produced by Leiber & Stoller. Also see Brenda & Herb. | | |
| 12/22/62+ | **5** | 11 | 1 **Tell Him** | *4* | United Art. 544 |
| 1/04/64 | **78** | 4 | 2 Do-Wah-Diddy <br> later, a #1 pop hit for Manfred Mann in 1964 | *Hot* | United Art. 662 |
| 1/16/65 | **98** | 1 | 3 I Want You To Be My Boy | *Hot* | Roulette 4591 |
| 3/08/69 | **49** | 2 | 4 You Don't Know What You're Missing (Till It's Gone) | | RCA 9723 |
| | | | **EXECUTIVE** | | |
| 4/18/81 | **66** | 6 | 1 You Got The Stuff | | 20th Century 2482 |
| | | | **EXECUTIVE SUITE** | | |
| | | | Vocal group from Camden, New Jersey, formed in 1969 as the Millionaires. Consisted of Henry Tuten, Billy Tyler, Charles Conyers and Vincent Unto. | | |
| 9/29/73 | **51** | 11 | 1 I'm A Winner Now | | Babylon 1109 |
| 2/09/74 | **48** | 9 | 2 When The Fuel Runs Out | | Babylon 1111 |
| 6/22/74 | **37** | 13 | 3 Your Love Is Paradise | | Babylon 1113 |
| | | | **THE EXITS** | | |
| 9/02/67 | **34** | 4 | 1 Under The Street Lamp | *116* | Gemini 1004 |
| | | | **EXPOSE** | | |
| | | | Miami-based dance/disco trio: Ann Curless, Jeanette Jurado and Gioia Carmen. | | |
| 1/31/87 | **14** | 15 | 1 Come Go With Me | *5* | Arista 9555 |
| 9/05/87 | **29** | 13 | 2 Let Me Be The One | *7* | Arista 9617 |
| 1/16/88 | **27** | 11 | 3 Seasons Change | *1* | Arista 9640 |
| | | | **EXTRA T'S** | | |
| 10/30/82 | **80** | 3 | 1 E.T. Boogie | | Sunnyview 3004 |

# F

| DEBUT DATE | PEAK POS | WKS CHR | ARTIST — Record Title | POP POS | Label & Number |
|---|---|---|---|---|---|

**FABIAN**
Born Fabian Forte on 2/6/43 in Philadelphia. Discovered at age 14 (because of his good looks and intriguing name) by a chance meeting with Bob Marcucci, owner of Chancellor Records. Began acting career in 1959 with "Hound Dog Man".

| DEBUT DATE | PEAK POS | WKS CHR | ARTIST — Record Title | POP POS | Label & Number |
|---|---|---|---|---|---|
| 7/27/59 | 15 | 4 | 1 Tiger .......................................................... | 3 | Chancellor 1037 |

**FABULOUS COUNTS**
Group from Detroit, discovered by John Barrow, produced by Ollie McLaughlin.

| 1/25/69 | 42 | 5 | 1 Jan Jan ..................................................... [I] | | Moira 103 |
| 4/25/70 | 32 | 9 | 2 Get Down People....................................... | 88 | Moira 108 |

**TOMMY FACENDA**
Born on 11/10/39 in Norfolk, Virginia. Back-up vocals with Gene Vincent from 1957-58. Nicknamed "Bubba". First recorded for Nasco in 1958.

| 11/23/59 | 30 | 1 | 1 High School U.S.A. ................................... [N] | 28 | Atlantic 51 to 78 |
| | | | Atlantic released 28 different versions of this record, each mentioning the names of high schools in various cities; original version on LeGrand | | |

**FACTS OF LIFE**
Trio formed by Millie Jackson, originally known as The Gospel Truth: Jean Davis (younger sister of Tyrone Davis), Keith William (formerly with the Imperials and Flamingos) and Chuck Carter.

| 5/22/76 | 13 | 13 | 1 Caught In The Act (Of Gettin' It On)................. | | Kayvette 5126 |
| 12/25/76+ | 3 | 22 | 2 **Sometimes** ............................................ | 31 | Kayvette 5128 |
| | | | produced by Millie Jackson | | |

**DONALD FAGEN**
Born on 1/10/48 in Passaic, New Jersey. Worked as back-up with Jay & The Americans. Fagen and Walter Becker founded Steely Dan.

| 12/04/82 | 54 | 9 | 1 I.G.Y. (What A Beautiful World) ...................... | 26 | Warner 29900 |
| | | | I.G.Y.: International Geo-physical Year (July '57-Dec. '58) | | |

**YVONNE FAIR**
Singer from Virginia. Toured with James Brown Revue. Appeared in the film "Lady Sings The Blues".

| 6/29/74 | 32 | 11 | 1 Funky Music Sho' Nuff Turns Me On................. | | Motown 1306 |
| 10/26/74 | 60 | 6 | 2 Walk Out The Door If You Wanna .................... | | Motown 1323 |
| 7/12/75 | 96 | 5 | 3 Love Ain't No Toy ....................................... | | Motown 1354 |

**FAITH, HOPE & CHARITY**
Trio from Tampa, Florida, originally consisting of Brenda Hilliard, Albert Bailey and Zulema Cusseaux. Zulema went solo in 1971, Hilliard and Bailey continued as a duo until 1974 when joined by Diane Destry.

| 4/25/70 | 14 | 8 | 1 So Much Love.............................................. | 51 | Maxwell 805 |
| 9/26/70 | 36 | 4 | 2 Baby Don't Take Your Love ........................... | 96 | Maxwell 808 |
| 8/16/75 | 1 [1] | 21 | 3 **To Each His Own** ..................................... | 50 | RCA 10343 |
| | | | all of the above written & produced by Van McCoy | | |
| 1/31/76 | 38 | 10 | 4 Don't Go Looking For Love ............................ | | RCA 10542 |
| 8/28/76 | 83 | 5 | 5 You're My Peace Of Mind............................. | | RCA 10749 |
| 1/29/77 | 65 | 7 | 6 Life Goes On .............................................. | | RCA 10865 |
| 6/03/78 | 20 | 15 | 7 Don't Pity Me ............................................ | | 20th Century 2370 |

**GENE FAITH**
Vocalist from Philadelphia. Lead singer of the Volcanos. Left for solo career, group became the Moods, later The Trampps.

| 3/21/70 | 48 | 2 | 1 My Baby's Missing....................................... | | Virtue 2512 |

**PERCY FAITH**
Born on 4/7/08 in Toronto, Canada. Moved to the United States in 1940. Joined Columbia Records in 1950 as conductor-arranger for their leading singers (Tony Bennett, Doris Day, Rosemary Clooney, Johnny Mathis, and others). Died on 2/9/76 (67).

| 2/15/60 | 2 [1] | 14 | 1●**The Theme From 'A Summer Place'** ........... [I] | 1 | Columbia 41490 |
| | | | from the film "A Summer Place" | | |

**LOLA FALANA**
Born Oletha Falana in Camden, New Jersey, in 1943. Actress/dancer/singer/protege of Sammy Davis, Jr. With Davis in the Broadway musical "Golden Boy" in 1964.

| 6/07/75 | 91 | 3 | 1 There's A Man Out There Somewhere .............. | | RCA 10267 |

| DEBUT DATE | PEAK POS | WKS CHR | ARTIST — Record Title | POP POS | Label & Number |
|---|---|---|---|---|---|
| | | | **FALCO** | | |
| | | | Falco (Johann Holzel) was born in Vienna, Austria. | | |
| 3/01/86 | **6** | 15 | 1 **Rock Me Amadeus** ................................. | *1* | A&M 2821 |
| | | | **THE FALCONS** | | |
| | | | Group from Detroit, formed in 1955: Eddie Floyd (lead), Bob Manardo, Arnett Robinson, Tom Shetler and Willie Schofield. Joe Stubbs (brother of Four Tops' Levi Stubbs) and Mack Rice replaced Manardo, Shetler and Robinson in 1957. Wilson Pickett joined the group in 1960. Disbanded in 1963. Name used by Carlis "Sonny" Monroe, James Gibson, Johnny Alvin and Alton Hollowell (formerly the Fabulous Playboys). | | |
| 4/06/59 | **2**[3] | 20 | 1 You're So Fine ................................. | *17* | Unart 2013 |
| 12/14/59 | **26** | 2 | 2 Just For Your Love ................................. | | Chess 1743 |
| 7/25/60 | **18** | 5 | 3 The Teacher ................................. | | United Art. 229 |
| | | | above 3: lead vocals by Joe Stubbs | | |
| 4/07/62 | **6** | 16 | 4 I Found A Love ................................. | *75* | LuPine 1003 |
| | | | lead vocal by Wilson Pickett | | |
| 10/29/66 | **29** | 6 | 5 Standing On Guard ................................. | *107* | Big Wheel 1967 |
| | | | lead vocal by Sonny Monroe | | |
| | | | **HAROLD FALTERMEYER** | | |
| | | | West German keyboardist/songwriter/arranger/producer. Arranged and played keyboards on the film scores of "Midnight Express" and "American Gigolo". | | |
| 4/06/85 | **13** | 14 | 1 Axel F ................................. [I] | *3* | MCA 52536 |
| | | | from the film "Beverly Hills Cop" - Eddie Murphy played Axel Foley | | |
| | | | **FAMILY** | | |
| | | | British quintet led by vocalist Roger Chapman. | | |
| 7/30/77 | **70** | 8 | 1 Music ................................. | | Little C. 10106 |
| | | | **THE FAMILY** | | |
| | | | Twin Cities quintet featuring Time members St. Paul (Paul Peterson), Jerome Benton and Jellybean Johnson. Female vocalist Susannah is the twin sister of Wendy Melvoin, member of Prince's Revolution. | | |
| 8/10/85 | **9** | 16 | 1 **The Screams Of Passion** ................................. | *63* | Paisley P. 28953 |
| 12/21/85+ | **34** | 12 | 2 High Fashion ................................. | | Paisley P. 28830 |
| | | | **FAMILY DREAM** | | |
| 6/13/87 | **75** | 7 | 1 Rescue Me ................................. | | Motown 1894 |
| | | | from the film "Police Academy 4: Citizens On Patrol" | | |
| | | | **FAMILY PLANN** | | |
| 6/28/75 | **71** | 11 | 1 Sexy Summer ................................. | | Drive 6242 |
| | | | **FANTASTIC FOUR** | | |
| | | | Group formed in Detroit in 1955. Consisted of "Sweet" James Epps, Robert and Joseph Pruitt, and Toby Childs. Robert Pruitt and Childs later replaced by Cleveland Horne and Ernest Newsome. Epps was cousin of the Tilmon brothers of the Detroit Emeralds. | | |
| 3/11/67 | **6** | 15 | 1 **The Whole World Is A Stage** ................................. | *63* | Ric-Tic 122 |
| 6/10/67 | **12** | 11 | 2 You Gave Me Something (And Everything's Alright) ................................. | *55* | Ric-Tic 128 |
| 8/26/67 | **38** | 4 | 3 As Long As I Live (I Live For You)/ | | Ric-Tic 130 |
| 9/30/67 | **30** | 5 | 4 To Share Your Love ................................. | *68* | Ric-Tic 130 |
| 1/06/68 | **39** | 5 | 5 Goddess Of Love ................................. | | Ric-Tic 134 |
| 5/18/68 | **23** | 10 | 6 I've Got To Have You ................................. | | Ric-Tic 139 |
| 9/28/68 | **12** | 12 | 7 I Love You Madly ................................. | *56* | Ric-Tic 144 |
| | | | also released on Soul 35052 | | |
| 2/09/74 | **77** | 8 | 8 I'm Falling In Love (I Feel Good All Over) ......... | | Eastbound 620 |
| 7/19/75 | **24** | 13 | 9 Alvin Stone (The Birth & Death Of A Gangster) ... | *74* | Westbound 5009 |
| 11/20/76+ | **56** | 12 | 10 Hideaway ................................. | | Westbound 5032 |
| 10/01/77 | **30** | 16 | 11 I Got To Have Your Love ................................. | | Westbound 55403 |
| 2/03/79 | **96** | 2 | 12 Sexy Lady ................................. | | Westbound 55417 |
| 4/14/79 | **77** | 3 | 13 B.Y.O.F. (Bring Your Own Funk) ................................. | | Westbound 55419 |
| | | | **THE FANTASTIC JOHNNY C** | | |
| | | | Born Johnny Corley on 4/28/43 in Greenwood, SC. Produced and managed by Jesse James. | | |
| 10/07/67 | **5** | 20 | 1 **Boogaloo Down Broadway** ................................. | *7* | Phil-L.A. 305 |
| 2/10/68 | **32** | 7 | 2 Got What You Need ................................. | *56* | Phil-L.A. 309 |
| 7/06/68 | **25** | 9 | 3 Hitch It To The Horse ................................. | *34* | Phil-L.A. 315 |

**143**

| DEBUT DATE | PEAK POS | WKS CHR | ARTIST — Record Title | POP POS | Label & Number |
|---|---|---|---|---|---|
| | | | **FANTASY** Vocal/dance group from New York City, consisting of Ken Roberson, Tamm E. Hunt, Rufus Jackson and Carolyn Edwards. | | |
| 2/07/81 | **28** | 13 | 1 You're Too Late .............................................. | *104* | Pavillion 6407 |
| 6/06/81 | **51** | 11 | 2 (Hey Who's Gotta) Funky Song........................ | | Pavillion 02098 |
| | | | **BILL FARRELL** Born William Fiorelli, in 1926, in Cleveland, Ohio. Long-time featured vocalist on the Bob Hope radio show from 1948. Similar style to Billy Eckstine. | | |
| 10/15/49 | **12** | 1 | 1 You've Changed .............................................. Juke Box #12 | | MGM 10519 |
| | | | **CEE FARROW** | | |
| 10/08/83 | **91** | 3 | 1 Should I Love You......................................... | *82* | Rocshire 95032 |
| | | | **THE FASCINATIONS** Group from Detroit, formed in 1960. Consisted of Shirley Walker, Joanne Levell, Bernadine Boswell and Fern Bledsoe. First recorded for ABC-Paramount in 1962. Disbanded in 1969, and re-formed in 1971 for tour of England. | | |
| 9/17/66 | **47** | 2 | 1 (Say It Isn't So) Say You'd Never Go ................ | | Mayfield 7711 |
| 1/14/67 | **13** | 10 | 2 Girls Are Out To Get You.............................. | *92* | Mayfield 7714 |
| 7/29/67 | **49** | 2 | 3 I Can't Stay Away From You .......................... all of above: written & produced by Curtis Mayfield for own label | | Mayfield 7716 |
| | | | **FATBACK** ★★**121**★★ 6-9 member band with fluctuating lineup. Originally consisted of Bill Curtis (drums), George Williams (trumpet), Johnny King (guitar), Johnny Flippin (bass), Earl Shelton (sax), and George Adam (flute). Nucleus of band, 1973-82, included Curtis, Williams, King, Flippin, Fred Demerey (sax), Gerry Thomas (synthesizer) and George Victory (guitar). In 1981-82, backed by female vocal trio, Wild Sugar (Robin Dunn, Linda Blakely and Janice Christie - who went solo in 1986). | | |
| | | | **FATBACK BAND:** | | |
| 6/23/73 | **26** | 9 | 1 Street Dance ................................................. | | Perception 526 |
| 10/06/73 | **56** | 11 | 2 Nija Walk (Street Walk) ................................. | | Perception 540 |
| 1/26/74 | **69** | 7 | 3 Soul March ................................................... | | Perception 520 |
| 9/14/74 | **50** | 9 | 4 Keep On Steppin' ........................................... | | Event 217 |
| 1/04/75 | **94** | 4 | 5 Wicki-Wacky ................................................ | | Event 219 |
| 9/13/75 | **80** | 5 | 6 Yum, Yum (Gimme Some) ............................. | | Event 226 |
| 11/22/75+ | **37** | 13 | 7 (Are You Ready) Do The Bus Stop .................... | | Event 227 |
| 3/20/76 | **12** | 12 | 8 Spanish Hustle ............................................. | *101* | Event 229 |
| 6/19/76 | **84** | 5 | 9 Party Time................................................... | | Spring 165 |
| 10/23/76 | **32** | 10 | 10 The Booty ................................................... | | Spring 168 |
| 2/19/77 | **52** | 13 | 11 Double Dutch .............................................. | | Spring 171 |
| | | | **FATBACK:** | | |
| 11/26/77 | **88** | 8 | 12 Master Booty ............................................... | | Spring 177 |
| 5/20/78 | **9** | 24 | 13 **I Like Girls** .............................................. | *101* | Spring 181 |
| 2/03/79 | **36** | 11 | 14 Freak The Freak The Funk (Rock) .................... | | Spring 191 |
| 9/08/79 | **67** | 4 | 15 You're My Candy Sweet/ | | |
| 10/06/79 | **26** | 11 | 16 King Tim III (Personality Jock) ...................... | | Spring 199 |
| 1/05/80 | **59** | 6 | 17 Love In Perfect Harmony ............................... | | Spring 3005 |
| 3/15/80 | **6** | 20 | 18 **Gotta Get My Hands On Some (Money)**........... | | Spring 3008 |
| 6/28/80 | **3** | 15 | 19 **Backstrokin'** ............................................. | | Spring 3012 |
| 10/18/80 | **55** | 9 | 20 Let's Do It Again ......................................... | | Spring 3015 |
| 1/31/81 | **67** | 6 | 21 Angel........................................................ | | Spring 3016 |
| 5/09/81 | **19** | 14 | 22 Take It Any Way You Want It ......................... | | Spring 3018 |
| 9/05/81 | **64** | 6 | 23 Kool Whip................................................... | | Spring 3020 |
| 11/28/81+ | **50** | 10 | 24 Rockin' To The Beat ...................................... | | Spring 3022 |
| 6/26/82 | **36** | 11 | 25 On The Floor ............................................... | | Spring 3025 |
| 10/02/82 | **76** | 5 | 26 She's My Shining Star ................................... | | Spring 3026 |
| 3/19/83 | **28** | 14 | 27 The Girl Is Fine (So Fine) .............................. | | Spring 3030 |
| 6/25/83 | **43** | 9 | 28 Is This The Future........................................ | | Spring 3032 |
| 5/19/84 | **70** | 7 | 29 Call Out My Name ....................................... | | Cotillion 99749 |
| 1/26/85 | **88** | 3 | 30 Spread Love................................................ lead vocal by Evelyn Thomas | | Spring 414 |
| 3/16/85 | **79** | 4 | 31 Girls On My Mind ........................................ | | Cotillion 99665 |

| DEBUT DATE | PEAK POS | WKS CHR | ARTIST — Record Title | POP POS | Label & Number |
|---|---|---|---|---|---|
| | | | **FAT BOYS** Brooklyn-born rap trio: Darren "The Human Beat Box" Robinson, Mark "Prince Markie Dee" Morales, & Damon "Kool Rock-ski" Wimbley. Combined weight of over 750 pounds. Appeared in the 1987 film "Disorderlies". Also see The Krush Groove All Stars. | | |
| 6/23/84 | 65 | 11 | 1 Fat Boys/ | | |
| | | 11 | 2 Human Beat Box............................................ above 2 shown as: **DISCO 3** | | Sutra 135 |
| 10/13/84 | 17 | 19 | 3 Jail House Rap ............................................ | *105* | Sutra 137 |
| 1/26/85 | 38 | 10 | 4 Can You Feel It ............................................ | *101* | Sutra 139 |
| 7/13/85 | 27 | 13 | 5 The Fat Boys Are Back .................................... | | Sutra 144 |
| 9/28/85 | 52 | 7 | 6 Hard Core Reggae......................................... | | Sutra 147 |
| 12/07/85 | 62 | 10 | 7 Don't Be Stupid ........................................... | | Sutra 148 |
| 4/26/86 | 23 | 13 | 8 Sex Machine.............................................. | | Sutra 152 |
| 7/26/86 | 51 | 9 | 9 In The House ............................................. | | Sutra 156 |
| 5/23/87 | 16 | 13 | 10 Falling In Love ........................................... | | Tin Pan 885766 |
| 8/01/87 | 10 | 14 | 11 **Wipeout**................................................. backing vocals by The Beach Boys | *12* | Tin Pan 885960 |
| 7/02/88 | 40 | 8 | 12 The Twist .................................................. **THE FAT BOYS with CHUBBY CHECKER** rap version of Checker's 1960/1962 hit | *16* | Tin Pan 887571 |
| | | | **FAT LARRY'S BAND** Group from Philadelphia, which included Art Capehart (trumpet, flute), Jimmy Lee (trombone, alto sax), Doug Jones (saxes), Erskine Williams (keyboards), Ted Cohen (guitar), Larry LaBes (bass), "Fat" Larry James (drums) and Darryl Grant (percussion). Leader/producer/songwriter "Fat" Larry (b: 8/2/49, Philadelphia) performed with the Delphonics and Blue Magic; also managed the group Slick. James died on 12/5/87 (38). | | |
| 4/15/78 | 94 | 2 | 1 Peaceful Journey ......................................... | | Stax 3204 |
| 2/10/79 | 43 | 11 | 2 Boogie Town .............................................. shown as: **FLB** | | Fantasy 849 |
| 10/06/79 | 47 | 8 | 3 Lookin' For Love .......................................... | | Fantasy 867 |
| 1/19/80 | 44 | 12 | 4 Here Comes The Sun ...................................... | | Fantasy 881 |
| 6/14/80 | 78 | 3 | 5 How Good Is Love ......................................... | | Fantasy 891 |
| 4/10/82 | 67 | 8 | 6 Act Like You Know ........................................ | | Fantasy 02798 |
| 4/05/86 | 89 | 3 | 7 Zoom ..................................................... | | Omni 99563 |
| | | | **TONY FAX** | | |
| 7/13/68 | 50 | 2 | 1 Lean On Me............................................... | | Calla 151 |
| | | | **ALMA FAYE** Real name: Alma Brooks, disco star from Canada. | | |
| 7/21/79 | 90 | 2 | 1 Don't Fall In Love ........................................ | | Casablanca 989 |
| | | | **FAZE-O** Chicago quintet consisting of Keith "Chop Chop" Harrison (keyboards), Ralph "Love" Aikens (guitar), Tyrone "Flye" Crum (bass), Roger "Dodger" Parker (drums) and Robert "Bip" Neal Jr. (percussion). | | |
| 3/04/78 | 9 | 18 | 1 **Riding High** ............................................. | | She 8700 |
| 11/25/78+ | 43 | 10 | 2 Good Thang .............................................. | | She 8701 |
| 11/03/79 | 63 | 8 | 3 Breakin' The Funk ........................................ | | She 800 |
| | | | **PHIL FEARON** | | |
| 12/13/86+ | 72 | 8 | 1 I Can Prove It ............................................ | | Cooltempo 43029 |
| 3/14/87 | 82 | 6 | 2 Ain't Nothing But A House Party ...................... | | Cooltempo 43073 |
| | | | **FEEL** | | |
| 8/21/82 | 58 | 8 | 1 Let's Rock (Over & Over Again)........................ | | Sutra 115 |
| | | | **WILTON FELDER** Born in Houston in 1940. Reed player, made debut at age 12. Co-founder of The Crusaders (originally known as The Swingsters, then as the Jazz Crusaders). | | |
| 12/16/78+ | 44 | 11 | 1 Let's Dance Together ..................................... | | ABC 12433 |
| 11/15/80 | 35 | 17 | 2 Inherit The Wind.......................................... vocal by Bobby Womack | | MCA 51024 |
| 1/26/85 | 2³ | 21 | 3 **(No Matter How High I Get) I'll Still Be Lookin' Up To You**.................................... vocals by Bobby Womack and Alltrinna Grayson | *102* | MCA 52467 |

| DEBUT DATE | PEAK POS | WKS CHR | ARTIST — Record Title | POP POS | Label & Number |
|---|---|---|---|---|---|
| | | | **JOSE FELICIANO**<br>Born on 9/8/45 in Puerto Rico. Blind since birth. Raised in New York City.<br>Virtuoso acoustic guitarist. Has acted in several TV shows. | | |
| 9/21/68 | **29** | 6 | 1 Light My Fire ................................................ | *3* | RCA 9550 |
| 11/02/68 | **44** | 5 | 2 Hi-Heel Sneakers.......................................... | *25* | RCA 9641 |
| 1/09/82 | **63** | 7 | 3 I Wanna Be Where You Are............................ | | Motown 1530 |
| | | | **FELIX & JARVIS** | | |
| 6/12/82 | **34** | 12 | 1 Flamethrower Rap......................................... | | Quality 7014 |
| 4/30/83 | **89** | 3 | 2 All Night Long .............................................. | | Quality 7035 |
| | | | **THE FELLOWS - see EUGENE CHURCH** | | |
| | | | **HELENA FERGUSON** | | |
| 11/11/67 | **27** | 6 | 1 Where Is The Party........................................ | *90* | Compass 7009 |
| | | | **MAYNARD FERGUSON**<br>Born on 5/4/28 in Verdun, Quebec, Canada. Moved to the United States in 1949. Played<br>trumpet for Charlie Barnet and then Stan Kenton's Band (1950-56). | | |
| 7/09/77 | **97** | 2 | 1 Gonna Fly Now (Theme From "Rocky").......... [I] | *28* | Columbia 10468 |
| | | | **FERRANTE & TEICHER**<br>Piano duo: Arthur Ferrante (b: 9/7/21, New York City) and Louis Teicher (b: 8/24/24,<br>Wilkes-Barre, PA). Met as children while attending the Juilliard School. | | |
| 10/17/60 | **24** | 1 | 1 Theme From The Apartment ........................ [I]<br>from the Billy Wilder film "The Apartment";<br>tune originally entitled "Jealous Lover" | *10* | United Art. 231 |
| 12/26/60+ | **6** | 11 | 2 **Exodus** ...................................................... [I]<br>theme from the Otto Preminger film of the same title | *2* | United Art. 274 |
| | | | **FERRARI** | | |
| 3/13/82 | **53** | 9 | 1 Let Your Mind Go Free.................................. | | Sugar Hill 573 |
| | | | **FESTIVALS**<br>Male vocal group from Philadelphia. | | |
| 8/22/70 | **28** | 7 | 1 You're Gonna Make It ................................... | *114* | Colossus 122 |
| 3/27/71 | **29** | 9 | 2 Baby Show It................................................. | *116* | Colossus 136 |
| | | | **SANDRA FEVA**<br>Detroit singer. | | |
| 7/14/79 | **80** | 7 | 1 The Need To Be ............................................ | | Venture 109 |
| 4/18/81 | **33** | 12 | 2 Tell 'Em I Heard It........................................ | | Venture 138 |
| 8/02/86 | **76** | 7 | 3 You Can't Come Up Here No More ................... | | Krisma 1005 |
| 1/10/87 | **65** | 10 | 4 Here Now..................................................... | | Catawba 0961 |
| | | | **FEVER**<br>Trio from Ohio consisting of Dale Reed (saxophone), Joe Bomback (keyboards) and<br>Dennis Waddington (bass). Vocals by Clydene Jackson. | | |
| 12/01/79 | **93** | 7 | 1 Beat Of The Night......................................... | | Fantasy 878 |
| | | | **ERNIE FIELDS**<br>Born on 8/26/05 in Nacogdoches, Texas. Trombonist/pianist/bandleader/arranger.<br>Formed own band in 1930, making Tulsa, Oklahoma its home base. First recorded<br>for Vocalion in 1939. Toured with big band until the early 50s. | | |
| 11/23/59 | **7** | 10 | 1 **In The Mood**............................................. [I]<br>revival of Glenn Miller's #1 hit from 1940 | *4* | Rendezvous 110 |
| | | | **ERNIE FIELDS JR. - see JIMMY BEE** | | |
| | | | **KIM FIELDS**<br>Born on 5/12/69 in Los Angeles. Singer/actress. Worked in commercials from an early<br>age. Played "Tootie" on the TV series "Facts Of Life" since age 9. Real life mother,<br>Chip Fields, plays her mother on the show. | | |
| 4/07/84 | **55** | 8 | 1 Dear Michael ............................................... <br>song addressed to Michael Jackson | | Critique 705 |
| | | | **LEE FIELDS** | | |
| 10/25/86 | **91** | 3 | 1 Stop Watch .................................................. | | BDA 999 |
| | | | **RICHARD "DIMPLES" FIELDS**<br>Vocalist/owner of the Cold Duck Music Lounge in San Francisco. | | |
| 6/13/81 | **81** | 3 | 1 Earth Angel ................................................. | | Boardwalk 02081 |
| 9/19/81 | **42** | 8 | 2 I've Got To Learn To Say No!.......................... | | Boardwalk 004 |

| DEBUT DATE | PEAK POS | WKS CHR | ARTIST — Record Title | POP POS | Label & Number |
|---|---|---|---|---|---|
| | | | **RICHARD "DIMPLES" FIELDS — Continued** | | |
| 2/20/82 | **1** [3] | 18 | 3  **If It Ain't One Thing...It's Another** .............. | *47* | Boardwalk 139 |
| 6/19/82 | **35** | 9 | 4  Taking Applications .................................... | | Boardwalk 143 |
| 11/13/82 | **32** | 11 | 5  People Treat You Funky (When Ya Ain't Got No Money!)............................................ | | Boardwalk 164 |
| 1/29/83 | **51** | 9 | 6  Don't Ever Stop Chasing Your Dreams (Pt.1) ...... | | Boardwalk 174 |
| 6/30/84 | **32** | 11 | 7  Your Wife Is Cheatin' On Us........................ | | RCA 13830 |
| 10/13/84 | **63** | 7 | 8  Jazzy Lady .............................................. | | RCA 13900 |
| 9/21/85 | **54** | 8 | 9  Shake 'Em Down........................................ <br> backing vocal by 9.9 | | RCA 14157 |
| 7/11/87 | **22** | 13 | 10  Tell It Like It Is .................................... | | Columbia 07188 |
| 11/28/87+ | **43** | 9 | 11  I Can't Live With Or Without You................... <br> above 3 shown only as: **DIMPLES** | | Columbia 07599 |
| | | | **FIESTA** | | |
| 12/16/78+ | **53** | 7 | 1  E.S.P.................................................... | | Arista 0369 |
| | | | **THE FIESTAS** <br> Newark, New Jersey vocal group: Tommy Bullock (lead), Eddie Morris (tenor), Sam Ingalls (baritone) and Preston Lane (bass). | | |
| 3/23/59 | **3** | 19 | 1  **So Fine**.............................................. | *11* | Old Town 1062 |
| 9/15/62 | **18** | 8 | 2  Broken Heart .......................................... | *81* | Old Town 1122 |
| | | | **FIFTH AVE.** | | |
| 9/19/87 | **86** | 4 | 1  Exception To The Rule................................ | | Paradise 4229 |
| | | | **5th AVE. SAX - see NINO TEMPO** | | |
| | | | **THE 5TH DIMENSION** <br> Los Angeles-based group formed in 1966. Consisted of Marilyn McCoo, Florence LaRue, Billy Davis, Jr., Lamont McLemore and Ron Townson. McLemore and McCoo had been in the Hi-Fi's; Townson and Davis had been with groups in St. Louis. First called the Versatiles. Davis and McCoo were married, 1969, and recorded as a duo from 1976. | | |
| 6/15/68 | **2** [4] | 14 | 1 ● Stoned Soul Picnic..................................... | *3* | Soul City 766 |
| 11/02/68 | **45** | 2 | 2  Sweet Blindness........................................ | *13* | Soul City 768 |
| 1/25/69 | **49** | 2 | 3  California Soul ........................................ | *25* | Soul City 770 |
| 3/29/69 | **6** | 11 | 4  **Aquarius/Let The Sunshine In** ..................... <br> from the Broadway rock musical "Hair" | *1* | Soul City 772 |
| 8/16/69 | **15** | 6 | 5  Workin' On A Groovy Thing .......................... | *20* | Soul City 776 |
| 10/25/69 | **23** | 8 | 6  Wedding Bell Blues.................................... | *1* | Soul City 779 |
| 7/04/70 | **41** | 2 | 7  Save The Country...................................... <br> 1-2, 6 & 7: written by Laura Nyro | *27* | Bell 895 |
| 11/28/70+ | **4** | 14 | 8  **One Less Bell To Answer** ........................... | *2* | Bell 940 |
| 3/13/71 | **28** | 5 | 9  Love's Lines, Angles And Rhymes.................... | *19* | Bell 965 |
| 10/30/71 | **45** | 5 | 10  Never My Love........................................ | *12* | Bell 45134 |
| 1/15/72 | **22** | 8 | 11  Together Let's Find Love............................ | *37* | Bell 45170 |
| 4/29/72 | **28** | 6 | 12  (Last Night) I Didn't Get To Sleep At All .......... | *8* | Bell 45195 |
| 8/11/73 | **54** | 8 | 13  Ashes To Ashes ...................................... | *52* | Bell 45380 |
| 12/22/73+ | **75** | 6 | 14  Flashback ............................................. <br> all of above: produced by Bones Howe | *82* | Bell 45425 |
| 12/14/74 | **87** | 4 | 15  Harlem ................................................ | | Bell 45612 |
| 4/03/76 | **39** | 7 | 16  Love Hangover ....................................... | *80* | ABC 12181 |
| 3/11/78 | **66** | 7 | 17  You Are The Reason (I Feel Like Dancing) ........ | | Motown 1437 |
| | | | **52ND STREET** <br> British disco group. | | |
| 5/03/86 | **8** | 14 | 1  **Tell Me (How It Feels)**.............................. | | MCA 52805 |
| 9/20/86 | **67** | 5 | 2  You're My Last Chance ............................... | | MCA 52887 |
| 10/17/87 | **79** | 7 | 3  I'll Return.............................................. | | MCA 53089 |
| | | | **FINISHED TOUCH** | | |
| 9/23/78 | **88** | 4 | 1  Sticks And Stones (But The Funk Won't Never Hurt You) ............................................ | | Motown 1445 |
| | | | **THE FIREBALLS - see JIMMY GILMER** | | |
| | | | **FIREFLY** | | |
| 11/15/75 | **57** | 9 | 1  Hey There Little Firefly - Part I...................... | *67* | A&M 1736 |

| DEBUT DATE | PEAK POS | WKS CHR | ARTIST — Record Title | POP POS | Label & Number |
|---|---|---|---|---|---|
| | | | **FIREFLY** | | |
| 4/18/81 | 49 | 10 | 1 Love (is gonna be on your side)..................... | | Emergency 4509 |
| | | | **FIRST CHOICE** Female trio from Philadelphia, formed as the Debronettes. Consisted of Rochelle Fleming, Annette Guest and Joyce Jones. | | |
| 3/31/73 | 11 | 11 | 1 Armed And Extremely Dangerous ..................... | 28 | Philly Groove 175 |
| 9/01/73 | 25 | 15 | 2 Smarty Pants ................................. | 56 | Philly Groove 179 |
| 2/16/74 | 35 | 11 | 3 Newsy Neighbors............................... | 97 | Philly Groove 183 |
| 8/17/74 | 7 | 13 | 4 **The Player - Part 1**........................ | 70 | Philly Groove 200 |
| 11/30/74+ | 19 | 12 | 5 Guilty ..................................... | 103 | Philly Groove 202 |
| 3/29/75 | 61 | 7 | 6 Love Freeze ................................. | | Philly Groove 204 |
| 5/29/76 | 64 | 7 | 7 Gotta Get Away (From You Baby).................... | | Warner 8214 |
| 9/18/76 | 97 | 3 | 8 Let Him Go .................................. | | Warner 8251 |
| 7/23/77 | 23 | 18 | 9 Doctor Love ................................. | 41 | Gold Mind 4004 |
| 11/26/77 | 68 | 10 | 10 Love Having You Around........................ | | Gold Mind 4009 |
| 2/03/79 | 73 | 5 | 11 Hold Your Horses ........................... | | Gold Mind 4017 |
| 4/28/79 | 60 | 5 | 12 Double Cross................................ | 104 | Gold Mind 4019 |
| | | | **FIRST CIRCLE** Group led by vocalist Albert Lee. Includes Larry Marsden, Glenn "Chango" Everette, Anthony McEwan and Richard Sinclair. | | |
| 3/14/87 | 49 | 14 | 1 Workin' Up A Sweat ........................... | | EMI America 8384 |
| | | | **FIRST CLASS** Group from Baltimore, Maryland, consisting of lead Harold Bell, Fred Marshall, Tony Yarbrough and Sylvester Redditt. | | |
| 5/11/74 | 85 | 4 | 1 What About Me............................... | | Today 1528 |
| 5/17/75 | 62 | 5 | 2 The Beginning Of My End ...................... | | Ebony Snds. 187 |
| 9/04/76 | 54 | 9 | 3 Me And My Gemini ............................ | | All Platinum 2365 |
| 4/30/77 | 89 | 4 | 4 This Is It................................... | | All Platinum 2368 |
| | | | **FIRST FAMILY** | | |
| 10/12/74 | 81 | 5 | 1 Control (People Go Where We Send You), Part 1.. | | Polydor 14250 |
| | | | **FIRST LOVE** Female group from Chicago consisting of Denise Austin, Demetrice Henrae, Martha Jackson and Lisa Hudson. | | |
| 12/27/80+ | 67 | 8 | 1 Don't Say Goodnight.......................... | | Dakar 4566 |
| 1/29/83 | 68 | 7 | 2 It's A Mystery To Me.......................... | | CIM 03533 |
| | | | **HERB FISHER TRIO** Later recorded for Imperial. | | |
| 7/15/50 | 4 | 4 | 1 **I'm Yours To Keep** ......................... Best Seller #4 / Juke Box #6 vocal by Herb Fisher | | Modern 753 |
| | | | **MISS TONI FISHER** Born in Los Angeles in 1931. | | |
| 2/01/60 | 16 | 7 | 1 The Big Hurt ................................ | 3 | Signet 275 |
| | | | **WILLIE FISHER** | | |
| 5/14/77 | 76 | 3 | 1 One Way Street.............................. | | Tigress 359 |
| | | | **THE FIT** Duo of producer/multi-instrumentalist Chuck Gentry and vocalist Vince Ebo. Gentry was a member of the Sweet Inspirations in 1979. | | |
| 2/13/88 | 22 | 15 | 1 Just Havin' Fun ............................. | | A&M 3007 |
| | | | **ELLA FITZGERALD**   ★★129★★ "The First Lady Of Jazz", born on 4/25/18 in Newport News, Virginia; raised in Yonkers, New York. Won amateur contests at the Harlem Opera House and Apollo Theater at age 16. Made professional debut in February of 1935 with Tiny Bradshaw. Vocalist with Chick Webb from 1932-41 and led the band for a year after Webb's death. Solo artist since 1942. In the films "Ride 'Em Cowboy", "Pete Kelly's Blues", "St. Louis Blues" and "Let No Man Write My Epitaph". Wrote "A-Tisket A-Tasket" in 1938. | | |
| 5/15/43 | 6 | 1 | 1 **My Heart And I Decided** ..................... with the Four Keys | | Decca 18530 |
| 2/26/44 | 1¹ | 12 | 2 **Cow-Cow Boogie**........................... | 10 | Decca 18587 |

| DEBUT DATE | PEAK POS | WKS CHR | ARTIST — Record Title | POP POS | Label & Number |
|---|---|---|---|---|---|
| | | | **ELLA FITZGERALD — Continued** | | |
| 10/28/44 | **1**[11] | 21 | 3 **Into Each Life Some Rain Must Fall/** | *1* | |
| 10/28/44+ | **2**[1] | 14 | 4 **I'm Making Believe** ..................................... | *1* | Decca 23356 |
| | | | above 3: **ELLA FITZGERALD & INK SPOTS** | | |
| | | | a reported million-seller | | |
| 8/18/45 | **4** | 2 | 5 **It's Only A Paper Moon** ........................... | *9* | Decca 23425 |
| | | | from the film "Take A Chance"; | | |
| | | | with the Delta Rhythm Boys | | |
| 4/13/46 | **4** | 2 | 6 **The Frim Fram Sauce** ............................... | | Decca 23496 |
| | | | **ELLA FITZGERALD & LOUIS ARMSTRONG** | | |
| 6/29/46 | **1**[5] | 20 | 7 **Stone Cold Dead In The Market (He Had It Coming)/** | *7* | |
| 7/27/46 | **3** | 2 | 8 **Petootie Pie** ........................................... | | Decca 23546 |
| | | | above 2: **ELLA FITZGERALD & LOUIS JORDAN** | | |
| 6/28/47 | **3** | 1 | 9 **That's My Desire** ..................................... | | Decca 23866 |
| | | | with the Bob Haggart Orchestra & the Andy Love Quintet | | |
| 8/07/48 | **8** | 5 | 10 **My Happiness** .......................................... | *6* | Decca 24446 |
| | | | Juke Box #8 / Best Seller #13 | | |
| | | | with the Song Spinners | | |
| 10/16/48 | **6** | 3 | 11 **It's Too Soon To Know** ............................ | | Decca 24497 |
| | | | Best Seller #6 / Juke Box #7 | | |
| 6/11/49 | **6** | 4 | 12 **Baby, It's Cold Outside** ............................ | *9* | Decca 24644 |
| | | | **ELLA FITZGERALD & LOUIS JORDAN** | | |
| | | | Juke Box #6 / Best Seller #12 | | |
| | | | from the film "Neptune's Daughter" | | |
| 11/04/50 | **7** | 2 | 13 **I'll Never Be Free** .................................... | | Decca 27200 |
| | | | **ELLA FITZGERALD & LOUIS JORDAN** | | |
| | | | Juke Box #7 | | |
| 9/15/51 | **3** | 12 | 14 **Smooth Sailing** ....................................... | *23* | Decca 27693 |
| | | | Juke Box #3 / Best Seller #5 | | |
| | | | one of Ella's most popular scat-singing performances; | | |
| | | | with The Ray Charles Singers and Bill Doggett on organ | | |
| 5/23/60 | **6** | 6 | 15 **Mack The Knife** .................................. [L] | *27* | Verve 10209 |
| | | | recorded on 2/13/60 with the Paul Smith Quartet, at | | |
| | | | The Deutschland-Halle, Berlin | | |

## FIVE BLIND BOYS

Gospel group also known as the Original Five Blind Boys Of Mississippi, and Jackson Harmoneers. First recorded in 1946 for Excelsior. Archie Brownlee, lead singer. Group also included Lawrence Abrams, Lloyd Woodard, Vance Powell, and J.T. Clinkscales. Still active into the 70s, with personnel changes.

| DEBUT DATE | PEAK POS | WKS CHR | ARTIST — Record Title | POP POS | Label & Number |
|---|---|---|---|---|---|
| 12/30/50 | **10** | 2 | 1 **Our Father** ............................................. | | Peacock 1550 |
| | | | Juke Box #10 | | |

## THE FIVE DU-TONES

Group from Patrick Henry High School in St. Louis, 1957: Willie Guest, Frank McCurrey, LeRoy Joyce, James West and Andrew Butler. Formed Five DuTones Revue, with Du-Ettes (Barbara Livsey & Mary-Francis Hayes) and Johnny Sayles. Group disbanded in 1967.

| DEBUT DATE | PEAK POS | WKS CHR | ARTIST — Record Title | POP POS | Label & Number |
|---|---|---|---|---|---|
| 7/13/63 | **28** | 2 | 1 Shake A Tail Feather .................................. | *51* | One-derful! 4815 |
| | | | lead vocal by Andrew Butler | | |

## THE FIVE KEYS

Group formed as the Sentimental Four in Newport News, Virginia, in the late 40s, consisting of two sets of brothers: Rudy & Bernie West and Ripley & Raphael Ingram. With Miller's Brownskin Models in 1949. Raphael Ingram left and Maryland Pierce and Dickie Smith were added. Group name changed to the Five Keys in 1949. Smith replaced by Ramon Loper in 1953. Rudy West replaced by Ulysses K. Hicks from 1953-54. Hicks died in 1954, and West rejoined group in 1956.

| DEBUT DATE | PEAK POS | WKS CHR | ARTIST — Record Title | POP POS | Label & Number |
|---|---|---|---|---|---|
| 8/18/51 | **1**[4] | 15 | 1 **The Glory Of Love** ................................... | | Aladdin 3099 |
| | | | Best Seller #1(4) / Juke Box #1(2) | | |
| 1/01/55 | **5** | 12 | 2 **Ling, Ting, Tong** ..................................... | *28* | Capitol F2945 |
| | | | Best Seller #5 / Jockey #8 | | |
| 3/05/55 | **5** | 16 | 3 **Close Your Eyes** ...................................... | | Capitol 3032 |
| | | | Jockey #5 / Best Seller #6 | | |
| 7/09/55 | **13** | 1 | 4 The Verdict ............................................. | | Capitol 3127 |
| | | | Jockey #13 | | |
| 12/03/55 | **12** | 2 | 5 'Cause You're My Lover/ | | |
| | | | Jockey #12 | | |
| 2/25/56 | **14** | 1 | 6 Gee Whittakers ......................................... | | Capitol 3267 |
| | | | Jockey #14 | | |
| 10/27/56 | **12** | 3 | 7 Out Of Sight, Out Of Mind ............................ | *23* | Capitol 3502 |
| | | | Jockey #12 | | |

| DEBUT DATE | PEAK POS | WKS CHR | ARTIST — Record Title | POP POS | Label & Number |
|---|---|---|---|---|---|
| | | | **THE FIVE RED CAPS** | | |
| | | | Formed as the Toppers in Los Angeles in 1938. Consisted of Steve Gibson, Emmett Matthews, Dave Patillo, Jimmy Springs and Romaine Brown. Also known as Steve Gibson's Red Caps. Damita Jo, married to Gibson for a time, was in the group from 1950-53. George Tindley was a member from 1959-60. | | |
| 2/19/44 | **3** | 15 | 1 **I've Learned A Lesson I'll Never Forget** ......... | *14* | Beacon 7120 |
| 3/25/44 | **10** | 1 | 2 **Boogie-Woogie Ball** ..................................... | | Beacon 7121 |
| 4/22/44 | **10** | 2 | 3 **Just For You**............................................. | | Beacon 7119 |
| 11/04/44 | **10** | 1 | 4 **No One Else Will Do** ................................... | | Beacon 7130 |
| | | | **THE "5" ROYALES** | | |
| | | | North Carolina group consisting of 3 cousins: Lowman and Clarence Pauling, and Johnny Tanner, with Obediah Carter and Johnny Moore. First recorded as The Royal Sons (gospel) for Apollo in 1951. Frequently confused with The Royals, until latter group changed name to The Midnighters. Lowman Pauling wrote "Dedicated To The One I Love". | | |
| 1/24/53 | **1** ³ | 16 | 1 **Baby, Don't Do It**...................................... | | Apollo 443 |
| | | | Best Seller #1(3) / Juke Box #1(3) | | |
| 5/16/53 | **1** ⁵ | 15 | 2 **Help Me Somebody/** | | |
| | | | Best Seller #1(5) / Juke Box #1(5) | | |
| 5/23/53 | **5** | 4 | 3 **Crazy, Crazy, Crazy** ................................. | | Apollo 446 |
| | | | Juke Box #5 / Best Seller #7 | | |
| 8/15/53 | **4** | 11 | 4 **Too Much Lovin'** ....................................... | | Apollo 448 |
| | | | Best Seller #4 / Juke Box #5 | | |
| 2/20/54 | **6** | 2 | 5 **I Do**...................................................... | | Apollo 452 |
| | | | Juke Box #6 | | |
| | | | all of above: with the Charlie "Little Jazz" Ferguson Orchestra | | |
| 7/15/57 | **9** | 1 | 6 **Tears Of Joy** ........................................... | | King 5032 |
| | | | Jockey #9 | | |
| 9/16/57 | **9** | 6 | 7 **Think**...................................................... | *66* | King 5053 |
| | | | Best Seller #9 / Jockey #11 | | |
| | | | **THE FIVE SATINS** | | |
| | | | Group from New Haven, Connecticut. Consisted of Fred Parris (lead), Al Denby, Jim Freeman, Eddie Martin and Jessie Murphy (piano). Parris was stationed in the Army in Japan when "Still Of The Nite" hit, and the group reformed with Bill Baker as lead singer. Parris returned in January of 1958, replacing Baker. Later releases on Ember consisted of Fred Parris, Richard Freeman, Wes Forbes, Lou Peebles, and Sylvester Hopkins. Also see Black Satin. | | |
| 9/01/56 | **3** | 17 | 1 **In The Still Of The Nite**............................. | *24* | Ember 1005 |
| | | | Jockey #3 / Best Seller #4 / Juke Box #4 | | |
| | | | written by Fred Parris - recorded in a New Haven church basement; a reported multi-million-seller; originally released on the Standord label | | |
| 7/15/57 | **5** | 9 | 2 **To The Aisle** .......................................... | *25* | Ember 1019 |
| | | | Best Seller #5 / Jockey #10 | | |
| | | | lead vocal by Bill Baker | | |
| 11/02/59 | **27** | 2 | 3 Shadows............................................... | *87* | Ember 1056 |
| | | | **FIVE SPECIAL** | | |
| | | | Detroit vocal group consisting of Bryan Banks (lead tenor), Greg Finley and Steve Harris (tenors), Steve Boyd (baritone) and Mike Petillo (bass). Banks is brother of Ron Banks of The Dramatics. | | |
| 5/12/79 | **9** | 23 | 1 **Why Leave Us Alone**.................................. | *55* | Elektra 46032 |
| 9/29/79 | **29** | 12 | 2 You're Something Special ............................... | | Elektra 46531 |
| 5/17/80 | **29** | 12 | 3 Jam (Let's Take It To The Streets) ................... | | Elektra 46620 |
| | | | **THE FIVE STAIRSTEPS** ★★165★★ | | |
| | | | Chicago group consisting of family members Clarence Jr., James, Aloha, Kenneth and Dennis Burke. Later joined by 5-year-old Cubie. Managed by their father and produced by Curtis Mayfield; later became the Invisible Man's Band. | | |
| 5/07/66 | **16** | 10 | 1 You Waited Too Long.................................... | *94* | Windy C 601 |
| 8/06/66 | **12** | 10 | 2 World Of Fantasy ...................................... | *49* | Windy C 602 |
| 11/05/66 | **15** | 9 | 3 Come Back ............................................. | *61* | Windy C 603 |
| 1/28/67 | **16** | 8 | 4 Danger! She's A Stranger............................. | *89* | Windy C 604 |
| 4/29/67 | **37** | 5 | 5 Ain't Gonna Rest (Till I Get You)...................... | *87* | Windy C 605 |
| 6/03/67 | **34** | 7 | 6 Ooh, Baby Baby ........................................ | *63* | Windy C 607 |
| | | | **FIVE STAIRSTEPS & CUBIE:** | | |
| 12/16/67+ | **17** | 8 | 7 Something's Missing ................................... | *88* | Buddah 20 |
| 2/10/68 | **28** | 7 | 8 A Million To One....................................... | *68* | Buddah 26 |
| 8/31/68 | **15** | 9 | 9 Don't Change Your Love................................ | *59* | Curtom 1931 |
| 2/15/69 | **12** | 9 | 10 Baby Make Me Feel So Good......................... | *101* | Curtom 1936 |

**150**

| DEBUT DATE | PEAK POS | WKS CHR | ARTIST — Record Title | POP POS | Label & Number |
|---|---|---|---|---|---|
| | | | **THE FIVE STAIRSTEPS — Continued** | | |
| 8/09/69 | **38** | 2 | 11 Madame Mary .......................................... | | Curtom 1944 |
| 10/25/69 | **17** | 7 | 12 We Must Be In Love ................................ | 88 | Curtom 1945 |
| | | | **THE FIVE STAIRSTEPS:** | | |
| 4/04/70 | **14** | 21 | 13●O-o-h Child/ | 8 | |
| | | 3 | 14 Dear Prudence ........................................... | | Buddah 165 |
| | | | **THE STAIRSTEPS:** | | |
| 2/13/71 | **32** | 6 | 15 Didn't It Look So Easy ............................. | 81 | Buddah 213 |
| 1/15/72 | **40** | 5 | 16 I Love You - Stop ...................................... | 115 | Buddah 277 |
| 1/10/76 | **10** | 17 | 17 **From Us To You** ...................................... | 102 | Dark Horse 10005 |
| | | | **FIVE STAR** | | |
| | | | Brother/sister quintet from Britain: Denicce (lead singer), Stedman, Doris, Lorraine and Delroy Pearson. | | |
| 7/27/85 | **16** | 19 | 1 All Fall Down ............................................ | 65 | RCA 14108 |
| 11/23/85+ | **2**[2] | 19 | 2 **Let Me Be The One** ................................. | 59 | RCA 14229 |
| 4/12/86 | **9** | 14 | 3 **Love Take Over** ...................................... | | RCA 14323 |
| 8/09/86 | **7** | 18 | 4 **Can't Wait Another Minute** ..................... | 41 | RCA 14421 |
| 12/13/86+ | **13** | 14 | 5 If I Say Yes .............................................. | 67 | RCA 5083 |
| 4/04/87 | **15** | 12 | 6 Are You Man Enough? ............................. | | RCA 5149 |
| 9/12/87 | **39** | 11 | 7 Whenever You're Ready ............................ | | RCA 5292 |
| | | | **FIZZY QWICK** | | |
| 6/28/86 | **71** | 5 | 1 Hangin' Out ............................................... | | Motown 1838 |
| | | | **ROBERTA FLACK** ★★89★★ | | |
| | | | Born on 2/10/39 in Asheville, North Carolina; raised in Arlington, Virginia. Played piano from an early age. Music scholarship to Howard University at age 15; classmate of Donny Hathaway. Discovered by Les McCann. Signed to Atlantic Records in 1969. Also see Sadao Watanabe. | | |
| 6/12/71 | **8** | 13 | 1 **You've Got A Friend** ............................... | 29 | Atlantic 2808 |
| 10/30/71 | **30** | 6 | 2 You've Lost That Lovin' Feelin' ................ | 71 | Atlantic 2837 |
| 1/29/72 | **38** | 3 | 3 Will You Still Love Me Tomorrow ............. | 76 | Atlantic 2851 |
| 4/01/72 | **4** | 12 | 4●**The First Time Ever I Saw Your Face** ..... | 1 | Atlantic 2864 |
| | | | popularized because of inclusion in the film "Play Misty For Me" | | |
| 6/17/72 | **1**[1] | 13 | 5●**Where Is The Love** .................................. | 5 | Atlantic 2879 |
| | | | 1, 2 & 5: **ROBERTA FLACK & DONNY HATHAWAY** | | |
| 2/03/73 | **2**[4] | 12 | 6●**Killing Me Softly With His Song** ............. | 1 | Atlantic 2940 |
| 9/29/73 | **19** | 10 | 7 Jesse ...................................................... | 30 | Atlantic 2982 |
| 6/22/74 | **1**[5] | 17 | 8●**Feel Like Makin' Love** .............................. | 1 | Atlantic 3025 |
| 6/14/75 | **25** | 10 | 9 Feelin' That Glow .................................... | 76 | Atlantic 3271 |
| 12/10/77+ | **52** | 8 | 10 25th Of Last December ............................. | | Atlantic 3441 |
| 2/11/78 | **1**[2] | 19 | 11●**The Closer I Get To You** ......................... | 2 | Atlantic 3463 |
| 6/03/78 | **37** | 9 | 12 If Ever I See You Again ............................ | 24 | Atlantic 3483 |
| 12/09/78 | **82** | 3 | 13 When It's Over ........................................ | | Atlantic 3521 |
| 3/03/79 | **98** | 2 | 14 You Are Everything .................................. | | Atlantic 3560 |
| 1/26/80 | **8** | 17 | 15 **You Are My Heaven** ................................ | 47 | Atlantic 3627 |
| 5/03/80 | **18** | 8 | 16 Back Together Again ................................ | 50 | Atlantic 3661 |
| | | | 11, 15 & 16: **ROBERTA FLACK with DONNY HATHAWAY** | | |
| 8/09/80 | **67** | 5 | 17 Don't Make Me Wait Too Long ................. | 104 | Atlantic 3753 |
| | | | written by Stevie Wonder | | |
| 12/06/80+ | **13** | 16 | 18 Make The World Stand Still ..................... | | Atlantic 3775 |
| | | | **ROBERTA FLACK & PEABO BRYSON** | | |
| 3/28/81 | **46** | 6 | 19 Love Is A Waiting Game ........................... | | Atlantic 3803 |
| | | | **ROBERTA FLACK & PEABO BRYSON** | | |
| 6/27/81 | **32** | 11 | 20 You Stopped Loving Me ........................... | 108 | MCA 51126 |
| | | | written by Luther Vandross; from the film "Bustin' Loose" | | |
| 3/06/82 | **29** | 17 | 21 Making Love ............................................ | 13 | Atlantic 4005 |
| | | | from the film of the same title | | |
| 7/10/82 | **24** | 14 | 22 I'm The One ............................................ | 42 | Atlantic 4068 |
| 12/11/82 | **80** | 3 | 23 In The Name Of Love .............................. | | Atlantic 89932 |
| 2/05/83 | **65** | 7 | 24 Our Love Will Stop The World .................. | | Atlantic 89931 |
| | | | **ERIC MERCURY & ROBERTA FLACK** | | |
| 7/09/83 | **5** | 20 | 25 **Tonight, I Celebrate My Love** ................. | 16 | Capitol 5242 |
| 11/05/83 | **68** | 6 | 26 Maybe .................................................... | | Capitol 5283 |
| 12/24/83+ | **41** | 12 | 27 You're Looking Like Love To Me ............. | 58 | Capitol 5307 |
| | | | above 3: **PEABO BRYSON/ROBERTA FLACK** | | |

**151**

| | | | **FLAKES** | | |
| 9/27/80 | **66** | 7 | 1 Hey There Lonely Girl................................... | | Salsoul 2130 |
| | | | **THE FLAMING EMBER** | | |
| | | | White soul/rock group from Detroit. Formed as the Flaming Embers: Joe Sladich (guitar), Bill Ellis (piano), Jim Bugnel (bass) and Jerry Plunk (drums). First recorded for Ric-Tic in 1968. | | |
| 5/23/70 | **15** | 13 | 1 Westbound #9.......................................... | *24* | Hot Wax 7003 |
| 10/31/70 | **12** | 8 | 2 I'm Not My Brothers Keeper ........................... | *34* | Hot Wax 7006 |
| 2/20/71 | **43** | 5 | 3 Stop The World And Let Me Off ...................... | *101* | Hot Wax 7010 |
| | | | also released on Radio Active Gold 115 | | |
| | | | **THE FLAMINGOS** | | |
| | | | Group formed in Chicago in 1952. Consisted of cousins Zeke & Jake Carey, and cousins Paul Wilson & Johnny Carter, with lead singer Sollie McElroy. First recorded for Chance Records in 1953. In 1954, Sollie departed and was replaced by Nate Nelson. Tommy Hunt and Terry Johnson joined in July of 1956, replacing Army-bound Zeke Carey and Johnny Carter. Carey returned in 1958 and group signed with End Records. Nelson joined The Platters in 1966; died of a heart attack on 6/1/84 (52). | | |
| 2/18/56 | **5** | 8 | 1 **I'll Be Home** ....................................... | | Checker 830 |
| | | | Juke Box #5 / Best Seller #10 / Jockey #15 | | |
| 6/09/56 | **12** | 2 | 2 A Kiss From Your Lips............................ | | Checker 837 |
| | | | Jockey #12 | | |
| 3/02/59 | **25** | 2 | 3 Lovers Never Say Goodbye......................... | *52* | End 1035 |
| 6/15/59 | **3** | 13 | 4 **I Only Have Eyes For You** ...................... | *11* | End 1046 |
| | | | a hit for Ben Selvin in 1934 (POS 2) | | |
| 5/23/60 | **23** | 3 | 5 Nobody Loves Me Like You ........................... | *30* | End 1068 |
| | | | written by Sam Cooke | | |
| 8/29/60 | **27** | 3 | 6 Mio Amore......................................... | *74* | End 1073 |
| 3/26/66 | **22** | 3 | 7 The Boogaloo Party ............................... | *93* | Philips 40347 |
| 9/27/69 | **48** | 2 | 8 Dealin' (Groovin' With Feelin') ...................... | | Julman 506 |
| 3/21/70 | **28** | 5 | 9 Buffalo Soldier........................................ | *86* | Polydor 14019 |
| | | | **THE FLARES** | | |
| | | | Group from Los Angeles, consisting of lead singer Aaron Collins, Willie Davis, Tommy Miller and George Hollis. Collins and Davis had been in the Cadets/Jacks; Miller and Hollis had been in The Ermines and Flairs. | | |
| 10/16/61 | **20** | 5 | 1 Foot Stompin' - Part 1 ................................. | *25* | Felsted 8624 |
| | | | **FLB - see FAT LARRY'S BAND** | | |
| | | | **THE FLEETWOODS** | | |
| | | | White vocal trio formed while in high school in Olympia, Washington, in 1958: Gary Troxel, Gretchen Christopher and Barbara Ellis. | | |
| 3/23/59 | **5** | 10 | 1 **Come Softly To Me** ..................................... | *1* | Dolphin 1 |
| 10/19/59 | **3** | 13 | 2 **Mr. Blue** .............................................. | *1* | Dolton 5 |
| | | | **WADE FLEMONS** | | |
| | | | Born on 9/25/40 in Coffeyville, Kansas. Electric pianist of Maurice White's pre-Earth, Wind & Fire group, the Salty Peppers. | | |
| 11/24/58+ | **19** | 12 | 1 Here I Stand.............................................. | *80* | Vee-Jay 295 |
| | | | backing vocals by The Newcomers | | |
| 5/02/60 | **10** | 3 | 2 **Easy Lovin'** ......................................... | *70* | Vee-Jay 344 |
| 9/11/61 | **20** | 4 | 3 Please Send Me Someone To Love ................... | | Vee-Jay 389 |
| | | | **JULIAN FLENOY** | | |
| 4/12/86 | **75** | 6 | 1 Turn Me Out............................................. | | KMA 005 |
| | | | **DARROW FLETCHER** | | |
| | | | Born on 1/23/51 in Inkster, Michigan. Moved to Chicago in 1954. Father, Johnny Haygood, produced his records. Freshman in high school at time of first hit. | | |
| 1/01/66 | **23** | 7 | 1 The Pain Gets A Little Deeper ........................ | *89* | Groovy 3001 |
| 3/07/70 | **47** | 3 | 2 I Think I'm Gonna Write A Song ..................... | | Congress 6011 |
| 3/06/76 | **99** | 3 | 3 We've Got To Get An Understanding................ | | Crossover 983 |
| | | | **DUSTY FLETCHER** | | |
| | | | Born Clinton Fletcher in Des Moines, Iowa. Comedian, long-time favorite at the Apollo Theater. | | |
| 2/08/47 | **2²** | 7 | 1 **Open The Door, Richard** ........................... [C] | *3* | National 4012 |
| | | | based on vaudeville routine originated by John "Spider Bruce" Mason; with Jimmy Jones' Orchestra | | |

### THE FLOATERS
Group from Detroit, consisting of Charles Clark (lead), Larry Cunningham, Paul and Ralph Mitchell and Jonathan "Mighty Midget" Murray.

| DEBUT DATE | PEAK POS | WKS CHR | ARTIST — Record Title | POP POS | Label & Number |
|---|---|---|---|---|---|
| 6/25/77 | **1**[6] | 20 | 1 ●Float On | 2 | ABC 12284 |
| 10/22/77 | **28** | 14 | 2 You Don't Have To Say You Love Me | | ABC 12314 |
| 5/27/78 | **36** | 9 | 3 I Just Want To Be With You | 103 | ABC 12364 |

### FLOS

| | | | | | |
|---|---|---|---|---|---|
| 4/18/87 | **58** | 8 | 1 We're Back | | Superstar I. 54 |

### EDDIE FLOYD ★★181★★
Born on 6/25/35 in Montgomery, Alabama. Raised in Detroit. Original member of The Falcons, 1955-63. Eddie's uncle, Robert West, founded the Lu Pine record label.

| DEBUT DATE | PEAK POS | WKS CHR | ARTIST — Record Title | POP POS | Label & Number |
|---|---|---|---|---|---|
| 8/27/66 | **1**[1] | 21 | 1 Knock On Wood | 28 | Stax 194 |
| 2/18/67 | **16** | 9 | 2 Raise Your Hand | 79 | Stax 208 |
| 8/26/67 | **30** | 5 | 3 Love Is A Doggone Good Thing | 97 | Stax 223 |
| 11/11/67 | **22** | 7 | 4 On A Saturday Night | 92 | Stax 233 |
| 7/13/68 | **2**[2] | 14 | 5 I've Never Found A Girl (To Love Me Like You Do) | 40 | Stax 0002 |
| 11/16/68 | **4** | 12 | 6 Bring It On Home To Me | 17 | Stax 0012 |
| 3/15/69 | **50** | 2 | 7 I've Got To Have Your Love | 102 | Stax 0025 |
| 6/28/69 | **18** | 7 | 8 Don't Tell Your Mama (Where You've Been) | 73 | Stax 0036 |
| 11/08/69 | **30** | 3 | 9 Why Is The Wine Sweeter (On The Other Side) | 98 | Stax 0051 |
| 2/21/70 | **11** | 13 | 10 California Girl | 45 | Stax 0060 |
| 7/18/70 | **43** | 5 | 11 My Girl | 116 | Stax 0072 |
| 10/17/70 | **29** | 6 | 12 The Best Years Of My Life | 118 | Stax 0077 |
| 9/11/71 | **33** | 6 | 13 Blood Is Thicker Than Water | | Stax 0095 |
| 3/18/72 | **49** | 2 | 14 Yum Yum Yum (I Want Some) | 122 | Stax 0109 |
| 8/25/73 | **50** | 8 | 15 Baby Lay Your Head Down/ first charted week listed as "Baby Let Me Take You In My Arms" | | |
| | | 4 | 16 Check Me Out | | Stax 0171 |
| 8/03/74 | **65** | 8 | 17 Soul Street | | Stax 0216 |
| 2/26/77 | **74** | 6 | 18 We Should Really Be In Love DOROTHY MOORE/EDDIE FLOYD | | Malaco 1040 |

### FOCUS

| | | | | | |
|---|---|---|---|---|---|
| 1/17/87 | **42** | 15 | 1 Zero In July | | EMI America 8366 |

### FORCE M.D.'S
Staten Island-based quintet: Antoine Maurice "T.C.D." Lundy, Stevie Lundy, Jesse Lee Daniels, Trisco Pearson and Charles Richard Nelson. Formed in 1980; worked at The Roxy, Harlem World and Afrika Bambaataa's Zulu Nation Party in 1982. Originally called Dr. Rock & The M.C.'s.

| DEBUT DATE | PEAK POS | WKS CHR | ARTIST — Record Title | POP POS | Label & Number |
|---|---|---|---|---|---|
| 5/19/84 | **49** | 10 | 1 Let Me Love You | | Tommy Boy 841 |
| 9/22/84 | **5** | 21 | 2 Tears | 102 | Tommy Boy 848 |
| 1/26/85 | **49** | 10 | 3 Forgive Me Girl | | Tommy Boy 851 |
| 6/01/85 | **13** | 16 | 4 Itchin' For A Scratch from the film "Rappin'" | 105 | Atlantic 89557 |
| 12/21/85+ | **4** | 22 | 5 Tender Love from the film "Krush Groove" | 10 | Warner 28818 |
| 4/19/86 | **18** | 15 | 6 Here I Go Again | | Tommy Boy 28742 |
| 8/23/86 | **29** | 11 | 7 One Plus One | | Tommy Boy 28619 |
| 11/22/86+ | **21** | 15 | 8 I Wanna Know Your Name | | Tommy Boy 890 |
| 7/04/87 | **1**[2] | 18 | 9 Love Is A House | 78 | Tommy Boy 28300 |
| 10/31/87 | **10** | 14 | 10 Touch And Go | | Tommy Boy 28181 |
| 2/27/88 | **23** | 12 | 11 Couldn't Care Less | | Tommy Boy 27978 |

### DEE DEE FORD - see DON GARDNER

### FRANKIE FORD
Born Frank Guzzo on 8/4/39 in Gretna, LA. Vocal training since age 6; appeared with Sophie Tucker, Ted Lewis, Carmen Miranda at local shows at an early age. Formed own band, Syncopators, in high school. Appeared in the film "American Hot Wax".

| DEBUT DATE | PEAK POS | WKS CHR | ARTIST — Record Title | POP POS | Label & Number |
|---|---|---|---|---|---|
| 4/13/59 | **11** | 7 | 1 Sea Cruise with Huey "Piano" Smith's group, The Clowns; Frankie's vocal, slightly sped up, was substituted for Huey Smith's | 14 | Ace 554 |

| DEBUT DATE | PEAK POS | WKS CHR | ARTIST — Record Title | POP POS | Label & Number |
|---|---|---|---|---|---|
| | | | **PENNYE FORD** | | |
| | | | Vocalist from Cincinnati, daughter of Gene Redd, Sr. (producer for James Brown), and Carolyn Ford (singer). Multi-instrumentalist, played piano from age 5. Winner of the Talented Teen Pageant in Cincinnati. Worked as a demo singer in Los Angeles. | | |
| 10/27/84+ | 25 | 21 | 1 Change Your Wicked Ways ........................... | | Total Exp. 2404 |
| 5/11/85 | 42 | 11 | 2 Dangerous ................................... | | Total Exp. 2413 |
| | | | **FORECAST** | | |
| 11/22/80 | 65 | 6 | 1 Non Stop ..................................... | | Ariola 811 |
| | | | **FOREIGNER** | | |
| | | | British/American rock group formed in New York City in 1976. | | |
| 2/02/85 | 85 | 4 | 1●I Want To Know What Love Is ........................ | *1* | Atlantic 89596 |
| | | | vocal backing by the New Jersey Mass Choir and Jennifer Holliday | | |
| | | | **EARL FOREST** | | |
| | | | Vocalist/drummer; member of the Beale Streeters band, with Bobby Bland and Johnny Ace. First recorded for Duke in 1952. Last name is also spelled Forrest. | | |
| 3/14/53 | 7 | 6 | 1 **Whoopin' And Hollerin'** .............................. | | Duke 108 |
| | | | Juke Box #7 | | |
| | | | with the Beale Streeters; Johnny Ace on piano | | |
| | | | **JIMMY FORREST** | | |
| | | | Born on 1/24/20 in St. Louis. Tenor saxophonist. Worked with Jay McShann in the early 40s, Andy Kirk from 1943-47, and Duke Ellington from 1949-50. Composer of the hit "Night Train". | | |
| 3/01/52 | 1 7 | 20 | 1 **Night Train** ................................ [I] | | United 110 |
| | | | Juke Box #1(7) / Best Seller #1(6) | | |
| 12/20/52+ | 3 | 2 | 2 **Hey Mrs. Jones** ............................. | | United 130 |
| | | | Juke Box #3 / Best Seller #8 | | |
| | | | **IAN FOSTER** | | |
| | | | Singer/songwriter born of Jamaican descent. Raised in London. Former leader of UK band, One Love. | | |
| 8/01/87 | 84 | 6 | 1 Out For The Count ...................... | | MCA 53059 |
| | | | **THE FOUNDATIONS** | | |
| | | | British integrated R&B/rock group. Lead singer Clem Curtis (from Trinidad) replaced by Colin Young (West Indies) in 1968. Disbanded in 1970. | | |
| 2/17/68 | 33 | 2 | 1 Baby, Now That I've Found You ...................... | *11* | Uni 55038 |
| | | | **FOUR BLAZES** | | |
| | | | Chicago group formed in 1940. First recorded as The Five Blazes for Aristocrat in 1947. Group on United label consisted of Tommy Braden (lead vocals - d: 1957), Shorty Hill, Floyd McDaniels and Paul Lindsley "Jelly" Holt. Eddie Chamblee, from the Sonny Thompson band, played on "Mary Jo" and subsequently joined the group. Also known as The Blazers. | | |
| 7/12/52 | 1 3 | 16 | 1 **Mary Jo** ..................................... | | United 114 |
| | | | Juke Box #1 / Best Seller #3 | | |
| 10/18/52 | 7 | 1 | 2 **Please Send Her Back To Me** ........................ | | United 127 |
| | | | Juke Box #7 | | |
| 11/28/53 | 5 | 2 | 3 **Perfect Woman** ............................... | | United 158 |
| | | | Juke Box #5 | | |
| | | | **THE FOUR BUDDIES** | | |
| | | | Group from Frederick Douglass High School in Baltimore. Consisted of Leon Harrison (lead, first tenor), Gregory Carroll (second tenor), Bert Palmer (baritone), and Tommy Smith (bass). First recorded as The Metronomes with Johnny Otis on Savoy. Name changed to the Four Buds, then Four Buddies. Harrison also led the Buddies on Glory and the Barons on Decca in 1954. Carroll joined the Orioles in 1954. Not to be confused with the Four Buddies on Club 51 in Chicago. | | |
| 4/14/51 | 2 1 | 12 | 1 **I Will Wait** ................................. | | Savoy 769 |
| | | | Juke Box #2 / Best Seller #3 | | |
| | | | **4 BY FOUR** | | |
| | | | Quartet from Queens, NY: Damen & Lance Heyward, Steve Gray and Jeraude Jackson. | | |
| 5/02/87 | 8 | 15 | 1 **Want You For My Girlfriend** ........................ | *79* | Capitol 5690 |
| 8/08/87 | 10 | 14 | 2 **Come Over** ................................. | | Capitol 44034 |
| 12/05/87 | 72 | 8 | 3 Don't Put The Blame On Me ........................... | | Capitol 44081 |

| DEBUT DATE | PEAK POS | WKS CHR | ARTIST — Record Title | POP POS | Label & Number |
|---|---|---|---|---|---|
| | | | **FOUR FELLOWS** | | |
| | | | Group from Brooklyn, formed in 1953. Consisted of Jimmy McGowan, Larry Banks, David Jones and Teddy Williams. First recorded for Derby Records in 1954. Banks was writer of The Moody Blues' 1964 pop hit "Go Now". Jones was later a member of The Rays. | | |
| 7/02/55 | **4** | 15 | 1 Soldier Boy .............................................. | | Glory 234 |
| | | | Best Seller #4 / Juke Box #7 / Jockey #8 with the Abie Baker Orchestra | | |
| | | | **450SL** | | |
| 8/31/85 | **76** | 7 | 1 The Rock .............................................. | | Golden Boy 7126 |
| | | | **FOUR JACKS** | | |
| 5/21/49 | **8** | 3 | 1 I Challenge Your Kiss ............................... | | Allen 21000 |
| | | | Juke Box #8 | | |
| | | | **FOUR KNIGHTS - see NAT KING COLE** | | |
| | | | **FOUR MINTS** | | |
| 9/01/73 | **84** | 6 | 1 Do You Really Love Me ............................. | | Capsoul 27 |
| 12/08/73+ | **80** | 6 | 2 You're My Desire .................................... | | Capsoul 28 |
| | | | **THE FOUR PENNIES - see THE CHIFFONS** | | |
| | | | **THE FOUR PREPS** | | |
| | | | White vocal group formed while at Hollywood High School: Bruce Belland, Glen Larson, Ed Cobb and Marvin Ingraham. Belland was later in duo with Dave Somerville of the Diamonds. | | |
| 3/03/58 | **6** | 8 | 1 26 Miles (Santa Catalina) ........................ | 2 | Capitol 3845 |
| | | | Best Seller #6 | | |
| 5/26/58 | **9** | 9 | 2 Big Man .............................................. | 3 | Capitol 3960 |
| | | | Jockey #9 / Best Seller #10 | | |
| | | | **THE 4 SEASONS** | | |
| | | | White vocal group formed in 1955, in Newark, New Jersey, as the Variatones. Several personnel and name changes later; known in 1961 as The 4 Seasons. 1961 lineup: lead singer Frankie Valli (Francis Castelluccio), Bob Gaudio (of the Royal Teens), Nick Massi and Tommy DeVito. Numerous personnel changes after 1965. | | |
| 9/08/62 | **1**[1] | 11 | 1 Sherry ................................................ | 1 | Vee-Jay 456 |
| 11/03/62 | **1**[3] | 13 | 2 Big Girls Don't Cry ................................ | 1 | Vee-Jay 465 |
| 2/09/63 | **3** | 12 | 3 Walk Like A Man ................................... | 1 | Vee-Jay 485 |
| 8/03/63 | **13** | 9 | 4 Candy Girl .......................................... | 3 | Vee-Jay 539 |
| | | | **THE FOUR SONICS** | | |
| | | | Quartet: Willie Frazier, Steve Gaston, Eddy Daniels and James "Jay" Johnson. | | |
| 3/02/68 | **32** | 5 | 1 You Don't Have To Say You Love Me ............. | 89 | Sport 110 |
| | | | **FOUR TOPS**   ★★17★★ | | |
| | | | Native Detroit group formed in 1954 as the Four Aims. Consisted of Levi Stubbs (lead singer), Renaldo "Obie" Benson, Lawrence Payton and Abdul "Duke" Fakir. First recorded for Chess in 1956, then Red Top and Columbia, before signing with Motown in 1963. Group has had no personnel changes since its formation. Stubbs is the voice of Audrey II (the voracious vegetation) in the 1986 film "Little Shop of Horrors". | | |
| 8/15/64 | **11** | 12 | 1 Baby I Need Your Loving ........................... | Hot | Motown 1062 |
| 11/28/64 | **43** | 5 | 2 Without The One You Love (Life's Not Worth While) ................................................ | Hot | Motown 1069 |
| 2/06/65 | **9** | 11 | 3 Ask The Lonely .................................... | 24 | Motown 1073 |
| 5/15/65 | **1**[9] | 18 | 4 I Can't Help Myself ............................... | 1 | Motown 1076 |
| 8/07/65 | **2**[4] | 13 | 5 It's The Same Old Song ........................... | 5 | Motown 1081 |
| 11/20/65 | **9** | 10 | 6 Something About You .............................. | 19 | Motown 1084 |
| 3/05/66 | **5** | 9 | 7 Shake Me, Wake Me (When It's Over) ............ | 18 | Motown 1090 |
| 6/18/66 | **12** | 7 | 8 Loving You Is Sweeter Than Ever ................. | 45 | Motown 1096 |
| 9/10/66 | **1**[2] | 14 | 9 Reach Out, I'll Be There .......................... | 1 | Motown 1098 |
| 12/24/66+ | **2**[2] | 12 | 10 Standing In The Shadows Of Love ............... | 6 | Motown 1102 |
| 3/18/67 | **3** | 11 | 11 Bernadette ......................................... | 4 | Motown 1104 |
| 6/03/67 | **10** | 9 | 12 7 Rooms Of Gloom/ | 14 | |
| 8/05/67 | **50** | 2 | 13 I'll Turn To Stone ............................... | 76 | Motown 1110 |
| 9/23/67 | **7** | 10 | 14 You Keep Running Away ........................... | 19 | Motown 1113 |
| 2/24/68 | **15** | 7 | 15 Walk Away Renee .................................. | 14 | Motown 1119 |
| 5/11/68 | **17** | 8 | 16 If I Were A Carpenter ............................ | 20 | Motown 1124 |

| DEBUT DATE | PEAK POS | WKS CHR | ARTIST — Record Title | POP POS | Label & Number |
|---|---|---|---|---|---|
| | | | **FOUR TOPS — Continued** | | |
| 8/10/68 | **31** | 6 | 17 Yesterday's Dreams................................ | *49* | Motown 1127 |
| 10/26/68 | **23** | 5 | 18 I'm In A Different World ........................... | *51* | Motown 1132 |
| 12/13/69 | **25** | 5 | 19 Don't Let Him Take Your Love From Me.......... | *45* | Motown 1159 |
| 5/02/70 | **6** | 13 | 20 It's All In The Game ................................. | *24* | Motown 1164 |
| 9/05/70 | **4** | 13 | 21 Still Water (Love)..................................... | *11* | Motown 1170 |
| 12/12/70+ | **7** | 9 | 22 River Deep-Mountain High........................ | *14* | Motown 1173 |
| | | | THE SUPREMES & FOUR TOPS | | |
| 1/30/71 | **9** | 9 | 23 Just Seven Numbers (Can Straighten Out My Life)................................................ | *40* | Motown 1175 |
| 6/19/71 | **41** | 4 | 24 You Gotta Have Love In Your Heart................ | *55* | Motown 1181 |
| | | | THE SUPREMES & FOUR TOPS | | |
| 7/03/71 | **28** | 7 | 25 In These Changing Times............................ | *70* | Motown 1185 |
| 9/18/71 | **27** | 7 | 26 MacArthur Park (Part II) ............................ | *38* | Motown 1189 |
| 2/12/72 | **34** | 3 | 27 A Simple Game........................................ | *90* | Motown 1196 |
| 9/09/72 | **8** | 9 | 28 (It's The Way) Nature Planned It .................. | *53* | Motown 1210 |
| 11/18/72 | **7** | 13 | 29 Keeper Of The Castle ............................... | *10* | Dunhill 4330 |
| 2/10/73 | **2**¹ | 14 | 30● Ain't No Woman (Like The One I've Got)........ | *4* | Dunhill 4339 |
| 6/23/73 | **2**¹ | 13 | 31 Are You Man Enough ............................... | *15* | Dunhill 4354 |
| | | | from the film "Shaft In Africa" | | |
| 10/13/73 | **10** | 13 | 32 Sweet Understanding Love ......................... | *33* | Dunhill 4366 |
| 1/19/74 | **18** | 14 | 33 I Just Can't Get You Out Of My Mind .............. | *62* | Dunhill 4377 |
| 4/20/74 | **3** | 15 | 34 One Chain Don't Make No Prison................... | *41* | Dunhill 4386 |
| 7/27/74 | **5** | 15 | 35 Midnight Flower ...................................... | *55* | Dunhill 15005 |
| 5/24/75 | **13** | 12 | 36 Seven Lonely Nights ................................ | *71* | ABC 12096 |
| 9/06/75 | **17** | 15 | 37 We All Gotta Stick Together......................... | *97* | ABC 12123 |
| 1/31/76 | **72** | 3 | 38 Mama You're All Right With Me/ | *107* | |
| | | 5 | 39 I'm Glad You Walked Into My Life ................. | | ABC 12155 |
| 9/04/76 | **7** | 21 | 40 Catfish ................................................. | *71* | ABC 12214 |
| 1/29/77 | **29** | 10 | 41 Feel Free .............................................. | | ABC 12236 |
| 11/19/77 | **84** | 6 | 42 The Show Must Go On ............................... | | ABC 12315 |
| 11/25/78+ | **38** | 11 | 43 H.E.L.P. ................................................ | | ABC 12427 |
| 8/15/81 | **1**² | 19 | 44 When She Was My Girl ............................. | *11* | Casablanca 2338 |
| 12/12/81 | **71** | 6 | 45 Let Me Set You Free ................................. | | Casablanca 2344 |
| 2/06/82 | **32** | 10 | 46 Tonight I'm Gonna Love You All Over .............. | | Casablanca 2345 |
| 8/14/82 | **40** | 8 | 47 Sad Hearts/ | *84* | |
| 12/11/82+ | **40** | 16 | 48 I Believe In You And Me ............................. | | Casablanca 2353 |
| 10/22/83 | **36** | 14 | 49 I Just Can't Walk Away................................ | *71* | Motown 1706 |
| 6/01/85 | **21** | 14 | 50 Sexy Ways ............................................. | | Motown 1790 |

## FOUR TUNES

New York City group formed in 1945 as Deek Watson & The Brown Dots. Consisted of Deek Watson (formerly with the Ink Spots), Pat Best, Jimmy Gordon and Jimmie Nabbie. First recorded for Regis in 1945. Recorded for Manor in 1946 as the Sentimentalists, without Watson. Danny Owens replaced Watson, group became the Four Tunes. Best and Watson wrote "I Love You For Sentimental Reasons" hit for Nat Cole, and others. Nabbie wrote hit "You Are My Love" for Joni James. Group active until 1963. Nabbie now fronts an "Ink Spots" group.

| DEBUT DATE | PEAK POS | WKS CHR | ARTIST — Record Title | POP POS | Label & Number |
|---|---|---|---|---|---|
| 11/21/53 | **2**¹ | 20 | 1 Marie ................................................... | *13* | Jubilee 5128 |
| | | | Juke Box #2 / Best Seller #7 | | |
| 6/05/54 | **7** | 7 | 2 I Understand Just How You Feel .................. | *6* | Jubilee 5132 |
| | | | Juke Box #7 / Best Seller #9 | | |
| | | | above 2: with the Sid Bass Orchestra; a reported million-seller | | |

## FOUR VAGABONDS

Group formed at Vashon High School, in St. Louis, in 1933. Consisted of John Jordan (lead), Robert O'Neal, Norval Taborn and Ray "Happy Pappy" Grant Jr. First recorded for Bluebird in 1941. Grant hosted the first all-black TV show on WENR-TV, Chicago, on 4/1/49.

| DEBUT DATE | PEAK POS | WKS CHR | ARTIST — Record Title | POP POS | Label & Number |
|---|---|---|---|---|---|
| 7/17/43 | **3** | 11 | 1 It Can't Be Wrong...................................... | | Bluebird 0815 |
| | | | from the film "Now, Voyager" | | |

## INEZ FOXX

Born on 9/9/42 in Greensboro, North Carolina. Sang with the Gospel Tide Chorus. First recorded for Brunswick in 1960 as "Inez Johnston", with brother Charlie (b: 10/23/39) until 1969. Solo thereafter.

| DEBUT DATE | PEAK POS | WKS CHR | ARTIST — Record Title | POP POS | Label & Number |
|---|---|---|---|---|---|
| 6/22/63 | **2**¹ | 19 | 1 Mockingbird............................................ | *7* | Symbol 919 |
| 12/07/63 | **98** | 1 | 2 Hi Diddle Diddle........................................ | *Hot* | Symbol 924 |

| DEBUT DATE | PEAK POS | WKS CHR | ARTIST — Record Title | POP POS | Label & Number |
|---|---|---|---|---|---|
| | | | **INEZ FOXX — Continued** | | |
| 1/25/64 | 91 | 3 | 3 Ask Me................................................ | *Hot* | Symbol 926 |
| 4/25/64 | 54 | 9 | 4 Hurt By Love........................................ | *Hot* | Symbol 20-001 |
| 10/29/66 | 49 | 2 | 5 No Stranger To Love ........................... | | Musicor 1201 |
| 5/27/67 | 41 | 6 | 6 I Stand Accused .................................. | *127* | Dynamo 104 |
| 9/02/67 | 32 | 4 | 7 You Are The Man ................................ | | Dynamo 109 |
| 12/30/67+ | 17 | 14 | 8 (1-2-3-4-5-6-7) Count The Days......................... | *76* | Dynamo 112 |
| | | | above 3 shown as: **INEZ & CHARLIE FOXX** | | |
| 1/23/71 | 50 | 2 | 9 You Shouldn't Have Set My Soul On Fire .......... | | Dynamo 144 |
| 12/22/73+ | 74 | 7 | 10 I Had A Talk With My Man........................... | | Volt 4101 |
| 6/22/74 | 83 | 5 | 11 Circuits Overloaded ...................................... | | Volt 4107 |
| | | | **FOXY** | | |
| | | | Group from Miami. Consisted of Ish Ledesma (lead vocals, guitar), Richie Puente (clarinet, percussion), Arnold Pasiero (bass), Charlie Murciano (keyboards, vibes) and Joe Galdo (drums). Puente is the son of famous bandleader Tito Puente. | | |
| 2/14/70 | 42 | 5 | 1 Call Me Later ..................................... | | Double Shot 145 |
| 4/24/76 | 39 | 10 | 2 Get Off Your Aahh! And Dance (Part 1) ............ | | Dash 5022 |
| 6/24/78 | 1² | 24 | 3 **Get Off** ................................................ | *9* | Dash 5046 |
| 2/17/79 | 4 | 20 | 4 **Hot Number** ...................................... | *21* | Dash 5050 |
| 9/15/79 | 22 | 14 | 5 Rrrrrrock........................................... | | Dash 5054 |
| | | | **CONNIE FRANCIS** | | |
| | | | Born Concetta Rosa Maria Franconero on 12/12/38 in Newark, New Jersey. First recorded for MGM in 1955. Films: "Where The Boys Are", "Follow The Boys", "Looking For Love" and "When The Boys Meet The Girls", 1961-65. Connie stopped performing after she was raped on 11/8/74, for which she was awarded $3,000,000 in damages. Began comeback with a performance on "Dick Clark's Live Wednesday" TV show in 1978. | | |
| 3/24/58 | 4 | 8 | 1 **Who's Sorry Now?**.................................... | *4* | MGM 12588 |
| | | | Best Seller #4 there were 5 Top 20 versions of this tune in 1923 | | |
| 1/05/59 | 11 | 10 | 2 My Happiness ................................... | *2* | MGM 12738 |
| | | | there were 5 Top 30 pop versions of this tune in 1948 | | |
| 3/23/59 | 29 | 2 | 3 If I Didn't Care.................................. | *22* | MGM 12769 |
| | | | tune popularized in 1939 by the Ink Spots (POS 2) | | |
| 6/08/59 | 10 | 12 | 4 **Lipstick On Your Collar/** | *5* | |
| 7/27/59 | 17 | 3 | 5 Frankie ............................................ | *9* | MGM 12793 |
| 1/11/60 | 10 | 5 | 6 **Among My Souvenirs**............................. | *7* | MGM 12841 |
| | | | there were 4 Top 20 versions of this song in 1928 | | |
| 5/30/60 | 2¹ | 11 | 7 **Everybody's Somebody's Fool** ....................... | *1* | MGM 12899 |
| 10/03/60 | 11 | 7 | 8 My Heart Has A Mind Of Its Own...................... | *1* | MGM 12923 |
| | | | **FRANKIE & THE SPINDLES** | | |
| 7/13/68 | 39 | 3 | 1 Candy ............................................. | | Roc-Ker 100 |
| | | | **ARETHA FRANKLIN**  ★★**2**★★ | | |
| | | | Born on 3/25/42 in Memphis; raised in Buffalo and Detroit. Daughter of Rev. Cecil L. Franklin, pastor of New Bethel Church in Detroit. First recorded for JVB/Battle in 1956. Signed to Columbia Records in 1960 by John Hammond, then dramatic turn in style and success after signing with Atlantic and working with producer Jerry Wexler. Appeared in the 1980 film "The Blues Brothers". The all-time Queen of Soul Music. | | |
| 10/24/60 | 10 | 12 | 1 **Today I Sing The Blues** ............................. | | Columbia 41793 |
| 2/13/61 | 7 | 8 | 2 **Won't Be Long** .................................... | *76* | Columbia 41923 |
| | | | with the Ray Bryant Combo | | |
| 10/09/61 | 6 | 12 | 3 **Operation Heartbreak** ............................. | | Columbia 42157 |
| 9/19/64 | 57 | 10 | 4 Runnin' Out Of Fools ........................... | *Hot* | Columbia 43113 |
| 1/30/65 | 96 | 2 | 5 Can't You Just See Me ......................... | *Hot* | Columbia 43203 |
| 5/15/65 | 18 | 5 | 6 One Step Ahead .................................. | *119* | Columbia 43241 |
| 11/19/66 | 27 | 8 | 7 Cry Like A Baby ................................. | *113* | Columbia 43827 |
| 3/11/67 | 1⁷ | 14 | 8 **I Never Loved A Man (The Way I Loved You)/** | *9* | |
| 6/03/67 | 37 | 4 | 9 Do Right Woman-Do Right Man...................... | | Atlantic 2386 |
| 5/06/67 | 1⁸ | 14 | 10●**Respect** ............................................ | *1* | Atlantic 2403 |
| 7/01/67 | 31 | 6 | 11 Lee Cross ........................................ | | Columbia 44181 |
| 7/29/67 | 1² | 13 | 12●**Baby I Love You** .................................. | *4* | Atlantic 2427 |
| 9/30/67 | 28 | 5 | 13 Take A Look ...................................... | *56* | Columbia 44270 |
| 10/07/67 | 2¹ | 13 | 14 **A Natural Woman (You Make Me Feel Like)**..... | *8* | Atlantic 2441 |
| 12/16/67+ | 1⁴ | 14 | 15●**Chain Of Fools** .................................. | *2* | Atlantic 2464 |

| DEBUT DATE | PEAK POS | WKS CHR | ARTIST — Record Title | POP POS | Label & Number |
|---|---|---|---|---|---|
| | | | **ARETHA FRANKLIN — Continued** | | |
| 3/02/68 | **1**³ | 13 | 16● (Sweet Sweet Baby) Since You've Been Gone/ | 5 | |
| 4/06/68 | **9** | 10 | 17   Ain't No Way.................................... | 16 | Atlantic 2486 |
| | | | written by Aretha's sister, Carolyn Franklin | | |
| 5/25/68 | **1**³ | 13 | 18● Think/ | 7 | |
| 6/22/68 | **28** | 9 | 19   You Send Me ................................... | 56 | Atlantic 2518 |
| 8/24/68 | **2**² | 10 | 20   **The House That Jack Built/** | 6 | |
| 8/31/68 | **3** | 12 | 21●  **I Say A Little Prayer** ...................... | 10 | Atlantic 2546 |
| 11/30/68+ | **9** | 9 | 22● **See Saw/** | 14 | |
| 12/07/68+ | **10** | 9 | 23   **My Song** ...................................... | 31 | Atlantic 2574 |
| 3/01/69 | **3** | 8 | 24   **The Weight/** | 19 | |
| 3/22/69 | **21** | 6 | 25   Tracks Of My Tears ........................ | 71 | Atlantic 2603 |
| 4/26/69 | **3** | 9 | 26   **I Can't See Myself Leaving You/** | 28 | |
| 5/17/69 | **50** | 1 | 27   Gentle On My Mind ......................... | 76 | Atlantic 2619 |
| 8/02/69 | **1**⁵ | 13 | 28   **Share Your Love With Me** ............... | 13 | Atlantic 2650 |
| 11/22/69 | **5** | 9 | 29   **Eleanor Rigby** ............................. | 17 | Atlantic 2683 |
| 2/14/70 | **1**² | 13 | 30   **Call Me** ..................................... | 13 | Atlantic 2706 |
| 5/30/70 | **3** | 10 | 31   **Spirit In The Dark/** | 23 | |
| | | 8 | 32   The Thrill Is Gone .......................... | | Atlantic 2731 |
| 8/15/70 | **1**³ | 12 | 33● Don't Play That Song ....................... | 11 | Atlantic 2751 |
| 11/28/70+ | **5** | 8 | 34   **Border Song (Holy Moses)/** | 37 | |
| | | | written by Elton John & Bernie Taupin | | |
| | | 6 | 35   You And Me .................................. | | Atlantic 2772 |
| | | | 31, 33 & 35: with The Dixie Flyers | | |
| 3/06/71 | **3** | 9 | 36   **You're All I Need To Get By** ............. | 19 | Atlantic 2787 |
| 4/24/71 | **1**² | 14 | 37● Bridge Over Troubled Water/ | 6 | |
| | | 8 | 38   Brand New Me .............................. | | Atlantic 2796 |
| 8/07/71 | **1**³ | 13 | 39   **Spanish Harlem** ........................... | 2 | Atlantic 2817 |
| 11/06/71 | **2**² | 12 | 40● Rock Steady ................................... | 9 | |
| | | 6 | 41   Oh Me Oh My (I'm A Fool For You Baby) ........ | 73 | Atlantic 2838 |
| 3/18/72 | **1**² | 12 | 42● Day Dreaming ................................ | 5 | Atlantic 2866 |
| 6/10/72 | **7** | 8 | 43   **All The King's Horses/** | 26 | |
| | | 1 | 44   April Fools .................................. | | Atlantic 2883 |
| 9/02/72 | **49** | 3 | 45   Wholy Holy .................................. | 81 | Atlantic 2901 |
| | | | with James Cleveland & The Southern California Community Choir | | |
| 2/17/73 | **8** | 10 | 46   **Master Of Eyes (The Deepness Of Your Eyes)** .. | 33 | Atlantic 2941 |
| 7/07/73 | **1**² | 12 | 47   **Angel** ........................................ | 20 | Atlantic 2969 |
| 11/17/73+ | **1**¹ | 17 | 48● Until You Come Back To Me (That's What I'm Gonna Do) ... | 3 | Atlantic 2995 |
| 4/06/74 | **1**² | 16 | 49   **I'm In Love** ................................. | 19 | Atlantic 2999 |
| 8/31/74 | **6** | 12 | 50   **Ain't Nothing Like The Real Thing** ........... | 47 | Atlantic 3200 |
| 11/16/74+ | **6** | 13 | 51   **Without Love** ............................... | 45 | Atlantic 3224 |
| | | | with the Ray Bryant Combo | | |
| 2/15/75 | **20** | 10 | 52   With Everything I Feel In Me ........... | | Atlantic 3249 |
| 9/20/75 | **13** | 11 | 53   **Mr. D.J. (5 For The D.J.)** ................. | 53 | Atlantic 3289 |
| 1/03/76 | **15** | 12 | 54   You .............................................. | | Atlantic 3311 |
| 5/22/76 | **1**⁴ | 19 | 55   **Something He Can Feel** ................... | 28 | Atlantic 3326 |
| 9/25/76 | **17** | 13 | 56   **Jump/** | 72 | |
| | | 13 | 57   Hooked On Your Love ..................... | | Atlantic 3358 |
| 1/15/77 | **10** | 13 | 58   **Look Into Your Heart** ..................... | 82 | Atlantic 3373 |
| 4/30/77 | **1**¹ | 14 | 59   **Break It To Me Gently** ................... | 85 | Atlantic 3393 |
| 8/13/77 | **16** | 14 | 60   When I Think About You .................. | | Atlantic 3418 |
| 4/29/78 | **12** | 12 | 61   Almighty Fire (Woman Of The Future) .............. | 103 | Atlantic 3468 |
| 7/22/78 | **51** | 9 | 62   More Than Just A Joy ..................... | | Atlantic 3495 |
| 8/25/79 | **33** | 11 | 63   Ladies Only.................................. | | Atlantic 3605 |
| 12/08/79+ | **65** | 6 | 64   Half A Love.................................. | | Atlantic 3632 |
| 11/15/80+ | **3** | 18 | 65   **United Together** .......................... | 56 | Arista 0569 |
| 2/21/81 | **17** | 12 | 66   What A Fool Believes....................... | | Arista 0591 |
| 5/16/81 | **39** | 9 | 67   Come To Me ................................. | 84 | Arista 0600 |
| 8/22/81 | **6** | 15 | 68   **Love All The Hurt Away** .................. | 46 | Arista 0624 |
| | | | **ARETHA FRANKLIN & GEORGE BENSON** | | |
| 11/14/81+ | **29** | 13 | 69   It's My Turn ................................. | | Arista 0646 |

| DEBUT DATE | PEAK POS | WKS CHR | ARTIST — Record Title | POP POS | Label & Number |
|---|---|---|---|---|---|
| | | | **ARETHA FRANKLIN — Continued** | | |
| 7/03/82 | **1**[4] | 20 | 70  **Jump To It** ............................................. | *24* | Arista 0699 |
| 11/27/82 | **22** | 11 | 71  Love Me Right ........................................... | | Arista 1023 |
| 3/26/83 | **63** | 5 | 72  This Is For Real ....................................... | | Arista 1043 |
| 7/02/83 | **1**[2] | 16 | 73  **Get It Right** .......................................... | *61* | Arista 9043 |
| 9/24/83 | **7** | 13 | 74  **Every Girl (Wants My Guy)**........................... | | Arista 9095 |
| 6/22/85 | **1**[5] | 17 | 75  **Freeway Of Love**..................................... | *3* | Arista 9354 |
| 9/14/85 | **2**[4] | 23 | 76  **Who's Zoomin' Who**................................ | *7* | Arista 9410 |
| 11/23/85 | **66** | 9 | 77  Sisters Are Doin' It For Themselves................. | *18* | RCA 14214 |
| | | | EURYTHMICS & ARETHA FRANKLIN | | |
| 1/25/86 | **9** | 16 | 78  **Another Night** ...................................... | *22* | Arista 9453 |
| 5/10/86 | **30** | 9 | 79  Ain't Nobody Ever Loved You ..................... | | Arista 9474 |
| 9/27/86 | **20** | 11 | 80  Jumpin' Jack Flash.................................... | *21* | Arista 9528 |
| | | | new version of Rolling Stones' 1968 pop hit (POS 3); from the film of the same title; produced by Keith Richards | | |
| 11/22/86+ | **2**[1] | 17 | 81  **Jimmy Lee** ........................................... | *28* | Arista 9546 |
| 2/21/87 | **5** | 14 | 82  **I Knew You Were Waiting (For Me)**................ | *1* | Arista 9559 |
| | | | ARETHA FRANKLIN & GEORGE MICHAEL | | |
| 5/23/87 | **25** | 13 | 83  Rock-A-Lott ........................................... | *82* | Arista 9574 |
| 10/03/87 | **88** | 4 | 84  If You Need My Love Tonight...................... | | Arista 9623 |
| | | | ARETHA FRANKLIN & LARRY GRAHAM | | |
| | | | **BOBBY FRANKLIN** | | |
| | | | Usually spelled "Boby". Singer/guitarist from Detroit. First recorded with own group, Insanity, for Thomas in 1969. Recorded as Boby Franklin & Friends for Lakeside in 1972. | | |
| 5/10/75 | **58** | 9 | 1  Whatever's Your Sign ............................... | | Baby 1123 |
| 3/13/76 | **93** | 4 | 2  Mutha's Love............................................ | | Columbia 10285 |
| | | | **CAROLYN FRANKLIN** | | |
| | | | Born in 1944 in Memphis. Died of cancer on 4/25/88 (43). Singer/songwriter/arranger. Youngest sister of Aretha. Worked as Aretha's back-up vocalist for 5 years, then went solo. Wrote "Baby Baby Baby", "Don't Wait Too Long", "Ain't No Way" and "Don't Catch The Dog's Bone". | | |
| 8/23/69 | **23** | 5 | 1  It's True I'm Gonna Miss You ........................ | *119* | RCA 0188 |
| 10/10/70 | **46** | 2 | 2  All I Want To Be Is Your Woman..................... | *108* | RCA 0373 |
| | | | **ERMA FRANKLIN** | | |
| | | | Born in 1943 in Memphis. Younger sister of Aretha. | | |
| 10/28/67 | **10** | 14 | 1  **Piece Of My Heart**................................... | *62* | Shout 221 |
| 4/05/69 | **40** | 3 | 2  Gotta Find Me A Lover (24 Hours A Day) .......... | | Brunswick 55403 |
| | | | **RODNEY FRANKLIN** | | |
| | | | Born on 9/16/58 in Berkeley, California. Jazz pianist. Played alto sax and organ from age 6. Toured with Bill Summers in 1977. Tours with Freddie Hubbard, Marlena Shaw and John Handy. | | |
| 4/26/80 | **41** | 9 | 1  The Groove ............................................. | | Columbia 11252 |
| 11/15/80 | **91** | 3 | 2  In The Center ......................................... | | Columbia 11371 |
| 1/31/81 | **89** | 4 | 3  Windy City ............................................. | | Columbia 11419 |
| 11/20/82 | **68** | 10 | 4  Enuff Is Enuff ........................................ | | Columbia 03273 |
| 2/26/83 | **64** | 7 | 5  That's The Way I Feel 'Bout Your Love ............ | | Columbia 03551 |
| 3/17/84 | **72** | 6 | 6  Stay On In The Groove ............................... | | Columbia 04390 |
| 8/23/86 | **59** | 8 | 7  Look What's Showing Through ....................... | | Columbia 06203 |
| | | | **FREDERICK** | | |
| 2/23/85 | **48** | 15 | 1  Gentle (Calling Your Name) ........................... | *108* | Heat 2022 |
| | | | **FREDERICK II** | | |
| 10/02/71 | **25** | 10 | 1  Groovin'Out On Life.................................. | | Vulture 5002 |
| | | | **FREE EXPRESSION** | | |
| 2/28/81 | **91** | 8 | 1  Chill-Out!............................................... | | Vanguard 35223 |
| | | | **FREE LIFE** | | |
| | | | Group included Carl Carwell, the brother of singer Sue Ann. | | |
| 2/03/79 | **81** | 3 | 1  Wish You Were Here................................... | | Epic 50642 |

| DEBUT DATE | PEAK POS | WKS CHR | ARTIST — Record Title | POP POS | Label & Number |
|---|---|---|---|---|---|
| | | | **THE FREE MOVEMENT** | | |
| | | | Group from Los Angeles, formed in 1971. Consisted of Godoy Colbert, formerly with the Pilgrim Travelers, Adrian and Claude Jefferson, Cheryl Conley, Jennifer Gates, and Josephine Brown, formerly with the Bells Of Joy. | | |
| 5/22/71 | 20 | 9 | 1 I've Found Someone Of My Own | 5 | Decca 32818 |
| 1/29/72 | 49 | 3 | 2 The Harder I Try (The Bluer I Get) | | Columbia 45512 |
| | | | **FREE SOUL - see JOE QUARTERMAN** | | |
| | | | **FREEDOM** | | |
| | | | 8-piece band from Jackson, Mississippi. | | |
| 6/16/79 | 62 | 8 | 1 Dance Sing Along | | Malaco 1057 |
| 11/24/79 | 82 | 4 | 2 Get Up And Dance | | Malaco 1060 |
| | | | **THE FREEDOM EXPRESS - see BUDDY MILES** | | |
| | | | **FREEEZ** | | |
| | | | John Rocca, lead singer; went solo in 1984. | | |
| 7/23/83 | 13 | 15 | 1 I.O.U. | *104* | Streetwise 1110 |
| 11/26/83+ | 47 | 11 | 2 Pop Goes My Love | *104* | Streetwise 1115 |
| | | | **BOBBY FREEMAN** | | |
| | | | Born on 6/13/40 in San Francisco. Formed vocal group, the Romancers, at age 14, and later formed the Vocaleers (not to be confused with the Harlem group on Red Robin). | | |
| 5/19/58 | 2² | 13 | 1 **Do You Want To Dance** | 5 | Josie 835 |
| | | | Best Seller #2 / Jockey #7 | | |
| 8/25/58 | 20 | 1 | 2 Betty Lou Got A New Pair Of Shoes | 37 | Josie 841 |
| | | | Best Seller #20 | | |
| 11/24/58 | 29 | 1 | 3 Need Your Love | 54 | Josie 844 |
| 7/11/64 | 5 | 12 | 4 **C'mon And Swim** | *Hot* | Autumn 2 |
| 10/31/64 | 56 | 6 | 5 S-W-I-M | *Hot* | Autumn 5 |
| | | | **ERNIE FREEMAN** | | |
| | | | Born on 8/16/22 in Cleveland. Died of a heart attack on 5/16/81. Pianist/arranger/producer. Prominent session man; on recordings by Frank Sinatra, Dean Martin, Sammy Davis, Jr. and Connie Francis. Recorded as "B. Bumble" on all records under that name except "Nut Rocker". Musical director at Reprise Records for 10 years. Retired in the late 70s. | | |
| 1/07/56 | 5 | 11 | 1 **Jivin' Around (Parts I & II)** [I] | | Cash 1017 |
| | | | Juke Box #5 / Best Seller #6 | | |
| 5/12/56 | 7 | 2 | 2 **Lost Dreams** [I] | | Imperial 5381 |
| | | | Juke Box #7 / Jockey #10 | | |
| 11/18/57+ | 1² | 13 | 3 **Raunchy** [I] | 4 | Imperial 5474 |
| | | | Jockey #1 / Best Seller #2 | | |
| | | | **JOHN FREEMAN** | | |
| 4/23/77 | 77 | 5 | 1 Dynamite | | Dakar 4562 |
| | | | **FREESTYLE** | | |
| | | | Miami-based trio led by vocalist Tony Butler. | | |
| 3/03/84 | 74 | 5 | 1 Freestyle | | Music Spec. 1102 |
| | | | **FREESTYLE EXPRESS** | | |
| 1/05/85 | 77 | 7 | 2 The Party Has Begun | | Music Spec. 108 |
| 2/01/86 | 83 | 6 | 3 Don't Stop The Rock | | Music Spec. 111 |
| | | | **FRESH 3 M.C.'S** | | |
| | | | Trio from the South Bronx. Also see Pumpkin & The Profile All-Stars. | | |
| 3/31/84 | 76 | 4 | 1 Fresh | | Profile 5037 |
| | | | **DOUG E. FRESH - see DOUG** | | |
| | | | **THE FRIENDS OF DISTINCTION** | | |
| | | | Los Angeles-based soul/MOR group: Floyd Butler (b: 6/5/41, San Diego); Harry Elston (b: 11/4/38, Dallas); Jessica Cleaves (b: 12/10/48, Los Angeles); Charlene Gibson (b: 5/6/47, Chicago); and Barbara Jean Love (b: 7/24/41, Los Angeles). Butler and Elston were in the Hi Fi's with LaMonte McLemore and Marilyn McCoo (later with The Fifth Dimension). | | |
| 4/05/69 | 5 | 17 | 1 ● **Grazing In The Grass** | 3 | RCA 0107 |
| | | | written by Harry Elston | | |
| 8/30/69 | 3 | 19 | 2 ● **Going In Circles** | 15 | RCA 0204 |
| 3/21/70 | 13 | 9 | 3 Love Or Let Me Be Lonely | 6 | RCA 0319 |
| 10/17/70 | 37 | 5 | 4 Time Waits For No One | 60 | RCA 0385 |
| 1/30/71 | 28 | 7 | 5 I Need You | 79 | RCA 0416 |

| DEBUT DATE | PEAK POS | WKS CHR | ARTIST — Record Title | POP POS | Label & Number |
|---|---|---|---|---|---|
| | | | **JOE FRITZ** | | |
| | | | Born on 11/3/24 in Houston. Vocalist/tenor saxophonist. Nicknamed "Papoose". Toured with Bobby Bland from 1955-57. Died in 1983. | | |
| 8/05/50 | **6** | 3 | 1 **I Love You, My Darlin'** .................................. | | Sittin' In 559 |
| | | | Juke Box #6 | | |
| | | | **FRANK FROST** | | |
| | | | Born on 4/15/36 in Augusta, Arkansas. Singer/multi-instrumentalist. To St. Louis in 1951. With Sonny Boy Williamson from 1956-59. Toured with Albert King, B.B. King, Carl Perkins and Conway Twitty in the 60s. | | |
| 8/06/66 | **43** | 3 | 1 My Back Scratcher ....................................... | | Jewel 765 |
| | | | **FULL FORCE** ★★175★★ | | |
| | | | Brooklyn band consisting of brothers Lucien "Lou", Paul Anthony and Brian "B-Fine" George. Included cousins Curtis Bedeau (guitar), Gerald Charles (keyboards) and Junior "Shy Shy" Clark (bass). Formed as the Amplifiers, renamed in 1978. Produced all of Lisa Lisa & Cult Jam's hits. Also see Lisa Lisa. | | |
| 5/18/85 | **6** | 22 | 1 **I Wonder If I Take You Home** ......................... | *34* | Columbia 04886 |
| | | | **LISA LISA & CULT JAM with FULL FORCE** | | |
| 8/10/85 | **79** | 8 | 2 Girl If You Take Me Home ............................. | | Columbia 05395 |
| 10/26/85+ | **16** | 18 | 3 Alice, I Want You Just For Me! ....................... | | Columbia 05623 |
| 11/09/85 | **40** | 25 | 4 Can You Feel The Beat.................................. | 69 | Columbia 05669 |
| | | | **LISA LISA & CULT JAM with FULL FORCE** | | |
| 2/22/86 | **34** | 13 | 5 Unselfish Lover ....................................... | | Columbia 05776 |
| 6/21/86 | **3** | 23 | 6 **All Cried Out** ........................................ | *8* | Columbia 05844 |
| | | | **LISA LISA & CULT JAM with FULL FORCE** featuring Paul Anthony & Bow Legged Lou | | |
| 6/21/86 | **12** | 17 | 7 Temporary Love Thing............................... | | Columbia 06116 |
| 10/11/86 | **20** | 15 | 8 Unfaithful So Much.................................. | | Columbia 06339 |
| 2/14/87 | **27** | 14 | 9 Old Flames Never Die................................ | | Columbia 06600 |
| 10/24/87 | **11** | 15 | 10 Love Is For Suckers (Like Me And You) ............ | | Columbia 07594 |
| 11/07/87+ | **7** | 15 | 11 **Someone To Love Me For Me** ....................... | *78* | Columbia 07619 |
| | | | **LISA LISA & CULT JAM** featuring **FULL FORCE** | | |
| 2/13/88 | **6** | 15 | 12 **All In My Mind** ...................................... | | Columbia 07705 |
| 3/12/88 | **9** | 12 | 13 **Everything Will B-Fine**............................. | | Columbia 07737 |
| | | | **LISA LISA & CULT JAM with FULL FORCE** | | |
| 6/11/88 | **24** | 10 | 14 Your Love Is So Def .................................. | | Columbia 07920 |
| | | | **LOWELL FULSON** ★★170★★ | | |
| | | | Born in March of 1921, in Tulsa, Oklahoma. Blues vocalist/guitarist. Also known as Tulsa Red. First recorded for Big Town in 1946. Teamed up with pianist Lloyd Glenn. Band, at one time, included Ray Charles, Stanley Turrentine and Billy Brooks. Also see Lloyd Glenn. | | |
| 10/02/48 | **6** | 1 | 1 **Three O'Clock Blues** ................................ | | Down Town 2002 |
| | | | Juke Box #6 | | |
| 8/13/49 | **13** | 4 | 2 Come Back Baby.......................................... | | Downbeat 230 |
| | | | Juke Box #13 / Best Seller #14 | | |
| 5/27/50 | **3** | 24 | 3 **Everyday I Have The Blues** ......................... | | Swingtime 196 |
| | | | **LOWELL FULSON** featuring **LLOYD GLENN AT THE "88"** Juke Box #3 / Best Seller #5 | | |
| 8/05/50 | **1**⁴ | 22 | 4 **Blue Shadows**......................................... | | Swingtime 226 |
| | | | Juke Box #1(4) / Best Seller #1(1) | | |
| 12/23/50+ | **7** | 2 | 5 **Lonesome Christmas (I & II)**..................... [X] | | Swingtime 242 |
| | | | Best Seller #7 | | |
| 12/30/50 | **8** | 3 | 6 **Low Society Blues**.................................. | | Swingtime 226 |
| | | | Juke Box #8 | | |
| 6/16/51 | **10** | 1 | 7 **I'm A Night Owl (I & II)** .......................... | | Swingtime 243 |
| | | | Best Seller #10 | | |
| 12/04/54 | **3** | 15 | 8 **Reconsider Baby**.................................... | | Checker 804 |
| | | | Best Seller #3 / Juke Box #3 / Jockey #5 | | |
| 5/07/55 | **14** | 1 | 9 **Loving You**......................................... | | Checker 812 |
| | | | Jockey #14 | | |
| 12/18/65+ | **11** | 12 | 10 Black Nights ......................................... | 91 | Kent 431 |
| 1/07/67 | **5** | 13 | 11 **Tramp**............................................... | 52 | Kent 456 |
| | | | written by Lowell Fulsom & Jimmy McCracklin | | |
| 4/01/67 | **20** | 7 | 12 Make A Little Love.................................. | 97 | Kent 463 |
| 10/07/67 | **38** | 2 | 13 I'm A Drifter ......................................... | 118 | Kent 474 |
| | | | above 4 shown as: **LOWELL FULSOM** | | |
| 2/07/76 | **78** | 7 | 14 Do You Love Me....................................... | | Granite 533 |

| DEBUT DATE | PEAK POS | WKS CHR | ARTIST — Record Title | POP POS | Label & Number |
|---|---|---|---|---|---|

## FUNKADELIC  ★★197★★

Funk aggregation formed in 1968, consisting of The Parliaments plus a backing band. While recording for Westbound, group also recorded for Invictus as Parliament in 1971. Formed corporation "A Parliafunkadelicament Thang" through which they recorded under both names. By 1974, leader/producer George Clinton reorganized the Parliament/Funkadelic corporation to include varying membership. 3 of the original members of The Parliaments left the corporation in 1977; recorded as Funkadelic for LAX Records in 1981, not in association with Clinton. Also see Parliament and The Parliaments.

| DEBUT DATE | PEAK POS | WKS CHR | ARTIST — Record Title | POP POS | Label & Number |
|---|---|---|---|---|---|
| 5/03/69 | 50 | 1 | 1 Music For My Mother | | Westbound 148 |
| 10/11/69 | 22 | 5 | 2 I'll Bet You | 63 | Westbound 150 |
| 4/04/70 | 30 | 6 | 3 I Got A Thing, You Got A Thing, Everybody's Got A Thing | 80 | Westbound 158 |
| 8/29/70 | 27 | 6 | 4 I Wanna Know If It's Good To You? | 81 | Westbound 167 |
| 5/01/71 | 42 | 3 | 5 You And Your Folks, Me And My Folks | 91 | Westbound 175 |
| 9/04/71 | 44 | 5 | 6 Can You Get To That | 93 | Westbound 185 |
| 9/16/72 | 38 | 4 | 7 Joyful Process/ | | |
| 3/17/73 | 49 | 3 | 8 Loose Booty | 118 | Westbound 205 |
| 6/29/74 | 27 | 15 | 9 On The Verge Of Getting It On | | Westbound 224 |
| 3/15/75 | 73 | 8 | 10 Red Hot Momma | | Westbound 5000 |
| 7/10/76 | 89 | 5 | 11 Let's Take It To The Stage | | Westbound 5026 |
| 9/25/76 | 30 | 12 | 12 Undisco Kidd | 102 | Westbound 5029 |
| 1/29/77 | 54 | 8 | 13 Comin' Round The Mountain | | Warner 8309 |
| 5/21/77 | 96 | 3 | 14 Smokey | | Warner 8367 |
| 8/19/78 | 1⁶ | 25 | 15● One Nation Under A Groove (Part 1) | 28 | Warner 8618 |
| 2/10/79 | 43 | 7 | 16 Cholly (Funk Getting Ready To Roll!) | | Warner 8735 |
| 8/25/79 | 1³ | 20 | 17 (not just) Knee Deep - Part 1 | 77 | Warner 49040 |
| 12/15/79+ | 53 | 8 | 18 Uncle Jam (Part 1) | | Warner 49117 |
| 4/11/81 | 60 | 6 | 19 The Electric Spanking Of War Babies | | Warner 49667 |

## FUNKADELIC

Group includes 3 members of The Parliaments: Clarence Haskins, Calvin Simon and Grady Thomas; no longer in association with George Clinton and the Parliament/Funkadelic corporation.

| DEBUT DATE | PEAK POS | WKS CHR | ARTIST — Record Title | POP POS | Label & Number |
|---|---|---|---|---|---|
| 3/07/81 | 68 | 12 | 1 Connections And Disconnections | | LAX 70055 |

## FUNK DELUXE

| DEBUT DATE | PEAK POS | WKS CHR | ARTIST — Record Title | POP POS | Label & Number |
|---|---|---|---|---|---|
| 5/12/84 | 77 | 6 | 1 This Time | | Salsoul 7071 |

## FUNN

Group led by Denzil "Broadway" Miller.

| DEBUT DATE | PEAK POS | WKS CHR | ARTIST — Record Title | POP POS | Label & Number |
|---|---|---|---|---|---|
| 10/31/81 | 53 | 7 | 1 School Daze | | Magic 93000 |

## HARVEY FUQUA - see ETTA JAMES/THE MOONGLOWS/ SPINNERS

## FURIOUS FIVE

Varying roster of rappers and dancers that recorded with Grandmaster Flash and Grandmaster Melle Mel.

| DEBUT DATE | PEAK POS | WKS CHR | ARTIST — Record Title | POP POS | Label & Number |
|---|---|---|---|---|---|
| 6/27/81 | 49 | 10 | 1 Showdown | | Sugar Hill 558 |
| | | | FURIOUS FIVE MEETS THE SUGARHILL GANG | | |
| 12/15/84+ | 48 | 10 | 2 Step Off | | Sugar Hill 32033 |
| | | | featuring Cowboy, Melle Mel, & Scorpio (Grandmaster Flash members) | | |

## FUTURE

| DEBUT DATE | PEAK POS | WKS CHR | ARTIST — Record Title | POP POS | Label & Number |
|---|---|---|---|---|---|
| 3/26/88 | 71 | 10 | 1 We're Going To Party | | Houston Int. 111 |

## THE FUTURES

Group from Philadelphia, consisting of James King, Kenny Crew, Harry McGilkerry, Frank Washington and Jon King.

| DEBUT DATE | PEAK POS | WKS CHR | ARTIST — Record Title | POP POS | Label & Number |
|---|---|---|---|---|---|
| 1/13/73 | 47 | 3 | 1 Love Is There | | Gamble 2502 |
| 8/09/75 | 35 | 11 | 2 Make It Last | | Buddah 481 |
| | | | BARBARA MASON & THE FUTURES | | |
| 1/13/79 | 94 | 2 | 3 Party Time Man | | Phil. Int. 3661 |
| 1/10/81 | 79 | 5 | 4 Silhouettes | | Phil. Int. 3119 |

## THE FUZZ

Trio from Washington, DC, consisting of Sheila Young, Barbara Gilliam and Val Williams. Originally called the Passionettes.

| DEBUT DATE | PEAK POS | WKS CHR | ARTIST — Record Title | POP POS | Label & Number |
|---|---|---|---|---|---|
| 1/02/71 | 10 | 12 | 1 I Love You For All Seasons | 21 | Calla 174 |
| | | | written by Sheila Young | | |

| DEBUT DATE | PEAK POS | WKS CHR | ARTIST — Record Title | POP POS | Label & Number |
|---|---|---|---|---|---|
| | | | **THE FUZZ — Continued** | | |
| 7/03/71 | 14 | 7 | 2 Like An Open Door......................................... | 77 | Calla 177 |
| 10/02/71 | 35 | 6 | 3 I'm So Glad ................................................. | 95 | Calla 179 |

# G

**PETER GABRIEL**
Born on 5/13/50 in London. Lead singer of Genesis from 1966-75.

| | | | | | |
|---|---|---|---|---|---|
| 10/30/82 | 64 | 6 | 1 Shock The Monkey ...................................... | 29 | Geffen 29883 |
| 7/05/86 | 61 | 8 | 2 Sledgehammer............................................. | 1 | Warner 28718 |

**JAMES GADSON**
Drummer with the Soul Runners and Watts 103rd St. Rhythm Band. Toured with Bill Withers.

| | | | | | |
|---|---|---|---|---|---|
| 4/08/72 | 36 | 6 | 1 Got To Find My Baby ................................... | | Cream 1014 |

**YVONNE GAGE**
Born in 1959 in Chicago. With the Soulettes (later: First Love), from 1973-80. Back-up singer with Captain Sky in 1980. First solo recording in 1981. Backup vocals for Ministry in 1981.

| | | | | | |
|---|---|---|---|---|---|
| 6/23/84 | 78 | 5 | 1 Doin' It In A Haunted House............................ | | CIM 04491 |

**SLIM GAILLARD TRIO**
Born Bulee Gaillard on 1/4/16 in Detroit. Vocalist/multi-instrumentalist. Formed duo with bassist Leroy "Slam" Stewart in 1937. Became known as the "Flat Foot Floogie Boys" from big hit of the same title. Gaillard invented "voot", a comical scat language he used on many recordings. Trio included Gaillard, Bam Brown and Zutty Singleton.

| | | | | | |
|---|---|---|---|---|---|
| 5/11/46 | 5 | 1 | 1 **Cement Mixer (Put-Ti, Put-Ti)**.................. [N] | 21 | Cadet CR 201 |

**ROSIE GAINES**

| | | | | | |
|---|---|---|---|---|---|
| 10/05/85 | 72 | 6 | 1 Skool-Ology (Ain't No Strain)......................... | | Epic 05589 |

**EARL GAINS**
Born Earl Gaines on 8/19/35 in Decatur, Alabama. Moved to Nashville in 1951, worked as vocalist with Louis Brooks. Also see Louis Brooks.

| | | | | | |
|---|---|---|---|---|---|
| 9/10/66 | 28 | 9 | 1 The Best Of Luck To You............................... | 133 | HBR 481 |
| 9/01/73 | 36 | 13 | 2 Hymn #5.................................................... | | Seventy 7 131 |

**SUNNY GALE - see EDDIE WILCOX**

**LEATA GALLOWAY**
Singer/Broadway actress, born in Brooklyn and raised in Harlem. In the original cast of "Hair".

| | | | | | |
|---|---|---|---|---|---|
| 6/04/88 | 69 | 6 | 1 With Every Beat Of My Heart.......................... | | Columbia 07786 |

**DEE DEE SHARP GAMBLE - see DEE DEE SHARP**

**GANG'S BACK**
Sextet from Fresno, California.

| | | | | | |
|---|---|---|---|---|---|
| 9/04/82 | 61 | 10 | 1 Got My Eye On You ...................................... | | Handshake 03199 |

**GANGSTERS**

| | | | | | |
|---|---|---|---|---|---|
| 8/04/79 | 36 | 14 | 1 I Feel You When You're Gone .......................... | | Heat 01978 |
| 2/16/80 | 77 | 5 | 2 Wop That Wandy ......................................... | | Heat 2001 |
| 6/27/81 | 80 | 3 | 3 Shake Your Body ......................................... | | Heat 2002 |
| 12/12/81 | 90 | 6 | 4 Strung Out On The Boogie .............................. | | Heat 2007 |

**CECIL GANT**
Born on 4/4/13 in Nashville. Died of pneumonia on 2/4/52 (38). Vocalist/pianist. Also recorded under the name Gunter Lee Carr. Billed as "The G.I. Sing-sation". Worked War Bond Rallies on the West Coast in 1944. Very prolific recording artist, with many releases on several labels.

| | | | | | |
|---|---|---|---|---|---|
| 10/21/44+ | 1 [2] | 28 | 1 I Wonder/<br>shown as: **PRIVATE CECIL GANT** | 20 | |
| 4/21/45 | 5 | 5 | 2 **Cecil's Boogie**.......................................... | | Gilt-Edge 500 |
| 7/21/45 | 7 | 1 | 3 **Grass Is Getting Greener Every Day** ............. | | Gilt-Edge 505 |
| 8/11/45 | 4 | 3 | 4 **I'm Tired** ................................................. | | Gilt-Edge 506 |
| 10/02/48 | 6 | 1 | 5 **Another Day-Another Dollar** ........................ | | Bullet 280 |
| | | | Juke Box #6 | | |

| DEBUT DATE | PEAK POS | WKS CHR | ARTIST — Record Title | POP POS | Label & Number |
|---|---|---|---|---|---|
| | | | **CECIL GANT — Continued** | | |
| 10/16/48 | **11** | 1 | 6 Special Delivery ............................................. | | Four Star 1176 |
| | | | Juke Box #11 | | |
| 4/02/49 | **12** | 1 | 7 I'm A Good Man But A Poor Man...................... | | Bullet 289 |
| | | | Best Seller #12 | | |
| | | | **THE GAP BAND** ★★**67**★★ | | |
| | | | Brother trio from Tulsa, Oklahoma: Charles, Ronnie and Robert Wilson. Named for three streets in Tulsa: Greenwood, Archer and Pine. Also see Billy & Baby Gap. | | |
| 3/12/77 | **42** | 11 | 1 Out Of The Blue (Can You Feel It).................... | | Tattoo 10884 |
| 6/25/77 | **95** | 3 | 2 Little Bit Of Love ........................................ | | Tattoo 10990 |
| 3/31/79 | **4** | 18 | 3 **Shake**.................................................... | *101* | Mercury 74053 |
| 7/28/79 | **13** | 14 | 4 Open Up Your Mind (Wide) ............................. | | Mercury 74080 |
| 12/01/79+ | **10** | 14 | 5 **Steppin' (Out)**.......................................... | *103* | Mercury 76021 |
| 2/16/80 | **4** | 16 | 6 **I Don't Believe You Want To Get Up And Dance (Oops, Up Side Your Head)** ............ | *102* | Mercury 76037 |
| 6/07/80 | **36** | 11 | 7 Party Lights............................................... | | Mercury 76062 |
| 12/06/80+ | **1** ² | 23 | 8 **Burn Rubber (Why You Wanna Hurt Me)**........ | 84 | Mercury 76091 |
| 3/28/81 | **5** | 18 | 9 **Yearning For Your Love** ............................. | 60 | Mercury 76101 |
| 7/18/81 | **60** | 6 | 10 Humpin'................................................... | | Mercury 76114 |
| 4/24/82 | **1** ³ | 24 | 11 **Early In The Morning**............................... | 24 | Total Exp. 8201 |
| 8/07/82 | **2** ⁴ | 15 | 12 **You Dropped A Bomb On Me** ...................... | 31 | Total Exp. 8203 |
| 12/04/82+ | **1** ¹ | 24 | 13 **Outstanding**............................................ | 51 | Total Exp. 8205 |
| 8/13/83 | **3** | 19 | 14 **Party Train**............................................ | *101* | Total Exp. 8209 |
| 11/19/83+ | **16** | 15 | 15 Jam The Motha'........................................... | | Total Exp. 8210 |
| 3/31/84 | **77** | 6 | 16 Not Guilty................................................. | | Mega 4005 |
| 4/14/84 | **74** | 5 | 17 I'm Ready (If You're Ready)........................... | | Total Exp. 8211 |
| 12/01/84+ | **2** ² | 18 | 18 **Beep A Freak** ......................................... | *103* | Total Exp. 2405 |
| 3/09/85 | **8** | 16 | 19 I Found My Baby ........................................ | | Total Exp. 2412 |
| 7/06/85 | **18** | 14 | 20 Disrespect ............................................... | | Total Exp. 2418 |
| 12/21/85+ | **46** | 9 | 21 Desire .................................................... | | Total Exp. 2427 |
| 2/08/86 | **2** ¹ | 17 | 22 **Going In Circles** ..................................... | | Total Exp. 2436 |
| 7/05/86 | **78** | 4 | 23 Automatic Brain ........................................ | | Total Exp. 2440 |
| 11/15/86+ | **8** | 18 | 24 **Big Fun** ................................................ | | Total Exp. 2700 |
| 3/21/87 | **15** | 12 | 25 Zibble, Zibble (Get The Money) (AKA: Get Loose, Get Funky) ............................................... | | Total Exp. 2703 |
| 10/03/87 | **40** | 14 | 26 Sweeter Than Candy/Penitentiary III ............... | | RCA 5305 |
| | | | from the film "Penitentiary III" | | |
| | | | **DON GARDNER & DEE DEE FORD** | | |
| | | | Vocal duo from Philadelphia. Gardner formed his own group, the Sonotones, in 1952 and recorded for Gotham and Bruce. Ford also plays organ and piano. Also see Baby Washington. | | |
| 6/09/62 | **4** | 14 | 1 **I Need Your Loving** ................................. | 20 | Fire 508 |
| | | | DON GARDNER & DEE DEE FORD | | |
| 9/29/62 | **7** | 8 | 2 **Don't You Worry**..................................... | 66 | Fire 513 |
| | | | DON GARDNER & DEE DEE FORD | | |
| 5/19/73 | **30** | 7 | 3 Forever ................................................... | *119* | Master 5 9103 |
| | | | BABY WASHINGTON & DON GARDNER | | |
| | | | **JOANNA GARDNER** | | |
| 6/08/85 | **77** | 5 | 1 Watching You............................................. | | Philly W. 99656 |
| | | | **REGGIE GARDNER** | | |
| 4/10/71 | **30** | 7 | 1 Teddy Bear .............................................. | | Capitol 3042 |
| | | | **TAANA GARDNER** | | |
| | | | Vocalist from Newark, New Jersey. Trained as opera singer from age 5. Lead singer of her own group, Taana & The Darnettes, at age 8. Performed with the Harlem Children's Theater. | | |
| 4/25/81 | **10** | 19 | 1 **Heartbeat** .............................................. | | West End 1232 |
| | | | **CLARENCE GARLOW** | | |
| | | | Born on 2/27/11 in Welsh, Louisiana; died on 7/24/86 (75). Vocalist/accordionist/ violinist/guitarist. Moved to Beaumont, Texas. Violinist from age 8, playing in father's string band. After hit "Bon Ton Roula", took nickname "Bon Ton". | | |
| 2/25/50 | **7** | 2 | 1 **Bon Ton Roula**......................................... | | Macy's 5002 |
| | | | Best Seller #7 / Juke Box #12 "Bon Ton Roula" is Cajun for "let the good times roll" | | |

| DEBUT DATE | PEAK POS | WKS CHR | ARTIST — Record Title | POP POS | Label & Number |
|---|---|---|---|---|---|
| | | | **ERROLL GARNER** | | |
| | | | Jazz pianist born on 6/15/21 in Pittsburgh. Died on 1/2/77 (53). No formal training on piano; could not read music. To New York City in 1944. Recorded with the Slam Stewart Trio, then own trio. Unique style was heard on dozens of records made for many labels during his freelance years from 1945-49. Composer of "Misty", later a hit for Johnny Mathis and others. | | |
| 10/08/49 | 8 | 1 | 1 I Cover The Waterfront ................................ [I] | | Savoy 688 |
| | | | Juke Box #8 | | |
| | | | featuring John Simmons (bass) and Alvin Stoller (drums) | | |
| | | | **LEE GARRETT** | | |
| | | | Vocalist/composer from Mississippi, blind since birth. Teamed with Stevie Wonder to write "It's A Shame" hit for the Spinners. | | |
| 5/22/76 | 85 | 4 | 1 You're My Everything .................................... | *58* | Chrysalis 2112 |
| | | | **SIEDAH GARRETT** | | |
| | | | Female singer/songwriter from North Hollywood. Prominent backing vocalist; toured with Sergio Mendes, worked with Quincy Jones since 1983. Co-wrote Michael Jackson's "Man In The Mirror". Also see Dennis Edwards and Michael Jackson. | | |
| 2/16/85 | 63 | 11 | 1 Do You Want It Right Now ............................. | | Qwest 29086 |
| | | | from the film "Fast Forward" | | |
| 11/07/87 | 44 | 15 | 2 Everchanging Times .................................... | | Qwest 28163 |
| | | | theme from the film "Baby Boom" | | |
| 6/25/88 | 16 | 13 | 3 K.I.S.S.I.N.G. ........................................... | *97* | Qwest 27928 |
| | | | **VERNON GARRETT** | | |
| | | | California-based singer. | | |
| 3/22/69 | 33 | 6 | 1 Without You............................................... | | Venture 632 |
| 9/10/77 | 38 | 20 | 2 I'm At The Crossroad (Part I).......................... | | ICA 003 |
| | | | **GARRETT'S CREW** | | |
| 7/23/83 | 59 | 9 | 1 Nasty Rock ............................................... | | Clockwork 80913 |
| | | | **GARY'S GANG** | | |
| | | | Septet from Queens, New York, led by Gary Turnier (drums) and Eric Matthew (guitar). | | |
| 2/10/79 | 15 | 14 | 1 Keep On Dancin' .......................................... | *41* | Columbia 10884 |
| | | | **MARVIN GAYE**  ★★**7**★★ | | |
| | | | Born Marvin Pentz Gay, Jr. on 4/2/39 in Washington, DC. Sang in his father's Apostolic church. In vocal groups the Rainbows and Marquees. Joined Harvey Fuqua in the reformed Moonglows. To Detroit in 1960. Session work as drummer at Motown; married to Berry Gordy's sister Anna, 1961-75. First recorded under own name for Tamla in 1961. In seclusion for several months following the death of Tammi Terrell, 1970. Problems with drugs and the IRS led to his moving to Europe for three years. Fatally shot by his father after a quarrel on 4/1/84 in Los Angeles. | | |
| 10/06/62 | 8 | 17 | 1 **Stubborn Kind Of Fellow** ............................. | *46* | Tamla 54068 |
| | | | backing vocals by Martha & The Vandellas | | |
| 2/09/63 | 12 | 8 | 2 Hitch Hike ............................................... | *30* | Tamla 54075 |
| 6/01/63 | 2³ | 16 | 3 **Pride And Joy** .......................................... | *10* | Tamla 54079 |
| 11/02/63 | 15 | 4 | 4 Can I Get A Witness ................................... | *22* | Tamla 54087 |
| 3/14/64 | 15 | 10 | 5 You're A Wonderful One............................... | *Hot* | Tamla 54093 |
| 5/02/64 | 19 | 9 | 6 Once Upon A Time/ | *Hot* | |
| 5/16/64 | 17 | 10 | 7 What's The Matter With You Baby ................. | *Hot* | Motown 1057 |
| | | | above 2: **MARVIN GAYE & MARY WELLS** | | |
| 6/06/64 | 15 | 11 | 8 Try It Baby ............................................... | *Hot* | Tamla 54095 |
| 9/19/64 | 27 | 9 | 9 Baby Don't You Do It ................................... | *Hot* | Tamla 54101 |
| 10/24/64 | 61 | 6 | 10 What Good Am I Without You ...................... | *Hot* | Tamla 54104 |
| | | | **MARVIN GAYE & KIM WESTON** | | |
| 1/30/65 | 4 | 8 | 11 **How Sweet It Is (To Be Loved By You)** ........... | *6* | Tamla 54107 |
| 3/20/65 | 1¹ | 15 | 12 **I'll Be Doggone** ....................................... | *8* | Tamla 54112 |
| 7/24/65 | 16 | 10 | 13 Pretty Little Baby ..................................... | *25* | Tamla 54117 |
| 10/09/65 | 1¹ | 19 | 14 **Ain't That Peculiar**.................................... | *8* | Tamla 54122 |
| 2/26/66 | 4 | 11 | 15 **One More Heartache**................................... | *29* | Tamla 54129 |
| 6/11/66 | 16 | 10 | 16 Take This Heart Of Mine............................... | *44* | Tamla 54132 |
| 8/27/66 | 10 | 9 | 17 **Little Darling, I Need You** ........................ | *47* | Tamla 54138 |
| 1/21/67 | 4 | 12 | 18 It Takes Two............................................. | *14* | Tamla 54141 |
| | | | **MARVIN GAYE & KIM WESTON** | | |
| 7/08/67 | 7 | 12 | 19 **Your Unchanging Love** .............................. | *33* | Tamla 54153 |
| 2/03/68 | 7 | 9 | 20 **You** ...................................................... | *34* | Tamla 54160 |
| 9/28/68 | 8 | 10 | 21 **Chained**................................................. | *32* | Tamla 54170 |
| 11/30/68 | 1⁷ | 14 | 22 **I Heard It Through The Grapevine** ............... | *1* | Tamla 54176 |

| DEBUT DATE | PEAK POS | WKS CHR | | ARTIST — Record Title | POP POS | Label & Number |
|---|---|---|---|---|---|---|
| | | | | **MARVIN GAYE — Continued** | | |
| 5/03/69 | **1** 6 | 15 | 23 | **Too Busy Thinking About My Baby**............... | 4 | Tamla 54181 |
| 9/06/69 | **2** 5 | 13 | 24 | **That's The Way Love Is**.............................. | 7 | Tamla 54185 |
| 1/17/70 | **18** | 7 | 25 | How Can I Forget You/ | 41 | |
| | | 9 | 26 | Gonna Give Her All The Love I've Got............ | 67 | Tamla 54190 |
| 6/20/70 | **7** | 9 | 27 | **The End Of Our Road**........................ | 40 | Tamla 54195 |
| 2/20/71 | **1** 5 | 15 | 28 | **What's Going On** ............................ | 2 | Tamla 54201 |
| 7/03/71 | **1** 2 | 13 | 29 | **Mercy Mercy Me (The Ecology)**.................... | 4 | Tamla 54207 |
| 10/09/71 | **1** 2 | 12 | 30 | **Inner City Blues (Make Me Wanna Holler)**....... | 9 | Tamla 54209 |
| 5/20/72 | **7** | 9 | 31 | **You're The Man**........................................ | 50 | Tamla 54221 |
| 12/23/72+ | **4** | 14 | 32 | **Trouble Man** .......................................... | 7 | Tamla 54228 |
| | | | | from the film of the same title | | |
| 7/14/73 | **1** 6 | 17 | 33 | **Let's Get It On** .................................. | 1 | Tamla 54234 |
| 9/29/73 | **4** | 15 | 34 | **You're A Special Part Of Me** .................... | 12 | Motown 1280 |
| 11/03/73 | **3** | 14 | 35 | **Come Get To This/** | 21 | |
| 1/19/74 | **13** | 14 | 36 | You Sure Love To Ball ........................ | 50 | Tamla 54244 |
| 2/09/74 | **15** | 14 | 37 | My Mistake (Was To Love You) ................ | 19 | Motown 1269 |
| 7/13/74 | **25** | 12 | 38 | Don't Knock My Love .......................... | 46 | Motown 1296 |
| | | | | 34, 37 & 38: **DIANA ROSS & MARVIN GAYE** | | |
| 9/28/74 | **12** | 13 | 39 | Distant Lover ................................. | 28 | Tamla 54253 |
| 4/24/76 | **1** 1 | 15 | 40 | **I Want You**................................... | 15 | Tamla 54264 |
| 8/07/76 | **14** | 10 | 41 | After The Dance ............................... | 74 | Tamla 54273 |
| 4/09/77 | **1** 5 | 21 | 42 | **Got To Give It Up (Pt. I)**...................... | 1 | Tamla 54280 |
| 1/27/79 | **26** | 11 | 43 | Pops, We Love You (A Tribute To Father) ......... | 59 | Motown 1455 |
| | | | | **DIANA ROSS, MARVIN GAYE, SMOKEY ROBINSON & STEVIE WONDER** | | |
| | | | | song written for Berry Gordy Sr.'s 90th birthday | | |
| 2/03/79 | **23** | 12 | 44 | A Funky Space Reincarnation (Part 1)............... | 106 | Tamla 54298 |
| 10/20/79 | **17** | 13 | 45 | Ego Tripping Out............................... | | Tamla 54305 |
| 2/21/81 | **18** | 12 | 46 | Praise ........................................ | 101 | Tamla 54322 |
| 5/16/81 | **61** | 6 | 47 | Heavy Love Affair ............................ | | Tamla 54326 |
| 10/16/82 | **1** 10 | 27 | 48● | **Sexual Healing** ............................ | 3 | Columbia 03302 |
| 2/19/83 | **31** | 10 | 49 | 'Til Tomorrow ................................ | | Columbia 03589 |
| 6/18/83 | **78** | 4 | 50 | Joy............................................ | | Columbia 03935 |
| 4/27/85 | **2** 3 | 15 | 51 | **Sanctified Lady** ............................ | 101 | Columbia 04861 |
| 7/27/85 | **55** | 8 | 52 | It's Madness................................. | | Columbia 05442 |
| | | | | **MARVIN GAYE & TAMMI TERRELL:** | | |
| 6/03/67 | **3** | 13 | 53 | **Ain't No Mountain High Enough**................... | 19 | Tamla 54149 |
| 9/30/67 | **2** 5 | 13 | 54 | **Your Precious Love** ......................... | 5 | Tamla 54156 |
| 12/16/67+ | **2** 2 | 14 | 55 | **If I Could Build My World Around You/** | 10 | |
| 3/02/68 | **27** | 7 | 56 | If This World Were Mine ...................... | 68 | Tamla 54161 |
| 4/27/68 | **1** 1 | 13 | 57 | **Ain't Nothing Like The Real Thing**.............. | 8 | Tamla 54163 |
| 8/03/68 | **1** 5 | 13 | 58 | **You're All I Need To Get By** ................. | 7 | Tamla 54169 |
| 10/19/68 | **11** | 8 | 59 | Keep On Lovin' Me Honey...................... | 24 | Tamla 54173 |
| 2/22/69 | **11** | 6 | 60 | Good Lovin' Ain't Easy To Come By ........... | 30 | Tamla 54179 |
| 12/13/69 | **6** | 7 | 61 | **What You Gave Me**.......................... | 49 | Tamla 54187 |
| 4/25/70 | **18** | 7 | 62 | The Onion Song ............................... | 50 | Tamla 54192 |
| | | | | **GLORIA GAYNOR** | | |
| | | | | Born on 9/7/49 in Newark, New Jersey. With the Soul Satisfiers group in 1971. | | |
| 4/06/74 | **55** | 7 | 1 | Honey Bee ..................................... | 103 | MGM 14706 |
| 12/21/74+ | **34** | 14 | 2 | Never Can Say Goodbye ....................... | 9 | MGM 14748 |
| 3/29/75 | **56** | 7 | 3 | Reach Out, I'll Be There ...................... | 60 | MGM 14790 |
| 9/06/75 | **24** | 12 | 4 | (If You Want It) Do It Yourself ............... | 98 | MGM 14823 |
| 11/29/75 | **73** | 5 | 5 | How High The Moon........................... | 75 | MGM 14838 |
| | | | | first popularized by Benny Goodman in 1940 (POS 6) | | |
| 11/27/76 | **95** | 2 | 6 | Let's Make A Deal............................. | | Polydor 14357 |
| 10/14/78 | **78** | 4 | 7 | Substitute/ | 107 | |
| 1/06/79 | **4** | 17 | 8 | **I Will Survive**................................ | 1 | Polydor 14508 |
| 5/05/79 | **16** | 14 | 9 | Anybody Wanna Party?........................ | 105 | Polydor 14558 |
| 10/13/79 | **61** | 5 | 10 | Let Me Know (I Have A Right)................. | 42 | Polydor 2021 |
| | | | | trumpet solo by Doc Severinsen | | |
| 7/11/81 | **76** | 3 | 11 | Let's Mend What's Been Broken .................... | | Polydor 2173 |

| DEBUT DATE | PEAK POS | WKS CHR | ARTIST — Record Title | POP POS | Label & Number |
|---|---|---|---|---|---|
| | | | **GLORIA GAYNOR — Continued** | | |
| 11/12/83 | 82 | 11 | 12 I Am What I Am ..................................... | *102* | Silver Blue 720 |
| | | | from Broadway's "La Cage Aux Folles"; also released on Silver Blue 04294 | | |
| | | | **MEL GAYNOR** | | |
| 12/24/55 | 14 | 1 | 1 Ebony Rhapsody ............................... | | Modern 977 |
| | | | **PAUL GAYTEN** | | |
| | | | Born on 1/29/20 in Kentwood, Louisiana. Vocalist/bandleader/pianist. Nephew of Little Brother Montgomery. Organized Army base band in Biloxi, Mississippi. First recorded for DeLuxe in 1947, with Edgar Blanchard, George Prior and Robert Green. Heard on many hits behind such artists as Larry Darnell, Clarence Henry, Bobby Charles, Sugar Boy Crawford and TV Slim. Moved to Los Angeles in the late 50s. Own label, Pzazz, from 1969, then inactive in music. Also see Clarence Henry, Annie Laurie and Chubby Newsom. | | |
| 10/04/47 | 3 | 8 | 1 Since I Fell For You ................................... | *20* | DeLuxe 1082 |
| | | | PAUL GAYTEN & HIS TRIO a pop hit for Lenny Welch in 1963 (POS 4); later released on Dixie 1082 | | |
| 10/18/47 | 5 | 1 | 2 True ............................................. | | DeLuxe 1063 |
| 4/29/50 | 4 | 8 | 3 I'll Never Be Free .......................................... | | Regal 3258 |
| | | | Juke Box #4 / Best Seller #8 1 & 3: vocals by Annie Laurie | | |
| 9/02/50 | 6 | 4 | 4 Goodnight Irene ...................................... | | Regal 3281 |
| | | | Juke Box #6 with the Coleman Brothers (vocal group) | | |
| | | | **THE G-CLEFS** | | |
| | | | Group from Roxbury, Massachusetts, consisting of brothers Teddy, Chris, Timmy and Arnold Scott, with Ray Gibson. | | |
| 10/20/56 | 9 | 2 | 1 Ka-Ding Dong .......................................... | *24* | Pilgrim 715 |
| | | | Juke Box #9 with Freddy Cannon on guitar | | |
| | | | **THE J. GEILS BAND** | | |
| | | | Rock group formed in Boston in 1967; named for guitarist Jerome Geils. Lead singer Peter "Wolf" Blankenfield left in Fall of 1983. | | |
| 3/06/82 | 25 | 10 | 1 Flamethrower/ | | |
| | | 10 | 2● Freeze-Frame ............................................. | *4* | EMI America 8108 |
| | | | **GENE & EUNICE** | | |
| | | | Duo of Forest Gene Wilson (from San Antonio), and Eunice Russ (from Texarkana, AR). Wilson recorded as "Gene Forrest". | | |
| 1/29/55 | 6 | 7 | 1 Ko Ko Mo ............................................ | | Combo 64 |
| | | | Juke Box #6 / Best Seller #7 / Jockey #10 also released on Aladdin 3276 | | |
| 5/21/55 | 8 | 8 | 2 This Is My Story .................... | | Aladdin 3282 |
| | | | Jockey #8 / Juke Box #10 / Best Seller #13 above 2: with Johnny's Combo | | |
| | | | **GENE & JERRY - see GENE CHANDLER and/or JERRY BUTLER** | | |
| | | | **GENE & WENDELL with THE SWEETHEARTS** | | |
| | | | Eugene Washington and Wendell Jones, with female backing group, the Sweethearts. | | |
| 11/27/61+ | 14 | 10 | 1 The Roach ................................. | *117* | Ray Starr 777 |
| | | | **GENERAL KANE** | | |
| | | | 8-member rap group led by Mitch "General Kane" McDowell. | | |
| 9/20/86 | 12 | 12 | 1 Crack Killed Applejack................................. | | Motown 1865 |
| 7/11/87 | 33 | 12 | 2 Girl Pulled The Dog ........................ | | Motown 1901 |
| | | | **GENTLEMEN & THEIR LADIES** | | |
| 2/16/74 | 50 | 11 | 1 Party Bump, Pt. 1........................... | | Jean 731 |
| | | | **BOBBIE GENTRY** | | |
| | | | Born Roberta Lee Streeter on 7/27/44 in Chickasaw County, Mississippi. Singer/ songwriter. Married singer Jim Stafford in 1978. | | |
| 9/16/67 | 8 | 9 | 1● Ode To Billie Joe ........................................ | *1* | Capitol 5950 |
| | | | written by Gentry and subsequently made into a film in 1976 | | |
| | | | **GENTY** | | |
| 10/18/80 | 51 | 10 | 1 You Don't Know Like I Know ......................... | | Venture 133 |
| | | | written and produced by Isaac Hayes | | |

| DEBUT DATE | PEAK POS | WKS CHR | ARTIST — Record Title | POP POS | Label & Number |
|---|---|---|---|---|---|
| | | | **BARBARA GEORGE**<br>Singer/songwriter, born on 8/16/42 in New Orleans. | | |
| 11/20/61+ | **1**⁴ | 19 | 1 I Know (You Don't Love Me No More) .............<br>cornet solo by Melvin Lastie | *3* | A.F.O. 302 |
| | | | **GEORGIO**<br>Los Angeles-based singer/songwriter/keyboardist/guitarist Georgio Allentini. | | |
| 2/14/87 | **16** | 15 | 1 Sexappeal ................................................... | *58* | Macolo 3563 |
| 5/30/87 | **5** | 18 | 2 **Tina Cherry** ............................................. | *96* | Motown 1892 |
| 10/03/87 | **26** | 15 | 3 Lover's Lane ............................................. | *59* | Motown 1906 |
| 2/20/88 | **37** | 12 | 4 Bedrock ................................................... | | Motown 1977 |
| | | | **DONNY GERRARD**<br>Lead singer of the Canadian group Skylark. | | |
| 6/28/75 | **65** | 8 | 1 (Baby) Don't Let It Mess Your Mind ................ | *104* | Rocket 40405 |
| 3/13/76 | **37** | 10 | 2 Words (Are Impossible)................................. | *87* | Greedy 101 |
| 9/25/76 | **92** | 2 | 3 He's Always Somewhere Around/ | | |
| 10/30/76 | **73** | 7 | 4    Greedy (For Your Love) ............................. | | Greedy 107 |
| 1/29/77 | **71** | 8 | 5 Stay Awhile With Me ................................... | | Greedy 109 |
| 6/18/77 | **88** | 6 | 6 Darlin' .................................................... | | Greedy 114 |
| | | | **GF & FRIENDS** | | |
| 4/23/77 | **87** | 5 | 1 Body Language.......................................... | | Monument 211 |
| | | | **ANDY GIBB**<br>Born Andrew Roy Gibb on 3/5/58 in Manchester, England. Moved to Australia when 6 months old, then back to England at age 9. Youngest brother of Barry, Robin and Maurice Gibb - The Bee Gees. Died on 3/30/88 (30) of an inflammatory heart virus in Oxford, England. | | |
| 8/13/77 | **19** | 13 | 1●I Just Want To Be Your Everything ................. | *1* | RSO 872 |
| 5/13/78 | **11** | 15 | 2 Shadow Dancing ........................................ | *1* | RSO 893 |
| 2/23/80 | **49** | 6 | 3 Desire...................................................... | *4* | RSO 1019 |
| | | | **DOUG GIBBS** | | |
| 9/09/72 | **25** | 5 | 1 Always Have You There ................................ | | Oak 108 |
| | | | **GIBSON BROTHERS**<br>Consisted of brothers Chris (guitar, percussion), Patrick (vocals, drums) and Alex Gibson (from the West Indies; vocals, keyboards). Based in Paris, France. | | |
| 6/16/79 | **64** | 6 | 1 Cuba....................................................... | *81* | Island 8832 |
| | | | **BEVERLY ANN GIBSON** | | |
| 3/09/59 | **17** | 3 | 1 Love's Burning Fire ..................................... | | Deb 506 |
| | | | **JOHNNY GILL**<br>Washington, DC singer discovered by Stacy Lattisaw. Sang in family group, Wings Of Of Faith, from age 5. Recorded solo at age 16 in 1983. Joined New Edition in 1988. | | |
| 6/11/83 | **29** | 11 | 1 Super Love ............................................... | | Cotillion 99859 |
| 8/27/83 | **57** | 7 | 2 When Something Is Wrong With My Baby ......... | | Cotillion 99840 |
| | | | **STACY LATTISAW & JOHNNY GILL:** | | |
| 2/18/84 | **10** | 15 | 3 **Perfect Combination** ................................... | *75* | Cotillion 99785 |
| 5/12/84 | **37** | 10 | 4 Baby It's You ............................................ | *102* | Cotillion 99750 |
| 7/14/84 | **63** | 7 | 5 Block Party............................................... | | Cotillion 99725 |
| | | | **JOHNNY GILL:** | | |
| 1/26/85 | **26** | 16 | 6 Half Crazy ............................................... | | Cotillion 99671 |
| 5/04/85 | **49** | 9 | 7 Can't Wait Til Tommorow ............................. | | Cotillion 99646 |
| | | | **DIZZY GILLESPIE**<br>Born John Birks Gillespie on 10/21/17 in Cheraw, South Carolina. Vocalist/trumpeter/ arranger. Worked with Cab Calloway, Ella Fitzgerald, Benny Carter, Charlie Barnet, Lucky Millinder, and Billy Eckstine. Formed own band in 1944. A pioneer of "bop". Own record label, DeeGee, in 1951. | | |
| 9/25/48 | **13** | 1 | 1 Manteca ..................................................<br>Juke Box #13 / Best Seller #15<br>vocal by Chano Pozo | | Victor 3023 |
| | | | **JIMMY GILMER & THE FIREBALLS**<br>Rock and roll band formed while high schoolers in Raton, New Mexico. Lead vocalist Chuck Tharp was replaced by Jimmy Gilmer in 1960. | | |
| 9/21/63 | **1**¹ | 10 | 1●Sugar Shack ............................................. | *1* | Dot 16487 |

| DEBUT DATE | PEAK POS | WKS CHR | ARTIST — Record Title | POP POS | Label & Number |
|---|---|---|---|---|---|
| | | | **JAMES GILREATH** | | |
| 5/11/63 | 19 | 4 | 1 Little Band Of Gold............................ | *21* | Joy 274 |
| | | | **JIM GILSTRAP** | | |
| | | | Backup singer from Texas; based in Los Angeles. | | |
| 2/22/75 | 10 | 13 | 1 **Swing Your Daddy**............................ | 55 | Roxbury 2006 |
| 8/16/75 | 64 | 4 | 2 House Of Strangers............................ | 93 | Roxbury 2013 |
| 10/25/75 | 20 | 10 | 3 I'm On Fire .................................... | 78 | Roxbury 2016 |
| 6/05/76 | 77 | 6 | 4 Move Me ....................................... | | Roxbury 2026 |
| 9/11/76 | 70 | 4 | 5 Love Talk ..................................... | | Roxbury 2029 |
| | | | **GINO & GINA** | | |
| 6/23/58 | 14 | 1 | 1 (It's Been A Long Time) Pretty Baby ................ | *20* | Mercury 71283 |
| | | | Jockey #14 | | |
| | | | **THE GIVENS FAMILY** | | |
| 11/23/85 | 74 | 9 | 1 Ain't That Much Love In The World.................. | | Sugar Hill 92018 |
| 9/13/86 | 77 | 5 | 2 Holding On.................................... | | PJ 542 |
| 12/20/86+ | 59 | 10 | 3 Someway, Somehow ............................ | | PJ 544 |
| 7/18/87 | 73 | 7 | 4 I'm Still Waiting................................ | | PJ 546 |
| | | | **THE GLADIOLAS** | | |
| | | | Group from Barr Street High School in Lancaster, South Carolina. Formed as the Royal Charms in 1955. Consisted of Maurice Williams (lead singer), Earl Gainey, William Massey, Willie Jones and Norman Wade. Name changed to Maurice Williams & The Zodiacs in 1959. Also see Maurice Williams. | | |
| 4/20/57 | 11 | 5 | 1 Little Darlin' .................................... | *41* | Excello 2101 |
| | | | Best Seller #11 | | |
| | | | **GLASS FAMILY** | | |
| 11/04/78 | 88 | 3 | 1 Mr. DJ You Know How To Make Me Dance......... | | JDC 428 |
| | | | **THE GLASS HOUSE** | | |
| | | | Vocal group from Detroit, consisting of Larry Mitchell, Pearl Jones, Sherrie Payne, Ty Hunter and Eric Dunham. Hunter (b: 1943; d: 2/24/81) was in group The Originals. Payne is the sister of Freda Payne (Supremes). | | |
| 9/27/69 | 7 | 12 | 1 **Crumbs Off The Table**................................ | 59 | Invictus 9071 |
| 6/13/70 | 33 | 8 | 2 I Can't Be You (You Can't Be Me) .................... | 90 | Invictus 9076 |
| 11/14/70+ | 42 | 8 | 3 Stealing Moments From Another Woman's Life/ | *121* | |
| | | 4 | 4 If It Ain't Love, It Don't Matter ...................... | | Invictus 9082 |
| 10/02/71 | 31 | 9 | 5 Look What We've Done To Love ...................... | *101* | Invictus 9097 |
| 10/21/72 | 47 | 3 | 6 Thanks I Needed That................................ | | Invictus 9229 |
| | | | **GARRY GLENN** | | |
| | | | Songwriter/singer/producer/keyboardist from Detroit. Brother of gospel singer Beverly Glenn. Former touring keyboardist for Anita Baker. | | |
| 8/29/87 | 37 | 11 | 1 Do You Have To Go ..................................... | | Motown 1904 |
| 12/05/87+ | 37 | 13 | 2 Feels Good To Feel Good ............................. | | Motown 1918 |
| | | | GARRY GLENN featuring SHEILA HUTCHINSON | | |
| | | | **LLOYD GLENN** | | |
| | | | Born on 11/21/09 in San Antonio, Texas. Died of a heart attack on 5/23/85. Pianist/arranger. To California in 1942. First recorded for Imperial in 1947. Member of the Kid Ory band from 1949-53. Much session work on the West Coast. Extensive touring with Joe Turner into the 80s. Glenn was backed by Earl Brown (alto sax), Bob Harvey (drums) and Billy Hadnott (bass). Also see Lowell Fulsom and Red Miller. | | |
| 11/18/50 | 3 | 10 | 1 **Old Time Shuffle Blues**............................ [I] | | Swingtime 237 |
| | | | LLOYD GLENN with TH' FULSON UNIT | | |
| | | | Juke Box #3 / Best Seller #5 | | |
| 4/14/51 | 1² | 15 | 2 **Chica Boo** ..................................... [I] | | Swingtime 254 |
| | | | LLOYD GLENN'S Combo | | |
| | | | Juke Box #1 / Best Seller #5 | | |
| | | | **THE GLITTER BAND** | | |
| | | | British backing group for Gary Glitter. | | |
| 11/27/76+ | 91 | 9 | 1 Makes You Blind.............................. [I] | *91* | Arista 0207 |
| | | | **G.L.O.B.E. & WHIZ KID** | | |
| | | | The rap master with the quick-cutter of Afrika Bambaataa & Soulsonic Force. | | |
| 10/29/83 | 68 | 7 | 1 Play That Beat Mr. D.J. ............................... | | Tommy Boy 836 |
| | | | all sound effects artificially done on a synthesizer | | |

**169**

| DEBUT DATE | PEAK POS | WKS CHR | ARTIST — Record Title | POP POS | Label & Number |
|---|---|---|---|---|---|
| | | | **THE GLORIES**<br>Trio led by Francis Yvonne Gearing (b: 12/17/44, Daytona Beach), with Betty Stokes and Mildred Vaney. Gearing and Vaney later joined Quiet Elegance. | | |
| 7/15/67 | 48 | 2 | 1 I Stand Accused (Of Loving You) ................... | 74 | Date 1553 |
| | | | **GO WEST**<br>British duo: Peter Cox & Richard Drummie. | | |
| 9/21/85 | 67 | 8 | 1 Eye To Eye ................................. | 73 | Chrysalis 42903 |
| | | | **JOHN GODFREY TRIO**<br>Vocalist/drummer. With Charlie Singleton band from 1950-52. | | |
| 10/20/51 | 6 | 7 | 1 **Hey, Little Girl**...........................<br>Juke Box #6<br>originally released on Hilltop 701 | | Chess 1478 |
| | | | **RAY GODFREY** | | |
| 7/18/70 | 40 | 7 | 1 I Gotta Get Away (From My Own Self) .............. | | Spring 104 |
| | | | **TERRI GONZALES** | | |
| 2/27/82 | 76 | 7 | 1 Treat Yourself To My Love........................... | | Becket 10 |
| | | | **GONZALEZ**<br>British soul/disco band. | | |
| 2/03/79 | 46 | 9 | 1 Haven't Stop Dancing Yet ...................... | 26 | Capitol 4674 |
| | | | **GOODIE** | | |
| 7/31/82 | 14 | 14 | 1 Do Something................................ | | Total Exp. 8202 |
| 12/25/82+ | 30 | 12 | 2 You And I ................................. | | Total Exp. 8206 |
| 9/29/84 | 67 | 7 | 3 Because Of You ............................ | | Total Exp. 2406 |
| | | | **CUBA GOODING**<br>Born on 4/27/44 in New York. Lead singer of The Main Ingredient. | | |
| 5/20/78 | 91 | 4 | 1 Mind Pleaser ................................. | | Motown 1440 |
| 8/23/80 | 69 | 5 | 2 Think Positive ................................. | | RCA 12060 |
| | | | **THE MAIN INGREDIENT featuring CUBA GOODING** | | |
| 11/19/83 | 43 | 12 | 3 Happiness Is Just Around The Bend ............... | | Streetwise 1114 |
| | | | **BENNY GOODMAN**<br>Born on 5/30/09 in Chicago. Nicknamed "King of Swing". Clarinetist/big band leader since the 30s. Fletcher Henderson arranged many of his early 30s hits. Died on 6/13/86 (77). | | |
| 2/13/43 | 4 | 5 | 1 **Why Don't You Do Right?**........................<br>vocal by Peggy Lee; from the film "Stage Door Canteen" | 4 | Columbia 36652 |
| 6/19/43 | 10 | 2 | 2 **Taking A Chance On Love** ........................<br>vocal by Helen Forrest; Cootie Williams on trumpet;<br>from the 1940 musical and 1943 film "Cabin In The Sky" | 1 | Columbia 35869 |
| 2/12/44 | 1[1] | 6 | 3 **Solo Flight**.............................. [I]<br>recorded on 3/4/41;<br>one of Charlie Christian's most famous guitar performances | 20 | Columbia 36684 |
| | | | **THE GOODTIMERS - see DON COVAY** | | |
| | | | **GOODY GOODY**<br>Vocalist Denise Montana with studio band from Philadelphia. | | |
| 11/25/78 | 97 | 2 | 1 #1 Dee Jay................................. | 82 | Atlantic 3504 |
| | | | **GOON SQUAD**<br>Vocalists Tina B., Lotti Golden, B.J. Nelson, and W. Downing. | | |
| 8/24/85 | 80 | 5 | 1 Eight Arms To Hold You.............................<br>from the film "The Goonies" | | Epic 05449 |
| | | | **FRESH GORDON - see CHOICE M.C.'s** | | |
| | | | **ROSCO GORDON**<br>Born in Memphis in 1934. Vocalist/guitarist/self-taught pianist. Own radio show on WDIA-Memphis, at age 16. Own record company, Bab-Roc, in the 70s. | | |
| 9/15/51+ | 9 | 5 | 1 **Saddle The Cow**...........................<br>Juke Box #9 | | RPM 324 |
| 2/09/52 | 1[1] | 13 | 2 **Booted**.................................<br>Best Seller #1 / Juke Box #2 | | Chess 1487 |
| 4/05/52 | 2[2] | 15 | 3 **No More Doggin'** ...........................<br>above 2 shown as: **ROSCOE GORDON**<br>Juke Box #2 / Best Seller #3 | | RPM 350 |
| 2/01/60 | 2[1] | 17 | 4 **Just A Little Bit**.............................. | 64 | Vee-Jay 332 |

| DEBUT DATE | PEAK POS | WKS CHR | ARTIST — Record Title | POP POS | Label & Number |
|---|---|---|---|---|---|
| | | | **LESLEY GORE**<br>Born on 5/2/46 in New York City. Raised in Tenafly, New Jersey. Discovered by Quincy Jones while singing at a hotel in Manhattan. In films "Girls On The Beach", "Ski Party" and "The T.A.M.I. Show". | | |
| 5/25/63 | **1**³ | 11 | 1 It's My Party............................................ | *1* | Mercury 72119 |
| 8/10/63 | **10** | 8 | 2 Judy's Turn To Cry ................................. | *5* | Mercury 72143 |
| 10/19/63 | **26** | 4 | 3 She's A Fool ........................................... | *5* | Mercury 72180 |
| | | | all of above: produced by Quincy Jones | | |
| | | | **EYDIE GORME**<br>Born on 8/16/31 in New York City. Vocalist with big bands of Tommy Tucker and Tex Beneke in the late 40s. Featured on Steve Allen's Tonight Show from 1953. Married to singer Steve Lawrence since 12/29/57. | | |
| 3/30/63 | **16** | 3 | 1 Blame It On The Bossa Nova ...................... | *7* | Columbia 42661 |
| | | | **GQ**<br>Group formed in the Bronx in 1968 as Sabu & The Survivors. Consisted of Emmanuel Rahiem LeBlanc (lead singer), Keith "Sabu" Crier, Herb Lane and Paul Service. At one time, Waymond Anderson (father of singer Suave) was a member. Group became a trio with the departure of Service in 1980. | | |
| 2/10/79 | **1**² | 22 | 1 ●Disco Nights (Rock-Freak) ......................... | *12* | Arista 0388 |
| 7/07/79 | **5** | 22 | 2 I Do Love You/ | *20* | Arista 0426 |
| | | 12 | 3    Make My Dreams A Reality .......................... | | Arista 0426 |
| 2/09/80 | **12** | 15 | 4 Standing Ovation .................................... | | Arista 0483 |
| 5/10/80 | **9** | 16 | 5 Sitting In The Park .................................. | *101* | Arista 0510 |
| 11/14/81 | **23** | 11 | 6 Shake ................................................. | | Arista 0603 |
| 2/13/82 | **39** | 8 | 7 Sad Girl............................................... | *93* | Arista 0659 |
| | | | **FREDI GRACE & RHINSTONE**<br>Trio from Atlanta. | | |
| 5/01/82 | **44** | 10 | 1 Help (...Save This Frantic Heart Of Mine) .......... | | RCA 13099 |
| | | | **LEDA GRACE** | | |
| 3/14/81 | **96** | 4 | 1 No George.............................................. | | Polydor 2156 |
| | | | **CHARLIE GRACIE**<br>Born Charles Graci on 5/14/36 in Philadelphia. Pop singer/guitarist. First recorded for Cadillac in 1951. | | |
| 3/09/57 | **10** | 5 | 1 Butterfly ............................................. | *1* | Cameo 105 |
| | | | Best Seller #10 / Jockey #12 | | |
| | | | **GRAHAM CENTRAL STATION - see LARRY GRAHAM** | | |
| | | | **JAKI GRAHAM** | | |
| 11/02/85 | **85** | 3 | 1 Round And Round...................................... | | Capitol 5516 |
| 2/22/86 | **60** | 8 | 2 Could It Be I'm Falling In Love ...................... | | Capitol 5553 |
| | | | **JAKI GRAHAM with DAVID GRANT** | | |
| | | | **LARRY GRAHAM**     ★★**117**★★<br>Born on 8/14/46 in Beaumont, Texas. To Oakland at the age of two. Bass player with Sly & The Family Stone from 1966-72. In 1973, formed Hot Chocolate (not to be confused with the English group of the same name); band later renamed Graham Central Station. Consisted of Graham (lead), Hershall Kennedy and Robert Sam (keyboards), Willie Sparks and Patrice Banks (percussion), and David Vega (guitar). Graham went solo in 1980. | | |
| | | | **GRAHAM CENTRAL STATION:** | | |
| 3/16/74 | **9** | 16 | 1 Can You Handle It?................................... | *49* | Warner 7782 |
| 10/19/74 | **56** | 8 | 2 Release Yourself ..................................... | | Warner 8025 |
| 12/28/74+ | **18** | 16 | 3 Feel The Need........................................ | | Warner 8061 |
| 7/05/75 | **1**¹ | 17 | 4 Your Love ............................................ | *38* | Warner 8105 |
| 11/08/75 | **19** | 13 | 5 It's Alright ........................................... | *92* | Warner 8148 |
| 2/14/76 | **15** | 10 | 6 The Jam ................................... [I] | *63* | Warner 8175 |
| 5/22/76 | **14** | 11 | 7 Love ................................................. | | Warner 8205 |
| 8/07/76 | **21** | 11 | 8 Entrow - Part 1 ...................................... | | Warner 8235 |
| 5/21/77 | **10** | 10 | 9 Now Do-U-Wanta Dance.............................. | | Warner 8378 |
| 7/23/77 | **25** | 11 | 10 Stomped Beat-Up & Whooped ........................ | | Warner 8417 |
| | | | **LARRY GRAHAM & GRAHAM CENTRAL STATION:** | | |
| 6/24/78 | **18** | 13 | 11 My Radio Sure Sounds Good To Me ................. | | Warner 86020 |
| 10/21/78 | **65** | 6 | 12 Is It Love? ........................................... | | Warner 8665 |
| | | | **LARRY GRAHAM with GRAHAM CENTRAL STATION:** | | |
| 5/12/79 | **37** | 10 | 13 (You're A) Foxy Lady ................................. | | Warner 8816 |

| DEBUT DATE | PEAK POS | WKS CHR | ARTIST — Record Title | POP POS | Label & Number |
|---|---|---|---|---|---|
| | | | **LARRY GRAHAM — Continued** | | |
| 8/11/79 | **85** | 2 | 14  Star Walk .................................................. | | Warner 49011 |
| | | | LARRY GRAHAM: | | |
| 5/03/80 | **1** [2] | 25 | 15●**One In A Million You**.......................... | *9* | Warner 49221 |
| 10/11/80 | **9** | 20 | 16  **When We Get Married** ......................... | *76* | Warner 49581 |
| 6/27/81 | **4** | 19 | 17  **Just Be My Lady**.................................. | *67* | Warner 49744 |
| 10/24/81 | **69** | 5 | 18  Guess Who ........................................... | | Warner 49833 |
| 5/08/82 | **16** | 11 | 19  Don't Stop When You're Hot ................. | *102* | Warner 50068 |
| 7/17/82 | **27** | 12 | 20  Sooner Or Later ................................... | *110* | Warner 29956 |
| 5/28/83 | **34** | 11 | 21  I Never Forgot Your Eyes...................... | | Warner 29620 |
| 10/03/87 | **88** | 4 | 22  If You Need My Love Tonight................. | | Arista 9623 |
| | | | ARETHA FRANKLIN & LARRY GRAHAM | | |
| | | | **GRAINGERS** | | |
| 7/11/81 | **29** | 16 | 1  Shine Your Light................................. | | BC 4009 |
| | | | **BILLY GRAMMER** | | |
| | | | Born on 8/28/25 in Benton, Illinois. Country singer/guitarist. Performed regularly on "The Jimmy Dean Show" from 1957-58. | | |
| 12/22/58+ | **14** | 12 | 1  Gotta Travel On ................................. | *4* | Monument 400 |
| | | | based on 19th century tune that originated in the British Isles | | |
| | | | **GRAND FUNK RAILROAD** | | |
| | | | Rock band formed in Flint, Michigan in 1968. Lineup included Mark Farner, Mel Schacher, Don Brewer and Craig Frost. Disbanded in 1976, re-formed in 1981 with Farner, Brewer and Dennis Bellinger. Disbanded again shortly thereafter. | | |
| 2/01/75 | **85** | 5 | 1  Some Kind Of Wonderful ...................... | *3* | Capitol 4002 |
| | | | produced by Jimmy Ienner | | |
| | | | **GRANDMASTER & MELLE MEL - see GRANDMASTER FLASH** | | |
| | | | **GRANDMASTER FLASH & THE FURIOUS FIVE** | | |
| | | | Grandmaster Flash is pioneer rap disk jockey/producer Joseph Saddler (born in Barbados; raised in the Bronx). The Furious Five is a group of rappers and dancers. The original Furious Five lineup - no relation to the August Darnell character), Rahiem (Guy Todd Williams), Cowboy (Keith Wiggins), Melle Mel (Melvin Glover) and Scorpio. In 1984, Melle Mel, Cowboy and Rahiem left; replaced by La Von Dukes, Broadway, Larry "Love" Parker, and Shame. Fluctuating personnel thereafter. Original lineup reunited in late 1987. Also see Furious Five and Grandmaster Melle Mel. | | |
| 9/13/80 | **19** | 11 | 1  Freedom............................................... | | Sugar Hill 549 |
| 2/28/81 | **36** | 9 | 2  The Birthday Party............................... | | Sugar Hill 759 |
| 5/23/81 | **55** | 9 | 3  The Adventures Of Grandmaster Flash On The     Wheels Of Steel ................................... | | Sugar Hill 557 |
| 2/06/82 | **22** | 12 | 4  It's Nasty (Genius Of Love).................. | | Sugar Hill 775 |
| 7/24/82 | **4** | 16 | 5  **The Message** ...................................... | *62* | Sugar Hill 584 |
| | | | features Melle Mel & Duke Bootee | | |
| 10/23/82 | **30** | 13 | 6  Scorpio .............................................. | | Sugar Hill 590 |
| 5/14/83 | **17** | 13 | 7  New York New York.............................. | | Sugar Hill 457 |
| | | | GRANDMASTER FLASH: | | |
| 2/02/85 | **55** | 9 | 8  Sign Of The Times ............................... | | Elektra 69677 |
| 5/11/85 | **54** | 10 | 9  Girls Love The Way He Spins ................ | | Elektra 69643 |
| 4/05/86 | **54** | 10 | 10  Style (Peter Gunn Theme) .................... | | Elektra 69552 |
| 3/21/87 | **57** | 9 | 11  U Know What Time It Is ...................... | | Elektra 69490 |
| | | | **GRANDMASTER MELLE MEL & THE FURIOUS FIVE** | | |
| | | | Melle Mel is rapper Melvin Glover. Under Glover's direction, the Furious Five included Cowboy (Keith Wiggins), King Lou, Scorpio, Grandmaster E-Z Mike, Dynamite, Tommy Gunn and Kami Kaze. Also see Furious Five, Grandmaster Flash and Chaka Khan. | | |
| 12/25/82+ | **32** | 12 | 1  Message II (Survival).......................... | | Sugar Hill 594 |
| | | | MELLE MEL & DUKE BOOTEE | | |
| 10/29/83 | **47** | 13 | 2  White Lines (Don't Do It) .................... | *101* | Sugar Hill 465 |
| | | | GRANDMASTER & MELLE MEL | | |
| 3/03/84 | **73** | 4 | 3  Jesse ................................................. | | Sugar Hill 32016 |
| | | | GRANDMASTER & MELLE MEL | | |
| 6/02/84 | **8** | 14 | 4  **Beat Street Breakdown - Part I**................ | *86* | Atlantic 89689 |
| | | | from the film "Beat Street" | | |
| 9/15/84 | **51** | 9 | 5  We Don't Work For Free........................ | | Sugar Hill 32025 |

| DEBUT DATE | PEAK POS | WKS CHR | ARTIST — Record Title | POP POS | Label & Number |
|---|---|---|---|---|---|
| | | | **GRANDMASTER MELLE MEL & THE FURIOUS FIVE — Continued** | | |
| 11/16/85 | **90** | 3 | 6 Vice............................................. shown only as: **GRANDMASTER MELLE MEL** from TV's "Miami Vice" soundtrack | | MCA 52740 |
| | | | **GRANDMIXER D.ST.** Former D.J. at the Roxy in New York (D.ST. = Delancey Street). | | |
| 12/17/83+ | **32** | 12 | 1 Crazy Cuts............................................. featuring vocals by Bernard Fowler | | Island 99803 |
| | | | **DAVID GRANT** British; co-founder of Linx. | | |
| 8/13/83 | **75** | 5 | 1 Stop And Go.............................................. | | Chrysalis 42712 |
| 2/22/86 | **60** | 8 | 2 Could It Be I'm Falling In Love ....................... **JAKI GRAHAM with DAVID GRANT** | | Capitol 5553 |
| | | | **EARL GRANT** Organist/pianist/vocalist born in Oklahoma City in 1931. First recorded for Decca in 1957. In the films "Tender Is The Night", "Imitation Of Life" and "Tokyo Night". Died in an automobile accident on 6/10/70 (39). | | |
| 10/13/58 | **16** | 9 | 1 The End ............................................ | 7 | Decca 30719 |
| 10/06/62 | **9** | 7 | 2 **Sweet Sixteen Bars** ................................ [I] | 55 | Decca 25574 |
| | | | **EDDY GRANT** Born Edmond Montague Grant on 3/5/48 in Plaisance, Guyana. Moved to London in 1960. Formed group, the Equals, in 1967. Own Ice Records in 1977. Moved to Barbados in 1982. | | |
| 11/03/79 | **86** | 3 | 1 Walking On Sunshine................................. | | Epic 50766 |
| 3/19/83 | **18** | 28 | 2●Electric Avenue ............................................ | 2 | Portrait 03793 |
| 5/26/84 | **68** | 8 | 3 Romancing The Stone ................................... written for the film of the same title, featured only momentarily; above 2: recorded in St. Phillip, Barbados | 26 | Portrait 04433 |
| | | | **ELEANOR GRANT** | | |
| 1/17/76 | **84** | 4 | 1 You Oughta' Be Here With Me ......................... | | Columbia 10268 |
| 10/08/77 | **80** | 9 | 2 This Time We're Really Through...................... | | Columbia 10617 |
| 1/08/83 | **71** | 6 | 3 (I Am Ready) Sexual Healing ........................... | | Catawba 8000 |
| 8/11/84 | **84** | 2 | 4 Lovin' Your Good Thing Away ......................... | | CBS Assoc. 04576 |
| 1/12/85 | **87** | 4 | 5 Don't Stop Until You Get Enough .................... | | CBS Assoc. 1968 |
| | | | **LOLA GRANT - see DEE BROWN** | | |
| | | | **TOM GRANT** Vocalist/keyboardist from Portland, Oregon. Worked with Joe Henderson in 1975. | | |
| 10/10/81 | **76** | 5 | 1 Heaven Is Waiting ...................................... | | WMOT 02128 |
| | | | **CARL GRAVES** Singer from Calgary, Alberta, Canada. Own band, Soul Unlimited, at age 17. With the group Skylark in 1973. | | |
| 11/23/74+ | **18** | 13 | 1 Baby, Hang Up The Phone ............................. | 50 | A&M 1620 |
| 1/03/76 | **26** | 11 | 2 Heart Be Still ................................................ | | A&M 1757 |
| 4/09/77 | **44** | 11 | 3 Sad Girl .................................................... | 83 | Ariola Am. 7660 |
| | | | **DIVA GRAY & OYSTER** Gray was a vocalist with the studio group Roundtree. | | |
| 2/09/80 | **72** | 4 | 1 Magic Carpet Ride ...................................... | | Columbia 11216 |
| | | | **DOBIE GRAY** Born Leonard Victor Ainsworth on 7/26/42 in Brookshire, Texas. Moved to Los Angeles in 1960. Worked as an actor on Broadway, and in the L.A. production of "Hair". Lead singer of Pollution in 1971. On soundtracks of the films "Uptown Saturday Night", "The Commitment" and "Casey's Shadow". Moved to Nashville in 1978. | | |
| 1/30/65 | **11** | 11 | 1 The "In" Crowd ....................................... | 13 | Charger 105 |
| 5/19/73 | **42** | 2 | 2●Drift Away ............................................... | 5 | Decca 33057 |
| 8/18/73 | **81** | 5 | 3 Loving Arms ............................................. above 2: produced by Mentor Williams (Paul Williams' brother) | 61 | MCA 40100 |
| 10/16/76 | **71** | 6 | 4 Find 'Em, Fool 'Em & Forget 'Em .................... | 94 | Capricorn 0259 |
| 12/16/78+ | **32** | 12 | 5 You Can Do It............................................. | 37 | Infinity 50003 |

| DEBUT DATE | PEAK POS | WKS CHR | ARTIST — Record Title | POP POS | Label & Number |
|---|---|---|---|---|---|
| | | | **GLEN GRAY & THE CASA LOMA ORCHESTRA** | | |
| | | | Swing band organized in 1929; named for a Toronto nightclub. Trombonist Pee Wee Hunt was its leading musician. Alto saxophonist/leader Glen Gray died on 8/23/63. | | |
| 1/22/44 | **7** | 1 | 1 **My Heart Tells Me** ..................................... | *1* | Decca 18567 |
| | | | vocal by Eugenie Baird; from the 1943 film "Sweet Rosie O'Grady" | | |
| | | | **"GREAT" GATES** | | |
| | | | Real name: Edward White. Vocalist/pianist, born in Philadelphia in 1918. Moved to California in 1932. Own NBC radio show in the mid-40s. Still active into the 80s, as "The Man In The Moon". | | |
| 9/17/49 | **6** | 1 | 1 **Late After Hours** ..................................... | | Selective 103 |
| | | | Juke Box #6 | | |
| | | | **R.B. GREAVES** | | |
| | | | Born Ronald Bertram Aloysius Greaves on 11/28/44 at the USAF Base in Georgetown, British Guyana. Half American Indian, raised on a Seminole reservation in California. Nephew of Sam Cooke. To England in 1963, as Sonny Childe & The TNT's. | | |
| 11/01/69 | **10** | 9 | 1●**Take A Letter Maria** ................................... | *2* | Atco 6714 |
| 2/21/70 | **50** | 2 | 2 Always Something There To Remind Me............ | *27* | Atco 6726 |
| 4/02/77 | **66** | 7 | 3 Who's Watching The Baby (Margie).................. | *115* | Bareback 523 |
| | | | **GREEN BERETS** | | |
| 3/07/70 | **31** | 4 | 1 (Lord) Send Me Somebody............................. | | Uni 55186 |
| | | | **AL GREEN** ★★**47**★★ | | |
| | | | Born on 4/13/46 in Forest City, Arkansas. Singer/songwriter. With gospel group, the Greene Brothers. To Grand Rapids, Michigan in 1959. First recorded for Fargo in 1960. In group, the Creations, from 1964-67. Sang with his brother Robert and Lee Virgins in the group Soul Mates from 1967-68. Went solo in 1969. Wrote most of his songs. Returned to gospel music in 1980. | | |
| 12/02/67+ | **5** | 14 | 1 **Back Up Train**...................................... | *41* | Hot Line 15000 |
| | | | **AL GREENE & THE SOUL MATES** | | |
| 2/07/70 | **28** | 9 | 2 **You Say It** ........................................ | | Hi 2172 |
| 6/27/70 | **23** | 8 | 3 Right Now, Right Now ................................. | | Hi 2177 |
| 11/07/70 | **11** | 13 | 4 I Can't Get Next To You................................ | *60* | Hi 2182 |
| 3/27/71 | **46** | 5 | 5 Driving Wheel........................................... | *115* | Hi 2188 |
| | | | recorded in Memphis | | |
| 7/10/71 | **7** | 20 | 6●**Tired Of Being Alone** .............................. | *11* | Hi 2194 |
| 12/04/71+ | **1**⁹ | 16 | 7●**Let's Stay Together** ............................... | *1* | Hi 2202 |
| 4/01/72 | **2**⁴ | 15 | 8●**Look What You Done For Me**...................... | *4* | Hi 2211 |
| 7/15/72 | **1**² | 12 | 9●**I'm Still In Love With You** ........................ | *3* | Hi 2216 |
| 9/23/72 | **29** | 10 | 10 Guilty .................................................. | *69* | Bell 45258 |
| 11/04/72 | **1**¹ | 14 | 11●**You Ought To Be With Me**......................... | *3* | Hi 2227 |
| 2/24/73 | **2**² | 11 | 12●**Call Me (Come Back Home)** ....................... | *10* | Hi 2235 |
| 7/07/73 | **2**³ | 15 | 13●**Here I Am (Come And Take Me)** ................... | *10* | Hi 2247 |
| 11/24/73+ | **1**¹ | 17 | 14 **Livin' For You** ..................................... | *19* | Hi 2257 |
| 3/23/74 | **3** | 18 | 15 Let's Get Married ..................................... | *32* | Hi 2262 |
| 10/05/74 | **2**² | 18 | 16●**Sha-La-La (Make Me Happy)**...................... | *7* | Hi 2274 |
| 3/01/75 | **1**² | 14 | 17 **L-O-V-E (Love)**.................................... | *13* | Hi 2282 |
| 7/05/75 | **7** | 12 | 18 Oh Me, Oh My (Dreams In My Arms)............... | *48* | Hi 2288 |
| 11/01/75 | **1**¹ | 15 | 19 **Full Of Fire** ....................................... | *28* | Hi 2300 |
| 5/01/76 | **16** | 12 | 20 Let It Shine............................................ | | Hi 2306 |
| 10/23/76 | **4** | 15 | 21 **Keep Me Cryin'**.................................... | *37* | Hi 2319 |
| | | | all of above Hi recordings produced by Willie Mitchell | | |
| 2/12/77 | **26** | 11 | 22 I Tried To Tell Myself................................. | *101* | Hi 2322 |
| 7/30/77 | **92** | 3 | 23 Love And Happiness .................................. | *104* | Hi 2324 |
| 10/29/77 | **9** | 17 | 24 **Belle**............................................... | *83* | Hi 77505 |
| 4/01/78 | **36** | 11 | 25 I Feel Good ............................................ | *103* | Hi 78511 |
| 1/06/79 | **71** | 5 | 26 To Sir With Love/ | | |
| 2/10/79 | **58** | 7 | 27     Wait Here .......................................... | | Hi 78522 |
| 3/28/87 | **22** | 14 | 28 Everything's Gonna Be Alright ...................... | | A&M 2919 |
| | | | **DARREN GREEN** | | |
| | | | Born on 12/31/59 in Washington, DC. Discovered by deejay Chuck McCool. Appeared in the musicals "Magnificent Thing To Be" and "The Me Nobody Knows". | | |
| 8/18/73 | **94** | 4 | 1 What Do You See In Him?............................. | | RCA 0016 |
| 12/22/73+ | **84** | 5 | 2 Beep-A-Boo ............................................ | | RCA 0154 |

| DEBUT DATE | PEAK POS | WKS CHR | ARTIST — Record Title | POP POS | Label & Number |
|---|---|---|---|---|---|
| | | | **GARLAND GREEN** | | |
| | | | Born on 6/24/42 in Leland, Mississippi. Vocalist/pianist. To Chicago in 1958. Attended Chicago Conservatory of Music. First recorded for Gamma in 1967. First produced by team of Mel Collins and Jo Armstead. To Los Angeles in 1979. | | |
| 8/23/69 | 5 | 16 | 1 **Jealous Kind Of Fella** | 20 | Uni 55143 |
| 1/17/70 | 42 | 2 | 2 Don't Think That I'm A Violent Guy | 113 | Uni 55188 |
| 3/13/71 | 17 | 11 | 3 Plain And Simple Girl | 109 | Cotillion 44098 |
| | | | arranged by Donny Hathaway | | |
| 1/12/74 | 67 | 8 | 4 He Didn't Know | | Spring 142 |
| 5/25/74 | 72 | 7 | 5 Sweet Loving Woman | | Spring 146 |
| 10/12/74 | 65 | 6 | 6 Let The Good Times Roll | | Spring 151 |
| 2/08/75 | 67 | 8 | 7 Let The Good Times Roll [R] | | Spring 151 |
| 5/17/75 | 72 | 6 | 8 Bumpin' And Stompin' | | Spring 158 |
| 3/12/77 | 93 | 3 | 9 Don't Let Love Walk Out On Us/ | | |
| | | 2 | 10 Ask Me For What You Want | | RCA 10889 |
| 10/08/83 | 63 | 10 | 11 Tryin' To Hold On | | Ocean Fr. 2000 |
| | | | **LIL GREEN** | | |
| | | | Born Lillian Green on 12/22/19 in Mississippi. Died of pneumonia on 4/14/54 (34). Left home at age 10; settled in Chicago. First recorded for Bluebird in 1940 with Big Bill Broonzy (guitar) and Jack Dupree (piano). | | |
| 10/24/42 | 8 | 1 | 1 **Let's Be Friends** | | Bluebird 8895 |
| | | | **SONNY GREEN** | | |
| 12/08/73 | 89 | 4 | 1 Don't Write A Check With Your Mouth | | Hill 339 |
| | | | **BARBARA GREENE** | | |
| | | | Chicago-based soprano. | | |
| 6/29/68 | 50 | 2 | 1 Young Boy | 86 | Renee 5001 |
| | | | **LAURA GREENE** | | |
| | | | Singer/actress from Cleveland, played piano from age 3. In films "Putney Swope" and "Sweet Monday". Prominent commercial jingle singer. | | |
| 3/29/80 | 90 | 3 | 1 Let Me Blow Your Whistle | | Sound Trek 103 |
| | | | **JOHN GREER & His Rhythm Rockers** | | |
| | | | Vocalist/tenor saxophonist, formerly with Lucky Millinder's band. His Rhythm Rockers featured Bill Doggett on piano and organ. Also see Annisteen Allen and Lucky Millinder. | | |
| 3/15/52 | 2[1] | 21 | 1 **Got You On My Mind** | | RCA 4348 |
| | | | Juke Box #2 / Best Seller #8 | | |
| | | | **BOBBY GREGG & His Friends** | | |
| | | | Bobby's real name is Robert Grego; jazz drummer from Philadelphia. Performed with Steve Gibson & The Red Caps from 1955-60. | | |
| 4/07/62 | 14 | 7 | 1 The Jam - Part 1 [I] | 29 | Cotton 1003 |
| | | | featuring Roy Buchanan on guitar | | |
| | | | **GREY & HANKS** | | |
| | | | Chicago-based vocal/songwriting duo of Zane Grey and Len Ron Hanks. With Jerry Butler in 1973. Moved to Los Angeles in 1976. Wrote "Back In Love Again" for L.T.D., "Never Had A Love Like This Before" for Tavares, and many others. | | |
| 9/09/78 | 19 | 16 | 1 You Fooled Me | 104 | RCA 11346 |
| 1/20/79 | 8 | 15 | 2 **Dancin'** | 83 | RCA 11460 |
| 3/15/80 | 57 | 9 | 3 Now I'm Fine | | RCA 11922 |
| | | | **GRIFFIN - see REGGIE GRIFFIN** | | |
| | | | **GRIFFIN BROTHERS** | | |
| | | | Band led by Jimmy Griffin (trombone) and Ernest "Buddy" Griffin (piano); from Norfolk, Virginia. Brother Wilbur was in the Progressive Four gospel group. Band included Wilbur Dyer (alto sax), Virgil Wilson (tenor sax), Jimmy Reeves (bass) and Emmett Shields (drums). By 1951, lineup was Dyer, Noble Watts (tenor sax), Wilbur Little (bass) and Belton Evans (drums). Group disbanded in 1954. | | |
| 11/25/50 | 7 | 3 | 1 **Street-Walkin' Daddy** | | Dot 1010 |
| | | | Juke Box #7 | | |
| 1/27/51 | 5 | 7 | 2 **Little Red Rooster** | | Dot 1019 |
| | | | Best Seller #5 / Juke Box #5 | | |
| | | | above 2: vocals by Margie Day | | |
| 7/28/51 | 7 | 8 | 3 **Tra La La/** | | |
| | | | Best Seller #7 / Juke Box #10 | | |
| 9/08/51 | 8 | 1 | 4 **Hoppin'** [I] | | Dot 1060 |
| | | | Juke Box #8 | | |

| DEBUT DATE | PEAK POS | WKS CHR | ARTIST — Record Title | POP POS | Label & Number |
|---|---|---|---|---|---|
| | | | **GRIFFIN BROTHERS — Continued** | | |
| 12/08/51+ | **1** [3] | 11 | 5 **Weepin' And Cryin'** .................................... | | Dot 1071 |
| | | | Juke Box #1 / Best Seller #3 | | |
| | | | 3 & 5: vocals by Tommy Brown | | |
| 12/29/51 | **10** | 1 | 6 **Pretty Baby** .................................... | | Dot 1070 |
| | | | Best Seller #10 | | |
| | | | vocals by Margie Day & Tommy Brown | | |
| | | | **BILLY GRIFFIN** | | |
| | | | Born on 8/15/50 in Baltimore. Sang with Last Dynasty. Replaced Smokey Robinson in The Miracles, 1972. Went solo in 1982. | | |
| 1/22/77 | **37** | 10 | 1 Spy For Brotherhood .................................... | *104* | Columbia 10464 |
| | | | THE MIRACLES featuring BILLY GRIFFIN | | |
| 5/06/78 | **55** | 10 | 2 Mean Machine .................................... | | Columbia 10706 |
| | | | THE MIRACLES featuring BILLY GRIFFIN | | |
| 10/15/83 | **61** | 7 | 3 Respect .................................... | | Columbia 04102 |
| 2/04/84 | **37** | 11 | 4 Serious.................................... | | Columbia 04321 |
| 9/06/86 | **66** | 6 | 5 Believe It Or Not .................................... | | Atlantic 89374 |
| | | | **REGGIE GRIFFIN & TECHNOFUNK** | | |
| | | | Vocalist/multi-instrumentalist Griffin was born on 10/27/55 in Indianapolis. Nephew of jazz trumpeter Clifford Brown. Lead vocalist of West Street Mob and leader of Manchild. Staff arranger for Sugarhill Records. | | |
| 12/25/82+ | **66** | 10 | 1 Mirda Rock .................................... | | Sweet Mt. 2001 |
| 7/28/84 | **52** | 9 | 2 Throw Down.................................... | | Qwest 29251 |
| | | | shown only as: **GRIFFIN** | | |
| | | | **JOHNNY GRIFFITH INC.** | | |
| 1/06/73 | **43** | 5 | 1 Grand Central Shuttle.................................... | | RCA 0805 |
| | | | **TINY GRIMES** | | |
| | | | Born Lloyd Grimes on 7/7/16 in Newport News, Virginia. Guitarist/vocalist. Member of Cats & The Fiddle and the Art Tatum Trio. Fronted own trio and band, the Rocking Highlanders, into the 50s. Important figure in the development of "bop". Also see Felix Gross. | | |
| 11/20/48 | **12** | 1 | 1 Midnight Special .................................... [I] | | Atlantic 865 |
| | | | Juke Box #12 | | |
| | | | featuring Red Prysock on tenor sax | | |
| | | | **DAN GRISSOM** | | |
| | | | Vocalist/alto saxophonist/clarinetist. With the Jimmy Lunceford Band from 1935-43. His brother is Jimmy Grissom. Also see Jimmy Lunceford. | | |
| 5/22/48 | **8** | 15 | 1 Recess In Heaven .................................... | | Jewel 2004 |
| | | | Juke Box #8 / Best Seller #10 | | |
| | | | with Buddy Harper's Orchestra | | |
| | | | **JIMMY GRISSOM with The Red Callender Sextet** | | |
| | | | Brother of Dan Grissom. With Duke Ellington from 1952-57. | | |
| 2/24/51 | **7** | 3 | 1 **Once There Lived A Fool** .................................... | | Hollywood 143 |
| | | | Juke Box #7 | | |
| | | | **FELIX GROSS** | | |
| | | | First recorded for Down Beat in 1945. Recorded in Los Angeles. | | |
| 12/31/49 | **9** | 1 | 1 **Love For Christmas** .................................... | | Savoy 720 |
| | | | Best Seller #9 / Juke Box #13 | | |
| | | | featuring Tiny Grimes on guitar | | |
| | | | **GROUND HOG** | | |
| | | | Ground Hog is vocalist/guitarist Joe Richardson. Born on 2/9/40 in Columbia, South Carolina. Toured extensively with the Shirelles. Also recorded as "Tender Slim" and "Tender Joe". Staff musician at All Platinum/Stang Records. | | |
| 11/30/74+ | **61** | 9 | 1 Bumpin .................................... | | Gemigo 100 |
| | | | **G.T.** | | |
| | | | Gary Taylor from Los Angeles. Worked as staff writer for Qwest Records. | | |
| 7/02/83 | **33** | 12 | 1 On The Line.................................... | | A&M 2554 |
| | | | **GUITAR SLIM** | | |
| | | | Born Eddie Jones on 12/10/26 in Greenwood, Mississippi. Died of pneumonia on 2/7/59 in New York City. Vocalist/guitarist. In 1949, formed trio with Huey "Piano" Smith; first recorded for Imperial in 1951. Electric guitar style was extremely influential on later musicians. | | |
| 1/16/54 | **1** [14] | 21 | 1 **Things That I Used To Do**.................................... | *23* | Specialty 482 |
| | | | Juke Box #1(14) / Best Seller #1(6) | | |
| | | | with Ray Charles on piano; a reported million-seller | | |

### ARTHUR GUNTER
Born on 5/23/26 in Nashville. Died of pneumonia on 3/16/76. Vocalist/guitarist. Sang in gospel group, the Gunter Brothers Quartet. First recorded for Excello in 1954. To Port Huron, Michigan in 1961. Won Michigan State Lottery in 1973.

| | | | | | |
|---|---|---|---|---|---|
| 1/29/55 | 12 | 3 | 1 Baby Let's Play House | | Excello 2047 |

Jockey #12
with Skippy Brooks on piano

### SHIRLEY GUNTER & "THE QUEENS"
Vocalist from Los Angeles. Sister of singer Cornell Gunter (Flairs, Coasters). Her vocal group, the Queens, included Zola Taylor, later with the Platters.

| | | | | | |
|---|---|---|---|---|---|
| 10/09/54 | 8 | 2 | 1 Oop Shoop | | Flair 1050 |

Best Seller #8 / Juke Box #10

### GWEN GUTHRIE
Singer/songwriter from New Jersey. Background vocalist for many top artists. Also see George Howard.

| | | | | | |
|---|---|---|---|---|---|
| 8/28/82 | 27 | 12 | 1 It Should Have Been You | | Island 150 |
| 4/30/83 | 83 | 3 | 2 Peanut Butter | | Island 99903 |
| 12/08/84+ | 17 | 15 | 3 Love In Moderation | 110 | Island 99685 |
| 4/06/85 | 53 | 9 | 4 Just For You | | Island 99660 |
| 6/29/85 | 25 | 14 | 5 Padlock | 102 | Garage 72001 |

featuring Sly Dunbar, Robbie Shakespeare, Wally Badarou & Darryl Thompson

| | | | | | |
|---|---|---|---|---|---|
| 11/09/85 | 75 | 4 | 6 Peanut Butter ... [R] | | Garage 72002 |
| 6/28/86 | 1¹ | 19 | 7 Ain't Nothin' Goin' On But The Rent | 42 | Polydor 885106 |
| 11/01/86 | 51 | 8 | 8 Outside In The Rain | | Polydor 885362 |
| 2/07/87 | 69 | 9 | 9 (They Long To Be) Close To You | | Polydor 885528 |
| 4/09/88 | 83 | 6 | 10 Can't Love You Tonight | | Warner 27990 |

### GUY
New York City trio formed and fronted by producer Teddy Riley. Includes brothers Aaron and Albert Damion Hall. Riley was a member of Kids At Work.

| | | | | | |
|---|---|---|---|---|---|
| 5/21/88 | 4 | 20 | 1 Groove Me | | Uptown 53300 |

### BUDDY GUY
Born George Guy on 7/30/36 in Lettsworth, Louisiana. Singer/self-taught guitarist. With Big Poppa John Tilley band in Baton Rouge, in 1953. To Chicago in 1957. Recorded with Magic Sam on Cobra in 1958. First solo recording for Artistic in 1958. With Junior Wells during the 60s.

| | | | | | |
|---|---|---|---|---|---|
| 2/24/62 | 12 | 6 | 1 Stone Crazy | | Chess 1812 |

featuring Otis Spann on piano

### GYPSIES
Group from New York City. Consisted of sisters Betty, Shirley and Earnestine Pearce from South Carolina and Lestine Johnson. In 1965, Shirley and Earnestine joined Viola Billups as the Flirtations.

| | | | | | |
|---|---|---|---|---|---|
| 5/29/65 | 33 | 3 | 1 Jerk It | 111 | Old Town 1180 |

also released on Janus Gold 720

# H

### CURTIS HAIRSTON

| | | | | | |
|---|---|---|---|---|---|
| 2/11/84 | 72 | 6 | 1 We All Are One | | Pretty P. 515 |
| 4/13/85 | 76 | 6 | 2 I Want Your Lovin' (Just A Little Bit) | | Pretty P. 0215 |
| 5/02/87 | 71 | 6 | 3 (You're My) Shining Star | | Atlantic 89283 |

### BILL HALEY & His Comets
Born William John Clifton Haley Jr. on 7/6/25 in Highland Park, Michigan. Began career as a singer with a New England country band, the "Down Homers". Formed the "Four Aces of Western Swing" in 1948. In 1949, formed the Saddlemen, who recorded on various labels before signing with the Essex label (as Bill Haley & The Comets) in 1952; signed with Decca in 1954. The original Comets band who backed Haley on "Rock Around The Clock" were: Danny Cedrone (lead guitar), Joey D'Ambrose (sax), Billy Williamson (steel guitar), Johnny Grande (piano), Marshall Lytle (bass) and Dick Richards (drums). Comets lineup on subsequent recordings included Williamson, Grande, Rudy Pompilli (sax), Al Rex (bass), Ralph Jones (drums) and Frannie Beecher (lead guitar). Bill died of a heart attack in Harlingen, Texas on 2/9/81.

| | | | | | |
|---|---|---|---|---|---|
| 1/22/55 | 10 | 3 | 1 Dim, Dim The Lights (I Want Some Atmosphere) | 11 | Decca 29317 |

Best Seller #10 / Jockey #14

| DEBUT DATE | PEAK POS | WKS CHR | ARTIST — Record Title | POP POS | Label & Number |
|---|---|---|---|---|---|
| | | | **BILL HALEY & His Comets — Continued** | | |
| 6/11/55 | 3 | 14 | 2 **Rock Around The Clock**........................ | *1* | Decca 29124 |
| | | | Jockey #3 / Juke Box #3 / Best Seller #4<br>recorded on 4/12/54; originally released in May of 1954;<br>featured in the film "Blackboard Jungle" | | |
| 11/19/55 | 9 | 3 | 3 **Burn That Candle**.......................... | *9* | Decca 29713 |
| | | | Jockey #9 | | |
| 2/11/56 | 7 | 4 | 4 **See You Later, Alligator**.................... | *6* | Decca 29791 |
| | | | Jockey #7 / Best Seller #14 | | |
| 8/25/56 | 15 | 1 | 5 R-O-C-K.................................... | *16* | Decca 29870 |
| | | | Jockey #15<br>featured in the film "Rock Around The Clock" | | |
| | | | **CAROL HALL - see ORBIT** | | |
| | | | **DARYL HALL** | | |
| | | | Born Daryl Franklin Hohl on 10/11/48 in Philadelphia. Half of Hall & Oates duo. | | |
| 12/13/86 | 91 | 6 | 1 Foolish Pride............................... | *33* | RCA 5038 |
| | | | **DARYL HALL & JOHN OATES** | | |
| | | | Daryl Hall (see above) & John Oates (b: 4/7/49 in New York City) met while students at Temple University in 1967. Hall sang backup for many top soul groups, before teaming up with Oates in 1972. Duo's sophisticated "blue-eyed soul" style has earned them the #2 ranking (behind the Everly Brothers) as the all-time top duo of the rock era. | | |
| 11/15/75 | 98 | 3 | 1 Alone Too Long ........................... | | RCA 10436 |
| 4/03/76 | 23 | 21 | 2● Sara Smile ............................... | *4* | RCA 10530 |
| 10/02/76 | 93 | 3 | 3 She's Gone......................... [R] | *7* | Atlantic 3332 |
| | | | released on Atlantic 2993 in 1974 (POS 60-Pop) | | |
| 11/06/76+ | 23 | 15 | 4 Do What You Want, Be What You Are.............. | *39* | RCA 10808 |
| 2/12/77 | 64 | 11 | 5● Rich Girl............................... | *1* | RCA 10860 |
| 5/28/77 | 70 | 6 | 6 Back Together Again ...................... | *28* | RCA 10970 |
| 11/28/81+ | 1¹ | 17 | 7 **I Can't Go For That (No Can Do)**.................... | *1* | RCA 12357 |
| 7/10/82 | 45 | 10 | 8 Your Imagination ......................... | *33* | RCA 13252 |
| 11/20/82 | 78 | 5 | 9● Maneater............................... | *1* | RCA 13354 |
| 2/12/83 | 8 | 17 | 10 **One On One**............................ | *7* | RCA 13421 |
| 6/11/83 | 81 | 5 | 11 Family Man .............................. | *6* | RCA 13507 |
| 11/12/83+ | 45 | 14 | 12 Say It Isn't So........................... | *2* | RCA 13654 |
| 3/03/84 | 50 | 11 | 13 Adult Education.......................... | *8* | RCA 13714 |
| 10/13/84 | 24 | 15 | 14 Out Of Touch............................ | *1* | RCA 13916 |
| 1/12/85 | 21 | 14 | 15 Method Of Modern Love.................... | *5* | RCA 13970 |
| 5/04/85 | 85 | 3 | 16 Some Things Are Better Left Unsaid............... | *18* | RCA 14035 |
| 6/22/85 | 69 | 6 | 17 Possession Obsession..................... | *30* | RCA 14098 |
| 9/14/85 | 40 | 9 | 18 A Nite At The Apollo Live! The Way You Do The Things You Do/My Girl ...................... | *20* | RCA 14178 |
| | | | **DARYL HALL JOHN OATES with DAVID RUFFIN & EDDIE KENDRICK**<br>recorded at the re-opening of New York's Apollo Theatre;<br>revival of two early Temptations' hits | | |
| 4/23/88 | 13 | 12 | 19 Everything Your Heart Desires ...................... | *3* | Arista 9684 |
| | | | **ELLIS HALL, JR.** | | |
| 1/29/83 | 67 | 8 | 1 Every Little Bit Hurts ................................... | | H.C.R.C. 3100 |
| | | | **RANDY HALL** | | |
| | | | Singer/guitarist. Wrote "Man With A Horn", recorded by Miles Davis. Toured with Diana Ross and Roberta Flack. | | |
| 7/14/84 | 18 | 16 | 1 I've Been Watching You (Jamie's Girl).............. | | MCA 52405 |
| 10/27/84 | 60 | 7 | 2 A Gentleman ............................. | | MCA 52477 |
| 4/09/88 | 36 | 12 | 3 Slow Starter .............................. | | MCA 53139 |
| | | | **HAMILTON, JOE FRANK & REYNOLDS** | | |
| | | | Dan Hamilton, Joe Frank Carollo and Tommy Reynolds. Trio were members of the T-Bones. Reynolds left group in 1972 and was replaced by Alan Dennison. Although Reynolds had left, group still recorded as Hamilton, Joe Frank & Reynolds until July of 1976. | | |
| 8/09/75 | 24 | 12 | 1● Fallin' In Love ............................ | *1* | Playboy 6024 |

| DEBUT DATE | PEAK POS | WKS CHR | ARTIST — Record Title | POP POS | Label & Number |
|---|---|---|---|---|---|
| | | | **ROY HAMILTON** | | |
| | | | Born on 4/16/29 in Leesburg, Georgia. Died of a stroke on 7/20/69 (40). Moved to Jersey City at age 14. Studied commercial art at Lincoln High School, boxed in Golden Gloves heavyweight division. First prize in Apollo amateur contest in 1947. Operatic and classical voice training. In gospel group, the Searchlight Singers. In retirement from 1956-58 due to exhaustion. | | |
| 2/20/54 | **1** [8] | 20 | 1 **You'll Never Walk Alone** .......................... | *21* | Epic 9015 |
| 6/12/54 | **4** | 7 | 2 **If I Loved You** ..................................... | *26* | Epic 9047 |
| | | | Best Seller #4 / Juke Box #6 | | |
| | | | above 2: from the Broadway musical "Carousel" | | |
| 9/11/54 | **5** | 9 | 3 **Ebb Tide** ........................................... | *30* | Epic 9068 |
| | | | Best Seller #5 / Juke Box #6 | | |
| 12/11/54+ | **8** | 7 | 4 **Hurt** ............................................... | | Epic 9086 |
| | | | Best Seller #8 / Juke Box #9 / Jockey #11 | | |
| | | | above 3: orchestra directed by O.B. Masingill | | |
| 4/30/55 | **1** [3] | 14 | 5 **Unchained Melody** ................................. | *6* | Epic 9102 |
| | | | Best Seller #1 / Jockey #2 / Juke Box #2 | | |
| | | | from the film "Unchained" | | |
| 7/30/55 | **10** | 2 | 6 **Forgive This Fool** ................................. | *45* | Epic 9111 |
| | | | Juke Box #10 / Best Seller #14 / Jockey #15 | | |
| 5/27/57 | **14** | 1 | 7 So Long ............................................. | | Epic 9212 |
| | | | Jockey #14 | | |
| 1/20/58 | **2** [3] | 12 | 8 **Don't Let Go** ...................................... | *13* | Epic 9257 |
| | | | Jockey #2 / Best Seller #3 | | |
| | | | with the Jesse Stone Orchestra | | |
| 4/27/59 | **14** | 7 | 9 I Need Your Lovin' ................................. | *62* | Epic 9307 |
| 2/06/61 | **6** | 12 | 10 **You Can Have Her** ............................... | *12* | Epic 9443 |
| | | | **RUSS HAMILTON** | | |
| | | | Singer/songwriter, born Ronald Hulme in Liverpool, England. | | |
| 9/23/57 | **10** | 3 | 1 **Rainbow** .......................................... | *4* | Kapp 184 |
| | | | Best Seller #10 / Jockey #10 | | |
| | | | **JAN HAMMER** | | |
| | | | Czechoslovakian-born, jazz/rock keyboard virtuoso. Toured with Sarah Vaughn as conductor/keyboardist. Member of Mahavishnu Orchestra until 1973. | | |
| 9/28/85 | **10** | 13 | 1 **Miami Vice Theme** ....................... [I] | *1* | MCA 52666 |
| | | | from TV's "Miami Vice" soundtrack | | |
| | | | **LIONEL HAMPTON & HIS ORCHESTRA** ★★**119**★★ | | |
| | | | Born on 4/12/09 in Louisville, Kentucky; raised in Birmingham and Chicago. Worked in Chicago clubs, then moved to Los Angeles in 1928. First recorded with the Reb Spikes band for Hollywood in 1924. Started as a drummer, added vibes in 1930. Worked with Les Hite, then Benny Goodman from 1936-40; own band thereafter. The first jazz musician to feature vibes. In the films "Depth Below", "Pennies From Heaven", "Hollywood Hotel", "A Song Is Born" and "The Benny Goodman Story". Wrote "Flying Home", "Midnight Sun", "Jack The Bellboy" and "Central Avenue Breakdown". | | |
| 5/01/43 | **3** | 4 | 1 **Flying Home** .............................. [I] | *23* | Decca 18394 |
| | | | most renowned version of Hampton's jazz classic, with tenor sax solo by Illinois Jacquet; Dexter Gordon also on tenor sax | | |
| 8/28/43 | **9** | 1 | 2 **Flying Home** .............................. [I] | *25* | Victor 26595 |
| | | | different version of above title, with Ziggy Elman on trumpet; originally released in 1940 | | |
| 1/29/44 | **10** | 1 | 3 **On The Sunnyside Of The Street** .................. | | Victor 25592 |
| | | | recorded in 1937 | | |
| 4/01/44 | **10** | 1 | 4 **Salty Papa Blues** .................................. | | Keynote 606 |
| | | | also released on Mercury 8044 | | |
| 4/22/44 | **9** | 2 | 5 **Evil Gal Blues** .................................... | | Keynote 605 |
| 8/12/44 | **1** [6] | 13 | 6 **Hamp's Boogie Woogie** ...................... [I] | *23* | Decca 18613 |
| 2/03/45 | **8** | 1 | 7 **Salty Papa Blues** .......................... [R] | | Keynot 606 |
| 12/08/45 | **2** [4] | 9 | 8 **Beulah's Boogie** ........................... [I] | | Decca 18719 |
| 3/02/46 | **1** [16] | 25 | 9 **Hey! Ba-Ba-Re-Bop** .............................. | *9* | Decca 18754 |
| 5/24/47 | **5** | 2 | 10 **Blow Top Blues** ................................. | *21* | Decca 23792 |
| | | | 4, 5, 7 & 10: vocals by Dinah Washington | | |
| 6/07/47 | **2** [1] | 11 | 11 **I Want To Be Loved** ....................... [I] | | Decca 23879 |
| | | | with His Hamptonians (quintet) | | |
| 7/10/48 | **13** | 2 | 12 Gone Again ........................................ | | Decca 24248 |
| | | | Juke Box #13 | | |
| | | | vocal by Wini Brown | | |
| 7/23/49 | **13** | 2 | 13 Drinkin' Wine Spo-Dee-O-Dee ............... [I] | | Decca 24642 |
| | | | Juke Box #13 | | |

| DEBUT DATE | PEAK POS | WKS CHR | ARTIST — Record Title | POP POS | Label & Number |
|---|---|---|---|---|---|
| | | | **LIONEL HAMPTON & HIS ORCHESTRA — Continued** | | |
| 8/13/49 | **12** | 1 | 14 Hucklebuck/ <br> Juke Box #12 <br> vocal by Betty Carter | | |
| 8/27/49 | **13** | 1 | 15 Lavender Coffin ............................................. <br> Juke Box #13 <br> vocals by Sonny Parker & Joe James | | Decca 24652 |
| 2/04/50 | **4** | 15 | 16 **Rag Mop** ............................................. <br> Best Seller #4 / Juke Box #4 <br> vocals by the Hamptones; with Wes Montgomery on guitar | **7** | Decca 24855 |
| 10/21/50 | **6** | 7 | 17 **Everybody's Somebody's Fool** ...................... <br> Juke Box #6 <br> vocal by Irma Curry | | Decca 27176 |
| | | | **HERBIE HANCOCK** <br> Born on 4/12/40 in Chicago. Jazz electronic keyboardist. Pianist with the Miles Davis band, 1963-68. Composed, conducted and produced the music for the critically-acclaimed 1986 film "Round Midnight" and the 1988 film "Colors". | | |
| 2/23/74 | **18** | 16 | 1 Chameleon................................................[I] | 42 | Columbia 46002 |
| 11/09/74 | **45** | 8 | 2 Palm Grease................................................ | | Columbia 10050 |
| 10/16/76 | **83** | 5 | 3 Doin' It...................................................... | *104* | Columbia 10408 |
| 8/05/78 | **85** | 4 | 4 I Thought It Was You.................................. | | Columbia 10781 |
| 4/07/79 | **25** | 14 | 5 Ready Or Not.............................................. | | Columbia 10936 |
| 4/12/80 | **33** | 12 | 6 Stars In Your Eyes ..................................... | | Columbia 11236 |
| 8/09/80 | **73** | 5 | 7 Making Love .............................................. | | Columbia 11323 |
| 8/15/81 | **46** | 11 | 8 Everybody's Broke ...................................... | | Columbia 02404 |
| 11/28/81 | **59** | 8 | 9 Magic Number ............................................ | | Columbia 02615 |
| 4/10/82 | **52** | 10 | 10 Lite Me Up ................................................ | | Columbia 02824 |
| 7/10/82 | **47** | 10 | 11 Gettin' To The Good Part............................ | | Columbia 03004 |
| 7/16/83 | **6** | 22 | 12 **Rockit**...............................................[I] | 71 | Columbia 04054 |
| 12/10/83+ | **26** | 14 | 13 Autodrive ................................................. | | Columbia 04268 |
| 5/19/84 | **36** | 9 | 14 Mega-Mix ...........................................[I] <br> includes: Rockit, Autodrive, Future Shock, TFS, Rough, & Chameleon '84 | *105* | Columbia 04473 |
| 8/11/84 | **41** | 8 | 15 Hardrock...............................................[I] | | Columbia 04565 |
| 4/30/88 | **25** | 10 | 16 Vibe Alive............................................... | | Columbia 07718 |
| | | | **JOHN HANDY** <br> Born in 1933 in Dallas. Jazz saxophonist. Own quintet in the mid-60s. | | |
| 6/05/76 | **13** | 17 | 1 Hard Work.............................................[I] | 46 | ABC/Impl. 31005 |
| | | | **HANSON & DAVIS** | | |
| 9/06/86 | **40** | 10 | 1 Hungry For Your Love ................................ | | Fresh 5 |
| | | | **PAUL HARDCASTLE** <br> Keyboardist/producer born in London on 12/10/57. | | |
| 11/24/84+ | **5** | 19 | 1 **Rain Forest**.........................................[I] | 57 | Profile 5059 |
| 4/27/85 | **32** | 11 | 2 King Tut................................................[I] | | Profile 5070 |
| 6/08/85 | **8** | 14 | 3 19............................................................ <br> title refers to the average age of U.S. soldiers in Vietnam | 15 | Chrysalis 42860 |
| 5/17/86 | **65** | 7 | 4 Don't Waste My Time.................................. | | Chrysalis 42965 |
| | | | **HARLEM RIVER DRIVE** | | |
| 9/27/75 | **60** | 8 | 1 Need You................................................... | | Arista 0142 |
| | | | **BEN HARNEY - see SHERYL LEE RALPH** | | |
| | | | **TONI HARPER & EDDIE BEALE SEXTET** <br> Born Rocquelle Toni Harper on 6/8/37 in Los Angeles. First recorded for Columbia in 1947. With Harry James from 1951-52. Active into the 70s on West Coast. | | |
| 8/07/48 | **15** | 1 | 1 Candy Store Blues....................................... <br> Juke Box #15 <br> Toni sang this tune in the film "Manhattan Angel" | 22 | Columbia 38229 |

| DEBUT DATE | PEAK POS | WKS CHR | ARTIST — Record Title | POP POS | Label & Number |
|---|---|---|---|---|---|
| | | | **SLIM HARPO** | | |
| | | | Born James Moore on 1/11/24 in Lobdell, Louisiana. Died of a heart attack on 1/31/70. Vocalist/harmonica player. Worked local clubs as "Harmonica Slim" into the 50s. Played on sessions with Lightnin' Slim (Otis Hicks) for Excello from 1955-56. Replaced by Lazy Lester (Leslie Johnson). First own recording as Slim Harpo, for Excello, in 1957. Operated trucking company in Baton Rouge from 1966. Wife Lovell co-wrote many of his songs. | | |
| 5/22/61 | 17 | 9 | 1 Rainin' In My Heart | 34 | Excello 2194 |
| | | | features blues guitarist Lightnin' Slim | | |
| 1/22/66 | 1² | 18 | 2 **Baby Scratch My Back** [I] | 16 | Excello 2273 |
| 7/08/67 | 37 | 4 | 3 Tip On In, Part 1 | 127 | Excello 2285 |
| 3/30/68 | 36 | 5 | 4 Te-Ni-Nee-Ni-Nu | | Excello 2294 |
| | | | **GRADY HARRELL** | | |
| | | | Los Angeles vocalist; singing professionally since age 9. With sister Rocquel in Papa's Results. Worked at Lorimar Productions. | | |
| 1/05/85 | 69 | 7 | 1 Belinda | | MCA 52485 |
| | | | **BETTY HARRIS** | | |
| | | | Born in 1943 in Orlando, Florida. Worked as maid to Big Maybelle, later brought on stage for duets with Maybelle. Worked as road manager for James Carr. | | |
| 9/28/63 | 10 | 9 | 1 **Cry To Me** | 23 | Jubilee 5456 |
| 1/04/64 | 89 | 4 | 2 His Kiss | Hot | Jubilee 5465 |
| 7/15/67 | 16 | 11 | 3 Nearer To You | 85 | Sansu 466 |
| 6/07/69 | 44 | 5 | 4 Cry To Me [R] | | Jubilee 5653 |
| | | | **BOBBY HARRIS** | | |
| 2/06/65 | 38 | 3 | 1 We Can't Believe You're Gone | 107 | Atlantic 2270 |
| | | | **BRENDA JO HARRIS** | | |
| 9/28/68 | 50 | 2 | 1 Standing On The Outside | 131 | Roulette 7021 |
| | | | **DAMON HARRIS** | | |
| | | | Vocalist from Baltimore. With the Vandalls vocal group. Lead singer of The Temptations from 1971-75. Re-formed the Vandalls as Impact. Went solo in 1978. | | |
| 2/10/79 | 96 | 4 | 1 It's Music | | WMOT 848 |
| | | | **DAVID HARRIS** | | |
| 5/25/74 | 82 | 7 | 1 (These Are) The Moments | | Pleasure 1104 |
| | | | **EDDIE HARRIS** | | |
| | | | Born in 1936 in Chicago. Jazz tenor saxophonist/vocalist. Noted for experimentation with electronic reed instruments. Les McCann (b: 9/23/35 in Lexington, KY) is a jazz keyboardist/vocalist. | | |
| 5/01/61 | 16 | 5 | 1 Exodus [I] | 36 | Vee-Jay 378 |
| | | | jazz version of the main theme from the film of the same title | | |
| 7/06/68 | 11 | 12 | 2 Listen Here [I] | 45 | Atlantic 2487 |
| 1/31/70 | 35 | 2 | 3 Compared To What/ | 85 | |
| 2/21/70 | 44 | 2 | 4 Cold Duck | | Atlantic 2694 |
| | | | above 2: **LES McCANN & EDDIE HARRIS** recorded live at Montreux Jazz Festival, Switzerland on 6/21/69 | | |
| 11/02/74 | 67 | 7 | 5 Is It In [I] | 107 | Atlantic 5120 |
| | | | also released on Atlantic 3216 | | |
| | | | **GENE HARRIS** | | |
| | | | Born in Benton Harbor, Michigan. Pianist; played professionally since age 7, own radio show at age 12. Formed own group, the Three Sounds, with Andrew Simpkins (bass) and William Dowdy (drums). First recorded for Blue Note in 1958. | | |
| 10/19/74 | 98 | 2 | 1 Higga-Boom | | Blue Note 551 |
| | | | **HUEY "BABY" HARRIS** | | |
| 9/07/85 | 58 | 10 | 1 You've Got To Be A Winner | | Profile 5075 |
| | | | **MAJOR HARRIS** | | |
| | | | Born on 2/9/47 in Richmond, Virginia. Sang with The Jarmels, Teenagers, and Impacts in the early 60s. With The Delfonics from 1971-74. Formed Boogie Blues Band with vocals by Allison Hobbs, Phyllis Newman and Karen Dempsey. | | |
| 1/11/75 | 98 | 2 | 1 Each Morning I Wake Up | | Atlantic 3217 |
| | | | shown as: **THE MAJOR HARRIS BOOGIE BLUES BAND** | | |
| 3/15/75 | 1¹ | 20 | 2●Love Won't Let Me Wait | 5 | Atlantic 3248 |
| 12/06/75+ | 24 | 12 | 3 I Got Over Love | | Atlantic 3303 |
| 4/03/76 | 46 | 8 | 4 Jealousy | 73 | Atlantic 3321 |
| 6/26/76 | 91 | 3 | 5 It's Got To Be Magic | | Atlantic 3336 |

| DEBUT DATE | PEAK POS | WKS CHR | ARTIST — Record Title | POP POS | Label & Number |
|---|---|---|---|---|---|
| | | | **MAJOR HARRIS — Continued** | | |
| 10/23/76 | **57** | 5 | 6 Laid Back Love......................................... | *91* | WMOT 4002 |
| 10/15/83 | **52** | 10 | 7 All My Life.............................................. | | Pop Art 1401 |
| | | | **PEPPERMINT HARRIS** | | |
| | | | Born Harrison D. Nelson on 7/17/25 in Texarkana, Texas. Vocalist/guitarist. Lightnin' Hopkins took him to Gold Star to record in 1948. First called self Peppermint Nelson. Still active in music in Houston. | | |
| 2/11/50 | **4** | 3 | 1 **Raining In My Heart** ................................. | | Sittin in 543 |
| | | | Juke Box #4 / Best Seller #6 | | |
| 9/15/51 | **1**² | 20 | 2 **I Got Loaded** ......................................... | | Aladdin 3097 |
| | | | Juke Box #1(2) / Best Seller #1(1) | | |
| | | | with Maxwell Davis and his All-Stars | | |
| | | | **PHIL HARRIS** | | |
| | | | Bandleader/drummer/radio-TV-movie personality. Co-hosted a radio program with his wife, actress Alice Faye, from 1947-54. | | |
| 9/07/46 | **4** | 1 | 1 **The Darktown Poker Club** ........................ [C] | *10* | ARA 116 |
| | | | from the Broadway musical "Ziegfield Follies of 1914" | | |
| | | | **ROLF HARRIS** | | |
| | | | Born in Perth, Australia on 3/30/30. Played piano from age nine. Moved to England in the mid-50s. Developed his unique "wobble board sound" out of a sheet of masonite. Had own BBC-TV series from 1970. | | |
| 7/20/63 | **19** | 5 | 1 Tie Me Kangaroo Down, Sport ..................... [N] | *3* | Epic 9596 |
| | | | **THURSTON HARRIS** | | |
| | | | Born on 7/11/31 in Indianapolis. First recorded with the Lamplighters in 1953. | | |
| 10/28/57 | **2**¹ | 11 | 1 **Little Bitty Pretty One**.............................. | *6* | Aladdin 3398 |
| | | | Jockey #2 / Best Seller #5 | | |
| | | | vocals by The Sharps | | |
| 2/03/58 | **14** | 2 | 2 Do What You Did ..................................... | *57* | Aladdin 3399 |
| | | | Jockey #14 | | |
| | | | **WYNONIE HARRIS**   ★★**132**★★ | | |
| | | | Born on 8/24/15 in Omaha, Nebraska. Died of cancer on 6/14/69 (53). Nicknamed "Mr. Blues". Vocalist/self-taught drummer. Worked as a dancer and comedian. To Los Angeles in 1940. Hired as singer by Lucky Millinder in 1944. First recorded for Decca in 1944. Original blues-shouter in the style of Joe Turner and Roy Brown, a pioneer of R&B. Left music from 1953-60; brief comeback in 1967. Also see Lucky Millinder. | | |
| 1/05/46 | **3** | 1 | 1 **Wynonie's Blues** ...................................... | | Apollo 362 |
| | | | with the Illinois Jacquet All-Stars | | |
| 9/28/46 | **2**¹ | 3 | 2 **Playful Baby** .......................................... | | Apollo 372 |
| | | | with the Johnnie Alston All-Stars | | |
| 5/01/48 | **1**¹ | 25 | 3 **Good Rockin' Tonight** ................................ | | King 4210 |
| | | | Best Seller #1(1) / Juke Box #1(1) | | |
| | | | widely considered a historic precursor of rock & roll | | |
| 7/17/48 | **8** | 9 | 4 **Lolly Pop Mama** ...................................... | | King 4226 |
| | | | Best Seller #8 / Juke Box #9 | | |
| 2/26/49 | **7** | 6 | 5 **Grandma Plays The Numbers/** | | King 4276 |
| | | | Best Seller #7 / Juke Box #8 | | |
| 2/26/49 | **10** | 3 | 6 **I Feel That Old Age Coming On**.................. | | |
| | | | Juke Box #10 / Best Seller #12 | | |
| 5/28/49 | **4** | 13 | 7 **Drinkin' Wine Spo-Dee-O-Dee**...................... | | King 4292 |
| | | | Best Seller #4 / Juke Box #4 | | |
| | | | with the Joe Morris Orchestra | | |
| 8/27/49 | **1**² | 18 | 8 **All She Wants To Do Is Rock/** | | |
| | | | Juke Box #1(2) / Best Seller #1(1) | | |
| 10/01/49 | **10** | 2 | 9 **I Want My Fanny Brown**............................ | | King 4304 |
| | | | Juke Box #10 | | |
| 1/14/50 | **3** | 8 | 10 **Sittin' On It All The Time** ........................ | | King 4330 |
| | | | Juke Box #3 / Best Seller #7 | | |
| 3/25/50 | **5** | 3 | 11 **I Like My Baby's Pudding**.......................... | | King 4342 |
| | | | Juke Box #5 / Best Seller #9 | | |
| 7/29/50 | **6** | 6 | 12 **Good Morning Judge** ................................ | | King 4378 |
| | | | Juke Box #6 | | |
| 12/02/50 | **7** | 2 | 13 **Oh Babe**.............................................. | | King 4418 |
| | | | Best Seller #7 / Juke Box #8 | | |
| | | | with the Lucky Millinder Orchestra | | |
| 8/18/51 | **6** | 11 | 14 **Bloodshot Eyes** ...................................... | | King 4461 |
| | | | Best Seller #6 / Juke Box #6 | | |
| | | | #4 Country hit for Hank Penny in 1950 | | |

| DEBUT DATE | PEAK POS | WKS CHR | ARTIST — Record Title | POP POS | Label & Number |
|---|---|---|---|---|---|
| | | | **WYNONIE HARRIS — Continued** | | |
| 1/05/52 | **5** | 3 | 15 Lovin' Machine.............................. | | King 4485 |
| | | | Juke Box #5 / Best Seller #7 | | |
| | | | with the Todd Rhodes Orchestra | | |
| | | | **SPENCER HARRISON - see NORMAN CONNORS** | | |
| | | | **WILBERT HARRISON** | | |
| | | | Born on 1/5/29 in Charlotte, North Carolina. Plays several instruments as a "one-man band". Joined W.C. Baker band. First recorded for Glades in 1952. | | |
| 4/20/59 | **1** 7 | 15 | 1 **Kansas City** .................................... *1* | | Fury 1023 |
| | | | written by Jerry Leiber & Mike Stoller in 1952 as "K.C. Lovin'" | | |
| | | | **DEBBIE HARRY** | | |
| | | | Born on 7/1/45 in New York City. Lead singer of Blondie. In films "Unmade Beds", "Union City", "Videodrome" and "Hairspray". | | |
| 9/19/81 | **71** | 5 | 1 Backfired.................................... *43* | | Chrysalis 2526 |
| | | | **DAN HARTMAN** | | |
| | | | Multi-instrumentalist/songwriter/producer from Harrisburg, Pennsylvania. Member of the Edgar Winter Group from 1972-76. Own studio called the Schoolhouse in Westport, Connecticut. | | |
| 11/11/78 | **44** | 11 | 1●Instant Replay............................ *29* | | Blue Sky 2772 |
| 5/26/84 | **60** | 13 | 2 I Can Dream About You................... *6* | | MCA 52378 |
| | | | from the film "Streets Of Fire" | | |
| 12/08/84+ | **58** | 10 | 3 We Are The Young ......................... *25* | | MCA 52471 |
| | | | **HARVEY & THE MOONGLOWS - see THE MOONGLOWS** | | |
| | | | **HASSAN & 7-11** | | |
| 5/12/84 | **65** | 7 | 1 City Life .................................... | | Easy St. 4508 |
| | | | **ROGER HATCHER** | | |
| | | | Born on 9/29/46 in Birmingham, Alabama. Brother of vocalists Edwin Starr and Willie Hatcher. First recorded as "Little" Roger Hatcher for Dotty's in 1964. | | |
| 2/28/76 | **92** | 4 | 1 We Gonna Make It........................... | | Brown Dog 9009 |
| | | | **DONNY HATHAWAY** ★★176★★ | | |
| | | | Born on 10/1/45 in Chicago; raised in St. Louis. Songwriter/keyboardist/producer/arranger; gospel singer since age 3. Attended Washington, DC's Howard University on a fine arts scholarship; classmate of Roberta Flack. Producer/writer for Aretha Franklin, Jerry Butler, The Staple Singers, Carla Thomas, and many others. Committed suicide by jumping from the 15th floor of New York City's Essex House hotel on 1/13/79 (33). | | |
| 2/22/69 | **45** | 2 | 1 I Thank You Baby ......................... | | Curtom 1935 |
| | | | JUNE (Conquest) **& DONNIE** | | |
| 1/10/70 | **23** | 11 | 2 The Ghetto (Part 1)...................... *87* | | Atco 6719 |
| 6/12/71 | **8** | 13 | 3 **You've Got A Friend** .................... *29* | | Atlantic 2808 |
| 10/30/71 | **30** | 6 | 4 You've Lost That Lovin' Feelin' ....... *71* | | Atlantic 2837 |
| 3/25/72 | **25** | 7 | 5 Little Ghetto Boy ........................ *109* | | Atco 6880 |
| 5/13/72 | **21** | 7 | 6 Giving Up ................................. *81* | | Atco 6884 |
| 6/17/72 | **1** 1 | 13 | 7●**Where Is The Love** ..................... *5* | | Atlantic 2879 |
| | | | 3-4 & 7: **ROBERTA FLACK & DONNY HATHAWAY** | | |
| 6/17/72 | **41** | 5 | 8 I Thank You........................[R] *94* | | Curtom 1071 |
| | | | **DONNY HATHAWAY & JUNE CONQUEST** | | |
| 10/21/72 | **20** | 10 | 9 I Love You More Than You'll Ever Know .......... *60* | | Atco 6903 |
| 6/30/73 | **16** | 11 | 10 Love, Love, Love....................... *44* | | Atco 6928 |
| 12/22/73+ | **67** | 9 | 11 Come Little Children .................. | | Atco 6951 |
| 2/11/78 | **1** 2 | 19 | 12●**The Closer I Get To You** ............... *2* | | Atlantic 3463 |
| 8/12/78 | **17** | 15 | 13 You Were Meant For Me ............... | | Atco 7092 |
| 1/26/80 | **8** | 17 | 14 **You Are My Heaven**................... *47* | | Atlantic 3627 |
| 5/03/80 | **18** | 8 | 15 Back Together Again ................... *56* | | Atlantic 3661 |
| | | | 12, 14 & 15: **ROBERTA FLACK with DONNY HATHAWAY** | | |
| | | | **COLEMAN HAWKINS** | | |
| | | | Born on 11/21/04 in St. Joseph, Missouri. Died on 5/19/69 (64). Tenor saxophonist/pianist/cellist. With Mamie Smith and Her Jazz Hounds from 1921-23, and Fletcher Henderson from 1924-34. European tours from 1934-39. Formed own band in 1939. Frequently toured with Jazz At The Philharmonic. Worked until the time of his death. | | |
| 7/01/44 | **4** | 9 | 1 **Body And Soul** .........................[I] *13* | | Bluebird 0825 |
| | | | jazz classic selected for NARAS Hall Of Fame; recorded in 1939 | | |

| DEBUT DATE | PEAK POS | WKS CHR | ARTIST — Record Title | POP POS | Label & Number |
|---|---|---|---|---|---|
| | | | **DALE HAWKINS** Born Delmar Allen Hawkins on 8/22/38 in Goldmine, Louisiana. Rockabilly vocalist/ guitarist. First recorded for Checker in 1956. Toured with R&B package shows. Record production work since 1965. | | |
| 6/10/57 | **7** | 2 | 1 **Susie-Q**...................................................... Jockey #7 with James Burton on guitar; recorded at KWKH radio in Shreveport, Louisiana | *27* | Checker 863 |
| | | | **THE EDWIN HAWKINS' SINGERS** Formed by Edwin Hawkins and Betty Watson in Oakland in 1967 as the Northern California State Youth Choir. Member Dorothy Morrison went on to a solo career. First recorded privately for fund-raising at concerts. | | |
| 5/10/69 | **2²** | 10 | 1●**Oh Happy Day**............................................. lead vocal by Dorothy Combs Morrison | *4* | Pavilion 20001 |
| | | | **ERSKINE HAWKINS & HIS ORCHESTRA** ★★**164**★★ Born on 7/26/14 in Birmingham, Alabama. Trumpeter/composer. Nicknamed the "Twentieth Century Gabriel Of The Trumpet". Member of the 'Bama State Collegians, at State Teacher's College, in Montgomery. Band became the Erskine Hawkins band in 1934. Very popular at the Savoy Ballroom in New York City. Active with own quartet into the 70s. | | |
| 12/26/42+ | **5** | 3 | 1 **Bicycle Bounce** ............................................ [I] | | Bluebird 11432 |
| 7/31/43 | **1¹⁴** | 29 | 2 **Don't Cry, Baby**........................................... recorded on 5/27/42 | *11* | Bluebird 0813 |
| 1/29/44 | **5** | 6 | 3 **Cherry**...................................................... recorded on 7/18/39 | *15* | Bluebird 0819 |
| 3/31/45 | **1⁶** | 25 | 4 **Tippin' In** ................................................. [I] | *9* | Victor 1639 |
| 5/19/45 | **2²** | 10 | 5 **Caldonia**................................................... vocal by Ace Harris | *12* | Victor 1659 |
| 10/13/45 | **4** | 1 | 6 **15 Years & I'm Still Serving Time**................. 2-3 & 6: vocals by Jimmy Mitchelle | | Victor 1685 |
| 6/29/46 | **5** | 2 | 7 **Sneakin' Out**.............................................. [I] | | Victor 1883 |
| 7/13/46 | **2¹** | 10 | 8 **I've Got A Right To Cry**............................... vocal by Laura Washington | | Victor 1902 |
| 11/16/46 | **3** | 4 | 9 **After Hours/** recorded in 1940 | [I] | |
| 5/03/47 | **2¹** | 8 | 10 **Hawk's Boogie**........................................... [I] | | Victor 2169 |
| 2/19/49 | **8** | 1 | 11 **Corn Bread** .............................................. Juke Box #8 / Best Seller #11 | | Victor 3326 |
| 12/30/50 | **6** | 1 | 12 **Tennessee Waltz**........................................ Best Seller #6 | | Coral 60313 |
| | | | **JENNELL HAWKINS** Keyboardist/vocalist from Los Angeles. First recorded with Richard Berry as Rickey & Jennell for Flair in 1954. | | |
| 12/11/61 | **16** | 4 | 1 Moments ................................................... | *50* | Amazon 1003 |
| 8/04/62 | **17** | 5 | 2 Money (That's What I Want) ........................... | | Amazon 708 |
| | | | **RONNIE HAWKINS** Born on 1/10/35 in Huntsville, AR. Formed The Hawks in 1952. To Canada in 1958; assembled group later known as "The Band". Back-up group became Crowbar in 1970. | | |
| 9/21/59 | **7** | 9 | 1 **Mary Lou** ................................................. | *26* | Roulette 4177 |
| | | | **ROY HAWKINS** Vocalist/pianist, active in the Oakland, California area since the mid-40s. First recorded for Cavatone in 1948. | | |
| 2/25/50 | **2²** | 19 | 1 **Why Do Things Happen To Me**....................... Juke Box #2 / Best Seller #3 also shown as "Why Do Everything Happen To Me" | | Modern 734 |
| 8/04/51 | **6** | 5 | 2 **Thrill Is Gone** ........................................... Best Seller #6 / Juke Box #8 original version of B.B. King's hit; written by Hawkins | | Modern 826 |
| | | | **SAM HAWKINS** | | |
| 5/29/65 | **10** | 10 | 1 **Hold On Baby**............................................. | *133* | Blue Cat 112 |
| | | | **EDGAR HAYES & HIS STARDUSTERS** Born on 5/23/04 in Lexington, Kentucky. Pianist/arranger. With small bands from 1924-30. With Mills Blue Rhythm Band from 1930-36, own big band from 1937-41. Band member, Joe Garland, wrote "In The Mood"; first recorded in 1938 by Hayes' band. Moved to Riverside, California in 1942. Led quartet, The Stardusters, until the early 50s. Active into the early 70s. | | |
| 2/26/49 | **11** | 2 | 1 Fat Meat And Greens ................................. [I] Juke Box #11 | | Exclusive 78 |

| DEBUT DATE | PEAK POS | WKS CHR | ARTIST — Record Title | POP POS | Label & Number |
|---|---|---|---|---|---|
| | | | **EDGAR HAYES & HIS STARDUSTERS — Continued** | | |
| 9/24/49 | **12** | 1 | 2 Blues At Dawn 1 & 2 ................................ [I]<br>Juke Box #12 | | Exclusive 110 |
| | | | **ISAAC HAYES**   ★★101★★ | | |
| | | | Born on 8/20/42 in Covington, Tennessee. Singer/songwriter/keyboardist/producer. Session musician for Otis Redding and other artists on the Stax label. Teamed with songwriter David Porter to compose "Soul Man", "Hold On! I'm A Comin'", and many others. Composed film score for "Shaft", "Tough Guys" and "Truck Turner". | | |
| 9/06/69 | **13** | 13 | 1 Walk On By/ | 30 | |
| 8/30/69 | **37** | 5 | 2  By The Time I Get To Phoenix ...................... | 37 | Enterprise 9003 |
| 9/19/70 | **23** | 7 | 3 I Stand Accused ........................................ | 42 | Enterprise 9017 |
| 5/22/71 | **5** | 9 | 4 **Never Can Say Goodbye** ............................ | 22 | Enterprise 9031 |
| 10/16/71 | **2**³ | 11 | 5 **Theme From Shaft** ................................ | 1 | Enterprise 0038 |
| | | | from the Richard Roundtree film "Shaft" | | |
| 2/26/72 | **3** | 9 | 6 **Do Your Thing** ...................................... | 30 | Enterprise 9042 |
| 4/08/72 | **25** | 8 | 7 Let's Stay Together ............................... [I] | 48 | Enterprise 9045 |
| 5/20/72 | **37** | 5 | 8 Ain't That Loving You (For More Reasons Than One) ..... | 86 | Enterprise 9049 |
| | | | **ISAAC HAYES & DAVID PORTER** | | |
| 10/14/72 | **19** | 11 | 9 Theme From The Men ........................... [I] | 38 | Enterprise 9058 |
| | | | from the ABC-TV series "The Men" | | |
| 12/15/73+ | **7** | 16 | 10 **Joy - Pt. I** | 30 | Enterprise 9085 |
| 4/27/74 | **18** | 13 | 11 Wonderful ........................................... | 71 | Enterprise 9095 |
| 8/03/74 | **72** | 4 | 12 Title Theme ........................................ | | Enterprise 9104 |
| | | | from the film "Three Tough Guys" | | |
| 8/09/75 | **13** | 11 | 13 Chocolate Chip ..................................... | 92 | HBS/ABC 12118 |
| 11/01/75 | **20** | 12 | 14 Come Live With Me ............................... | | HBS/ABC 12138 |
| 3/13/76 | **60** | 7 | 15 Disco Connection .................................. | | HBS/ABC 12171 |
| | | | shown as: **ISAAC HAYES MOVEMENT** | | |
| 4/17/76 | **58** | 5 | 16 Rock Me Easy Baby (Pt. 1) ...................... | | HBS/ABC 12176 |
| 3/19/77 | **65** | 7 | 17 By The Time I Get To Phoenix/Say A Little Prayer ............................. | | ABC 12253 |
| | | | **ISAAC HAYES & DIONNE WARWICK** | | |
| 1/21/78 | **42** | 10 | 18 Out Of The Ghetto ............................... | 107 | Polydor 14446 |
| 5/06/78 | **96** | 2 | 19 Moonlight Lovin' ................................... | | Polydor 14464 |
| 12/16/78+ | **19** | 11 | 20 Zeke The Freak .................................... | | Polydor 14521 |
| 9/15/79 | **11** | 22 | 21 Don't Let Go ....................................... | 18 | Polydor 2011 |
| 12/01/79+ | **30** | 11 | 22 Do You Wanna Make Love ...................... | | Spring 2036 |
| | | | **MILLIE JACKSON & ISAAC HAYES** | | |
| 3/22/80 | **78** | 4 | 23 You Never Cross My Mind ...................... | | Spring 2063 |
| | | | **MILLIE JACKSON & ISAAC HAYES** | | |
| 4/19/80 | **89** | 2 | 24 A Few More Kisses To Go ....................... | | Polydor 2068 |
| 5/24/80 | **49** | 9 | 25 I Ain't Never ........................................ | | Polydor 2090 |
| 8/23/80 | **86** | 2 | 26 It's All In The Game ............................. | 107 | Polydor 2102 |
| 10/25/86 | **9** | 16 | 27 Ike's Rap/ | | |
| | | 16 | 28  Hey Girl ........................................... | | Columbia 06363 |
| 2/14/87 | **43** | 10 | 29 Thing For You ...................................... | | Columbia 06655 |
| | | | **LINDA HAYES** | | |
| | | | Born Bertha Williams on 12/10/23 in Linden, New Jersey. Sister of Tony Williams, lead singer of The Platters. | | |
| 2/07/53 | **2**² | 7 | 1 **Yes I Know (What You're Putting Down)** ........<br>Juke Box #2 / Best Seller #3<br>with the Red Callender Sextet;<br>answer song to Willie Mabon's "I Don't Know" | | R-I-H 244 |
| 1/02/54 | **10** | 1 | 2 **Take Me Back** ..................................<br>Juke Box #10<br>with the Monroe Tucker Orchestra | | Hollywood 1003 |
| | | | **DICK HAYMES** | | |
| | | | Born on 9/13/16 in Buenos Aires, Argentina; raised in U.S. Ballad singer; sang with Harry James, Benny Goodman, and Tommy Dorsey in the early 40s, and appeared in various movies from 1944-53. Married briefly to actress Rita Hayworth. Died on 3/28/80. | | |
| 6/26/43 | **2**¹ | 10 | 1 **It Can't Be Wrong** ...................................<br>from the film "Now, Voyager" | 1 | Decca 18557 |
| 7/10/43 | **1**⁴ | 16 | 2 **You'll Never Know** .....................................<br>from the film "Hello, Frisco, Hello"; won an Oscar in 1943 | 1 | Decca 18556 |

| DEBUT DATE | PEAK POS | WKS CHR | ARTIST — Record Title | POP POS | Label & Number |
|---|---|---|---|---|---|
| | | | **DICK HAYMES — Continued** | | |
| 10/16/43 | 8 | 1 | 3 I Heard You Cried Last Night ....................... | *13* | Decca 18558 |
| | | | from the film "Cinderella Swings It"; all of the above with the Song Spinners | | |
| | | | **LEON HAYWOOD** ★★149★★ | | |
| | | | Born on 2/11/42 in Houston. Singer/keyboardist. With Big Jay McNeely and Sam Cooke in the early 60s. | | |
| 10/30/65 | 13 | 7 | 1 She's With Her Other Love............................. | *92* | Imperial 66123 |
| | | | shown as: **LEON HAYWARD** | | |
| 7/29/67 | 21 | 13 | 2 It's Got To Be Mellow.................................. | *63* | Decca 32164 |
| 1/06/68 | 35 | 7 | 3 Mellow Moonlight ....................................... | *92* | Decca 32230 |
| 2/02/74 | 11 | 15 | 4 Keep It In The Family/ | *50* | |
| 4/20/74 | 63 | 9 | 5 Long As There's You (I Got Love)................... | | 20th Century 2065 |
| 8/03/74 | 35 | 10 | 6 Sugar Lump ............................................. | *108* | 20th Century 2103 |
| 12/07/74+ | 21 | 16 | 7 Believe Half Of What You See (And None Of What You Hear)....................................... | *94* | 20th Century 2146 |
| 5/24/75 | 19 | 17 | 8 Come An' Get Yourself Some........................ | *83* | 20th Century 2191 |
| 9/13/75 | 7 | 15 | 9 I Want'a Do Something Freaky To You .......... | *15* | 20th Century 2228 |
| 1/03/76 | 26 | 13 | 10 Just Your Fool ......................................... | *102* | 20th Century 2264 |
| 5/15/76 | 13 | 13 | 11 Strokin' (Pt. II)........................................ | *101* | 20th Century 2285 |
| 10/16/76 | 63 | 6 | 12 The Streets Will Love You To Death - Part 1 ...... | *107* | Columbia 10413 |
| 10/01/77 | 54 | 12 | 13 Super Sexy ............................................. | | MCA 40793 |
| 2/11/78 | 91 | 5 | 14 Double My Pleasure .................................. | | MCA 40849 |
| 5/06/78 | 84 | 4 | 15 Fine And Healthy Thing ............................. | | MCA 40889 |
| 9/02/78 | 24 | 15 | 16 Party .................................................... | | MCA 40941 |
| 2/16/80 | 2² | 19 | 17 Don't Push It Don't Force It ...................... | *49* | 20th Century 2443 |
| 7/05/80 | 67 | 5 | 18 If You're Lookin' For A Night Of Fun (Look Past Me, I'm Not The One) ............................... | | 20th Century 2454 |
| 5/14/83 | 27 | 12 | 19 I'm Out To Catch............................... | | Casablanca 812164 |
| 10/22/83 | 83 | 4 | 20 T.V. Mama ............................................. | | Casablanca 814217 |
| 9/08/84 | 22 | 13 | 21 Tenderoni ............................................. | | Modern 99708 |
| | | | **HAZE** | | |
| 3/15/75 | 89 | 6 | 1 I Do Love My Lady ................................... | | ASI 202 |
| | | | **MURRAY HEAD** | | |
| | | | British singer/actor. Played juvenile lead in 1971 film "Sunday, Bloody Sunday". | | |
| 5/18/85 | 89 | 3 | 1 One Night In Bangkok............................... | *3* | Chess 13988 |
| | | | from the Tim Rice, Benny Andersson & Bjorn Ulvaeus musical "Chess" | | |
| | | | **ROY HEAD & THE TRAITS** | | |
| | | | Born on 1/9/53 in Three Rivers, Texas. Rock-country singer/guitarist. | | |
| 9/18/65 | 2¹ | 14 | 1 Treat Her Right.............................. | *2* | Back Beat 546 |
| | | | **THE HEART & SOUL ORCHESTRA** | | |
| | | | 33-piece disco act assembled by former disc jockey Frankie Crocker. | | |
| 3/05/77 | 85 | 5 | 1 Love In "C" Minor ..................................... [I] | *46* | Casablanca 876 |
| | | | **THE HEARTBEATS** | | |
| | | | Group formed in 1954 in Queens, New York. Consisted of James "Shep" Sheppard, Wally Roker, Walter Crump, Robbie Adams, and Vernon Walker. Group disbanded in 1960. Sheppard formed Shep & The Limelites in 1961; was murdered on 1/24/70. | | |
| 11/17/56+ | 5 | 15 | 1 A Thousand Miles Away ............................. | *53* | Rama 216 |
| | | | Best Seller #5 / Jockey #6 with the Al Browne Orchestra; originally released on Hull 720 | | |
| | | | **THE HEARTS** | | |
| | | | Female group formed in New York City in 1954. Consisted of Joyce James, Joyce Peterson, Jeanette "Baby" Washington, and Zell Sanders. Sanders, the mother of Johnnylouise Richardson of Johnnie & Joe, produced their records. Not to be confused with Lee Andrews' male group of the same name. | | |
| 3/26/55 | 8 | 15 | 1 Lonely Nights................................ | | Baton 208 |
| | | | Best Seller #8 / Jockey #10 with the Al Sears Orchestra | | |

| DEBUT DATE | PEAK POS | WKS CHR | ARTIST — Record Title | POP POS | Label & Number |
|---|---|---|---|---|---|
| | | | **JOHNNY HEARTSMAN** Born on 2/9/37 in San Fernando, California. Singer/guitarist/pianist. Popular session man. First recorded for Rhythm in 1953. | | |
| 6/10/57 | **13** | 1 | 1  Johnny's House Party (Pts. I & II)...................... Best Seller #13 with the Gaylarks (vocal group) | | Music City 807 |
| | | | **HEAT** | | |
| 4/12/80 | **45** | 8 | 1  Baby (This Love That We've Found)................. | | MCA 41203 |
| 7/19/80 | **57** | 7 | 2  Just Like You........................................ | | MCA 41267 |
| | | | **HEATH BROTHERS** | | |
| 5/02/81 | **76** | 5 | 1  Dreamin'........................................... | | Columbia 02014 |
| | | | **WALTER HEATH** | | |
| 11/09/74+ | **51** | 12 | 1  I Am Your Leader................................... | | Buddah 435 |
| | | | **HEATWAVE** Multi-national, inter-racial group formed in Germany by Johnnie and Keith Wilder of Dayton, OH. Johnnie injured in auto accident in 1979, paralyzed from neck down. | | |
| 7/02/77 | **5** | 26 | 1▲Boogie Nights..................................... | 2 | Epic 50370 |
| 12/24/77+ | **2**² | 17 | 2●Always And Forever............................... | 18 | Epic 50490 |
| 4/08/78 | **3** | 19 | 3▲The Groove Line.................................. | 7 | Epic 50524 |
| 9/02/78 | **49** | 10 | 4  Mind Blowing Decisions........................... | | Epic 50586 |
| 5/05/79 | **30** | 11 | 5  Eyeballin'......................................... | | Epic 50699 |
| 11/01/80 | **21** | 15 | 6  Gangsters Of The Groove........................... | 110 | Epic 50945 |
| 2/21/81 | **74** | 7 | 7  Where Did I Go Wrong............................. | | Epic 51005 |
| 6/12/82 | **54** | 8 | 8  Lettin' It Loose................................... | | Epic 02904 |
| | | | **HEAVEN & EARTH** Chicago vocal group, consisting of brothers Dwight (falsetto lead) & James (bass) Dukes, Keith Steward (tenor), and Michael Brown (baritone). Brown was replaced by Dean Williams from 1978-79 and Greg Rose from 1979-81. Steward joined Cashmere in 1982. | | |
| 3/13/76 | **83** | 5 | 1  I Can't Seem To Forget You ....................... | | Gec 1000 |
| 8/12/78 | **42** | 12 | 2  Guess Who's Back In Town ........................ | | Mercury 74013 |
| 8/11/79 | **78** | 6 | 3  I Feel A Groove Under My Feet .................... | | Mercury 74081 |
| 10/20/79 | **63** | 7 | 4  I Only Have Eyes For You ......................... | | Mercury 76012 |
| 5/02/81 | **47** | 10 | 5  I Really Love You.................................. | | WMOT 02028 |
| | | | **HEAVY D. & THE BOYZ** Rap quartet from Mt. Vernon, New York: Leader Heavy D. (Dwight Meyers), G. Whiz (Glen Parrish), Trouble T-Roy (Troy Dixon) & DJ Eddie F (Edward Ferrell). | | |
| 12/20/86+ | **60** | 14 | 1  Mr. Big Stuff.................................... | | MCA 52962 |
| 2/27/88 | **12** | 13 | 2  Don't You Know ................................. | | MCA 53255 |
| | | | **BOBBY HEBB** Born on 7/26/41 in Nashville. Singer/songwriter/multi-instrumentalist. Featured on the Grand Ole Opry at age 12. His brother Hal was a member of the Marigolds. | | |
| 6/25/66 | **3** | 16 | 1●Sunny............................................ | 2 | Philips 40365 |
| 10/22/66 | **40** | 3 | 2  A Satisfied Mind ................................. | 39 | Philips 40400 |
| 1/10/76 | **94** | 2 | 3  Sunny 76 ......................................... | | Laurie 3638 |
| | | | **DONALD HEIGHT** Also see the Hollywood Flames. | | |
| 11/26/66+ | **20** | 8 | 1  My Baby's Gone.................................. | | Shout 204 |
| 3/29/69 | **47** | 3 | 2  Games People Play ............................... | | Jubilee 5648 |
| | | | **BOBBY HELMS** Born on 8/15/33 in Bloomington, Indiana. Singer/guitarist. Appeared on father's local TV show for 6 years. | | |
| 11/04/57 | **8** | 9 | 1  My Special Angel ................................. Best Seller #8 | 7 | Decca 30423 |
| | | | **JIMMY HELMS** Born in 1944 in Florida. Singer/trumpeter. Moved to Columbus, Ohio at an early age. In Fort Jackson Army Band. Formed own record company, Oracle. Frequent appearances on the Merv Griffin TV show. In the musical "Hair". | | |
| 7/28/73 | **92** | 3 | 1  Gonna Make You An Offer ........................ | | MGM 14540 |

| DEBUT DATE | PEAK POS | WKS CHR | ARTIST — Record Title | POP POS | Label & Number |
|---|---|---|---|---|---|
| | | | **FINIS HENDERSON** | | |
| | | | Vocalist from Chicago. Former lead singer in Weapons Of Peace. Later moved to Los Angeles. | | |
| 6/25/83 | 48 | 13 | 1  Skip To My Lou ............................................... | | Motown 1669 |
| | | | **JOE HENDERSON** | | |
| | | | Born in 1938 in Como, Mississippi; raised in Gary, Indiana. Died in 1966. Moved to Nashville in 1958. With the Fairfield Four gospel group. | | |
| 2/03/62 | 7 | 10 | 1  **Baby Don't Leave Me**.................................... | *106* | Todd 1066 |
| 5/19/62 | 2[1] | 16 | 2  **Snap Your Fingers**.................................... | 8 | Todd 1072 |
| | | | **MICHAEL HENDERSON** | | |
| | | | Born in 1951 in Yazoo City, Mississippi. Singer/bass player. To Detroit in the early 60s. Worked as session musician. Toured with Stevie Wonder, Aretha Franklin and Miles Davis. Also see Norman Connors. | | |
| 12/18/76+ | 23 | 13 | 1  Be My Girl ................................................... | *101* | Buddah 552 |
| 4/16/77 | 80 | 4 | 2  You Haven't Made It To The Top...................... | | Buddah 565 |
| 7/30/77 | 27 | 14 | 3  I Can't Help It.............................................. | *103* | Buddah 578 |
| 12/03/77 | 82 | 8 | 4  Won't You Be Mine........................................ | | Buddah 586 |
| 7/01/78 | 3 | 20 | 5  **Take Me I'm Yours**...................................... | 88 | Buddah 597 |
| 10/28/78 | 15 | 13 | 6  In The Night-Time ......................................... | | Buddah 600 |
| 8/04/79 | 56 | 7 | 7  Do It All ...................................................... | | Buddah 609 |
| 10/20/79 | 62 | 8 | 8  To Be Loved ................................................. | | Buddah 615 |
| 7/05/80 | 4 | 24 | 9  **Wide Receiver Part 1** ................................. | | Buddah 622 |
| 11/01/80 | 27 | 15 | 10  Prove It ....................................................... | | Buddah 623 |
| 2/28/81 | 78 | 4 | 11  Reach Out For Me ......................................... | | Buddah 626 |
| 11/14/81 | 51 | 7 | 12  (We Are Here To) Geek You Up ......................... | | Buddah 629 |
| 1/23/82 | 68 | 6 | 13  Make It Easy On Yourself .............................. | | Buddah 630 |
| 4/23/83 | 33 | 10 | 14  Fickle ......................................................... | | Buddah 800 |
| 3/15/86 | 17 | 14 | 15  Do It To Me Good (Tonight) ............................. | | EMI America 8312 |
| 6/21/86 | 86 | 2 | 16  Tin Soldier................................................... | | EMI America 8324 |
| | | | **RON HENDERSON & CHOICE OF COLOUR** | | |
| 9/24/77 | 74 | 5 | 1  Don't Take Her For Granted............................ | | Chelsea 3067 |
| | | | **WAYNE HENDERSON** | | |
| | | | Trombone player; original member of the Jazz Crusaders. Left group for a solo career in 1975. Produced the Los Angeles group Side Effect. | | |
| 8/05/78 | 91 | 3 | 1  Hot Stuff ..................................................... | | Polydor 14485 |
| 12/23/78+ | 59 | 8 | 2  Heat Of The Beat .......................................... | | Polydor 14523 |
| | | | ROY AYERS/WAYNE HENDERSON | | |
| | | | **WILLIE HENDERSON** | | |
| | | | Born on 8/9/41 in Pensacola, Florida. Producer and music director for Brunswick/Dakar in Chicago for 5 years. | | |
| 2/21/70 | 22 | 6 | 1  Funky Chicken (Part 1) ............................... [I] | 91 | Brunswick 55429 |
| | | | WILLIE HENDERSON & THE SOUL EXPLOSIONS | | |
| 6/29/74 | 18 | 11 | 2  Dance Master ........................................... [I] | 73 | Playboy 50057 |
| 10/05/74 | 50 | 9 | 3  Gangster Boogie Bump.................................. | | Playboy 6011 |
| | | | **BOBBY HENDRICKS** | | |
| | | | Born on 2/22/38 in Columbus, Ohio. With the Swallows in 1956. First recorded with the Flyers for Atco in 1957. With The Drifters in 1958. Went solo. Rejoined The Drifters with Bill Pinkney in 1964. | | |
| 9/15/58 | 5 | 5 | 1  **Itchy Twitchy Feeling** ............................... | 25 | Sue 706 |
| | | | Jockey #5 / Best Seller #12 backing vocals by The Coasters; with the Jimmy Oliver Orchestra | | |
| | | | **PATTI HENDRIX** | | |
| 8/19/78 | 65 | 10 | 1  Lighting A Fire (That You Can't Put Out).......... | | Hilltak 7801 |
| | | | **NONA HENDRYX** | | |
| | | | Born on 8/18/45 in Trenton, New Jersey. Member of "Patti LaBelle & The Blue-Belles" and "LaBelle" from 1961-77. | | |
| 3/19/83 | 22 | 15 | 1  Keep It Confidential...................................... | 91 | RCA 13437 |
| 7/16/83 | 40 | 12 | 2  Transformation............................................ | | RCA 13559 |
| 3/31/84 | 28 | 14 | 3  I Sweat (Going Through The Motions)............... | | RCA 13759 |
| 10/05/85 | 71 | 7 | 4  If Looks Could Kill (D.O.A.) ............................ | | RCA 14168 |
| 2/15/86 | 68 | 5 | 5  I Need Love................................................... | | RCA 14275 |
| 4/11/87 | 5 | 15 | 6  **Why Should I Cry?**...................................... | 58 | EMI America 8382 |

| DEBUT DATE | PEAK POS | WKS CHR | ARTIST — Record Title | POP POS | Label & Number |
|---|---|---|---|---|---|
| 8/08/87 | 60 | 7 | **NONA HENDRYX — Continued**<br>7 Baby Go-Go ................................................. | | EMI Amer. 43028 |
| | | | **DON HENLEY**<br>Born on 7/22/47 in Gilmer, Texas. Singer/songwriter/drummer. Worked with Glenn Frey backing Linda Ronstadt before forming the Eagles in 1971. Went solo in 1982. | | |
| 5/04/85 | 65 | 6 | 1 All She Wants To Do Is Dance ........................ | 9 | Geffen 29065 |
| | | | **CLARENCE "Frogman" HENRY**<br>Born on 3/19/37 in Algiers, Louisiana. Vocalist/pianist/trombonist. With Bobby Mitchell's R&B band from 1953-55. Nicknamed "Frogman" from hit "Ain't Got No Home". | | |
| 12/08/56+ | 3 | 12 | 1 Ain't Got No Home ................................. [N]<br>Best Seller #3 / Jockey #4<br>with the Paul Gayten Orchestra | 20 | Argo 5259 |
| 3/06/61 | 9 | 11 | 2 But I Do .........................................................<br>also titled "I Don't Know Why" | 4 | Argo 5378 |
| 5/29/61 | 11 | 7 | 3 You Always Hurt The One You Love ................ | 12 | Argo 5388 |
| 8/07/61 | 19 | 5 | 4 Lonely Street ................................................ | 57 | Argo 5395 |
| | | | **HERB THE "K"** | | |
| 5/04/85 | 78 | 3 | 1 (Breakin') Super Turf .................................... | | Private I 04850 |
| | | | **WOODY HERMAN & HIS ORCHESTRA**<br>Born Woodrow Charles Herman on 5/16/13 in Milwaukee. Saxophonist/clarinetist in dance bands beginning in 1929. Formed own band in 1936. Band dubbed The Herman Herd in 1944. One of the most innovative and contemporary of all big-band leaders. Died on 10/29/87 of cardiac arrest. | | |
| 2/19/44 | 4 | 4 | 1 **Do Nothin' Till You Hear From Me** ................ | 7 | Decca 18578 |
| 8/31/46 | 4 | 1 | 2 Fan It ...............................................................<br>above 2: vocals by Woody Herman | | Columbia 37059 |
| | | | **THE HESITATIONS**<br>Cleveland group. Lead singer George "King" Scott was accidentally killed by a bullet from a gun owned by tenor Fred Deal in February of 1968. | | |
| 1/14/67 | 42 | 2 | 1 Soul Superman ............................................. | | Kapp 790 |
| 1/13/68 | 4 | 11 | 2 **Born Free** ......................................................<br>from the film of the same title | 38 | Kapp 878 |
| 3/23/68 | 14 | 9 | 3 The Impossible Dream ....................................<br>from the Broadway musical "Man Of La Mancha" | 42 | Kapp 899 |
| 7/13/68 | 34 | 3 | 4 Who Will Answer ......................................... | 112 | Kapp 926 |
| | | | **HOWARD HEWETT**<br>Lead vocalist of Shalamar, 1979-1985. Born and raised in Akron, Ohio. | | |
| 8/24/85 | 90 | 3 | 1 Obsession ..................................................... | | Elektra 69620 |
| 8/09/86 | 2² | 20 | 2 I'm For Real ...................................................<br>backing musicians: George Duke, Stanley Clarke & Wilton Felder | 90 | Elektra 69527 |
| 12/13/86+ | 8 | 18 | 3 **Stay** .............................................................. | | Elektra 69499 |
| 4/25/87 | 12 | 14 | 4 I Commit To Love ........................................... | | Elektra 69477 |
| 8/29/87 | 54 | 10 | 5 Say Amen ...................................................... | | Elektra 69441 |
| 2/13/88 | 42 | 9 | 6 Another Chance To Love ...............................<br>**DIONNE WARWICK & HOWARD HEWETT** | | Arista 9656 |
| 3/19/88 | 9 | 14 | 7 **Strange Relationship** ................................. | | Elektra 96415 |
| 6/25/88 | 15 | 17 | 8 Once, Twice, Three Time .............................. | | Elektra 69390 |
| | | | **EDDIE HEYWOOD - see HUGO WINTERHALTER** | | |
| | | | **AL HIBBLER**<br>Born on 8/16/15 in Little Rock, Arkansas. Blind since birth, studied voice at Little Rock's Conservatory for the Blind. First recorded with Jay McShann for Decca in 1942. With Duke Ellington, 1943-51. Also recorded with Harry Carney, Tab Smith, Mercer Ellington and Billy Strayhorn. Also see Jay McShann. | | |
| 12/18/48+ | 3 | 14 | 1 **Trees/**<br>Best Seller #3 / Juke Box #3 | | |
| 2/19/49 | 9 | 1 | 2 Lover Come Back To Me ...........................<br>Juke Box #9<br>also released on Chess 1456 | | Miracle 501 |
| 8/12/50 | 9 | 1 | 3 Danny Boy .....................................................<br>Juke Box #9<br>with Billy Kyle's Orchestra | | Atlantic 911 |
| 5/12/51 | 9 | 1 | 4 **What Will I Tell My Heart** ...........................<br>Juke Box #9<br>recorded in 1948 | | Chess 1455 |

| DEBUT DATE | PEAK POS | WKS CHR | ARTIST — Record Title | POP POS | Label & Number |
|---|---|---|---|---|---|
| | | | **AL HIBBLER — Continued** | | |
| 4/23/55 | **1**¹ | 14 | 5 **Unchained Melody**........................ | *3* | Decca 29441 |
| | | | Juke Box #1 / Best Seller #2 / Jockey #6 from the film "Unchained" | | |
| 10/22/55 | **13** | 3 | 6 He ............................ | *4* | Decca 29660 |
| | | | Best Seller #13 with the Jack Pleis Orchestra | | |
| | | | **HIDDEN STRENGTH** | | |
| 2/28/76 | **35** | 16 | 1 Hustle On Up (Do The Bump) ................ | *105* | United Art. 733 |
| 9/25/76 | **78** | 5 | 2 I Don't Want To Be A Lone Ranger ............ | | United Art. 847 |
| | | | **MONK HIGGINS** | | |
| | | | Born Milton Bland in 1936 in Menifee, Arkansas. Died on 7/3/86 in Los Angeles. Keyboardist/arranger/leader. Taught music in Missouri and Chicago. Music director at One-Derful Records. | | |
| 8/13/66 | **30** | 8 | 1 Who-Dun-It?........................[I] | *117* | St. Lawrence 1013 |
| 5/06/72 | **22** | 8 | 2 Gotta Be Funky ............................ | *105* | United Art. 50897 |
| | | | **HIGH FASHION** | | |
| | | | Trio from New York City. | | |
| 5/15/82 | **32** | 14 | 1 Feelin' Lucky Lately........................ | | Capitol 5104 |
| | | | **HIGH INERGY** | | |
| | | | Female group from Pasadena, California, consisting of Barbara Mitchell, Linda Howard, Michelle Rumph and Vernessa Mitchell. Vernessa left group in 1978; group continued as a trio. Smokey Robinson recorded with Barbara Mitchell in 1983. | | |
| 9/03/77 | **2**⁴ | 24 | 1 **You Can't Turn Me Off (In The Middle Of Turning Me On)**........................ | *12* | Gordy 7155 |
| 2/18/78 | **20** | 13 | 2 Love Is All You Need ...................... | *89* | Gordy 7157 |
| 6/24/78 | **77** | 7 | 3 We Are The Future........................ | | Gordy 7160 |
| 9/09/78 | **51** | 9 | 4 Lovin' Fever ............................ | | Gordy 7161 |
| 5/19/79 | **50** | 8 | 5 Shoulda Gone Dancin'...................... | *101* | Gordy 7166 |
| 8/30/80 | **68** | 6 | 6 Make Me Yours .......................... | | Gordy 7187 |
| 8/15/81 | **73** | 5 | 7 Goin Thru The Motions .................... | | Gordy 7207 |
| 5/08/82 | **50** | 10 | 8 First Impressions ........................ | | Gordy 1613 |
| 2/26/83 | **62** | 11 | 9 He's A Pretender........................ | *82* | Gordy 1662 |
| | | | **WILLIE HIGHTOWER** | | |
| 4/05/69 | **33** | 7 | 1 It's A Miracle............................ | *130* | Capitol 2226 |
| 4/25/70 | **26** | 8 | 2 Walk A Mile In My Shoes .................. | *107* | Fame 1465 |
| | | | **BOBBY HILL** | | |
| 12/20/69 | **43** | 5 | 1 The Children ............................ | | LoLo 2305 |
| | | | **BUNKER HILL** | | |
| | | | Born David Walker on 5/5/41 in Washington, DC. Professional boxer. Ex-lead singer with the gospel group, Mighty Clouds Of Joy. | | |
| 9/22/62 | **27** | 1 | 1 Hide & Go Seek, Part I .................... | *33* | Mala 451 |
| | | | **JESSIE HILL** | | |
| | | | Born on 12/9/32 in New Orleans. Singer/pianist/drummer. With Huey Smith until 1958. | | |
| 5/02/60 | **3** | 11 | 1 **Ooh Poo Pah Doo - Part II**........................[I] | *28* | Minit 607 |
| | | | **LONNIE HILL** | | |
| 12/22/84+ | **53** | 12 | 1 Hard Times ............................ | | Urban Sound 779 |
| 5/18/85 | **76** | 6 | 2 You Got Me Running........................ | | Urban Sound 780 |
| 10/19/85 | **64** | 9 | 3 Could It Be Love ........................ | | Urban Sound 785 |
| | | | **Z.Z. HILL** | | |
| | | | Born Arzel Hill on 9/30/35 in Naples, Texas. Blues vocalist; first recorded for MH in 1963. Formed own Hill Records in 1970. Died of a heart attack on 4/27/84. | | |
| 3/07/64 | **100** | 1 | 1 You Were Wrong.......................... | *Hot* | M.H. 200 |
| 2/13/71 | **17** | 8 | 2 Don't Make Me Pay For His Mistakes ......... | *62* | Hill 222 |
| 5/22/71 | **30** | 7 | 3 I Need Someone (To Love Me) .............. | *86* | Kent 4547 |
| | | | recorded in 1964 | | |
| 10/09/71 | **30** | 8 | 4 Chokin' Kind............................ | *108* | Mankind 12017 |
| 6/24/72 | **39** | 12 | 5 Second Chance .......................... | | Mankind 12012 |
| 11/04/72 | **34** | 5 | 6 It Ain't No Use............................ | | Mankind 12015 |
| 6/02/73 | **37** | 7 | 7 Ain't Nothing You Can Do.................. | *114* | Hill/UA 225 |

| DEBUT DATE | PEAK POS | WKS CHR | ARTIST — Record Title | POP POS | Label & Number |
|---|---|---|---|---|---|
| | | | **Z.Z. HILL — Continued** | | |
| 9/15/73 | **63** | 8 | 8 I Don't Need Half A Love ................................ | | Hill/UA 307 |
| 1/05/74 | **74** | 8 | 9 Let Them Talk.................................................. | | Hill/UA 365 |
| 4/13/74 | **84** | 6 | 10 Am I Groovin' You........................................... | | Hill/UA 412 |
| 9/14/74 | **39** | 11 | 11 I Keep On Lovin' You....................................... | *104* | Hill/UA 536 |
| 8/09/75 | **40** | 11 | 12 I Created A Monster ....................................... | *109* | Hill/UA 631 |
| 6/25/77 | **15** | 18 | 13 Love Is So Good When You're Stealing It ........... | *102* | Columbia 10552 |
| 2/25/78 | **42** | 13 | 14 This Time They Told The Truth ...................... | | Columbia 10680 |
| 4/24/82 | **19** | 20 | 15 Cheating In The Next Room ........................... | | Malaco 2079 |
| 1/28/84 | **85** | 3 | 16 Get A Little, Give A Little.............................. | | Malaco 2094 |
| | | | **HINDSIGHT** | | |
| 2/20/88 | **16** | 15 | 1 Stand Up ...................................................... | | Virgin 99391 |
| | | | **ANN HINES - see J. BLACKFOOT** | | |
| | | | **EARL HINES & HIS ORCHESTRA** | | |
| | | | Born on 12/28/05 in Duquesne, Pennsylvania. Died of a heart attack on 4/22/83 (78). Vocalist/pianist. Nicknamed "Fatha" or "Father". Piano style inspired by Louis Armstrong's trumpet work. Recorded solo for QRS in 1928. Own bands until 1948. With Louis Armstrong from 1948-51, then own sextet. Many overseas tours. | | |
| 10/24/42 | **1**¹ | 14 | 1 **Stormy Monday Blues**................................ vocal by Billy Eckstine | *23* | Bluebird 11567 |
| | | | **GREGORY HINES** | | |
| | | | Dancer/actor/singer from New York. At age 5, began touring nationally in a professional dance duo, The Hines Kids, with his brother Maurice. In 1980, appeared in the Broadway musicals "Eubie" and "Comin' Uptown". Appeared in the films "The Deal Of The Century" (1983), "The Cotton Club" (1984), "White Nights" (1985), "Running Scared" (1986), and "Tap" (1988). | | |
| 3/07/87 | **1**¹ | 17 | 1 **There's Nothing Better Than Love**................ LUTHER VANDROSS with GREGORY HINES | *50* | Epic 06978 |
| 6/11/88 | **6** | 16 | 2 **That Girl Wants To Dance With Me** .............. | | Epic 07793 |
| | | | **J. HINES & THE FELLOWS** | | |
| 8/18/73 | **71** | 5 | 1 Camelot Time................................................ | | DeLuxe 509 |
| | | | **JOE HINTON** | | |
| | | | Born in 1929; died on 8/13/68 in Boston. With the Chosen Gospel Singers; lead singer of the Spirits Of Memphis (gospel group). | | |
| 6/22/63 | **20** | 5 | 1 You Know It Ain't Right .................................. | *88* | Back Beat 537 |
| 10/12/63 | **89** | 1 | 2 Better To Give Than Receive.......................... | *Hot* | Back Beat 539 |
| 8/15/64 | **13** | 12 | 3 Funny.......................................................... | *Hot* | Back Beat 541 |
| 1/30/65 | **34** | 1 | 4 I Want A Little Girl ........................................ | *132* | Back Beat 545 |
| | | | **HIROSHIMA** | | |
| | | | Los Angeles jazz/pop band founded in 1974 by Dan Kuramoto, with varying membership. | | |
| 3/15/80 | **80** | 5 | 1 Roomful Of Mirrors......................................... | | Arista 0487 |
| 1/10/81 | **79** | 4 | 2 Warriors...................................................... | | Arista 0574 |
| 7/30/83 | **68** | 4 | 3 San Say....................................................... | | Epic 03921 |
| 10/22/83 | **79** | 4 | 4 Heavenly Angel ............................................ | | Epic 04146 |
| | | | **HITMAN HOWIE TEE - see THE REAL ROXANNE** | | |
| | | | **HODGES, JAMES & SMITH** | | |
| | | | Trio formed in Los Angeles. Consisted of Pat Hodges, Denita James and Jessica Smith. Appeared on Richard Pryor's TV specials. | | |
| 7/16/77 | **24** | 14 | 1 Since I Fell For You/I'm Falling In Love ........... medley produced by William "Mickey" Stevenson (Jessica was his secretary) | *96* | London 256 |
| 12/17/77 | **90** | 5 | 2 Don't Take Away Your Love............................ | | London 260 |
| 7/21/79 | **85** | 3 | 3 Dancing In The Street .................................. | | London 274 |
| | | | **CHARLES HODGES** | | |
| | | | Born on 6/29/47 in Memphis. With the Nightingales, and own group, Christianaires. | | |
| 1/31/70 | **25** | 6 | 1 Slip Around .................................................. | | Calla 168 |
| 7/25/70 | **47** | 2 | 2 The Day He Made You....:.............................. | | Calla 171 |

| DEBUT DATE | PEAK POS | WKS CHR | ARTIST — Record Title | POP POS | Label & Number |
|---|---|---|---|---|---|

### JOHNNY HODGES & HIS ORCHESTRA
Born on 7/25/06 in Cambridge, Massachusetts. Died of a heart attack on 5/11/70 (63). Nicknamed Rabbit. Alto and soprano saxophonist/clarinetist. Joined Duke Ellington band in May of 1928; remained until March of 1951. Own small groups, rejoined Ellington in 1955, until the time of his death. Many freelance recordings with own bands. Also see Ivory Joe Hunter.

| DEBUT DATE | PEAK POS | WKS CHR | ARTIST — Record Title | POP POS | Label & Number |
|---|---|---|---|---|---|
| 10/07/44 | 10 | 1 | 1 Going Out The Back Way ........................... [I] <br> recorded in 1941 | | Bluebird 0817 |
| 7/07/51 | 4 | 9 | 2 Castle Rock .................................................. [I] <br> Juke Box #4 / Best Seller #5 <br> with Big Al Sears on tenor sax and Duke Ellington's trombonist, <br> Lawrence Brown | 28 | Mercury 8944 |
| 3/22/52 | 4 | 5 | 3 A Pound Of Blues ..................................... [I] <br> Juke Box #4 | | Mercury 8961 |

### SMOKEY HOGG
Born Andrew Hogg on 1/27/14 in Westconnie, Texas. Died on 5/1/60 (ulcer hemorrhage). Guitarist/pianist/vocalist. Also known as Little Peetie Wheatstraw. Cousin of Lightnin' Hopkins and John Hogg. First recorded for Decca in 1937.

| 8/14/48 | 9 | 1 | 1 Long Tall Mama ........................................... <br> Juke Box #9 | | Modern 574 |
| 1/07/50 | 5 | 5 | 2 Little School Girl ....................................... <br> Juke Box #5 / Best Seller #9 <br> above 2: with the Hadda Brooks Trio | | Modern 704 |

### RON HOLDEN with THE THUNDERBIRDS
Born on 8/7/39 in Seattle. In group, the Playboys, in 1957. With Little Willie & The Thunderbirds, first recorded for Night Owl in 1959. Worked as Emcee at Art Laboe's "Oldies But Goodies" club from 1972-77.

| 5/16/60 | 11 | 9 | 1 Love You So .................................................. | 7 | Donna 1315 |
| 3/30/74 | 49 | 10 | 2 Can You Talk ................................................ | | Now 6 |

### BILLIE HOLIDAY
Born Eleanor Gough on 4/7/15 in Baltimore. Died on 7/17/59 in New York City (drug addiction). Nicknamed Lady Day. Singing at age 15 in Harlem Clubs, heard by John Hammond, who arranged for her to record with Benny Goodman in 1933. With Teddy Wilson from 1935-39, Count Basie from 1937-38, Artie Shaw in 1938, then solo work. Final appearance on 5/25/59 in New York City. Subject of the 1972 film "Lady Sings The Blues" starring Diana Ross. Also see Paul Whiteman.

| 5/12/45 | 5 | 1 | 1 Lover Man (Oh, Where Can You Be) ................ <br> with Toots Camarata & His Orchestra | 16 | Decca 23391 |

### JIMMY HOLIDAY
Born on 7/24/34 in Durant, Mississippi; raised in Waterloo, Iowa. Singer/songwriter. Died of heart failure on 2/15/87 in Waterloo.

| 3/16/63 | 8 | 9 | 1 How Can I Forget ........................................ | 57 | Everest 2022 |
| 7/30/66 | 21 | 9 | 2 Baby I Love You ......................................... | 98 | Minit 32002 |
| 3/18/67 | 36 | 11 | 3 Everybody Needs Help ................................. | 116 | Minit 32016 |
| 6/15/68 | 35 | 4 | 4 Spread Your Love ........................................ | | Minit 32040 |

### THE HOLIDAYS
Group from Detroit, consisting of Edwin Starr, J.J. Barnes and Steve Mancha. Later recordings by group consisting of Jimmy & Jack Holland, Jay Reid and Tony Hestor.

| 4/09/66 | 7 | 16 | 1 I'll Love You Forever .................................... | 63 | Golden World 36 |

### BRIAN HOLLAND
Born on 2/15/41 in Detroit. Singer/songwriter/producer. Teamed with brother Eddie Lamont Dozier in successful songwriting and production team for Motown; wrote many of Motown's all-time greatest hits. Trio left Motown in 1968 and formed own Invictus/Hot Wax label. Recorded in duo with Lamont Dozier in 1973.

| 12/30/72+ | 13 | 13 | 1 Don't Leave Me Starvin' For Your Love (Part 1) .. | 52 | Invictus 9133 |
| 7/21/73 | 46 | 10 | 2 Slipping Away ............................................. <br> HOLLAND-DOZIER | | Invictus 1253 |
| 9/29/73 | 61 | 8 | 3 New Kind Of Woman .................................... <br> HOLLAND-DOZIER | | Invictus 1254 |

### EDDIE HOLLAND
Born on 10/30/39 in Detroit. Singer/songwriter/producer. Member of Motown's hit-production trio with brother Brian Holland and Lamont Dozier. Co-founder of the Invictus/Hot Wax label.

| 1/13/62 | 6 | 19 | 1 Jamie ........................................................... | 30 | Motown 1021 |
| 2/08/64 | 76 | 5 | 2 Leaving Here ............................................... | Hot | Motown 1052 |
| 5/23/64 | 54 | 7 | 3 Just Ain't Enough Love ................................ | Hot | Motown 1058 |
| 8/29/64 | 58 | 6 | 4 Candy To Me ............................................... | Hot | Motown 1063 |

| DEBUT DATE | PEAK POS | WKS CHR | ARTIST — Record Title | POP POS | Label & Number |
|---|---|---|---|---|---|
| | | | **HOLLAND-DOZIER - see BRIAN HOLLAND and/or LAMONT DOZIER** | | |
| | | | **JENNIFER HOLLIDAY** | | |
| | | | Born on 10/19/60 in Houston. Sang in Pleasant Grove Baptist Church choir. Lead in the Broadway show "Your Arm's Too Short To Box With God", in 1978. Tony award winner for Best Actress in Broadway's "Dreamgirls". In the Broadway show "Sing, Mahalia, Sing", in 1985. Appeared on the Love Boat TV series in 1986. Also see Foreigner. | | |
| 6/05/82 | 1⁴ | 20 | 1 **And I Am Telling You I'm Not Going** | 22 | Geffen 29983 |
| 9/25/82 | 29 | 10 | 2 I Am Changing | | Geffen 29910 |
| | | | above 2: from the original Broadway cast "Dreamgirls" | | |
| 9/03/83 | 2² | 22 | 3 **I Am Love** | 49 | Geffen 29525 |
| 12/10/83+ | 24 | 13 | 4 Just Let Me Wait | 103 | Geffen 29432 |
| 8/17/85 | 17 | 15 | 5 Hard Times For Lovers | 69 | Geffen 28958 |
| 12/14/85+ | 29 | 14 | 6 No Frills Love | 87 | Geffen 28845 |
| 8/01/87 | 48 | 10 | 7 Heart On The Line | | Geffen 28298 |
| | | | **BRENDA HOLLOWAY** | | |
| | | | Born on 6/21/46 in Atascadero, California. Singer/songwriter. Later a back-up singer for Joe Cocker. | | |
| 5/02/64 | 13 | 10 | 1 Every Little Bit Hurts | *Hot* | Tamla 54094 |
| 8/08/64 | 60 | 5 | 2 I'll Always Love You | *Hot* | Tamla 54099 |
| 3/06/65 | 12 | 13 | 3 When I'm Gone | 25 | Tamla 54111 |
| 6/26/65 | 36 | 2 | 4 Operator | 78 | Tamla 54115 |
| 4/29/67 | 21 | 11 | 5 Just Look What You've Done | 69 | Tamla 54148 |
| 11/04/67 | 40 | 5 | 6 You've Made Me So Very Happy | 39 | Tamla 54155 |
| | | | **LOLEATTA HOLLOWAY** | | |
| | | | Singer from Chicago. Former member of the Caravans gospel troupe. Also see Salsoul Orchestra. | | |
| 7/21/73 | 43 | 8 | 1 Mother Of Shame/ | | |
| | | 4 | 2 Our Love | | Aware 6001 |
| 2/01/75 | 10 | 15 | 3 **Cry To Me** | 68 | Aware 047 |
| 6/21/75 | 69 | 5 | 4 I Know Where You're Coming From | | Aware 050 |
| 11/20/76+ | 25 | 13 | 5 Worn Out Broken Heart | | Gold Mind 4000 |
| 4/09/77 | 56 | 7 | 6 Hit And Run | | Gold Mind 4001 |
| 8/19/78 | 11 | 15 | 7 Only You | 87 | Gold Mind 4012 |
| | | | **LOLEATTA HOLLOWAY & BUNNY SIGLER** | | |
| 12/23/78+ | 92 | 4 | 8 Catch Me On The Rebound | | Gold Mind 4016 |
| 8/04/84 | 86 | 3 | 9 Crash Goes Love | | Streetwise 1130 |
| | | | **BUDDY HOLLY - see THE CRICKETS** | | |
| | | | **HOLLYWOOD ARGYLES** | | |
| | | | Gary Paxton recorded "Alley-Oop" as a solo artist; since he was still under contract to Brent Records, where he recorded as Flip of "Skip & Flip", he made up the name of the Hollywood Argyles. After the song was a hit, Gary assembled a Hollywood Argyles group, included Bobby Rey, Ted Winter, Gary Webb, Ted Marsh and Deary Weaver. | | |
| 6/13/60 | 3 | 9 | 1 **Alley-Oop** [N] | *1* | Lute 5905 |
| | | | written by Dallas Frazier | | |
| | | | **HOLLYWOOD FLAMES** | | |
| | | | Los Angeles-based group formed in 1950 by Bobby Day. Also known as The Flames, Four Flames, Hollywood Four Flames, and The Satellites. Many personnel changes. Group lineup in 1957: Earl Nelson (of Bob & Earl), Bobby Byrd, David Ford, Clyde Tillis and Curtis Williams (former member of the Penguins; wrote "Earth Angel"). | | |
| 11/25/57 | 5 | 7 | 1 **Buzz-Buzz-Buzz** | 11 | Ebb 119 |
| | | | Jockey #5 / Best Seller #11 | | |
| | | | lead vocal by Earl "Jackie" Nelson | | |
| 6/26/61 | 26 | 3 | 2 Gee | | Chess 1787 |
| | | | lead vocal by Donald Height | | |
| | | | **EDDIE HOLMAN** | | |
| | | | Born on 6/3/46 in Norfolk, Virginia. Attended Victoria School Of Music in New York and Cheyney State College in Philadelphia. | | |
| 12/25/65+ | 17 | 16 | 1 This Can't Be True | 57 | Parkway 960 |
| 11/12/66 | 17 | 9 | 2 Am I A Loser | 101 | Parkway 106 |
| 6/21/69 | 30 | 5 | 3 I Love You | | ABC 11149 |

| DEBUT DATE | PEAK POS | WKS CHR | ARTIST — Record Title | POP POS | Label & Number |
|---|---|---|---|---|---|
| | | | **EDDIE HOLMAN — Continued** | | |
| 12/06/69+ | **4** | 17 | 4●Hey There Lonely Girl ............................ | 2 | ABC 11240 |
| | | | recorded in 1963 by Ruby & The Romantics as "Hey There Lonely Boy" (POS 27-Pop) | | |
| 4/18/70 | **24** | 4 | 5 Don't Stop Now............................................. | 48 | ABC 11261 |
| 11/14/70 | **28** | 6 | 6 Cathy Called ................................................. | | ABC 11276 |
| 9/09/72 | **20** | 9 | 7 My Mind Keeps Telling Me ............................. | | GSF 6873 |
| 3/23/74 | **73** | 6 | 8 You're My Lady ............................................. | | Silver Blue 807 |
| 4/30/77 | **25** | 12 | 9 This Will Be A Night To Remember.................. | 90 | Salsoul 2026 |
| 9/17/77 | **96** | 2 | 10 You Make My Life Complete ........................... | | Salsoul 2043 |
| | | | **JAN HOLMES** | | |
| 3/02/85 | **83** | 5 | 1 I'm Your Superman ....................................... | | Jay Jay 1005 |
| | | | **RICHARD "GROOVE" HOLMES** | | |
| | | | Born on 5/2/31 in Camden, New Jersey. Jazz organist. | | |
| 7/16/66 | **12** | 11 | 1 Misty .................................................... [I] | 44 | Prestige 401 |
| | | | with Gene Edwards (guitar) and Jimmie Smith (drums) | | |
| | | | **THE HONEY CONE** | | |
| | | | Female trio formed in Los Angeles in 1969. Consisted of prominent backup singers: Carolyn Willis (member of The Girlfriends and Bob B. Soxx & The Blue Jeans), Edna Wright (sister of Darlene Love - member of The Blossoms and Bob B. Soxx & The Blue Jeans) and Shellie Clark (former Ikette and regular on the TV series "The Jim Nabors Hour" from 1969-70). | | |
| 7/05/69 | **26** | 8 | 1 While You're Out Looking For Sugar? .............. | 62 | Hot Wax 6901 |
| 10/11/69 | **8** | 9 | 2 Girls It Ain't Easy ......................................... | 68 | Hot Wax 6903 |
| 4/18/70 | **28** | 4 | 3 Take Me With You.......................................... | 108 | Hot Wax 7001 |
| 4/17/71 | **1**³ | 14 | 4●Want Ads................................................... | 1 | Hot Wax 7011 |
| 8/14/71 | **1**² | 13 | 5●Stick-Up.................................................... | 11 | Hot Wax 7106 |
| 11/27/71+ | **5** | 12 | 6 One Monkey Don't Stop No Show (Part I)........ | 15 | Hot Wax 7110 |
| 2/19/72 | **8** | 10 | 7 The Day I Found Myself................................. | 23 | Hot Wax 7113 |
| 7/29/72 | **33** | 6 | 8 Sittin' On A Time Bomb (Waitin' For The Hurt To Come)................................................. | 96 | Hot Wax 7205 |
| 10/14/72 | **37** | 3 | 9 Innocent Til Proven Guilty............................. | 101 | Hot Wax 7208 |
| | | | **MIKI HONEYCUTT** | | |
| 3/05/77 | **97** | 2 | 1 Make Up For Lost Time ................................. | | Paula 422 |
| | | | **FRANK HOOKER & POSITIVE PEOPLE** | | |
| | | | 7-piece, male/female ensemble. | | |
| 8/25/79 | **82** | 8 | 1 Rock Me........................................................ | | Panorama 11634 |
| 5/24/80 | **40** | 9 | 2 I Wanna Know Your Name ............................. | | Panorama 11984 |
| 12/20/80+ | **62** | 8 | 3 Like Sister And Brother ................................. | | Panorama 12132 |
| 4/11/81 | **79** | 4 | 4 Ooh Suga Wooga .......................................... | | Panorama 12196 |
| | | | **JOHN LEE HOOKER** | | |
| | | | Born on 8/22/17 in Clarksdale, Mississippi. Vocalist/internationally-known blues guitarist. Worked in Memphis with Robert Nighthawk and others from 1931-33. To Cincinnati in the mid-30s. With gospel groups including the Fairfield Four in 1938. To Detroit in 1943. Own small band in Detroit in 1949. First recorded for Modern in 1948. Featured in the 1980 movie "The Blues Brothers". | | |
| 1/08/49 | **1**¹ | 18 | 1 Boogie Chillen' ........................................... | | Modern 627 |
| | | | Juke Box #1 / Best Seller #2 | | |
| 5/07/49 | **5** | 8 | 2 Hobo Blues/ | | |
| | | | Juke Box #5 / Best Seller #8 | | |
| 4/30/49 | **9** | 4 | 3 Hoogie Boogie ...................................... [I] | | Modern 663 |
| | | | Juke Box #9 / Best Seller #13 | | |
| 12/03/49 | **6** | 5 | 4 Crawling King Snake Blues .......................... | | Modern 714 |
| | | | Juke Box #6 / Best Seller #11 | | |
| 2/11/50 | **15** | 1 | 5 Huckle Up, Baby .......................................... | | Sensation 26 |
| | | | Juke Box #15 | | |
| 10/13/51 | **1**⁴ | 15 | 6 I'm In The Mood .......................................... | 30 | Modern 835 |
| | | | Juke Box #1 / Best Seller #2 | | |
| 12/08/58 | **29** | 1 | 7 I Love You Honey.......................................... | | Vee-Jay 293 |
| 7/25/60 | **21** | 2 | 8 No Shoes ..................................................... | | Vee-Jay 349 |
| 6/16/62 | **16** | 8 | 9 Boom Boom .................................................. | 60 | Vee-Jay 438 |

| DEBUT DATE | PEAK POS | WKS CHR | ARTIST — Record Title | POP POS | Label & Number |
|---|---|---|---|---|---|
| | | | **STIX HOOPER** | | |
| | | | Born Nesbert Hooper in 1939 in Houston. Drummer with The Crusaders. | | |
| 1/12/80 | 49 | 8 | 1 Brazos River Breakdown ............................... | | MCA 41165 |
| | | | **LYNN HOPE QUINTET** | | |
| | | | Born on 9/26/26 in Alabama. Tenor saxophonist. Played from age 9. In the William "King Kolax" Little Band during the 40s. Own band in 1950. Muslim name Hajji Ahmad. | | |
| 8/12/50 | 8 | 2 | 1 **Tenderly**.................................................. [I] *19* | | Premium 851 |
| | | | Juke Box #8 / Best Seller #9 | | |
| | | | **LIGHTNIN' HOPKINS** | | |
| | | | Born Sam Hopkins on 3/15/12 in Centerville, Texas. Died of cancer on 1/30/82 (69). Vocalist/guitarist, cousin of Smokey Hogg. With Texas Alexander in the late 1920s to 1937, and again from 1945-50s. First recorded for Aladdin in 1946, with Wilson "Thunder" Smith. Prolific recording for many labels. Highly esteemed as an unspoiled singer of the blues; active until his death. | | |
| 2/12/49 | 13 | 1 | 1 Tim Moore's Farm ............................... | | Modern 673 |
| | | | Juke Box #13 | | |
| | | | originally released on Goldstar 640 | | |
| 10/08/49 | 8 | 1 | 2 "T" Model Blues.................................... | | Goldstar 662 |
| | | | Juke Box #8 | | |
| | | | also released on S-I-W 644 | | |
| 9/30/50 | 5 | 4 | 3 **Shotgun Blues**.................................... | | Aladdin 3063 |
| | | | Best Seller #5 | | |
| 2/23/52 | 6 | 6 | 4 **Give Me Central 209**................................... | | Sittin' In 621 |
| | | | Juke Box #6 | | |
| | | | also known as "Hello Central" | | |
| 3/29/52 | 6 | 2 | 5 **Coffee Blues**........................................ | | Sittin' In 635 |
| | | | Juke Box #6 | | |
| | | | also released on Jax 635 | | |
| | | | **LINDA HOPKINS - see JACKIE WILSON** | | |
| | | | **EDDIE HORAN** | | |
| 8/19/78 | 91 | 3 | 1 Love The Way You Love Me ........................ | | HDM 506 |
| | | | **PAUL HORN** | | |
| 11/11/78 | 95 | 2 | 1 Witch Doctor ................................. | | Mushroom 7037 |
| | | | **TREVOR HORN - see THE ART OF NOISE** | | |
| | | | **JIMMY "BO" HORNE** | | |
| | | | Singer/dancer from Miami. | | |
| 7/26/75 | 47 | 10 | 1 Gimme Some (Part One)................................ | | Alston 3714 |
| 5/07/77 | 46 | 8 | 2 Get Happy............................................ | | Alston 3729 |
| 3/18/78 | 8 | 21 | 3 **Dance Across The Floor** ....................... *38* | | Sunshine S. 1003 |
| | | | written and produced by Harry "KC" Casey | | |
| 10/14/78 | 60 | 7 | 4 Let Me (Let Me Be Your Lover)....................... | | Sunshine S. 1005 |
| 1/20/79 | 55 | 9 | 5 Spank ............................................ | | Sunshine S. 1007 |
| 8/25/79 | 18 | 15 | 6 You Get Me Hot ................................ *101* | | Sunshine S. 1014 |
| 2/09/80 | 78 | 3 | 7 Without You........................................ | | Sunshine S. 1015 |
| 10/04/80 | 77 | 6 | 8 Is It In................................................ | | Sunshine S. 1018 |
| | | | **LENA HORNE** | | |
| | | | Born on 6/00/17 in Brooklyn. Broadway and movie musical star, long married to bandleader Lennie Hayton. Her career reached a new peak in the 1980s with her one-woman Broadway show. | | |
| 11/23/63 | 92 | 2 | 1 Now! .............................................. *Hot* | | 20th Century 449 |
| | | | **THE HORNY HORNS - see FRED WESLEY** | | |
| | | | **JOHNNY HORTON** | | |
| | | | Country singer born on 4/3/29 in Tyler, Texas. Married to Billie Jean Jones, widow of Country music superstar Hank Williams. Killed in an auto accident on 11/5/60. | | |
| 5/18/59 | 3 | 16 | 1 ●Battle Of New Orleans............................... *1* | | Columbia 41339 |
| | | | original melody written in celebration of the final battle of the War of 1812 | | |
| 11/21/60+ | 10 | 11 | 2 **North To Alaska** ............................... *4* | | Columbia 41782 |
| | | | from the John Wayne film of the same title | | |
| | | | **HOSANNA** | | |
| 2/07/76 | 45 | 8 | 1 Hipit - Part 1 ................................. | | Calla 12078 |

| DEBUT DATE | PEAK POS | WKS CHR | ARTIST — Record Title | POP POS | Label & Number |
|---|---|---|---|---|---|
| | | | **HOT** | | |
| | | | Integrated female trio consisting of Gwen Owens, Cathy Carson and Juanita Curiel. First known as Sugar & Spice. | | |
| 3/05/77 | **29** | 20 | 1● Angel In Your Arms................................ | 6 | Big Tree 16085 |
| 9/03/77 | **58** | 6 | 2 The Right Feeling At The Wrong Time .............. | 65 | Big Tree 16099 |
| | | | **HOTBOX** | | |
| | | | New York City trio: Pete Rojas, Lisa Vidal and Michelle Zangara. | | |
| 2/18/84 | **60** | 7 | 1 Do You Wanna Lover ................................... | | Polydor 817034 |
| | | | **HOT CHOCOLATE** | | |
| | | | Interracial rock-soul group formed in England by lead singer Errol Brown in 1970. Included Harvey Hinsley (guitar), Larry Ferguson (keyboards), Tony Wilson (bass), Patrick Olive (congas) and Tony Connor (drums). Wilson left in 1975, Olive switched to bass. | | |
| 5/31/75 | **40** | 11 | 1 Disco Queen................................................. | 28 | Big Tree 16038 |
| 11/01/75+ | **6** | 19 | 2● You Sexy Thing ......................................... | 3 | Big Tree 16047 |
| 4/17/76 | **43** | 9 | 3 Don't Stop It Now ...................................... | 42 | Big Tree 16060 |
| 7/30/77 | **82** | 9 | 4 So You Win Again ....................................... | 31 | Big Tree 16096 |
| 11/18/78+ | **7** | 18 | 5● Every 1's A Winner ..................................... | 6 | Infinity 50002 |
| 7/28/79 | **43** | 8 | 6 Going Through The Motions ......................... | 53 | Infinity 50016 |
| 12/25/82+ | **50** | 10 | 7 Are You Getting Enough Happiness ................. | 65 | EMI America 8143 |
| | | | all of above: produced by Mickie Most | | |
| | | | **HOT CUISINE** | | |
| 8/29/81 | **53** | 9 | 1 Who's Been Kissing You? .............................. | | Prelude 8035 |
| | | | **HOT LINE** | | |
| 10/26/74 | **47** | 9 | 1 Juice It Up, Pt. 2.......................................... | | Red Coach 808 |
| | | | **HOT SAUCE** | | |
| | | | Hot Sauce is Rhonda Washington. Produced by Al Perkins. | | |
| 4/29/72 | **35** | 6 | 1 Bring It Home (And Give It To Me) .................... | 96 | Volt 4076 |
| 6/22/74 | **78** | 4 | 2 Stop Doggin' Me ......................................... | | Volt 4109 |
| | | | **HOT-TODDYS - see THE REBELS** | | |
| | | | **CISSY HOUSTON** | | |
| | | | Real name: Emily Houston. Began career singing with a family gospel group, the Drinkard Singers, which included her nieces Dionne and Dee Dee Warwick. Lead singer of the Sweet Inspirations, 1967-70. Mother of Whitney Houston. Also see Herbie Mann. | | |
| 6/13/70 | **45** | 2 | 1 I'll Be There ................................................ | 125 | Commonw. 3010 |
| 3/13/71 | **31** | 8 | 2 Be My Baby................................................ | 92 | Janus 145 |
| 3/26/77 | **97** | 4 | 3 Love Is Something That Leads You .................. | | Private S. 45137 |
| 7/16/77 | **74** | 7 | 4 Tomorrow ................................................... | | Private S. 45153 |
| 8/12/78 | **32** | 10 | 5 Think It Over.............................................. | 106 | Private S. 45204 |
| | | | produced & arranged by Michael Zager | | |
| | | | **JOE HOUSTON** | | |
| | | | Born in Austin, Texas. Tenor saxophonist. With Amos Milburn's and Joe Turner's touring bands in the late 40s. First recorded for Freedom in 1949, with small band. Active on the West Coast since 1952. | | |
| 2/23/52 | **10** | 1 | 1 **Worry, Worry, Worry** ............................... [I] | | Mercury 8248 |
| | | | Juke Box #10 | | |
| | | | originally released on Sphinx 122 | | |
| | | | **THELMA HOUSTON** | | |
| | | | Singer/actress from Leland, Mississippi. In the films "Norman...Is That You?", "Death Scream" and "The Seventh Dwarf". | | |
| 9/07/74 | **64** | 6 | 1 You've Been Doin' Wrong For So Long .............. | | Motown 1316 |
| 12/25/76+ | **1** [1] | 19 | 2 **Don't Leave Me This Way** ........................... | 1 | Tamla 54278 |
| 5/07/77 | **12** | 13 | 3 If It's The Last Thing I Do............................. | 47 | Tamla 54283 |
| 9/24/77 | **84** | 3 | 4 It's A Lifetime Thing................................... | | Motown 1422 |
| 10/15/77 | **21** | 17 | 5 I'm Here Again ........................................... | | Tamla 54287 |
| 2/17/79 | **19** | 17 | 6 Saturday Night, Sunday Morning..................... | 34 | Tamla 54297 |
| 4/25/81 | **35** | 13 | 7 If You Feel It ............................................. | | RCA 12215 |
| 10/03/81 | **76** | 5 | 8 96 Tears .................................................... | | RCA 12285 |
| 4/02/83 | **46** | 8 | 9 Working Girl .............................................. | | MCA 52196 |
| 8/13/83 | **80** | 5 | 10 Just Like All The Rest ................................. | | MCA 52239 |
| 11/10/84+ | **13** | 15 | 11 You Used To Hold Me So Tight........................ | | MCA 52491 |

| DEBUT DATE | PEAK POS | WKS CHR | ARTIST — Record Title | POP POS | Label & Number |
|---|---|---|---|---|---|
| 3/02/85 | **59** | 9 | **THELMA HOUSTON — Continued**<br>12 (I Guess) It Must Be Love ............................... | | MCA 52489 |
| | | | **WHITNEY HOUSTON** ★★**193**★★<br>Born in 1963 in New Jersey. Billboard's "Artist of the Year" for 1986. Daughter of Cissy Houston and cousin of Dionne Warwick. Began career as a fashion model, then worked as a backing vocalist. Also see Teddy Pendergrass. | | |
| 3/09/85 | **1**¹ | 28 | 1 **You Give Good Love** ................................... | *3* | Arista 9274 |
| 6/29/85 | **1**¹ | 21 | 2 **Saving All My Love For You**......................... | *1* | Arista 9381 |
| 10/19/85 | **10** | 15 | 3 **Thinking About You** ................................... | | Arista 9412 |
| 12/28/85+ | **1**¹ | 19 | 4 **How Will I Know** ...................................... | *1* | Arista 9434 |
| 4/05/86 | **3** | 17 | 5 **Greatest Love Of All** ................................<br>originally released on the flip side of "You Give Good Love" | *1* | Arista 9466 |
| 5/16/87 | **2**² | 15 | 6●**I Wanna Dance With Somebody (Who Loves Me)** ................................................ | 1 | Arista 9598 |
| 8/01/87 | **2**¹ | 16 | 7 **Didn't We Almost Have It All** ...................... | *1* | Arista 9616 |
| 11/07/87+ | **5** | 14 | 8 **So Emotional** ........................................... | *1* | Arista 9642 |
| 3/05/88 | **2**¹ | 15 | 9 **Where Do Broken Hearts Go**........................ | *1* | Arista 9674 |
| 7/02/88 | **5** | 14 | 10 **Love Will Save The Day** ............................. | *9* | Arista 9720 |
| | | | **CAMILLE HOWARD TRIO**<br>Vocalist/pianist. With Roy Milton's group, The Solid Senders, on string of hits, starting in 1945. Led own trio and small bands from 1948, based in Los Angeles. Trio included Dallas Bartley and Roy Milton. Also see Roy Milton. | | |
| 5/22/48 | **7** | 2 | 1 **X-Temperaneous Boogie/**               [I]<br>Juke Box #7 | | |
| 6/26/48 | **12** | 3 | 2 You Don't Love Me ................................... [I]<br>Best Seller #12 / Juke Box #12 | | Specialty 307 |
| 9/24/49 | **12** | 1 | 3 Fiesta In Old Mexico ............................... [I]<br>Juke Box #12 | | Specialty 332 |
| 9/15/51 | **10** | 1 | 4 **Money Blues**........................................<br>**CAMILLE HOWARD & HER BOY FRIENDS**<br>Best Seller #10 | | Specialty 401 |
| | | | **GEORGE HOWARD**<br>Pop/jazz musician from Philadelphia. Played clarinet from age 6. Attended the Settlement School Of Music. Toured with Grover Washington. | | |
| 4/09/83 | **82** | 4 | 1 The Preacher ........................................ | | Palo Alto 8035 |
| 6/23/84 | **76** | 6 | 2 Steppin' Out......................................<br>vocal by Gwen Guthrie | | TBA 701 |
| 6/15/85 | **80** | 5 | 3 Love Will Find A Way ........................... [I] | | TBA 705 |
| | | | **MIKI HOWARD**<br>Session singer/songwriter from Chicago. Former lead singer of Side Effect. | | |
| 10/25/86+ | **5** | 23 | 1 **Come Share My Love** ................................. | | Atlantic 89351 |
| 3/07/87 | **13** | 16 | 2 Imagination.......................................... | | Atlantic 89284 |
| 6/20/87 | **33** | 11 | 3 Come Back To Me Lover ........................... | | Atlantic 89232 |
| 10/31/87+ | **5** | 20 | 4 **Baby Be Mine** ....................................... | | Atlantic 89165 |
| 2/20/88 | **4** | 16 | 5 **That's What Love Is** ...............................<br>**MIKI HOWARD with GERALD LEVERT** | | Atlantic 89123 |
| 7/02/88 | **38** | 10 | 6 Crazy................................................. | | Atlantic 89068 |
| | | | **ROSETTA HOWARD**<br>Born in 1914 in Chicago. Singing professionally since 1932. First recorded for Decca in 1937, with the Harlem Hamfats. With Sonny Thompson in 1941. Died in 1974. | | |
| 3/27/48 | **8** | 4 | 1 **Ebony Rhapsody**.................................... *21*<br>with the Big Three Trio, including bassist/songwriter Willie Dixon | | Columbia 37573 |
| | | | **HOWLIN' WOLF**<br>Born Chester Arthur Burnett on 6/10/10 in West Point, Mississippi. Died of cancer on 1/10/76 (65). Vocalist/guitarist/harmonica player. With Robert Johnson and Sonny Boy Williamson (Alex "Rice Miller" Ford) in the early 30s. Continued work as a farmer during early career. Own band in 1948. Internationally known as premier blues singer. | | |
| 11/10/51 | **10** | 1 | 1 **Moanin' At Midnight/**<br>Juke Box #10 | | |
| 12/08/51 | **4** | 11 | 2 **How Many More Years**..............................<br>above 2 shown as: **THE HOWLIN' WOLF**<br>Juke Box #4 / Best Seller #8<br>with Ike Turner on piano | | Chess 1479 |
| 6/04/55 | **14** | 1 | 3 Who Will Be Next ................................... [I]<br>Jockey #14<br>with Jody Williams & Hubert Sumlin on guitars | | Chess 1593 |

| DEBUT DATE | PEAK POS | WKS CHR | ARTIST — Record Title | POP POS | Label & Number |
|---|---|---|---|---|---|
| | | | **HOWLIN' WOLF — Continued** | | |
| 3/17/56 | **8** | 3 | 4 **Smoke Stack Lightning** ................................ | | Chess 1618 |
| | | | Juke Box #8 / Best Seller #11 | | |
| | | | with Willie Johnson & Hubert Sumlin on guitars | | |
| 11/10/56 | **8** | 1 | 5 **I Asked For Water** ..................................... | | Chess 1632 |
| | | | Juke Box #8 | | |
| | | | with Willie Johnson & Smokey Smothers on guitars | | |
| 4/12/69 | **43** | 2 | 6 Evil ................................................. | | Cadet Con. 7013 |
| | | | with Hubert Sumlin, Gene Barge and Phil Upchurch | | |
| | | | **R.B. HUDMON** | | |
| | | | Born in West Point, Georgia. | | |
| 3/13/76 | **73** | 4 | 1 How Can I Be A Witness ........................... | | Atlantic 3318 |
| 1/08/77 | **61** | 6 | 2 Whatever Makes You Happy ......................... | | Atlantic 3366 |
| 8/13/77 | **42** | 12 | 3 This Could Be The Night............................ | | Atlantic 3413 |
| 3/11/78 | **47** | 9 | 4 Cause You're Mine Now .............................. | | Cotillion 44232 |
| | | | **AL HUDSON & THE SOUL PARTNERS** | | |
| | | | Detroit singer. His backing band, The Soul Partners, became One Way in 1979. | | |
| 11/20/76+ | **64** | 10 | 1 I Got A Notion ..................................... | | ABC 12230 |
| 9/10/77 | **83** | 5 | 2 Why Must We Say Goodbye.......................... | | ABC 12294 |
| 12/10/77+ | **78** | 10 | 3 If You Feel Like Dancin' ............................ | | ABC 12317 |
| 9/02/78 | **75** | 3 | 4 Spread Love....................................... | | ABC 12385 |
| 11/11/78 | **51** | 7 | 5 How Do You Do.................................... | | ABC 12424 |
| 3/24/79 | **52** | 23 | 6 You Can Do It..................................... | *101* | ABC 12459 |
| | | | shown only as: **AL HUDSON & THE PARTNERS** | | |
| | | | **DAVID HUDSON** | | |
| 5/10/80 | **37** | 14 | 1 Honey, Honey..................................... | *59* | Alston 3750 |
| | | | **THE HUES CORPORATION** | | |
| | | | Vocal trio formed in Los Angeles in 1969. Consisted of H. Ann Kelley (soprano), Fleming Williams (tenor) and Bernard "St. Clair Lee" Henderson (baritone). Williams replaced by Tom Brown after "Rock The Boat". Brown replaced by Karl Russell in 1975. | | |
| 5/04/74 | **2²** | 21 | 1 ●**Rock The Boat**.................................... | *1* | RCA 0232 |
| 10/19/74 | **6** | 15 | 2 Rockin' Soul ...................................... | *18* | RCA 10066 |
| 2/15/75 | **15** | 11 | 3 Love Corporation .................................. | *62* | RCA 10200 |
| 5/14/77 | **61** | 11 | 4 I Caught Your Act ................................. | *92* | Warner 8334 |
| | | | **LEON HUFF** | | |
| | | | Born in Camden, New Jersey. Session pianist in New York City and Philadelphia. Formed band, the Locomotions. Wrote "Mixed-Up Shook-Up Girl" for Patty & The Emblems in 1964. Joined the Romeos in 1965. Formed Gamble Records with Kenny Gamble in 1965. One of the foremost Philly-sound producers. | | |
| 8/02/80 | **68** | 5 | 1 Tight Money ....................................... | | Phil. Int. 3109 |
| 1/10/81 | **57** | 7 | 2 I Ain't Jivin', I'm Jammin' (Part 1) .................. | | Phil. Int. 3122 |
| | | | **TERRY HUFF** | | |
| 5/01/76 | **11** | 17 | 1 The Lonely One .................................... | *75* | Mainstream 5581 |
| | | | **SPECIAL DELIVERY featuring TERRY HUFF** | | |
| 9/11/76 | **91** | 5 | 2 That's When It Hurts ............................... | | Mainstream 5585 |
| | | | **FRED HUGHES** | | |
| | | | Singer from Arkansas. To Los Angeles, formed own band, the Creators. Went solo in 1965. | | |
| 5/22/65 | **3** | 15 | 1 **Oo Wee Baby, I Love You** ............................ | *23* | Vee-Jay 684 |
| 9/11/65 | **12** | 12 | 2 You Can't Take It Away ............................. | *96* | Vee-Jay 703 |
| 7/06/68 | **20** | 10 | 3 Send My Baby Back................................. | *94* | Wand 1182 |
| 12/13/69+ | **25** | 8 | 4 Baby Boy.......................................... | | Brunswick 55419 |
| 7/18/70 | **45** | 3 | 5 I Understand ...................................... | | Brunswick 55439 |
| | | | **JIMMY HUGHES** | | |
| | | | Singer from Florence, Alabama. With the Singing Clouds gospel group to 1962. Cousin of Percy Sledge. | | |
| 6/20/64 | **17** | 12 | 1 Steal Away ........................................ | *Hot* | Fame 6401 |
| 9/26/64 | **65** | 4 | 2 Try Me ............................................ | *Hot* | Fame 6403 |
| 5/28/66 | **4** | 12 | 3 **Neighbor, Neighbor**................................ | *65* | Fame 1003 |
| 9/17/66 | **25** | 5 | 4 I Worship The Ground You Walk On ................. | | Fame 1006 |
| 2/11/67 | **5** | 12 | 5 **Why Not Tonight** ................................... | *90* | Fame 1011 |

| DEBUT DATE | PEAK POS | WKS CHR | ARTIST — Record Title | POP POS | Label & Number |
|---|---|---|---|---|---|
| | | | **JIMMY HUGHES — Continued** | | |
| 1/20/68 | 43 | 3 | 6 It Ain't What You Got ..................................... | | Atlantic 2454 |
| 9/14/68 | 21 | 9 | 7 I Like Everything About You .......................... | | Volt 4002 |
| | | | **RHETTA HUGHES** | | |
| | | | Sister of keyboardist Tennyson Stephens. With Stephens as duo in Dallas. Worked at Caesar's Palace in Las Vegas, and at Redd Foxx's club in Los Angeles. Toured with Bill Cosby. | | |
| 2/08/69 | 36 | 6 | 1 Light My Fire ......................................... | *102* | Tetragramm. 1513 |
| | | | #1 pop hit for The Doors in 1967 | | |
| 5/28/83 | 88 | 3 | 2 Angel Man ..................................... | | Aria 1208 |
| | | | **HUMAN BODY** | | |
| 5/19/84 | 84 | 2 | 1 Make You Shake It .................................. | | Bearsville 29296 |
| | | | **THE HUMAN LEAGUE** | | |
| | | | Electro-pop band from Sheffield, England, featuring lead singer/synthesizer player Philip Oakey, with vocalists Joanne Catherall and Susanne Sulley. | | |
| 7/02/83 | 56 | 11 | 1 (Keep Feeling) Fascination ............................ | 8 | A&M 2547 |
| 9/20/86 | 3 | 16 | 2 **Human** ..................................... | *1* | A&M 2861 |
| 12/20/86+ | 52 | 9 | 3 I Need Your Loving................................. | 44 | A&M 2893 |
| | | | **HELEN HUMES** | | |
| | | | Born on 6/23/13 in Louisville, Kentucky. Died in 9/13/81. Vocalist/pianist. First recorded for Okeh in 1927. With Al Sears band in Buffalo, New York, and at the Cotton Club in Cincinnati. Recorded with Harry James for Brunswick in 1937. Signed by Count Basie to replace Billie Holiday from 1938-41, then went solo. To the West Coast in the mid-40s. Left music from 1967-74. | | |
| 12/15/45 | 3 | 8 | 1 **Be Baba Leba** ..................................... | | Philo 106 |
| | | | with Bill Doggett Octet; also released on Aladdin 106 | | |
| 10/28/50 | 6 | 4 | 2 **Million Dollar Secret**................................. | | Modern 779 |
| | | | Best Seller #6 / Juke Box #7 with Roy Milton's Band; recorded live at "Blues Jubilee", Los Angeles in August of 1950 | | |
| | | | **BOBBI HUMPHREY** | | |
| | | | Born on 4/25/50 in Dallas. Jazz Flutist. Studied at Southern Methodist and Texas Southern University. First recorded for Blue Note in 1971. | | |
| 4/06/74 | 49 | 9 | 1 Chicago, Damn ....................................... | *106* | Blue Note 395 |
| 8/24/74 | 86 | 5 | 2 Harlem River Drive .................................. | | Blue Note 455 |
| 3/08/75 | 82 | 4 | 3 Fun House ............................................ | | Blue Note 592 |
| 5/01/76 | 82 | 4 | 4 Uno Esta ............................................. | | Blue Note 785 |
| 5/27/78 | 60 | 11 | 5 Home-Made Jam ..................................... | | Epic 50529 |
| | | | with Stevie Wonder on harmonica | | |
| 9/08/79 | 90 | 2 | 6 Love When I'm In Your Arms ......................... | | Epic 50745 |
| | | | **DELLA HUMPHREY** | | |
| 11/16/68 | 18 | 7 | 1 Don't Make The Good Girls Go Bad.................. | 79 | Arctic 144 |
| | | | **PAUL HUMPHREY & HIS COOL AID CHEMISTS** | | |
| | | | Paul was born on 10/12/35 in Detroit. Session drummer. With Wes Montgomery, Les McCann, Kai Winding, Charlie Mingus, Lee Konitz and Gene Ammons in the early 60s. | | |
| 3/06/71 | 14 | 11 | 1 Cool Aid ............................................ [I] | 29 | Lizard 21006 |
| 8/07/71 | 45 | 4 | 2 Funky L.A. ............................................. | *109* | Lizard 1009 |
| | | | written by Nolan Porter | | |
| | | | **TEDDY HUMPHRIES** | | |
| 3/16/59 | 16 | 6 | 1 What Makes You So Tough .......................... | | King 5182 |
| | | | with Mickey Baker (guitar) and Milt Hinton (bass) | | |
| | | | **GERALDINE HUNT** | | |
| | | | Vocalist from Chicago, attended Hyde Park High School with Minnie Riperton. Toured with the International Ink Spots, settled in Montreal. Daughter Rosalind was in the group Cheri. | | |
| 10/24/70 | 45 | 3 | 1 You & I ............................................. | | Calla 173 |
| 8/05/72 | 47 | 3 | 2 Baby, I Need Your Loving ........................... | | Roulette 7129 |
| 11/24/73 | 78 | 4 | 3 You Brought Joy..................................... | | Roulette 7149 |
| 10/11/80 | 58 | 9 | 4 Can't Fake The Feeling ............................. | | Prism 315 |
| 10/24/81 | 67 | 7 | 5 Heart Heart........................................ | | Prism 323 |

| DEBUT DATE | PEAK POS | WKS CHR | ARTIST — Record Title | POP POS | Label & Number |
|---|---|---|---|---|---|
| | | | **TOMMY HUNT** | | |
| | | | Vocalist from Pittsburgh. Real name: Charles Hunt. While a member of The Five Echoes (from 1952-53), recorded for Sabre in 1953. In The Flamingos from 1958-61. First solo recording for Wand in 1961. Moved to Wales, UK in 1970. | | |
| 9/25/61 | **5** | 11 | 1 **Human** .................................................... | *48* | Scepter 1219 |
| 11/09/63 | **71** | 5 | 2 I Am A Witness.......................................... | *Hot* | Scepter 1261 |
| 2/25/67 | **29** | 4 | 3 The Biggest Man ...................................... | *124* | Dynamo 101 |
| | | | **IVORY JOE HUNTER** ★★**76**★★ | | |
| | | | Born on 10/10/14 in Kirbyville, Texas. Died of lung cancer on 11/8/74. Vocalist/ pianist/composer. First recorded in 1933, a cylinder record for the Library of Congress in Wiergate, Texas. Own radio shows, KFDM-Beaumont in the early 40s. To West Coast in 1942. Own record companies, Ivory and Pacific, in 1944. Signed by King Records in 1947, MGM in 1950. Popular Country artist in later years. | | |
| 12/15/45 | **3** | 2 | 1 **Blues At Sunrise** ..................................... | | Exclusive 209 |
| | | | with Johnny Moore's Three Blazers | | |
| 6/05/48 | **1**³ | 25 | 2 **Pretty Mama Blues** ................................ | | Pacific 637 |
| | | | Best Seller #1(3) / Juke Box #1(3) also released on Four Star 1254 | | |
| 6/05/48 | **8** | 13 | 3 **Don't Fall In Love With Me**...................... | | King 4220 |
| | | | Juke Box #8 / Best Seller #9 | | |
| 10/23/48 | **9** | 2 | 4 **What Did You Do To Me**............................ | | King 4232 |
| | | | Juke Box #9 | | |
| 12/25/48 | **14** | 1 | 5 **I Like It** ................................................ | | King 4255 |
| | | | Juke Box #14 / Best Seller #15 above 3: with Tyree Glenn, Russell Procope & Oscar Pettiford | | |
| 9/10/49 | **5** | 4 | 6 **Waiting In Vain**...................................... | | King 4291 |
| | | | Juke Box #5 | | |
| 9/10/49 | **10** | 1 | 7 **Blues At Midnight** .................................. | | 4 Star 1283 |
| | | | Juke Box #10 recorded in 1947; originally released on Pacific 630 | | |
| 10/08/49 | **2**² | 12 | 8 **Guess Who/** | | |
| | | | Juke Box #2 / Best Seller #5 6 & 8: with Ray Nance, Tyree Glenn, Russell Procope & Oscar Pettiford | | |
| 10/15/49 | **6** | 5 | 9 **Landlord Blues**...................................... | | King 4306 |
| | | | Juke Box #6 / Best Seller #7 with Owen Bradley on guitar | | |
| 11/12/49 | **2**¹ | 10 | 10 **Jealous Heart**......................................... | | King 4314 |
| | | | Juke Box #2 / Best Seller #15 | | |
| 1/07/50 | **1**⁵ | 24 | 11 **I Almost Lost My Mind** ............................ | | MGM 10578 |
| | | | Juke Box #1(5) / Best Seller #1(2) with Taft Jordan on trumpet | | |
| 1/14/50 | **4** | 9 | 12 **I Quit My Pretty Mama**............................. | | King 4326 |
| | | | Juke Box #4 / Best Seller #5 with Johnny Hodges on alto sax | | |
| 2/25/50 | **9** | 3 | 13 **S.P. Blues** ............................................. | | MGM 10618 |
| | | | Juke Box #9 / Best Seller #13 with Taft Jordan on trumpet | | |
| 4/29/50 | **1**² | 21 | 14 **I Need You So**.......................................... | | MGM 10663 |
| | | | Juke Box #1 / Best Seller #2 | | |
| 12/02/50 | **10** | 1 | 15 **It's A Sin**............................................... | | MGM 10818 |
| | | | Juke Box #10 | | |
| 4/30/55 | **14** | 1 | 16 **It May Sound Silly**................................... | | Atlantic 1049 |
| | | | Jockey #14 with his Ivory Tones and the Budd Johnson Orchestra | | |
| 3/17/56 | **15** | 1 | 17 A Tear Fell ............................................. | | Atlantic 1086 |
| | | | Jockey #15 | | |
| 12/01/56+ | **1**³ | 18 | 18 **Since I Met You Baby** .............................. | *12* | Atlantic 1111 |
| | | | Juke Box #1(3) / Jockey #1(1) / Best Seller #2 | | |
| 4/06/57 | **2**¹ | 8 | 19 **Empty Arms/** | *43* | |
| | | | Jockey #2 / Juke Box #5 / Best Seller #10 | | |
| 4/13/57 | **7** | 5 | 20 **Love's A Hurting Game** ........................... | | Atlantic 1128 |
| | | | Jockey #7 above 3: with the Ray Ellis Orchestra & Chorus | | |
| 10/20/58 | **13** | 3 | 21 Yes I Want You ....................................... | *94* | Atlantic 1191 |
| | | | with saxophonists Budd Johnson and Dave McRae | | |
| | | | **TAB HUNTER** | | |
| | | | Born Arthur Andrew Kelm on 7/11/31 in New York City. Sportsman turned actor in 1952. Very popular on film and TV. | | |
| 1/26/57 | **8** | 6 | 1 **Young Love**............................................. | *1* | Dot 15533 |
| | | | Jockey #8 / Juke Box #8 / Best Seller #9 | | |

| DEBUT DATE | PEAK POS | WKS CHR | ARTIST — Record Title | POP POS | Label & Number |
|---|---|---|---|---|---|
| | | | **TY HUNTER** | | |
| | | | Born in 1943; died on 2/24/81. Former lead singer of the Voice Masters. Joined The Originals in 1971. | | |
| 7/04/60 | 18 | 4 | 1 Everthing About You ..................................... | | Anna 1114 |
| 12/29/62 | 22 | 1 | 2 Lonely Baby................................................. | | Check-Mate 1015 |
| | | | **DEBRA HURD** | | |
| 4/16/83 | 50 | 7 | 1 Hug Me, Squeeze Me ...................................... | | Geffen 29710 |
| 7/16/83 | 62 | 6 | 2 Gotta Broken Heart Again ............................. | | Geffen 29581 |
| | | | **HURT 'EM BAD & THE S.C. BAND** | | |
| 11/13/82 | 87 | 3 | 1 Monday Night Football .................................. | | Profile 5011 |
| | | | **WILLIE HUTCH** | | |
| | | | Born Willie McKinley Hutchinson in 1946 in Los Angeles; raised in Dallas. Producer/writer for Motown from 1970. Debut as performer with "The Mack" soundtrack album in 1973. | | |
| 5/05/73 | 18 | 11 | 1 Brother's Gonna Work It Out........................ | 67 | Motown 1222 |
| 7/28/73 | 18 | 10 | 2 Slick........................................................ | 65 | Motown 1252 |
| | | | above 2: from the film "The Mack" | | |
| 11/24/73 | 72 | 6 | 3 Sunshine Lady .......................................... | | Motown 1282 |
| 3/02/74 | 70 | 6 | 4 If You Ain't Got No Money ........................... | | Motown 1287 |
| 6/08/74 | 64 | 6 | 5 Theme Of Foxy Brown................................. | | Motown 1292 |
| 3/08/75 | 24 | 11 | 6 Get Ready For The Get Down ....................... | | Motown 1339 |
| 8/09/75 | 8 | 20 | 7 **Love Power** ............................................. | 41 | Motown 1360 |
| 2/28/76 | 19 | 15 | 8 Party Down .............................................. | | Motown 1371 |
| 11/13/76 | 95 | 2 | 9 Let Me Be The One Baby ............................. | | Motown 1406 |
| 12/25/76+ | 60 | 9 | 10 Shake It, Shake It ..................................... | | Motown 1411 |
| 8/27/77 | 49 | 12 | 11 We Gonna Party Tonight ............................ | | Motown 1424 |
| 1/21/78 | 40 | 9 | 12 What You Gonna Do After The Party ............. | | Motown 1433 |
| 8/05/78 | 62 | 8 | 13 All American Funkathon ............................. | | Whitfield 8615 |
| 11/18/78 | 74 | 4 | 14 Paradise ................................................... | | Whitfield 8689 |
| 10/23/82 | 55 | 10 | 15 In And Out ............................................... | | Motown 1637 |
| | | | **SHEILA HUTCHINSON - see GARRY GLENN** | | |
| | | | **LeROY HUTSON** | | |
| | | | Born on 6/4/45 in Newark, New Jersey. Lead singer with The Impressions from 1971-73. | | |
| 7/14/73 | 75 | 2 | 1 Love Oh Love ............................................ | | Curtom 1983 |
| 10/06/73 | 81 | 5 | 2 When You Smile ........................................ | | Curtom 1989 |
| 6/15/74 | 81 | 5 | 3 Ella Wheeze .............................................. | | Curtom 1996 |
| 3/01/75 | 31 | 12 | 4 All Because Of You...................................... | | Curtom 0100 |
| 9/27/75 | 66 | 8 | 5 Can't Stay Away ........................................ | | Curtom 0107 |
| 2/07/76 | 25 | 10 | 6 Feel The Spirit (In '76)................................ | | Curtom 0112 |
| 5/22/76 | 68 | 7 | 7 Lover's Holiday ......................................... | | Curtom 0117 |
| 11/13/76+ | 55 | 13 | 8 I Do, I Do (Want To Make Love To You) ............. | | Curtom 0121 |
| 5/07/77 | 82 | 3 | 9 Blackberry Jam ......................................... | | Curtom 0124 |
| 3/04/78 | 45 | 11 | 10 Where Did Love Go ..................................... | | Curtom 0134 |
| 5/20/78 | 56 | 7 | 11 In The Mood............................................. | | Curtom 0139 |
| 11/10/79 | 47 | 10 | 12 Right Or Wrong.......................................... | | RSO 1011 |
| | | | **BRIAN HYLAND** | | |
| | | | Born on 11/12/43 in Queens, New York. Own group, the Delphis, at age 12. In production company with Del Shannon in 1970. | | |
| 7/25/60 | 10 | 9 | 1 **Itsy Bitsy Teenie Weenie Yellow Polka Dot Bikini** ............................................... [N] | 1 | Leader 805 |
| | | | Brian was a high school sophomore at the time of this recording | | |
| | | | **DICK HYMAN & HIS ELECTRIC ECLECTICS** | | |
| | | | Born on 3/8/27 in New York City. Pianist/composer/conductor/arranger who toured Europe with Benny Goodman in 1950. Staff pianist at WMCA and WNBC-New York from 1951-57. Music director of the Arthur Godfrey Show from 1958-62. | | |
| 6/21/69 | 27 | 5 | 1 The Minotaur ............................................. [I] | 38 | Command 4126 |
| | | | **PHYLLIS HYMAN** | | |
| | | | Philadelphia-born singer/actress/fashion model. Raised in Pittsburgh. Sang in All-City Choir. With the group New Direction in 1971. Toured with Norman Connors. In the Broadway musical "Sophisticated Ladies" in 1981. Also see Norman Connors. | | |
| 8/21/76 | 76 | 6 | 1 Baby I'm Gonna Love You ............................. | | Desert Mn. 6402 |

| DEBUT DATE | PEAK POS | WKS CHR | ARTIST — Record Title | POP POS | Label & Number |
|---|---|---|---|---|---|
| | | | **PHYLLIS HYMAN — Continued** | | |
| 4/09/77 | **32** | 12 | 2 Loving You - Losing You.................................... | *103* | Buddah 567 |
| 7/23/77 | **58** | 10 | 3 No One Can Love You More........................... | | Buddah 577 |
| 12/23/78+ | **12** | 16 | 4 Somewhere In My Lifetime........................... | | Arista 0380 |
| 10/20/79 | **12** | 21 | 5 You Know How To Love Me.......................... produced by James Mtume and Reggie Lucas | *101* | Arista 0463 |
| 3/08/80 | **37** | 11 | 6 Under Your Spell....................................... | | Arista 0495 |
| 7/11/81 | **9** | 15 | 7 **Can't We Fall In Love Again** ..................... | | Arista 0606 |
| 10/24/81 | **22** | 10 | 8 Tonight You And Me................................... | | Arista 0637 |
| 2/06/82 | **76** | 3 | 9 You Sure Look Good To Me.......................... | | Arista 0656 |
| 5/28/83 | **30** | 13 | 10 Riding The Tiger........................................ | | Arista 9023 |
| 9/24/83 | **74** | 4 | 11 Why Did You Turn Me On ........................... | | Arista 9071 |
| 8/30/86 | **14** | 16 | 12 Old Friend ............................................... | | Phil. Int. 53031 |
| 12/20/86+ | **12** | 17 | 13 Living All Alone......................................... | | Phil. Int. 50059 |
| 5/09/87 | **29** | 12 | 14 Ain't You Had Enough Love ......................... | | Phil. Int. 50070 |

# I

## ICE-T
Los Angeles-based rapper, Tracy Morrow. In films, "Breakin'" and "Breakin' II".

| | | | | | |
|---|---|---|---|---|---|
| 6/25/88 | **77** | 4 | 1 Colors........................................................ from the film of the same title | *70* | Sire 27902 |

## IDEALS
Group from Crane High School in Chicago. Formed in 1952 as the Mel-tones. Included Major Lance for a short time. First recorded for Paso in 1961. Group that recorded "Kissin'" consisted of Reggie Jackson, Leonard Mitchell and Sam Stewart.

| | | | | | |
|---|---|---|---|---|---|
| 2/26/66 | **40** | 1 | 1 Kissin' ...................................................... | | Satellite 2009 |

## JULIO IGLESIAS - see DIANA ROSS and STEVIE WONDER

## THE IKETTES
Female trio formed for the Ike & Tina Turner Revue. Atco group consisted of Delores Johnson (lead), Eloise Hester and "Joshie" Jo Armstead. Various personnel; group on Modern consisted of Vanetta Fields, Robbie Montgomery and Jessie Smith; they were later known as The Mirettes.

| | | | | | |
|---|---|---|---|---|---|
| 1/13/62 | **3** | 13 | 1 **I'm Blue (The Gong-Gong Song)** ................... | *19* | Atco 6212 |
| 3/20/65 | **28** | 8 | 2 Peaches 'N' Cream...................................... | *36* | Modern 1005 |
| 10/02/65 | **12** | 12 | 3 I'm So Thankful ......................................... | *74* | Modern 1011 |
| | | | **IKE & TINA TURNER & THE IKETTES:** | | |
| 5/04/68 | **50** | 2 | 4 So Fine .................................................... | *117* | Innis 6667 |
| 2/07/70 | **21** | 8 | 5 Come Together .......................................... | *57* | Minit 32087 |
| 6/13/70 | **25** | 5 | 6 I Want To Take You Higher.......................... | *34* | Liberty 56177 |

## ILLUSION
Jazz-rock sextet formed by members of Renaissance.

| | | | | | |
|---|---|---|---|---|---|
| 6/26/82 | **60** | 5 | 1 Why Can't We Live Together ......................... | | Sugar Hill 785 |

## IMAGINATION
London trio formed in 1981: Leee John (vocals), Ashley Ingram (keyboards) and Errol Kennedy (drums). Group name is tribute to John Lennon and his song "Imagine".

| | | | | | |
|---|---|---|---|---|---|
| 2/20/82 | **68** | 6 | 1 Burnin' Up................................................. | | MCA 52007 |
| 6/05/82 | **27** | 16 | 2 Just An Illusion.......................................... | *102* | MCA 52067 |
| 11/27/82+ | **52** | 9 | 3 Music And Lights ....................................... | | MCA 52129 |
| 3/12/83 | **46** | 7 | 4 Changes ................................................... | | MCA 52174 |
| 8/06/83 | **64** | 6 | 5 Looking At Midnight.................................... | | Elektra 69815 |
| 1/28/84 | **29** | 11 | 6 This Means War (Shoobedoodah Dabba Doobee).. | | Elektra 69763 |
| 12/12/87 | **88** | 5 | 7 The Last Time ............................................ | | RCA 5296 |

## IMPACT
Baltimore group formed as the Vandalls: Damon Otis Harris (lead vocals), John Simms, Charles Timmons and Donald Tilghman. Harris was in The Temptations from 1971-75, then returned to the Vandalls (re-named Impact).

| | | | | | |
|---|---|---|---|---|---|
| 5/22/76 | **42** | 10 | 1 Happy Man (Pt. I)....................................... | *94* | Atco 7049 |
| 8/14/76 | **36** | 9 | 2 Give A Broken Heart A Break........................ | *102* | Atco 7056 |
| 9/03/77 | **90** | 5 | 3 Rainy Days, Stormy Nights Pt. 1 ................... | | Fantasy 798 |
| 1/21/78 | **49** | 10 | 4 Sister Fine ................................................ | | Fantasy 813 |

| DEBUT DATE | PEAK POS | WKS CHR | ARTIST — Record Title | POP POS | Label & Number |
|---|---|---|---|---|---|
| | | | **THE IMPALAS** | | |
| | | | Pop vocal quartet from Brooklyn: Joe "Speedo" Frazier, Richard Wagner, Lenny Renda and Tony Carlucci. All members, except black lead singer Frazier, are white. Group disbanded by early 1961. | | |
| 5/11/59 | 14 | 5 | 1 Sorry (I Ran All The Way Home) ..................... | 2 | Cub 9022 |
| | | | **IMPERIALS** | | |
| 6/10/78 | 73 | 6 | 1 Who's Gonna Love Me................................. | | Omni 5501 |
| | | | **THE IMPRESSIONS** ★★18★★ | | |
| | | | Chicago group, formed in 1957. Originally known as The Roosters; consisted of Jerry Butler, Curtis Mayfield, Sam Gooden and brothers Arthur and Richard Brooks. Butler left for a solo career in 1958, replaced by Fred Cash. The Brooks brothers left in 1962, leaving Mayfield as the trio's leader. Mayfield left in 1970 for a solo career, replaced by Leroy Hutson. In 1973, Hutson was replaced by Reggie Torian and Ralph Johnson. In 1976, Johnson joined Mystique. Did film soundtrack for "Three The Hard Way". Butler, Mayfield, Gooden and Cash reunited for a tour in 1983. | | |
| 7/28/58 | 3 | 7 | 1 **For Your Precious Love** ............................... JERRY BUTLER & THE IMPRESSIONS | 11 | Abner/Falcon 1013 |
| | | | Jockey #3 / Best Seller #10 | | |
| 10/20/58 | 29 | 1 | 2 Come Back My Love ...................................... THE IMPRESSIONS featuring JERRY BUTLER | | Abner/Falcon 1017 |
| 11/13/61 | 2¹ | 11 | 3 **Gypsy Woman**................................................ | 20 | ABC-Para. 10241 |
| 10/05/63 | 1² | 8 | 4 **It's All Right**.............................................. | 4 | ABC-Para. 10487 |
| 1/18/64 | 12 | 9 | 5 Talking About My Baby............................... | Hot | ABC-Para. 10511 |
| 4/04/64 | 14 | 11 | 6 I'm So Proud .............................................. | Hot | ABC-Para. 10544 |
| 6/06/64 | 10 | 13 | 7 **Keep On Pushing** ....................................... | Hot | ABC-Para. 10554 |
| 9/05/64 | 15 | 10 | 8 You Must Believe Me.................................. | Hot | ABC-Para. 10581 |
| 1/30/65 | 17 | 2 | 9 Amen/ | 7 | |
| | | | featured in the film "Lillies Of The Field" | | |
| 1/30/65 | 35 | 1 | 10 Long, Long Winter ..................................... | | ABC-Para. 10602 |
| 2/20/65 | 3 | 10 | 11 **People Get Ready/** | 14 | |
| 3/13/65 | 35 | 2 | 12 I've Been Trying ....................................... | 133 | ABC-Para. 10622 |
| 4/17/65 | 9 | 7 | 13 **Woman's Got Soul**.................................... | 29 | ABC-Para. 10647 |
| 6/12/65 | 12 | 9 | 14 Meeting Over Yonder ................................ | 48 | ABC-Para. 10670 |
| 9/11/65 | 26 | 7 | 15 I Need You/ | 64 | |
| 10/02/65 | 35 | 4 | 16 Never Could You Be................................... | | ABC-Para. 10710 |
| 12/04/65+ | 12 | 11 | 17 You've Been Cheatin'................................. | 33 | ABC-Para. 10750 |
| 8/27/66 | 12 | 12 | 18 Can't Satisfy ............................................ | 65 | ABC 10831 |
| 3/11/67 | 20 | 11 | 19 You Always Hurt Me .................................. | 96 | ABC 10900 |
| 7/01/67 | 50 | 2 | 20 You Got Me Running.................................. | | ABC 10932 |
| 9/30/67 | 34 | 6 | 21 I Can't Stay Away From You ...................... | 80 | ABC 10964 |
| 1/06/68 | 1¹ | 17 | 22 **We're A Winner** ...................................... | 14 | ABC 11022 |
| 5/04/68 | 17 | 7 | 23 We're Rolling On (Part 1) ........................... | 59 | ABC 11071 |
| 7/27/68 | 9 | 9 | 24 **I Loved And I Lost** .................................. | 61 | ABC 11103 |
| 9/21/68 | 3 | 12 | 25 **Fool For You** ........................................... | 22 | Curtom 1932 |
| 12/07/68+ | 8 | 11 | 26 **This Is My Country** ................................. | 25 | Curtom 1934 |
| 12/07/68 | 44 | 3 | 27 Don't Cry My Love ..................................... | 71 | ABC 11135 |
| 3/08/69 | 23 | 6 | 28 My Deceiving Heart .................................... | 104 | Curtom 1937 |
| 4/19/69 | 15 | 7 | 29 Seven Years .............................................. | 84 | Curtom 1940 |
| 6/28/69 | 1¹ | 13 | 30 **Choice Of Colors** .................................... | 21 | Curtom 1943 |
| 10/18/69 | 10 | 10 | 31 **Say You Love Me** .................................... | 58 | Curtom 1946 |
| 1/10/70 | 44 | 2 | 32 Amen (1970)/ | 110 | |
| 1/24/70 | 31 | 4 | 33 Wherever She Leadeth Me ............................ | 128 | Curtom 1948 |
| 5/16/70 | 3 | 12 | 34 **Check Out Your Mind**................................ | 28 | Curtom 1951 |
| 9/05/70 | 6 | 10 | 35 **(Baby) Turn On To Me** ............................ | 56 | Curtom 1954 |
| 2/20/71 | 12 | 10 | 36 Ain't Got Time............................................ | 53 | Curtom 1957 |
| 7/24/71 | 25 | 5 | 37 Love Me ................................................... | 94 | Curtom 1959 |
| | | | all of above (except #1 & 5): written by Curtis Mayfield | | |
| 4/22/72 | 41 | 3 | 38 This Love's For Real .................................. | | Curtom 1970 |
| 12/29/73+ | 26 | 13 | 39 If It's In You To Do Wrong ......................... | | Curtom 1994 |
| 4/27/74 | 1² | 17 | 40 **Finally Got Myself Together (I'm A Changed Man)** ...................................................... | 17 | Curtom 1997 |
| 9/21/74 | 28 | 11 | 41 Something's Mighty, Mighty Wrong.................. | | Curtom 2003 |
| 4/26/75 | 3 | 19 | 42 **Sooner Or Later** ..................................... | 68 | Curtom 0103 |

| DEBUT DATE | PEAK POS | WKS CHR | ARTIST — Record Title | POP POS | Label & Number |
|---|---|---|---|---|---|
| | | | **THE IMPRESSIONS — Continued** | | |
| 9/06/75 | 3 | 15 | 43 Same Thing It Took ..................................... | 75 | Curtom 0106 |
| 12/13/75+ | 11 | 13 | 44 Loving Power ................................................. | 103 | Curtom 0110 |
| 5/08/76 | 36 | 9 | 45 Sunshine ...................................................... | | Curtom 0116 |
| 11/20/76+ | 40 | 11 | 46 This Time....................................................... | | Cotillion 44210 |
| 3/12/77 | 99 | 1 | 47 You'll Never Find ......................................... | | Cotillion 44214 |
| 7/30/77 | 42 | 8 | 48 Can't Get Along ........................................... | | Cotillion 44222 |
| 5/23/81 | 58 | 10 | 49 For Your Precious Love.............................. | | Chi-Sound 2491 |
| | | | new version of #1 above | | |
| 2/14/87 | 91 | 2 | 50 Can't Wait 'Til Tomorrow ............................. | | MCA 52995 |
| | | | **THE INCREDIBLE BONGO BAND** | | |
| | | | Studio band assembled in Canada by producer Michael Viner. | | |
| 6/30/73 | 42 | 7 | 1 Bongo Rock .............................................. [I] | 57 | MGM 14588 |
| 10/20/73 | 90 | 6 | 2 Let There Be Drums ................................. [I] | 107 | MGM 14635 |
| 9/28/74 | 96 | 4 | 3 Kiburi............................................................ | | Pride 7601 |
| | | | **INCREDIBLES** | | |
| | | | Group from Los Angeles, formed in 1963. Consisted of Cal Waymon, Carl Gilbert Jean Smith and Alda Denise Edwards. Waymon, Gilbert and Smith met at Jefferson High School in Los Angeles. Edwards had been with the Vi-Dels group. | | |
| 10/29/66 | 39 | 5 | 1 I'll Make It Easy (If You'll Come On Home) ......... | 108 | Audio Ar. 60001 |
| 7/29/67 | 45 | 4 | 2 Heart And Soul.............................................. | 122 | Audio Ar. 60007 |
| | | | **INDEEP** | | |
| | | | Michael Cleveland, leader. | | |
| 1/08/83 | 10 | 7 | 1 Last Night A D.J. Saved My Life ................... | 101 | Snd. of NY 602 |
| 4/23/83 | 32 | 13 | 2 When Boys Talk............................................. | | Snd. of NY 604 |
| 7/23/83 | 81 | 4 | 3 Buffalo Bill .................................................... | | Snd. of NY 607 |
| 1/07/84 | 45 | 9 | 4 The Record Keeps Spinning ......................... | | Snd. of NY 610 |
| | | | **THE INDEPENDENTS** | | |
| | | | Group consisting of Chuck Jackson, Maurice Jackson, Helen Curry, and Eric Thomas. Jackson (no relation to solo singer Chuck Jackson) and Marvin Yancey, Jr. were producers/writers for the group, later teamed in production work (Natalie Cole). | | |
| 4/15/72 | 8 | 11 | 1 Just As Long As You Need Me, Part 1 ........... | 84 | Wand 11245 |
| 10/14/72 | 38 | 5 | 2 I Just Want To Be There ................................ | 113 | Wand 11249 |
| 3/31/73 | 1¹ | 13 | 3●Leaving Me .................................................. | 21 | Wand 11252 |
| 7/14/73 | 4 | 13 | 4 Baby I've Been Missing You .......................... | 41 | Wand 11258 |
| 11/03/73 | 12 | 13 | 5 It's All Over .................................................. | 65 | Wand 11263 |
| 1/05/74 | 20 | 13 | 6 The First Time We Met.................................. | 103 | Wand 11267 |
| 5/04/74 | 19 | 13 | 7 Arise And Shine (Let's Get In On).................... | | Wand 11273 |
| 9/07/74 | 7 | 14 | 8 Let This Be A Lesson To You ......................... | 88 | Wand 11279 |
| | | | **THE INDIGOS** | | |
| 12/03/66 | 47 | 2 | 1 Tired Of Crying Over You............................... | | Date 1531 |
| | | | **INDIVIDUALS** | | |
| 11/08/75 | 70 | 6 | 1 Gotta Make A Move ...................................... | | P.I.P. 6510 |
| | | | **INFINITY - see BILLY BUTLER** | | |
| | | | **JORGEN INGMANN & HIS GUITAR** | | |
| | | | Born Jorgen Ingmann-Pedersen on 4/26/25 in Copenhagen, Denmark. | | |
| 2/27/61 | 9 | 11 | 1 Apache.................................................... [I] | 2 | Atco 6184 |
| | | | **INGRAM** | | |
| 12/03/77 | 97 | 4 | 1 Get Your Stuff Off ........................................ | | H&L 4689 |
| | | | **JAMES INGRAM** | | |
| | | | Vocalist/multi-instrumentalist/composer from Akron, Ohio. To Los Angeles in the late 70s, with the band Revelation Funk. Vocalist Phillip Ingram (member of Deco) is his brother. Also see Donna Summer. | | |
| 8/22/81 | 11 | 18 | 1 Just Once .................................................. | 17 | A&M 2357 |
| | | | QUINCY JONES featuring JAMES INGRAM | | |
| 12/26/81+ | 10 | 23 | 2 One Hundred Ways ...................................... | 14 | A&M 2387 |
| | | | QUINCY JONES featuring JAMES INGRAM | | |
| 3/27/82+ | 9 | 38 | 3●Baby, Come To Me ....................................... | 1 | Qwest 50036 |
| | | | PATTI AUSTIN with JAMES INGRAM | | |

| DEBUT DATE | PEAK POS | WKS CHR | ARTIST — Record Title | POP POS | Label & Number |
|---|---|---|---|---|---|
| | | | **JAMES INGRAM — Continued** | | |
| 5/14/83 | 6 | 21 | 4 How Do You Keep The Music Playing ............. | 45 | Qwest 29618 |
| | | | JAMES INGRAM & PATTI AUSTIN | | |
| 10/08/83 | 21 | 15 | 5 Party Animal................................................. | 101 | Qwest 29493 |
| 12/17/83+ | 5 | 19 | 6 Yah Mo B There.......................................... | 19 | Qwest 29394 |
| | | | JAMES INGRAM with MICHAEL McDONALD | | |
| 3/24/84 | 14 | 15 | 7 There's No Easy Way .................................. | 58 | Qwest 29316 |
| 8/04/84 | 59 | 8 | 8 She Loves Me (The Best That I Can Be) ............ | | Qwest 29235 |
| 10/06/84 | 57 | 9 | 9 What About Me? ........................................ | 15 | RCA 13899 |
| | | | KENNY ROGERS with KIM CARNES & JAMES INGRAM | | |
| 7/26/86 | 27 | 14 | 10 Always ..................................................... | | Qwest 28669 |
| 12/06/86 | 86 | 5 | 11 Never Felt So Good.................................... | | Qwest 28537 |
| 7/04/87 | 66 | 5 | 12 Better Way .............................................. | | MCA 53125 |
| | | | from the film "Beverly Hills Cop II" | | |
| | | | **LUTHER INGRAM**   ★★147★★ | | |
| | | | Born on 11/30/44 in Jackson, Tennessee. Singer/songwriter. Sang in a gospel group with his brothers. First recorded for Smash in 1965. Appeared in the film "Wattstax". | | |
| 5/24/69 | 39 | 5 | 1 Pity For The Lonely.................................... | | KoKo 2102 |
| 12/06/69 | 19 | 11 | 2 My Honey And Me ...................................... | 55 | KoKo 2104 |
| 5/16/70 | 6 | 11 | 3 Ain't That Loving You (For More Reasons Than One)............................................... | 45 | KoKo 2105 |
| 10/24/70 | 22 | 10 | 4 To The Other Man ...................................... | 110 | KoKo 2106 |
| 5/08/71 | 21 | 8 | 5 Be Good To Me Baby................................... | 97 | KoKo 2107 |
| 9/25/71 | 39 | 5 | 6 I'll Love You Until The End........................ | | KoKo 2108 |
| 2/12/72 | 18 | 9 | 7 You Were Made For Me/ | 93 | |
| | | 4 | 8 Missing You ............................................. | 108 | KoKo 2110 |
| 6/03/72 | 1⁴ | 15 | 9 (If Loving You Is Wrong) I Don't Want To Be Right .................................................. | 3 | KoKo 2111 |
| 12/02/72+ | 9 | 12 | 10 I'll Be Your Shelter (In Time Of Storm) ......... | 40 | KoKo 2113 |
| 4/07/73 | 11 | 7 | 11 Always .................................................... | 64 | KoKo 2115 |
| 7/14/73 | 23 | 8 | 12 Love Ain't Gonna Run Me Away ..................... | | KoKo 2116 |
| 7/17/76 | 44 | 12 | 13 Ain't Good For Nothing .............................. | | KoKo 721 |
| 2/19/77 | 33 | 13 | 14 Let's Steal Away To The Hideaway................. | | KoKo 724 |
| 6/04/77 | 35 | 12 | 15 I Like The Feeling .................................... | | KoKo 725 |
| 1/21/78 | 13 | 16 | 16 Do You Love Somebody .............................. | | KoKo 728 |
| 5/13/78 | 41 | 16 | 17 Get To Me ............................................... | | KoKo 731 |
| 11/29/86+ | 29 | 13 | 18 Baby Don't Go Too Far.............................. | | Profile 5125 |
| 2/28/87 | 55 | 9 | 19 Don't Turn Around .................................... | | Profile 5132 |
| 6/06/87 | 89 | 5 | 20 Gotta Serve Somebody ............................... | | Profile 5143 |
| | | | **PHILLIP INGRAM - see SCHERRIE PAYNE** | | |
| | | | **INK SPOTS**   ★★109★★ | | |
| | | | Group from Indianapolis, formed in 1931 as the King, Jack & Jesters. Consisted of Ivory "Deek" Watson (d: 1969), Charlie Fuqua (d: 1971), Orville "Hoppy" Jones (d: 1944) and Jerry Daniels. Name changed to the Ink Spots in 1932. In film "What A Business" in 1934. First recorded for Victor in 1935. Daniels left in 1936, replaced by Bill Kenny (d: 1978). Watson left in 1945, formed new group, the Brown Dots (later called the Four Tunes). Kenny went solo in 1952. Fuqua was the uncle of Harvey Fuqua, leader of The Moonglows. Although many groups have used the name since 1952, there are no original members left singing. | | |
| 10/24/42+ | 1² | 28 | 1 Don't Get Around Much Anymore ................. | 2 | Decca 18503 |
| 10/24/42 | 6 | 4 | 2 Ev'ry Night About This Time...................... | 17 | Decca 18461 |
| 10/24/42 | 10 | 1 | 3 Just As Though You Were Here/ | | |
| 10/31/42 | 9 | 1 | 4 This Is Worth Fighting For ....................... | | Decca 18466 |
| 1/16/43 | 10 | 1 | 5 If I Cared A Little Bit Less .......................... | 20 | Decca 18528 |
| 4/17/43 | 1⁷ | 16 | 6 I Can't Stand Losing You ........................... | 19 | Decca 18542 |
| 2/26/44 | 1¹ | 12 | 7 Cow Cow Boogie (Cuma-Ti-Yi-Yi-Ay) ............ | 10 | Decca 18587 |
| | | | ELLA FITZGERALD & INK SPOTS | | |
| 3/18/44 | 6 | 3 | 8 Don't Believe Everything You Dream ............ | 14 | Decca 18583 |
| | | | from the film "Around The World" | | |
| 5/13/44 | 4 | 14 | 9 I'll Get By (As Long As I Have You)................ | 7 | Decca 18579 |
| | | | from the film "A Guy Named Joe" | | |

| DEBUT DATE | PEAK POS | WKS CHR | ARTIST — Record Title | POP POS | Label & Number |
|---|---|---|---|---|---|
| | | | **INK SPOTS — Continued** | | |
| 10/28/44 | **1** 11 | 21 | 10 **Into Each Life Some Rain Must Fall/** | *1* | |
| 10/28/44+ | **2** 1 | 14 | 11 **I'm Making Believe** ..................... | *1* | Decca 23356 |
| | | | above 2: **ELLA FITZGERALD & INK SPOTS** from the film "Sweet And Low-Down"; a reported million-seller | | |
| 6/01/46 | **1** 3 | 13 | 12 **The Gypsy** ..................................... | *1* | Decca 18817 |
| | | | British song; a reported million-seller | | |
| 7/06/46 | **5** | 1 | 13 **Prisoner Of Love**............................. | *9* | Decca 18864 |
| 9/28/46 | **3** | 3 | 14 **To Each His Own**............................. | *1* | Decca 23615 |
| | | | written for, but not used in the film of the same title; a reported million-seller | | |
| 8/30/47 | **5** | 1 | 15 **Ask Anyone Who Knows** .................. | *17* | Decca 23900 |
| 3/06/48 | **10** | 1 | 16 **The Best Things In Life Are Free** ......... | | Decca 24327 |
| 11/06/48 | **15** | 1 | 17 **You Were Only Fooling (While I Was Falling In Love)**....... | *8* | Decca 24507 |
| | | | Best Seller #15 | | |
| | | | **INNER CITY JAM BAND** | | |
| 11/05/77 | **59** | 11 | 1 What I Did For Love ..................... | | Bareback 535 |
| | | | **INNER LIFE** | | |
| | | | Vocal group led by Jocelyn Brown (former back-up singer). | | |
| 12/15/79+ | **22** | 15 | 1 I'm Caught Up (In A One Night Love Affair)....... | | Prelude 8004 |
| 3/31/84 | **93** | 2 | 2 No Way ..................................... | | Personal 19805 |
| | | | **INNERVISION** | | |
| 4/05/75 | **58** | 8 | 1 Honey Baby (Be Mine) ................... | *106* | Private S. 45015 |
| 7/30/77 | **97** | 3 | 2 Gotta Find A Way To Get Back Home ............. | | Ariola Am. 7657 |
| | | | **THE INNOCENTS** | | |
| | | | Pop trio from Sun Valley, California: James West, Al Candelaria and Darron Stankey. First recorded as The Echoes for Andex in 1959. Back-up vocal group for Kathy Young (b: 10/21/45 in Santa Ana, CA). Group named after their car club. | | |
| 10/24/60+ | **6** | 11 | 1 **A Thousand Stars**............................. | *3* | Indigo 108 |
| | | | **KATHY YOUNG with THE INNOCENTS** | | |
| 1/23/61 | **15** | 5 | 2 Gee Whiz.................................. | *28* | Indigo 111 |
| | | | **INSTANT FUNK** | | |
| | | | Ten-man band from Philadelphia, formed in 1977. Formerly back-up band for Bunny Sigler. Included: Kim Miller (guitar), Raymond Earl (bass), Scotty Miller (drums), Dennis Richardson (piano) and Charles Williams (congas). Also included James Carmichael (percussion, lead vocals), Larry Davis (trumpet), Johnny Onderline (saxes), Eric Huff (trombone) and George Bell (guitar). | | |
| 1/06/79 | **1** 3 | 23 | 1 ● I Got My Mind Made Up (You Can Get It Girl).. | *20* | Salsoul 2078 |
| 6/09/79 | **41** | 11 | 2 Crying..................................... | | Salsoul 2088 |
| 11/17/79 | **35** | 10 | 3 Witch Doctor.............................. | | Salsoul 2108 |
| 1/26/80 | **41** | 10 | 4 Bodyshine................................. | *103* | Salsoul 2112 |
| 11/29/80 | **87** | 3 | 5 The Funk Is On............................ | | Salsoul 2131 |
| 3/13/82 | **59** | 9 | 6 Why Don't You Think About Me............. | | Salsoul 7021 |
| 2/05/83 | **32** | 16 | 7 No Stoppin' That Rockin'................... | | Salsoul 7041 |
| 5/21/83 | **70** | 6 | 8 Who Took Away The Funk.................. | | Salsoul 7046 |
| 10/22/83 | **71** | 8 | 9 (Just Because) You'll Be Mine............... | | Salsoul 7062 |
| | | | **INSTRUMENTAL - see AL KENT** | | |
| | | | **INTERLUDE** | | |
| 5/24/80 | **64** | 6 | 1 Gee Whiz .................................. | | Star Vis. 1103 |
| | | | **THE INTRIGUES** | | |
| | | | Philadelphia trio. | | |
| 8/23/69 | **10** | 10 | 1 In A Moment ............................. | *31* | Yew 1001 |
| 5/22/71 | **21** | 8 | 2 The Language Of Love .................... | *100* | Yew 1012 |
| 3/16/85 | **80** | 5 | 3 Fly Girl .................................... | | World Trd. 1000 |
| | | | **INTRIQUE** | | |
| 9/05/87 | **85** | 3 | 1 Together Forever ......................... | | Cooltempo 43140 |

| DEBUT DATE | PEAK POS | WKS CHR | ARTIST — Record Title | POP POS | Label & Number |
|---|---|---|---|---|---|
| | | | **THE INTRUDERS** ★★90★★ | | |
| | | | Group formed in Philadelphia in 1960. Consisted of Sam "Little Sonny" Brown, Eugene "Bird" Daughtry, Phil Terry and Robert "Big Sonny" Edwards. First recorded for Gowen in 1961. Not to be confused with the white rock trio of the same name. | | |
| 7/09/66 | **14** | 8 | 1 (We'll Be) United ................................... | 78 | Gamble 201 |
| 11/19/66 | **29** | 6 | 2 Devil With Angel's Smile ........................... | | Gamble 203 |
| 4/15/67 | **9** | 11 | 3 **Together** ............................................... | 48 | Gamble 205 |
| 9/16/67 | **28** | 6 | 4 Baby, I'm Lonely/ | 70 | |
| 12/02/67+ | **35** | 8 | 5 A Love That's Real ................................... | 82 | Gamble 209 |
| 3/23/68 | **1**¹ | 14 | 6● Cowboys To Girls ................................... | 6 | Gamble 214 |
| 7/20/68 | **4** | 11 | 7 **(Love Is Like A) Baseball Game** ................ | 26 | Gamble 217 |
| 11/30/68 | **12** | 10 | 8 Slow Drag ........................................... | 54 | Gamble 221 |
| 2/15/69 | **23** | 5 | 9 Give Her A Transplant ............................. | 104 | Gamble 223 |
| 5/03/69 | **41** | 4 | 10 Me Tarzan You Jane ................................ | | Gamble 225 |
| 6/14/69 | **22** | 6 | 11 Lollipop (I Like You) .............................. | 101 | Gamble 231 |
| 8/23/69 | **14** | 11 | 12 Sad Girl ............................................. | 47 | Gamble 235 |
| 12/06/69 | **35** | 4 | 13 Old Love ............................................. | | Gamble 240 |
| 3/14/70 | **25** | 5 | 14 Tender (Was The Love We Knew) ................. | 119 | Gamble 4001 |
| 6/06/70 | **8** | 11 | 15 **When We Get Married** ............................ | 45 | Gamble 4004 |
| 10/17/70 | **22** | 8 | 16 This Is My Love Song .............................. | 85 | Gamble 4007 |
| 2/27/71 | **16** | 9 | 17 I'm Girl Scoutin' ................................... | 88 | Gamble 4009 |
| | | | Little Sonny replaced by Bobby Starr (this record only) | | |
| 6/26/71 | **25** | 6 | 18 Pray For Me ......................................... | 105 | Gamble 4014 |
| 9/25/71 | **20** | 13 | 19 I Bet He Don't Love You (Like I Love You) ........ | 92 | Gamble 4016 |
| 8/19/72 | **12** | 10 | 20 (Win, Place Or Show) She's A Winner ............. | | Gamble 672 |
| 5/12/73 | **6** | 13 | 21 **I'll Always Love My Mama (Part 1)** ............... | 36 | Gamble 2506 |
| 10/13/73 | **9** | 15 | 22 **I Wanna Know Your Name** ....................... | 60 | Gamble 2508 |
| 10/12/74 | **21** | 14 | 23 A Nice Girl Like You ............................... | | TSOP 4758 |
| 5/03/75 | **81** | 5 | 24 Rainy Days And Mondays ........................... | | TSOP 4766 |
| | | | **THE INVINCIBLES** | | |
| | | | Trio formed in Los Angeles, with David Richardson, Lester Johnson and Clifton Knight. Richardson had been in the Invincible Songbirds gospel group. | | |
| 3/27/65 | **31** | 6 | 1 Heart Full Of Love ................................. | | Warner 5495 |
| 6/18/66 | **38** | 2 | 2 Can't Win ........................................... | | Loma 2032 |
| | | | **THE INVISIBLE MAN'S BAND** | | |
| | | | Group evolved from The Five Stairsteps. Consisted of Clarence, Kenneth, Dennis and James Burke. | | |
| 3/15/80 | **9** | 22 | 1 **All Night Thing** ................................... | 45 | Mango 103 |
| 3/06/82 | **79** | 4 | 2 Really Wanna See You .............................. | | Boardwalk 137 |
| 8/27/83 | **77** | 7 | 3 Sunday Afternoon ................................... | | Move'n N G. 004 |
| | | | **INVITATIONS** | | |
| | | | Group from New York City, formed as the Tip-Toppers. Consisted of lead Herman Colefield, Gary Gant, Billy Morris and Bobby Rivers. Recorded for Dyno-Voice in 1965. Several tours of England as the "Original Drifters" in the 60s. | | |
| 5/19/73 | **17** | 9 | 1 They Say The Girl's Crazy ......................... | 110 | Silver Blue 801 |
| 5/25/74 | **79** | 6 | 2 Living Together Is Keeping Us Apart .............. | | Silver Blue 809 |
| 11/09/74 | **43** | 10 | 3 Look On The Good Side ............................. | | Silver Blue 818 |
| | | | **INXS** | | |
| | | | Rock sextet formed in Sydney, Australia: Michael Hutchence (lead singer), Kirk Pengilly, Garry Beers, and brothers Tim, Andy and Jon Farriss. Hutchence starred in the 1987 film "Dogs In Space". | | |
| 2/06/88 | **73** | 6 | 1 Need You Tonight ................................... | 1 | Atlantic 89188 |
| | | | **GLORIA IRVING & SAX KARI** | | |
| | | | Irving is a Detroit native. With the Isaac "Sax" Kari Orchestra. | | |
| 4/11/53 | **8** | 2 | 1 **(Daughter) That's Your Red Wagon** .............. | | States 115 |
| | | | Best Seller #8 / Juke Box #9 | | |
| | | | answer song to Ruth Brown's "Mama He Treats Your Daughter Mean" | | |

| DEBUT DATE | PEAK POS | WKS CHR | ARTIST — Record Title | POP POS | Label & Number |
|---|---|---|---|---|---|
| | | | **THE ISLEY BROTHERS**   ★★12★★ | | |
| | | | Trio of brothers from Cincinatti. Formed in the early 1950s as a gospel group. Consisted of O'Kelly, Ronald and Rudolph Isley. Moved to New York in 1957 and first recorded for Teenage Records. Trio added their younger brothers Ernie (guitar, drums), and Marvin Isley (bass, percussion) and cousin Chris Jasper (keyboards), from 1973-84. Formed own label T-Neck, in 1969. Ernie, Marvin and Chris began recording as the trio Isley, Jasper, Isley, in 1984. O'Kelly died of a heart attack on 3/31/86 at age 48. | | |
| 6/16/62 | 2² | 19 | 1  Twist And Shout | 17 | Wand 124 |
| 2/26/66 | 6 | 13 | 2  This Old Heart Of Mine (Is Weak For You) | 12 | Tamla 54128 |
| 8/06/66 | 31 | 6 | 3  I Guess I'll Always Love You | 61 | Tamla 54135 |
| 5/13/67 | 47 | 3 | 4  Got To Have You Back | 93 | Tamla 54146 |
| | | | written by Leon Ware | | |
| 4/20/68 | 22 | 4 | 5  Take Me In Your Arms (Rock Me A Little While) | 121 | Tamla 54164 |
| 3/15/69 | 1⁴ | 14 | 6 ● It's Your Thing | 2 | T-Neck 901 |
| 6/07/69 | 6 | 11 | 7  I Turned You On | 23 | T-Neck 902 |
| 9/06/69 | 43 | 4 | 8  Black Berries - Pt. 1 | 79 | T-Neck 906 |
| 10/04/69 | 33 | 5 | 9  Was It Good To You | 83 | T-Neck 908 |
| 12/06/69 | 29 | 4 | 10  Bless Your Heart | 105 | T-Neck 912 |
| 2/07/70 | 17 | 8 | 11  Keep On Doin' | 75 | T-Neck 914 |
| 4/25/70 | 21 | 7 | 12  If He Can, You Can | 113 | T-Neck 919 |
| 7/25/70 | 21 | 6 | 13  Girls Will Be Girls, Boys Will Be Boys | 75 | T-Neck 921 |
| 10/03/70 | 25 | 5 | 14  Get Into Something | 89 | T-Neck 924 |
| 12/26/70+ | 16 | 11 | 15  Freedom | 72 | T-Neck 927 |
| 4/03/71 | 17 | 6 | 16  Warpath | 111 | T-Neck 929 |
| 6/19/71 | 3 | 13 | 17  Love The One You're With | 18 | T-Neck 930 |
| 10/02/71 | 14 | 8 | 18  Spill The Wine | 49 | T-Neck 932 |
| 12/04/71 | 29 | 7 | 19  Lay Lady Lay | 71 | T-Neck 933 |
| 3/11/72 | 6 | 11 | 20  Lay-Away | 54 | T-Neck 934 |
| 7/01/72 | 3 | 14 | 21  Pop That Thang | 24 | T-Neck 935 |
| 11/04/72 | 11 | 10 | 22  Work To Do | 51 | T-Neck 936 |
| 5/26/73 | 39 | 4 | 23  It's Too Late | | T-Neck 937 |
| 7/07/73 | 2² | 17 | 24 ● That Lady (Part 1) | 6 | T-Neck 2251 |
| 12/15/73+ | 5 | 14 | 25  What It Comes Down To | 55 | T-Neck 2252 |
| 3/23/74 | 10 | 14 | 26  Summer Breeze (Part 1) | 60 | T-Neck 2253 |
| 7/20/74 | 4 | 17 | 27  Live It Up (Part 1) | 52 | T-Neck 2254 |
| 12/21/74+ | 8 | 14 | 28  Midnight Sky (Part 1) | 73 | T-Neck 2255 |
| 5/31/75 | 1³ | 19 | 29 ● Fight The Power (Part 1) | 4 | T-Neck 2256 |
| 11/08/75 | 10 | 12 | 30  For The Love Of You (Part 1 & 2) | 22 | T-Neck 2259 |
| 5/08/76 | 3 | 16 | 31  Who Loves You Better (Part 1) | 47 | T-Neck 2260 |
| 8/21/76 | 9 | 13 | 32  Harvest For The World | 63 | T-Neck 2261 |
| 3/12/77 | 1¹ | 15 | 33  The Pride (Part 1) | 63 | T-Neck 2262 |
| 6/18/77 | 4 | 14 | 34  Livin' In The Life | 40 | T-Neck 2264 |
| 11/05/77 | 50 | 10 | 35  Voyage To Atlantis | | T-Neck 2270 |
| 4/01/78 | 1² | 18 | 36  Take Me To The Next Phase (Part 1) | | T-Neck 2272 |
| 7/01/78 | 16 | 11 | 37  Groove With You | | T-Neck 2277 |
| 4/14/79 | 1¹ | 17 | 38  I Wanna Be With You (Part 1) | | T-Neck 2279 |
| 7/21/79 | 38 | 7 | 39  Winner Takes All | | T-Neck 2284 |
| 9/08/79 | 27 | 11 | 40  It's A Disco Night (Rock Don't Stop) | 90 | T-Neck 2287 |
| 3/08/80 | 1⁴ | 17 | 41  Don't Say Goodnight (It's Time For Love) (Parts 1 & 2) | 39 | T-Neck 2290 |
| 6/14/80 | 11 | 14 | 42  Here We Go Again (Part 1) | | T-Neck 2291 |
| 12/27/80+ | 20 | 15 | 43  Who Said? | | T-Neck 2293 |
| 4/18/81 | 17 | 10 | 44  Hurry Up And Wait | 58 | T-Neck 02033 |
| 7/04/81 | 57 | 7 | 45  I Once Had Your Love (And I Can't Let Go) | | T-Neck 02179 |
| 10/03/81 | 10 | 16 | 46  Inside You (Part 1) | | T-Neck 02531 |
| 2/20/82 | 45 | 9 | 47  Welcome To My Heart | | T-Neck 02705 |
| 6/26/82 | 14 | 15 | 48  The Real Deal | | T-Neck 02985 |
| 10/16/82 | 59 | 6 | 49  It's Alright With Me | | T-Neck 03281 |
| 12/25/82+ | 67 | 6 | 50  All In My Lover's Eyes | | T-Neck 03420 |
| 4/09/83 | 3 | 20 | 51  Between The Sheets | 101 | T-Neck 03797 |
| 7/09/83 | 6 | 15 | 52  Choosey Lover | | T-Neck 03994 |

| DEBUT DATE | PEAK POS | WKS CHR | ARTIST — Record Title | POP POS | Label & Number |
|---|---|---|---|---|---|
| | | | **THE ISLEY BROTHERS — Continued** | | |
| 11/02/85+ | 12 | 17 | 53 Colder Are My Nights.................................... | | Warner 28860 |
| 3/15/86 | 42 | 9 | 54 May I?................................................... | | Warner 28764 |
| 5/16/87 | 3 | 16 | 55 **Smooth Sailin' Tonight** .......................... | | Warner 28385 |
| 9/26/87 | 71 | 7 | 56 Come My Way........................................ | | Warner 28241 |
| 1/16/88 | 74 | 7 | 57 I Wish................................................ | | Warner 28129 |
| | | | **ISLEY, JASPER, ISLEY** | | |
| | | | Ernie Isley, Chris Jasper, Marvin Isley - see above Isley Brothers biography. | | |
| 10/13/84 | 14 | 17 | 1 Look The Other Way.............................. | | CBS Assoc. 04642 |
| 1/12/85 | 52 | 10 | 2 Kiss And Tell .................................... | 63 | CBS Assoc. 04741 |
| 9/21/85 | 1³ | 24 | 3 **Caravan Of Love**.............................. | 51 | CBS Assoc. 05611 |
| 1/18/86 | 13 | 15 | 4 Insatiable Woman ................................ | | CBS Assoc. 05760 |
| 4/04/87 | 18 | 14 | 5 8th Wonder Of The World ........................ | | CBS Assoc. 07018 |
| 7/11/87 | 15 | 13 | 6 Givin' You Back The Love ........................ | | CBS Assoc. 07254 |
| | | | **IVY** | | |
| 5/17/86 | 74 | 9 | 1 Tell Me........................................... | | Heat 2032 |
| | | | **THE IVY THREE** | | |
| | | | Formed in 1959 at Adelphi College in New York. Consisted of Charles Koppelman (lead), Art Berkowitz and Don Rubin. | | |
| 10/10/60 | 22 | 1 | 1 Yogi....................................... [N] | 8 | Shell 720 |
| | | | based on a character from TV's "Huckleberry Hound" show | | |

# J

| DEBUT DATE | PEAK POS | WKS CHR | ARTIST — Record Title | POP POS | Label & Number |
|---|---|---|---|---|---|
| | | | **JACKIE & THE STARLITES** | | |
| | | | Group consisting of lead Jackie Rue, Alton Thomas (tenor), John Felix (baritone) and Billy Montgomery (bass). | | |
| 4/21/62 | 17 | 3 | 1 I Found Out Too Late................................. | | Fury 1057 |
| | | | **THE JACKS** | | |
| | | | Quintet - see The Cadets for complete biography. | | |
| 8/06/55 | 3 | 14 | 1 **Why Don't You Write Me?**..................... | 82 | RPM 428 |
| | | | Jockey #3 / Best Seller #4 / Juke Box #5 | | |
| | | | **JACKSON SISTERS** | | |
| | | | Family group from Compton, California. Consisted of Gennie, Rae, Pat, Lyn and Jackie Jackson. Ages ranged from 11 to 16. | | |
| 9/29/73 | 89 | 5 | 1 I Believe In Miracles ............................. | | Prophesy 3005 |
| | | | **BRIAN JACKSON - see GIL SCOTT-HERON** | | |
| | | | **BULL MOOSE JACKSON & HIS BUFFALO BEARCATS** ★★174★★ | | |
| | | | Born Benjamin Jackson in 1919 in Cleveland, Ohio. Vocalist/saxophonist/violinist/ clarinetist. Formed combo "Harlem Hotshots" with Freddie Webster in high school. Joined Lucky Millinder band in 1943; first sang as replacement for Wynonie Harris. Own band with Millinder sidemen in 1947. Recorded for Bogus Records in 1984. Toured Europe in 1985. One of the first major stars of R&B. | | |
| 6/29/46 | 4 | 7 | 1 I Know Who Threw The Whiskey In The Well .. | | Queen 4116 |
| | | | BULL MOOSE JACKSON | | |
| | | | answer song to "Who Threw The Whiskey In The Well" | | |
| 12/20/47+ | 1³ | 26 | 2 **I Love You, Yes I Do/** | 21 | |
| | | | Juke Box #1 / Best Seller #8 | | |
| 3/27/48 | 10 | 1 | 3 **Sneaky Pete** .................................. | | King 4181 |
| 3/13/48 | 3 | 17 | 4 **All My Love Belongs To You/** | | |
| | | | Juke Box #3 / Best Seller #4 | | |
| 4/10/48 | 5 | 11 | 5 **I Want A Bowlegged Woman**...................... | | King 4189 |
| | | | Juke Box #5 / Best Seller #11 | | |
| 7/17/48 | 1⁸ | 17 | 6 **I Can't Go On Without You** ....................... | | King 4230 |
| | | | Best Seller #1(8) / Juke Box #1(4) | | |
| 11/27/48 | 12 | 1 | 7 Cleveland, Ohio Blues ............................ | | King 4244 |
| | | | Juke Box #12 | | |
| | | | recorded in 1945; first released on King 4165 | | |
| 12/04/48 | 12 | 1 | 8 Love Me Tonight.................................. | | King 4250 |
| | | | Juke Box #12 | | |
| 4/02/49 | 12 | 1 | 9 Don't Ask Me Why................................. | | King 4280 |
| | | | Best Seller #12 | | |

| DEBUT DATE | PEAK POS | WKS CHR | | ARTIST — Record Title | POP POS | Label & Number |
|---|---|---|---|---|---|---|
| | | | | **BULL MOOSE JACKSON & HIS BUFFALO BEARCATS — Continued** | | |
| 4/30/49 | 2⁵ | 20 | 10 | Little Girl, Don't Cry ................................... | | King 4288 |
| | | | | Best Seller #2 / Juke Box #2 | | |
| 10/22/49 | 2² | 12 | 11 | Why Don't You Haul Off And Love Me? ......... | | King 4322 |
| | | | | Best Seller #2 / Juke Box #2 | | |
| 8/28/61 | 10 | 9 | 12 | I Love You Yes I Do................................... | 98 | 7 Arts 705 |
| | | | | BULL MOOSE JACKSON<br>new version of his 1947 hit | | |
| | | | | **CHUCK JACKSON**   ★★143★★ | | |
| | | | | Born on 7/22/37 in Latta, South Carolina. Cousin of singer Ann Sexton. Moved to Pittsburgh as a child. Left college in 1957 to work with the Raspberry Singers gospel group. With The Dell-Vikings from 1957-59. First recorded as a solo for Beltone in 1960. | | |
| 2/13/61 | 5 | 14 | 1 | I Don't Want To Cry................................... | 36 | Wand 106 |
| 5/29/61 | 22 | 2 | 2 | (It Never Happens) In Real Life ...................... | 46 | Wand 108 |
| 8/28/61 | 13 | 10 | 3 | I Wake Up Crying ...................................... | 59 | Wand 110 |
| 5/12/62 | 2³ | 16 | 4 | Any Day Now (My Wild Beautiful Bird) .......... | 23 | Wand 122 |
| 2/23/63 | 12 | 10 | 5 | Tell Him I'm Not Home ............................... | 42 | Wand 132 |
| 6/15/63 | 29 | 1 | 6 | I Will Never Turn My Back On You ................... | 110 | Wand 138 |
| 11/02/63 | 81 | 5 | 7 | Any Other Way ......................................... | Hot | Wand 141 |
| 3/28/64 | 92 | 3 | 8 | Hand It Over ........................................... | Hot | Wand 149 |
| 5/23/64 | 45 | 10 | 9 | Beg Me .................................................. | Hot | Wand 154 |
| 10/03/64 | 93 | 2 | 10 | Somebody New .......................................... | Hot | Wand 161 |
| 11/14/64 | 47 | 8 | 11 | Since I Don't Have You................................ | Hot | Wand 169 |
| 5/08/65 | 10 | 11 | 12 | Something You Got ..................................... | 55 | Wand 181 |
| 5/08/65 | 22 | 3 | 13 | I Need You ............................................. | 75 | Wand 179 |
| 9/11/65 | 18 | 7 | 14 | If I Didn't Love You .................................. | 46 | Wand 188 |
| 3/04/67 | 20 | 7 | 15 | Hold On I'm Coming.................................... | 91 | Wand 1148 |
| 6/03/67 | 46 | 3 | 16 | Daddy's Home ........................................... | 91 | Wand 1155 |
| | | | | 12, 15 & 16:  CHUCK JACKSON & MAXINE BROWN | | |
| 11/11/67 | 40 | 5 | 17 | Shame On Me ........................................... | 76 | Wand 1166 |
| 4/19/69 | 27 | 4 | 18 | Are You Lonely For Me Baby........................... | 107 | Motown 1144 |
| 9/20/69 | 43 | 4 | 19 | Honey Come Back ...................................... | | Motown 1152 |
| 6/30/73 | 35 | 6 | 20 | I Only Get This Feeling................................ | 117 | ABC 11368 |
| 12/01/73+ | 62 | 8 | 21 | I Can't Break Away .................................... | | ABC 11398 |
| 12/20/75+ | 30 | 12 | 22 | I'm Needing You, Wanting You ........................ | | All Platinum 2360 |
| 6/07/80 | 90 | 2 | 23 | I Wanna Give You Some Love .......................... | | EMI America 8042 |
| | | | | written by Bob Marley | | |
| | | | | **CLARENCE JACKSON** | | |
| 1/05/85 | 95 | 3 | 1 | Our Love Will Last Forever ........................... | | R&R 934 |
| | | | | **DEON JACKSON** | | |
| | | | | Born on 1/26/46 in Ann Arbor, Michigan. Singer/clarinetist/drummer. Discovered by producer Ollie McLaughlin. | | |
| 1/22/66 | 3 | 18 | 1 | Love Makes The World Go Round................... | 11 | Carla 2526 |
| 12/02/67 | 28 | 6 | 2 | Ooh Baby.............................................. | 65 | Carla 2537 |
| | | | | **EARNEST JACKSON** | | |
| 5/05/73 | 22 | 9 | 1 | Love And Happiness ................................... | 58 | Stone 200 |
| | | | | **FREDDIE JACKSON**   ★★182★★ | | |
| | | | | Singer/songwriter born and raised in Harlem. Backup singer for Melba Moore, Evelyn King, and others. Member of Mystic Merlin. Also see Paul Laurence. | | |
| 4/06/85 | 1⁶ | 26 | 1 | Rock Me Tonight (For Old Times Sake) .......... | 18 | Capitol 5459 |
| 8/10/85 | 1² | 24 | 2 | You Are My Lady....................................... | 12 | Capitol 5495 |
| 12/07/85+ | 8 | 17 | 3 | He'll Never Love You (Like I Do) ................... | 25 | Capitol 5535 |
| 3/15/86 | 9 | 14 | 4 | Love Is Just A Touch Away .......................... | | Capitol 5565 |
| 9/06/86 | 1¹ | 20 | 5 | A Little Bit More ..................................... | | Capitol 5632 |
| | | | | MELBA MOORE with FREDDIE JACKSON | | |
| 9/27/86 | 1⁴ | 20 | 6 | Tasty Love ............................................. | 41 | Capitol 5616 |
| 12/20/86+ | 1² | 18 | 7 | Have You Ever Loved Somebody ...................... | 69 | Capitol 5661 |
| 3/28/87 | 2¹ | 16 | 8 | I Don't Want To Lose Your Love...................... | | Capitol 5680 |
| 6/20/87 | 1¹ | 15 | 9 | Jam Tonight ........................................... | 32 | Capitol 44037 |
| 10/31/87 | 69 | 7 | 10 | Look Around ........................................... | | Capitol 44075 |

| DEBUT DATE | PEAK POS | WKS CHR | ARTIST — Record Title | POP POS | Label & Number |
|---|---|---|---|---|---|
| | | | **FREDDIE JACKSON — Continued** | | |
| 5/14/88 | **12** | 14 | 11 I Can't Complain ........................................ | | Capitol 44148 |
| | | | MELBA MOORE with FREDDIE JACKSON | | |
| | | | **GEORGE JACKSON** | | |
| | | | Born in Greenville, Mississippi in 1936. First recorded for Prann in 1963. Vocalist with the Ovations; wrote their hit "It's Wonderful To Be In Love", in 1965. Recorded as "Bart Jackson" for Decca in 1968. Wrote hits "Too Weak To Fight" for Clarence Carter, "A Man And A Half" for Wilson Pickett, "Down Home Blues" for Z.Z. Hill, "One Bad Apple" for the Osmond Brothers, and "Old Time Rock & Roll" for Bob Seger. Staff writer for Malaco Records. | | |
| 6/27/70 | **48** | 3 | 1 That's How Much You Mean To Me .................. | | Fame 1468 |
| 5/27/72 | **38** | 4 | 2 Aretha, Sing One For Me ............................. | | Hi 2212 |
| | | | **JANET JACKSON**   ★★186★★ | | |
| | | | Born on 5/16/66 in Gary, Indiana. Sister of The Jacksons (youngest of 9 children). Debuted at age 7 at the MGM Grand in Las Vegas with her brothers. At age 10, she played Penny Gordon in the TV series "Good Times" (1977-79); in the cast of "Diff'rent Strokes" (1981-82). | | |
| 10/09/82 | **6** | 20 | 1 **Young Love** ............................................. | *64* | A&M 2440 |
| 1/29/83 | **17** | 15 | 2 Come Give Your Love To Me ......................... | *58* | A&M 2522 |
| 5/14/83 | **15** | 13 | 3 Say You Do ............................................... | | A&M 2545 |
| 8/18/84+ | **9** | 15 | 4 **Don't Stand Another Chance** ..................... | *101* | A&M 2660 |
| 12/08/84+ | **40** | 12 | 5 Fast Girls ................................................. | | A&M 2693 |
| 1/25/86 | **1** ² | 20 | 6 **What Have You Done For Me Lately** .............. | *4* | A&M 2812 |
| 4/19/86 | **1** ² | 22 | 7 **Nasty** ..................................................... | *3* | A&M 2830 |
| 8/09/86 | **3** | 16 | 8 **When I Think Of You** ................................ | *1* | A&M 2855 |
| 11/01/86+ | **1** ¹ | 19 | 9 **Control** .................................................. | *5* | A&M 2877 |
| 1/24/87 | **1** ¹ | 18 | 10 **Let's Wait Awhile** ................................... | *2* | A&M 2906 |
| 5/23/87 | **1** ¹ | 17 | 11 **The Pleasure Principle** ............................. | *14* | A&M 2927 |
| | | | **JENNY JACKSON** | | |
| 10/02/76 | **75** | 6 | 1 Shoora Shoora ........................................... | | Farr 008 |
| | | | **JERMAINE JACKSON**   ★★131★★ | | |
| | | | Born on 12/11/54 in Gary, Indiana. Fourth oldest of the Jackson family. Vocalist/ bassist for The Jackson 5 until group left Motown in 1976. Married Hazel Joy Gordy, daughter of Berry Gordy Jr., on 12/15/73. | | |
| 9/30/72 | **23** | 9 | 1 That's How Love Goes ................................. | *46* | Motown 1201 |
| 12/30/72+ | **3** | 13 | 2 **Daddy's Home** .......................................... | *9* | Motown 1216 |
| 10/13/73 | **35** | 11 | 3 You're In Good Hands ................................. | *79* | Motown 1244 |
| 9/04/76 | **19** | 16 | 4 Let's Be Young Tonight ................................ | *55* | Motown 1401 |
| 11/05/77 | **75** | 7 | 5 You Need To Be Loved ................................. | | Motown 1409 |
| 7/15/78 | **38** | 10 | 6 Castles Of Sand ......................................... | | Motown 1441 |
| 3/22/80 | **1** ⁶ | 22 | 7 **Let's Get Serious** ..................................... | *9* | Motown 1469 |
| 7/19/80 | **32** | 11 | 8 You're Supposed To Keep Your Love For Me ...... | *34* | Motown 1490 |
| | | | above 2: written, produced & arranged by Stevie Wonder | | |
| 11/15/80+ | **17** | 18 | 9 Little Girl Don't You Worry ........................... | | Motown 1499 |
| 2/28/81 | **13** | 16 | 10 You Like Me Don't You ................................ | *50* | Motown 1503 |
| 10/31/81 | **29** | 12 | 11 I'm Just Too Shy......................................... | *60* | Motown 1525 |
| 2/06/82 | **60** | 6 | 12 Paradise In Your Eyes ................................. | | Motown 1600 |
| 7/24/82 | **5** | 17 | 13 **Let Me Tickle Your Fancy**............................ | *18* | Motown 1628 |
| | | | backing vocals by Devo | | |
| 11/06/82 | **54** | 10 | 14 Very Special Part ....................................... | | Motown 1649 |
| 7/28/84 | **8** | 17 | 15 **Dynamite** ............................................... | *15* | Arista 9190 |
| 11/10/84+ | **14** | 17 | 16 Do What You Do ......................................... | *13* | Arista 9279 |
| 3/02/85 | **61** | 9 | 17 When The Rain Begins To Fall....................... | *54* | Curb 52521 |
| | | | JERMAINE JACKSON/PIA ZADORA   from the film "Voyage of the Rock Aliens" | | |
| 6/22/85 | **63** | 6 | 18 (Closest Thing To) Perfect ............................ | *67* | Arista 9356 |
| | | | from the film "Perfect" | | |
| 2/15/86 | **14** | 16 | 19 I Think It's Love ......................................... | *16* | Arista 9444 |
| 6/07/86 | **40** | 10 | 20 Do You Remember Me? ................................ | *71* | Arista 9502 |
| 1/17/87 | **90** | 4 | 21 Words Into Action ....................................... | | Arista 9495 |

| DEBUT DATE | PEAK POS | WKS CHR | ARTIST — Record Title | POP POS | Label & Number |
|---|---|---|---|---|---|
| | | | **J.J. JACKSON** | | |
| | | | Born Jerome Louis Jackson on 4/8/41 in Brooklyn; raised in the Bronx. Worked on the New York Daily News in 1958. With the Cordials from 1959, recorded for Seven Arts in 1961. Worked as an arranger. Became permanent resident of England in 1969. Not the same person as the MTV-VJ. | | |
| 10/01/66 | 4 | 15 | 1 But It's Alright ........................................... | 22 | Calla 119 |
| | | | originally recorded in London on Polydor 56718 | | |
| 1/14/67 | 19 | 5 | 2 I Dig Girls ............................................... | 83 | Calla 125 |
| 6/17/67 | 17 | 9 | 3 Four Walls (Three Windows and Two Doors)....... | 123 | Calla 133 |
| | | | **LA TOYA JACKSON** | | |
| | | | Born in 1955 in Gary, Indiana. Backup vocals for her brothers' group, The Jackson 5. Solo since 1979. The fifth of 9 children. | | |
| 9/06/80 | 59 | 8 | 1 Night Time Lover ....................................... | | Polydor 2117 |
| 11/08/80 | 40 | 14 | 2 If You Feel The Funk .................................. | 103 | Polydor 2137 |
| 7/18/81 | 31 | 11 | 3 Stay The Night ......................................... | | Polydor 2177 |
| 7/30/83 | 22 | 11 | 4 Bet'cha Gonna Need My Lovin' ....................... | | Larc 81025 |
| 5/12/84 | 29 | 11 | 5 Heart Don't Lie ........................................ | 56 | Private I 04439 |
| 8/18/84 | 43 | 11 | 6 Hot Potato .............................................. | | Private I 04572 |
| 2/22/86 | 76 | 4 | 7 He's A Pretender........................................ | | Private I 05783 |
| 11/22/86 | 89 | 2 | 8 Oops, Oh No ............................................ | | Palass 0934 |
| | | | CERRONE & LaTOYA JACKSON | | |
| | | | **LITTLE SON JACKSON** | | |
| | | | Born Melvin Jackson on 8/16/15 in Barry, Texas. Died of cancer on 5/30/76 (60). Vocalist/guitarist. With Blue Eagle Four gospel group in the 30s. Retired from music in 1954. Recorded for Arhoolie in 1960. | | |
| 10/16/48 | 7 | 1 | 1 **Freedom Train Blues**................................ | | Gold Star 638 |
| | | | Juke Box #7 | | |
| | | | **MARLON JACKSON** | | |
| | | | Born on 3/12/57 in Gary, Indiana. Sixth oldest of the Jackson family. Vocalist/ guitarist of his brothers' group, The Jackson 5. | | |
| 9/12/87 | 2[1] | 14 | 1 **Don't Go** .............................................. | | Capitol 44047 |
| 12/19/87+ | 57 | 10 | 2 Baby Tonight .......................................... | | Capitol 44092 |
| | | | **MICHAEL JACKSON**   ★★40★★ | | |
| | | | Born on 8/29/58 in Gary, Indiana; seventh of 9 children. Became lead singer of his brothers' group, The Jackson 5 (later known as The Jacksons), at age 5. His 1982 "Thriller" album, with sales of 40 million+ copies, is the best-selling album in history. Internationally-recognized as the most popular artist since 1983. Also see Rockwell, Diana Ross, and Donna Summer. | | |
| 11/06/71 | 4 | 13 | 1 **Got To Be There** ..................................... | 4 | Motown 1191 |
| 3/18/72 | 2[1] | 9 | 2 **Rockin' Robin** ........................................ | 2 | Motown 1197 |
| 6/03/72 | 2[2] | 12 | 3 **I Wanna Be Where You Are** ......................... | 16 | Motown 1202 |
| 8/19/72 | 5 | 14 | 4 **Ben** ................................................... | 1 | Motown 1207 |
| | | | title song from the film about a trained rat | | |
| 5/12/73 | 14 | 10 | 5 With A Child's Heart.................................... | 50 | Motown 1218 |
| 3/01/75 | 7 | 13 | 6 **We're Almost There** ................................. | 54 | Motown 1341 |
| 5/24/75 | 4 | 15 | 7 **Just A Little Bit Of You** ............................ | 23 | Motown 1349 |
| 9/16/78 | 17 | 13 | 8 Ease On Down The Road................................ | 41 | MCA 40947 |
| | | | DIANA ROSS & MICHAEL JACKSON | | |
| | | | from the film "The Wiz", starring Diana Ross & Michael Jackson | | |
| 1/20/79 | 42 | 10 | 9 You Can't Win (Part 1) ................................ | 81 | Epic 50654 |
| 7/28/79 | 1[5] | 20 | 10● **Don't Stop 'Til You Get Enough** ................... | 1 | Epic 50742 |
| 11/03/79+ | 1[6] | 25 | 11● **Rock With You** ........................................ | 1 | Epic 50797 |
| 2/23/80 | 5 | 13 | 12 **Off The Wall** ......................................... | 10 | Epic 50838 |
| 5/03/80 | 43 | 8 | 13 She's Out Of My Life .................................. | 10 | Epic 50871 |
| 4/25/81 | 42 | 10 | 14 One Day In Your Life .................................. | 55 | Motown 1512 |
| | | | recorded in 1975 | | |
| 11/13/82+ | 1[3] | 20 | 15● **The Girl Is Mine** ..................................... | 2 | Epic 03288 |
| | | | MICHAEL JACKSON/PAUL McCARTNEY | | |
| 1/29/83 | 1[9] | 23 | 16● **Billie Jean** ............................................ | 1 | Epic 03509 |
| 4/02/83 | 1[1] | 19 | 17● **Beat It** ................................................ | 1 | Epic 03759 |
| | | | featuring Eddie Van Halen on lead guitar | | |
| 6/04/83 | 5 | 17 | 18 **Wanna Be Startin' Somethin'**........................ | 5 | Epic 03914 |
| 7/30/83 | 27 | 12 | 19 Human Nature .......................................... | 7 | Epic 04026 |
| 10/22/83 | 2[4] | 20 | 20● **Say Say Say** ........................................... | 1 | Columbia 04168 |
| | | | PAUL McCARTNEY & MICHAEL JACKSON | | |
| 10/29/83 | 46 | 8 | 21 P.Y.T. (Pretty Young Thing)............................ | 10 | Epic 04165 |

| DEBUT DATE | PEAK POS | WKS CHR | ARTIST — Record Title | POP POS | Label & Number |
|---|---|---|---|---|---|
| | | | **MICHAEL JACKSON — Continued** | | |
| 2/18/84 | **3** | 14 | 22 **Thriller** ................................................ | *4* | Epic 04364 |
| | | | all of above Epic recordings produced by Quincy Jones | | |
| 6/09/84 | **37** | 10 | 23 Farewell My Summer Love........................... | *38* | Motown 1739 |
| | | | re-mix of a recording from 8/31/73 | | |
| 8/08/87 | **1**¹ | 11 | 24●**I Just Can't Stop Loving You**.................... | *1* | Epic 07253 |
| | | | backing vocal by Siedah Garrett | | |
| 9/19/87 | **1**³ | 11 | 25 **Bad** ...................................................... | *1* | Epic 07418 |
| | | | organ solo by Jimmy Smith | | |
| 11/21/87 | **1**⁴ | 13 | 26 **The Way You Make Me Feel**..................... | *1* | Epic 07645 |
| 2/06/88 | **1**¹ | 14 | 27 **Man In The Mirror** ............................... | *1* | Epic 07668 |
| | | | backing vocals by Siedah Garrett, The Winans, and The Andrae Crouch Choir | | |
| 4/23/88 | **4** | 11 | 28 **Get It** ................................................... | *80* | Motown 1930 |
| | | | **STEVIE WONDER & MICHAEL JACKSON** | | |
| 4/30/88 | **5** | 13 | 29 **Dirty Diana** .......................................... | *1* | Epic 07739 |
| | | | features Steve Stevens (Billy Idol's guitarist) | | |
| | | | **MILLIE JACKSON** ★★59★★ | | |
| | | | Born on 7/15/44 in Thompson, Georgia. Singer/songwriter. To Newark, New Jersey in 1958. Worked as a model in New York City. Professional singing debut at Club Zanzibar in Hoboken, New Jersey in 1964. First recorded for MGM in 1970. Founded and produced the trio, Facts Of Life. | | |
| 11/06/71 | **22** | 7 | 1 A Child Of God (It's Hard To Believe) .............. | *102* | Spring 119 |
| 3/18/72 | **4** | 15 | 2 **Ask Me What You Want**............................. | *27* | Spring 123 |
| 8/05/72 | **7** | 13 | 3 **My Man, A Sweet Man** ............................. | *42* | Spring 127 |
| 12/09/72+ | **22** | 10 | 4 I Miss You Baby ........................................ | *95* | Spring 131 |
| 4/21/73 | **16** | 8 | 5 Breakaway............................................... | *110* | Spring 134 |
| 8/11/73 | **3** | 18 | 6 **Hurts So Good** ........................................ | *24* | Spring 139 |
| | | | from the film "Cleopatra Jones" | | |
| 2/23/74 | **21** | 14 | 7 I Got To Try It One Time ............................. | | Spring 144 |
| 6/01/74 | **11** | 14 | 8 How Do You Feel The Morning After ................ | *77* | Spring 147 |
| 1/18/75 | **42** | 11 | 9 The Rap/ | | |
| | | 11 | 10    (If Loving You Is Wrong) I Don't Want To Be Right ................................................... | *42* | Spring 155 |
| 5/17/75 | **58** | 4 | 11 I'm Through Trying To Prove My Love To You.... | | Spring 157 |
| 9/27/75 | **17** | 13 | 12 Leftovers/ | *87* | |
| | | 1 | 13    Loving Arms ........................................ | | Spring 161 |
| 6/19/76 | **24** | 11 | 14 Bad Risk/ | | |
| | | 11 | 15    There You Are ...................................... | | Spring 164 |
| 9/18/76 | **71** | 4 | 16 Feel Like Making Love ............................... | | Spring 167 |
| 2/19/77 | **40** | 12 | 17 I Can't Say Goodbye ................................. | | Spring 170 |
| 5/28/77 | **87** | 6 | 18 A Love Of Your Own ................................. | | Spring 173 |
| 9/03/77 | **5** | 23 | 19 **If You're Not Back In Love By Monday** .......... | *43* | Spring 175 |
| 2/18/78 | **12** | 15 | 20 All The Way Lover ..................................... | *102* | Spring 179 |
| 9/09/78 | **33** | 10 | 21 Sweet Music Man ...................................... | | Spring 185 |
| 12/23/78+ | **83** | 4 | 22 Keep The Home Fire Burnin' ........................ | | Spring 189 |
| 4/07/79 | **33** | 12 | 23 Never Change Lovers In The Middle Of The Night | | Spring 192 |
| 7/21/79 | **70** | 4 | 24 A Moment's Pleasure .................................. | | Spring 197 |
| 9/08/79 | **56** | 8 | 25 We Got To Hit It Off.................................. | | Spring 3002 |
| 12/01/79+ | **30** | 11 | 26 Do You Wanna Make Love ........................... | | Spring 2036 |
| | | | **MILLIE JACKSON & ISAAC HAYES** | | |
| 2/02/80 | **49** | 8 | 27 Didn't I Blow Your Mind ............................. | | Spring 3007 |
| 3/22/80 | **78** | 4 | 28 You Never Cross My Mind ........................... | | Spring 2063 |
| | | | **MILLIE JACKSON & ISAAC HAYES** | | |
| 6/28/80 | **61** | 5 | 29 Despair .................................................. | | Spring 3011 |
| 9/27/80 | **88** | 3 | 30 This Is It (Part 1)...................................... | | Spring 3013 |
| 8/01/81 | **62** | 6 | 31 I Can't Stop Loving You .............................. | | Spring 3019 |
| 10/30/82 | **51** | 11 | 32 Special Occasion ....................................... | | Spring 3028 |
| 10/29/83 | **58** | 13 | 33 I Feel Like Walking In The Rain..................... | | Spring 3034 |
| 9/20/86 | **9** | 16 | 34 **Hot! Wild! Unrestricted! Crazy Love** ............. | | Jive 1007 |
| 1/17/87 | **6** | 16 | 35 **Love Is A Dangerous Game** ....................... | | Jive 1009 |
| 5/09/87 | **58** | 7 | 36 An Imitation Of Love ................................. | | Jive 1040 |
| 8/22/87 | **79** | 5 | 37 It's A Thang............................................. | | Jive 1056 |
| 9/19/87 | **20** | 11 | 38 Be Yourself.............................................. | | Jive 9629 |
| | | | **WHODINI featuring MILLIE JACKSON** | | |

| DEBUT DATE | PEAK POS | WKS CHR | ARTIST — Record Title | POP POS | Label & Number |
|---|---|---|---|---|---|
| | | | **MILLIE JACKSON — Continued** | | |
| 5/14/88 | 45 | 11 | 39 Something You Can Feel .............................. | | Jive 1111 |
| | | | **PAUL JACKSON, JR.** | | |
| | | | Multi-instrumentalist/producer/prominent session guitarist (since age 16). | | |
| 5/07/88 | 67 | 7 | 1 I Came To Play ........................................ | | Atlantic 89095 |
| | | | **RANDY JACKSON** | | |
| | | | Born on 10/29/61 in Gary, Indiana; eighth of 9 children. Member of his brothers' group, The Jacksons, replacing Jermaine as bassist, in 1976. | | |
| 9/09/78 | 91 | 2 | 1 How Can I Be Sure ..................................... | | Epic 50576 |
| | | | **REBBIE JACKSON** | | |
| | | | Born Maureen Jackson on 5/29/50 in Gary, Indiana. Eldest of the 9-sibbling Jackson family. Worked with The Jacksons from 1974-77, then went solo. | | |
| 9/08/84 | 4 | 21 | 1 **Centipede** ..................................... | 24 | Columbia 04547 |
| | | | written & produced by Michael Jackson | | |
| 2/02/85 | 40 | 10 | 2 A Fork In The Road ................................... | | Columbia 04765 |
| 8/23/86 | 16 | 13 | 3 Reaction................................................ | | Columbia 06197 |
| 12/20/86+ | 50 | 10 | 4 You Send The Rain Away ............................. | | Columbia 06563 |
| | | | **REBBIE JACKSON with ROBIN ZANDER** | | |
| | | | Robin is lead singer of the rock group, Cheap Trick | | |
| 1/23/88 | 8 | 13 | 5 **Plaything**............................................ | | Columbia 07685 |
| 6/25/88 | 78 | 5 | 6 R U Tuff Enuff ....................................... | | Columbia 07799 |
| | | | with rap by Melle Mel | | |
| | | | **SHAWN JACKSON** | | |
| | | | Female singer from Toronto. Sang in kid group, the Sneakers, at age 13. Vocalist with the house band at the Blue Note in Toronto. Worked as a model in New York City. | | |
| 6/15/74 | 98 | 3 | 1 Just As Bad As You .................................. | | Playboy 50053 |
| | | | **STONEWALL JACKSON** | | |
| | | | His real name. Born on 11/6/32 in Tabor City, North Carolina. Country singer/songwriter/guitarist. Named after the Confederate general. | | |
| 7/06/59 | 11 | 7 | 1 Waterloo ............................................. | 4 | Columbia 41393 |
| | | | **WALTER JACKSON** | | |
| | | | Born on 3/19/38 in Pensacola, Florida; died of a cerebral hemorrhage on 6/20/83. Moved to Detroit. Contracted polio at an early age, performed on crutches. Lead singer in the Velvetones, recorded for Deb in 1959. First recorded for Columbia in 1962. Inactive from 1973-76. | | |
| 11/21/64 | 67 | 6 | 1 It's All Over ......................................... | Hot | Okeh 7204 |
| 1/30/65 | 13 | 10 | 2 Suddenly I'm All Alone ................................ | 96 | Okeh 7215 |
| 5/29/65 | 15 | 9 | 3 Welcome Home ....................................... | 95 | Okeh 7219 |
| 6/25/66 | 11 | 7 | 4 It's An Uphill Climb To The Bottom................... | 88 | Okeh 7247 |
| 10/01/66 | 40 | 4 | 5 After You There Can Be Nothing...................... | 130 | Okeh 7256 |
| 11/19/66 | 46 | 2 | 6 A Corner In The Sun................................. | 83 | Okeh 7260 |
| 3/04/67 | 22 | 14 | 7 Speak Her Name ..................................... | 89 | Okeh 7272 |
| 7/08/67 | 43 | 3 | 8 Deep In The Heart Of Harlem........................ | 110 | Okeh 7285 |
| 11/29/69 | 37 | 5 | 9 Anyway That You Want Me............................ | 111 | Cotillion 44053 |
| 11/10/73 | 91 | 4 | 10 It Doesn't Take Much................................ | | Brunswick 55520 |
| 11/27/76+ | 9 | 15 | 11 **Feelings**............................................ | 93 | Chi-Sound 908 |
| 4/02/77 | 19 | 13 | 12 Baby, I Love Your Way............................... | | Chi-Sound 964 |
| 8/27/77 | 75 | 7 | 13 It's All Over ......................................... | | Chi-Sound 1044 |
| | | | new version of #1 above | | |
| 3/11/78 | 68 | 10 | 14 If I Had My Way ..................................... | | Chi-Sound 1140 |
| 5/02/81 | 28 | 13 | 15 Tell Me Where It Hurts............................... | | Columbia 02037 |
| 1/08/83 | 83 | 5 | 16 If I Had A Chance .................................... | | Kelli-Arts 1006 |

| DEBUT DATE | PEAK POS | WKS CHR | ARTIST — Record Title | POP POS | Label & Number |
|---|---|---|---|---|---|
| | | | **THE JACKSONS** ★★**36**★★ | | |
| | | | Quintet of brothers formed and managed by their father beginning in 1966 in Gary, Indiana. Consisted of Sigmund "Jackie" (b: 5/4/51), Toriano "Tito" (b: 10/15/53), Jermaine (b: 12/11/54), Marlon (b: 3/12/57) and lead singer Michael (b: 8/29/58). First recorded for Steeltown in 1968. Known as The Jackson 5 from 1968-75. Jermaine replaced by Randy (b: 10/29/61) in 1976. Jermaine rejoined the group for 1984's highly publicized "Victory" album and tour. Since 1971, Michael has also recorded solo; a phenomenally popular entertainer since 1983. Marlon left for a solo career in 1987. Their sisters Rebbie, La Toya and Janet backed the group; each had a string of solo hits. Also see Stevie Wonder. | | |
| | | | THE JACKSON 5: | | |
| 11/22/69+ | 1⁴ | 18 | 1 **I Want You Back/** | *1* | |
| | | 7 | 2 Who's Loving You ............................... | | Motown 1157 |
| 3/21/70 | 1⁴ | 12 | 3 **ABC** ................................................ | *1* | Motown 1163 |
| 6/06/70 | 1⁶ | 14 | 4 **The Love You Save/** | *1* | |
| | | 4 | 5 I Found That Girl ............................ | | Motown 1166 |
| 9/26/70 | 1⁶ | 13 | 6 **I'll Be There** ................................... | *1* | Motown 1171 |
| 2/06/71 | 2² | 11 | 7 **Mama's Pearl** ................................. | *2* | Motown 1177 |
| 4/10/71 | 1³ | 13 | 8 **Never Can Say Goodbye** ................. | *2* | Motown 1179 |
| 7/24/71 | 3 | 8 | 9 **Maybe Tomorrow** ........................... | *20* | Motown 1186 |
| 12/18/71+ | 3 | 11 | 10 **Sugar Daddy** ................................. | *10* | Motown 1194 |
| 4/29/72 | 8 | 8 | 11 **Little Bitty Pretty One** ................. | *13* | Motown 1199 |
| 7/22/72 | 5 | 11 | 12 **Lookin' Through The Windows** ...... | *16* | Motown 1205 |
| 11/11/72 | 9 | 11 | 13 **Corner Of The Sky** ....................... | *18* | Motown 1214 |
| | | | from the Broadway musical "Pippin" | | |
| 3/24/73 | 10 | 8 | 14 **Hallelujah Day** .............................. | *28* | Motown 1224 |
| 8/25/73 | 2² | 18 | 15 **Get It Together** ............................. | *28* | Motown 1277 |
| 3/09/74 | 1¹ | 20 | 16 **Dancing Machine** ......................... | *2* | Motown 1286 |
| 10/26/74 | 3 | 15 | 17 **Whatever You Got, I Want** ........... | *38* | Motown 1308 |
| 1/25/75 | 5 | 12 | 18 **I Am Love (Parts I & II)** ............... | *15* | Motown 1310 |
| 6/28/75 | 6 | 13 | 19 **Forever Came Today/** | *60* | |
| 11/01/75 | 50 | 7 | 20 All I Do Is Think Of You ................ | | Motown 1356 |
| | | | THE JACKSONS: | | |
| 10/16/76 | 2² | 20 | 21 ● Enjoy Yourself ........................... | *6* | Epic 50289 |
| 4/02/77 | 6 | 14 | 22 **Show You The Way To Go** ............. | *28* | Epic 50350 |
| 10/08/77 | 8 | 15 | 23 **Goin' Places** ................................. | *52* | Epic 50454 |
| 2/04/78 | 38 | 12 | 24 Find Me A Girl ............................. | | Epic 50496 |
| 9/02/78 | 3 | 16 | 25 **Blame It On The Boogie** ............... | *54* | Epic 50595 |
| 1/27/79 | 3 | 23 | 26 ▲ **Shake Your Body (Down To The Ground)** ....... | *7* | Epic 50656 |
| 10/04/80 | 2² | 18 | 27 **Lovely One** ................................... | *12* | Epic 50938 |
| 12/06/80+ | 2⁵ | 17 | 28 **Heartbreak Hotel** ......................... | *22* | Epic 50959 |
| 4/11/81 | 30 | 9 | 29 Can You Feel It ............................. | *77* | Epic 01032 |
| 6/27/81 | 50 | 10 | 30 Walk Right Now ........................... | *73* | Epic 02132 |
| 6/30/84 | 4 | 14 | 31 ● **State Of Shock** ........................... | *3* | Epic 04503 |
| | | | lead vocals by Michael Jackson & Mick Jagger | | |
| 8/25/84 | 12 | 13 | 32 Torture ........................................ | *17* | Epic 04575 |
| | | | lead vocals by Jermaine & Michael Jackson | | |
| 11/03/84 | 39 | 9 | 33 Body ........................................... | *47* | Epic 04673 |
| | | | lead vocal by Marlon Jackson | | |
| 2/14/87 | 88 | 5 | 34 Time Out For The Burglar ............. | | MCA 53032 |
| | | | from the film "Burglar" | | |
| | | | **DEBBIE JACOBS** | | |
| | | | Disco-oriented singer from Baltimore. | | |
| 9/01/79 | 66 | 7 | 1 Don't You Want My Love ............. | *106* | MCA 41102 |
| | | | **HANK JACOBS** | | |
| 1/18/64 | 91 | 3 | 1 So Far Away ............................. [I] | *Hot* | Sue 795 |
| | | | **ILLINOIS JACQUET & HIS ORCHESTRA** | | |
| | | | Born Battiste Illinois Jacquet on 10/31/22 in Broussard, Louisiana. Saxophonist. Raised in Houston. To West Coast in 1941. With Lionel Hampton from 1941-42. With Cab Calloway, 1943-44, then led brother Russell's band. With Jazz At The Philharmonic until the early 50s. Originator of the big honking tenor sax style. Also see Wynonie Harris. | | |
| 10/25/52 | 3 | 11 | 1 **Port Of Rico** ............................. [I] | | Mercury 89001 |
| | | | Juke Box #3 / Best Seller #7 Count Basie on organ | | |

| DEBUT DATE | PEAK POS | WKS CHR | ARTIST — Record Title | POP POS | Label & Number |
|---|---|---|---|---|---|
| | | | **MICK JAGGER** | | |
| | | | Born Michael Phillip Jagger on 7/26/43 in Dartford, England. Lead singer of The Rolling Stones. Also see the Jacksons' "State Of Shock". | | |
| 3/09/85 | 83 | 4 | 1 Just Another Night........................................ | *12* | Columbia 04743 |
| | | | **JAISUN** | | |
| 4/15/78 | 42 | 13 | 1 Try And Understand....................................... | | Jett Sett 101 |
| | | | **JAK** | | |
| | | | Vocalist/guitarist/keyboardist from Albuquerque, New Mexico. | | |
| 3/16/85 | 88 | 2 | 1 I Go Wild ................................................... | | Epic 04751 |
| | | | **THE JAMAICA BOYS** | | |
| | | | Trio from Jamaica, Queens. Composer/multi-instrumentalist Marcus Miller is a noted producer (Luther Vandross, David Sanborn). Drummer Lenny White was an original member of Chick Corea's band. Singer Mark Stevens is Chaka Khan's brother. | | |
| 9/12/87 | 67 | 7 | 1 (It's That) Lovin' Feeling................................ | | Warner 28381 |
| 4/09/88 | 76 | 6 | 2 Spend Some Time With Me............................. | | Warner 28137 |
| | | | **AHMAD JAMAL** | | |
| | | | Born Fritz Jones on 7/2/30 in Pittsburgh. Pianist/leader. With George Hudson. Formed own trio, the Three Strings with Ray Crawford (guitar), Eddie Calhoun (bass). Recorded for Okeh in 1951. | | |
| 11/24/58 | 18 | 3 | 1 Secret Love................................................ [I] | | Argo 5317 |
| | | | recorded at the Spotlite Club in Washington, DC on 9/5/58, with Israel Crosby (bass) and Vernell Fournier (drums) | | |
| 3/29/80 | 79 | 4 | 2 Don't Ask My Neighbors ............................. | | 20th Century 2448 |
| | | | **THE JAMES BOYS** | | |
| | | | Studio band produced by Jesse James of Philadelphia. Arranged by pianist Bobby Martin, also included Norman Harris, Roland and Karl Chambers, Ronnie Baker and Earl Young. Later became Family, MFSB. | | |
| 8/17/68 | 23 | 6 | 1 The Mule/ | [I] *82* | |
| 8/24/68 | 49 | 3 | 2 The Horse................................................. [I] | | Phil-L.A. 316 |
| | | | originally used as flip side of Cliff Nobles vocal track | | |
| | | | **ELMORE JAMES** | | |
| | | | Born Elmore Brooks on 1/27/18 in Richland, Mississippi. Died of a heart attack on 5/24/63 (45). Singer/guitarist. Toured with Sonny Boy Williamson II (Alex [Rice] Miller) to 1942. Appeared on radio shows in the late 40s. Frequent appearances in Chicago until his death. | | |
| 4/05/52 | 9 | 1 | 1 Dust My Broom........................................... | | Trumpet 146 |
| | | | shown as: **ELMO JAMES** Best Seller #9 with Rice Miller on harmonica | | |
| 2/14/53 | 9 | 3 | 2 I Believe ................................................... | | Meteor 5000 |
| | | | Best Seller #9 | | |
| 5/02/60 | 15 | 5 | 3 The Sky Is Crying....................................... | | Fire 1016 |
| 4/24/65 | 25 | 8 | 4 It Hurts Me Too .......................................... | *106* | Enjoy 2015 |
| | | | **ETTA JAMES** ★★**63**★★ | | |
| | | | Born Jamesetta Hawkins on 1/25/38 in Los Angeles. Nicknamed Miss Peaches. First recorded for Modern in 1954. Frequent bouts with heroin addiction; finally cured in the late 70s. Still active into the 80s, makes many anti-drug abuse appearances. | | |
| 2/19/55 | 1⁴ | 19 | 1 **The Wallflower** ....................................... | | Modern 947 |
| | | | Jockey #1 / Best Seller #2 / Juke Box #4 a #1 pop hit for Georgia Gibbs in 1955 as "Dance With Me Henry"; with the Peaches (vocal group); male voice: Richard Berry | | |
| 11/05/55 | 6 | 3 | 2 **Good Rockin' Daddy**................................ | | Modern 962 |
| | | | Juke Box #6 / Jockey #8 / Best Seller #12 with the Dreamers (vocal group), including Jesse Belvin | | |
| 5/02/60 | 2¹ | 15 | 3 **All I Could Do Was Cry**............................ | *33* | Argo 5359 |
| 8/15/60 | 6 | 10 | 4 **If I Can't Have You** ................................. | *52* | Chess 1760 |
| | | | **ETTA & HARVEY** (Harvey Fuqua of The Moonglows) | | |
| 9/19/60 | 5 | 17 | 5 **My Dearest Darling**................................. | *34* | Argo 5368 |
| 12/26/60+ | 12 | 6 | 6 **Spoonful**................................................ | *78* | Chess 1771 |
| | | | **ETTA & HARVEY** | | |
| 1/16/61 | 2¹ | 13 | 7 **At Last**................................................... | *47* | Argo 5380 |
| | | | popularized in 1942 by Glenn Miller (POS 9) | | |
| 4/03/61 | 4 | 9 | 8 **Trust In Me**............................................. | *30* | Argo 5385 |
| | | | Wayne King and Mildred Bailey both had Top 5 versions in 1937 | | |
| 6/05/61 | 14 | 6 | 9 Fool That I Am ........................................... | *50* | Argo 5390 |
| 8/07/61 | 6 | 12 | 10 **Don't Cry, Baby**....................................... | *39* | Argo 5393 |

| DEBUT DATE | PEAK POS | WKS CHR | ARTIST — Record Title | POP POS | Label & Number |
|---|---|---|---|---|---|
| | | | **ETTA JAMES — Continued** | | |
| 3/03/62 | **4** | 15 | 11 **Something's Got A Hold On Me** | 37 | Argo 5409 |
| 8/04/62 | **6** | 11 | 12 **Stop The Wedding** | 34 | Argo 5418 |
| 10/27/62 | **13** | 7 | 13 **Next Door To The Blues** | 71 | Argo 5424 |
| 5/04/63 | **7** | 10 | 14 **Pushover** | 25 | Argo 5437 |
| | | | recorded in Nashville | | |
| 10/05/63 | **63** | 4 | 15 Two Sides (To Every Story) | Hot | Argo 5452 |
| 2/01/64 | **82** | 3 | 16 Baby What You Want Me To Do | Hot | Argo 5459 |
| 4/18/64 | **65** | 6 | 17 Loving You More Every Day | Hot | Argo 5465 |
| 8/13/66 | **37** | 6 | 18 In The Basement - Part 1 | 97 | Cadet 5539 |
| | | | **ETTA JAMES & SUGAR PIE DeSANTO** | | |
| 1/28/67 | **42** | 4 | 19 I Prefer You | | Cadet 5552 |
| 11/18/67+ | **10** | 16 | 20 **Tell Mama** | 23 | Cadet 5578 |
| 3/09/68 | **11** | 9 | 21 **Security** | 35 | Cadet 5594 |
| 6/01/68 | **32** | 6 | 22 I Got You Babe | 69 | Cadet 5606 |
| 1/11/69 | **32** | 11 | 23 Almost Persuaded | 79 | Cadet 5630 |
| 10/10/70 | **26** | 7 | 24 Losers Weepers - Part 1 | 94 | Cadet 5676 |
| 5/20/72 | **31** | 6 | 25 I Found A Love | 108 | Chess 2125 |
| 9/29/73 | **29** | 13 | 26 All The Way Down | 101 | Chess 2144 |
| 3/16/74 | **76** | 5 | 27 Leave Your Hat On | | Chess 2148 |
| 8/10/74 | **84** | 3 | 28 Out On The Street, Again | | Chess 2153 |
| 7/24/76 | **92** | 2 | 29 Jump Into Love | | Chess 30001 |
| 6/03/78 | **93** | 3 | 30 Piece Of My Heart | | Warner 8545 |

## HARRY JAMES

Born on 3/15/16 in Albany, Georgia; died on 7/5/83 (67). Star trumpet player and bandleader. Achieved fame playing with Benny Goodman in the late 30s. His own band was very popular during the 40s.

| DEBUT DATE | PEAK POS | WKS CHR | ARTIST — Record Title | POP POS | Label & Number |
|---|---|---|---|---|---|
| 1/30/43 | **4** | 7 | 1 **I Had The Craziest Dream** | 1 | Columbia 36659 |
| | | | from the film "Springtime In The Rockies" | | |
| 2/06/43 | **1**[1] | 10 | 2 **I've Heard That Song Before** | 1 | Columbia 36668 |
| | | | from the film "Youth On Parade" | | |
| | | | above 2: vocals by Helen Forrest | | |
| 5/08/43 | **5** | 6 | 3 **Velvet Moon** [I] | 2 | Columbia 36672 |
| 7/17/43 | **8** | 2 | 4 **All Or Nothing At All/** | 1 | |
| | | | **FRANK SINATRA with HARRY JAMES & HIS ORCHESTRA** | | |
| | | | recorded on 9/17/39; a reported million-seller | | |
| 7/24/43 | **10** | 1 | 5 **Flash** [I] | 19 | Columbia 35587 |
| | | | recorded on 11/8/39 | | |
| 1/15/44 | **9** | 2 | 6 **Jump Town/** [I] | 21 | |
| 2/05/44 | **10** | 1 | 7 **Cherry** [I] | 4 | Columbia 36683 |
| | | | above 2: recorded on 7/22/42 | | |

## JESSE JAMES

Real name: James McClelland; born in 1943. Singer/producer from Eldora, Arkansas. First recorded for Shirley in 1961.

| DEBUT DATE | PEAK POS | WKS CHR | ARTIST — Record Title | POP POS | Label & Number |
|---|---|---|---|---|---|
| 9/09/67 | **42** | 7 | 1 Believe In Me Baby - Part I | 92 | 20th Century 6684 |
| 8/01/70 | **18** | 7 | 2 Don't Nobody Want To Get Married (Part II) | | Zea 50000 |
| 4/10/71 | **47** | 4 | 3 I Need You Baby | | Zea 50003 |
| 12/04/71+ | **25** | 11 | 4 At Last | | Zea 30002 |
| 7/05/75 | **73** | 8 | 5 If You Want A Love Affair | | 20th Century 2201 |
| 6/20/87 | **61** | 13 | 6 I Can Do Bad By Myself | | T.T.E.D. 3026 |

## JIMMY JAMES & THE VAGABONDS

Band from London. Vocals by Jimmy James and Count Prince Miller.

| DEBUT DATE | PEAK POS | WKS CHR | ARTIST — Record Title | POP POS | Label & Number |
|---|---|---|---|---|---|
| 3/09/68 | **44** | 2 | 1 Come To Me Softly | 76 | Atco 6551 |
| 1/24/76 | **62** | 8 | 2 I Am Somebody | 94 | Pye 71057 |

## RICK JAMES ★★57★★

Born James Johnson on 2/1/52 in Buffalo. "Punk funk" singer/songwriter/guitarist. In Mynah Birds band with Neil Young in the late 60s. To London; formed the band Main Line. Returned to the US and formed Stone City Band; produced Teena Marie, Mary Jane Girls, Eddie Murphy, and others.

| DEBUT DATE | PEAK POS | WKS CHR | ARTIST — Record Title | POP POS | Label & Number |
|---|---|---|---|---|---|
| 5/20/78 | **1**[2] | 22 | 1 **You And I** | 13 | Gordy 7156 |
| 9/30/78 | **3** | 17 | 2 **Mary Jane** | 41 | Gordy 7162 |
| 2/24/79 | **12** | 13 | 3 High On Your Love Suite | 72 | Gordy 7164 |
| 4/28/79 | **8** | 13 | 4 **Bustin' Out** | 71 | Gordy 7167 |
| 8/18/79 | **35** | 10 | 5 Fool On The Street | | Gordy 7171 |

| DEBUT DATE | PEAK POS | WKS CHR | ARTIST — Record Title | POP POS | Label & Number |
|---|---|---|---|---|---|
| | | | **RICK JAMES — Continued** | | |
| 11/03/79 | **13** | 12 | 6 Love Gun............................................. | | Gordy 7176 |
| 2/09/80 | **26** | 11 | 7 Come Into My Life (Part 1) ........................ | | Gordy 7177 |
| 7/12/80 | **17** | 17 | 8 Big Time............................................. | | Gordy 7185 |
| 3/28/81 | **1** ⁵ | 25 | 9 **Give It To Me Baby** ............................ | 40 | Gordy 7197 |
| 8/01/81 | **3** | 17 | 10 **Super Freak (Part 1)**.......................... | 16 | Gordy 7205 |
| 11/21/81+ | **38** | 10 | 11 Ghetto Life ........................................ | 102 | Gordy 7215 |
| 4/24/82 | **6** | 17 | 12 **Standing On The Top - Part 1**................ | 66 | Gordy 1616 |
| | | | THE TEMPTATIONS featuring RICK JAMES | | |
| 5/15/82 | **3** | 17 | 13 **Dance Wit' Me (Part 1)** ...................... | 64 | Gordy 1619 |
| 7/31/82 | **15** | 13 | 14 Hard To Get ...................................... | | Gordy 1634 |
| 11/06/82 | **62** | 6 | 15 She Blew My Mind (69 Times) ................... | | Gordy 1646 |
| 7/23/83 | **1** ⁶ | 19 | 16 **Cold Blooded**.................................. | 40 | Gordy 1687 |
| 10/22/83 | **16** | 14 | 17 U Bring The Freak Out............................ | 101 | Gordy 1703 |
| 12/17/83+ | **22** | 11 | 18 Ebony Eyes........................................ | 43 | Gordy 1714 |
| | | | RICK JAMES featuring SMOKEY ROBINSON | | |
| 7/14/84 | **6** | 16 | 19 **17**............................................... | 36 | Gordy 1730 |
| 10/20/84 | **31** | 11 | 20 You Turn Me On .................................. | | Gordy 1763 |
| 4/06/85 | **10** | 12 | 21 **Can't Stop** ..................................... | 50 | Gordy 1776 |
| | | | from the film "Beverly Hills Cop" | | |
| 6/15/85 | **5** | 15 | 22 **Glow**............................................. | 106 | Gordy 1796 |
| 9/21/85 | **41** | 10 | 23 Spend The Night With Me ........................ | | Gordy 1806 |
| 5/24/86 | **6** | 15 | 24 **Sweet And Sexy Thing** ....................... | | Motown 1844 |
| 6/18/88 | **1** ¹ | 16 | 25 **Loosey's Rap**.................................. | | Reprise 27885 |
| | | | RICK JAMES featuring ROXANNE SHANTE | | |

## SONNY JAMES

Born Sonny James Loden on 5/1/29 in Hacklesburg, Alabama. Country singer/songwriter/guitarist. Nicknamed "The Southern Gentleman". Brought to Capitol Records in Nashville by Chet Atkins.

| DEBUT DATE | PEAK POS | WKS CHR | ARTIST — Record Title | POP POS | Label & Number |
|---|---|---|---|---|---|
| 2/23/57 | **3** | 4 | 1 **Young Love**................................. | 1 | Capitol 3602 |
| | | | Juke Box #3 | | |

## TOMMY JAMES & THE SHONDELLS

Pop group formed by Tommy "James" Jackson (b: 4/29/47 in Dayton, OH), at age 12, in Niles, Michigan. After the song "Hanky Panky" was popularized by a Pittsburgh disc jockey, the original master was sold to Roulette. James recruited a Pittsburgh group, The Raconteurs, to become the official Shondells.

| DEBUT DATE | PEAK POS | WKS CHR | ARTIST — Record Title | POP POS | Label & Number |
|---|---|---|---|---|---|
| 7/16/66 | **39** | 2 | 1 ● Hanky Panky .................................. | 1 | Roulette 4686 |
| | | | recorded on the Snap label in 1963 | | |

## JAMMERS

| DEBUT DATE | PEAK POS | WKS CHR | ARTIST — Record Title | POP POS | Label & Number |
|---|---|---|---|---|---|
| 10/16/82 | **65** | 6 | 1 And You Know That .............................. | | Salsoul 7036 |
| 1/29/83 | **76** | 4 | 2 Be Mine Tonight.................................. | | Salsoul 7044 |

## JAN & DEAN

Los Angeles pop duo: Jan Berry (b: 4/3/41) and Dean Torrence (b: 3/10/40). While Dean was in the Army Reserve for 6 months, Jan recorded "Jennie Lee" with Arnie Ginsburg. Dean returned and Arnie joined the Navy. Jan was critically injured in a car accident on 4/19/66. Duo made a comeback in 1978, after their biographical film "Dead Man's Curve" aired on TV.

| DEBUT DATE | PEAK POS | WKS CHR | ARTIST — Record Title | POP POS | Label & Number |
|---|---|---|---|---|---|
| 5/26/58 | **4** | 10 | 1 **Jennie Lee** ..................................... | 8 | Arwin 108 |
| | | | shown as: **JAN & ARNIE** | | |
| | | | Jockey #4 / Best Seller #5 | | |
| 9/14/59 | **28** | 2 | 2 Baby Talk........................................... | 10 | Dore 522 |
| 7/06/63 | **3** | 11 | 3 **Surf City** ....................................... | 1 | Liberty 55580 |
| | | | Brian Wilson (Beach Boys) helped on words & vocals for this tune | | |

## JANICE

| DEBUT DATE | PEAK POS | WKS CHR | ARTIST — Record Title | POP POS | Label & Number |
|---|---|---|---|---|---|
| 5/24/86 | **48** | 11 | 1 Bye-Bye............................................. | | 4th & B'way 7424 |

## CHAS JANKEL

Formerly with Ian Dury & The Blockheads.

| DEBUT DATE | PEAK POS | WKS CHR | ARTIST — Record Title | POP POS | Label & Number |
|---|---|---|---|---|---|
| 2/27/82 | **57** | 8 | 1 Glad To Know You ................................ | 102 | A&M 2396 |

## THE JARMELS

Group from Richmond, Virginia. Consisted of Nathaniel Ruff, Ray Smith, Paul Burnett, Earl Christian and Tom Eldridge.

| DEBUT DATE | PEAK POS | WKS CHR | ARTIST — Record Title | POP POS | Label & Number |
|---|---|---|---|---|---|
| 8/28/61 | **7** | 13 | 1 **A Little Bit Of Soap** ........................... | 12 | Laurie 3098 |

| DEBUT DATE | PEAK POS | WKS CHR | ARTIST — Record Title | POP POS | Label & Number |
|---|---|---|---|---|---|
| | | | **AL JARREAU** ★★**195**★★ | | |
| | | | Born on 3/12/40 in Milwaukee. Winner of 4 Grammy Awards. Has masters degree in psychology from the University of Iowa. Worked clubs in San Francisco with George Duke. | | |
| 11/20/76 | **92** | 3 | 1 Rainbow In Your Eyes........................................ | | Reprise 1374 |
| 10/08/77 | **91** | 6 | 2 Take Five ....................................................... | | Warner 8443 |
| 11/11/78 | **55** | 9 | 3 Thinkin' About It Too ...................................... | | Warner 8677 |
| 5/24/80 | **26** | 13 | 4 Never Givin' Up............................................... | 102 | Warner 49234 |
| 9/06/80 | **63** | 5 | 5 Gimme What You Got ...................................... | | Warner 49538 |
| 11/01/80 | **61** | 6 | 6 Distracted...................................................... | | Warner 49588 |
| 7/18/81 | **6** | 19 | 7 **We're In This Love Together**........................ | 15 | Warner 49746 |
| 11/28/81+ | **25** | 12 | 8 Breakin' Away ................................................ | 43 | Warner 49842 |
| 3/20/82 | **51** | 8 | 9 Teach Me Tonight .......................................... | 70 | Warner 50032 |
| 10/09/82 | **16** | 15 | 10 Your Precious Love ....................................... | 102 | Warner 29893 |
| | | | **AL JARREAU & RANDY CRAWFORD** | | |
| 3/12/83 | **6** | 16 | 11 **Mornin'** ...................................................... | 21 | Warner 29720 |
| 5/28/83 | **9** | 17 | 12 **Boogie Down** .............................................. | 77 | Warner 29624 |
| 9/24/83 | **66** | 5 | 13 Trouble In Paradise ...................................... | 63 | Warner 29501 |
| | | | above 3 shown only as: **JARREAU** | | |
| 10/20/84 | **26** | 14 | 14 After All...................................................... | 69 | Warner 29262 |
| 3/02/85 | **42** | 10 | 15 Raging Waters .............................................. | | Warner 29091 |
| 8/30/86 | **42** | 9 | 16 L Is For Lover .............................................. | | Warner 28686 |
| 11/15/86 | **37** | 12 | 17 Tell Me What I Gotta Do ................................ | | Warner 28538 |
| 6/20/87 | **32** | 10 | 18 Moonlighting ................................................ | 23 | MCA 53124 |
| | | | theme from the TV series of the same title | | |
| | | | **MARION JARVIS** | | |
| 8/10/74 | **26** | 15 | 1 Hell Of A Fix ................................................ | | Roxbury 2000 |
| | | | **CHRIS JASPER** | | |
| | | | Member of the group, The Isley Brothers, from 1973-84. Formed trio (Isley, Jasper, Isley) with cousins Ernie and Marvin Isley. | | |
| 12/05/87+ | **3** | 16 | 1 **Superbad** ................................................... | | CBS Assoc. 07657 |
| 3/26/88 | **12** | 11 | 2 One Time Love .............................................. | | CBS Assoc. 07733 |
| | | | **JAY & THE TECHNIQUES** | | |
| | | | Integrated R&B/rock group from Allentown, Pennsylvania: Jay Proctor (lead singer), Karl Landis, Ronnie Goosly, John Walsh, George Lloyd, Chuck Crowl and Dante Dancho. | | |
| 9/09/67 | **8** | 10 | 1 **Apple, Peaches, Pumpkin Pie** ...................... | 6 | Smash 2086 |
| 2/14/76 | **94** | 3 | 2 Number Onederful ........................................ | | Event 228 |
| | | | **MILES JAYE** | | |
| | | | Singer/songwriter born Miles Davis in Brooklyn. Classical violinist until launching his singing career as lead vocalist of the Air Force Band. Commercial jingle singer. | | |
| 9/12/87 | **5** | 21 | 1 **Let's Start Love Over**................................. | | Island 99413 |
| 2/06/88 | **10** | 16 | 2 **I've Been A Fool For You** ............................. | | Island 99379 |
| | | | **THE JAYHAWKS** | | |
| | | | Los Angeles group formed at Jefferson High School in 1955. Consisted of James Johnson, Carlton Fisher, Dave Govan and Carver Bunkum. Changed name to The Vibrations in 1960. Also recorded as The Marathons. | | |
| 7/14/56 | **9** | 3 | 1 **Stranded In The Jungle** .........................[N] | 18 | Flash 109 |
| | | | Best Seller #9 / Juke Box #10 | | |
| | | | **THE JAYNETTS** | | |
| | | | New York City female group formed by producer/composer Zelma "Zell" Sanders. Consisted of Johnnielouise Richardson (ex-Johnnie & Joe), Ethel Davis, Mary Sue Wells, Yvonne Bushnell and Ada Ray. Richardson left after first release. | | |
| 9/14/63 | **4** | 9 | 1 **Sally, Go 'Round The Roses** ....................... | 2 | Tuff 369 |
| | | | **JAZZ AT THE PHILHARMONIC** | | |
| | | | Orchestra with varying membership. First recorded under the direction of Norman Granz for Granz's Clef label in 1944. Lineup (on 9/27/47): Howard McGhee, Bill Harris, Illinois Jacquet, Flip Phillips, Hank Jones, Ray Brown, and Jo Jones. | | |
| 4/02/49 | **14** | 1 | 1 Mordido................................................[I] | | Mercury 11013 |
| | | | Juke Box #14 | | |
| | | | recorded at Carnegie Hall on 9/27/47, and released in 4 parts | | |
| | | | **JAZZ CRUSADERS - see THE CRUSADERS** | | |

| DEBUT DATE | PEAK POS | WKS CHR | ARTIST — Record Title | POP POS | Label & Number |
|---|---|---|---|---|---|
| | | | **JAZZY JAY** | | |
| | | | Rap disc jockey; member of Afrika Bambaataa's Soulsonic Force. | | |
| 9/29/84 | **70** | 5 | 1 Son Of Beat Street............................................ | | Atlantic 89620 |
| | | | from the film "Beat Street" | | |
| | | | **JAZZY JEFF & FRESH PRINCE - see D.J. JAZZY JEFF** | | |
| | | | **THE J.B.'s - see JAMES BROWN/"BOOTSY" COLLINS/NAT KENDRICK/MACEO & THE MACKS/FRED WESLEY** | | |
| | | | **J.E. THE P.C. FROM D.C.** | | |
| | | | Family group from Washington D.C., two nephews and a brother to producer Jonah Ellis: Glenn Ellis (lead vocals), Ronnie McLeod and John "Bob" Ellis. | | |
| 11/14/87 | **81** | 5 | 1 Hello Rochelle ............................................... | | Profile 5167 |
| | | | **JEFF & ALETA** | | |
| 9/13/80 | **48** | 8 | 1 Love Touch.................................................... | | SRI 00007 |
| | | | **MORRIS JEFFERSON** | | |
| 12/10/77+ | **34** | 15 | 1 Spank Your Blank Blank .............................. | | Parachute 504 |
| | | | **JEFFREE** | | |
| | | | Singer/composer/keyboardist. | | |
| 11/18/78 | **53** | 11 | 1 Mr. Fix-It ..................................................... | | MCA 40955 |
| | | | **JELLYBEAN** | | |
| | | | John "Jellybean" Benitez is a reknown Manhattan club DJ/remixer/producer. | | |
| 2/01/86 | **51** | 9 | 1 Sidewalk Talk .............................................. | 18 | EMI America 8297 |
| | | | written by Madonna | | |
| 9/26/87 | **49** | 12 | 2 The Real Thing............................................. | 82 | Chrysalis 43167 |
| | | | vocal by Steve Dante | | |
| | | | **THE JELLY BEANS** | | |
| | | | Quintet from Jersey City: sisters Elyse & Maxine Herbert, Alma Brewer, Diane Taylor and Charles Thomas. | | |
| 6/20/64 | **9** | 12 | 1 I Wanna Love Him So Bad............................ | *Hot* | Red Bird 10003 |
| 9/26/64 | **51** | 7 | 2 Baby Be Mine ............................................... | *Hot* | Red Bird 10011 |
| | | | **KECHIA JENKINS** | | |
| | | | Female singer/off-Broadway actress. | | |
| 3/05/88 | **55** | 9 | 1 I Need Somebody........................................... | | Profile 7180 |
| | | | **NORMA JENKINS** | | |
| 1/24/76 | **92** | 4 | 1 Gimme Some (Of Your Love)........................... | | Desert Mn. 6400 |
| | | | **JERRYO** | | |
| | | | Real name: Jerry Murray. Singer/dancer from Chicago. | | |
| 9/16/67 | **16** | 11 | 1 Karate-Boo-Ga-Loo ...................................... | 51 | Shout 217 |
| 1/27/68 | **40** | 4 | 2 Funky Boo-Ga-Loo........................................ | | Shout 225 |
| | | | **JESSE & MARVIN - see JESSE BELVIN** | | |
| | | | **JESSE'S GANG** | | |
| | | | Chicago dance band led by Jesse Saunders. | | |
| 8/29/87 | **90** | 2 | 1 Back-Up ........................................................ | | Geffen 28449 |
| | | | vocal by Nadine Lewis | | |
| | | | **GENOBIA JETER** | | |
| 8/30/86 | **30** | 12 | 1 All Of My Love............................................. | | RCA 14415 |
| 2/07/87 | **42** | 10 | 2 Together........................................................ | | RCA 5098 |
| | | | GENOBIA JETER & GLENN JONES | | |
| | | | **THE JETS** | | |
| | | | Minneapolis-based family band consisting of eight brothers and sisters: Leroy, Eddie, Eugene, Haini, Rudy, Kathi, Elizabeth and Moana Wolfgramm. Their parents are from the South Pacific country of Tonga. All members play at least two instruments. In 1985, ranged in age from 13 to 21. | | |
| 10/12/85 | **8** | 19 | 1 Curiosity ..................................................... | | MCA 52682 |
| 3/01/86 | **4** | 21 | 2 Crush On You.............................................. | 3 | MCA 52774 |
| 7/05/86 | **28** | 13 | 3 Private Number............................................ | 47 | MCA 52846 |
| 11/22/86+ | **2**[1] | 23 | 4 You Got It All.............................................. | 3 | MCA 52968 |
| 7/04/87 | **11** | 12 | 5 Cross My Broken Heart ............................... | 7 | MCA 53123 |
| | | | from the film "Beverly Hills Cop II" | | |

| DEBUT DATE | PEAK POS | WKS CHR | ARTIST — Record Title | POP POS | Label & Number |
|---|---|---|---|---|---|
| | | | **THE JETS — Continued** | | |
| 10/24/87 | **19** | 13 | 6  I Do You .................................................. | 20 | MCA 53193 |
| 1/23/88 | **5** | 14 | 7  **Rocket 2 U**........................................... | 6 | MCA 53254 |
| 5/07/88 | **24** | 12 | 8  Make It Real.......................................... | 4 | MCA 53311 |
| | | | **THE JEWELS** | | |
| 10/10/64 | **64** | 10 | 1  Opportunity ......................................... | *Hot* | Dimension 1034 |
| | | | **JIMMY G. & THE TACKHEADS** | | |
| 1/25/86 | **48** | 12 | 1  Break My Heart ................................. | | Capitol 5543 |
| | | | **GUS JINKINS** | | |
| | | | Born Gus Jenkins on 3/24/31 in Birmingham, Alabama. Pianist, also known as "Little Temple". First own recording in 1952 for Combo. | | |
| 12/15/56 | **2¹** | 4 | 1  **Tricky** .................................................. [I] | 79 | Flash 115 |
| | | | Juke Box #2 / Jockey #7 | | |
| | | | **THE JIVE BOMBERS** | | |
| | | | New York City group formed in the mid-40s from elements of Sonny Austin & The Jive Bombers, and the Palmer Brothers. Recorded for Coral as The Sparrows in 1949, and for Citation as The Jive Bombers in 1952. Lineup in 1957: Earl Johnson, Al Tinney, William "Pee Wee" Tinney and Clarence Palmer. | | |
| 3/02/57 | **7** | 4 | 1  **Bad Boy**.............................................. | 36 | Savoy 1508 |
| | | | Juke Box #7 <br> written & recorded by Lil Armstrong as "Brown Gal" in 1936 | | |
| | | | **THE JIVE FIVE** | | |
| | | | Brooklyn group formed in 1959 with lead singer Eugene Pitt (b: 11/6/37), Jerome Hanna, Billy Prophet, Richard Harris and Norman Johnson. After Johnson's death in 1970, group name changed to Jyve Fyve. Also recorded as the Corvairs on Leopard. | | |
| 6/26/61 | **1³** | 20 | 1  **My True Story**................................. | 3 | Beltone 1006 |
| 12/22/62 | **27** | 1 | 2  These Golden Rings ......................... | | Beltone 2029 |
| 7/31/65 | **26** | 6 | 3  I'm A Happy Man ............................. | 36 | United Art. 853 |
| 6/01/68 | **34** | 4 | 4  Sugar (Don't Take Away My Candy)................ | 119 | Musicor 1305 |
| | | | THE JIVE FIVE featuring EUGENE PITT | | |
| 12/05/70 | **50** | 2 | 5  I Want You To Be My Baby ........................... | | Decca 32736 |
| | | | **J.J. FAD** | | |
| | | | Los Angeles female rap trio: M.C.J.B. (Juana Burns), Baby-D (Dania Birks) and Sassy C (Michelle Franklin). | | |
| 5/28/88 | **22** | 14 | 1  Supersonic.......................................... | 30 | Ruthless 99328 |
| | | | **JO ANN & TROY** | | |
| | | | Jo Ann Campbell and husband Troy Seals. | | |
| 2/06/65 | **32** | 3 | 1  I Found A Love Oh What A Love ..................... | 67 | Atlantic 2256 |
| | | | **DAMITA JO** | | |
| | | | Born Damita Jo DuBlanc on 8/5/40 in Austin, Texas. Featured singer with Steve Gibson & The Red Caps (married to Gibson), 1951-53 and 1959-60. Regular on the Redd Foxx TV variety series in 1977. | | |
| 11/28/60 | **16** | 3 | 1  I'll Save The Last Dance For You ..................... | 22 | Mercury 71690 |
| | | | answer song to "Save The Last Dance For Me" | | |
| 7/17/61 | **15** | 6 | 2  I'll Be There ....................................... | 12 | Mercury 71840 |
| | | | **JOE & ANN** | | |
| 12/12/60 | **14** | 4 | 1  Gee Baby ........................................... | 108 | Ace 577 |
| | | | **JOESKI LOVE** | | |
| 5/03/86 | **16** | 15 | 1  Pee-Wee's Dance ................................. | | Vintertn. 69535 |
| | | | **JOHN & ERNEST** | | |
| | | | Duo of John Free and Ernest Smith - a Dickie Goodman production. | | |
| 4/14/73 | **17** | 7 | 1  Super Fly Meets Shaft ................................ [N] | 31 | Rainy Wed. 201 |
| 8/25/73 | **78** | 3 | 2  Soul President Number One ......................... | | Rainy Wed. 203 |
| | | | **ELTON JOHN** | | |
| | | | Born Reginald Kenneth Dwight on 3/25/47 in Pinner, Middlesex, England. Formed his first group, Bluesology, in 1966. Group backed visiting U.S. soul artists and later became Long John Baldry's backing band. Took the name of Elton John from the first names of Bluesology members Elton Dean and John Baldry. Performed as "The Pinball Wizard" in the film version of "Tommy". Also see Dionne Warwick. | | |
| 3/30/74 | **15** | 13 | 1 ● Bennie And The Jets ................................. | 1 | MCA 40198 |
| 4/26/75 | **32** | 12 | 2 ● Philadelphia Freedom ................................. | 1 | MCA 40365 |
| | | | ELTON JOHN BAND | | |

| DEBUT DATE | PEAK POS | WKS CHR | ARTIST — Record Title | POP POS | Label & Number |
|---|---|---|---|---|---|
| | | | **ELTON JOHN — Continued** | | |
| 7/21/79 | **36** | 9 | 3●Mama Can't Buy You Love .............................. | 9 | MCA 41042 |
| | | | all of above: written by Elton John and lyricist Bernie Taupin | | |
| | | | **LITTLE WILLIE JOHN** ★★**124**★★ | | |
| | | | Born William Edgar John on 11/15/37 in Cullendale, Arkansas. Raised in Detroit. Brother of Mabel John (of the Raeletts). First recorded for Prize in 1953. Convicted of manslaughter in 1966; died of a heart attack in Washington State Prison on 5/26/68. | | |
| 9/17/55 | **5** | 16 | 1 **All Around The World** .................................. | | King 4818 |
| | | | Jockey #5 / Best Seller #6 / Juke Box #8 | | |
| | | | song also known as "Grits Ain't Groceries" | | |
| 1/07/56 | **5** | 16 | 2 **Need Your Love So Bad/** | | |
| | | | Best Seller #5 / Jockey #11 | | |
| 1/28/56 | **6** | 1 | 3 **Home At Last** ............................................. | | King 4841 |
| | | | Jockey #6 | | |
| 5/19/56 | **1**[5] | 23 | 4 **Fever/** | 24 | |
| | | | Jockey #1(5) / Best Seller #1(3) / Juke Box #1(1) | | |
| 7/21/56 | **10** | 4 | 5 **Letter From My Darling** ........................... | | King 4935 |
| | | | Jockey #10 | | |
| 11/24/56 | **15** | 1 | 6 Do Something For Me .................................. | | King 4960 |
| | | | Jockey #15 | | |
| 4/14/58 | **5** | 14 | 7 **Talk To Me, Talk To Me** ............................ | 20 | King 5108 |
| | | | Jockey #5 / Best Seller #10 | | |
| 8/25/58 | **14** | 2 | 8 You're A Sweetheart.................................... | 66 | King 5142 |
| | | | Jockey #14 / Best Seller #19 | | |
| 9/15/58 | **12** | 5 | 9 Tell It Like It Is ....................................... | | King 5147 |
| | | | Jockey #12 / Top 30 #19 | | |
| | | | recorded in 1956 | | |
| 8/10/59 | **13** | 9 | 10 Leave My Kitten Alone............................... | 60 | King 5219 |
| 11/23/59+ | **11** | 14 | 11 Let Them Talk.......................................... | 100 | King 5274 |
| 6/20/60 | **11** | 13 | 12 Heartbreak (It's Hurtin' Me)...................... | 38 | King 5356 |
| 10/10/60 | **10** | 9 | 13 **Sleep** ...................................................... | 13 | King 5394 |
| | | | #1 hit for Fred Waring's Pennsylvanians in 1924 | | |
| 2/06/61 | **21** | 2 | 14 Walk Slow ............................................... | 48 | King 5428 |
| 5/29/61 | **25** | 1 | 15 (I've Got) Spring Fever/ | 71 | |
| 6/05/61 | **17** | 2 | 16 Flamingo ................................................. | | King 5503 |
| 7/31/61 | **5** | 11 | 17 **Take My Love (I Want To Give It All To You)** .. | 87 | King 5516 |
| | | | **MABLE JOHN** | | |
| | | | Vocalist, member of the Raeletts. Sister of Little Willie John. | | |
| 7/16/66 | **6** | 10 | 1 **Your Good Thing (Is About To End)** .............. | 95 | Stax 192 |
| | | | **JOHNNIE & JOE** | | |
| | | | Duo consisting of Johnnylouise Richardson and Joe Rivers. Richardson, daughter of Zell Sanders, later with Jaynettes on "Sally Go 'Round The Roses", in 1963. | | |
| 1/12/57 | **10** | 1 | 1 **I'll Be Spinning** ..................................... | | Chess 1641 |
| | | | Jockey #10 | | |
| | | | originally released on J&S 1762 | | |
| 5/06/57 | **3** | 16 | 2 **Over The Mountain; Across The Sea/** | 8 | |
| | | | Best Seller #3 / Jockey #6 | | |
| 7/29/57 | **15** | 1 | 3 My Baby's Gone, On, On ............................. | | Chess 1654 |
| | | | Jockey #15 | | |
| | | | above 2: originally released on J&S 1664 | | |
| | | | **JOHNNY & THE EXPRESSIONS** | | |
| | | | Group led by Johnny Matthews. | | |
| 1/01/66 | **14** | 10 | 1 Something I Want To Tell You....................... | 79 | Josie 946 |
| | | | **JOHNNY & THE HURRICANES** | | |
| | | | Rock and roll instrumental band formed as the Orbits in Toledo, Ohio, in 1958; led by saxophonist John Pocisk "Paris". First recorded for Twirl in 1959. Paris had own label, Attila, from 1965-70. | | |
| 8/24/59 | **5** | 14 | 1 **Red River Rock** ............................... [I] | 5 | Warwick 509 |
| | | | rock version of "Red River Valley" | | |
| 11/23/59 | **17** | 6 | 2 Reveille Rock ............................... [I] | 25 | Warwick 513 |
| | | | rock version of the Army bugle call "Reveille" | | |
| | | | **AL JOHNSON** | | |
| 3/01/80 | **26** | 15 | 1 I'm Back For More....................................... | | Columbia 11207 |
| | | | with Jean Carne | | |
| 6/21/80 | **58** | 8 | 2 I've Got My Second Wind ............................. | | Columbia 11287 |

| DEBUT DATE | PEAK POS | WKS CHR | ARTIST — Record Title | POP POS | Label & Number |
|---|---|---|---|---|---|
| | | | **BENNY JOHNSON** | | |
| 9/22/73 | **79** | 6 | 1 Visions Of Paradise ....................................... | | Today 1525 |
| 12/22/73+ | **68** | 9 | 2 Baby I Love You ........................................... | | Today 1527 |
| | | | **BILL JOHNSON & HIS MUSICAL NOTES** | | |
| | | | Born on 9/30/12 in Jacksonville, Florida. Died of cancer on 7/5/60. Vocalist/ alto saxophonist/clarinetist/arranger. Performed with Jimmy Dudley, Jabbo Smith, Baron Lee, Sam Marshall and Tiny Bradshaw. Joined Erskine Hawkins from 1936-43. Wrote "Tuxedo Junction". Own band in 1946 (recorded for Alert). Own quartet, Bill Johnson & His Musical Notes, from 1947; shared vocals with Gus Gordon (drums). | | |
| 9/13/47 | **3** | 2 | 1 **Don't You Think I Ought To Know** .............. | | Victor 2225 |
| 9/13/47 | **3** | 2 | 2 **Don't You Think I Oughta Know** .................. | | Queen 4171 |
| | | | different version of #1 above; originally released on Harlem 1011; also released on King 4171 | | |
| | | | **BUBBER JOHNSON** | | |
| | | | Vocalist/pianist Robert Johnson. Not to be confused with bandleader Buddy Johnson. | | |
| 10/22/55 | **9** | 5 | 1 **Come Home** .................................................. | *92* | King 4822 |
| | | | Best Seller #9 / Jockey #9 / Juke Box #9 | | |
| | | | **BUDDY JOHNSON**      ★★**145**★★ | | |
| | | | Born Woodrow Wilson Johnson on 1/10/15 in Darlington, South Carolina. Died of a brain tumor on 2/9/77 (62). Vocalist/pianist/composer. Pianist since age 4. Moved to New York City in 1938. With Cotton Club Revue to Europe in 1939. Expelled from Nazi, Germany; returned to New York. First recorded for Decca in late 1939. Joined by sister Ella, in 1940, as vocalist. Prolific composer, wrote "Since I Fell For You", "Please Mr. Johnson" and "Fine Brown Fame". Band toured continuously. Joined by vocalist Arthur Prysock in 1943. Wrote blues concerto in 1946, portion released as "Far Cry" (Decca 48076). Performed concerto at Carnegie Hall in September of 1948, with "Southland Suite". Recorded into the early 60s. Johnson's son Bud was a member of The Chanters. Not to be confused with sax player/bandleader Budd Johnson. | | |
| 2/06/43 | **2**² | 24 | 1 **Let's Beat Out Some Love** ........................... | | Decca 8647 |
| | | | vocal by Buddy Johnson | | |
| 4/03/43 | **3** | 6 | 2 **Baby Don't You Cry** .................................... | | Decca 8632 |
| | | | vocal by Warren Evans | | |
| 2/26/44 | **1**¹ | 24 | 3 **When My Man Comes Home** ........................ | *23* | Decca 8655 |
| 7/14/45 | **2**² | 11 | 4 **That's The Stuff You Gotta Watch** ............... | *14* | Decca 8671 |
| 7/06/46 | **5** | 1 | 5 **They All Say I'm The Biggest Fool** ............... | | Decca 11000 |
| | | | vocal by Arthur Prysock | | |
| 2/12/49 | **11** | 2 | 6 I Don't Care Who Knows .............................. | | Decca 48088 |
| | | | Best Seller #11 | | |
| 8/20/49 | **13** | 2 | 7 Did You See Jackie Robinson Hit The Ball? ....... | *17* | Decca 24675 |
| | | | Juke Box #13 / Best Seller #15 vocal by Buddy Johnson | | |
| 3/18/50 | **8** | 1 | 8 **Because, Pts. 1 & 2** ................................... | | Decca 24842 |
| | | | Best Seller #8 vocal by Arthur Prysock | | |
| 5/16/53 | **6** | 7 | 9 **Hittin' On Me** .......................................... | | Mercury 70116 |
| | | | Juke Box #6 / Best Seller #9 | | |
| 1/09/54 | **6** | 8 | 10 **I'm Just Your Fool** .................................... | | Mercury 70251 |
| | | | Best Seller #6 | | |
| 2/26/55 | **13** | 1 | 11 (Gotta Go) Upside Your Head ........................ | | Mercury 70523 |
| | | | Best Seller #13 | | |
| 2/25/56 | **14** | 3 | 12 I Don't Want Nobody (To Have My Love But You) | | Mercury 70775 |
| | | | Best Seller #14 | | |
| 3/10/56 | **15** | 1 | 13 I Don't Want Nobody (To Have My Love But You) ................................................... [R] | | Wing 90064 |
| | | | Jockey #15 above 2: same song - Mercury also distributed title on its subsidiary label, Wing; reissued in 1960 as "Ella Johnson with Buddy Johnson" on Mercury 71723 (POS 78-Pop) | | |
| 12/08/56 | **9** | 1 | 14 **Bring It Home To Me** .................................. | | Mercury 70912 |
| | | | Jockey #9 3-4 & 9-14: vocals by Ella Johnson | | |
| 5/06/57 | **13** | 1 | 15 Rock On ..................................................... | | Mercury 71068 |
| | | | Jockey #13 vocal by Buddy Johnson | | |
| | | | **DANNY JOHNSON** | | |
| | | | Born in Chicago, raised in Robbins, Illinois. Lead singer for the Chi-Lites from 1976-77. | | |
| 3/24/79 | **92** | 4 | 1 Future Past ................................................ | | 1st American 108 |

| DEBUT DATE | PEAK POS | WKS CHR | ARTIST — Record Title | POP POS | Label & Number |
|---|---|---|---|---|---|
| | | | **DON JOHNSON BAND** | | |
| | | | Trumpet player. | | |
| 4/16/49 | **14** | 1 | 1 Jackson's Blues.............................................. [I] | | Specialty 323 |
| | | | Juke Box #14 | | |
| | | | **ELLA JOHNSON - see BUDDY JOHNSON** | | |
| | | | **GENERAL JOHNSON** | | |
| | | | General Norman Johnson, singer/songwriter from Norfolk, Virginia. Leader of The Showmen from 1961-67, and Chairmen Of The Board from 1969-74. Wrote Clarence Carter's hit "Patches". | | |
| 3/27/76 | **22** | 12 | 1 All In The Family .................................... | | Arista 0177 |
| 7/04/76 | **36** | 9 | 2 We The People........................................ | | Arista 0192 |
| 10/23/76 | **42** | 10 | 3 Don't Walk Away .................................... | | Arista 0203 |
| 9/17/77 | **78** | 7 | 4 Let's Fool Around .................................... | | Arista 0264 |
| 11/04/78 | **79** | 5 | 5 Can't Nobody Love Me Like You Do ................. | | Arista 0359 |
| | | | **HOWARD JOHNSON** | | |
| | | | Born in Miami. First recorded with Tornader, which became Nite Flyte. | | |
| 6/19/82 | **6** | 19 | 1 **So Fine** .......................................... *105* | | A&M 2415 |
| 10/30/82 | **47** | 11 | 2 Keepin' Love New.................................... | | A&M 2448 |
| | | | written by Kashif | | |
| 12/03/83+ | **30** | 12 | 3 Let's Take Time Out .................................... | | A&M 2588 |
| 3/17/84 | **58** | 7 | 4 Let This Dream Be Real ............................. | | A&M 2611 |
| 8/03/85 | **29** | 14 | 5 Stand Up ............................................. | | A&M 2752 |
| | | | **JAMES ARTHUR JOHNSON** | | |
| 11/15/86 | **73** | 5 | 1 Too Much Is Never Enough ........................... | | Tux. Music 3005 |
| | | | **JANICE MARIE JOHNSON** | | |
| | | | Vocalist/bass player from Los Angeles. Formerly half of duo, A Taste Of Honey. | | |
| 7/07/84 | **67** | 7 | 1 Love Me Tonite....................................... | | Capitol 5359 |
| | | | **JESSE JOHNSON** | | |
| | | | Jesse was lead guitarist with The Time. | | |
| | | | **JESSE JOHNSON'S REVUE:** | | |
| 2/09/85 | **4** | 18 | 1 **Be Your Man** .................................... *61* | | A&M 2702 |
| 5/04/85 | **3** | 16 | 2 **Can You Help Me** ............................. *110* | | A&M 2730 |
| 7/06/85 | **7** | 15 | 3 **I Want My Girl** ................................. *76* | | A&M 2749 |
| 11/16/85 | **87** | 3 | 4 Let's Have Some Fun ............................... | | A&M 2778 |
| 9/27/86 | **2**¹ | 18 | 5 **Crazay** .......................................... *53* | | A&M 2878 |
| | | | **JESSE JOHNSON featuring SLY STONE** | | |
| | | | **JESSE JOHNSON:** | | |
| 12/27/86+ | **28** | 13 | 6 She (I Can't Resist) ................................. | | A&M 2901 |
| 4/18/87 | **23** | 13 | 7 Baby Let's Kiss...................................... | | A&M 2912 |
| 4/02/88 | **4** | 14 | 8 **Love Struck** .................................... *78* | | A&M 3020 |
| 6/25/88 | **19** | 14 | 9 Every Shade Of Love................................. | | A&M 1214 |
| | | | **JIMMY JOHNSON & His Band featuring HANK ALEXANDER** | | |
| | | | Bluesman from Los Angeles. | | |
| 2/06/65 | **16** | 5 | 1 Don't Answer The Door ................................ *128* | | Magnum 719 |
| | | | **L.V. JOHNSON** | | |
| | | | Singer/guitarist from Chicago, formerly with Tyrone Davis. Wrote "Are You Serious", and "True Love Is Hard To Find" for Davis, "Country Love" for Bobby Bland, and "Standing Ovation" for the Dells. | | |
| 1/05/80 | **44** | 12 | 1 It's Not My Time ...................................... | | ICA 026 |
| 5/23/81 | **51** | 11 | 2 I Don't Really Care ................................... | | ICA 027 |
| | | | **LONNIE JOHNSON** | | |
| | | | Born Alonzo Johnson on 2/8/1889 in New Orleans. Died of a stroke on 6/16/70 in Toronto, Canada. Vocalist/guitarist/pianist/violinist. Worked Storyville district in New Orleans from 1910-17, riverboat bands, and theater circuits in the 20s. Staff musician at Okeh from 1925-32. Recorded with Louis Armstrong, and Duke Ellington; toured with Bessie Smith. Active into the late 60s. Guitar style highly influential to later jazz and blues guitarists. | | |
| 2/28/48 | **1**⁷ | 33 | 1 **Tomorrow Night** ........................... *19* | | King 4201 |
| | | | Best Seller #1(7) / Juke Box #1(7) | | |
| | | | written in 1939 | | |

| DEBUT DATE | PEAK POS | WKS CHR | ARTIST — Record Title | POP POS | Label & Number |
|---|---|---|---|---|---|
| | | | **LONNIE JOHNSON — Continued** | | |
| 10/23/48 | **2**¹ | 10 | 2 **Pleasing You (As Long As I Live)** .................. | | King 4245 |
| | | | Best Seller #2 / Juke Box #2 | | |
| 2/19/49 | **9** | 5 | 3 **So Tired** ............................................... | | King 4263 |
| | | | Juke Box #9 | | |
| 2/04/50 | **11** | 3 | 4 Confused ............................................... | | King 4336 |
| | | | Best Seller #11 / Juke Box #15 | | |
| | | | 1 & 4: featuring pianist Simeon Hatch | | |
| | | | **LOU JOHNSON** | | |
| 10/19/63 | **74** | 8 | 1 Reach Out For Me ..................................... | *Hot* | Big Top 3153 |
| 8/22/64 | **49** | 7 | 2 (There's) Always Something There To Remind Me ...................................................... | *Hot* | Big Hill 552 |
| | | | **MARV JOHNSON** | | |
| | | | Born on 10/15/38 in Detroit. Singer/songwriter/pianist. With Jr. Serenaders vocal group, mid-50s. First recorded for Kudo in 1958. Worked in sales and promotion for Motown in the early 70s. | | |
| 3/09/59 | **6** | 15 | 1 **Come To Me** ........................................ | 30 | United Art. 160 |
| | | | released regionally on Tamla 101 - Barry Gordy's first release | | |
| 8/10/59 | **23** | 3 | 2 I'm Coming Home ..................................... | 82 | United Art. 175 |
| 10/19/59+ | **2**² | 22 | 3 **You Got What It Takes** ........................... | 10 | United Art. 185 |
| 3/07/60 | **2**¹ | 12 | 4 **I Love The Way You Love** ........................ | 9 | United Art. 208 |
| 9/26/60 | **12** | 3 | 5 (You've Got To) Move Two Mountains .............. | 20 | United Art. 241 |
| 12/12/60+ | **7** | 9 | 6 **Happy Days** ........................................ | 58 | United Art. 273 |
| 3/13/61 | **26** | 3 | 7 Merry-Go-Round ...................................... | 61 | United Art. 294 |
| 4/09/66 | **39** | 2 | 8 I Miss You, Baby (How I Miss You) ................. | | Gordy 7051 |
| | | | **MICHAEL JOHNSON** | | |
| | | | Born on 8/8/44 in Denver. Pop singer/guitarist. Member of the Chad Mitchell Trio from 1967-68. | | |
| 11/11/78 | **91** | 2 | 1 Almost Like Being In Love ........................... | 32 | EMI America 8004 |
| | | | **DR. PERRI JOHNSON - see HAMILTON BOHANNON** | | |
| | | | **PETE JOHNSON ALL-STAR ORCHESTRA** | | |
| | | | Born Kermit Johnson on 3/24/04 in Kansas City, Missouri. Died of a heart attack on 3/23/67 (62). Pianist/drummer. Raised in an orphanage. Popular figure in Kansas City from 1926-38, frequently teamed with vocalist Joe Turner. To New York with Turner in 1938. Key figure in boogie woogie revival in the late 30s. Active into the late 50s, primarily around his home in Buffalo. | | |
| 3/17/45 | **3** | 6 | 1 **S.K. Blues, Pt 1&2** ................................. | | National 9010 |
| | | | vocal by Joe Turner | | |
| | | | **PAUL JOHNSON** | | |
| 3/12/88 | **56** | 9 | 1 When Love Comes Calling ............................ | | Epic 07707 |
| | | | **ROZETTA JOHNSON** | | |
| | | | Singer from Tuscaloosa, Alabama. | | |
| 12/19/70 | **39** | 3 | 1 A Woman's Way ....................................... | 94 | Clintone 001 |
| 4/17/71 | **45** | 3 | 2 Who Are You Gonna Love ............................ | | Clintone 003 |
| | | | **RUBY JOHNSON** | | |
| | | | Singer from Memphis. First recorded for V-Tone in 1960. | | |
| 5/07/66 | **31** | 4 | 1 I'll Run Your Hurt Away .............................. | | Volt 133 |
| | | | **SYL JOHNSON**  ★★183★★ | | |
| | | | Born Syl Thompson on 7/1/39 in Holly Springs, Mississippi. Singer/guitarist/ harmonica player/producer. Brothers Mac Thompson and Jimmy Johnson were also musicians. With Magic Sam, Billy Boy Arnold and Junior Wells in the late 50s. Recorded with Jimmy Reed for Vee-Jay in 1959. First solo recording for Federal in 1959. Johnson's backing band, The Deacons, recorded in 1968. | | |
| 7/15/67 | **12** | 12 | 1 Come On Sock It To Me ............................... | 97 | Twilight 100 |
| 9/23/67 | **17** | 10 | 2 Different Strokes ...................................... | 95 | Twilight 103 |
| 11/23/68 | **36** | 9 | 3 Dresses Too Short ..................................... | | Twinight 110 |
| 11/08/69+ | **11** | 14 | 4 Is It Because I'm Black ................................ | 68 | Twinight 125 |
| 2/28/70 | **29** | 7 | 5 Concrete Reservation ................................. | | Twinight 129 |
| 6/27/70 | **24** | 9 | 6 One Way Ticket To Nowhere ......................... | 125 | Twinight 134 |
| 4/17/71 | **34** | 5 | 7 Get Ready ............................................... | | Twinight 149 |
| 1/08/72 | **43** | 3 | 8 The Love You Left Behind ............................ | | Hi 2208 |
| 12/09/72+ | **23** | 16 | 9 We Did It ............................................... | 95 | Hi 2229 |
| 9/08/73 | **16** | 14 | 10 Back For A Taste Of Your Love ...................... | 72 | Hi 2250 |

| DEBUT DATE | PEAK POS | WKS CHR | ARTIST — Record Title | POP POS | Label & Number |
|---|---|---|---|---|---|
| | | | **SYL JOHNSON — Continued** | | |
| 3/02/74 | **68** | 6 | 11  I'm Yours............................................ | | Hi 3260 |
| 8/03/74 | **54** | 8 | 12  Let Yourself Go ............................... | | Hi 2269 |
| 11/16/74+ | **40** | 13 | 13  I Want To Take You Home (To See Mama)......... | | Hi 2275 |
| 4/19/75 | **7** | 18 | 14  **Take Me To The River**...................... | 48 | Hi 2285 |
| 9/13/75 | **15** | 14 | 15  I Only Have Love............................... | | Hi 2295 |
| 3/20/76 | **89** | 4 | 16  Star Bright, Star Lite ......................... | | Hi 2304 |
| 6/12/76 | **94** | 4 | 17  Bout To Make Me Leave Home..................... | | Hi 2308 |
| 6/18/77 | **93** | 4 | 18  Goodie-Goodie-Good Times....................... | | Shama 1235 |
| 11/13/82 | **60** | 9 | 19  Ms. Fine Brown Frame .......................... | | Boardwalk 99904 |
| | | | **TROY JOHNSON** | | |
| 4/19/86 | **65** | 8 | 1  It's You...................................... | | Kallista 1831 |
| | | | **FRANCE JOLI** | | |
| | | | French-Canadian singer from Montreal. Age 16 in 1979. | | |
| 9/22/79 | **36** | 10 | 1  Come To Me................................... | 15 | Prelude 8001 |
| | | | **THE JONES GIRLS** | | |
| | | | Detroit trio consisting of sisters Shirley, Brenda and Valorie Jones. First recorded for GM in 1968. Backup singers for Lou Rawls, Teddy Pendergrass and Aretha Franklin. With Diana Ross from 1975-78. Sang with Le Pamplemousse. | | |
| 5/12/79 | **5** | 22 | 1 ● You Gonna Make Me Love Somebody Else....... | 38 | Phil. Int. 3680 |
| 11/24/79 | **78** | 4 | 2  We're A Melody ............................... | | Phil. Int. 3722 |
| 1/19/80 | **77** | 5 | 3  I'm At Your Mercy............................. | | Phil. Int. 3735 |
| 8/02/80 | **22** | 15 | 4  Dance Turned Into A Romance .................. | | Phil. Int. 3111 |
| 11/29/80+ | **9** | 21 | 5  **I Just Love The Man** ...................... | | Phil. Int. 3121 |
| 11/14/81+ | **20** | 14 | 6  (I Found) That Man Of Mine ................... | | Phil. Int. 02618 |
| 2/13/82 | **23** | 11 | 7  Nights Over Egypt ............................ | | Phil. Int. 02713 |
| 9/24/83 | **43** | 11 | 8  On Target .................................... | | RCA 13619 |
| 12/10/83+ | **47** | 10 | 9  2 Win U Back ................................. | | RCA 13686 |
| | | | **BRENDA JONES** | | |
| 10/09/82 | **85** | 4 | 1  My Heart's Not In It ......................... | | Wave 1215 |
| | | | **ETTA JONES** | | |
| | | | Born on 11/25/28 in Aiken, South Carolina. Jazz singer with Earl Hines' orchestra from 1949-52. First recorded for Black & White in 1944. | | |
| 11/21/60 | **5** | 11 | 1  **Don't Go To Strangers** .................... | 36 | Prestige 180 |
| | | | **GLENN JONES** | | |
| | | | Vocalist from Jacksonville, Florida. Sang with the gospel group, Bivens Special, from age 8. Had own gospel group, the Modulations, from age 14. In the Broadway musical "Sing Mahalia, Sing". | | |
| 2/12/83 | **30** | 14 | 1  I Am Somebody ............................... | | RCA 13435 |
| 5/21/83 | **51** | 3 | 2  Keep On Doin' ................................ | | RCA 13519 |
| 9/22/84 | **3** | 23 | 3  **Show Me** .................................. | | RCA 13873 |
| 2/09/85 | **47** | 10 | 4  Finder Of Lost Loves ......................... | | Arista 9281 |
| | | | **DIONNE WARWICK & GLENN JONES** from the TV series of the same title | | |
| 3/09/85 | **18** | 17 | 5  Bring Back Your Love......................... | | RCA 13999 |
| 12/28/85+ | **85** | 6 | 6  Everlasting Love.............................. | | RCA 14241 |
| 7/12/86 | **19** | 15 | 7  Giving Myself To You ......................... | | RCA 14395 |
| 11/01/86 | **69** | 6 | 8  Stay.......................................... | | RCA 5040 |
| 2/07/87 | **42** | 10 | 9  Together...................................... | | RCA 5098 |
| | | | **GENOBIA JETER & GLENN JONES** | | |
| 8/01/87 | **2²** | 20 | 10  **We've Only Just Begun (The Romance Is Not Over)**.......................................... | 66 | Jive 1049 |
| 12/05/87+ | **38** | 12 | 11  Oh Girl ...................................... | | Jive 5364 |
| 3/26/88 | **34** | 10 | 12  Living In The Limelight....................... | | Jive 1090 |
| | | | **GRACE JONES** | | |
| | | | Model/film actress/singer, born on 5/19/52 in Spanishtown, Jamaica. Moved to Syracuse, New York in 1964. | | |
| 8/30/80 | **87** | 4 | 1  The Hunter Gets Captured By The Game .......... | | Island 49531 |
| 4/11/81 | **5** | 21 | 2  **Pull Up To The Bumper** .................... | 101 | Island 49697 |
| 11/06/82 | **17** | 14 | 3  Nipple To The Bottle ......................... | 103 | Island 99963 |
| 3/05/83 | **64** | 8 | 4  Cry Now, Laugh Later ......................... | | Island 99917 |

| DEBUT DATE | PEAK POS | WKS CHR | ARTIST — Record Title | POP POS | Label & Number |
|---|---|---|---|---|---|
| | | | **GRACE JONES — Continued** | | |
| 11/23/85+ | 20 | 16 | 5 Slave To The Rhythm ............................. | | Manhattan 50020 |
| 11/08/86+ | 9 | 15 | 6 I'm Not Perfect (But I'm Perfect For You) ....... | 69 | Manhattan 50052 |
| | | | **GRANT JONES** | | |
| 6/16/51 | 8 | 3 | 1 I'd Rather Drink Muddy Water..................... | | Decca 48192 |
| | | | Juke Box #8 | | |
| | | | with Brown's Blues Blowers | | |
| | | | **HOWARD JONES** | | |
| | | | Born on 2/23/55 in Southampton, England. Pop singer/songwriter/synth wizard. | | |
| 4/27/85 | 54 | 11 | 1 Things Can Only Get Better ...................... | 5 | Elektra 69651 |
| | | | **JIMMY JONES** | | |
| | | | Born on 6/2/37 in Birmingham, Alabama. Singer/dancer. Worked as a tap-dancer in touring show during the early 50s. Joined vocal group, Sparks Of Rhythm in 1955. Formed own group, the Savoys (later: Pretenders), in 1956. Cut demo record of Otis Blackwell's "Handy Man", released by MGM/Cub. | | |
| 2/01/60 | 3 | 12 | 1 Handy Man ..................................... | 2 | Cub 9049 |
| 5/23/60 | 8 | 8 | 2 Good Timin' ................................... | 3 | Cub 9067 |
| | | | **JIMMY JONES** | | |
| | | | Singer from Chicago, worked as staff writer/producer for One-Derful Records during the 60s. | | |
| 10/30/76 | 98 | 3 | 1 Ain't Nothin' Wrong With Makin' Love The First Time........................................ | | Conchillo 101 |
| | | | **JOE JONES** | | |
| | | | Born on 8/12/26 in New Orleans. Pianist/valet for B.B. King in the early 50s. First recorded for Capitol in 1954. Produced The Dixie Cups and Alvin Robinson. | | |
| 10/03/60 | 9 | 12 | 1 You Talk Too Much.............................. | 3 | Roulette 4304 |
| | | | **JOHNNY JONES** | | |
| | | | Vocalist from Nashville. | | |
| 7/27/68 | 49 | 2 | 1 Tennessee Waltz................................ | | Fury 5050 |
| | | | **LINDA JONES** | | |
| | | | Born on 1/14/44 in Newark, New Jersey. Died of diabetes on 3/14/72. Sang in family gospel group from age 6. | | |
| 6/17/67 | 4 | 15 | 1 Hypnotized ..................................... | 21 | Loma 2070 |
| 10/07/67 | 8 | 10 | 2 What've I Done (To Make You Mad)................ | 61 | Loma 2077 |
| 1/20/68 | 34 | 2 | 3 Give My Love A Try.............................. | 93 | Loma 2085 |
| 4/13/68 | 50 | 2 | 4 My Heart Needs A Break ......................... | | Loma 2091 |
| 12/20/69+ | 40 | 2 | 5 That's When I'll Stop Loving You/ | | |
| | | 5 | 6 I'll Be Sweeter Tomorrow ......................... | | Neptune 17 |
| 6/19/71 | 47 | 2 | 7 Stay With Me Forever ........................... | | Turbo 012 |
| 2/19/72 | 15 | 10 | 8 Your Precious Love ............................. | 74 | Turbo 021 |
| 6/03/72 | 32 | 5 | 9 Not On The Outside ............................. | | Turbo 024 |
| | | | all of above: produced by George Kerr | | |
| | | | **ORAN "JUICE" JONES** | | |
| | | | Singer born in Houston; raised in Harlem. | | |
| 5/31/86 | 75 | 5 | 1 You Can't Hide From Love ....................... | | Def Jam 05870 |
| | | | shown only as: **JUICE** | | |
| 7/19/86 | 1² | 21 | 2 The Rain........................................ | 9 | Def Jam 06209 |
| 11/29/86 | 45 | 9 | 3 Curiosity ...................................... | | Def Jam 06389 |
| 2/28/87 | 45 | 10 | 4 Here I Go Again ................................ | | Def Jam 06687 |
| 9/19/87 | 41 | 11 | 5 Cold Spendin' My $ Money ....................... | | Def Jam 07391 |
| | | | **QUINCY JONES** | | |
| | | | Born Quincy Delight Jones, Jr. on 3/14/33 in Chicago. Composer/conductor/arranger/producer. Began as a jazz trumpeter, with Lionel Hampton, 1950-53. Music Director for Mercury Records in 1961, then Vice President in 1964. Wrote scores for many films, 1965-73. Scored TV series "Roots" in 1977. Produced Michael Jackson's 1982 "Thriller" album. Arranger and producer for hundreds of successful singers and orchestras. Winner of 19 Grammy Awards. | | |
| 5/02/70 | 47 | 4 | 1 Killer Joe ..................................... [I] | 74 | A&M 1163 |
| 4/01/72 | 46 | 4 | 2 Money Runner .................................. [I] | 57 | Reprise 1062 |
| | | | from the film "$" | | |
| 9/21/74 | 71 | 6 | 3 If I Ever Lose This Heaven ...................... | | A&M 1606 |
| 11/23/74 | 70 | 6 | 4 Boogie Joe, The Grinder ........................ | | A&M 1638 |
| 4/05/75 | 85 | 6 | 5 Body Heat ..................................... | | A&M 1663 |

| DEBUT DATE | PEAK POS | WKS CHR | ARTIST — Record Title | POP POS | Label & Number |
|---|---|---|---|---|---|
| | | | **QUINCY JONES — Continued** | | |
| 10/04/75 | **18** | 13 | 6 Is It Love That We're Missin' ........................... | 70 | A&M 1743 |
| | | | vocals by The Brothers Johnson | | |
| 3/13/76 | **82** | 4 | 7 Mellow Madness ............................................. | | A&M 1791 |
| 11/13/76 | **47** | 10 | 8 Midnight Soul Patrol ..................................... | 104 | A&M 1878 |
| 3/12/77 | **32** | 9 | 9 "Roots" Medley .............................. [I] | 57 | A&M 1909 |
| | | | Motherland/Theme From "Roots" (Roots Mural Theme) | | |
| 5/20/78 | **1**[1] | 20 | 10 **Stuff Like That** ......................................... | 21 | A&M 2043 |
| | | | vocals by Ashford & Simpson and Chaka Khan | | |
| 9/30/78 | **60** | 8 | 11 Love, I Never Had It So Good .......................... | | A&M 2080 |
| | | | vocals by Patti Austin & Charles May | | |
| 2/21/81 | **10** | 17 | 12 **Ai No Corrida** ............................................ | 28 | A&M 2309 |
| | | | vocals by Dune | | |
| 6/06/81 | **17** | 12 | 13 Razzamatazz ................................................ | | A&M 2334 |
| | | | vocals by Patti Austin | | |
| 8/22/81 | **11** | 18 | 14 Just Once .................................................... | 17 | A&M 2357 |
| | | | QUINCY JONES featuring JAMES INGRAM | | |
| 12/26/81+ | **10** | 23 | 15 **One Hundred Ways** ..................................... | 14 | A&M 2387 |
| | | | QUINCY JONES featuring JAMES INGRAM | | |
| | | | **RICKIE LEE JONES** | | |
| | | | Born on 11/8/54 in Chicago. Pop jazz-styled singer/songwriter. Moved to Los Angeles in 1977. | | |
| 7/07/79 | **79** | 5 | 1 Chuck E.'s In Love ........................................ | 4 | Warner 8825 |
| | | | **SHIRLEY JONES** | | |
| | | | Born and raised in Detroit. Lead singer of The Jones Girls. | | |
| 6/07/86 | **1**[2] | 20 | 1 **Do You Get Enough Love** ............................. | | Phil. Int. 50034 |
| 9/20/86 | **36** | 13 | 2 Last Night I Needed Somebody ........................ | | Phil. Int. 50046 |
| 1/31/87 | **80** | 6 | 3 She Knew About Me ...................................... | | Phil. Int. 50062 |
| | | | **SPENCER JONES** | | |
| 7/26/86 | **84** | 7 | 1 How To Win Your Love.................................... | | Profile 7105 |
| | | | **TAMIKO JONES** | | |
| | | | Born Barbara Tamiko Ferguson in 1945 in Kyle, West Virginia; raised in Detroit. First recorded for Atlantic in 1966. Moved to London; married to John Abbey (publisher of "Blues & Soul" magazine). | | |
| 3/01/75 | **12** | 15 | 1 Touch Me Baby (Reaching Out For Your Love).... | 60 | Arista 0110 |
| 8/09/75 | **78** | 5 | 2 Just You And Me ........................................... | | Arista 0134 |
| 12/11/76+ | **76** | 10 | 3 Let It Flow .................................................. | | Contempo 7001 |
| 4/16/77 | **92** | 2 | 4 Cloudy ....................................................... | | Atlantis 716 |
| 8/18/79 | **70** | 7 | 5 Can't Live Without Your Love .......................... | | Polydor 14580 |
| 9/27/86 | **81** | 6 | 6 I Want You ................................................. | | Sutra 157 |
| | | | **THELMA JONES** | | |
| | | | Vocalist from Fayetteville, North Carolina. | | |
| 2/18/67 | **49** | 2 | 1 Never Leave Me ............................................ | | Barry 1010 |
| 10/07/78 | **74** | 6 | 2 I Second That Emotion................................... | | Columbia 10814 |
| | | | **TOM JONES** | | |
| | | | Pop singer, born Thomas Jones Woodward on 6/7/40 in Pontypridd, Wales, England. Host of his own TV musical variety series from 1969-71. | | |
| 5/29/65 | **26** | 4 | 1 It's Not Unusual............................................ | 10 | Parrot 9737 |
| 2/07/70 | **41** | 2 | 2●Without Love (There Is Nothing)..................... | 5 | Parrot 40045 |
| 3/20/71 | **42** | 2 | 3●She's A Lady ............................................... | 2 | Parrot 40058 |
| | | | written by Paul Anka | | |
| | | | **THE JONESES** | | |
| | | | Group from Pittsburgh. Consisted of Glenn Dorsey, Harold Taylor, Cy Brooks and Ernest Holt. To New York in 1971. Taylor and Holt replaced by Reginald and Wendell Noble. Samuel White and Larry Noble (guitar), added. | | |
| 3/16/74 | **18** | 17 | 1 Hey Babe.................................................... | | Mercury 72458 |
| 8/31/74 | **10** | 14 | 2 **Sugar Pie Guy - Pt. 1** ................................. | 47 | Mercury 73614 |
| 2/22/75 | **28** | 10 | 3 I Can't See What You See In Me ....................... | | Mercury 73663 |
| 6/28/75 | **47** | 8 | 4 Love Inflation (Pt. 1) ..................................... | | Mercury 73689 |
| | | | featuring Harold Taylor & Jimmy Richardson | | |
| 11/01/75 | **35** | 9 | 5 Name Of The Game (Pt. 1) ............................. | | Mercury 73719 |
| 4/03/76 | **55** | 8 | 6 In A Good Groove/ | | |
| | | 8 | 7 Child Of Mine ............................................. | | Mercury 73778 |

| DEBUT DATE | PEAK POS | WKS CHR | | ARTIST — Record Title | POP POS | Label & Number |
|---|---|---|---|---|---|---|
| | | | | **THE JONZUN CREW** | | |
| | | | | Electronic instrumentation group formed in Boston by ex-Florida brothers Michael and Soni Johnson, with Steve Thorpe and Gordy Worthy. Michael recorded solo in 1986. | | |
| 9/11/82 | **13** | 12 | 1 | Pack Jam (Look Out For The OVC) ................. | *108* | Tommy Boy 826 |
| 12/25/82+ | **31** | 14 | 2 | Space Is The Place ..................................... | | Tommy Boy 828 |
| 4/16/83 | **12** | 17 | 3 | Space Cowboy ........................................... | | Tommy Boy 833 |
| 7/02/83 | **37** | 9 | 4 | We Are The Jonzun Crew ........................... | | Tommy Boy 834 |
| 8/18/84 | **66** | 9 | 5 | Time Is Running Out.................................. | | Tommy Boy 845 |
| 12/01/84+ | **40** | 14 | 6 | Lovin' ....................................................... | | Tommy Boy 850 |
| | | | | THE JONZUN CREW featuring Michael Jonzun | | |
| | | | | **MICHAEL JONZUN** | | |
| | | | | Leader of The Jonzun Crew. Discovered New Edition; wrote and produced their hit "Candy Girl". | | |
| 7/19/86 | **83** | 2 | 1 | Burning Up ............................................... | | A&M 2840 |
| | | | | **LONNIE JORDAN** | | |
| | | | | Born Leroy Jordan on 11/21/48 in San Diego. Singer/keyboardist. Member of War. | | |
| 10/16/76 | **35** | 10 | 1 | Grey Rainy Days........................................ | | United Art. 873 |
| 5/15/82 | **73** | 6 | 2 | I Think You're Out Of This World.................... | | Boardwalk 11141 |
| | | | | **LOUIS JORDAN** ★★5★★ | | |
| | | | | Born on 7/8/08 in Brinkley, Arkansas. Died of a heart attack on 2/4/75 (66). Vocalist/saxophonist. First recorded for Brunswick in 1929, with the Jungle Band. With Clarence Williams in New York, early 30s, and Chick Webb from 1936-38. Formed own band at Elk's Rendezvous in 1938; later known as The Tympany Five, the backing band on many of his recordings. Innovative, extremely popular vocal style. | | |
| 10/24/42 | **3** | 3 | 1 | I'm Gonna Leave You At The Outskirts Of Town...................................................... | | Decca 8638 |
| 11/14/42+ | **1**¹ | 14 | 2 | What's The Use Of Getting Sober/ | | |
| 1/30/43 | **10** | 1 | 3 | The Chicks I Pick Are Slender And Tender And Tall........................................ | | Decca 8645 |
| 10/09/43 | **3** | 10 | 4 | Five Guys Named Moe/ | | |
| 10/23/43 | **8** | 1 | 5 | That'll Just About Knock Me Out................. | | Decca 8653 |
| 12/18/43+ | **1**¹ | 21 | 6 | Ration Blues ............................................. | *11* | Decca 8654 |
| 4/29/44 | **1**⁶ | 26 | 7 | G.I. Jive/ | *1* | |
| 6/17/44 | **3** | 16 | 8 | Is You Is Or Is You Ain't (Ma' Baby) ............ | *2* | Decca 8659 |
| | | | | from the film "Follow The Boys" | | |
| 2/10/45 | **1**¹ | 17 | 9 | Mop Mop/ | | |
| 2/17/45 | **2**⁴ | 13 | 10 | You Can't Get That No More..................... | *11* | Decca 8668 |
| 5/12/45 | **1**⁷ | 26 | 11 | Caldonia/ | *6* | |
| 6/23/45 | **3** | 10 | 12 | Somebody Done Changed The Lock On My Door ..................................................... | | Decca 8670 |
| 1/12/46 | **1**⁹ | 13 | 13 | Buzz Me/ | *9* | |
| 1/26/46 | **1**¹ | 11 | 14 | Don't Worry 'Bout That Mule..................... | | Decca 18734 |
| 3/02/46 | **2**⁶ | 15 | 15 | Salt Pork, W.Va./ | | |
| 3/09/46 | **2**² | 7 | 16 | Reconversion Blues................................... | | Decca 18762 |
| 5/04/46 | **2**¹ | 9 | 17 | Beware/ | *20* | |
| 6/01/46 | **3** | 8 | 18 | Don't Let The Sun Catch You Cryin' .......... | | Decca 18818 |
| 6/29/46 | **1**⁵ | 20 | 19 | Stone Cold Dead In The Market (He Had It Coming)/ | *7* | |
| 7/27/46 | **3** | 2 | 20 | Petootie Pie ............................................. | | Decca 23546 |
| | | | | above 2: ELLA FITZGERALD & LOUIS JORDAN | | |
| 8/17/46 | **1**¹⁸ | 26 | 21 | Choo Choo Ch'Boogie/ | *7* | |
| 8/31/46 | **3** | 11 | 22 | That Chick's Too Young To Fry ................. | | Decca 23610 |
| 10/19/46 | **1**² | 17 | 23 | Ain't That Just Like A Woman ................... | *17* | Decca 23669 |
| 12/14/46+ | **1**¹⁷ | 27 | 24 | Ain't Nobody Here But Us Chickens/ | *6* | |
| 12/21/46+ | **2**⁴ | 23 | 25 | Let The Good Times Roll ........................... | | Decca 23741 |
| 3/01/47 | **1**² | 15 | 26 | Texas And Pacific.................................... | *20* | Decca 23810 |
| 3/08/47 | **2**⁴ | 6 | 27 | Open The Door, Richard ...................... [C] | *6* | Decca 23841 |
| 6/07/47 | **1**⁷ | 20 | 28 | Jack, You're Dead .................................... | *21* | Decca 23901 |
| 6/07/47 | **5** | 1 | 29 | I Like 'Em Fat Like That............................ | | Decca 23810 |
| | | | | recorded in 1944 | | |
| 6/28/47 | **3** | 4 | 30 | I Know What You're Putting Down ............. | | Decca 23901 |
| 8/30/47 | **1**¹⁴ | 24 | 31 | Boogie Woogie Blue Plate.......................... | *21* | Decca 24104 |

| DEBUT DATE | PEAK POS | WKS CHR | | ARTIST — Record Title | POP POS | Label & Number |
|---|---|---|---|---|---|---|
| | | | | **LOUIS JORDAN — Continued** | | |
| 10/25/47 | 5 | 6 | 32 | **Look Out/** | | |
| 11/15/47 | 3 | 10 | 33 | **Early In The Morning**............................. | | Decca 24155 |
| 2/14/48 | 2 [4] | 13 | 34 | **Barnyard Boogie/** | | |
| 3/06/48 | 9 | 1 | 35 | **How Long Must I Wait For You** ................. | | Decca 24300 |
| | | | | recorded in 1945 | | |
| 4/17/48 | 4 | 6 | 36 | **Reet, Petite, And Gone**............................. | | Decca 24381 |
| | | | | recorded in 1946 | | |
| 6/26/48 | 1 [2] | 15 | 37 | **Run, Joe/** | 23 | |
| | | | | Juke Box #1 / Best Seller #3 | | |
| | | | | vocals by The Calypso Boys | | |
| 7/24/48 | 13 | 1 | 38 | **All For The Love Of Lil** ............................. | | Decca 24448 |
| | | | | Juke Box #13 | | |
| | | | | above 2: recorded in 1946 | | |
| 8/07/48 | 14 | 1 | 39 | Pinetop's Boogie Woogie............................. [I] | | Decca 25394 |
| | | | | Juke Box # 14 | | |
| | | | | recorded in 1941 | | |
| 9/04/48 | 4 | 7 | 40 | **Don't Burn The Candle At Both Ends/** | | |
| | | | | Best Seller #4 / Juke Box #6 | | |
| 9/11/48 | 14 | 1 | 41 | We Can't Agree........................................... | | Decca 24483 |
| | | | | Juke Box #14 | | |
| 10/30/48+ | 7 | 5 | 42 | **Daddy-O** | | Decca 24502 |
| | | | | Best Seller #7 / Juke Box #9 | | |
| | | | | 40 & 42: vocals by Martha Davis | | |
| 12/25/48 | 5 | 6 | 43 | **Pettin' And Pokin'** .................................. | | Decca 24527 |
| | | | | Best Seller #5 / Juke Box #12 | | |
| 3/26/49 | 10 | 2 | 44 | **Roamin' Blues** ........................................ | | Decca 24571 |
| | | | | Juke Box #10 / Best Seller #2 | | |
| 4/02/49 | 3 | 2 | 45 | **You Broke Your Promise**.......................... | | Decca 24587 |
| | | | | Juke Box #3 | | |
| 5/28/49 | 7 | 10 | 46 | **Cole Slaw/** | | |
| | | | | Best Seller #7 / Juke Box #10 | | |
| 6/25/49 | 10 | 2 | 47 | **Every Man To His Own Profession** .............. | | Decca 24633 |
| | | | | Juke Box #10 | | |
| | | | | recorded in 1947 | | |
| 6/11/49 | 6 | 4 | 48 | **Baby, It's Cold Outside** ........................... | 9 | Decca 24644 |
| | | | | **ELLA FITZGERALD & LOUIS JORDAN** | | |
| | | | | Juke Box #6 / Best Seller #12 | | |
| | | | | from the film "Neptune's Daughter" | | |
| 8/06/49 | 1 [1] | 11 | 49 | **Beans And Corn Bread** ........................... | | Decca 24673 |
| | | | | Best Seller #1 / Juke Box #8 | | |
| 10/08/49 | 1 [12] | 23 | 50 | **Saturday Night Fish Fry (Part I)** .................. | 21 | Decca 24725 |
| | | | | Best Seller #1(12) / Juke Box #1(11) | | |
| 1/14/50 | 5 | 7 | 51 | **School Days** ........................................... | | Decca 24815 |
| | | | | Juke Box #5 / Best Seller #7 | | |
| 8/05/50 | 1 [7] | 16 | 52 | **Blue Light Boogie - Parts 1 & 2** ................... | | Decca 27114 |
| | | | | Best Seller #1(7) / Juke Box #1(4) | | |
| 11/04/50 | 7 | 2 | 53 | **I'll Never Be Free**.................................... | | Decca 27200 |
| | | | | **ELLA FITZGERALD & LOUIS JORDAN** | | |
| | | | | Juke Box #7 | | |
| 11/04/50 | 10 | 1 | 54 | **Tamburitza Boogie** ................................. | | Decca 27203 |
| | | | | Best Seller #10 | | |
| | | | | with Bill Doggett on organ | | |
| 1/13/51 | 6 | 3 | 55 | **Lemonade** ............................................. | | Decca 27324 |
| | | | | Best Seller #6 / Juke Box #7 | | |
| | | | | 45-46, 49-52 & 55: with Bill Doggett on piano | | |
| 3/17/51 | 4 | 2 | 56 | **Tear Drops From My Eyes** ......................... | | Decca 27424 |
| | | | | Best Seller #4 / Juke Box #8 | | |
| 5/12/51 | 5 | 2 | 57 | **Weak Minded Blues** ................................ | | Decca 27547 |
| | | | | Best Seller #5 / Juke Box #10 | | |
| | | | | **TENITA JORDAN** | | |
| 8/10/85 | 89 | 3 | 1 | I Don't Wanna Think About It ........................ | | CBS Assoc. 05427 |
| | | | | **DAVID JOSEPH** | | |
| | | | | British. | | |
| 4/30/83 | 72 | 6 | 1 | You Can't Hide ......................................... | | Mango 7804 |
| 8/13/83 | 84 | 3 | 2 | Let's Live It Up ........................................ | | Mango 7806 |

| DEBUT DATE | PEAK POS | WKS CHR | ARTIST — Record Title | POP POS | Label & Number |
|---|---|---|---|---|---|
| | | | **MARGIE JOSEPH** | | |
| | | | Born in Gautier, Mississippi in 1950. Attended Dillard University in New Orleans during the mid-60s. Worked as a teacher. First recorded for Okeh in 1967. | | |
| 6/20/70 | 46 | 2 | 1 Your Sweet Loving .............................. | | Volt 4037 |
| 4/10/71 | 38 | 2 | 2 Stop! In The Name Of Love.......................... | 96 | Volt 4056 |
| 4/28/73 | 43 | 2 | 3 Let's Stay Together .............................. | | Atlantic 2954 |
| 10/27/73 | 32 | 10 | 4 Come Lay Some Lovin' On Me ................. | | Atlantic 2988 |
| 5/25/74 | 10 | 13 | 5 **My Love** .............................. | 69 | Atlantic 3032 |
| 11/02/74 | 27 | 13 | 6 Words (Are Impossible).......................... | 91 | Atlantic 3220 |
| 9/06/75 | 34 | 10 | 7 Stay Still .............................. | | Atlantic 3290 |
| 11/01/75 | 11 | 14 | 8 What's Come Over Me .............................. | | Atco 7030 |
| | | | with Blue Magic (vocal group) | | |
| 5/22/76 | 18 | 15 | 9 Hear The Words, Feel The Feeling................. | | Cotillion 44201 |
| 9/11/76 | 46 | 9 | 10 Don't Turn The Lights Off.......................... | | Cotillion 44207 |
| 4/29/78 | 85 | 7 | 11 Come On Back To Me Lover ................. | | Atlantic 3445 |
| 9/16/78 | 94 | 3 | 12 I Feel His Love Getting Stronger ................. | | Atlantic 3509 |
| 11/20/82+ | 12 | 24 | 13 Knockout .............................. | | H.C.R.C. 03337 |
| 4/28/84 | 69 | 6 | 14 Ready For The Night.......................... | | Cotillion 99771 |
| | | | **RODDIE JOY** | | |
| 3/27/65 | 21 | 5 | 1 Come Back Baby.......................... | 86 | Red Bird 10021 |
| | | | **JUBALAIRES - see ANDY KIRK** | | |
| | | | **JUICE - see ORAN "JUICE" JONES** | | |
| | | | **JUICY** | | |
| | | | Brother and sister duo of Jerry and Katreese Barnes. | | |
| 2/12/83 | 75 | 6 | 1 Love's A Merry-Go-'Round ................. | | Arista 1032 |
| 8/04/84 | 76 | 4 | 2 Beat Street Strut.......................... | 107 | Atlantic 89655 |
| | | | from the film "Beat Street" | | |
| 7/06/85 | 41 | 12 | 3 Bad Boy .............................. | | Private I 05422 |
| 12/07/85 | 72 | 8 | 4 It Takes Two .............................. | | Private I 05694 |
| 2/01/86 | 13 | 14 | 5 Sugar Free .............................. | | Private I 05793 |
| 5/17/86 | 59 | 9 | 6 Nobody But You.......................... | | CBS Assoc. 05891 |
| | | | **JUMBO** | | |
| 5/14/77 | 98 | 3 | 1 Turn On To Love.......................... | | Prelude 71088 |
| | | | **JUNE & DONNIE - see DONNIE HATHAWAY** | | |
| | | | **JUNIE** | | |
| | | | Born Walter Morrison. Keyboardist, formerly with the Ohio Players and the Parliament/Funkadelic organization. | | |
| 2/16/74 | 84 | 6 | 1 Tightrope.............................. | | Eastbound 619 |
| 4/04/81 | 74 | 6 | 2 Rappin About Rappin (Uh-Uh-Uh) ................. | | Columbia 60520 |
| 11/17/84 | 71 | 7 | 3 Tease Me .............................. | | Island 99693 |
| | | | JUNIE MORRISON | | |
| | | | **JUNIOR** | | |
| | | | Full name: Junior Giscombe. Funk singer/songwriter from England. | | |
| 1/09/82 | 2² | 21 | 1 **Mama Used To Say**.......................... | 30 | Mercury 76132 |
| 5/15/82 | 8 | 18 | 2 **Too Late**.......................... | 102 | Mercury 76150 |
| 6/04/83 | 40 | 10 | 3 Communication Breakdown ................. | | Mercury 812397 |
| 9/24/83 | 72 | 4 | 4 Baby I Want You Back ................. | | Mercury 814226 |
| 11/26/83+ | 44 | 11 | 5 Unison ................. | | Casablanca 814725 |
| 9/29/84 | 47 | 10 | 6 Somebody ................. | | London 882008 |
| 3/22/86 | 14 | 16 | 7 Oh Louise ................. | | Mercury 886037 |
| 8/02/86 | 76 | 8 | 8 Not Tonight.......................... | | Mercury 886064 |
| 4/09/88 | 24 | 11 | 9 Yes (If You Want Me).......................... | | London 886169 |
| | | | **JU-PAR UNIVERSAL ORCHESTRA** | | |
| 6/04/77 | 32 | 12 | 1 Funky Music ................. | 101 | Ju-Par 8002 |

| DEBUT DATE | PEAK POS | WKS CHR | ARTIST — Record Title | POP POS | Label & Number |
|---|---|---|---|---|---|
| | | | **BILL JUSTIS**<br>Born on 10/14/26 in Birmingham, Alabama. Died on 7/15/82 in Nashville. Session saxophonist/arranger/producer. Led house band for Sun Records. | | |
| 11/25/57+ | 1 1 | 11 | 1 **Raunchy** ........................................... [I]<br>Jockey #1 / Best Seller #3<br>with Bill Justis (sax) and Sid Manker (guitar) | 2 | Phil. Int. 3519 |

# K

| | | | **BERT KAEMPFERT**<br>Born on 10/16/23 in Hamburg, Germany. Multi-instrumentalist/bandleader/producer/composer/arranger for Polydor Records in Germany. Produced the first Beatles' recording session. Died on 6/21/80 in Zug, Switzerland. | | |
|---|---|---|---|---|---|
| 12/12/60 | 5 | 12 | 1 **Wonderland By Night** ........................ [I]<br>trumpet solo by Charly Tabor | 1 | Decca 31141 |
| | | | **KALIN TWINS**<br>Herbert and Harold Kalin, born on 2/16/39 in Port Jervis, New York. | | |
| 8/04/58 | 1 1 | 5 | 1 **When** .................................................<br>Jockcy #1 / Best Seller #9 | 5 | Decca 30642 |
| | | | **KALYAN**<br>14-man soul/calypso band from Trinidad. | | |
| 4/30/77 | 92 | 3 | 1 Disco Reggae (Tony's Groove) Part 1 .................<br>recorded in Canada | 102 | MCA 40699 |
| | | | **KANO**<br>Italian disco band. | | |
| 11/22/80+ | 21 | 19 | 1 I'm Ready ................................................ | | Emergency 4504 |
| 11/28/81+ | 35 | 14 | 2 Can't Hold Back (Your Loving) ....................... | 89 | Mirage 3878 |
| | | | **PAUL KANTNER**<br>Original member of the rock group Jefferson Airplane, later known as Jefferson Starship. | | |
| 8/11/79 | 26 | 12 | 1 Groove Me ............................................... | | Malaco 1058 |
| | | | **SAX KARI - see GLORIA IRVING** | | |
| | | | **FRANKIE KARL & THE DREAMS** | | |
| 11/16/68 | 23 | 14 | 1 Don't Be Afraid (Do As I Say) ....................... | 93 | D.C. 180 |
| | | | **KARMA** | | |
| 4/16/77 | 100 | 2 | 1 Funk De Mambo ........................................ | | A&M/Horizon 111 |
| | | | **KARTOON KREW** | | |
| 12/28/85+ | 53 | 10 | 1 Inspector Gadget ....................................... | | Profile 5087 |
| | | | **KaSANDRA**<br>Born John W. Anderson in 1935 in Panama City, Florida. To Buffalo, New York in the early 50s, sang with the Cherokees group. | | |
| 12/21/68+ | 43 | 5 | 1 Don't Pat Me On The Back And Call Me Brother .<br>................................................. [S] | 91 | Capitol 2342 |
| | | | **KASHIF**    ★★198★★<br>Techno-funk musician, born Michael Jones in Brooklyn, in 1959. In B.T. Express at age 15. Member of Stephanie Mills' touring band. | | |
| 2/12/83 | 5 | 20 | 1 **I Just Gotta Have You (Lover Turn Me On)** ..... | 103 | Arista 1042 |
| 6/04/83 | 22 | 12 | 2 Stone Love ............................................... | | Arista 9033 |
| 8/06/83 | 28 | 12 | 3 Help Yourself To My Love ............................. | | Arista 9063 |
| 6/16/84 | 6 | 16 | 4 **Baby Don't Break Your Baby's Heart** ............. | 108 | Arista 9200 |
| 9/22/84 | 25 | 12 | 5 Are You The Woman ................................... | | Arista 9263 |
| 1/12/85 | 75 | 6 | 6 Ooh Love .............................................. | | Arista 9300 |
| 5/04/85 | 24 | 13 | 7 Love On The Rise ...................................<br>KENNY G & KASHIF | | Arista 9336 |
| 11/02/85 | 34 | 15 | 8 Condition Of The Heart ............................. | | Arista 9415 |
| 2/01/86 | 36 | 9 | 9 Dancing In The Dark (Heart To Heart) ............. | | Arista 9447 |
| 6/21/86 | 5 | 15 | 10 **Love The One I'm With (A Lot Of Love)** ..........<br>MELBA (Moore) & KASHIF | | Capitol 5577 |
| 10/17/87 | 20 | 15 | 11 Reservations For Two ................................<br>DIONNE (Warwick) & KASHIF | 62 | Arista 9638 |

| DEBUT DATE | PEAK POS | WKS CHR | ARTIST — Record Title | POP POS | Label & Number |
|---|---|---|---|---|---|
| | | | **KASHIF — Continued** | | |
| 11/07/87+ | **2**[1] | 19 | 12 Love Changes ........................................<br>KASHIF & MELI'SA MORGAN | | Arista 9626 |
| 3/19/88 | **14** | 13 | 13 Love Me All Over ................................... | | Arista 9680 |
| | | | **THE KAY-GEES**<br>8-man unit formed in Jersey City, New Jersey. Produced by Ronald Bell of Kool & The Gang, and named for that group. Consisted of Ray Wright, Peter Duart, Dennis White, Kevin Bell, Kevin Lassiter, Michel Cheek, Callie Cheek and Wilson Beckett. | | |
| 6/15/74 | **41** | 10 | 1 You Got To Keep On Bumpin' ...................... | | Gang 1321 |
| 11/30/74 | **60** | 7 | 2 Master Plan.......................................... | | Gang 1322 |
| 3/08/75 | **40** | 10 | 3 Get Down............................................. | | Gang 1323 |
| 9/06/75 | **56** | 8 | 4 Hustle Wit Every Muscle...........................<br>theme from the TV show "Party" | | Gang 1325 |
| 6/05/76 | **52** | 13 | 5 Waiting At The Bus Stop (Part 1)..................... | | Gang 1326 |
| 7/29/78 | **75** | 6 | 6 Cheek To Cheek..................................... | | De-Lite 906 |
| | | | **KC & THE SUNSHINE BAND**     ★★125★★<br>Band formed in Florida in 1973 by lead singer/keyboardist Harry "KC" Casey and bassist Richard Finch. Integrated band contained from 7 to 11 members. Casey and Finch wrote, arranged and produced all of their hits. Also see Terry DeSario. | | |
| 9/08/73 | **27** | 12 | 1 Blow Your Whistle.................................. | | T.K. 1001 |
| 2/02/74 | **21** | 15 | 2 Sound Your Funky Horn............................ | | T.K. 1003 |
| 1/04/75 | **57** | 8 | 3 I'm A Pushover ..................................... | | T.K. 1008 |
| 4/12/75 | **1**[1] | 23 | 4 **Get Down Tonight**............................... | 1 | T.K. 1009 |
| 9/20/75 | **25** | 11 | 5 Shotgun Shuffle ................................ [I]<br>THE SUNSHINE BAND | 88 | T.K. 1010 |
| 10/25/75 | **1**[1] | 16 | 6 **That's The Way (I Like It)**..................... | 1 | T.K. 1015 |
| 1/24/76 | **70** | 6 | 7 Rock Your Baby ................................ [I]<br>THE SUNSHINE BAND | | T.K. 1018 |
| 3/06/76 | **25** | 10 | 8 Queen Of Clubs ..................................... | 66 | T.K. 1005 |
| 7/10/76 | **1**[4] | 18 | 9 **(Shake, Shake, Shake) Shake Your Booty** ....... | 1 | T.K. 1019 |
| 12/04/76+ | **4** | 14 | 10 I Like To Do It ..................................... | 37 | T.K. 1020 |
| 2/26/77 | **3** | 17 | 11 **I'm Your Boogie Man**............................ | 1 | T.K. 1022 |
| 7/30/77 | **1**[1] | 17 | 12 **Keep It Comin' Love**............................ | 2 | T.K. 1023 |
| 11/19/77+ | **24** | 13 | 13 Wrap Your Arms Around Me ......................<br>originally released as the "B" side of "I'm Your Boogie Man" | 48 | T.K. 1022 |
| 3/04/78 | **29** | 10 | 14 Boogie Shoes........................................ | 35 | T.K. 1025 |
| 4/01/78 | **75** | 8 | 15 Black Water Gold................................ [I]<br>THE SUNSHINE BAND | | T.K. 1026 |
| 5/20/78 | **30** | 10 | 16 It's The Same Old Song ........................... | 35 | T.K. 1028 |
| 10/14/78 | **62** | 4 | 17 Do You Feel All Right ............................. | 63 | T.K. 1030 |
| 1/13/79 | **88** | 3 | 18 Who Do Ya Love ................................... | 68 | T.K. 1031 |
| 3/31/79 | **8** | 23 | 19 **Do You Wanna Go Party** ......................... | 50 | T.K. 1033 |
| 9/01/79 | **25** | 17 | 20 I Betcha Didn't Know That........................<br>flip side "Please Don't Go" hit POS 1 on the pop charts in 1980 | | T.K. 1035 |
| | | | **ERNIE K-DOE**<br>Born Ernest Kador, Jr. on 2/22/36 in New Orleans. With the Blue Diamonds, recorded for Savoy in 1954. Group included Huey "Piano" Smith, Billy Tate, Frank Fields and Earl Palmer. Name legally changed to K-Doe. | | |
| 4/03/61 | **1**[5] | 16 | 1 **Mother-In-Law** ..........................................<br>bass vocal by Benny Spellman | 1 | Minit 623 |
| 7/03/61 | **21** | 4 | 2 Te-Ta-Te-Ta-Ta .................................. | 53 | Minit 627 |
| 4/08/67 | **37** | 4 | 3 Later For Tomorrow ............................. | 122 | Duke 411 |
| 11/04/67 | **48** | 3 | 4 Until The Real Thing Comes Along ................. | | Duke 423 |
| | | | **ROGER KELLAWAY - see HOUSTON PERSON** | | |
| | | | **KELLY BROTHERS - see THE KING PINS** | | |
| | | | **HERMAN KELLY & LIFE** | | |
| 11/04/78 | **92** | 3 | 1 Dance To The Drummer's Beat ...................... | | Alston 3742 |
| | | | **PAUL KELLY**<br>Born on 6/19/40 in Miami. With vocal groups the Spades and Valadeers. First solo recording for T.K. in 1960. | | |
| 6/20/70 | **14** | 12 | 1 Stealing In The Name Of The Lord................... | 49 | Happy Tiger 541 |
| 1/20/73 | **35** | 7 | 2 Don't Burn Me ..................................... | 79 | Warner 7657 |

| DEBUT DATE | PEAK POS | WKS CHR | ARTIST — Record Title | POP POS | Label & Number |
|---|---|---|---|---|---|
| | | | **PAUL KELLY — Continued** | | |
| 7/14/73 | 95 | 2 | 3 Come Lay Some Lovin' On Me ........................ | | Warner 7707 |
| 2/16/74 | 84 | 5 | 4 I'm Into Something I Can't Shake ..................... | | Warner 7765 |
| 7/27/74 | 30 | 14 | 5 Hooked, Hogtied And Collared ........................ | | Warner 7823 |
| 11/16/74 | 55 | 9 | 6 Let Your Love Come Down (Let It Fall On Me) .... | | Warner 8040 |
| 3/01/75 | 33 | 11 | 7 Take It Away From Him (Put It On Me) ............. | | Warner 8067 |
| 10/04/75 | 98 | 2 | 8 Get Sexy .......................................................... | | Warner 8120 |
| 5/01/76 | 99 | 2 | 9 Play Me A Love Song .................................... | | Warner 8187 |
| | | | **REV. KELSEY'S CONGREGATION** | | |
| | | | Congregation of the Washington, DC Temple, Church Of God In Christ, led by Reverend (later: Bishop) Samuel Kelsey. | | |
| 7/17/48 | 13 | 1 | 1 Little Boy ....................................................... Juke Box #13 | | Super Disc 1057 |
| | | | **J. KELY & PREMIERS** | | |
| 2/02/74 | 46 | 14 | 1 She Calls Me Baby ........................................ | | Roadshow 7005 |
| | | | **JOHNNY KEMP** | | |
| | | | Singer/dancer/actor/songwriter, began performing in nightclubs in his native Nassau, Bahamas, at the age of 13. Moved to Harlem in 1979. | | |
| 4/05/86 | 14 | 17 | 1 Just Another Lover ........................................ | | Columbia 05853 |
| 4/09/88 | 1 ² | 23 | 2 **Just Got Paid** ................................................ | 10 | Columbia 07744 |
| | | | **THE KENDALL SISTERS** | | |
| 3/17/58 | 13 | 1 | 1 Yea, Yea .......................................................... Jockey #13 also released on Checker 889 | 73 | Argo 5291 |
| | | | **NAT KENDRICK & THE SWANS** | | |
| | | | James Brown's back-up band, also known as the JB's. Consisted of J.C. Adams, Bobby Roach, Fats Gonder, Bernard Odum and Nat Kendrick (drums). Also see Fred Wesley. | | |
| 2/15/60 | 8 | 11 | 1 **(Do The) Mashed Potatoes (Part 1)** ................ vocal shouts by Miami deejay "King" Coleman | 84 | Dade 1804 |
| | | | **EDDIE KENDRICKS**    ★★**77**★★ | | |
| | | | Born on 12/17/39 in Union Springs, Alabama; raised in Birmingham. Joined group the Primes in Detroit in the late 50s. Group later evolved into The Temptations. Eddie was their lead singer from 1960-71. Eddie later dropped the letter "s" from his last name. | | |
| 5/15/71 | 37 | 6 | 1 It's So Hard For Me To Say Good-Bye ............... | 88 | Tamla 54203 |
| 12/04/71 | 37 | 3 | 2 Can I ............................................................... | 101 | Tamla 54210 |
| 6/03/72 | 35 | 6 | 3 Eddie's Love .................................................... | 77 | Tamla 54218 |
| 9/16/72 | 17 | 14 | 4 If You Let Me ................................................. | 66 | Tamla 54222 |
| 2/17/73 | 13 | 8 | 5 Girl You Need A Change Of Mind (Part 1) .......... | 87 | Tamla 54230 |
| 6/16/73 | 26 | 8 | 6 Darling Come Back Home ................................ | 67 | Tamla 54236 |
| 8/18/73 | 1 ² | 16 | 7 **Keep On Truckin' (Part 1)** ............................. | 1 | Tamla 54238 |
| 12/29/73+ | 1 ³ | 19 | 8 **Boogie Down** ................................................ | 2 | Tamla 54243 |
| 5/11/74 | 5 | 14 | 9 **Son Of Sagittarius** ....................................... | 28 | Tamla 54247 |
| 7/27/74 | 8 | 15 | 10 **Tell Her Love Has Felt The Need** ................. | 50 | Tamla 54249 |
| 12/07/74+ | 8 | 11 | 11 **One Tear** ..................................................... | 71 | Tamla 54255 |
| 2/08/75 | 1 ¹ | 16 | 12 **Shoeshine Boy** ............................................ | 18 | Tamla 54257 |
| 7/19/75 | 7 | 14 | 13 **Get The Cream Off The Top** ........................ | 50 | Tamla 54260 |
| 10/11/75 | 8 | 16 | 14 **Happy** ......................................................... | 66 | Tamla 54263 |
| 2/07/76 | 2 ³ | 16 | 15 **He's A Friend** .............................................. | 36 | Tamla 54266 |
| 6/19/76 | 24 | 14 | 16 Get It While It's Hot ...................................... | | Tamla 54270 |
| 11/27/76+ | 30 | 14 | 17 Goin' Up In Smoke ........................................ | | Tamla 54277 |
| 1/21/78 | 24 | 14 | 18 Intimate Friends ........................................... | | Tamla 54290 |
| 4/29/78 | 13 | 14 | 19 Ain't No Smoke Without Fire ......................... | | Arista 0325 |
| 8/05/78 | 49 | 12 | 20 The Best Of Strangers Now ............................ | | Arista 0346 |
| 1/12/80 | 87 | 3 | 21 I Just Want To Be The One In Your Life ........... | | Arista 0466 |
| 7/04/81 | 41 | 8 | 22 (Oh I) Need Your Lovin' ................................. | | Atlantic 3796 |
| 7/07/84 | 87 | 6 | 23 Surprise Attack ............................................ | | Corner St. 3001 |
| 9/14/85 | 40 | 9 | 24 A Nite At The Apollo Live! The Way You Do The Things You Do/My Girl ............................ DARYL HALL JOHN OATES with DAVID RUFFIN & EDDIE KENDRICK recorded at the re-opening of New York's Apollo Theatre; revival of two early Temptations' hits | 20 | RCA 14178 |

| DEBUT DATE | PEAK POS | WKS CHR | ARTIST — Record Title | POP POS | Label & Number |
|---|---|---|---|---|---|
| | | | **EDDIE KENDRICKS — Continued** | | |
| 10/17/87 | **14** | 16 | 25 I Couldn't Believe It......................................... | | RCA 5313 |
| | | | DAVID RUFFIN & EDDIE KENDRICK | | |
| 2/06/88 | **43** | 10 | 26 One More For The Lonely Hearts Club ............. | | RCA 6925 |
| | | | DAVID RUFFIN & EDDIE KENDRICK | | |
| | | | **JOYCE KENNEDY** | | |
| | | | Vocalist from Chicago. With Glenn Murdock in duo. Formed group, Mother's Finest, in 1968. | | |
| 7/28/84 | **2**¹ | 18 | 1 **The Last Time I Made Love**.......................... | 40 | A&M 2656 |
| | | | JOYCE KENNEDY & JEFFREY OSBORNE | | |
| 10/27/84 | **30** | 15 | 2 Stronger Than Before.................................... | | A&M 2685 |
| 11/23/85 | **72** | 9 | 3 Hold On (For Love's Sake)............................. | | A&M 2790 |
| | | | **CHRIS KENNER** | | |
| | | | Born on 12/25/29 in Kenner, Louisiana. Died of a heart attack on 1/25/77 (46). Singer/composer. First recorded for Baton in 1956. | | |
| 8/05/57 | **13** | 2 | 1 Sick And Tired ............................................. | | Imperial 5448 |
| | | | Jockey #13 | | |
| 6/05/61 | **2**¹ | 17 | 2 **I Like It Like That, Part 1**.......................... | 2 | Instant 3229 |
| | | | **KENNY & JOHNNY - see WHITEHEAD** | | |
| | | | **KENNY G** | | |
| | | | Kenny Gorelick - fusion saxophonist from Seattle. With Barry White's Love Unlimited Orchestra at age 17. Worked with Jeff Lorber. | | |
| 2/25/84 | **23** | 14 | 1 Hi, How Ya Doin'? ........................................ | | Arista 9105 |
| 6/09/84 | **74** | 5 | 2 I've Been Missin' You.................................... | | Arista 9207 |
| 5/04/85 | **24** | 13 | 3 Love On The Rise.......................................... | | Arista 9336 |
| | | | KENNY G & KASHIF | | |
| 8/30/86 | **15** | 12 | 4 What Does It Take (To Win Your Love)............. | | Arista 9516 |
| | | | vocal by Ellis Hall | | |
| 12/13/86 | **77** | 5 | 5 Don't Make Me Wait For Love.......................... | | Arista 9544 |
| | | | vocal by Lenny Williams (original lead singer for Tower Of Power) | | |
| 4/18/87 | **23** | 15 | 6 Songbird.................................................[I] | 4 | Arista 9588 |
| 9/19/87 | **17** | 12 | 7 Don't Make Me Wait For Love....................[R] | 15 | Arista 9625 |
| | | | **AL KENT** | | |
| | | | Born Al Hamilton in 1937 in Detroit. Singer/guitarist/producer. With the Nitecaps group (brothers Ronnie "Ronnie Savoy" Hamilton, Bob Hamilton and Freddy Price), recorded for Groove in 1955. Arranger/writer for Golden World in 1961 and for Ric-Tic from 1964-68. Wrote "S.O.S.", hit for Edwin Starr. | | |
| 8/12/67 | **22** | 7 | 1 You've Got To Pay The Price.......................[I] | 49 | Ric-Tic 127 |
| | | | artist shown only as: INSTRUMENTAL | | |
| | | | "B" side of an Al Kent vocal recording; Dennis Coffey on guitar | | |
| | | | **STAN KENTON** | | |
| | | | Born on 2/19/12 in Wichita, Kansas. Died in Los Angeles on 8/25/79. Organized his first jazz band in 1941. Third person named to the Jazz Hall of Fame. | | |
| 4/01/44 | **8** | 1 | 1 **Do Nothin' Till You Hear From Me**................. | 10 | Capitol 145 |
| | | | vocal by Red Dorris | | |
| 8/08/60 | **12** | 4 | 2 My Love ...................................................... | 47 | Capitol 4393 |
| | | | NAT KING COLE-STAN KENTON | | |
| | | | **GEORGE KERR** | | |
| | | | Singer/producer for Motown, All Platinum/Stang, and many Philadelphia soul records. | | |
| 4/18/70 | **15** | 7 | 1 3 Minutes 2 - Hey Girl ................................. | 124 | All Platinum 2316 |
| | | | **TROY KEYES** | | |
| | | | Born in 1945. Lead singer with the High Keys (included Jimmy Williams, Bobby Haggard and Cliff Rise). Recorded for Atco in 1963. | | |
| 2/10/68 | **43** | 3 | 1 Love Explosion ............................................ | 92 | ABC 11027 |
| | | | **CHAKA KHAN** ★★**146**★★ | | |
| | | | Born Yvette Marie Stevens on 3/23/53 in Great Lakes, Illinois. Became lead singer of Rufus in 1972. Recorded solo and with Rufus since 1978. Sister of vocalists Taka Boom and Mark Stevens (Jamaica Boys). Also see Rufus. | | |
| 10/07/78 | **1**³ | 20 | 1 **I'm Every Woman**........................................ | 21 | Warner 8683 |
| 2/17/79 | **40** | 8 | 2 Life Is A Dance ........................................... | | Warner 8740 |
| 4/26/80 | **10** | 14 | 3 **Clouds**..................................................... | 103 | Warner 49216 |
| 7/12/80 | **22** | 14 | 4 Papillon (aka Hot Butterfly)........................... | | Warner 49256 |
| 10/18/80 | **48** | 7 | 5 Get Ready, Get Set ...................................... | | Warner 49571 |
| 3/21/81 | **1**² | 20 | 6 **What Cha' Gonna Do For Me** ........................ | 53 | Warner 49692 |

| DEBUT DATE | PEAK POS | WKS CHR | ARTIST — Record Title | POP POS | Label & Number |
|---|---|---|---|---|---|
| | | | **CHAKA KHAN — Continued** | | |
| 7/11/81 | **34** | 8 | 7 We Can Work It Out...................................... | | Warner 49759 |
| 9/19/81 | **68** | 4 | 8 Any Old Sunday.......................................... | | Warner 49804 |
| 11/06/82+ | **5** | 23 | 9 **Got To Be There** ...................................... | *67* | Warner 29881 |
| 4/09/83 | **48** | 8 | 10 Tearin' It Up .......................................... | | Warner 29745 |
| 9/15/84 | **1**³ | 21 | 111 **I Feel For You**.................................... | *3* | Warner 29195 |
| | | | with Grandmaster Melle Mel (rap) and Stevie Wonder (harmonica); written by Prince | | |
| 1/19/85 | **11** | 14 | 12 This Is My Night........................................ | *60* | Warner 29097 |
| 4/13/85 | **15** | 17 | 13 Through The Fire....................................... | *60* | Warner 29025 |
| 9/14/85 | **18** | 14 | 14 (Krush Groove) Can't Stop The Street .............. | | Warner 28923 |
| | | | from the film "Krush Groove" | | |
| 12/28/85+ | **66** | 9 | 15 Own The Night.......................................... | *57* | MCA 52730 |
| | | | from the TV series "Miami Vice" | | |
| 3/29/86 | **81** | 4 | 16 The Other Side Of The World........................ | | Atlantic 89449 |
| | | | from the film "White Nights" | | |
| 7/12/86 | **21** | 13 | 17 Love Of A Lifetime ..................................... | *53* | Warner 28671 |
| 10/25/86 | **28** | 13 | 18 Tight Fit ................................................ | | Warner 28576 |
| 3/07/87 | **93** | 3 | 19 Earth To Mickey ....................................... | | Warner 28459 |
| | | | **KHEMISTRY** | | |
| | | | Vocal trio from Washington, DC. Consisted of Shirl Hayes, Kimus Knight and Marie Council. Council had been in the Soulful Strutters. | | |
| 9/18/82 | **75** | 5 | 1 I Got A Feeling ......................................... | | Columbia 03156 |
| | | | **KIARA** | | |
| | | | Detroit duo formed in 1982: Greg Charley and John Winston. | | |
| 12/28/85 | **88** | 4 | 1 Quiet Guy................................................ | | Warlock 001 |
| | | | **K.I.D.** | | |
| 4/25/81 | **47** | 10 | 1 Don't Stop ............................................... | | Sam 5018 |
| | | | **KID CREOLE & THE COCONUTS** | | |
| | | | Born Augustus Darnell Browder on 8/12/50 in Montreal. Singer/songwriter/producer. With brother Stony in Dr. Buzzard's Original Savannah Band during the mid-70s. Formed The Coconuts with his wife, Addy and Andy "Coati Mundi" Hernandez. | | |
| 5/29/82 | **44** | 13 | 1 I'm A Wonderful Thing, Baby ........................ | | Sire 50069 |
| | | | **KIDDO** | | |
| | | | Band from Long Beach, California. Consisted of Donnie Sterling, Leroy Davis, Arthur Brown, Fred "Juice" Johnson, Leon "Rock" Goodin, and Willie Jenkins. Sterling had been in the Parliament/Funkadelic organization. | | |
| 2/26/83 | **24** | 13 | 1 Try My Loving (Gimme Just Enough) .............. | | A&M 2529 |
| 11/24/84 | **87** | 4 | 2 She's Got The Body ..................................... | | A&M 2679 |
| | | | **KIDS AT WORK** | | |
| | | | New York City trio: Clurel Henderson (lead), Teddy Riley (keyboards) and Timmy Gatling (bass). All had been in the group Fame from 1980-83. In 1988, 20-year-old Riley, already a renown producer, formed and fronted the trio, Guy. | | |
| 8/11/84 | **50** | 7 | 1 Sugar Baby .............................................. | | CBS Assoc. 04543 |
| 11/10/84 | **64** | 8 | 2 Singing Hey Yea......................................... | | CBS Assoc. 04661 |
| | | | **GREG KIHN BAND** | | |
| | | | Greg is a rock singer/songwriter/guitarist from Baltimore. Formed band in Berkeley, California, in 1975. | | |
| 3/26/83 | **48** | 9 | 1 Jeopardy ................................................. | *2* | Beserkley 69847 |
| | | | **THEOLA KILGORE** | | |
| | | | Born in Shreveport, Louisiana; raised in Oakland. Sang gospel from age 7. Discovered by Ed Townsend. | | |
| 4/20/63 | **3** | 15 | 1 **The Love Of My Man** ................................. | *21* | Serock 2004 |
| | | | **NEAL KIMBLE** | | |
| | | | Born on 3/18/34 in New Orleans. | | |
| 3/09/68 | **50** | 2 | 1 I've Made A Reservation (In My Life For You) ..... | | Venture 607 |
| | | | **KING COLE TRIO - see NAT KING COLE** | | |

| DEBUT DATE | PEAK POS | WKS CHR | ARTIST — Record Title | POP POS | Label & Number |
|---|---|---|---|---|---|
| | | | **KING CURTIS** Born Curtis Ousley on 2/7/34 in Fort Worth, Texas. Stabbed to death on 8/13/71 in New York City. Saxophonist, with Lionel Hampton in 1950. Moved to New York City, did session work. First own recording on Gem in 1953. Played on sessions for Bobby Darin, Aretha Franklin, Brook Benton, Nat Cole, McGuire Sisters, Andy Williams, The Coasters, The Shirelles, and hundreds of others. Also see Ruth Brown, Herbie Mann, and the Ramrods. | | |
| 2/17/62 | 1² | 19 | 1 **Soul Twist** ..................................................[I] **KING CURTIS & THE NOBLE KNIGHTS** | *17* | Enjoy 1000 |
| 3/07/64 | 51 | 12 | 2 Soul Serenade ..............................................[I] | *Hot* | Capitol 5109 |
| 2/18/67 | 31 | 5 | 3 Something On Your Mind......................[I] recorded at "Small's Paradise", New York City on 7/22/66 | | Atco 6457 |
| 9/16/67 | 6 | 10 | 4 **Memphis Soul Stew**....................................[I] | *33* | Atco 6511 |
| 9/30/67 | 6 | 9 | 5 **Ode To Billie Joe** .......................................[I] shown as: **THE KINGPINS** **KING CURTIS & THE KINGPINS:** | *28* | Atco 6516 |
| 2/03/68 | 49 | 2 | 6 I Was Made To Love Her...........................[I] | *76* | Atco 6547 |
| 6/21/69 | 35 | 2 | 7 Instant Groove ..............................................[I] | *127* | Atco 6680 |
| 8/01/70 | 46 | 2 | 8 Get Ready..................................................... | | Atco 6762 |
| 2/06/71 | 43 | 4 | 9 Whole Lotta Love...........................................[I] | *64* | Atco 6779 |
| | | | **KING DREAM CHORUS & HOLIDAY CREW** Featuring: El DeBarge, Whitney Houston, Stacy Lattisaw, Lisa Lisa and Full Force, Teena Marie, Menudo, Stephanie Mills, New Edition, James "J.T." Taylor, Kurtis Blow, the Fat Boys, Grandmaster Melle Mel, Run-D.M.C., and Whodini. | | |
| 2/01/86 | 30 | 8 | 1 King Holiday .................................................. tribute to Martin Luther King, Jr. - all proceeds benefit the Martin Luther King, Jr. Center for Non-Violent Social Change | | Mercury 884442 |
| | | | **KING FLOYD** Born on 2/13/45 in New Orleans. Singing since age 11, professional debut in 1961. In US Army from 1961-63. To New York City from 1963-64. To Los Angeles in 1964. First recorded for Original Sound in 1965. To New Orleans in 1969. | | |
| 10/10/70+ | 1⁴ | 22 | 1 ● **Groove Me** ................................................. | *6* | Chimneyville 435 |
| 3/27/71 | 5 | 9 | 2 **Baby Let Me Kiss You** .................................. | | Chimneyville 437 |
| 8/07/71 | 35 | 5 | 3 Got To Have Your Lovin' ................................. | *101* | Chimneyville 439 |
| 8/26/72 | 3 | 15 | 4 **Woman Don't Go Astray** .............................. | | Chimneyville 443 |
| 4/07/73 | 49 | 2 | 5 Think About It................................................ | | Chimneyville 446 |
| 1/05/74 | 95 | 4 | 6 So Much Confusion ........................................ | | Chimneyville 1779 |
| 7/06/74 | 35 | 12 | 7 I Feel Like Dynamite ...................................... | | Chimneyville 10202 |
| 12/21/74 | 96 | 2 | 8 Don't Cry No More.......................................... | | Chimneyville 10205 |
| 10/18/75 | 76 | 6 | 9 We Can Love ................................................. | | Chimneyville 10207 |
| 11/06/76+ | 25 | 16 | 10 Body English................................................. | | Chimneyville 10212 |
| | | | **KING HANNIBAL** Jimmy Shaw from Columbus, Georgia. First recorded in 1959. | | |
| 1/06/73 | 37 | 10 | 1 The Truth Shall Make You Free ...................... | *105* | Aware 027 |
| | | | **THE KING KOLAX ORCHESTRA - see JOE WILLIAMS** | | |
| | | | **THE KING PINS** Group from Clarksdale, Mississippi. Formed as gospel group, the Kelly Brothers. Consisted of Andrew, Curtis, and Robert Kelly, Charles Lee and Offe Reece. Changed name in 1958. Later returned to gospel music. | | |
| 7/20/63 | 13 | 12 | 1 It Won't Be This Way (Always).......................... | *89* | Federal 12484 |
| 3/19/66 | 39 | 3 | 2 Falling In Love Again................................... shown as: **KELLY BROTHERS** | | Sims 265 |
| | | | **THE KINGPINS - see KING CURTIS** | | |
| | | | **KING PLEASURE** Born Clarence Beeks on 3/24/22 in Oakdale, Tennessee. Died in 1981. Developed technique of setting lyrics to jazz solos. Debuted in 1951. | | |
| 5/17/52 | 2¹ | 16 | 1 **Moody Mood For Love**................................... Juke Box #2 / Best Seller #5 vocal version of James Moody's "I'm In The Mood For Love"; vocal by Blossom Dearie | | Prestige 924 |

| DEBUT DATE | PEAK POS | WKS CHR | ARTIST — Record Title | POP POS | Label & Number |
|---|---|---|---|---|---|
| | | | **KING PLEASURE — Continued** | | |
| 4/04/53 | **3** | 12 | 2 Red Top.............................................. | | Prestige 821 |
| | | | Best Seller #3 / Juke Box #3 | | |
| | | | vocal by Betty Carter; with the Charlie Ferguson Orchestra | | |
| | | | **KING SUN-D MOET** | | |
| 5/23/87 | **69** | 9 | 1 Hey Love ........................................ | | Zakia 5139 |
| | | | **AL KING** | | |
| | | | Real name: Alvin K. Smith. | | |
| 4/16/66 | **36** | 2 | 1 Think Twice Before You Speak ...................... | | Sahara 111 |
| | | | **ALBERT KING** | | |
| | | | Born Albert Nelson on 4/25/23 in Indianola, Mississippi. Blues-based singer/ guitarist/drummer. With Harmony Kings gospel group from 1949-51. First recorded for Parrot in 1953. Formed own band in St. Louis, in 1956. | | |
| 12/04/61 | **14** | 9 | 1 Don't Throw Your Love On Me So Strong........... | | King 5575 |
| | | | originally released on Bobbin 131 | | |
| 6/25/66 | **29** | 5 | 2 Laundromat Blues................................ | | Stax 190 |
| 1/07/67 | **34** | 6 | 3 Crosscut Saw ................................... | | Stax 201 |
| 8/26/67 | **49** | 2 | 4 Born Under A Bad Sign .......................... | | Stax 217 |
| 1/27/68 | **20** | 8 | 5 Cold Feet................................[S-I] | 67 | Stax 241 |
| 5/18/68 | **46** | 3 | 6 (I Love) Lucy .................................. | | Stax 252 |
| | | | above 5: with Booker T. & The MG's | | |
| 7/11/70 | **50** | 2 | 7 Can't You See What You're Doing To Me ........... | *127* | Stax 0069 |
| 10/02/71 | **38** | 6 | 8 Everybody Wants To Go To Heaven ................. | *103* | Stax 0101 |
| 4/29/72 | **42** | 3 | 9 Angel Of Mercy ................................. | | Stax 0121 |
| 8/19/72 | **31** | 8 | 10 I'll Play The Blues For You ..................... | | Stax 0135 |
| 12/16/72+ | **35** | 8 | 11 Breaking Up Somebody's Home..................... | *91* | Stax 0147 |
| 1/05/74 | **15** | 12 | 12 That's What The Blues Is All About................ | | Stax 0189 |
| 3/13/76 | **40** | 10 | 13 Cadillac Assembly Line ......................... | | Utopia 10544 |
| 7/17/76 | **80** | 5 | 14 Sensation, Communication Together ............... | | Utopia 10682 |
| 11/13/76 | **79** | 4 | 15 Guitar Man .................................... | | Utopia 10770 |
| 4/23/77 | **95** | 4 | 16 Ain't Nothing You Can Do....................... | | Utopia 10879 |
| 1/28/78 | **72** | 7 | 17 Call My Job.................................... | | Tomato 10001 |
| 5/06/78 | **72** | 8 | 18 Chump Change ................................. | | Tomato 10002 |
| 4/28/79 | **87** | 3 | 19 The Very Thought Of You ....................... | | Tomato 10009 |
| | | | **ANNA KING** | | |
| 1/04/64 | **67** | 6 | 1 If Somebody Told You .................................. | *Hot* | Smash 1858 |
| 4/04/64 | **52** | 6 | 2 Baby Baby Baby ......................................... | *Hot* | Smash 1884 |
| | | | **ANNA KING-BOBBY BYRD** | | |
| | | | written by Carolyn Franklin; above 2: produced by James Brown | | |
| | | | **B.B. KING** ★★8★★ | | |
| | | | Born Riley B. King on 9/16/25 in Itta Bena, Mississippi. Moved to Memphis in 1946. Own radio show from 1949-50, where he was dubbed "The Beale Street Blues Boy", later shortened to "Blues Boy", then simply "B.B.". First recorded for Bullet in 1949. Appeared in the 1987 film "Amazon Women On The Moon". The most famous blues singer/guitarist in the world today. | | |
| 12/29/51+ | **1** 5 | 17 | 1 Three O'Clock Blues ............................ | | RPM 339 |
| | | | Best Seller #1(5) / Juke Box #1(5) | | |
| 9/13/52 | **1** 2 | 18 | 2 You Know I Love You ............................ | | RPM 363 |
| | | | Best Seller #1 / Juke Box #2 | | |
| 12/27/52 | **9** | 1 | 3 Story From My Heart And Soul ................... | | RPM 374 |
| | | | Best Seller #9 | | |
| | | | with Ike Turner on piano | | |
| 3/14/53 | **3** | 8 | 4 Woke Up This Morning ........................... | | RPM 380 |
| | | | Juke Box #3 / Best Seller #5 | | |
| 6/27/53 | **1** 3 | 16 | 5 Please Love Me ................................. | | RPM 386 |
| | | | Juke Box #1 / Best Seller #2 | | |
| 10/03/53 | **4** | 5 | 6 Please Hurry Home ............................. | | RPM 391 |
| | | | Juke Box #4 / Best Seller #8 | | |
| 9/11/54 | **8** | 3 | 7 When My Heart Beats Like A Hammer .......... | | RPM 412 |
| | | | Juke Box #8 | | |
| 11/06/54 | **1** 2 | 12 | 8 You Upset Me Baby/ | | |
| | | | Juke Box #1 / Best Seller #2 / Jockey #7 | | |
| 11/13/54 | **8** | 3 | 9 Whole Lotta' Love.............................. | | RPM 416 |
| | | | Best Seller #8 | | |

**238**

| DEBUT DATE | PEAK POS | WKS CHR | ARTIST — Record Title | POP POS | Label & Number |
|---|---|---|---|---|---|
| | | | **B.B. KING — Continued** | | |
| 1/29/55 | 8 | 5 | 10 **Every Day I Have The Blues/** Juke Box #8 / Best Seller #10 / Jockey #10 King's theme song; remake of the 1948 Memphis Slim song "Nobody Loves Me" | | |
| 2/05/55 | 14 | 3 | 11 Sneakin' Around.......................................... Jockey #14 / Best Seller #15 | | RPM 421 |
| 10/01/55 | 9 | 3 | 12 Ten Long Years ........................................ Juke Box #9 / Best Seller #12 / Jockey #14 | | RPM 437 |
| 2/04/56 | 15 | 1 | 13 Cryin' Won't Help You .............................. Best Seller #15 / Jockey #15 | | RPM 451 |
| 9/08/56 | 3 | 8 | 14 **Bad Luck/** Juke Box #3 / Best Seller #6 / Jockey #13 | | |
| 11/03/56 | 8 | 2 | 15 **Sweet Little Angel**................................... Jockcy #8 | | RPM 468 |
| 11/17/56 | 3 | 10 | 16 **On My Word Of Honor** ........................... Jockey #3 / Juke Box #6 / Best Seller #11 | | RPM 479 |
| 5/06/57 | 13 | 3 | 17 Troubles, Troubles, Troubles/ Best Seller #13 | | |
| | | 3 | 18 I Want To Get Married .............................. Best Seller flip | | RPM 492 |
| 11/03/58 | 16 | 4 | 19 You've Been An Angel/ | | |
| 11/10/58 | 9 | 14 | 20 **Please Accept My Love**........................... | | Kent 315 |
| 1/18/60 | 2[1] | 14 | 21 **Sweet Sixteen, Pt. 1**.............................. | | Kent 330 |
| 5/30/60 | 8 | 3 | 22 **Got A Right To Love My Baby** .................. | | Kent 333 |
| 7/11/60 | 8 | 13 | 23 **Partin' Time** ........................................ | | Kent 346 |
| 10/03/60 | 23 | 2 | 24 Walkin' Dr. Bill ...................................... | | Kent 350 |
| 6/12/61 | 16 | 2 | 25 Someday/ | | |
| 6/19/61 | 7 | 8 | 26 **Peace Of Mind** ..................................... | 119 | Kent 360 |
| 2/10/62 | 24 | 5 | 27 My Sometimes Baby .................................. | | Kent 365 |
| 5/05/62 | 17 | 5 | 28 Gonna Miss You Around Here...................... | | Kent 372 |
| 3/28/64 | 97 | 2 | 29 How Blue Can You Get .............................. | Hot | ABC-Para. 10527 |
| 5/09/64 | 34 | 8 | 30 Rock Me Baby ........................................ | Hot | Kent 393 |
| 6/27/64 | 98 | 2 | 31 Help The Poor ........................................ | Hot | ABC-Para. 10552 |
| 11/07/64 | 82 | 3 | 32 Beautician Blues ..................................... | Hot | Kent 403 |
| 11/07/64 | 90 | 3 | 33 Never Trust A Woman................................ | Hot | ABC-Para. 10599 |
| 6/12/65 | 25 | 8 | 34 Blue Shadows ......................................... | 97 | Kent 426 |
| 2/19/66 | 31 | 6 | 35 Eyesight To The Blind .............................. | | Kent 441 |
| 9/24/66 | 45 | 2 | 36 I Stay In The Mood ................................. recorded in 1956 | | Kent 450 |
| 10/15/66 | 2[2] | 13 | 37 **Don't Answer The Door - Part 1** .................... | 72 | ABC 10856 |
| 1/28/67 | 49 | 2 | 38 It's A Mean World ................................... recorded in 1961 | | Kent 458 |
| 3/25/67 | 17 | 7 | 39 The Jungle ............................................ recorded in 1962 | 94 | Kent 462 |
| 4/06/68 | 10 | 12 | 40 **Paying The Cost To Be Boss**...................... | 39 | BluesWay 61015 |
| 8/03/68 | 26 | 6 | 41 I'm Gonna Do What They Do To Me ................ | 74 | BluesWay 61018 |
| 8/03/68 | 31 | 3 | 42 The Woman I Love ................................... recorded in 1959 | 94 | Kent 492 |
| 10/26/68 | 25 | 4 | 43 You Put It On Me..................................... from the film "For Love Of Ivy" | 82 | BluesWay 61019 |
| 5/03/69 | 13 | 14 | 44 Why I Sing The Blues.............................. | 61 | BluesWay 61024 |
| 8/16/69 | 34 | 5 | 45 I Want You So Bad/ | 127 | |
| 8/30/69 | 32 | 8 | 46 Get Off My Back Woman............................ | 74 | BluesWay 61026 |
| 11/01/69 | 15 | 8 | 47 Just A Little Love ................................... | 76 | BluesWay 61029 |
| 1/03/70 | 3 | 14 | 48 **The Thrill Is Gone** ................................ | 15 | BluesWay 61032 |
| 4/18/70 | 14 | 7 | 49 So Excited ............................................ | 54 | BluesWay 61035 |
| 8/01/70 | 25 | 7 | 50 Hummingbird ........................................ | 48 | ABC 11268 |
| 8/08/70 | 48 | 2 | 51 Worried Life........................................... recorded in 1960 | | Kent 4526 |
| 11/07/70 | 6 | 9 | 52 **Chains And Things** ................................ with Carole King on piano | 45 | ABC 11280 |
| 2/27/71 | 18 | 9 | 53 Ask Me No Questions ............................... | 40 | ABC 11290 |
| 3/27/71 | 34 | 7 | 54 That Evil Child ...................................... recorded in 1962 | 97 | Kent 4542 |

| DEBUT DATE | PEAK POS | WKS CHR | ARTIST — Record Title | POP POS | Label & Number |
|---|---|---|---|---|---|
| | | | **B.B. KING — Continued** | | |
| 6/12/71 | **36** | 3 | 55 Help The Poor .................................................. [I] | 90 | ABC 11302 |
| | | | instrumental version of King's 1964 hit | | |
| 9/11/71 | **25** | 7 | 56 Ghetto Woman.................................................. | 68 | ABC 11310 |
| 11/27/71+ | **28** | 9 | 57 Ain't Nobody Home ......................................... | 46 | ABC 11316 |
| 3/25/72 | **37** | 3 | 58 Sweet Sixteen.................................................. | 93 | ABC 11319 |
| | | | new version of #21 above | | |
| 5/20/72 | **28** | 5 | 59 I Got Some Help I Don't Need ......................... | 92 | ABC 11321 |
| 9/09/72 | **21** | 7 | 60 Guess Who....................................................... | 62 | ABC 11330 |
| 7/21/73 | **12** | 13 | 61 To Know You Is To Love You ............................ | 38 | ABC 11373 |
| 12/15/73+ | **6** | 19 | 62 **I Like To Live The Love**................................ | 28 | ABC 11406 |
| 5/25/74 | **27** | 12 | 63 Who Are You.................................................... | 78 | ABC 11433 |
| 10/05/74 | **19** | 12 | 64 Philadelphia.............................................. [I] | 64 | ABC 12029 |
| 4/05/75 | **34** | 9 | 65 Friends ........................................................... | | ABC 12053 |
| 1/24/76 | **22** | 12 | 66 When I'm Wrong ............................................. | | ABC 12158 |
| 7/31/76 | **20** | 11 | 67 Let The Good Times Roll ................................. | 101 | ABC/Impulse |
| | | | **BOBBY BLAND & B.B. KING** | | 31006 |
| 3/26/77 | **88** | 3 | 68 Slow And Easy ................................................ | | ABC 12247 |
| 6/24/78 | **19** | 17 | 69 Never Make A Move Too Soon ......................... | 102 | ABC 12380 |
| 11/04/78 | **90** | 3 | 70 I Just Can't Leave Your Love Alone ................. | | ABC 12412 |
| 7/21/79 | **30** | 16 | 71 Better Not Look Down..................................... | 110 | MCA 41062 |
| 5/30/81 | **91** | 5 | 72 There Must Be A Better World Somewhere ........ | | MCA 51101 |
| 2/23/85 | **15** | 15 | 73 Into The Night ............................................... | 107 | MCA 52530 |
| | | | from the film of the same title | | |
| 10/12/85 | **62** | 7 | 74 Big Boss Man.................................................. | | MCA 52675 |

**BEN E. KING**     ★★108★★

Born Benjamin Earl Nelson on 9/23/38 in Henderson, North Carolina. To New York in 1947. Worked with The Moonglows for six months while still in high school. Joined the Five Crowns in 1957, who became the new Drifters in 1959. Wrote lyrics to "There Goes My Baby", his first lead performance with The Drifters. Went solo in May of 1960. Also see The Soul Clan.

| DEBUT DATE | PEAK POS | WKS CHR | ARTIST — Record Title | POP POS | Label & Number |
|---|---|---|---|---|---|
| 1/23/61 | **15** | 13 | 1 Spanish Harlem ............................................... | 10 | Atco 6185 |
| 5/15/61 | **1**⁴ | 12 | 2 **Stand By Me** ................................................. | 4 | Atco 6194 |
| | | | re-released on Atlantic 89361 in 1986, after inclusion in film of the same title (POS 9-Pop) | | |
| 8/21/61 | **10** | 6 | 3 Amor ................................................................ | 18 | Atco 6203 |
| 5/12/62 | **2**⁴ | 14 | 4 **Don't Play That Song (You Lied)** ................... | 11 | Atco 6222 |
| 1/12/63 | **29** | 2 | 5 Tell Daddy ....................................................... | 122 | Atco 6246 |
| 3/23/63 | **23** | 1 | 6 How Can I Forget ............................................. | 85 | Atco 6256 |
| 8/03/63 | **16** | 9 | 7 I (Who Have Nothing) ...................................... | 29 | Atco 6267 |
| 11/02/63 | **72** | 4 | 8 I Could Have Danced All Night......................... | Hot | Atco 6275 |
| | | | from the musical "My Fair Lady" | | |
| 4/04/64 | **63** | 7 | 9 That's When It Hurts ....................................... | Hot | Atco 6288 |
| 9/12/64 | **72** | 5 | 10 It's All Over ..................................................... | Hot | Atco 6315 |
| 1/30/65 | **11** | 4 | 11 Seven Letters ................................................... | 45 | Atco 6328 |
| 4/17/65 | **24** | 4 | 12 The Record (Baby I Love You)........................... | 84 | Atco 6343 |
| 9/24/66 | **35** | 4 | 13 I Swear By Stars Above .................................... | | Atco 6431 |
| 1/14/67 | **38** | 2 | 14 What Is Soul .................................................... | | Atco 6454 |
| 4/29/67 | **34** | 4 | 15 Tears, Tears, Tears .......................................... | 93 | Atco 6472 |
| 5/04/68 | **44** | 2 | 16 Don't Take Your Love From Me ........................ | 117 | Atco 6571 |
| 1/11/69 | **37** | 4 | 17 Til I Can't Take It Anymore .............................. | 134 | Atco 6637 |
| 1/17/70 | **45** | 2 | 18 I Can't Take It Like A Man............................... | | Maxwell 800 |
| 1/25/75 | **1**¹ | 16 | 19 **Supernatural Thing - Part I**.......................... | 5 | Atlantic 3241 |
| 6/07/75 | **4** | 14 | 20 **Do It In The Name Of Love**........................... | 60 | Atlantic 3274 |
| 1/03/76 | **23** | 11 | 21 I Had A Love ................................................... | | Atlantic 3308 |
| 6/04/77 | **21** | 14 | 22 Get It Up ......................................................... | | Atlantic 3402 |
| | | | **BEN E. KING & AWB** | | |
| 9/10/77 | **25** | 12 | 23 A Star In The Ghetto ....................................... | | Atlantic 3427 |
| | | | **AWB & BEN E. KING** | | |
| 2/16/80 | **29** | 13 | 24 Music Trance................................................... | | Atlantic 3635 |

**BOBBY KING - see ALFIE SILAS**

| DEBUT DATE | PEAK POS | WKS CHR | ARTIST — Record Title | POP POS | Label & Number |
|---|---|---|---|---|---|
| | | | **CLYDIE KING** | | |
| | | | Member of the Raeletts. Recorded as Little Clydie; later as Brown Sugar. | | |
| 5/01/71 | 45 | 4 | 1 'Bout Love ................................................ | | Lizard 21007 |
| 7/07/73 | 44 | 7 | 2 Loneliness (Will Bring Us Together Again) ......... *107* | | Chelsea 0125 |
| | | | BROWN SUGAR | | |
| | | | **EARL KING** | | |
| | | | Born Earl Connelly on 11/19/29 in Philadelphia. Graduate of Temple University in 1952. . | | |
| 6/18/55 | 7 | 10 | 1 **Don't Take It So Hard**................................... | | King 4780 |
| | | | Jockey #7 / Juke Box #10 / Best Seller #12 | | |
| | | | **EARL KING** | | |
| | | | Born Earl Silas Johnson on 2/7/34 in New Orleans. Vocalist/guitarist. In band, as "Earl Johnson", with Huey Smith; recorded for Savoy in 1953. His own band, The Kings, recorded for Specialty from 1953-55. Also recorded as "Handsome Earl". Active into the 80s. | | |
| 8/20/55 | 7 | 11 | 1 **Those Lonely Lonely Nights** .......................... | | Ace 509 |
| | | | Jockey #7 / Juke Box #10 | | |
| 3/17/62 | 17 | 5 | 2 Always A First Time.................................... | | Imperial 5811 |
| | | | **EVELYN "CHAMPAGNE" KING**   ★★112★★ | | |
| | | | Born on 6/29/60 in the Bronx. To Philadelphia in 1970. Employed as cleaning woman at Sigma Studios when discovered. | | |
| 4/29/78 | 7 | 21 | 1 ●Shame................................................. | 9 | RCA 11122 |
| 10/21/78+ | 7 | 25 | 2 ●I Don't Know If It's Right ......................... | 23 | RCA 11386 |
| 5/26/79 | 14 | 13 | 3 Music Box ............................................ | 75 | RCA 11586 |
| 8/11/79 | 34 | 9 | 4 Out There ............................................ | | RCA 11680 |
| 9/20/80 | 34 | 9 | 5 Let's Get Funky Tonight............................. | | RCA 12075 |
| 6/20/81 | 1¹ | 18 | 6 **I'm In Love** ......................................... | 40 | RCA 12243 |
| 10/24/81 | 28 | 13 | 7 Don't Hide Our Love ................................ | | RCA 12322 |
| 1/30/82 | 51 | 8 | 8 Spirit Of The Dancer ................................ | | RCA 13017 |
| 8/07/82 | 1⁵ | 21 | 9 **Love Come Down**................................... | 17 | RCA 13273 |
| 11/13/82+ | 2³ | 23 | 10 **Betcha She Don't Love You**....................... | 49 | RCA 13380 |
| | | | above 5 shown only as: **EVELYN KING** | | |
| 4/02/83 | 61 | 7 | 11 Get Loose ............................................ | | RCA 13461 |
| 12/17/83+ | 16 | 15 | 12 Action................................................ | 75 | RCA 13682 |
| 3/10/84 | 12 | 14 | 13 Shake Down .......................................... | *107* | RCA 13748 |
| 6/16/84 | 28 | 13 | 14 Teenager ............................................. | | RCA 13825 |
| 10/06/84 | 16 | 15 | 15 Just For The Night .................................. | *107* | RCA 13914 |
| 1/19/85 | 54 | 8 | 16 Out Of Control ...................................... | | RCA 13980 |
| 4/27/85 | 57 | 7 | 17 Till Midnight ........................................ | | RCA 14048 |
| 11/02/85+ | 9 | 18 | 18 **Your Personal Touch**.............................. | 86 | RCA 14201 |
| 3/15/86 | 19 | 12 | 19 High Horse........................................... | | RCA 14308 |
| 6/14/86 | 81 | 4 | 20 Slow Down ........................................... | | RCA 14373 |
| 4/02/88 | 3 | 15 | 21 Flirt .................................................. | | EMI-Man. 50101 |
| | | | shown only as: **EVELYN KING** | | |
| | | | **FREDDY KING** | | |
| | | | Born Freddie Christian on 9/30/34 in Gilmer, Texas. Died on 12/28/76 of a heart attack, hepatitis. Vocalist/guitarist. To Chicago in 1950, worked local clubs with own band, the Every Hour Blues Boys. Session work for Parrot and Chess. First own recording for El-Bee in 1956. Settled in Dallas in 1963. | | |
| 3/13/61 | 5 | 19 | 1 **Hide Away** ................................... [I] | 29 | Federal 12401 |
| | | | named for Mel's Hide Away Lounge in Chicago | | |
| 5/29/61 | 8 | 10 | 2 **Lonesome Whistle Blues** ........................... | 88 | Federal 12415 |
| 8/07/61 | 4 | 8 | 3 **San-Ho-Zay**................................... [I] | 47 | Federal 12428 |
| 10/23/61 | 5 | 10 | 4 **I'm Tore Down**...................................... | | Federal 12432 |
| 10/30/61 | 21 | 4 | 5 See See Baby......................................... | | Federal 12428 |
| 12/25/61 | 26 | 1 | 6 Christmas Tears ..................................... | | Federal 12439 |
| | | | **JEWEL KING** | | |
| | | | Mary Jewel King from New Orleans. | | |
| 3/04/50 | 4 | 14 | 1 **3 X 7 = 21**............................................ | | Imperial 5055 |
| | | | Juke Box #4 / Best Seller #15 | | |
| | | | with the Dave Bartholomew Orchestra | | |

| DEBUT DATE | PEAK POS | WKS CHR | ARTIST — Record Title | POP POS | Label & Number |
|---|---|---|---|---|---|
| | | | **KID KING'S COMBO** | | |
| | | | Small band led by vocalist/pianist Ed "Skippy" Brooks. | | |
| 11/14/53 | 6 | 2 | 1 **Banana Split** ............................................... [I] | | Excello 2009 |
| | | | Juke Box #6 | | |
| | | | **MARVA KING - see CHUCK CISSEL** | | |
| | | | **SAUNDERS KING** | | |
| | | | Born on 3/13/09 in Staple, Louisiana. Vocalist/guitarist. With Southern Harmony Four on NBC in San Francisco in 1938. Own band in 1942. | | |
| 3/19/49 | 9 | 2 | 1 **Empty Bedroom Blues** ................................. | | Modern 20-659 |
| | | | Best Seller #9 / Juke Box #11 | | |
| 3/19/49 | 14 | 1 | 2 Stay Gone Blues ........................................... | | Rhythm 301 |
| | | | Juke Box #14 | | |
| | | | **SLEEPY KING** | | |
| | | | Vocalist/organist. | | |
| 1/06/62 | 27 | 3 | 1 Pushin' Your Luck ...................................... | *92* | Joy 257 |
| | | | with the Morton Garson Orchestra | | |
| | | | **WILL KING** | | |
| | | | Vocalist from Los Angeles. Toured Europe with his group, Redd Eye Express, before going solo. | | |
| 5/18/85 | 26 | 14 | 1 I'm Sorry ................................................... | | Total Exp. 2417 |
| | | | **WILL KING** | | |
| 7/28/73 | 88 | 3 | 1 Lady Be Mine ............................................. | | Capitol 3644 |
| | | | **THE KINGSMEN** | | |
| | | | America's premier Sixties garage rock band formed in Portland in 1957. Recorded the original 1963, #2 pop hit "Louie Louie". | | |
| 3/14/64 | 16 | 11 | 1 Money ...................................................... | *Hot* | Wand 150 |
| 7/11/64 | 46 | 9 | 2 Little Latin Lupe Lu ................................... | *Hot* | Wand 157 |
| 9/12/64 | 42 | 9 | 3 Death Of An Angel ..................................... | *Hot* | Wand 164 |
| 1/30/65 | 25 | 1 | 4 The Jolly Green Giant................................ | *4* | Wand 172 |
| | | | same tune (different lyrics) as The Olympics' "Big Boy Pete" | | |
| | | | **THE KINGSTON TRIO** | | |
| | | | Folk trio formed in San Francisco in 1957. Consisted of Dave Guard, Bob Shane and Nick Reynolds. John Stewart replaced Guard in 1961. Disbanded in 1968. The originators of the folk music craze of the 60s. | | |
| 12/01/58 | 9 | 8 | 1 ● **Tom Dooley** ............................................. | *1* | Capitol 4049 |
| | | | traditional American folk song written in 1866 as "Tom Dula" | | |
| 5/11/63 | 15 | 5 | 2 Reverend Mr. Black ..................................... | *8* | Capitol 4951 |
| | | | **FERN KINNEY** | | |
| | | | Fern Kinney-Lewis, vocalist from Jackson, Mississippi. Formerly in the Poppies. Did background vocals for Malaco and North American Records. | | |
| 8/11/79 | 26 | 12 | 1 Groove Me ................................................. | *54* | Malaco 1058 |
| | | | **KINSMAN DAZZ - see DAZZ BAND** | | |
| | | | **ANDY KIRK & HIS TWELVE CLOUDS OF JOY** | | |
| | | | Born on 5/28/1898 in Newport, Kentucky. Bass saxophonist/bandleader. From 1929, led the Dark Clouds Of Joy, featuring Mary Lou Williams (arranger, piano). Group disbanded in 1948. The Jubalaires, formed as the Royal Harmony Singers (a.k.a. Royal Harmony Quartet) in 1936, consisted of Orville Brooks (lead), Caleb "J.C." Ginyard (d: 1978) and Theodore Brooks (baritones), and George McFadden (bass). Ginyard later formed the Dixieaires, and Du Droppers, then with Golden Gate Quartet from 1955-71. Also see the Shadows. | | |
| 10/24/42 | 1[1] | 5 | 1 **Take It And Git** ....................................... | | Decca 4366 |
| 6/26/43 | 4 | 8 | 2 **Hey Lawdy Mama**........................................ | | Decca 4405 |
| 5/04/46 | 2[4] | 16 | 3 **I Know**..................................................... | *14* | Decca 18782 |
| | | | **JUBALAIRES with ANDY KIRK & HIS ORCHESTRA** | | |
| 11/09/46 | 5 | 1 | 4 **I Don't Know What I'd Do Without You** ......... | | Decca 18916 |
| | | | **JUBALAIRES with ANDY KIRK & HIS ORCHESTRA** | | |
| 3/19/49 | 14 | 1 | 5 47th St. Jive ............................................. | | Coral 60021 |
| | | | Juke Box #14 | | |
| | | | 2 & 5: vocals by June Richmond | | |
| | | | **BO KIRKLAND** | | |
| | | | Born Mike James Kirkland on 10/11/46 in Yazoo City, Mississippi. Began recording duo with Ruth Davis in 1976. | | |
| 10/11/75 | 80 | 7 | 1 Grandfather Clock....................................... | | Claridge 409 |

| DEBUT DATE | PEAK POS | WKS CHR | ARTIST — Record Title | POP POS | Label & Number |
|---|---|---|---|---|---|
| | | | **BO KIRKLAND & RUTH DAVIS** | | |
| 3/20/76 | **38** | 18 | 1　Easy Lovin'/ | | |
| | | 6 | 2　We Got The Recipe ................................... | | Claridge 414 |
| 10/16/76 | **77** | 10 | 3　I Feel Love In This Room Tonight/ | | |
| | | 7 | 4　To Make You Love Me.............................. | | Claridge 421 |
| 2/05/77 | **66** | 9 | 5　You're Gonna Get To Me............................ | | Claridge 424 |
| 9/17/77 | **72** | 9 | 6　Loving Arms ....................................... | | Claridge 427 |
| 1/14/78 | **63** | 9 | 7　Stand By My Side.................................. | | Claridge 432 |
| | | | **LEW KIRTON** | | |
| | | | Born in Barbados. Toured with the Blue Rhythm Combo in the Caribbean. To Ottawa, Canada while a teenager; worked on local TV shows. Worked as drummer for Sam & Dave. | | |
| 3/26/77 | **94** | 4 | 1　Do What You Want, Be What You Are.............. | | Marlin 3311 |
| 8/20/83 | **31** | 12 | 2　Talk To Me ........................................ | | Believe 04058 |
| 12/03/83 | **71** | 8 | 3　Don't Give Up Your Dream (Hang On In There).... | | Believe 04233 |
| | | | **KITTY & THE HAYWOODS** | | |
| | | | Family vocal group from Chicago. Consisted of sisters Kitty, Vivian and Mary Ann Haywood - prolific commercial jingle singers. Joined in 1976 by Vivian's daughter, Cynthia. Produced by the Ohio Players. | | |
| 8/20/77 | **84** | 4 | 1　Love Shock ....................................... | | Mercury 73931 |
| | | | **KLEEER** | | |
| | | | Group formed in New York City in 1972 as Pipeline. Consisted of Paul Crutchfield (vocals, percussion), Richard Lee (guitar), Norman Durham (bass) and Woody Cunningham (drums). Became the Jam Band in the mid-70s; recorded and toured as the Universal Robot Band in 1977. Included vocalists Isabelle Coles, Melanie Moore and Yvette Flowers. | | |
| 3/10/79 | **60** | 13 | 1　Keeep Your Body Workin'............................ | *101* | Atlantic 3559 |
| 6/30/79 | **33** | 12 | 2　Tonight's The Night (Good Time) ..................... | | Atlantic 3586 |
| 4/05/80 | **23** | 13 | 3　Winners ........................................... | | Atlantic 3650 |
| 8/09/80 | **86** | 2 | 4　Open Your Mind .................................. | | Atlantic 3750 |
| 2/14/81 | **15** | 17 | 5　Get Tough.......................................... | | Atlantic 3788 |
| 7/04/81 | **69** | 4 | 6　Running Back To You ............................. | | Atlantic 3823 |
| 3/20/82 | **55** | 8 | 7　Taste The Music .................................. | | Atlantic 4024 |
| 5/29/82 | **74** | 5 | 8　De Ting Continues................................. | | Atlantic 4046 |
| 12/11/82+ | **84** | 5 | 9　She Said She Loves Me............................ | | Atlantic 89924 |
| 3/17/84 | **79** | 5 | 10　Next Time It's For Real ........................... | | Atlantic 89699 |
| 6/16/84 | **48** | 12 | 11　Intimate Connection .............................. | | Atlantic 89663 |
| 6/22/85 | **62** | 10 | 12　Take Your Heart Away ............................. | | Atlantic 89549 |
| | | | **KLIQUE** | | |
| | | | Trio consisting of Howard Huntsberry, Isaac Suthers and his sister Deborah Hunter. | | |
| 5/09/81 | **24** | 15 | 1　Love's Dance....................................... | | MCA 51099 |
| 9/19/81 | **45** | 9 | 2　Middle Of A Slow Dance ................................. | | MCA 51158 |
| 5/01/82 | **39** | 10 | 3　Dance Like Crazy ................................. | | MCA 52035 |
| 8/14/82 | **47** | 8 | 4　I Can't Shake This Feeling ........................ | | MCA 52083 |
| 1/15/83 | **83** | 2 | 5　Pump Your Rump.................................. | | MCA 52132 |
| 8/13/83 | **2**⁴ | 24 | 6　**Stop Doggin' Me Around**............................ | *50* | MCA 52250 |
| | | | re-make of Jackie Wilson's 1960 hit "Doggin' Around" | | |
| 12/24/83+ | **59** | 9 | 7　Flashback ......................................... | | MCA 52303 |
| 2/09/85 | **56** | 9 | 8　Be Ready For Love ................................ | | MCA 52483 |
| 4/27/85 | **15** | 16 | 9　A Woman, A Lover, A Friend........................ | | MCA 52566 |
| | | | **KLOCKWISE** | | |
| 11/10/84 | **86** | 3 | 1　Cruzamatic ........................................ | | Sinban 0025 |
| 4/27/85 | **85** | 6 | 2　Kiss Me Now....................................... | | Sinban 0028 |
| | | | **EARL KLUGH** | | |
| | | | Born on 9/16/53 in Detroit. Guitarist/pianist. Taught guitar from age 16. Worked Baker's Keyboard Lounge. Toured with George Benson and Chick Corea. First solo recording for Blue Note in 1976. | | |
| 2/05/77 | **93** | 2 | 1　Living Inside Your Love ............................ | | Blue Note 924 |
| 12/05/81+ | **59** | 10 | 2　Twinkle............................................. | | Liberty 1431 |

| DEBUT DATE | PEAK POS | WKS CHR | | ARTIST — Record Title | POP POS | Label & Number |
|---|---|---|---|---|---|---|
| | | | | **KLYMAXX** | | |
| | | | | Female group from Los Angeles. Consisted of Lorena Porter Hardiman (lead vocals), M. Ann Williams, Cheryl Cooley, & Robbin Grider (guitars), Joyce "Fenderetta" Irby (vocals, bass), Lynn Malsby (keyboards), Judy Takeuchi (percussion) and Bernadette Cooper (drums). In 1987, Cooper founded and produced Madame X. | | |
| 6/06/81 | 74 | 6 | 1 | Never Underestimate The Power Of A Woman .... | | Solar 47931 |
| 11/06/82 | 78 | 5 | 2 | Wild Girls ..................................................... | | Solar 69955 |
| 11/10/84+ | 5 | 23 | 3 | The Men All Pause ......................................... | 105 | Constell. 52486 |
| | | | | hit the pop charts on 2/15/86 and peaked at POS 80 | | |
| 3/23/85 | 4 | 17 | 4 | Meeting In The Ladies Room .......................... | 59 | Constell. 52545 |
| 7/20/85 | 11 | 18 | 5 | I Miss You..................................................... | 5 | Constell. 52606 |
| 11/23/85+ | 47 | 14 | 6 | Lock And Key ................................................ | | Constell. 52714 |
| 7/19/86 | 43 | 10 | 7 | Man Size Love ............................................... | 15 | MCA 52841 |
| | | | | from the film "Running Scared" | | |
| 11/01/86 | 18 | 15 | 8 | Sexy .............................................................. | | Constell. 52934 |
| 2/21/87 | 7 | 19 | 9 | I'd Still Say Yes ............................................. | 18 | Constell. 53028 |
| 7/11/87 | 14 | 13 | 10 | Divas Need Love Too ...................................... | | Constell. 53117 |
| | | | | **THE KNIGHT BROS.** | | |
| | | | | Washington, DC duo: Richard Dunbar (b: 5/31/39) and Jerry Diggs (b: 1937). In vocal group, the Starfires, in 1956; recorded for Decca in 1958. Group disbanded in 1961. Duo first recorded for Chess/Checker in 1963; split in 1968. Dunbar sang in an Orioles group in the early 80s. | | |
| 5/22/65 | 12 | 8 | 1 | Temptation 'Bout To Get Me ......................... | 70 | Checker 1107 |
| | | | | **FREDERICK KNIGHT** | | |
| | | | | Born on 8/15/44 in Alabama. Singer/producer. Produced Anita Ward for TK Records. | | |
| 4/15/72 | 8 | 14 | 1 | I've Been Lonely For So Long......................... | 27 | Stax 0117 |
| | | | | written by Fred's wife Posie, and Jerry Weaver | | |
| 3/01/75 | 27 | 15 | 2 | I Betcha Didn't Know That.............................. | | Truth 3216 |
| 11/07/81 | 74 | 8 | 3 | The Old Songs .............................................. | | Juana 3700 |
| | | | | **GLADYS KNIGHT & THE PIPS** ★★10★★ | | |
| | | | | Atlanta family group formed in 1952. Consisted of Gladys (b: 5/28/44 in Atlanta), her brother Merald "Bubba" Knight and sister Brenda, and cousins William & Eleanor Guest. Named "Pips" for their manager, cousin James "Pip" Woods. First recorded for Brunswick in 1958. Brenda and Eleanor replaced by cousins Edward Patten and Langston George in 1959. Langston left group in 1962 and group has remained a quartet with the same members ever since. Hosted own variety television show in July of 1975. Due to legal problems, Gladys could not record with the Pips from 1977-80. Gladys was a cast member of the 1985 TV series "Charlie & Co.". Also see Dionne Warwick. | | |
| 5/29/61 | 1¹ | 12 | 1 | Every Beat Of My Heart ................................. | 6 | Vee-Jay 386 |
| | | | | shown only as: **PIPS** | | |
| 5/29/61 | 15 | 3 | 2 | Every Beat Of My Heart.................................. | 45 | Fury 1050 |
| | | | | song first released on Huntom label; re-recorded for Fury; Huntom master sold to Vee-Jay and released as Pips | | |
| 12/25/61+ | 3 | 15 | 3 | Letter Full Of Tears........................................ | 19 | Fury 1054 |
| 5/09/64 | 38 | 10 | 4 | Giving Up ..................................................... | Hot | Maxx 326 |
| 8/22/64 | 89 | 5 | 5 | Lovers Always Forgive ................................... | Hot | Maxx 329 |
| 7/15/67 | 3 | 14 | 6 | Everybody Needs Love.................................... | 39 | Soul 35034 |
| 10/28/67 | 1⁶ | 17 | 7 | I Heard It Through The Grapevine ................. | 2 | Soul 35039 |
| 2/24/68 | 5 | 11 | 8 | The End Of Our Road..................................... | 15 | Soul 35042 |
| 6/29/68 | 9 | 9 | 9 | It Should Have Been Me................................. | 40 | Soul 35045 |
| 9/14/68 | 15 | 9 | 10 | I Wish It Would Rain...................................... | 41 | Soul 35047 |
| 3/22/69 | 11 | 9 | 11 | Didn't You Know (You'd Have To Cry Sometime). | 63 | Soul 35057 |
| 7/26/69 | 2² | 13 | 12 | The Nitty Gritty ............................................ | 19 | Soul 35063 |
| 11/08/69 | 2¹ | 13 | 13 | Friendship Train ............................................ | 17 | Soul 35068 |
| 4/04/70 | 3 | 10 | 14 | You Need Love Like I Do (Don't You).............. | 25 | Soul 35071 |
| 11/28/70+ | 1¹ | 15 | 15 | If I Were Your Woman ................................... | 9 | Soul 35078 |
| 6/05/71 | 2⁴ | 12 | 16 | I Don't Want To Do Wrong ............................. | 17 | Soul 35083 |
| 12/18/71+ | 3 | 13 | 17 | Make Me The Woman That You Go Home To ... | 27 | Soul 35091 |
| 3/25/72 | 13 | 9 | 18 | Help Me Make It Through The Night ............... | 33 | Soul 35094 |
| 1/27/73 | 1⁴ | 16 | 19 | Neither One Of Us (Wants To Be The First To Say Goodbye) ........................................... | 2 | Soul 35098 |
| 5/05/73 | 2² | 14 | 20 | Daddy Could Swear, I Declare........................ | 19 | Soul 35105 |
| 6/23/73 | 6 | 11 | 21 | Where Peaceful Waters Flow .......................... | 28 | Buddah 363 |
| 8/04/73 | 28 | 10 | 22 | All I Need Is Time.......................................... | 61 | Soul 35107 |
| 8/25/73 | 1⁴ | 18 | 23 | ● Midnight Train To Georgia ........................... | 1 | Buddah 383 |

| DEBUT DATE | PEAK POS | WKS CHR | ARTIST — Record Title | POP POS | Label & Number |
|---|---|---|---|---|---|
| | | | **GLADYS KNIGHT & THE PIPS — Continued** | | |
| 11/24/73+ | **1**[1] | 16 | 24●I've Got To Use My Imagination ................... | *4* | Buddah 393 |
| 2/16/74 | **1**[2] | 19 | 25●Best Thing That Ever Happened To Me ......... | *3* | Buddah 403 |
| 5/18/74 | **2**[4] | 15 | 26●On And On ............................................ | *5* | Buddah 423 |
| | | | from the film "Claudine" | | |
| 6/22/74 | **45** | 10 | 27 Between Her Goodbye And My Hello ................ | *57* | Soul 35111 |
| 10/12/74 | **1**[2] | 17 | 28 I Feel A Song (In My Heart) ...................... | *21* | Buddah 433 |
| 2/15/75 | **3** | 12 | 29 Love Finds It's Own Way ...................... | *47* | Buddah 453 |
| 5/03/75 | **6** | 16 | 30 The Way We Were/Try To Remember ............ | *11* | Buddah 463 |
| 8/23/75 | **4** | 11 | 31 Money............................................... | *50* | Buddah 487 |
| 11/01/75 | **4** | 14 | 32 Part Time Love ................................. | *22* | Buddah 513 |
| 3/13/76 | **18** | 12 | 33 Make Yours A Happy Home ................... | | Buddah 523 |
| 10/09/76 | **12** | 16 | 34 So Sad The Song ............................... | *47* | Buddah 544 |
| | | | from the film "Pipe Dreams" starring Gladys Knight | | |
| 5/28/77 | **10** | 14 | 35 Baby Don't Change Your Mind ................ | *52* | Buddah 569 |
| 11/05/77+ | **24** | 16 | 36 Sorry Doesn't Always Make It Right ................ | | Buddah 584 |
| 3/18/78 | **40** | 10 | 37 The One And Only ........................... | | Buddah 592 |
| 8/12/78 | **16** | 13 | 38 It's A Better Than Good Time ................ | | Buddah 598 |
| 11/25/78 | **54** | 9 | 39 I'm Coming Home Again ...................... | | Buddah 601 |
| 3/17/79 | **45** | 9 | 40 Am I Too Late ................................ | | Columbia 10922 |
| | | | above 2 shown only as: **GLADYS KNIGHT** | | |
| 4/19/80 | **3** | 20 | 41 Landlord ....................................... | *46* | Columbia 11239 |
| 8/09/80 | **38** | 9 | 42 Taste Of Bitter Love ......................... | | Columbia 11330 |
| 10/25/80 | **45** | 9 | 43 Bourgie', Bourgie' ............................ | | Columbia 11375 |
| 6/06/81 | **52** | 7 | 44 Forever Yesterday (For The Children) .............. | | Columbia 02113 |
| 8/08/81 | **37** | 13 | 45 If That'll Make You Happy ................... | | Columbia 02413 |
| 10/31/81 | **21** | 14 | 46 I Will Fight.................................... | | Columbia 02549 |
| 2/20/82 | **50** | 9 | 47 A Friend Of Mine.............................. | | Columbia 02706 |
| 4/09/83 | **1**[1] | 25 | 48 Save The Overtime (For Me) ................. | *66* | Columbia 03761 |
| 7/30/83 | **5** | 19 | 49 You're Number One (In My Book) ................ | | Columbia 04033 |
| 11/26/83+ | **64** | 11 | 50 Hero ............................................ | *104* | Columbia 04219 |
| | | | a.k.a.: "Wind Beneath My Wings" | | |
| 2/25/84 | **42** | 10 | 51 When You're Far Away ...................... | | Columbia 04369 |
| 2/09/85 | **16** | 14 | 52 My Time ........................................ | *102* | Columbia 04761 |
| 4/27/85 | **31** | 11 | 53 Keep Givin' Me Love ......................... | | Columbia 04873 |
| 11/30/85 | **85** | 4 | 54 Till I See You Again.......................... | | Columbia 05679 |
| 12/27/86+ | **14** | 13 | 55 Send It To Me ................................ | | MCA 53002 |
| 11/14/87+ | **1**[1] | 15 | 56 Love Overboard ............................... | *13* | MCA 53210 |
| 2/27/88 | **3** | 13 | 57 Lovin' On Next To Nothin' ................... | | MCA 53211 |
| 6/11/88 | **29** | 10 | 58 It's Gonna Take All Our Love ............... | | MCA 53351 |
| | | | **JEAN KNIGHT** | | |
| | | | Born on 6/26/43 in New Orleans. | | |
| 5/22/71 | **1**[5] | 16 | 1 Mr. Big Stuff ................................. | *2* | Stax 0088 |
| 10/16/71 | **19** | 7 | 2 You Think You're Hot Stuff........................ | *57* | Stax 0105 |
| 3/04/72 | **44** | 1 | 3 Carry On ...................................... | | Stax 0116 |
| 8/29/81 | **56** | 7 | 4 You Got The Papers (But I Got The Man) .......... | | Cotillion 46020 |
| | | | **JEAN KNIGHT & PREMIUM** | | |
| 5/18/85 | **59** | 6 | 5 My Toot Toot................................. | *50* | Mirage 99643 |
| | | | **JERRY KNIGHT** | | |
| | | | Bass player, founding member (with Ray Parker) of Raydio. | | |
| 4/05/80 | **17** | 16 | 1 Overnight Sensation ......................... | *103* | A&M 2215 |
| 8/30/80 | **87** | 3 | 2 Joy Ride...................................... | | A&M 2248 |
| 2/07/81 | **16** | 15 | 3 Perfect Fit ................................... | | A&M 2304 |
| 5/23/81 | **65** | 6 | 4 Turn It Out .................................. | | A&M 2336 |
| 2/05/83 | **71** | 7 | 5 She's Got To Be (A Dancer) ................. | | A&M 2519 |
| | | | **MARIE KNIGHT** | | |
| | | | Born on 6/1/25 in Brooklyn. Teamed with Rosetta Tharpe on gospel records from 1947-54, later recorded for Mercury/Wing, Baton, and others. | | |
| 2/19/49 | **9** | 1 | 1 Gospel Train ................................. | | Decca 48092 |
| | | | Juke Box #9 | | |
| | | | with the Dependable Boys (vocal group) and the Sam Price Group | | |
| 4/17/65 | **35** | 3 | 2 Cry Me A River .............................. | *124* | Musicor 1076 |

| DEBUT DATE | PEAK POS | WKS CHR | ARTIST — Record Title | POP POS | Label & Number |
|---|---|---|---|---|---|
| | | | **ROBERT KNIGHT** | | |
| | | | Born on 4/21/45 in Franklin, Tennessee. With the Paramounts group (included Clarence Holland, Richard Sammons, Neil Hooper and Kenneth Buttrick). Recorded for Dot in 1960. | | |
| 10/07/67 | **14** | 11 | 1 Everlasting Love ............................................... | *13* | Rising Sons 705 |
| | | | **SONNY KNIGHT** | | |
| | | | Born Joseph C. Smith in 1934 in Maywood, Illinois. Vocalist/pianist/composer. Also recorded as Joe Smith. Wrote hit "Vicious, Vicious Vodka" for Amos Milburn. Wrote book "The Day The Music Died" in the late 70s under real name. | | |
| 11/24/56 | **8** | 5 | 1 **Confidential**.............................................. | *17* | Dot 15507 |
| | | | Jockey #8 / Juke Box #8 with the Jack Collier Orchestra | | |
| 10/10/64 | **71** | 9 | 2 If You Want This Love ................................... | *Hot* | Aura 403 |
| | | | **BUDDY KNOX with THE RHYTHM ORCHIDS** | | |
| | | | Born Buddy Wayne Knox on 7/20/33 in Happy, Texas. Formed The Rhythm Orchids at West Texas State University: Knox, Jimmy Bowen, Don Lanier, and Dave "Dickey Doo" Alldred. Formed own label, Triple-D, named after KDDD radio in Dumas, Texas. | | |
| 3/09/57 | **3** | 11 | 1 **Party Doll**............................................... | *1* | Roulette 4002 |
| | | | Jockey #3 / Best Seller #5 / Juke Box #6 originally released on Triple-D 797 (flip side by Jimmy Bowen) | | |
| 10/14/57 | **13** | 2 | 2 Hula Love ............................................... | *9* | Roulette 4018 |
| | | | Jockey #13 / Best Seller #14 | | |
| | | | **KOKOMO** | | |
| | | | English jazz/rock nine-member band. | | |
| 8/07/76 | **81** | 5 | 1 Use Your Imagination ................................... | | Columbia 10380 |
| | | | **KOKO-POP** | | |
| | | | Quartet from Columbus, Ohio. Consisted of Chris Powell (saxophone), Eric O'Neal (keyboards), Keith Alexander (guitar) and Recco Philmore (bass). Powell had been in Rick James' Punk Funk Horns. | | |
| 6/30/84 | **51** | 9 | 1 Baby Sister ........................................ | | Motown 1733 |
| 11/17/84 | **62** | 10 | 2 I'm In Love With You................................... | | Motown 1759 |
| 10/05/85 | **84** | 4 | 3 Brand New Beat (Part 1) ................................ | | Motown 1803 |
| | | | **KOMIKO** | | |
| 4/10/82 | **83** | 4 | 1 Feel Alright................................................ | | Sam 5025 |
| | | | **KOOL & THE GANG**   ★★**19**★★ | | |
| | | | Group formed in Jersey City, New Jersey in 1964 by bass player Robert "Kool" Bell as the Jazziacs. Session work in New York City, 1964-68. First recorded for De-Lite in 1969. Added lead singer James "J.T." Taylor in 1979. Members include brothers Robert and Ronald Bell (sax, keyboards), George Brown (drums), Curtis "Fitz" Williams (keyboards) and Charles Smith (guitar). Taylor left group in 1988. | | |
| 9/13/69 | **19** | 9 | 1 Kool And The Gang ................................... [I] | *59* | De-Lite 519 |
| 1/17/70 | **37** | 4 | 2 The Gangs Back Again/   [I] | *85* | |
| | | 2 | 3   Kool's Back Again................................ | | De-Lite 523 |
| 6/20/70 | **19** | 9 | 4 Let The Music Take Your Mind ........................ | *78* | De-Lite 529 |
| 9/19/70 | **16** | 9 | 5 Funky Man ........................................ | *87* | De-Lite 534 |
| 1/23/71 | **28** | 5 | 6 Who's Gonna Take The Weight (Part One).......... | *113* | De-Lite 538 |
| 6/12/71 | **35** | 5 | 7 I Want To Take You Higher............................... | *105* | De-Lite 540 |
| 2/19/72 | **31** | 8 | 8 Love The Life You Live (Part I) ........................ | *107* | De-Lite 546 |
| 8/11/73 | **5** | 19 | 9 **Funky Stuff** ........................................ | *29* | De-Lite 557 |
| 12/01/73+ | **2**[2] | 22 | 10●**Jungle Boogie**........................................ | *4* | De-Lite 559 |
| 4/13/74 | **1**[1] | 17 | 11●**Hollywood Swinging**............................... | *6* | De-Lite 561 |
| 8/31/74 | **1**[1] | 14 | 12 **Higher Plane** ........................................ | *37* | De-Lite 1562 |
| 12/14/74+ | **3** | 16 | 13 **Rhyme Tyme People**............................... | *63* | De-Lite 1563 |
| 4/05/75 | **1**[1] | 16 | 14 **Spirit Of The Boogie/** | *35* | |
| 6/21/75 | **36** | 5 | 15   Summer Madness................................ | | De-Lite 1567 |
| 10/18/75 | **6** | 16 | 16 **Caribbean Festival** ............................. [I] | *55* | De-Lite 1573 |
| 3/06/76 | **8** | 15 | 17 **Love And Understanding (Come Together)**...... | *77* | De-Lite 1579 |
| 6/26/76 | **71** | 7 | 18 Universal Sound ........................................ | *101* | De-Lite 1583 |
| 10/30/76 | **6** | 18 | 19 **Open Sesame-Part 1** ............................. [I] | *55* | De-Lite 1586 |
| 3/12/77 | **17** | 13 | 20 Super Band ........................................ | *101* | De-Lite 1590 |
| 3/04/78 | **19** | 16 | 21 Slick Superchick....................................... | *102* | De-Lite 901 |
| 12/16/78+ | **65** | 8 | 22 Everybody's Dancin'................................ | | De-Lite 910 |
| 9/08/79 | **1**[3] | 21 | 23●**Ladies Night** ........................................ | *8* | De-Lite 801 |
| 1/05/80 | **3** | 20 | 24 **Too Hot** ........................................ | *5* | De-Lite 802 |

| DEBUT DATE | PEAK POS | WKS CHR | ARTIST — Record Title | POP POS | Label & Number |
|---|---|---|---|---|---|
| | | | **KOOL & THE GANG — Continued** | | |
| 5/17/80 | **36** | 8 | 25 Hangin' Out..................................... | *103* | De-Lite 804 |
| 10/18/80 | **1**[6] | 24 | 26▲Celebration.................................... | *1* | De-Lite 807 |
| 2/28/81 | **11** | 14 | 27 Take It To The Top............................ | | De-Lite 810 |
| 5/23/81 | **33** | 12 | 28 Jones Vs. Jones.............................. | *39* | De-Lite 813 |
| 10/03/81 | **1**[1] | 21 | 29 **Take My Heart (You Can Have It If You Want It)**................................................ | *17* | De-Lite 815 |
| 1/30/82 | **12** | 10 | 30 Steppin' Out................................. | *89* | De-Lite 816 |
| 3/13/82 | **4** | 13 | 31 **Get Down On It**........................... | *10* | De-Lite 818 |
| 8/28/82 | **6** | 14 | 32 **Big Fun**................................. | *21* | De-Lite 822 |
| 11/06/82 | **7** | 17 | 33 **Let's Go Dancin' (Ooh La, La, La)**........ | *30* | De-Lite 824 |
| 3/19/83 | **78** | 4 | 34 Street Kids................................. | | De-Lite 825 |
| 11/05/83+ | **1**[2] | 23 | 35 **Joanna**.................................. | *2* | De-Lite 829 |
| 2/18/84 | **7** | 17 | 36 **Tonight**................................. | *13* | De-Lite 830 |
| 6/23/84 | **49** | 8 | 37 Straight Ahead............................. | *103* | De-Lite 831 |
| 11/24/84+ | **3** | 20 | 38 **Misled**.................................. | *10* | De-Lite 880431 |
| 3/16/85 | **1**[1] | 19 | 39 **Fresh**................................... | *9* | De-Lite 880623 |
| 7/13/85 | **1**[1] | 18 | 40 **Cherish**................................. | *2* | De-Lite 880869 |
| 10/26/85 | **7** | 16 | 41 **Emergency**............................... | *18* | De-Lite 884199 |
| 11/01/86 | **2**[2] | 18 | 42 **Victory**................................. | *10* | Mercury 888074 |
| 1/31/87 | **4** | 17 | 43 **Stone Love**.............................. | *10* | Mercury 888292 |
| 6/27/87 | **9** | 13 | 44 **Holiday**................................. | *66* | Mercury 888712 |
| | | | **KOOL MOE DEE** | | |
| | | | Rapper from Harlem. Real name: Mohandas Dewese. Formerly with the Treacherous Three. | | |
| 11/07/87+ | **22** | 18 | 1 How Ya Like Me Now ......................... | | Jive 1050 |
| 3/05/88 | **4** | 16 | 2 **Wild, Wild West**.......................... | *62* | Jive 1086 |
| | | | **KOPPER** | | |
| 3/01/86 | **88** | 2 | 1 Time To Say Goodbye ........................ | | KMA 003 |
| 5/24/86 | **84** | 4 | 2 Velocity................................... | | KMA 008 |
| 5/09/87 | **94** | 3 | 3 Speaking Japanese .......................... | | KMA 014 |
| | | | **KRAFTWERK** | | |
| | | | German all-electronic duo: Ralf Hutter and Florian Schneider. | | |
| 11/07/81+ | **22** | 15 | 1 Numbers................................... | *103* | Warner 49795 |
| | | | **GEORGE KRANZ** | | |
| | | | German. | | |
| 1/07/84 | **61** | 9 | 1 Trommeltanz (Din Daa Daa) ............ [I] | *110* | Personal 19804 |
| | | | **THE KRUSH GROOVE ALL STARS** | | |
| | | | Fat Boys, Run-D.M.C., Sheila E. and Kurtis Blow (these artists starred in the film "Krush Groove"). | | |
| 12/07/85 | **87** | 5 | 1 Krush Groovin'............................. | | Warner 28843 |
| | | | from the film "Krush Groove" | | |
| | | | **KRYSTAL GENERATION** | | |
| | | | Chicago group consisting of Joyce Smith, Darlene Arnold, Mary Shelley and Mary Lead. | | |
| 9/25/71 | **49** | 2 | 1 Wanted Dead Or Alive....................... | | Mr. Chand 8006 |
| | | | **KRYSTOL** | | |
| | | | Female trio consisting of Tina Scott, Roberta Stiger and Robbie Danzie. | | |
| 6/09/84 | **87** | 4 | 1 Nobody's Gonna Get This Lovin' But You ......... | | Epic 04412 |
| 8/17/85 | **86** | 5 | 2 Love Is Like An Itchin' In My Heart................. | | Epic 04941 |
| 1/11/86 | **90** | 5 | 3 The Things That Men Do ..................... | | Epic 05715 |
| 7/12/86 | **18** | 16 | 4 Passion From A Woman ...................... | | Epic 06046 |
| 11/01/86 | **25** | 13 | 5 Precious, Precious......................... | | Epic 06382 |
| | | | **KWICK** | | |
| | | | Memphis vocal group formed at Booker T. Washington High School. Consisted of Terry Bartlett, Bertram Brown and William Sumlin. Recorded as The Newcomers from 1971-78. Changed name to Kwick with the addition of Vince Williams. | | |
| 4/12/80 | **20** | 13 | 1 Let This Moment Be Forever ......................... | | EMI America 8037 |
| 9/06/80 | **68** | 7 | 2 Can't Help Myself ............................. | | EMI America 8048 |
| 10/10/81 | **64** | 9 | 3 Nightlife .................................. | | EMI America 8091 |
| 2/13/82 | **73** | 6 | 4 Shake Till Your Body Break...................... | | EMI America 8105 |

| DEBUT DATE | PEAK POS | WKS CHR | ARTIST — Record Title | POP POS | Label & Number |
|---|---|---|---|---|---|
| 9/15/84 | 67 | 8 | **KYM**<br>1 Give Me The Dance............................................. | | Award 7784008 |

# L

| DEBUT DATE | PEAK POS | WKS CHR | ARTIST — Record Title | POP POS | Label & Number |
|---|---|---|---|---|---|
| | | | **L.A. BOPPERS**<br>Formed in Los Angeles as back-up band for Side Effect. Consisted of Stan Martin (trumpet, flugelhorn), Kenny Styles (guitar), Ed "Funky Thumbs" Reddick (bass), and Vance "Mad Dog" Tennort (lead vocals, percussion). | | |
| 2/09/80 | 28 | 14 | 1 Is This The Best (Bop-Doo-Wah) ....................... | 103 | Mercury 76038 |
| 4/18/81 | 77 | 4 | 2 La La Means I Love You ................................... | | Mercury 76096 |
| 2/06/82 | 57 | 9 | 3 Where Do The Bop Go? ................................... | | MCA 51232 |
| | | | **L.A. DREAM TEAM**<br>West Coast rap group led by Rudy Pardee (from Cleveland) and Chris Wilson (from Watts). | | |
| 8/02/86 | 50 | 10 | 1 Nursery Rhymes .......................................... | | MCA 52860 |
| | | | **L.A. EXPRESS - see TOM SCOTT** | | |
| | | | **L.A. STREET BAND - see JIMMY LEWIS** | | |
| | | | **PATTI LaBELLE** ★★58★★<br>Patti, born Patricia Holt on 5/24/44 in Philadelphia, began singing career as leader of The Blue Belles. The quartet, formed in Philadelphia in 1962, included Nona Hendryx, Sarah Dash and Cindy Birdsong. Cindy left in 1967 to join The Supremes. Group continued as a trio. In 1971, they shortened their name to LaBelle. In 1977, group disbanded and Patti recorded solo. | | |
| | | | **THE BLUE-BELLES:** | | |
| 5/26/62 | 13 | 7 | 1 I Sold My Heart To The Junkman.....................<br><small>label incorrectly listed artist as The Blue-Belles; The Starlets are the real vocalists on this song</small> | 15 | Newtown 5000 |
| | | | **PATTI LaBELLE & THE BLUE BELLES:** | | |
| 8/31/63 | 14 | 11 | 2 Down The Aisle (Wedding Song) ....................... | 37 | Newtown 5777 |
| 1/04/64 | 34 | 8 | 3 You'll Never Walk Alone...................................<br><small>from the musical "Carousel"</small> | Hot | Parkway 896 |
| 12/19/64+ | 76 | 4 | 4 Danny Boy.....................................................<br><small>based on the traditional Irish tune "Londonderry Air" of 1855</small> | Hot | Parkway 935 |
| 10/01/66 | 36 | 7 | 5 I'm Still Waiting ............................................ | | Atlantic 2347 |
| 1/14/67 | 36 | 4 | 6 Take Me For A Little While ............................. | 89 | Atlantic 2373 |
| | | | **LaBELLE:** | | |
| 12/14/74+ | 1¹ | 18 | 7●Lady Marmalade............................................ | 1 | Epic 50048 |
| 5/10/75 | 8 | 14 | 8 What Can I Do For You? ................................. | 48 | Epic 50097 |
| 9/06/75 | 19 | 12 | 9 Messin' With My Mind ................................... | | Epic 50140 |
| 12/06/75 | 99 | 1 | 10 Far As We Felt Like Goin'.............................. | | Epic 50168 |
| 10/16/76 | 50 | 9 | 11 Get You Somebody New................................. | 102 | Epic 50262 |
| | | | **PATTI LaBELLE:** | | |
| 10/08/77 | 31 | 15 | 12 Joy To Have Your Love ................................. | | Epic 50445 |
| 1/21/78 | 61 | 6 | 13 You Are My Friend ...................................... | | Epic 50487 |
| 6/10/78 | 51 | 8 | 14 Teach Me Tonight (Me Gusta Tu Baile) ............. | | Epic 50550 |
| 8/12/78 | 60 | 7 | 15 Little Girls .............................................. | | Epic 50583 |
| 3/10/79 | 34 | 11 | 16 It's Alright With Me/ | | |
| 5/19/79 | 81 | 5 | 17 Music Is My Way Of Life ............................. | | Epic 50659 |
| 3/08/80 | 61 | 7 | 18 Release (The Tension) ................................. | | Epic 50852 |
| 5/03/80 | 26 | 12 | 19 I Don't Go Shopping................................... | | Epic 50872 |
| 12/11/82+ | 14 | 19 | 20 The Best Is Yet To Come ............................. | 104 | Elektra 69887 |
| | | | **GROVER WASHINGTON, JR. with PATTI LaBELLE** | | |
| 11/05/83+ | 1⁴ | 26 | 21 If Only You Knew ....................................... | 46 | Phil. Int. 04248 |
| 2/11/84 | 3 | 17 | 22 Love Has Finally Come At Last ...................... | 88 | Beverly Glen 2012 |
| | | | **BOBBY WOMACK & PATTI LaBELLE** | | |
| 3/24/84 | 10 | 17 | 23 Love, Need And Want You............................. | | Phil. Int. 04399 |
| 11/03/84 | 76 | 7 | 24 It Takes A Lot Of Strength To Say Goodbye ....... | | Beverly Glen 2018 |
| | | | **BOBBY WOMACK & PATTI LaBELLE** | | |
| 2/09/85 | 3 | 19 | 25 New Attitude................................................ | 17 | MCA 52517 |
| 6/29/85 | 5 | 14 | 26 Stir It Up.....................................................<br><small>above 2: from the film "Beverly Hills Cop"</small> | 41 | MCA 52610 |

| DEBUT DATE | PEAK POS | WKS CHR | ARTIST — Record Title | POP POS | Label & Number |
|---|---|---|---|---|---|
| | | | **PATTI LaBELLE — Continued** | | |
| 8/03/85 | 63 | 10 | 27 I Can't Forget You............................. | | Phil. Int. 05436 |
| 1/25/86 | 79 | 6 | 28 If You Don't Know Me By Now - Part 1 ............. | | Phil. Int. 05755 |
| 3/29/86 | 1⁴ | 21 | 29●On My Own ........................................... | 1 | MCA 52770 |
| | | | PATTI LaBELLE & MICHAEL McDONALD | | |
| 7/12/86 | 7 | 12 | 30 **Oh, People** ........................................ | 29 | MCA 52877 |
| 10/11/86 | 13 | 16 | 31 Kiss Away The Pain ........................... | | MCA 52945 |
| 1/31/87 | 50 | 8 | 32 Something Special (Is Gonna Happen Tonight).... | | MCA 52876 |
| | | | theme from the film "Outrageous Fortune" | | |
| 6/27/87 | 33 | 11 | 33 Just The Facts ................................. | | MCA 53100 |
| | | | theme from the film "Dragnet" | | |
| | | | **LABYRINTH featuring JULIE LOCO** | | |
| 12/07/85 | 83 | 6 | 1 Help Me Out ................................. | | 21 Records 99601 |
| | | | **LACE** | | |
| | | | Washington, D.C.-based, female trio: Kathy Merrick, Vivian Ross and Lisa Frazier. | | |
| 9/05/87 | 10 | 14 | 1 **My Love Is Deep** ............................ | | Wing 887042 |
| 12/19/87+ | 37 | 12 | 2 Since You Came Over Me ............................. | | Wing 887248 |
| | | | **LADIES' CHOICE** | | |
| 9/24/83 | 70 | 6 | 1 Girl's Night Out.............................. | | Streetwise 2212 |
| | | | **LADY** | | |
| 4/24/82 | 76 | 6 | 1 Number One.................................. | | Mega 100 |
| | | | **LA FLAVOUR** | | |
| | | | Pop/disco assemblage featuring lead singer Craig DeBock. | | |
| 6/09/79 | 89 | 3 | 1 When The Whistle Blows (Anything Goes).......... | | Mercury 74055 |
| 5/31/80 | 63 | 6 | 2 Only The Lonely (Have A Reason To Be Sad)...... | 91 | Sweet City 7377 |
| | | | **LAID BACK** | | |
| | | | Vocal/instrumental duo from Denmark. Consisted of Tim Stahl (keyboards) and John Guldberg (guitar). Highly successful in Europe for three years before their US debut. | | |
| 2/18/84 | 5 | 17 | 1 **White Horse** ................................. | 26 | Sire 29346 |
| | | | **FRANKIE LAINE** | | |
| | | | Born Frank Paul LoVecchio on 3/30/13 in Chicago. To Los Angeles in the early 40s. First recorded for Exclusive in 1945. With Johnny Moore's Three Blazers. | | |
| 5/17/47 | 3 | 11 | 1 **That's My Desire** ........................... | 4 | Mercury 5007 |
| | | | with Mannie Klein's All Stars; a reported million-seller | | |
| 1/08/49 | 15 | 1 | 2 You're All I Want For Christmas.................. [X] | 11 | Mercury 5177 |
| | | | Juke Box #15 | | |
| | | | with Carl Fischer's Orchestra | | |
| | | | **LAKESIDE** ★★159★★ | | |
| | | | Funk group from Dayton, Ohio, formed in 1969. Consisted of Tiemeyer McCain, Thomas Oliver Shelby, Otis Stokes and Mark Woods (vocals), Steve Shockley (guitar), Norman Beavers (keyboards), Marvin Craig (bass), Fred Alexander (drums) and Fred Lewis (percussion). | | |
| 11/18/78 | 4 | 22 | 1 **It's All The Way Live (Part 1)** ...................... | 102 | Solar 11380 |
| 6/02/79 | 73 | 9 | 2 Given In To Love.............................. | | Solar 11589 |
| 11/10/79+ | 31 | 15 | 3 Pull My Strings ................................. | | Solar 11746 |
| 3/29/80 | 44 | 10 | 4 From 9:00 Until ................................. | | Solar 11931 |
| 11/15/80+ | 1² | 22 | 5 **Fantastic Voyage**............................ | 55 | Solar 12129 |
| 3/21/81 | 14 | 15 | 6 Your Love Is On The One...................... | | Solar 12188 |
| 11/14/81 | 44 | 7 | 7 We Want You (On The Floor) ................ | | Solar 12334 |
| 1/09/82 | 5 | 18 | 8 **I Want To Hold Your Hand** .................. | 102 | Solar 47954 |
| 5/01/82 | 25 | 13 | 9 Something About That Woman ................ | 110 | Solar 48009 |
| 4/02/83 | 8 | 16 | 10 **Raid**.................................... | | Solar 69836 |
| 7/02/83 | 38 | 12 | 11 Turn The Music Up........................... | | Solar 69816 |
| 9/17/83 | 17 | 13 | 12 Real Love ................................. | | Solar 69796 |
| 6/16/84 | 7 | 14 | 13 **Outrageous**................................. | 101 | Solar 69716 |
| 9/08/84 | 37 | 11 | 14 Make My Day................................. | | Solar 69695 |
| 4/04/87 | 24 | 12 | 15 Relationship................................. | | Solar 70005 |
| 7/25/87 | 33 | 14 | 16 Bullseye.................................... | | Solar 70010 |

| DEBUT DATE | PEAK POS | WKS CHR | ARTIST — Record Title | POP POS | Label & Number |
|---|---|---|---|---|---|
| | | | **LA LA** | | |
| | | | La Forrest Cope, writer of Whitney Houston's 1985 hit "You Give Good Love". Producer/backing vocalist/piano protege. Played Carnegie Hall at age 9. | | |
| 5/09/87 | **22** | 12 | 1 (If You) Love Me Just A Little .......................... | | Arista 9568 |
| 8/29/87 | **48** | 8 | 2 My Love Is On The Money .............................. | | Arista 9620 |
| | | | **LEE LAMONT** | | |
| 1/30/65 | **30** | 2 | 1 Crying Man ....................................... | | Back Beat 542 |
| | | | **LAMP SISTERS** | | |
| 4/06/68 | **20** | 8 | 1 Woman With The Blues......................... | | Duke 427 |
| | | | **HERB LANCE & THE CLASSICS** | | |
| 4/09/49 | **4** | 18 | 1 **Close Your Eyes**............................. | | Sittin' in 514 |
| | | | Best Seller #4 / Juke Box #5 | | |
| 7/16/49 | **8** | 2 | 2 **Because** ...................................... | | Sittin' in 519 |
| | | | Juke Box #8 | | |
| 10/22/49 | **6** | 2 | 3 **That Lucky Old Sun**.......................... | | Sittin' in 524 |
| | | | Juke Box #6 | | |
| | | | **MAJOR LANCE**  ★★**158**★★ | | |
| | | | Singer, born on 4/4/42 in Chicago. Amateur boxer. Dancer on The Jim Lounsbury and Record Hop TV shows. Sang with The Five Gospel Harmonaires. Member of the Ideals. First recorded for Mercury in 1959. Lived in Britain from 1972-74. Own label, Osiris, with Al Jackson of the MG's in 1975. In prison from 1978-81 for selling cocaine. | | |
| 8/03/63 | **2** [2] | 15 | 1 **The Monkey Time** ...................................... | 8 | Okeh 7175 |
| 11/09/63 | **12** | 3 | 2 Hey Little Girl ..................................... | *13* | Okeh 7181 |
| 1/04/64 | **5** | 11 | 3 **Um, Um, Um, Um, Um, Um**........................... | *Hot* | Okeh 7187 |
| 3/28/64 | **20** | 8 | 4 The Matador........................................ | *Hot* | Okeh 7191 |
| 6/06/64 | **68** | 8 | 5 It Ain't No Use/ | *Hot* | |
| 6/27/64 | **68** | 6 | 6 Girls .............................................. | *Hot* | Okeh 7197 |
| 8/22/64 | **24** | 10 | 7 Rhythm ............................................ | *Hot* | Okeh 7203 |
| 1/30/65 | **13** | 5 | 8 Sometimes I Wonder ............................... | 64 | Okeh 7209 |
| 3/06/65 | **20** | 10 | 9 Come See.......................................... | 40 | Okeh 7216 |
| 6/19/65 | **20** | 6 | 10 Ain't It A Shame .................................. | 91 | Okeh 7223 |
| 9/18/65 | **32** | 4 | 11 Too Hot To Hold .................................. | 93 | Okeh 7226 |
| 9/24/66 | **37** | 5 | 12 It's The Beat ...................................... | 128 | Okeh 7255 |
| 1/20/68 | **49** | 2 | 13 Without A Doubt................................... | | Okeh 7298 |
| 6/21/69 | **28** | 8 | 14 Follow The Leader................................. | 125 | Dakar 608 |
| 7/11/70 | **13** | 13 | 15 Stay Away From Me (I Love You Too Much)........ | 67 | Curtom 1953 |
| | | | all of above (except #4 & 11): written by Curtis Mayfield | | |
| 1/02/71 | **31** | 6 | 16 Must Be Love Coming Down ......................... | 119 | Curtom 1956 |
| 10/26/74 | **59** | 9 | 17 Um, Um, Um, Um, Um, Um .............................. | | Playboy 6017 |
| | | | new version of #3 above | | |
| 3/15/75 | **58** | 8 | 18 Sweeter........................................... | | Playboy 6020 |
| 7/05/75 | **50** | 11 | 19 You're Everything I Need............................ | | Osiris 001 |
| | | | **LANIER & CO.** | | |
| | | | Group led by Farris Lanier, Jr. | | |
| 11/13/82+ | **26** | 17 | 1 After I Cry Tonight..................................... | 48 | Larc 81010 |
| 3/05/83 | **47** | 10 | 2 I Just Got To Have You ............................... | | Larc 81017 |
| 5/21/83 | **57** | 7 | 3 Share Your Love With Me ............................ | | Larc 81021 |
| | | | **LARKS** | | |
| 7/28/51 | **5** | 1 | 1 **Eyesight To The Blind** ............................. | | Apollo 427 |
| | | | Best Seller #5 | | |
| 10/06/51 | **10** | 1 | 2 **Little Side Car** .......................................... | | Apollo 429 |
| | | | Best Seller #10 | | |
| | | | **THE LARKS** | | |
| | | | Group from Los Angeles formed by Don Julian as the Meadowlarks in 1953. First recorded for RPM in 1954. Group on hit "The Jerk" consisted of Don Julian, Ted Walters and Charles Morrison. (Not to be confused with East Coast groups of same name.) | | |
| 1/30/65 | **9** | 4 | 1 The Jerk.............................................. | *7* | Money 106 |

| DEBUT DATE | PEAK POS | WKS CHR | ARTIST — Record Title | POP POS | Label & Number |
|---|---|---|---|---|---|
| | | | **NICOLETTE LARSON** | | |
| | | | Born on 7/17/52 in Helena, Montana; raised in Kansas City. To San Francisco in 1974. Prominent pop session vocalist. | | |
| 3/15/80 | 96 | 2 | 1  Let Me Go, Love ............................................. | 35 | Warner 49130 |
| | | | duet with Michael McDonald | | |
| | | | **DENISE LaSALLE** | | |
| | | | Born Denise Craig on 7/16/39 in LeFlore County, Mississippi. Singer/songwriter. Moved to Chicago in the early 50s. First recorded for Tarpen (Chess) in 1967. Own Crajon Productions with husband Bill Jones from 1969. | | |
| 8/21/71 | 1¹ | 16 | 1 ● Trapped By A Thing Called Love ................. | 13 | Westbound 182 |
| 2/05/72 | 3 | 12 | 2  Now Run And Tell That ............................... | 46 | Westbound 201 |
| 10/07/72 | 4 | 13 | 3  Man Sized Job .......................................... | 55 | Westbound 206 |
| 5/05/73 | 31 | 7 | 4  What It Takes To Get A Good Woman (That's What It's Gonna Take To Keep Her) .......... | | Westbound 215 |
| 10/06/73 | 92 | 3 | 5  Your Man And Your Best Friend .................... | | Westbound 219 |
| 1/12/74 | 67 | 7 | 6  Don't Nobody Live Here (By The Name Of Fool)... | | Westbound 221 |
| 6/08/74 | 96 | 4 | 7  Get Up Off My Mind ................................... | | Westbound 223 |
| 4/12/75 | 55 | 9 | 8  My Brand On You ...................................... | | Westbound 5004 |
| 3/27/76 | 16 | 17 | 9  Married, But Not To Each Other .................... | 102 | Westbound 5019 |
| 4/09/77 | 100 | 1 | 10  Freedom To Express Yourself ....................... | | ABC 12238 |
| 11/26/77+ | 10 | 21 | 11  Love Me Right .......................................... | 80 | ABC 12312 |
| 5/20/78 | 87 | 5 | 12  One Life To Live ....................................... | | ABC 12353 |
| 10/28/78 | 70 | 6 | 13  Workin' Overtime ...................................... | | ABC 12419 |
| 2/10/79 | 90 | 2 | 14  P.A.R.T.Y. (Where It Is) .............................. | | ABC 12443 |
| 5/17/80 | 82 | 5 | 15  I'm So Hot ............................................... | | MCA 41222 |
| 6/01/85 | 79 | 5 | 16  My Tu-Tu ................................................. | | Malaco 2112 |
| | | | **DAVID LASLEY** | | |
| | | | Born on 8/20/47 in Sault St. Marie, Michigan. Backup singer for James Taylor and others. Member of the studio group Roundtree. | | |
| 4/17/82 | 56 | 8 | 1  If I Had My Wish Tonight ............................. | 36 | EMI America 8111 |
| | | | **LATIMORE** | | |
| | | | Born Benjamin Latimore on 9/7/39 in Charleston, Tennessee. Singer/songwriter. | | |
| 10/13/73+ | 27 | 16 | 1  Stormy Monday ......................................... | 102 | Glades 1716 |
| 4/13/74 | 70 | 5 | 2  If You Were My Woman ............................... | | Glades 1720 |
| 9/07/74 | 1² | 20 | 3  Let's Straighten It Out ............................... | 31 | Glades 1722 |
| 4/05/75 | 5 | 16 | 4  Keep The Home Fire Burnin' ......................... | | Glades 1726 |
| 9/13/75 | 36 | 10 | 5  There's A Red-Neck In The Soul Band ............... | | Glades 1729 |
| 2/07/76 | 43 | 11 | 6  Qualified Man .......................................... | | Glades 1733 |
| 12/18/76+ | 7 | 19 | 7  Somethin' 'Bout 'Cha ................................. | 37 | Glades 1739 |
| 6/11/77 | 30 | 9 | 8  I Get Lifted .............................................. | 104 | Glades 1742 |
| 11/05/77 | 49 | 12 | 9  Let Me Live The Life I Love ........................... | | Glades 1744 |
| 12/02/78+ | 42 | 11 | 10  Dig A Little Deeper ................................... | | Glades 1750 |
| 4/14/79 | 75 | 4 | 11  Long Distance Love ................................... | | Glades 1752 |
| 7/28/79 | 82 | 4 | 12  Goodbye Heartache ................................... | | Glades 1755 |
| 12/22/79+ | 68 | 10 | 13  Discoed To Death ..................................... | | Glades 1756 |
| 11/15/86 | 76 | 6 | 14  Sunshine Lady.......................................... | | Malaco 2130 |
| | | | **STACY LATTISAW**   ★★144★★ | | |
| | | | Born on 11/25/66 in Washington, DC. Recorded her first album at age 12. | | |
| 6/09/79 | 91 | 4 | 1  When You're Young And In Love ..................... | | Cotillion 44250 |
| 5/17/80 | 8 | 20 | 2  Dynamite! ............................................... | | Cotillion 45015 |
| 8/02/80 | 8 | 20 | 3  Let Me Be Your Angel ................................. | 21 | Cotillion 46001 |
| 6/06/81 | 2⁴ | 18 | 4  Love On A Two Way Street ........................... | 26 | Cotillion 46015 |
| 9/26/81 | 61 | 5 | 5  It Was So Easy ......................................... | | Cotillion 46024 |
| 11/07/81 | 71 | 4 | 6  Feel My Love Tonight ................................. | | Cotillion 46026 |
| 7/10/82 | 9 | 16 | 7  Don't Throw It All Away............................... | 101 | Cotillion 47011 |
| 9/25/82 | 14 | 13 | 8  Attack Of The Name Game........................ [N] | 70 | Cotillion 99968 |
| 12/18/82+ | 71 | 8 | 9  Hey There Lonely Boy................................. | 108 | Cotillion 99943 |
| 7/02/83 | 13 | 17 | 10  Miracles ................................................. | 40 | Cotillion 99855 |
| 11/19/83 | 52 | 12 | 11  Million Dollar Babe.................................... | | Cotillion 99819 |
| | | | **STACY LATTISAW & JOHNNY GILL:** | | |
| 2/18/84 | 10 | 15 | 12  Perfect Combination ................................. | 75 | Cotillion 99785 |

| DEBUT DATE | PEAK POS | WKS CHR | ARTIST — Record Title | POP POS | Label & Number |
|---|---|---|---|---|---|
| | | | **STACY LATTISAW — Continued** | | |
| 5/12/84 | 37 | 10 | 13 Baby It's You ................................................. | *102* | Cotillion 99750 |
| 7/14/84 | 63 | 7 | 14 Block Party ...................................................... | | Cotillion 99725 |
| | | | **STACY LATTISAW:** | | |
| 7/06/85 | 52 | 9 | 15 I'm Not The Same Girl........................................ | | Cotillion 99635 |
| 9/13/86 | 4 | 18 | 16 **Nail It To The Wall** ........................................ | 48 | Motown 1859 |
| 1/24/87 | 13 | 12 | 17 Jump Into My Life ............................................ | | Motown 1874 |
| 1/09/88 | 8 | 16 | 18 **Every Drop Of Your Love**............................... | | Motown 1912 |
| 4/30/88 | 11 | 14 | 19 Let Me Take You Down ..................................... | | Motown 1934 |
| | | | **CYNDI LAUPER** | | |
| | | | Born on 6/20/53 in Queens, New York. Recorded an album for Polydor Records in 1980 with the group, Blue Angel. Won a Grammy in 1984 as Best New Artist. | | |
| 4/07/84 | 80 | 5 | 1●Girls Just Want To Have Fun ......................... | 2 | Portrait 04120 |
| 5/19/84 | 78 | 5 | 2 Time After Time ............................................. | 1 | Portrait 04432 |
| | | | **LAURA & JOHNNY** | | |
| 3/22/69 | 49 | 2 | 1 Pledging My Love............................................ | | Silver Fox 1 |
| | | | **PAUL LAURENCE** | | |
| 10/05/85 | 50 | 9 | 1 She's Not A Sleaze ......................................... | | Capitol 5507 |
| | | | with Lillo Thomas & Freddie Jackson | | |
| 2/01/86 | 55 | 9 | 2 You Hooked Me.............................................. | | Capitol 5545 |
| 4/26/86 | 48 | 10 | 3 Strung Out..................................................... | | Capitol 5564 |
| | | | **ANNIE LAURIE** | | |
| | | | Native of Atlanta. Sang with the Dallas Brockley, Snookum Russell bands before joining Paul Gayten in 1948. Made a brief comeback in 1957. Also see Paul Gayten. | | |
| 12/03/49 | 6 | 3 | 1 **Cuttin' Out**................................................ | | Regal 3235 |
| | | | Juke Box #6 | | |
| | | | with the Paul Gayten Orchestra | | |
| 3/02/57 | 3 | 11 | 2 **It Hurts To Be In Love** ................................. | 61 | DeLuxe 6107 |
| | | | Best Seller #3 / Jockey #7 / Juke Box #9 | | |
| 7/11/60 | 17 | 11 | 3 If You're Lonely ............................................. | *104* | DeLuxe 6189 |
| | | | **BETTY LaVETTE** | | |
| | | | Born Betty Haskin in 1946 in Muskegon, Michigan. With Don Gardner & Dee Dee Ford revue in the mid-60s. In the Broadway musical "Bubbling Brown Sugar". | | |
| 11/24/62+ | 7 | 8 | 1 My Man - He's A Lovin' Man ......................... | *101* | Atlantic 2160 |
| 4/24/65 | 20 | 8 | 2 Let Me Down Easy .......................................... | *103* | Calla 102 |
| 12/06/69+ | 25 | 7 | 3 He Made A Woman Out Of Me.......................... | | Silver Fox 17 |
| 3/21/70 | 38 | 5 | 4 Do Your Duty ................................................ | | Silver Fox 21 |
| 10/18/75 | 94 | 2 | 5 Thank You For Loving Me................................ | | Epic 50143 |
| 1/30/82 | 35 | 12 | 6 Right In The Middle (Of Falling In Love)............. | *103* | Motown 1532 |
| | | | shown as: **BETTYE LaVETTE** | | |
| | | | **STEVE LAWRENCE** | | |
| | | | Born Sam Leibowitz on 7/8/35 in Brooklyn. Regular performer on the Steve Allen "Tonight Show" for 5 years. First recorded for King in 1953. Married to singer Eydie Gorme since 12/29/57. | | |
| 1/05/63 | 14 | 9 | 1 Go Away Little Girl ....................................... | 1 | Columbia 42601 |
| | | | **DEBRA LAWS** | | |
| | | | Born in Houston, younger sister of Ronnie, Hubert and Eloise Laws. | | |
| 1/31/81 | 31 | 15 | 1 Be Yourself.................................................... | | Elektra 47084 |
| 5/23/81 | 11 | 19 | 2 Very Special................................................... | 90 | Elektra 47142 |
| | | | male vocal by Ronnie Laws | | |
| 9/26/81 | 47 | 9 | 3 Meant For You............................................... | | Elektra 47198 |
| | | | **ELOISE LAWS** | | |
| | | | Born in 1949 in Houston. Sister of Hubert, Ronnie and Debra Laws. First recorded for Columbia in 1969. | | |
| 4/15/78 | 78 | 5 | 1 Number One................................................... | 97 | ABC 12341 |
| 11/22/80+ | 33 | 15 | 2 Strength Of A Woman ..................................... | | Liberty 1388 |
| 3/21/81 | 53 | 8 | 3 You Are Everything ......................................... | | Liberty 1399 |
| | | | **HUBERT LAWS** | | |
| | | | Born in 1939 in Houston. Oldest brother of Ronnie, Eloise and Debra Laws. Jazz flutist. With the Swingsters (later the Jazz Crusaders), in 1954. With Mongo Santamaria from 1958. | | |
| 8/23/75 | 53 | 9 | 1 The Chicago Theme (Love Loop) ...................... | | CTI 27 |

**252**

| DEBUT DATE | PEAK POS | WKS CHR | ARTIST — Record Title | POP POS | Label & Number |
|---|---|---|---|---|---|
| | | | **HUBERT LAWS — Continued** | | |
| 10/18/80 | 74 | 5 | 2 Family ......................................... | | Columbia 11368 |
| | | | **RONNIE LAWS** | | |
| | | | Saxophonist, born on 10/3/50 in Houston. Brother of Hubert, Eloise and Debra Laws. Member of Earth, Wind & Fire from 1972-73. Also see Debra Laws and Pressure. | | |
| 12/06/75+ | 45 | 12 | 1 Always There ............................... | | Blue Note 738 |
| | | | **RONNIE LAWS & PRESSURE** | | |
| 12/09/78+ | 57 | 10 | 2 Love Is Here ................................. | | United Art. 1264 |
| 4/28/79 | 93 | 2 | 3 All For You .................................. | | United Art. 1278 |
| 1/26/80 | 12 | 17 | 4 Every Generation .......................... | | United Art. 1334 |
| 8/22/81 | 19 | 18 | 5 Stay Awake.................................. | 60 | Liberty 1424 |
| 12/26/81+ | 75 | 6 | 6 There's A Way............................... | | Liberty 1442 |
| 6/25/83 | 31 | 14 | 7 In The Groove............................... | | Capitol 5241 |
| 10/08/83 | 80 | 4 | 8 Mr. Nice Guy ................................ | | Capitol 5274 |
| 12/01/84+ | 31 | 14 | 9 City Girl ..................................... | | Capitol 5421 |
| | | | **LE PAMPLEMOUSSE** | | |
| | | | Disco band featuring vocals by The Jones Girls. | | |
| 11/26/77+ | 13 | 19 | 1 Le Spank/ | [I] 58 | |
| 5/13/78 | 76 | 9 | 2 Monkey See, Monkey Do................... | | AVI 153 |
| | | | **OTIS LEAVILLE** | | |
| | | | Born Otis Leavill Cobb on 2/8/41 in Atlanta. Singer/songwriter/producer. To Chicago in 1943. Sang in Cobb Quartet, family gospel group. Formed group, the Floats, with Major Lance and Barbara Tyson. Wrote "I'm A Soldier Boy" for Dee Clark. Toured with Lance on Dick Clark's Caravan Of Stars. Own label, Chi-Sound, in 1976. | | |
| 2/06/65 | 31 | 3 | 1 Let Her Love Me ........................... | 116 | Blue Rock 4002 |
| 11/22/69+ | 10 | 10 | 2 I Love You ................................... | 63 | Dakar 614 |
| 9/05/70 | 19 | 11 | 3 Love Uprising............................... | 72 | Dakar 620 |
| | | | **CALVIN LEAVY** | | |
| | | | Vocalist/guitarist from Scott, Arkansas. | | |
| 5/02/70 | 40 | 5 | 1 Cummins Prison Farm ..................... | | Blue Fox 100 |
| | | | **BOBBY LEE** | | |
| 8/27/66 | 41 | 5 | 1 I Was A Born Loser ........................ | | Sue 144 |
| | | | **BRENDA LEE** | | |
| | | | Born Brenda Mae Tarpley on 12/11/44 in Lithonia, Georgia. Professional singer since age six. Signed to Decca Records in 1956. Became known as "Little Miss Dynamite". Successful Country singer since 1971. | | |
| 3/28/60 | 12 | 9 | 1 Sweet Nothin's.............................. | 4 | Decca 30967 |
| 6/13/60 | 4 | 12 | 2 I'm Sorry/ | 1 | |
| | | | above 2: written by Ronnie Self | | |
| 6/27/60 | 19 | 2 | 3 That's All You Gotta Do ................... | 6 | Decca 31093 |
| 10/17/60 | 7 | 8 | 4 I Want To Be Wanted ...................... | 1 | Decca 31149 |
| 5/01/61 | 25 | 3 | 5 You Can Depend On Me ................... | 6 | Decca 31231 |
| 5/25/63 | 13 | 5 | 6 Losing You ................................... | 6 | Decca 31478 |
| | | | **DICKEY LEE** | | |
| | | | Born Dickey Lipscomb on 9/21/41 in Memphis. Pop-country singer/songwriter. First recorded for Sun Records in 1957. | | |
| 9/22/62 | 10 | 8 | 1 Patches ...................................... | 6 | Smash 1758 |
| 1/19/63 | 12 | 4 | 2 I Saw Linda Yesterday .................... | 14 | Smash 1791 |
| | | | **JACKIE LEE** | | |
| | | | Real name: Earl Nelson (of Bob & Earl). Took name from his wife's middle name, Jackie, and his middle name, Lee. Sang lead on Hollywood Flames' "Buzz-Buzz-Buzz". | | |
| 12/04/65+ | 4 | 18 | 1 The Duck..................................... | 14 | Mirwood 5502 |
| 4/27/68 | 43 | 2 | 2 African Boo-Ga-Loo ........................ | 121 | Keymen 114 |
| 8/22/70 | 47 | 3 | 3 The Chicken.................................. | | Uni 55206 |
| | | | **JIMMIE LEE & ARTIS** | | |
| | | | Vocal duo of Jimmie Lee and Artis Brewster, husband and wife, from Texarkana, Texas. | | |
| 7/19/52 | 7 | 6 | 1 My Heart's Desire .......................... | | Modern 870 |
| | | | Best Seller #7 / Juke Box #10 with Jay Franks & His Rockettes of Rhythm | | |

| DEBUT DATE | PEAK POS | WKS CHR | | ARTIST — Record Title | POP POS | Label & Number |
|---|---|---|---|---|---|---|
| | | | | **JULIA LEE & HER BOYFRIENDS** | | |
| | | | | Born on 10/31/02 in Boonville, Missouri. Died of a heart attack on 12/8/58 (56). Vocalist/pianist. With father's band from age four. Joined brother George E. Lee's band from 1920-33. First recorded for Merritt in 1927. Worked up until the time of her death. Noted for her risque style of recordings. | | |
| 11/16/46 | **3** | 7 | 1 | **Gotta Gimme Whatcha Got** ........................... | | Capitol 308 |
| 5/24/47 | **5** | 1 | 2 | **I'll Get Along Somehow** .............................. | | Capitol 379 |
| 10/11/47 | **1** [12] | 28 | 3 | **Snatch And Grab It** ................................ [N] | 24 | Capitol A. 40028 |
| 2/14/48 | **1** [9] | 28 | 4 | **King Size Papa**...................................... | 15 | Capitol A. 40082 |
| | | | | Juke Box #1 / Best Seller #5 with Benny Carter (alto sax); above 2: Dave Cavanaugh (tenor sax) | | |
| 5/29/48 | **6** | 3 | 5 | **That's What I Like** ................................. | | Capitol 15060 |
| | | | | Juke Box #6 | | |
| 8/07/48 | **9** | 3 | 6 | **Tell Me Daddy**...................................... | | Capitol 15144 |
| | | | | Juke Box #9 / Best Seller #12 | | |
| 1/08/49 | **14** | 1 | 7 | Christmas Spirits ..................................... [X] | | Capitol 15203 |
| | | | | Best Seller #14 | | |
| 3/12/49 | **4** | 2 | 8 | **I Didn't Like It The First Time** .................... | 29 | Capitol 15367 |
| | | | | Juke Box #4 / Best Seller #9 | | |
| 9/03/49 | **13** | 1 | 9 | Tonight's The Night................................... | | Capitol 70013 |
| | | | | Juke Box #13 | | |
| 11/12/49 | **9** | 1 | 10 | **You Ain't Got It No More**........................... | | Capitol 70031 |
| | | | | Best Seller #9 | | |
| | | | | **LAURA LEE** | | |
| | | | | Born Laure Lee Rundless in 1945 in Chicago. Singer/songwriter. In Meditation Singers gospel group, in Detroit until 1965. | | |
| 9/16/67 | **13** | 11 | 1 | Dirty Man ............................................ | 68 | Chess 2013 |
| 12/30/67+ | **16** | 7 | 2 | Up Tight, Good Man................................... | 93 | Chess 2030 |
| 4/27/68 | **31** | 5 | 3 | As Long As I Got You ................................ | 123 | Chess 2041 |
| 8/03/68 | **44** | 5 | 4 | Need To Belong....................................... | | Chess 2052 |
| 1/04/69 | **48** | 3 | 5 | Hang It Up ........................................... | | Chess 2062 |
| 1/09/71 | **37** | 3 | 6 | Wedlock Is A Padlock ................................ | | Hot Wax 7007 |
| 8/07/71 | **11** | 16 | 7 | Women's Love Rights.................................. | 36 | Hot Wax 7105 |
| 12/25/71+ | **23** | 6 | 8 | Love And Liberty ..................................... | 94 | Hot Wax 7111 |
| 3/04/72 | **24** | 6 | 9 | Since I Fell For You .................................. | 76 | Hot Wax 7201 |
| 6/03/72 | **3** | 12 | 10 | **Rip Off** ............................................. | 68 | Hot Wax 7204 |
| 10/07/72 | **31** | 6 | 11 | If You Can Beat Me Rockin' (You Can Have My Chair) ............................................. | 65 | Hot Wax 7207 |
| 12/23/72+ | **40** | 5 | 12 | Crumbs Off The Table ................................ | 107 | Hot Wax 7210 |
| 9/08/73 | **49** | 12 | 13 | I'll Catch You When You Fall ......................... | | Hot Wax 7305 |
| 7/13/74 | **55** | 10 | 14 | I Need It Just As Bad As You ......................... | | Invictus 1264 |
| 11/27/76 | **61** | 8 | 15 | Love's Got Me Tired (But I Ain't Tired Of Love)... | | Ariola Am. 7652 |
| | | | | **LEON LEE** | | |
| | | | | Formerly with People's Choice. | | |
| 9/28/74 | **75** | 4 | 1 | He Was The Man, Part 1 ............................. | | Crossover 977 |
| | | | | **NICKIE LEE** | | |
| 11/23/68 | **50** | 3 | 1 | And Black Is Beautiful................................ | | Mala 12025 |
| | | | | **PEGGY LEE** | | |
| | | | | Big band jazz singer/actress, born Norma Jean Egstrom on 5/26/20 in Jamestown, North Dakota. Co-wrote many songs with husband Dave Barbour. | | |
| 8/11/58 | **5** | 6 | 1 | **Fever**............................................... | 8 | Capitol 3998 |
| | | | | Jockey #5 / Best Seller #12 | | |
| | | | | **TONEY LEE** | | |
| 4/27/85 | **64** | 9 | 1 | Teaser............................................... | | Critique 712 |
| | | | | **LEGACY** | | |
| 7/31/82 | **71** | 7 | 1 | Word Up ............................................. | | Brunswick 222 |
| 3/09/85 | **44** | 12 | 2 | Don't Waste The Night ............................... | | Private I 04794 |
| 10/12/85 | **71** | 6 | 3 | Someone Else's Girl.................................. | | Private I 05630 |

| DEBUT DATE | PEAK POS | WKS CHR | ARTIST — Record Title | POP POS | Label & Number |
|---|---|---|---|---|---|
| | | | **J.B. LENORE** | | |
| | | | Correct spelling: Lenoir. Born on 3/5/29 in Monticello, Mississippi. Died on 5/29/67 (auto accident, heart attack). Singer/guitarist/harmonica player. Moved to Chicago in 1949. With Memphis Minnie and Muddy Waters. Own band, the Bayou Boys, from 1950. First recorded for Chess in 1951. Overseas tour, 1965-66. | | |
| 7/23/55 | **11** | 2 | 1 Mama, Talk To Your Daughter........................ | | Parrot 809 |
| | | | Jockey #11 | | |
| | | | **ANNE LeSEAR** | | |
| | | | Vocalist from Houston. Singing from age 13. Worked as a programmer on local radio and in record promotion. | | |
| 4/14/84 | **94** | 3 | 1 Take Him Back (Taxi)................................. | | H.C.R.C. 3190 |
| | | | **KETTY LESTER** | | |
| | | | Born Revoyda Frierson on 8/16/34 in Hope, Arkansas. To Los Angeles in 1955. Acted in several TV shows. | | |
| 3/10/62 | **2**¹ | 14 | 1 **Love Letters**........................................ | 5 | Era 3068 |
| | | | Dick Haymes' version hit pop charts in 1945 (POS 11) | | |
| | | | **LEVERT** | | |
| | | | Trio from Ohio: Gerald & Sean Levert (sons of the O'Jays' Eddie Levert) and Marc Gordon. | | |
| 3/09/85 | **70** | 8 | 1 I'm Still................................................ | | Tempre 5505 |
| 7/19/86 | **1**¹ | 18 | 2 **(Pop, Pop, Pop, Pop) Goes My Mind**.............. | | Atlantic 89389 |
| 10/11/86 | **14** | 16 | 3 Let's Go Out Tonight ............................... | | Atlantic 89350 |
| 2/07/87 | **26** | 11 | 4 Fascination ........................................... | | Atlantic 89311 |
| 7/04/87 | **1**² | 20 | 5 **Casanova**.......................................... | 5 | Atlantic 89217 |
| 10/10/87 | **2**⁴ | 19 | 6 **My Forever Love**................................... | | Atlantic 89182 |
| 2/13/88 | **4** | 15 | 7 **Sweet Sensation** ................................... | | Atlantic 89124 |
| | | | **GERALD LEVERT - see MIKI HOWARD** | | |
| | | | **BARBARA LEWIS** | | |
| | | | Born on 2/9/43 in South Lyon, Michigan. Singer/multi-instrumentalist/songwriter (since age 9). First recorded in Chicago in 1961. Inactive since the early 70s. | | |
| 5/25/63 | **1**² | 14 | 1 **Hello Stranger**..................................... | 3 | Atlantic 2184 |
| | | | with The Dells | | |
| 12/28/63+ | **71** | 5 | 2 Snap Your Fingers/ | Hot | |
| 1/11/64 | **38** | 12 | 3 Puppy Love ........................................... | Hot | Atlantic 2214 |
| 6/26/65 | **5** | 17 | 4 **Baby, I'm Yours** ................................... | 11 | Atlantic 2283 |
| 10/23/65 | **9** | 10 | 5 **Make Me Your Baby** .............................. | 11 | Atlantic 2300 |
| 8/20/66 | **36** | 5 | 6 Make Me Belong To You ............................. | 28 | Atlantic 2346 |
| | | | **BOBBY LEWIS** | | |
| | | | Singer, born on 2/17/33 in Indianapolis. Grew up in an orphanage, adopted by a Detroit family at age 12. First recorded for the Parrot label in 1952. | | |
| 5/29/61 | **1**¹⁰ | 19 | 1 **Tossin' And Turnin'** ................................ | 1 | Beltone 1002 |
| 9/04/61 | **8** | 11 | 2 **One Track Mind** ................................... | 9 | Beltone 1012 |
| | | | above 2: with the Joe Rene Orchestra | | |
| | | | **HUEY LEWIS & THE NEWS** | | |
| | | | San Francisco 6-man pop/rock band formed in 1980 by Huey Lewis (born Hugh Cregg III on 7/5/50 in New York City). | | |
| 9/07/85 | **81** | 4 | 1 The Power Of Love ................................. | 1 | Chrysalis 42876 |
| | | | from the film "Back To The Future" | | |
| | | | **J.G. LEWIS** | | |
| 1/31/76 | **81** | 8 | 1 Let The Music Play................................... | | IX Chains 7014 |
| | | | **JERRY LEE LEWIS** | | |
| | | | Rock 'n' roll singer/pianist, born on 9/29/35 in Ferriday, Louisiana. First recorded for Sun in 1956. Career plagued by tragedy and controversy. Cousin of country singer Mickey Gilley and televangelist Jimmy Swaggart. | | |
| 8/19/57 | **1**² | 10 | 1 **Whole Lotta Shakin' Going On** ..................... | 3 | Sun 267 |
| | | | Best Seller #1(2) / Jockey #1(1) | | |
| 12/09/57 | **3** | 12 | 2 **Great Balls Of Fire/** | 2 | |
| | | | Best Seller #3 / Jockey #3 | | |
| | | 1 | 3 You Win Again ....................................... | 95 | Sun 281 |
| | | | Best Seller flip written by Hank Williams; #13 pop hit for Tommy Edwards in 1952 | | |
| 3/17/58 | **3** | 7 | 4 **Breathless** ......................................... | 7 | Sun 288 |
| | | | Jockey #3 / Best Seller #6 | | |

| DEBUT DATE | PEAK POS | WKS CHR | ARTIST — Record Title | POP POS | Label & Number |
|---|---|---|---|---|---|
| | | | **JERRY LEE LEWIS — Continued** | | |
| 6/23/58 | **5** | 4 | 5 **High School Confidential/** <br> Jockey #5 / Best Seller #16 | *21* | |
| 7/14/58 | **11** | 1 | 6 Fools Like Me............................................. <br> Jockey #11 | | Sun 296 |
| 5/22/61 | **26** | 1 | 7 What'd I Say ........................................... | *30* | Sun 356 |
| | | | **JIMMY LEWIS** <br> Jimmy was born in Itta Bena, Mississippi. Singer/songwriter/arranger. <br> First recorded in 1963. | | |
| 1/11/69 | **21** | 7 | 1 If It Wasn't For Bad Luck ............................ <br> RAY CHARLES & JIMMY LEWIS | *77* | ABC 11170 |
| 4/05/75 | **95** | 3 | 2 Help Me Understand You ............................... | | Hotlanta 307 |
| 5/26/84 | **50** | 10 | 3 Street Freeks ........................................... <br> JIMMY LEWIS & The L.A. Street Band | | MCA 52384 |
| | | | **LENNY LEWIS & HIS ORCHESTRA** <br> Big band led by clarinetist Lenny Lewis. | | |
| 12/28/46 | **5** | 1 | 1 **Blue Flame**....................................[I] | | Queen 4133 |
| | | | **LINDA LEWIS** <br> Singer/actress from London. Appeared in the films "Taste Of Honey" and "A Hard Day's <br> Night" before solo debut in 1971. | | |
| 7/12/75 | **96** | 2 | 1 It's In His Kiss (The Shoop Shoop Song)............. | *107* | Arista 0129 |
| | | | **RAMSEY LEWIS** <br> Ramsey formed the Gentlemen Of Swing, a jazz-oriented trio, in 1956 in Chicago. <br> Consisted of Ramsey (b: 5/27/35, Chicago; piano), Eldee Young (bass) and <br> Isaac "Red" Holt (drums). All had been in The Clefs in the early 50s. First recorded <br> for Chess/Argo in 1956. Disbanded in 1965; Young and Holt then formed the Young-Holt <br> Trio. Lewis re-formed his trio with Cleveland Eaton (bass) and Maurice White (later <br> with Earth, Wind & Fire; drums). Reunited with Young and Holt in 1983. | | |
| | | | **THE RAMSEY LEWIS TRIO:** | | |
| 10/10/64 | **63** | 6 | 1 Something You Got ...........................[I] *Hot* | | Argo 5481 |
| 8/21/65 | **2**³ | 14 | 2 **The "In" Crowd**...............................[I] | *5* | Argo 5506 |
| 11/27/65 | **6** | 10 | 3 **Hang On Sloopy**..............................[I] | *11* | Cadet 5522 |
| 2/05/66 | **29** | 6 | 4 A Hard Day's Night............................[I] | *29* | Cadet 5525 |
| | | | **RAMSEY LEWIS:** | | |
| 7/30/66 | **3** | 14 | 5 **Wade In The Water**..........................[I] | *19* | Cadet 5541 |
| 10/22/66 | **30** | 5 | 6 Up Tight...........................................[I] | *49* | Cadet 5547 |
| 9/27/69 | **37** | 6 | 7 Julia................................................[I] <br> written by John Lennon & Paul McCartney | *76* | Cadet 5640 |
| 9/02/72 | **44** | 3 | 8 Slipping Into Darkness.............................. | *101* | Columbia 45634 |
| 11/30/74+ | **61** | 11 | 9 Hot Dawgit........................................[I] <br> RAMSEY LEWIS and EARTH, WIND & FIRE | *50* | Columbia 10056 |
| 3/15/75 | **20** | 12 | 10 Sun Goddess .....................................[I] <br> RAMSEY LEWIS and EARTH, WIND & FIRE | *44* | Columbia 10103 |
| 11/29/75+ | **50** | 13 | 11 What's The Name Of This Funk (Spider Man)...... | *69* | Columbia 10235 |
| 4/10/76 | **99** | 1 | 12 Don't It Feel Good ................................ | | Columbia 10293 |
| 8/07/76 | **88** | 3 | 13 Brazilica.......................................... | | Columbia 10382 |
| 7/09/77 | **85** | 3 | 14 Spring High....................................... | | Columbia 10571 |
| 6/13/81 | **93** | 3 | 15 So Much More..................................... | | Columbia 02043 |
| 3/06/82 | **64** | 6 | 16 You Never Know .................................. <br> vocals by Alice Echols & Morris Gray | | Columbia 02704 |
| 7/21/84 | **56** | 9 | 17 The Two Of Us.................................... <br> vocals by Nancy Wilson & Daryl Coley | | Columbia 04524 |
| 12/07/85 | **88** | 2 | 18 This Ain't No Fantasy ............................ | | Columbia 05640 |
| 6/27/87 | **67** | 9 | 19 7-11............................................[I] | | Columbia 07220 |
| | | | **SMILEY LEWIS** <br> Born Overton Amos Lemons on 7/5/13 in DeQuincy, Louisiana. Died of cancer on <br> 10/7/66 (53). Vocalist/guitarist. First recorded for DeLuxe in 1947, as Smiling <br> Lewis. His version of "Shame Shame Shame" was used in the 1956 movie soundtrack <br> "Baby Doll". | | |
| 9/06/52 | **10** | 2 | 1 Bells Are Ringing ............................... <br> THE SMILEY LEWIS BAND <br> Best Seller #10 | | Imperial 5194 |
| 9/03/55 | **2**² | 18 | 2 I Hear You Knocking............................... <br> Best Seller #2 / Jockey #2 / Juke Box #3 <br> with the Dave Bartholomew Band | | Imperial 5356 |

| DEBUT DATE | PEAK POS | WKS CHR | ARTIST — Record Title | POP POS | Label & Number |
|---|---|---|---|---|---|
| | | | **SMILEY LEWIS — Continued** | | |
| 3/31/56 | **11** | 3 | 3 One Night ............................................ | | Imperial 5380 |
| | | | Jockey #11 | | |
| 6/16/56 | **9** | 2 | 4 **Please Listen To Me** .................................. | | Imperial 5389 |
| | | | Jockey #9 | | |
| | | | **WEBSTER LEWIS** | | |
| | | | Keyboardist from Baltimore. Toured with Dionne Warwick, Sonny Rollins and Dizzy Gillespie. Former conductor for Lola Falana. Leader of the 65-piece New England Conservatory Post-Pop Orchestra, member of the Piano Choir. Assistant Dean, Director of Community Service at the New England Conservatory of Music. | | |
| 2/09/80 | **41** | 13 | 1 Give Me Some Emotion................................. | *107* | Epic 50832 |
| 3/28/81 | **64** | 8 | 2 Let Me Be The One ..................................... | | Epic 51014 |
| 6/20/81 | **69** | 5 | 3 Kemo-Kimo.............................................. | | Epic 02112 |
| | | | **LIFESTYLE** | | |
| 6/04/77 | **86** | 3 | 1 Katrina ................................................. | | MCA 40722 |
| | | | **JIMMY LIGGINS** | | |
| | | | Born on 10/14/22 in Newby, Oklahoma. Vocalist/guitarist. Younger brother of Joe Liggins. To San Diego in 1932. Professional boxer; trained with Archie Moore. Driver for Joe Liggins band. Self-taught on guitar. First recorded for Specialty in 1947. Own Duplex Records from 1958-78. To Durham, North Carolina in 1975; operated music school. | | |
| 7/31/48 | **7** | 4 | 1 **Tear Drop Blues** ..................................... | | Specialty 521 |
| | | | Juke Box #7 / Best Seller #14 | | |
| 4/16/49 | **15** | 1 | 2 Careful Love ........................................... | | Specialty 319 |
| | | | Best Seller #15 | | |
| 12/03/49 | **9** | 4 | 3 **Don't Put Me Down** ................................. | | Specialty 339 |
| | | | Best Seller #9 / Juke Box #9 | | |
| 10/03/53 | **4** | 8 | 4 **Drunk** ................................................ | | Specialty 470 |
| | | | **JIMMY LIGGINS & HIS 3-D MUSIC** | | |
| | | | Juke Box #4 / Best Seller #7 | | |
| | | | **JOE LIGGINS & HIS "HONEYDRIPPERS"** ★★**142**★★ | | |
| | | | Born in 1915 in Guthrie, Oklahoma; died of a stroke on 8/1/87. Vocalist/pianist/composer/leader. Pianist from age 8. Moved to San Diego in 1932. Achieved "big band" sound with small combos. Recording actively until his death. | | |
| 8/11/45 | **1**¹⁸ | 27 | 1 **The Honeydripper** ................................... | *13* | Exclusive 207 |
| | | | written by Liggins in 1942; a reported million-seller | | |
| 11/10/45 | **2**¹ | 4 | 2 **Left A Good Deal In Mobile** ......................... | | Exclusive 208 |
| 1/05/46 | **2**² | 12 | 3 **Got A Right To Cry**................................ [I] | *12* | Exclusive 210 |
| 10/05/46 | **3** | 9 | 4 **Tanya**................................................ | | Exclusive 231 |
| 8/09/47 | **3** | 2 | 5 **Blow Mr. Jackson** .................................... | | Exclusive 244 |
| 7/10/48 | **7** | 1 | 6 **Sweet Georgia Brown/** | | |
| | | | Juke Box #7 | | |
| 7/31/48 | **9** | 1 | 7 **Dripper's Blues** ..................................... | | Exclusive 271 |
| | | | Juke Box #9 | | |
| 8/28/48 | **14** | 1 | 8 Sweet And Lovely/ | | |
| | | | Juke Box #14 | | |
| 10/02/48 | **9** | 2 | 9 **Roll 'Em** ............................................. | | Exclusive 41 |
| | | | Juke Box #9 | | |
| 10/16/48 | **7** | 1 | 10 **The Darktown Strutters' Ball** ...................... | | Exclusive 49 |
| | | | Juke Box #7 | | |
| 2/18/50 | **4** | 5 | 11 **Rag Mop** ............................................. | | Specialty 350 |
| | | | Juke Box #4 / Best Seller #6 | | |
| 5/06/50 | **1**¹³ | 25 | 12 **Pink Champagne** ..................................... | *30* | Specialty 355 |
| | | | Juke Box #1(13) / Best Seller #1(11) | | |
| 1/13/51 | **5** | 3 | 13 **Little Joe's Boogie**................................ [I] | | Specialty 379 |
| | | | Juke Box #5 | | |
| 2/17/51 | **9** | 1 | 14 **Frankie Lee** ......................................... | | Specialty 392 |
| | | | Juke Box #9 | | |
| | | | **LIGHTNIN' SLIM** | | |
| | | | Blues guitarist, born Otis Hicks on 3/13/13 in St. Louis; died of cancer on 7/27/74 in Detroit. Also see Slim Harpo. | | |
| 11/30/59 | **23** | 1 | 1 Rooster Blues............................................ | | Excello 2169 |
| | | | **THE LIMIT** | | |
| | | | Dutch band. | | |
| 9/18/82 | **44** | 8 | 1 She's So Divine.......................................... | | Arista 1003 |
| 12/01/84 | **81** | 5 | 2 Say Yeah ............................................... | | Portrait 04671 |

| DEBUT DATE | PEAK POS | WKS CHR | ARTIST — Record Title | POP POS | Label & Number |
|---|---|---|---|---|---|
| | | | **LIMMIE & FAMILY COOKIN'** | | |
| | | | Pop family trio from Canton, Ohio: sisters Martha Stewart and Jimmy Thomas, and brother Limmie Snell. | | |
| 1/06/73 | 42 | 4 | 1 You Can Do Magic ........................................ | 84 | Avco 4602 |
| | | | **LINK-EDDY COMBO** | | |
| | | | Instrumental studio group from Los Angeles. Formed by Lincoln Mayorga & Eddie Cobb. | | |
| 5/01/61 | 28 | 2 | 1 Big Mr. C. .................................................. | | Reprise 20002 |
| | | | **LINX** | | |
| | | | London group consisting of David Grant (vocals), Peter "Sketch" Martin (bass), Bob Carter (keyboards) and Andy Duncan (drums). | | |
| 2/28/81 | 27 | 14 | 1 You're Lying ............................................. | | Chrysalis 2461 |
| 6/06/81 | 45 | 9 | 2 Together We Can Shine ............................... | | Chrysalis 2521 |
| | | | **LIPPS, INC.** | | |
| | | | Funk project from Minneapolis formed by producer/songwriter/multi-instrumentalist Steven Greenberg. Vocals by Miss Black Minnesota U.S.A. of 1976, Cynthia Johnson. | | |
| 3/22/80 | 2⁵ | 22 | 1▲Funkytown................................................ | 1 | Casablanca 2233 |
| 8/16/80 | 85 | 2 | 2 Rock It..................................................... | 64 | Casablanca 2281 |
| 10/18/80 | 29 | 14 | 3 How Long ................................................. | | Casablanca 2303 |
| 11/28/81 | 70 | 8 | 4 Hold Me Down .......................................... | | Casablanca 2342 |
| 9/17/83 | 78 | 4 | 5 Addicted To The Night ............................... | | Casablanca 812900 |
| | | | **LIQUID GOLD** | | |
| | | | English disco quartet led by vocalist Ellie Hope. | | |
| 8/27/83 | 52 | 7 | 1 What's She Got .......................................... | 86 | Critique 701 |
| | | | **LISA LISA & CULT JAM with FULL FORCE** | | |
| | | | Harlem trio: Lisa Velez, Mike Hughes and Alex "Spanador" Moseley. All of their hits were produced by Full Force. | | |
| 5/18/85 | 6 | 22 | 1 I Wonder If I Take You Home ....................... | 34 | Columbia 04886 |
| 11/09/85 | 40 | 25 | 2 Can You Feel The Beat................................. | 69 | Columbia 05669 |
| 6/21/86 | 3 | 23 | 3 All Cried Out ........................................... | 8 | Columbia 05844 |
| | | | featuring Paul Anthony & Bow Legged Lou | | |
| 4/04/87 | 1² | 17 | 4 Head To Toe............................................. | 1 | Columbia 07008 |
| | | | LISA LISA & CULT JAM | | |
| 8/01/87 | 1¹ | 17 | 5 Lost In Emotion......................................... | 1 | Columbia 07267 |
| | | | LISA LISA & CULT JAM | | |
| 11/07/87+ | 7 | 15 | 6 Someone To Love Me For Me ......................... | 78 | Columbia 07619 |
| 3/12/88 | 9 | 12 | 7 Everything Will B-Fine................................ | | Columbia 07737 |
| | | | **LITTLE ANTHONY & THE IMPERIALS** | | |
| | | | Group formed in 1957 in Brooklyn. Consisted of Anthony Gourdine (b: 1/8/40), Ernest Wright, Jr., Tracy Lord, Glouster Rogers and Clarence Collins. Anthony first recorded on Winley in 1955 with The DuPonts. Formed The Chesters in 1957, who changed name to The Imperials in 1958. Sammy Strain, who joined group in 1964, left in 1975 to join The O'Jays. | | |
| 9/08/58 | 2¹ | 12 | 1 Tears On My Pillow.................................... | 4 | End 1027 |
| 1/19/59 | 24 | 1 | 2 So Much .................................................. | 87 | End 1036 |
| 1/18/60 | 14 | 10 | 3 Shimmy, Shimmy, Ko-Ko-Bop ......................... | 24 | End 1060 |
| 8/22/64 | 15 | 10 | 4 I'm On The Outside (Looking In)..................... | Hot | DCP 1104 |
| 1/30/65 | 22 | 1 | 5 Goin' Out Of My Head ................................ | 6 | DCP 1119 |
| 2/06/65 | 3 | 11 | 6 Hurt So Bad ............................................ | 10 | DCP 1128 |
| 7/31/65 | 15 | 10 | 7 Take Me Back............................................ | 16 | DCP 1136 |
| 11/06/65 | 23 | 5 | 8 I Miss You So ........................................... | 34 | DCP 1149 |
| 8/23/69 | 38 | 4 | 9 Out Of Sight, Out Of Mind ......................... | 52 | United Art. 50552 |
| 11/21/70+ | 32 | 10 | 10 Help Me Find A Way (To Say I Love You) .......... | 92 | United Art. 50720 |
| 4/27/74 | 25 | 13 | 11 I'm Falling In Love With You........................ | 86 | Avco 4635 |
| 4/05/75 | 79 | 5 | 12 Hold On (Just A Little Bit Longer) .................... | 106 | Avco 4651 |
| | | | shown as: ANTHONY & THE IMPERIALS | | |
| | | | **LITTLE BEAVER** | | |
| | | | Born Willie Hale on 8/15/45 in Forest City, Arkansas. Singer/guitarist. Played professionally from age 13. With Birdlegs & Pauline in 1962, session work from 1964. First recorded for Phil-L.A. Of Soul. Played guitar on Betty Wright's "Clean-up Woman". | | |
| 2/05/72 | 48 | 1 | 1 Joey ...................................................... | | Cat 1977 |
| 1/12/74 | 72 | 9 | 2 Wish I Had A Little Girl Like You.................... | | Cat 1991 |

| DEBUT DATE | PEAK POS | WKS CHR | ARTIST — Record Title | POP POS | Label & Number |
|---|---|---|---|---|---|
| | | | **LITTLE BEAVER — Continued** | | |
| 8/17/74 | **2**¹ | 19 | 3 **Party Down - Part 1**............................ | | Cat 1993 |
| 3/15/75 | **34** | 10 | 4 Let The Good Times Roll Everybody ................ | | Cat 1995 |
| 6/19/76 | **91** | 4 | 5 Little Girl Blue ........................................ | | Cat 2003 |
| | | | **LITTLE CAESAR** | | |
| | | | Born Horace "Harry" Caesar on 2/18/26 in Pittsburgh. Vocalist/actor. To Youngstown, Ohio at an early age. Acted in many films and television series ("Tarzan", "Hill Street Blues" and "Cagney & Lacey"). With the Turbans and Robins vocal groups. | | |
| 10/11/52 | **5** | 8 | 1 **Goodbye Baby** ........................................ Best Seller #5 instrumental backing by Que Martyn | | Hollywood 235 |
| | | | **LITTLE CAESAR & THE ROMANS** | | |
| | | | Los Angeles quintet: David "Little Caesar" Johnson, Carl Burnett, Johnny Simmons, Early Harris and Leroy Sanders. Formed as the Up-Fronts, all were veterans of other groups. | | |
| 7/10/61 | **28** | 2 | 1 Those Oldies But Goodies (Remind Me Of You).... | 9 | Del-Fi 4158 |
| | | | **LITTLE ESTHER - see ESTHER PHILLIPS** | | |
| | | | **LITTLE EVA** | | |
| | | | Born Eva Narcissus Boyd on 6/29/45 in Bellhaven, North Carolina. Discovered by songwriters Carole King and Gerry Goffin. | | |
| 8/04/62 | **1**³ | 12 | 1 **The Loco-Motion**....................................... | 1 | Dimension 1000 |
| 11/24/62 | **6** | 10 | 2 **Keep Your Hands Off My Baby** ..................... | 12 | Dimension 1003 |
| 2/23/63 | **16** | 9 | 3 Let's Turkey Trot...................................... | 20 | Dimension 1006 |
| | | | **LITTLE JOE BLUE** | | |
| | | | Born Joseph Valery, Jr. on 9/23/34 in Vicksburg, Mississippi. Singer/guitarist. Raised in Tallulah, Louisiana in 1951. Formed own band in the late 50s. To Los Angeles in 1961. With James Brown Revue in 1975. | | |
| 7/23/66 | **40** | 1 | 1 Dirty Work Going On ................................... | 111 | Checker 1141 |
| | | | **LITTLE JUNIOR - see LITTLE JUNIOR PARKER** | | |
| | | | **LITTLE MAC & THE BOSS SOUNDS** | | |
| | | | Band from Ranstoff, North Carolina. | | |
| 12/25/65+ | **37** | 3 | 1 In The Midnight Hour................................. [I] | | Atlantic 2309 |
| | | | **LITTLE MILTON** ★★83★★ | | |
| | | | Born Milton Campbell, Jr. on 9/7/34 in Inverness, Mississippi. Blues singer/guitarist. Own band in Memphis, in 1951. Recorded with Ike Turner for Sun Records from 1953-54. In the 1972 concert film "Wattstax". Also see Herbie Mann. | | |
| 1/13/62 | **14** | 5 | 1 So Mean To Me ......................................... | | Checker 994 |
| 1/02/65 | **86** | 4 | 2 Blind Man ................................................ | Hot | Checker 1096 |
| 3/27/65 | **1**³ | 15 | 3 **We're Gonna Make It**.................................. | 25 | Checker 1105 |
| 6/12/65 | **4** | 10 | 4 **Who's Cheating Who?**................................. | 43 | Checker 1113 |
| 9/03/66 | **45** | 2 | 5 Man Loves Two .......................................... | 127 | Checker 1149 |
| 1/21/67 | **7** | 15 | 6 **Feel So Bad** ............................................ | 91 | Checker 1162 |
| 6/03/67 | **31** | 4 | 7 I'll Never Turn My Back On You...................... | | Checker 1172 |
| 12/16/67+ | **45** | 5 | 8 More And More ......................................... | | Checker 1189 |
| 10/12/68 | **27** | 11 | 9 Let Me Down Easy ...................................... | | Checker 1208 |
| 1/18/69 | **13** | 8 | 10 Grits Ain't Groceries (All Around The World) ..... | 73 | Checker 1212 |
| 4/26/69 | **13** | 8 | 11 Just A Little Bit........................................ | 97 | Checker 1217 |
| 7/19/69 | **13** | 9 | 12 Let's Get Together ...................................... | | Checker 1225 |
| 10/04/69 | **18** | 7 | 13 Poor Man ................................................. | 103 | Checker 1221 |
| 12/27/69+ | **10** | 11 | 14 **If Walls Could Talk** .................................. | 71 | Checker 1226 |
| 4/11/70 | **6** | 9 | 15 **Baby I Love You** ...................................... | 82 | Checker 1227 |
| 7/25/70 | **22** | 5 | 16 Somebody's Changin' My Sweet Baby's Mind...... | | Checker 1231 |
| 5/01/71 | **37** | 3 | 17 I Play Dirty .............................................. | | Checker 1239 |
| 10/02/71 | **41** | 2 | 18 If That Ain't A Reason (For Your Woman To Leave You) ............................................ | | Stax 0100 |
| 2/05/72 | **9** | 9 | 19 **That's What Love Will Make You Do** ............. | 59 | Stax 0111 |
| 9/15/73 | **51** | 9 | 20 What It Is ................................................ | | Stax 0174 |
| 2/23/74 | **51** | 11 | 21 Tin Pan Alley ........................................... | | Stax 0191 |
| 5/11/74 | **31** | 12 | 22 Behind Closed Doors.................................... | | Stax 0210 |
| 11/02/74 | **38** | 11 | 23 Let Me Back In .......................................... | | Stax 0229 |
| 5/24/75 | **34** | 13 | 24 If You Talk In You Sleep............................... | | Stax 0238 |

| DEBUT DATE | PEAK POS | WKS CHR | | ARTIST — Record Title | POP POS | Label & Number |
|---|---|---|---|---|---|---|
| | | | | **LITTLE MILTON — Continued** | | |
| 4/24/76 | **15** | 13 | 25 | Friend Of Mine.................... | | Glades 1734 |
| 1/08/77 | **94** | 2 | 26 | Baby It Ain't No Way .................... | | Glades 1738 |
| 3/12/77 | **59** | 11 | 27 | Just One Step.................... | | Glades 1741 |
| 8/20/77 | **47** | 12 | 28 | Loving You (Is The Best Thing To Happen To Me) | | Glades 1743 |
| 4/16/83 | **89** | 4 | 29 | Age Ain't Nothin' But A Number .................... | | MCA 52184 |

**LITTLE RICHARD**  ★★82★★

Born Richard Wayne Penniman on 12/5/32 in Macon, Georgia. R&B/rock and roll singer/pianist. Talent contest win led to first recordings for RCA-Victor in 1951. Worked with the Tempo Toppers, 1953-55. Earned degree in Theology in 1961 and was ordained a minister. Left R&B for Gospel music, 1959-62 and again in mid-70s. The key figure in the transition from R&B to rock 'n' roll. Appeared in 3 early rock & roll films: "Don't Knock The Rock", "The Girl Can't Help It" and "Mister Rock 'n' Roll; and in the 1986 film "Down & Out In Beverly Hills". Also see New Edition.

| DEBUT DATE | PEAK POS | WKS CHR | | ARTIST — Record Title | POP POS | Label & Number |
|---|---|---|---|---|---|---|
| 11/26/55+ | **2**[6] | 21 | 1 | **Tutti-Frutti**.................... | *17* | Specialty 561 |
| | | | | Best Seller #2 / Jockey #2 / Juke Box #2 | | |
| 4/07/56 | **1**[8] | 16 | 2 | **Long Tall Sally/** | *6* | |
| | | | | Juke Box #1(8) / Best Seller #1(6) / Jockey #1(5) | | |
| 4/14/56 | **2**[2] | 12 | 3 | **Slippin' And Slidin' (Peepin' And Hidin')** ..... | *33* | Specialty 572 |
| | | | | Jockey #2 | | |
| 6/30/56 | **1**[2] | 17 | 4 | **Rip It Up/** | *17* | |
| | | | | Best Seller #1(2) / Juke Box #1(1) / Jockey #2 | | |
| 7/07/56 | **8** | 8 | 5 | **Ready Teddy** .................... | *44* | Specialty 579 |
| | | | | Jockey #8 | | |
| 10/27/56 | **9** | 5 | 6 | **She's Got It/** | | |
| | | | | Jockey #9 / Best Seller #15 | | |
| 11/03/56 | **7** | 3 | 7 | **Heebie Jeebies** .................... | | Specialty 584 |
| | | | | Juke Box #7 | | |
| 12/29/56+ | **7** | 9 | 8 | **The Girl Can't Help It/** | *49* | |
| | | | | Juke Box #7 / Jockey #8 / Best Seller #11 | | |
| | | | | from the Jayne Mansfield film of the same title | | |
| 1/19/57 | **13** | 1 | 9 | All Around The World.................... | | Specialty 591 |
| | | | | Jockey #13 | | |
| 3/16/57 | **1**[2] | 13 | 10 | **Lucille/** | *21* | |
| | | | | Juke Box #1 / Best Seller #2 / Jockey #2 | | |
| 4/13/57 | **3** | 11 | 11 | **Send Me Some Lovin'** .................... | *54* | Specialty 598 |
| | | | | Jockey #3 | | |
| 6/17/57 | **2**[2] | 12 | 12 | **Jenny, Jenny/** | *10* | |
| | | | | Best Seller #2 / Jockey #5 / Juke Box #10 | | |
| 6/24/57 | **6** | 6 | 13 | **Miss Ann** .................... | *56* | Specialty 606 |
| | | | | Jockey #6 | | |
| 9/30/57 | **2**[1] | 9 | 14 | **Keep A Knockin'**.................... | *8* | Specialty 611 |
| | | | | Jockey #2 / Best Seller #5 | | |
| 2/24/58 | **4** | 8 | 15 | **Good Golly, Miss Molly** .................... | *10* | Specialty 624 |
| | | | | Jockey #4 / Best Seller #6 | | |
| 6/30/58 | **15** | 4 | 16 | **Ooh! My Soul/** | *31* | |
| | | | | Best Seller #15 | | |
| | | 4 | 17 | **True, Fine Mama**.................... | *68* | Specialty 633 |
| | | | | Best Seller flip | | |
| 9/22/58 | **12** | 7 | 18 | Baby Face.................... | *41* | Specialty 645 |
| | | | | Jockey #12 / Hot R&B #12 | | |
| | | | | there were 4 Top 10 versions of this tune in 1926 | | |
| 7/18/64 | **82** | 4 | 19 | Bama Lama Bama Loo .................... | *Hot* | Specialty 692 |
| 11/20/65 | **12** | 8 | 20 | I Don't Know What You've Got But It's Got Me - Part I.................... | *92* | Vee-Jay 698 |
| 8/27/66 | **41** | 4 | 21 | Poor Dog (Who Can't Wag His Own Tail) ........... | *121* | Okeh 7251 |
| 6/13/70 | **28** | 4 | 22 | Freedom Blues.................... | *47* | Reprise 0907 |
| 8/11/73 | **71** | 9 | 23 | In The Middle Of The Night .................... | | Green Mt. 413 |

**LITTLE ROYAL & THE SWINGMASTERS**

| DEBUT DATE | PEAK POS | WKS CHR | | ARTIST — Record Title | POP POS | Label & Number |
|---|---|---|---|---|---|---|
| 5/27/72 | **15** | 13 | 1 | **Jealous**.................... | | Tri-Us 912 |
| 7/14/73 | **88** | 2 | 2 | I'm Glad To Do It .................... | | Tri-Us 916 |

**LITTLE SISTER**

Female trio organized by Sly Stone, consisting of Vanetta Stewart (Sly's sister), Mary Rand and Elva Melton.

| DEBUT DATE | PEAK POS | WKS CHR | | ARTIST — Record Title | POP POS | Label & Number |
|---|---|---|---|---|---|---|
| 2/28/70 | **4** | 13 | 1 | **You're The One - Part I** .................... | *22* | Stone Flower 9000 |
| 11/28/70+ | **8** | 14 | 2 | **Somebody's Watching You/** | *32* | |
| 2/19/72 | **44** | 2 | 3 | Stanga .................... | | Stone Flower 9001 |

| DEBUT DATE | PEAK POS | WKS CHR | ARTIST — Record Title | POP POS | Label & Number |
|---|---|---|---|---|---|
| | | | **LITTLE WALTER** ★★136★★ | | |
| | | | Born Marion Walter Jacobs on 5/1/30 in Marksville, Louisiana. Died on 2/15/68 (injuries from street fight). Vocalist/guitarist/harmonica player. Left home at age 12 to work in New Orleans. To Chicago in 1946. First recorded for Ora-Nelle in 1947. Important figure in the Chicago blues scene. Toured England with the Rolling Stones in 1964. Also see Muddy Waters. | | |
| | | | **LITTLE WALTER with His Night Cats:** | | |
| 9/06/52 | 1⁸ | 20 | 1 **Juke**........................................................ [I] | | Checker 758 |
| | | | Juke Box #1(8) / Best Seller #1(1) | | |
| 12/13/52 | 2² | 10 | 2 **Sad Hours/** | | |
| | | | Juke Box #2 / Best Seller #3 | | |
| 1/03/53 | 6 | 6 | 3 **Mean Old World**.................................... | | Checker 764 |
| | | | Juke Box #6 / Best Seller #10 | | |
| | | | **LITTLE WALTER & his Jukes:** | | |
| 4/25/53 | 10 | 2 | 4 **Tell Me, Mama/** | | |
| | | | Juke Box #10 | | |
| 5/16/53 | 8 | 2 | 5 **Off The Wall** ...................................... | | Checker 770 |
| | | | Juke Box #8 | | |
| 10/10/53 | 2² | 11 | 6 **Blues With A Feeling** .......................... | | Checker 780 |
| | | | Juke Box #2 / Best Seller #6 | | |
| 1/02/54 | 2³ | 12 | 7 **You're So Fine**.................................... | | Checker 786 |
| | | | Juke Box #2 / Best Seller #4 | | |
| 5/01/54 | 8 | 1 | 8 **Oh, Baby**............................................. | | Checker 793 |
| | | | Juke Box #8 | | |
| 9/18/54 | 8 | 4 | 9 **You Better Watch Yourself** ........................ | | Checker 799 |
| | | | Juke Box #8 / Best Seller #10 | | |
| 12/18/54 | 6 | 4 | 10 **Last Night** ...................................... | | Checker 805 |
| | | | Juke Box #6 | | |
| 3/12/55 | 1⁵ | 19 | 11 **My Babe** ............................................. | *106* | Checker 811 |
| | | | Juke Box #1(5) / Best Seller #1(4) / Jockey #1(2) based on the spiritual tune "This Train" | | |
| 7/09/55 | 6 | 2 | 12 **Roller Coaster** .................................... | | Checker 817 |
| | | | Juke Box #6 | | |
| 3/31/56 | 7 | 3 | 13 **Who** .................................................... | | Checker 833 |
| | | | Juke Box #7 / Best Seller #13 | | |
| 10/20/58 | 6 | 14 | 14 **Key To The Highway** ................................ | | Checker 904 |
| 9/14/59 | 25 | 2 | 15 Everything Gonna Be Alright........................ | | Checker 930 |
| | | | LITTLE WALTER | | |
| | | | **RICH LITTLE** | | |
| | | | Comedian/impressionist. | | |
| 6/12/82 | 39 | 8 | 1 President Rap's ...................................... [N] | *105* | Boardwalk 99901 |
| | | | **LITTLE WILLIE LITTLEFIELD** | | |
| | | | Born on 9/16/31 in El Campo, Texas. Vocalist/pianist/guitarist. First recorded for Eddie's in 1946. To Los Angeles in 1949. Recorded original version of "Kansas City" as "K.C. Lovin'", for Federal in 1952. | | |
| 8/20/49 | 3 | 13 | 1 **It's Midnight**........................................ | | Modern 686 |
| | | | Best Seller #3 / Juke Box #3 | | |
| 11/19/49 | 5 | 2 | 2 **Farewell** ............................................. | | Modern 709 |
| | | | Juke Box #5 | | |
| 8/25/51 | 10 | 1 | 3 **I've Been Lost** ...................................... | | Modern 801 |
| | | | Juke Box #10 | | |
| | | | **LIVE** | | |
| 12/26/81+ | 65 | 8 | 1 Strut Your Stuff...................................... | | T.S.O.B. 2006 |
| | | | **LIVIN' PROOF** | | |
| | | | Chicago trio formed in 1976 as Flavor. Consisted of Stan Sheppard and twin brothers Steven and Sterling Rice from Elkhart, Illinois. Also recorded as Triple "S" Connection. Sheppard later formed Skool Boyz. | | |
| 12/24/77+ | 34 | 14 | 1 You And I ............................................ | | Jupar 532 |
| | | | **LIVING IN A BOX** | | |
| | | | Soul-styled, pop trio from England: Richard Darbyshire (vocals), Marcus Vere (keyboards) and Anthony "Tich" Critchlow (drums). | | |
| 7/18/87 | 74 | 9 | 1 Living In A Box........................................ | *17* | Chrysalis 43104 |
| | | | **LIVING PROOF** | | |
| | | | Detroit quintet. | | |
| 3/21/87 | 85 | 4 | 1 Hold On To Your Dreams ............................ | | Fantasy 977 |

| DEBUT DATE | PEAK POS | WKS CHR | ARTIST — Record Title | POP POS | Label & Number |
|---|---|---|---|---|---|
| | | | **L.L. COOL J** | | |
| | | | Real name: James Todd Smith. 19-year-old rap artist from Queens, New York. | | |
| 11/23/85+ | **15** | 18 | 1 I Can't Live Without My Radio........................ | | Def Jam 05665 |
| 3/08/86 | **17** | 15 | 2 Rock The Bells ............................................... | | Def Jam 05840 |
| 6/21/86 | **59** | 7 | 3 You'll Rock ..................................................... | | Def Jam 06061 |
| 5/23/87 | **4** | 14 | 4 I'm Bad ......................................................... | | Def Jam 07120 |
| 8/08/87 | **1**¹ | 13 | 5 I Need Love.................................................... | *14* | Def Jam 07350 |
| 2/06/88 | **12** | 14 | 6 Going Back To Cali........................................ | *31* | Def Jam 07679 |
| | | | from the film "Less Than Zero" | | |
| | | | **LOCKSMITH** | | |
| | | | Former sidemen with Grover Washington, Jr. Consisted of John Blake, Jr., Richard "Lee" Steacker, James "Sid" Simmons, Tyrone Brown, Leonard "Doc" Gibbs, and Millard "Pete" Vinson. | | |
| 8/23/80 | **49** | 10 | 1 Unlock The Funk ........................................... | | Arista 0543 |
| | | | **JULIE LOCO - see LABYRINTH** | | |
| | | | **LOGG** | | |
| 8/29/81 | **80** | 4 | 1 I Know You Will............................................. | | Salsoul 2146 |
| | | | **KENNY LOGGINS** | | |
| | | | Pop singer/guitarist, born on 1/7/48 in Everett, Washington. In duo with Jim Messina from 1972-76. Also see Donna Summer. | | |
| 1/05/80 | **19** | 14 | 1 This Is It....................................................... | *11* | Columbia 11109 |
| 1/15/83 | **71** | 8 | 2 Heart To Heart ............................................. | *15* | Columbia 03377 |
| | | | **LAURIE LONDON** | | |
| | | | Male vocalist, born on 1/19/44 in London. Recorded only hit record at age 13. | | |
| 4/07/58 | **3** | 11 | 1●He's Got The Whole World (In His Hands)....... | *1* | Capitol 3891 |
| | | | Best Seller #3 / Jockey #3 | | |
| | | | traditional Gospel song | | |
| | | | **SHORTY LONG** | | |
| | | | Born Frederick Earl Long on 5/20/40 in Birmingham, Alabama. Singer/songwriter/pianist. Moved to Detroit in 1959. First recorded for Tri-Phi in 1962. Drowned on 6/29/69 in Ontario, Canada. | | |
| 10/01/66 | **42** | 9 | 1 Function At The Junction ............................. | *97* | Soul 35021 |
| 3/09/68 | **42** | 5 | 2 Night Fo' Last............................................... | *75* | Soul 35040 |
| 6/15/68 | **4** | 10 | 3 Here Comes The Judge............................[N] | *8* | Soul 35044 |
| | | | **WILBERT LONGMIRE** | | |
| | | | Singer/guitarist from Cincinnati. Studied to be a barber. | | |
| 2/16/80 | **92** | 3 | 1 Music Speaks Louder Than Words................... | | Tap.Zee 11189 |
| | | | **LOOSE CHANGE** | | |
| | | | Female trio consisting of Leah Gwin, Donna Beene and Becky Anderson. Produced by Tom Moulton. | | |
| 1/05/80 | **54** | 6 | 1 Straight From The Heart ............................... | | Casablanca 2219 |
| | | | **LOOSE ENDS** | | |
| | | | London trio formed in 1985: Carl McIntosh (lead vocals, guitar), Steve Nichol and Jayne Eugene. | | |
| 5/04/85 | **1**¹ | 21 | 1 Hangin' On A String (Contemplating) ............ | *43* | MCA 52570 |
| 8/10/85 | **47** | 11 | 2 Choose Me .................................................... | | MCA 52637 |
| 8/09/86 | **18** | 14 | 3 Stay A Little While, Child .............................. | | MCA 52820 |
| 11/29/86+ | **1**¹ | 21 | 4 Slow Down .................................................... | | MCA 52976 |
| 5/02/87 | **32** | 13 | 5 You Can't Stop The Rain ............................... | | MCA 53060 |
| 9/05/87 | **58** | 8 | 6 Nights Of Pleasure........................................ | | MCA 53170 |
| 6/25/88 | **2**¹ | 17 | 7 Watching You................................................ | | MCA 53304 |
| | | | **TRINI LOPEZ** | | |
| | | | Born on 5/15/37 in Dallas. Pop-folk singer/guitarist. Discovered by Don Costa while performing at PJs nightclub in Los Angeles. | | |
| 9/07/63 | **12** | 7 | 1 If I Had A Hammer ....................................... | *3* | Reprise 20198 |
| | | | **JEFF LORBER** | | |
| | | | Lorber is a jazz fusion keyboardist. Los Angeles native White is a prominent session singer. | | |
| 2/16/85 | **31** | 15 | 1 Step By Step ................................................. | *105* | Arista 9307 |
| | | | **JEFF LORBER featuring Audrey Wheeler** | | |
| 10/18/86 | **17** | 18 | 2 Facts Of Love................................................ | *27* | Warner 28588 |
| | | | **JEFF LORBER featuring KARYN WHITE** | | |

| DEBUT DATE | PEAK POS | WKS CHR | ARTIST — Record Title | POP POS | Label & Number |
|---|---|---|---|---|---|
| | | | **JEFF LORBER — Continued** | | |
| 4/18/87 | 88 | 4 | 3  True Confessions ........................................... | | Warner 28446 |
| | | | JEFF LORBER & KARYN WHITE | | |
| | | | **C.M. LORD** | | |
| 1/09/82 | 89 | 6 | 1  Flashback.................................................... | | Montage 1209 |
| | | | **BRYAN LOREN** | | |
| 3/03/84 | 23 | 17 | 1  Lollipop Luv................................................. | *105* | Philly W. 99760 |
| 7/21/84 | 68 | 7 | 2  Do You Really Love Me ................................ | | Philly W. 99739 |
| | | | **GLORIA LORING - see CARL ANDERSON** | | |
| | | | **LOS POP TOPS** | | |
| | | | Vocal septet based in Spain. Lead singer Phil Tris is from the West Indies. | | |
| 9/14/68 | 35 | 7 | 1  Oh Lord, Why Lord........................................ | *78* | Calla 154 |
| | | | medley based on Pachelbel's "Canon in D Major" | | |
| | | | **THE LOST GENERATION** | | |
| | | | Chicago quartet: Lowrell Simon (lead), his brother Fred Simon, Larry Brownlee (of The C.O.D.'s) and Jesse Dean. Lowrell and Dean had been in vocal group the Vondells. Disbanded in 1974. Fred Simon and Brownlee were later in Mystique. Brownlee died in 1978. Lowrell began solo career in 1978; recorded as Lowrell. | | |
| 5/30/70 | 14 | 13 | 1  The Sly, Slick, And The Wicked....................... | 30 | Brunswick 55436 |
| 11/07/70 | 25 | 5 | 2  Wait A Minute .............................................. | *127* | Brunswick 55441 |
| 2/20/71 | 48 | 2 | 3  Someday .................................................... | | Brunswick 55445 |
| 7/03/71 | 35 | 6 | 4  Talking The Teen Age Language ...................... | | Brunswick 55453 |
| 9/14/74 | 65 | 7 | 5  Your Mission (If You Decide To Accept It) Pt. 1 ... | | Innovation 800 |
| | | | **LOVE & KISSES** | | |
| | | | Studio group assembled by European disco producer Alec Costandinos. Consisted of Don Daniels, Elaine Hill, Dianne Brooks and Jean Graham. | | |
| 6/03/78 | 23 | 12 | 1  Thank God It's Friday .................................... | 22 | Casablanca 925 |
| | | | from the film of the same title | | |
| | | | **LOVE BUG STARSKI** | | |
| | | | Kevin Smith from the Bronx. Rapper and deejay; worked at the Disco Fever club from 1979-85. | | |
| 5/25/85 | 68 | 7 | 1  Rappin' ...................................................... | | Atlantic 89566 |
| | | | **LOVE CHILDS AFRO CUBAN BLUES BAND** | | |
| | | | Studio group assembled by New York disco producer Michael Zager. | | |
| 7/05/75 | 48 | 9 | 1  Life And Death In G&A ............................. [I] | 90 | Roulette 7172 |
| | | | **LOVE COMMITTEE** | | |
| | | | Philadelphia group formerly known as the Ethics, led by Ronald "Tyson" Presson. | | |
| 3/20/76 | 32 | 9 | 1  Heaven Only Knows....................................... | | Ariola Am. 7609 |
| 11/19/77 | 57 | 11 | 2  Cheaters Never Win....................................... | | Gold Mind 4003 |
| 7/01/78 | 97 | 4 | 3  Law And Order ............................................ | | Gold Mind 4011 |
| | | | **THE LOVELITES** | | |
| | | | Group from Carver High in Chicago. Consisted of Patti Hamilton, sister Rozena Petty and Barbara Peterman. Peterman replaced by Ardell "Dell" McDaniel in 1968; Petty replaced by Joni Berlman in 1970. McDaniel replaced by Rhonda Grayson in 1971. Had own Lovelite label from 1970-73. Disbanded in 1973. | | |
| 11/08/69 | 15 | 15 | 1  How Can I Tell My Mom & Dad........................ | 60 | Uni 55181 |
| 1/16/71 | 36 | 12 | 2  My Conscience.............................................. | | Lovelite 01 |
| | | | **LOVE NOTES** | | |
| 6/17/57 | 13 | 1 | 1  United........................................................ | | Holiday 2605 |
| | | | Jockey #13 | | |
| | | | **LOVE, PEACE & HAPPINESS** | | |
| | | | One of the two vocal groups that were part of New Birth, Inc. (formerly known as The Nite-Liters). Consisted of Melvin Wilson, Leslie Wilson and Ann Bogan (formerly with Harvey Fuqua in the duo "Harvey & Ann"). Also see The New Birth. | | |
| 8/12/72 | 41 | 3 | 1  I Don't Want To Do Wrong ............................. | | RCA 0740 |
| | | | **LOVE PATROL** | | |
| 12/21/85+ | 69 | 9 | 1  Love Patrol ................................................. | | 4th & B'way 7419 |

| DEBUT DATE | PEAK POS | WKS CHR | ARTIST — Record Title | POP POS | Label & Number |
|---|---|---|---|---|---|
| | | | **LOVE UNLIMITED** | | |
| | | | Female trio from San Pedro, California: sisters Glodean & Linda James, and Diane Taylor. Barry White, who married Glodean on 7/4/74, was their manager and producer. Glodean recorded duets with Barry in 1981. | | |
| 3/25/72 | 6 | 14 | 1 ● Walkin' In The Rain With The One I Love....... | 14 | Uni 55319 |
| 7/14/73 | 70 | 7 | 2 Yes, We Finally Made It.................................... | 101 | 20th Century 2025 |
| 12/01/73+ | 35 | 13 | 3 It May Be Winter Outside, (But In My Heart It's Spring)..................... | 83 | 20th Century 2062 |
| | | | written by Barry White | | |
| 4/06/74 | 70 | 7 | 4 Under The Influence Of Love........................... | 76 | 20th Century 2082 |
| 11/09/74+ | 1¹ | 21 | 5 I Belong To You............................................... | 27 | 20th Century 2141 |
| 5/21/77 | 66 | 7 | 6 I Did It For Love............................................. | | Un. Gold 7001 |
| 9/29/79 | 45 | 13 | 7 High Steppin', Hip Dressin' Fella (You Got It Together)....................... | | Un. Gold 1409 |
| 3/01/80 | 96 | 2 | 8 I'm So Glad That I'm A Woman...................... | | Un. Gold 1412 |
| 8/16/80 | 71 | 5 | 9 If You Want Me, Say It ................................... | | Un. Gold 1417 |
| | | | **LOVE UNLIMITED ORCHESTRA** | | |
| | | | 40-piece orchestra formed by conductor/producer/arranger/songwriter/singer Barry White, to back Love Unlimited. The orchestra is also heard on some of White's solo hits. | | |
| 12/15/73+ | 10 | 16 | 1 ● Love's Theme .................................... [I] | 1 | 20th Century 2069 |
| 4/20/74 | 48 | 9 | 2 Rhapsody In White ..................................... [I] | 63 | 20th Century 2090 |
| 2/08/75 | 23 | 11 | 3 Satin Soul.................................................... [I] | 22 | 20th Century 2162 |
| 4/19/75 | 21 | 9 | 4 Share A Little Love In Your Heart.................... | | 20th Century 2183 |
| 5/24/75 | 22 | 13 | 5 Forever In Love ............................................ | | 20th Century 2197 |
| 5/15/76 | 91 | 3 | 6 Midnight Groove ........................................ [I] | 108 | 20th Century 2281 |
| 9/11/76 | 28 | 11 | 7 My Sweet Summer Suite............................. [I] | 48 | 20th Century 2301 |
| 1/22/77 | 15 | 12 | 8 Theme From King Kong (Pt. I) ..................... [I] | 68 | 20th Century 2325 |
| | | | from the Dino DeLaurentiis film "King Kong" | | |
| | | | **CANDACE LOVE** | | |
| | | | Chicago-born soprano. | | |
| 8/16/69 | 25 | 10 | 1 Uh! Uh! Boy, That's A No No ......................... | | Aquarius 4010 |
| | | | **LE JUAN LOVE** | | |
| 2/27/88 | 78 | 6 | 1 Everybody Say Yeah...................................... | | Luke Sky. 110 |
| | | | **MARY LOVE** | | |
| | | | Born Mary Ann Varney on 7/27/43 in Sacramento, California. | | |
| 8/27/66 | 48 | 2 | 1 Move A Little Closer ..................................... | | Modern 1020 |
| 11/30/68 | 46 | 2 | 2 The Hurt Is Just Beginning ........................... | | Josie 999 |
| | | | **RONNIE LOVE** | | |
| 1/16/61 | 15 | 3 | 1 Chills And Fever............................................ | 72 | Dot 16144 |
| | | | **RUDY LOVE & THE LOVE FAMILY** | | |
| 2/21/76 | 66 | 10 | 1 Does Your Mama Know ................................. | | Calla 107 |
| 10/09/76 | 75 | 7 | 2 Ain't Nuthin' Spooky .................................... | | Calla 112 |
| | | | **VIKKI LOVE - see NUANCE** | | |
| | | | **IKE LOVELY** | | |
| 12/22/73+ | 72 | 7 | 1 Fool's Hall Of Fame ...................................... | | Wand 11266 |
| | | | **THE LOVERS** | | |
| | | | Duo of Alden "Tarheel Slim" Bunn (b: 9/24/24, Bailey, NC; d: 8/21/77 of pneumonia) and wife Anna "Little Ann" Sandford. Bunn played guitar since age 12. With Gospel Four group, own Southern Harmoneers, the Selah Singers, Larks, and Wheels. Formed duo with wife in 1954. | | |
| 11/25/57 | 15 | 1 | 1 Darling It's Wonderful................................... | 48 | Lamp 2005 |
| | | | Jockey #15 with the Ray Ellis Orchestra | | |
| 8/24/59 | 20 | 8 | 2 It's Too Late ................................................. | | Fire 1000 |
| | | | TARHEEL SLIM & LITTLE ANN | | |
| | | | **MICHAEL LOVESMITH** | | |
| 7/16/83 | 80 | 6 | 1 Baby I Will.................................................... | | Motown 1685 |
| 8/10/85 | 82 | 4 | 2 Break The Ice................................................ | | Motown 1794 |

**264**

| DEBUT DATE | PEAK POS | WKS CHR | ARTIST — Record Title | POP POS | Label & Number |
|---|---|---|---|---|---|
| | | | **JIM LOWE** | | |
| | | | Born 5/7/27 in Springfield, Missouri. Vocalist/pianist/composer. Disc jockey in New York City when he recorded "Green Door". | | |
| 9/24/55 | **13** | 1 | 1 Maybelline .................................................... | | Dot 15407 |
| | | | Jockey #13 | | |
| 10/20/56 | **5** | 14 | 2 **Green Door** .................................................. | *1* | Dot 15486 |
| | | | Best Seller #5 / Juke Box #7 / Jockey #9 with Bob Davie on piano | | |
| | | | **LOWRELL** | | |
| | | | Lowrell Simon, lead singer of the Chicago quartet, The Lost Generation, from 1970-74. His brother Fred, also a member of The Lost Generation, was in Mystique. | | |
| 11/04/78 | **89** | 3 | 1 Overdose Of Love ...................................... | | AVI 235 |
| 10/06/79 | **32** | 15 | 2 Mellow, Mellow Right On ............................. | | AVI 300 |
| 5/17/80 | **87** | 3 | 3 You're Playing Dirty ................................... | | AVI 314 |
| 12/12/81+ | **58** | 10 | 4 Love Massage ............................................ | | Zoo York 1324 |
| | | | shown as: **LOWRELL SIMON** | | |
| | | | **L.T.D.** ★★163★★ | | |
| | | | Group from North Carolina, backed Sam & Dave. Acquired lead vocalist/drummer Jeffrey Osborne in Providence, Rhode Island. To California; back-up singer for Merry Clayton in 1971. Osborne left in 1980, replaced by Leslie Wilson and Andre Ray. First called Love Men, Ltd.; then Love, Ltd. Name means "Love, Togetherness, and Devotion". | | |
| 8/28/76 | **1**² | 22 | 1 Love Ballad ............................................... | *20* | A&M 1847 |
| 1/22/77 | **27** | 10 | 2 Love To The World ...................................... | *91* | A&M 1897 |
| 9/10/77 | **1**² | 22 | 3● **(Every Time I Turn Around) Back In Love Again** ...................................................... | *4* | A&M 1974 |
| 2/18/78 | **8** | 14 | 4 **Never Get Enough Of Your Love** ................... | *56* | A&M 2005 |
| 7/15/78 | **1**² | 17 | 5 **Holding On (When Love Is Gone)** .................... | *49* | A&M 2057 |
| 11/04/78 | **19** | 13 | 6 We Both Deserve Each Other's Love ................. | *107* | A&M 2095 |
| 6/16/79 | **15** | 15 | 7 Dance "N" Sing "N" ..................................... | | A&M 2142 |
| 9/22/79 | **69** | 3 | 8 Share My Love ........................................... | | A&M 2176 |
| 10/13/79 | **14** | 17 | 9 Stranger .................................................. | | A&M 2192 |
| 8/09/80 | **7** | 20 | 10 **Where Did We Go Wrong** ............................. | | A&M 2250 |
| 11/15/80+ | **19** | 18 | 11 Shine On .................................................. | *40* | A&M 2283 |
| 11/14/81+ | **10** | 14 | 12 **Kickin' Back** ............................................ | *102* | A&M 2382 |
| 2/13/82 | **28** | 15 | 13 April Love ................................................ | | A&M 2395 |
| 7/16/83 | **50** | 11 | 14 For You .................................................... | | Montage 908 |
| | | | **LTG EXCHANGE** | | |
| | | | Band from Jersey City, New Jersey. Formed by Walter Chiles (keyboards). Other members included Kevin Beverly, Melvyn Barton, Bruce Slade and Victor Santos. Chiles recorded with Clarence Pettiford and Al Harewood for Atlantic in 1965. | | |
| 2/16/74 | **66** | 5 | 1 Corazon .................................................. | | Wand 11269 |
| 6/29/74 | **79** | 6 | 2 Waterbed (Part 1) ...................................... | | Wand 11275 |
| | | | **BUDDY LUCAS with his Band of Tomorrow** | | |
| | | | Vocalist/tenor saxophonist/leader Buddy Lucas led house band at Jubilee Records from the early 50s. Later led house band at Gone/End Records. Vocalist/pianist Edna McGriff was from Harlem, New York. McGriff first recorded with Benny Green's Band for Jubilee in 1951; sang duets with Sonny Til of The Orioles. She recorded "Heavenly Father" at age 16. | | |
| 4/05/52 | **4** | 13 | 1 **Heavenly Father** ....................................... | | Jubilee 5073 |
| | | | **EDNA McGRIFF with BUDDY LUCAS & His Band of Tomorrow** Best Seller #4 / Juke Box #5 | | |
| 4/12/52 | **2**¹ | 3 | 2 **Diane** ............................................... [I] | | Jubilee 5070 |
| | | | Juke Box #2 | | |
| | | | **CARRIE LUCAS** | | |
| | | | Former back-up singer with The Whispers; from Los Angeles. | | |
| 4/09/77 | **44** | 11 | 1 I Gotta Keep Dancin' .................................. | *64* | Soul Train 10891 |
| | | | shown only as: **CARRIE** | | |
| 3/17/79 | **27** | 16 | 2 Dance With You .......................................... | *70* | Solar 11482 |
| 10/11/80 | **74** | 3 | 3 It's Not What You Got (It's How You Use It) ........ | | Solar 12085 |
| 12/20/80+ | **55** | 10 | 4 Career Girl ............................................... | | Solar 12143 |
| 5/29/82 | **23** | 15 | 5 Show Me Where You're Coming From ............... | | Solar 48010 |
| 9/22/84 | **84** | 3 | 6 Summer In The Street ................................. | | Constell. 52449 |
| 7/13/85 | **20** | 14 | 7 Hello Stranger ........................................... | | Constell. 52602 |
| | | | featuring The Whispers | | |

| DEBUT DATE | PEAK POS | WKS CHR | ARTIST — Record Title | POP POS | Label & Number |
|---|---|---|---|---|---|
| | | | **FRANK LUCAS** | | |
| | | | Singer from San Bernardino, California. | | |
| 2/19/77 | **9** | 28 | 1 **Good Thing Man** ........................................ | *92* | ICA 001 |
| 2/04/78 | **85** | 5 | 2 Don't Put Out The Fire................................. | | ICA 011 |
| | | | shown as: **GOOD THING MAN FRANK LUCAS** | | |
| | | | **ROBIN LUKE** | | |
| | | | Born on 3/19/42 in Los Angeles. Recorded "Susie Darlin'" in Hawaii, inspired by his younger sister, Susie. | | |
| 9/15/58 | **6** | 7 | 1 **Susie Darlin'**.............................................. | *5* | Dot 15781 |
| | | | Best Seller #6 / Jockey #8 | | |
| | | | **LULU** | | |
| | | | Born Marie Lawrie on 11/3/48 near Glasgow, Scotland. Married to Maurice Gibb (Bee Gees) from 1969-73. | | |
| 10/21/67 | **9** | 8 | 1●**To Sir With Love** ..................................... | *1* | Epic 10187 |
| | | | from the film of the same title (starring Lulu) | | |
| | | | **BOB LUMAN** | | |
| | | | Born on 4/15/37 in Nacogdoches, Texas. Died on 12/27/78 in Nashville. Country-rockabilly singer/songwriter/guitarist. | | |
| 10/24/60 | **14** | 6 | 1 Let's Think About Living........................... [N] | *7* | Warner 5172 |
| | | | **LUNAR FUNK** | | |
| 2/12/72 | **29** | 8 | 1 Mr. Penguin - Pt. I ..................................... [I] | *63* | Bell 45172 |
| | | | **JIMMIE LUNCEFORD** | | |
| | | | Bandleader born on 6/6/02 in Fulton, Mississippi. Died on 7/12/47 in Seaside, Oregon. His band was one of the most influential big black bands during the swing era. | | |
| 12/12/42 | **9** | 1 | 1 **It Had To Be You** ..................................... | | Decca 18504 |
| | | | vocals by Trummy Young, Willie Smith, Dan Grissom & Joe Thomas | | |
| 11/03/45 | **2**[8] | 9 | 2 **The Honeydripper** ................................... | *10* | Decca 23451 |
| | | | vocals by the Delta Rhythm Boys | | |
| | | | **PAT LUNDI** | | |
| 7/28/73 | **90** | 4 | 1 He's The Father Of My Children ....................... | | RCA 0951 |
| 9/13/75 | **65** | 8 | 2 Party Music................................................ | *78* | Vigor 1723 |
| 4/24/76 | **94** | 3 | 3 Ain't No Pity In The Naked City/ | | |
| | | 3 | 4 Let's Get Down To Business........................... | | Pyramid 8001 |
| | | | shown as: **PAT LUNDY** | | |
| | | | **LUSHUS DAIM & The Pretty Vain** | | |
| | | | Female vocalist born in Los Angeles, raised in Germany and on military bases around the world. Debut album produced by Leon Sylvers. | | |
| 10/19/85 | **53** | 8 | 1 More Than You Can Handle .......................... | | Motown 1801 |
| 2/08/86 | **33** | 10 | 2 The One You Love....................................... | | Motown 1826 |
| | | | **JOE LUTCHER** | | |
| | | | Vocalist/saxophonist. Brother of Nellie Lutcher. | | |
| 3/06/48 | **10** | 1 | 1 **Shuffle Woogie** ....................................... [I] | | Capitol 40071 |
| 9/25/48 | **14** | 1 | 2 Rockin' Boogie ......................................... [I] | | Specialty 303 |
| | | | **JOE LUTCHER with his Society Cats** Juke Box #14 | | |
| 9/03/49 | **13** | 1 | 3 Mardi Gras................................................ | | Modern 672 |
| | | | Juke Box #13 | | |
| | | | **NELLIE LUTCHER** | | |
| | | | Born on 10/15/15 in Lake Charles, Louisiana. Vocalist/pianist/composer. Her brother is vocalist/saxophonist Joe Lutcher. With the Clarence Hart band in 1930. To the West Coast in 1935. Heard by Dave Dexter (Capitol Records), on a broadcast of a March Of Dimes Benefit Concert in 1957. Recorded into the early 60s. Once featured on Ralph Edward's "This Is Your Life" TV show. Also see Nat King Cole. | | |
| 8/16/47 | **2**[3] | 18 | 1 **Hurry On Down** ....................................... | *20* | Capitol 40002 |
| 9/27/47 | **2**[3] | 23 | 2 **He's A Real Gone Guy** ............................. | *15* | Capitol A. 40017 |
| 1/31/48 | **3** | 4 | 3 **The Song Is Ended (But The Melody Lingers On)** ...................................................... | *23* | Capitol 40063 |
| 1/31/48 | **9** | 2 | 4 **Do You Or Don't You Love Me** ...................... | | Capitol A. 40063 |
| 3/13/48 | **2**[3] | 17 | 5 **Fine Brown Frame** ................................... | *21* | Capitol 15032 |
| | | | Juke Box #2 / Best Seller #4 | | |
| 5/15/48 | **6** | 4 | 6 **Come And Get It Honey** ............................ | | Capitol 15064 |
| | | | Juke Box #6 | | |

| DEBUT DATE | PEAK POS | WKS CHR | ARTIST — Record Title | POP POS | Label & Number |
|---|---|---|---|---|---|
| | | | **NELLIE LUTCHER — Continued** | | |
| 8/07/48 | **7** | 3 | 7 Cool Water/<br>Juke Box #7 / Best Seller #10 | | |
| 8/07/48 | **13** | 1 | 8 Lake Charles Boogie.................................<br>Juke Box #13 | | Capitol 15148 |
| 10/02/48 | **13** | 1 | 9 Alexander's Rag-Time Band ...........................<br>Best Seller #13 | | Capitol 15180 |
| 1/01/49 | **13** | 1 | 10 I Wish I Was In Walla Walla ...........................<br>Best Seller #13 | | Capitol 15279 |
| 2/18/50 | **8** | 3 | 11 **For You, My Love**....................................<br>NAT KING COLE TRIO with NELLIE LUTCHER<br>Juke Box #8 / Best Seller #12 | | Capitol 847 |
| | | | **LUTHER - see LUTHER VANDROSS** | | |
| | | | **BOBBY LYLE**<br>Jazz keyboardist from Minnesota; prominent session musician in Los Angeles. | | |
| 12/23/78 | **98** | 3 | 1 Groove ............................................ | | Capitol 4657 |
| | | | **FRANKIE LYMON & THE TEENAGERS**<br>Group formed as The Premiers in the Bronx, in 1955. Lead singer Lymon was born on 9/30/42 in New York City; died of a drug overdose on 2/28/68 at the age of 25. Other members included Herman Santiago & Jimmy Merchant (tenors), Joe Negroni (baritone; d: 9/5/78) and Sherman Garnes (bass; d: 2/26/77). Group appeared in the films "Rock, Rock, Rock" and "Mister Rock 'n' Roll". | | |
| 2/18/56 | **1**⁵ | 17 | 1 **Why Do Fools Fall In Love** ...................... | 6 | Gee 1002 |
| | | | THE TEENAGERS featuring FRANKIE LYMON<br>Best Seller #1(5) / Jockey #1(2) / Juke Box #2 | | |
| 5/05/56 | **3** | 13 | 2 **I Want You To Be My Girl**..........................<br>Best Seller #3 / Jockey #3 / Juke Box #5 | 13 | Gee 1012 |
| 8/11/56 | **10** | 3 | 3 **I Promise To Remember/**<br>Best Seller #10 / Jockey #14<br>written by Jimmy Castor | 57 | |
| 8/18/56 | **7** | 4 | 4 **Who Can Explain?** ...............................<br>Juke Box #7 | | Gee 1018 |
| 10/20/56 | **8** | 3 | 5 **The ABC's Of Love**...............................<br>Jockey #8 / Best Seller #14 | 77 | Gee 1022 |
| 7/08/57 | **10** | 1 | 6 **Out In The Cold Again** ...........................<br>Jockey #10 | | Gee 1036 |
| | | | **LINDA LYNDELL** | | |
| 8/24/68 | **50** | 2 | 1 What A Man ..................................... | | Volt 4001 |
| | | | **BARBARA LYNN**<br>Born Barbara Lynn Ozen on 1/16/42 in Beaumont, Texas. Singer/songwriter/guitarist. Records produced by Huey Meaux, recorded in New Orleans and Clinton, Mississippi. | | |
| 6/23/62 | **1**³ | 15 | 1 **You'll Lose A Good Thing** ........................... | 8 | Jamie 1220 |
| 1/19/63 | **13** | 6 | 2 You're Gonna Need Me ........................... | 65 | Jamie 1240 |
| 6/20/64 | **69** | 8 | 3 Oh! Baby (We Got A Good Thing Goin')............. | Hot | Jamie 1277 |
| 10/03/64 | **93** | 3 | 4 Don't Spread It Around ................................ | Hot | Jamie 1286 |
| 1/30/65 | **26** | 2 | 5 It's Better To Have It ............................. | 95 | Jamie 1292 |
| 10/22/66 | **42** | 3 | 6 You Left The Water Running.......................... | 110 | Tribe 8319 |
| 2/17/68 | **39** | 6 | 7 This Is The Thanks I Get .......................... | 65 | Atlantic 2450 |
| 7/31/71 | **31** | 9 | 8 (Until Then) I'll Suffer ........................... | | Atlantic 2812 |
| | | | **CHERYL LYNN** ★★189★★<br>Born on 3/11/57 in Los Angeles. Discovered on TV's "Gong Show". | | |
| 9/09/78+ | **1**¹ | 26 | 1●**Got To Be Real** ............................... | 12 | Columbia 10808 |
| 2/24/79 | **16** | 15 | 2 Star Love ....................................... | 62 | Columbia 10907 |
| 1/12/80 | **41** | 10 | 3 I've Got Faith In You ............................ | | Columbia 11174 |
| 5/30/81 | **5** | 19 | 4 **Shake It Up Tonight** ........................... | 70 | Columbia 02102 |
| 10/17/81 | **79** | 4 | 5 In The Night ................................... | | Columbia 02511 |
| 6/05/82 | **16** | 16 | 6 Instant Love.................................... | 105 | Columbia 02905 |
| 9/04/82 | **4** | 16 | 7 **If This World Were Mine** ...................... | 101 | Columbia 03204 |
| | | | CHERYL LYNN & LUTHER VANDROSS | | |
| 1/15/83 | **77** | 5 | 8 Look Before You Leap............................ | | Columbia 03475 |
| 10/22/83 | **85** | 4 | 9 Preppie ........................................ | | Columbia 04153 |
| 12/10/83+ | **1**¹ | 22 | 10 **Encore** ....................................... | 69 | Columbia 04256 |
| 4/14/84 | **49** | 10 | 11 This Time ..................................... | | Columbia 04429 |
| 1/26/85 | **34** | 10 | 12 At Last You're Mine ........................... | | Private I 04736 |
| | | | from the film "Heavenly Bodies" | | |

| DEBUT DATE | PEAK POS | WKS CHR | ARTIST — Record Title | POP POS | Label & Number |
|---|---|---|---|---|---|
| | | | **CHERYL LYNN — Continued** | | |
| 6/08/85 | **25** | 13 | 13 Fidelity .................................................. | | Columbia 04932 |
| 10/12/85 | **85** | 3 | 14 Fade To Black ....................................... | | Columbia 05605 |
| 2/21/87 | **34** | 11 | 15 New Dress............................................. | | Manhattan 50056 |
| 6/13/87 | **11** | 13 | 16 If You Were Mine ................................. | | Manhattan 50074 |
| | | | **GINIE LYNN** | | |
| 7/15/78 | **95** | 6 | 1 I Love The Way You Love ..................... | | ABC 12386 |
| | | | **JAIME LYNN - see GENE CHANDLER** | | |
| | | | **GLORIA LYNNE** | | |
| | | | Born on 11/23/31 in New York City. Jazz-styled vocalist. | | |
| 10/23/61 | **16** | 7 | 1 Impossible ............................................ | *95* | Everest 19418 |
| 1/11/64 | **28** | 12 | 2 I Wish You Love.................................... | *Hot* | Everest 2036 |
| 4/04/64 | **64** | 5 | 3 I Should Care ....................................... | *Hot* | Everest 2042 |
| | | | there were 4 Top 20-Pop versions of this tune in 1945 | | |
| 4/04/64 | **88** | 4 | 4 Be Anything (But Be Mine)................... | *Hot* | Fontana 1890 |
| 7/04/64 | **76** | 3 | 5 Don't Take Your Love From Me ............ | *Hot* | Everest 2044 |
| 6/12/65 | **8** | 9 | 6 **Watermelon Man**................................. | *62* | Fontana 1511 |

# M

**MOMS MABLEY**
Born Loretta Mary Aiken on 3/19/1894 in Brevard, North Carolina. Died on 5/23/75. Bawdy comedienne. Toured with Butterbeans & Susie in 1921. Charted 13 comedy albums on Billboard's pop albums charts. In the films "Boarding House Blues", "Emperor Jones" and "Amazing Grace".

| | | | | | |
|---|---|---|---|---|---|
| 7/05/69 | **18** | 6 | 1 Abraham, Martin And John ........................... | *35* | Mercury 72935 |

**WILLIE MABON**
Born on 10/24/25 in Hollywood, Tennessee. Died in Paris, France on 4/19/85 (59). Vocalist/pianist/harmonica player. To Chicago in 1942. Formed Blues Rockers band in Chicago in 1947. First recorded for Apollo in 1949, as "Big Willie".

| | | | | | |
|---|---|---|---|---|---|
| 12/06/52+ | **1**⁸ | 19 | 1 **I Don't Know**........................................... | | Chess 1531 |
| | | | Best Seller #1(8) / Juke Box #1(7) | | |
| 4/25/53 | **1**² | 14 | 2 **I'm Mad** .................................................. | | Chess 1538 |
| | | | Best Seller #1 / Juke Box #2 | | |
| 12/11/54 | **7** | 9 | 3 **Poison Ivy**.............................................. | | Chess 1580 |
| | | | Juke Box #7 / Best Seller #8 / Jockey #10 | | |

**MAC BAND Featuring THE McCAMPBELL BROTHERS**
Dallas-based, 8-member group from Flint, Michigan. Vocalist brothers Charles, Derrick, Kelvin and Ray McCampbell, backed by Ray Flippin (bass), Rodney Frazier (keyboards), Slye Fuller (drums) and Mark Harper (guitar).

| | | | | | |
|---|---|---|---|---|---|
| 5/14/88 | **1**¹ | 17 | 1 **Roses Are Red** ........................................ | | MCA 53177 |

**RALPH MacDONALD**
Session percussionist/leader. Formerly with Roberta Flack and the jazz sextet, The Writers.

| | | | | | |
|---|---|---|---|---|---|
| 2/12/77 | **76** | 5 | 1 Where Is The Love ...................................... | | Marlin 3308 |
| 6/11/77 | **42** | 13 | 2 Jam On The Groove ..................................... | | Marlin 3312 |
| 5/13/78 | **90** | 3 | 3 The Path (Part Two)..................................... | | Marlin 3319 |
| 8/25/84 | **13** | 15 | 4 In The Name Of Love ................................... | *58* | Polydor 881221 |
| | | | **RALPH MacDONALD with BILL WITHERS** | | |

**MACEO & THE MACKS**
JB's spin-off funk group led by Maceo Parker (tenor sax), who was a member of the Parliament/Funkadelic organization.

| | | | | | |
|---|---|---|---|---|---|
| 11/28/70 | **41** | 2 | 1 Gotta Get 'Cha............................................. | | House of Fox 1 |
| 8/04/73 | **24** | 9 | 2 Parrty - Part I ...................................... [I] | *71* | People 624 |
| 12/08/73+ | **20** | 15 | 3 Soul Power 74 - Part I ................................. | *109* | People 631 |
| | | | above 2: written, produced & arranged by James Brown | | |
| 4/06/74 | **73** | 7 | 4 I Can Play (Just For You And Me).................. | | People 634 |

**MACHINE**
Disco group consisting of Jay Stovall (vocals, lead guitar), Kevin Nance (keyboards), Melvin Lee (bass), Lonnie Ferguson (drums) and Clare Bathe (vocals).

| | | | | | |
|---|---|---|---|---|---|
| 3/24/79 | **91** | 5 | 1 There But For The Grace Of God Go I............... | *77* | RCA 11456 |

| DEBUT DATE | PEAK POS | WKS CHR | ARTIST — Record Title | POP POS | Label & Number |
|---|---|---|---|---|---|
| | | | **LONNIE MACK** | | |
| | | | Born Lonnie McIntosh on 7/18/41 in Aurora, Indiana. Singer/guitarist (since age 5). Own Country band in 1954. With Troy Seals in the early 60s. Re-discovered in 1968. Retired from music, 1971-85. | | |
| 6/29/63 | 4 | 8 | 1 **Memphis** .................................................. [I] | 5 | Fraternity 906 |
| | | | **THE MAD LADS** | | |
| | | | Consisted of John Gary Williams, Julius Green, William Brown and Robert Phillips. Williams and Brown replaced by Sam Nelson and Quincy Clifton Billops, Jr. (later with Ollie & The Nightingales, The Ovations) from 1966-69. Brown's brother Bertrand was a member of The Newcomers (later known as Kwick). | | |
| 10/16/65 | 11 | 11 | 1 Don't Have To Shop Around ........................... | 93 | Volt 127 |
| 2/12/66 | 10 | 13 | 2 **I Want Someone** .......................................... | 74 | Volt 131 |
| 7/30/66 | 16 | 7 | 3 I Want A Girl .............................................. | | Volt 137 |
| 12/03/66 | 41 | 2 | 4 Patch My Heart ........................................... | | Volt 139 |
| 5/25/68 | 31 | 7 | 5 Whatever Hurts You ..................................... | | Volt 162 |
| 10/12/68 | 35 | 4 | 6 So Nice..................................................... | | Volt 4003 |
| 7/19/69 | 28 | 7 | 7 By The Time I Get To Phoenix ........................ | 84 | Volt 4016 |
| | | | **MADAGASCAR** | | |
| | | | Studio group produced by John Barnes. Included vocals by Barnes and Marva King. | | |
| 10/03/81 | 61 | 9 | 1 Baby Not Tonight ........................................ | | Arista 0625 |
| 1/09/82 | 55 | 9 | 2 Rainbow .................................................... | | Arista 0654 |
| | | | **MADAME X** | | |
| | | | West Coast-based female trio created by producer Bernadette Cooper (founding member of Klymaxx): Iris Parker, Valerie Victoria and Alisa Randolph. Madame X is the code name of the 45 rpm record development project in the 1950s. | | |
| 8/01/87 | 4 | 17 | 1 **Just That Type Of Girl** ............................... | | Atlantic 89216 |
| 12/26/87+ | 56 | 11 | 2 I Want Your Body......................................... | | Atlantic 89149 |
| 3/12/88 | 83 | 4 | 3 Action Jackson ........................................... | | Lorimar 99368 |
| | | | from the film of the same title | | |
| | | | **MADE IN U.S.A.** | | |
| 10/22/77 | 60 | 12 | 1 Melodies..................................................... | | De-Lite 1594 |
| | | | **MADHOUSE** | | |
| | | | Jazz-fusion quartet led by Eric Leeds (sax man in Prince's band, The Revolution). | | |
| 2/07/87 | 5 | 13 | 1 6.............................................................. [I] | | Paisley P. 28485 |
| 11/14/87 | 66 | 10 | 2 (The Perfect) 10 ........................................... [I] | | Paisley P. 28182 |
| | | | **MADONNA** | | |
| | | | Born Madonna Louise Ciccone on 8/16/58 in Bay City, Michigan. Singer/film actress. Married actor Sean Penn in 1985. | | |
| 10/29/83+ | 25 | 18 | 1 Holiday ...................................................... | 16 | Sire 29478 |
| 9/29/84 | 42 | 8 | 2 Lucky Star.................................................. | 4 | Sire 29177 |
| 12/01/84+ | 9 | 15 | 3●Like A Virgin .............................................. | 1 | Sire 29210 |
| 3/02/85 | 49 | 10 | 4 Material Girl............................................... | 2 | Sire 29083 |
| 5/11/85 | 80 | 3 | 5●Crazy For You ............................................. | 1 | Geffen 29051 |
| | | | from the film "Vision Quest" | | |
| 6/01/85 | 71 | 6 | 6●Angel........................................................ | 5 | Sire 29008 |
| 6/29/85 | 19 | 10 | 7 Into The Groove ........................................... | | Sire 20335 |
| 8/31/85 | 64 | 9 | 8 Dress You Up .............................................. | 5 | Sire 28919 |
| 8/22/87 | 78 | 5 | 9 Who's That Girl ........................................... | 1 | Sire 28341 |
| | | | from the film of the same title | | |
| | | | **MAGIC LADY** | | |
| | | | Female trio from Detroit: Linda Stokes, Jackie Steele, and Kimberly Ball. Worked as back-up singers for Enchantment, Shirley Caesar, Soul Searchers, Bob Seger, and Keith Barrow. | | |
| 9/25/82 | 52 | 6 | 1 Red Hot Stuff ............................................. | | A&M 2436 |
| 4/09/88 | 45 | 10 | 2 Betcha Can't Lose (With My Love) ................... | | Motown 1929 |
| | | | **MAGIC TOUCH** | | |
| | | | Group led by Diana Tyler. | | |
| 6/19/71 | 36 | 6 | 1 Step Into My World (Part 2) ........................... | 114 | Black F. 19102 |
| 7/21/73 | 82 | 7 | 2 Baby You Belong To Me................................. | | Roulette 7143 |

| DEBUT DATE | PEAK POS | WKS CHR | ARTIST — Record Title | POP POS | Label & Number |
|---|---|---|---|---|---|

## MAGNIFICENTS
Vocal group formed at Hyde Park High School in Chicago, in 1953: Johnny Keyes, Thurman "Ray" Ramsey, Fred Rakestraw and Willie Myles. Originally called the Tams, name changed by disc jockey "The Magnificent" Montague. Later, Barbara Arrington was added, and Charles "L.C." Cooke (brother of Sam Cooke), replaced Ramsey.

| | | | | | |
|---|---|---|---|---|---|
| 7/14/56 | 9 | 1 | 1 Up On The Mountain .................................... | | Vee-Jay 183 |
| | | | Juke Box #9 / Best Seller #14 / Jockey #15 | | |

## MAGNUM FORCE
8-man group from Chicago, formerly known as Seville. Led by Rory "Star" Sizemore.

| | | | | | |
|---|---|---|---|---|---|
| 1/26/85 | 72 | 7 | 1 Cool Out................................................... | | Paula 1244 |

## SKIP MAHONEY & THE CASUALS
Group from Washington, DC. Consisted of Skip Mahoney, Tracy Reid, Julius Jerome Rogers and Elwood Morgan.

| | | | | | |
|---|---|---|---|---|---|
| 3/16/74 | 80 | 5 | 1 Your Funny Moods ................................ | 113 | D.C. Int. 5003 |
| | | | SKIP & THE CASUALS | | |
| 7/27/74 | 88 | 7 | 2 Seems Like The Love We Have Is Dead And Gone ...................................................... | | D.C. Int. 5007 |
| 6/19/76 | 60 | 9 | 3 Where Ever You Go ................................ | | Abet 9465 |
| 9/11/76 | 40 | 15 | 4 Bless My Soul................................................ | | Abet 9466 |

## MAI TAI
Dutch trio: Jettie Well, Carolien De Windt and Mildred Douglas.

| | | | | | |
|---|---|---|---|---|---|
| 6/29/85 | 37 | 12 | 1 History.................................................... | 109 | Critique 715 |
| 12/14/85 | 69 | 7 | 2 What, When, Where, Who .......................... | | Critique 718 |
| 4/19/86 | 49 | 10 | 3 Female Intuition ..................................... | 71 | Critique 722 |

## THE MAIN ATTRACTION

| | | | | | |
|---|---|---|---|---|---|
| 5/17/86 | 69 | 7 | 1 Reconsider................................................ | | RCA 14321 |

## THE MAIN INGREDIENT    ★★172★★
New York trio, formed as the Poets in 1964. Consisted of Donald McPherson (d: 7/4/71), Luther Simmons, Jr. and Tony Sylvester. First recorded as the Poets for Red Bird in 1965. McPherson replaced by Cuba Gooding in 1971.

| | | | | | |
|---|---|---|---|---|---|
| 6/13/70 | 25 | 10 | 1 You've Been My Inspiration .......................... | 64 | RCA 0340 |
| 12/19/70+ | 13 | 14 | 2 I'm So Proud ......................................... | 49 | RCA 0401 |
| 4/24/71 | 7 | 12 | 3 Spinning Around (I Must Be Falling In Love) .. | 52 | RCA 0456 |
| 9/04/71 | 15 | 9 | 4 Black Seeds Keep On Growing ........................ | 97 | RCA 0517 |
| 7/15/72 | 2³ | 19 | 5●Everybody Plays The Fool ......................... | 3 | RCA 0731 |
| 1/06/73 | 18 | 12 | 6 You've Got To Take It (If You Want It)............... | 46 | RCA 0856 |
| 6/09/73 | 34 | 6 | 7 You Can Call Me Rover................................... | 101 | RCA 0939 |
| 9/01/73 | 51 | 11 | 8 Girl Blue................................................ | 119 | RCA 0046 |
| 1/26/74 | 8 | 20 | 9●Just Don't Want To Be Lonely ...................... | | RCA 0205 |
| 6/15/74 | 7 | 16 | 10 Happiness Is Just Around The Bend .............. | 35 | RCA 0305 |
| 11/02/74 | 48 | 9 | 11 California My Way ................................... | 75 | RCA 10095 |
| 3/22/75 | 7 | 14 | 12 Rolling Down A Mountainside ...................... | 92 | RCA 10224 |
| 8/02/75 | 45 | 9 | 13 The Good Old Days.................................. | | RCA 10334 |
| 11/29/75+ | 20 | 15 | 14 Shame On The World ................................ | | RCA 10431 |
| 4/17/76 | 96 | 2 | 15 Instant Love............................................ | | RCA 10606 |
| 8/23/80 | 69 | 5 | 16 Think Positive ....................................... | | RCA 12060 |
| | | | THE MAIN INGREDIENT featuring CUBA GOODING | | |
| 8/30/86 | 75 | 5 | 17 Do Me Right ......................................... | | Zakia 015 |

## MAINSTREETERS
Also see Joe Simon's "Theme From Cleopatra Jones".

| | | | | | |
|---|---|---|---|---|---|
| 10/20/73 | 91 | 3 | 1 It's My Life ............................................ | | Event 212 |

## MAJESTY

| | | | | | |
|---|---|---|---|---|---|
| 6/08/85 | 74 | 6 | 1 Tell Me Whatchu Want................................ | | Golden Boy 7125 |

## THE MAJORS
Philadelphia group, consisted of Ricky Cordo (lead), Eugene Glass, Frank Troutt, Ronald Gathers and Idella Morris. Produced by Jerry Ragavoy.

| | | | | | |
|---|---|---|---|---|---|
| 10/13/62 | 23 | 1 | 1 A Wonderful Dream.................................... | 22 | Imperial 5855 |

| DEBUT DATE | PEAK POS | WKS CHR | ARTIST — Record Title | POP POS | Label & Number |
|---|---|---|---|---|---|
| | | | **MIRIAM MAKEBA** Born Zensi Miriam Makeba on 3/4/32 in Johannesburg, South Africa. Formerly married to Hugh Masekela. | | |
| 10/07/67 | **7** | 13 | 1 **Pata Pata** .............................................. [F] | *12* | Reprise 0606 |
| | | | **MALCOLM X** | | |
| 1/28/84 | **75** | 5 | 1 No Sell Out ...................................... | | Tommy Boy 840 |
| | | | **STEVE MANCHA** Born Clyde Wilson on 12/25/45 in Walhall, South Carolina. Moved to Detroit in 1954. Ex-lead of 100 Proof Aged In Soul. First recorded with Wilbert Jackson as "Two Friends" for HPC in 1960. Known as "Steve Mancha" since 1965. Member of The Holidays in 1966. | | |
| 7/02/66 | **34** | 3 | 1 I Don't Want To Lose You............................ | | Groovesville 1002 |
| 2/25/67 | **34** | 3 | 2 Don't Make Me A Story Teller........................ | | Groovesville 1005 |
| | | | **MELISSA MANCHESTER - see PEABO BRYSON** | | |
| | | | **MANCHILD** Formed in Indianapolis in 1974 by Reggie Griffin (reeds) and Anthony "A.J." Johnson (bass). In 1977, group included Kenny Edmonds, Chuckie Bush, Daryl Simmons, Robert Parson and Flash Ferrell (vocals). | | |
| 12/17/77 | **70** | 8 | 1 Especially For You ....................................... | | Chi-Sound 1112 |
| | | | **MIKE MANDELL** | | |
| 2/14/81 | **93** | 3 | 1 Don't Cha Give Up.................................... | | Vanguard 35221 |
| | | | **MANDRE** Disco-funk artist Andre Lewis; formerly with Maxayn, Buddy Miles and Frank Zappa. | | |
| 11/05/77 | **87** | 6 | 1 Solar Flight (Opus 1) ..................................... | | Motown 1429 |
| | | | **MANDRILL** Brooklyn Latin jazz/rock septet formed in 1968 by brothers Louis "Sweet Lou", Richard "Dr. Ric", and Carlos "Mad Dog" Wilson. Included Omar Mesa, Claude "Coffee" Cave, Charlie Pardo, and Fudgie Kae. The seven men played 20 different instruments. Moved to Los Angeles in 1975. | | |
| 9/09/72 | **37** | 2 | 1 Get It All ................................................ | | Polydor 14142 |
| 4/07/73 | **19** | 11 | 2 Fencewalk ............................................. | *52* | Polydor 14163 |
| 7/14/73 | **25** | 11 | 3 Hang Loose............................................ [I] | *83* | Polydor 14187 |
| 11/03/73+ | **40** | 12 | 4 Mango Meat ........................................... | *107* | Polydor 14200 |
| 1/19/74 | **65** | 7 | 5 Love Song............................................. | | Polydor 14214 |
| 5/18/74 | **29** | 11 | 6 Positive Thing ....................................... | | Polydor 14235 |
| 11/09/74 | **82** | 4 | 7 The Road To Love .................................... | | Polydor 14257 |
| 7/02/77 | **69** | 4 | 8 Ali Bom-Ba-Ye I ..................................... [I] | | Arista 0250 |
| | | | MICHAEL MASSER & MANDRILL | | |
| 10/29/77 | **45** | 14 | 9 Funky Monkey....................................... | | Arista 0274 |
| 2/04/78 | **43** | 11 | 10 Can You Get It (Suzie Caesar)....................... | | Arista 0304 |
| 5/27/78 | **99** | 2 | 11 Happy Beat .......................................... | | Arista 0326 |
| 12/09/78+ | **37** | 12 | 12 Too Late.............................................. | | Arista 0375 |
| 10/30/82 | **83** | 4 | 13 Put Your Money Where The Funk Is ................ | | Montage 1222 |
| | | | **CHUCK MANGIONE** Born on 11/29/40 in Rochester, New York. Flugelhorn/bandleader/composer. Recorded with older brother Gaspare ("Gap") as the Jazz Brothers for Riverside in 1960. To New York City in 1965, with Maynard Ferguson, Kai Winding, and Art Blakey's Jazz Messengers. | | |
| 2/11/78 | **68** | 7 | 1 Feels So Good......................................... [I] | *4* | A&M 2001 |
| 2/02/80 | **32** | 12 | 2 Give It All You Got ................................... [I] | *18* | A&M 2211 |
| | | | featured song by ABC sports for the 1980 Winter Olympics | | |
| 8/07/82 | **80** | 4 | 3 Steppin' Out............................................. | | Columbia 03008 |
| | | | **THE MANHATTAN TRANSFER** Versatile vocal harmony quartet formed in New York City in 1972: Tim Hauser, Alan Paul, Janis Siegel and Cheryl Bentyne (replaced Laurel Masse in 1979). | | |
| 9/17/83 | **32** | 11 | 1 Spice Of Life.............................................. | *40* | Atlantic 89786 |
| 5/19/84 | **80** | 5 | 2 Mystery .................................................. | *102* | Atlantic 89695 |

| DEBUT DATE | PEAK POS | WKS CHR | ARTIST — Record Title | POP POS | Label & Number |
|---|---|---|---|---|---|
| | | | **THE MANHATTANS**  ★★31★★ | | |
| | | | Group from Jersey City, New Jersey. First recorded for Piney in 1962. Consisted of George "Smitty" Smith (lead; d: 1970, spinal meningitis), Winfred "Blue" Lovett (bass), Edward "Sonny" Bivins and Kenneth "Wally" Kelly (tenors), and Richard Taylor (baritone). Smith replaced by Gerald Alston in 1971. Taylor (a.k.a.: Abdul Rashid Talhah) left in 1976; died on 12/7/87 (47) following a lengthy illness. Featured female vocalist Regina Belle began solo career in 1987. | | |
| 1/30/65 | 12 | 9 | 1 I Wanna Be (Your Everything) | 68 | Carnival 507 |
| 6/05/65 | 20 | 5 | 2 Searchin' For My Baby | 135 | Carnival 509 |
| 12/04/65 | 20 | 5 | 3 Follow Your Heart | 92 | Carnival 512 |
| 3/19/66 | 22 | 7 | 4 Baby I Need You | 96 | Carnival 514 |
| 8/06/66 | 23 | 7 | 5 Can I | | Carnival 517 |
| 11/05/66 | 23 | 8 | 6 I Bet'cha (Couldn't Love Me) | 128 | Carnival 522 |
| 7/22/67 | 31 | 6 | 7 When We're Made As One | | Carnival 529 |
| 11/25/67+ | 24 | 9 | 8 I Call It Love | 96 | Carnival 533 |
| 1/10/70 | 36 | 5 | 9 It's Gonna Take A Lot To Bring Me Back | | DeLuxe 115 |
| 6/06/70 | 30 | 6 | 10 If My Heart Could Speak | 98 | DeLuxe 122 |
| 10/31/70 | 48 | 2 | 11 From Atlanta To Goodbye | 113 | DeLuxe 129 |
| 1/15/72 | 47 | 6 | 12 A Million To One | 114 | DeLuxe 8459 |
| 9/02/72 | 3 | 18 | 13 **One Life To Live** | 102 | DeLuxe 139 |
| 1/13/73 | 19 | 8 | 14 Back Up | 107 | DeLuxe 144 |
| 5/26/73 | 3 | 14 | 15 **There's No Me Without You** | 43 | Columbia 45838 |
| 8/25/73 | 40 | 11 | 16 Do You Ever | | DeLuxe 152 |
| 9/22/73 | 18 | 11 | 17 You'd Better Believe It | 77 | Columbia 45927 |
| 12/08/73+ | 19 | 16 | 18 Wish That You Were Mine | | Columbia 45971 |
| 7/27/74 | 45 | 10 | 19 Summertime In The City | | Columbia 46081 |
| 11/02/74+ | 7 | 19 | 20 **Don't Take Your Love** | 37 | Columbia 10045 |
| 5/24/75 | 10 | 13 | 21 Hurt | 97 | Columbia 10140 |
| 4/03/76 | 1¹ | 26 | 22▲Kiss And Say Goodbye | 1 | Columbia 10310 |
| 10/30/76 | 7 | 18 | 23 I Kinda Miss You | 46 | Columbia 10430 |
| 3/19/77 | 6 | 19 | 24 **It Feels So Good To Be Loved So Bad** | 66 | Columbia 10495 |
| 7/23/77 | 10 | 18 | 25 **We Never Danced To A Love Song** | 93 | Columbia 10586 |
| 1/28/78 | 6 | 17 | 26 **Am I Losing You** | 101 | Columbia 10674 |
| 7/01/78 | 65 | 9 | 27 Everybody Has A Dream | | Columbia 10766 |
| 3/10/79 | 29 | 13 | 28 Here Comes The Hurt Again | | Columbia 10921 |
| 7/21/79 | 33 | 12 | 29 The Way We Were/Memories | | Columbia 11024 |
| 3/15/80 | 4 | 24 | 30●Shining Star | 5 | Columbia 11222 |
| | | | written by Paul Richmond, leader of Amuzement Park | | |
| 7/26/80 | 30 | 12 | 31 Girl Of My Dream | | Columbia 11321 |
| 11/08/80 | 12 | 18 | 32 I'll Never Find Another (Find Another Like You) | 109 | Columbia 11398 |
| 7/04/81 | 19 | 13 | 33 Just One Moment Away | | Columbia 02191 |
| 11/07/81 | 77 | 4 | 34 Let Your Love Come Down | | Columbia 02548 |
| 1/23/82 | 25 | 15 | 35 Honey, Honey | | Columbia 02666 |
| 6/18/83 | 4 | 16 | 36 **Crazy** | 72 | Columbia 03939 |
| 10/01/83 | 30 | 11 | 37 Forever By Your Side | | Columbia 04110 |
| 2/23/85 | 20 | 14 | 38 You Send Me | 81 | Columbia 04754 |
| 6/08/85 | 60 | 8 | 39 Don't Say No | | Columbia 04930 |
| 11/08/86 | 42 | 13 | 40 Where Did We Go Wrong? | | Columbia 06376 |
| | | | vocal by Regina Belle | | |
| 3/28/87 | 41 | 9 | 41 All I Need | | Columbia 07010 |
| | | | **CARL MANN** | | |
| | | | Born on 8/24/42 in Huntingdon, Tennessee. Rockabilly singer/pianist. Own band at age 12, radio show on WHDM in Marion, Tennessee. Worked in Carl Perkins' band from 1962-74. Left music from 1967-74. | | |
| 7/27/59 | 24 | 2 | 1 Mona Lisa | 25 | Phillips 3539 |
| | | | **CHARLES MANN** | | |
| | | | Born on 12/29/49 in Atlanta. Singer/songwriter/pianist/woodwinds. | | |
| 4/28/73 | 36 | 5 | 1 Say You Love Me Too | | ABC 11347 |

| DEBUT DATE | PEAK POS | WKS CHR | ARTIST — Record Title | POP POS | Label & Number |
|---|---|---|---|---|---|
| | | | **HERBIE MANN** <br> Born Herbert Jay Solomon on 4/16/30 in Brooklyn. Saxophonist/flutist/reeds. First recorded with Mat Mathews Quintet for Brunswick in 1953. First recorded as a solo for Bethlehem in 1954. | | |
| 10/08/66 | 36 | 3 | 1 Philly Dog ................................................ [I] <br> featuring King Curtis on sax | 93 | Atlantic 5074 |
| 6/28/69 | 42 | 6 | 2 Memphis Underground ............................... [I] <br> featuring Roy Ayers on vibes | 44 | Atlantic 2621 |
| 11/08/69 | 41 | 3 | 3 It's A Funky Thing-Right On (Part 1) ................ <br> vocal version of "Memphis Underground" (featuring Little Milton) | 95 | Atlantic 2671 |
| 3/08/75 | 24 | 16 | 4 Hijack ................................................... | 14 | Atlantic 3246 |
| 9/20/75 | 53 | 7 | 5 Waterbed ............................................... | | Atlantic 3282 |
| 7/24/76 | 94 | 3 | 6 Cajun Moon ............................................ <br> vocal by Cissy Houston | | Atlantic 3343 |
| 2/10/79 | 63 | 9 | 7 Superman ............................................... | 26 | Atlantic 3547 |
| | | | **MANTRA** <br> 6-piece band from Orlando, Florida, led by Roger Harris. | | |
| 5/02/81 | 79 | 4 | 1 Doin' It To The Bone ................................... | | Casablanca 2329 |
| | | | **MANTRONIX** <br> New York rap duo of producer/instrumentalist Mantronik (Curtis Kahleel - born in New Jersey and raised in Canada) and lyricist/vocalist M.C. Tee (a Bronx native). | | |
| 3/14/87 | 68 | 11 | 1 Who Is It ............................................... | | Sleeping Bag 25 |
| | | | **THE MARATHONS - see THE VIBRATIONS** | | |
| | | | **THE MARCELS** <br> Vocal group from Pittsburgh: Cornelius "Nini" Harp (lead singer), Ronald "Bingo" Mundy & Gene Bricker (tenors), Richard Knauss (baritone) and Fred Johnson (bass). Knauss replaced by Allen Johnson and Bricker replaced by Walt Maddox in mid-1961. Mundy left in late 1961. | | |
| 3/13/61 | 1² | 11 | 1 **Blue Moon** ............................................ <br> there were 3 Top 10 versions of this classic tune in 1935 | 1 | Colpix 186 |
| 12/11/61 | 19 | 3 | 2 Heartaches ............................................. <br> #12 hit for Guy Lombardo in 1931; #1 pop hit for Ted Weems in 1947 | 7 | Colpix 612 |
| | | | **LITTLE PEGGY MARCH** <br> Born Margaret Battavio on 3/7/48 in Lansdale, Pennsylvania. Youngest female singer to have a #1 single on the pop charts. | | |
| 4/06/63 | 1¹ | 12 | 1 **I Will Follow Him** .................................... | 1 | RCA 8139 |
| | | | **BOBBY MARCHAN** <br> Born on 4/30/30 in Youngstown, Ohio. Worked with the Powder Box Revue, troupe of female impersonators. With Huey "Piano" Smith & The Clowns. Toured with Shirley & Lee in the mid-50s. Formed own band, the Tick Tocks in 1959. | | |
| 6/13/60 | 1¹ | 15 | 1 **There's Something On Your Mind, Part 2** ... [N] | 31 | Fire 1022 |
| 10/08/66 | 14 | 11 | 2 Shake Your Tambourine ............................... | | Cameo 429 |
| | | | **BOBBY MARDIS** | | |
| 3/08/86 | 85 | 3 | 1 Keep On ................................................ | | Profile 5085 |
| | | | **ERNIE MARESCA** <br> Born on 4/21/39 in the Bronx. Songwriter/vocalist. Wrote "Runaround Sue" and "The Wanderer". | | |
| 6/02/62 | 25 | 3 | 1 Shout! Shout! (Knock Yourself Out) ................. <br> with the Del Satins (vocal group) | 6 | Seville 117 |
| | | | **TEENA MARIE** ★★154★★ <br> White singer/composer/guitarist/keyboardist/producer/actress born Mary Christine Brockert in Santa Monica, in 1957. Raised in Venice, California. Produces the group, Ozone. | | |
| 5/19/79 | 8 | 21 | 1 **I'm A Sucker For Your Love** ........................ | 102 | Gordy 7169 |
| 10/06/79 | 91 | 4 | 2 Don't Look Back ........................................ | | Gordy 7173 |
| 3/01/80 | 57 | 9 | 3 Can It Be Love ......................................... | | Gordy 7180 |
| 5/03/80 | 21 | 13 | 4 Behind The Groove ..................................... | | Gordy 7184 |
| 8/30/80 | 9 | 23 | 5 **I Need Your Lovin'** .................................. | 37 | Gordy 7189 |
| 2/14/81 | 41 | 10 | 6 Young Love ............................................. | | Gordy 7194 |
| 6/20/81 | 3 | 19 | 7 **Square Biz** ........................................... | 50 | Gordy 7202 |
| 10/17/81 | 30 | 9 | 8 It Must Be Magic ....................................... | | Gordy 7212 |
| 11/21/81+ | 54 | 10 | 9 Portuguese Love ........................................ | | Gordy 7216 |
| 10/01/83 | 21 | 12 | 10 Fix It (Part 1) .......................................... | | Epic 04124 |

| DEBUT DATE | PEAK POS | WKS CHR | ARTIST — Record Title | POP POS | Label & Number |
|---|---|---|---|---|---|
| | | | **TEENA MARIE — Continued** | | |
| 12/17/83+ | **36** | 15 | 11 Midnight Magnet .......................................... | | Epic 04271 |
| 4/28/84 | **77** | 4 | 12 Dear Lover ................................................ | | Epic 04415 |
| 10/27/84+ | **9** | 19 | 13 **Lovergirl** .................................................. | *4* | Epic 04619 |
| 4/06/85 | **45** | 10 | 14 Jammin ...................................................... | *81* | Epic 04738 |
| 6/22/85 | **56** | 9 | 15 Out On A Limb ............................................ | | Epic 04943 |
| 10/12/85 | **87** | 3 | 16 14K .......................................................... | | Epic 05599 |
| 5/31/86 | **28** | 12 | 17 Lips To Find You .......................................... | | Epic 05872 |
| 9/27/86 | **76** | 4 | 18 Love Me Down Easy ...................................... | | Epic 06292 |
| 2/06/88 | **1** [1] | 16 | 19 **Ooo La La La** ............................................ | *85* | Epic 07708 |
| 5/28/88 | **10** | 14 | 20 **Work It** .................................................... | | Epic 07902 |
| | | | **MARIGOLDS** | | |
| | | | Group formed at Tennessee State Penitentiary in 1955. Consisted of Johnny Bragg, Hal Hebb (brother of Bobby Hebb), Willie Wilson, Al Brooks, and Henry Jones. | | |
| 6/04/55 | **8** | 8 | 1 **Rollin' Stone** ............................................ | | Excello 2057 |
| | | | Juke Box #8 / Best Seller #12 | | |
| | | | **MARK IV** | | |
| | | | New York City group, formed as the Attractions in 1970. Consisted of lead Jimmy Ponder, Lawrence Jones, Candido Antomade and Walter Moreland. Group was managed by vocalist Roy "C". | | |
| 8/19/72 | **13** | 12 | 1 Honey I Still Love You ................................. | | Mercury 73319 |
| 1/20/73 | **33** | 10 | 2 My Everything You Are ................................. | | Mercury 73353 |
| 6/30/73 | **54** | 3 | 3 Got To Get Back (To My Baby's Love) .............. | | Mercury 73378 |
| | | | **MAR-KEYS** | | |
| | | | Instrumental group formed in Memphis in 1958. Consisted of Charles Axton, Wayne Jackson, Don Nix, Jerry Lee "Smoochie" Smith, Steve Cropper, Donald "Duck" Dunn, and Terry Johnson. Staff musicians at Stax/Volt. Cropper and Dunn also worked with Booker T. & The MG's. Jackson joined The Memphis Horns. Axton later joined The Packers. | | |
| 7/10/61 | **2** [3] | 15 | 1 **Last Night** ................................................ [I] | *3* | Satellite 107 |
| 2/26/66 | **19** | 16 | 2 Philly Dog .................................................. [I] | *89* | Stax 185 |
| | | | **PIGMEAT MARKHAM** | | |
| | | | Born Dewey Markham in Durham, North Carolina, in 1906. Died on 12/13/81 in the Bronx. Stage and TV comedian. | | |
| 6/29/68 | **4** | 9 | 1 **Here Comes The Judge** ............................ [N] | *19* | Chess 2049 |
| | | | **BOB MARLEY & THE WAILERS** | | |
| | | | Singer/guitarist born on 2/6/45 in Rhoden Hall, Jamaica. Died of brain cancer on 5/11/81. With Winston Hubert "Peter Tosh" McIntosh (murdered on 9/11/87 [42]), Neville "Bunny Wailer" O'Reilly, , Beverly Kelso and Junior Braithewaite in the Wailin' Wailers; recorded for Studio One. Also recorded as Wailin' Rudies. The Wailers included Marley, Tosh, Wailer, Aston "Familyman" Barrett and his brother Carlton. Tosh and Wailer left in 1975, replaced by Al Anderson, Bernard "Touter" Harvey, and vocalists Rita Marley, Judy Mowatt and Marcia Griffiths. Assassination attempt in Jamaica, in December of 1976, wounded Marley and wife Rita. Celebrated as the masters of reggae. | | |
| 6/19/76 | **37** | 9 | 1 Roots, Rock, Reggae ..................................... | *51* | Island 060 |
| 7/16/77 | **19** | 10 | 2 Exodus....................................................... | *103* | Island 089 |
| 9/24/77 | **38** | 10 | 3 Waiting In Vain............................................ | | Island 092 |
| 11/24/79 | **93** | 3 | 4 Wake Up And Live........................................ | | Island 49080 |
| 9/13/80 | **56** | 8 | 5 Could You Be Loved ...................................... | | Island 49547 |
| 10/03/81 | **66** | 6 | 6 Reggae On Broadway ................................... | | Cotillion 46023 . |
| 6/18/83 | **71** | 6 | 7 Buffalo Soldier............................................. | | Island 99882 |
| | | | **M/A/R/R/S** | | |
| | | | U.K.-based, electro-funk group featuring 2 pairs of brothers: Martyn & Steve Young, with Alex & Rudi Kane. Includes mixers: Chris "CJ" Mackintosh and DJ Dave Dorrell. | | |
| 12/12/87+ | **8** | 16 | 1● **Pump Up The Volume** ............................... | *13* | 4th & B'way 7452 |
| | | | **MITZI MARS** | | |
| | | | Vocalist with William "King Kolax" Little's band. Kolax (trumpet) was with Ernie Fields in 1942. | | |
| 6/06/53 | **9** | 3 | 1 **I'm Glad** .................................................. | | Checker 773 |
| | | | Juke Box #9 answer song to "I'm Mad" by Willie Mabon | | |

| DEBUT DATE | PEAK POS | WKS CHR | ARTIST — Record Title | POP POS | Label & Number |
|---|---|---|---|---|---|
| | | | **MARTHA & THE VANDELLAS** ★★86★★ | | |
| | | | Detroit group organized by Martha Reeves (b: 7/18/41) in 1962 with Annette Beard and Rosalind Ashford. Reeves had been in the Del-Phis, recorded for Checkmate. Worked at Motown as A&R secretary, sang back-up. Vandellas did back-up on Marvin Gaye's "Stubborn Kind Of Fellow". Beard left group in 1964, replaced by Betty Kelly (former member of The Velvelettes). Group disbanded from 1969-71; re-formed with Martha and her sister Lois Reeves, and Sandra Tilley in 1971. Martha Reeves went solo in 1972. Lois joined Quiet Elegance. | | |
| 4/27/63 | 6 | 13 | 1 Come And Get These Memories...................... | 29 | Gordy 7014 |
| 8/10/63 | 1⁴ | 16 | 2 Heat Wave ..................................................... | 4 | Gordy 7022 |
| 11/23/63+ | 8 | 12 | 3 Quicksand ..................................................... | Hot | Gordy 7025 |
| 2/08/64 | 42 | 7 | 4 Live Wire...................................................... | Hot | Gordy 7027 |
| 4/11/64 | 44 | 6 | 5 In My Lonely Room ......................................... | Hot | Gordy 7031 |
| 8/22/64 | 2² | 14 | 6 Dancing In The Street...................................... | Hot | Gordy 7033 |
| 12/05/64+ | 34 | 7 | 7 Wild One ....................................................... | Hot | Gordy 7036 |
| 2/27/65 | 5 | 15 | 8 Nowhere To Run .............................................. | 8 | Gordy 7039 |
| 9/18/65 | 25 | 9 | 9 You've Been In Love Too Long/ | 36 | |
| 10/23/65+ | 22 | 13 | 10 Love (Makes Me Do Foolish Things) ................. | 70 | Gordy 7045 |
| 2/05/66 | 3 | 13 | 11 My Baby Loves Me ......................................... | 22 | Gordy 7048 |
| 11/12/66 | 2¹ | 11 | 12 I'm Ready For Love .......................................... | 9 | Gordy 7056 |
| 3/04/67 | 1¹ | 15 | 13 Jimmy Mack................................................... | 10 | Gordy 7058 |
| | | | 1-5, 8, 10, 12-13: written by Holland, Dozier, Holland | | |
| 9/16/67 | 14 | 7 | 14 Love Bug Leave My Heart Alone ...................... | 25 | Gordy 7062 |
| | | | **MARTHA REEVES & THE VANDELLAS:** | | |
| 11/25/67+ | 5 | 13 | 15 Honey Chile .................................................. | 11 | Gordy 7067 |
| 5/18/68 | 36 | 3 | 16 I Promise To Wait My Love .............................. | 62 | Gordy 7070 |
| 8/24/68 | 24 | 8 | 17 I Can't Dance To That Music You're Playin' ....... | 42 | Gordy 7075 |
| 11/30/68 | 45 | 2 | 18 Sweet Darlin'................................................. | 80 | Gordy 7080 |
| 4/26/69 | 27 | 8 | 19 (We've Got) Honey Love .................................. | 56 | Gordy 7085 |
| 9/20/69 | 44 | 3 | 20 Taking My Love (And Leaving Me).................... | 102 | Gordy 7094 |
| 11/14/70 | 43 | 3 | 21 I Gotta Let You Go .......................................... | 93 | Gordy 7103 |
| 10/23/71 | 29 | 5 | 22 Bless You ...................................................... | 53 | Gordy 7110 |
| 1/29/72 | 22 | 11 | 23 In And Out Of My Life ..................................... | 102 | Gordy 7113 |
| 7/15/72 | 37 | 4 | 24 Tear It On Down ............................................. | 103 | Gordy 7118 |
| | | | **DEREK MARTIN** | | |
| | | | Singer formerly with the Pearls (Five Pearls). | | |
| 8/07/65 | 25 | 5 | 1 You Better Go................................................ | 78 | Roulette 4631 |
| | | | **KENNY MARTIN** | | |
| 11/03/58 | 19 | 2 | 1 I'm Sorry ...................................................... | | Federal 12330 |
| | | | **NANCY MARTIN** | | |
| 11/06/82 | 70 | 6 | 1 Can't Believe................................................. | | Atlantic 89957 |
| | | | **PAUL MARTIN** | | |
| 5/01/65 | 27 | 8 | 1 Snake In The Grass ........................................ | | Ascot 2172 |
| | | | **AL MARTINO** | | |
| | | | Born Alfred Cini on 10/7/27 in Philadelphia. Encouraged by success of boyhood friend, Mario Lanza. Winner on Arthur Godfrey's "Talent Scouts" in 1952. Portrayed singer Johnny Fontane in the 1972 film "The Godfather". | | |
| 9/07/59 | 27 | 1 | 1 Darling, I Love You......................................... | 63 | 20th Fox 153 |
| | | | **THE MARVELETTES** ★★103★★ | | |
| | | | Group from Inkster High School, Inkster, Michigan. Formed in 1960 by Gladys Horton, with Georgeanna Marie Tillman Gordon (died of lupus on 1/6/80), Wanda Young, Katherine Anderson and Juanita Cowart. Cowart and Gordon left in 1965, Horton left in 1967, replaced by Anne Bogan. Disbanded, 1969. | | |
| 9/11/61 | 1⁷ | 23 | 1 Please Mr. Postman ........................................ | 1 | Tamla 54046 |
| 2/17/62 | 13 | 6 | 2 Twistin' Postman .......................................... | 34 | Tamla 54054 |
| 5/26/62 | 4 | 13 | 3 Playboy ........................................................ | 7 | Tamla 54060 |
| 8/18/62 | 7 | 11 | 4 Beechwood 4-5789/ | 17 | |
| 9/15/62 | 8 | 12 | 5 Someday, Someway .................................... | | Tamla 54065 |
| 12/29/62+ | 10 | 10 | 6 Strange I Know ............................................. | 49 | Tamla 54072 |
| 5/04/63 | 25 | 1 | 7 Locking Up My Heart/ | 44 | |
| 6/15/63 | 24 | 4 | 8 Forever ....................................................... | 78 | Tamla 54077 |
| 11/09/63 | 47 | 13 | 9 As Long As I Know He's Mine.......................... | Hot | Tamla 54088 |

| DEBUT DATE | PEAK POS | WKS CHR | ARTIST — Record Title | POP POS | Label & Number |
|---|---|---|---|---|---|
| | | | **THE MARVELETTES — Continued** | | |
| 2/22/64 | 55 | 7 | 10 He's A Good Guy (Yes He Is) | *Hot* | Tamla 54091 |
| 7/04/64 | 48 | 7 | 11 You're My Remedy | *Hot* | Tamla 54097 |
| 1/30/65 | 15 | 1 | 12 Too Many Fish In The Sea | 25 | Tamla 54105 |
| 6/19/65 | 11 | 8 | 13 I'll Keep Holding On | 34 | Tamla 54116 |
| 9/11/65 | 11 | 8 | 14 Danger Heartbreak Dead Ahead | 61 | Tamla 54120 |
| 1/15/66 | 3 | 15 | 15 **Don't Mess With Bill** | 7 | Tamla 54126 |
| 5/21/66 | 20 | 5 | 16 You're The One | 48 | Tamla 54131 |
| 2/04/67 | 2³ | 14 | 17 **The Hunter Gets Captured By The Game** | 13 | Tamla 54143 |
| 5/13/67 | 9 | 10 | 18 **When You're Young And In Love** | 23 | Tamla 54150 |
| 12/30/67+ | 8 | 12 | 19 **My Baby Must Be A Magician** | 17 | Tamla 54158 |
| 6/22/68 | 14 | 9 | 20 Here I Am Baby | 44 | Tamla 54166 |
| 10/12/68 | 28 | 7 | 21 Destination: Anywhere | 63 | Tamla 54171 |
| | | | **THE MARVELOWS** | | |
| | | | Group from Chicago Heights, Illinois. Formed in 1959 with Melvin Mason, Willie "Sonny" Stevenson, Frank Paden and Johnny Paden. First known as the Mystics. Added Jesse Smith in 1964, became the Marvelows. Disbanded in 1969. Re-formed, 1974-75. | | |
| 5/15/65 | 7 | 10 | 1 I Do | 37 | ABC-Para. 10629 |
| 3/23/68 | 24 | 10 | 2 In The Morning | 105 | ABC-Para. 11011 |
| | | | MIGHTY MARVELOWS | | |
| | | | **MARVIN & JOHNNY** | | |
| | | | Vocal duo: Marvin Phillips (from Guthrie, OK) and Emory "Johnny" Perry (from Sherman, TX). Phillips had been with Jesse Belvin as "Jesse & Marvin". | | |
| 12/05/53 | 9 | 1 | 1 **Baby Doll** | | Specialty 479 |
| | | | Juke Box #9 | | |
| 9/18/54 | 9 | 3 | 2 **Tick Tock** | | Modern 933 |
| | | | Best Seller #9 | | |
| | | | **MARY JANE GIRLS** | | |
| | | | Female "funk & roll" quartet: Joanne McDuffie, Candice Ghant, Kim Wuletick and Yvette Marine. Formed and produced by Rick James. | | |
| 4/09/83 | 23 | 18 | 1 Candy Man | 101 | Gordy 1670 |
| 7/23/83 | 11 | 18 | 2 All Night Long | 101 | Gordy 1690 |
| 10/15/83 | 29 | 17 | 3 Boys | 102 | Gordy 1704 |
| 3/10/84 | 84 | 3 | 4 Jealousy | 106 | Gordy 1721 |
| 2/23/85 | 3 | 22 | 5 **In My House** | 7 | Gordy 1741 |
| 6/29/85 | 10 | 14 | 6 **Wild And Crazy Love** | 42 | Gordy 1798 |
| 11/16/85 | 79 | 2 | 7 Break It Up | | Gordy 1816 |
| 8/02/86 | 91 | 8 | 8 Walk Like A Man | 41 | Motown 1851 |
| | | | from the film "A Fine Mess" | | |
| | | | **HUGH MASEKELA** | | |
| | | | Born Hugh Ramapolo Masekela on 4/4/39 in Wilbank, South Africa. Trumpeter/ bandleader/arranger. Played trumpet since age 14. To England in 1959; New York City in 1960. Formerly married to Miriam Makeba. Formed own band in 1964. | | |
| 1/06/68 | 47 | 2 | 1 Up-Up And Away [I] | 71 | Uni 55037 |
| 6/15/68 | 1⁴ | 14 | 2 **Grazing In The Grass** [I] | 1 | Uni 55066 |
| 2/08/69 | 21 | 6 | 3 Riot [I] | 55 | Uni 55102 |
| 4/29/78 | 87 | 5 | 4 Skokiaan [I] | | Horizon 115 |
| | | | HERB ALPERT/HUGH MASEKELA | | |
| 6/23/84 | 67 | 7 | 5 Don't Go Lose It Baby [I] | | Jive Afrika 9193 |
| | | | **THE MASKMAN & THE AGENTS** | | |
| | | | Group formed by vocalist Harmon Bethea, former member of the Cap-Tans vocal group solo in 1973. | | |
| 12/07/68+ | 20 | 13 | 1 One Eye Open | 95 | Dynamo 125 |
| 5/03/69 | 22 | 9 | 2 My Wife, My Dog, My Cat | 91 | Dynamo 131 |
| | | | above 2: with The Billy Clark Orchestra | | |
| | | | **MASON** | | |
| 6/27/87 | 73 | 10 | 1 Pour It On | | Elektra 69471 |
| | | | **MASON DIXON DANCE BAND** | | |
| 1/06/79 | 95 | 3 | 1 Southern Comfort | | Alex. 010 |

276

| DEBUT DATE | PEAK POS | WKS CHR | | ARTIST — Record Title | POP POS | Label & Number |
|---|---|---|---|---|---|---|
| | | | | **BARBARA MASON**  ★★**177**★★ | | |
| | | | | Born on 8/9/47 in Philadelphia. First recorded for Crusader in 1964. Wrote all of her Arctic hits. | | |
| 1/30/65 | **31** | 1 | 1 | Girls Have Feelings Too................................. | | Arctic 102 |
| 5/08/65 | **2**³ | 18 | 2 | **Yes, I'm Ready** ....................................... | 125 | Arctic 105 |
| 9/04/65 | **12** | 9 | 3 | Sad, Sad Girl ........................................... | 27 | Arctic 108 |
| 6/25/66 | **25** | 5 | 4 | I Need Love ............................................. | 98 | Arctic 120 |
| 1/06/68 | **11** | 9 | 5 | Oh, How It Hurts ....................................... | 59 | Arctic 137 |
| 5/30/70 | **38** | 5 | 6 | Raindrops Keep Fallin' On My Head/ | 112 | |
| | | 5 | 7 | If You Knew Him Like I Do ........................... | | National G. 005 |
| 6/17/72 | **24** | 8 | 8 | Bed And Board .......................................... | 70 | Buddah 296 |
| 12/16/72+ | **9** | 16 | 9 | **Give Me Your Love** ................................... | 31 | Buddah 331 |
| 9/01/73 | **79** | 5 | 10 | Child Of Tomorrow ..................................... | | Buddah 375 |
| 11/23/74+ | **3** | 13 | 11 | **From His Woman To You** ........................... | 28 | Buddah 441 |
| 3/29/75 | **9** | 18 | 12 | **Shackin' Up** .......................................... | 91 | Buddah 459 |
| 8/09/75 | **35** | 11 | 13 | We Got Each Other/ | | |
| | | 3 | 14 | Make It Last............................................ | | Buddah 481 |
| | | | | **BARBARA MASON & THE FUTURES** | | |
| 4/29/78 | **14** | 15 | 15 | I Am Your Woman, She Is Your Wife................. | | Prelude 71103 |
| 12/20/80+ | **54** | 9 | 16 | I'll Never Love The Same Way Twice ................ | | WMOT 5352 |
| 8/29/81 | **29** | 10 | 17 | She's Got The Papers (But I Got The Man)......... | | WMOT 02506 |
| 1/21/84 | **68** | 7 | 18 | Another Man ............................................ | | West End 22164 |
| | | | | **DAVE MASON** | | |
| | | | | Born on 5/10/46 in Worchester, England. Vocalist/composer/guitarist. Original member of the rock group Traffic. | | |
| 8/30/80 | **70** | 5 | 1 | Save Me................................................. | 71 | Columbia 11289 |
| | | | | **HARVEY MASON** | | |
| | | | | Born on 2/22/47 in Atlantic City, New Jersey. Drummer/percussionist. Much session and production work, including Esther Phillips, Herbie Hancock, Deodata, Shirley Brown and Stanley Clarke. | | |
| 2/21/76 | **93** | 4 | 1 | Marching In The Street................................ | | Arista 0167 |
| 4/29/78 | **57** | 9 | 2 | Till You Take My Love ................................ | | Arista 0323 |
| 6/09/79 | **58** | 9 | 3 | Groovin' You ........................................... | | Arista 0403 |
| 5/09/81 | **55** | 8 | 4 | We Can Start Tonight ................................. | | Arista 0593 |
| | | | | **VAUGHAN MASON & CREW** | | |
| | | | | East Coast disco/funk group. Jerome Bell, lead singer. Three members of the Crew later joined AM-FM. | | |
| 1/19/80 | **5** | 19 | 1 | **Bounce, Rock, Skate, Roll Pt. 1**..................... | 81 | Brunswick 55548 |
| 6/07/80 | **52** | 7 | 2 | Roller Skate............................................. | | Brunswick 212 |
| 8/22/81 | **65** | 9 | 3 | Jammin' Big Guitar ..................................... | | Brunswick 220 |
| | | | | **VAUGHAN MASON featuring BUTCH DAYO:** | | |
| 12/18/82+ | **45** | 10 | 4 | You Can Do It ........................................... | | Salsoul 7042 |
| 5/21/83 | **83** | 4 | 5 | Party On The Corner.................................... | | Salsoul 7052 |
| | | | | **THE MASQUERADERS** | | |
| | | | | Texas group: Lee Hatim, Robert Wrightsill, David Sanders, Harold Thomas and Sammie Hutchins. | | |
| 9/07/68 | **7** | 13 | 1 | **I Ain't Got To Love Nobody Else**.................... | 57 | Bell 733 |
| 1/18/69 | **24** | 11 | 2 | I'm Just An Average Guy .............................. | | AGP 108 |
| 11/29/75+ | **76** | 7 | 3 | Baby It's You ........................................... | | Hot Bt. So. 12141 |
| 1/24/76 | **32** | 16 | 4 | (Call Me) The Traveling Man.......................... | 101 | Hot Bt. So. 12157 |
| 3/01/80 | **38** | 11 | 5 | Desire .................................................... | | Bang 4806 |
| | | | | **MASS PRODUCTION** | | |
| | | | | Group from Richmond, Virginia: Agnes "Tiny" Kelly, Larry Marshall, Ricardo Williams (vocals), Gregory McCoy, James Drumgole, LeCoy Bryant, Tyrone Williams, Kevin Douglas, Emmanuel Redding and Samuel Williams. | | |
| 2/12/77 | **32** | 11 | 1 | Welcome To Our World (Of Merry Music)........... | 68 | Cotillion 44213 |
| 10/01/77 | **60** | 10 | 2 | I Believe In Music ..................................... | | Cotillion 44221 |
| 12/10/77 | **92** | 3 | 3 | Cosmic Lust............................................. | | Cotillion 44225 |
| 5/06/78 | **46** | 13 | 4 | Just Wanna Make A Dream Come True (Mass In F Minor) ........................................... | | Cotillion 44233 |
| 8/26/78 | **85** | 4 | 5 | Sky High ................................................ | | Cotillion 44239 |
| 3/31/79 | **43** | 9 | 6 | Can't You See I'm Fired Up ........................... | | Cotillion 44248 |

| DEBUT DATE | PEAK POS | WKS CHR | ARTIST — Record Title | POP POS | Label & Number |
|---|---|---|---|---|---|
| | | | **MASS PRODUCTION — Continued** | | |
| 6/23/79 | **4** | 21 | 7  Firecracker | *43* | Cotillion 44254 |
| 3/29/80 | **42** | 11 | 8  Forever | | Cotillion 45009 |
| 6/21/80 | **49** | 7 | 9  Shante | | Cotillion 45018 |
| 4/25/81 | **90** | 2 | 10  I Can't Believe You're Going Away | | Cotillion 46011 |
| 5/09/81 | **36** | 13 | 11  Turn Up The Music | | Cotillion 46013 |
| 4/03/82 | **61** | 7 | 12  Inner City | | Cotillion 47004 |
| | | | **MICHAEL MASSER - see MANDRILL** | | |
| | | | **MASTER OF CEREMONY featuring DON BARRON** | | |
| 4/25/87 | **92** | 3 | 1  Sexy | | 4th & B'way 473 |
| | | | **THE MASTERDON COMMITTEE** | | |
| 4/19/86 | **79** | 5 | 1  Get Off My Tip! | | Profile 5097 |
| | | | **MASTERPIECE** | | |
| | | | 5-member band from Los Angeles. | | |
| 4/26/80 | **81** | 8 | 1  The Girl's Alright With Me | | Whitfield 49218 |
| | | | **JOHNNY MATHIS** | | |
| | | | Born on 9/30/35 in San Francisco. Studied opera from age 13. Track scholarship at the San Francisco State College. Invited to Olympic try-outs, chose singing career instead. To New York City in 1956. Ranks behind only Elvis Presley and Frank Sinatra as the top album artist of the rock era. | | |
| 11/25/57 | **12** | 3 | 1  Chances Are | *1* | Columbia 40993 |
| | | | Best Seller #12 / Jockey #15 | | |
| 11/09/59 | **10** | 7 | 2  Misty | *12* | Columbia 41483 |
| | | | the Erroll Garner classic charted at POS 30-Pop in 1954 | | |
| 3/09/63 | **21** | 3 | 3  What Will Mary Say | *9* | Columbia 42666 |
| 10/06/73 | **92** | 5 | 4  I'm Coming Home | *75* | Columbia 45908 |
| 1/26/74 | **65** | 8 | 5  Life Is A Song Worth Singing | *54* | Columbia 45975 |
| 3/04/78 | **1** [4] | 20 | 6● **Too Much, Too Little, Too Late** | *1* | Columbia 10693 |
| | | | JOHNNY MATHIS/DENIECE WILLIAMS | | |
| 7/08/78 | **10** | 12 | 7  **You're All I Need To Get By** | *47* | Columbia 10772 |
| | | | JOHNNY MATHIS & DENIECE WILLIAMS | | |
| 8/09/80 | **81** | 4 | 8  Different Kinda Different | | Columbia 11313 |
| | | | duet with Paulette | | |
| 4/17/82 | **22** | 13 | 9  Friends In Love | *38* | Arista 0673 |
| | | | DIONNE WARWICK & JOHNNY MATHIS | | |
| 2/25/84 | **32** | 12 | 10  Love Won't Let Me Wait | *106* | Columbia 04379 |
| | | | JOHNNY MATHIS & DENIECE WILLIAMS | | |
| 5/19/84 | **43** | 12 | 11  Simple | *81* | Columbia 04468 |
| | | | **KATHY MATHIS** | | |
| 5/09/87 | **40** | 11 | 1  Late Night Hour | | Tabu 07046 |
| | | | **RONN MATLOCK** | | |
| | | | Born on 9/15/47 in Detroit. Singer/songwriter. Writer for teen magazines while still in high school. | | |
| 9/22/79 | **87** | 2 | 1  Let Me Dance | | Cotillion 45002 |
| | | | **MILT MATTHEWS** | | |
| 2/18/78 | **61** | 11 | 1  Trust Me | | H&L 4692 |
| | | | **MAXAYN** | | |
| | | | Group formed in 1970: Maxayn Lewis, Andre Lewis, Marlo Henderson and Emilio Thomas. Maxayn was with the Ikettes and Bobby Bland. Andre and Henderson were with Buddy Miles. Andre later recorded as "Mandre". | | |
| 6/02/73 | **35** | 3 | 1  Check Out Your Mind | | Capricorn 0017 |
| | | | **MAXINE TRIO - see RAY CHARLES** | | |
| | | | **LEE MAYE - see COUNTRY BOYS** | | |
| | | | **NATHANIEL MAYER & The Fabulous Twilights** | | |
| | | | Vocalist from Detroit. | | |
| 5/26/62 | **16** | 5 | 1  Village Of Love | *22* | Fortune 449 |

| DEBUT DATE | PEAK POS | WKS CHR | ARTIST — Record Title | POP POS | Label & Number |
|---|---|---|---|---|---|
| | | | **CURTIS MAYFIELD** ★★70★★ | | |
| | | | Born on 6/3/42 in Chicago. Singer/songwriter/producer. With Jerry Butler in the gospel group Northern Jubilee Singers. Joined The Impressions in 1957. Wrote most of the hits for The Impressions, Jerry Butler, and himself. Own labels: Windy C, Mayfield, and Curtom. Went solo in 1970. Scored "Superfly", "Claudine", "A Piece Of The Action", "Short Eyes" film soundtracks. Appeared in "Short Eyes". | | |
| 11/28/70+ | 3 | 13 | 1 **(Don't Worry) If There's A Hell Below We're All Going To Go** | 29 | Curtom 1955 |
| 11/06/71 | 13 | 9 | 2 Get Down | 69 | Curtom 1966 |
| 2/26/72 | 32 | 5 | 3 We Got To Have Peace | 115 | Curtom 1968 |
| 5/27/72 | 45 | 2 | 4 Beautiful Brother Of Mine | | Curtom 1972 |
| 8/12/72 | 2⁴ | 17 | 5 ●Freddie's Dead | 4 | Curtom 1975 |
| 11/25/72+ | 5 | 15 | 6 ●Superfly | 8 | Curtom 1978 |
| | | | above 2: from the film "Superfly" | | |
| 7/14/73 | 11 | 11 | 7 Future Shock | 39 | Curtom 1987 |
| 10/20/73 | 22 | 11 | 8 If I Were Only A Child Again | 71 | Curtom 1991 |
| 12/01/73+ | 16 | 12 | 9 Can't Say Nothin' | 88 | Curtom 1993 |
| 6/22/74 | 3 | 16 | 10 **Kung Fu** | 40 | Curtom 1999 |
| 10/26/74 | 32 | 8 | 11 Sweet Exorcist | | Curtom 2005 |
| 1/18/75 | 15 | 11 | 12 Mother's Son | | Curtom 2006 |
| 8/09/75 | 9 | 18 | 13 **So In Love** | 67 | Curtom 0105 |
| 8/07/76 | 8 | 13 | 14 **Only You Babe** | | Curtom 0118 |
| 11/20/76+ | 39 | 11 | 15 Party Night | | Curtom 0211 |
| 4/30/77 | 41 | 9 | 16 Show Me Love | | Curtom 0125 |
| 10/15/77 | 29 | 16 | 17 Do Do Wap Is Strong In Here | | Curtom 0131 |
| 4/01/78 | 34 | 12 | 18 You Are, You Are | | Curtom 0135 |
| 9/30/78 | 96 | 3 | 19 Do It All Night | | Curtom 0141 |
| 3/03/79 | 40 | 8 | 20 This Year | | RSO 919 |
| 8/18/79 | 14 | 18 | 21 Between You Baby And Me/ <br> **CURTIS MAYFIELD & LINDA CLIFFORD** | | |
| 12/01/79+ | 46 | 9 | 22 You're So Good To Me | | RSO 941 |
| 5/17/80 | 34 | 11 | 23 Love's Sweet Sensation <br> **CURTIS MAYFIELD & LINDA CLIFFORD** | | RSO 1029 |
| 6/28/80 | 48 | 9 | 24 Love Me, Love Me Now | | RSO 1036 |
| 9/06/80 | 46 | 10 | 25 Tripping Out | | RSO 1046 |
| 9/12/81 | 15 | 15 | 26 She Don't Let Nobody (But Me) | 103 | Boardwalk 122 |
| 12/12/81+ | 22 | 13 | 27 Toot An'Toot An'Toot | | Boardwalk 132 |
| 10/09/82 | 68 | 8 | 28 Hey Baby (Give It All To Me) | | Boardwalk 155 |
| 9/14/85 | 69 | 9 | 29 Baby It's You | | CRC 001 |
| | | | **PERCY MAYFIELD** | | |
| | | | Born on 8/12/20 in Minden, Louisiana. Died of a heart attack on 8/11/84 (63). Vocalist/pianist/composer. To Los Angeles in 1942. Own band from 1950. Staff writer for Ray Charles. Wrote "Hit The Road, Jack". Active into the 80s. | | |
| 10/28/50 | 1² | 27 | 1 **Please Send Me Someone To Love/** <br> Best Seller #1(2) / Juke Box #1(1) <br> a reported million-seller | 26 | |
| 1/13/51 | 7 | 2 | 2 **Strange Things Happening** <br> Juke Box #7 | | Specialty 375 |
| 2/17/51 | 2³ | 17 | 3 **Lost Love** <br> Best Seller #2 / Juke Box #2 | | Specialty 390 |
| 6/16/51 | 8 | 2 | 4 **What A Fool I Was** <br> Best Seller #8 / Juke Box #8 | | Specialty 400 |
| 11/03/51 | 9 | 2 | 5 **Prayin' For Your Return** <br> Juke Box #9 | | Specialty 408 |
| 1/12/52 | 9 | 1 | 6 **Cry Baby** <br> Best Seller #9 | | Specialty 416 |
| 4/05/52 | 6 | 2 | 7 **Big Question** <br> Juke Box #6 / Best Seller #9 | | Specialty 425 |
| 7/13/63 | 25 | 4 | 8 River's Invitation | 99 | Tangerine 931 |
| 3/14/70 | 41 | 3 | 9 To Live In The Past | | RCA 0307 |
| 9/07/74 | 64 | 5 | 10 I Don't Want To Be President | | Atlantic 3207 |
| | | | **MAZARATI** | | |
| | | | Minneapolis funk/rock septet - Sir Casey Terry, lead singer. Group formed and produced by Prince's bassist, Brownmark. | | |
| 3/29/86 | 79 | 6 | 1 Player's Ball | | Paisley P. 28759 |

**279**

| DEBUT DATE | PEAK POS | WKS CHR | ARTIST — Record Title | POP POS | Label & Number |
|---|---|---|---|---|---|
| | | | **MAZARATI — Continued** | | |
| 5/17/86 | 19 | 14 | 2  100 MPH.......................................... | | Paisley P. 28705 |
| | | | **MAZE Featuring FRANKIE BEVERLY**  ★★**111**★★ | | |
| | | | Group from Philadelphia, formed as the Butlers (later, Raw Soul). To San Francisco in the mid-70s. Re-formed as Maze, consisting of Frankie Beverly, Wayne Thomas, Sam Porter, Robin Duke, Roame Lowry, McKinley Williams, and Joe Provost. Provost replaced by Ahaguna G. Sun. Sun replaced by Billy "Shoes" Johnson, Thomas replaced by Ron Smith. Philip Woo added in 1980. | | |
| 4/02/77 | 21 | 17 | 1  While I'm Alone.......................................... | 89 | Capitol 4392 |
| 8/06/77 | 13 | 17 | 2  Lady Of Magic .......................................... | 108 | Capitol 4456 |
| 1/21/78 | 9 | 17 | 3  Workin' Together .......................................... | | Capitol 4531 |
| 5/27/78 | 39 | 9 | 4  Golden Time Of Day/ | | Capitol 4580 |
| | | 9 | 5  Travelin' Man.......................................... | | |
| 9/30/78 | 61 | 8 | 6  I Wish You Well .......................................... | | Capitol 4629 |
| 3/03/79 | 7 | 20 | 7  **Feel That You're Feelin'**.......................... | 67 | Capitol 4686 |
| 7/14/79 | 55 | 10 | 8  Timin'.......................................... | | Capitol 4742 |
| 7/19/80 | 9 | 18 | 9  **Southern Girl**.......................................... | | Capitol 4891 |
| 11/15/80+ | 29 | 16 | 10  The Look In Your Eyes.......................... | | Capitol 4942 |
| 5/16/81 | 7 | 17 | 11  **Running Away**.......................................... | | Capitol 5000 |
| 8/22/81 | 13 | 16 | 12  Before I Let Go.......................................... | | Capitol 5031 |
| 1/23/82 | 29 | 9 | 13  We Need Love To Live.......................... | | Capitol 5072 |
| 4/30/83 | 5 | 17 | 14  **Love Is The Key**.......................................... | 80 | Capitol 5221 |
| 8/06/83 | 26 | 10 | 15  Never Let You Down.......................... | | Capitol 5255 |
| 10/29/83 | 47 | 12 | 16  We Are One.......................................... | | Capitol 5285 |
| 2/04/84 | 59 | 8 | 17  I Wanna Thank You.......................... | | Capitol 5312 |
| 2/23/85 | 1[2] | 16 | 18  **Back In Stride**.......................................... | 88 | Capitol 5431 |
| 5/18/85 | 5 | 14 | 19  **Too Many Games** .......................................... | 103 | Capitol 5474 |
| 8/31/85 | 28 | 13 | 20  I Want To Feel I'm Wanted.......................... | | Capitol 5510 |
| 8/09/86 | 12 | 14 | 21  I Wanna Be With You.......................... | | Capitol 5599 |
| 11/08/86 | 38 | 12 | 22  When You Love Someone .......................... | | Capitol 5643 |
| | | | **LETTA MBULU** | | |
| | | | Singer from South Africa. Toured with Harry Belafonte for 4 years. Background vocals by her husband, Caiphus Semenya. | | |
| 4/16/77 | 97 | 2 | 1  Music Man .......................................... | | A&M 1915 |
| | | | **M.C. CHILL** | | |
| 2/15/86 | 70 | 9 | 1  Bust This Rhyme .......................................... | | Fever 808 |
| | | | **M.C. SHAN featuring T.J. SWAN** | | |
| 11/14/87 | 71 | 9 | 1  Left Me - Lonely.......................................... | | Cold Chill. 28123 |
| | | | **AL McCALL** | | |
| | | | New Jersey native. | | |
| 11/19/83 | 80 | 4 | 1  If You Ever Knew .......................................... | | Profile 7026 |
| | | | **CASH McCALL** | | |
| | | | Real name: Maurice Dollison. Singer/guitarist. With Gospel Songbirds vocal group in the early 60s; recorded for Nashboro. Wrote hit "That's How It Is" for Otis Clay. | | |
| 7/09/66 | 19 | 10 | 1  When You Wake Up.......................................... | 102 | Thomas 307 |
| | | | **TOUSSAINT McCALL** | | |
| | | | Organist/vocalist born in Monroe, Louisiana in 1934. Attended Southern University, later worked as a teacher. | | |
| 3/18/67 | 5 | 15 | 1  **Nothing Takes The Place Of You** .................. | 52 | Ronn 3 |
| 7/08/67 | 26 | 7 | 2  I'll Do It For You.......................................... | 77 | Ronn 9 |
| | | | **LES McCANN - see EDDIE HARRIS** | | |
| | | | **PAUL McCARTNEY** | | |
| | | | Founding member/bass guitarist of the world's #1 rock group, The Beatles; born on 6/18/42 in Liverpool, England. Writer of over 50 Top 10 pop singles. First solo album in 1970. Formed group, Wings, in 1971. | | |
| 4/17/82 | 8 | 19 | 1●Ebony And Ivory.......................................... **PAUL McCARTNEY with STEVIE WONDER** | 1 | Columbia 02860 |
| 11/13/82+ | 1[3] | 20 | 2●The Girl Is Mine .......................................... **MICHAEL JACKSON/PAUL McCARTNEY** | 2 | Epic 03288 |

| DEBUT DATE | PEAK POS | WKS CHR | ARTIST — Record Title | POP POS | Label & Number |
|---|---|---|---|---|---|
| | | | **PAUL McCARTNEY — Continued** | | |
| 10/22/83 | **2**⁴ | 20 | 3 ● Say Say Say ............................................ | 1 | Columbia 04168 |
| | | | PAUL McCARTNEY & MICHAEL JACKSON | | |
| | | | 1 & 3: produced by George Martin (Beatles' producer) | | |
| | | | **ALTON McCLAIN & DESTINY** | | |
| | | | Female trio: Alton McClain with Destiny (D'Marie Warren and Robyrda Stiger). | | |
| 2/10/79 | **10** | 20 | 1 It Must Be Love ......................................... | 32 | Polydor 14532 |
| 7/28/79 | **69** | 6 | 2 Crazy Love .............................................. | | Polydor 14574 |
| 2/02/80 | **73** | 3 | 3 Hang On In There Baby ............................... | | Polydor 2050 |
| | | | Bristol's solo version originally charted in 1974 | | |
| | | | ALTON & JOHNNY (Bristol) | | |
| 4/19/80 | **76** | 4 | 4 I Don't Want To Be With Nobody Else .............. | | Polydor 2073 |
| 5/02/81 | **81** | 5 | 5 My Destiny .............................................. | | Polydor 2162 |
| | | | **JANICE McCLAIN** | | |
| | | | Singer from Philadelphia, daughter of Sandra McClain, formerly with the Fashions. | | |
| 1/26/80 | **91** | 2 | 1 Smack Dab In The Middle ............................. | | RFC 49103 |
| 11/29/86 | **75** | 8 | 2 Passion And Pain ...................................... | | MCA 52821 |
| | | | **THOMAS McCLARY** | | |
| | | | Vocalist/former guitarist with the Commodores. | | |
| 12/15/84+ | **57** | 10 | 1 Thin Walls ............................................... | | Motown 1768 |
| | | | **O.B. McCLINTON** | | |
| | | | Born Osbie Burnett McClinton on 4/25/40 in Senatobia, Mississippi. Died of abdominal cancer on 9/23/87. Worked on WDIA-Memphis and as staff writer for Stax/Volt Records. First recorded for Stax in 1971. One of the few black country stars. | | |
| 11/27/76 | **86** | 7 | 1 Black Speck ............................................. | | Mercury 73817 |
| | | | **BOBBY McCLURE** | | |
| | | | Born on 4/21/42 in Chicago; raised in East St. Louis. Sang in gospel group, the Spirit Of Illinois, from age 9. Sang with the Big Daddy Jenkins band in St. Louis. Worked as band singer with Oliver Sain. Solo work since 1966. | | |
| 2/06/65 | **5** | 15 | 1 Don't Mess Up A Good Thing ......................... | 33 | Checker 1097 |
| | | | FONTELLA BASS & BOBBY McCLURE | | |
| 6/19/65 | **27** | 6 | 2 You'll Miss Me (When I'm Gone) .................... | 91 | Checker 1111 |
| | | | FONTELLA BASS & BOBBY McCLURE | | |
| 11/12/66 | **16** | 10 | 3 Peak Of Love ........................................... | 97 | Checker 1152 |
| | | | **MARILYN McCOO** | | |
| | | | Former vocalist with the Hi-Fi's and The 5th Dimension. Married 5th Dimension member Billy Davis, Jr. in 1969; began recording as a duo in 1976. Host of the TV show "Sold Gold". | | |
| 12/03/83 | **76** | 7 | 1 Heart Stop Beating In Time ........................... | | RCA 13677 |
| | | | **MARILYN McCOO & BILLY DAVIS, JR.** | | |
| | | | Husband/wife duo; both were members of The 5th Dimension. Each recorded solo. | | |
| 4/17/76 | **37** | 16 | 1 I Hope We Get To Love In Time ...................... | 91 | ABC 12170 |
| 9/18/76 | **1**¹ | 21 | 2 ● You Don't Have To Be A Star (To Be In My Show) .................................................. | 1 | ABC 12208 |
| 3/26/77 | **9** | 12 | 3 Your Love .............................................. | 15 | ABC 12262 |
| 8/20/77 | **27** | 11 | 4 Look What You've Done To My Heart ............... | 51 | ABC 12298 |
| 11/19/77 | **76** | 9 | 5 Wonderful .............................................. | | ABC 12316 |
| 2/11/78 | **92** | 3 | 6 My Reason To Be Is You .............................. | | ABC 12324 |
| 9/16/78 | **86** | 4 | 7 Shine On Silver Moon ................................. | | Columbia 10806 |
| | | | **VAN McCOY** | | |
| | | | Born on 1/6/44 in Washington, DC; died of a heart attack on 7/6/79. Singer/pianist/producer. Sang with the Marylanders, own group the Starliters, recorded for End, in 1959. Had own Rock'N label in 1960. A&R man at Scepter/Wand, from 1961-64, produced the Shirelles, Gladys Knight and the Drifters. Own MAXX label in the mid-60s. Formed Van McCoy Productions in 1968. Discovered Faith, Hope & Charity, produced for the Stylistics and Brenda & The Tabulations. | | |
| 8/24/74 | **77** | 5 | 1 Love Is The Answer .................................... | | Avco 4639 |
| 2/01/75 | **67** | 5 | 2 Boogie Down ........................................... | | Avco 4648 |
| 4/26/75 | **1**¹ | 19 | 3 ● The Hustle ........................................ [I] | 1 | Avco 4653 |
| 10/11/75 | **6** | 14 | 4 Change With The Times ............................... | 46 | Avco 4660 |
| | | | all of above: with the Soul City Symphony | | |
| 4/17/76 | **51** | 7 | 5 Night Walk .......................................... [I] | 96 | H&L 4667 |
| 6/12/76 | **20** | 13 | 6 Party .................................................... | 69 | H&L 4670 |
| 12/25/76+ | **79** | 8 | 7 The Shuffle ............................................. | 105 | H&L 4677 |

| DEBUT DATE | PEAK POS | WKS CHR | ARTIST — Record Title | POP POS | Label & Number |
|---|---|---|---|---|---|
| | | | **VAN McCOY — Continued** | | |
| 4/29/78 | 76 | 8 | 8  My Favorite Fantasy | | MCA 40885 |
| | | | **JIMMY McCRACKLIN** | | |
| | | | Born on 8/13/21 in St. Louis. Singer/harmonica player. Settled in Los Angeles. Professional boxer in the mid-40s. First recorded for Globe in 1945. Own band, the Blues Blasters, in 1949. | | |
| 3/10/58 | 5 | 8 | 1  The Walk | 7 | Checker 885 |
| | | | Best Seller #5 / Jockey #7 | | |
| 10/16/61 | 2² | 19 | 2  Just Got To Know | 64 | Art-Tone 825 |
| 3/03/62 | 17 | 5 | 3  Shame, Shame, Shame | | Art-Tone 827 |
| 4/03/65 | 19 | 7 | 4  Every Night, Every Day | 91 | Imperial 66094 |
| 10/16/65 | 7 | 13 | 5  Think | 95 | Imperial 66129 |
| 1/29/66 | 11 | 11 | 6  My Answer | 92 | Imperial 66147 |
| 6/11/66 | 32 | 3 | 7  Come On Home | | Imperial 66168 |
| | | | **GEORGE McCRAE** | | |
| | | | Born on 10/19/44 in West Palm Beach, Florida; died on 1/24/86 of cancer. Duets with wife Gwen McCrae, became her manager. Also see Gwen McCrae. | | |
| 5/11/74 | 1² | 19 | 1  Rock Your Baby | 1 | T.K. 1004 |
| 10/12/74 | 10 | 12 | 2  I Can't Leave You Alone/ | 50 | |
| 12/28/74+ | 8 | 18 | 3   I Get Lifted | 37 | T.K. 1007 |
| 4/26/75 | 31 | 8 | 4  Look At You | 95 | T.K. 1011 |
| 8/23/75 | 31 | 10 | 5  I Ain't Lyin' | | T.K. 1014 |
| 12/20/75+ | 18 | 14 | 6  Honey I | 65 | T.K. 1016 |
| | | | all of above: written & produced by Harry Wayne Casey and Richard Finch of KC & The Sunshine Band | | |
| 4/17/76 | 44 | 7 | 7  Winners Together Or Losers Apart | | Cat 2002 |
| | | | **GEORGE & GWEN McCRAE** | | |
| 11/12/77 | 57 | 11 | 8  Kiss Me (The Way I Like It) | 110 | T.K. 1024 |
| 6/24/78 | 93 | 3 | 9  Let's Dance | | T.K. 1029 |
| 2/03/79 | 91 | 3 | 10  I Want You Around Me | | T.K. 1032 |
| | | | **GWEN McCRAE** | | |
| | | | Born on 12/21/43 in Pensacola, Florida. Married George McCrae, who later became her manager. First recorded with George for Alston in 1969. | | |
| 11/07/70 | 32 | 6 | 1  Lead Me On | 102 | Columbia 45214 |
| 9/29/73 | 17 | 15 | 2  For Your Love | | Cat 1989 |
| 4/27/74 | 66 | 8 | 3  It's Worth The Hurt | | Cat 1992 |
| 3/22/75 | 1¹ | 20 | 4  Rockin' Chair | 9 | Cat 1996 |
| | | | backing vocal by George McCrae | | |
| 9/27/75 | 16 | 13 | 5  Love Insurance | | Cat 1999 |
| 3/06/76 | 53 | 6 | 6  Cradle Of Love | | Cat 2000 |
| 4/17/76 | 44 | 7 | 7  Winners Together Or Losers Apart | | Cat 2002 |
| | | | **GEORGE & GWEN McCRAE** | | |
| 12/18/76+ | 72 | 7 | 8  Damn Right It's Good | | Cat 2005 |
| 9/19/81 | 22 | 19 | 9  Funky Sensation | | Atlantic 3853 |
| 1/08/83 | 60 | 8 | 10  Keep The Fire Burning | | Atlantic 89910 |
| 5/12/84 | 83 | 5 | 11  Do You Know What I Mean | | Black Jack 0021 |
| | | | **THE McCRARYS** | | |
| | | | Siblings Linda, Charity, Alfred and Sam McCrary. | | |
| 5/27/78 | 9 | 22 | 1  You | 45 | Portrait 70014 |
| 10/28/78 | 40 | 8 | 2  Don't Wear Your Self Out | | Portrait 70022 |
| 4/07/79 | 35 | 12 | 3  Lost In Loving You | | Portrait 70028 |
| 6/26/82 | 72 | 5 | 4  Love On A Summer Night | | Capitol 5122 |
| | | | **ULLANDA McCULLOUGH** | | |
| | | | Vocalist from Detroit. Toured for four years with Ashford & Simpson. Popular session singer in New York City. | | |
| 3/21/81 | 36 | 11 | 1  Bad Company | | Atlantic 3804 |
| | | | **GENE McDANIELS** | | |
| | | | Born Eugene B. McDaniels on 2/12/35 in Kansas City. To Omaha, early 1940s, sang in choirs, attended Omaha Conservatory of Music. Own band, early 50s. Appeared in the film "It's Trad, Dad" in 1962. | | |
| 5/01/61 | 11 | 5 | 1  A Hundred Pounds Of Clay | 3 | Liberty 55308 |
| 11/13/61 | 5 | 8 | 2  Tower Of Strength | 5 | Liberty 55371 |

| DEBUT DATE | PEAK POS | WKS CHR | ARTIST — Record Title | POP POS | Label & Number |
|---|---|---|---|---|---|
| | | | **GENE McDANIELS — Continued** | | |
| 9/15/62 | **23** | 4 | 3 Point Of No Return ............................................... | *21* | Liberty 55480 |
| | | | above 2: with The Johnny Mann Singers | | |
| | | | all of above: produced by Snuff Garrett | | |
| | | | **MICHAEL McDONALD** | | |
| | | | Keyboardist from St. Louis, Missouri. Formerly with Steely Dan and The Doobie Brothers. Married to singer Amy Holland. Also see Nicolette Larson. | | |
| 8/21/82 | **7** | 17 | 1 **I Keep Forgettin' (Every Time You're Near)** .... | *4* | Warner 29933 |
| 12/17/83+ | **5** | 19 | 2 **Yah Mo B There** ................................................... | *19* | Qwest 29394 |
| | | | **JAMES INGRAM with MICHAEL McDONALD** | | |
| 3/29/86 | **1**⁴ | 21 | 3●**On My Own** ........................................................... | *1* | MCA 52770 |
| | | | **PATTI LaBELLE & MICHAEL McDONALD** | | |
| 6/28/86 | **17** | 13 | 4 Sweet Freedom ................................................... | *7* | MCA 52857 |
| | | | from the film "Running Scared" | | |
| | | | **CARRIE McDOWELL** | | |
| | | | Vocalist from Des Moines, Iowa. At the age of 10, made 3 appearances on the "Tonight Show" and was the opening act for George Burns, Liberace, and Danny Thomas. | | |
| 4/18/87 | **65** | 9 | 1 Uh Uh, No No Casual Sex (Pt. 1) ..................... | | Motown 1885 |
| | | | originally titled only as "Casual Sex" | | |
| | | | **BROTHER JACK McDUFF** | | |
| | | | Born Eugene McDuffy on 9/17/26 in Champaign, Illinois. Organist, with Schoolboy Porter in 1946; Jimmy Coe and Willis Jackson from 1958-59. First recorded for Prestige in 1960. | | |
| 10/05/68 | **42** | 3 | 1 Let My People Go ........................................ [I] | | Cadet 5614 |
| 1/03/70 | **48** | 2 | 2 Theme From Electric Surfboard ................... [I] | *95* | Blue Note 1953 |
| | | | **McFADDEN & WHITEHEAD** | | |
| | | | Duo of Gene McFadden and John Whitehead from Philadelphia. Wrote and produced songs for many Philadelphia soul acts; defined "The Sound Of Philadelphia". While teenagers, were members of band, The Epsilons, that toured with and were managed by Otis Redding until his death in 1967. Whitehead recorded solo in 1988. | | |
| 4/07/79 | **1**¹ | 22 | 1 **Ain't No Stoppin' Us Now** ............................. | *13* | Phil. Int. 3681 |
| 12/15/79+ | **73** | 7 | 2 I've Been Pushed Aside ................................. | | Phil. Int. 3725 |
| 8/02/80 | **23** | 15 | 3 I Heard It In A Love Song ............................. | | TSOP 4788 |
| 11/20/82 | **58** | 10 | 4 One More Time ............................................... | | Capitol 5176 |
| | | | **BROWNIE McGHEE** | | |
| | | | Born Walter Brown McGhee on 11/30/15 in Knoxville, Tennessee. Vocalist/pianist/ guitarist. Older brother of Stick McGhee. Diagnosed with polio at age 4. With father in gospel group, Golden Voices, from 1934-36. Formed a vocal duo with Sonny Terry in 1939. Appeared in many films and TV shows (in USA and overseas). Active into the 80s. | | |
| 10/09/48 | **2**¹ | 8 | 1 **My Fault** ...................................................... | | Savoy 5551 |
| | | | Juke Box #2 / Best Seller #11 | | |
| | | | with Hal Singer on tenor sax | | |
| | | | **JACCI McGHEE - see KEITH SWEAT** | | |
| | | | **STICK McGHEE & HIS BUDDIES** | | |
| | | | Born Granville H. McGhee on 3/23/18 in Knoxville, Tennessee. Died of cancer on 8/15/61 (43). Vocalist/guitarist. Younger brother of Brownie McGhee (present on many of his recordings). Also known as "Globetrotter" and "Sticks". | | |
| 4/02/49 | **2**⁴ | 23 | 1 **Drinking Wine, Spo-Dee-O-Dee, Drinking Wine** .................................................... | *26* | Atlantic 873 |
| | | | Juke Box #2 / Best Seller #3 | | |
| 3/31/51 | **2**¹ | 6 | 2 **Tennessee Waltz Blues** ............................. [I] | | Atlantic 926 |
| | | | Best Seller #2 / Juke Box #5 | | |
| | | | **ROLLIE McGILL** | | |
| | | | Vocalist/pianist/saxophonist. | | |
| 8/06/55 | **10** | 2 | 1 **There Goes That Train** ............................... | | Mercury 70582 |
| | | | Jockey #10 / Juke Box #10 | | |
| | | | **EDNA McGRIFF - see BUDDY LUCAS** | | |
| | | | **JIMMY McGRIFF** | | |
| | | | Born on 4/3/36 in Philadelphia. Organist/multi-instrumentalist. Toured with Don Gardner and Arthur Prysock. | | |
| 10/27/62 | **5** | 11 | 1 **I've Got A Woman, Part 1** ......................... [I] | *20* | Sue 770 |
| | | | originally released on Jell | | |
| 2/02/63 | **12** | 4 | 2 All About My Girl .................................... [I] | *50* | Sue 777 |
| 5/16/64 | **79** | 4 | 3 Kiko ........................................................ [I] | *Hot* | Sue 10001 |

| DEBUT DATE | PEAK POS | WKS CHR | ARTIST — Record Title | POP POS | Label & Number |
|---|---|---|---|---|---|
| | | | **JIMMY McGRIFF — Continued** | | |
| 12/07/68+ | **28** | 7 | 4  The Worm........................................ [I] | *97* | Solid State 2524 |
| | | | originally released on Jell | | |
| | | | **LONETT McKEE** | | |
| | | | Born in 1945 in Detroit. Singer/pianist/actress. Sang with the Soul Sisters on Jonathan Winters' TV show. In the films "Sparkle", "Cotton Club" and "Which Way Is Up". | | |
| 11/23/74 | **96** | 3 | 1  Save It ................................................. | | Sussex 624 |
| | | | **MALCOLM McLAREN - see THE WORLD'S FAMOUS SUPREME TEAM** | | |
| | | | **PENNY McLEAN** | | |
| 1/03/76 | **90** | 5 | 1  Lady Bump ......................................... | *48* | Atco 7038 |
| | | | **BIG JAY McNEELY & BAND** | | |
| | | | Born Cecil James McNeely on 4/29/27 in Los Angeles. Tenor saxophonist/leader. Originator of the acrobatic, wild honking sax style. Toured with small band, usually with brothers Bob & Dillard McNeely, Melvin Glass and Leonard "Tight" Hardiman. Active into the 80s. | | |
| 1/29/49 | **1**[1] | 14 | 1  Deacon's Hop ................................ [I] | | Savoy 685 |
| | | | Best Seller #1(1) / Juke Box #1(1) | | |
| 2/26/49 | **12** | 1 | 2  Wild Wig.......................................... [I] | | Savoy 682 |
| | | | Juke Box #12 | | |
| | | | above 2: with His Blue Jays | | |
| 6/01/59 | **5** | 25 | 3  There Is Something On Your Mind................ | *44* | Swingin' 614 |
| | | | vocal by Little Sonny Warner | | |
| | | | **RONNIE McNEIR** | | |
| | | | Born in Camden, Alabama; raised in Pontiac, Michigan. Vocalist/keyboardist. First recorded at age 14. Moved to Hollywood in 1971, discovered by Kim Weston. | | |
| 5/17/75 | **51** | 10 | 1  Wendy Is Gone .................................. | | Prodigal 0614 |
| 12/27/75+ | **63** | 8 | 2  Saggitarian Affair............................. | | Prodigal 0620 |
| 4/21/84 | **76** | 5 | 3  Come Be With Me.............................. | | Capitol 5318 |
| | | | **CLYDE McPHATTER**   ★★138★★ | | |
| | | | Born Clyde Lensley McPhatter on 11/15/32 in Durham, North Carolina. Died on 6/13/72 in New York City (heart attack). Signed by Billy Ward for the Dominoes in 1950. Left the Dominoes in June, 1953 to form own group, The Drifters. Drafted in 1954, returned to sing solo. One of the most influential and distinctive male voices of the R&B era. | | |
| 12/03/55 | **8** | 3 | 1  Love Has Joined Us Together...................... | | Atlantic 1077 |
| | | | RUTH BROWN & CLYDE McPHATTER Jockey #8 | | |
| 1/07/56 | **2**[4] | 13 | 2  Seven Days ........................................ | *44* | Atlantic 1081 |
| | | | Jockey #2 / Juke Box #2 / Best Seller #3 | | |
| 5/26/56 | **1**[1] | 13 | 3  Treasure Of Love................................. | *16* | Atlantic 1092 |
| | | | Juke Box #1 / Jockey #2 / Best Seller #3 | | |
| 1/12/57 | **4** | 11 | 4  Without Love (There Is Nothing)................... | *19* | Atlantic 1117 |
| | | | Jockey #4 / Juke Box #4 / Best Seller #6 | | |
| 4/29/57 | **6** | 11 | 5  Just To Hold My Hand ........................... | *26* | Atlantic 1133 |
| | | | Jockey #6 / Juke Box #7 / Best Seller #8 | | |
| 8/05/57 | **1**[1] | 9 | 6  Long Lonely Nights.............................. | *49* | Atlantic 1149 |
| | | | Jockey #1 / Best Seller #9 | | |
| 6/16/58 | **3** | 5 | 7  Come What May ................................. | *43* | Atlantic 1185 |
| | | | Jockey #3 / Best Seller #20 | | |
| 10/20/58 | **1**[1] | 23 | 8  A Lover's Question ............................... | *6* | Atlantic 1199 |
| 4/13/59 | **12** | 6 | 9  Lovey Dovey ...................................... | *49* | Atlantic 2018 |
| 6/15/59 | **14** | 12 | 10  Since You've Been Gone ...................... | *38* | Atlantic 2028 |
| 10/19/59 | **13** | 6 | 11  You Went Back On Your Word................ | *72* | Atlantic 2038 |
| 1/04/60 | **13** | 4 | 12  Let's Try Again.................................. | *48* | MGM 12843 |
| 8/15/60 | **7** | 10 | 13  Ta Ta ............................................. | *23* | Mercury 71660 |
| 7/17/61 | **17** | 6 | 14  I Never Knew .................................... | *56* | Mercury 71841 |
| 1/04/64 | **90** | 5 | 15  Deep In The Heart Of Harlem.................... | *Hot* | Mercury 72220 |
| 4/17/65 | **22** | 5 | 16  Crying Won't Help You Now .................... | *117* | Mercury 72407 |
| | | | **WYATT (EARP) McPHERSON** | | |
| 6/05/61 | **26** | 1 | 1  Here's My Confession................................ | *97* | Savoy 1599 |

| DEBUT DATE | PEAK POS | WKS CHR | ARTIST — Record Title | POP POS | Label & Number |
|---|---|---|---|---|---|
| | | | **JAY McSHANN**<br>Born on 1/12/09 in Muskogee, Oklahoma. Nicknamed Hootie. Pianist/leader. Played since age 12. With Eddie Hill in the early 30s. Formed own band in Kansas City in 1937, which included Charlie Parker. First recorded for Decca in 1941. | | |
| 7/17/43 | **7** | 8 | 1 **Get Me On Your Mind**.................................<br>vocal by Al Hibbler | *18* | Decca 4418 |
| 1/15/49 | **9** | 7 | 2 **Hot Biscuits**.............................. [I]<br>Best Seller #9 / Juke Box #12 | | Downbeat 165 |
| 4/16/49 | **15** | 1 | 3 Buttermilk............................. [I]<br>Best Seller #15 | | Downbeat 172 |
| 11/05/55 | **1**³ | 16 | 4 **Hands Off**.............................<br>Best Seller #1(3) / Jockey #1(2) / Juke Box #1(2)<br>vocal by Priscilla Bowman (d: 7/24/88) | | Vee-Jay 155 |
| | | | **JACK McVEA**<br>Born on 11/5/14 in Los Angeles. Vocalist/saxophonist/clarinetist. In father's band at age 11. With Walter "Dootsie" William's Harlem Dukes from 1932-34. With Lionel Hampton from 1940-43, then formed own band in 1944. Featured in the film "Sarge Goes To College". In later years, led trio at Disneyland. | | |
| 2/08/47 | **2**² | 7 | 1 **Open The Door, Richard!**......................... [C]<br>vocals by McVea & John "Red" Kelly | *3* | Blk. & Wht. 792 |
| | | | **PAULETTE McWILLIAMS**<br>Singer from Chicago. Appeared on the Patricia Vance TV show at age 11. Joined the rock quartet American Breed in 1969, which evolved into Ask Rufus (later known as Rufus). Went solo in 1972; replaced by Chaka Khan. Made many radio and TV commercials. | | |
| 2/19/77 | **97** | 2 | 1 Dancin' .......................................... | | Fantasy 786 |
| | | | **MEADOWS BROTHERS**<br>Family trio led by Wilson Meadows. | | |
| 9/24/77 | **76** | 6 | 1 I Can't Understand ................................. | | Kayvette 5132 |
| | | | **MEAN MACHINE** | | |
| 10/03/81 | **42** | 10 | 1 Disco Dream................................. | | Sugar Hill 768 |
| | | | **MEATLOAF - see STONEY** | | |
| | | | **MECO**<br>Discofied instrumentals by producer Meco Monardo; born on 11/29/39 in Johnsonburg, Pennsylvania. | | |
| 9/03/77 | **8** | 15 | 1▲**Star Wars Theme/Cantina Band**................ [I] | *1* | Millennium 604 |
| 2/04/78 | **76** | 5 | 2 Theme From Close Encounters ................... [I] | *25* | Millennium 608 |
| | | | **BILL MEDLEY**<br>Born on 9/19/40 in Santa Ana, California. Baritone of the Righteous Brothers duo. | | |
| 9/07/68 | **37** | 7 | 1 Brown Eyed Woman ..................................... | *43* | MGM 13959 |
| | | | **MEL & KIM**<br>British dance/disco sister duo. | | |
| 1/24/87 | **23** | 13 | 1 Showing Out (Get Fresh at the Weekend)........... | *78* | Atlantic 89329 |
| | | | **MEL & TIM**<br>Cousins Mel Hardin and Tim McPherson, from Holly Springs, Mississippi. | | |
| 10/18/69 | **3** | 14 | 1●Backfield In Motion ................................. | *10* | Bamboo 107 |
| 2/07/70 | **17** | 8 | 2 Good Guys Only Win In The Movies ................. | *45* | Bamboo 109 |
| 7/08/72 | **4** | 14 | 3 Starting All Over Again ............................. | *19* | Stax 0127 |
| 3/10/73 | **33** | 4 | 4 I May Not Be What You Want ......................... | *113* | Stax 0154 |
| 10/05/74 | **79** | 2<br>3 | 5 Forever And A Day/<br>6 That's The Way I Want To Live My Life........... | | Stax 0224 |
| | | | **MELBA & KASHIF - see MELBA MOORE and/or KASHIF** | | |
| | | | **MELLE MEL - see DUKE BOOTEE/GRANDMASTER/REBBIE JACKSON/CHAKA KHAN** | | |
| | | | **MELLAA** | | |
| 4/02/83 | **58** | 8 | 1 Makin' Love In The Fast Lane ......................... | | Larc 81014 |

| DEBUT DATE | PEAK POS | WKS CHR | ARTIST — Record Title | POP POS | Label & Number |
|---|---|---|---|---|---|
| | | | **MELLOW MOODS** | | |
| | | | Also known as Mello-Moods or Mellomoods. New York City group formed in 1950: Ray "Buddy" Wooten, Bobby Williams, Monteith "Monte" Owens, Alvin "Bobby" Baylor and Jimmy Bethea. Baylor, Owens and Williams were later in the Solitaires. | | |
| 2/23/52 | **7** | 1 | **1  Where Are You? (Now That I Need You)** .......... | | Robin 105 |
| | | | Best Seller #7 | | |
| | | | with The Schubert Swanston Trio | | |
| | | | **HAROLD MELVIN & THE BLUE NOTES**   ★★**104**★★ | | |
| | | | Philadelphia group formed in 1954. Consisted of Harold Melvin, Bernard Williams, Jesse Gillis, Jr., Franklin Peaker and Roosevelt Brodie. First recorded for Josie in 1956. Numerous personnel changes to 1970, when Teddy Pendergrass joined as drummer and lead singer. Pendergrass went solo in 1975, relaced by David Ebo. | | |
| 10/31/60 | **19** | 7 | **1  My Hero** ........................................ | *78* | Val-ue 213 |
| | | | THE BLUE NOTES | | |
| 1/30/65 | **38** | 1 | **2**  Get Out ...................................... | *125* | Landa 703 |
| | | | lead vocal by John Atkins | | |
| 6/17/72 | **7** | 15 | **3  I Miss You (Part I)** ........................ | *58* | Phil. Int. 3516 |
| 10/14/72 | **1** ² | 16 | **4 ●If You Don't Know Me By Now** ............... | *3* | Phil. Int. 3520 |
| 3/31/73 | **12** | 8 | **5**  Yesterday I Had The Blues ................... | *63* | Phil. Int. 3525 |
| 9/22/73 | **1** ² | 17 | **6 ●The Love I Lost (Part 1)** .................. | *7* | Phil. Int. 3533 |
| 3/23/74 | **6** | 16 | **7**  Satisfaction Guaranteed (Or Take Your Love Back)/ | *58* | |
| | | 1 | **8**  I'm Weak For You ........................... | | Phil. Int. 3543 |
| 11/02/74 | **8** | 13 | **9  Where Are All My Friends** ............... | *80* | Phil. Int. 3552 |
| 3/15/75 | **4** | 15 | **10  Bad Luck (Part 1)** ........................ | *15* | Phil. Int. 3562 |
| 6/21/75 | **1** ¹ | 16 | **11  Hope That We Can Be Together Soon** ............ | *42* | Phil. Int. 3569 |
| | | | SHARON PAIGE and HAROLD MELVIN & THE BLUE NOTES | | |
| 11/15/75+ | **1** ² | 17 | **12  Wake Up Everybody (Part 1)** ................. | *12* | Phil. Int. 3579 |
| 3/20/76 | **7** | 11 | **13**  Tell The World How I Feel About 'Cha Baby ... | *94* | Phil. Int. 3588 |
| | | | all of above (except #1 & 2): produced by Kenny Gamble & Leon Huff | | |
| 1/29/77 | **6** | 15 | **14  Reaching For The World** .................... | *74* | ABC 12240 |
| 5/07/77 | **15** | 12 | **15**  After You Love Me, Why Do You Leave Me ........ | *102* | ABC 12268 |
| | | | HAROLD MELVIN & THE BLUE NOTES featuring SHARON PAGE | | |
| 1/28/78 | **36** | 10 | **16**  Baby, You Got My Nose Open .............. | | ABC 12327 |
| 12/15/79+ | **18** | 20 | **17**  Prayin' .................................... | | Source 41156 |
| 2/23/80 | **61** | 7 | **18**  Tonight's The Night ...................... | | Source 41157 |
| | | | SHARON PAIGE and HAROLD MELVIN & THE BLUE NOTES | | |
| 5/10/80 | **25** | 12 | **19**  I Should Be Your Lover ................... | | Source 41231 |
| 10/17/81 | **52** | 9 | **20**  Hang On In There ........................ | | MCA 51190 |
| 5/26/84 | **85** | 4 | **21**  Don't Give Me Up ........................ | | Philly W. 99761 |
| 9/01/84 | **81** | 4 | **22**  Today's Your Lucky Day .................. | | Philly W. 99735 |
| | | | featuring Nikko | | |
| 11/17/84 | **81** | 4 | **23**  I Really Love You ........................ | | Philly W. 99709 |
| | | | **THE MEMPHIS HORNS** | | |
| | | | Studio group including Wayne Jackson, Andrew Love, Floyd Newman, Jimmy Brown, Don Chandler, Charlie Freeman, Tommy McClure and Sammy Creason. Jackson was a member of the Mar-Keys. Also see Jackie Moore. | | |
| 12/11/76+ | **61** | 11 | **1**  Get Up And Dance .......................... | *108* | RCA 10836 |
| 7/02/77 | **83** | 3 | **2**  What The Funk ............................. | | RCA 10999 |
| 9/03/77 | **17** | 20 | **3**  Just For Your Love ........................ | *101* | RCA 11064 |
| 7/29/78 | **42** | 11 | **4**  Our Love Will Survive ..................... | | RCA 11309 |
| | | | **MEMPHIS SLIM** | | |
| | | | Born Peter Chatman, Jr. on 9/3/15 in Memphis. Self-taught pianist/organist/vocalist. To Chicago in 1937. Worked with Bill Broonzy. First recorded for Okeh in 1940. Moved to Paris in 1961. Died of kidney failure on 2/24/88 (72) in Paris. | | |
| 5/22/48 | **1** ² | 18 | **1  Messin' Around** ............................ | | Miracle 125 |
| | | | Juke Box #1 / Best Seller #5 | | |
| 2/26/49 | **11** | 1 | **2  Frisco Bay** ................................ | | Miracle 132 |
| | | | Best Seller #11 / Juke Box #12 | | |
| 7/16/49 | **2** ² | 11 | **3  Blue And Lonesome/** | | |
| | | | Juke Box #2 / Best Seller #3 | | |
| 9/17/49 | **9** | 1 | **4   Help Me Some** ............................. | | Miracle 136 |
| | | | Juke Box #9 | | |
| 11/19/49 | **6** | 5 | **5  Angel Child** ............................... | | Miracle 145 |
| | | | Juke Box #6 / Best Seller #7 | | |
| 1/20/51 | **7** | 3 | **6  Mother Earth** .............................. | | Premium 867 |
| | | | Juke Box #7 | | |

| DEBUT DATE | PEAK POS | WKS CHR | ARTIST — Record Title | POP POS | Label & Number |
|---|---|---|---|---|---|
| | | | **MEMPHIS SLIM — Continued** | | |
| 11/07/53 | **3** | 1 | 7 **The Come Back**.............................................<br>Juke Box #3 | | United 156 |
| | | | **SERGIO MENDES**<br>Born on 2/11/41 in Niteroi, Brazil. Pianist/bandleader. Resident in U.S. since the mid-60s. Originator of the "bossa nova" style. | | |
| 8/06/77 | **51** | 11 | 1 The Real Thing .............................................. | | Elektra 45416 |
| 12/22/79+ | **49** | 11 | 2 I'll Tell You........................................<br>**SERGIO MENDES, BRASIL '88** | | Elektra 46567 |
| 4/23/83 | **28** | 19 | 3 Never Gonna Let You Go ........................<br>vocals by Joe Pizzulo & Leza Miller | *4* | A&M 2540 |
| | | | **MENUDO**<br>Puerto Rican teen quintet. The superstar group of Latin America. | | |
| 7/28/84 | **36** | 12 | 1 If You're Not Here (By My Side)..................... | *102* | RCA 13771 |
| 6/01/85 | **61** | 8 | 2 Hold Me........................................................ | *62* | RCA 14087 |
| | | | **MERC & MONK**<br>Eric Mercury and Thelonious S. Monk III. | | |
| 5/04/85 | **76** | 5 | 1 Baby Face ................................................. | | Manhattan 50003 |
| | | | **JOHNNY MERCER**<br>Born on 11/18/09 in Savannah, Georgia. Legendary lyricist of more than 1000 songs, including "Blues In The Night", "That Old Black Magic" and "Moon River". Founded Capitol Records in 1942. Died on 6/25/76 (66). | | |
| 1/08/44 | **1**¹ | 6 | 1 **G.I. Jive** ................................................. | *11* | Capitol 141 |
| 1/27/45 | **4** | 3 | 2 **Ac-Cent-Tchu-Ate The Positive**....................<br>accompanied by Paul Weston's Orchestra;<br>from the film "Here Come The Waves" | *1* | Capitol 180 |
| | | | **ERIC MERCURY - see ROBERTA FLACK** | | |
| | | | **MERCY DEE**<br>Born Mercy Dee Walton on 8/3/15 in Waco, Texas. Died on 12/2/62 (cerebral hemorrhage). Vocalist/pianist. To Oakland, California in the late 30s. Toured with Big Jay McNeely band. Active until the time of his death. | | |
| 12/03/49+ | **7** | 5 | 1 **Lonesome Cabin Blues**................................<br>Best Seller #7 | | Spire 001 |
| 6/06/53 | **8** | 3 | 2 **One Room Country Shack** ...........................<br>Juke Box #8 | | Specialty 458 |
| | | | **MERGE**<br>Sextet from Chicago, formed as 357 Python in 1975. Included: Randy Alexander, Marion Mathis, Reginald Morris, Carlton Johnson, Marc Reaux and Debbie Alexander (vocals). | | |
| 3/27/82 | **67** | 5 | 1 Take It To The Top..................................... | | RCA 13050 |
| | | | **MES'AY** | | |
| 2/28/87 | **71** | 7 | 1 Climb The Walls ....................................... | | Superstar I. 51 |
| | | | **THE METERS**<br>Instrumental group formed in New Orleans in 1966. Consisted of Arthur Lanon Neville, Leo Nocentelli, Joseph "Zigaboo" Modeliste and George Porter. Neville, brother of Aaron Neville, had been in the Hawketts vocal group. Backed Fats Domino, Lee Dorsey, Betty Harris, Irma Thomas, and many others. Toured with the Rolling Stones in 1975, back up for Robert Palmer and Paul McCartney. Group disbanded in 1977 when Art, Aaron and brothers Charles and Cyril formed the Neville Brothers. | | |
| 2/01/69 | **7** | 10 | 1 Sophisticated Cissy ................................. [I] | *34* | Josie 1001 |
| 4/19/69 | **4** | 12 | 2 Cissy Strut .............................................. [I] | *23* | Josie 1005 |
| 7/19/69 | **20** | 7 | 3 Ease Back................................................ [I] | *61* | Josie 1008 |
| 11/01/69 | **39** | 3 | 4 Dry Spell ................................................ [I] | | Josie 1013 |
| 12/06/69+ | **11** | 9 | 5 Look-Ka Py Py ........................................ [I] | *56* | Josie 1015 |
| 4/04/70 | **11** | 8 | 6 Chicken Strut ......................................... [I] | *50* | Josie 1018 |
| 6/20/70 | **26** | 8 | 7 Hand Clapping Song ................................ | *89* | Josie 1021 |
| 9/12/70 | **21** | 7 | 8 A Message From The Meters....................... | | Josie 1024 |
| 2/06/71 | **42** | 3 | 9 Stretch Your Rubber Band ........................ | | Josie 1026 |
| 6/12/71 | **47** | 4 | 10 Doodle Oop ............................................ | | Josie 1029 |
| 9/07/74 | **31** | 12 | 11 Hey, Pokey-A-Way.................................. | | Reprise 1307 |
| 12/28/74+ | **52** | 11 | 12 People Say ............................................ | | Reprise 1314 |
| 8/14/76 | **87** | 4 | 13 Disco Is The Thing Today ........................ | | Reprise 1357 |
| 10/01/77 | **78** | 8 | 14 Be My Lady............................................ | *78* | Warner 8434 |

| DEBUT DATE | PEAK POS | WKS CHR | ARTIST — Record Title | POP POS | Label & Number |
|---|---|---|---|---|---|
| | | | **THE METROS** | | |
| 2/25/67 | **44** | 3 | 1  Sweetest One................................................ | *88* | RCA 8994 |
| | | | **MFSB** | | |
| | | | Large racially-mixed studio band formed by producers Kenny Gamble and Leon Huff. Also recorded as The James Boys, and Family. Name means "Mothers, Fathers, Sisters, Brothers". Also see The Music Makers. | | |
| 3/02/74 | **1**¹ | 17 | 1 ● **TSOP (The Sound Of Philadelphia)** ............. [I]<br>MFSB featuring THE THREE DEGREES<br>theme from the TV show "Soul Train" | *1* | Phil. Int. 3540 |
| 7/13/74 | **42** | 7 | 2  Love Is The Message......................................<br>MFSB featuring THE THREE DEGREES | *85* | Phil. Int. 3547 |
| 5/31/75 | **2**² | 17 | 3  **Sexy**............................................................. [I] | *42* | Phil. Int. 3567 |
| 9/27/75 | **54** | 6 | 4  T.L.C. (Tender Lovin' Care) ............................ | | Phil. Int. 3576 |
| 11/22/75 | **72** | 6 | 5  The Zip ...................................................... [I] | *91* | Phil. Int. 3578 |
| 8/28/76 | **65** | 4 | 6  Summertime And I'm Feelin' Mellow................ | | Phil. Int. 3600 |
| 8/05/78 | **94** | 2 | 7  Use Ta Be My Guy ....................................... | | Phil. Int. 3650 |
| | | | **M.G.'s - see BOOKER T.** | | |
| | | | **MIAMI** | | |
| 9/28/74 | **51** | 9 | 1  Party Freaks .................................................<br>MIAMI featuring Robert Moore | | Drive 6234 |
| 8/14/76 | **42** | 10 | 2  Kill That Roach ........................................... | *102* | Drive 6251 |
| | | | **MIAMI DISCO BAND featuring Beverly Barkley** | | |
| 3/17/79 | **96** | 3 | 1  (I Wanna) Go Home With You ..:..................... | | Salsoul 2084 |
| | | | **MIAMI SOUND MACHINE** | | |
| | | | Lead singer Gloria Estefan, with husband Emilio Estefan, Marcos Avila and Kiki Garcia. | | |
| 12/14/85+ | **60** | 14 | 1  Conga ......................................................... | *10* | Epic 05457 |
| 4/26/86 | **74** | 8 | 2  Bad Boy ...................................................... | *8* | Epic 05805 |
| 6/25/88 | **54** | 11 | 3  1 - 2 - 3 ....................................................<br>GLORIA ESTEFAN & MIAMI SOUND MACHINE | *3* | Epic 07921 |
| | | | **GEORGE MICHAEL** | | |
| | | | Born Georgios Kyriacos Panayiotou in Bushey, England. Former lead singer of Wham!. | | |
| 2/21/87 | **5** | 14 | 1  **I Knew You Were Waiting (For Me)**................<br>ARETHA FRANKLIN & GEORGE MICHAEL | *1* | Arista 9559 |
| 6/13/87 | **43** | 13 | 2  I Want Your Sex...........................................<br>from the film "Beverly Hills Cop II" | *2* | Columbia 07164 |
| 10/17/87 | **21** | 14 | 3  Hard Day ....................................................<br>available only on CD | | Columbia 07466 |
| 1/23/88 | **6** | 14 | 4  **Father Figure** ............................................ | *1* | Columbia 07682 |
| 4/23/88 | **1**¹ | ,17 | 5  **One More Try** ............................................ | *1* | Columbia 07773 |
| | | | **MICKEY & SYLVIA** | | |
| | | | McHouston "Mickey" Baker and Sylvia Vanderpool. Mickey (b: 10/15/25, Louisville) was a prolific session man on guitar for Atlantic, Savoy, King, Aladdin, and many others. Sylvia (b: 3/6/36, New York City), owner of Sugar Hill Records, first recorded as "Little Sylvia" with Hot Lips Page for Columbia in 1950. Began her solo career in 1973, recorded as Sylvia. | | |
| 12/22/56+ | **1**² | 15 | 1  **Love Is Strange** ..........................................<br>Jockey #1 / Best Seller #2 / Juke Box #2 | *11* | Groove 0175 |
| 4/13/57 | **8** | 3 | 2  **There Oughta Be A Law** ..............................<br>Jockey #8 / Juke Box #8 / Best Seller #15 | *47* | Vik 0267 |
| 9/25/61 | **27** | 3 | 3  Baby You're So Fine ..................................... | *52* | Willow 23000 |
| | | | **MICO WAVE** | | |
| | | | Singer/songwriter born on 12/27/61 in Champaign, Illinois. | | |
| 11/07/87 | **70** | 11 | 1  Misunderstood............................................. | | Columbia 07354 |
| 2/20/88 | **15** | 15 | 2  Instant Replay............................................. | | Columbia 07702 |
| | | | **MIDNIGHT STAR** | | |
| | | | Group from Louisville, Kentucky, formed in 1976. Consisted of Reginald Calloway, Vincent Calloway, Jeffrey Cooper, Kenneth Gant, Melvin Gantry, William Simmons and Boas Watson. Lead vocals by Belinda Lipscomb. Reginald Calloway produced many hits for Midnight Star and The Deele. | | |
| 4/05/80 | **85** | 4 | 1  Make It Last.............................................. | | Solar 11903 |
| 7/04/81 | **36** | 11 | 2  I've Been Watching You .............................. | | Solar 47933 |
| 11/21/81 | **60** | 9 | 3  Tuff.......................................................... | | Solar 47948 |

| DEBUT DATE | PEAK POS | WKS CHR | ARTIST — Record Title | POP POS | Label & Number |
|---|---|---|---|---|---|
| | | | **MIDNIGHT STAR — Continued** | | |
| 7/24/82 | 35 | 12 | 4 Hot Spot .................................................... | *108* | Solar 48012 |
| 11/20/82 | 83 | 4 | 5 Victory ..................................................... | | Solar 69932 |
| 6/11/83 | 2⁴ | 20 | 6 **Freak-A-Zoid** ........................................... | 66 | Solar 69828 |
| 10/15/83 | 8 | 17 | 7 **Wet My Whistle** ....................................... | 61 | Solar 69790 |
| 2/25/84 | 43 | 13 | 8 No Parking (On The Dance Floor) ...................... | 81 | Solar 69753 |
| 11/10/84 | 1⁵ | 17 | 9 **Operator** ................................................ | 18 | Solar 69684 |
| 2/23/85 | 16 | 12 | 10 Scientific Love............................................. | 80 | Solar 69659 |
| 6/01/85 | 31 | 10 | 11 Body Snatchers ......................................... | | Solar 69638 |
| 5/03/86 | 3 | 18 | 12 **Headlines**................................................ | 69 | Solar 69547 |
| 8/02/86 | 7 | 18 | 13 **Midas Touch** ........................................... | 42 | Solar 69525 |
| 12/27/86+ | 11 | 15 | 14 Engine No. 9............................................... | | Solar 69501 |

## THE MIDNIGHTERS - see HANK BALLARD

## MIDWAY

| | | | | | |
|---|---|---|---|---|---|
| 10/06/84 | 80 | 5 | 1 Set It Out.................................... | | Personal 49811 |

## MIGHTY CLOUDS OF JOY
Gospel group formed in Los Angeles in 1959: Willie Joe Ligon & Johnny Martin (leads), Elmo Franklin (baritone) and Richard Wallace (bass). Later joined by Leon Polk and David Walker. First recorded for Peacock in 1960. Early lead singer Bunker Hill recorded solo in 1962. Also see Roger.

| | | | | | |
|---|---|---|---|---|---|
| 10/05/74 | 32 | 11 | 1 Time.......................................... | *102* | ABC/Dunhill 15012 |
| 2/15/75 | 47 | 8 | 2 Mighty Cloud Of Joy ...................................... | | ABC/Dunhill 15025 |
| 2/14/76 | 22 | 11 | 3 Mighty High ................................. | 69 | ABC 12164 |
| 1/29/77 | 53 | 10 | 4 There's Love In The World (Tell The Lonely People).................................................. | | ABC 12241 |
| 2/20/82 | 63 | 5 | 5 Glow Love.................................... | | Myrrh 241 |

## MIGHTY FIRE
Quintet from Los Angeles: Mel Bolton, Alfred D'Lanie McQuaig, Harry Kim, Darryl Roberts and Perry Peyton. Bolton had been with Motown as a producer and writer.

| | | | | | |
|---|---|---|---|---|---|
| 1/26/80 | 66 | 9 | 1 Country Freakin' ........................... | | Zephyr 001 |
| 4/04/81 | 60 | 8 | 2 Love Attack ................................. | | Elektra 47108 |
| 10/24/81 | 91 | 3 | 3 I Could Write A Love Song........................... | | Elektra 47199 |
| 4/24/82 | 58 | 7 | 4 Sixth Street (Turn It Up) ........................... | | Elektra 47426 |

## MIGHTY FLEA

| | | | | | |
|---|---|---|---|---|---|
| 1/20/68 | 46 | 2 | 1 Ode To Billy Joe ........................... | | Eldo 155 |

## THE MIGHTY HANNIBAL
Real name is James T. Shaw.

| | | | | | |
|---|---|---|---|---|---|
| 11/12/66 | 21 | 8 | 1 Hymn No. 5.................................. | *115* | Shurfine 021 |

## MIGHTY MARVELOWS - see THE MARVELOWS

## MIGHTY POPE

| | | | | | |
|---|---|---|---|---|---|
| 9/03/77 | 93 | 4 | 1 Heaven On The Seventh Floor ...................... | | Private S. 45157 |

## MIKE & BILL
Songwriting duo of Michael Felder (guitar) and William Daniels (piano), formed in New York City. Felder sang in Romeo Four while in US Army at Fort Dix and in Germany. Wrote score for the film "The Long Night".

| | | | | | |
|---|---|---|---|---|---|
| 10/04/75 | 78 | 6 | 1 Somebody's Gotta Go (Sho Ain't Me) ................ | | Arista 0139 |

## MIKKI

| | | | | | |
|---|---|---|---|---|---|
| 11/27/82+ | 67 | 13 | 1 Itching For Love ........................... | | Emerald I. 101 |
| 4/23/83 | 82 | 4 | 2 Look Before You Leap.............................. | | Emerald I. 71003 |
| 9/01/84 | 59 | 8 | 3 Love Emergency ........................... | | Pop Art 1404 |

| DEBUT DATE | PEAK POS | WKS CHR | ARTIST — Record Title | POP POS | Label & Number |
|---|---|---|---|---|---|
| | | | **AMOS MILBURN** ★★**84**★★ | | |
| | | | Born on 4/1/27 in Houston, Texas. Died of a stroke on 1/3/80 (52). Vocalist/pianist. In US Navy from 1942-45. Own band in Houston in 1945. First recorded for Aladdin in 1946. Frequently worked with Charles Brown in the late 50s. Suffered first stroke in 1970. Largely in retirement until his death. | | |
| 11/20/48 | **1**⁵ | 23 | 1 **Chicken Shack Boogie**/ <br> Juke Box #1(5) / Best Seller #1(4) | | |
| 12/04/48 | **6** | 2 | 2 **It Took A Long, Long Time**...................... <br> Juke Box #6 / Best Seller #9 | | Aladdin 3014 |
| 12/11/48 | **1**³ | 16 | 3 **Bewildered**/ <br> Best Seller #1(3) / Juke Box #1(2) | | |
| 1/22/49 | **9** | 1 | 4 **A&M Blues**........................................ <br> Juke Box #9 | | Aladdin 3018 |
| 4/23/49 | **2**² | 15 | 5 **Hold Me, Baby**................................ <br> Juke Box #2 / Best Seller #2 | | Aladdin 3023 |
| 6/11/49 | **3** | 12 | 6 **In The Middle Of The Night** ........................ <br> Juke Box #3 / Best Seller #6 | | Aladdin 3026 |
| 9/10/49 | **1**² | 11 | 7 **Roomin' House Boogie**/ <br> Juke Box #1 / Best Seller #2 | | |
| 9/24/49 | **4** | 10 | 8 **Empty Arms Blues**............................ <br> Best Seller #4 / Juke Box #6 | | Aladdin 3032 |
| 11/26/49+ | **3** | 6 | 9 **Let's Make Christmas Merry, Baby**............ [X] <br> Best Seller #3 / Juke Box #5 | | Aladdin 3037 |
| | | | **AMOS MILBURN & HIS ALADDIN CHICKENSHACKERS:** | | |
| 12/10/49 | **9** | 2 | 10 **Real Pretty Mama Blues** ............................... <br> Juke Box #9 / Best Seller #13 | | Aladdin 3038 |
| 5/06/50 | **8** | 1 | 11 **Walking Blues** ....................................... <br> Best Seller #8 / Juke Box #8 | | Aladdin 3049 |
| 9/30/50 | **9** | 1 | 12 **Sax Shack Boogie** ............................... <br> Juke Box #9 | | Aladdin 3064 |
| 11/11/50+ | **1**³ | 19 | 13 **Bad, Bad Whiskey**.............................. <br> Juke Box #1(3) / Best Seller #1(1) | | Aladdin 3068 |
| 4/07/51 | **3** | 3 | 14 **Let's Rock A While**/ <br> Juke Box #3 / Best Seller #6 | | |
| 4/14/51 | **5** | 5 | 15 **Tears, Tears, Tears** ............................ <br> Best Seller #5 / Juke Box #8 | | Aladdin 3080 |
| 3/22/52 | **8** | 1 | 16 **Thinking And Drinking**............................... <br> Best Seller #8 | | Aladdin 3124 |
| 2/28/53 | **3** | 10 | 17 **Let Me Go Home Whiskey**............................ <br> Best Seller #3 / Juke Box #6 | | Aladdin 3164 |
| 9/26/53 | **2**² | 14 | 18 **One Scotch, One Bourbon, One Beer** ............. <br> Best Seller #2 / Juke Box #2 | | Aladdin 3197 |
| 2/06/54 | **5** | 3 | 19 **Good Good Whiskey** ............................... <br> Juke Box #5 | | Aladdin 3218 |
| | | | **BUDDY MILES** | | |
| | | | Born George Miles on 9/5/46 in Omaha. Vocalist/drummer. Prominent session musician. Worked as sideman in the Dick Clark Revue from 1963-64; with Wilson Pickett from 1965-66. In Michael Bloomfield's Electric Flag in 1967. With Jimi Hendrix's Band Of Gypsys from 1969-70. In 1987, was the voice of The California Raisins, the claymation TV ad characters. | | |
| 4/04/70 | **36** | 4 | 1 Them Changes............................................ <br> **BUDDY MILES & THE FREEDOM EXPRESS** | *81* | Mercury 73008 |
| 1/16/71 | **47** | 2 | 2 We Got To Live Together - Part I...................... | *86* | Mercury 73159 |
| 5/29/71 | **49** | 4 | 3 Wholesale Love ................................ | *71* | Mercury 73205 |
| 4/26/75 | **83** | 5 | 4 Pull Yourself Together .............................. | | Mercury 10089 |
| 8/23/75 | **33** | 12 | 5 Rockin' And Rollin' On The Streets Of <br> Hollywood ............................................... | *91* | Casablanca 839 |
| | | | **JOHN MILES** | | |
| | | | Born on 4/23/49 in Jarrow, England. Rock vocalist/guitarist/keyboardist. | | |
| 5/21/77 | **100** | 3 | 1 Slowdown .................................................. | *34* | London 20092 |
| | | | **LENNY MILES** | | |
| | | | Born on 12/22/34 in Fort Worth, Texas. | | |
| 3/13/61 | **28** | 1 | 1 Don't Believe Him, Donna ............................. | *41* | Scepter 1212 |
| | | | **BOBBY MILITELLO - see JEAN CARNE** | | |

| DEBUT DATE | PEAK POS | WKS CHR | ARTIST — Record Title | POP POS | Label & Number |
|---|---|---|---|---|---|
| | | | **GLENN MILLER & His Orchestra** | | |
| | | | #1 dance band of all-time. Glenn disappeared on a plane flight from England to France on 12/15/44 (40). | | |
| 10/23/43 | 6 | 8 | 1 **Rhapsody In Blue** ..................................... [I] | *13* | Victor 1529 |
| | | | featured solos by Bobby Hackett & Tex Beneke | | |
| 1/08/44 | 2² | 9 | 2 **It Must Be Jelly ('cause Jam Don't Shake Like That)** ..................................... | *12* | Victor 1546 |
| | | | vocals by The Modernaires | | |
| | | | above 2: recorded July 15-16, 1942 | | |
| | | | **MARCUS MILLER** | | |
| 3/05/83 | 55 | 8 | 1 Lovin' You..................................... | | Warner 29768 |
| 5/26/84 | 53 | 10 | 2 My Best Friend's Girlfriend .......................... | | Warner 29275 |
| | | | **RED MILLER TRIO** | | |
| | | | Vocalist backed by Lloyd Glenn & His Trio, which featured: Glenn (piano), Tiny Webb (guitar), Ralph Hamilton (bass) and Robert Harvey (drums). Miller later recorded for King with Tiny Bradshaw, and for Savoy with the Emmitt Slay Trio. | | |
| 11/20/48 | 1⁵ | 21 | 1 **Bewildered** ..................................... | | Bullet 295 |
| | | | Juke Box #1(5) / Best Seller #1(4) | | |
| | | | **STEVE MILLER BAND** | | |
| | | | Blues-rock singer/songwriter/guitarist, Steve was born on 10/5/43 in Milwaukee; raised in Dallas. The Steve Miller Band, which featured fluctuating lineup, formed in 1966, in San Francisco. | | |
| 3/19/77 | 20 | 11 | 1●Fly Like An Eagle ................................... | *2* | Capitol 4372 |
| | | | shown only as: **STEVE MILLER** | | |
| 9/04/82 | 26 | 11 | 2●Abracadabra ..................................... | *1* | Capitol 5126 |
| | | | **LUCKY MILLINDER** | | |
| | | | Born Lucius Millinder on 8/8/1900 in Anniston, Alabama. Died on 9/28/66 in New York City (66). Vocalist/bandleader. Raised in Chicago, worked as emcee in the late 20s. First led band for RKO theater tour in 1931. Toured Europe in 1933. Led Mills Blue Rhythm Band in 1934, Bill Doggett Band in 1938. Led own band from 1940-52. Band included many future stars of R&B and jazz, including Wynonie Harris, Bullmoose Jackson, Rosetta Tharpe, Tab Smith, Dizzy Gillespie, Lockjaw Davis, Annisteen Allen, and John Greer. Later, disc jockey in New York, and public relations for a distillery. Band recorded soundtrack for the film "Paradise In Harlem". Also see Wynonie Harris. | | |
| 10/24/42 | 1² | 17 | 1 **When The Lights Go On Again (All Over The World)** ..................................... | *12* | Decca 18496 |
| | | | with Dizzy Gillespie (trumpet) | | |
| 2/13/43 | 1² | 17 | 2 **Apollo Jump**.......................................... [I] | | Decca 18529 |
| 12/11/43 | 1¹ | 19 | 3 **Sweet Slumber** ..................................... | *12* | Decca 18569 |
| | | | 1 & 3: vocals by Trevor Bacon | | |
| 6/09/45 | 1⁸ | 20 | 4 **Who Threw The Whiskey In The Well?** .......... | *7* | Decca 18674 |
| | | | vocal by Wynonie Harris | | |
| 6/08/46 | 4 | 4 | 5 **Shorty's Got To Go** ..................................... | | Decca 18867 |
| | | | vocal by Lucky Millinder | | |
| 4/02/49 | 4 | 12 | 6 **D'Natural Blues/** [I] | | |
| | | | Juke Box #4 / Best Seller #6 | | |
| | | | vocal by Doris Davis | | |
| 7/30/49 | 15 | 1 | 7 Little Girl Don't Cry ................................... | | Victor 20-3351 |
| | | | Juke Box #15 | | |
| | | | vocal by John Greer | | |
| 1/06/51 | 8 | 2 | 8 **I'll Never Be Free**..................................... | | RCA 3128 |
| | | | Best Seller #8 | | |
| | | | vocal by Annisteen Allen; also issued on 78 rpm (#20-3622) | | |
| 6/09/51 | 2⁸ | 21 | 9 **I'm Waiting Just For You** ........................... | *19* | King 4453 |
| | | | Juke Box #2 / Best Seller #2 | | |
| | | | vocals by Annisteen Allen and John Carol | | |
| | | | **MILLS BROTHERS** ★★192★★ | | |
| | | | Smooth vocal group from Piqua, Ohio. Consisted of John Jr. (b: 1911, d: 1936), Herbert (b: 1912), Harry (b: 1913, d: 6/28/82) and Donald (b: 1915). Originally featured unusual vocal style of imitating instruments. Achieved national fame via radio broadcasts and appearances in films. Father, John Sr., joined group in 1936, replacing John Jr., remained in group until 1956 (d: 12/8/67). Group continued as trio until 1982. Presently, Donald is singing with his son, John III. | | |
| 5/29/43 | 2⁵ | 28 | 1 **Paper Doll**.......................................... | *1* | Decca 18318 |
| | | | biggest non-holiday hit of the decade, with sales over 6 million; written in 1915 | | |
| 6/03/44 | 1¹ | 20 | 2 **Till Then/** | *8* | |
| 8/05/44 | 5 | 24 | 3 **You Always Hurt The One You Love** ........... | *1* | Decca 18599 |
| | | | a reported million-seller | | |

| DEBUT DATE | PEAK POS | WKS CHR | ARTIST — Record Title | POP POS | Label & Number |
|---|---|---|---|---|---|
| | | | **MILLS BROTHERS — Continued** | | |
| 5/26/45 | 4 | 3 | 4  Put Another Chair At The Table/ | 14 | |
| 6/02/45 | 4 | 3 | 5    I Wish ................................................ | 6 | Decca 18663 |
| 3/30/46 | 3 | 8 | 6  Don't Be A Baby, Baby .......................... | 12 | Decca 18753 |
| 6/07/47 | 2¹ | 12 | 7  Across The Alley From The Alamo/ | 2 | |
| 6/07/47 | 5 | 1 | 8    Dream Dream Dream.............................. | | Decca 23863 |
| 2/28/48 | 10 | 1 | 9  Manana .............................................. | | Decca 24333 |
| 4/24/48 | 10 | 1 | 10  Shine ................................................. | | Decca 24382 |
| 4/09/49 | 8 | 1 | 11  I Love You So Much It Hurts........................ | 8 | Decca 24550 |
| | | | Juke Box #8 | | |
| | | | **STEPHANIE MILLS**    ★★**94**★★ | | |
| | | | Born in 1957 in Brooklyn. In Cornerstone Baptist Church choir at age 3. Appeared in the Broadway musical "Maggie Flynn" at age 7. In 1967, appeared for 4 weeks at the Apollo Theater with The Isley Brothers. First recorded for ABC in 1974. At age 15, she won starring role of Dorothy in the hit Broadway show "The Wiz". Played role for 4 years. Briefly married to Jeffrey Daniels of Shalamar in 1980. | | |
| 4/28/79 | 8 | 24 | 1  What Cha Gonna Do With My Lovin' ............. | 22 | 20th Century 2403 |
| 11/17/79 | 55 | 8 | 2  You Can Get Over ................................. | 101 | 20th Century 2427 |
| 4/05/80 | 3 | 21 | 3  Sweet Sensation ................................. | 52 | 20th Century 2449 |
| 8/09/80 | 12 | 21 | 4● Never Knew Love Like This Before.................. | 6 | 20th Century 2460 |
| 4/25/81 | 3 | 19 | 5  Two Hearts ....................................... | 40 | 20th Century 2492 |
| | | | STEPHANIE MILLS featuring TEDDY PENDERGRASS | | |
| 8/22/81 | 33 | 11 | 6  Night Games ...................................... | | 20th Century 2506 |
| 7/10/82 | 14 | 16 | 7  Last Night........................................ | 101 | Casablanca 2352 |
| 9/25/82 | 13 | 17 | 8  Keep Away Girls .................................. | | Casablanca 2354 |
| 2/12/83 | 59 | 8 | 9  You Can't Run From My Love ..................... | | Casablanca 810336 |
| 8/20/83 | 12 | 15 | 10  Pilot Error ........................................ | | Casablanca 814142 |
| 11/12/83 | 12 | 14 | 11  How Come U Don't Call Me Anymore?.............. | | Casablanca 814747 |
| | | | written by Prince | | |
| 8/25/84 | 8 | 17 | 12  The Medicine Song................................ | 65 | Casabln. 880180 |
| 12/22/84+ | 47 | 10 | 13  Edge Of The Razor ............................... | | Casabln. 880445 |
| 7/13/85 | 52 | 9 | 14  Bit By Bit ......................................... | 78 | MCA 52617 |
| | | | theme from the film "Fletch" | | |
| 12/14/85+ | 15 | 14 | 15  Stand Back ........................................ | | MCA 52731 |
| 3/01/86 | 1² | 20 | 16  I Have Learned To Respect The Power Of Love..................................................... | | MCA 52799 |
| 6/14/86 | 11 | 14 | 17  Rising Desire ..................................... | | MCA 52843 |
| 5/02/87 | 1³ | 18 | 18  I Feel Good All Over.............................. | | MCA 53056 |
| 8/08/87 | 1¹ | 16 | 19  (You're Puttin') A Rush On Me ................... | 85 | MCA 53151 |
| 11/14/87+ | 7 | 17 | 20  Secret Lady ....................................... | | MCA 53209 |
| 3/19/88 | 19 | 13 | 21  If I Were Your Woman............................. | | MCA 53275 |
| | | | **RONNIE MILSAP** | | |
| | | | Born on 1/16/46 in Robbinsville, North Carolina. Country singer/pianist/guitarist. Blind since birth, multi-instrumentalist by age 12. With J.J. Cale band, own band from 1965. | | |
| 10/30/65 | 19 | 8 | 1  Never Had It So Good................................. | 106 | Scepter 12109 |
| | | | **ROY MILTON**    ★★**80**★★ | | |
| | | | Born on 7/31/07 in Tulsa, Oklahoma. Died of a stroke in September, 1983. Vocalist/drummer/leader. With Ernie Fields as vocalist in 1928. To West Coast in 1935; formed own band. Formed new group, The Solid Senders, in the mid-40s. First recorded for HampTone in 1945. Vocalist/pianist Camille Howard was a member of The Solid Senders. Milton was also a member of the Camille Howard Trio. Had series own labels from 1946-48. Remained active in music into the 80s. | | |
| 4/20/46 | 2² | 25 | 1  R.M. Blues ......................................... | 20 | Juke Box 504 |
| 12/14/46 | 4 | 1 | 2  Milton's Boogie.................................... | | Juke Box 503 |
| 8/09/47 | 4 | 5 | 3  True Blues ......................................... | | Specialty 510 |
| 11/15/47 | 5 | 1 | 4  Thrill Me .......................................... | | Specialty 518 |
| | | | vocal by Camille Howard | | |
| 3/27/48 | 8 | 1 | 5  Keep A Dollar In Your Pocket ................... | | Specialty 522 |
| 9/18/48 | 5 | 8 | 6  Everything I Do Is Wrong/ | | |
| | | | Juke Box #5 / Best Seller #7 | | |
| 10/02/48 | 3 | 11 | 7  Hop, Skip And Jump................................ | | Specialty 314 |
| | | | Best Seller #3 / Juke Box #3 | | |

| DEBUT DATE | PEAK POS | WKS CHR | ARTIST — Record Title | POP POS | Label & Number |
|---|---|---|---|---|---|
| | | | **ROY MILTON — Continued** | | |
| 4/16/49 | 5 | 14 | 8 Hucklebuck............................................<br>Best Seller #5 / Juke Box #11 | | Specialty 328 |
| 2/25/50 | 2¹ | 10 | 9 **Information Blues**...............................<br>Juke Box #2 / Best Seller #3 | | Specialty 349 |
| 7/01/50 | 10 | 1 | 10 **Where There Is No Love/**<br>Juke Box #10 | | |
| 7/15/50 | 10 | 1 | 11 **Junior Jive**..................................... [I] | | Specialty 358 |
| | | | Juke Box #10 | | |
| 12/02/50 | 5 | 4 | 12 **Oh Babe**.........................................<br>Juke Box #5 / Best Seller #8 | | Specialty 381 |
| 6/02/51 | 10 | 1 | 13 **It's Later Than You Think**..................<br>Juke Box #10 | | Specialty 403 |
| 8/04/51 | 7 | 4 | 14 **I Have News For You/**<br>Juke Box #7 | | |
| 9/08/51 | 6 | 3 | 15 **T-Town Twist** ............................. [I] | | Specialty 407 |
| | | | Best Seller #6 | | |
| 11/24/51+ | 2¹ | 14 | 16 **Best Wishes** ..................................<br>Best Seller #2 / Juke Box #2 | | Specialty 414 |
| 5/31/52 | 6 | 9 | 17 **So Tired** .......................................<br>Juke Box #6 / Best Seller #7 | | Specialty 429 |
| 9/13/52 | 5 | 2 | 18 **Night And Day (I Miss You So)** ...........<br>Juke Box #5 / Best Seller #10 | | Specialty 438 |
| 7/04/53 | 9 | 2 | 19 **Early In The Morning**.......................<br>Juke Box #9 | | Specialty 464 |
| 8/07/61 | 27 | 3 | 20 Red Light ...................................... | | Warwick 662 |
| 10/16/61 | 21 | 4 | 21 Baby You Don't Know ........................<br>recorded in 1953 | | Specialty 480 |

## GARNET MIMMS

Born Garrett Mimms on 11/16/33 in Ashland, West Virginia. Sang in gospel groups the Evening Stars, Norfolk Four, Harmonizing Four. Formed group the Gainors in 1958.

**GARNET MIMMS & THE ENCHANTERS:**

| DEBUT DATE | PEAK POS | WKS CHR | ARTIST — Record Title | POP POS | Label & Number |
|---|---|---|---|---|---|
| 9/07/63 | 1³ | 12 | 1 **Cry Baby** .......................................... | 4 | United Art. 629 |
| 11/23/63+ | 26 | 9 | 2 For Your Precious Love/ | *Hot* | |
| 11/16/63 | 30 | 9 | 3 Baby Don't You Weep ......................... | *Hot* | United Art. 658 |
| | | | **GARNET MIMMS:** | | |
| 2/15/64 | 69 | 7 | 4 Tell Me Baby ..................................... | *Hot* | United Art. 694 |
| 5/16/64 | 67 | 4 | 5 One Girl/ | | |
| 7/18/64 | 78 | 7 | 6 A Quiet Place ................................... | *Hot* | United Art. 715 |
| | | | **GARNET MIMMS & THE ENCHANTERS** | | |
| 10/17/64 | 73 | 5 | 7 Look Away ........................................ | *Hot* | United Art. 773 |
| 1/02/65 | 95 | 1 | 8 A Little Bit Of Soap ........................... | *Hot* | United Art. 796 |
| 4/09/66 | 15 | 10 | 9 I'll Take Good Care Of You................... | 30 | United Art. 995 |
| 4/16/77 | 38 | 10 | 10 What It Is ........................................ | | Arista 0239 |
| | | | **GARNET MIMMS & TRUCKIN' COMPANY** | | |

## MINNEAPOLIS GENIUS 94 EAST

| DEBUT DATE | PEAK POS | WKS CHR | ARTIST — Record Title | POP POS | Label & Number |
|---|---|---|---|---|---|
| 3/22/86 | 80 | 5 | 1 Just Another Sucker ...................................... | | Hot Pink 3223 |

## THE MIRACLES  ★★14★★

Group formed at Northern High School in Detroit in 1955. Consisted of William "Smokey" Robinson (lead), Emerson and Bobby Rogers (tenors), Ronnie White (baritone) and Warren "Pete" Moore (bass). Emerson Rogers left in 1956 for US Army, replaced by Claudette Rogers Robinson, Smokey's wife. First recorded for End in 1958. Claudette retired in 1964. Smokey wrote many hit songs for his group and other Motown artists. Smokey went solo in 1972, replaced by William Griffin.

| DEBUT DATE | PEAK POS | WKS CHR | ARTIST — Record Title | POP POS | Label & Number |
|---|---|---|---|---|---|
| 12/12/60+ | 1⁸ | 16 | 1 **Shop Around** .................................... | 2 | Tamla 54034 |
| 4/17/61 | 15 | 6 | 2 Ain't It, Baby .................................... | 49 | Tamla 54036 |
| 7/24/61 | 21 | 3 | 3 Mighty Good Lovin' ............................ | 51 | Tamla 54044 |
| 11/20/61 | 11 | 7 | 4 Everybody's Gotta Pay Some Dues .......... | 52 | Tamla 54048 |
| 1/13/62 | 16 | 13 | 5 What's So Good About Good-by .......... | 35 | Tamla 54053 |
| 5/19/62 | 11 | 10 | 6 I'll Try Something New....................... | 39 | Tamla 54059 |
| 12/29/62+ | 1¹ | 14 | 7 **You've Really Got A Hold On Me**.......... | 8 | Tamla 54073 |
| 4/27/63 | 21 | 4 | 8 A Love She Can Count On .................. | 31 | Tamla 54078 |
| 8/31/63 | 3 | 11 | 9 **Mickey's Monkey** ............................. | 8 | Tamla 54083 |
| 11/23/63+ | 35 | 10 | 10 I Gotta Dance To Keep From Crying .......... | *Hot* | Tamla 54089 |
| 3/07/64 | 59 | 5 | 11 (You Can't Let The Boy Overpower) The Man In You.............................................. | *Hot* | Tamla 54092 |

| DEBUT DATE | PEAK POS | WKS CHR | ARTIST — Record Title | POP POS | Label & Number |
|---|---|---|---|---|---|
| | | | **THE MIRACLES — Continued** | | |
| 6/27/64 | **27** | 9 | 12 I Like It Like That................................ | *Hot* | Tamla 54098 |
| 9/19/64 | **35** | 6 | 13 That's What Love Is Made Of................... | *Hot* | Tamla 54102 |
| 12/12/64+ | **50** | 8 | 14 Come On Do The Jerk............................ | *Hot* | Tamla 54109 |
| 4/03/65 | **4** | 14 | 15 **Ooo Baby Baby**.................................. | *16* | Tamla 54113 |
| 7/10/65 | **2**¹ | 18 | 16 **The Tracks Of My Tears**..................... | *16* | Tamla 54118 |
| 10/16/65 | **3** | 14 | 17 **My Girl Has Gone**............................. | *14* | Tamla 54123 |
| 1/01/66 | **2**² | 15 | 18 **Going To A Go-Go/** | *11* | |
| 3/12/66 | **35** | 2 | 19    Choosey Beggar .............................. | | Tamla 54127 |
| 6/25/66 | **20** | 7 | 20 Whole Lot Of Shakin' In My Heart (Since I Met You)......................................... | *46* | Tamla 54134 |
| 11/26/66 | **4** | 10 | 21 (Come 'Round Here) I'm The One You Need ..... | *17* | Tamla 54140 |
| | | | **SMOKEY ROBINSON & THE MIRACLES:** | | |
| 3/04/67 | **10** | 10 | 22 **The Love I Saw In You Was Just A Mirage** ..... | *20* | Tamla 54145 |
| 6/24/67 | **5** | 14 | 23 **More Love**...................................... | *23* | Tamla 54152 |
| 11/18/67+ | **1**¹ | 15 | 24 **I Second That Emotion**......................... | *4* | Tamla 54159 |
| 3/09/68 | **3** | 12 | 25 **If You Can Want**............................... | *11* | Tamla 54162 |
| 6/15/68 | **9** | 8 | 26 **Yester Love**.................................... | *31* | Tamla 54167 |
| 8/31/68 | **4** | 11 | 27 **Special Occasion**.............................. | *26* | Tamla 54172 |
| 1/18/69 | **3** | 12 | 28 **Baby, Baby Don't Cry**.......................... | *8* | Tamla 54178 |
| 6/28/69 | **7** | 11 | 29 **Doggone Right/** | *32* | |
| 9/06/69 | **15** | 8 | 30    Here I Go Again .............................. | *37* | Tamla 54183 |
| 7/12/69 | **16** | 6 | 31 Abraham, Martin & John....................... | *33* | Tamla 54184 |
| 12/20/69+ | **4** | 10 | 32 **Point It Out**.................................. | *37* | Tamla 54189 |
| 6/06/70 | **9** | 8 | 33 **Who's Gonna Take The Blame**................. | *46* | Tamla 54194 |
| 10/24/70 | **1**³ | 14 | 34 **The Tears Of A Clown**........................ | *1* | Tamla 54199 |
| 3/27/71 | **7** | 10 | 35 **I Don't Blame You At All**..................... | *18* | Tamla 54205 |
| 7/17/71 | **20** | 7 | 36 Crazy About The La La La...................... | *56* | Tamla 54206 |
| 11/27/71+ | **20** | 7 | 37 Satisfaction.................................... | *49* | Tamla 54211 |
| 6/10/72 | **9** | 12 | 38 **We've Come Too Far To End It Now** .............. | *46* | Tamla 54220 |
| 12/30/72+ | **21** | 8 | 39 I Can't Stand To See You Cry ................... | *45* | Tamla 54225 |
| | | | **THE MIRACLES:** | | |
| 7/28/73 | **26** | 12 | 40 Don't Let It End ('Til You Let It Begin) .............. | *56* | Tamla 54237 |
| 12/01/73+ | **47** | 12 | 41 Give Me Just Another Day ...................... | *111* | Tamla 54240 |
| 7/13/74 | **4** | 19 | 42 **Do It Baby** .................................... | *13* | Tamla 54248 |
| 12/14/74+ | **4** | 15 | 43 **Don't Cha Love It** ............................ | *78* | Tamla 54256 |
| 4/26/75 | **43** | 8 | 44 Gemini ........................................ | *101* | Tamla 54259 |
| 10/18/75+ | **5** | 21 | 45 **Love Machine (Part 1)** ........................ | *1* | Tamla 54262 |
| 5/22/76 | **60** | 5 | 46 Night Life ..................................... | | Tamla 54268 |
| 1/22/77 | **37** | 10 | 47 Spy For Brotherhood ........................... | *104* | Columbia 10464 |
| | | | **THE MIRACLES featuring BILLY GRIFFIN** | | |
| 5/06/78 | **55** | 10 | 48 Mean Machine ................................. | | Columbia 10706 |
| | | | **THE MIRACLES featuring BILLY GRIFFIN** | | |
| | | | **WAYNE MIRAN & RUSH RELEASE** | | |
| 9/27/75 | **68** | 6 | 1 Oh Baby ..................................... | *104* | Roulette 7176 |
| | | | **THE MIRETTES** | | |
| | | | Former Ikettes Vanetta Fields, Jessie Smith and Robbie Montgomery. | | |
| 2/03/68 | **18** | 10 | 1 In The Midnight Hour................................... | *45* | Revue 11004 |
| | | | **MISS THANG** | | |
| 9/20/86 | **48** | 9 | 1 Thunder And Lightning.......................... | | Tommy Boy 889 |
| | | | **MISSION** | | |
| | | | 7-member group from Philadelphia, led by guitarist Randall Bowland. | | |
| 10/03/87 | **33** | 17 | 1 Show A Little Love............................. | | Columbia 07189 |
| 3/26/88 | **64** | 9 | 2 Lover For Life ................................ | | Columbia 07742 |
| | | | **MISSION** | | |
| 6/29/74 | **61** | 11 | 1 Fear No Evil................................. | | Paramount 0288 |

| DEBUT DATE | PEAK POS | WKS CHR | ARTIST — Record Title | POP POS | Label & Number |
|---|---|---|---|---|---|
| | | | **MR. T**<br>Born Lawrence Tero on 5/21/52 in Chicago. Entertainer/actor. First worked as a bodyguard and bouncer in Chicago. In the film "Rocky III", and feature player in the TV show "The A-Team". | | |
| 9/22/84 | 75 | 7 | 1 Mr. T's Commandment ............................... [N] | | Columbia 04589 |
| | | | **BARBARA MITCHELL - see SMOKEY ROBINSON** | | |
| | | | **THE BILLY MITCHELL GROUP** | | |
| 7/05/69 | 41 | 6 | 1 Oh Happy Day ............................................. [I] | *115* | Calla 165 |
| 11/01/69 | 49 | 3 | 2 Too Busy Thinking 'Bout My Baby ................. | | Calla 167 |
| | | | **BOBBY MITCHELL**<br>Born on 8/16/35 in Algiers, Louisiana. Formed group, the Toppers in 1950, at L. B. Landry High School. Discovered by Dave Bartholomew. Went solo and formed own band in 1954. Had original version of "I'm Gonna Be A Wheel Someday". Became pathologist and teacher in 1963. Still active in music in New Orleans. | | |
| 3/24/56 | 14 | 2 | 1 Try Rock And Roll ....................................<br>Best Seller #14 | | Imperial 5378 |
| | | | **FREDDIE MITCHELL**<br>Tenor saxophonist. Worked with Benny Carter and Fletcher Henderson in 1941. | | |
| 8/27/49 | 4 | 5 | 1 **Doby's Boogie**............................................. [I]<br>Best Seller #4 / Juke Box #10<br>featuring Joe Blake on piano; dedicated to Larry Doby, the first<br>Black baseball player in the American League | | Derby 713 |
| 4/08/50 | 7 | 1 | 2 **Easter Parade** ...................................... [I]<br>Best Seller #7 / Juke Box #8 | | Derby 733 |
| | | | **GUY MITCHELL**<br>Born Al Cernik on 2/27/27 in Detroit. Sang briefly with Carmen Cavallaro's orchestra in the late 40s. Appearances in several films and TV series. | | |
| 12/15/56+ | 4 | 9 | 1 **Singing The Blues** ...................................<br>Best Seller #4 / Juke Box #6 / Jockey #12 | *1* | Columbia 40769 |
| 11/30/59+ | 19 | 6 | 2 Heartaches By The Number........................... | *1* | Columbia 41476 |
| | | | **McKINLEY MITCHELL**<br>Born on 12/25/34 in Jackson, Mississippi; died on 1/18/86. In gospel group, Hearts Of Harmony, in 1950. To Springfield, Massachusetts with this group in the early 50s. Own gospel group, the Mitchellairs, in 1956. To Chicago in 1958. Returned to Jackson from 1976-84, then back to Chicago. | | |
| 4/14/62 | 8 | 9 | 1 **The Town I Live In**.................................... | *115* | One-derful! 2030 |
| 12/24/77+ | 71 | 10 | 2 The End Of The Rainbow ............................. | | Chimneyville 10219 |
| | | | **PRINCE PHILLIP MITCHELL**<br>Born on 6/27/44 in Louisville. Singer/songwriter/guitarist/pianist. With the Premiers and The Checkmates (not the same as Sonny Charles' group) until 1962. Dancer with the Bean Brothers in Los Angeles. Wrote hits for Mel & Tim, Millie Jackson, Norman Connors, Joe Simon and Candi Staton. Also see Norman Connors. | | |
| 3/01/75 | 58 | 8 | 1 There's Another In My Life ............................ | | Event 223 |
| 6/03/78 | 32 | 11 | 2 One On One................................................ | | Atlantic 3480 |
| 5/12/79 | 90 | 4 | 3 Let's Get Wet ............................................. | | Atlantic 3569 |
| 8/11/79 | 76 | 4 | 4 If It Ain't Love, It'll Go Away......................... | | Atlantic 3587 |
| 12/20/86+ | 74 | 11 | 5 You're Gonna Come Back To Love .................. | | Ichiban 111 |
| | | | **WILLIE MITCHELL**<br>Born in Ashland, Mississippi in 1928. Trumpeter/keyboardist/composer/arranger/producer. To Memphis at an early age. With Tuff Green and Al Jackson in the early 50s. Formed own band in 1954, became house band at Home Of The Blues and Hi Records. Eventually became president of Hi Records. | | |
| 8/29/64 | 31 | 10 | 1 20-75 .................................................. [I]<br>title refers to the record's label number | *Hot* | Hi 2075 |
| 12/19/64+ | 85 | 3 | 2 Percolatin'............................................... [I] | *Hot* | Hi 2066 |
| 7/03/65 | 29 | 5 | 3 Buster Browne........................................... [I] | *96* | Hi 2091 |
| 6/04/66 | 23 | 5 | 4 Bad Eye................................................... [I] | *92* | Hi 2103 |
| 3/02/68 | 10 | 13 | 5 **Soul Serenade** ......................................... [I] | *23* | Hi 2140 |
| 8/10/68 | 23 | 6 | 6 Prayer Meetin'........................................... [I] | *45* | Hi 2147 |
| 1/25/69 | 31 | 6 | 7 30-60-90................................................... [I] | *69* | Hi 2154 |
| 10/18/69 | 37 | 5 | 8 My Babe ................................................... [I] | *115* | Hi 2167 |
| | | | **MODERN MAN - see CHARLIE SINGLETON** | | |

| DEBUT DATE | PEAK POS | WKS CHR | ARTIST — Record Title | POP POS | Label & Number |
|---|---|---|---|---|---|
| | | | **DOMENICO MODUGNO** | | |
| | | | Born on 1/9/28 in Polignano a Mare, Italy. Singer/actor. | | |
| 9/01/58 | 2¹ | 7 | 1 **Nel Blu Dipinto Di Blu (Volare)**.................. [F] | *1* | Decca 30677 |
| | | | Best Seller #2 | | |
| | | | **MODULATIONS** | | |
| 9/07/74 | 65 | 9 | 1 I Can't Fight Your Love ................................... | | Buddah 418 |
| 10/25/75 | 79 | 5 | 2 Worth Your Weight In Gold ............................ | | Buddah 497 |
| | | | **MOMENT OF TRUTH** | | |
| | | | Vocal group consisting of Billy Jones (lead), Ivory "Caprice" Bell & Michael Garrison (tenors), and Norris Harris (baritone). Jones had been with Kool & The Gang and Freda Payne; Harris with Chain Reaction and Family Brick. | | |
| 9/14/74 | 68 | 5 | 1 Your Love.................................................... | | Roulette 7158 |
| 3/29/75 | 74 | 8 | 2 Helplessly.................................................. | | Roulette 7164 |
| | | | **THE MOMENTS**   ★★**61**★★ | | |
| | | | Trio from Hackensack, New Jersey featuring Mark Greene. Greene left after first record, replaced by William Brown and Al Goodman. Harry Ray joined after "Love On A Two-Way Street" in 1970. Brown had been with Lenny Welch in the Broadways, later in the Uniques. Goodman had been in the Corvettes and Vipers. Ray had sung with the Establishment. Became "Ray, Goodman & Brown" in 1978. | | |
| 11/30/68+ | 13 | 14 | 1 Not On The Outside ...................................... | *57* | Stang 5000 |
| 4/12/69 | 13 | 8 | 2 Sunday....................................................... | *90* | Stang 5003 |
| 7/19/69 | 10 | 10 | 3 **I Do**......................................................... | *62* | Stang 5005 |
| 11/01/69 | 43 | 4 | 4 I'm So Lost ................................................. | | Stang 5008 |
| 12/20/69+ | 14 | 10 | 5 Lovely Way She Loves .................................. | *120* | Stang 5009 |
| 3/28/70 | 1⁵ | 17 | 6●**Love On A Two-Way Street**........................ | *3* | Stang 5012 |
| 8/22/70 | 7 | 10 | 7 If I Didn't Care............................................ | *44* | Stang 5016 |
| 11/21/70 | 9 | 11 | 8 **All I Have**.................................................. | *56* | Stang 5017 |
| 2/27/71 | 27 | 6 | 9 I Can't Help It............................................. | *108* | Stang 5020 |
| 5/22/71 | 34 | 4 | 10 That's How It Feels..................................... | *115* | Stang 5024 |
| 8/14/71 | 31 | 7 | 11 Lucky Me .................................................. | *98* | Stang 5031 |
| | | | all of above: produced by Sylvia (Robinson) | | |
| 11/27/71 | 36 | 7 | 12 To You With Love ....................................... | *107* | Stang 5033 |
| 4/15/72 | 41 | 2 | 13 Thanks A Lot ............................................. | | Stang 5036 |
| 7/22/72 | 25 | 7 | 14 Just Because He Wants To Make Love (Doesn't Mean He Loves You) ............................... | | Stang 5041 |
| 12/02/72+ | 19 | 10 | 15 My Thing ................................................... | | Stang 5045 |
| 7/28/73 | 16 | 12 | 16 Gotta Find A Way ....................................... | *68* | Stang 5050 |
| 12/08/73+ | 3 | 20 | 17 **Sexy Mama**.............................................. | *17* | Stang 5052 |
| 4/27/74 | 45 | 11 | 18 Sho Nuff Boogie (Part I) ............................. | *80* | All Platinum 2350 |
| | | | **SYLVIA & THE MOMENTS** | | |
| 6/22/74 | 29 | 10 | 19 Sweet Sweet Lady ...................................... | | Stang 5054 |
| 9/07/74 | 28 | 13 | 20 What's Your Name ...................................... | | Stang 5056 |
| 12/07/74+ | 25 | 14 | 21 Girls (Part I) .............................................. | | Stang 5057 |
| | | | **MOMENTS & WHATNAUTS** | | |
| 4/19/75 | 1¹ | 19 | 22 **Look At Me (I'm In Love)**............................ | *39* | Stang 5060 |
| 5/08/76 | 44 | 10 | 23 Nine Times................................................ | | Stang 5066 |
| 10/02/76 | 14 | 18 | 24 With You ................................................... | | Stang 5068 |
| 3/19/77 | 79 | 7 | 25 We Don't Cry Out Loud ............................... | | Stang 5071 |
| 7/09/77 | 18 | 15 | 26 I Don't Wanna Go....................................... | | Stang 5073 |
| 2/18/78 | 20 | 16 | 27 I Could Have Loved You .............................. | | Stang 5075 |
| 11/29/80+ | 39 | 13 | 28 Baby Let's Rap Now (Pt.1)........................... | | Sugar Hill 551 |
| | | | **MONDAY AFTER** | | |
| 2/07/76 | 20 | 9 | 1 Merry-Go-Round, Pt. I ................................. | *106* | Buddah 512 |
| 9/04/76 | 98 | 4 | 2 He Who Laughs Last Laughs The Best ............. | | Buddah 540 |
| | | | **MONET** | | |
| 4/25/87 | 48 | 8 | 1 My Heart Gets All The Breaks ........................ | | Ligosa 501 |
| 11/07/87 | 76 | 7 | 2 Leave The Lights On..................................... | | Ligosa 51 |
| | | | **MONET with NOLAN THOMAS** | | |
| | | | **THE MONITORS** | | |
| | | | Group consisting of Sandra and John "Maurice" Fagin, Warren Harris and Richard Street. Street, formerly with the Distants, joined The Temptations in 1971. | | |
| 1/08/66 | 36 | 3 | 1 Say You ..................................................... | | V.I.P. 25028 |

| DEBUT DATE | PEAK POS | WKS CHR | ARTIST — Record Title | POP POS | Label & Number |
|---|---|---|---|---|---|
| | | | **THE MONITORS — Continued** | | |
| 4/30/66 | 21 | 9 | 2 Greetings (This Is Uncle Sam) ........................... *100* | | V.I.P. 25032 |
| | | | **T.S. MONK** | | |
| | | | Thelonious Monk Jr. (son of the legendary jazz artist), sister Boo Boo, and Yvonne Fletcher. | | |
| 12/13/80+ | 11 | 23 | 1 Bon Bon Vie (Gimme The Good Life) ................. | 63 | Mirage 3780 |
| 5/09/81 | 69 | 7 | 2 Candidate For Love ...................................... | | Mirage 3812 |
| 12/12/81+ | 56 | 11 | 3 Too Much Too Soon ...................................... | | Mirage 3875 |
| 3/20/82 | 75 | 4 | 4 More To Love ............................................. | | Mirage 4014 |
| | | | **THE MONOTONES** | | |
| | | | Group from Newark, New Jersey: Charles Patrick (lead vocals), Warren Davis, George Malone, Warren Ryanes, John Smith, and John Ryanes (d: 5/30/72 [31]). | | |
| 4/07/58 | 3 | 11 | 1 Book Of Love ............................................... | 5 | Argo 5290 |
| | | | Jockey #3 / Best Seller #4 | | |
| | | | originally released on Mascot 124 | | |
| | | | **MONTCLAIRS** | | |
| | | | Group from East St. Louis. Consisted of Kevin Sanlin, Phil Perry, George McLellan, David Frye and Clifford "Scotty" Williams. First recorded for Arch in 1969. | | |
| 5/27/72 | 34 | 7 | 1 Dreaming Out Of Season............................... | | Paula 363 |
| 10/28/72 | 33 | 9 | 2 Beggin' Is Hard To Do .................................. | | Paula 375 |
| 7/14/73 | 70 | 2 | 3 Prelude To A Heartbreak.............................. | | Paula 382 |
| 3/30/74 | 46 | 18 | 4 Make Up For Lost Time ................................ | | Paula 381 |
| 11/16/74+ | 40 | 12 | 5 Baby You Know (I'm Gonna Miss You)-Part 1...... | | Paula 409 |
| | | | **LOU MONTE** | | |
| | | | Born on 4/2/17 in Lynhurst, New Jersey. Vocalist/guitarist. | | |
| 6/09/58 | 14 | 1 | 1 Lazy Mary ................................. [F] | *12* | Victor 7160 |
| | | | Jockey #14 | | |
| | | | **CHRIS MONTEZ** | | |
| | | | Born Christopher Montanez on 1/17/43 in Los Angeles. Protege of Ritchie Valens. | | |
| 9/08/62 | 15 | 9 | 1●Let's Dance............................................... | 4 | Monogram 505 |
| | | | **WES MONTGOMERY** | | |
| | | | Jazz guitarist; brother of bassist Monk, and pianist Buddy Montgomery. Wes died on 6/15/68 (43). Also see Lionel Hampton. | | |
| 12/30/67+ | 48 | 3 | 1 Windy .............................................. [I] | 44 | A&M 883 |
| | | | **JACKIE MONTRE-EL** | | |
| 2/10/68 | 34 | 2 | 1 I Worship The Ground You Walk On ................. | | ABC 11035 |
| | | | **THE MOONGLOWS** | | |
| | | | Group from Louisville, Kentucky: Bobby Lester (b: 1/13/30, d: 10/15/80), Harvey Fuqua (b: 7/27/29), Alexander "Pete" Graves (b: 4/17/36), and Prentiss Barnes (b: 1921). Billy Johnson (b: 1924) played guitar. Barnes is brother of James "Pookie" Hudson of the Spaniels. Originally called the Crazy Sounds, re-named by deejay Alan Freed. Also recorded as The Moonlighters. Fuqua, nephew of Charlie Fuqua of the Ink Spots, left in 1958, and recorded as Harvey & The Moonglows with Marvin Gaye, Reese Palmer, James Knowland and Chester Simmons. Fuqua founded own Tri-Phi label, and created and produced new group, the Spinners, in 1961. The Moonglows' reunited lineup in 1972: Fuqua, Lester, Graves, Doc Williams and Chuck Lewis. | | |
| 12/04/54+ | 1² | 20 | 1 Sincerely ..................................... | 20 | Chess 1581 |
| | | | Juke Box #1(2) / Jockey #1(1) / Best Seller #2 | | |
| 4/09/55 | 5 | 11 | 2 Most Of All ................................... | | Chess 1589 |
| | | | Jockey #5 / Juke Box #9 / Best Seller #11 | | |
| 6/02/56 | 9 | 2 | 3 We Go Together............................... | | Chess 1619 |
| | | | Jockey #9 / Juke Box #9 | | |
| 9/15/56 | 6 | 7 | 4 See Saw/ | 25 | |
| | | | Juke Box #6 / Jockey #8 / Best Seller #11 | | |
| 9/15/56 | 15 | 1 | 5 When I'm With You ..................................... | | Chess 1629 |
| | | | Best Seller #15 | | |
| 7/01/57 | 5 | 6 | 6 Please Send Me Someone To Love ................... | 73 | Chess 1661 |
| | | | Jockey #5 / Best Seller #12 | | |
| 10/06/58 | 9 | 9 | 7 Ten Commandments Of Love ......................... | 22 | Chess 1705 |
| | | | **HARVEY & THE MOONGLOWS** | | |
| 8/26/72 | 43 | 4 | 8 Sincerely '72 ............................................. | | RCA 0759 |
| | | | new version of #1 above; originally released on Big P 101 | | |

| DEBUT DATE | PEAK POS | WKS CHR | ARTIST — Record Title | POP POS | Label & Number |
|---|---|---|---|---|---|
| | | | **BILL MOORE** | | |
| | | | Tenor saxophonist nicknamed "Wild Bill". First recorded for Apollo in 1945. Hit "We're Gonna Rock" was recorded in Detroit with band including Paul Williams (baritone sax) and Phil Gilbeaux (trumpet). Not to be confused with several others of the same name. Also see Paul Williams. | | |
| 7/24/48 | **14** | 1 | 1  We're Gonna Rock, We're Gonna Roll ............... | | Savoy 666 |
| | | | Best Seller #14 / Juke Box #15 | | |
| | | | **BOB MOORE** | | |
| | | | Born on 11/30/32 in Nashville. Top session bass player. Led the band on Roy Orbison's sessions for Monument Records. Also worked as sideman for Elvis Presley, Brenda Lee, Pat Boone and others. | | |
| 10/23/61 | **22** | 4 | 1  Mexico ............................................... [I] | 7 | Monument 446 |
| | | | **BOBBY MOORE** | | |
| 7/19/75 | **78** | 10 | 1  (Call Me Your) Anything Man.......................... | 99 | Scepter 12405 |
| 1/31/76 | **94** | 3 | 2  Try To Hold On................................... | | Scepter 12417 |
| | | | **BOBBY MOORE & THE RHYTHM ACES** | | |
| | | | Formed in Montgomery, Alabama in 1961 by Bobby Moore (tenor sax). Included Chico Jenkins (lead vocalist), Larry Moore, Joe Frank, Clifford Laws, Marion Sledge and John Baldwin, Jr. | | |
| 3/05/66 | **7** | 17 | 1  **Searching For My Love**........................... | 27 | Checker 1129 |
| 12/03/66 | **40** | 3 | 2  Try My Love Again ............................... | 97 | Checker 1156 |
| 8/12/67 | **49** | 2 | 3  Chained To Your Heart ......................... | | Checker 1180 |
| | | | **DOROTHY MOORE** | | |
| | | | Born in 1946 in Jackson, Mississippi. Lead singer of pop group, The Poppies; formed at Jackson State University. | | |
| 11/17/73 | **79** | 5 | 1  Cry Like A Baby ................................ | | GSF 6908 |
| 2/14/76 | **2**[2] | 23 | 2  **Misty Blue** ..................................... | 3 | Malaco 1029 |
| 7/17/76 | **7** | 13 | 3  **Funny How Time Slips Away**.................... | 58 | Malaco 1033 |
| 11/06/76 | **53** | 12 | 4  For Old Time Sake............................. | | Malaco 1037 |
| 2/26/77 | **74** | 6 | 5  We Should Really Be In Love................... | | Malaco 1040 |
| | | | DOROTHY MOORE/EDDIE FLOYD | | |
| 6/25/77 | **5** | 21 | 6  **I Believe You** ................................ | 27 | Malaco 1042 |
| 12/03/77+ | **12** | 17 | 7  With Pen In Hand............................. | 101 | Malaco 1047 |
| | | | written by Bobby Goldsboro | | |
| 4/29/78 | **50** | 9 | 8  Let The Music Play/ | | |
| 7/08/78 | **93** | 5 | 9  1-2-3 (You And Me) .......................... | | Malaco 1048 |
| 8/26/78 | **30** | 16 | 10  Special Occasion............................. | | Malaco 1052 |
| 1/06/79 | **81** | 5 | 11  (We Need More) Loving Time ................. | | Malaco 1054 |
| 3/15/80 | **87** | 4 | 12  Talk To Me/Every Beat Of My Heart ........ | | Malaco 2062 |
| 7/03/82 | **90** | 2 | 13  What's Forever For............................ | | Handshake 02879 |
| | | | **JACKIE MOORE** | | |
| | | | Singer from Jacksonville, Florida. | | |
| 12/05/70+ | **12** | 15 | 1 ●Precious, Precious........................... | 30 | Atlantic 2681 |
| | | | with The Memphis Horns | | |
| 5/22/71 | **19** | 6 | 2  Sometimes It's Got To Rain (In Your Life) ......... | | Atlantic 2798 |
| | | | JACKIE MOORE with THE DIXIE FLYERS | | |
| 3/11/72 | **22** | 8 | 3  Darling Baby ................................. | 106 | Atlantic 2861 |
| 11/04/72 | **39** | 6 | 4  Time......................................... | | Atlantic 2830 |
| | | | with Dr. John & The Memphis Horns | | |
| 6/09/73 | **15** | 13 | 5  Sweet Charlie Babe ......................... | 42 | Atlantic 2956 |
| 11/10/73+ | **28** | 13 | 6  Both Ends Against The Middle................ | 102 | Atlantic 2989 |
| 6/28/75 | **6** | 16 | 7  **Make Me Feel Like A Woman**.............. | | Kayvette 5122 |
| 12/13/75+ | **37** | 9 | 8  Puttin' It Down To You...................... | | Kayvette 5124 |
| 6/12/76 | **74** | 8 | 9  It's Harder To Leave ....................... | | Kayvette 5125 |
| 10/02/76 | **36** | 10 | 10  Disco Body (Shake It To The East, Shake It To The West).................................. | | Kayvette 5127 |
| 4/30/77 | **72** | 7 | 11  Make Me Yours .............................. | | Kayvette 5129 |
| 8/26/78 | **92** | 4 | 12  Personally ................................... | | Columbia 10779 |
| 7/07/79 | **24** | 14 | 13  This Time Baby .............................. | | Columbia 10993 |
| 10/25/80 | **78** | 4 | 14  Love Won't Let Me Wait ..................... | | Columbia 11363 |
| 3/12/83 | **73** | 7 | 15  Holding Back................................. | | Catawba 1010 |

| DEBUT DATE | PEAK POS | WKS CHR | ARTIST — Record Title | POP POS | Label & Number |
|---|---|---|---|---|---|
| | | | **JOHNNY MOORE'S THREE BLAZERS** ★★**134**★★ | | |
| | | | Group formed in Los Angeles in 1944. Consisted of Charles Brown (piano, vocals), Johnny Moore (guitar) and Eddie Williams (bass). Joined by Moore's brother Oscar in 1947, who was formerly with the King Cole Trio. Brown left to pursue highly successful solo career in 1948. Replaced by Billy Valentine. Group disbanded in the early 50s. Also see Floyd Dixon and Ivory Joe Hunter. | | |
| 2/23/46 | 2¹ | 23 | 1 **Drifting Blues** ............................................... | | Philo 112 |
| 11/16/46 | 4 | 4 | 2 **Sunny Road** .................................................. | | Exclusive 233 |
| 11/30/46 | 4 | 1 | 3 **So Long** ...................................................... | | Modern Mus. 143 |
| 6/28/47 | 2¹ | 13 | 4 **New Orleans Blues** ........................................ | | Exclusive 240 |
| 11/01/47 | 5 | 1 | 5 **Changeable Woman Blues** ............................... | | Exclusive 251 |
| 12/20/47+ | 3 | 2 | 6 **Merry Christmas Baby** ............................. [X] | | Exclusive 254 |
| 6/12/48 | 10 | 2 | 7 **Groovy Movie Blues**...................................... Juke Box #10 | | Exclusive 265 |
| 8/28/48 | 11 | 1 | 8 Jilted Blues ............................................... Juke Box #11 | | Exclusive 40X |
| 10/16/48 | 4 | 1 | 9 **More Than You Know** ................................... Juke Box #4 | | Modern 20-599 |
| 11/20/48 | 15 | 1 | 10 Lonesome Blues.......................................... Juke Box #15 | | Exclusive 53X |
| 12/04/48 | 8 | 4 | 11 **Merry Christmas Baby** ....................... [X-R] Best Seller #8 / Juke Box #15 | | Exclusive 63X |
| 4/09/49 | 8 | 1 | 12 **Where Can I Find My Baby** ......................... Juke Box #8 | | Exclusive 69X |
| 10/08/49 | 7 | 3 | 13 **Walkin' Blues**............................................ Best Seller #7 / Juke Box #13 vocal by Billy Valentine; also issued on 45 rpm (#50-0026) | | Victor 22-0042 |
| 12/24/49+ | 9 | 2 | 14 **Merry Christmas Baby** ....................... [X-R] Best Seller #9 | | Exclusive 63X |
| 8/22/53 | 8 | 2 | 15 **Dragnet Blues** .......................................... Juke Box #8 | | Modern 910 |
| 3/05/55 | 15 | 1 | 16 Johnny Ace's Last Letter ............................... Jockey #15 a tribute to Johnny Ace; above 2: vocals by Frankie Ervin | | Hollywood 1031 |
| | | | **LEE MOORE** | | |
| 8/25/79 | 48 | 11 | 1 Reachin' Out (For Your Love) Pt. 1 .................. | | Source 41068 |
| | | | **MELBA MOORE** ★★**73**★★ | | |
| | | | Singer/actress from New York City. Appeared in the Broadway production of "Hair"; award winning performer as Lutiebelle in the musical "Purlie". | | |
| 6/28/75 | 82 | 6 | 1 I Am His Lady ......................................... | | Buddah 452 |
| 4/03/76 | 18 | 13 | 2 This Is It................................................ | 91 | Buddah 519 |
| 7/24/76 | 17 | 17 | 3 Lean On Me ........................................... | | Buddah 535 |
| 2/12/77 | 62 | 8 | 4 The Way You Make Me Feel ...................... | 108 | Buddah 562 |
| 5/14/77 | 94 | 3 | 5 Long And Winding Road ........................... | | Buddah 568 |
| 1/07/78 | 69 | 5 | 6 Standing Right Here .............................. | | Buddah 589 |
| 10/21/78 | 17 | 18 | 7 You Stepped Into My Life...................... | 47 | Epic 50600 |
| 3/24/79 | 85 | 6 | 8 Pick Me Up, I'll Dance ........................ | 103 | Epic 50663 |
| 11/03/79 | 90 | 2 | 9 Miss Thing .......................................... | | Epic 50762 |
| 8/23/80 | 47 | 12 | 10 Everything So Good About You.................. | | Epic 50909 |
| 9/12/81 | 15 | 16 | 11 Take My Love........................................ | | EMI America 8092 |
| 12/26/81+ | 44 | 11 | 12 Let's Stand Together ............................ | | EMI America 8104 |
| 8/21/82 | 5 | 19 | 13 **Love's Comin' At Ya** ........................... | 104 | EMI America 8126 |
| 11/27/82+ | 25 | 17 | 14 Mind Up Tonight .................................. | | Capitol 5180 |
| 3/12/83 | 35 | 11 | 15 Underlove........................................... | | Capitol 5208 |
| 10/29/83 | 14 | 15 | 16 Keepin' My Lover Satisfied .................... | | Capitol 5288 |
| 1/21/84 | 6 | 17 | 17 **Livin' For Your Love**........................... | 108 | Capitol 5308 |
| 4/21/84 | 15 | 13 | 18 Love Me Right ..................................... | | Capitol 5343 |
| 10/27/84 | 28 | 14 | 19 (Can't Take Half) All Of You .................. LILLO THOMAS & MELBA MOORE | | Capitol 5415 |
| 3/09/85 | 12 | 15 | 20 Read My Lips ....................................... | 104 | Capitol 5437 |
| 6/15/85 | 14 | 16 | 21 When You Love Me Like This ................... | 106 | Capitol 5484 |
| 9/28/85 | 29 | 12 | 22 I Can't Believe It (It's Over) .................. | | Capitol 5520 |
| 6/21/86 | 5 | 15 | 23 **Love The One I'm With (A Lot Of Love)**.......... MELBA & KASHIF | | Capitol 5577 |

| DEBUT DATE | PEAK POS | WKS CHR | ARTIST — Record Title | POP POS | Label & Number |
|---|---|---|---|---|---|
| | | | **MELBA MOORE — Continued** | | |
| 9/06/86 | 1¹ | 20 | 24 A Little Bit More ........................................ | | Capitol 5632 |
| | | | MELBA MOORE with FREDDIE JACKSON | | |
| 11/29/86+ | 1¹ | 19 | 25 Falling ..................................................... | | Capitol 5651 |
| 3/14/87 | 6 | 15 | 26 It's Been So Long ...................................... | | Capitol 5681 |
| 6/20/87 | 26 | 9 | 27 I'm Not Gonna Let You Go ........................... | | Capitol 44012 |
| 5/14/88 | 12 | 14 | 28 I Can't Complain ...................................... | | Capitol 44148 |
| | | | MELBA MOORE with FREDDIE JACKSON | | |
| | | | **ROBERT MOORE - see MIAMI** | | |
| | | | **DENROY MORGAN** | | |
| | | | Vocalist from Jamaica. Formed own band, the Black Eagles, in New York City. | | |
| 7/04/81 | 9 | 20 | 1 I'll Do Anything For You ............................. | | Becket 5 |
| 11/28/81+ | 47 | 14 | 2 Sweet Tender Love ...................................... | | Becket 8 |
| 11/27/82 | 74 | 5 | 3 Happy Feeling ........................................... | | Becket 14 |
| | | | **LEE MORGAN** | | |
| | | | Born on 7/10/38 in Philadelphia; fatally shot on 2/19/72. Jazz trumpeter. | | |
| 12/19/64+ | 81 | 4 | 1 The Sidewinder, Part I ................... [I] *Hot* | | Blue Note 1911 |
| | | | **MELI'SA MORGAN** | | |
| | | | Meli'sa (pronounced Me-Lee-Sa) is a Queens, New York native. Back-up singer for Melba Moore, Whitney Houston, Kashif & Chaka Khan. Formal training at Julliard. | | |
| 11/30/85+ | 1³ | 24 | 1 Do Me Baby.............................................. | *46* | Capitol 5523 |
| | | | written by Prince | | |
| 3/29/86 | 5 | 19 | 2 Do You Still Love Me? ................................. | | Capitol 5567 |
| 7/19/86 | 24 | 12 | 3 Fool's Paradise ......................................... | | Capitol 5600 |
| 1/24/87 | 74 | 7 | 4 Deeper Love ............................................. | | Capitol 5674 |
| | | | from the film "The Golden Child" | | |
| 10/24/87+ | 2¹ | 18 | 5 If You Can Do It: I Can Too!!......................... | | Capitol 44088 |
| 11/07/87+ | 2¹ | 19 | 6 Love Changes ........................................... | | Arista 9626 |
| | | | KASHIF & MELI'SA MORGAN | | |
| 2/13/88 | 17 | 13 | 7 Here Comes The Night................................. | | Capitol 44022 |
| | | | **JOHNNIE MORISETTE** | | |
| | | | Born in 1935 in Montu Island, South Pacific. Sang with Medallions as "Johnny Twovoice". First recorded for Dootone in 1955. Moved to Dallas in 1973. | | |
| 4/21/62 | 18 | 4 | 1 Meet Me At The Twistin' Place........................ | *63* | Sar 126 |
| | | | **PAUL MORLEY - see THE ART OF NOISE** | | |
| | | | **MORNING, NOON, & NIGHT** | | |
| 6/25/77 | 48 | 10 | 1 Bite Your Granny........................................ | | Roadshow 1003 |
| | | | **DAVID MORRIS JR.** | | |
| 3/27/76 | 72 | 8 | 1 Midnight Lady, Pt. II ................................... | | Buddah 518 |
| | | | **JOE MORRIS** | | |
| | | | Born in 1922 in Montgomery, Alabama. Died in November of 1958 (cerebral hemorrhage). Vocalist/trumpeter/leader. With Lionel Hampton from 1942-46, HampTone All Stars, and Buddy Rich, in 1946. Formed own band in 1946. One of the first artists on the Atlantic label. Active up until death. Also see Wynonie Harris. | | |
| 10/07/50 | 1⁴ | 22 | 1 Anytime, Any Place, Anywhere ..................... | | Atlantic 914 |
| | | | Best Seller #1(4) / Juke Box #1(3) | | |
| 3/24/51 | 3 | 10 | 2 Don't Take Your Love Away From Me ............ | | Atlantic 923 |
| | | | Best Seller #3 / Juke Box #3 | | |
| | | | above 2: vocals by Laurie Tate | | |
| 11/14/53 | 3 | 12 | 3 I Had A Notion ......................................... | | Herald 417 |
| | | | Best Seller #3 / Juke Box #5 | | |
| | | | vocal by Al Savage | | |
| | | | **DOROTHY MORRISON** | | |
| | | | Born in 1945 in Longview, Texas. Former lead vocalist with The Edwin Hawkins' Singers. | | |
| 8/08/70 | 43 | 3 | 1 Border Song (Holy Moses) ............................. | *114* | Buddah 184 |
| | | | written by Elton John and lyricist Bernie Taupin | | |
| | | | **JUNIE MORRISON - see JUNIE** | | |

| DEBUT DATE | PEAK POS | WKS CHR | ARTIST — Record Title | POP POS | Label & Number |
|---|---|---|---|---|---|
| | | | **ELLA MAE MORSE** Born on 9/12/24 in Mansfield, Texas. Sang on radio since age 12. Briefly with Jimmy Dorsey's band in 1939. With the Freddie Slack's band from 1941-42, then solo career. Appeared in many films. Largely inactive since the early 50s. Also see Freddie Slack. | | |
| 12/18/43 | 1² | 13 | 1 **Shoo Shoo Baby**.......... sung by Morse in the film "South Of Dixie"; also in the film "Three Cheers For The Boys" | *4* | Capitol 143 |
| 1/26/46 | 2³ | 3 | 2 **Buzz Me**.......... with Billy May's Orchestra | *15* | Capitol 226 |
| | | | **BILL MOSS** Leader/pianist for family group, the Celestials, which included Essie Moss and Theresa Moss (vocals). | | |
| 4/19/69 | 49 | 2 | 1 Sock It To 'Em Soul Brother.......... | | Bell 771 |
| | | | **MOTHER'S FINEST** Sextet consisting of vocalists Glenn Murdock, Joyce Kennedy (husband & wife), Gary "Mo" Moore, guitar; Jerry "Wizard" Seay, bass; Barry "B.B." Borden, drums; and Michael Keck, keyboards. | | |
| 8/13/77 | 79 | 3 | 1 Baby Love.......... | *58* | Epic 50407 |
| 9/23/78 | 54 | 11 | 2 Don't Wanna Come Back.......... | | Epic 50596 |
| 11/25/78+ | 26 | 15 | 3 Love Changes.......... | | Epic 50641 |
| | | | **MOTIVATION** | | |
| 7/09/83 | 34 | 13 | 1 Crazy Daze.......... | | De-Lite 827 |
| 11/19/83 | 84 | 4 | 2 Please Don't Say No.......... | | De-Lite 828 |
| | | | **ALPHONSE MOUZON** Born on 11/21/48 in Charleston, South Carolina. Singer/pianist/drummer. With Chubby Checker in 1965, Freddie Hubbard and Roy Ayers in 1970, Weather Report in 1971. Also with Les McCann, Roberta Flack and Stevie Wonder. Own recordings from 1971. | | |
| 10/02/82+ | 16 | 17 | 1 The Lady In Red/ | | |
| | | 8 | 2 I Don't Want To Lose This Feeling.......... | | Highrise 2000 |
| 8/18/84 | 80 | 5 | 3 Our Love Is Hot.......... featuring Carol Dennis | | Private I 04545 |
| | | | **THE MOVIES** | | |
| 9/20/86 | 88 | 5 | 1 Juke Box.......... | | CBS Assoc. 06276 |
| | | | **MTUME** Progressive funk band led by James Mtume (pronounced Em-too-may, vocals, percussion). Mtume had been a percussionist with Miles Davis in the early 70s. Included Tawatha Agee (vocals), Phil Fields (keyboards) and Raymond Johnson (bass). Agee also backed Roxy Music; recorded solo, in 1987, as Tawatha. | | |
| 8/05/78 | 93 | 5 | 1 Just Funnin'.......... | | Epic 50558 |
| 8/23/80 | 26 | 12 | 2 Give It On Up (If You Want To).......... | | Epic 50917 |
| 12/06/80+ | 60 | 10 | 3 So You Wanna Be A Star.......... | | Epic 50952 |
| 4/09/83 | 1⁸ | 25 | 4● **Juicy Fruit**.......... | *45* | Epic 03578 |
| 9/10/83 | 11 | 17 | 5 Would You Like To (Fool Around).......... | | Epic 04087 |
| 1/21/84 | 66 | 6 | 6 Green Light.......... | | Epic 04277 |
| 6/30/84 | 2¹ | 22 | 7 **You, Me And He**.......... | *83* | Epic 04504 |
| 10/20/84 | 20 | 15 | 8 C.O.D. (I'll Deliver).......... | *104* | Epic 04057 |
| 5/17/86 | 9 | 16 | 9 **Breathless**.......... | | Epic 05899 |
| 9/27/86 | 39 | 9 | 10 P.O.P. (Pursuits Of Pleasure) Generation.......... | | Epic 06283 |
| 1/10/87 | 71 | 5 | 11 Body & Soul (Take Me).......... | | Epic 06560 |
| | | | **IDRIS MUHAMMAD** Born Leo Morris in New Orleans, 1939. Prolific session drummer since early 60s. | | |
| 7/16/77 | 21 | 12 | 1 Turn This Mutha Out (Part I).......... | *102* | Kudu 940 |
| 10/08/77 | 68 | 8 | 2 Could Heaven Ever Be Like This (Part 1).......... | *76* | Kudu 939 |
| 10/11/80 | 57 | 8 | 3 I Believe In You.......... lead vocal by Claytoven | | Fantasy 902 |
| | | | **NICK MUNDY** | | |
| 12/22/84 | 89 | 5 | 1 Ain't It All Right.......... | | Columbia 04689 |
| | | | **LYDIA MURDOCK** New Jersey native. | | |
| 10/01/83 | 58 | 6 | 1 Superstar.......... | | Teen Ent. 3001 |

| DEBUT DATE | PEAK POS | WKS CHR | ARTIST — Record Title | POP POS | Label & Number |
|---|---|---|---|---|---|
| | | | **SHIRLEY MURDOCK** Former gospel singer from Toledo. Discovered by Roger Troutman (aka Roger) who hired her as backup singer for his family funk group, Zapp. | | |
| 2/15/86 | **24** | 15 | 1　No More........................................ | | Elektra 69590 |
| 10/18/86+ | **5** | 28 | 2　**As We Lay**.................................... | 23 | Elektra 69518 |
| 3/21/87 | **5** | 17 | 3　**Go On Without You**...................... | | Elektra 69480 |
| 9/05/87 | **86** | 4 | 4　Be Free ...................................... | | Elektra 69450 |
| 6/18/88 | **5** | 20 | 5　**Husband**.................................... | | Elektra 69396 |
| | | | **EDDIE MURPHY** Born on 4/3/61 in Hempstead, New York. Comedian/actor. Former cast member of TV's "Saturday Night Live". Starred in the films "Beverly Hills Cop (I & II)", "Trading Places", "48 Hours", "The Golden Child" and "Coming To America". | | |
| 9/18/82 | **56** | 8 | 1　Boogie In Your Butt........................... [N] | | Columbia 03209 |
| 9/14/85 | **8** | 23 | 2●**Party All The Time**....................... written, produced & arranged by Rick James | 2 | Columbia 05609 |
| 2/15/86 | **63** | 9 | 3　How Could It Be............................ | | Columbia 05772 |
| | | | **ROSE MURPHY** Born in Xenia, Ohio. Vocalist/pianist. Nicknamed the Chee-Chee Girl for unique vocal style. | | |
| 1/31/48 | **3** | 8 | 1　**I Can't Give You Anything But Love/** from the Broadway musical "Blackbirds of 1928" | 13 | |
| 2/14/48 | **10** | 1 | 2　**When I Grow Too Old To Dream** ................. | | Majestic 1204 |
| 3/13/48 | **10** | 1 | 3　**Cecilia**...................................... | | Majestic 1213 |
| | | | **WALTER MURPHY** Born in 1952 in New York City. Studied classical and jazz piano at Manhattan School of Music. Former arranger for Doc Severinsen and "The Tonight Show" orchestra. | | |
| 8/14/76 | **10** | 15 | 1●**A Fifth Of Beethoven** .............................. [I] based on Beethoven's Fifth Symphony | 1 | Private S. 45073 |
| | | | **MURPHY'S** | | |
| 7/03/82 | **80** | 4 | 1　Murphy's Jive Law ....................................... | | Venture 5020 |
| | | | **MICKEY MURRAY** | | |
| 9/30/67 | **11** | 10 | 1　Shout Bamalama........................... | 54 | SSS Int'l. 715 |
| | | | **MUSCLE SHOALS HORNS** Studio band from Muscle Shoals, Alabama. | | |
| 3/13/76 | **8** | 16 | 1　**Born To Get Down (Born To Mess Around)** ...... | 105 | Bang 721 |
| 7/24/76 | **47** | 9 | 2　Open Up Your Heart ....................................... | | Bang 725 |
| 10/23/76 | **63** | 9 | 3　Bump De Bump Yo Boodie ............................ | | Bang 728 |
| 11/26/77+ | **57** | 12 | 4　Dance To The Music ................................... | | Ariola Am. 7674 |
| | | | **THE MUSIC MAKERS** Studio band, evolved into MFSB. | | |
| 1/06/68 | **48** | 3 | 1　United (Part I)................................ [I] instrumental version of The Intruders' "(We'll Be) United" | 78 | Gamble 210 |
| | | | **MUSICAL YOUTH** 5 schoolboys (ages 11 to 16) from Birmingham, England: Dennis Seaton (lead), brothers Kelvin (guitar) and Michael Grant (keyboards), and brothers Patrick (bass) and Junior Waite (drums). Also see Donna Summer. | | |
| 12/18/82+ | **8** | 19 | 1　**Pass The Dutchie**........................... Dutchie: a Jamaican cooking pot | 10 | MCA 52149 |
| 5/28/83 | **68** | 6 | 2　Heartbreaker................................. | | MCA 52216 |
| 12/17/83+ | **25** | 13 | 3　She's Trouble ................................... | 65 | MCA 52312 |
| 4/28/84 | **81** | 5 | 4　Whatcha Talking 'Bout ............................ | | MCA 52364 |
| | | | **MUSIQUE** Disco trio: Christine Wiltshire, Gina Tharps and Mary Seymour. | | |
| 10/07/78 | **29** | 12 | 1　In The Bush ....................................... | 58 | Prelude 71110 |
| 2/10/79 | **81** | 3 | 2　Keep On Jumpin' ................................. | | Prelude 71114 |
| | | | **ALICIA MYERS** Former lead singer of One Way. | | |
| 9/18/82 | **37** | 11 | 1　I Want To Thank You........................... | | MCA 52107 |
| 8/04/84 | **5** | 17 | 2　**You Get The Best From Me (say, say, say)**....... | 105 | MCA 52425 |
| 11/10/84 | **38** | 11 | 3　Appreciation .................................... | | MCA 52490 |

| DEBUT DATE | PEAK POS | WKS CHR | ARTIST — Record Title | POP POS | Label & Number |
|---|---|---|---|---|---|
| | | | **BILLY MYLES** | | |
| | | | New York singer/songwriter. Wrote the Mello-Kings' pop hit "Tonite, Tonite". | | |
| 1/20/58 | **13** | 1 | 1 The Joker (That's What They Call Me) ............. | 25 | Ember 1026 |
| | | | Jockey #13 | | |
| | | | **MYSTIC MERLIN** | | |
| | | | Group from Brooklyn, consisting of Clyde Bullard, Jerry Anderson, Barry Strutt, Sly Randolph and Keith Gonzales (vocals). Freddie Jackson was later a member. | | |
| 3/21/81 | **82** | 4 | 1 Got To Make It Better .................................... | | Capitol 4961 |
| 5/30/81 | **76** | 3 | 2 Sixty Thrills A Minute.................................... | | Capitol 4992 |
| | | | **THE MYSTIC MOODS** | | |
| | | | Hollywood studio orchestra produced by Brad Miller. | | |
| 12/25/76+ | **95** | 4 | 1 Being With You............................................ | | Sound Blvd 5004 |
| | | | **MYSTIQUE** | | |
| | | | Chicago group consisting of Ralph "Preacherman" Johnson, Charles Fowler, Fred Simon and Larry Brownlee. Johnson had been in The Impressions from 1973-76. Simon and Brownlee were in The Lost Generation. Brownlee died in 1978. | | |
| 3/12/77 | **59** | 7 | 1 What Would The World Be Without Music ......... | | Curtom 0123 |
| 5/28/77 | **77** | 4 | 2 Is It Really You ........................................... | | Curtom 0126 |
| 10/01/77 | **71** | 10 | 3 It Took A Woman Like You............................. | | Curtom 0130 |

# N

| DEBUT DATE | PEAK POS | WKS CHR | ARTIST — Record Title | POP POS | Label & Number |
|---|---|---|---|---|---|
| | | | **NAIROBI & The Awesome Foursome** | | |
| 12/25/82+ | **68** | 7 | 1 Funky Soul Makossa...................................... | | Streetwise 2205 |
| | | | **NAJEE** | | |
| | | | Jazz saxophonist born and raised in Queens, New York. Session work for George Benson, Kashif and Lillo Thomas. Also see Vanesse Thomas. | | |
| 1/10/87 | **55** | 7 | 1 Sweet Love ............................................... [I] | | EMI America 8362 |
| 4/11/87 | **72** | 6 | 2 Feel So Good To Me .................................... [I] | | EMI America 8381 |
| 7/18/87 | **45** | 11 | 3 Betcha Don't Know .................................... [I] | | EMI Amer. 43019 |
| 11/28/87+ | **33** | 13 | 4 Mysterious ............................................... [I] | | EMI Amer. 50130 |
| | | | above 4: primarily instrumentals with limited vocal chorus | | |
| | | | **NARADA - see NARADA MICHAEL WALDEN** | | |
| | | | **JOHNNY NASH** | | |
| | | | Born on 8/19/40 in Houston. Vocalist/guitarist/actor. Appeared on local TV from age 13. With Arthur Godfrey, TV and radio, from 1956-63. In the film "Take A Giant Step" in 1959. Own label, JoDa, in 1965. Began recording in Jamaica, late 60s. | | |
| 9/25/65 | **4** | 13 | 1 Let's Move & Groove (Together).................... | 88 | JoDa 102 |
| 5/14/66 | **35** | 5 | 2 Somewhere .............................................. | 120 | JoDa 106 |
| 10/05/68 | **21** | 8 | 3 Hold Me Tight............................................ | 5 | JAD 207 |
| 12/28/68+ | **46** | 3 | 4 You Got Soul ............................................ | 58 | JAD 209 |
| 10/21/72 | **38** | 6 | 5● I Can See Clearly Now ................................ | 1 | Epic 10902 |
| 2/02/74 | **40** | 14 | 6 Loving You ............................................... | 91 | Epic 11070 |
| 9/14/74 | **38** | 9 | 7 You Can't Go Halfway ................................. | 105 | Epic 50021 |
| 5/08/76 | **66** | 6 | 8 (What A) Wonderful World ........................... | 103 | Epic 50219 |
| 9/15/79 | **74** | 9 | 9 Closer .................................................... | | Epic 50737 |
| | | | **NATIVE** | | |
| 11/17/84 | **79** | 5 | 1 Love Ain't No Holiday .................................. | | Jamaica 9003 |
| | | | **NATURAL FOUR** | | |
| | | | Group led by Chris James, formed in San Francisco in 1967, includes Darryl Canady, Steve Striplin and Delmos Whitley. | | |
| 5/03/69 | **31** | 8 | 1 Why Should We Stop Now .............................. | | ABC 11205 |
| 11/24/73+ | **10** | 18 | 2 Can This Be Real ....................................... | 31 | Curtom 1990 |
| 4/06/74 | **23** | 12 | 3 Love That Really Counts ............................... | 98 | Curtom 1995 |
| 7/13/74 | **20** | 12 | 4 You Bring Out The Best In Me ....................... | | Curtom 2000 |
| 3/08/75 | **68** | 6 | 5 Heaven Right Here On Earth .......................... | | Curtom 0101 |
| 8/02/75 | **87** | 5 | 6 Love's So Wonderful ................................... | | Curtom 0104 |
| 4/10/76 | **82** | 5 | 7 It's The Music............................................ | | Curtom 0114 |
| 7/24/76 | **71** | 5 | 8 Free..................................................... | | Curtom 0119 |

| DEBUT DATE | PEAK POS | WKS CHR | ARTIST — Record Title | POP POS | Label & Number |
|---|---|---|---|---|---|
| | | | **NATURALS** Group consisting of Johnny Simon (formerly in the Wallace Brothers), William Thomas, Robert Fitzpatrick and Michael Williams. | | |
| 1/29/72 | **41** | 4 | 1  I Can't Share You............................................ | | Calla 181 |
| | | | **NATURE ZONE** | | |
| 7/17/76 | **68** | 10 | 1  Porcupine.................................................. [I] | | London 235 |
| | | | **NATURE'S DIVINE** 10-member group from Detroit. | | |
| 9/15/79 | **6** | 15 | 1  **I Just Can't Control Myself**......................... | *65* | Infinity 50027 |
| | | | **NATURE'S GIFT** | | |
| 5/04/74 | **94** | 4 | 1  Secret Affair ............................................... | | ABC 11422 |
| | | | **NAYOBE** Female singer. | | |
| 12/13/86 | **74** | 9 | 1  Good Things Come To Those Who Wait ............ | | Fever 1910 |
| | | | **NAZTY** Detroit group formed in 1968: Artwell Matthews, Jr., Mark Patterson, Audrey Matthews, Jackie Casper, Mike Judkins, Larry Thomas and Alice Myers. | | |
| 7/31/76 | **100** | 2 | 1  It's Summertime ............................................ | | Mankind 12024 |
| | | | **N.C.C.U.** | | |
| 5/21/77 | **91** | 6 | 1  Bull City Party ............................................. | | United Art. 990 |
| | | | **N'COLE** | | |
| 8/12/78 | **60** | 12 | 1  I'm Gonna Need This Love ............................. | | Millennium 617 |
| | | | **NDUGU & THE CHOCOLATE JAM COMPANY** Group led by Leon Ndugu Chancler. | | |
| 3/22/80 | **91** | 3 | 1  Shadow Dancing .......................................... | | Epic 50837 |
| | | | **JIMMY NELSON** Vocalist from Houston. | | |
| 7/28/51 | **1**[1] | 21 | 1  "T" 99 Blues ................................................. Juke Box #1 / Best Seller #6 with the Peter Rabbit Trio | | RPM 325 |
| | | | **PHYLLIS NELSON** Dance/disco singer from Philadelphia. | | |
| 12/21/85+ | **65** | 14 | 1  I Like You.................................................... | *61* | Carrere 05719 |
| | | | **RICKY NELSON** Born Eric Hilliard Nelson on 5/8/40 in Teaneck, New Jersey. Died on 12/31/85 in a plane crash in DeKalb, Texas. Son of bandleader Ozzie Nelson and vocalist Harriet Hilliard. Rick and brother David appeared on Nelson's radio show from March, 1949, later on TV, 1952 to 1966. Formed own Stone Canyon Band in 1969. Films "Rio Bravo", "Wackiest Ship In The Army", and "Love And Kisses". One of the first teen idols of the rock era. | | |
| 7/08/57 | **10** | 1 | 1  **I'm Walking** .............................................. orchestra directed by Barney Kessel Jockey #10 | *17* | Verve 10047 |
| 10/28/57 | **5** | 8 | 2  **Be-Bop Baby** ............................................. Best Seller #5 / Jockey #10 | *3* | Imperial 5463 |
| 1/20/58 | **4** | 8 | 3  **Stood Up/** Jockey #4 / Best Seller #8 | *2* | |
| 2/24/58 | **12** | 1 | 4  Waitin' In School ....................................... Jockey #12 | *18* | Imperial 5483 |
| 4/21/58 | **6** | 5 | 5  **Believe What You Say/** Jockey #6 / Best Seller #9 above 2: written by Johnny & Dorsey Burnette | *4* | |
| | | 4 | 6  My Bucket's Got A Hole In It...................... Best Seller flip | *18* | Imperial 5503 |
| 6/30/58 | **3** | 13 | 7  **Poor Little Fool** ......................................... Best Seller #3 / Jockey #5 | *1* | Imperial 5528 |
| 11/24/58+ | **15** | 6 | 8  Lonesome Town............................................ written by Baker Knight | *7* | Imperial 5545 |
| 3/09/59 | **30** | 1 | 9  It's Late .................................................... written by Dorsey Burnette | *9* | Imperial 5565 |
| 6/06/60 | **28** | 2 | 10  Young Emotions.......................................... | *12* | Imperial 5663 |
| 2/16/63 | **24** | 5 | 11  It's Up To You ........................................... | *6* | Imperial 5901 |

| DEBUT DATE | PEAK POS | WKS CHR | ARTIST — Record Title | POP POS | Label & Number |
|---|---|---|---|---|---|
| | | | **RICKY NELSON — Continued** | | |
| 11/02/63 | 24 | 3 | 12 Fools Rush In ................................ | *12* | Decca 31533 |
| | | | #1 hit for Glenn Miller in 1940 | | |
| | | | **SANDY NELSON** | | |
| | | | Born Sander Nelson on 12/1/38 in Santa Monica, California. Prominent studio rock drummer. In 1963, lost portion of his right leg in a motorcycle accident. Returned to performing in 1964. | | |
| 9/28/59 | 17 | 7 | 1 Teen Beat .................................... [I] | *4* | Orig. Sound 5 |
| | | | **TYKA NELSON** | | |
| | | | Minneapolis singer/songwriter, sister of Prince. | | |
| 5/21/88 | 33 | 11 | 1 Marc Anthony's Tune ...................... | | Cooltempo 43228 |
| | | | **ROBBIE NEVIL** | | |
| 11/22/86+ | 7 | 17 | 1 C'est La Vie ................................ | *2* | Manhattan 50047 |
| 6/13/87 | 69 | 9 | 2 Wot's It To Ya ............................. | *10* | Manhattan 50075 |
| | | | **AARON NEVILLE** | | |
| | | | Born in 1941 in New Orleans. Member of the New Orleans' family group, The Neville Brothers. Brother Art was keyboardist of The Meters. His son Ivan began recording career in 1988. | | |
| 9/26/60 | 21 | 2 | 1 Over You ................................... | *111* | Minit 612 |
| | | | shown as: **ARRON NEVILLE** | | |
| 12/03/66+ | 1⁵ | 17 | 2 Tell It Like It Is .......................... | *2* | Par-Lo 101 |
| | | | **THE NEW BIRTH** | | |
| | | | Vocal group portion of New Birth, Inc. (see The Nite-Liters). Original group consisted of vocalists Londee Loren, Bobby Downs, Melvin Wilson, Leslie Wilson, Ann Bogan and soloist Alan Frye, with instrumental backing by The Nite-Liters. Melvin, Leslie and Ann recorded as Love, Peace & Happiness in 1972. | | |
| 9/18/71 | 12 | 14 | 1 It's Impossible ............................. | *52* | RCA 0520 |
| 4/22/72 | 45 | 2 | 2 Umh Song .................................. | | RCA 0657 |
| 3/24/73 | 4 | 12 | 3 I Can Understand It ....................... | *35* | RCA 0912 |
| 7/14/73 | 21 | 10 | 4 Until It's Time For You To Go............... | *97* | RCA 0003 |
| 1/26/74 | 9 | 17 | 5 It's Been A Long Time...................... | *66* | RCA 0185 |
| 5/11/74 | 17 | 13 | 6 Wildflower ................................. | *45* | RCA 0265 |
| 8/24/74 | 46 | 9 | 7 I Wash My Hands Of The Whole Damn Deal, Part I........................................ | *88* | RCA 10017 |
| 11/30/74+ | 76 | 8 | 8 Comin' From All Ends...................... | | RCA 10110 |
| 4/12/75 | 28 | 9 | 9 Granddaddy (Part 1) ...................... | *95* | Buddah 464 |
| 6/21/75 | 1¹ | 16 | 10 Dream Merchant .......................... | *36* | Buddah 470 |
| 7/04/76 | 91 | 5 | 11 The Long And Winding Road ............... | | Warner 8217 |
| 9/25/76 | 51 | 6 | 12 Fallin' In Love - Part 1 ................... | | Warner 8256 |
| 9/17/77 | 65 | 10 | 13 Deeper ................................... | | Warner 8422 |
| 1/07/78 | 49 | 7 | 14 The Mighty Army ......................... | | Warner 8499 |
| 8/18/79 | 28 | 11 | 15 I Love You ................................ | | Ariola 7760 |
| | | | **NEW CENSATION** | | |
| 4/06/74 | 61 | 8 | 1 Come Down To Earth ...................... | | Pride 406 |
| 11/30/74 | 79 | 6 | 2 First Round Knockout...................... | | Pride 7000 |
| | | | **NEW CHOICE** | | |
| | | | Sacramento-based, female vocal quintet formed by producer/label owner Jay King. In 1987, members' ages ranged from 18 to 21. | | |
| 9/19/87 | 69 | 10 | 1 Cold Stupid ............................... | | RCA 5290 |
| | | | from the film "Penitentiary III" | | |
| | | | **THE NEWCOMERS** | | |
| | | | Trio from Memphis: Terry Bartlett, William Somlin and Bertrand Brown. Brown's brother William was in The Mad Lads. First recorded for Stax/Volt in 1970. Became a quartet with the addition of Vince Williams; group recorded as Kwick in 1980. | | |
| 9/11/71 | 28 | 9 | 1 Pin The Tail On The Donkey .............. | *74* | Stax 0099 |
| | | | instrumental backing by The Bar-Kays | | |
| 9/21/74 | 66 | 8 | 2 Keep An Eye On Your Close Friends ........ | | Truth 3204 |
| 1/11/75 | 74 | 9 | 3 (Too Little In Common To Be Lovers) Too Much Going To Say Good-Bye.......................... | | Truth 3213 |
| 8/19/78 | 84 | 8 | 4 Do Yourself A Favor ...................... | | Mercury 74011 |

| DEBUT DATE | PEAK POS | WKS CHR | ARTIST — Record Title | POP POS | Label & Number |
|---|---|---|---|---|---|
| | | | **NEW EDITION** ★★**130**★★ | | |
| | | | Group formed in Boston in 1982, consisting of Ralph Tresvant (b: 5/16/68), Ronald DeVoe (b: 11/17/67), Michael Bivins (b: 10/10/68), Ricky Bell (b: 9/18/67) and Bobby Brown (B: 2/5/69). Brown left for solo career in 1986; replaced by Johnny Gill in 1988. | | |
| 4/02/83 | 1¹ | 18 | 1 **Candy Girl** | 46 | Streetwise 1108 |
| 7/16/83 | 8 | 19 | 2 **Is This The End** | 85 | Streetwise 1111 |
| 11/12/83 | 25 | 14 | 3 Popcorn Love/ | 101 | |
| | | 14 | 4 Jealous Girl | | Streetwise 1116 |
| 9/08/84 | 1¹ | 23 | 5●**Cool It Now** | 4 | MCA 52455 |
| 12/15/84+ | 1³ | 17 | 6 **Mr. Telephone Man** | 12 | MCA 52484 |
| 3/23/85 | 6 | 15 | 7 **Lost In Love** | 35 | MCA 52553 |
| 7/06/85 | 87 | 2 | 8 Kind Of Girls We Like | | MCA 23544 |
| 7/20/85 | 27 | 12 | 9 My Secret (Didja Gitit Yet?) | 103 | MCA 52627 |
| 11/02/85 | 2² | 17 | 10 **Count Me Out** | 51 | MCA 52703 |
| 2/15/86 | 3 | 15 | 11 **A Little Bit Of Love (Is All It Takes)** | 38 | MCA 52768 |
| 5/17/86 | 7 | 15 | 12 **With You All The Way** | 51 | MCA 52829 |
| 8/23/86 | 3 | 14 | 13 **Earth Angel** | 21 | MCA 52905 |
| | | | from the film "The Karate Kid Part II" | | |
| 10/25/86 | 10 | 16 | 14 **Once In A Lifetime Groove** | | MCA 52959 |
| | | | from the film "Running Scared" | | |
| 1/31/87 | 41 | 8 | 15 Tears On My Pillow | | MCA 53019 |
| | | | featuring vocals by Little Richard | | |
| 8/01/87 | 20 | 11 | 16 Helplessly In Love | | MCA 53164 |
| | | | from the film "Dragnet" | | |
| 6/04/88 | 2¹ | 19 | 17 **If It Isn't Love** | 7 | MCA 53264 |
| | | | **NEW GUYS ON THE BLOCK Featuring: Lane** | | |
| 6/04/83 | 63 | 7 | 1 On The Dance Floor | | Sugar Hill 797 |
| | | | **NEW HORIZONS** | | |
| | | | Family band from Dayton, Ohio, formed as Horizon. Included the Thomas brothers: Mark (lead), Varges (keyboards), Bart (bass) and Art (percussion); with cousin Timothy Abrams (guitar). Discovered by Roger Troutman. | | |
| 5/28/83 | 39 | 14 | 1 Your Thing Is Your Thing - Part I | | Columbia 03887 |
| | | | **THE NEW INGREDIENT - see TONY SYLVESTER** | | |
| | | | **NEW JERSEY MASS CHOIR** | | |
| | | | Gospel choir that backed Foreigner on the original hit version. | | |
| 2/23/85 | 37 | 12 | 1 I Want To Know What Love Is | 101 | Savoy 0004 |
| | | | featuring Donnie Harper, Donald Malloy & Sherry McGee | | |
| | | | **NEW KIDS ON THE BLOCK** | | |
| | | | White, Boston teen quintet formed in the summer of 1984: Joe McIntyre (13-year-old lead singer), Donny Wahlberg, Danny Wood, and brothers Jordan and Jon Knight. | | |
| 6/07/86 | 90 | 2 | 1 Be My Girl | | Columbia 05883 |
| 4/02/88 | 55 | 11 | 2 Please Don't Go Girl | 10 | Columbia 07700 |
| | | | **THE NEW MARKETTS** | | |
| | | | Studio group from Los Angeles; included Tommy Tedesco (guitar). | | |
| 6/26/76 | 50 | 11 | 1 Song From M*A*S*H | [I] | Farr 007 |
| | | | new version of theme from the movie and TV series "M*A*S*H"; originally released on Seminole 501 | | |
| | | | **NEW ORDER** | | |
| | | | Electro-pop quartet formed in Manchester, England with the name, Warsaw, in April, 1979. Changed name to Joy Division. After suicide of vocalist Ian Curtis (May 1980), name changed to New Order. Lineup since 1986: Bernard Sumner, Stephen Morris, Peter Hook and Gillian Gilbert. | | |
| 10/29/83 | 71 | 6 | 1 Confusion | | Streetwise 2213 |
| | | | **NEW YORK CITI PEECH BOYS** | | |
| | | | Percussive funk-rock band formed at the Paradise Garage club in New York City. Consisted of Robert Kaspar, Michael de Benedictus, Darryl Short, Steven Brown and R. Bernard Fowler (vocals). Re-mixed by club DJ Levan. | | |
| 6/05/82 | 89 | 5 | 1 Don't Make Me Wait | | West End 1240 |
| | | | shown only as: **PEECH BOYS** | | |
| 2/12/83 | 74 | 7 | 2 Life Is Something Special | 108 | Island 99926 |
| 10/15/83 | 56 | 6 | 3 On A Journey | | Island 99822 |
| | | | shown only as: **PEECH BOYS** | | |

| DEBUT DATE | PEAK POS | WKS CHR | ARTIST — Record Title | POP POS | Label & Number |
|---|---|---|---|---|---|
| | | | **NEW YORK CITY** | | |
| | | | New York City quartet: Tim McQueen, John Brown, Ed Shell and Claude Johnston. First recorded for Buddah as Triboro Exchange. Name changed in 1972. | | |
| 3/31/73 | **14** | 11 | 1 I'm Doin' Fine Now ........................................ | *17* | Chelsea 0113 |
| 8/11/73 | **44** | 12 | 2 Make Me Twice The Man ............................... | *93* | Chelsea 0025 |
| 12/01/73+ | **19** | 16 | 3 Quick, Fast, In A Hurry ............................... | *79* | Chelsea 0150 |
| 7/20/74 | **20** | 14 | 4 Happiness Is................................................ | | Chelsea 3000 |
| 12/14/74+ | **41** | 9 | 5 Love Is What You Make It............................ ... | *104* | Chelsea 3008 |
| 4/12/75 | **76** | 7 | 6 Got To Get You Back In My Life....................∴... | *105* | Chelsea 3010 |
| | | | **NEW YORK COMMUNITY CHOIR** | | |
| 7/30/77 | **76** | 6 | 1 Express Yourself ......................................... | | RCA 11035 |
| | | | **NEW YOUNG HEARTS** | | |
| 11/07/70 | **40** | 3 | 1 The Young Hearts Get Lonely Too.................... | *123* | Zea 50001 |
| | | | written by Richard "Dimples" Fields | | |
| | | | **BOOKER NEWBERRY III** | | |
| 4/30/83 | **46** | 10 | 1 Love Town.................................................. | | Boardwalk 99905 |
| 5/10/86 | **61** | 8 | 2 Take A Piece Of Me ..................................... | | Omni 96820 |
| | | | **NEWCLEUS** | | |
| | | | New York rap group. | | |
| 8/06/83 | **26** | 11 | 1 Jam On Revenge (The Wikki-Wikki Song) ...... [N] | | Sunnyview 3007 |
| 3/24/84 | **9** | 22 | 2 **Jam On It** ............................................... [N] | *56* | Sunnyview 3010 |
| 8/11/84 | **31** | 12 | 3 Computer Age (Push the Button)..................... | | Sunnyview 3013 |
| 6/01/85 | **74** | 4 | 4 I Wanna Be A B-Boy ................................... | | Sunnyview 425 |
| 7/27/85 | **74** | 7 | 5 Let's Jam ................................................... | | Sunnyview 3024 |
| 4/05/86 | **77** | 5 | 6 Na Na Beat................................................. | | Sunnyview 3031 |
| | | | **JIMMY NEWMAN** | | |
| | | | Born on 8/27/27 in Big Mamou, Louisiana. Cajun-country singer/guitarist. | | |
| 7/01/57 | **7** | 1 | 1 **A Fallen Star** ............................................. | *23* | Dot 15574 |
| | | | Jockey #7 | | |
| | | | **CHUBBY NEWSOM & Her Hip Shakers** | | |
| | | | Female vocalist from New Orleans. The Hip Shakers were Paul Gayten's band. | | |
| 2/26/49 | **8** | 4 | 1 **Hip Shakin' Mama** ........................................ | | DeLuxe 3199 |
| | | | Juke Box #8 / Best Seller #12 | | |
| | | | featuring Lee Allen on tenor sax; also released on Miltone 3199 | | |
| | | | **BOBBY NEWSOME** | | |
| 6/03/72 | **47** | 3 | 1 Jody, Come Back And Get Your Shoes ............. | | Spring 125 |
| | | | **FRANKIE NEWSOME** | | |
| | | | Singer from Chicago; also recorded as "Willie Parker". | | |
| 11/15/69 | **42** | 3 | 1 My Lucky Day ............................................. | | GWP 515 |
| | | | **OLIVIA NEWTON-JOHN** | | |
| | | | Pop/country singer born on 9/26/48 in Cambridge, England; raised in Australia. Co-starred in the films "Grease", "Xanadu" and "Two Of A Kind". | | |
| 1/23/82 | **28** | 8 | 1▲Physical ...................................,,,................ | *1* | MCA 51182 |
| | | | **NEXT MOVEMENT** | | |
| | | | Group from Chicago, formed in 1971. Consisted of Samuel Thomas, Jr., Guy Sutton, Earl Shelby, Carnell Haywood and Alonzo Pickens. | | |
| 8/25/84 | **69** | 8 | 1 All I Do ................................................... | | Nuance 745 |
| | | | **NICOLE** | | |
| | | | Vocalist/songwriter Nicole McCloud, from Rochester, New York. | | |
| 10/26/85 | **66** | 7 | 1 Always And Forever ..................................... | | Portrait 05434 |
| 3/01/86 | **66** | 11 | 2 Don't You Want My Love ............................. | | Portrait 05761 |
| 6/14/86 | **52** | 10 | 3 What About Me............................................ | | Portrait 06044 |
| 6/18/88 | **93** | 2 | 4 Jam Packed (At The Wall)............................. | | Epic 07778 |
| | | | **NIGHTHAWK** | | |
| 8/28/82 | **71** | 4 | 1 Eye Of The Tiger ......................................... | | Quality 7020 |
| | | | new version of theme from the film "Rocky III" | | |

| DEBUT DATE | PEAK POS | WKS CHR | ARTIST — Record Title | POP POS | Label & Number |
|---|---|---|---|---|---|
| | | | **NIGHTHAWKS** | | |
| | | | Blues band led by Robert Nighthawk. Born Robert Lee McCollum on 11/30/09 in Helena, Arkansas. Died of a heart attack on 11/5/67 (57). First recorded as Lee McCoy for Bluebird in 1937. Also known as Peetie's Boy and Rambling Bob. Assumed name Nighthawk from first record, "Prowling Night Hawk". Toured with own Nighthawks Trio into the 50s. Active until his death. | | |
| 12/31/49 | **13** | 1 | 1  Annie Lee Blues ............................................ | | Aristocrat 2301 |
| | | | Juke Box #13 with Willie Dixon on bass | | |
| | | | **MAXINE NIGHTINGALE** | | |
| | | | Born on 11/2/52 in Wembly, England. First recorded in 1968. In productions of "Hair", "Jesus Christ Superstar", "Godspell" and "Savages", in the early 70s. | | |
| 4/17/76 | **46** | 11 | 1●Right Back Where We Started From ................. | *2* | United Art. 752 |
| 5/26/79 | **37** | 15 | 2●Lead Me On................................................. | *5* | Windsong 11530 |
| 11/13/82+ | **17** | 15 | 3  Turn To Me ................................................ | | Highrise 2004 |
| | | | MAXINE NIGHTINGALE featuring JIMMY RUFFIN | | |
| | | | **OLLIE NIGHTINGALE** | | |
| | | | Born Ollie Hoskins in Memphis. Formed gospel group, the Dixie Nightingales, in 1950; became Ollie & The Nightingales in 1968. Went solo in 1970. Other Nightingales became The Ovations. Also see Ollie & The Nightingales. | | |
| 5/08/71 | **23** | 9 | 1  It's A Sad Thing........................................... | | Memphis 104 |
| 9/23/72 | **39** | 11 | 2  May The Best Man Win.................................. | | Pride 1002 |
| | | | **9.9** | | |
| | | | Trio from Boston: Margot Thunder, Leslie Jones and Wanda Perry. Also see Richard "Dimples" Fields. | | |
| 6/29/85 | **5** | 20 | 1  **All Of Me For All Of You**............................. | *51* | RCA 14082 |
| 11/16/85+ | **30** | 14 | 2  I Like The Way You Dance.............................. | | RCA 14203 |
| | | | **NINTH CREATION** | | |
| 6/04/77 | **98** | 2 | 1  Why Not Today............................................. | | Prelude 71085 |
| 11/10/79 | **45** | 11 | 2  Let's Dance................................................. | | Hilltak 7901 |
| | | | **THE NITE-LITERS** | | |
| | | | Band formed in 1963 in Louisville, Kentucky, by Harvey Fuqua and Tony Churchill. Expanded to 17 members with two vocal groups and band. Renamed New Birth, Inc. Band consisted of Churchill, Austin Lander, James Baker, Robert "Lurch" Jackson, Leroy Taylor and Robin Russell. Later included Ben Boxtel, Roger Voice & James Hall. Also see Love, Peace & Happiness. | | |
| 7/03/71 | **17** | 13 | 1  K-Jee.......................................................[I] | *39* | RCA 0461 |
| 1/01/72 | **24** | 15 | 2  Afro-Strut/ [I] | *49* | |
| | | 3 | 3  (We've Got To) Pull Together ......................... | | RCA 0591 |
| | | | **NITEFLYTE** | | |
| | | | Disco group led by Howard Johnson and Sandy Torano. | | |
| 4/28/79 | **21** | 16 | 1  If You Want It............................................... | *37* | Ariola 7747 |
| 6/07/80 | **97** | 2 | 2  All About Love ............................................ | | Ariola 800 |
| 3/21/81 | **79** | 4 | 3  You Are...................................................... | | Ariola 814 |
| | | | **PAMELA NIVENS** | | |
| 6/25/83 | **58** | 8 | 1  It's You I Love .............................................. | | Sun Valley 8401 |
| | | | **THE NOBLE KNIGHTS - see KING CURTIS** | | |
| | | | **CLIFF NOBLES & CO.** | | |
| | | | Cliff was born in 1944 in Mobile, Alabama. Vocalist/bandleader. | | |
| 6/01/68 | **2**² | 15 | 1●The Horse................................................[I] | | Phil-L.A. 313 |
| 2/15/69 | **22** | 6 | 2  Switch It On ............................................[I] | *93* | Phil-L.A. 324 |
| | | | above 2: written & produced by Jesse James | | |
| 6/02/73 | **42** | 5 | 3  Feeling Of Loneliness.................................... | | Roulette 7142 |
| | | | **NOCERA** | | |
| | | | Female dance/disco singer from Italy. | | |
| 11/08/86 | **47** | 13 | 1  Summertime, Summertime............................. | *84* | Sleeping Bag 22 |
| 12/12/87 | **70** | 10 | 2  Let's Go ..................................................... | | Sleeping Bag 29 |
| | | | **NOEL** | | |
| | | | Real name: Noel Pagan; 21-year-old Latin singer from the Bronx. | | |
| 5/14/88 | **88** | 6 | 1  Like A Child................................................ | *67* | 4th & B'way 7458 |
| | | | **NOLAN - see NOLAN PORTER** | | |

| DEBUT DATE | PEAK POS | WKS CHR | ARTIST — Record Title | POP POS | Label & Number |
|---|---|---|---|---|---|
| | | | **KENNY NOLAN** Los Angeles-based singer/songwriter. Wrote "My Eyes Adored You", "Lady Marmalade" and "Get Dancin'". Also see The Eleventh Hour. | | |
| 2/23/80 | 89 | 4 | 1  Us And Love (We Go Together) ...................... | 44 | Casablanca 2234 |
| | | | **NORMA JEAN** Born Norma Jean Wright in Elyria, Ohio. Sang in female trio, the Topettes. Attended Ohio State University. Toured for a short time with the Spinners. Moved to New York. Former lead singer of Chic. | | |
| 7/15/78 | 15 | 14 | 1  Saturday ........................................ | | Bearsville 0326 |
| 11/18/78 | 83 | 5 | 2  Having A Party ................................. | | Bearsville 0331 |
| 12/22/79+ | 19 | 14 | 3  High Society.................................... | | Bearsville 49119 |
| | | | **JIMMY NORMAN** Singer, born on 8/12/37 in Nashville. Member of The Chargers and The Dyna-Sores. Currently tours as one of The Coasters. | | |
| 7/14/62 | 21 | 6 | 1  I Don't Love You No More (I Don't Care About You) .......................................... | 47 | Little Star 113 |
| 10/22/66 | 35 | 5 | 2  Can You Blame Me ............................. | | Samar 116 |
| | | | **FREDDIE NORTH** Vocalist from Nashville. Worked in sales and promotion for Nashboro Records. Disc jockey on "Night Train", WLAC-Nashville. | | |
| 8/21/71 | 10 | 17 | 1  **She's All I Got**.............................. | 39 | Mankind 12004 |
| 2/05/72 | 26 | 9 | 2  You And Me Together Forever ...................... | 116 | Mankind 12009 |
| | | | **NORWOOD** Singer/songwriter Norwood B. Young from Trenton, New Jersey. | | |
| 3/21/87 | 30 | 11 | 1  I Can't Let You Go.............................. | | Magnolia 52929 |
| | | | **DOROTHY NORWOOD** Formerly with the Caravans. Own group, the Dorothy Norwood Singers. | | |
| 12/29/73+ | 21 | 13 | 1  There's Got To Be Rain In Your Life (To Appreciate The Sunshine) ...................... | 88 | GRC 1011 |
| 6/07/75 | 96 | 3 | 2  Let Your Feet Down Easy ............................ | | GRC 2057 |
| | | | **NOTATIONS** Group from Chicago, formed in 1965. Consisted of Clifford Curry, LaSalle Matthews, Bobby Thomas and Jimmy Stroud. First recorded for Tad in the late 60s. Stroud replaced by Walter Jones in 1973. Jones left in 1976. | | |
| 12/05/70+ | 26 | 15 | 1  I'm Still Here................................... | | Twinight 141 |
| 3/22/75 | 27 | 12 | 2  It Only Hurts For A Little While.................... | | Gemigo 103 |
| 8/16/75 | 93 | 3 | 3  Think Before You Stop .......................... | | Gemigo 0500 |
| 11/22/75 | 42 | 10 | 4  It's Alright (This Feeling) ......................... | | Gemigo 0503 |
| 4/10/76 | 91 | 3 | 5  Make Me Twice The Man ......................... | | Gemigo 0506 |
| | | | **NU ROMANCE CREW** | | |
| 5/02/87 | 59 | 8 | 1  Tonight ........................................ | | EMI America 8387 |
| | | | **NU SHOOZ** Portland, Oregon group centered around husband and wife team of guitarist/ songwriter John Smith and lead singer Valerie Day. | | |
| 2/15/86 | 2[3] | 34 | 1  **I Can't Wait** ................................. | 3 | Atlantic 89446 |
| 7/12/86 | 36 | 15 | 2  Point Of No Return ............................. | 28 | Atlantic 89392 |
| 4/30/88 | 17 | 14 | 3  Should I Say Yes? .............................. | 41 | Atlantic 89108 |
| | | | **NUANCE featuring VIKKI LOVE** | | |
| 7/14/84 | 23 | 17 | 1  Take A Chance ................................. | | 4th & B'way 403 |
| 12/01/84+ | 34 | 14 | 2  Loveride ....................................... | | 4th & B'Way 7409 |
| 9/21/85 | 36 | 12 | 3  Stop Playing On Me ............................ shown as: **VIKKI LOVE with Nuance** | | 4th & B'way 418 |
| | | | **NUGGETS** | | |
| 6/30/79 | 74 | 3 | 1  New York....................................... | | Mercury 74067 |
| | | | **NUMONICS** | | |
| 3/10/84 | 80 | 5 | 1  Sexy Chile ..................................... | | Hodisk 008 |
| 8/25/84 | 66 | 7 | 2  Fox Trappin (Part 1)............................ | | Hodisk 8009 |

| DEBUT DATE | PEAK POS | WKS CHR | ARTIST — Record Title | POP POS | Label & Number |
|---|---|---|---|---|---|
| | | | **BOBBY NUNN** Vocalist/keyboardist from Buffalo, New York. Performed on Rick James' debut LP "Come Get It". Moved to Los Angeles, formed own band, Splendor. | | |
| 9/25/82 | **15** | 13 | 1 She's Just A Groupie | *104* | Motown 1643 |
| 12/25/82+ | **36** | 10 | 2 Got To Get Up On It | | Motown 1653 |
| 10/08/83 | **66** | 8 | 3 Private Party | | Motown 1695 |
| 12/24/83+ | **50** | 12 | 4 Hangin' Out At The Mall | | Motown 1711 |
| | | | **NUTMEGS** Vocal group from New Haven, Connecticut. Formed as the Lyres in 1954. Consisted of Leroy Griffin, James "Sonny" Griffin, James "CoCo" Tyson, Billy Emery and Leroy McNeil. Re-named for the Nutmeg State. Also recorded as The Rajahs. | | |
| 6/04/55 | **2**[1] | 13 | 1 **Story Untold** Best Seller #2 / Jockey #5 / Juke Box #5 | | Herald 452 |
| 10/01/55 | **13** | 2 | 2 Ship Of Love Jockey #13 | | Herald 459 |
| | | | **THE NUTTY SQUIRRELS** Creators and voices: Don Elliot (from Sommerville, NJ) and Sascha Burland (from New York City). | | |
| 12/07/59 | **9** | 6 | 1 Uh! Oh! Part 2 [N] | *14* | Hanover 4540 |
| | | | **NYTRO** 8-piece group originally from Columbus, Ohio, formed as the Soul Superbs in 1972. Became the Ohio Silver, moved to Los Angeles in 1974 and renamed Nytro. Consisted of Chris Powell, Earnest "Pepper" Reed Jr., Robert "Frankie" Justice (lead), Ted Willingham, Kenneth Scott, Lamorris Payne, Ron Allen Smith and John Jackson. | | |
| 4/23/77 | **74** | 5 | 1 What It Is | | Whitfield 8356 |

# O

| DEBUT DATE | PEAK POS | WKS CHR | ARTIST — Record Title | POP POS | Label & Number |
|---|---|---|---|---|---|
| | | | **O'BRYAN** Born O'Bryan Burnett II from Sneads Ferry, North Carolina. | | |
| 1/30/82 | **5** | 17 | 1 **The Gigolo** | *57* | Capitol 5067 |
| 5/22/82 | **23** | 13 | 2 Still Water (Love) | | Capitol 5117 |
| 2/05/83 | **15** | 18 | 3 I'm Freaky | | Capitol 5203 |
| 5/14/83 | **19** | 17 | 4 You And I | | Capitol 5224 |
| 4/07/84 | **1**[1] | 21 | 5 **Lovelite** | *101* | Capitol 5329 |
| 8/04/84 | **32** | 10 | 6 Breakin' Together | | Capitol 5376 |
| 10/13/84 | **62** | 8 | 7 Go On And Cry | | Capitol 5414 |
| 11/22/86+ | **35** | 13 | 8 Tenderoni | | Capitol 5617 |
| 3/14/87 | **60** | 7 | 9 Driving Force | | Capitol 5673 |
| | | | **BILLY OCEAN**    ★★156★★ Born Leslie Sebastian Charles on 1/21/50 in Trinidad. Raised in England, worked as a tailor. Did session work in London. Moved to the United States in the late 70s. | | |
| 8/07/76 | **55** | 7 | 1 L.O.D. (Love On Delivery) | *106* | Ariola Am. 7630 |
| 5/16/81 | **7** | 19 | 2 **Night (Feel Like Getting Down)** | *103* | Epic 02053 |
| 9/12/81 | **66** | 6 | 3 Another Day Won't Matter | | Epic 02485 |
| 6/19/82 | **72** | 5 | 4 Calypso Funkin' | | Epic 02942 |
| 6/30/84 | **1**[4] | 27 | 5●**Caribbean Queen (No More Love On The Run)** . | *1* | Jive 9199 |
| 11/17/84+ | **20** | 20 | 6 Loverboy | *2* | Jive 9284 |
| 3/30/85 | **5** | 20 | 7 **Suddenly** | *4* | Jive 9323 |
| 7/20/85 | **10** | 14 | 8 **Mystery Lady** | *24* | Jive 9374 |
| 12/07/85+ | **6** | 19 | 9 **When The Going Gets Tough, The Tough Get Going** from the film "The Jewel of the Nile" | *2* | Jive 9432 |
| 4/19/86 | **1**[2] | 21 | 10 **There'll Be Sad Songs (To Make You Cry)** | *1* | Jive 9465 |
| 7/12/86 | **1**[1] | 15 | 11 **Love Zone** | *10* | Jive 9510 |
| 10/25/86 | **10** | 16 | 12 **Love Is Forever** | *16* | Jive 9540 |
| 2/20/88 | **1**[1] | 16 | 13 **Get Outta My Dreams, Get Into My Car** | *1* | Jive 9678 |
| 6/04/88 | **10** | 13 | 14 **The Colour Of Love** | *17* | Jive 9707 |
| | | | **OCTAVIA** | | |
| 11/15/86 | **68** | 9 | 1 2 The Limit | | Pow Wow 415 |

| DEBUT DATE | PEAK POS | WKS CHR | ARTIST — Record Title | POP POS | Label & Number |
|---|---|---|---|---|---|
| | | | **ODDS & ENDS** | | |
| 9/19/70 | 38 | 6 | 1 Let Me Try.................................................. | | Today 1001 |
| 3/06/71 | 28 | 8 | 2 Love Makes The World Go Round.................... | 83 | Today 1003 |
| | | | **BROOKS O'DELL** | | |
| | | | Male vocalist from Philadelphia; sang lead with the Commanders, and with own group, the Majestics. | | |
| 12/14/63+ | 58 | 9 | 1 Watch Your Step......................................... | Hot | Gold 214 |
| | | | **ODYSSEY** | | |
| | | | Vocal trio from Connecticut. Formed as The Lopez Sisters, with Lillian, Louise and Carmen Lopez (originally from the Virgin Islands). Carmen left in 1968, replaced by Manila-born Tony Reynolds. | | |
| 10/15/77 | 6 | 20 | 1 Native New Yorker..................................... | 21 | RCA 11129 |
| 4/29/78 | 37 | 12 | 2 Weekend Lover........................................... | 57 | RCA 11245 |
| 5/10/80 | 44 | 10 | 3 Don't Tell Me, Tell Her.............................. | 105 | RCA 11962 |
| 6/20/81 | 68 | 8 | 4 Going Back To My Roots ............................. | | RCA 12240 |
| 6/12/82 | 12 | 18 | 5 Inside Out................................................. | 104 | RCA 13217 |
| | | | **LILLIAN OFFITT** | | |
| | | | Born on 11/4/38 in Nashville. To Chicago in 1958. Largely outside of music since the early 70s. | | |
| 7/15/57 | 8 | 3 | 1 Miss You So ............................................... | 66 | Excello 2104 |
| | | | Jockey #8 / Best Seller #11 | | |
| | | | **LENNY O'HENRY** | | |
| 5/30/64 | 98 | 1 | 1 Across The Street ...................................... | Hot | Atco 6291 |
| | | | **OHIO PLAYERS**    ★★78★★ | | |
| | | | Originally an instrumental group called the Ohio Untouchables. Formed in Dayton in 1959. Back-up on The Falcons' records. First recorded for Lupine in 1962. Members during prime (1974-79): Marshall Jones, Clarence "Satch" Satchell, Jimmy "Diamond" Williams, Marvin "Merv" Pierce, Billy Beck, Ralph "Pee Wee" Middlebrook and Leroy "Sugarfoot" Bonner. In 1979, Williams and Beck formed Shadow with Clarence "Chet" Willis. | | |
| 2/24/68 | 50 | 2 | 1 Trespassin'................................................ | | Compass 7015 |
| 12/04/71+ | 35 | 13 | 2 Pain (Part I)............................................. | 64 | Westbound 188 |
| 7/08/72 | 45 | 4 | 3 Got Pleasure ............................................. | | Westbound 204 |
| 3/10/73 | 1¹ | 13 | 4●Funky Worm ........................................ [N] | 15 | Westbound 214 |
| 8/11/73 | 12 | 16 | 5 Ecstasy ..................................................... | 31 | Westbound 216 |
| 5/04/74 | 6 | 15 | 6 Jive Turkey (Part 1).................................. | 47 | Mercury 73480 |
| 8/10/74 | 2¹ | 15 | 7●Skin Tight.............................................. | 13 | Mercury 73609 |
| 12/14/74+ | 1² | 18 | 8●Fire....................................................... | 1 | Mercury 73643 |
| 4/12/75 | 6 | 12 | 9 I Want To Be Free..................................... | 44 | Mercury 73675 |
| 9/20/75 | 1¹ | 11 | 10 Sweet Sticky Thing.................................. | 33 | Mercury 73713 |
| 11/15/75 | 1¹ | 15 | 11●Love Rollercoaster................................. | 1 | Mercury 73734 |
| 2/21/76 | 69 | 4 | 12 Rattlesnake ......................................... [I] | 90 | Westbound 5018 |
| 2/28/76 | 9 | 12 | 13 Fopp ...................................................... | 30 | Mercury 73775 |
| 6/26/76 | 1¹ | 17 | 14 Who'd She Coo?....................................... | 18 | Mercury 73814 |
| 11/06/76 | 26 | 11 | 15 Far East Mississippi................................. | | Mercury 73860 |
| 1/22/77 | 31 | 9 | 16 Feel The Beat (Everybody Disco) ................. | 61 | Mercury 73881 |
| 4/30/77 | 19 | 9 | 17 Body Vibes.............................................. | | Mercury 73913 |
| 7/02/77 | 9 | 18 | 18 O-H-I-O ............................................... [I] | 45 | Mercury 73932 |
| 11/12/77 | 77 | 5 | 19 Merry Go Round....................................... | | Mercury 73956 |
| 12/24/77+ | 51 | 10 | 20 Good Luck Charm (Part I) ......................... | 101 | Mercury 73974 |
| 4/01/78 | 93 | 4 | 21 Magic Trick ............................................. | | Mercury 73983 |
| 7/29/78 | 27 | 13 | 22 Funk-O-Nots............................................ | 105 | Mercury 74014 |
| 11/11/78 | 53 | 6 | 23 Time Slips Away....................................... | | Mercury 74031 |
| 5/05/79 | 33 | 9 | 24 Everybody Up........................................... | | Arista 0408 |
| 2/28/81 | 40 | 10 | 25 Try A Little Tenderness ............................ | | Boardwalk 5708 |
| 5/16/81 | 46 | 10 | 26 Skinny ................................................... | | Boardwalk 02063 |
| 5/26/84 | 83 | 5 | 27 Sight For Sore Eyes .................................. | | Air City 402 |
| 6/04/88 | 50 | 9 | 28 Sweat..................................................... | | Track 58816 |

| DEBUT DATE | PEAK POS | WKS CHR | ARTIST — Record Title | POP POS | Label & Number |
|---|---|---|---|---|---|
| | | | **THE O'JAYS**  ★★20★★ | | |
| | | | Group from Canton, Ohio; formed in 1958 as the Triumphs. Consisted of Eddie Levert, Walter Williams, William Powell, Bobby Massey and Bill Isles. Recorded as the Mascots for King in 1961. Re-named by Cleveland dee-jay, Eddie O'Jay. Isles left in 1965. Massey left to become a record producer in 1971. Levert, Williams and Powell continued as a trio. Powell retired from touring due to illness, late 1975 (d: 5/26/77), replaced by Sammy Strain, formerly with Little Anthony & The Imperials. Kenneth Gamble and Leon Huff wrote many of The O'Jays' hits since 1969. Levert's sons, Gerald and Sean, are members of the trio Levert. | | |
| 9/14/63 | 93 | 3 | 1 Lonely Drifter.................................................... | *Hot* | Imperial 5976 |
| 5/22/65 | 28 | 3 | 2 Lipstick Traces (On A Cigarette) ...................... | 48 | Imperial 66102 |
| 10/02/65 | 28 | 7 | 3 Let It All Out..................................................... | | Imperial 66131 |
| 9/24/66 | 12 | 12 | 4 Stand In For Love ............................................. | 95 | Imperial 66197 |
| 11/25/67 | 8 | 11 | 5 I'll Be Sweeter Tomorrow (Than I Was Today). | 66 | Bell 691 |
| 6/01/68 | 27 | 8 | 6 Look Over Your Shoulder .................................. | 89 | Bell 704 |
| 10/05/68 | 41 | 2 | 7 The Choice........................................................ | 94 | Bell 737 |
| 7/05/69 | 15 | 10 | 8 One Night Affair ............................................... | 68 | Neptune 12 |
| 11/01/69 | 41 | 4 | 9 Branded Bad ..................................................... | | Neptune 18 |
| 3/14/70 | 21 | 7 | 10 Deeper (In Love With You) ............................... | 64 | Neptune 22 |
| 8/01/70 | 17 | 8 | 11 Looky Looky (Look At Me Girl)......................... | 98 | Neptune 31 |
| 7/08/72 | 1¹ | 17 | 12● Back Stabbers.................................................. | 3 | Phil. Int. 3517 |
| | | | written by Gene McFadden & John Whitehead | | |
| 11/18/72 | 13 | 9 | 13 992 Arguments.................................................. | 57 | Phil. Int. 3522 |
| 1/20/73 | 1⁴ | 13 | 14● Love Train........................................................ | 1 | Phil. Int. 3524 |
| 5/19/73 | 2² | 13 | 15 Time To Get Down ............................................ | 33 | Phil. Int. 3531 |
| 12/22/73+ | 2² | 19 | 16 Put Your Hands Together .................................. | 10 | Phil. Int. 3535 |
| 4/13/74 | 3 | 15 | 17● For The Love Of Money................................... | 9 | Phil. Int. 3544 |
| 8/24/74 | 65 | 4 | 18 Peace............................................................... | | Astroscope 112 |
| 12/21/74+ | 17 | 13 | 19 Sunshine Part II............................................... | 48 | Phil. Int. 3558 |
| 4/26/75 | 1¹ | 16 | 20 Give The People What They Want .................... | 45 | Phil. Int. 3565 |
| 8/16/75 | 10 | 11 | 21 Let Me Make Love To You/ | 75 | |
| | | 11 | 22    Survival ........................................................ | | Phil. Int. 3573 |
| 11/01/75 | 1¹ | 18 | 23● I Love Music (Part 1)....................................... | 5 | Phil. Int. 3577 |
| 3/13/76 | 1² | 15 | 24 Livin' For The Weekend/ | 20 | |
| | | 13 | 25    Stairway To Heaven ..................................... | | Phil. Int. 3587 |
| 7/04/76 | 45 | 6 | 26 Family Reunion ................................................ | | Phil. Int. 3596 |
| 9/04/76 | 1¹ | 13 | 27 Message In Our Music ...................................... | 49 | Phil. Int. 3601 |
| 11/27/76+ | 1¹ | 16 | 28 Darlin' Darlin' Baby (Sweet, Tender, Love)..... | 72 | Phil. Int. 3610 |
| 7/23/77 | 7 | 17 | 29 Work On Me ...................................................... | | Phil. Int. 3631 |
| 4/08/78 | 1⁵ | 21 | 30● Use Ta Be My Girl............................................ | 4 | Phil. Int. 3642 |
| 8/05/78 | 21 | 13 | 31 Brandy.............................................................. | 79 | Phil. Int. 3652 |
| 8/04/79 | 7 | 14 | 32 Sing A Happy Song ........................................... | 102 | Phil. Int. 3707 |
| 11/17/79 | 49 | 8 | 33 I Want You Here With Me ................................. | | Phil. Int. 3726 |
| 12/01/79+ | 4 | 15 | 34 Forever Mine.................................................... | 28 | Phil. Int. 3727 |
| 7/26/80 | 3 | 17 | 35 Girl, Don't Let It Get You Down ...................... | 55 | TSOP 4790 |
| 11/15/80 | 44 | 11 | 36 Once Is Not Enough .......................................... | | TSOP 4791 |
| 3/27/82 | 15 | 15 | 37 I Just Want To Satisfy ..................................... | 101 | Phil. Int. 02834 |
| 7/03/82 | 13 | 17 | 38 Your Body's Here With Me (But Your Mind's On The Other Side Of Town) ......................... | | Phil. Int. 03009 |
| 6/11/83 | 35 | 11 | 39 I Can't Stand The Pain ..................................... | | Phil. Int. 03892 |
| 8/27/83 | 35 | 9 | 40 Put Our Heads Together ................................... | | Phil. Int. 04069 |
| 4/21/84 | 26 | 12 | 41 Extraordinary Girl............................................ | | Phil. Int. 04437 |
| 8/04/84 | 75 | 5 | 42 Let Me Show You (How Much I Really Love You). | | Phil. Int. 04535 |
| 8/24/85 | 18 | 13 | 43 Just Another Lonely Night ............................... | | Phil. Int. 50013 |
| 11/23/85+ | 38 | 12 | 44 What A Woman ................................................. | | Phil. Int. 50021 |
| 5/16/87 | 60 | 8 | 45 Don't Take Your Love Away............................. | | Phil. Int. 50067 |
| 8/22/87 | 1¹ | 20 | 46 Lovin' You ........................................................ | | Phil. Int. 50084 |
| 12/05/87+ | 5 | 15 | 47 Let Me Touch You............................................. | | Phil. Int. 50104 |
| | | | **THE O'KAYSIONS** | | |
| | | | North Carolina sextet: Donny Weaver (lead), Ron Turner, Jim Spidel, Wayne Pittman, Jimmy Hennant and Bruce Joyner. Originally known as The Kays. | | |
| 8/10/68 | 6 | 16 | 1● Girl Watcher................................................. | 5 | ABC 11094 |

| DEBUT DATE | PEAK POS | WKS CHR | ARTIST — Record Title | POP POS | Label & Number |
|---|---|---|---|---|---|
| | | | **DAVID OLIVER** | | |
| | | | Singer from Florida. Teamed with Gene Godfrey (piano). Moved to Los Angeles in 1967, worked with Five Days And Three Nights. Toured with Mighty Joe Hicks from 1973-75. | | |
| 3/25/78 | 13 | 19 | 1 Ms............................................................ | | Mercury 73973 |
| 2/10/79 | 27 | 13 | 2 I Wanna Write You A Love Song .................... | | Mercury 74043 |
| 9/22/79 | 56 | 8 | 3 Summer Love .............................................. | | Mercury 76006 |
| 11/24/79+ | 57 | 9 | 4 Never Seen A Girl Like You.......................... | | Mercury 76022 |
| 7/12/80 | 77 | 3 | 5 Love TKO .................................................. | | Mercury 76067 |
| | | | **OLLIE & JERRY** | | |
| | | | Duo of Ollie Brown and Jerry Knight (former member of Raydio). | | |
| 6/09/84 | 3 | 16 | 1 **Breakin'...There's No Stopping Us**............... | *9* | Polydor 821708 |
| | | | from the film "Breakin'" | | |
| 12/01/84+ | 45 | 12 | 2 Electric Boogaloo ...................................... | | Polydor 881461 |
| | | | from the film "Breakin' 2 Electric Boogaloo" | | |
| | | | **OLLIE & THE NIGHTINGALES** | | |
| | | | Formed as the Dixie Nightingales in 1950. Consisted of Ollie Nightingale (Ollie Hoskins), Quincy Clifton Billops Jr., Bill Davis, Nelson Lesure and Rochester Neal. Billops was a member of The Mad Lads. Hoskins went solo in 1970, replaced by Sir Mack Rice. Neal, Billops and Davis were in The Ovations in 1972. Also see Ollie Nightingale. | | |
| 4/13/68 | 16 | 7 | 1 I Got A Sure Thing ..................................... | *73* | Stax 245 |
| 12/14/68+ | 47 | 5 | 2 You're Leaving Me...................................... | | Stax 0014 |
| 8/30/69 | 45 | 2 | 3 I've Got A Feeling ...................................... | | Stax 0045 |
| | | | **OLYMPIC RUNNERS** | | |
| | | | Group from England, consisting of Joe Jammer (guitar), Pete Wingfield (keyboards), DeLisle Harper (bass), Glen LeFleur (drums) and George Chandler (vocals). Additional vocals and percussion by producer Mike Vernon. | | |
| 6/15/74 | 72 | 7 | 1 Do It Over/ | *107* | |
| 8/31/74 | 72 | 7 | 2 Put The Music Where Your Mouth Is.............. | *103* | London 202 |
| 1/18/75 | 73 | 6 | 3 Grab It .................................................... | *103* | London 216 |
| 8/23/75 | 92 | 3 | 4 Drag It Over Here ..................................... | *109* | London 219 |
| 6/05/76 | 97 | 2 | 5 Party Time Is Here To Stay ........................... | | London 233 |
| | | | **THE OLYMPICS** | | |
| | | | Group formed at Centennial High School in Compton, California in 1954 as the Challengers. Consisted of Walter Ward (lead), Eddie Lewis (tenor), Charles Fizer (baritone) and Walter Hammond (baritone). Recorded as the Challengers for Melatone in 1956. Melvin King replaced Fizer in 1958, remained in group as replacement for Hammond when Fizer returned in 1959. Fizer was killed during the Watts rioting; replaced by Julius McMichael ("Mack Starr"), former lead of the Paragons. King left in 1966. Kenny Sinclair, formerly of The Six Teens, joined in 1970. | | |
| 8/11/58 | 7 | 7 | 1 **Western Movies** ................................. [N] | *8* | Demon 1508 |
| | | | Best Seller #7 / Jockey #14 | | |
| 6/06/60 | 10 | 17 | 2 **Big Boy Pete** ........................................ | *50* | Arvee 595 |
| | | | lyrically altered by The Kingsmen as "The Jolly Green Giant" | | |
| 6/29/63 | 22 | 1 | 3 The Bounce............................................... | *40* | Tri Disc 106 |
| 5/21/66 | 25 | 6 | 4 Mine Exclusively ....................................... | *99* | Mirwood 5513 |
| 9/24/66 | 20 | 10 | 5 Baby, Do The Philly Dog.............................. | *63* | Mirwood 5523 |
| | | | **ALEXANDER O'NEAL** | | |
| | | | Born in 1955 in Minneapolis. Had own band, Alexander, in the late 70s. Lead singer of Flyte Tyme. Went solo in 1980. Teamed with James "Jimmy Jam" Harris III, produced "Control", hit for Janet Jackson. | | |
| 2/23/85 | 11 | 18 | 1 Innocent................................................... | *101* | Tabu 04718 |
| 6/29/85 | 17 | 17 | 2 If You Were Here Tonight .............................. | | Tabu 05418 |
| 11/02/85 | 62 | 7 | 3 A Broken Heart Can Mend ............................ | | Tabu 05646 |
| 1/25/86 | 2³ | 19 | 4 **Saturday Love**............................................ | *26* | Tabu 05767 |
| | | | **CHERRELLE with ALEXANDER O'NEAL** | | |
| 3/29/86 | 8 | 16 | 5 **What's Missing**........................................ | | Tabu 05850 |
| 5/30/87 | 1² | 20 | 6 **Fake**..................................................... | *25* | Tabu 07100 |
| 9/26/87 | 4 | 17 | 7 **Criticize**................................................ | *70* | Tabu 07600 |
| 1/23/88 | 2² | 14 | 8 **Never Knew Love Like This**...................... | *28* | Tabu 07646 |
| | | | **ALEXANDER O'NEAL featuring CHERRELLE** | | |
| 5/14/88 | 41 | 10 | 9 The Lovers ............................................... | | Tabu 07795 |
| | | | **ONE ON ONE** | | |
| 11/03/84 | 77 | 6 | 1 Gotta Thang.............................................. | | Kee Wee 8449 |

**313**

| DEBUT DATE | PEAK POS | WKS CHR | ARTIST — Record Title | POP POS | Label & Number |
|---|---|---|---|---|---|
| | | | **100 PROOF Aged In Soul**<br>Group from Detroit: Clyde Wilson ("Steve Mancha"), lead; Joe Stubbs and Eddie Anderson ("Eddie Holiday"). Stubbs, brother of Levi Stubbs of the Four Tops, had been in The Contours and The Falcons. | | |
| 11/15/69 | **24** | 8 | 1  Too Many Cooks (Spoil The Soup).................... | 94 | Hot Wax 6904 |
| 8/29/70 | **6** | 14 | 2● Somebody's Been Sleeping ........................... | 8 | Hot Wax 7004 |
| 3/13/71 | **37** | 4 | 3  One Man's Leftovers (Is Another Man's Feast) .... | 96 | Hot Wax 7009 |
| 6/26/71 | **33** | 4 | 4  Driveway ..................................................... | 121 | Hot Wax 7104 |
| 11/06/71 | **34** | 4 | 5  90 Day Freeze ............................................. | | Hot Wax 7108 |
| 3/18/72 | **15** | 13 | 6  Everything Good Is Bad................................. | 45 | Hot Wax 7202 |
| | | | **ONE WAY**  ★★126★★<br>Group led by Al Hudson, formerly known as the Soul Partners. Consisted of Alicia Myers (vocals - replaced by Candyce Edwards in 1980), Dave Robertson and Cortez Harris (guitars), Kevin McCord (bass), Gregory Green and Jonathan Meadows (drums). Myers began solo career in 1982. Also see Al Hudson. | | |
| | | | **ONE WAY featuring AL HUDSON:** | | |
| 1/26/80 | **36** | 10 | 1  Music.......................................................... | | MCA 41170 |
| 5/24/80 | **36** | 10 | 2  Do Your Thang ............................................. | | MCA 41238 |
| 8/16/80 | **20** | 13 | 3  Pop It......................................................... | | MCA 41298 |
| 11/29/80 | **76** | 5 | 4  Something In The Past ................................... | | MCA 51021 |
| | | | **ONE WAY:** | | |
| 2/21/81 | **52** | 8 | 5  My Lady ...................................................... | | MCA 51054 |
| 5/09/81 | **12** | 16 | 6  Push .......................................................... | | MCA 51110 |
| 9/05/81 | **12** | 21 | 7  Pull Fancy Dancer/Pull-Part 1 ....................... | | MCA 51165 |
| 2/20/82 | **34** | 12 | 8  Who's Foolin' Who ......................................... | | MCA 52004 |
| 5/08/82 | **4** | 18 | 9  **Cutie Pie**.................................................... | 61 | MCA 52049 |
| 10/02/82 | **83** | 4 | 10 Runnin' Away............................................... | | MCA 52112 |
| 11/06/82 | **36** | 12 | 11 Wild Night .................................................. | | MCA 52133 |
| 2/19/83 | **43** | 10 | 12 Can I.......................................................... | | MCA 52164 |
| 6/18/83 | **24** | 15 | 13 Shine On Me................................................ | | MCA 52228 |
| 10/01/83 | **44** | 11 | 14 Let's Get Together ........................................ | | MCA 52278 |
| 3/24/84 | **5** | 21 | 15 **Lady You Are** ............................................. | | MCA 52348 |
| 6/23/84 | **8** | 13 | 16 **Mr. Groove** ................................................ | | MCA 52409 |
| 10/27/84 | **51** | 10 | 17 Don't Stop .................................................. | | MCA 52480 |
| 8/03/85 | **66** | 7 | 18 Serving It.................................................... | | MCA 52631 |
| 10/19/85 | **52** | 8 | 19 More Than Friends, Less Than Lovers ............. | | MCA 52699 |
| 9/27/86 | **5** | 17 | 20 **Don't Think About It** .................................. | | MCA 52893 |
| 1/24/87 | **6** | 17 | 21 **You Better Quit**.......................................... | | MCA 53020 |
| 5/23/87 | **25** | 11 | 22 Whammy ..................................................... | | MCA 53005 |
| | | | **OPUS SEVEN**<br>7-piece band from Atlanta. | | |
| 10/27/79 | **76** | 12 | 1  Bussle......................................................... | | Source 41121 |
| | | | **OPUS 10** | | |
| 3/23/85 | **48** | 10 | 1  Love's Calling............................................... | | Pandisc 012 |
| | | | **ROY ORBISON**<br>Born on 4/23/36 in Vernon, Texas. Had own band, the Wink Westerners in 1952. Attended North Texas University with Pat Boone. First recorded for Jewel in early 1956. Toured with Sun Records shows to 1958. Toured with The Beatles in 1963. | | |
| 8/08/60 | **14** | 7 | 1  Only The Lonely (Know How I Feel) ................. | 2 | Monument 421 |
| 10/10/60 | **23** | 4 | 2  Blue Angel................................................... | 9 | Monument 425 |
| 3/23/63 | **19** | 3 | 3  In Dreams..................................................... | 7 | Monument 806 |
| | | | his 1986 version was featured in the film "Blue Velvet" | | |
| 10/19/63 | **8** | 6 | 4  **Mean Woman Blues/** | 5 | |
| 11/09/63 | **26** | 3 | 5  Blue Bayou ................................................. | 29 | Monument 824 |
| | | | 1, 2 & 5: written by Roy Orbison & Joe Melson | | |
| | | | **ORBIT featuring Carol Hall** | | |
| 12/04/82+ | **24** | 17 | 1  The Beat Goes On ....................................... | | Quality 7025 |
| | | | new version of Sonny & Cher's 1967 pop hit (POS 6) | | |
| 10/15/83 | **75** | 5 | 2  All Shook Up................................................ | | Quality 047 |
| 4/28/84 | **66** | 6 | 3  Too Busy Thinking About My Baby ................. | | Quality 058 |

| DEBUT DATE | PEAK POS | WKS CHR | ARTIST — Record Title | POP POS | Label & Number |
|---|---|---|---|---|---|
| | | | **THE ORIGINAL CASUALS** Dallas vocal trio: Gary Mears (lead), Jay Joe Adams and Paul Kearney. | | |
| 3/03/58 | 6 | 4 | 1 **So Tough** ............................ *Jockey #6* | *42* | Back Beat 503 |
| | | | **ORIGINAL CONCEPT** | | |
| 4/26/86 | 78 | 4 | 1 Can You Feel It? ............................ | | Def Jam 2308 |
| | | | **THE ORIGINALS** Group formed in Detroit in 1966. Consisted of Freddie Gorman, bass; Crathman Spencer, Henry Dixon, tenors; and Walter Gaines, baritone. Gorman was with the Quailtones (recorded for Josie in 1955), and solo (recorded for Miracle in 1961). Spencer and Gaines were in the Voice Masters and with Dixon in the Five Stars. Gorman wrote "Please Mr. Postman" and "Just Like Romeo And Juliet"; back-up work for Motown recordings. Spencer left in 1971, replaced by former Voice Masters' lead singer, Ty Hunter. Group based in Los Angeles since 1974. | | |
| 9/27/69 | 1⁵ | 17 | 1 **Baby I'm For Real** ........................... | *14* | Soul 35066 |
| 2/14/70 | 4 | 13 | 2 **The Bells** ................................ | *12* | Soul 35069 |
| 8/15/70 | 20 | 9 | 3 We Can Make It Baby/ *above 3: written & produced by Marvin Gaye* | *74* | |
| | | 8 | 4 I Like Your Style............................ | | Soul 35074 |
| 1/02/71 | 14 | 12 | 5 God Bless Whoever Sent You.................... | *53* | Soul 35079 |
| 6/28/75 | 53 | 8 | 6 Good Lovin' Is Just A Dime Away .................. | | Motown 1355 |
| 10/09/76 | 93 | 8 | 7 Down To Love Town ......................... | *47* | Soul 35119 |
| 2/14/81 | 74 | 7 | 8 Waitin' On A Letter/Mr. Postman .................... | | Phase II 5653 |
| | | | **THE ORIOLES** ★★**196**★★ Group from Baltimore, formed in 1947. Consisted of Earlington Carl Tilghman ("Sonny Til" d: 12/9/81 [heart attack - 51]), lead; Alexander Sharp (tenor), George Nelson, baritone; Johnny Reed, bass; and Tommy Gaither, guitar. Originally called the Vibra-Naires. Appeared twice on Arthur Godfrey's Talent Scouts. Gregory Carroll, formerly with the Four Buddies, joined in 1954. Name changed to the Maryland state bird. Considered to be the first R&B vocal group. | | |
| 9/11/48 | 1¹ | 17 | 1 **It's Too Soon To Know** ............................... *Juke Box #1 / Best Seller #2* | *13* | Natural 5000 |
| 12/25/48 | 8 | 2 | 2 **(It's Gonna Be A) Lonely Christmas** ........... [X] *Juke Box #8* | | Jubilee 5001 |
| 4/23/49 | 1¹ | 26 | 3 **Tell Me So**................................ *Best Seller #1 / Juke Box #2* | | Jubilee 5005 |
| 8/27/49 | 12 | 2 | 4 A Kiss And A Rose.................... *Best Seller #12 / Juke Box #13* | | Jubilee 5009 |
| 11/05/49 | 11 | 1 | 5 I Challenge Your Kiss ........................ *Juke Box #11* | | Jubilee 5008 |
| 11/12/49 | 5 | 9 | 6 **Forgive And Forget**........................ *Best Seller #5 / Juke Box #12* | | Jubilee 5016 |
| 12/24/49 | 9 | 2 | 7 **What Are You Doing New Year's Eve/** *Best Seller #9* | | |
| 12/31/49 | 5 | 1 | 8 **(It's Gonna Be A) Lonely Christmas** ...... [X-R] *Best Seller #5* | | Jubilee 5017 |
| 2/09/52 | 8 | 2 | 9 **Baby, Please Don't Go** .................... *Best Seller #8* | | Jubilee 5065 |
| 8/01/53 | 1⁵ | 18 | 10 **Crying In The Chapel**................... *Juke Box #1(5) / Best Seller #1(4)* *a reported million-seller* | *11* | Jubilee 5122 |
| 10/17/53 | 7 | 4 | 11 **In The Mission Of St. Augustine**.................. *Juke Box #7* | | Jubilee 5217 |
| | | | **THE ORLONS** Group from Philadelphia. Consisted of lead Rosetta Hightower, Marlena Davis, Steve Caldwell and Shirley Brickley (d: 10/13/77 [32], gun shot wound). Davis and Caldwell left in 1964 and were replaced by Audrey Brickley. Disbanded in 1968, when Hightower moved to England. | | |
| 6/23/62 | 5 | 13 | 1 **The Wah Watusi** ............................. | *2* | Cameo 218 |
| 11/10/62 | 3 | 9 | 2 **Don't Hang Up**............................ | *4* | Cameo 231 |
| 3/02/63 | 4 | 12 | 3 **South Street** .............................. | *3* | Cameo 243 |
| 6/29/63 | 8 | 9 | 4 **Not Me**.................................... | *12* | Cameo 257 |
| 11/16/63 | 25 | 2 | 5 Cross Fire! ............................. | *19* | Cameo 273 |
| 12/14/63+ | 55 | 6 | 6 Bon-Doo-Wah ........................... | *Hot* | Cameo 287 |
| 2/01/64 | 66 | 5 | 7 Shimmy Shimmy ......................... | *Hot* | Cameo 295 |
| 5/16/64 | 66 | 6 | 8 Rules Of Love ............................. *1-3, 5-6 & 8: written by Kal Mann & Dave Appell* | *Hot* | Cameo 319 |
| 8/29/64 | 64 | 6 | 9 Knock! Knock! (Who's There?)............... | *Hot* | Cameo 332 |

| DEBUT DATE | PEAK POS | WKS CHR | ARTIST — Record Title | POP POS | Label & Number |
|---|---|---|---|---|---|
| | | | **OSBORNE & GILES** Duo of Billy Osborne and Attala Zane Giles. | | |
| 8/10/85 | 67 | 9 | 1 Strangers In The Night | | Red Label 71000 |
| 11/16/85 | 84 | 4 | 2 I'll Make You An Offer | | Red Label 71010 |
| | | | **JEFFREY OSBORNE**  ★★**148**★★ Born on 3/9/48 in Providence, Rhode Island. Singer/songwriter/drummer. Lead singer of L.T.D. until 1980. | | |
| 5/08/82 | 3 | 23 | 1 **I Really Don't Need No Light** | 39 | A&M 2410 |
| 9/11/82 | 13 | 15 | 2 On The Wings Of Love | 29 | A&M 2434 |
| 7/16/83 | 3 | 19 | 3 **Don't You Get So Mad** | 25 | A&M 2561 |
| 10/08/83 | 4 | 20 | 4 **Stay With Me Tonight** | 30 | A&M 2591 |
| 1/21/84 | 10 | 13 | 5 Plane Love | | A&M 12089 |
| 3/10/84 | 16 | 14 | 6 We're Going All The Way | 48 | A&M 2618 |
| 7/28/84 | 2¹ | 18 | 7 **The Last Time I Made Love** JOYCE KENNEDY & JEFFREY OSBORNE | 40 | A&M 2656 |
| 10/06/84 | 6 | 17 | 8 **Don't Stop** | 44 | A&M 2687 |
| 12/22/84+ | 7 | 16 | 9 **The Borderlines** | 38 | A&M 2695 |
| 4/20/85 | 44 | 9 | 10 Let Me Know | | A&M 2724 |
| 5/24/86 | 2² | 19 | 11 **You Should Be Mine (The Woo Woo Song)** | 13 | A&M 2814 |
| 7/26/86 | 18 | 13 | 12 Soweto | | A&M 2863 |
| 9/27/86 | 29 | 9 | 13 Room With A View | | A&M 2866 |
| 12/13/86+ | 82 | 6 | 14 In Your Eyes | | A&M 2894 |
| 7/11/87 | 5 | 14 | 15 **Love Power** DIONNE WARWICK & JEFFREY OSBORNE | 12 | Arista 9567 |
| | | | **OSIBISA** Band from Great Britain, founded by Ghanaians Teddy Osei (reeds, percussion), Sol Amarifo (drums), Mac Tontoh (bass, percussion) and West Indian Wendell Richardson (guitar). Frequent personnel changes in the mid-70s. | | |
| 3/27/76 | 61 | 9 | 1 Sunshine Day | 108 | Island 053 |
| | | | **OSIRIS** 9-piece band from Washington, DC, formed in 1977 by Osiris Marsh. | | |
| 3/03/79 | 77 | 6 | 1 Consistency | | Warner 8758 |
| | | | **LEE OSKAR** Born on 3/24/48 in Copenhagen, Denmark. Harmonica player. Studio musician in Los Angeles. Original member of War. | | |
| 6/05/76 | 23 | 10 | 1 BLT  [I] | 59 | United Art. 807 |
| 12/04/76 | 85 | 4 | 2 Sunshine Keri | | United Art. 861 |
| 12/02/78 | 91 | 2 | 3 Before The Rain | | Elektra 45538 |
| 2/24/79 | 89 | 2 | 4 Feelin' Happy | | Elektra 46002 |
| | | | **THE OSMONDS** Pop family group: Alan, Wayne, Merrill, Jay and Donny Osmond from Ogden, Utah. Singing professionally since 1959. Alan, Wayne, Merrill and Jay are currently a hot Country act. | | |
| 2/06/71 | 6 | 10 | 1 ● One Bad Apple | 1 | MGM 14193 |
| | | | **OTIS & CARLA - see OTIS REDDING and/or CARLA THOMAS** | | |
| | | | **JOHNNY OTIS ORCHESTRA**   ★★**114**★★ Born John Veliotes on 12/28/21 in Vallejo, California. Vocalist/drummer/vibes/ composer/leader. Worked in Oakland with Otis "Count" Matthews, 1940, Willard Marsh's Collegians, in 1941. Also with Lloyd Hunter and Harlan Leonard in the early 40s. Formed own big band in 1945. Own first recording for Excelsior in 1945. Co-owner of Barrelhouse nightclub in 1948. Discovered Charles Brown, Little Esther, Mel Walker (real name: Melvin Lightsey), Devonia "Lady Dee" Williams, The Robins, and many others. National tours with the Rhythm & Blues Caravan in the early 50s. Recorded in the 50s as Johnny Otis Quintette; Orchestra; Congregation; and Show. Own Dig label in 1955. Johnny's son, Shuggie, had a hit in 1975. Still active in Los Angeles as musician/minister/producer/politician. Also see Esther Phillips, The Robins, Joe Swift and Willie Mae Thornton. | | |
| 2/04/50 | 1⁹ | 22 | 1 **Double Crossing Blues** Best Seller #1(9) / Juke Box #1(5) vocals by The Robins & Little Esther | | Savoy 731 |
| 4/08/50 | 1⁴ | 16 | 2 **Mistrustin' Blues/** Best Seller #1(4) / Juke Box #1(4) vocals by Little Esther & Mel Walker | | |
| 4/15/50 | 9 | 1 | 3 **Misery** Juke Box #9 vocal by Little Esther | | Savoy 735 |

| DEBUT DATE | PEAK POS | WKS CHR | ARTIST — Record Title | POP POS | Label & Number |
|---|---|---|---|---|---|
| | | | **JOHNNY OTIS ORCHESTRA — Continued** | | |
| 4/29/50 | **6** | 6 | 4 **Cry Baby** .............................................. <br> Juke Box #6 <br> vocals by Mel Walker & The Quintones | | Regent 1016 |
| 6/10/50 | **1**¹ | 17 | 5 **Cupid's Boogie** .................................... <br> Juke Box #1 / Best Seller #2 <br> vocal by Little Esther | | Savoy 750 |
| 9/09/50 | **4** | 6 | 6 **Deceivin' Blues**.................................... <br> Best Seller #4 <br> vocals by Little Esther & Mel Walker | | Savoy 759 |
| 9/09/50 | **8** | 1 | 7 **Dreamin' Blues**.................................... <br> Best Seller #8 <br> vocal by Mel Walker; also released on Savoy 748 | | Regent 1018 |
| 11/11/50 | **6** | 4 | 8 **Wedding Boogie/** <br> Best Seller #6 <br> vocals by Little Esther, Mel Walker & Lee Graves | | |
| 12/09/50 | **6** | 4 | 9 **Faraway Blues** ................................... <br> Best Seller #6 <br> also known as "Christmas Blues"; <br> vocals by Little Esther & Mel Walker | | Savoy 764 |
| 12/30/50+ | **2**⁶ | 22 | 10 **Rockin' Blues** ..................................... <br> Juke Box #2 / Best Seller #2 <br> vocal by Mel Walker | | Savoy 766 |
| 3/17/51 | **4** | 5 | 11 **Mambo Boogie/**             [I] <br> Juke Box #4 / Best Seller #9 | | |
| 4/07/51 | **2**¹ | 5 | 12 **Gee Baby** ........................................... <br> Best Seller #2 / Juke Box #7 <br> vocal by Mel Walker | | Savoy 777 |
| 8/25/51 | **6** | 4 | 13 **All Nite Long**...................................... <br> Best Seller #6 / Juke Box #6 <br> vocals by Johnny Otis & George Washington | | Savoy 788 |
| 1/19/52 | **10** | 1 | 14 **Sunset To Dawn** ................................. <br> Best Seller #10 <br> vocal by Mel Walker | | Savoy 821 |
| 8/16/52 | **4** | 4 | 15 **Call Operator 210** ............................. <br> Juke Box #4 <br> vocal by Mel Walker | | Mercury 8289 |
| 6/30/58 | **3** | 13 | 16 **Willie And The Hand Jive**.................. <br> Jockey #3 / Best Seller #5 | 9 | Capitol 3966 |
| 3/22/69 | **29** | 6 | 17 Country Girl............................................ <br> shown only as: **JOHNNY OTIS** | | Kent 506 |
| | | | **SHUGGIE OTIS** <br> Born on 11/30/53 in Los Angeles. Multi-instrumentalist. Son of Johnny Otis. <br> Professional debut in 1965. | | |
| 2/01/75 | **56** | 10 | 1 Inspiration Information ....................... | | Epic 50054 |
| | | | **OUTPUT** | | |
| 3/10/84 | **88** | 3 | 1 Move For Me........................................ | | Tuff City 04229 |
| | | | **THE OVATIONS** <br> Group led by Louis Williams. Re-formed in 1972 with former members of Ollie & The <br> Nightingales: Rochester Neal, Bill Davis and Quincy Billops, Jr. | | |
| 5/22/65 | **22** | 5 | 1 It's Wonderful To Be In Love........................ | 61 | Goldwax 113 |
| 2/25/67 | **40** | 2 | 2 Me And My Imagination............................... | | Goldwax 314 |
| 7/01/72 | **19** | 10 | 3 Touching Me ....................................... <br> shown only as: **OVATION** | 104 | Snds. of M. 708 |
| 9/08/73 | **7** | 17 | 4 **Having A Party** ........................ [N] <br> remake of Sam Cooke's hit infused with a line or two of other <br> top soul hits | 56 | MGM 14623 |
| | | | **DANNY OVERBEA** | | |
| 3/07/53 | **7** | 2 | 1 **Train, Train, Train**............................. <br> Juke Box #7 <br> with the Sax Mallard Orchestra | | Checker 768 |
| | | | **C.B. OVERTON** | | |
| 2/18/78 | **72** | 8 | 1 If I Can't Stop You............................... | | Shock 9 |
| | | | **GWEN OWENS** | | |
| 8/09/69 | **40** | 3 | 1 Keep On Living .................................... | | Josie 1009 |
| | | | **TONY OWENS** | | |
| 1/30/71 | **39** | 4 | 1 Confessin' A Feeling .......................... | | Cotillion 44103 |

| DEBUT DATE | PEAK POS | WKS CHR | ARTIST — Record Title | POP POS | Label & Number |
|---|---|---|---|---|---|
| | | | **OZONE** | | |
| | | | Formed in Nashville in 1977. Consisted of Thomas Bumpass, William White, Ray Woodard, Greg Hargrove, Benny Wallace, Jimmy Stewart, Charles Glenn and Paul Hines. Stewart, Wallace and Glenn had been in the Endeavors. Produced by Teena Marie. | | |
| 7/26/80 | 94 | 2 | 1  Walk On ...................................................... [I] | | Motown 1487 |
| 12/19/81+ | 73 | 7 | 2  Gigolette ......................................................... | | Motown 1521 |
| 7/31/82 | 59 | 9 | 3  Li'l Suzy ......................................................... | 109 | Motown 1627 |
| 4/16/83 | 55 | 13 | 4  Strutt My Thang .......................................... | | Motown 1668 |

# P

| | | | **PABLO CRUISE** | | |
|---|---|---|---|---|---|
| | | | San Francisco pop/rock band, formed in 1973, led by vocalist Dave Jenkins. | | |
| 5/07/77 | 46 | 16 | 1  Whatcha Gonna Do? ..................................... | 6 | A&M 1920 |
| 8/22/81 | 78 | 4 | 2  Cool Love ....................................................... | 13 | A&M 2349 |
| | | | **PACIFIC GAS & ELECTRIC** | | |
| | | | West Coast blues-rock quintet; Charles Allen, lead singer. | | |
| 7/04/70 | 49 | 3 | 1  Are You Ready? ............................................. | 14 | Columbia 45158 |
| | | | vocal backing by The Blackberries | | |
| 3/04/72 | 50 | 2 | 2  Thank God For You Baby ............................. | 97 | Columbia 45519 |
| | | | shown as: **PG&E** | | |
| | | | **THE PACKERS** | | |
| | | | Band formed by Charles "Packy" Axton (tenor sax). Axton, son of Estelle Axton, co-owner of Stax/Volt, had been in the Mar-Keys. | | |
| 11/13/65 | 5 | 15 | 1  **Hole In The Wall** ....................................... [I] | 43 | Pure Soul 1107 |
| | | | **BRUNI PAGAN** | | |
| | | | Female vocalist born in Puerto Rico, raised in New York City. Toured with Herbie Mann. | | |
| 8/18/79 | 53 | 10 | 1  Fantasy ............................................ | | Elektra 46501 |
| | | | **RALFI PAGAN** | | |
| 7/10/71 | 32 | 11 | 1  Make It With You ......................................... | 104 | Fania 567 |
| 8/18/73 | 39 | 7 | 2  Soul Je T'Aime ............................................. | 99 | Vibration 525 |
| | | | **SYLVIA** (Vanderpool) **& RALFI PAGAN** | | |
| | | | **GENE PAGE** | | |
| | | | Keyboardist/arranger/conductor from Los Angeles. Staff arranger with Reprise and Motown Records. | | |
| 1/21/78 | 30 | 10 | 1  Close Encounters Of The Third Kind............. [I] | | Arista 0302 |
| | | | new version of theme from the film of the same title | | |
| | | | **SHARON PAIGE - see HAROLD MELVIN & THE BLUE NOTES** | | |
| | | | **GLADYS PALMER** | | |
| | | | Singer/pianist. Nicknamed the "First Lady Of The Ivories" and "The High Priestess Of Jive". | | |
| 9/13/47 | 3 | 1 | 1  **Fool That I Am** ............................................. | | Miracle 104 |
| | | | with the Floyd Hunt Orchestra | | |
| | | | **PANIC BUTTON** | | |
| 5/10/69 | 48 | 2 | 1  O Wow ....................................................... | | Gamble 230 |
| | | | **PARADISE EXPRESS** | | |
| | | | Husband-and-wife team of Vi-Ann and Herb Jimmerson. Originally known as Organized Confusion. | | |
| 2/24/79 | 71 | 4 | 1  Dance ....................................................... | | Fantasy 845 |
| | | | **THE PARADONS** | | |
| | | | Vocal group from Bakersfield, California. West Tyler (lead), Chuck Weldon, Billy Myers and William Powers. | | |
| 10/03/60 | 27 | 3 | 1  Diamonds And Pearls .................................. | 18 | Milestone 2003 |

| DEBUT DATE | PEAK POS | WKS CHR | ARTIST — Record Title | POP POS | Label & Number |
|---|---|---|---|---|---|

### CHARLIE PARKER

Born on 8/29/20 in Kansas City, Missouri. Died on 3/12/55 in New York City (drug addiction). Alto saxophonist/composer; founder of progressive jazz. Nicknames: "Bird" and "Yardbird". With Jay McShann and Harlan Leonard in the late 30s. With Earl Hines, Cootie Williams and Andy Kirk in the early 40s. Toured with Billy Eckstine in 1944; with own small combos thereafter. With the Jazz Philharmonic in 1947, overseas tours from 1949-50. Innovative sessions with strings and woodwinds in 1950.

| DEBUT DATE | PEAK POS | WKS CHR | ARTIST — Record Title | POP POS | Label & Number |
|---|---|---|---|---|---|
| 12/18/48 | 15 | 1 | 1 Barbados .................................................. [I] <br> Juke Box #15 <br> with Miles Davis on trumpet | | Savoy 936 |

### LITTLE JUNIOR PARKER    ★★185★★

Born Herman Parker, Jr. on 3/3/27 in West Memphis, Arkansas. Died of a brain tumor on 11/18/71 in Blue Island, Illinois. Blues singer/harmonica player. With The Howlin' Wolf Band from 1949-50; Beale Streeters in 1951. Own band, Little Junior's Blue Flames, in 1951. First recorded for Modern in 1952. With Johnny Ace Revue from 1953-54.

| DEBUT DATE | PEAK POS | WKS CHR | ARTIST — Record Title | POP POS | Label & Number |
|---|---|---|---|---|---|
| 10/03/53 | 5 | 6 | 1 Feelin' Good ............................................... <br> LITTLE JUNIOR'S BLUE FLAMES <br> Best Seller #5 | | Sun 187 |
| 3/16/57 | 7 | 16 | 2 Next Time You See Me ................................ <br> Best Seller #7 / Jockey #10 / Juke Box #10 | 74 | Duke 164 |
| 12/08/58+ | 13 | 10 | 3 Sweet Home Chicago.................................. | | Duke 301 |
| 5/04/59 | 13 | 3 | 4 Five Long Years ......................................... | | Duke 306 |
| 1/23/61 | 11 | 5 | 5 Stand By Me .............................................. | | Duke 330 |
| 5/15/61 | 5 | 11 | 6 Driving Wheel ........................................... | 85 | Duke 335 |
| 11/06/61 | 7 | 9 | 7 In The Dark .............................................. | | Duke 341 |
| 2/10/62 | 28 | 2 | 8 How Long Can This Go On ......................... | | Duke 340 |
| 3/17/62 | 6 | 14 | 9 Annie Get Your Yo-Yo ............................... <br> JUNIOR PARKER: | 51 | Duke 345 |
| 2/08/64 | 99 | 2 | 10 Strange Things Happening ......................... | Hot | Duke 371 |
| 6/05/65 | 36 | 2 | 11 Crying For My Baby .................................. | | Duke 389 |
| 12/24/66+ | 27 | 10 | 12 Man Or Mouse .......................................... | | Duke 413 |
| 8/26/67 | 48 | 2 | 13 I Can't Put My Finger On It ....................... | | Mercury 72699 |
| 5/24/69 | 48 | 2 | 14 Ain't Gon' Be No Cutting Loose ................. | | Blue Rock 4080 |
| 12/27/69+ | 34 | 4 | 15 Worried Life Blues .................................... | | Minit 32080 |
| 1/23/71 | 48 | 2 | 16 Drowning On Dry Land............................. | 114 | Capitol 2997 |

### RAY PARKER JR.    ★★81★★

Born on 5/1/54 in Detroit. Prominent session guitarist in California, worked with Stevie Wonder, Barry White and others. Formed band Raydio in 1977 with Arnell Carmichael, Jerry Knight, Larry Tolbert, Darren Carmichael and Charles Fearing. In 1984, Knight recorded in the duo, Ollie & Jerry.

| DEBUT DATE | PEAK POS | WKS CHR | ARTIST — Record Title | POP POS | Label & Number |
|---|---|---|---|---|---|
| | | | RAYDIO: | | |
| 11/19/77+ | 5 | 25 | 1● Jack And Jill ............................................ | 8 | Arista 0283 |
| 5/20/78 | 20 | 12 | 2 Is This A Love Thing ................................. | | Arista 0328 |
| 8/12/78 | 43 | 9 | 3 Honey I'm Rich ......................................... | 102 | Arista 0353 |
| 3/10/79 | 3 | 19 | 4 You Can't Change That ............................. | 9 | Arista 0399 |
| 9/01/79 | 25 | 13 | 5 More Than One Way To Love A Woman............ <br> RAY PARKER JR. & RAYDIO: | 103 | Arista 0441 |
| 3/15/80 | 6 | 18 | 6 Two Places At The Same Time ..................... | 30 | Arista 0494 |
| 6/28/80 | 14 | 12 | 7 For Those Who Like To Groove.................... | | Arista 0522 |
| 9/20/80 | 57 | 6 | 8 Can't Keep You From Cryin'....................... | | Arista 0554 |
| 3/07/81 | 1² | 21 | 9 A Woman Needs Love (Just Like You Do) ........ | 4 | Arista 0592 |
| 7/18/81 | 26 | 11 | 10 That Old Song ......................................... | 21 | Arista 0616 |
| 10/24/81 | 73 | 5 | 11 It's Your Night ........................................ <br> RAY PARKER JR.: | | Arista 0641 |
| 3/20/82 | 2⁴ | 19 | 12 The Other Woman .................................... | 4 | Arista 0669 |
| 6/19/82 | 3 | 19 | 13 Let Me Go ............................................... | 38 | Arista 0695 |
| 10/09/82 | 44 | 7 | 14 It's Our Own Affair .................................. | 106 | Arista 1014 |
| 12/04/82+ | 6 | 21 | 15 Bad Boy .................................................. | 35 | Arista 1030 |
| 3/26/83 | 60 | 7 | 16 The People Next Door .............................. | | Arista 1051 |
| 11/12/83+ | 12 | 18 | 17 I Still Can't Get Over Loving You ............... | 12 | Arista 9116 |
| 3/03/84 | 71 | 4 | 18 Woman Out Of Control ............................ | | Arista 9048 |
| 5/05/84 | 64 | 5 | 19 In The Heat Of The Night......................... | | Arista 9198 |
| 6/30/84 | 1² | 19 | 20● Ghostbusters ........................................... <br> from 1984's #1 box office hit of the same title | 1 | Arista 9212 |

| DEBUT DATE | PEAK POS | WKS CHR | ARTIST — Record Title | POP POS | Label & Number |
|---|---|---|---|---|---|
| | | | **RAY PARKER JR. — Continued** | | |
| 11/24/84+ | **12** | 14 | 21 Jamie | *14* | Arista 9293 |
| 10/12/85 | **21** | 11 | 22 Girls Are More Fun | *34* | Arista 9352 |
| 8/29/87 | **5** | 13 | 23 **I Don't Think That Man Should Sleep Alone** | *68* | Geffen 28417 |
| 12/05/87+ | **10** | 16 | 24 **Over You** | | Geffen 28152 |
| | | | RAY PARKER JR. with NATALIE COLE | | |
| | | | **ROBERT PARKER** | | |
| | | | Born on 10/14/30 in New Orleans. Saxophonist/vocalist/bandleader. In Professor Longhair's (Roy Byrd) band from 1949. Led house band at Club Tijuana, New Orleans. Prolific session work. | | |
| 4/30/66 | **2**¹ | 17 | 1 **Barefootin'** | *7* | Nola 721 |
| 2/11/67 | **48** | 3 | 2 Tip Toe | *83* | Nola 729 |
| | | | **WINFIELD PARKER** | | |
| 9/04/71 | **48** | 3 | 1 S.O.S. | | Spring 116 |
| | | | **PARLET** | | |
| | | | Vocal trio portion of the Parliament/Funkadelic organization. Mahalia Franklin and Shirley Hayden were members. | | |
| 4/22/78 | **66** | 7 | 1 Pleasure Principle | | Casablanca 919 |
| 6/02/79 | **49** | 9 | 2 Ridin' High | | Casablanca 975 |
| 5/24/80 | **67** | 7 | 3 Wolf Tickets | | Casablanca 2260 |
| | | | PARLET featuring Jeanette Washington | | |
| 9/06/80 | **73** | 4 | 4 Help From My Friends | | Casablanca 2293 |
| | | | **PARLIAMENT**   ★★135★★ | | |
| | | | The funk group Funkadelic, which evolved from the Detroit-based group, The Parliaments, recorded under the name Parliament for Invictus in 1971. The original members of The Parliaments, led by producer/singer/songwriter George Clinton, founded the corporation, "A Parliafunkadelicament Thang". By the time Parliament signed to Casablanca in 1974, Clinton headed and reorganized the New York-based corporation to include a varying roster of nearly 40 musicians which recorded under the names of Parliament and Funkadelic. 3 members of The Parliaments split from Clinton. Parliament/Funkadelic spawned various offshoots: Bootsy's Rubber Band, The Brides Of Funkenstein, Parlet and the P.Funk All Stars. Also see Funkadelic. | | |
| 8/07/71 | **30** | 5 | 1 The Breakdown | *107* | Invictus 9095 |
| 7/06/74 | **10** | 16 | 2 **Up For The Down Stroke** | *63* | Casablanca 0104 |
| 12/07/74 | **77** | 5 | 3 Testify | | Casablanca 811 |
| | | | new version of The Parliaments' 1967 hit "(I Wanna) Testify" | | |
| 5/24/75 | **24** | 14 | 4 Chocolate City [S] | *94* | Casablanca 831 |
| 9/20/75 | **64** | 7 | 5 Ride On | | Casablanca 843 |
| 2/21/76 | **33** | 10 | 6 P. Funk (Wants To Get Funked Up) | | Casablanca 852 |
| 4/24/76 | **5** | 16 | 7●**Tear The Roof Off The Sucker (Give Up The Funk)** | *15* | Casablanca 856 |
| 9/04/76 | **26** | 10 | 8 Star Child | | Casablanca 864 |
| 11/06/76+ | **22** | 15 | 9 Do That Stuff | | Casablanca 871 |
| 2/12/77 | **43** | 8 | 10 Dr. Funkenstein | *102* | Casablanca 875 |
| 7/30/77 | **54** | 10 | 11 Fantasy Is Reality | | Casablanca 892 |
| 10/29/77 | **14** | 15 | 12 Bop Gun (Endangered Species) | *102* | Casablanca 900 |
| 1/28/78 | **1**³ | 20 | 13●**Flash Light** | *16* | Casablanca 909 |
| 6/03/78 | **27** | 10 | 14 Funkentelechy | | Casablanca 921 |
| 12/09/78+ | **1**⁴ | 18 | 15 **Aqua Boogie (A Psychoalphadiscobetabioaquadoloop)** | *89* | Casablanca 950 |
| 4/21/79 | **63** | 5 | 16 Rumpofsteelskin | | Casablanca 976 |
| 11/17/79 | **39** | 10 | 17 Party People | | Casablanca 2222 |
| 1/19/80 | **8** | 16 | 18 **Theme From The Black Hole** | | Casablanca 2235 |
| 4/12/80 | **50** | 7 | 19 The Big Bang Theory [I] | | Casablanca 2250 |
| 11/22/80+ | **7** | 14 | 20 **Agony Of DeFeet** | | Casablanca 2317 |

| DEBUT DATE | PEAK POS | WKS CHR | ARTIST — Record Title | POP POS | Label & Number |
|---|---|---|---|---|---|

### THE PARLIAMENTS

Detroit vocal group founded in 1955. Consisted of George Clinton (lead), Raymond Davis, Calvin Simon, Clarence "Fuzzy" Haskins and Grady Thomas. First recorded for ABC in 1956. In 1967, a legal battle over group's name ensued when they left Revilot before their contract expired. They recruited a backing band and signed with Westbound Records under the name Funkadelic. Continued to record as Funkadelic when they signed with Invictus as Parliament in 1971. Formed a corporation called "A Parliafunkadelicament Thang". By 1974, Clinton assembled various musicians into the corporation to record as Parliament and Funkadelic. In 1977, Haskins, Simon and Thomas split from the corporation; in 1981, they recorded as Funkadelic for LAX Records.

| 7/01/67 | 3 | 15 | 1 (I Wanna) Testify ................................ | 20 | Revilot 207 |
| | | | recorded by Parliament in 1974 as "Testify" | | |
| 11/04/67 | 21 | 8 | 2 All Your Goodies Are Gone (The Loser's Seat) .... | 80 | Revilot 211 |
| 5/24/69 | 44 | 2 | 3 A New Day Begins ............................... | | Atco 6675 |

### FRED PARRIS - see BLACK SATIN and THE FIVE SATINS

### MAN PARRISH

| 1/15/83 | 66 | 8 | 1 Hip Hop, Be Bop (Don't Stop) ...................... | | Importe/12 321 |
| 2/16/85 | 76 | 3 | 2 Boogie Down Bronx ............................. | | Sugar Scoop 132 |

### BILL PARSONS - see BOBBY BARE

### THE PARTNERS - see AL HUDSON

### THE PASTELS

Vocal group formed at Air Force base in Narsarssuak, Greenland, in 1954. Consisted of lead vocalist "Big Dee Irwin" (DiFosco Ervin), lead; Richard Travis, Tony Thomas and Jimmy Willingham. Group disbanded in 1959. Ervin recorded solo as "DiFosco" in 1976.

| 3/10/58 | 4 | 5 | 1 Been So Long ................................ | 24 | Argo 5287 |
| | | | Jockey #4 / Best Seller #15 | | |
| | | | originally released on Mascot 123 | | |

### JOHNNY PATE QUINTET

Born in Chicago Heights, Illinois in 1923. Leader/arranger/bass player. With Coleridge Davs and Stuff Smith in the late 40s. With Eddie South to 1952.

| 3/03/58 | 17 | 2 | 1 Swinging Shepherd Blues ................. [I] | 43 | Federal 12312 |
| | | | Best Seller #17 | | |
| | | | featuring Lennie Druss on flute | | |

### PATIENCE

| 9/20/80 | 78 | 3 | 1 Shame On You.............................. | | Columbia 11334 |

### KEITH PATRICK

| 10/25/86 | 61 | 8 | 1 Night To Remember ........................ | | Omni 99505 |

### BOBBY PATTERSON

Born on 3/13/44 in Dallas, Texas. Singer/guitarist/drummer. Had own band, the Royal Rockers, in the mid-50s. First recorded for Abnak in 1962. Co-owner of Soul Power label.

| 4/26/69 | 36 | 5 | 1 T.C.B. Or T.Y.A. .............................. | | Jetstar 114 |
| 4/24/76 | 60 | 11 | 2 If He Hadn't Slipped And Got Caught ............... | | Granite 536 |
| 9/10/77 | 68 | 11 | 3 Right Place, Wrong Time ................... | | All Platinum 2371 |

### KELLEE PATTERSON

Born in Gary, Indiana. Crowned Miss Indiana in 1972. The second black contestant in the history of the Miss America Pageant. Moved to Hollywood in 1973. Worked in commercials.

| 6/04/77 | 74 | 10 | 1 Turn On The Lights (Phase 1) ........................ | | Shady Brook 1037 |
| 9/10/77 | 10 | 24 | 2 If It Don't Fit, Don't Force It.................... | 75 | Shady Brook 1041 |

### PATTY & THE EMBLEMS

Pat Russell, lead singer.

| 6/20/64 | 37 | 11 | 1 Mixed-Up, Shook-Up, Girl............................ | Hot | Herald 590 |

### PAUL & PAULA

Real names: Ray Hildebrand (b: 12/21/40, Joshua, TX) and Jill Jackson (b: 5/20/42, McCaney, TX). Formed duo at Howard Payne College, Brownwood, TX.

| 2/02/63 | 1² | 10 | 1 Hey Paula .................................... | 1 | Phillips 40084 |
| | | | written by Hildebrand; first released on LeCam as by "Jill & Ray" | | |
| 4/20/63 | 14 | 5 | 2 Young Lovers .............................. | 6 | Phillips 40096 |

| DEBUT DATE | PEAK POS | WKS CHR | ARTIST — Record Title | POP POS | Label & Number |
|---|---|---|---|---|---|
| | | | **BILLY PAUL** | | |
| | | | Born Paul Williams on 12/1/34 in Philadelphia. Attended West Philadelphia Music School and Granoff Music School. Sang on Philadelphia radio broadcasts at age 12. First recorded for Jubilee in 1952. Kenny Gamble and Leon Huff produced many of his hits. Also see the Philadelphia International All Stars. | | |
| 10/28/72 | 1⁴ | 18 | 1 ● Me And Mrs. Jones .................................... | 1 | Phil. Int. 3521 |
| 4/07/73 | 29 | 6 | 2 Am I Black Enough For You.......................... | 79 | Phil. Int. 3526 |
| 1/26/74 | 9 | 17 | 3 **Thanks For Saving My Life**...................... | 37 | Phil. Int. 3538 |
| 10/26/74 | 37 | 8 | 4 Be Truthful To Me ................................ | | Phil. Int. 3551 |
| 4/05/75 | 52 | 7 | 5 Billy's Back Home ................................ | | Phil. Int. 3563 |
| 2/28/76 | 18 | 13 | 6 Let's Make A Baby ................................ | 83 | Phil. Int. 3584 |
| 6/19/76 | 82 | 4 | 7 People Power..................................... | | Phil. Int. 3593 |
| 2/26/77 | 50 | 8 | 8 How Good Is Your Game .......................... | | Phil. Int. 3613 |
| 5/07/77 | 91 | 4 | 9 Let 'Em In ...................................... | | Phil. Int. 3621 |
| 8/27/77 | 79 | 3 | 10 I Trust You ..................................... | | Phil. Int. 3630 |
| 12/10/77+ | 68 | 10 | 11 Only The Strong Survive ......................... | | Phil. Int. 3635 |
| 5/12/79 | 90 | 3 | 12 Bring The Family Back............................ | | Phil. Int. 3676 |
| 1/26/80 | 69 | 5 | 13 You're My Sweetness ............................ | | Phil. Int. 3736 |
| | | | **LES PAUL & MARY FORD** | | |
| | | | Guitarist Les was born Lester Polfus on 6/9/16 in Waukesha, Wisconsin. Vocalist Mary was born Colleen Summer on 7/7/28 in Pasadena; died on 9/30/77. Paul had own trio in 1936; with Fred Waring from 1938-41. Innovator in electric guitar and multi-track recordings. Les & Mary married on 12/29/49; divorced in 1963. | | |
| 5/12/51 | 2¹ | 6 | 1 **How High The Moon** ............................... Juke Box #2 / Best Seller #5 record selected for NARAS Hall Of Fame; a reported million-seller; from the Broadway musical "Two for the Show" | 1 | Capitol 1451 |
| | | | **CECIL PAYNE ORCHESTRA** | | |
| | | | Born on 12/14/22 in Brooklyn, New York. Baritone and alto saxes. With Roy Elridge in 1946, and Dizzy Gillespie from 1946-49. With Illinois Jacquet from 1952-54. European tours with Randy Weston and Lionel Hampton in the 60s. | | |
| 3/04/50 | 12 | 1 | 1 Block Buster Boogie ............................... [I] with Billy Taylor on piano Juke Box #12 | | Decca 48127 |
| | | | **FREDA PAYNE** | | |
| | | | Born on 9/19/45 in Detroit. Attended The Institute Of Musical Arts. To New York in 1963. Performed with Pearl Bailey, Duke Ellington and Quincy Jones. First recorded for Impulse in 1965. Hosted the syndicated TV talk show "For You, Black Woman" in the early 80s. Sister is singer Scherrie Payne. | | |
| 12/27/69+ | 43 | 3 | 1 The Unhooked Generation ........................... | | Invictus 9073 |
| 4/04/70 | 20 | 16 | 2 ● Band Of Gold............................... | 3 | Invictus 9075 |
| 9/26/70 | 9 | 9 | 3 **Deeper & Deeper** ................................ | 24 | Invictus 9080 |
| 2/27/71 | 11 | 7 | 4 Cherish What Is Dear To You (While It's Near To You) .......................................... | 44 | Invictus 9085 |
| 6/05/71 | 3 | 13 | 5 ● **Bring The Boys Home**............................ | 12 | Invictus 9092 |
| 10/16/71 | 21 | 6 | 6 You Brought The Joy................................ | 52 | Invictus 9100 |
| 8/25/73 | 75 | 3 | 7 Two Wrongs Don't Make A Right.................... | | Invictus 1255 |
| 12/07/74+ | 81 | 7 | 8 It's Yours To Have................................ | | ABC/Dunhill 15018 |
| 10/22/77 | 85 | 8 | 9 Love Magnet ..................................... | | Capitol 4494 |
| 10/30/82 | 63 | 6 | 10 In Motion....................................... | | Sutra 117 |
| | | | **SCHERRIE PAYNE** | | |
| | | | Sister of Freda Payne. Member of The Glass House; joined The Supremes in mid-70s. | | |
| 1/31/87 | 57 | 10 | 1 Incredible ......................................... SCHERRIE PAYNE & PHILLIP INGRAM (member of Deco) | | Superstar I. 12 |
| 5/16/87 | 67 | 8 | 2 Testify .......................................... | | Superstar I. 55 |
| | | | **LAWRENCE PAYTON** | | |
| | | | Singer from Detroit; member of the Four Tops. | | |
| 2/09/74 | 63 | 10 | 1 One Woman Man...................................... | | Dunhill 4376 |
| | | | **"P" CREW** | | |
| 8/06/83 | 74 | 6 | 1 Nasty Rock ....................................... | | Prelude 586 |

| DEBUT DATE | PEAK POS | WKS CHR | | ARTIST — Record Title | POP POS | Label & Number |
|---|---|---|---|---|---|---|
| | | | | **PEACHES & HERB** ★★120★★ | | |
| | | | | Duo from Washington, DC: Herb Fame (born Herbert Feemster, 1942) and Francine Barker (born Francine Hurd, 1947). Fame had been recording solo; Francine sang in vocal group, Sweet Things. Marlene Mack filled in for Francine, 1968-69. Re-formed with Fame and Linda Green in 1977. | | |
| 12/03/66+ | 11 | 18 | 1 | Let's Fall In Love .......................................... | 21 | Date 1523 |
| 4/08/67 | 4 | 13 | 2 | **Close Your Eyes**.......................................... | 8 | Date 1549 |
| 7/01/67 | 10 | 9 | 3 | **For Your Love**............................................ | 20 | Date 1563 |
| 10/28/67 | 16 | 8 | 4 | Love Is Strange ........................................... | 13 | Date 1574 |
| 12/30/67+ | 25 | 7 | 5 | Two Little Kids ........................................... | 31 | Date 1586 |
| 3/23/68 | 25 | 6 | 6 | Ten Commandments Of Love.......................... | 55 | Date 1592 |
| 6/01/68 | 11 | 9 | 7 | United...................................................... | 46 | Date 1603 |
| 11/16/68 | 34 | 3 | 8 | Let's Make A Promise .................................. | 75 | Date 1623 |
| 3/08/09 | 10 | 9 | 9 | **When He Touches Me (Nothing Else Matters)** .. | 49 | Date 1637 |
| 8/23/69 | 40 | 3 | 10 | Let Me Be The One ...................................... | 74 | Date 1649 |
| 5/30/70 | 50 | 2 | 11 | It's Just A Game, Love.................................. | 110 | Date 1669 |
| | | | | from the film "The Split" | | |
| 6/25/77 | 98 | 2 | 12 | We're Still Together..................................... | 107 | MCA 40701 |
| 10/28/78+ | 4 | 22 | 13● | **Shake Your Groove Thing**........................... | 5 | Polydor 14514 |
| 3/24/79 | 1⁴ | 17 | 14▲ | **Reunited**................................................. | 1 | Polydor 14547 |
| 7/14/79 | 25 | 12 | 15 | We've Got Love ........................................... | 44 | Polydor 14577 |
| 10/27/79 | 30 | 9 | 16 | Roller-Skatin' Mate (Part I) ......................... | 66 | Polydor 2031 |
| 1/05/80 | 37 | 11 | 17 | I Pledge My Love......................................... | 19 | Polydor 2053 |
| | | | | above 5: produced by Freddie Perren | | |
| 8/09/80 | 37 | 10 | 18 | Funtime (Part 1).......................................... | | Polydor 2115 |
| 11/29/80 | 51 | 10 | 19 | One Child Of Love ....................................... | | Polydor 2140 |
| 3/14/81 | 77 | 4 | 20 | Surrender .................................................. | | Polydor 2157 |
| 8/01/81 | 37 | 10 | 21 | Freeway .................................................... | | Polydor 2178 |
| 11/14/81 | 45 | 7 | 22 | Bluer Than Blue .......................................... | | Polydor 2187 |
| 5/21/83 | 35 | 10 | 23 | Remember .................................................. | | Columbia 03872 |
| | | | | **MR. DANNY PEARSON** | | |
| | | | | Born in Racine, Wisconsin. Moved to California in 1974, discovered by Barry White. | | |
| 12/02/78+ | 16 | 17 | 1 | What's Your Sign Girl?................................. | 106 | Un. Gold 1400 |
| | | | | **PEBBLES** | | |
| | | | | Her real name is Perri McKissack. Native of Oakland. Worked with Con Funk Shun in the early 80s while still a teenager. Her cousin is vocalist Cherrelle. | | |
| 11/07/87+ | 1² | 21 | 1 | **Girlfriend** ............................................... | 5 | MCA 53185 |
| | | | | written by Babyface and L.A. Reid (of The Deele) | | |
| 3/19/88 | 1¹ | 18 | 2 | **Mercedes Boy** ........................................... | 2 | MCA 53279 |
| | | | | **ANN PEEBLES** | | |
| | | | | Born on 4/27/47 in East St. Louis. Sang in family gospel group the Peebles Choir from age 8. Married to singer Don Bryant. | | |
| 4/19/69 | 22 | 7 | 1 | Walk Away ................................................. | | Hi 2157 |
| 9/27/69 | 45 | 3 | 2 | Give Me Some Credit.................................... | | Hi 2165 |
| 9/19/70 | 7 | 13 | 3 | Part Time Love............................................ | 45 | Hi 2178 |
| 3/06/71 | 18 | 7 | 4 | I Pity The Fool............................................ | 85 | Hi 2186 |
| 9/18/71 | 42 | 2 | 5 | Slipped, Tripped And Fell In Love .................. | 113 | Hi 2198 |
| 2/19/72 | 13 | 12 | 6 | Breaking Up Somebody's Home........................ | 101 | Hi 2205 |
| 8/05/72 | 32 | 8 | 7 | Somebody's On Your Case ............................. | 117 | Hi 2219 |
| 2/03/73 | 31 | 9 | 8 | I'm Gonna Tear Your Playhouse Down ............. | 111 | Hi 2232 |
| 8/11/73 | 6 | 18 | 9 | **I Can't Stand The Rain** .............................. | 38 | Hi 2248 |
| 5/04/74 | 37 | 11 | 10 | (You Keep Me) Hangin' On............................. | 102 | Hi 2265 |
| 7/20/74 | 57 | 8 | 11 | Do I Need You............................................. | | Hi 2271 |
| 4/19/75 | 69 | 10 | 12 | Beware...................................................... | | Hi 2284 |
| 10/18/75 | 62 | 14 | 13 | Come To Mama ........................................... | | Hi 2294 |
| 2/14/76 | 57 | 8 | 14 | Dr. Love Power ........................................... | | Hi 2302 |
| 12/18/76+ | 96 | 5 | 15 | Fill This World With Love ............................ | | Hi 2320 |
| 7/09/77 | 64 | 8 | 16 | If This Is Heaven ........................................ | | Hi 77502 |
| 3/11/78 | 54 | 15 | 17 | Old Man With Young Ideas ........................... | | Hi 78509 |
| 7/29/78 | 55 | 10 | 18 | Didn't Take Your Man.................................. | | Hi 78518 |
| 3/24/79 | 95 | 4 | 19 | If You Got The Time (I've Got The Love) ........... | | Hi 79528 |

| DEBUT DATE | PEAK POS | WKS CHR | ARTIST — Record Title | POP POS | Label & Number |
|---|---|---|---|---|---|
| | | | **PEECH BOYS - see NEW YORK CITI PEECH BOYS** | | |
| | | | **NIA PEEPLES** | | |
| | | | Singer/actress. Played Nicole Chapman for 3 seasons on the TV series "Fame". Hosted "Top Of The Pops" TV show. | | |
| 4/30/88 | 71 | 8 | 1 Trouble | 35 | Mercury 870154 |
| | | | **TEDDY PENDERGRASS** ★★**79**★★ | | |
| | | | Born on 3/26/50 in Philadelphia. Worked local clubs, became drummer for Harold Melvin's Blue Notes in 1969; vocalist with same group in 1970. Went solo in 1976. Auto accident on 3/18/82 left him partially paralyzed. Also see Philadelphia International All Stars. | | |
| 4/30/77 | 5 | 17 | 1 **I Don't Love You Anymore** | 41 | Phil. Int. 3622 |
| 9/03/77 | 16 | 16 | 2 The Whole Town's Laughing At Me | 102 | Phil. Int. 3633 |
| 5/27/78 | 1² | 19 | 3● **Close The Door** | 25 | Phil. Int. 3648 |
| 10/07/78 | 22 | 11 | 4 Only You | 106 | Phil. Int. 3657 |
| 6/09/79 | 2⁴ | 20 | 5 **Turn Off The Lights** | 48 | Phil. Int. 3696 |
| 9/01/79 | 14 | 10 | 6 Come Go With Me | | Phil. Int. 3717 |
| 12/22/79+ | 21 | 10 | 7 Shout And Scream | | Phil. Int. 3733 |
| 3/01/80 | 44 | 9 | 8 It's You I Love | | Phil. Int. 3742 |
| 7/05/80 | 3 | 16 | 9 **Can't We Try** | 52 | Phil. Int. 3107 |
| 10/18/80 | 2⁶ | 18 | 10 **Love T.K.O.** | 44 | Phil. Int. 3116 |
| 4/25/81 | 3 | 19 | 11 **Two Hearts** | 40 | 20th Century 2492 |
| | | | STEPHANIE MILLS featuring TEDDY PENDERGRASS | | |
| 8/29/81 | 10 | 16 | 12 **I Can't Live Without Your Love** | 103 | Phil. Int. 02462 |
| 11/21/81+ | 4 | 17 | 13 **You're My Latest, My Greatest Inspiration** | 43 | Phil. Int. 02619 |
| 5/15/82 | 31 | 10 | 14 This Gift Of Life/ | | |
| | | 10 | 15 Nine Times Out Of Ten | | Phil. Int. 02856 |
| 10/02/82 | 32 | 10 | 16 I Can't Win For Losing | | Phil. Int. 03284 |
| 1/21/84 | 61 | 6 | 17 I Want My Baby Back | | Phil. Int. 04302 |
| 6/02/84 | 5 | 16 | 18 **Hold Me** | 46 | Asylum 69720 |
| | | | female vocal by Whitney Houston | | |
| 9/01/84 | 15 | 15 | 19 You're My Choice Tonight (Choose Me) | | Asylum 69696 |
| 7/13/85 | 76 | 6 | 20 Somewhere I Belong | | Asylum 69628 |
| | | | from the film "D.A.R.Y.L." | | |
| 10/12/85 | 21 | 15 | 21 Never Felt Like Dancin' | | Asylum 69595 |
| 2/15/86 | 6 | 16 | 22 **Love 4/2** | | Asylum 69568 |
| 6/14/86 | 67 | 7 | 23 Let Me Be Closer | | Asylum 69538 |
| 4/23/88 | 1² | 18 | 24 **Joy** | 77 | Asylum 69401 |
| | | | **THE PENGUINS** | | |
| | | | Group from Los Angeles in 1954. Consisted of Cleveland Duncan (lead), Dexter Tisby (tenor), Bruce Tate (baritone) and Curtis Williams (bass). Group named for trademark on Kool cigarettes. | | |
| 12/18/54+ | 1³ | 19 | 1 **Earth Angel (Will You Be Mine)** | 8 | DooTone 348 |
| | | | Best Seller #1(3) / Juke Box #1(3) / Jockey #1(1) written by Curtis Williams; considered to be the top R&B record of all time in terms of continuous popularity | | |
| 5/13/57 | 15 | 1 | 2 Pledge Of Love | | Atlantic 1132 |
| | | | Jockey #15 | | |
| | | | **PEOPLE'S CHOICE** | | |
| | | | Philadelphia group formed in 1971. Consisted of Frankie Brunson (vocals), Stanley Burton, Roger Andrews, Dave Thompson and Leon Lee. Brunson sang with Lynn Hope's band, and with Andrews and Thompson in the vocal group, the Fashions. Lee recorded solo in 1974. | | |
| 7/03/71 | 9 | 12 | 1 I Likes To Do It [I] | 38 | Phil-L.A. 349 |
| 1/13/73 | 45 | 4 | 2 Let Me Do My Thing | | Phil-L.A. 358 |
| 12/21/74+ | 45 | 14 | 3 Party Is A Groovy Thing | | TSOP 4759 |
| 7/19/75 | 1¹ | 18 | 4● **Do It Any Way You Wanna** [I] | 11 | TSOP 4769 |
| 12/13/75+ | 22 | 15 | 5 Nursery Rhymes (Part I) | 93 | TSOP 4773 |
| 6/19/76 | 52 | 7 | 6 Here We Go Again [I] | | TSOP 4781 |
| 8/21/76 | 52 | 8 | 7 Movin' In All Directions | | TSOP 4782 |
| 1/15/77 | 83 | 3 | 8 Cold Blooded & Down-Right-Funky | | TSOP 4784 |
| 4/30/77 | 76 | 7 | 9 If You Gonna Do It (Put Your Mind To It) (Part 1). | | TSOP 4786 |
| 12/20/80+ | 77 | 6 | 10 My Feet Won't Move, But My Shoes Did The Boogie | | Casablanca 2322 |

| DEBUT DATE | PEAK POS | WKS CHR | ARTIST — Record Title | POP POS | Label & Number |
|---|---|---|---|---|---|
| | | | **THE PEPPERS** | | |
| | | | Paris studio duo: Mat Camison (synthesizer) and Pierre Dahan (drums). | | |
| 3/02/74 | 34 | 11 | 1 Pepper Box ................................................. [I] | 76 | Event 213 |
| 8/10/74 | 76 | 4 | 2 Hot Caramel................................................. | | Event 215 |
| 1/11/75 | 100 | 2 | 3 Do It, Do It ............................................ [I] | | Event 221 |
| | | | **PERCY & THEM** | | |
| | | | Led by Percy Hargrove from Detroit. | | |
| 1/19/74 | 94 | 4 | 1 Sing A Sad Song ......................................... | | Playboy 50048 |
| | | | **AL PERKINS** | | |
| | | | Born on 8/1/30 in Brookhaven, Mississippi. Died from a gunshot on 2/13/83. Singer/producer/manager/bass player. Own band in Chicago from 1957-64. First recorded for C.J. in 1960. Deejay in Milwaukee, Little Rock and Memphis. Produced Al Hudson & Soul Partners, Hot Sauce, One Way, Oliver Cheatham and Little Milton. Al's sister is singer Vee Allen. | | |
| 8/02/69 | 48 | 2 | 1 Yes, My Goodness, Yes................................... | | Atco 6693 |
| | | | **CARL PERKINS** | | |
| | | | Born on 4/9/32 in Tiptonville, Tennessee. Rockabilly singer/guitarist/songwriter. Member of Johnny Cash's touring troupe from 1965-75. The Beatles recorded his songs "Matchbox", "Honey Don't" and "Everybody's Trying To Be My Baby". | | |
| 3/10/56 | 2⁴ | 16 | 1 Blue Suede Shoes............................................. Juke Box #2 / Best Seller #2 / Jockey #6 | 2 | Sun 234 |
| | | | **GEORGE PERKINS & THE SILVER STARS** | | |
| 3/07/70 | 12 | 12 | 1 Cryin' In The Streets (Part 1).......................... | 61 | Silver Fox 18 |
| | | | **PERRY & SANLIN** | | |
| 6/07/80 | 81 | 3 | 1 Just To Make You Happy............................... | | Capitol 4852 |
| | | | **GREG PERRY** | | |
| | | | Vocalist/songwriter from North Dakota. | | |
| 8/17/74 | 81 | 6 | 1 Boogie Man ............................................... | | Casablanca 0019 |
| 2/15/75 | 24 | 16 | 2 Come On Down (Get Your Head Out Of The Clouds) .................................................. | | Casablanca 817 |
| 7/05/75 | 48 | 7 | 3 I'll Be Comin Back...................................... | | Casablanca 835 |
| 4/10/82 | 53 | 7 | 4 It Takes Heart .......................................... | | Alfa 7016 |
| | | | **JEFF PERRY** | | |
| | | | Born on 10/23/51 in Chicago. Vocalist, formerly in Three Of A Kind. | | |
| 8/30/75 | 19 | 13 | 1 Love Don't Come No Stronger (Than Yours And Mine) ................................................... | 108 | Arista 0133 |
| | | | **LINDA PERRY** | | |
| 12/29/73+ | 54 | 10 | 1 I Need Someone ......................................... | | Mainstream 5550 |
| | | | **PERSIANS** | | |
| | | | Group consisting of James Gill, Leroy Priester, Freddie Lewis, James Harlee and Jim Brown. | | |
| 7/13/68 | 17 | 5 | 1 Too Much Pride ......................................... | | ABC 11087 |
| 8/02/69 | 48 | 3 | 2 Don't Know How (To Fall Out Of Love) ............. | | GWP 509 |
| 3/28/70 | 50 | 2 | 3 Detour ................................................... | | Grapevine 201 |
| 1/29/72 | 39 | 5 | 4 Your Love................................................ | 108 | Capitol 3230 |
| | | | **HOUSTON PERSON** | | |
| | | | Born on 11/10/34 in Florence, South Carolina. Tenor saxophonist. | | |
| 11/22/75+ | 30 | 14 | 1 Disco Sax/ ............................................ [I] | 91 | |
| | | 10 | 2 For The Love Of You ............................... [I] | | Westbound 5015 |
| 2/09/85 | 89 | 2 | 3 Moon ..................................................... ROGER KELLAWAY/HOUSTON PERSON | | Green St. 703 |
| | | | **THE PERSUADERS** | | |
| | | | Group formed in New York City in 1969. Consisted of lead Douglas "Smokey" Scott, Willie Holland, James "B.J." Barnes and Charles Stodghill. In 1974, lineup consisted of Thomas Lee Hill, Douglas Scott, Richard Gant and Willie Coleman. | | |
| 8/14/71 | 1² | 16 | 1● Thin Line Between Love & Hate .................. | 15 | Atco 6822 |
| 12/18/71+ | 8 | 12 | 2 Love Gonna Pack Up (And Walk Out) ........... | 64 | Win Or Lose 220 |
| 4/15/72 | 27 | 3 | 3 If This Is What You Call Love (I Don't Want No Part Of It) ........................................ all of above: accompanied by the vocal group Young, Gifted & Bad | | Win Or Lose 222 |
| 10/14/72 | 21 | 12 | 4 Peace In The Valley Of Love........................... | 104 | Win Or Lose 225 |

| DEBUT DATE | PEAK POS | WKS CHR | ARTIST — Record Title | POP POS | Label & Number |
|---|---|---|---|---|---|
| | | | **THE PERSUADERS — Continued** | | |
| 4/28/73 | 24 | 6 | 5 Bad, Bold And Beautiful Girl | *105* | Atco 6919 |
| 9/29/73 | 7 | 15 | 6 **Some Guys Have All The Luck** | 39 | Atco 6943 |
| 2/09/74 | 29 | 11 | 7 Best Thing That Ever Happened To Me | 85 | Atco 6956 |
| 7/20/74 | 32 | 12 | 8 All Strung Out On You | | Atco 6964 |
| 6/25/77 | 34 | 12 | 9 I Need Love | | Calla 3006 |
| | | | **PERSUASIONS** | | |
| | | | A cappella quintet from Bedford-Stuyvesant, New York, formed in 1966. Consisted of Jerry Lawson (lead), Joseph "Jesse" Russell and Jayotis Washington (tenors), Herbert "Tubo" Rhoad (baritone) and Jimmy "Bro" Hayes (bass). | | |
| 7/06/74 | 56 | 11 | 1 I Really Got It Bad For You | | A&M 1531 |
| 8/09/75 | 84 | 5 | 2 One Thing On My Mind | | A&M 1698 |
| | | | **PET SHOP BOYS** | | |
| | | | British duo: Neil Tennant (vocals) and Chris Lowe. Tennant was a writer for the British fan magazine "Smash Hits". Lowe studied to be an architect. | | |
| 4/19/86 | 36 | 12 | 1 West End Girls | *1* | EMI America 8307 |
| | | | **PETER, PAUL & MARY** | | |
| | | | Folk group formed in New York City in 1961. Consisted of Mary Travers, Peter Yarrow and Paul Stookey. Disbanded in 1971; reunited in 1978. | | |
| 4/27/63 | 10 | 7 | 1 **Puff (The Magic Dragon)** | *2* | Warner 5348 |
| | | | **PAUL PETERSEN** | | |
| | | | Born on 9/23/45 in Glendale, California. Member of Disney's "Mouseketeers" and played Jeff Stone on TV's "Donna Reed Show". | | |
| 1/05/63 | 19 | 5 | 1 My Dad | 6 | Colpix 663 |
| | | | **BOBBY PETERSON** | | |
| | | | Pianist/vocalist from Chester, Pennsylvania. Leader of own quintet. | | |
| 9/26/60 | 15 | 4 | 1 Irresistable You | *96* | V-Tone 214 |
| | | | **LUCKY PETERSON BLUES BAND** | | |
| | | | Chicago band produced by Willie Dixon and featuring 5-year-old Lucky Peterson - lead singer singer/organist born on 12/13/64 in Buffalo, New York. | | |
| 8/21/71 | 40 | 4 | 1 1-2-3-4 | *102* | Today 1503 |
| | | | **PETITE** | | |
| 3/08/86 | 86 | 2 | 1 So Fine | | York's 786 |
| | | | **GIORGE PETTUS** | | |
| | | | Minneapolis-based singer born in Southampton, Long Island. | | |
| 9/19/87 | 40 | 14 | 1 My Night For Love | | MCA 52894 |
| 3/19/88 | 42 | 11 | 2 Can You Wait | | MCA 53296 |
| | | | **P.FUNK ALL STARS** | | |
| | | | Group led by George Clinton, containing elements of Parliament/Funkadelic. Also see Parliament. | | |
| 1/09/82 | 66 | 8 | 1 Hydraulic Pump | | Hump 1 |
| 7/24/82 | 77 | 5 | 2 One Of Those Summers | | Hump 3 |
| 10/01/83 | 62 | 8 | 3 Generator Pop | | CBS Assoc. 04032 |
| | | | **PG&E - see PACIFIC GAS & ELECTRIC** | | |
| | | | **JAMES PHELPS** | | |
| | | | Gospel vocalist from Shreveport, LA. Member of The Soul Stirrers from 1964-65. | | |
| 5/01/65 | 12 | 7 | 1 Love Is A 5-Letter Word | 66 | Argo 5499 |
| | | | **PHILADELPHIA INTERNATIONAL ALL STARS** | | |
| | | | Supergroup of Philadelphia International artists: Lou Rawls, Billy Paul, Teddy Pendergrass, The O'Jays, Archie Bell and Dee Dee Sharp. | | |
| 7/02/77 | 4 | 18 | 1 **Let's Clean Up The Ghetto** | 91 | Phil. Int. 3627 |
| | | | all profits were committed to a five-year charity project | | |
| | | | **PHILADELPHIA STORY** | | |
| 3/05/77 | 99 | 1 | 1 People Users | | H&L 4679 |
| | | | **THE PHILARMONICS** | | |
| | | | Group of top British session musicians. Steve Gray, conductor/arranger. | | |
| 2/26/77 | 91 | 4 | 1 For Elise [I] | *100* | Capricorn 0268 |
| | | | an adaptation of Beethoven's "Fur Elise" | | |

| DEBUT DATE | PEAK POS | WKS CHR | ARTIST — Record Title | POP POS | Label & Number |
|---|---|---|---|---|---|
| | | | **GREG PHILLINGANES**<br>Keyboardist from Detroit. Worked with Stevie Wonder from 1976-81. | | |
| 5/09/81 | 72 | 5 | 1 Baby, I Do Love You .................................... | | Planet 47928 |
| 3/02/85 | 77 | 8 | 2 Behind The Mask ...................................... | | Planet 13943 |
| | | | **ESTHER PHILLIPS** ★★128★★<br>Born Esther Mae Jones on 12/23/35 in Galveston, Texas. Died on 8/7/84 in Los Angeles (liver, kidney failure). Vocalist/multi-instrumentalist. Moved to Los Angeles in 1940. Discovered by Johnny Otis. Toured and recorded with Otis to 1954. One of the first female superstars of R&B. Assumed name "Esther Phillips" in 1962. Bouts with drug addiction frequently interrupted her career and eventually led to her death. Youngest female singer to have a #1 hit on the R&B charts. | | |
| | | | LITTLE ESTHER with THE JOHNNY OTIS ORCHESTRA: | | |
| 2/04/50 | 1⁹ | 22 | 1 **Double Crossing Blues**............................<br>Best Seller #1(9) / Juke Box #1(5)<br>backing vocals by The Robins | | Savoy 731 |
| 4/08/50 | 1⁴ | 16 | 2 **Mistrustin' Blues/**<br>Best Seller #1(4) / Juke Box #1(4)<br>with vocals by Mel Walker | | |
| 4/15/50 | 9 | 1 | 3 **Misery**.................................................<br>Juke Box #9 | | Savoy 735 |
| 6/10/50 | 1¹ | 17 | 4 **Cupid's Boogie** ....................................<br>Juke Box #1 / Best Seller #2 | | Savoy 750 |
| 9/09/50 | 4 | 6 | 5 **Deceivin' Blues**...................................<br>Best Seller #4 / Juke Box #9<br>with vocals by Mel Walker | | Savoy 759 |
| 11/11/50 | 6 | 4 | 6 **Wedding Boogie/**<br>Best Seller #6<br>with vocals by Mel Walker & Lee Graves | | |
| 12/09/50 | 6 | 4 | 7 **Faraway Blues** .....................................<br>Best Seller #6<br>with vocals by Mel Walker; also known as "Christmas Blues" | | Savoy 764 |
| 2/23/52 | 8 | 2 | 8 **Ring-A-Ding-Doo** ................................<br>Best Seller #8<br>with vocals by Mel Walker | | Federal 12055 |
| | | | ESTHER PHILLIPS: | | |
| 11/10/62 | 1³ | 13 | 9 **Release Me**...............................................| 8 | Lenox 5555 |
| 4/17/65 | 11 | 9 | 10 And I Love Him................................... | 54 | Atlantic 2281 |
| 5/28/66 | 26 | 8 | 11 When A Woman Loves A Man ............... | 73 | Atlantic 2335 |
| 3/08/69 | 35 | 5 | 12 Too Late To Worry, Too Blue To Cry ........<br>orchestra conducted by Ernie Freeman | 121 | Roulette 7031 |
| 8/08/70 | 39 | 6 | 13 Set Me Free................................................<br>ESTHER PHILLIPS with The Dixie Flyers | 118 | Atlantic 2745 |
| 4/01/72 | 40 | 6 | 14 Home Is Where The Hatred Is ...................... | 122 | Kudu 904 |
| 6/24/72 | 38 | 6 | 15 Baby I'm For Real ..................................... | | Kudu 906 |
| 12/02/72 | 17 | 9 | 16 I've Never Found A Man (To Love Me Like You Do)...................................... | 106 | Kudu 910 |
| 7/19/75 | 10 | 18 | 17 **What A Diff'rence A Day Makes** ................... | 20 | Kudu 925 |
| 2/28/76 | 98 | 2 | 18 For All We Know........................................ | | Kudu 929 |
| 7/02/83 | 85 | 3 | 19 Turn Me Out.............................................. | | Winning 1001 |
| | | | **PHIL PHILLIPS with The Twilights**<br>Born John Phillip Baptiste on 3/14/31 in Lake Charles, Louisiana. Singer/guitarist. With gospel Gateway Quartet. Became a deejay in Louisiana. | | |
| 8/17/59 | 1¹ | 13 | 1 **Sea Of Love**...........................................<br>originally released on Khoury's 711 | 2 | Mercury 71465 |
| | | | **WES PHILLIPS** | | |
| 2/25/84 | 53 | 9 | 1 (I'm Just A) Sucker For A Pretty Face.............. | | Quality 7053 |
| | | | **PHILLY CREAM**<br>Philadelphia session band. | | |
| 6/30/79 | 46 | 8 | 1 Motown Review......................................... | 67 | Fant./WMOT 862 |
| 10/11/80 | 72 | 4 | 2 Cowboys To Girls ..................................... | | WMOT 5350 |
| | | | **PHILLY DEVOTIONS**<br>Quartet from Philadelphia: Ellis "Butch" Hill, Ernest "Chucky" Gibson, Morris Taylor and Matthew Coginton. | | |
| 2/15/75 | 81 | 7 | 1 I Just Can't Say Goodbye ............................ | 95 | Columbia 10076 |
| 6/14/75 | 67 | 9 | 2 We're Gonna Make It ................................. | | Columbia 10143 |
| 3/27/76 | 94 | 3 | 3 Hurt So Bad .............................................<br>new version of Little Anthony & The Imperials' classic | | Columbia 10292 |

| DEBUT DATE | PEAK POS | WKS CHR | ARTIST — Record Title | POP POS | Label & Number |
|---|---|---|---|---|---|
| | | | **PIANO RED** | | |
| | | | Born William Lee Perryman on 10/19/11 in Hampton, Georgia; raised in Atlanta. Died of cancer on 7/25/85 (73). Also known as Doctor Feelgood. Vocalist/pianist. Younger brother of Rufus "Speckled Red" Perryman. Formed Dr. Feelgood & The Interns. Overseas tours from 1974-77. | | |
| 12/30/50+ | 5 | 6 | 1 **Rockin' With Red/** <br> Best Seller #5 | | |
| 2/10/51 | 4 | 9 | 2 **Red's Boogie** ........................................... <br> Best Seller #4 / Juke Box #7 | | RCA 0099 |
| 5/26/51 | 10 | 1 | 3 **The Wrong Yo Yo**................................... <br> Best Seller #10 | | RCA 0106 |
| 7/28/51 | 10 | 1 | 4 **Just Right Bounce**................................ <br> Best Seller #10 | | RCA 0118 |
| 9/15/51 | 8 | 1 | 5 **Laying The Boogie** ............................... <br> Best Seller #8 | | RCA 0130 |
| | | | **BOBBY "BORIS" PICKETT & The Crypt-Kickers** | | |
| | | | Born on 2/11/40 in Somerville, Massachusetts. Began recording career in Hollywood while aspiring to be an actor. | | |
| 10/06/62 | 9 | 9 | 1 ● **Monster Mash**........................................ [N] | 1 | Garpax 44167 |
| 12/29/62+ | 18 | 2 | 2 Monsters' Holiday ................................. [X-N] | 30 | Garpax 44171 |
| | | | **WILSON PICKETT**  ★★21★★ | | |
| | | | Born on 3/18/41 in Prattville, Alabama. Singer/songwriter. Sang in local gospel groups. To Detroit in 1955. With The Falcons, 1961-63. Career took off after recording in Memphis with guitarist/producer Steve Cropper. | | |
| 5/18/63 | 30 | 1 | 1 If You Need Me ........................................ | 64 | Double-L 713 |
| 8/10/63 | 7 | 12 | 2 It's Too Late .............................................. | 49 | Double-L 717 |
| 11/09/63 | 95 | 4 | 3 I'm Down To My Last Heartbreak ..................... | Hot | Double-L 724 |
| 6/26/65 | 1¹ | 23 | 4 **In The Midnight Hour** ............................ | 21 | Atlantic 2289 |
| 11/20/65 | 4 | 13 | 5 **Don't Fight It**........................................ | 53 | Atlantic 2306 |
| 2/19/66 | 1⁷ | 16 | 6 **634-5789 (Soulsville, U.S.A.)**...................... | 13 | Atlantic 2320 |
| 6/11/66 | 13 | 8 | 7 **Ninety-Nine And A Half (Won't Do)** ................. | 53 | Atlantic 2334 |
| 8/06/66 | 1¹ | 12 | 8 **Land Of 1,000 Dances** .............................. | 6 | Atlantic 2348 |
| 12/03/66+ | 6 | 12 | 9 **Mustang Sally** ....................................... | 23 | Atlantic 2365 |
| 2/18/67 | 19 | 7 | 10 Everybody Needs Somebody To Love ............... | 29 | Atlantic 2381 |
| 4/08/67 | 6 | 11 | 11 **I Found A Love - Part 1**............................. | 32 | Atlantic 2394 |
| 6/24/67 | 10 | 8 | 12 **Soul Dance Number Three/** | 55 | |
| 6/17/67 | 26 | 3 | 13  You Can't Stand Alone............................. | 70 | Atlantic 2412 |
| 8/12/67 | 1¹ | 13 | 14 **Funky Broadway** ................................... | 8 | Atlantic 2430 |
| 11/11/67 | 13 | 7 | 15 Stag-O-Lee/ <br> remake of Archibald's "Stack-A-Lee" | 22 | |
| 12/02/67 | 4 | 13 | 16 **I'm In Love** ............................................ | 45 | Atlantic 2448 |
| 3/09/68 | 18 | 6 | 17 Jealous Love/ | 50 | |
| 3/30/68 | 46 | 3 | 18  I've Come A Long Way ............................ | 101 | Atlantic 2484 |
| 4/20/68 | 7 | 12 | 19 She's Lookin' Good .................................. | 15 | Atlantic 2504 |
| 7/06/68 | 6 | 10 | 20 **I'm A Midnight Mover** ............................ | 24 | Atlantic 2528 |
| 9/28/68 | 11 | 9 | 21 I Found A True Love................................. | 42 | Atlantic 2558 |
| 11/23/68 | 20 | 7 | 22 A Man And A Half .................................. | 42 | Atlantic 2575 |
| 1/04/69 | 13 | 7 | 23 Hey Jude................................................ | 23 | Atlantic 2591 |
| 4/05/69 | 19 | 5 | 24 Mini-Skirt Minnie .................................. | 50 | Atlantic 2611 |
| 5/31/69 | 41 | 4 | 25 Born To Be Wild ..................................... | 64 | Atlantic 2631 |
| 7/12/69 | 29 | 6 | 26 Hey Joe.................................................. | 59 | Atlantic 2648 |
| 12/13/69 | 16 | 5 | 27 You Keep Me Hanging On ......................... | 92 | Atlantic 2682 |
| 4/11/70 | 4 | 13 | 28 **Sugar Sugar/** | 25 | |
| | | 5 | 29  Cole, Cooke & Redding............................ | | Atlantic 2722 |
| 8/22/70 | 20 | 6 | 30 She Said Yes .......................................... | 68 | Atlantic 2753 |
| 10/03/70 | 3 | 14 | 31 **Engine Number 9** .................................. | 14 | Atlantic 2765 |
| 1/23/71 | 2² | 13 | 32 ● **Don't Let The Green Grass Fool You**............. | 17 | Atlantic 2781 |
| 5/01/71 | 1¹ | 14 | 33 ● **Don't Knock My Love - Pt. 1**..................... | 13 | Atlantic 2797 |
| 8/28/71 | 10 | 9 | 34 **Call My Name, I'll Be There** ..................... | 52 | Atlantic 2824 |
| 1/01/72 | 2² | 12 | 35 **Fire And Water** .................................... | 24 | Atlantic 2852 |
| 5/27/72 | 11 | 9 | 36 Funk Factory ......................................... | 58 | Atlantic 2878 |
| 11/11/72 | 16 | 7 | 37 Mama Told Me Not To Come....................... | 99 | Atlantic 2909 |
| 3/17/73 | 16 | 8 | 38 Mr. Magic Man ...................................... | 98 | RCA 0898 |

| DEBUT DATE | PEAK POS | WKS CHR | ARTIST — Record Title | POP POS | Label & Number |
|---|---|---|---|---|---|
| | | | **WILSON PICKETT — Continued** | | |
| 5/05/73 | 30 | 6 | 39 International Playboy | *104* | Atlantic 2961 |
| 9/08/73 | 17 | 12 | 40 Take A Closer Look At The Woman You're With. | *90* | RCA 0049 |
| 11/24/73+ | 20 | 13 | 41 Soft Soul Boogie Woogie | *103* | RCA 0174 |
| 7/06/74 | 68 | 8 | 42 Take Your Pleasure Where You Find It | | RCA 0309 |
| 11/29/75+ | 26 | 12 | 43 The Best Part Of A Man | | Wicked 8101 |
| 3/27/76 | 69 | 7 | 44 Love Will Keep Us Together | | Wicked 8102 |
| | | | new version of Captain & Tennille's 1975 pop hit (POS 1) | | |
| 6/17/78 | 59 | 7 | 45 Who Turned You On | | Big Tree 16121 |
| 11/04/78 | 94 | 2 | 46 Groovin' | | Big Tree 16129 |
| 11/10/79 | 41 | 13 | 47 I Want You | | EMI America 8027 |
| 3/01/80 | 95 | 2 | 48 Live With Me | | EMI America 8034 |
| 8/15/87 | 74 | 6 | 49 Don't Turn Away | | Motown 1898 |
| | | | **PICTURE PERFECT** | | |
| | | | Female, teenage dance trio from Boston: LaTamra Smith, Durana Billings and Gennyfer Hall. | | |
| 3/28/87 | 66 | 8 | 1 Prove It, Boy | | Atlantic 89308 |
| | | | **PIECES OF A DREAM** | | |
| | | | Jazz trio from Philadelphia, formed in 1975 as Touch Of Class. Consisted of James Lloyd (keyboards), Cedric Napoleon (bass) and Curtis Harmon (drums). Ages in 1981 were 17, 19 and 19, respectively. Worked as house band for "City Lights" TV series at KYW-Philadelphia. | | |
| 9/26/81 | 54 | 8 | 1 Warm Weather | | Elektra 47181 |
| 9/18/82 | 33 | 14 | 2 Mt. Airy Groove | | Elektra 47482 |
| | | | rap version released on Elektra 69884 | | |
| 12/10/83+ | 15 | 16 | 3 Fo-Fi-Fo | *107* | Elektra 69771 |
| 3/24/84 | 65 | 7 | 4 It's Time For Love | | Elektra 69750 |
| 6/21/86 | 16 | 14 | 5 Say La La | | Manhattan 50038 |
| 10/11/86 | 65 | 8 | 6 Joyride | | Manhattan 50049 |
| 7/02/88 | 71 | 8 | 7 Ain't My Love Enough | | EMI Man. 50124 |
| | | | **WARDELL PIPER** | | |
| | | | Female disco singer from Philadelphia. Sang in family gospel group, the Pipers, from age 5. In vocal group First Choice, recorded for Scepter and Philly Groove. | | |
| 2/03/79 | 33 | 11 | 1 Captain Boogie | | Midsong Int. 1001 |
| 6/16/79 | 20 | 15 | 2 Super Sweet | | Midsong Int. 1005 |
| 4/19/80 | 53 | 6 | 3 Gimme Something Real | | Midsong Int. 72000 |
| | | | **PIPS - see GLADYS KNIGHT** | | |
| | | | **DONNELL PITMAN** | | |
| 4/26/86 | 82 | 4 | 1 Your Love Is Dynamite | | After Five 710 |
| | | | backing vocals: The Chi-Lites | | |
| 10/18/86 | 63 | 9 | 2 Chocolate Lover | | After Five 1210 |
| | | | **GENE PITNEY** | | |
| | | | Born on 2/17/41 in Rockville, Connecticut. Prolific pop singer/songwriter. Recorded for Decca in 1959, with Ginny Arnell as Jamie & Jane. Recorded for Blaze in 1960 as Billy Bryan. First recorded under own name for Festival in 1960. | | |
| 11/24/62 | 16 | 2 | 1 Only Love Can Break A Heart | 2 | Musicor 1022 |
| | | | **EUGENE PITT - see THE JIVE FIVE** | | |
| | | | **PLANET PATROL** | | |
| 10/30/82 | 21 | 14 | 1 Play At Your Own Risk [I] | | Tommy Boy 825 |
| 8/27/83 | 30 | 10 | 2 Cheap Thrills | | Tommy Boy 835 |
| 12/24/83+ | 62 | 9 | 3 I Didn't Know I Loved You (Till I Saw You Rock & Roll) | | Tommy Boy 837 |
| | | | **EDDIE PLATT** | | |
| | | | Saxophonist/bandleader from Cleveland. | | |
| 3/24/58 | 11 | 5 | 1 Tequila [I] | 20 | ABC-Para. 9899 |
| | | | Best Seller #11 / Jockey #11 | | |

**329**

| DEBUT DATE | PEAK POS | WKS CHR | | ARTIST — Record Title | POP POS | Label & Number |
|---|---|---|---|---|---|---|
| | | | | **THE PLATTERS** ★★87★★ | | |
| | | | | Group formed in Los Angeles in 1953. Consisted of Tony Williams (b: 4/5/28, Elizabeth, NJ), lead; David Lynch, tenor; Paul Robi, baritone; Herb Reed, bass; and Zola Taylor. Taylor had formerly sung with Shirley Gunter's Queens. Group first recorded for Federal in 1954, with Alex Hodge instead of Robi, and without Zola Taylor. Hit "Only You" was written by manager Buck Ram and first recorded for Federal, who did not want to use it. To Mercury in 1955, re-recorded "Only You". Williams left to go solo, replaced by Sonny Turner in 1961. Taylor replaced by Sandra Dawn; Robi replaced by Nate Nelson (formerly in The Flamingos) in 1966. Several unrelated groups use this famous name today. | | |
| 7/30/55 | **1**[7] | 30 | 1 | **Only You (And You Alone)**.............................. Best Seller #1(7) / Juke Box #1(6) / Jockey #1(5) | **5** | Mercury 70633 |
| 12/17/55+ | **1**[11] | 20 | 2 | **The Great Pretender**.................................... Jockey #1(11) / Best Seller #1(10) / Juke Box #1(9) | *1* | Mercury 70753 |
| 4/07/56 | **4** | 12 | 3 | **(You've Got) The Magic Touch**...................... Best Seller #4 / Jockey #4 / Juke Box #4 | *4* | Mercury 70819 |
| 7/14/56 | **1**[2] | 17 | 4 | **My Prayer/** Jockey #1(2) / Juke Box #1(2) / Best Seller #2 #2 hit for Glenn Miller in 1939 | *1* | |
| 9/15/56 | **13** | 3 | 5 | **Heaven On Earth**.............................. Jockey #13 | *39* | Mercury 70893 |
| 11/03/56 | **9** | 3 | 6 | **You'll Never Never Know/** Juke Box #9 / Jockey #10 | *11* | |
| 11/03/56 | **10** | 4 | 7 | **It Isn't Right** .............................. Best Seller #10 | *23* | Mercury 70948 |
| 12/29/56+ | **7** | 6 | 8 | **On My Word Of Honor/** Juke Box #7 / Jockey #8 / Best Seller #11 | *20* | |
| | | 2 | 9 | **One In A Million**.............................. Best Seller flip / Juke Box flip | *31* | Mercury 71011 |
| 4/06/57 | **15** | 1 | 10 | I'm Sorry/ Jockey #15 | *11* | |
| 4/29/57 | **5** | 5 | 11 | **He's Mine**.............................. Juke Box #5 / Jockey #9 | *23* | Mercury 71032 |
| 6/10/57 | **7** | 2 | 12 | **My Dream**.............................. Jockey #7 / Best Seller #11 | *24* | Mercury 71093 |
| 4/14/58 | **1**[3] | 14 | 13 | **Twilight Time** .............................. Best Seller #1 / Jockey #2 | *1* | Mercury 71289 |
| 12/15/58 | **3** | 15 | 14 | **Smoke Gets In Your Eyes** .............................. #1 hit in 1934 for Paul Whiteman | *1* | Mercury 71383 |
| 4/27/59 | **9** | 5 | 15 | **Enchanted** .............................. | *12* | Mercury 71427 |
| 2/29/60 | **15** | 9 | 16 | Harbor Lights .............................. there were 5 pop Top 10 versions of this tune in 1950 | *8* | Mercury 71563 |
| 8/14/61 | **17** | 3 | 17 | I'll Never Smile Again .............................. Tommy Dorsey's version hit POS 1 in 1940 | *25* | Mercury 71847 |
| 5/14/66 | **6** | 16 | 18 | **I Love You 1000 Times** .............................. | *31* | Musicor 1166 |
| 3/04/67 | **12** | 13 | 19 | With This Ring .............................. | *14* | Musicor 1229 |
| 7/08/67 | **29** | 9 | 20 | Washed Ashore (On A Lonely Island In The Sea). | *56* | Musicor 1251 |
| 11/04/67 | **32** | 5 | 21 | Sweet, Sweet Lovin'.............................. | *70* | Musicor 1275 |
| | | | | **PLAYER** | | |
| | | | | Pop/rock group formed in Los Angeles: Peter Becket (lead), John Crowley, Ronn Mass, John Friesen and Wayne Cooke. Moss joined the cast of the TV soap opera "The Bold & The Beautiful". | | |
| 12/03/77+ | **10** | 18 | 1●**Baby Come Back**.............................. | *1* | RSO 879 |
| | | | | **PLAYERS** | | |
| | | | | Group led by Herbert Butler. | | |
| 8/06/66 | **24** | 16 | 1 | He'll Be Back ............................. | *107* | Minit 32001 |
| 12/03/66 | **32** | 5 | 2 | I'm Glad I Waited ......................................... | *130* | Minit 32012 |
| | | | | **PLAYERS ASSOCIATION** | | |
| | | | | Band consisted of Joe Farrell (tenor sax), Jon Faddis (trumpet, flugelhorn) and Chris Hills (vocals, clarinet, keyboards, drums, guitar). | | |
| 4/05/80 | **59** | 7 | 1 | The Get-Down Mellow Sound ......................... | | Vanguard 35214 |
| | | | | **PLEASURE** | | |
| | | | | Formed in 1970 in Portland, Oregon. Consisted of Sherman Davis (lead), with Nate and Marlon McClain, Michael and Donald Hepburn, Bruce Smith, Bruce Carter and Dennis Springer. | | |
| 9/11/76 | **71** | 8 | 1 | Ghettos Of The Mind......................................... | | Fantasy 774 |
| 5/28/77 | **35** | 16 | 2 | Joyous....................................................... | | Fantasy 793 |
| 9/08/79 | **75** | 4 | 3 | Future Now.................................................. | | Fantasy 864 |

| DEBUT DATE | PEAK POS | WKS CHR | ARTIST — Record Title | POP POS | Label & Number |
|---|---|---|---|---|---|
| | | | **PLEASURE — Continued** | | |
| 10/06/79 | **10** | 20 | 4 Glide .................... | 55 | Fantasy 874 |
| 3/22/80 | **65** | 5 | 5 The Real Thing ..................... | | Fantasy 882 |
| 6/28/80 | **30** | 13 | 6 Yearnin' Burnin' ...................... | | Fantasy 893 |
| 10/04/80 | **56** | 7 | 7 Now You Choose Me ......................... | | Fantasy 900 |
| 3/13/82 | **27** | 16 | 8 Sending My Love ........................ | | RCA 13067 |
| 7/17/82 | **80** | 4 | 9 Give It Up ....................... | | RCA 13241 |
| | | | **PLUSH** | | |
| 6/26/82 | **62** | 8 | 1 Burnin' Love ...................... | | RCA 13228 |
| | | | **POCKETS** | | |
| | | | Group from Baltimore, Maryland: Al McKinney (lead), Larry Jacobs, Gary Grainger, Charles C. Williams, Kevin Barnes, George Gray, Irving Madison and Jacob R. Sheffer. | | |
| 11/05/77+ | **17** | 18 | 1 Come Go With Me.................... | 84 | Columbia 10632 |
| 3/11/78 | **65** | 7 | 2 Pasado ...................... | | Columbia 10687 |
| 8/26/78 | **24** | 14 | 3 Take It On Up........................ | 106 | Columbia 10755 |
| 11/25/78+ | **51** | 11 | 4 Happy For Love ....................... | | Columbia 10859 |
| 8/04/79 | **69** | 10 | 5 Catch Me ........................ | | ARC 10954 |
| 11/17/79+ | **34** | 11 | 6 So Delicious ...................... | | ARC 11121 |
| | | | **THE POETS** | | |
| | | | Quartet consisting of Ronnie Lewis (lead), Melvin Bradford, Paul Fulton and Johnny James. | | |
| 4/02/66 | **2**[2] | 13 | 1 **She Blew A Good Thing** ............................. | 45 | Symbol 214 |
| | | | **POINTER SISTERS**  ★★66★★ | | |
| | | | Group formed in Oakland in 1971. Consisted of sisters Ruth, Anita, Bonnie and June Pointer. Parents were ministers. Group was originally a trio, joined by youngest sister June, in the early 70s. First recorded for Atlantic in 1971. Back-up work for Cold Blood, Elvin Bishop, Boz Scaggs, Grace Slick, and many others. Sang in nostalgic 1940s style, 1973-77. In the film "Car Wash", 1976. Bonnie went solo in 1978, group continued as trio in new musical style. | | |
| 8/25/73 | **12** | 15 | 1 Yes We Can Can ......................... | 11 | Blue Thumb 229 |
| 12/29/73+ | **24** | 10 | 2 Wang Dang Doodle ................... | 61 | Blue Thumb 243 |
| 7/26/75 | **1**[2] | 14 | 3 **How Long (Betcha' Got A Chick On The Side)** . | 20 | Blue Thumb 265 |
| 11/22/75+ | **16** | 12 | 4 Going Down Slowly ................... | 61 | Blue Thumb 268 |
| 11/27/76+ | **14** | 13 | 5 You Gotta Believe ..................... | 103 | Blue Thumb 271 |
| 10/22/77 | **62** | 13 | 6 Having A Party ....................... | | Blue Thumb 275 |
| | | | new version of Sam Cooke's 1962 hit all of above: produced by David Rubinson | | |
| 1/20/79 | **14** | 11 | 7● Fire ....................... | 2 | Planet 45901 |
| | | | written by Bruce Springsteen | | |
| 3/17/79 | **20** | 12 | 8 Happiness....................... | 30 | Planet 45902 |
| 8/02/80 | **10** | 20 | 9● **He's So Shy**........................ | 3 | Planet 47916 |
| 11/08/80 | **22** | 14 | 10 Could I Be Dreaming ................. | 52 | Planet 47920 |
| 6/13/81 | **7** | 20 | 11● **Slow Hand** ..................... | 2 | Planet 47929 |
| 10/24/81 | **52** | 5 | 12 What A Surprise ................... | | Planet 47937 |
| 7/10/82 | **23** | 14 | 13 American Music .................... | 16 | Planet 13254 |
| 10/02/82 | **46** | 9 | 14 I'm So Excited ..................... | 30 | Planet 13327 |
| | | | new version released in 1984, hit POS 9 on pop charts | | |
| 3/05/83 | **44** | 9 | 15 If You Wanna Get Back Your Lady ................... | 67 | Planet 13430 |
| 10/15/83 | **13** | 16 | 16 I Need You .................... | 48 | Planet 13639 |
| 1/28/84 | **2**[3] | 18 | 17 **Automatic**.................... | 5 | Planet 13730 |
| 4/28/84 | **3** | 20 | 18 **Jump (For My Love)** ..................... | 3 | Planet 13780 |
| 12/08/84+ | **13** | 21 | 19 Neutron Dance ................... | 6 | Planet 13951 |
| | | | from the film "Beverly Hills Cop" | | |
| 4/13/85 | **24** | 14 | 20 Baby Come And Get It.................... | 44 | Planet 14041 |
| 7/20/85 | **6** | 17 | 21 **Dare Me** ...................... | 11 | RCA 14126 |
| 11/16/85+ | **25** | 15 | 22 Freedom ...................... | 59 | RCA 14224 |
| 3/08/86 | **61** | 6 | 23 Twist My Arm ................... | 83 | RCA 14197 |
| 11/08/86+ | **17** | 14 | 24 Goldmine ..................... | 33 | RCA 5062 |
| 2/21/87 | **69** | 7 | 25 All I Know Is The Way I Feel ...................... | 93 | RCA 5112 |
| 6/20/87 | **49** | 8 | 26 Mercury Rising ..................... | | RCA 5230 |
| 2/06/88 | **39** | 9 | 27 He Turned Me Out ..................... | | RCA 6865 |
| | | | from the film "Action Jackson" | | |
| 6/18/88 | **67** | 5 | 28 I'm In Love ..................... | | RCA 8378 |

| DEBUT DATE | PEAK POS | WKS CHR | ARTIST — Record Title | POP POS | Label & Number |
|---|---|---|---|---|---|
| | | | **ANITA POINTER** | | |
| | | | Second eldest of the Pointer Sisters, born in 1948. | | |
| 10/10/87 | **41** | 14 | 1 Overnight Success.................................... | | RCA 5291 |
| 6/18/88 | **73** | 6 | 2 More Than A Memory ................................ | | RCA 6847 |
| | | | **BONNIE POINTER** | | |
| | | | Born on 7/11/51 in East Oakland, California. One of the Pointer Sisters. | | |
| 11/04/78+ | **10** | 18 | 1 **Free Me From My Freedom/Tie Me To A Tree (Handcuff Me)**...................................... | 58 | Motown 1451 |
| 5/12/79 | **52** | 14 | 2 Heaven Must Have Sent You......................... | 11 | Motown 1459 |
| 12/22/79+ | **42** | 11 | 3 I Can't Help Myself (Sugar Pie, Honey Bunch) ..... | 40 | Motown 1478 |
| 7/14/84 | **35** | 13 | 4 Your Touch.............................................. | | Private I 04449 |
| 11/03/84 | **84** | 4 | 5 Premonition ........................................... | | Private I 04658 |
| 3/16/85 | **87** | 3 | 6 The Beast In Me....................................... | | Private I 04819 |
| | | | **JUNE POINTER** | | |
| | | | Youngest member of The Pointer Sisters. | | |
| 5/28/83 | **28** | 8 | 1 Ready For Some Action.............................. | | Planet 13522 |
| | | | **NOEL POINTER** | | |
| | | | Jazz-fusion violin prodigy from Brooklyn. | | |
| 10/27/79 | **73** | 4 | 1 For You (A Disco Concerto) Part 1 ................... | | United Art. 1311 |
| 4/25/81 | **38** | 11 | 2 All The Reasons Why.................................. | | Liberty 1403 |
| 7/25/81 | **46** | 10 | 3 Classy Lady ............................................ | | Liberty 1421 |
| | | | **POISON** | | |
| | | | Funk outfit, not to be confused with the heavy metal quartet of the same name. | | |
| 8/09/75 | **27** | 11 | 1 Let Me Lay My Funk On You .......................... | | Roulette 7174 |
| | | | **KEITH POLE** | | |
| 4/06/85 | **86** | 5 | 1 Fulfill Your Fantasy ................................. | | Supertronics 005 |
| | | | **POLITICIANS** | | |
| | | | Band formed by writer/producer McKinley Jackson. | | |
| 4/15/72 | **33** | 3 | 1 Free Your Mind........................................ [I] | 110 | Hot Wax 7114 |
| | | | **PONDEROSA TWINS + ONE** | | |
| | | | Cleveland group, consisting of two sets of twins: Alvin & Alfred Pelham, and Keith & Kirk Gardner, plus Ricky Spencer. Produced by Bobby Massey of The O'Jays. | | |
| 9/04/71 | **12** | 12 | 1 You Send Me ............................................ | 78 | Horoscope 102 |
| 1/01/72 | **41** | 6 | 2 Bound.................................................... | 102 | Horoscope 103 |
| 5/27/72 | **40** | 3 | 3 Why Do Fools Fall In Love ........................... | 102 | Horoscope 104 |
| 10/27/73 | **82** | 6 | 4 Tomorrow's Train ..................................... | | Astroscope 114 |
| | | | **PONI-TAILS** | | |
| | | | Pop female trio from Brush High School in Lyndhurst, Ohio. Consisted of Toni Cistone (lead), LaVerne Novak (high harmony) and Patti McCabe. First recorded for Point in 1957. | | |
| 9/15/58 | **11** | 4 | 1 Born Too Late .......................................... Jockey #11 / Best Seller #13 | 7 | ABC-Para. 9934 |
| | | | **SERGE PONSAR - see SERGE!** | | |
| | | | **DAVID PORTER** | | |
| | | | Born on 11/21/41 in Memphis. Songwriter, teamed with Isaac Hayes, wrote "Hold On I'm Coming", "B-A-B-Y", "I Got To Love Somebody's Baby", and many others. | | |
| 5/30/70 | **29** | 5 | 1 Can't See You When I Want To ....................... | 105 | Enterprise 9014 |
| 5/20/72 | **37** | 5 | 2 Ain't That Loving You (For More Reasons Than One) ................................................... ISAAC HAYES & DAVID PORTER | 86 | Enterprise 9049 |
| | | | **NOLAN PORTER** | | |
| | | | Born in 1949 in Los Angeles. Also worked as Nolan and N.F. Porter. Produced by Gabriel Mekler. | | |
| 7/10/71 | **40** | 8 | 1 I Like What You Give................................... shown only as: **NOLAN** | 70 | Lizard 1008 |
| 12/11/71+ | **39** | 7 | 2 Keep On Keepin On ................................... | 77 | Lizard 1010 |
| 2/24/73 | **29** | 8 | 3 If I Could Only Be Sure................................ | 89 | ABC 11343 |

| DEBUT DATE | PEAK POS | WKS CHR | ARTIST — Record Title | POP POS | Label & Number |
|---|---|---|---|---|---|
| | | | **FRANCK POURCEL'S FRENCH FIDDLES** | | |
| | | | Frank was born on 1/1/15 in Marseilles, France. String orchestra leader/composer/arranger/violinist. | | |
| 5/25/59 | **18** | 4 | 1 Only You ................................................. [I] | 9 | Capitol 4165 |
| | | | **BOBBY POWELL** | | |
| | | | Blind singer from Baton Rouge, Louisiana. Attended Southern University for the Blind. | | |
| 11/13/65+ | **12** | 13 | 1 C.C. Rider ........................................... | 76 | Whit 714 |
| 4/16/66 | **39** | 3 | 2 Do Something For Yourself ............................ | 120 | Whit 715 |
| 3/13/71 | **45** | 5 | 3 The Bells ............................................ | | Whit 6907 |
| | | | **PEREZ PRADO** | | |
| | | | Domase Perez Pradio, born on 11/13/18 in Mantanzas, Cuba. Moved to Mexico City in 1948 and formed a big band. Toured and worked in the U.S.A. beginning in 1954. In the film "Underwater". "The King Of Mambo" died on 12/4/83 (65). | | |
| 7/28/58 | **1** ² | 11 | 1 ●Patricia ............................................ [I] | 1 | Victor 7245 |
| | | | Best Seller #1(2) / Jockey #1(1) | | |
| | | | **THE PRECISIONS** | | |
| | | | Group led by Bobby Brooks. | | |
| 5/27/67 | **28** | 7 | 1 Why Girl ............................................. | | Drew 1002 |
| 9/30/67 | **26** | 5 | 2 If This Is Love (I'd Rather Be Lonely) .............. | 60 | Drew 1003 |
| 6/08/68 | **50** | 2 | 3 A Place ............................................. | | Drew 1005 |
| | | | **PREMIUM - see JEAN KNIGHT** | | |
| | | | **THE PREPARATIONS** | | |
| | | | Trio from New York City. Consisted of Frank McLeod, Gregory Reel and Henry Sollis. First worked as the Spiders. | | |
| 3/09/68 | **30** | 6 | 1 Get-E-Up (The Horse) ................................ | 134 | Heart & So. 201 |
| | | | **THE PRESIDENTS** | | |
| | | | Group consisting of Archie Powell, Bill Shorter and Tony Boyd. | | |
| 6/27/70 | **45** | 2 | 1 For You ............................................. | | Sussex 200 |
| 9/26/70 | **5** | 15 | 2 5-10-15-20 (25-30 Years Of Love) ................... | 11 | Sussex 207 |
| 2/06/71 | **16** | 7 | 3 Triangle Of Love (Hey Diddle Diddle) ............... | 68 | Sussex 212 |
| 5/22/71 | **30** | 3 | 4 The Sweetest Thing This Side Of Heaven ............ | | Sussex 217 |
| | | | **ELVIS PRESLEY** ★★**32**★★ | | |
| | | | "The King of Rock & Roll". Born on 1/8/35 in Tupelo, Mississippi. Died on 8/16/77 in Memphis at the age of 42 due to heart failure caused by drug abuse. Won talent contest at age eight, singing "Old Shep". First played guitar at age eleven. Moved to Memphis in 1948. Sang in high school shows. Worked as an usher and truck driver after graduation. First recorded on Sun in 1954. Signed to RCA Records on 11/22/55. First film, "Love Me Tender" in 1956. In US Army from 3/24/58 to 3/5/60. In many films thereafter. NBC-TV special in 1968. Married Priscilla Beaulieu on 5/1/67; divorced on 10/11/73. Only child Lisa Marie, born on 2/1/68. Elvis' last live performance was in Indianapolis on 6/26/77. | | |
| 3/31/56 | **3** | 13 | 1 **Heartbreak Hotel** ................................. | 1 | RCA 47-6420 |
| | | | Juke Box #3 / Jockey #4 / Best Seller #5 | | |
| 6/02/56 | **3** | 12 | 2 **I Want You, I Need You, I Love You/** | 1 | |
| | | | Juke Box #3 / Jockey #7 / Best Seller #10 | | |
| | | 4 | 3 My Baby Left Me ..................................... | 31 | RCA 47-6540 |
| | | | Juke Box flip | | |
| | | | written & recorded on RCA by Arthur "Big Boy" Crudup in 1950 | | |
| 8/11/56 | **1** ⁶ | 14 | 4 **Hound Dog/** | 1 | |
| | | | Juke Box #1 / Jockey #2 | | |
| | | | #1 for 7 weeks for Big Mama Thornton in 1953 | | |
| 8/25/56 | **1** ¹ | 17 | 5 **Don't Be Cruel** ................................... | 1 | RCA 47-6604 |
| | | | Best Seller #1 / Jockey #2 | | |
| 10/20/56 | **3** | 13 | 6 **Love Me Tender/** | 1 | |
| | | | Jockey #3 / Best Seller #4 / Juke Box #6 | | |
| | | | from Elvis' first movie - tune adapted from "Aura Lee" of 1861 | | |
| 12/15/56 | **12** | 1 | 7 Anyway You Want Me (That's How I Will Be).... | 20 | RCA 47-6643 |
| | | | Jockey #12 | | |
| 12/01/56 | **7** | 6 | 8 **Love Me** ........................................... | 2 | RCA EPA-992 |
| | | | Jockey #7 | | |
| | | | from the E.P. "Elvis" | | |
| 2/02/57 | **3** | 10 | 9 **Too Much** .......................................... | 1 | RCA 47-6800 |
| | | | Jockey #3 / Juke Box #6 / Best Seller #7 | | |
| 4/13/57 | **1** ⁴ | 14 | 10 **All Shook Up** ...................................... | 1 | RCA 47-6870 |
| | | | Best Seller #1(4) / Juke Box #1(4) / Jockey #1(2) | | |

| DEBUT DATE | PEAK POS | WKS CHR | ARTIST — Record Title | POP POS | Label & Number |
|---|---|---|---|---|---|
| | | | **ELVIS PRESLEY — Continued** | | |
| 7/01/57 | **1** [1] | 15 | 11 **(Let Me Be Your) Teddy Bear/** | *1* | |
| | | | Best Seller #1 / Jockey #2 | | |
| | | 8 | 12 Loving You ................................. | 20 | RCA 47-7000 |
| | | | Best Seller flip | | |
| 9/16/57 | **11** | 1 | 13 Mean Woman Blues ..................... | | RCA EPA-2-1515 |
| | | | Jockey #11 | | |
| | | | above 3: from the film "Loving You"; | | |
| | | | from the E.P. "Loving You, Vol. II" | | |
| 10/14/57 | **1** [5] | 15 | 14 **Jailhouse Rock/** | *1* | |
| | | | Best Seller #1(5) / Jockey #1(3) | | |
| 11/04/57 | **7** | 5 | 15 **Treat Me Nice** ........................ | 18 | RCA 47-7035 |
| | | | Jockey #7 | | |
| 1/20/58 | **14** | 1 | 16 (You're So Square) Baby I Don't Care ............... | | RCA EPA-4114 |
| | | | Jockey #14 | | |
| | | | above 3: from the film "Jailhouse Rock"; | | |
| | | | from the E.P. "Jailhouse Rock" | | |
| 2/03/58 | **4** | 10 | 17●**Don't/** | *1* | |
| | | | Best Seller #4 / Jockey #6 | | |
| 2/10/58 | **5** | 4 | 18 **I Beg Of You** ......................... | 8 | RCA 47-7150 |
| | | | Jockey #5 | | |
| 4/21/58 | **1** [3] | 11 | 19●**Wear My Ring Around Your Neck/** | 2 | |
| | | | Jockey #1 / Best Seller #7 | | |
| 5/12/58 | **10** | 2 | 20 **Doncha' Think It's Time** ........................... | 15 | RCA 47-7240 |
| | | | Jockey #10 | | |
| 6/30/58 | **2** [2] | 10 | 21●**Hard Headed Woman/** | *1* | |
| | | | Best Seller #2 / Jockey #6 | | |
| 7/28/58 | **9** | 2 | 22 **Don't Ask Me Why** ................................. | 25 | RCA 47-7280 |
| | | | Jockey #9 | | |
| | | | above 2: from the film "King Creole" | | |
| 11/17/58+ | **10** | 15 | 23 **One Night** ............................ | 4 | RCA 47-7410 |
| 4/20/59 | **16** | 7 | 24●(Now And Then There's) A Fool Such As I ......... | 2 | RCA 47-7056 |
| | | | #4 hit in 1953 on the Country charts for Hank Snow | | |
| 7/27/59 | **10** | 7 | 25 **A Big Hunk O' Love/** | *1* | |
| 8/10/59 | **15** | 3 | 26 My Wish Came True .................................. | 12 | RCA 47-7600 |
| 5/02/60 | **6** | 9 | 27 **Stuck On You**.................................. | *1* | RCA 47-7740 |
| | | | recorded 15 days after his Army discharge | | |
| 8/08/60 | **7** | 7 | 28●**It's Now Or Never** ............................ | *1* | RCA 47-7777 |
| | | | adapted from the Italian song "O Sole Mio" of 1899 | | |
| 11/28/60 | **3** | 10 | 29●**Are You Lonesome To-night?** ..................... | *1* | RCA 47-7810 |
| | | | #4 hit in 1927 for Vaughn Deleath | | |
| 6/05/61 | **15** | 3 | 30 **I Feel So Bad**............................ | 5 | RCA 47-7880 |
| 9/08/62 | **13** | 5 | 31 She's Not You............................ | 5 | RCA 47-8041 |
| 11/10/62 | **5** | 12 | 32●**Return To Sender** ............................ | 2 | RCA 47-8100 |
| | | | from the film "Girls! Girls! Girls!" | | |
| 3/23/63 | **21** | 4 | 33 One Broken Heart For Sale .......... | 11 | RCA 47-8134 |
| | | | from the film "It Happened At The Worlds Fair" | | |
| 7/27/63 | **9** | 8 | 34 **(You're the) Devil In Disguise**....................... | 3 | RCA 47-8188 |
| 11/16/63 | **20** | 2 | 35 Bossa Nova Baby ........................ | 8 | RCA 47-8243 |
| | | | from the film "Fun In Acapulco" | | |
| | | | **PRESSURE** | | |
| | | | Sextet, produced by Ronnie Laws. | | |
| 12/06/75+ | **45** | 12 | 1 Always There............................ | | Blue Note 738 |
| | | | **RONNIE LAWS & PRESSURE** | | |
| 2/23/80 | **54** | 11 | 2 Can You Feel It............................ | | MCA 41179 |
| | | | **PRESSURE DROP** | | |
| 10/09/82 | **74** | 7 | 1 Rock The House (You'll Never Be) ................... | | Tommy Boy 827 |
| | | | **BILLY PRESTON**   ★★**166**★★ | | |
| | | | Born on 9/9/46 in Houston. Vocalist/keyboardist. Moved to Los Angeles at an early age. With Mahalia Jackson in 1956. Played piano in film "St. Louis Blues", 1958. Regular on "Shindig" TV show. Recorded with The Beatles on "Get Back" and "Let It Be"; worked Concert For Bangladesh in 1969. Prominent session man, played on Sly & The Family Stone hits. With The Rolling Stones USA tour in 1975. | | |
| 1/16/71 | **23** | 8 | 1 My Sweet Lord............................ | 90 | Apple 1826 |
| | | | produced by George Harrison | | |
| 4/15/72 | **43** | 2 | 2 The Bus.................................. | | A&M 1340 |
| 5/06/72 | **1** [1] | 15 | 3 **Outa-Space** .............................. [I] | 2 | A&M 1320 |

| DEBUT DATE | PEAK POS | WKS CHR | ARTIST — Record Title | POP POS | Label & Number |
|---|---|---|---|---|---|
| | | | **BILLY PRESTON — Continued** | | |
| 9/16/72 | **17** | 10 | 4  Slaughter.................................................. | *50* | A&M 1380 |
| | | | from the film of the same title | | |
| 3/31/73 | **10** | 16 | 5  **Will It Go Round In Circles** ......................... | *1* | A&M 1411 |
| 9/22/73 | **1** ¹ | 15 | 6  **Space Race** .............................................. [I] | *4* | A&M 1463 |
| 1/12/74 | **11** | 12 | 7  You're So Unique ...................................... | *48* | A&M 1492 |
| 7/13/74 | **8** | 17 | 8  **Nothing From Nothing** .............................. | *1* | A&M 1544 |
| 12/14/74+ | **11** | 14 | 9  Struttin' .................................................... [I] | *22* | A&M 1644 |
| 9/27/75 | **23** | 10 | 10  Fancy Lady............................................... | *71* | A&M 1735 |
| 12/27/75+ | **58** | 7 | 11  Do It While You Can ................................. | | A&M 1768 |
| 2/05/77 | **48** | 7 | 12  I've Got The Spirit/ | | |
| | | 7 | 13    Do What You Want................................... | | A&M 1892 |
| 4/30/77 | **44** | 12 | 14  Girl........................................................... | | A&M 1925 |
| 11/19/77 | **33** | 13 | 15  Wide Stride .............................................. | | A&M 1980 |
| 4/01/78 | **59** | 9 | 16  I'm Really Gonna Miss You ......................... | | A&M 2012 |
| 1/19/80 | **86** | 3 | 17  With You I'm Born Again............................. | *4* | Motown 1477 |
| | | | **BILLY PRESTON & SYREETA** | | |
| 6/28/80 | **72** | 7 | 18  One More Time For Love ............................. | *52* | Tamla 54312 |
| | | | **BILLY PRESTON & SYREETA** | | |
| 7/24/82 | **64** | 9 | 19  I'm Never Gonna Say Goodbye........................ | *88* | Motown 1625 |
| | | | **JIMMY PRESTON** | | |
| | | | Vocalist/alto saxophonist. | | |
| 4/09/49 | **4** | 8 | 1  **Hucklebuck Daddy**............................... | | Gotham 175 |
| | | | Best Seller #4 / Juke Box #4 | | |
| 9/17/49 | **6** | 2 | 2  **Rock The Joint**...................................... | | Gotham 188 |
| | | | Juke Box #6 / Best Seller #11 | | |
| 11/11/50 | **5** | 4 | 3  **Oh Babe** .................................................. | | Derby 748 |
| | | | Best Seller #5 | | |
| | | | vocal by Burnetta Evans | | |
| | | | **JOHNNY PRESTON** | | |
| | | | Born John Preston Courville on 8/18/39 in Port Arthur, Texas. Discovered by J.P. "Big Bopper" Richardson. | | |
| 1/04/60 | **3** | 13 | 1  **Running Bear** ......................................... | *1* | Mercury 71474 |
| | | | Indian sounds by the Big Bopper and George Jones; written by the Big Bopper (J.P. Richardson) | | |
| 5/02/60 | **15** | 6 | 2  Cradle Of Love............................................ | *7* | Mercury 71598 |
| | | | **PRETTY POISON** | | |
| | | | Five-piece Philadelphia dance band founded by Camden, New Jersey natives: Jade Starling (vocals) and Whey Cooler. | | |
| 10/27/84 | **82** | 4 | 1  Nightime................................................... | | Svengali 8403 |
| 9/26/87 | **13** | 19 | 2  Catch Me (I'm Falling) ................................ | *8* | Virgin 99416 |
| | | | from the film "Hiding Out" | | |
| 5/07/88 | **83** | 5 | 3  Nightime ................................................. [R] | *36* | Virgin 99350 |
| | | | remix of their 1984 hit | | |
| | | | **PRETTY TONY** | | |
| | | | Real name is Tony Butler. | | |
| 5/26/84 | **63** | 8 | 1  Fix It In The Mix ...................................., | | Music Spec. 1104 |
| | | | **ANDRE PREVIN - see DAVID ROSE** | | |
| | | | **RON PREYER** | | |
| 4/29/78 | **84** | 8 | 1  Baltimore ................................................. | | Shock 10 |
| | | | **LLOYD PRICE**  ★★**75**★★ | | |
| | | | Born on 3/9/33 in Kenner, Louisiana. Vocalist/pianist/composer. Own band in 1949. In US Army from 1953-56. Formed own record company, KRC, in 1957. Signed to ABC Records in 1958. Own label, Double-L, in the mid-60s. In later years, continued in production and booking agency work. | | |
| 5/17/52 | **1** ⁷ | 26 | 1  **Lawdy Miss Clawdy**................................... | | Specialty 428 |
| | | | Best Seller #1(7) / Juke Box #1(1) based on singing commercial; features Fats Domino on piano | | |
| 10/11/52 | **4** | 10 | 2  **Oooh, Oooh, Oooh**/ | | |
| | | | Juke Box #4 / Best Seller #5 | | |
| 10/11/52 | **5** | 4 | 3  **Restless Heart**......................................... | | Specialty 440 |
| | | | Juke Box #5 / Best Seller #8 | | |

| DEBUT DATE | PEAK POS | WKS CHR | ARTIST — Record Title | POP POS | Label & Number |
|---|---|---|---|---|---|
| | | | **LLOYD PRICE — Continued** | | |
| 1/31/53 | **8** | 2 | 4 **Tell Me Pretty Baby/** | | |
| | | | Juke Box #8 | | |
| 2/07/53 | **6** | 5 | 5 **Ain't It A Shame** ........................... | | Specialty 452 |
| | | | Juke Box #6 / Best Seller #7 | | |
| 12/05/53 | **4** | 4 | 6 **Ain't It A Shame** .......................... [R] | | Specialty 452 |
| | | | Juke Box #4 | | |
| 3/09/57 | **3** | 12 | 7 **Just Because**.............................. | 29 | ABC-Para. 9792 |
| | | | Juke Box #3 / Best Seller #4 / Jockey #8 | | |
| | | | originally released on KRC 587 | | |
| 12/15/58+ | **1**[4] | 19 | 8 **Stagger Lee** ............................... | 1 | ABC-Para. 9927 |
| | | | remake of Archibald's "Stack-A-Lee" | | |
| 3/23/59 | **4** | 8 | 9 **Where Were You (On Our Wedding Day)?** ........ | 23 | ABC-Para. 9997 |
| 5/18/59 | **1**[4] | 16 | 10 **Personality** ............................. | 2 | ABC-Para. 10018 |
| 8/17/59 | **1**[3] | 13 | 11 **I'm Gonna Get Married/** | 3 | |
| 10/05/59 | **15** | 4 | 12 Three Little Pigs ...................... | | ABC-Para. 10032 |
| 11/23/59 | **2**[2] | 13 | 13 **Come Into My Heart/** | 20 | |
| 11/23/59+ | **6** | 11 | 14 Wont'cha Come Home...................... | 43 | ABC-Para. 10062 |
| 2/15/60 | **3** | 12 | 15 **Lady Luck/** | 14 | |
| 5/02/60 | **26** | 2 | 16 Never Let Me Go ...................... | 82 | ABC-Para. 10075 |
| 5/02/60 | **16** | 3 | 17 No If's-No And's ...................... | 40 | ABC-Para. 10102 |
| 7/11/60 | **5** | 12 | 18 Question............................... | 19 | ABC-Para. 10123 |
| 10/19/63 | **11** | 6 | 19 Misty .................................. | 21 | Double-L 722 |
| 1/11/64 | **84** | 3 | 20 Billie Baby ........................... | Hot | Double-L 729 |
| 10/18/69 | **21** | 8 | 21 Bad Conditions ....................... | | Turntable 506 |
| 7/28/73 | **32** | 10 | 22 Trying To Slip (Away) ................. | | GSF 6904 |
| 8/07/76 | **99** | 2 | 23 What Did You Do With Your Love .......... | | LPG 111 |
| | | | **PRISCILLA PRICE** | | |
| 7/14/73 | **70** | 7 | 1 Funny................................. | | BASF 15151 |

## LOUIS PRIMA

Born on 12/7/11 in New Orleans. Vocalist/trumpeter/composer/leader. Worked with Red Nichols in 1932. First recorded for Bluebird in 1933. Own band in 1934. Film work in Los Angeles from 1936-39. Wrote "Sing Sing Sing" in 1936. Married to jazz-styled vocalist Dorothy "Keely" Smith (b: 3/9/32 in Norfolk, VA) from 1952-61. The popular Las Vegas duo was backed by Sam Butera & The Witnesses. Louis was the voice for the cartoon character King Louis in Disney's "Jungle Book", in 1969. Surgery for a brain tumor in 1975 left him in a coma until his death on 8/24/78.

| DEBUT DATE | PEAK POS | WKS CHR | ARTIST — Record Title | POP POS | Label & Number |
|---|---|---|---|---|---|
| 10/21/44 | **9** | 1 | 1 **I'll Walk Alone** .............................. | | Hit 7083 |
| | | | from the film "Follow The Boys" | | |
| 12/16/44+ | **9** | 3 | 2 **White Cliffs Of Dover** ...................... | | Hit 7109 |
| 1/13/45 | **10** | 1 | 3 **Robin Hood** ............................... | | Hit 7083 |
| 12/15/58 | **26** | 2 | 4 That Old Black Magic.................... | 18 | Capitol 4063 |
| | | | **LOUIS PRIMA & KEELY SMITH** | | |

## PRIME TIME

Los Angeles quartet formed in 1974 with Dale Hightower (lead, percussion), Jimmy Hamilton (keyboards), Maurice Hayes (bass, guitar) and Frankie Hamilton (drums). (drums).

| DEBUT DATE | PEAK POS | WKS CHR | ARTIST — Record Title | POP POS | Label & Number |
|---|---|---|---|---|---|
| 6/23/84 | **88** | 3 | 1 Love Talk .............................. | | Total Exp. 2402 |
| 9/01/84 | **21** | 16 | 2 I Owe It To Myself ...................... | | Total Exp. 2407 |

## PRINCE ★★44★★

Born Prince Roger Nelson on 6/7/58 in Minneapolis. Vocalist/multi-instrumentalist/ composer/producer/actor. Named for the Prince Roger Trio, led by his father. Self-taught musician - own band, Grand Central, in junior high school. Self-produced first album in 1978. Starred in the films "Purple Rain" (1984), "Under The Cherry Moon" (1986) and the concert film "Sign "O" The Times" (1987). Founded own label, Paisley Park. Prince's backing band, The Revolution, featured Lisa Coleman (keyboards), Wendy Melvoin (guitar - twin sister of The Family's vocalist, Susannah), Bobby Z (percussion), Matt "Dr." Fink (keyboards), Eric Leeds (saxophone) and Andre Cymone (bass, replaced by Brownmark in 1981). In 1986, Brownmark founded the band Mazarati (who also backed Prince); recorded solo in 1988. Leeds formed Madhouse in 1987. Coleman and Melvoin recorded as the duo, Wendy & Lisa, in 1988. Percussionist Sheila E. joined Prince's band in 1986.

| DEBUT DATE | PEAK POS | WKS CHR | ARTIST — Record Title | POP POS | Label & Number |
|---|---|---|---|---|---|
| 7/29/78 | **12** | 20 | 1 Soft And Wet ........................... | 92 | Warner 8619 |
| 12/23/78+ | **91** | 7 | 2 Just As Long As We're Together.................... | | Warner 8713 |
| 9/22/79 | **1**[2] | 23 | 3 ●I Wanna Be Your Lover .............................. | 11 | Warner 49050 |
| 2/09/80 | **13** | 15 | 4 Why You Wanna Treat Me So Bad? .................. | | Warner 49178 |
| 4/26/80 | **65** | 8 | 5 Still Waiting.............................. | | Warner 49226 |

| DEBUT DATE | PEAK POS | WKS CHR | ARTIST — Record Title | POP POS | Label & Number |
|---|---|---|---|---|---|
| | | | **PRINCE — Continued** | | |
| 10/04/80 | 5 | 18 | 6 Uptown.................................................. | *101* | Warner 49559 |
| 1/17/81 | 65 | 6 | 7 Dirty Mind | | Warner 49638 |
| 9/26/81 | 3 | 20 | 8 Controversy ......................................... | 70 | Warner 49808 |
| 1/23/82 | 9 | 16 | 9 Let's Work .......................................... | *104* | Warner 50002 |
| 10/16/82 | 4 | 19 | 10 1999 .................................................. | *12* | Warner 29896 |
| 3/12/83 | 15 | 17 | 11 Little Red Corvette .............................. | *6* | Warner 29746 |
| 9/24/83 | 18 | 15 | 12 Delirious ........................................... | *8* | Warner 29503 |
| 1/07/84 | 55 | 8 | 13 Let's Pretend We're Married/ | *52* | |
| | | 8 | 14    Irresistible Bitch .......................... | | Warner 29548 |
| 6/09/84 | 1[8] | 20 | 15▲When Doves Cry ................................ | *1* | Warner 29286 |
| | | | **PRINCE & THE REVOLUTION:** | | |
| 8/11/84 | 1[1] | 17 | 16●Let's Go Crazy .................................. | *1* | Warner 29216 |
| 10/13/84 | 4 | 14 | 17●Purple Rain ...................................... | *2* | Warner 29174 |
| 12/22/84+ | 11 | 11 | 18 I Would Die 4 U .................................. | *8* | Warner 29121 |
| 2/23/85 | 40 | 9 | 19 Take Me With U ................................. | *25* | Warner 29079 |
| | | |    female vocals by Apollonia;<br>   above 5: from his semi-autobiographical film "Purple Rain" | | |
| 5/25/85 | 3 | 14 | 20 Raspberry Beret ................................. | *2* | Paisley P. 28972 |
| 8/03/85 | 8 | 13 | 21 Pop Life ............................................ | *7* | Paisley P. 28998 |
| 11/02/85 | 35 | 8 | 22 America ............................................. | *46* | Paisley P. 28999 |
| 3/01/86 | 1[4] | 17 | 23●Kiss ................................................. | *1* | Paisley P. 28751 |
| 5/31/86 | 15 | 12 | 24 Mountains ......................................... | *23* | Paisley P. 28711 |
| 7/19/86 | 18 | 12 | 25 Anotherloverholenyohead........................ | *63* | Paisley P. 28620 |
| | | |    above 3: from the film "Under The Cherry Moon" | | |
| | | | **PRINCE:** | | |
| 3/07/87 | 1[3] | 14 | 26 Sign 'O' The Times ............................. | *3* | Paisley P. 28399 |
| 5/30/87 | 12 | 12 | 27 If I Was Your Girlfriend ....................... | *67* | Paisley P. 28334 |
| 8/01/87 | 11 | 14 | 28 U Got The Look ................................. | *2* | Paisley P. 28289 |
| | | |    backing vocals by Sheena Easton | | |
| 12/12/87+ | 14 | 14 | 29 Hot Thing ......................................... | *63* | Paisley P. 28288 |
| | | |    flip side of his Hot 100 hit "I Could Never Take The Place Of Your<br>   Man"; above 4: from the concert film "Sign "O" The Times" | | |
| 4/30/88 | 3 | 14 | 30 Alphabet St. ...................................... | *8* | Paisley P. 27900 |
| | | |    all of above: written & produced by Prince | | |
| | | | **PRINCE BUSTER** | | |
| | | |    Born Buster Campbell on 5/24/38 in Kingston, Jamaica. Owned ten record stores<br>   in the Caribbean. | | |
| 2/04/67 | 17 | 6 | 1 Ten Commandments ................................... [S] | *81* | Philips 40427 |
| | | | **PRINCE HAROLD** | | |
| | | |    Vocalist from Lexington, Kentucky. Raised in New York. Sang in All-City Choir<br>   while attending Jamaica High School. | | |
| 11/26/66 | 25 | 6 | 1 Forget About Me ................................... | *114* | Mercury 72621 |
| | | | **PRINCE LA LA** | | |
| | | |    Born Lawrence Nelson. Singer/guitarist, from New Orleans. Brother of guitarist<br>   Walter "Papoose" Nelson, cousin of prolific New Orleans session musicians David<br>   and Melvin Lastie. | | |
| 9/25/61 | 28 | 4 | 1 She Put The Hurt On Me.............................. | *119* | A.F.O. 301 |
| | | | **PRINCESS** | | |
| 10/05/85 | 20 | 20 | 1 Say I'm Your Number One............................. | | Next Plat. 50035 |
| 1/25/86 | 41 | 11 | 2 After The Love Has Gone............................. | | Next Plat. 50037 |
| 8/15/87 | 78 | 4 | 3 Red Hot ............................................ | | Polydor 885885 |
| | | | **JEROME "SECRET WEAPON" PRISTER** | | |
| 6/04/88 | 89 | 4 | 1 Say You'll Be...................................... | | Tuff City 12008 |
| | | | **PROCESS & THE DOO RAGS** | | |
| | | |    Vocal group from Buffalo, New York, created by Rick James. Consisted of leader<br>   James "Bunty" Hawkins, Stacy Lattimore, Henry "Gumps" Graham, Dennis "Shorty"<br>   Andrews and Michael "Smoothie" Gibson. Hawkins was a back-up singer for Rick James. | | |
| 3/23/85 | 73 | 6 | 1 Stomp And Shout................................... | | Columbia 04825 |
| 5/02/87 | 80 | 3 | 2 I Promise To Remember ........................... | | Columbia 6612 |
| 8/29/87 | 71 | 6 | 3 Call Me Up ........................................ | | Columbia 07204 |

| DEBUT DATE | PEAK POS | WKS CHR | ARTIST — Record Title | POP POS | Label & Number |
|---|---|---|---|---|---|
| | | | **PROCOL HARUM** | | |
| | | | British rock group led by Gary Brooker (vocals/piano) & Robin Trower (guitar). | | |
| 7/22/67 | **22** | 8 | 1 A Whiter Shade Of Pale | 5 | Deram 7507 |
| | | | **PROFESSOR FUNK & HIS EIGHTH STREET FUNK BAND** | | |
| 12/15/73 | **89** | 4 | 1 Love Is Such A Good Thing | | Roxbury 0076 |
| | | | **PROFESSOR LONGHAIR - see ROY BYRD** | | |
| | | | **THE PROFILES** | | |
| 9/28/68 | **30** | 5 | 1 If I Didn't Love You | | Duo 7449 |
| 4/26/69 | **43** | 2 | 2 Got To Be Love (Something Stupid) | | Bamboo 104 |
| | | | **PROJECT FUTURE** | | |
| 9/24/83 | **89** | 3 | 1 Ray-Gun-Omics | | Capitol 8555 |
| | | | **PROPHECY** | | |
| 5/17/75 | **74** | 5 | 1 What Ever's Your Sign - Part I (You Got To Be Mine) | | Mainstream 5565 |
| 8/23/75 | **97** | 3 | 2 Betcha Can't Guess My Sign | | Mainstream 5569 |
| | | | **ARTHUR PRYSOCK** | | |
| | | | Born on 1/2/29 in Spartanburg, South Carolina. First recorded with Buddy Johnson on Decca in 1944. Solo since 1952. Very popular night club act, frequently appearing with his brother, saxophonist Wilbert "Red" Prysock. Also see Buddy Johnson. | | |
| 2/02/52 | **5** | 5 | 1 **I Didn't Sleep A Wink Last Night** | | Decca 27871 |
| | | | Best Seller #5 with the Sy Oliver Orchestra | | |
| 5/30/60 | **19** | 2 | 2 The Very Thought Of You | | Old Town 1079 |
| 8/14/61 | **30** | 2 | 3 One More Time | | Old Town 1106 |
| 7/10/65 | **11** | 11 | 4 It's Too Late, Baby Too Late | 56 | Old Town 1183 |
| 9/08/73 | **36** | 12 | 5 In The Rain | 110 | Old Town 100 |
| 11/06/76+ | **10** | 18 | 6 **When Love Is New** | 64 | Old Town 1000 |
| 3/12/77 | **43** | 9 | 7 I Wantcha Baby | | Old Town 1001 |
| 8/20/77 | **33** | 12 | 8 You Can Do It | | Old Town 1002 |
| | | | **PUBLIC ENEMY** | | |
| | | | Rap group led by Chuck D. Includes MC Flavor-Flave (William Drayton) and deejay Terminator X (Norman Rogers). | | |
| 2/06/88 | **56** | 10 | 1 Bring The Noise | | Def Jam 07491 |
| | | | **PULSE** | | |
| 4/17/82 | **96** | 2 | 1 Don't Stop The Magic | | Silver Cloud 5 |
| | | | **PUMPKIN & THE PROFILE ALL-STARS** | | |
| 6/30/84 | **57** | 7 | 1 Here Comes That Beat! | | Profile 5047 |
| | | | featuring: Dr. Jeckyll & Mr. Hyde, Fresh 3 M.C.'s, Greg G & Mr. Troy (Disco 4), George "Galaxy" Llado and Fly Ty-rone | | |
| | | | **PRETTY PURDIE** | | |
| | | | Born Bernard Purdie on 6/11/39 in Elkton, MD. Highly regarded session drummer. | | |
| 10/07/67 | **48** | 2 | 1 Funky Donkey [I] | 87 | Date 1568 |
| 3/02/68 | **45** | 2 | 2 Modern Jive [I] | | Date 1587 |
| | | | **PURE ENERGY** | | |
| | | | Curtis and Lisa Hudson. | | |
| 7/26/80 | **93** | 4 | 1 Party On | | Prism 311 |
| | | | **JAMES & BOBBY PURIFY** | | |
| | | | Duo of cousins James Purify (b: 5/12/44, Pensacola, FL) and Robert Lee Dickey (b: 9/2/39, Tallahassee, FL). Dickey left, late 1960's. Purify worked as solo until 1974, when Ben Moore became "Bobby Purify". | | |
| 9/24/66 | **5** | 17 | 1 **I'm Your Puppet** | 6 | Bell 648 |
| 2/11/67 | **27** | 7 | 2 Wish You Didn't Have To Go | 38 | Bell 660 |
| 5/13/67 | **15** | 7 | 3 Shake A Tail Feather | 25 | Bell 669 |
| 8/05/67 | **23** | 5 | 4 I Take What I Want | 41 | Bell 680 |
| 10/07/67 | **18** | 8 | 5 Let Love Come Between Us | 23 | Bell 685 |
| 2/03/68 | **38** | 4 | 6 Do Unto Me | 73 | Bell 700 |
| 5/18/68 | **42** | 2 | 7 I Can Remember | 51 | Bell 721 |
| 8/31/68 | **31** | 5 | 8 Help Yourself (To All Of My Lovin') | 94 | Bell 735 |

| DEBUT DATE | PEAK POS | WKS CHR | ARTIST — Record Title | POP POS | Label & Number |
|---|---|---|---|---|---|
| | | | **JAMES & BOBBY PURIFY — Continued** | | |
| 12/28/68+ | 47 | 4 | 9 Untie Me............................................ | | Bell 751 |
| 11/23/74+ | 30 | 12 | 10 Do Your Thing...................................... | *101* | Casablanca 812 |
| | | | **BILL PURSELL** | | |
| | | | Pianist from Tulare, California. Appeared with the Nashville Symphony Orchestra. Taught musical composition at Vanderbilt University. | | |
| 4/06/63 | 20 | 2 | 1 Our Winter Love ............................... [I] | 9 | Columbia 42619 |

# Q

| DEBUT DATE | PEAK POS | WKS CHR | ARTIST — Record Title | POP POS | Label & Number |
|---|---|---|---|---|---|
| | | | **QUADRANT SIX** | | |
| 2/05/83 | 72 | 9 | 1 Body Mechanic ............................... | | Atlantic 89892 |
| | | | **QUADROPHONICS** | | |
| 8/17/74 | 51 | 9 | 1 Betcha If You Check It Out .................... | | Warner 7826 |
| | | | **SIDNEY JOE QUALIS** | | |
| | | | Vocalist from Jacknash, Arkansas; aka: Sydney Qualls. | | |
| 3/02/74 | 65 | 10 | 1 Where The Lillies Grow ...................... | | Dakar 4530 |
| 10/19/74 | 47 | 5 | 2 How Can You Say Goodbye/ | | |
| | | 7 | 3 I Enjoy Loving You............................. | | Dakar 4537 |
| | | | **JOE QUARTERMAN** | | |
| 11/25/72+ | 30 | 8 | 1 (I Got) So Much Trouble In My Mind ................ | | GSF 6879 |
| 9/15/73 | 96 | 3 | 2 This Girl Of Mine (She's Good To Me) ............. | | GSF 6903 |
| 1/19/74 | 82 | 6 | 3 Thanks Dad, Pt. 1 ............................. | | GSF 6911 |
| 1/04/75 | 59 | 8 | 4 Get Down Baby, Pt. 1 .......................... | | Mercury 73637 |
| | | | **JOE QUARTERMAN & Free Soul** | | |
| | | | **QUARTZ** | | |
| 11/18/78+ | 52 | 11 | 1 Beyond The Clouds ......................... [I] | | Marlin 3328 |
| | | | **QUAZAR** | | |
| | | | Band from New Jersey. Consisted of Kevin Goins, Harvey Banks, Monica Peteres, Darryl "Major D" Dixon, Gregory Fitz, Richard "Shiadi" Banks, Eugene "Moochie" Jackson, Jeffrey Adams, Darryl de Lomberto and Peachena. | | |
| 9/16/78 | 11 | 18 | 1 Funk 'n' Roll (Dancin' In The "Funkshine") ........ | | Arista 0349 |
| | | | **QUEEN** | | |
| | | | Rock group formed in England in 1972. Consisted of Freddie Mercury (vocals), Brian May (guitar), John Deacon (bass) and Roger Taylor (drums). | | |
| 8/23/80 | 2³ | 18 | 1▲Another One Bites The Dust ....................... | *1* | Elektra 47031 |
| 5/15/82 | 30 | 10 | 2 Body Language............................... | *11* | Elektra 47452 |
| | | | **THE QUICK** | | |
| 9/19/81 | 60 | 9 | 1 Zulu ......................................... | | Pavillion 02455 |
| | | | **THE QUICKEST WAY OUT** | | |
| 12/27/75+ | 67 | 9 | 1 Thank You Baby For Loving Me .................... | | Warner 0103 |
| | | | **QUIET ELEGANCE** | | |
| | | | Trio of Frankie Gearing (lead), Mildred Vaney and Lois Reeves. Gearing and Vaney had been in The Glories. Reeves, sister of Martha Reeves, had been in The Vandellas. | | |
| 7/14/73 | 54 | 8 | 1 You've Got My Message ...................... | | Hi 2245 |
| | | | also listed on chart as "You've Got My Mind Messed Up" (4 weeks) and "You've Got My Mind Made Up" (1 week) | | |
| | | | **THE QUIN-TONES** | | |
| | | | Group from York, Pennsylvania, consisting of Roberta Haymon (lead), Ronnie Scott, Phyllis Carr, Caroline Holmes, Kenneth Sexton and Eunice Cristi. | | |
| 9/22/58 | 5 | 7 | 1 **Down The Aisle Of Love**............................. | *18* | Hunt 321 |
| | | | Jockey #5 / Best Seller #6 originally released on Red Top 108 | | |
| | | | **QUINELLA** | | |
| 1/10/81 | 78 | 5 | 1 Your Place Or Mine........................... | | Becket 3 |

# R

| DEBUT DATE | PEAK POS | WKS CHR | ARTIST — Record Title | POP POS | Label & Number |
|---|---|---|---|---|---|
| | | | **RACE** | | |
| 12/17/83+ | 54 | 9 | 1 What Is Race............................................... | | Ocean Fr. 2003 |
| | | | **RADIANCE** | | |
| | | | Group from Oakland, California. Consisted of Kenneth Taylor and Frank Funchess (keyboards), Byron Gipson (guitar), Eric Young (bass), Leonard Polk (drums) and vocalists Tyrone Tiggs and Kenneth Mitchell. | | |
| 7/20/85 | 81 | 6 | 1 All Night..................................................... | | Warner 28981 |
| | | | **THE RADIANTS** | | |
| | | | Group formed at The Greater Harvest Baptist Church in Chicago in 1960. Consisted of Maurice McAlister (lead), Jerome Brooks and Green "Mac" McLauren (tenors), Wallace Sampson (baritone) and Elzie Butler (bass). Recorded as trio with McAlister, Sampson and Leonard Caston, Jr. in 1964. | | |
| 1/30/65 | 16 | 3 | 1 Voice Your Choice..................................... | 51 | Chess 1904 |
| 5/01/65 | 14 | 6 | 2 It Ain't No Big Thing................................. | 91 | Chess 1925 |
| 4/01/67 | 47 | 2 | 3 Feel Kind Of Bad...................................... | | Chess 1986 |
| 4/20/68 | 35 | 7 | 4 Hold On................................................... | 68 | Chess 2037 |
| | | | **MARK RADICE** | | |
| | | | Born on 11/23/57 in Newark, New Jersey. Pianist/composer. First recorded at age 9. Toured with Donovan and Aerosmith. | | |
| 8/14/76 | 55 | 11 | 1 If You Can't Beat 'Em, Join 'Em..................... | 110 | United Art. 840 |
| | | | **FONDA RAE** | | |
| | | | Also see Wish. | | |
| 8/07/82 | 75 | 6 | 1 Over Like A Fat Rat.................................... | | Vanguard 35230 |
| 12/22/84+ | 70 | 9 | 2 Touch Me (All Night Long) ......................... | | Personal 1001 |
| | | | WISH featuring FONDA RAE | | |
| | | | **THE RAELETTS** | | |
| | | | Originally formed as The Cookies, later became the back-up group for Ray Charles. From 1967-69, group included Merry Clayton (lead), Clydie King, Minnie Riperton, Gwendolyn Berry and Alexandra Brown. In 1970, the group consisted of Mabel John, Susaye Green, Vernita Amoss and Estella Yarbrough. | | |
| 4/08/67 | 24 | 7 | 1 One Hurt Deserves Another ........................ | 76 | Tangerine 972 |
| 5/11/68 | 23 | 8 | 2 I'm Gett'n Long Alright .............................. | | Tangerine 984 |
| | | | shown as: THE RAELETTES | | |
| 10/26/68 | 47 | 2 | 3 I Want To Thank You.................................. | | Tangerine 986 |
| 5/09/70 | 30 | 6 | 4 I Want To (Do Everything For You) ................. | 96 | Tangerine 1006 |
| 12/19/70+ | 40 | 7 | 5 Bad Water ............................................... | 58 | Tangerine 1014 |
| | | | **THE RAINDROPS** | | |
| | | | Songwriting team of Ellie Greenwich (b: 10/23/40) and husband Jeff Barry (b: 4/3/38). Barry wrote "Tell Laura I Love Her"; team wrote "Be My Baby", "Da Doo Ron Ron", "Chapel Of Love", "River Deep-Mountain High", "Hanky Panky", "Leader Of The Pack", and many others. | | |
| 6/08/63 | 25 | 2 | 1 What A Guy ............................................. | 41 | Jubilee 5444 |
| 9/07/63 | 27 | 3 | 2 The Kind Of Boy You Can't Forget ................. | 17 | Jubilee 5455 |
| 3/14/64 | 62 | 7 | 3 Book Of Love............................................ | Hot | Jubilee 5469 |
| | | | **RAKE** | | |
| | | | Rake is Keith Rose. | | |
| 8/06/83 | 63 | 7 | 1 Street Justice........................................... | | Profile 7024 |
| | | | **SHERYL LEE RALPH** | | |
| | | | Singer/actress born in 1954 in New York. Miss Black Teen-Age New York in 1973. Medical student at Rutgers University. Named Best College Actress in 1974. Performed on USO tour of the Far East. Appeared in the film "A Piece Of The Action". Performed in the Broadway musical "Dreamgirls" and on the TV shows "Search For Tomorrow", "The Jeffersons", "Good Times" and "Wonder Woman". | | |
| 4/02/83 | 50 | 6 | 1 When I First Saw You ................................ | | Geffen 29734 |
| | | | BEN HARNEY & SHERYL LEE RALPH from the original Broadway cast "Dreamgirls" | | |
| 3/09/85 | 84 | 4 | 2 You're So Romantic.................................... | | New York 7001 |
| | | | **RAMRODS** | | |
| | | | Studio group featuring tenor saxophonist King Curtis. | | |
| 7/08/72 | 41 | 5 | 1 Soul Train, Pts. 1 & 2 .................................. [I] originally released in 1962 on Enjoy 1010 as "Hot Potato" | | Rampage 1000 |

| DEBUT DATE | PEAK POS | WKS CHR | ARTIST — Record Title | POP POS | Label & Number |
|---|---|---|---|---|---|
| | | | **THE RAN-DELLS** | | |
| | | | Cousins Steve Rappaport and John Spirt from Villas, New Jersey. | | |
| 8/24/63 | **27** | 2 | 1 Martian Hop ........................................ [N] | *16* | Chairman 4403 |
| | | | **BOOTS RANDOLPH** | | |
| | | | Born Homer Louis Randolph III in Paducah, Kentucky. Saxophone virtuoso. Did prolific session work in Nashville. | | |
| 3/09/63 | **29** | 2 | 1 Yakety Sax ........................................ [I] | *35* | Monument 804 |
| | | | **RANDY & THE RAINBOWS** | | |
| | | | Group from Queens, New York, originally called Jr. And The Counts. Consisted of Dominick "Randy" Safuto (lead), Frank Safuto, Mike and Sal Zero, and Ken Arcipowski. Disbanded in 1966; re-formed in 1982. Safuto brothers recorded for Goldisc as the Dialtones in 1960. | | |
| 9/14/63 | **18** | 3 | 1 Denise ........................................ | *10* | Rust 5059 |
| | | | **RAPPIN' DUKE** | | |
| 8/16/86 | **47** | 7 | 1 Duke Is Back ........................................ | | Tommy Boy 881 |
| | | | **RARE EARTH** | | |
| | | | Rock group from Detroit. Nucleus consisted of Gil Bridges (saxophone, flute), John Persh (trombone, bass) and Pete Rivera (drums). Worked as Sunliners in the 60s. Added Ed Guzman (percussion), in 1970, and Ray Monette (replaced Rob Richards - guitar). Mark Olson replaced Kenneth James (keyboards) in 1971. Many changes thereafter. | | |
| 5/02/70 | **20** | 5 | 1 Get Ready ........................................ | *4* | Rare Earth 5012 |
| 8/22/70 | **20** | 9 | 2 (I Know) I'm Losing You ........................................ | *7* | Rare Earth 5017 |
| 2/06/71 | **48** | 2 | 3 Born To Wander ........................................ | *17* | Rare Earth 5021 |
| 9/04/71 | **30** | 5 | 4 I Just Want To Celebrate ........................................ | *7* | Rare Earth 5031 |
| 12/18/71+ | **40** | 6 | 5 Hey Big Brother ........................................ | *19* | Rare Earth 5038 |
| 10/06/73 | **95** | 3 | 6 Hum Along And Dance ........................................ | *110* | Rare Earth 5054 |
| | | | **RARE ESSENCE** | | |
| | | | Male vocal group led by Reginald Boyd, Jr. | | |
| 3/27/82 | **75** | 6 | 1 Body Moves ........................................ | | Fantasy 205 |
| | | | **THE RASCALS** | | |
| | | | Blue-eyed soul/pop quartet formed in New York City in 1964. Consisted of Felix Cavaliere, Dino Danelli, Eddie Brigati and Gene Cornish. All except Danelli had been in Joey Dee's Starliters. Brigati and Cornish left in 1971, replaced by Robert Popwell, Buzzy Feiten and Ann Sutton. Group disbanded in 1972. Cavaliere, Cornish and Danelli reunited in June of 1988. | | |
| | | | **THE YOUNG RASCALS:** | | |
| 3/04/67 | **33** | 7 | 1 I've Been Lonely Too Long ........................................ | *16* | Atlantic 2377 |
| 5/13/67 | **3** | 11 | 2●Groovin' ........................................ | *1* | Atlantic 2401 |
| | | | **THE RASCALS:** | | |
| 5/25/68 | **36** | 6 | 3●A Beautiful Morning ........................................ | *3* | Atlantic 2493 |
| 8/10/68 | **14** | 9 | 4●People Got To Be Free ........................................ | *1* | Atlantic 2537 |
| 1/11/69 | **36** | 2 | 5 A Ray Of Hope ........................................ | *24* | Atlantic 2584 |
| | | | all of above: written by Cavaliere & Brigati | | |
| | | | **THE RAVENS** | | |
| | | | Group formed in New York City in 1945. Consisted of Ollie Jones (tenor), Leonard Puzey (tenor), Warren Suttles (baritone) and Jimmy "Ricky" Ricks (bass). First recorded for Hub in 1946. Jones replaced by Maithe Marshall in 1946. Bass voice of Ricks contrasted with the high tenor of Marshall gave group a unique sound, often imitated by other groups. Many personnel changes culminated with Ricks' departure for a solo career in 1956. | | |
| 1/10/48 | **5** | 12 | 1 **Write Me A Letter** ........................................ | *24* | National 9038 |
| | | | Juke Box #5 / Best Seller #10 | | |
| 2/07/48 | **10** | 1 | 2 **Ol' Man River** ........................................ | | National 9035 |
| 7/03/48 | **5** | 11 | 3 **Send For Me If You Need Me** ........................................ | | National 9045 |
| | | | Best Seller #5 / Juke Box #7 | | |
| 8/21/48 | **8** | 3 | 4 **Bye Bye Baby Blues** ........................................ | | King 4234 |
| | | | Best Seller #8 / Juke Box #13 | | |
| 11/06/48 | **13** | 1 | 5 **Be On Your Merry Way/** | | |
| | | | Juke Box #13 | | |
| 11/20/48 | **11** | 1 | 6 **It's Too Soon To Know** ........................................ | | National 9056 |
| | | | Best Seller #11 | | |
| 12/25/48 | **8** | 1 | 7 **Silent Night/** [X] | | |
| | | | Juke Box #8 | | |
| 1/08/49 | **9** | 1 | 8 **White Christmas** ........................................ [X] | | National 9063 |
| | | | Juke Box #9 / Best Seller #14 | | |

| DEBUT DATE | PEAK POS | WKS CHR | ARTIST — Record Title | POP POS | Label & Number |
|---|---|---|---|---|---|
| | | | **THE RAVENS — Continued** | | |
| 6/11/49 | **8** | 1 | 9 Ricky's Blues ...................................... | | National 9073 |
| | | | Juke Box #8 / Best Seller #13 | | |
| 2/18/50 | **9** | 2 | 10 **Don't Have To Ride No More** ...................... | | National 9101 |
| | | | Best Seller #9 / Juke Box #13 | | |
| | | | all of above: with the Howard Biggs Orchestra | | |
| 9/20/52 | **4** | 8 | 11 **Rock Me All Night Long**............................. | | Mercury 8291 |
| | | | Juke Box #4 / Best Seller #8 | | |
| | | | **RAW SILK** | | |
| 9/25/82 | **65** | 7 | 1 Do It To The Music ..................................... | | West End 22148 |
| | | | **LOU RAWLS**  ★★96★★ | | |
| | | | Born on 12/1/35 in Chicago. Vocalist/actor. With gospel groups the Teenage Kings Of Harmony, Holy Wonders, and Chosen Gospel Singers. With Pilgrim Travelers gospel group from 1957-59. Recorded for Capitol in 1961. Summer replacement TV show "Lou Rawls & The Golddiggers" in 1969. In the films "Angel Angel, Down We Go" and "Believe In Me". Voice of many Budweiser beer ads. Also see Sam Cooke and the Philadelphia International All Stars. | | |
| 7/23/66 | **33** | 2 | 1 The Shadow Of Your Smile........................... | | Capitol 5655 |
| 9/03/66 | **1**¹ | 16 | 2 **Love Is A Hurtin' Thing** ........................... | 13 | Capitol 5709 |
| 12/17/66+ | **35** | 5 | 3 You Can Bring Me All Your Heartaches ........... | 55 | Capitol 5790 |
| 4/15/67 | **3** | 13 | 4 **Dead End Street** .................................... | 29 | Capitol 5869 |
| 7/22/67 | **25** | 5 | 5 Show Business........................................ | 45 | Capitol 5941 |
| 7/26/69 | **3** | 15 | 6 **Your Good Thing (Is About To End)** .............. | 18 | Capitol 2550 |
| 12/20/69 | **33** | 3 | 7 I Can't Make It Alone .............................. | 63 | Capitol 2668 |
| 3/28/70 | **32** | 5 | 8 You've Made Me So Very Happy .................. | 95 | Capitol 2734 |
| 8/08/70 | **45** | 3 | 9 Bring It On Home ................................... | 96 | Capitol 2856 |
| | | | all of above: produced by David Axelrod | | |
| 8/28/71 | **17** | 13 | 10 A Natural Man ...................................... | 17 | MGM 14262 |
| 3/04/72 | **44** | 3 | 11 His Song Shall Be Sung .......................... | 105 | MGM 14349 |
| 10/19/74 | **81** | 7 | 12 She's Gone........................................... | | Bell 45608 |
| | | | written by Daryl Hall and John Oates | | |
| 5/15/76 | **1**² | 22 | 13● **You'll Never Find Another Love Like Mine** ..... | 2 | Phil. Int. 3592 |
| 10/16/76 | **19** | 13 | 14 Groovy People/ | 64 | |
| 2/12/77 | **74** | 4 | 15 This Song Will Last Forever ...................... | | Phil. Int. 3604 |
| 5/28/77 | **8** | 18 | 16 **See You When I Git There**........................ | 66 | Phil. Int. 3623 |
| 12/17/77+ | **21** | 18 | 17 Lady Love ............................................ | 24 | Phil. Int. 3634 |
| 5/20/78 | **32** | 11 | 18 One Life To Live .................................... | | Phil. Int. 3643 |
| 8/19/78 | **76** | 3 | 19 There Will Be Love ................................ | | Phil. Int. 3653 |
| 4/21/79 | **11** | 18 | 20 Let Me Be Good To You ........................... | | Phil. Int. 3684 |
| 12/22/79+ | **26** | 17 | 21 Sit Down And Talk To Me ........................ | | Phil. Int. 3738 |
| 4/26/80 | **57** | 7 | 22 Ain't That Loving You (For More Reasons Than One) ......................................... | | Phil. Int. 3102 |
| 10/11/80 | **37** | 12 | 23 I Go Crazy ........................................... | | Phil. Int. 3114 |
| 7/17/82 | **54** | 10 | 24 Will You Kiss Me One More Time ................ | | Epic 02999 |
| 3/26/83 | **60** | 8 | 25 Wind Beneath My Wings......................... | 65 | Epic 03758 |
| 8/11/84 | **67** | 8 | 26 All Time Lover ...................................... | | Epic 04550 |
| 12/07/85 | **71** | 9 | 27 Learn To Love Again .............................. | | Epic 05714 |
| | | | duet with Tata Vega | | |
| 11/28/87+ | **28** | 16 | 28 I Wish You Belonged To Me.......................... | | Gamble & H. 310 |
| | | | **THE RAY-O-VACS** | | |
| | | | New York group formed in the late 40s. First recorded for Coleman in 1948. Vocals by Lester Harris (real name: Harry Lester - died of pneumonia in March of 1953 [33]). Group had unique "stop-time" rhythm" delivery. Harris left in 1952 for a solo career, replaced by Herb Milliner. Active until the mid-50s. | | |
| 1/22/49 | **8** | 2 | 1 I'll Always Be In Love With You ................... | | Savoy 681 |
| | | | Best Seller #8 / Juke Box #15 | | |
| 10/21/50 | **5** | 8 | 2 Besame Mucho (Kiss Me Much)/ | | |
| | | | Best Seller #5 / Juke Box #5 | | |
| 11/25/50 | **8** | 1 | 3 **You Gotta Love Me Baby Too** ..................... | | Decca 48162 |
| | | | Juke Box #8 | | |
| | | | **RAY, GOODMAN & BROWN** | | |
| | | | Group consisting of Harry Ray (tenor), Al Goodman (bass) and Billy Brown (falsetto). Formerly known as The Moments. | | |
| 11/24/79+ | **1**¹ | 23 | 1● **Special Lady** .............................................. | 5 | Polydor 2033 |
| 3/29/80 | **14** | 13 | 2 Inside Of You ........................................ | 76 | Polydor 2077 |

| DEBUT DATE | PEAK POS | WKS CHR | ARTIST — Record Title | POP POS | Label & Number |
|---|---|---|---|---|---|
| | | | **RAY, GOODMAN & BROWN — Continued** | | |
| 8/30/80 | **31** | 10 | 3 My Prayer............................................... | *47* | Polydor 2116 |
| 11/01/80 | **16** | 16 | 4 Happy Anniversary................................. | | Polydor 2135 |
| 3/28/81 | **67** | 5 | 5 Shoestrings............................................ | | Polydor 2159 |
| 12/05/81+ | **30** | 14 | 6 How Can Love So Right (Be So Wrong) ............ | | Polydor 2191 |
| 1/05/85 | **59** | 10 | 7 Who's Gonna Make The First Move.................. | | Panoramic 201 |
| 11/29/86+ | **8** | 18 | 8 **Take It To The Limit** ................................. | | EMI America 8365 |
| 4/04/87 | **34** | 11 | 9 Celebrate Our Love.................................. | | EMI America 8378 |
| | | | **HARRY RAY**<br>Born on 12/15/46 in Hackensack, New Jersey. Member of Ray, Goodman & Brown and The Moments. | | |
| 11/06/82 | **37** | 12 | 1 Sweet Baby ................................................ | | Sugar Hill 789 |
| | | | **JAMES RAY**<br>Born James Ray Raymond in 1941, in Washington DC. | | |
| 1/13/62 | **10** | 7 | 1 **If You Gotta Make A Fool Of Somebody**......... | *22* | Caprice 110 |
| | | | with the Hutch Davie Orchestra | | |
| | | | **JOHNNIE RAY**<br>Born on 1/10/27 in Dallas, Oregon. Has worn hearing aid since age 14. First recorded for Okeh in 1951. Famous for emotion-packed delivery, with R&B influences. Appeared in three films. Active into the 80s. Now lives in Hollywood. | | |
| 12/22/51+ | **1**[1] | 15 | 1 Cry/ | *1* |  |
| | | | Best Seller #1(1) / Juke Box #1(1)<br>reportedly sold over 2 million copies; Johnnie's trademark song | | |
| 2/23/52 | **6** | 4 | 2 **The Little White Cloud That Cried** ............. | *2* | Okeh 6840 |
| | | | Juke Box #6<br>above 2: with the Four Lads | | |
| | | | **RAYDIO - see RAY PARKER JR.** | | |
| | | | **THE RAYS**<br>Group formed in New York City in 1955. Consisted of Harold Miller (lead), Walter Ford & David Jones (tenors) and Harry James (baritone). First recorded for Chess in 1955. Jones had been in the Four Fellows. | | |
| 10/28/57 | **3** | 14 | 1 Silhouettes/ | *3* |  |
| | | | Best Seller #3 / Jockey #3 | | |
| | | 1 | 2 Daddy Cool ................................................ | | Cameo 117 |
| | | | Best Seller flip | | |
| | | | **THE RAYS**<br>Female trio. | | |
| 5/28/88 | **83** | 6 | 1 Be Alone Tonight ....................................... | | EMI-Man. 50129 |
| | | | from the film "School Daze" | | |
| | | | **RCR**<br>Rock trio: Donna and Sandra Rhodes and Charles Chalmers. | | |
| 7/12/80 | **89** | 7 | 1 Give It To You ........................................... | *108* | Radio 712 |
| | | | **READY FOR THE WORLD**<br>Group from Flint, Michigan, formed in 1982. Consisted of Melvin Riley, Jr. (lead), Gordon Strozier, Gregory Potts, Willie Triplett, John Eaton and Gerald Valentine. First recorded for own Blue Lake label. | | |
| 12/15/84+ | **6** | 22 | 1 **Tonight** ..................................................... | *103* | MCA 52507 |
| | | | originally released on Blue Lake | | |
| 4/20/85 | **6** | 16 | 2 **Deep Inside Your Love**............................... | | MCA 52561 |
| 7/20/85 | **1**[2] | 19 | 3 **Oh Sheila**.................................................. | *1* | MCA 52636 |
| 11/16/85+ | **4** | 18 | 4 **Digital Display** ........................................ | *21* | MCA 52734 |
| 3/15/86 | **57** | 8 | 5 Slide Over ................................................. | | MCA 52713 |
| 6/07/86 | **82** | 3 | 6 Ceramic Girl............................................. | | MCA 23618 |
| 10/11/86 | **1**[2] | 22 | 7 **Love You Down** ........................................ | *9* | MCA 52947 |
| 2/07/87 | **23** | 12 | 8 Mary Goes 'Round ..................................... | | MCA 53004 |
| 6/06/87 | **54** | 7 | 9 Long Time Coming ..................................... | | MCA 53099 |
| | | | **THE REAL ROXANNE with HITMAN HOWIE TEE** | | |
| 8/17/85 | **64** | 8 | 1 Romeo Part 1 & Part 2 ................................ | | Select 62260 |
| 6/21/86 | **24** | 13 | 2 Bang Zoom (Let's Go-Go)/ | | |
| | | 12 | 3 Howie's Teed Off......................................... | | Select 62269 |

| DEBUT DATE | PEAK POS | WKS CHR | ARTIST — Record Title | POP POS | Label & Number |
|---|---|---|---|---|---|
| | | | **THE REAL THING** | | |
| | | | Group from Liverpool, England, formed in 1970. Consisted of Chris Amoo, Ray Lake, Dave Smith and Kenny Davis. Davis replaced by Eddie Amoo in the early 70s. In film "The Stud", in 1978. | | |
| 7/24/76 | **28** | 11 | 1 You To Me Are Everything ............................ | *64* | United Art. 833 |
| | | | **REAL TO REEL** | | |
| | | | Group formed by the Leslie brothers: Dominic (lead, guitar), Matthew (lead guitar), and Peter (guitar). Other members included Billy Smith, Daniel Morgan, Marques "Hami" Hair, and Isaias Gamboa. Produced by Leon Sylvers III. | | |
| 3/17/84 | **36** | 12 | 1 Love Me Like This...................................... | | Arista 9167 |
| | | | **PAULETTE REAVES** | | |
| 3/19/77 | **89** | 3 | 1 Your Real Good Thing's About To Come To An End ...................................................... | | Blue Cndl. 1518 |
| 1/21/78 | **88** | 6 | 2 Jazz Freak.............................................. | | Blue Cndl. 1526 |
| | | | **THE REBELS** | | |
| | | | Buffalo disc jockey Tom Shannon and producer Phil Todaro (Shan-Todd label) recruited the Buffalo group, The Rebels (aka: The Rockin' Rebels) to record Shannon's theme song "Wild Weekend". Consisted of twins Mickey & Jim Kipler, Paul Balon and Tom Gorman. Later Swan recordings, which were billed as The Rockin' Rebels, were by a different group. | | |
| 3/16/63 | **28** | 2 | 1 Wild Weekend ............................................ [I] | *8* | Swan 4125 |
| | | | originally released on Marlee 0094; recorded in 1959 | | |
| | | | **EUGENE RECORD** | | |
| | | | Born on 12/23/40 in Chicago. Singer/songwriter, formerly with The Chi-Lites. | | |
| 2/26/77 | **24** | 15 | 1 Laying Beside You...................................... | | Warner 8322 |
| | | | **REDBONE** | | |
| | | | American Indian group formed in Los Angeles in 1968. Consisted of brothers Lolly (lead vocals, guitar) & Pat Vegas, Anthony Bellamy and Peter De Poe. | | |
| 5/04/74 | **75** | 5 | 1●Come And Get Your Love ............................. | *5* | Epic 11035 |
| | | | **REDD** | | |
| | | | Born Albert Cottle III on 8/2/69 in Atlanta. Redd joined his father's group, The Tams, at age 7. | | |
| 5/30/87 | **90** | 3 | 1 Mr. D.J.................................................. | | RCA 5114 |
| | | | **REDD HOT** | | |
| 12/12/81+ | **63** | 12 | 1 Big Fat Bottom ......................................... | | Venture 148 |
| | | | **SHARON REDD** | | |
| | | | Born on 10/19/45 in New York City. Former member of Bette Midler's backup group, the Harlettes, with Ula Hedwig and Charlotte Crossley. | | |
| 2/07/81 | **57** | 9 | 1 Can You Handle It ...................................... | | Prelude 8024 |
| 9/18/82 | **41** | 9 | 2 Beat The Street ......................................... | | Prelude 8058 |
| | | | **GENE REDDING** | | |
| | | | Born in Anderson, IN, 1945. Discovered by Etta James at USO Club, Anchorage, Alaska. | | |
| 3/09/74 | **31** | 13 | 1 This Heart .............................................. | *24* | Haven 7000 |
| 9/21/74 | **80** | 5 | 2 Blood Brothers ......................................... | | Haven 7003 |
| | | | **OTIS REDDING** ★★**50**★★ | | |
| | | | Born on 9/9/41 in Dawson, Georgia. Killed in a plane crash in Lake Monona in Madison, Wisconsin on 12/10/67. Singer/songwriter/producer/pianist. First recorded with Johnny Jenkins & The Pinetoppers for Confederate in 1960. Own label, Jotis. Plane crash also took the lives of four members of the Bar-Kays. | | |
| 3/23/63 | **20** | 1 | 1 These Arms Of Mine ................................... | *85* | Volt 103 |
| 10/05/63 | **27** | 2 | 2 That's What My Heart Needs .......................... | | Volt 109 |
| 11/23/63+ | **61** | 11 | 3 Pain In My Heart........................................ | *Hot* | Volt 112 |
| 3/21/64 | **69** | 7 | 4 Come To Me ............................................ | *Hot* | Volt 116 |
| 5/23/64 | **97** | 1 | 5 Security .................................................. | *Hot* | Volt 117 |
| 10/24/64 | **70** | 7 | 6 Chained And Bound ..................................... | *Hot* | Volt 121 |
| 1/30/65 | **18** | 6 | 7 That's How Strong My Love Is/ | *74* | |
| 2/06/65 | **10** | 13 | 8 **Mr. Pitiful** ............................................ | *41* | Volt 124 |
| 5/15/65 | **2**¹ | 12 | 9 **I've Been Loving You Too Long (To Stop Now)**. | *21* | Volt 126 |
| 9/04/65 | **4** | 16 | 10 **Respect** ............................................... | *35* | Volt 128 |
| 12/25/65+ | **11** | 8 | 11 I Can't Turn You Lose/ | | |
| 12/25/65+ | **15** | 9 | 12 Just One More Day...................................... | *85* | Volt 130 |
| 3/19/66 | **4** | 12 | 13 **Satisfaction** ........................................... | *31* | Volt 132 |

| DEBUT DATE | PEAK POS | WKS CHR | ARTIST — Record Title | POP POS | Label & Number |
|---|---|---|---|---|---|
| | | | **OTIS REDDING — Continued** | | |
| 6/11/66 | **10** | 10 | 14 **My Lover's Prayer** ............................................ | *61* | Volt 136 |
| 10/08/66 | **12** | 10 | 15 Fa-Fa-Fa-Fa-Fa (Sad Song) ............................ | *29* | Volt 138 |
| 12/10/66+ | **4** | 12 | 16 **Try A Little Tenderness** ............................... | *25* | Volt 141 |
| 4/29/67 | **30** | 3 | 17 I Love You More Than Words Can Say ............. | *78* | Volt 146 |
| 5/13/67 | **2**¹ | 13 | 18 **Tramp** ........................................................ | *26* | Stax 216 |
| | | | OTIS & CARLA (Thomas) | | |
| 6/03/67 | **16** | 7 | 19 Shake ......................................................... | *47* | Volt 149 |
| 7/29/67 | **19** | 7 | 20 Glory Of Love ............................................ | *60* | Volt 152 |
| 9/02/67 | **8** | 8 | 21 Knock On Wood .......................................... | *30* | Stax 228 |
| | | | OTIS & CARLA | | |
| 2/03/68 | **1**³ | 15 | 22● **(Sittin' On) The Dock Of The Bay** ................ | *1* | Volt 157 |
| | | | recorded 3 days before his death | | |
| 3/02/08 | **21** | 7 | 23 Lovey Dovey ............................................... | *60* | Stax 244 |
| | | | OTIS & CARLA | | |
| 5/04/68 | **10** | 9 | 24 **The Happy Song (Dum-Dum)** ......................... | *25* | Volt 163 |
| 7/13/68 | **15** | 8 | 25 Amen/ | *36* | |
| 8/03/68 | **38** | 4 | 26   Hard To Handle ....................................... | *51* | Atco 6592 |
| 10/05/68 | **6** | 9 | 27 **I've Got Dreams To Remember** ..................... | *41* | Atco 6612 |
| 12/07/68+ | **10** | 10 | 28 Papa's Got A Brand New Bag ...................... | *21* | Atco 6636 |
| 3/15/69 | **20** | 5 | 29 A Lover's Question .................................... | *48* | Atco 6654 |
| 5/31/69 | **17** | 7 | 30 Love Man................................................... | *72* | Atco 6677 |
| 8/16/69 | **30** | 5 | 31 Free Me .................................................... | *103* | Atco 6700 |
| | | | **THE REDDINGS** | | |
| | | | Consisted of Otis Redding's sons Dexter (vocals, bass) and Otis III (guitar), and cousin Mark Locket (vocals, drums, keyboards). | | |
| 10/11/80+ | **6** | 20 | 1 **Remote Control** ......................................... | *89* | Believe 5600 |
| 2/14/81 | **50** | 8 | 2 I Want It .................................................. | | Believe 5602 |
| 6/13/81 | **48** | 10 | 3 You're The Only One ................................. | | Believe 02066 |
| 8/29/81 | **63** | 8 | 4 Class (Is What You Got) ............................ | | Believe 02437 |
| 3/27/82 | **32** | 12 | 5 I Know You Got Another ............................ | | Believe 02767 |
| 6/05/82 | **21** | 12 | 6 (Sittin' On) The Dock Of The Bay.................... | *55* | Believe 02836 |
| 7/30/83 | **76** | 7 | 7 Hand Dance ............................................. | | Believe 04067 |
| 3/16/85 | **37** | 11 | 8 Where Did Our Love Go/ | | |
| 7/06/85 | **70** | 8 | 9   Parasite ................................................. | | Polydor 881767 |
| 4/30/88 | **60** | 8 | 10 So In Love With You................................. | | Polydor 887395 |
| | | | **REDDS & THE BOYS** | | |
| | | | Group from Randall Junior High School in Washington, DC. Consisted of Redds (vocals, lead guitar), Shake & Bake and Dr. P. (keyboards), CJ (saxophone, flute), Too Tall Steve (trumpet), Hollywood (bass), Funky Foot (drums) and Li'l Beats (congas). | | |
| 3/30/85 | **58** | 8 | 1 Movin' & Groovin' ..................................... | | 4th & B'way 205 |
| | | | **HELEN REDDY** | | |
| | | | Pop vocalist born on 10/25/42 in Melbourne, Australia. Own TV series in the early 60s. Moved to New York in 1966. | | |
| 7/28/79 | **59** | 7 | 1 Make Love To Me ...................................... | *60* | Capitol 4712 |
| | | | **JIMMY REED**   ★★**113**★★ | | |
| | | | Born Mathis James Reed on 9/6/25 in Dunleith, Mississippi. Died from an epileptic seizure on 8/29/76. Vocalist/guitarist/harmonica/composer. Taught guitar by Eddie Taylor at age 7. First recorded for Chance in 1953. Afflicted with epilepsy since 1957. Distinctive and influential blues singer, active until death. | | |
| 3/05/55 | **5** | 10 | 1 **You Don't Have To Go** .............................. | | Vee-Jay 119 |
| | | | Juke Box #5 / Jockey #6 / Best Seller #9 | | |
| 9/24/55+ | **12** | 2 | 2 I Don't Go For That .................................. | | Vee-Jay 153 |
| | | | Jockey #12 | | |
| 2/11/56 | **3** | 11 | 3 **Ain't That Lovin' You Baby** ......................... | | Vee-Jay 168 |
| | | | Jockey #3 / Best Seller #7 / Juke Box #7 | | |
| 6/09/56 | **10** | 4 | 4 **Can't Stand To See You Go**.......................... | | Vee-Jay 186 |
| | | | Jockey #10 | | |
| 9/15/56 | **13** | 2 | 5 I Love You Baby ....................................... | | Vee-Jay 203 |
| | | | Jockey #13 | | |
| 12/15/56+ | **3** | 9 | 6 **You've Got Me Dizzy** ................................. | | Vee-Jay 226 |
| | | | Jockey #3 / Best Seller #6 / Juke Box #9 | | |

| DEBUT DATE | PEAK POS | WKS CHR | ARTIST — Record Title | POP POS | Label & Number |
|---|---|---|---|---|---|
| | | | **JIMMY REED — Continued** | | |
| 3/30/57 | **13** | 1 | 7 Honey Where You Going/ | | |
| | | | *Jockey #13* | | |
| 4/13/57 | **7** | 2 | **8 Little Rain**.................................................... | | Vee-Jay 237 |
| | | | *Juke Box #7* | | |
| 6/24/57 | **12** | 2 | 9 The Sun Is Shining ...................................... | *65* | Vee-Jay 248 |
| | | | *Best Seller #12* | | |
| 10/14/57 | **4** | 8 | 10 Honest I Do............................................... | *32* | Vee-Jay 253 |
| | | | *Jockey #4 / Best Seller #10* | | |
| 10/20/58 | **5** | 13 | **11 I'm Gonna Get My Baby**............................... | | Vee-Jay 298 |
| 1/05/59 | **19** | 6 | 12 I Told You Baby ......................................... | | Vee-Jay 304 |
| 3/07/60 | **10** | 6 | **13 Baby What Do You Want Me To Do** ............... | 37 | Vee-Jay 333 |
| 6/13/60 | **16** | 5 | 14 Found Love............................................... | 88 | Vee-Jay 347 |
| 10/24/60 | **18** | 8 | 15 Hush-Hush ............................................... | 75 | Vee-Jay 357 |
| 2/06/61 | **12** | 6 | 16 Close Together ......................................... | 68 | Vee-Jay 373 |
| 5/01/61 | **13** | 8 | 17 Big Boss Man............................................ | 78 | Vee-Jay 380 |
| 9/04/61 | **3** | 13 | **18 Bright Lights Big City** ............................... | 58 | Vee-Jay 398 |
| 6/11/66 | **39** | 2 | 19 Knockin' At Your Door................................ | | Exodus 2005 |
| | | | **VIVIAN REED** | | |
| | | | Born in 1945 in Pittsburgh; attended the Pittsburgh Musical Institute and Juilliard School of Music in New York City. Lead in touring company of Broadway show "Don't Bother Me, I Can't Cope". Award-winning performance in the musical "Bubbling Brown Sugar". | | |
| 6/15/68 | **44** | 5 | 1 Yours Until Tomorrow ................................... | *113* | Epic 10319 |
| 10/07/78 | **74** | 5 | 2 It's Alright (This Feeling I'm Feeling) ............... | | United Art. 1239 |
| 3/10/79 | **95** | 2 | 3 Start Dancin'............................................... | | United Art. 1267 |
| | | | **DELLA REESE** | | |
| | | | Born Delloreese Patricia Early on 7/6/31 in Detroit. With Mahalia Jackson troupe from 1945-49, and Erskine Hawkins in the early 50s. Solo since 1957. Actress/singer on many TV shows. Own series "Della" in 1970. Played Della Rogers on the TV series "Chico & The Man" from 1976-78. Appeared in the film "Let's Rock" in 1958. | | |
| 10/12/59 | **1** [2] | 14 | **1 Don't You Know**........................................... | *2* | RCA 7591 |
| 1/25/60 | **13** | 6 | 2 Not One Minute More ................................... | *16* | RCA 7644 |
| | | | **DIANNE REEVES** | | |
| | | | Jazz singer born in Detroit in 1956, raised in Denver. Principal vocalist for Sergio Mendes. Niece of jazz bassist Charles Burrell. | | |
| 5/28/88 | **44** | 12 | 1 Better Days................................................. | | Blue Note 50119 |
| | | | **JIM REEVES** | | |
| | | | Country singer born on 8/20/24 in Panola County, Texas. Killed in a plane crash on 7/31/64. Joined the Grand Ole Opry in 1955. Own TV series in 1957. In the film "Kimberly Jim" in 1963. | | |
| 5/16/60 | **13** | 3 | 1 He'll Have To Go ......................................... | *2* | RCA 7643 |
| | | | **MARTHA REEVES** | | |
| | | | Born on 7/18/41 in Detroit. Leader of Martha & The Vandellas from 1962-72. Early in career recorded for Checkmates as a member of the Del-Phis. Worked at Motown as an A&R secretary and backup singer. | | |
| 3/02/74 | **27** | 13 | 1 Power Of Love ............................................. | *76* | MCA 40194 |
| 8/24/74 | **74** | 7 | 2 Wild Night ................................................. | | MCA 40274 |
| 5/31/75 | **61** | 6 | 3 Love Blind ................................................. | | Arista 0124 |
| | | | **THE REFLECTIONS** | | |
| | | | Group formed in 1971 in New York City. Consisted of Herman Edwards, Josh Pridgen, Edmund "Butch" Simmons and John Simmons. Toured as back-up group with Melba Moore in 1972. | | |
| 6/07/75 | **9** | 14 | **1 Three Steps From True Love**......................... | *94* | Capitol 4078 |
| 10/04/75 | **58** | 10 | 2 Love On Delivery (L.O.D.)................................ | | Capitol 4137 |
| 2/21/76 | **37** | 9 | 3 Day After Day (Night After Night)..................... | | Capitol 4222 |
| 12/25/76+ | **66** | 8 | 4 Gift Wrap My Love ....................................... | | Capitol 4358 |
| | | | **THE REGAL DEWY** | | |
| 8/20/77 | **86** | 5 | 1 Love Music ................................................. | | Millennium 603 |

| DEBUT DATE | PEAK POS | WKS CHR | ARTIST — Record Title | POP POS | Label & Number |
|---|---|---|---|---|---|
| | | | **THE REGENTS** | | |
| | | | Bronx vocal group formed as the Desires in 1958. Consisted of Guy Villari (lead), Sal Cuomo, Charles Fassert, Don Jacobucci and Tony "Hot Rod" Gravagna. "Barbara-Ann", written for Fassert's sister, was first recorded as a demo in 1958. Group had disbanded by the time "Barbara-Ann" was released. | | |
| 5/29/61 | **7** | 3 | 1 **Barbara-Ann** ............................................ | *13* | Gee 1065 |
| | | | originally released on Cousins 1002 | | |
| 7/31/61 | **30** | 1 | 2 Runaround ............................................... | *28* | Gee 1071 |
| | | | **REGINA** | | |
| | | | New York native, Regina Richards. | | |
| 5/24/86 | **30** | 18 | 1 Baby Love ............................................... | *10* | Atlantic 89417 |
| | | | **THE REGISTERS - see ALVIN CASH** | | |
| | | | **CLARENCE REID** | | |
| | | | Born on 2/14/45 in Cochran, Georgia. Singer/songwriter/arranger/producer. With Miami vocal group, the Delmiros; recorded for Dade in the early 60s. Also recorded as "Blowfly". | | |
| 7/05/69 | **7** | 15 | 1 **Nobody But You Babe** ............................... | *40* | Alston 4574 |
| 1/22/72 | **38** | 6 | 2 Good Old Days ......................................... | | Alston 4603 |
| 6/01/74 | **17** | 14 | 3 Funky Party ............................................. | *99* | Alston 4621 |
| | | | **JACQUES RENARD & HIS ORCHESTRA** | | |
| | | | Violinist/leader. Led a popular radio dance band from the mid-20s to 1940. | | |
| 4/24/43 | **8** | 1 | 1 **As Time Goes By** ..................................... | *3* | Brunswick 6205 |
| | | | originally released in 1931; from the Broadway musical "Everybody's Welcome"; featured in the 1942 film "Casablanca" | | |
| | | | **RUDY RENDER** | | |
| | | | Vocalist from Indiana. | | |
| 10/08/49 | **2**² | 15 | 1 **Sneakin' Around** ...................................... | | London 17000 |
| | | | Best Seller #2 / Juke Box #2 | | |
| | | | **RENE & ANGELA** | | |
| | | | Duo of Rene Moore and Angela Winbush, formed in Los Angeles in 1977. Moore, brother of Bobby Watson of Rufus, had worked with Brothers Johnson. Winbush had sung back-up for Jean Carn, Lenny Williams and Dolly Parton. | | |
| 6/14/80 | **43** | 11 | 1 Do You Really Love Me ............................. | | Capitol 4851 |
| 10/04/80 | **39** | 9 | 2 Everything We Do ..................................... | | Capitol 4925 |
| 6/27/81 | **14** | 17 | 3 I Love You More ....................................... | | Capitol 5010 |
| 10/17/81 | **37** | 9 | 4 Wall To Wall ............................................ | | Capitol 5052 |
| 1/30/82 | **26** | 10 | 5 Imaginary Playmates ................................ | | Capitol 5081 |
| 5/07/83 | **33** | 10 | 6 Banging The Boogie ................................. | | Capitol 5220 |
| 10/01/83 | **12** | 18 | 7 My First Love ........................................... | | Capitol 5272 |
| 5/18/85 | **1**² | 17 | 8 **Save Your Love (For #1)** ........................ | *101* | Mercury 880731 |
| 8/24/85 | **4** | 18 | 9 **I'll Be Good** .......................................... | *47* | Mercury 884009 |
| 12/21/85+ | **1**¹ | 21 | 10 **Your Smile** ........................................... | *62* | Mercury 884271 |
| 4/19/86 | **2**¹ | 19 | 11 **You Don't Have To Cry** .......................... | *75* | Mercury 884587 |
| 9/13/86 | **29** | 10 | 12 No How-No Way ...................................... | | Mercury 884972 |
| | | | **DELIA RENE** | | |
| 12/12/81 | **94** | 6 | 1 You're Gonna Want Me Back ...................... | | Airwave 94963 |
| | | | **GOOGIE RENE Combo** | | |
| | | | Born Raphael Rene. Bandleader/keyboardist. Son of songwriter/producer Leon Rene. First recorded for Class in 1956. | | |
| 12/31/60+ | **20** | 4 | 1 The Slide ................................................ [I] | *105* | Rendezvous 134 |
| 1/26/63 | **25** | 1 | 2 Flapjacks - Part I ................................... [I] | | Class 305 |
| 2/19/66 | **35** | 4 | 3 Smokey Joe's La La ................................ [I] | *77* | Class 1517 |
| | | | **ANTHONY C. RENFRO, ORCHESTRA** | | |
| 12/25/76+ | **98** | 4 | 1 Gloria's Theme ......................................... | | Renfro 43 |
| | | | **REO SPEEDWAGON** | | |
| | | | Graham Lear. Group named after a 1911 fire truck. Pop quintet from Champaign, Illinois, led by Kevin Cronin. Name taken from 1911 fire truck. | | |
| 3/09/85 | **89** | 3 | 1 Can't Fight This Feeling ........................... | *1* | Epic 04713 |

| DEBUT DATE | PEAK POS | WKS CHR | ARTIST — Record Title | POP POS | Label & Number |
|---|---|---|---|---|---|
| | | | **REVELATION** | | |
| | | | Disco quartet: Phillip Ballou, Benny Driggs, Arthur Freeman and Arnold McCuller. | | |
| 7/31/76 | **83** | 4 | 1 You To Me Are Everything, Part I.................... | *98* | RSO 854 |
| 12/06/80 | **80** | 6 | 2 When I Fall In Love/ | | |
| 3/07/81 | **51** | 9 | 3 Feel It ................................................ | | Handshake 5305 |
| 8/22/81 | **89** | 3 | 4 Stand Up .............................................. | | Handshake 02139 |
| | | | **THE REVELS** | | |
| | | | Philadelphia group formed in high school, led by John Kelly. Included John Grant, Henry Colclough, John Jones and Bill Jackson. | | |
| 11/02/59 | **20** | 3 | 1 Midnight Stroll ...................................... | *35* | Norgolde 103 |
| | | | **DEBBIE REYNOLDS** | | |
| | | | Born Mary Reynolds on 4/1/32 in El Paso, Texas. Leading lady of 50s musicals and later in comedies. Married actor/singer Eddie Fisher on 9/26/55; divorced by 1959. Mother of actress Carrie Fisher. | | |
| 4/18/60 | **13** | 4 | 1 Am I That Easy To Forget.......................... | *25* | Dot 15985 |
| | | | **JEANNIE REYNOLDS** | | |
| | | | Sister of L. J. Reynolds. Committed suicide in July of 1980, after taking the lives of her two children. | | |
| 6/14/75 | **10** | 15 | 1 The Phones Been Jumping All Day ................ | | Casablanca 834 |
| 10/18/75 | **46** | 12 | 2 Lay Some Lovin' On Me.............................. | | Casablanca 846 |
| | | | **JODY REYNOLDS** | | |
| | | | Rockabilly singer/guitarist from Yuma, Arizona. | | |
| 6/02/58 | **5** | 11 | 1 Endless Sleep.......................................... | *5* | Demon 1507 |
| | | | Best Seller #5 / Jockey #6 | | |
| | | | **L.J. REYNOLDS** | | |
| | | | Singer/songwriter/producer Larry J. Reynolds. Brother of Jeannie Reynolds. Member of Chocolate Syrup (1971-73); joined The Dramatics in 1973. Began solo career in 1981. | | |
| 11/13/71 | **31** | 9 | 1 Let One Hurt Do .................................... | *104* | Law-Ton 1553 |
| | | | **L.J. REYNOLDS & CHOCOLATE SYRUP** | | |
| 6/20/81 | **59** | 9 | 2 Ain't No Woman Like My Baby ...................... | | Capitol 4998 |
| 9/19/81 | **69** | 6 | 3 Key To The World ................................... | | Capitol 5035 |
| 7/31/82 | **84** | 4 | 4 Special Effects ...................................... | | Capitol 5136 |
| 5/05/84 | **27** | 13 | 5 Touch Down........................................... | | Mercury 818791 |
| 11/30/85 | **81** | 4 | 6 Tomorrow ............................................. | | Fantasy 962 |
| 5/09/87 | **79** | 10 | 7 Tell Me You Will ..................................... | | Fantasy 976 |
| | | | **TODD RHODES** | | |
| | | | Born on 8/31/1900 in Hopkinsville, Kentucky. Died in 1965 in Flint, Michigan. Pianist/arranger/leader. Moved to Detroit. Own band in 1946. First own recording for Vitacoustic in 1947. Band's vocalists included Connie Allen, LaVern Baker, Pinocchio James and Kitty Stevenson. Also see Wynonie Harris. | | |
| 10/23/48+ | **4** | 16 | 1 Blues For The Red Boy.............................. [I] | | King 4240 |
| | | | Best Seller #4 / Juke Box #4 | | |
| 5/21/49 | **3** | 11 | 2 Pot Likker ............................................ [I] | | King 4287 |
| | | | Juke Box #3 / Best Seller #9 originally released on Sensation 15 | | |
| | | | **RHYTHM** | | |
| | | | Group formed in Boston in 1971. Consisted of Troy Robinson, Suzanne Swan (vocals), Kingsley Swan (guitar), Jerry Pritchette (keyboards), Kevin Parham (bass) and Grayling Wallace (drums). The Swans, husband and wife, are from Bermuda. | | |
| 1/10/76 | **97** | 2 | 1 Find Yourself Somebody To Love ..................... | | Polydor 14288 |
| | | | **THE RHYTHM ACES - see BOBBY MOORE** | | |
| | | | **RHYTHM HERITAGE** | | |
| | | | Los Angeles studio group assembled by producers Steve Barri and Michael Omartian (keyboards). Vocals by Oren and Luther Waters. | | |
| 11/22/75+ | **11** | 20 | 1 ● Theme From S.W.A.T. ................................. [I] | *1* | ABC 12135 |
| | | | from the ABC-TV series "S.W.A.T." | | |
| 4/10/76 | **19** | 12 | 2 Baretta's Theme ("Keep Your Eye On The Sparrow") ...................................... | *20* | ABC 12177 |
| | | | from the Robert Blake TV series "Baretta" | | |
| 8/21/76 | **80** | 3 | 3 Disco-Fied............................................... | *101* | ABC 12205 |
| 2/26/77 | **78** | 5 | 4 Theme From Rocky (Gonna Fly Now) ............. [I] | *94* | ABC 12243 |
| | | | from the Sylvester Stallone film "Rocky" | | |
| 10/08/77 | **93** | 7 | 5 Theme From Starsky & Hutch ...................... [I] | | ABC 12273 |
| | | | from the TV series "Starsky & Hutch" | | |

| DEBUT DATE | PEAK POS | WKS CHR | ARTIST — Record Title | POP POS | Label & Number |
|---|---|---|---|---|---|
| | | | **RHYTHM HERITAGE — Continued** | | |
| 3/18/78 | **92** | 5 | 6  Holdin' Out (For Your Love) ............................ | | ABC 12334 |
| | | | **RHYTHM MAKERS** | | |
| | | | Group originally called Third Chance. Consisted of Rahiem LeBlanc (guitar), Herb Cane (keyboards), Sabo Crier (bass) and Kenny Banks (drums). | | |
| 4/17/76 | **92** | 3 | 1  Zone ...................................................... [I] | | Vigor 1726 |
| | | | **RHYZE** | | |
| | | | 7-member band from New York City. | | |
| 6/07/80 | **92** | 4 | 1  Just How Sweet Is Your Love ......................... | | Sam 5014 |
| | | | **ALFONSO RIBEIRO** | | |
| | | | Young star of Broadway's "Tap Dance Kid" and a regular on TV's "Silver Spoons". | | |
| 3/02/85 | **69** | 8 | 1  Not Too Young (To Fall In Love)....................... | | Prism 99661 |
| | | | **SIR MACK RICE** | | |
| | | | Singer from Detroit. With the Five Scalders vocal group, recorded for Drummond in 1956. In the Falcons from 1957-63. Became road manager for new Falcons group (formerly the Fabulous Playboys) in late 1963. | | |
| 5/15/65 | **15** | 6 | 1  Mustang Sally................................................ | *108* | Blue Rock 4014 |
| 3/29/69 | **48** | 3 | 2  Coal Man ..................................................... | *135* | Atco 6645 |
| | | | shown only as: **MACK RICE** | | |
| | | | **DIANE RICHARDS** | | |
| 3/05/83 | **44** | 12 | 1  Listen To Your Heart ................................. | | Zoo York 03535 |
| | | | **LIONEL RICHIE**   ★★127★★ | | |
| | | | Born on 6/20/49 in Tuskegee, Alabama. Grew up on the campus of Tuskegee Institute where his grandfather worked. Former lead singer of the Commodores. Appeared in the film "Thank God It's Friday" with Donna Summer. Wrote "Three Times A Lady" as tribute to his wife, Brenda. Also see Donna Summer. | | |
| 7/11/81 | **1**⁷ | 24 | 1▲Endless Love................................................ | *1* | Motown 1519 |
| | | | **DIANA ROSS & LIONEL RICHIE** from the film of the same title | | |
| 10/16/82 | **2**⁹ | 23 | 2●Truly........................................................ | *1* | Motown 1644 |
| 1/22/83 | **2**³ | 23 | 3  You Are..................................................... | *4* | Motown 1657 |
| 4/16/83 | **6** | 15 | 4  My Love .................................................... | *5* | Motown 1677 |
| 9/24/83 | **1**⁷ | 22 | 5●All Night Long (All Night)............................ | *1* | Motown 1698 |
| 12/03/83+ | **6** | 19 | 6  Running With The Night ............................ | *7* | Motown 1710 |
| 3/10/84 | **1**³ | 21 | 7●Hello ....................................................... | *1* | Motown 1722 |
| 7/07/84 | **8** | 16 | 8  Stuck On You.............................................. | *3* | Motown 1746 |
| 10/13/84 | **8** | 14 | 9  Penny Lover ............................................... | *8* | Motown 1762 |
| 11/16/85+ | **1**² | 18 | 10●Say You, Say Me........................................... | *1* | Motown 1819 |
| | | | featured in the film (not album) "White Nights" | | |
| 7/19/86 | **6** | 14 | 11  Dancing On The Ceiling .............................. | *2* | Motown 1843 |
| 10/04/86 | **2**² | 17 | 12  Love Will Conquer All ................................. | *9* | Motown 1866 |
| 12/13/86+ | **5** | 16 | 13  Ballerina Girl ........................................... | *7* | Motown 1873 |
| 3/28/87 | **12** | 13 | 14  Se La .......................................................... | *20* | Motown 1883 |
| | | | **RICHIE'S ROOM 222 GANG** | | |
| | | | Group named after the TV series "Room 222". Included Howard "Richie" Rice (vocals, guitar), actor in that series; brothers Jerome and Alfred Rice (guitars) and cousin Dennis Hughes (piano). Howard and Jerome appeared as the Rice Brothers in the early 60s. | | |
| 3/20/71 | **48** | 2 | 1  I'd Rather Stay A Child ................................. | | Scepter 12305 |
| | | | **RICHMOND EXTENSION** | | |
| 6/29/74 | **75** | 4 | 1  Everything's Coming Up Love......................... | | Silver Blue 811 |
| | | | **THE RIGHT CHOICE** | | |
| | | | Memphis-based trio: Archie Love (vocals), Eric Shotwell (vocals) and Tony DeCarlos Black (keyboards). | | |
| 4/09/88 | **13** | 13 | 1  Tired Of Being Alone ................................. | | Motown 1931 |
| | | | **RIGHT KIND** | | |
| 2/24/68 | **49** | 2 | 1  Why Do You Have To Lie? ............................ | | Galaxy 759 |

| DEBUT DATE | PEAK POS | WKS CHR | ARTIST — Record Title | POP POS | Label & Number |
|---|---|---|---|---|---|
| | | | **THE RIGHTEOUS BROTHERS** | | |
| | | | Blue-eyed soul duo: Bill Medley (b: 9/19/40, Santa Ana, CA), baritone; and Bobby Hatfield (b: 8/10/40, Beaver Dam, WI), tenor. Both sang in local Los Angeles groups, formed duo in 1962. First recorded as the Paramours for Smash in 1962. On "Hullaballoo" and "Shindig" TV shows. Split up, 1968-74, Medley went solo, replaced by Billy Walker, then rejoined Hatfield in 1974. | | |
| 1/30/65 | **3** | 9 | 1 **You've Lost That Lovin' Feelin'** .................... | *1* | Philles 124 |
| 4/17/65 | **26** | 5 | 2 Just Once In My Life................................. | *9* | Philles 127 |
| 8/14/65 | **6** | 12 | 3 **Unchained Melody**................................. | *4* | Philles 129 |
| 12/18/65+ | **13** | 7 | 4 Ebb Tide............................................. | *5* | Philles 130 |
| | | | all of above: produced by Phil Spector | | |
| 4/02/66 | **13** | 9 | 5●(You're My) Soul And Inspiration ..................... | *1* | Verve 10383 |
| | | | **RIMSHOTS** | | |
| 12/09/72+ | **36** | 7 | 1 Save That Thang............................. | | A-1 4002 |
| 1/03/76 | **93** | 4 | 2 Do What You Feel ............................... | | Stang 5065 |
| 6/12/76 | **49** | 17 | 3 Super Disco............................................. | | Stang 5067 |
| | | | **THE RINKY-DINKS - see BOBBY DARIN** | | |
| | | | **MINNIE RIPERTON** | | |
| | | | Born on 11/8/47 in Chicago; died of cancer on 7/12/79 in Los Angeles. Recorded as "Andrea Davis" on Chess in 1966. In Rotary Connection, 1967-70. In Stevie Wonder's back-up group, Wonderlove, in 1973. | | |
| 1/25/75 | **3** | 17 | 1●**Lovin' You** ........................................ | *1* | Epic 50057 |
| 8/16/75 | **26** | 9 | 2 Inside My Love .................................. | *76* | Epic 50128 |
| 11/15/75 | **70** | 8 | 3 Simple Things .................................. | | Epic 50166 |
| 2/14/76 | **72** | 6 | 4 Adventures In Paradise ........................... | | Epic 50190 |
| 2/19/77 | **57** | 11 | 5 Stick Together (Part One) ....................... | | Epic 50337 |
| 4/28/79 | **16** | 22 | 6 Memory Lane ................................... | | Capitol 4706 |
| 8/25/79 | **20** | 13 | 7 Lover And Friend ................................ | | Capitol 4761 |
| 8/23/80 | **14** | 14 | 8 Here We Go..................................... | | Capitol 4902 |
| 1/10/81 | **75** | 5 | 9 Give Me Time .................................. | | Capitol 4955 |
| | | | **RIPPLE** | | |
| | | | Chicago-based integrated progressive septet, originally from Kalamazoo, Michigan. Consisted of Dave Ferguson, Bill Hull, Keith "Doc" Samuels, Curtis Reynolds, Ken Carter, Walter Carter and Brian Sherrer. | | |
| 9/08/73 | **11** | 15 | 1 I Don't Know What It Is, But It Sure Is Funky..... | *67* | GRC 1004 |
| 2/16/74 | **27** | 11 | 2 Willie Pass The Water ............................ | *108* | GRC 1013 |
| 5/18/74 | **41** | 12 | 3 A Funky Song ................................... | | GRC 2017 |
| 9/14/74 | **51** | 7 | 4 You Were Right On Time ........................ | | GRC 2030 |
| 6/07/75 | **81** | 5 | 5 This Ain't No Time To Be Giving Up ................ | | GRC 2060 |
| 3/25/78 | **91** | 6 | 6 The Beat Goes On & On ......................... | | Salsoul 2057 |
| | | | **THE RITCHIE FAMILY** | | |
| | | | Philadelphia disco group named for producer Ritchie Rome. Consisted of Cheryl Mason Jackson, Cassandra Ann Wooten and Gwendolyn Oliver. Later consisted of Jacqueline Smith-Lee, Theodosia "Dodie" Draher and Ednah Holt. | | |
| 8/09/75 | **13** | 16 | 1 Brazil.......................................... | *11* | 20th Century 2218 |
| 12/27/75+ | **74** | 6 | 2 I Want To Dance With You (Dance With Me)....... | *84* | 20th Century 2252 |
| 8/21/76 | **12** | 14 | 3 The Best Disco In Town......................... | *17* | Marlin 3306 |
| 3/26/77 | **74** | 4 | 4 Life Is Music................................... | *102* | Marlin 3309 |
| 9/24/77 | **68** | 7 | 5 Quiet Village .................................. | | Marlin 3316 |
| 6/21/80 | **80** | 4 | 6 Give Me A Break ............................... | | Casablanca 2259 |
| 5/08/82 | **27** | 13 | 7 I'll Do My Best (For You Baby) ................. | | RCA 13092 |
| 8/13/83 | **77** | 4 | 8 All Night All Right............................... | | RCA 13550 |
| | | | **LEE RITENOUR** | | |
| | | | Born on 1/11/52 in Los Angeles. Guitarist/composer/arranger. Top session guitarist, has appeared on more than 200 albums. Nicknamed "Captain Fingers". | | |
| 4/25/81 | **27** | 16 | 1 Is It You ...................................... | *15* | Elektra 47124 |
| | | | vocal by Eric Tagg | | |
| | | | **HECTOR RIVERA** | | |
| 12/31/66+ | **26** | 8 | 1 At The Party ................................... | *104* | Barry! 1011 |

| DEBUT DATE | PEAK POS | WKS CHR | ARTIST — Record Title | POP POS | Label & Number |
|---|---|---|---|---|---|
| | | | **THE RIVINGTONS** Los Angeles vocal group, formed in 1957 as The Sharps. Consisted of Carl White (d: 1/7/80), John "Sonny" Harris, Turner "Rocky" Wilson Jr. and Al Frazier. Back-up on Paul Anka's first recording, Duane Eddy's "Rebel Rouser" and "Little Bitty Pretty One" by Thurston Harris. | | |
| 6/08/63 | 27 | 1 | 1 The Bird's The Word................................. | 52 | Liberty 55553 |
| | | | **JERRY RIX** | | |
| 6/11/77 | 92 | 7 | 1 Disco Train .................................. | | AVI 131 |
| | | | **R.J.'S LATEST ARRIVAL** R.J. is keyboardist Ralph James Rice from Detroit. | | |
| 2/28/81 | 59 | 8 | 1 Wind Me Up ................................ | | Buddah 625 |
| 10/17/81 | 72 | 4 | 2 Body Snatcher ............................... | | Sutra 109 |
| 5/01/82 | 35 | 14 | 3 (Acrobic Dancin) Keep Dancin ................... | | Zoo York 1393 |
| 10/09/82 | 62 | 10 | 4 Stay With Me................................ | | Zoo York 03228 |
| 4/30/83 | 44 | 10 | 5 Movin' On Up............................... | | Larc 81020 |
| 4/14/84 | 6 | 20 | 6 **Shackles** ................................. | | Golden Boy 7059 |
| 9/29/84 | 48 | 8 | 7 Harmony .................................. | | Golden Boy 7122 |
| 12/15/84+ | 61 | 10 | 8 Cry Like A Wolf ............................. | | Golden Boy 7124 |
| 6/22/85 | 27 | 12 | 9 Swing Low ................................. | 107 | Atlantic 89551 |
| 9/21/85 | 25 | 13 | 10 Baby I'm Sorry ............................ | | Atlantic 89510 |
| 8/23/86 | 12 | 14 | 11 Heaven In Your Arms........................ | | Manhattan 50040 |
| 11/29/86+ | 9 | 20 | 12 **Hold On** ................................ | | Manhattan 50058 |
| 4/18/87 | 15 | 13 | 13 Rhythm Method ........................... | | Manhattan 50071 |
| 5/28/88 | 6 | 17 | 14 **Off The Hook (With Your Love)**.................... | | EMI-Man. 50132 |
| | | | **ROB BASE & D.J. E-Z ROCK** Harlem rap duo: Robert Ginyard with deejay Rodney "Skip" Bryce. | | |
| 5/21/88 | 17 | 25 | 1 It Takes Two ............................... | 36 | Profile 7186 |
| | | | **ROCKIE ROBBINS** Born Edward W. Robbins, Jr. in Minneapolis. Inactive in music from 1981-85. | | |
| 10/13/79 | 67 | 6 | 1 Be Ever Wonderful .......................... | | A&M 2180 |
| 4/26/80 | 9 | 22 | 2 You And Me ................................ | 80 | A&M 2231 |
| 10/04/80 | 70 | 5 | 3 Hang Tough ................................ | | A&M 2264 |
| 12/06/80+ | 59 | 9 | 4 After Loving You ............................ | | A&M 2287 |
| 9/05/81 | 32 | 11 | 5 Time To Think.............................. | | A&M 2355 |
| 11/14/81+ | 30 | 13 | 6 I Believe In Love ............................ | | A&M 2380 |
| 2/02/85 | 45 | 11 | 7 We Belong Together ......................... | | MCA 52516 |
| | | | **ROBE** | | |
| 11/21/87 | 70 | 9 | 1 Turn On The Moon .......................... | | 2000 AD 4 |
| | | | **ROBERT & JOHNNY** Bronx duo: Robert Carr and Johnny Mitchell. | | |
| 5/05/58 | 12 | 2 | 1 We Belong Together ......................... Jockey #12 / Best Seller #18 | 32 | Old Town 1047 |
| | | | **JOHN ROBERTS** | | |
| 11/25/67+ | 19 | 9 | 1 Sockin' 1-2-3-4............................. | 71 | Duke 425 |
| | | | **LEA ROBERTS** Leatha Roberta Hicks from Dayton. Moved to Newark in 1968, discovered by producer George Butler. | | |
| 8/09/69 | 39 | 4 | 1 Prove It .................................. | | Minit 32069 |
| 7/14/73 | 94 | 2 | 2 (If You Don't Want My Love) Give It Back ......... | | United Art. 222 |
| 9/28/74 | 69 | 6 | 3 Laughter In The Rain.................... | 109 | United Art. 539 |
| 4/19/75 | 54 | 6 | 4 All Right Now .............................. | 92 | United Art. 626 |
| | | | **THE ROBINS** Group formed in Los Angeles in 1947: Ty Terrell, Billy Richards, Roy Richard and Bobby Nunn. First known as the Four Bluebirds. Carl Gardner and Grady Chapman added in 1954. Gardner and Nunn formed The Coasters in 1955. Also see the Johnny Otis Orchestra. | | |
| 1/28/50 | 10 | 2 | 1 **If It's So, Baby**......................... Juke Box #10 / Best Seller #14 with the Johnny Otis Band | | Savoy 726 |

| DEBUT DATE | PEAK POS | WKS CHR | ARTIST — Record Title | POP POS | Label & Number |
|---|---|---|---|---|---|
| | | | **THE ROBINS — Continued** | | |
| 12/03/55 | 10 | 2 | 2 Smokey Joe's Cafe ....................................... | *79* | Atco 6059 |
| | | | Juke Box #10 / Best Seller #13 | | |
| | | | originally released on Spark 122 | | |
| | | | **JIMMY ROBINS** | | |
| | | | Born James Robbins in Chicago. First recorded for Federal in 1963. | | |
| 1/14/67 | 21 | 6 | 1 I Can't Please You......................................... | *131* | Jerhart 207 |
| | | | **ALVIN ROBINSON** | | |
| | | | Session guitarist/vocalist. | | |
| 6/06/64 | 52 | 8 | 1 Something You Got........................................ | *Hot* | Tiger 104 |
| | | | **BERT ROBINSON** | | |
| | | | Vocalist from Detroit. | | |
| 6/27/87 | 44 | 10 | 1 All The Way With You .................................. | | Capitol 44014 |
| | | | **PEGGI BLU with BERT ROBINSON** | | |
| 8/22/87 | 5 | 15 | 2 **Heart Of Gold**............................................ | | Capitol 44013 |
| | | | **DUTCH ROBINSON** | | |
| 12/22/84 | 90 | 5 | 1 Happy .......................................................... | | CBS Assoc. 1969 |
| 6/22/85 | 86 | 3 | 2 Change Your Mind...................................... | | CBS Assoc. 04888 |
| | | | **ED ROBINSON** | | |
| 8/29/70 | 44 | 4 | 1 Hey Blackman ............................................. | | Cotillion 44090 |
| | | | **FAT MAN ROBINSON** | | |
| | | | Real name is Paul Robinson. Prominent tenor sax player in Boston into the mid-60s. | | |
| 5/21/49 | 9 | 1 | 1 **Lavender Coffin**....................................... | | Motif 2001 |
| | | | Juke Box #9 | | |
| | | | **FLOYD ROBINSON** | | |
| | | | Born in 1937 in Nashville. Singer/guitarist/composer. Worked on local radio with his high school band, the Eagle Rangers, at age 12. Own programs on WLAC and WSM-Nashville. | | |
| 10/12/59 | 27 | 3 | 1 Makin' Love ................................................ | *20* | RCA 7529 |
| | | | **FREDDY ROBINSON** | | |
| | | | Born in Memphis in 1939. Guitarist/bass player with Little Walter, Howlin' Wolf and Jerry Butler. Worked with Ray Charles in 1968. With John Mayall in the early 70s. | | |
| 8/08/70 | 29 | 8 | 1 Black Fox .................................................... [I] | *56* | World P.J. 88155 |
| | | | **JACKIE ROBINSON** | | |
| 5/01/76 | 61 | 7 | 1 Movin' Like A Superstar ............................... | | Ariola Am. 7618 |
| | | | **JAMES ROBINSON** | | |
| 7/18/87 | 79 | 6 | 1 Can We Do It Again .................................... | | Tabu 7122 |
| | | | **J.P. ROBINSON** | | |
| 11/22/69 | 46 | 2 | 1 You Got Your Thing On A String...................... | | Alston 4577 |
| 3/28/70 | 39 | 5 | 2 What Can I Tell Her....................................... | | Alston 4583 |
| | | | **ROSCOE ROBINSON** | | |
| | | | Born on 5/22/28 in Dumont, Arkansas. Singer/producer. Moved to Gary, Indiana in 1938. Veteran of many gospel groups, including the Five Trumpets, Southern Sons, Highway QC's, Fairfield Four and Five Blind Boys. First recorded for Trumpet, 1951. | | |
| 7/02/66 | 7 | 13 | 1 **That's Enough** ........................................... | *62* | Wand 1125 |
| 12/03/66 | 39 | 5 | 2 How Much Pressure (Do You Think I Can Stand)/ | *125* | |
| 12/17/66+ | 40 | 4 | 3 Do It Right Now ......................................... | | Wand 1143 |
| 7/05/69 | 42 | 4 | 4 Oo Wee Baby I Love You ............................. | | Atlantic 2637 |
| | | | **SMOKEY ROBINSON**   ★★38★★ | | |
| | | | Born William Robinson on 2/19/40 in Detroit. Formed The Miracles (then called the Matadors) at Northern High School in 1955. First recorded for End in 1958. Married Miracles' member Claudette Rogers in 1963. Left The Miracles on 1/29/72. Wrote dozens of hit songs for Motown artists. Vice President of Motown Records. | | |
| 7/14/73 | 31 | 12 | 1 Sweet Harmony ......................................... | *48* | Tamla 54233 |
| 11/10/73+ | 7 | 17 | 2 **Baby Come Close** .................................... | *27* | Tamla 54239 |
| 5/18/74 | 29 | 11 | 3 It's Her Turn To Live ................................. | *82* | Tamla 54246 |
| 8/10/74 | 12 | 14 | 4 Virgin Man .............................................. | *56* | Tamla 54250 |
| 11/30/74+ | 6 | 16 | 5 **I Am I Am** .............................................. | *56* | Tamla 54251 |
| 3/15/75 | 1¹ | 16 | 6 **Baby That's Backatcha** ........................... | *26* | Tamla 54258 |
| 8/23/75 | 7 | 16 | 7 **The Agony And The Ecstasy** ....................... | *36* | Tamla 54261 |

| DEBUT DATE | PEAK POS | WKS CHR | ARTIST — Record Title | POP POS | Label & Number |
|---|---|---|---|---|---|
| | | | **SMOKEY ROBINSON — Continued** | | |
| 12/20/75+ | 25 | 11 | 8 Quiet Storm ................................................ | 61 | Tamla 54265 |
| 4/17/76 | 10 | 13 | 9 **Open** ...................................................... | 81 | Tamla 54267 |
| 2/12/77 | 7 | 17 | 10 **There Will Come A Day (I'm Gonna Happen To You)** .......................................................... | 42 | Tamla 54279 |
| 6/18/77 | 18 | 13 | 11 Vitamin U ................................................. | 101 | Tamla 54284 |
| 9/17/77 | 38 | 11 | 12 Theme From Big Time Pt. 1.......................... | | Tamla 54288 |
| 3/18/78 | 9 | 16 | 13 **Daylight And Darkness/** | 75 | |
| | | 5 | 14 Why You Wanna See My Bad Side ................. | | Tamla 54293 |
| 11/11/78 | 68 | 5 | 15 Shoe Soul ................................................. | | Tamla 54296 |
| 1/27/79 | 26 | 11 | 16 Pops, We Love You (A Tribute To Father) .......... | 59 | Motown 1455 |
| | | | DIANA ROSS, MARVIN GAYE, SMOKEY ROBINSON & STEVIE WONDER song written for Berry Gordy Sr.'s 90th birthday | | |
| 7/14/79 | 82 | 4 | 17 Get Ready ................................................. | | Tamla 54301 |
| 9/01/79 | 4 | 28 | 18 **Cruisin'** .................................................. | 4 | Tamla 54306 |
| 3/22/80 | 4 | 17 | 19 **Let Me Be The Clock** ................................ | 31 | Tamla 54311 |
| 6/21/80 | 34 | 10 | 20 Heavy On Pride (Light On Love) ..................... | | Tamla 54313 |
| 2/14/81 | 1⁵ | 21 | 21 ●**Being With You** ...................................... | 2 | Tamla 54321 |
| 6/20/81 | 31 | 9 | 22 You Are Forever ......................................... | 59 | Tamla 54327 |
| 9/05/81 | 62 | 6 | 23 Who's Sad.................................................. | | Tamla 54332 |
| 1/23/82 | 3 | 17 | 24 **Tell Me Tomorrow - Part I** ......................... | 33 | Tamla 1601 |
| 4/17/82 | 17 | 12 | 25 Old Fashioned Love .................................... | 60 | Tamla 1615 |
| 1/22/83 | 8 | 15 | 26 **I've Made Love To You A Thousand Times**...... | 101 | Tamla 1655 |
| 5/07/83 | 68 | 7 | 27 Touch The Sky .......................................... | 110 | Tamla 1678 |
| 7/09/83 | 35 | 12 | 28 Blame It On Love ....................................... | 48 | Tamla 1684 |
| | | | SMOKEY ROBINSON & BARBARA MITCHELL (member of High Energy) | | |
| 12/03/83 | 75 | 8 | 29 Don't Play Another Love Song....................... | 103 | Tamla 1700 |
| 12/17/83+ | 22 | 11 | 30 Ebony Eyes ............................................... | 43 | Gordy 1714 |
| | | | RICK JAMES featuring SMOKEY ROBINSON | | |
| 5/19/84 | 33 | 12 | 31 And I Don't Love You ................................. | 106 | Tamla 1735 |
| 9/01/84 | 41 | 13 | 32 I Can't Find............................................... | 109 | Tamla 1756 |
| 1/25/86 | 11 | 12 | 33 Hold On To Your Love................................. | | Tamla 1828 |
| 5/03/86 | 51 | 10 | 34 Sleepless Nights......................................... | | Tamla 1839 |
| 2/28/87 | 2¹ | 19 | 35 **Just To See Her** ...................................... | 8 | Motown 1877 |
| 6/20/87 | 3 | 18 | 36 **One Heartbeat** ........................................ | 10 | Motown 1897 |
| 10/17/87 | 16 | 14 | 37 What's Too Much ....................................... | 79 | Motown 1911 |
| 2/06/88 | 31 | 13 | 38 Love Don't Give No Reason .......................... | | Motown 1925 |
| | | | **SUGAR CHILE ROBINSON** Born Frankie Robinson in 1940 in Detroit. Vocalist/pianist. Child prodigy on piano since age two. Worked with Frankie Carle and Lionel Hampton. Performed for President Truman at age 7. Appeared in the film "No Leave, No Love". | | |
| 10/01/49 | 4 | 17 | 1 **Numbers Boogie**...................................... | | Capitol 70037 |
| | | | Best Seller #4 / Juke Box #9 | | |
| 12/17/49 | 14 | 1 | 2 Caldonia................................................... | | Capitol 70056 |
| | | | Best Seller #14 / Juke Box #14 | | |
| | | | **VICKI SUE ROBINSON** Born in 1955 in Philadelphia. In the original Broadway productions of "Hair" and "Jesus Christ Superstar". | | |
| 5/29/76 | 73 | 8 | 1 Turn The Beat Around ................................. | 10 | RCA 10562 |
| 11/13/76 | 91 | 2 | 2 Daylight .................................................. | 63 | RCA 10775 |
| 8/27/77 | 91 | 3 | 3 Hold Tight ................................................ | 67 | RCA 11028 |
| | | | **ALEXANDER ROBOTNICK** | | |
| 7/27/85 | 84 | 6 | 1 Problemes D'Amour.................................. [F] | | Sire 28967 |
| | | | **JOHN ROCCA** Lead singer of Freeez. | | |
| 5/05/84 | 55 | 8 | 1 I Want It To Be Real ................................... | | Streetwise 1125 |
| | | | **ROCHELL & THE CANDLES** Los Angeles-based group, formed in 1958. Consisted of Johnny Wyatt (b: 1938; d: 1983) Rochell Henderson, Melvin Sasso and T.C. Henderson. | | |
| 3/27/61 | 20 | 3 | 1 Once Upon A Time ...................................... | 26 | Swingin' 623 |
| | | | featuring Marvin Phillips on piano | | |

| DEBUT DATE | PEAK POS | WKS CHR | ARTIST — Record Title | POP POS | Label & Number |
|---|---|---|---|---|---|
| | | | **ROCK MASTER SCOTT & THE DYNAMIC THREE** | | |
| 12/08/84+ | **21** | 14 | 1　Request Line ................................................. | *103* | Reality 951 |
| 7/06/85 | **45** | 12 | 2　The Roof Is On Fire (Scratchin') ....................... | | Reality 955 |
| | | | **ROCKER'S REVENGE** | | |
| 9/18/82 | **63** | 8 | 1　Walking On Sunshine................................. | | Streetwise 2203 |
| 2/11/84 | **69** | 6 | 2　There Goes My Heart ............................... | | Streetwise 2218 |
| | | | **ROCKET** | | |
| 5/07/83 | **72** | 9 | 1　Here Comes My Love ................................. | | Quality 033 |
| | | | **ROCKIN' REBELS - see THE REBELS** | | |
| | | | **ROCKWELL** | | |
| | | | Born Kennedy Gordy on 3/15/64 in Detroit. Son of Motown chairman, Berry Gordy, Jr. | | |
| 1/28/84 | **1**⁵ | 17 | 1●**Somebody's Watching Me** ........................... <br> background vocals by Michael Jackson | 2 | Motown 1702 |
| 5/12/84 | **9** | 14 | 2　**Obscene Phone Caller**............................ | 35 | Motown 1731 |
| 1/26/85 | **65** | 6 | 3　He's A Cobra ....................................... | *108* | Motown 1772 |
| 6/14/86 | **46** | 9 | 4　Carme (Part 1) ...................................... | | Motown 1845 |
| | | | **ROD** | | |
| 7/26/80 | **49** | 11 | 1　Shake It Up (Do The Boogaloo)....................... | | Prelude 8014 |
| | | | **JIMMIE RODGERS** | | |
| | | | Pop vocalist/guitarist/pianist born on 9/18/33 in Camas, Washington. Own NBC-TV series in 1959. Career hampered following mysterious assault in Los Angeles on 12/1/67, which left him with a fractured skull. Returned to performing on 1/28/69. | | |
| 9/09/57 | **1**² | 13 | 1　**Honeycomb** ......................................... <br> Best Seller #1(2) / Jockey #1(1) | *1* | Roulette 4015 |
| 12/09/57+ | **8** | 6 | 2　**Kisses Sweeter Than Wine**........................ <br> Best Seller #8 | *3* | Roulette 4031 |
| 3/17/58 | **19** | 2 | 3　Oh-Oh, I'm Falling In Love Again .................... <br> Best Seller #19 | *7* | Roulette 4045 |
| 6/02/58 | **7** | 10 | 4　**Secretly/** <br> Best Seller #7 / Jockey #11 | *3* | |
| | | 2 | 5　Make Me A Miracle................................... <br> Best Seller flip <br> all of above: with Hugo Peretti & His Orchestra | *16* | Roulette 4070 |
| | | | **NILE RODGERS** | | |
| | | | Born on 9/19/52 in New York City. Guitarist/producer, member of Chic and The Honeydrippers. Produced Madonna's "Like A Virgin" single. | | |
| 5/25/85 | **35** | 10 | 1　Let's Go Out Tonight ..................................... | *88* | Warner 29049 |
| | | | **TOMMY ROE** | | |
| | | | Born on 5/9/42 in Atlanta. Pop-rock singer/guitarist/composer. Formed band, The Satins in the late 50s. Moved to Britain in the mid-60s; returned in 1969. | | |
| 8/18/62 | **6** | 10 | 1●**Sheila**................................................... <br> originally released on Judd 1022 | *1* | ABC-Para. 10329 |
| | | | **ROGER** | | |
| | | | Roger Troutman from Hamilton, Ohio. Leader of the family group Zapp. Worked with Sly Stone and George Clinton. | | |
| 8/22/81 | **1**² | 23 | 1　**I Heard It Through The Grapevine** ............... | *79* | Warner 49786 |
| 12/19/81+ | **24** | 14 | 2　Do It Roger ........................................ | | Warner 49883 |
| 5/12/84 | **10** | 15 | 3　**In The Mix** ...................................... | | Warner 29271 |
| 7/28/84 | **34** | 10 | 4　Midnight Hour - Part I ............................... <br> featuring The Mighty Clouds Of Joy | | Warner 29231 |
| 1/26/85 | **79** | 4 | 5　Girl, Cut It Out ..................................... <br> featuring Shirley Murdock | | Warner 29123 |
| 10/03/87 | **1**¹ | 19 | 6　**I Want To Be Your Man** .............................. | *3* | Reprise 28229 |
| 2/20/88 | **27** | 10 | 7　Thrill Seekers................................................ | | Reprise 27982 |
| | | | **D.J. ROGERS** | | |
| | | | DeWayne Julius Rogers - vocalist/keyboardist/composer from Los Angeles; the brother-in-law of Michael Wycoff. Worked with James Cleveland, the director of Watts Community Choir. Also a member of the Los Angeles Community Choir. | | |
| 3/06/76 | **51** | 17 | 1　Say You Love Me ........................................ | *98* | RCA 10568 |
| 9/18/76 | **78** | 5 | 2　Let My Life Shine.................................... | | RCA 10760 |
| 7/15/78 | **20** | 15 | 3　Love Brought Me Back ............................... | | Columbia 10754 |
| 11/25/78 | **87** | 5 | 4　All My Love (Part 1)................................. | | Columbia 10836 |

| DEBUT DATE | PEAK POS | WKS CHR | ARTIST — Record Title | POP POS | Label & Number |
|---|---|---|---|---|---|
| | | | **D.J. ROGERS — Continued** | | |
| 5/19/79 | **68** | 8 | 5 Trust Me (Part 1)........................................... | | ARC 10963 |
| 5/10/80 | **44** | 8 | 6 Love Cycles ................................................. | | ARC 11254 |
| 6/07/80 | **47** | 7 | 7 Givin' It Up Is Givin' Up................................ | | Elektra 46647 |
| | | | **PATRICE RUSHEN & D.J. ROGERS** | | |
| 8/16/80 | **66** | 4 | 8 She Believes In Me ...................................... | | ARC 11324 |
| | | | **JIMMY ROGERS** | | |
| | | | Born James A. Lane on 6/3/24 in Ruleville, Mississippi; raised in Atlanta. Singer/ guitarist/pianist/harmonica player. To Chicago in 1941. First recorded for Ora-Nelle in 1947. Much session work. Active into the late 70s. Also see Muddy Waters. | | |
| 2/16/57 | **14** | 1 | 1 Walking By Myself......................................... | | Chess 1643 |
| | | | Best Seller #14 with Big Walter Horton on harmonica | | |
| | | | **KENNY ROGERS** | | |
| | | | Pop-country singer/actor born on 8/21/38 in Houston. In Kirby Stone Four and The New Christy Minstrels, mid-60s. Formed The First Edition in 1967. Went solo in 1973. Appeared in the films "The Gambler", "Coward Of The County" and "Six Pack". | | |
| 11/08/80 | **42** | 10 | 1 ● Lady ........................................................ | 1 | Liberty 1380 |
| | | | written by Lionel Richie | | |
| 10/06/84 | **57** | 9 | 2 What About Me? ......................................... | 15 | RCA 13899 |
| | | | **KENNY ROGERS with KIM CARNES & JAMES INGRAM** | | |
| | | | **LEE ROGERS** | | |
| 1/30/65 | **17** | 7 | 1 I Want You To Have Everything ...................... | 114 | D-Town 1035 |
| | | | **THE ROLLERS** | | |
| | | | San Bernardino quartet consisting of Eddie Wilson, Don Sampson, Al Wilson and Willie Willingham. Wilson had solo hits in the late 60s. | | |
| 5/22/61 | **28** | 1 | 1 The Continental Walk ................................... | 80 | Liberty 55320 |
| | | | **THE ROLLING STONES** | | |
| | | | R&B-influenced rock group formed in London in January of 1963. Consisted of Mick Jagger, Keith Richards, Brian Jones, Bill Wyman and Charlie Watts. Took name from a Muddy Waters' tune. Jones left group shortly before drowning on 7/3/69; replaced by Mick Taylor. Ron Wood replaced Taylor in 1975. Considered by many as the world's greatest rock band of all-time. | | |
| 7/24/65 | **19** | 7 | 1 ● (I Can't Get No) Satisfaction ......................... | 1 | London 9766 |
| 4/02/66 | **32** | 2 | 2 19th Nervous Breakdown.............................. | 2 | London 9823 |
| | | | above 2: produced by Andrew Loog Oldham | | |
| 8/07/76 | **84** | 4 | 3 Hot Stuff .................................................. | 49 | Rolling S. 19304 |
| 6/17/78 | **33** | 13 | 4 ● Miss You ................................................. | 1 | Rolling S. 19307 |
| | | | all of above: written by Jagger & Richards | | |
| | | | **LYN ROMAN** | | |
| 11/22/86 | **78** | 8 | 1 Don't Look Back .......................................... | | Ichiban 110 |
| | | | **ROMEO** | | |
| 7/18/87 | **67** | 9 | 1 Ooh Baby Baby ........................................... | | Triple 706 |
| | | | **THE ROMEOS** | | |
| | | | Philadelphia group featuring producers Kenny Gamble and Thom Bell, with Roland and Karl Chambers and Winnie Walford. Gamble was a member of the Voice Masters. | | |
| 4/08/67 | **31** | 9 | 1 Precious Memories ................................... [I] | 67 | Mark II 101 |
| | | | **THE RONETTES** | | |
| | | | Formed in New York City as the Darling Sisters in 1958. Consisted of Veronica "Ronnie" Bennett Spector (b: 8/10/45), sister Estelle Bennett Vann (b: 7/22/44), and cousin Nedra Talley Ross (b: 1/27/46). Sang professionally since junior high school. Recorded as Ronnie & The Relatives for Colpix/May in 1961. Worked as the Rondettes at Peppermint Lounges, Miami and New York, in 1961. Back-up work for Phil Spector in 1962. Group disbanded in 1966. Veronica married to Phil Spector from 1968-74. | | |
| 9/21/63 | **4** | 10 | 1 Be My Baby ............................................... | 2 | Philles 116 |
| 12/21/63+ | **24** | 9 | 2 Baby, I Love You .......................................... | Hot | Philles 118 |
| 4/04/64 | **39** | 8 | 3 (The Best Part Of) Breakin' Up........................ | Hot | Philles 120 |
| 6/20/64 | **34** | 9 | 4 Do I Love You? ........................................... | Hot | Philles 121 |
| 1/30/65 | **28** | 1 | 5 Walking In The Rain ..................................... | 23 | Philles 123 |
| | | | all of above: produced by Phil Spector | | |
| | | | **LINDA RONSTADT** | | |
| | | | Pop vocalist born on 7/15/46 in Tucson, Arizona. Successful in folk, country, rock, opera and adult contemporary. | | |
| 1/20/79 | **77** | 4 | 1 Ooh Baby Baby ........................................... | 7 | Asylum 45546 |

| DEBUT DATE | PEAK POS | WKS CHR | ARTIST — Record Title | POP POS | Label & Number |
|---|---|---|---|---|---|
| | | | **THE ROOFTOP SINGERS** | | |
| | | | Folk trio consisting of Erik Darling, Willard Svanoe and Lynne Taylor (d: 1982). Group disbanded in 1967. Darling was a member of The Tarriers in 1956, and The Weavers from 1958-62. | | |
| 1/26/63 | 4 | 9 | 1 **Walk Right In**.............................................. | *1* | Vanguard 35017 |
| 5/04/63 | 30 | 1 | 2 Tom Cat ...................................................... | 20 | Vanguard 35019 |
| | | | **ROSCOE & MABLE** | | |
| 2/19/77 | 92 | 2 | 1 United We Stand.......................................... | | Choc. City 007 |
| | | | **THE ROSE BROTHERS** | | |
| | | | Quartet consists of brothers Bobby, Greg, Kenny and Larry Rose. | | |
| 3/22/86 | 28 | 16 | 1 I Get Off On You........................................... | | Muscle Sh. 102 |
| 8/02/86 | 93 | 4 | 2 Wall To Wall Freaks ..................................... | | Muscle Sh. 103 |
| 12/20/86+ | 29 | 15 | 3 Easy Lover.................................................... | | Muscle Sh. 3003 |
| 4/18/87 | 66 | 8 | 4 I Get A Rush ................................................ | | Muscle Sh. 105 |
| 12/19/87+ | 68 | 11 | 5 I Put My Money Where My Mouth Is.................. | | Muscle Sh. 108 |
| 3/19/88 | 69 | 10 | 6 In The Mix .................................................. | | Muscle Sh. 109 |
| | | | **ROSE ROYCE**   ★★171★★ | | |
| | | | Los Angeles group formed as a backing band. Consisted of Kenji Brown (guitar), Victor Nix (keyboards), Kenny Copeland, Freddie Dunn (trumpets), Michael Moore (saxophone), Lequient "Duke" Jobe (bass), Henry Garner and Terral Santiel (drums). Backed Edwin Starr as Total Concept Unlimited in 1973; Yvonne Fair as Magic Wand. Backed The Temptations. Became regular band for Undisputed Truth. Vocalist Gwen Dickey added, name changed to Rose Royce in 1976. Did soundtrack for the film "Car Wash". Nix replaced by Michael Nash in 1976. Dickey and Brown replaced by Richee Benson and Walter McKinney in 1980. | | |
| 10/09/76 | 1 [2] | 22 | 1▲**Car Wash**................................................ | *1* | MCA 40615 |
| 2/26/77 | 3 | 13 | 2 I Wanna Get Next To You ............................. | 10 | MCA 40662 |
| 5/14/77 | 10 | 12 | 3 **I'm Going Down**........................................ | 70 | MCA 40721 |
| | | | above 3: from the film "Car Wash" | | |
| 9/03/77 | 4 | 17 | 4 **Do Your Dance - Part 1** .............................. | 39 | Whitfield 8440 |
| 11/19/77+ | 3 | 14 | 5 **Ooh Boy**.................................................... | 72 | Whitfield 8491 |
| | | | all of above: written & produced by Norman Whitfield | | |
| 2/25/78 | 52 | 7 | 6 Wishing On A Star........................................ | 101 | Whitfield 8531 |
| 8/05/78 | 5 | 17 | 7 **I'm In Love (And I Love The Feeling)**............. | | Whitfield 8629 |
| 10/28/78 | 5 | 16 | 8 **Love Don't Live Here Anymore**...................... | 32 | Whitfield 8712 |
| 4/14/79 | 65 | 6 | 9 First Come, First Serve ................................. | | Whitfield 8789 |
| 9/08/79 | 31 | 10 | 10 Is It Love You're After ................................ | 105 | Whitfield 49049 |
| 7/19/80 | 60 | 9 | 11 Pop Your Fingers ....................................... | | Whitfield 49274 |
| 3/14/81 | 56 | 10 | 12 Golden Touch............................................ | | Whitfield 49681 |
| 4/10/82 | 64 | 8 | 13 Best Love .................................................. | | Epic 02818 |
| 8/04/84 | 77 | 7 | 14 Magic Touch.............................................. | | C&R 7684 |
| 12/06/86+ | 22 | 14 | 15 Doesn't Have To Be This Way........................ | | Omni 99488 |
| 3/07/87 | 45 | 11 | 16 Lonely Road.............................................. | | Omni 99476 |
| | | | sax solo by Grover Washington, Jr. | | |
| 8/15/87 | 69 | 7 | 17 If Walls Could Talk ..................................... | | Omni 96754 |
| | | | **DAVID ROSE** | | |
| | | | Rose was born on 6/15/10 in London; moved to Chicago at an early age. Conductor/composer/arranger for numerous film and television scores. Pianist/composer/conductor/arranger Previn was born on 4/6/29 in Berlin, Germany; came to the U.S. in 1939. He also scored many films. | | |
| 7/20/59 | 22 | 3 | 1 Like Young ........................................ [I] | 46 | MGM 12792 |
| | | | **ANDRE PREVIN & DAVID ROSE** | | |
| 7/14/62 | 12 | 7 | 2 The Stripper.................................... [I] | *1* | MGM 13064 |
| | | | **ROSIE & THE ORIGINALS** | | |
| | | | San Diego group - Rosalie Hamlin, lead singer. | | |
| 1/16/61 | 5 | 8 | 1 Angel Baby ................................................ | *5* | Highland 1011 |
| | | | **DIANA ROSS**   ★★23★★ | | |
| | | | Born Diane Earle on 3/26/44 in Detroit. In vocal group, the Primettes, first recorded for LuPine in 1960. Lead singer of The Supremes from 1961-69. Went solo in late 1969. Oscar nominee for the 1972 film "Lady Sings The Blues". Appeared in the films "Mahogany" and "The Wiz". Also see The Supremes. | | |
| 5/02/70 | 7 | 9 | 1 **Reach Out And Touch (Somebody's Hand)** ...... | 20 | Motown 1165 |
| 8/15/70 | 1 [1] | 12 | 2 **Ain't No Mountain High Enough**.................. | *1* | Motown 1169 |
| 1/09/71 | 10 | 8 | 3 **Remember Me**............................................ | 16 | Motown 1176 |

| DEBUT DATE | PEAK POS | WKS CHR | ARTIST — Record Title | POP POS | Label & Number |
|---|---|---|---|---|---|
| | | | **DIANA ROSS — Continued** | | |
| 5/08/71 | 17 | 6 | 4 Reach Out I'll Be There | 29 | Motown 1184 |
| 9/11/71 | 16 | 5 | 5 Surrender | 38 | Motown 1188 |
| 11/27/71 | 40 | 3 | 6 I'm Still Waiting | 63 | Motown 1192 |
| 2/10/73 | 20 | 8 | 7 Good Morning Heartache | 34 | Motown 1211 |
| | | | from the film "Lady Sings The Blues" | | |
| 6/09/73 | 5 | 14 | 8 **Touch Me In The Morning** | 1 | Motown 1239 |
| 9/29/73 | 4 | 15 | 9 **You're A Special Part Of Me** | 12 | Motown 1280 |
| 12/29/73+ | 15 | 13 | 10 Last Time I Saw Him | 14 | Motown 1278 |
| 2/09/74 | 15 | 14 | 11 My Mistake (Was To Love You) | 19 | Motown 1269 |
| 4/20/74 | 50 | 9 | 12 Sleepin' | 70 | Motown 1295 |
| 7/13/74 | 25 | 12 | 13 Don't Knock My Love | 46 | Motown 1296 |
| | | | 9, 11 & 13: **DIANA ROSS & MARVIN GAYE** | | |
| 11/01/75 | 14 | 17 | 14 Theme From Mahogany (Do You Know Where You're Going To) | 1 | Motown 1377 |
| | | | from the film "Mahogany" | | |
| 3/20/76 | 61 | 3 | 15 I Thought It Took A Little Time (But Today I Fell In Love) | 47 | Motown 1387 |
| 4/03/76 | 1¹ | 17 | 16 **Love Hangover** | 1 | Motown 1392 |
| 7/31/76 | 10 | 13 | 17 **One Love In My Lifetime** | 25 | Motown 1398 |
| 11/05/77 | 16 | 15 | 18 Gettin' Ready For Love | 27 | Motown 1427 |
| 2/25/78 | 16 | 11 | 19 Your Love Is So Good For Me | 49 | Motown 1436 |
| 5/13/78 | 39 | 9 | 20 You Got It | 49 | Motown 1442 |
| 9/16/78 | 17 | 13 | 21 Ease On Down The Road | 41 | MCA 40947 |
| | | | **DIANA ROSS & MICHAEL JACKSON** | | |
| | | | from the film "The Wiz" | | |
| 1/27/79 | 26 | 11 | 22 Pops, We Love You (A Tribute To Father) | 59 | Motown 1455 |
| | | | **DIANA ROSS, MARVIN GAYE, SMOKEY ROBINSON & STEVIE WONDER** | | |
| | | | song written for Berry Gordy Sr.'s 90th birthday | | |
| 1/27/79 | 86 | 3 | 23 What You Gave Me | | Motown 1456 |
| 6/09/79 | 12 | 21 | 24 The Boss | 19 | Motown 1462 |
| 11/10/79 | 27 | 15 | 25 It's My House | | Motown 1471 |
| 7/12/80 | 1⁴ | 19 | 26● Upside Down | 1 | Motown 1494 |
| 9/13/80 | 6 | 16 | 27 I'm Coming Out | 5 | Motown 1491 |
| 11/08/80 | 14 | 15 | 28 It's My Turn | 9 | Motown 1496 |
| | | | from the film of the same title | | |
| 4/04/81 | 54 | 7 | 29 One More Chance | 79 | Motown 1508 |
| 7/11/81 | 1⁷ | 24 | 30▲ Endless Love | 1 | Motown 1519 |
| | | | **DIANA ROSS & LIONEL RICHIE** | | |
| | | | from the film of the same title; written by Lionel Richie | | |
| 10/24/81 | 6 | 17 | 31 **Why Do Fools Fall In Love** | 7 | RCA 12349 |
| 1/09/82 | 2³ | 15 | 32 **Mirror, Mirror** | 8 | RCA 13021 |
| 4/24/82 | 34 | 9 | 33 Work That Body | 44 | RCA 13201 |
| 10/09/82 | 4 | 18 | 34 **Muscles** | 10 | RCA 13348 |
| | | | written by Michael Jackson | | |
| 3/05/83 | 76 | 4 | 35 So Close | 40 | RCA 13424 |
| 7/02/83 | 15 | 14 | 36 Pieces Of Ice | 31 | RCA 13549 |
| 10/01/83 | 60 | 5 | 37 Up Front | | RCA 13624 |
| 12/17/83+ | 52 | 9 | 08 Let's Go Up | 77 | RCA 13671 |
| 7/21/84 | 38 | 11 | 39 All Of You | 19 | Columbia 04507 |
| | | | **JULIO IGLESIAS & DIANA ROSS** | | |
| 9/01/84 | 3 | 16 | 40 **Swept Away** | 19 | RCA 13864 |
| | | | written & produced by Daryl Hall | | |
| 12/08/84+ | 1³ | 24 | 41 **Missing You** | 10 | RCA 13966 |
| | | | dedicated to Marvin Gaye; written & produced by Lionel Richie | | |
| 6/01/85 | 13 | 12 | 42 Telephone | | RCA 14032 |
| 9/28/85 | 10 | 12 | 43 **Eaten Alive** | 77 | RCA 14181 |
| | | | background vocal by Michael Jackson | | |
| 12/21/85 | 85 | 5 | 44 Chain Reaction | 95 | RCA 14244 |
| | | | a new mix was released in 1986; hit POS 66 on the pop charts | | |
| 5/23/87 | 12 | 11 | 45 Dirty Looks | | RCA 5172 |
| | | | **JACKIE ROSS** | | |
| | | | Born on 1/30/46 in St. Louis. Sang gospel on parent's radio show at age 3. Moved to Chicago in 1954. First recorded for Sar in 1962. | | |
| 8/01/64 | 11 | 10 | 1 Selfish One | *Hot* | Chess 1903 |

| DEBUT DATE | PEAK POS | WKS CHR | ARTIST — Record Title | POP POS | Label & Number |
|---|---|---|---|---|---|
| | | | **JACKIE ROSS — Continued** | | |
| 11/14/64 | 89 | 2 | 2 I've Got The Skill ........................................ | *Hot* | Chess 1913 |
| 1/30/65 | 85 | 4 | 3 Jerk And Twine ........................................... | *Hot* | Chess 1920 |
| | | | **JIMMY ROSS** | | |
| 10/03/81 | 50 | 11 | 1 First True Love Affair .................................... | | RFC 7002 |
| | | | **ROUGE - see DESMOND CHILD** | | |
| | | | **ROUNDTREE** | | |
| | | | 38-member studio group produced, arranged and conducted by Kenny Lehman (horns). Members included bassist Bernard Edwards (Chic), vocalists Diva Gray, David Lasley and Luther Vandross. | | |
| 9/30/78 | 76 | 3 | 1 Get On Up (Get On Down)............................. | | Island 8646 |
| | | | **RICHARD ROUNDTREE** | | |
| | | | Born on 7/9/42 in New Rochelle, New York. In the films "What Do You Say To A Naked Lady?" and "Parachute To Paradise" In the TV series "Shaft" from 1973-74. Starred in the TV mini-series "Roots". | | |
| 6/05/76 | 90 | 2 | 1 This Magic Moment ...................................... | | Art. Of Am. 115 |
| | | | **ROXANNE - see UTFO** | | |
| | | | **ROY "C"** | | |
| | | | Born Roy Charles Hammond in 1943 in New York City. With the Genies in the early 60s. Managed the group Mark IV. | | |
| 10/30/65 | 14 | 9 | 1 Shotgun Wedding ........................................ | | Black Hawk 12101 |
| 6/12/71 | 45 | 4 | 2 Got To Get Enough (Of Your Sweet Love Stuff).... | | Alaga 1006 |
| 8/04/73 | 56 | 9 | 3 Don't Blame The Man .................................. | | Mercury 73391 |
| 10/12/74 | 48 | 13 | 4 Loneliness Had Got A Hold On Me/ | | |
| | | 9 | 5 If I Could Love You Forever ......................... | | Mercury 73605 |
| 5/10/75 | 46 | 9 | 6 Love Me Till Tomorrow Comes........................ | | Mercury 73672 |
| | | | **BARBARA ROY** | | |
| | | | Lead singer of Ecstasy, Passion & Pain. Native of Kingston, North Carolina. | | |
| 10/11/86 | 83 | 7 | 1 Gotta See You Tonight ................................. | | RCA 14404 |
| | | | **ROYALCASH** | | |
| 10/15/83 | 35 | 16 | 1 Radio Activity (Part 1).................................. | | Sutra 126 |
| | | | **THE ROYALETTES** | | |
| | | | Baltimore family group: sisters Anita and Sheila Ross, Terry Jones and Ronnie Brown. First recorded for Chancellor in 1962. | | |
| 8/07/65 | 28 | 6 | 1 It's Gonna Take A Miracle ........................... | *41* | MGM 13366 |
| 11/27/65 | 26 | 5 | 2 I Want To Meet Him..................................... | *72* | MGM 13405 |
| | | | **ROYAL HARMONY QUARTET** | | |
| | | | Group which later recorded as the Jubalaires. Formed in 1936; consisted of Caleb "J.C." Ginyard, Jr. (lead; d: 1978), Orville Brooks (tenor), Theodore Brooks (baritone) and George McFadden (bass). Ginyard left Jubalaires in 1946 and formed the Dixieaires. In 1952, he formed the Du Droppers. Also see the Shadows. | | |
| 11/14/42 | 10 | 1 | 1 **Praise The Lord And Pass The Ammunition ...** inspired by words of US Navy Chaplain William MacGuire at Pearl Harbor attack | | Keynote 101 |
| | | | **ROYAL HOUSE** | | |
| 2/27/88 | 84 | 6 | 1 Party People............................................... | | Idlers War 015 |
| | | | **ROYAL TEENS** | | |
| | | | Quartet from Fort Lee, New Jersey. Consisted of Bob Gaudio, Bill Crandall, Billy Dalton and Tom Austin. Crandall was replaced by Larry Qualiano, and Joseph "Joe Villa" Francavilla joined as vocalist in late 1958. In 1960, Gaudio joined The 4 Seasons. Al Kooper joined the group for a short time in 1959. | | |
| 2/10/58 | 2[1] | 10 | 1 **Short Shorts** ........................................... Jockey #2 / Best Seller #3 originally released on Power 215 | *3* | ABC-Para. 9882 |
| | | | **THE ROYALS - see HANK BALLARD & THE MIDNIGHTERS** | | |
| | | | **RUBY & THE PARTY GANG** | | |
| 12/11/71 | 29 | 5 | 1 Hey Ruby (Shut Your Mouth)......................... | *105* | Law-Ton 1554 |

| DEBUT DATE | PEAK POS | WKS CHR | ARTIST — Record Title | POP POS | Label & Number |
|---|---|---|---|---|---|
| | | | ### RUBY & THE ROMANTICS | | |
| | | | Formed in 1961 in Akron, Ohio. Consisted of Ruby Nash Curtis (b: 11/12/39, lead), Ed Roberts and George Lee (tenors), Ronald Mosley (baritone) and Leroy Fann (d: 1973, bass). The male members had been working in Akron as the Supremes. In 1966, group consisted of Ruby, Richard Pryor, Vincent McLeod, Robert Lewis, Ronald Jackson and Bill Evans. Became all-female trio in 1968 with Denise Lewis and Cheryl Thomas. | | |
| 3/02/63 | 1² | 12 | 1  **Our Day Will Come**.................................... | *1* | Kapp 501 |
| 10/26/63 | 47 | 8 | 2  Young Wings Can Fly (Higher Than You Know)... | *Hot* | Kapp 557 |
| 3/21/64 | 64 | 6 | 3  Our Everlasting Love ...................................... | *Hot* | Kapp 578 |
| 7/18/64 | 75 | 4 | 4  Baby Come Home.......................................... | *Hot* | Kapp 601 |
| 10/03/64 | 48 | 8 | 5  When You're Young And In Love .................... | *Hot* | Kapp 615 |
| | | | ### RUE | | |
| 3/14/87 | 84 | 4 | 1  I Need Your Loving ...................................... | | Asiana 1002 |
| | | | ### DAVID RUFFIN     ★★173★★ | | |
| | | | Born on 1/18/41 in Meridian, Mississippi. Brother of Jimmy Ruffin. With the Dixie Nightingales gospel group. Recorded for Anna in 1960. Co-lead singer of The Temptations from 1963-68. | | |
| 2/22/69 | 2¹ | 11 | 1  **My Whole World Ended (The Moment You Left Me)** .................................................... | 9 | Motown 1140 |
| 7/19/69 | 11 | 8 | 2  I've Lost Everything I've Ever Loved................ | 58 | Motown 1149 |
| 12/20/69+ | 18 | 7 | 3  I'm So Glad I Fell For You............................. | 53 | Motown 1158 |
| 10/31/70 | 24 | 7 | 4  Stand By Me.............................................. DAVID & JIMMY RUFFIN | 61 | Soul 35076 |
| 7/28/73 | 84 | 3 | 5  Common Man ............................................ | | Motown 1259 |
| 11/15/75+ | 1¹ | 17 | 6  **Walk Away From Love**.............................. | 9 | Motown 1376 |
| 3/06/76 | 8 | 13 | 7  **Heavy Love** ............................................ | 47 | Motown 1388 |
| 6/12/76 | 8 | 14 | 8  **Everything's Coming Up Love** ........................ | 49 | Motown 1393 |
| 10/30/76 | 48 | 8 | 9  On And Off................................................ above 4: produced by Van McCoy | | Motown 1405 |
| 7/30/77 | 18 | 16 | 10  Just Let Me Hold You For A Night.................... | 106 | Motown 1420 |
| 2/04/78 | 71 | 5 | 11  You're My Peace Of Mind ............................. | | Motown 1435 |
| 8/18/79 | 9 | 17 | 12  **Break My Heart** ...................................... | | Warner 49030 |
| 12/08/79 | 79 | 6 | 13  I Get Excited ............................................ | | Warner 49123 |
| 7/26/80 | 63 | 8 | 14  Slow Dance .............................................. | | Warner 49277 |
| 9/14/85 | 40 | 9 | 15  A Nite At The Apollo Live! The Way You Do The Things You Do/My Girl ............................. DARYL HALL JOHN OATES with DAVID RUFFIN & EDDIE KENDRICK recorded at the re-opening of New York's Apollo Theatre; revival of two early Temptations' hits | 20 | RCA 14178 |
| 10/17/87 | 14 | 16 | 16  I Couldn't Believe It.................................... DAVID RUFFIN & EDDIE KENDRICK | | RCA 5313 |
| 2/06/88 | 43 | 10 | 17  One More For The Lonely Hearts Club ............. DAVID RUFFIN & EDDIE KENDRICK | | RCA 6925 |
| | | | ### JIMMY RUFFIN | | |
| | | | Born on 5/7/39 in Collinsville, Mississippi. Brother of David Ruffin. Back-up work at Motown in the early 60s. First recorded for Miracle in 1961. | | |
| 8/06/66 | 6 | 21 | 1  **What Becomes Of The Brokenhearted** ........... | 7 | Soul 35022 |
| 12/24/66+ | 10 | 10 | 2  **I've Passed This Way Before** ........................ | 17 | Soul 35027 |
| 4/08/67 | 14 | 8 | 3  Gonna Give Her All The Love I've Got .............. | 29 | Soul 35032 |
| 8/19/67 | 27 | 6 | 4  Don't You Miss Me A Little Bit Baby................ | 68 | Soul 35035 |
| 10/31/70 | 24 | 7 | 5  Stand By Me............................................... DAVID & JIMMY RUFFIN | 61 | Soul 35076 |
| 12/14/74+ | 42 | 11 | 6  Tell Me What You Want................................ | | Chess 2160 |
| 3/15/80 | 29 | 12 | 7  Hold On To My Love ................................... written & produced by Robin Gibb | 10 | RSO 1021 |
| 11/13/82+ | 17 | 15 | 8  Turn To Me ............................................... MAXINE NIGHTINGALE featuring JIMMY RUFFIN | | Highrise 2004 |
| | | | ### RUFUS Featuring CHAKA KHAN     ★★64★★ | | |
| | | | Chicago group that evolved from members of the rock quartet American Breed. First known as Smoke, then Ask Rufus. Varying membership. Group included Chaka Khan (lead), Tony Maiden (guitar), Nate Morgan & Kevin Murphy (keyboards), Bobby Watson (bass) and Andre Fischer (drums). Khan recorded solo and with Rufus since 1978. After 1978, Maiden and David Wolinski also sang lead. Watson's brother, Rene Moore, recorded in the duo, Rene & Angela, with Angela Winbush. | | |
| 7/28/73 | 40 | 9 | 1  Whoever's Thrilling You (Is Killing Me)............. | | ABC 11376 |

| DEBUT DATE | PEAK POS | WKS CHR | ARTIST — Record Title | POP POS | Label & Number |
|---|---|---|---|---|---|
| | | | **RUFUS Featuring CHAKA KHAN — Continued** | | |
| 11/17/73+ | 45 | 10 | 2 Feel Good ................................................ | | ABC 11394 |
| 6/01/74 | 3 | 19 | 3● Tell Me Something Good .......................... | 3 | ABC 11427 |
| | | | shown only as: **RUFUS** written by Stevie Wonder | | |
| 10/19/74 | 1¹ | 15 | 4 **You Got The Love** ...................................... | 11 | ABC 12032 |
| 2/08/75 | 4 | 17 | 5 Once You Get Started .............................. | 10 | ABC 12066 |
| 5/31/75 | 6 | 13 | 6 **Please Pardon Me (You Remind Me Of A Friend)**.............................................. | 48 | ABC 12099 |
| 12/20/75+ | 1² | 19 | 7● Sweet Thing.......................................... | 5 | ABC 12149 |
| 4/17/76 | 5 | 13 | 8 Dance Wit Me ........................................ | 39 | ABC 12179 |
| 7/31/76 | 35 | 11 | 9 Jive Talkin' ............................................ | | ABC 12197 |
| | | | #1 pop hit for The Bee Gees in 1975 | | |
| 2/05/77 | 1² | 15 | 10 **At Midnight (My Love Will Lift You Up)**.......... | 30 | ABC 12239 |
| 4/30/77 | 3 | 12 | 11 Hollywood ............................................ | 32 | ABC 12269 |
| | | | **RUFUS & CHAKA KHAN:** | | |
| 8/06/77 | 17 | 13 | 12 Everlasting Love .................................... | | ABC 12296 |
| 3/25/78 | 3 | 18 | 13 Stay.................................................... | 38 | ABC 12349 |
| 7/29/78 | 34 | 9 | 14 Blue Love .............................................. | 105 | ABC 12390 |
| 1/20/79 | 16 | 12 | 15 Keep It Togcther (Declaration Of Love)............... | 109 | ABC 12444 |
| | | | shown only as: **RUFUS** | | |
| 10/13/79 | 1³ | 23 | 16 **Do You Love What You Feel** ...................... | 30 | MCA 41131 |
| 3/01/80 | 24 | 10 | 17 Any Love.............................................. | 102 | MCA 41191 |
| 5/17/80 | 43 | 8 | 18 I'm Dancing For Your Love ...................... | | MCA 41230 |
| 3/07/81 | 18 | 16 | 19 Tonight We Love .................................... | | MCA 51070 |
| | | | shown only as: **RUFUS** | | |
| 6/27/81 | 56 | 7 | 20 Hold On To A Friend................................ | | MCA 51125 |
| | | | only shown as: **RUFUS** | | |
| 10/31/81 | 8 | 14 | 21 **Sharing The Love** .................................... | 91 | MCA 51203 |
| 2/20/82 | 66 | 5 | 22 Better Together ...................................... | | MCA 52002 |
| | | | vocals by Chaka Khan and Tony Maiden | | |
| 2/05/83 | 47 | 9 | 23 Take It To The Hop ................................ | | Warner 29790 |
| | | | shown only as: **RUFUS** | | |
| 7/30/83 | 1¹ | 27 | 24 **Ain't Nobody**........................................ | 22 | Warner 29555 |
| 1/28/84 | 37 | 11 | 25 One Million Kisses.................................. | 102 | Warner 29406 |

## RUFUS & CARLA - see RUFUS THOMAS and/or CARLA THOMAS

## RUN-D.M.C.  ★★178★★

Rap trio from Queens, New York: Rappers Joseph Simmons (Run), Darryl McDaniels (DMC) and deejay Jason Mizell (Jam Master Jay). Also see The Krush Groove All Stars.

| DEBUT DATE | PEAK POS | WKS CHR | ARTIST — Record Title | POP POS | Label & Number |
|---|---|---|---|---|---|
| 5/21/83 | 15 | 20 | 1 It's Like That ........................................ | | Profile 5019 |
| 1/07/84 | 11 | 16 | 2 Hard Times/ | | |
| | | 16 | 3 Jam-Master Jay...................................... | | Profile 5036 |
| | | | above 2: music by Orange Krush | | |
| 4/28/84 | 22 | 13 | 4 Rock Box................................................ | | Profile 5045 |
| 7/28/84 | 16 | 13 | 5 30 Days................................................ | | Profile 5051 |
| 11/10/84 | 65 | 6 | 6 Hollis Crew ............................................ | | Profile 5058 |
| 2/09/85 | 14 | 14 | 7 King Of Rock .......................................... | 108 | Profile 5064 |
| 5/04/85 | 19 | 14 | 8 You Talk Too Much .................................. | 107 | Profile 5069 |
| 9/14/85 | 53 | 8 | 9 Jam-Master Jammin' ................................ | | Profile 7080 |
| 12/07/85+ | 19 | 16 | 10 Can You Rock It Like This .......................... | | Profile 7088 |
| | | | from the film "Krush Groove" | | |
| 5/17/86 | 5 | 16 | 11 **My Adidas**.............................................. | | Profile 5102 |
| 8/02/86 | 8 | 14 | 12 **Walk This Way** ...................................... | 4 | Profile 5112 |
| | | | featuring Aerosmith's Steve Tyler (vocals) & Joe Perry (guitar) | | |
| 10/25/86 | 12 | 16 | 13 You Be Illin'............................................ | 29 | Profile 5119 |
| 2/21/87 | 21 | 13 | 14 It's Tricky.............................................. | 57 | Profile 5131 |
| 4/30/88 | 10 | 12 | 15 **Run's House** .......................................... | | Profile 5202 |

## RUSH RELEASE - see WAYNE MIRAN

| DEBUT DATE | PEAK POS | WKS CHR | ARTIST — Record Title | POP POS | Label & Number |
|---|---|---|---|---|---|
| | | | **BOBBY RUSH** Born Emmett Ellis, Jr. on 11/10/40 in Homer, Louisiana. Singer/keyboardist/ guitarist/bassist/drummer/composer. To Chicago in 1953. Currently active in Jackson, Mississippi. | | |
| 7/10/71 | **34** | 8 | 1 Chicken Heads.............................................. | | Galaxy 778 |
| 7/28/79 | **75** | 5 | 2 I Wanna Do The Do ...................................... | | Phil. Int. 3695 |
| | | | **OTIS RUSH** Born on 4/29/34 in Philadelphia, Mississippi. Vocalist/guitarist/harmonica player. Moved to Chicago in 1948. Own group as Little Otis from 1955-60. | | |
| 10/13/56 | **6** | 6 | 1 **I Can't Quit You Baby**............................... Juke Box #6 / Best Seller #9 | | Cobra 5000 |
| | | | **PATRICE RUSHEN** Born on 9/30/54 in Los Angeles. Vocalist/pianist/songwriter. Much session work with Jean Luc-Ponty, Lee Ritenour and Stanley Turrentine. | | |
| 12/16/78+ | **16** | 15 | 1 Hang It Up ................................................. | | Elektra 45549 |
| 4/14/79 | **87** | 2 | 2 When I Found You....................................... | | Elektra 46024 |
| 11/10/79+ | **7** | 22 | 3 **Haven't You Heard** ................................... | 42 | Elektra 46551 |
| 4/05/80 | **50** | 7 | 4 Let The Music Take Me ............................... | | Elektra 46604 |
| 6/07/80 | **47** | 7 | 5 Givin' It Up Is Givin' Up.............................. | | Elektra 46647 |
| | | | **PATRICE RUSHEN & D.J. ROGERS** | | |
| 10/25/80 | **13** | 17 | 6 Look Up ..................................................... | 102 | Elektra 47067 |
| 2/21/81 | **30** | 9 | 7 Never Gonna Give You Up (Part 1) .................... | | Elektra 47113 |
| 3/13/82 | **4** | 23 | 8 **Forget Me Nots**........................................ | 23 | Elektra 47427 |
| 8/07/82 | **46** | 8 | 9 Breakout! ................................................... | | Elektra 69992 |
| 12/04/82 | **79** | 4 | 10 I Was Tired Of Being Alone (Glad I Got Cha)....... | | Elektra 69930 |
| 5/12/84 | **3** | 17 | 11 **Feels So Real (Won't Let Go)** ...................... | 78 | Elektra 69742 |
| 8/18/84 | **26** | 12 | 12 Get Off (You Fascinate Me) ........................... | | Elektra 69702 |
| 3/07/87 | **9** | 16 | 13 **Watch Out** .............................................. | | Arista 9562 |
| 7/25/87 | **51** | 8 | 14 Anything Can Happen .................................. | | Arista 9604 |
| 12/05/87+ | **65** | 10 | 15 Come Back To Me ....................................... | | Arista 9644 |
| | | | **BRENDA RUSSELL** Singer/keyboardist/composer born Brenda Gordon in Brooklyn, New York. To Toronto at age 12. Recorded as duo, Brian & Brenda, with former husband Brian Russell in 1978; co-hosted the Canadian TV series "Music Machine". Session work for Barbra Streisand, Elton John, Bette Midler, and many others. | | |
| 8/25/79 | **15** | 18 | 1 So Good, So Right ....................................... | 30 | Horizon 123 |
| 2/02/80 | **42** | 9 | 2 Way Back When........................................... | | A&M 2207 |
| 4/25/81 | **50** | 9 | 3 If You Love (The One You Lose) ....................... | | A&M 2326 |
| 3/05/88 | **8** | 19 | 4 **Piano In The Dark** .................................... features male vocals by Joe Esposito (Brooklyn Dreams) | 6 | A&M 3003 |
| | | | **LUIS RUSSELL** Born on 8/5/02 in Careening Cay, Panama. Died of cancer on 12/11/63. Pianist/ arranger/leader. To New Orleans in 1919. To Chicago in 1924. With King Oliver from 1925-27. Own band in New York in 1927, became the Louis Armstrong band from 1935-44. Formed another band from 1944-48 in New York. | | |
| 10/05/46 | **3** | 3 | 1 **The Very Thought Of You**........................... [I] | | Apollo 1012 |
| | | | **SAM RUSSELL** | | |
| 11/03/73 | **70** | 8 | 1 It's So Nice .............................................. | | Playboy 50031 |
| | | | **BOBBY RYDELL** Pop singer/actor born Robert Riderelli on 4/26/42 in Philadelphia. Regular on Paul Whiteman's amateur TV show from 1951-54. Drummer with Rocco & The Saints, which included Frankie Avalon on trumpet in 1956. | | |
| 9/28/59 | **29** | 1 | 1 Kissin' Time................................................ | 11 | Cameo 167 |
| 2/15/60 | **10** | 11 | 2 **Wild One**................................................ | 2 | Cameo 171 |
| 8/15/60 | **9** | 9 | 3 **Volare** ................................................... | 4 | Cameo 179 |

# S

| DEBUT DATE | PEAK POS | WKS CHR | ARTIST — Record Title | POP POS | Label & Number |
|---|---|---|---|---|---|
| | | | **SADANE** | | |
| | | | Marc Sadane, singer/dancer from Savannah, Georgia. Studied fashion design at the Fashion Institute of Technology in New York City. Lead singer for Tungsten Steele. Left for solo career in 1977. Vocalist for the house band at Mikell's in New York City. Toured with Stephanie Mills. | | |
| 2/21/81 | 34 | 13 | 1 One-Way Love Affair.................................... | | Warner 49663 |
| 5/23/81 | 78 | 5 | 2 Sit Up ..................................................... | | Warner 49727 |
| 6/19/82 | 78 | 3 | 3 One Minute From Love.............................. | | Warner 29985 |
| 8/28/82 | 64 | 6 | 4 Exciting.................................................. | | Warner 29946 |
| | | | MARC SADANE all of above: written & produced by James Mtume and Reggie Lucas | | |
| | | | **SADE** | | |
| | | | Born Helen Folasade Adu on 1/16/59 in Nigeria; moved to London at age 4. Appeared in the 1986 film "Absolute Beginners". A former designer of menswear. | | |
| 11/24/84+ | 14 | 19 | 1 Hang On To Your Love................................. | 102 | Portrait 04664 |
| 3/09/85 | 5 | 17 | 2 **Smooth Operator** ........................................ | 5 | Portrait 04807 |
| 6/29/85 | 35 | 12 | 3 Your Love Is King ...................................... | 54 | Portrait 05408 |
| 11/30/85+ | 3 | 20 | 4 **The Sweetest Taboo** ................................... | 5 | Portrait 05713 |
| 3/22/86 | 8 | 14 | 5 **Never As Good As The First Time**................. | 20 | Portrait 05846 |
| 7/05/86 | 55 | 7 | 6 Is It A Crime ............................................ | | Portrait 06121 |
| 5/14/88 | 1¹ | 14 | 7 **Paradise** ................................................. | 16 | Epic 07904 |
| | | | **OLIVER SAIN** | | |
| | | | Born on 3/1/32 in Dundee, Mississippi. Bandleader/saxophonist/drummer. Moved to St. Louis in 1960. First band featured Little Milton (vocals). Discovered Fontella Bass and Bobby McClure. | | |
| 4/05/75 | 78 | 4 | 1 Booty Bumpin' (The Double Bump)............... [I] | | Abet 9458 |
| 1/24/76 | 16 | 12 | 2 Party Hearty ............................................ | 103 | Abet 9463 |
| 4/30/77 | 100 | 3 | 3 Feel Like Dancing ...................................... | | Abet 9472 |
| | | | **JON ST. JAMES** | | |
| 4/21/84 | 89 | 3 | 1 Oogity Boogity.......................................... | 105 | EMI America 8198 |
| | | | **ST. PAUL** | | |
| | | | Paul Peterson from Minneapolis. Joined The Time at age 16. Co-founder and leader of The Family. Performed in the Prince film "Purple Rain". | | |
| 10/24/87 | 32 | 16 | 1 Rich Man.................................................. | | MCA 53110 |
| | | | **SAINT TROPEZ** | | |
| | | | Disco studio production by W. Michael Lewis and Laurin Rinder. | | |
| 5/12/79 | 90 | 4 | 1 One More Minute........................................ | 49 | Butterfly 41080 |
| 3/27/82 | 71 | 5 | 2 I Want To Do Something Freaky To You........... | | Destiny 2007 |
| | | | shown as: **ST. TROPEZ** | | |
| 5/15/82 | 43 | 11 | 3 Femmes Fatales........................................ | | Destiny 2010 |
| | | | **KYU SAKAMOTO** | | |
| | | | Native of Kawasaki, Japan. One of 520 people killed in the crash of the Japan Airlines 747 near Tokyo on 8/12/85 (43). | | |
| 6/08/63 | 18 | 4 | 1 Sukiyaki................................................ [F] | 1 | Capitol 4945 |
| | | | released in Japan as "Ue O Muite Aruko" (I Look Up When I Walk) | | |
| | | | **SALSOUL ORCHESTRA** | | |
| | | | Disco orchestra conducted by Philadelphia producer/arranger Vincent Montana, Jr. Vocalists included Phyllis Rhodes, Ronni Tyson, Carl Helm and Philip Hurt. | | |
| 9/13/75 | 44 | 9 | 1 Salsoul Hustle .......................................... [I] | 76 | Salsoul 2002 |
| 1/17/76 | 36 | 11 | 2 Tangerine................................................ [I] | 18 | Salsoul 2004 |
| | | | Jimmy Dorsey's version hit #1 on the pop charts in 1942 | | |
| 5/08/76 | 76 | 5 | 3 You're Just The Right Size ........................... | 88 | Salsoul 2007 |
| 8/28/76 | 20 | 14 | 4 Nice 'N' Naasty ......................................... | 30 | Salsoul 2011 |
| 6/18/77 | 33 | 11 | 5 Getaway.................................................. [I] | 105 | Salsoul 2038 |
| 11/12/77 | 84 | 6 | 6 Run Away ................................................ | | Salsoul 2045 |
| | | | featuring Loleatta Holloway | | |
| 4/22/78 | 68 | 5 | 7 West Side Encounter - West Side Story (Medley).. | | Salsoul 2064 |
| 10/27/79 | 66 | 7 | 8 How High................................................. | 105 | Salsoul 2096 |
| | | | THE SALSOUL ORCHESTRA featuring COGNAC | | |
| 6/05/82 | 52 | 12 | 9 Take Some Time Out (For Love) ...................... | | Salsoul 7026 |

| DEBUT DATE | PEAK POS | WKS CHR | ARTIST — Record Title | POP POS | Label & Number |
|---|---|---|---|---|---|
| | | | **SALT-N-PEPA** | | |
| | | | Queens-based female rap trio: Cheryl "Salt" James and Sandy "Pepa" Denton (from Kingston, Jamaica) with DJ Spinderella (LaToya). | | |
| 3/21/87 | 41 | 13 | 1 My Mike Sounds Nice | | Next Plat. 50055 |
| 7/18/87 | 21 | 16 | 2 Tramp | | Next Plat. 50063 |
| 12/19/87+ | 55 | 10 | 3 Chick On The Side | | Next Plat. 50071 |
| 1/30/88 | 28 | 10 | 4●Push It | 19 | Next Plat. 315 |
| | | | **SAM & BILL** | | |
| | | | Duo of Bill Johnson (b: 10/16/32, August, GA) and Sam Gary. In 1959, Bill recorded for Sun, with own band, the Steps Of Rhythm. Teamed with Sam, guitarist for the Soul Brothers, in 1962. | | |
| 8/21/65 | 14 | 14 | 1 For Your Love | 95 | JoDa 100 |
| 2/26/66 | 38 | 1 | 2 Fly Me To The Moon | 98 | JoDa 104 |
| | | | **SAM & DAVE**   ★★169★★ | | |
| | | | Samuel Moore (b: 10/12/35, Miami) and David Prater (b: 5/9/37, Ocilla, GA). Sam had been with the Melionaires gospel group, and Dave was a solo artist prior to their meeting in Miami in 1961. First recorded for Alston in 1962. Duo produced by Isaac Hayes and David Porter. Dave was killed in a car crash on 4/11/88. | | |
| 1/01/66 | 7 | 14 | 1 **You Don't Know Like I Know** | 90 | Stax 180 |
| 4/09/66 | 1 [1] | 20 | 2 **Hold On! I'm A Comin'** | 21 | Stax 189 |
| 9/24/66 | 8 | 10 | 3 **Said I Wasn't Gonna Tell Nobody** | 64 | Stax 198 |
| 12/10/66+ | 7 | 10 | 4 **You Got Me Hummin'** | 77 | Stax 204 |
| 2/25/67 | 2 [1] | 14 | 5 **When Something Is Wrong With My Baby** | 42 | Stax 210 |
| 7/01/67 | 16 | 8 | 6 **Soothe Me** | 56 | Stax 218 |
| 9/16/67 | 1 [7] | 18 | 7●**Soul Man** | 2 | Stax 231 |
| 2/03/68 | 4 | 14 | 8 **I Thank You** | 9 | Stax 242 |
| 6/01/68 | 20 | 8 | 9 You Don't Know What You Mean To Me | 48 | Atlantic 2517 |
| 8/17/68 | 19 | 6 | 10 Can't You Find Another Way (Of Doing It) | 54 | Atlantic 2540 |
| 1/04/69 | 18 | 7 | 11 Soul Sister, Brown Sugar | 41 | Atlantic 2590 |
| 3/22/69 | 27 | 6 | 12 Born Again | 92 | Atlantic 2608 |
| | | | 1-5, 8-9, 11-12: written by Isaac Hayes & David Porter | | |
| 11/13/71 | 36 | 4 | 13 Don't Pull Your Love | 102 | Atlantic 2839 |
| 6/22/74 | 89 | 4 | 14 A Little Bit Of Good (Cures A Whole Lot Of Bad) | | United Art. 14022 |
| 8/10/85 | 92 | 4 | 15 The Sam & Dave Medley | | 21 Records 99636 |
| | | | STARS on 45 featuring SAM & DAVE  You Don't Know What You Mean To Me/Soul Sister (You're Brown Sugar)/Soul Man/Hold On, I'm Coming/I Thank You | | |
| | | | **SAM THE SHAM & THE PHAROAHS** | | |
| | | | Rock group from Arlington College, Texas. Formed by vocalist Domingo "Sam" Samudio. Included Ray Stinnet, David Martin, Jerry Patterson and Butch Gibson. | | |
| 6/19/65 | 31 | 5 | 1●Wooly Bully | 2 | MGM 13322 |
| | | | **BUTCH SAM & THE STATION BAND** | | |
| 1/05/85 | 78 | 6 | 1 Say That You Will | | Private I 04720 |
| | | | **DAVID SANBORN** | | |
| | | | Born in 1945 in Tampa, Florida; raised in St. Louis. Saxophonist/flutist. Stricken with polio as a child. Played with Paul Butterfield from 1967-71; Stevie Wonder from 1972-73. Formed own group in 1975. | | |
| 12/04/76 | 98 | 3 | 1 Smile | | Warner 8272 |
| 4/26/80 | 75 | 4 | 2 Anything You Want [I] | | Warner 49219 |
| 11/05/83 | 56 | 11 | 3 Neither One Of Us | | Warner 29473 |
| 4/14/84 | 91 | 2 | 4 I Told U So [I] | | Warner 29331 |
| 3/09/85 | 66 | 8 | 5 Love & Happiness | 103 | Warner 29087 |
| | | | lead vocal by Hamish Stuart | | |
| 3/28/87 | 35 | 12 | 6 Chicago Song [I] | | Warner 28392 |
| 7/02/88 | 50 | 9 | 7 Slam [I] | | Reprise 27857 |
| | | | **THE SANDPEBBLES** | | |
| | | | Consisted of Calvin White, Andrea Bolden and Lonzine Wright. White had been lead singer of the Gospel Wonders. Group name changed to C & The Shells in 1968. | | |
| 8/05/67 | 10 | 11 | 1 **Forget It** | 81 | Calla 134 |
| 11/25/67 | 14 | 10 | 2 Love Power | 22 | Calla 141 |
| | | | above 2: produced by Teddy Vann | | |
| 4/20/68 | 42 | 4 | 3 If You Didn't Hear Me The First Time (I'll Say It Again) | 122 | Calla 148 |

| DEBUT DATE | PEAK POS | WKS CHR | ARTIST — Record Title | POP POS | Label & Number |
|---|---|---|---|---|---|
| | | | **TOMMY SANDS**<br>Born on 8/27/37 in Chicago. Pop singer/actor. Mother was a vocalist with Art Kassel's band. Married Nancy Sinatra in 1960; divorced in 1965. In the films "Sing Boy Sing", "Mardi Gras", "Babes In Toyland" and "The Longest Day". | | |
| 3/09/57 | 10 | 3 | 1 **Teen-Age Crush**.......................................<br>Jockey #10<br>from the 1957 TV play "The Singing Idol" (starring Sands) | 2 | Capitol 3639 |
| | | | **SAMANTHA SANG**<br>Born Cheryl Gray on 8/5/53 in Melbourne, Australia. Began career on Melbourne radio at age 8. | | |
| 2/11/78 | 42 | 12 | 1▲Emotion ...............................................<br>backing vocal by Barry Gibb;<br>written by Barry & Robin Gibb (of The Bee Gees) | 3 | Private S. 45178 |
| | | | **MONGO SANTAMARIA**<br>Born Ramon Santamaria on 4/7/22 in Havana, Cuba. Percussionist, toured with Perez Prado, Tito Puente and Cal Tjader. Own group from 1961. In the film "Made In Paris" in 1966. | | |
| 3/30/63 | 8 | 10 | 1 **Watermelon Man**.............................. [I] | 10 | Battle 45909 |
| 7/13/68 | 49 | 3 | 2 Cold Sweat................................ [I] | | Columbia 44502 |
| 2/22/69 | 33 | 5 | 3 Cloud Nine................................ [I] | 32 | Columbia 44740 |
| 11/08/69 | 40 | 3 | 4 We Got Latin Soul ....................... | 132 | Columbia 44998 |
| | | | **SANTANA**<br>Latin-rock group formed in San Francisco in 1966. Consisted of Carlos Santana (b: 7/20/47, Autlan de Navarro, Mexico), vocals, guitar; Gregg Rolie, keyboards; and David Brown, bass. Added percussionists Michael Carabello, Jose Chepitos Areas and Michael Shrieve in 1969. Worked Fillmore West and Woodstock in 1969. Neal Schon, guitar, added in 1971. Santana began solo work in 1972. Schon and Rolie formed Journey. | | |
| 3/27/71 | 32 | 6 | 1 Oye Como Va .............................. [F] | 13 | Columbia 45330 |
| 11/20/71 | 39 | 5 | 2 Everybody's Everything.................... | 12 | Columbia 45472 |
| 5/15/76 | 78 | 5 | 3 Let It Shine............................... | 77 | Columbia 10336 |
| 6/30/79 | 68 | 3 | 4 One Chain (Don't Make No Prison)........ | 59 | Columbia 10938 |
| | | | **JORGE SANTANA** | | |
| 1/13/79 | 92 | 3 | 1 Love The Way .......................... | | Tomato 10006 |
| | | | **SANTIAGO** | | |
| 8/28/76 | 66 | 8 | 1 Nice & Slow............................. | | Amherst 715 |
| | | | **SANTO & JOHNNY**<br>Brooklyn-born guitar duo: Santo Farina (b: 10/24/37) on steel guitar, and his brother Johnny (b: 4/30/41) on rhythm guitar. | | |
| 8/31/59 | 4 | 9 | 1 **Sleep Walk**.............................. [I] | 1 | Canadian A. 103 |
| 1/11/60 | 17 | 2 | 2 Tear Drop................................ [I] | 23 | Canadian A. 107 |
| | | | **THE SAPPHIRES**<br>Philadelphia trio: Carol Jackson (lead), George Gainer and Joe Livingston. | | |
| 1/11/64 | 25 | 12 | 1 Who Do You Love......................... | Hot | Swan 4162 |
| 5/08/65 | 33 | 3 | 2 Gotta Have Your Love.................... | 77 | ABC-Para. 10639 |
| | | | **SASS** | | |
| 2/05/77 | 88 | 4 | 1 I Only Wanted To Love You .............. | | 20th Century 2318 |
| | | | **THE SATISFACTIONS**<br>Group from Washington, DC, consisting of James "Junior" Isom (lead), Lorenzo Hines (tenor), Earl Jones (baritone) and Fletcher Lee (bass). | | |
| 7/04/70 | 36 | 5 | 1 This Bitter Earth.......................... | 96 | Lionel 3201 |
| 10/10/70 | 21 | 7 | 2 One Light Two Lights..................... | 94 | Lionel 3205 |
| | | | **SATURDAY NIGHT BAND**<br>A Jesse Boyce & Moses Dillard disco production. | | |
| 6/03/78 | 70 | 7 | 1 Come On Dance, Dance ................. | | Prelude 71104 |
| | | | **RODNEY SAULSBERRY**<br>Singer/actor from Detroit. Appeared in "M.A.S.H.", "Taxi" and "Dynasty" TV series. Played Jeff Johnson on the TV soap opera "Capitol" from 1982-83. | | |
| 8/25/84 | 55 | 10 | 1 I Wonder ............................... | | Allegiance 3919 |
| 12/15/84+ | 68 | 9 | 2 Look Whatcha Done Now............... | | Allegiance 3923 |
| 2/06/88 | 27 | 14 | 3 Who Do You Love....................... | | Ryan 1001 |

| DEBUT DATE | PEAK POS | WKS CHR | ARTIST — Record Title | POP POS | Label & Number |
|---|---|---|---|---|---|
| | | | **LEO SAYER** Born Gerard Sayer on 5/21/48 in Shoreham, England. With Patches in the early 70s. Songwriting team with David Courtney from 1972-75. Own TV show in England in the early 80s. | | |
| 1/22/77 | **43** | 9 | 1 ● You Make Me Feel Like Dancing ..................... | *1* | Warner 8283 |
| 6/18/77 | **94** | 3 | 2 ● When I Need You ......................................... | *1* | Warner 8332 |
| | | | **BOZ SCAGGS** Born William Royce Scaggs on 6/8/44 in Ohio; raised in Texas. Joined Steve Miller's band, The Marksmen, in 1959. Joined band, The Wigs, in 1963. Moved to Europe in 1964, toured as a folksinger. Rejoined Miller in 1967, solo since 1969. | | |
| 7/10/76 | **5** | 19 | 1 ● Lowdown ................................................... | *3* | Columbia 10367 |
| 12/11/76+ | **68** | 9 | 2 What Can I Say............................................. | *42* | Columbia 10440 |
| 6/21/80 | **17** | 14 | 3 JoJo ......................................................... | *17* | Columbia 11281 |
| | | | **HARVEY SCALES & THE SEVEN SOUNDS** Group formed in Milwaukee in 1961. Consisted of Scales (b: 1941, Memphis; lead), Monny Smith, Bill Purtie, Rudy Jacobs, Al Vance, Bill Stonewall and Ray Armstead. Scales was formerly with The Esquires. | | |
| 10/28/67 | **32** | 4 | 1 Get Down....................................................... | *79* | Magic Touch 2007 |
| | | | **THE SCHOOLBOYS** Harlem group consisting of Leslie Martin (lead), Roger Hayes (tenor), James McKay (baritone) and Renaldo Gamble (bass). | | |
| 2/23/57 | **15** | 1 | 1 Shirley/ *Jockey #15* | *91* | |
| 3/23/57 | **13** | 1 | 2 Please Say You Want Me ............................... *Jockey #13* *above 2: with the Leroy Kirkland Orchestra* | | Okeh 7076 |
| | | | **FREDDIE SCOTT** Born on 4/24/33 in Providence, Rhode Island. Attended Cooper High School in New York City. Recorded first hit while working as a songwriter for Columbia Music. | | |
| 8/03/63 | **10** | 11 | 1 Hey, Girl....................................................... | *10* | Colpix 692 |
| 11/02/63 | **48** | 7 | 2 I Got A Woman ............................................. | *Hot* | Colpix 709 |
| 3/14/64 | **82** | 7 | 3 Where Does Love Go....................................... | *Hot* | Colpix 724 |
| 12/17/66+ | **1** ⁴ | 17 | 4 Are You Lonely For Me ................................... | *39* | Shout 207 |
| 3/25/67 | **40** | 5 | 5 Cry To Me ..................................................... | *70* | Shout 211 |
| 5/27/67 | **25** | 6 | 6 Am I Grooving You ......................................... | *71* | Shout 212 |
| 11/11/67 | **24** | 8 | 7 He Ain't Give You None................................... | *100* | Shout 220 |
| 8/31/68 | **27** | 8 | 8 (You) Got What I Need .................................. | | Shout 233 |
| 6/20/70 | **40** | 2 | 9 I Shall Be Released......................................... | | Probe 481 |
| | | | **GLORIA SCOTT** | | |
| 4/27/74 | **74** | 5 | 1 What Am I Gonna Do ..................................... | | Casablanca 0005 |
| 1/04/75 | **14** | 14 | 2 Just As Long As We're Together (In My Life There Will Never Be Another).................... *above 2: produced by Barry White* | | Casablanca 815 |
| | | | **JACK SCOTT** Born Jack Scafone, Jr. on 1/24/36 in Windsor, Canada. Rock and roll-ballad singer/ songwriter/guitarist. Moved to Hazel Park, Michigan in 1946. First recorded for ABC-Paramount in 1957. Still active into the 80s in Detroit area. | | |
| 7/14/58 | **5** | 13 | 1 My True Love/ *Best Seller #5 / Jockey #7* | *3* | |
| | | 6 | 2 Leroy........................................................... *Best Seller flip* | *25* | Carlton 462 |
| 2/15/60 | **7** | 8 | 3 What In The World's Come Over You ............. | *5* | Top Rank 2028 |
| 5/30/60 | **5** | 6 | 4 Burning Bridges ........................................... | *3* | Top Rank 2041 |
| | | | **LINDA SCOTT** Born Linda Joy Sampson on 6/1/45 in Queens, NY. Moved to Teaneck, NJ at age 11. | | |
| 4/10/61 | **22** | 3 | 1 I've Told Every Little Star............................... *from the 1932 stage production "Music In The Air"* | *3* | Canadian A. 123 |
| | | | **MABEL SCOTT** Born on 4/30/15 in Richmond, Virginia. Moved to New York City in 1921. Professional debut in 1932. Moved to Cleveland in 1936, then to Los Angeles in 1942. Married to Charles Brown from 1949-51. Active into the late 50s. | | |
| 7/31/48 | **6** | 5 | 1 Elevator Boogie .......................................... *Juke Box #6 / Best Seller #11* *with Charles Brown on piano* | | Exclusive 35X |

| DEBUT DATE | PEAK POS | WKS CHR | ARTIST — Record Title | POP POS | Label & Number |
|---|---|---|---|---|---|
| | | | **MABEL SCOTT — Continued** | | |
| 12/25/48+ | **12** | 2 | 2  Boogie Woogie Santa Claus ........................ [X] | | Exclusive 75X |
| | | | Best Seller #12 | | |
| | | | **MARILYN SCOTT** | | |
| | | | Born Mary DeLoatch. Vocalist/guitarist from the Carolinas. | | |
| 9/03/83 | **55** | 9 | 1  Only You ...................................................... | | Mercury 812962 |
| 3/10/84 | **83** | 6 | 2  10 X 10 ...................................................... | | Mercury 814959 |
| | | | above 2: produced by Michael Sembello | | |
| | | | **MILLIE SCOTT** | | |
| | | | Singer from Savannah, Georgia. Former member of Cut Glass. | | |
| 5/03/86 | **78** | 4 | 1  Prisoner Of Love ...................................... | | 4th & B'way 421 |
| | | | shown as: **MILDRED SCOTT** | | |
| 1/31/87 | **11** | 15 | 2  Every Little Bit................................... | | 4th & B'way 7432 |
| 6/06/87 | **40** | 11 | 3  Love Me Right ....................................... | | 4th & B'way 7433 |
| 9/05/87 | **49** | 10 | 4  Automatic ............................................. | | 4th & B'way 7427 |
| | | | **PEGGY SCOTT & JO JO BENSON** | | |
| | | | Jo Jo formerly sang with Chuck Willis and The Blue Notes. | | |
| 4/20/68 | **8** | 19 | 1  **Lover's Holiday** ......................................... | *31* | SSS Int'l. 736 |
| 10/19/68 | **8** | 12 | 2  **Pickin' Wild Mountain Berries** ..................... | *27* | SSS Int'l. 748 |
| 2/15/69 | **13** | 7 | 3  Soul Shake ........................................ | *37* | SSS Int'l. 761 |
| 5/10/69 | **24** | 6 | 4  I Want To Love You Baby ........................... | *81* | SSS Int'l. 769 |
| | | | **RENA SCOTT** | | |
| 7/21/79 | **92** | 4 | 1  Super Lover ......................................... | | Buddah 607 |
| | | | written & produced by James Mtume and Reggie Lucas | | |
| 1/16/88 | **55** | 9 | 2  Do That To Me One More Time ........................ | | Sedona 75030 |
| | | | **TOM SCOTT** | | |
| | | | Born on 5/19/48 in Los Angeles. Pop-jazz-fusion saxophonist. Session work for Joni Mitchell, Steely Dan, Carole King and others. Composer of films and TV scores. | | |
| 8/03/74 | **72** | 6 | 1  Jump Back .......................................... | | Ode 66048 |
| | | | **TOM SCOTT & THE L.A. EXPRESS featuring MERRY CLAYTON** | | |
| 1/25/75 | **93** | 6 | 2  Tom Cat ........................................... [I] | | Ode 66105 |
| | | | **TOM SCOTT & THE L.A. EXPRESS** | | |
| 2/14/76 | **65** | 5 | 3  Uptown & Country ..................................... [I] | 80 | Ode 66118 |
| 5/29/76 | **100** | 1 | 4  Time And Love ..................................... [I] | | Ode 66121 |
| 11/12/83 | **80** | 6 | 5  Come Back To Me .................................. | | Atlantic 89763 |
| | | | **GIL SCOTT-HERON** | | |
| | | | Born on 4/1/49 in Chicago. Composer/keyboardist/author/poet. Raised in Jackson, Tennessee. Attended Lincoln University in Pennsylvania; met bass guitarist Brian Jackson. Masters in creative writing, taught at Columbia University. First novel published in 1968. Began converting his poems to songs. Went solo in 1980. | | |
| | | | **GIL SCOTT-HERON & BRIAN JACKSON:** | | |
| 10/04/75 | **29** | 10 | 1  Johannesburg ...................................... | | Arista 0152 |
| 2/12/77 | **98** | 2 | 2  The Bottle - Part 1................................ | | Arista 0225 |
| | | | above 2: composed by Brian Jackson | | |
| | | | **GIL SCOTT-HERON:** | | |
| 10/21/78 | **15** | 16 | 3  Angel Dust ........................................ | | Arista 0366 |
| 3/03/79 | **83** | 3 | 4  Show Bizness ...................................... | | Arista 0390 |
| 2/02/80 | **68** | 7 | 5  Shut 'Um Down..................................... | | Arista 0488 |
| 1/17/81 | **86** | 5 | 6  Legend In His Own Mind .............................. | | Arista 0583 |
| 12/05/81+ | **49** | 12 | 7  "B" Movie ......................................... [S] | | Arista 0647 |
| 9/15/84 | **72** | 6 | 8  Re-Ron............................................ [S] | | Arista 9253 |
| | | | inspired by the 1984 presidential election | | |
| | | | **SCRITTI POLITTI** | | |
| | | | British soul/pop trio: vocalist Green Gartside, drummer Fred Maher and keyboardist David Gamson. Italian group means "political writing". | | |
| 11/30/85 | **85** | 3 | 1  Perfect Way ....................................... | *11* | Warner 28949 |
| | | | **SEA LEVEL** | | |
| | | | Jazzy blues-rock 7-man band formed by 3 members of The Allman Brothers Band. | | |
| 3/17/79 | **91** | 2 | 1  Sneakers (Fifty-Four) ................................ [I] | | Capricorn 0314 |

| DEBUT DATE | PEAK POS | WKS CHR | ARTIST — Record Title | POP POS | Label & Number |
|---|---|---|---|---|---|
| | | | **SEAWIND** | | |
| | | | Group from Hawaii, formed in 1972 as Ox. Consisted of Pauline Wilson (lead), husband Bob Wilson, Larry Williams, Jerry Hey, Kim Hutchcroft, Bud Nuanez and Ken Wild. Paulette is the only native Hawaiian in the group. Moved to Los Angeles in 1976, changed name to Seawind. | | |
| 4/28/79 | 70 | 5 | 1 Hold On To Love ........................................ | | Horizon 120 |
| 10/25/80 | 18 | 15 | 2 What Cha Doin' ......................................... | | A&M 2274 |
| 3/07/81 | 85 | 2 | 3 The Two Of Us.......................................... | | A&M 2302 |
| | | | **SECOND VERSE** | | |
| 8/24/74 | 92 | 3 | 1 Be Here In The Morning................................ | | 9 Chains 7004 |
| | | | **SECRET WEAPON** | | |
| | | | Septet from New York, founded by Jerome Pfister. | | |
| 1/30/82 | 24 | 19 | 1 Must Be The Music ..................................... | | Prelude 8036 |
| 3/19/83 | 73 | 5 | 2 "DJ" Man............................................... | | Prelude 8066 |
| | | | **NEIL SEDAKA** | | |
| | | | Born on 3/13/39 in Brooklyn. Pop singer/songwriter/pianist. Formed songwriting team with lyricist Howard Greenfield while attending Lincoln High School (partnership lasted over 20 years). Recorded with The Tokens on Melba in 1956. Attended Juilliard School for classical piano. Career revived in 1974 after signing with Elton John's new Rocket label. Also see the Willows. | | |
| 2/16/59 | 25 | 2 | 1 The Diary ............................................. | *14* | RCA 7408 |
| 11/23/59 | 27 | 2 | 2 Oh! Carol ............................................. | *9* | RCA 7595 |
| | | | written for singer/songwriter Carole King | | |
| 5/23/60 | 16 | 2 | 3 Stairway To Heaven..................................... | *9* | RCA 7709 |
| 2/20/61 | 22 | 3 | 4 Calendar Girl.......................................... | *4* | RCA 7829 |
| 9/01/62 | 12 | 6 | 5 Breaking Up Is Hard To Do ............................ | *1* | RCA 8046 |
| 11/03/62 | 19 | 5 | 6 Next Door To An Angel ................................ | *5* | RCA 8086 |
| 6/15/63 | 21 | 2 | 7 Let's Go Steady Again.................................. | *26* | RCA 8169 |
| | | | all of above: written by Sedaka and Greenfield, produced by Al Nevins and Don Kirshner | | |
| | | | **MICHAEL SEMBELLO** | | |
| | | | Born on 4/17/54 in Philadelphia. Session guitarist/producer/composer/arranger/vocalist. Guitarist on Stevie Wonder's albums from 1974-79. | | |
| 8/30/86 | 79 | 4 | 1 Wonder Where You Are................................ | | A&M 2850 |
| | | | **EDDY SENAY** | | |
| 4/15/72 | 39 | 6 | 1 Hot Thang ................................ [I] | *104* | Sussex 230 |
| 8/18/73 | 82 | 6 | 2 Safari.................................................. | | Sussex 260 |
| | | | **SENOR SOUL** | | |
| 5/24/69 | 39 | 6 | 1 It's Your Thing ......................................... | | Whiz 611 |
| | | | **THE SENSATIONS** | | |
| | | | Group from Philadelphia, formed in 1954 as the Cavaliers. Contained dual lead singers Yvonne Mills Baker and Tommy Wicks. Group re-formed in 1961, with Baker and Alphonso Howell, bassist of the original group, plus Richard Curtain (tenor) and Sam Armstrong (baritone). | | |
| 2/18/56 | 15 | 1 | 1 Yes Sir, That's My Baby ............................... | | Atco 6056 |
| | | | Best Seller #15 | | |
| 5/19/56 | 13 | 1 | 2 Please Mr. Disc Jockey.................................. | | Atco 6067 |
| | | | Jockey #13 — lead vocal by Yvonne Mills Baker | | |
| 8/14/61 | 12 | 7 | 3 Music, Music, Music.................................... | *54* | Argo 5391 |
| 2/03/62 | 2¹ | 14 | 4 Let Me In ............................................. | *4* | Argo 5405 |
| | | | **SEQUENCE** | | |
| | | | Female funk trio. | | |
| 1/05/80 | 15 | 15 | 1 Funk You Up .......................................... | | Sugar Hill 543 |
| 8/29/81 | 39 | 13 | 2 Funky Sound (Tear The Roof Off) ..................... | | Sugar Hill 767 |
| 5/29/82 | 40 | 11 | 3 I Don't Need Your Love ................................ | | Sugar Hill 783 |
| | | | **THE SEQUINS** | | |
| | | | Trio from Harlan High School in Chicago. Consisted of Veronica "Ronnie" Gonzalez, Linda Jackson and Dottie Hayes. Group disbanded in 1973. | | |
| 8/22/70 | 34 | 10 | 1 Hey Romeo ............................................. | | Gold Star 101 |
| | | | **SERGE!** | | |
| | | | Serge Ponsar, born in Toulon, France. Played in local band, Les Smarts. | | |
| 8/13/83 | 56 | 9 | 1 Out In The Night ....................................... | | Warner 29580 |

| DEBUT DATE | PEAK POS | WKS CHR | ARTIST — Record Title | POP POS | Label & Number |
|---|---|---|---|---|---|
| | | | **TAJA SEVELLE** Female vocalist/disc jockey from Minneapolis. Studied at Boston's Berklee School Of Music. | | |
| 10/31/87 | **58** | 15 | 1 Love Is Contagious ......................................... | *62* | Paisley P. 28257 |
| 2/20/88 | **61** | 9 | 2 Wouldn't You Love To Love Me? ...................... | | Reprise 28127 |
| | | | **SEVEN SEAS** | | |
| 8/16/75 | **48** | 9 | 1 Super "Jaws" ............................................... | *104* | Glades 1728 |
| | | | **THE SEVEN SOUNDS - see HARVEY SCALES** | | |
| | | | **7TH WONDER** Group from Tuskegee, Alabama. Consisted of Wilbert Cox, Allen Williams, and Deborah Matthews (vocals), William Butler, Lloyd Obie (horns), Julius Chislom (keyboards), Marvin Patton (guitar), Jerome Thornton (bass) and Johnnie Hammon (drums). | | |
| 12/08/73+ | **51** | 12 | 1 For The Good Times ...................................... | | Abet 9454 |
| 6/24/78 | **78** | 10 | 2 Words Don't Say Enough ................................ | | Parachute 510 |
| 11/18/78 | **51** | 10 | 3 My Love Ain't Never Been This Strong .............. | | Parachute 519 |
| 8/25/79 | **49** | 11 | 4 Do It With Your Body.................................... | | Parachute 527 |
| 6/28/80 | **33** | 13 | 5 I Enjoy Ya................................................. shown as: **SEVENTH WONDER** | | Choc. City 3207 |
| 9/27/80 | **39** | 9 | 6 The Tilt.................................................... | | Choc. City 3212 |
| | | | **DOC SEVERINSEN** Born Carl H. Severinsen on 7/7/27 in Arlington, Oregon. Trumpet virtuoso - leader of the "Tonight Show" orchestra. With Charlie Barnet (1947-49), Tommy Dorsey (1949-50), and Sauter-Finegan (1952-53) bands. Also see Gloria Gaynor. | | |
| 5/29/76 | **97** | 2 | 1 I Wanna Be With You..................................... | | Epic 50220 |
| | | | **DAVID SEVILLE** Born Ross Bagdasarian on 1/27/19 in Fresno, California. Died on 1/16/72 (52). Singer/songwriter/actor. To Los Angeles in 1950. Creator of The Chipmunks (all named for Liberty Records' executives: Theodore Keep, Alvin Bennett and Simon Waronker). | | |
| 4/21/58 | **1**¹ | 14 | 1 **Witch Doctor**............................................. [N] Jockey #1 / Best Seller #2 | *1* | Liberty 55132 |
| 12/15/58+ | **5** | 9 | 2 **Chipmunk Song**................................... [X-N] **THE CHIPMUNKS** | *1* | Liberty 55168 |
| 8/03/59 | **29** | 1 | 3 Ragtime Cowboy Joe .............................. [N] **DAVID SEVILLE & THE CHIPMUNKS** | *16* | Liberty 55200 |
| | | | **ANN SEXTON** Born on 2/5/50 in Greenville, South Carolina. Cousin of songwriter/singer Chuck Jackson. Married to sax player/vocalist Melvin Burton. First recorded for Impel in 1971. | | |
| 9/29/73 | **47** | 8 | 1 You're Gonna Miss Me.................................... | *77* | Records 133 |
| 2/12/77 | **79** | 5 | 2 I'm His Wife (You're Just A Friend) ................. | | Sound Stage 2504 |
| | | | **BILLY SHA-RAE** | | |
| 4/17/71 | **50** | 2 | 1 Do It....................................................... | | Spectrum 114 |
| | | | **SHACK** | | |
| 1/16/71 | **23** | 9 | 1 Too Many Lovers ........................................ | *118* | Volt 4051 |
| | | | **SHADES OF BLUE** White male-female quartet, discovered by Edwin Starr. | | |
| 5/28/66 | **16** | 9 | 1 Oh How Happy............................................. | *12* | Impact 1007 |
| | | | **SHADES OF LOVE** | | |
| 7/10/82 | **52** | 10 | 1 Keep In Touch ............................................ | | Venture 5021 |
| | | | **SHADOW** Former members of the Ohio Players: James "Diamond" Williams, Clarence "Chet" Willis and Billy Beck. | | |
| 11/24/79+ | **77** | 8 | 1 I Need Love .............................................. | | Elektra 46540 |
| 2/23/80 | **72** | 3 | 2 No Better Love ........................................... | | Elektra 46605 |
| 8/09/80 | **68** | 5 | 3 Mystery Dancer/ | | |
| 10/18/80 | **75** | 4 | 4 Hot City ................................................. | | Elektra 47002 |

| DEBUT DATE | PEAK POS | WKS CHR | ARTIST — Record Title | POP POS | Label & Number |
|---|---|---|---|---|---|
| | | | **SHADOWS** | | |
| | | | Group from New Haven, Connecticut, formed in 1946 as the Melody Kings. Consisted of Scott King (lead), Raymond Reid (tenor), Sam McClure (baritone) and Jasper Edwards (bass). All except King had toured with Andy Kirk and Orville Brooks as The Jubalaires in 1946. Disbanded in 1958. | | |
| 1/21/50 | 7 | 5 | 1 **I've Been A Fool** ............................... *Juke Box #7 / Best Seller #9* | | Lee 200 |
| | | | **SHALAMAR** ★★115★★ | | |
| | | | Vocal trio formed in 1977 by Don Cornelius, the producer/host of TV's "Soul Train". Consisted of vocalists/dancers Jody Watley and Jeffrey Daniels, with Gerald Brown. Howard Hewett replaced Brown in early 1978. Watley and Daniels (former husband of Stephanie Mills) pursued solo careers in 1984; replaced by Delisa Davis and Micki Free. Hewett left in 1985, replaced by Sidney Justin. | | |
| 3/26/77 | 10 | 16 | 1 **Uptown Festival** ....................................... *Going To A Go-Go/I Can't Help Myself/Uptight (Everything's Alright/Stop! In The Name Of Love/It's The Same Old Song* | 25 | Soul Train 10885 |
| 8/27/77 | 59 | 10 | 2 Ooh Baby, Baby ........................................... | | Soul Train 11045 |
| 10/21/78+ | 11 | 18 | 3 Take That To The Bank ............................... | 79 | Solar 11379 |
| 9/29/79+ | 1¹ | 32 | 4● **The Second Time Around** ..................... | 8 | Solar 11709 |
| 3/29/80 | 22 | 13 | 5 Right In The Socket ..................................... | | Solar 11929 |
| 7/26/80 | 60 | 6 | 6 I Owe You One ............................................ | | Solar 12049 |
| 12/20/80+ | 24 | 14 | 7 Full Of Fire ................................................ | 55 | Solar 12152 |
| 3/14/81 | 6 | 19 | 8 **Make That Move** ...................................... | 60 | Solar 12192 |
| 6/27/81 | 17 | 15 | 9 This Is For The Lover In You ..................... | | Solar 12250 |
| 10/31/81 | 19 | 14 | 10 Sweeter As The Days Go By ....................... | | Solar 12329 |
| 3/13/82 | 8 | 16 | 11 **A Night To Remember** ............................ | 44 | Solar 48005 |
| 7/03/82 | 33 | 13 | 12 I Can Make You Feel Good ......................... | 102 | Solar 48013 |
| 7/02/83 | 10 | 16 | 13 **Dead Giveaway** ....................................... | 22 | Solar 69819 |
| 10/15/83 | 26 | 15 | 14 Over And Over ............................................ | | Solar 69787 |
| 1/28/84 | 34 | 10 | 15 Deadline U.S.A. .......................................... *from the film "D.C. Cab"* | | MCA 52335 |
| 2/11/84 | 77 | 4 | 16 You Can Count On Me ................................ | 101 | Solar 69765 |
| 2/25/84 | 18 | 17 | 17 Dancing In The Sheets .............................. *from the film "Footloose"* | 17 | Columbia 04372 |
| 11/17/84 | 49 | 11 | 18 Amnesia ...................................................... | 73 | Solar 69682 |
| 2/16/85 | 22 | 15 | 19 My Girl Loves Me ....................................... | 106 | Solar 69660 |
| 6/22/85 | 79 | 5 | 20 Don't Get Stopped In Beverly Hills .................. *from the film "Beverly Hills Cop"* | | MCA 52594 |
| 6/20/87 | 30 | 12 | 21 Circumstantial Evidence ............................ | | Solar 70008 |
| 9/26/87 | 11 | 17 | 22 Games ......................................................... | | Solar 70013 |
| | | | **THE SHANGRI-LAS** | | |
| | | | "Girl group" formed at Andrew Jackson High School in Queens, New York. Consisted of two sets of sisters: Mary (lead singer) & Betty Weiss and twins Mary Ann & Marge Ganser. Mary Ann died of encephalitis in 1971 and Marge died of a drug overdose. | | |
| 8/22/64 | 5 | 11 | 1 **Remember (Walkin' In The Sand)** .................. | *Hot* | Red Bird 008 |
| 10/10/64 | 1¹ | 12 | 2 **Leader Of The Pack** ................................. | *Hot* | Red Bird 014 |
| | | | **SHANNON** | | |
| | | | Brenda Shannon Greene from Washington, DC. Began singing career at York University. | | |
| 11/05/83+ | 2² | 25 | 1● **Let The Music Play** ................................. | 8 | Mirage 99810 |
| 3/31/84 | 6 | 15 | 2 **Give Me Tonight** ...................................... | 46 | Mirage 99775 |
| 7/14/84 | 48 | 9 | 3 My Heart's Divided ..................................... | | Mirage 99738 |
| 4/06/85 | 13 | 16 | 4 Do You Wanna Get Away ............................ | 49 | Mirage 99655 |
| 7/27/85 | 26 | 12 | 5 Stronger Together ....................................... | 103 | Mirage 99631 |
| 11/09/85 | 68 | 7 | 6 Urgent ........................................................ | | Mirage 99602 |
| 11/15/86 | 82 | 3 | 7 Prove Me Right ........................................... | | Atlantic 89352 |
| | | | **DEL SHANNON** | | |
| | | | Pop singer born Charles Westover on 12/30/39 in Coopersville, Michigan. Wrote "I Go To Pieces" for Peter & Gordon. To Los Angeles in 1966, production work. | | |
| 4/17/61 | 3 | 6 | 1 **Runaway** .................................................. *electric organ (musitron) solo by co-writer Max Crook* | 1 | Big Top 3067 |
| | | | **ROXANNE SHANTE** | | |
| | | | Female rapper, born Lolita Gooden, from Long Island City, New York. Discovered by producer Marley Marl. | | |
| 2/02/85 | 22 | 12 | 1 Roxanne's Revenge ..................................... *answer song to "Roxanne, Roxanne" by UTFO* | 109 | Pop Art 7546 |

| DEBUT DATE | PEAK POS | WKS CHR | ARTIST — Record Title | POP POS | Label & Number |
|---|---|---|---|---|---|
| | | | **ROXANNE SHANTE — Continued** | | |
| 4/13/85 | **49** | 10 | 2  Queen Of Rox (Shante Rox On).......................... | | Pop Art 7547 |
| 9/21/85 | **84** | 4 | 3  Bite This ................................................. | | Pop Art 1411 |
| 6/18/88 | **1** [1] | 16 | 4  **Loosey's Rap**.......................................... | | Reprise 27885 |
| | | | RICK JAMES featuring ROXANNE SHANTE | | |
| | | | **SHANTELLE** | | |
| 6/22/85 | **73** | 7 | 1  Love Attack .................................... | | Pandisc 011 |
| | | | **DEE DEE SHARP** | | |
| | | | Born Dione LaRue on 9/9/45 in Philadelphia. Backing vocalist at Cameo Records in 1961. Married record producer Kenny Gamble in 1967, recorded as Dee Dee Sharp Gamble. Also see Chubby Checker and the Philadelphia International All Stars. | | |
| 3/31/62 | **1** [4] | 16 | 1  **Mashed Potato Time** ........................... | 2 | Cameo 212 |
| 6/23/62 | **11** | 10 | 2  Gravy (For My Mashed Potatoes) ...................... | 9 | Cameo 219 |
| 12/01/62 | **7** | 7 | 3  **Ride!** ...................................... | 5 | Cameo 230 |
| 3/30/63 | **8** | 6 | 4  **Do The Bird** ................................. | 10 | Cameo 244 |
| 11/09/63 | **25** | 1 | 5  Wild! ........................................ | 33 | Cameo 274 |
| 2/01/64 | **82** | 4 | 6  Where Did I Go Wrong/ | Hot | |
| | | | above 3: written by Kal Mann & Dave Appell | | |
| 2/29/64 | **97** | 1 | 7  Willyam, Willyam....................................... | Hot | Cameo 296 |
| 1/15/66 | **37** | 2 | 8  I Really Love You .................................. | 78 | Cameo 375 |
| | | | DEE DEE SHARP GAMBLE: | | |
| 4/17/76 | **62** | 10 | 9  I'm Not In Love ................................. | | TSOP 4778 |
| 3/14/81 | **79** | 3 | 10  I Love You Anyway ......................................... | | Phil. Int. 70058 |
| | | | also released on Phil. Int. 02041 | | |
| | | | **RAY SHARPE** | | |
| | | | Born on 2/8/38 in Fort Worth, Texas. Rockabilly singer/guitarist. First recorded for Hamilton in 1958. Long residency at the Skyliner Ballroom in Fort Worth. | | |
| 8/03/59 | **11** | 9 | 1  Linda Lu ................................................... | 46 | Jamie 1128 |
| | | | with guitarists Duane Eddy and Al Casey | | |
| | | | **ARTIE SHAW** | | |
| | | | Famed clarinetist/bandleader/theatrical producer. Born Arthur Arshawsky on 5/23/10 in New York City. Married 8 times; wives included actresses Lana Turner and Ava Gardner. | | |
| 10/31/42 | **8** | 1 | 1  **Just Kiddin' Around** ................................. [I] | | Victor 27806 |
| | | | arranged by Ray Conniff | | |
| | | | **MARLENA SHAW** | | |
| | | | Born Marlena Burgess in New Rochelle, New York in 1944. Appeared at the Apollo Theater at age 10. Band vocalist with Count Basie from 1967-72. | | |
| 3/18/67 | **33** | 7 | 1  Mercy, Mercy, Mercy..................................... | 58 | Cadet 5557 |
| 5/08/76 | **74** | 6 | 2  It's Better Than Walkin' Out/ | 103 | |
| | | 3 | 3  Be For Real ...................................... | | Blue Note 790 |
| 5/21/77 | **21** | 11 | 4  Yu-Ma/Go Away Little Boy............................. | | Columbia 10542 |
| 5/21/83 | **91** | 4 | 5  Never Give Up On You................................... | | South Bay 22004 |
| | | | **TIMMY SHAW** | | |
| 1/25/64 | **41** | 7 | 1  Gonna Send You Back To Georgia .................... | Hot | Wand 146 |
| | | | **DAMON SHAWN** | | |
| 5/13/72 | **42** | 3 | 1  Feel The Need............................................. | 105 | Westbound 193 |
| | | | **BOBBY SHEEN** | | |
| | | | Vocalist from Los Angeles. Recorded as "Bob B. Soxx" in the 60s. With Bobby Nunn's Coasters in the 80s. | | |
| 12/20/75+ | **53** | 7 | 1  Love Stealing ................................... | | Chelsea 3034 |
| | | | **SHEILA & B. DEVOTION** | | |
| | | | Born Anny Chancel in Paris in 1946. Also performed as Sheila. | | |
| 5/17/80 | **28** | 13 | 1  Spacer ...................................... | | Carrere 7209 |
| 9/27/80 | **75** | 3 | 2  Your Love Is Good............................ | | Carrere 7304 |
| | | | **SHEILA E.** | | |
| | | | Born Sheila Escovedo on 12/12/59 in San Francisco. Singer/percussionist. With father Pete Escovedo in the band, Azteca, in the mid-70s. Toured with Lionel Richie; since 1986, toured and recorded with Prince. Brother Peto was in Con Funk Shun. Uncle Coke Escovedo is a noted percussionist. Also see The Krush Groove All Stars. | | |
| 6/02/84 | **9** | 23 | 1  **The Glamorous Life** ..................................... | 7 | Warner 29285 |

| DEBUT DATE | PEAK POS | WKS CHR | | ARTIST — Record Title | POP POS | Label & Number |
|---|---|---|---|---|---|---|
| | | | | **SHEILA E. — Continued** | | |
| 11/24/84 | **68** | 6 | 2 | The Belle Of St. Mark ........................... | *34* | Warner 29180 |
| 8/10/85 | **36** | 11 | 3 | Sister Fate ........................... | *102* | Warner 28955 |
| 10/19/85 | **2**¹ | 21 | 4 | **A Love Bizarre** ........................... | *11* | Paisley P. 28890 |
| | | | | from the film "Krush Groove"; backing vocal by Prince | | |
| 1/31/87 | **3** | 14 | 5 | **Hold Me** ........................... | *68* | Paisley P. 28580 |
| 5/30/87 | **35** | 11 | 6 | Koo Koo ........................... | | Paisley P. 28348 |
| | | | | **ROSCOE SHELTON** | | |
| | | | | Born on 8/22/31 in Lynchburg, Tennessee. | | |
| 2/06/65 | **25** | 7 | 1 | Strain On My Heart ........................... | *109* | Sims 217 |
| 2/19/66 | **32** | 6 | 2 | Easy Going Fellow ........................... | *102* | Sound Stage 7 2555 |
| | | | | **SHEP & THE LIMELITES** | | |
| | | | | New York City vocal trio: James "Shep" Sheppard, lead (formerly with The Heartbeats) and tenors Clarence Bassett and Charles Baskerville (formerly in the Videos). Group disbanded after Sheppard's death in 1970. | | |
| 4/03/61 | **4** | 12 | 1 | **Daddy's Home** ........................... | *2* | Hull 740 |
| | | | | answer song to The Heartbeats' "A Thousand Miles Away" | | |
| 2/24/62 | **7** | 13 | 2 | **Our Anniversary** ........................... | *59* | Hull 748 |
| | | | | **SHERRICK** | | |
| | | | | Session vocalist/songwriter/multi-instrumentalist born in Austin, Texas. Fronted Motown group Kagny. | | |
| 7/25/87 | **8** | 16 | 1 | **Just Call** ........................... | | Warner 28380 |
| 11/28/87 | **53** | 13 | 2 | Baby I'm For Real ........................... | | Warner 28150 |
| | | | | **THE SHERRYS** | | |
| | | | | Female group from Philadelphia. Formed by Little Joe Cook, and included his daughters Delthine (lead) and Dinell, with Charlotte Butler and Delores "Honey" Wylie. | | |
| 11/17/62 | **25** | 4 | 1 | Pop Pop Pop-Pie ........................... | *35* | Guyden 2068 |
| | | | | **THE SHIELDS** | | |
| | | | | Group formed in Los Angeles in 1958 by Jesse Belvin solely to record "You Cheated". Lead singer was Frankie Ervin (b: 3/27/26 in Blythe, CA). Personnel fluctuated on later releases, other singers performed group's live appearances. | | |
| 9/01/58 | **11** | 8 | 1 | You Cheated ........................... | *12* | Tender 513 |
| | | | | Best Seller #11 / Jockey #12 also released on Dot 15805 | | |
| | | | | **THE SHIRELLES** ★★**157**★★ | | |
| | | | | Female group from Passaic, New Jersey. Consisted of Shirley Owens Alston (b: 6/10/41), Beverly Lee (b: 8/3/41), Doris Kenner (b: 8/2/41) and Addie "Micki" Harris (b: 1/22/40; d: 6/10/82). Formed in junior high school as the Poquellos. First recorded for Tiara in 1958. Kenner left group in 1968; returned in 1975. Alston left for solo career in 1975, recorded as "Lady Rose". | | |
| 10/10/60 | **14** | 9 | 1 | Tonight's The Night ........................... | *39* | Scepter 1208 |
| 12/31/60+ | **2**⁴ | 12 | 2 | **Will You Love Me Tomorrow** ........................... | *1* | Scepter 1211 |
| 2/27/61 | **2**² | 9 | 3 | **Dedicated To The One I Love** ........................... | *3* | Scepter 1203 |
| | | | | originally released in 1959 (POS 83-Pop) | | |
| 5/01/61 | **2**¹ | 8 | 4 | **Mama Said** ........................... | *4* | Scepter 1217 |
| 8/28/61 | **26** | 2 | 5 | A Thing Of The Past ........................... | *41* | Scepter 1220 |
| 10/23/61 | **2**¹ | 9 | 6 | **Big John** ........................... | *21* | Scepter 1223 |
| 1/07/62 | **3** | 13 | 7 | **Baby It's You** ........................... | *8* | Scepter 1227 |
| 4/14/62 | **3** | 13 | 8 | **Soldier Boy** ........................... | *1* | Scepter 1228 |
| 7/21/62 | **20** | 6 | 9 | Welcome Home Baby ........................... | *22* | Scepter 1234 |
| 12/29/62+ | **15** | 7 | 10 | Everybody Loves A Lover ........................... | *19* | Scepter 1243 |
| 4/13/63 | **9** | 11 | 11 | **Foolish Little Girl** ........................... | *4* | Scepter 1248 |
| 9/07/63 | **53** | 6 | 12 | What Does A Girl Do? ........................... | *Hot* | Scepter 1259 |
| 10/19/63 | **92** | 2 | 13 | It's A Mad, Mad, Mad, Mad World/ | *Hot* | |
| 11/02/63 | **97** | 1 | 14 | 31 Flavors ........................... | *Hot* | Scepter 1260 |
| | | | | above 2: from the film "It's A Mad, Mad, Mad, Mad World" | | |
| 1/11/64 | **57** | 5 | 15 | Tonight You're Gonna Fall In Love With Me ....... | *Hot* | Scepter 1264 |
| 3/21/64 | **69** | 4 | 16 | Sha-La-La ........................... | *Hot* | Scepter 1267 |
| 7/18/64 | **63** | 7 | 17 | Thank You Baby ........................... | *Hot* | Scepter 1278 |
| 10/31/64 | **88** | 2 | 18 | Maybe Tonight ........................... | *Hot* | Scepter 1284 |
| 12/26/64+ | **91** | 4 | 19 | Are You Still My Baby ........................... | *Hot* | Scepter 1292 |
| 8/12/67 | **41** | 5 | 20 | Last Minute Miracle ........................... | *99* | Scepter 12198 |

| DEBUT DATE | PEAK POS | WKS CHR | ARTIST — Record Title | POP POS | Label & Number |
|---|---|---|---|---|---|
| | | | **SHIRLEY & COMPANY** | | |
| | | | Shirley Goodman (formerly of Shirley & Lee), and a group of studio musicians. Included Kenny Jeremiah of the Soul Survivors. | | |
| 1/11/75 | **1**¹ | 15 | 1 Shame, Shame, Shame ................................. | *12* | Vibration 532 |
| | | | vocal by Jesus Alvarez | | |
| 5/24/75 | **38** | 7 | 2 Cry Cry Cry............................................ | *91* | Vibration 535 |
| | | | above 2: written & produced by Sylvia Robinson (Mickey & Sylvia) | | |
| 4/24/76 | **91** | 2 | 3 I Like To Dance ...................................... | | Vibration 542 |
| | | | **SHIRLEY & LEE** | | |
| | | | New Orleans duo formed in the early 50s. Shirley Goodman (b: 6/19/36) and Leonard Lee (b: 6/29/36; d: 10/23/76). Billed as "The Sweethearts Of The Blues", recorded fulltime until 1963. Goodman did backup work on the West Coast, made comeback in 1975 with recordings for Sylvia Robinson's Vibration label. | | |
| 12/20/52+ | **2**³ | 11 | 1 I'm Gone ............................................. | | Aladdin 3153 |
| | | | Best Seller #2 / Juke Box #4 | | |
| 8/27/55 | **2**³ | 25 | 2 Feel So Good .......................................... | | Aladdin 3289 |
| | | | Juke Box #2 / Best Seller #5 / Jockey #7 | | |
| | | | Johnny Preston's version "Feel So Fine" hit POS 14-Pop in 1960 | | |
| 7/28/56 | **1**³ | 19 | 3 Let The Good Times Roll ............................ | *20* | Aladdin 3325 |
| | | | Jockey #1(3) / Juke Box #1(3) / Best Seller #2 | | |
| 11/24/56 | **3** | 10 | 4 I Feel Good ........................................... | *38* | Aladdin 3338 |
| | | | Jockey #3 / Juke Box #4 / Best Seller #5 | | |
| 3/02/57 | **14** | 1 | 5 When I Saw You........................................ | | Aladdin 3363 |
| | | | Jockey #14 | | |
| | | | **SHO-NUFF** | | |
| | | | Funk band formed at Jackson State University, Mississippi, in 1975. Consisted of Frederick Young (lead), Lawrence Lewis (guitar), James Lewis (keyboards), Sky Chambers (bass), Bruce Means (drums), Albert Bell (congas) and Jerod Minnis. | | |
| 10/21/78 | **93** | 3 | 1 I Live Across The Street .............................. | | Stax 3212 |
| 5/23/81 | **82** | 5 | 2 What Am I Gonna Do ................................... | | Malaco 2072 |
| | | | **SHOCK** | | |
| | | | Group from Portland, Oregon. Consisted of brothers Roger and Steve Sause, Steve Snyder, Steve Liddle, Ricky Ollison, Scott Boyd, Joe Plass, Johnny Riley, Billy Bradford and Malcolm Noble. First recorded for Nebula in 1979. | | |
| 9/05/81 | **52** | 10 | 1 Let's Get Crackin' ..................................... | | Fantasy 916 |
| 1/09/82 | **85** | 7 | 2 Let Your Body Do The Talkin' ......................... | | Fantasy 922 |
| 7/03/82 | **58** | 11 | 3 Electrophonic Phunk .................................. | | Fantasy 926 |
| 4/30/83 | **81** | 5 | 4 Waitin' On Your Love/ | | |
| | | 5 | 5 Nite Life .............................................. | | Fantasy 936 |
| 7/09/83 | **80** | 4 | 6 San Juan............................................... [I] | | Fantasy 938 |
| | | | **THE SHONDELLS - see TOMMY JAMES** | | |
| | | | **DINAH SHORE** | | |
| | | | Born Frances Shore on 3/1/17 in Winchester, Tennessee. One of the most popular female vocalists of the 1940 to mid-50s era. Own TV variety show, 1951-62, and own morning talk show "Dinah's Place", 1970-74. Married to actor George Montgomery from 1943-62. | | |
| 5/01/43 | **10** | 1 | 1 You'd Be So Nice To Come Home To .............. | *3* | Victor 1519 |
| | | | from the film "Something To Shout About" accompanied by Paul Weston's Orchestra | | |
| 11/18/44 | **10** | 2 | 2 I'll Walk Alone ....................................... | *1* | Victor 1586 |
| | | | with a mixed chorus; from the film "Follow The Boys" | | |
| | | | **SHOTGUN** | | |
| | | | Detroit group consisting of Richard Sebastian (trumpet), Greg Ingram (saxophone), Billy Talbert (keyboards, lead guitar), Ernest Latimore (guitar), Larry Austin (bass), Tyrone Steels (drums, vocals) and Leslie Carter (percussion). Toured with Rick James. | | |
| 4/23/77 | **87** | 7 | 1 Hot Line .............................................. | | ABC 12264 |
| 8/13/77 | **67** | 8 | 2 Mutha Funk ........................................... | | ABC 12292 |
| 5/27/78 | **38** | 14 | 3 Good, Bad And Funky ................................. | | ABC 12363 |
| 9/02/78 | **40** | 11 | 4 Love Attack ........................................... | | ABC 12395 |
| 2/10/79 | **35** | 16 | 5 Don't You Wanna Make Love? ........................ | | ABC 12452 |
| 9/20/80 | **69** | 7 | 6 Bad Babe ............................................. | | MCA 41312 |
| 4/10/82 | **41** | 12 | 7 Ladies Choice ......................................... | | Montage 1214 |
| 8/28/82 | **83** | 5 | 8 Shake And Pop ........................................ | | Montage 1221 |
| | | | **SHOWDOWN** | | |
| 9/10/77 | **90** | 5 | 1 Keep Doing It - Pt. 1 ................................. | | Honey Bee 2005 |

| DEBUT DATE | PEAK POS | WKS CHR | ARTIST — Record Title | POP POS | Label & Number |
|---|---|---|---|---|---|
| | | | **THE SHOWMEN** | | |
| | | | Group from Norfolk, Virginia, led by General Norman Johnson (member of Chairmen Of The Board). Included Milton Wells, Gene & Dorsey Knight, and Leslie Felton. | | |
| 7/04/64 | **80** | 3 | 1  It Will Stand........................................ [R] *Hot* | | Imperial 66033 |
| | | | first charted in 1961 on pop charts (POS 61); originally released on Minit 632 | | |
| | | | **SIDE EFFECT** | | |
| | | | Los Angeles group, formed in 1972. Produced by Wayne Henderson. Consisted of Augie Johnson (lead), Louis Patton, Gregory Matta and Sylvia Nabors. Nabors was replaced by Helen Lowe, who was replaced by Sylvia St. James in 1977. Miki Howard was lead singer, at one time. | | |
| 6/12/76 | **56** | 11 | 1  Always There............................................. | | Fantasy 769 |
| 12/04/76+ | **88** | 8 | 2  S.O.S........................................................ | | Fantasy 784 |
| 3/26/77 | **22** | 14 | 3  Keep That Same Old Feeling ........................ | | Fantasy 792 |
| 9/03/77 | **85** | 3 | 4  Finally Found Someone............................... | | Fantasy 796 |
| 3/11/78 | **18** | 14 | 5  It's All In Your Mind ................................. | | Fantasy 818 |
| 1/27/79 | **68** | 7 | 6  She's A Lady............................................. | | Fantasy 850 |
| 5/24/80 | **64** | 5 | 7  Superwoman .............................................. | | Elektra 46637 |
| 8/16/80 | **77** | 3 | 8  Georgy Porgy............................................. | | Elektra 47007 |
| | | | new version of Toto's 1979 pop hit (POS 48) | | |
| 4/04/81 | **26** | 14 | 9  Make You Mine ......................................... | | Elektra 47112 |
| | | | **LABI SIFFRE** | | |
| 5/09/87 | **49** | 10 | 1  (Something Inside) So Strong........................ | | China 43102 |
| | | | **BUNNY SIGLER** | | |
| | | | Born Walter Sigler on 3/27/41 in Philadelphia. Vocalist/multi-instrumentalist/composer/producer. Own group, the Opals, with brother James, Ritchie Rome and Jack Faith. First recorded for V-Tone in 1959. | | |
| 7/22/67 | **20** | 7 | 1  Let The Good Times Roll & Feel So Good.......... | 22 | Parkway 153 |
| 2/10/73 | **38** | 6 | 2  Tossin' And Turnin'.................................... | 97 | Phil. Int. 3523 |
| 6/15/74 | **28** | 9 | 3  Love Train (Part One)................................. | | Phil. Int. 3545 |
| 11/23/74 | **46** | 10 | 4  Keep Smilin' ............................................. | | Phil. Int. 3554 |
| 7/24/76 | **98** | 2 | 5  My Music .................................................. | | Phil. Int. 3597 |
| 1/07/78 | **8** | 19 | 6  **Let Me Party With You (Party, Party, Party) - Part 1** ..................................................... | 43 | Gold Mind 4008 |
| 5/27/78 | **42** | 11 | 7  I Got What You Need .................................. | | Gold Mind 4010 |
| 8/19/78 | **11** | 15 | 8  Only You .................................................. | 87 | Gold Mind 4012 |
| | | | LOLEATTA HOLLOWAY & BUNNY SIGLER | | |
| 12/02/78 | **94** | 2 | 9  Don't Even Try (Give It Up) ......................... | | Gold Mind 4014 |
| 3/24/79 | **37** | 9 | 10  By The Way You Dance (I Knew It Was You) ...... | | Gold Mind 4018 |
| | | | **ALFIE SILAS** | | |
| | | | Female singer from Los Angeles. Sang in gospel group, We, while at Los Angeles City College. Sang backup for Martha Reeves and Gino Vannelli. | | |
| 10/02/82 | **77** | 5 | 1  A Puppet To You......................................... | | RCA 13304 |
| 11/20/82+ | **28** | 12 | 2  There I Go ................................................ | | RCA 13387 |
| 2/25/84 | **77** | 4 | 3  Be Yourself............................................... | | RCA 13727 |
| 8/18/84 | **73** | 5 | 4  Close To Me .............................................. | | Motown 1747 |
| | | | BOBBY KING featuring ALFIE SILAS | | |
| | | | ALFIE: | | |
| 4/20/85 | **68** | 6 | 5  Star......................................................... | | Motown 1777 |
| | | | from the film "The Last Dragon" | | |
| 3/22/86 | **71** | 7 | 6  Just Gets Better With Time........................... | | Motown 1827 |
| | | | **SILENT UNDERDOG** | | |
| 7/20/85 | **69** | 6 | 1  Papa's Got A Brand New Pig Bag.................... | | Profile 7072 |
| | | | **THE SILHOUETTES** | | |
| | | | Group from Philadelphia, formed as the Tornadoes. Consisted of William Horton (lead), Richard "Rick" Lewis, Earl Beal and Raymond Edwards. | | |
| 1/20/58 | **1**[6] | 11 | 1  **Get A Job** ............................................... | 1 | Ember 1029 |
| | | | Jockey #1(6)/ Best Seller #1(4) originally released on Junior 391 | | |
| | | | **SILK** | | |
| | | | 7-member band from Philadelphia, formerly known as Ujima and Anglo Saxon Brown. Vocals by Debbie Henry. | | |
| 3/05/77 | **81** | 5 | 1  Party - Pt. 1 ............................................. | | Prelude 71084 |

| DEBUT DATE | PEAK POS | WKS CHR | ARTIST — Record Title | POP POS | Label & Number |
|---|---|---|---|---|---|
| | | | **SILK — Continued** | | |
| 1/26/80 | 87 | 3 | 2  I Can't Stop (Turning You On)........................., | | Phil. Int. 3730 |
| | | | **SILVER CONVENTION** | | |
| | | | German studio disco act assembled by producer Michael Kunze and writer/arranger Silvester Levay. Female vocal trio formed in 1976 consisting of Penny McLean, Ramona Wolf and Linda Thompson. | | |
| 10/04/75 | 1¹ | 18 | 1●Fly, Robin, Fly ............................... [I] | 1 | Midland 10339 |
| 3/20/76 | 5 | 18 | 2●Get Up And Boogie (That's Right)................. | 2 | Midland 10571 |
| 8/07/76 | 34 | 9 | 3  No, No, Joe .................................... | 60 | Midland 10723 |
| 12/18/76+ | 80 | 6 | 4  Dancing In The Aisles (Take Me Higher) ........... | 102 | Midland 10849 |
| 6/17/78 | 80 | 6 | 5  Spend The Night With Me ....................... | | Midsong Int. 40896 |
| | | | **SILVER PLATINUM** | | |
| 12/20/80+ | 25 | 15 | 1  Dance ......................................... | | Spector 00009 |
| 6/06/81 | 93 | 2 | 2  One More Chance ............................ | | Spector 00011 |
| | | | **SILVER, PLATINUM & GOLD** | | |
| 2/22/75 | 92 | 4 | 1  La-La-Love Chains ............................. | | Warner 8057 |
| 11/13/76 | 63 | 10 | 2  Just Friends.................................... | | Farr 011 |
| | | | **DOOLEY SILVERSPOON** | | |
| | | | Recorded as Little Dooley on Philadelphia's North Bay label. | | |
| 2/15/75 | 20 | 12 | 1  Bump Me Baby (Part 1)........................... | 80 | Cotton 636 |
| | | | **SILVETTI** | | |
| | | | Argentinian Bebu Silvetti. | | |
| 3/12/77 | 77 | 6 | 1  Spring Rain................................. [I] | 39 | Salsoul 2014 |
| | | | **CHANDRA SIMMONS** | | |
| 9/26/87 | 60 | 9 | 1  Never Gonna' Let You Go ...................... | | Fresh 0013 |
| | | | **PATRICK SIMMONS** | | |
| | | | Born on 1/23/50 in Aberdeen, Washington; raised in San Jose, California. Vocalist/ guitarist. Original member of The Doobie Brothers, he wrote their hit "Black Water". | | |
| 4/09/83 | 77 | 5 | 1  So Wrong.................................... | 30 | Elektra 69839 |
| | | | **SIMTEC SIMMONS** | | |
| | | | Born Walter Simmons on 12/19/44 in Chicago. Singer/guitarist. Formed Tea Boxes Band at Loop Junior College in 1964. Merged with Wylie Dixon & The Wheels in 1967, forming Simtec & Wylie. | | |
| 1/18/75 | 66 | 7 | 1  Some Other Time ........................... | | Innovation 8047 |
| | | | **JOHN & ARTHUR SIMMS** | | |
| 4/05/80 | 39 | 11 | 1  That Thang Of Yours ...................... | | Casablanca 2251 |
| | | | **SIMON SAID** | | |
| 6/07/75 | 61 | 6 | 1  Love Song..................................... | | Roulette 7167 |
| | | | **JOE SIMON**  ★★24★★ | | |
| | | | Born on 9/2/43 in Simmesport, Louisiana. Moved to Oakland in 1959. First recorded with vocal group, the Golden Tones, for Hush in 1960. | | |
| 8/21/65 | 13 | 17 | 1  Let's Do It Over .............................. | | Vee-Jay 694 |
| 6/11/66 | 11 | 12 | 2  Teenager's Prayer ........................... | 66 | Snd. St. 7 2564 |
| 1/14/67 | 17 | 12 | 3  My Special Prayer ........................... | 87 | Snd. St. 7 2577 |
| 6/17/67 | 47 | 5 | 4  Put Your Trust In Me (Depend On Me) .............. | 129 | Snd. St. 7 2583 |
| 9/30/67 | 19 | 11 | 5  Nine Pound Steel.............................. | 70 | Snd. St. 7 2589 |
| 1/13/68 | 22 | 8 | 6  No Sad Songs ............................... | 49 | Snd. St. 7 2602 |
| 4/27/68 | 11 | 14 | 7  (You Keep Me) Hangin' On........................ | 25 | Snd. St. 7 2608 |
| 9/14/68 | 31 | 7 | 8  Message From Maria ........................... | 75 | Snd. St. 7 2617 |
| 12/21/68+ | 42 | 7 | 9  Looking Back ................................ | 70 | Snd. St. 7 2622 |
| 3/29/69 | 1³ | 13 | 10●The Chokin' Kind .............................. | 13 | Snd. St. 7 2628 |
| 7/05/69 | 16 | 7 | 11  Baby, Don't Be Looking In My Mind................. | 72 | Snd. St. 7 2634 |
| 9/27/69 | 29 | 3 | 12  San Francisco Is A Lonely Town/ | 79 | |
| 10/18/69 | 26 | 10 | 13    It's Hard To Get Along ....................... | 87 | Snd. St. 7 2641 |
| 1/03/70 | 11 | 13 | 14  Moon Walk - Part 1............................ | 54 | Snd. St. 7 2651 |
| 4/25/70 | 7 | 8 | 15  Farther On Down The Road ........................ | 56 | Snd. St. 7 2656 |
| 8/08/70 | 10 | 9 | 16  Yours Love................................... | 78 | Snd. St. 7 2664 |
| 10/31/70 | 27 | 6 | 17  That's The Way I Want Our Love ................... | 93 | Snd. St. 7 2667 |

| DEBUT DATE | PEAK POS | WKS CHR | ARTIST — Record Title | POP POS | Label & Number |
|---|---|---|---|---|---|
| | | | **JOE SIMON** — Continued | | |
| 12/12/70+ | **3** | 14 | 18 **Your Time To Cry** | 40 | Spring 108 |
| 5/01/71 | **13** | 8 | 19 Help Me Make It Through The Night/ | 69 | |
| | | 2 | 20    To Lay Down Beside You | 117 | Spring 113 |
| 7/17/71 | **12** | 9 | 21 You're The One For Me | 71 | Spring 115 |
| 9/18/71 | **19** | 6 | 22 All My Hard Times/ | 93 | |
| | | 4 | 23    Georgia Blues | | Spring 118 |
| | | | all of above: produced by John Richbourg | | |
| 11/20/71+ | **3** | 15 | 24● **Drowning In The Sea Of Love** | 11 | Spring 120 |
| 4/01/72 | **13** | 9 | 25 Pool Of Bad Luck | 42 | Spring 124 |
| 7/15/72 | **1**² | 13 | 26● **Power Of Love** | 11 | Spring 128 |
| 10/21/72 | **47** | 5 | 27 Misty Blue | 91 | Sound Stage 1508 |
| 11/11/72 | **5** | 10 | 28 **Trouble In My Home/** | 50 | |
| | | 13 | 29    I Found My Dad | | Spring 130 |
| 3/03/73 | **6** | 11 | 30 **Step By Step** | 37 | Spring 133 |
| 7/14/73 | **3** | 14 | 31 **Theme From Cleopatra Jones** | 18 | Spring 138 |
| | | | featuring The Mainstreeters; from the film of the same title | | |
| 11/03/73 | **6** | 13 | 32 **River** | 62 | Spring 141 |
| 3/16/74 | **12** | 13 | 33 Carry Me | | Spring 145 |
| 6/22/74 | **15** | 12 | 34 Best Time Of My Life | | Spring 149 |
| 3/22/75 | **1**² | 17 | 35 **Get Down, Get Down (Get On The Floor)** | 8 | Spring 156 |
| 8/09/75 | **7** | 14 | 36 **Music In My Bones** | 92 | Spring 159 |
| 1/03/76 | **5** | 12 | 37 **I Need You, You Need Me** | | Spring 163 |
| 8/14/76 | **22** | 11 | 38 Come Get To This | 102 | Spring 166 |
| 12/11/76+ | **12** | 15 | 39 Easy To Love | | Spring 169 |
| 5/28/77 | **62** | 7 | 40 You Didn't Have To Play No Games | | Spring 172 |
| 9/24/77 | **28** | 15 | 41 One Step At A Time | | Spring 176 |
| 1/07/78 | **27** | 12 | 42 For Your Love, Love, Love | | Spring 178 |
| 7/22/78 | **71** | 8 | 43 I.O.U. | | Spring 184 |
| 11/25/78+ | **15** | 15 | 44 Love Vibration | | Spring 190 |
| 5/05/79 | **78** | 4 | 45 Going Through These Changes | | Spring 194 |
| 10/20/79 | **87** | 4 | 46 I Wanna Taste Your Love | | Spring 3003 |
| 8/02/80 | **60** | 8 | 47 Baby, When Love Is In Your Heart (It's In Your Eyes) | | Posse 5001 |
| 12/27/80+ | **43** | 12 | 48 Glad You Came My Way | | Posse 5005 |
| 5/16/81 | **52** | 11 | 49 Are We Breaking Up | | Posse 5010 |
| | | | **LOWRELL SIMON - see LOWRELL** | | |
| | | | **NINA SIMONE** | | |
| | | | Born Eunice Waymon on 2/21/33 in Tryon, South Carolina. Jazz-influenced vocalist/pianist/composer. Attended Juilliard School of Music in New York City. Devoted more time to political activism in the 70s, infrequent recording. | | |
| 6/22/59 | **2**¹ | 21 | 1 **I Loves You, Porgy** | 18 | Bethlehem 11021 |
| | | | from the film "Porgy And Bess" | | |
| 8/15/60 | **23** | 6 | 2 Nobody Knows You When You're Down And Out. | 93 | Colpix 158 |
| 1/09/61 | **11** | 6 | 3 Trouble In Mind | 92 | Colpix 175 |
| 7/03/65 | **23** | 7 | 4 I Put A Spell On You | 120 | Philips 40286 |
| 9/28/68 | **43** | 6 | 5 Do What You Gotta Do | 83 | RCA 9602 |
| 4/12/69 | **41** | 2 | 6 Revolution | | RCA 9730 |
| 11/22/69+ | **8** | 9 | 7 **To Be Young, Gifted And Black** | 76 | RCA 0269 |
| | | | **SIMPLY RED** | | |
| | | | British pop sextet led by vocalist Mick "Red" Hucknall. | | |
| 5/31/86 | **29** | 16 | 1 Holding Back The Years | 1 | Elektra 69564 |
| | | | **VALERIE SIMPSON** | | |
| | | | Born on 8/26/46 in New York City. Half of vocal/songwriting/producing duo Ashford & Simpson. | | |
| 12/16/72 | **24** | 11 | 1 Silly Wasn't I | 63 | Tamla 54224 |
| | | | **SIMS TWINS** | | |
| | | | Los Angeles duo of brothers Bobby and Kenneth Sims. | | |
| 10/02/61 | **4** | 22 | 1 Soothe Me | 42 | Sar 117 |
| | | | originally released on Karate 508 | | |

| DEBUT DATE | PEAK POS | WKS CHR | ARTIST — Record Title | POP POS | Label & Number |
|---|---|---|---|---|---|
| | | | **JOYCE SIMS** Dance singer, born and raised in Rochester, New York. | | |
| 4/26/86 | 69 | 12 | 1 (You Are My) All And All ................................ | | Sleeping Bag 17 |
| 5/30/87 | 23 | 16 | 2 Lifetime Love ............................................ | | Sleeping Bag 24 |
| 11/21/87+ | 10 | 18 | 3 **Come Into My Life**.................................... | | Sleeping Bag 28 |
| 4/16/88 | 29 | 11 | 4 Love Makes A Woman.................................. JOYCE SIMS featuring JIMMY CASTOR | | Sleeping Bag 40134 |
| | | | **MARVIN L. SIMS** Born on 12/11/44 in Sedalia, Missouri. Singer/songwriter. First recorded in 1962. Has master's degree in psychotherapy. | | |
| 9/07/68 | 50 | 3 | 1 Talkin About Soul ........................................ | | Revue 11024 |
| | | | **SIMTEC & WYLIE** Group formed in Chicago in 1967. Consisted of Walter "Simtec" Simmons and Wylie Dixon, Bobby Pointer, Ronald Simmons and Fred White. White, brother of Maurice White, left for Ramsey Lewis' band and Earth, Wind & Fire. Replaced by Wilbur "June" Mhoon. Group disbanded in 1973, some members became The South Side Movement. Simmons recorded solo in 1975. | | |
| 2/14/70 | 49 | 2 | 1 Do It Like Mama ......................................... | | Shama 4003 |
| 7/24/71 | 29 | 9 | 2 Gotta' Get Over The Hump............................ | *101* | Mr. Chand 8005 |
| | | | **FRANK SINATRA** Born Francis Albert Sinatra on 12/12/15 in Hoboken, New Jersey. With Harry James from 1939-40, first recorded for Brunswick in 1939; with Tommy Dorsey, 1940-42. Went solo in late 1942 and charted 40 Top 10 hits through 1954. Appeared in many films from 1941 on. Won an Oscar for the film "From Here To Eternity" in 1953. Own TV show in 1957. Own record company, Reprise, 1961, sold to Warner Bros. in 1963. Announced his retirement in 1970, but made comeback in 1973. Regarded by many as the greatest popular singer of the 20th century. | | |
| 7/17/43 | 8 | 2 | 1 All Or Nothing At All ................................ FRANK SINATRA with HARRY JAMES & HIS ORCHESTRA recorded on 9/17/39; a reported million-seller | *1* | Columbia 35587 |
| 8/17/59 | 20 | 2 | 2 High Hopes ............................................... with Nelson Riddle & His Orchestra; from the film "A Hole In The Head" | *30* | Capitol 4214 |
| 12/17/66+ | 25 | 6 | 3 That's Life ............................................... | *4* | Reprise 0531 |
| | | | **HAL SINGER** Born Harold Singer on 10/8/19 in Tulsa, Oklahoma. Tenor saxophonist. With Ernie Fields in 1938, Lloyd Hunter, Nat Towles, Tommy Douglas in 1939, and Jay McShann in 1941. Moved to New York in 1942. With Roy Eldridge, Earl Bostic, Lucky Millinder and Duke Ellington. Own band from 1949-58. One of the originators of the honking rock 'n' roll sax style. | | |
| 9/04/48 | 1[4] | 22 | 1 Corn Bread ................................................ [I] Best Seller #1(4) / Juke Box #1(4) | | Savoy 671 |
| 3/19/49 | 11 | 1 | 2 Beef Stew ................................................ [I] Best Seller #11 | | Savoy 686 |
| | | | **CHARLIE SINGLETON** Vocalist/guitarist from Louisiana. Member of Cameo - former guitarist with Billy Cobham's group. | | |
| 8/31/85 | 19 | 13 | 1 Make Your Move On Me Baby (with Rap!) .......... | | Arista 9386 |
| 10/24/87 | 22 | 15 | 2 Nothing Ventured-Nothing Gained .................... CHARLIE SINGLETON & MODERN MAN | | Epic 07429 |
| 3/19/88 | 81 | 6 | 3 Thank You (falettinmebemicelfagain)................ CHARLIE SINGLETON & MODERN MAN | | Epic 07719 |
| | | | **SINITTA** Vocalist born in Seattle of American-Indian descent. Daughter of singer/dancer Miquel Brown. Starred in musicals & TV shows. Appeared in the films "Shock Treatment" (1981) and "Foreign Bodies". | | |
| 4/04/87 | 63 | 7 | 1 Feels Like The First Time ............................. | | Omni 99477 |
| | | | **SINNAMON** | | |
| 5/22/82 | 44 | 11 | 1 Thanks To You ........................................... | | Becket 11 |
| | | | **SIREN** | | |
| 9/22/79 | 79 | 5 | 1 Open Up For Love ...................................... | | Midsong Int. 1006 |
| | | | **THE SISTER & BROTHERS** Mixed male-female vocal group from Chicago. | | |
| 7/11/70 | 28 | 6 | 1 Dear Ike (Remember I'm John's Girl) ............ [S] | *131* | Uni 55238 |
| 4/17/71 | 43 | 3 | 2 Ack-A-Fool................................................ | | Calla 175 |

| DEBUT DATE | PEAK POS | WKS CHR | ARTIST — Record Title | POP POS | Label & Number |
|---|---|---|---|---|---|
| | | | **SISTER SLEDGE** ★★162★★ | | |
| | | | Sisters Debra, Joan, Kim and Kathie Sledge from North Philadelphia. First recorded as Sisters Sledge for Money Back in 1971. Worked as back-up vocalists. Began producing their own albums in 1981. Also see Percy Sledge. | | |
| 12/28/74+ | **31** | 13 | 1 Love Don't You Go Through No Changes On Me .. | 92 | Atco 7008 |
| 7/17/76 | **78** | 5 | 2 Thank You For Today | | Cotillion 44202 |
| 1/08/77 | **100** | 2 | 3 Cream Of The Crop | | Cotillion 44208 |
| 7/09/77 | **61** | 6 | 4 Blockbuster Boy | | Cotillion 44220 |
| 1/27/79 | **1**¹ | 17 | 5 **He's The Greatest Dancer** | 9 | Cotillion 44245 |
| 5/05/79 | **1**¹ | 13 | 6●**We Are Family** | 2 | Cotillion 44251 |
| 8/04/79 | **35** | 9 | 7 Lost In Music | | Cotillion 45001 |
| 1/05/80 | **6** | 15 | 8 **Got To Love Somebody** | 64 | Cotillion 45007 |
| 3/29/80 | **21** | 12 | 9 Reach Your Peak | 101 | Cotillion 45013 |
| 6/21/80 | **63** | 5 | 10 Let's Go On Vacation | | Cotillion 45020 |
| 1/31/81 | **3** | 16 | 11 **All American Girls** | 79 | Cotillion 46007 |
| 4/18/81 | **28** | 14 | 12 Next Time You'll Know | 82 | Cotillion 46012 |
| 7/25/81 | **32** | 9 | 13 He's Just A Runaway | | Cotillion 46017 |
| 1/23/82 | **14** | 15 | 14 My Guy | 23 | Cotillion 47000 |
| 5/15/82 | **45** | 10 | 15 All The Man I Need | | Cotillion 47007 |
| | | | featuring David Simmons | | |
| 5/07/83 | **22** | 14 | 16 B.Y.O.B. (Bring Your Own Baby) | | Cotillion 99885 |
| 9/17/83 | **56** | 7 | 17 Gotta Get Back To Love | | Cotillion 99834 |
| 6/08/85 | **32** | 10 | 18 Frankie | 75 | Atlantic 89547 |
| 9/21/85 | **71** | 6 | 19 Dancing On The Jagged Edge | | Atlantic 89520 |
| | | | **SISTERS LOVE** | | |
| | | | Group consisting of Merry Clayton, Odia Coates, Gwen Berry and Lillian Fort. All except Fort had been in The Raeletts. | | |
| 5/29/71 | **20** | 11 | 1 Are You Lonely? | 108 | A&M 1259 |
| | | | **THE SIX TEENS** | | |
| | | | Group formed in 1956 in Los Angeles. Consisted of Ed Wells and Trudy Williams (leads), Richard Owens, Darryl Lewis, Beverly Pecot and Louise Williams. In 1956, members ranged in age from 14 to 19. | | |
| 6/09/56 | **7** | 10 | 1 **A Casual Look** | 25 | Flip 315 |
| | | | Best Seller #7 / Jockey #8 | | |
| | | | **SKIP & FLIP** | | |
| | | | Gary "Flip" Paxton and Clyde "Skip" Battin. Met at the University of Arizona, and appeared on "Arizona Jubilee" in 1958 as the Rockabillies. Paxton formed The Hollywood Argyles, and later started own Garpax record label. | | |
| 4/25/60 | **27** | 1 | 1 Cherry Pie | 11 | Brent 7010 |
| | | | **SKIP & THE CASUALS - see SKIP MAHONEY** | | |
| | | | **SKIPWORTH & TURNER** | | |
| | | | Duo of Rodney Skipworth (from Syracuse, keyboards) and Phil Turner (from Memphis; raised in Buffalo, vocals). | | |
| 5/04/85 | **10** | 19 | 1 **Thinking About Your Love** | 104 | 4th & B'way 7414 |
| 8/23/86 | **63** | 7 | 2 Can't Give Her Up | | Warner 28695 |
| | | | **SKOOL BOYZ** | | |
| | | | Trio formed in Los Angeles, featuring Stan Sheppard, formerly with Triple "S" Connection and Livin' Proof (vocals, percussion). Included Billy Sheppard (vocals, guitar) and Chauncy Matthews (guitar, keyboards). | | |
| 11/28/81 | **57** | 9 | 1 Your Love | | Destiny 2001 |
| 2/27/82 | **54** | 10 | 2 This Feeling Must Be Real | | Destiny 2006 |
| 10/29/83 | **63** | 8 | 3 Before You Go | | Cross Rds. 1063 |
| 6/16/84 | **47** | 10 | 4 Slip Away | | Columbia 04481 |
| 7/20/85 | **86** | 4 | 5 Superfine (From Behind) | | Columbia 04942 |
| | | | **THE SKWARES** | | |
| | | | Six-man band from Memphis. Includes: Johnny Adkinson (vocals), Willie Bonds, Michael Anderson, Bryan Jones, William Polk and Tony Smith. | | |
| 2/27/88 | **33** | 11 | 1 Don't Mess With My Heart | | Mercury 870115 |
| | | | **SKYLARK** | | |
| | | | Group from Vancouver: lead singers Donny Gerrard & B.J. (Bonnie Jean) Cook, with David Foster, Duris Maxwell, Norman McPherson, Steven Pugsley and Carl Graves. Keyboardist Foster recorded solo in the mid-80s. | | |
| 12/15/73+ | **55** | 9 | 1 If That's The Way You Want It | | Capitol 3773 |

| DEBUT DATE | PEAK POS | WKS CHR | ARTIST — Record Title | POP POS | Label & Number |
|---|---|---|---|---|---|
| | | | **THE SKYLINERS** | | |
| | | | Pittsburgh vocal quintet: Jimmy Beaumont (b: 10/21/40), lead; Janet Vogel (d: 2/21/80, suicide) & Wally Lester, tenors; Joe VerScharen, baritone; and Jackie Taylor, bass voice/guitarist. Beaumont, Lester and Taylor had been in the Crescents group. Vogel and VerScharen had been in the El Rios. | | |
| 3/16/59 | 3 | 13 | 1 **Since I Don't Have You**............................ | 12 | Calico 103 |
| 7/20/59 | 20 | 3 | 2 This I Swear................................................ | 26 | Calico 106 |
| 7/10/65 | 34 | 9 | 3 The Loser ................................................... | 72 | Jubilee 5506 |
| | | | **SKYY** ★★191★★ | | |
| | | | Octet from New York City. Consisted of the Dunning Sisters [Denise, Delores and Bonnie (vocals)], Solomon Roberts & Anibal Anthony Sierra (guitars), Larry Greenberg (keyboards), Gerald LaBon (bass) and Tommy McConnell (drums). Organized by Randy Muller, former leader of Brass Construction. | | |
| 5/19/79 | 20 | 14 | 1 First Time Around........................................ | | Salsoul 2087 |
| 9/08/79 | 65 | 9 | 2 Let's Turn It Out......................................... | | Salsoul 2102 |
| 2/23/80 | 13 | 16 | 3 High .......................................................... | 102 | Salsoul 2113 |
| 5/31/80 | 32 | 11 | 4 Skyyzoo..................................................... | | Salsoul 2121 |
| 12/06/80+ | 23 | 18 | 5 Here's To You............................................. | | Salsoul 2132 |
| 3/28/81 | 31 | 10 | 6 Superlove .................................................. | | Salsoul 2136 |
| 11/07/81 | 1² | 24 | 7 **Call Me**.................................................... | 26 | Salsoul 2152 |
| 3/20/82 | 16 | 15 | 8 Let's Celebrate ........................................... | | Salsoul 7020 |
| 6/26/82 | 43 | 10 | 9 When You Touch Me .................................... | | Salsoul 7029 |
| 10/30/82 | 26 | 14 | 10 Movin' Violation........................................ | | Salsoul 7038 |
| 1/22/83 | 39 | 9 | 11 Let Love Shine .......................................... | | Salsoul 7045 |
| 6/18/83 | 33 | 11 | 12 Bad Boy ................................................... | | Salsoul 7057 |
| 10/08/83 | 35 | 11 | 13 Show Me The Way ..................................... | | Salsoul 7061 |
| 12/22/84+ | 49 | 10 | 14 Dancin' To Be Dancin' ............................... | | Salsoul 7077 |
| 5/24/86 | 8 | 17 | 15 **Givin' It (To You)**..................................... | | Capitol 5560 |
| | | | **FREDDIE SLACK** | | |
| | | | Born on 8/7/10 in Westby, Wisconsin. Died of diabetes on 8/10/65. Pianist/composer/drummer. Moved to Chicago in 1927, with Johnny Tobin. Moved to Los Angeles in 1931. With Ben Pollack from 1934-39, and Jimmy Dorsey from 1939-41. Own band in 1942; featured vocalists Ella Mae Morse and Margaret Whiting. In the films "The Sky's The Limit", "Reveille With Beverly", "Keep 'Em Flying", "Babes On Swing Street" and "Follow The Boys". | | |
| 10/24/42 | 1² | 14 | 1 **Mr. Five By Five**........................................ | 10 | Capitol 115 |
| | | | from the film "Behind The 8-Ball" | | |
| 10/31/42+ | 6 | 9 | 2 **Cow Cow Boogie**....................................... | 9 | Capitol 102 |
| | | | from the film "Ride 'Em, Cowboy"; sung by Morse in the film "Reveille With Beverly"; above 2: vocals by Ella Mae Morse | | |
| 4/17/43 | 3 | 7 | 3 **Riffette**.................................................[I] | 19 | Capitol 129 |
| | | | from the film "Star-Spangled Rhythm"; with T-Bone Walker on guitar | | |
| | | | **SLAVE** ★★187★★ | | |
| | | | Group formed by Steve Washington (trumpet), in Dayton, Ohio, in 1975. With Floyd Miller (vocals), Tom Lockett, Jr., Charles Bradley, Mark Adams, Mark Hicks, Danny Webster, Orion Wilhoite and Tim Dozier. Vocalists Steve Arrington and Starleana Young added in 1978. Arrington became lead vocalist; Young, Washington and Lockett left to form Aurra in 1979. Other members after 1980 included Charles C. Carter, Delburt Taylor, Sam Carter, Kevin Johnson & Roger Parker. Young and Jones formed Deja in 1987. | | |
| 5/21/77 | 1¹ | 20 | 1 **Slide** ...................................................[I] | 32 | Cotillion 44218 |
| 2/04/78 | 22 | 10 | 2 The Party Song............................................ | 110 | Cotillion 44231 |
| 6/03/78 | 74 | 4 | 3 Baby Sinister ...........................................[I] | | Cotillion 44235 |
| 7/08/78 | 14 | 17 | 4 Stellar Fungk ............................................. | | Cotillion 44238 |
| 11/11/78 | 64 | 5 | 5 Just Freak ................................................. | 110 | Cotillion 44242 |
| 10/20/79+ | 9 | 22 | 6 **Just A Touch Of Love**................................ | | Cotillion 45005 |
| 3/15/80 | 55 | 7 | 7 Foxy Lady (Funky Lady)................................ | | Cotillion 45011 |
| 11/08/80 | 57 | 7 | 8 Sizzlin' Hot ................................................ | | Cotillion 46004 |
| 12/13/80+ | 6 | 24 | 9 **Watching You**........................................... | 78 | Cotillion 46006 |
| 6/06/81 | 62 | 6 | 10 Feel My Love ............................................ | | Cotillion 46014 |
| 9/12/81 | 6 | 20 | 11 **Snap Shot**.............................................. | 91 | Cotillion 46022 |
| 12/19/81+ | 20 | 13 | 12 Wait For Me ............................................. | 103 | Cotillion 46028 |
| 12/11/82 | 81 | 3 | 13 Intro (Come To Blow Ya Mind) ......................... | | Cotillion 99953 |
| 1/22/83 | 73 | 5 | 14 Do You Like It...(Girl) ................................. | | Cotillion 99927 |
| 9/03/83 | 22 | 13 | 15 Shake It Up .............................................. | | Cotillion 99838 |
| 12/10/83+ | 73 | 7 | 16 Steppin' Out ............................................. | | Cotillion 99804 |

| DEBUT DATE | PEAK POS | WKS CHR | ARTIST — Record Title | POP POS | Label & Number |
|---|---|---|---|---|---|
| | | | **SLAVE — Continued** | | |
| 10/20/84 | **41** | 9 | 17 Ooohh .......................................................... | | Atlantic 99696 |
| 4/19/86 | **84** | 2 | 18 Thrill Me ...................................................... | | Ichiban 105 |
| 6/28/86 | **85** | 4 | 19 All We Need Is Time ..................................... | | Ichiban 107 |
| 7/11/87 | **83** | 8 | 20 Juicy-O ........................................................ | | Ichiban 120 |
| | | | **EMITT SLAY TRIO** | | |
| | | | Detroit singer/guitarist Emmitt Slay, with Bob White (vocals, organ) and Lawrence Jackson (drums). | | |
| 3/21/53 | **9** | 2 | 1 **My Kind Of Woman** .................................. | | Savoy 886 |
| | | | Best Seller #9 | | |
| | | | **PERCY SLEDGE** | | |
| | | | Born in 1941 in Leighton, Alabama. Worked local clubs with Esquires Combo until going solo. Wrote "When A Man Loves A Woman" with Cameron Lewis (bass) and Andrew Wright (organ). Cousin of Jimmy Hughes. | | |
| 4/16/66 | **1**[4] | 16 | 1●**When A Man Loves A Woman** ....................... | *1* | Atlantic 2326 |
| 7/30/66 | **5** | 11 | 2 **Warm And Tender Love** ................................ | *17* | Atlantic 2342 |
| 11/05/66 | **7** | 13 | 3 **It Tears Me Up** ........................................... | *20* | Atlantic 2358 |
| 3/18/67 | **44** | 2 | 4 Baby, Help Me .............................................. | *87* | Atlantic 2383 |
| 4/15/67 | **25** | 10 | 5 Out Of Left Field .......................................... | *59* | Atlantic 2396 |
| 7/08/67 | **35** | 7 | 6 Love Me Tender ............................................. | *40* | Atlantic 2414 |
| 12/23/67+ | **39** | 3 | 7 Cover Me ...................................................... | *42* | Atlantic 2453 |
| 3/30/68 | **6** | 12 | 8 **Take Time To Know Her** ............................. | *11* | Atlantic 2490 |
| 8/10/68 | **41** | 4 | 9 Sudden Stop ................................................. | *63* | Atlantic 2539 |
| 2/15/69 | **44** | 3 | 10 My Special Prayer ......................................... | *93* | Atlantic 2594 |
| 4/19/69 | **35** | 4 | 11 Any Day Now ................................................ | *86* | Atlantic 2616 |
| | | | all of above: produced by Quin Ivy and Marlin Greene | | |
| 8/04/73 | **89** | 3 | 12 Sunshine ...................................................... | | Atlantic 2963 |
| | | | backing vocals by Sister Sledge | | |
| 10/26/74 | **15** | 12 | 13 I'll Be Your Everything ................................. | *62* | Capricorn 0209 |
| | | | **SLICK** | | |
| | | | Vocal group from Philadelphia, originally known as Breeze. Lead singer Brandi Wells. | | |
| 8/23/80 | **46** | 13 | 1 Sunrise ........................................................ | | Fantasy 892 |
| | | | **SLINGSHOT** | | |
| | | | Detroit studio musicians. | | |
| 7/23/83 | **25** | 11 | 1 Do It Again/Billie Jean (medley)...................... | | Quality 7044 |
| | | | **SLY & THE FAMILY STONE**   ★★**140**★★ | | |
| | | | San Francisco interracial "psychedelic soul" group formed by Sylvester "Sly Stone" Stewart (b: 3/15/44, Dallas; lead singer/keyboards). Included Sly's brother Freddie Stone (guitar), Cynthia Robinson (trumpet), Jerry Martini (saxophone), Sly's sister Rosie Stone (vocalist/piano), Larry Graham (bass) and Gregg Errico (drums). Sly recorded gospel at age 4. With vocal group, the Viscanes, while in high school. Producer/writer for Bobby Freeman, the Mojo Men, and the Beau Brummels. Formed own groups, The Stoners in 1966 and the Family Stone in 1967. Worked Woodstock Festival in 1969. With George Clinton in 1982. Graham formed and fronted Graham Central Station in 1973; began solo career in 1980. Also see Sly Stone. | | |
| 1/27/68 | **9** | 18 | 1 **Dance To The Music** ................................... | *8* | Epic 10256 |
| 12/21/68+ | **1**[2] | 15 | 2●**Everyday People/** | *1* | |
| 1/25/69 | **28** | 10 | 3 Sing A Simple Song ..................................... | *89* | Epic 10407 |
| 4/19/69 | **14** | 9 | 4 **Stand!/** | *22* | |
| 5/24/69 | **24** | 7 | 5 I Want To Take You Higher............................ | *60* | Epic 10450 |
| 8/23/69 | **3** | 15 | 6 **Hot Fun In The Summertime** ....................... | *2* | Epic 10497 |
| 1/10/70 | **1**[5] | 14 | 7●**Thank You (Falettinme Be Mice Elf Agin)** ....... | *1* | Epic 10555 |
| 11/13/71 | **1**[5] | 13 | 8●**Family Affair** ............................................. | *1* | Epic 10805 |
| 2/19/72 | **15** | 7 | 9 Runnin' Away................................................. | *23* | Epic 10829 |
| 4/29/72 | **21** | 7 | 10 Smilin' ......................................................... | *42* | Epic 10850 |
| 6/30/73 | **3** | 16 | 11●**If You Want Me To Stay** ............................. | *12* | Epic 11017 |
| 11/17/73 | **28** | 8 | 12 **Frisky/** | *79* | |
| 1/12/74 | **57** | 10 | 13 If It Were Left Up To Me ............................... | | Epic 11060 |
| 6/22/74 | **10** | 15 | 14 **Time For Livin'** .......................................... | *32* | Epic 11140 |
| 10/12/74 | **22** | 11 | 15 Loose Booty .................................................. | *84* | Epic 50033 |
| 2/26/77 | **85** | 3 | 16 Family Again.................................................. | | Epic 50331 |
| | | | all of above: written & produced by Sly Stone | | |
| 9/29/79 | **38** | 11 | 17 Remember Who You Are ................................. | *104* | Warner 49062 |

| DEBUT DATE | PEAK POS | WKS CHR | ARTIST — Record Title | POP POS | Label & Number |
|---|---|---|---|---|---|
| | | | **SLY FOX** | | |
| | | | Black-and-white duo: Gary "Mudbone" Cooper (P-Funk) and Michael Camacho. | | |
| 3/29/86 | **57** | 9 | 1 Let's Go All The Way .......................................... | 7 | Capitol 5552 |
| | | | based on the same groove as the Boogie Boys' "Fly Girl" | | |
| | | | **KAREN SMALL** | | |
| 5/28/66 | **37** | 6 | 1 Boys Are Made To Love.................................. | *123* | Venus 1066 |
| | | | **MILLIE SMALL** | | |
| | | | Born Millicent Smith on 10/6/46 in Jamaica. Nicknamed "The Blue Beat Girl". | | |
| 5/23/64 | **2**¹ | 12 | 1 **My Boy Lollipop**............................................. | *Hot* | Smash 1893 |
| 8/08/64 | **40** | 7 | 2 Sweet William ......................................... | *Hot* | Smash 1920 |
| | | | **SMITH CONNECTION** | | |
| | | | Family group including Michael L. and Louis Smith. Michael wrote and arranged for 100 Proof Aged In Soul, Honey Cone, Jermaine Jackson, Stevie Wonder, Thelma Houston, and others. | | |
| 1/27/73 | **28** | 8 | 1 I've Been A Winner, I've Been A Loser ............. | | Music Mer. 1012 |
| | | | **DAWSON SMITH** | | |
| 2/08/75 | **79** | 6 | 1 I Don't Know If I Can Make It (Part 1)................ | | Scepter 12400 |
| | | | **EFFIE SMITH** | | |
| | | | Singer/comedienne. Died of cancer in March, 1977. Recorded with Three Shades of Rhythm and Lionel Hampton in the 30s. First solo recording for G&G in 1945. Promotion work for Stax in Memphis and Los Angeles in the early 70s. | | |
| 1/30/65 | **36** | 1 | 1 Dial That Telephone ................................. | | Duo Disc 107 |
| 11/02/68 | **43** | 5 | 2 Harper Valley P.T.A. Gossip ........................... | | Eee Cee 100 |
| | | | **FRANKIE SMITH** | | |
| | | | Philadelphia native. Wrote and produced for Philadelphia International in the late 70s, and later for WMOT. | | |
| 2/28/81 | **1**⁴ | 31 | 1●**Double Dutch Bus**..................................... | *30* | WMOT 5356 |
| | | | based on the double-dutch jump rope game; certified gold for both 7" and 12" singles | | |
| | | | **HELENE SMITH** | | |
| | | | Vocalist from Miami, produced by Willie Clark and Clarence Reid. | | |
| 8/12/67 | **20** | 5 | 1 A Woman Will Do Wrong ............................... | *128* | Phil-L.A. 300 |
| | | | **HUEY "PIANO" SMITH & THE CLOWNS** | | |
| | | | Huey was born on 1/26/34 in New Orleans. With Earl King in the early 50s. Recorded with Eddie "Guitar Slim" Jones' band from 1951-54. Much session work in New Orleans. Own band, The Clowns, in 1957, with Bobby Marchan (vocals). Marchan left in 1959, replaced by Curly Smith. Also see Frankie Ford. | | |
| 7/15/57 | **5** | 7 | 1 **Rocking Pneumonia And The Boogie Woogie Flu** .................................................... | *52* | Ace 530 |
| | | | Jockey #5 / Best Seller #9 | | |
| 3/31/58 | **4** | 9 | 2 **Don't You Just Know It**............................... | *9* | Ace 545 |
| | | | Best Seller #4 / Jockey #11 | | |
| | | | **JIMMY SMITH** | | |
| | | | Born on 12/8/25 in Norristown, Pennsylvania. Pioneer jazz organist. Won Major Bowes Amateur Show in 1934. With father (James, Sr.) in song and dance team, 1942. With Don Gardner & The Sonotones, recorded for Bruce in 1953. Smith first recorded with own trio for Blue Note in 1956. Began doing vocals in 1966. Also see Richard Holmes and Michael Jackson. | | |
| 3/03/62 | **13** | 10 | 1 Midnight Special, Part I................................ [I] | *69* | Blue Note 1819 |
| | | | with Stanley Turrentine on tenor sax | | |
| 6/02/62 | **4** | 12 | 2 **Walk On The Wild Side - Part 1** ................ [I] | *21* | Verve 10255 |
| | | | with Oliver Nelson's Orchestra from the film of the same title | | |
| 11/02/63 | **96** | 1 | 3 Theme From "Any Number Can Win"............ [I] | *Hot* | Verve 10299 |
| 4/25/64 | **72** | 5 | 4 Who's Afraid Of Virginia Woolf? ................... [I] | *Hot* | Verve 10314 |
| | | | from the film of the same title | | |
| 9/05/64 | **67** | 6 | 5 The Cat .............................................. [I] | *Hot* | Verve 10330 |
| | | | from the film "Joy House" | | |
| 4/16/66 | **17** | 9 | 6 Got My Mojo Working (Part I)........................... | *51* | Verve 10393 |
| 8/20/66 | **49** | 2 | 7 I'm Your Hoochie Cooche Man (Part 1) ............. | *94* | Verve 10426 |
| | | | above 4: produced by Creed Taylor | | |
| | | | **KEELY SMITH** - see **LOUIS PRIMA** | | |
| | | | **LESLIE SMITH** - see **MERRY CLAYTON** | | |

| DEBUT DATE | PEAK POS | WKS CHR | ARTIST — Record Title | POP POS | Label & Number |
|---|---|---|---|---|---|
| | | | **LONNIE LISTON SMITH** | | |
| | | | Born in December of 1940 in Richmond, Virginia. Keyboardist/trumpeter/tuba. With Art Blakey's Jazz Messengers in 1965, Roland Kirk, Pharoah Sanders, Norman Connors, Stanley Turrentine and Gato Barbieri. With Miles Davis from 1972-73. Formed own group, the Cosmic Echoes. | | |
| 7/19/75 | 79 | 6 | 1 Expansions ..................................... | | Fly. Dut. 10214 |
| 11/08/75 | 81 | 7 | 2 Afrodesia.................................... | | Groove M. 1034 |
| | | | LONNIE SMITH | | |
| 12/06/75 | 91 | 5 | 3 A Chance For Peace ......................... | | Fly. Dut. 10392 |
| | | | LONNIE LISTON SMITH & The Cosmic Echoes | | |
| 6/24/78 | 92 | 2 | 4 Journey Into Love............................ | | Columbia 10747 |
| 2/24/79 | 86 | 2 | 5 Space Princess .............................. | | Columbia 10903 |
| | | | **O.C. SMITH** | | |
| | | | Born Ocie Lee Smith on 6/21/36 in Mansfield, Louisiana. To Los Angeles in 1939. Sang while in US Air Force from 1953-57. First recorded for Cadence in 1956. With Count Basie from 1961-63. | | |
| 3/16/68 | 32 | 9 | 1 The Son Of Hickory Holler's Tramp ................. | 40 | Columbia 44425 |
| 9/14/68 | 2² | 14 | 2 ● Little Green Apples ......................... | 2 | Columbia 44616 |
| 12/28/68+ | 40 | 4 | 3 Isn't It Lonely Together..................... | 63 | Columbia 44705 |
| 3/01/69 | 44 | 3 | 4 Honey (I Miss You).......................... | 44 | Columbia 44751 |
| 6/21/69 | 25 | 4 | 5 Friend, Lover, Woman, Wife ................ | 47 | Columbia 44859 |
| 9/06/69 | 9 | 7 | 6 **Daddy's Little Man** ...................... | 34 | Columbia 44948 |
| 12/20/69 | 38 | 3 | 7 Me And You .............................. | 103 | Columbia 45038 |
| 9/12/70 | 30 | 7 | 8 Baby, I Need Your Loving ................. | 52 | Columbia 45206 |
| 10/23/71 | 38 | 8 | 9 Help Me Make It Through The Night ................ | 91 | Columbia 45435 |
| | | | all of above: produced by Jerry Fuller | | |
| 9/28/74 | 27 | 9 | 10 La La Peace Song................. | 62 | Columbia 10031 |
| 11/27/76+ | 62 | 11 | 11 Together.................................. | | Caribou 9017 |
| 9/23/78 | 34 | 13 | 12 Love To Burn ............................ | | Shady Brook 1045 |
| 11/22/80 | 92 | 3 | 13 Dreams Come True ...................... | | Family 5000 |
| 6/19/82 | 68 | 7 | 14 Love Changes........................... | | Motown 1623 |
| | | | originally released on South Bay 1003 | | |
| 6/28/86 | 53 | 14 | 15 What'cha Gonna Do..................... | | Rendezvous 1019 |
| 10/11/86 | 52 | 10 | 16 You're The First, My Last, My Everything......... | | Rendezvous 102 |
| 1/17/87 | 58 | 11 | 17 Brenda ................................. | | Rendezvous 1038 |
| | | | **RICHARD JON SMITH** | | |
| | | | South African. | | |
| 4/24/82 | 54 | 7 | 1 Stay With Me Tonight - Part 1 ..................... | | Jive 101 |
| | | | **TAB SMITH** | | |
| | | | Born Talmadge Smith on 1/11/09 in Kinston, North Carolina; died on 8/17/71. Jazz alto saxophonist with the Mills Rhythm Band (1936-38), Count Basie (1940-42) and Lucky Millinder (1942-44). | | |
| 2/03/45 | 7 | 1 | 1 **I'll Live True To You**.................. | | Decca 8661 |
| | | | vocal by Trevor Bacon | | |
| 11/10/51 | 1² | 11 | 2 **Because Of You** ...................... [I] | 20 | United 104 |
| | | | TAB SMITH, HIS FABULOUS ALTO, & ORCHESTRA Best Seller #1 / Juke Box #9 also released on Checker 033 | | |
| | | | **SMOKE CITY** | | |
| | | | Chicago group consisting of Charles Radcliff (guitar), Michael Sterling (trumpet), Gerard Allen Matthews (saxophone), Michael Watkins (keyboards), Candyce Barr (bass, vocals) and Fernando Romero (percussion). | | |
| 5/25/85 | 82 | 4 | 1 I Really Want You ........................ | | Epic 04866 |
| 9/28/85 | 67 | 10 | 2 Dreams ................................. | | Epic 05448 |
| | | | **LOIS SNEAD** | | |
| | | | Singer from Florida. Sang in gospel groups from age 6. With Clara Ward from 1960-62. Moved to Philadelphia, recorded with Evangelist Rosie Wallace Brown. With the Dorothy Norwood Singers from 1967-75. | | |
| 10/27/73 | 95 | 2 | 1 This Little Woman........................ | | Capitol 3722 |
| | | | **ANNETTE SNELL** | | |
| 9/08/73 | 19 | 15 | 1 You Oughta' Be Here With Me ........... | 102 | Dial 1023 |
| 1/05/74 | 44 | 9 | 2 Get Your Thing Together ................ | | Dial 1014 |
| 6/29/74 | 71 | 6 | 3 Just As Hooked As I've Been ........... | | Dial 1028 |

| DEBUT DATE | PEAK POS | WKS CHR | ARTIST — Record Title | POP POS | Label & Number |
|---|---|---|---|---|---|
| | | | **PHOEBE SNOW** Born Phoebe Laub on 7/17/52 in New York City; raised in New Jersey. Vocalist/guitarist/songwriter. Began performing in Greenwich Village in the early 70s. | | |
| 1/21/78 | 87 | 7 | 1 Love Makes A Woman............................... | | Columbia 10654 |
| | | | **GINO SOCCIO** Techno-disco vocalist/multi instrumentalist, born in 1955 in Montreal. Producer of Witch Queen and Kebekelektrik. | | |
| 4/07/79 | 60 | 10 | 1 Dancer......................................... | *48* | RFC 8757 |
| 5/09/81 | 22 | 15 | 2 Try It Out..................................... | *103* | Atlantic 3813 |
| 6/26/82 | 60 | 8 | 3 It's Alright.................................... | *108* | Atlantic 4052 |
| | | | **SOFTONES** | | |
| 4/14/73 | 44 | 2 | 1 I'm Gonna Prove It ........................... | | Avco 4616 |
| 7/21/73 | 56 | 7 | 2 Can't Help Fallin' In Love ..................... | | Avco 4619 |
| 12/15/73 | 69 | 4 | 3 First Day .................................... | | Avco 4626 |
| 12/27/75+ | 29 | 13 | 4 That Old Black Magic......................... | | Avco 4663 |
| | | | **SOFT TOUCH** | | |
| 10/10/87 | 83 | 6 | 1 Please, Please Me ............................ | | Pow Wow 424 |
| | | | **SOLARIS** 6-piece group led by Mavis Washington and James Anderson. | | |
| 3/08/80 | 71 | 10 | 1 You And Me ................................. | | Dana 00131 |
| 9/06/80 | 92 | 3 | 2 Right In The Middle Of Falling In Love ............. | | Dana 1416 |
| | | | **SONNY & CHER** Husband and wife duo: Sonny and Cher Bono. Session singers for Phil Spector. First recorded as Caesar & Cleo for Vault in 1963. Married in 1963; divorced in 1974. In the films "Good Times" (1966) and "Chastity" (1968). Own CBS-TV variety series from 1971-74. Brief TV reunion in 1975. Each recorded solo. | | |
| 8/14/65 | 19 | 6 | 1●I Got You Babe .............................. | *1* | Atco 6359 |
| | | | **SONS OF CHAMPLIN** San Francisco 7-man rock band led by Bill Champlin. | | |
| 7/17/76 | 88 | 4 | 1 Hold On....................................... | *47* | Ariola Am. 7627 |
| | | | **SOPHISTICATED LADIES** Female disco group. | | |
| 7/23/77 | 78 | 11 | 1 Check It Out (Part 1)............................ | | Mayhew 532 |
| | | | **THE S.O.S. BAND** ★★153★★ Formed in Atlanta by Mary Davis (vocals, keyboards). Included Willie "Sonny" Killebrew (saxophone), Billy Ellis (flute), Jason "T.C." Bryant (keyboards), Bruno Speight (guitar), John Simpson (bass) and James Earl Jones III (drums). Jones was replaced by Jerome Thomas in 1981, and Abdul Raoof (horns) was added in 1981. Davis went solo in 1987, replaced by Pennye Ford from Cincinnati, formerly in Reach. | | |
| 4/19/80 | 1[5] | 24 | 1▲Take Your Time (Do It Right) Part 1 ............. | *3* | Tabu 5522 |
| 9/27/80 | 20 | 13 | 2 S.O.S. (Dit Dit Dit Dash Dash Dash Dit Dit Dit).... | | Tabu 5526 |
| 1/24/81 | 87 | 4 | 3 What's Wrong With Our Love Affair?................ | | Tabu 5527 |
| 7/18/81 | 15 | 16 | 4 Do It Now (Part 1)............................. | | Tabu 02125 |
| 11/21/81 | 64 | 6 | 5 You ......................................... | | Tabu 02569 |
| 10/09/82 | 25 | 17 | 6 High Hopes .................................. | | Tabu 03248 |
| 2/26/83 | 57 | 6 | 7 Have It Your Way............................. | | Tabu 03527 |
| 6/25/83 | 2[3] | 22 | 8 Just Be Good To Me .......................... | *55* | Tabu 03955 |
| 10/15/83 | 5 | 18 | 9 Tell Me If You Still Care...................... | *65* | Tabu 04160 |
| 2/18/84 | 34 | 11 | 10 For Your Love ............................... | | Tabu 04348 |
| 7/21/84 | 6 | 17 | 11 Just The Way You Like It....................... | *64* | Tabu 04523 |
| 11/03/84 | 15 | 14 | 12 No One's Gonna Love You...................... | *102* | Tabu 04665 |
| 2/16/85 | 40 | 12 | 13 Weekend Girl ............................... | | Tabu 04776 |
| 3/22/86 | 2[2] | 20 | 14 The Finest ................................. | *44* | Tabu 05848 |
| 7/05/86 | 14 | 13 | 15 Borrowed Love .............................. | | Tabu 06164 |
| 10/18/86 | 34 | 10 | 16 Even When You Sleep ........................ | | Tabu 06333 |
| | | | 6-16 (except #7): written by Jimmy Jam & Terry Lewis 8-16: produced by Jimmy Jam & Terry Lewis | | |
| 2/14/87 | 43 | 10 | 17 No Lies...................................... | | Tabu 06649 |
| | | | **S.O.U.L.** | | |
| 5/26/73 | 44 | 9 | 1 This Time Around ............................ | | Musicor 1472 |

| DEBUT DATE | PEAK POS | WKS CHR | ARTIST — Record Title | POP POS | Label & Number |
|---|---|---|---|---|---|
| 1/18/75 | 65 | 10 | **S.O.U.L. — Continued**<br>2  The Joneses (Part I)............................................. | | Musicor 1500 |
| | | | **THE SOUL CHILDREN**<br>Group formed by songwriters Isaac Hayes and David Porter. Consisted of Anita Louis, Shelbra Bennett, John Colbert and Norman West. Colbert later recorded as J. Blackfoot. | | |
| 11/02/68 | 40 | 3 | 1  Give 'Em Love ............................................. | | Stax 0008 |
| 2/08/69 | 29 | 7 | 2  I'll Understand .......................................... | | Stax 0018 |
| 5/31/69 | 49 | 2 | 3  Tighten Up My Thang........................... | | Stax 0030 |
| 9/20/69 | 7 | 13 | 4  **The Sweeter He Is - Part I** ....................... | 52 | Stax 0050 |
| 4/11/70 | 48 | 2 | 5  Hold On, I'm Coming........................... | | Stax 0062 |
| 3/04/72 | 5 | 13 | 6  **Hearsay**.................................................. | 44 | Stax 0119 |
| 7/29/72 | 14 | 11 | 7  Don't Take My Kindness For Weakness............ | 102 | Stax 0132 |
| 2/24/73 | 11 | 10 | 8  It Ain't Always What You Do (It's Who You Let See You Do It)............................ | 105 | Stax 0152 |
| 7/14/73 | 59 | 7 | 9  Love Is A Hurtin' Thing............................. | | Stax 0170 |
| 12/22/73+ | 3 | 19 | 10  **I'll Be The Other Woman** ........................ | 36 | Stax 0182 |
| 8/03/74 | 47 | 11 | 11  Love Makes It Right............................. | | Stax 0218 |
| 2/07/76 | 49 | 11 | 12  Finders Keepers ............................. | | Epic 50178 |
| 6/26/76 | 99 | 2 | 13  If You Move I'll Fall ............................. | | Epic 50236 |
| 4/30/77 | 96 | 3 | 14  Where Is Your Woman Tonight ................. | | Epic 50345 |
| 5/27/78 | 19 | 14 | 15  Can't Give Up A Good Thing................... | | Stax 3206 |
| | | | **THE SOUL CLAN**<br>Top soul stars: Solomon Burke, Arthur Conley, Don Covay, Ben E. King and Joe Tex. | | |
| 7/20/68 | 34 | 6 | 1  Soul Meeting .................................. [N] | 91 | Atlantic 2530 |
| | | | **SOUL DOG** | | |
| 5/15/76 | 65 | 11 | 1  Soul Dog, Part 1............................. | | Amherst 711 |
| | | | **THE SOUL EXPLOSIONS - see WILLIE HENDERSON** | | |
| | | | **SOUL GENERATION** | | |
| 4/29/72 | 27 | 11 | 1  That's The Way It's Got To Be Body And Soul.... | 115 | Ebony Snds. 175 |
| 3/10/73 | 45 | 4 | 2  Million Dollars ................................. | | Ebony Snds. 176 |
| | | | **THE SOUL PARTNERS - see AL HUDSON** | | |
| | | | **SOUL RUNNERS**<br>Los Angeles group. Became Watts 103rd Street Rhythm Band in 1967. Included Charles Wright (vocals), James Gadson (drums), Bernard Blackman and Raymond Jackson (trombones) and Melvin Dunlap (bass). Backed Bill Cosby and Bill Withers. | | |
| 2/11/67 | 33 | 5 | 1  Grits 'N Corn Bread ................................. [I] | 103 | MoSoul 101 |
| | | | **SOUL SEARCHERS**<br>Washington, DC group formed in 1968. Consisted of Chuck Brown (guitar), John Ewell (bass) and Frank Wellman (drums). Expanded to an 8-piece unit by 1972. Brown later led the Soul Partners. | | |
| 7/29/72 | 40 | 6 | 1  We The People............................. | | Sussex 236 |
| 4/28/73 | 13 | 5 | 2  Think.................................. | | Sussex 253 |
| 6/29/74 | 31 | 10 | 3  Blow Your Whistle................................. | | Sussex 517 |
| 10/19/74 | 74 | 6 | 4  If It Ain't Funky............................. | | Sussex 627 |
| 9/13/75 | 93 | 5 | 5  Boogie Up The Nation Part I ................... | | Polydor 14277 |
| | | | **THE SOUL SISTERS**<br>Vocal duo: Thresia Cleveland and Ann Gissendanner. | | |
| 2/29/64 | 46 | 9 | 1  I Can't Stand It............................. | Hot | Sue 799 |
| 6/13/64 | 98 | 1 | 2  Good Time Tonight................................. | Hot | Sue 005 |
| 10/10/64 | 100 | 1 | 3  Just A Moment Ago............................. | Hot | Sue 111 |
| | | | above 3: written by Smokey McAlister | | |
| | | | **SOUL SURVIVORS**<br>White-soul band from New York City and Philadelphia. Formed by the Ingui brothers, Charles & Richard, and Kenny Jeremiah. Re-formed by the Inguis in 1972. Jeremiah was later with Shirley Goodman in Shirley & Company. | | |
| 9/09/67 | 3 | 15 | 1  **Expressway To Your Heart** ......................... | 4 | Crimson 1010 |
| 1/13/68 | 45 | 3 | 2  Explosion In Your Soul................................. | 33 | Crimson 1012 |
| 10/05/74 | 75 | 6 | 3  City Of Brotherly Love ............................. | | TSOP 4756 |
| | | | all of above: produced by Kenny Gamble & Leon Huff | | |

| DEBUT DATE | PEAK POS | WKS CHR | ARTIST — Record Title | POP POS | Label & Number |
|---|---|---|---|---|---|
| | | | **SOUL TORANODOES** | | |
| 11/29/69 | 39 | 4 | 1 Go For Yourself ............................................ | | Burt 4000 |
| | | | **SOUL TRAIN GANG** Studio singers from the syndicated TV show "Soul Train". | | |
| 10/11/75 | 9 | 16 | 1 **Soul Train '75'**............................................ | 75 | Soul Train 10400 |
| 11/20/76 | 62 | 6 | 2 Ooh Cha ..................................................... | 107 | Soul Train 10792 |
| | | | **JIMMY SOUL** Born James McCleese in New York City in 1942; raised in North Carolina and Portsmouth, Virginia. Worked with gospel groups, including the Nightingales, billed as "The Wonder Boy". | | |
| 6/16/62 | 20 | 1 | 1 Twistin' Matilda.......................................... | 22 | S.P.Q.R. 3300 |
| 4/27/63 | 1¹ | 12 | 2 **If You Wanna Be Happy**.............................. | 1 | S.P.Q.R. 3305 |
| | | | **GEORGE SOULE** | | |
| 10/13/73 | 35 | 12 | 1 Get Involved............................................... | | Fame 302 |
| | | | **THE SOULFUL STRINGS** Chicago studio group with Lennie Druss (oboe, flute), Bobby Christian (vibes), Phil Upchurch and Ron Steel (guitars). | | |
| 2/24/68 | 36 | 5 | 1 Burning Spear ............................................. [I] | 64 | Cadet 5576 |
| | | | **SOUND EXPERIENCE** Formed in Baltimore in 1970 at Morgan State College. Consisted of Reginal Wright, Melvin Miles, Johnny Forman, Gregory Holmes, James Lindsey, Everett Harris, Leroy Frailing, Anton Scott, Rodney Parks and vocalist Arthur Grant. | | |
| 8/10/74 | 61 | 4 | 1 Don't Fight The Feeling................................. | | Soulville 14024 |
| | | | **THE SOURCE - see CANDI STATON** | | |
| | | | **SOUTH SHORE COMMISSION** Formed in 1960 in Washington, DC as the Exciters. Worked as back-up band for the Five DuTones. Lead vocals by Frank McCurry from the Five DuTones and Sheryl Henry. | | |
| 5/17/75 | 9 | 16 | 1 **Free Man**..................................................... | 61 | Wand 11287 |
| 10/25/75 | 30 | 14 | 2 We're On The Right Track .............................. | 94 | Wand 11291 |
| 2/07/76 | 35 | 8 | 3 Train Called Freedom .................................... | 86 | Wand 11294 |
| | | | **THE SOUTH SIDE MOVEMENT** Includes former members of the group Simtec & Wylie. | | |
| 3/03/73 | 14 | 14 | 1 I Been Watchin' You..................................... | 61 | Wand 11251 |
| 8/11/73 | 56 | 7 | 2 Can You Get To That .................................... | | Wand 11259 |
| | | | **SOUTHERN SONS** Group formed in 1940 by William "Highpockets" Langford, former first tenor with the Golden Gate Quartet. Consisted of James K. Baxter, Wesley Hill, Charles H. Wilson and Clifford Givens. Also recorded as the Knites Of Rhythm for Bluebird. | | |
| 11/21/42 | 7 | 6 | 1 **Praise The Lord And Pass The Ammunition** ... inspired by words of US Navy Chaplain William MacGuire at Pearl Harbor attack | | Bluebird 0806 |
| | | | **SOUTHROAD CONNECTION** From White Plains, New York. Consisted of Eugene Faffley, Delwin Gillman, Harold Hutton, Ellsworth Forrester, Jerry Jenkins, Steven Fields and vocalists Linda Watson & Michael Jones. Originally known as Exact Change. | | |
| 2/11/78 | 88 | 5 | 1 You Like It, We Love It ................................. | | Mahogany 12772 |
| 2/16/80 | 93 | 3 | 2 In The Morning............................................ | | United Art. 1333 |
| 9/06/80 | 79 | 4 | 3 We Came To Funk You Out ............................ | | United Art. 1361 |
| | | | **SOUTHSIDE JOHNNY & THE JUKES** Rock band formed in Asbury Park, NJ; led by Johnny Lyon (b: 12/4/48, Neptune, NJ). | | |
| 12/03/83+ | 55 | 10 | 1 Get Your Body On The Job ............................ | | Mirage 99802 |
| | | | **THE SPACEMEN** | | |
| 11/02/59 | 1³ | 18 | 1 **The Clouds** ................................................ [I] | 41 | Alton 254 |
| | | | **JOANNE SPAIN** | | |
| 2/05/77 | 95 | 3 | 1 Elevator ..................................................... | | Casino 077 |
| | | | **SPANDAU BALLET** English quintet: Tony Hadley (lead singer), Gary Kemp (guitar), Steve Norman (sax), Martin Kemp (bass) and John Keeble (drums). | | |
| 8/27/83 | 76 | 8 | 1 **True** ......................................................... | 4 | Chrysalis 42720 |

| DEBUT DATE | PEAK POS | WKS CHR | ARTIST — Record Title | POP POS | Label & Number |
|---|---|---|---|---|---|
| | | | **THE SPANIELS** | | |
| | | | Group formed at Roosevelt High School in Gary, Indiana in 1952. Consisted of James "Pookie" Hudson (lead), Ernest Warren, Opal Courtney, Willie Jackson and Gerald Gregory. Group changed membership in 1955: Courtney replaced by James "Dimples" Cochran, and Warren left. Hudson also left briefly, and returned in 1956. Other personnel changes up until Hudson left for solo career in 1961. Own label, North American, in the late 60s to early 70s. Formed new Spaniels group in 1975. Hudson's brother, Prentiss Barnes, was a member of The Moonglows. | | |
| 9/05/53 | 10 | 2 | 1 **Baby, It's You** .............................. Best Seller #10 / Juke Box #10 also released on Vee-Jay 101 | | Chance 1141 |
| 5/01/54 | 5 | 16 | 2 **Goodnite Sweetheart, Goodnite** ..................... Best Seller #5 / Juke Box #5 | 24 | Vee-Jay 107 |
| 10/15/55 | 13 | 1 | 3 You Painted Pictures ................................... Best Seller #13 | | Vee-Jay 154 |
| 7/08/57 | 13 | 2 | 4 Everyone's Laughing ................................... Best Seller #13 | 69 | Vee-Jay 246 |
| 8/01/60 | 23 | 6 | 5 I Know ............................................... | | Vee-Jay 350 |
| 9/12/70 | 45 | 2 | 6 Fairy Tales ........................................... | | Calla 172 |
| | | | **JOHNNY SPARROW & HIS BOWS & ARROWS** | | |
| | | | Tenor saxophonist. | | |
| 1/28/50 | 12 | 1 | 1 Sparrow's Flight ......................................... [I] Juke Box #12 | | Melford 253 |
| | | | **SPECIAL DELIVERY** | | |
| 10/18/75+ | 62 | 19 | 1 I Destroyed Your Love - Part 1 ...................... | | Mainstream 5573 |
| 5/01/76 | 11 | 17 | 2 The Lonely One ....................................... SPECIAL DELIVERY featuring TERRY HUFF | 75 | Mainstream 5581 |
| 7/23/77 | 22 | 17 | 3 Oh Let Me Know (Pt. 1)................................ | 107 | Shield 6307 |
| 12/09/78 | 93 | 2 | 4 This Kind Of Love ..................................... | | Shield 6311 |
| | | | **THE SPELLBINDERS** | | |
| | | | Group from Jersey City. Consisted of Bob Shivers, Jimmy Wright, Ben Grant, McArthur Munford and Elouise Pennington. | | |
| 12/04/65+ | 23 | 10 | 1 For You.............................................. | 93 | Columbia 43384 |
| | | | **BENNY SPELLMAN** | | |
| | | | Born in 1938 in Pensacola, Florida. Worked with Huey Smith & The Clowns in New Orleans. Frequent session work as back-up singer. Bass vocalist on Ernie K-Doe's "Mother-In-Law". Left music in the late 60s to work in beer promotion. | | |
| 6/16/62 | 28 | 1 | 1 Lipstick Traces (On A Cigarette) ..................... | 80 | Minit 644 |
| | | | **TRACIE SPENCER** | | |
| | | | Native of Waterloo, Iowa. 12 years old at time of first hit in 1988. | | |
| 5/14/88 | 11 | 15 | 1 Symptons Of True Love ................................ | | Capitol 44140 |
| | | | **SPIDERS** | | |
| | | | Group from New Orleans, formed as the Zion City Harmonizers in 1947. Radio work as the Delta Southernaires from 1952-53. Consisted of Hayward "Chuck" Carbo (lead), Joe Maxon, Matthew "Mac" West, Oliver Howard and Leonard "Chick" Carbo. After 1956, both Carbo brothers went on to solo careers. | | |
| 2/20/54 | 3 | 17 | 1 **I Didn't Want To Do It/** Juke Box #3 / Best Seller #3 | | |
| 4/17/54 | 8 | 3 | 2 **You're The One** ........................................ Best Seller #8 / Juke Box #9 | | Imperial 5265 |
| 7/31/54 | 6 | 4 | 3 **I'm Slippin' In**............................................ Juke Box #6 | | Imperial 5291 |
| 1/08/55 | 9 | 1 | 4 **Twenty One**............................................ Juke Box #9 | | Imperial 5318 |
| 12/03/55+ | 5 | 11 | 5 **Witchcraft** ............................................ Jockey #5 / Best Seller #7 | | Imperial 5366 |
| | | | **SPINNERS** ★★29★★ | | |
| | | | Vocal group from Ferndale High School near Detroit, originally known as the Domingoes. Discovered by producer/lead singer of The Moonglows, Harvey Fuqua, and became the Spinners in 1961. First recorded on Fuqua's Tri-Phi label. Consisted of Bobby Smith, Billy Henderson, Henry Fambrough and Pervis Jackson. G.C. Cameron was lead singer from 1968-72. Phillippe Wynne was added in 1971. Wynne (d: 7/14/84) left group in 1977 and toured with Parliament/Funkadelic; replaced by John Edwards. Many personnel changes since then. | | |
| 6/19/61 | 5 | 10 | 1 **That's What Girls Are Made For** .................. lead vocal by Harvey Fuqua | 27 | Tri-Phi 1001 |
| 7/10/65 | 8 | 11 | 2 **I'll Always Love You** ................................. | 35 | Motown 1078 |
| 5/21/66 | 16 | 7 | 3 Truly Yours ............................................ | 111 | Motown 1093 |

**385**

| DEBUT DATE | PEAK POS | WKS CHR | ARTIST — Record Title | POP POS | Label & Number |
|---|---|---|---|---|---|
| | | | **SPINNERS — Continued** | | |
| 7/25/70 | **4** | 15 | 4 It's A Shame | *14* | V.I.P. 25057 |
| 1/30/71 | **20** | 7 | 5 We'll Have It Made | *89* | V.I.P. 25060 |
| | | | above 2: produced by Stevie Wonder | | |
| 8/19/72 | **1** ⁵ | 14 | 6●I'll Be Around/ | *3* | |
| | | 10 | 7 How Could I Let You Get Away | | Atlantic 2904 |
| 12/30/72+ | **1** ¹ | 15 | 8●Could It Be I'm Falling In Love | *4* | Atlantic 2927 |
| 4/28/73 | **1** ⁴ | 14 | 9●One Of A Kind (Love Affair) | *11* | Atlantic 2962 |
| 8/11/73 | **4** | 11 | 10 Ghetto Child | *29* | Atlantic 2973 |
| 1/19/74 | **1** ² | 17 | 11 Mighty Love-Pt. 1 | *20* | Atlantic 3006 |
| 5/18/74 | **3** | 13 | 12 I'm Coming Home | *18* | Atlantic 3027 |
| 7/20/74 | **2** ² | 15 | 13●Then Came You | *1* | Atlantic 3202 |
| | | | **DIONNE WARWICK & SPINNERS** | | |
| 9/28/74 | **4** | 15 | 14 Love Don't Love Nobody - Pt. I | *15* | Atlantic 3206 |
| 3/01/75 | **7** | 12 | 15 Living A Little, Laughing A Little | *37* | Atlantic 3252 |
| 5/10/75 | **7** | 11 | 16 Sadie | *54* | Atlantic 3268 |
| 8/02/75 | **1** ¹ | 20 | 17●They Just Can't Stop It the (Games People Play) | *5* | Atlantic 3284 |
| 12/20/75+ | **8** | 14 | 18 Love Or Leave | *36* | Atlantic 3309 |
| 6/26/76 | **11** | 12 | 19 Wake Up Susan | *56* | Atlantic 3341 |
| 9/04/76 | **1** ¹ | 21 | 20●The Rubberband Man | *2* | Atlantic 3355 |
| 3/19/77 | **5** | 13 | 21 You're Throwing A Good Love Away | *43* | Atlantic 3382 |
| 6/18/77 | **39** | 8 | 22 Me And My Music | | Atlantic 3400 |
| 9/03/77 | **23** | 14 | 23 Heaven On Earth (So Fine) | *89* | Atlantic 3425 |
| 2/11/78 | **46** | 9 | 24 Easy Come, Easy Go | | Atlantic 3462 |
| 7/15/78 | **17** | 12 | 25 If You Wanna Do A Dance | *49* | Atlantic 3493 |
| 3/24/79 | **25** | 13 | 26 Are You Ready For Love | | Atlantic 3546 |
| | | | 6-26: produced & arranged by Thom Bell | | |
| 10/06/79 | **35** | 11 | 27 Body Language | *103* | Atlantic 3619 |
| 12/22/79+ | **6** | 21 | 28●Working My Way Back To You/Forgive Me, Girl | *2* | Atlantic 3637 |
| 5/24/80 | **5** | 15 | 29 Cupid/I've Loved You For A Long Time | *4* | Atlantic 3664 |
| 9/13/80 | **25** | 15 | 30 Now That You're Mine Again | | Atlantic 3757 |
| 12/06/80 | **75** | 4 | 31 I Just Want To Fall In Love | | Atlantic 3765 |
| 2/21/81 | **32** | 10 | 32 Yesterday Once More/Nothing Remains The Same | *52* | Atlantic 3798 |
| 5/02/81 | **64** | 5 | 33 Long Live Soul Music | | Atlantic 3814 |
| 10/17/81 | **39** | 8 | 34 You Go Your Way (I'll Go Mine) | *110* | Atlantic 3865 |
| | | | produced by James Mtume & Reggie Lucas | | |
| 12/19/81+ | **68** | 8 | 35 Love Connection (Raise The Window Down) | *107* | Atlantic 3882 |
| 10/09/82 | **30** | 10 | 36 Magic In The Moonlight | | Atlantic 89962 |
| 12/04/82+ | **43** | 11 | 37 Funny How Time Slips Away | *67* | Atlantic 89922 |
| 3/24/84 | **22** | 14 | 38 Right Or Wrong | *104* | Atlantic 89689 |
| | | | **SPOONBREAD** | | |
| | | | Kid group from Germany, produced by Joe Robinson. | | |
| 9/23/72 | **33** | 5 | 1 How Can You Mend A Broken Heart | | Stang 5043 |
| | | | **SPOONIE GEE** | | |
| | | | Rapper from New York City, formerly in the Treacherous 3. Went solo in 1979. | | |
| 12/24/83+ | **69** | 8 | 1 The Big Beat | | Tuff City 04190 |
| | | | **SPRING** | | |
| 12/29/73+ | **55** | 11 | 1 Talk To The Rain | | 9 Chains 401 |
| | | | **SPRINGERS** | | |
| 2/06/65 | **23** | 6 | 1 I Know Why | | Way Out 2699 |
| | | | **SPUNK** | | |
| 10/03/81 | **72** | 4 | 1 Get What You Want | | Gold Coast 1101 |
| | | | **SPYDER-D** | | |
| 11/09/85 | **78** | 4 | 1 Rap Is Here To Stay | | Profile 7078 |
| 6/07/86 | **65** | 7 | 2 I Can't Wait (To Rock The Mike) | | Profile 5103 |
| | | | **SPYDER-D** (featuring D.J. DOC) rap version of the Nu Shooz hit | | |

| DEBUT DATE | PEAK POS | WKS CHR | ARTIST — Record Title | POP POS | Label & Number |
|---|---|---|---|---|---|
| | | | **SPYRO GYRA** | | |
| | | | Jazz-pop band formed in 1975 in Buffalo, New York. Led by saxophonist Jay Beckenstein (b: 5/14/51). | | |
| 5/13/78 | 90 | 9 | 1 Shaker Song.................................... [I] | 90 | Amherst 730 |
| 5/12/79 | 60 | 8 | 2 Morning Dance ............................... [I] | 24 | Infinity 50011 |
| 12/01/79 | 92 | 4 | 3 Jubilee........................................... [I] | | Infinity 50041 |
| | | | **S.S.O.** | | |
| 10/18/75 | 59 | 14 | 1 Tonight's The Night.............................. | 99 | Shady Brook 019 |
| | | | **STACEY Q** | | |
| | | | Dance/disco singer from Los Angeles. Real name: Stacey Swain. | | |
| 9/06/86 | 56 | 9 | 1 Two Of Hearts .................................. | 3 | Atlantic 89381 |
| | | | **STAIRSTEPS - see THE FIVE STAIRSTEPS** | | |
| | | | **CHUCK STANLEY** | | |
| | | | Former back-up singer from Hollis, Queens, New York. Backed the Crown Heights Affair while still in high school. | | |
| 2/28/87 | 29 | 14 | 1 Day By Day ..................................... | | Def Jam 06610 |
| 6/20/87 | 19 | 12 | 2 Jammin To The Bells............................ | | Def Jam 07184 |
| 10/24/87 | 66 | 8 | 3 Make You Mine Tonight........................ | | Def Jam 07425 |
| | | | CHUCK STANLEY introducing ALYSON WILLIAMS | | |
| | | | **THE STAPLE SINGERS** ★★88★★ | | |
| | | | Family group consisting of Roebuck "Pop" Staples (b: 12/28/15, Winoma, MS), with his son Pervis (who left in 1971) and daughters Cleotha, Yvonne, and lead singer Mavis Staples. Roebuck was a blues guitarist in his teens, later with the Golden Trumpets gospel group. Moved to Chicago in 1935. Formed own gospel group in the early 50s. First recorded for United in 1953. Mavis recorded solo, early 70s. | | |
| 12/19/70+ | 6 | 13 | 1 **Heavy Makes You Happy (Sha-Na-Boom Boom)/** | 27 | |
| | | 5 | 2 Love Is Plentiful ............................... | | Stax 0083 |
| 7/03/71 | 11 | 9 | 3 You've Got To Earn It .......................... | 97 | Stax 0093 |
| 10/09/71 | 2² | 17 | 4 **Respect Yourself**................................ | 12 | Stax 0104 |
| 4/01/72 | 1⁴ | 16 | 5 **I'll Take You There**............................ | 1 | Stax 0125 |
| 8/05/72 | 6 | 11 | 6 **This World**.................................... | 38 | Stax 0137 |
| 3/10/73 | 4 | 9 | 7 **Oh La De Da**.................................. | 33 | Stax 0156 |
| 6/16/73 | 18 | 8 | 8 Be What You Are ............................... | 66 | Stax 0164 |
| 10/20/73 | 1³ | 17 | 9● **If You're Ready (Come Go With Me)**.............. | 9 | Stax 0179 |
| 2/23/74 | 3 | 18 | 10 **Touch A Hand, Make A Friend** .................... | 23 | Stax 0196 |
| 7/13/74 | 4 | 13 | 11 **City In The Sky**............................... | 79 | Stax 0215 |
| 12/14/74+ | 18 | 12 | 12 My Main Man .................................. | 76 | Stax 0227 |
| | | | all of above Stax recordings produced by Al Bell | | |
| 10/11/75 | 1² | 18 | 13● **Let's Do It Again**.............................. | 1 | Curtom 0109 |
| 2/07/76 | 4 | 13 | 14 **New Orleans**.................................. | 70 | Curtom 0113 |
| | | | above 2: from the film "Let's Do It Again" | | |
| | | | THE STAPLES: | | |
| 11/06/76+ | 11 | 14 | 15 Love Me, Love Me, Love Me...................... | | Warner 8279 |
| 2/19/77 | 52 | 5 | 16 Sweeter Than The Sweet ....................... | | Warner 8317 |
| 10/22/77 | 77 | 5 | 17 See A Little Further (Than My Bed) ............. | | Warner 8460 |
| 1/07/78 | 68 | 6 | 18 I Honestly Love You ........................... | | Warner 8510 |
| | | | originally a #1 pop hit for Olivia Newton-John (1974) | | |
| 9/23/78 | 16 | 14 | 19 Unlock Your Mind ............................. | | Warner 8669 |
| 2/24/79 | 82 | 3 | 20 Chica Boom ................................... | | Warner 8748 |
| | | | THE STAPLE SINGERS: | | |
| 4/14/84 | 46 | 8 | 21 H-A-T-E (Don't Live Here Anymore) ............. | | Private I 04384 |
| 9/08/84 | 22 | 14 | 22 Slippery People ............................... | 109 | Private I 04583 |
| 12/01/84+ | 50 | 12 | 23 This Is Our Night............................... | | Private I 04711 |
| 9/07/85 | 39 | 11 | 24 Are You Ready?................................. | | Private I 05565 |
| 12/28/85+ | 89 | 7 | 25 Nobody Can Make It On Their Own ............... | | Private I 05727 |
| | | | **MAVIS STAPLES** | | |
| | | | Born in 1940 in Chicago. Lead singer of The Staple Singers. | | |
| 8/22/70 | 13 | 11 | 1 I Have Learned To Do Without You ............... | 87 | Volt 4044 |
| 9/16/72 | 30 | 9 | 2 Endlessly..................................... | 109 | Volt 4086 |
| 11/12/77 | 47 | 12 | 3 A Piece Of The Action.......................... | | Curtom 0132 |
| 7/21/79 | 91 | 4 | 4 Tonight I Feel Like Dancing .................... | | Warner 8838 |

| DEBUT DATE | PEAK POS | WKS CHR | ARTIST — Record Title | POP POS | Label & Number |
|---|---|---|---|---|---|
| | | | **MAVIS STAPLES — Continued** | | |
| 1/07/84 | 75 | 7 | 5  Love Gone Bad .................................................... | | Phono 1051 |
| 3/08/86 | 68 | 6 | 6  Show Me How It Works.................................... | | Warner 28765 |
| | | | **STARGARD** | | |
| | | | Disco trio: Rochelle Runnells, Debra Anderson and Janice Williams. Appeared as "The Diamonds" in film "Sgt. Pepper's Lonely Hearts Club Band". Anderson left group in 1980, group continued as a duo. | | |
| 12/03/77+ | 1 ² | 21 | 1  **Theme Song From "Which Way Is Up"** ........... | 21 | MCA 40825 |
| | | | from the film of the same title | | |
| 5/13/78 | 75 | 8 | 2  Love Is So Easy ............................................... | | MCA 40890 |
| 7/22/78 | 4 | 18 | 3  **What You Waitin' For** ................................... | | MCA 40932 |
| 12/16/78+ | 81 | 5 | 4  Sensuous Woman............................................ | | MCA 40980 |
| 10/13/79 | 43 | 11 | 5  Wear It Out....................................................... | | Warner 49066 |
| 2/02/80 | 61 | 6 | 6  Runnin' From The Law .................................... | | Warner 49165 |
| 6/06/81 | 70 | 7 | 7  High On The Boogie.......................................... | | Warner 49731 |
| | | | **THE STARLETS** | | |
| | | | Female group from Chicago: Liz "Dynetta Bonne" Walker, Jane Hall, Mickey McKinney, Maxine Edwards and Bernice Williams. Also see Patti LaBelle & The Blue Belles. | | |
| 6/19/61 | 24 | 2 | 1  **Better Tell Him No** ......................................... | 38 | Pam 1003 |
| | | | lead vocal by Maxine Edwards | | |
| | | | **STARPOINT** ★★168★★ | | |
| | | | Sextet from Maryland: brothers Ernest, George, Orlando and Gregory Phillips, with Renee Diggs and Kayode Adeyemo. Formed as Lycindiana, did session work for Motown and All-Platinum Records. | | |
| 7/05/80 | 19 | 14 | 1  I Just Wanna Dance With You .......................... | | Choc. City 3208 |
| 2/28/81 | 28 | 16 | 2  Keep On It ........................................................ | | Choc. City 3223 |
| 6/20/81 | 67 | 7 | 3  I Want You Closer ............................................ | | Choc. City 3226 |
| 10/31/81 | 66 | 7 | 4  Wanting You .................................................... | | Choc. City 3229 |
| 2/13/82 | 50 | 8 | 5  Angel................................................................. | | Choc. City 3230 |
| 5/08/82 | 56 | 8 | 6  Do What You Wanna Do .................................. | | Choc. City 3232 |
| 7/24/82 | 76 | 5 | 7  Get Your Body Up ............................................ | | Choc. City 3234 |
| 10/30/82 | 69 | 6 | 8  All Night Long.................................................. | | Choc. City 3236 |
| 5/14/83 | 14 | 14 | 9  Don't Be So Serious ........................................ | 107 | Boardwalk 178 |
| 10/01/83 | 79 | 4 | 10  It's So Delicious .............................................. | | Elektra 69793 |
| 2/18/84 | 17 | 14 | 11  It's All Yours.................................................... | | Elektra 69751 |
| 6/02/84 | 73 | 6 | 12  Breakout .......................................................... | | Elektra 69726 |
| 7/28/84 | 59 | 9 | 13  Am I Still The One............................................ | | Elektra 69711 |
| 7/27/85 | 8 | 22 | 14  **Object Of My Desire** ....................................... | 25 | Elektra 69621 |
| 11/09/85+ | 9 | 18 | 15  **What You Been Missin'** ................................... | | Elektra 69588 |
| 3/08/86 | 11 | 14 | 16  Restless ............................................................ | 46 | Elektra 69561 |
| 6/14/86 | 64 | 10 | 17  Till The End Of Time ....................................... | | Elektra 69534 |
| 2/07/87 | 9 | 15 | 18  **He Wants My Body** ......................................... | 89 | Elektra 69489 |
| 5/16/87 | 25 | 10 | 19  D.Y.B.O. ........................................................... | | Elektra 69467 |
| | | | D.Y.B.O.: dance your butt off | | |
| 8/15/87 | 30 | 11 | 20  The More We Love............................................ | | Elektra 69451 |
| | | | **BRENDA K. STARR** | | |
| | | | Real name: Brenda Kaplan. Singer/film actress from New York City of Puerto Rican heritage. Daughter of Harvey Kaplan (member of Spiral Staircase). | | |
| 10/05/85 | 83 | 4 | 1  Pickin' Up Pieces ............................................ | | Mirage 99618 |
| | | | **EDWIN STARR** ★★150★★ | | |
| | | | Born Charles Hatcher on 1/21/42 in Nashville; raised in Cleveland. Brother of singers Roger and Willie Hatcher. In vocal group, the Futuretones; recorded for Tress in 1957. With Bill Doggett Combo from 1963-65. First recorded as "Edwin Starr" for Ric-Tic in 1965. Member of the Detroit trio, The Holidays, in 1966. Recorded duets with Sandra "Blinky" Williams in 1970. | | |
| 7/31/65 | 8 | 16 | 1  **Agent Double-O-Soul**.................................... | 21 | Ric-Tic 103 |
| 1/15/66 | 33 | 2 | 2  Back Street........................................................ | 95 | Ric-Tic 107 |
| 2/19/66 | 9 | 12 | 3  **Stop Her On Sight (S.O.S.)**............................ | 48 | Ric-Tic 109 |
| 5/11/68 | 45 | 2 | 4  I Am The Man For You Baby ........................... | 112 | Gordy 7071 |
| 2/22/69 | 6 | 13 | 5  **Twenty-Five Miles** ......................................... | 6 | Gordy 7083 |
| 6/28/69 | 27 | 6 | 6  I'm Still A Struggling Man.............................. | 80 | Gordy 7087 |
| 2/28/70 | 39 | 4 | 7  Time.................................................................. | 117 | Gordy 7097 |
| 7/18/70 | 3 | 13 | 8  **War** .................................................................. | 1 | Gordy 7101 |

| DEBUT DATE | PEAK POS | WKS CHR | ARTIST — Record Title | POP POS | Label & Number |
|---|---|---|---|---|---|
| | | | **EDWIN STARR — Continued** | | |
| 12/26/70+ | 5 | 9 | 9 Stop The War Now ...................................... | 26 | Gordy 7104 |
| 5/01/71 | 6 | 9 | 10 Funky Music Sho Nuff Turns Me On ............. | 64 | Gordy 7107 |
| 6/02/73 | 12 | 9 | 11 There You Go ........................................ | 80 | Soul 35103 |
| 9/29/73 | 40 | 11 | 12 You've Got My Soul On Fire ........................... | | Motown 1276 |
| 5/17/75 | 25 | 13 | 13 Pain................................................... | | Granite 522 |
| 10/04/75 | 51 | 10 | 14 Stay With Me........................................ | | Granite 528 |
| 12/27/75+ | 25 | 12 | 15 Abyssinia Jones ....................................... | 98 | Granite 532 |
| 6/04/77 | 94 | 4 | 16 I Just Wanna Do My Thing........................ | | 20th Century 2338 |
| 1/20/79 | 13 | 12 | 17 Contact .............................................. | 65 | 20th Century 2396 |
| 6/02/79 | 28 | 14 | 18 H.A.P.P.Y. Radio ................................... | 79 | 20th Century 2408 |
| | | | **STARS on 45** | | |
| | | | Dutch session vocalists and musicians assembled by producer Jaap Eggermont. | | |
| 4/03/82 | 44 | 8 | 1 Stars on 45 III ...................................... | 28 | Radio 4019 |
| | | | tribute to Stevie Wonder; Uptight Everything's All Right/My Cherie Amour/Yester Me, Yester You/Master Blaster/You Are The Sunshine Of My Life/Isn't She Lovely/Sir Duke/I Wish/I Was Made To Love Her/Superstition/Fingertips | | |
| 8/10/85 | 92 | 4 | 2 The Sam & Dave Medley .............................. | | 21 Records 99636 |
| | | | **STARS on 45 featuring SAM & DAVE** You Don't Know What You Mean To Me/Soul Sister (You're Brown Sugar)/Soul Man/Hold On, I'm Coming/I Thank You | | |
| | | | **CANDI STATON**  ★★100★★ | | |
| | | | Born in Hanceville, Alabama. Sang with the Jewel Gospel Trio from age 10. Went solo in 1968. Married for a time to Clarence Carter. | | |
| 6/14/69 | 9 | 10 | 1 **I'd Rather Be An Old Man's Sweetheart (Than A Young Man's Fool)**............................... | 46 | Fame 1456 |
| 9/20/69 | 22 | 4 | 2 Never In Public ....................................... | 124 | Fame 1459 |
| 1/03/70 | 13 | 11 | 3 I'm Just A Prisoner (Of Your Good Lovin') ......... | 56 | Fame 1460 |
| 5/09/70 | 5 | 10 | 4 **Sweet Feeling** ........................................ | 60 | Fame 1466 |
| 8/29/70 | 4 | 17 | 5 **Stand By Your Man** .................................. | 24 | Fame 1472 |
| 1/02/71 | 9 | 11 | 6 **He Called Me Baby**.................................. | 52 | Fame 1476 |
| 4/17/71 | 20 | 8 | 7 Mr. And Mrs. Untrue/ | 109 | |
| | | 4 | 8 Too Hurt To Cry ................................... | | Fame 1478 |
| 6/24/72 | 12 | 12 | 9 In The Ghetto ....................................... | 48 | Fame 91000 |
| 11/18/72 | 40 | 6 | 10 Lovin' You, Lovin' Me ................................ | 83 | Fame 91005 |
| 1/20/73 | 17 | 12 | 11 Do It In The Name Of Love ........................ | 63 | Fame 91009 |
| 7/14/73 | 83 | 2 | 12 Something's Burning ................................. | | Fame 256 |
| 10/27/73 | 31 | 11 | 13 Love Chain .......................................... | | Fame 328 |
| 11/09/74+ | 6 | 16 | 14 **As Long As He Takes Care Of Home**.............. | 51 | Warner 8038 |
| 4/19/75 | 35 | 9 | 15 Here I Am Again ..................................... | | Warner 8078 |
| 7/12/75 | 86 | 5 | 16 Six Nights And A Day ............................... | | Warner 8112 |
| 3/27/76 | 1[1] | 21 | 17 **Young Hearts Run Free** ............................. | 20 | Warner 8181 |
| 9/18/76 | 26 | 12 | 18 Run To Me ........................................... | | Warner 8249 |
| 2/26/77 | 37 | 11 | 19 A Dreamer Of A Dream ............................. | | Warner 8320 |
| 6/04/77 | 16 | 18 | 20 Nights On Broadway ................................. | 102 | Warner 8387 |
| | | | written by Barry, Robin & Maurice Gibb (The Bee Gees) | | |
| 11/26/77 | 90 | 4 | 21 Listen To The Music ................................. | | Warner 8477 |
| | | | originally a #11 pop hit for The Doobie Brothers (1972) | | |
| 6/17/78 | 17 | 22 | 22 Victim .............................................. | | Warner 8582 |
| 12/09/78 | 77 | 3 | 23 Honest I Do Love You ............................... | | Warner 8691 |
| 6/02/79 | 13 | 17 | 24 When You Wake Up Tomorrow ...................... | | Warner 8821 |
| 6/07/80 | 42 | 11 | 25 Looking For Love.................................... | | Warner 49240 |
| 5/30/81 | 78 | 7 | 26 Without You I Cry .................................... | | LA 0080 |
| 12/19/81 | 82 | 5 | 27 Count On Me ......................................... | | Sugar Hill 770 |
| 11/29/86 | 88 | 9 | 28 You Got The Love .................................... | | Source 9001 |
| | | | **THE SOURCE featuring CANDI STATON** | | |
| | | | **STEAM** | | |
| | | | Studio group from New York City, with vocals by Garrett Scott, Tom Zuke, Hank Schorz and Bill Steer. | | |
| 11/15/69 | 20 | 8 | 1●Na Na Hey Hey Kiss Him Goodbye ................... | 1 | Fontana 1667 |
| | | | **JAKE & JEFF STEEL** | | |
| 7/06/74 | 81 | 4 | 1 The Impeachment Story ............................. | | Peach-Mint 6065 |

| DEBUT DATE | PEAK POS | WKS CHR | ARTIST — Record Title | POP POS | Label & Number |
|---|---|---|---|---|---|
| | | | **THE STEELERS** Vocal group from Chicago: Leonard "Red" Truss, Wales Wallace, Wes "Preach" Wells, Alonzo "Cool" Wells and George "Flue" Wells. | | |
| 12/13/69 | **46** | 2 | 1 Get It From The Bottom ................................. | *56* | Date 1642 |
| | | | **STEELY DAN** Los Angeles-based pop/jazz-styled group formed by Donald Fagen (keyboards, vocals) and Walter Becker (bass, vocals). Group, primarily known as a studio unit, featured Fagen and Becker with various studio musicians. Duo went their separate ways, 1981. | | |
| 1/24/81 | **68** | 7 | 1 Hey Nineteen............................................ | *10* | MCA 51036 |
| | | | **TENISON STEPHENS** Keyboardist Tennyson Stephens from Texas. Younger brother of Rhetta Hughes. | | |
| 11/15/69 | **43** | 5 | 1 Hurry Change............................................ | | Aries 2076 |
| | | | **STEPTOE** | | |
| 11/13/82 | **73** | 7 | 1 Sureyoureright ........................................... | | Fantasy 930 |
| | | | **THE STEREOS** Group from Steubenville, Ohio. Originally called the Buckeyes. Consisted of Bruce Robinson, Nathaniel Hicks, Sam Profit, George Otis and Ronnie Collins. Group disbanded in 1968. | | |
| 10/16/61 | **15** | 7 | 1 I Really Love You........................................ lead vocal by Ronnie Collins | *29* | Cub 9095 |
| | | | **MICHAEL STERLING** | | |
| 9/24/83 | **66** | 7 | 1 Desperate .................................................. | | Success 02686 |
| | | | **STETSASONIC** Rap sextet formed in 1982 in Bedford-Stuyvesant, Brooklyn, New York, led by Daddy-O. Evolved from quartet known as The Stetson Brothers. | | |
| 6/11/88 | **25** | 14 | 1 Sally......................................................... | | Tommy Boy 912 |
| | | | **CAT STEVENS** Pop-folk singer born Steven Georgiou on 7/21/47 in London. Converted to Muslim religion in late 1979; took name Yusef Islam. | | |
| 12/03/77+ | **53** | 10 | 1 Was Dog A Doughnut................................. [I] | *70* | A&M 1971 |
| | | | **CONNIE STEVENS** Born Concetta Ingolia on 4/8/38 in Brooklyn. Played Cricket Blake on TV's "Hawaiian Eye" from 1959-63. Appeared in the films "Eighteen And Anxious", "Rockabye Baby", "Parrish", "Never Too Late", and others. | | |
| 6/29/59 | **30** | 1 | 1 Kookie, Kookie (Lend Me Your Comb) ........... [N] EDWARD BYRNES & CONNIE STEVENS | *4* | Warner 5047 |
| 4/11/60 | **10** | 7 | 2 **Sixteen Reasons** ........................................ | *3* | Warner 5137 |
| | | | **DODIE STEVENS** Born Geraldine Pasquale on 2/17/46 in Chicago; raised in California. | | |
| 4/20/59 | **5** | 8 | 1 **Pink Shoe Laces** ........................................ | *3* | Crystalette 724 |
| | | | **RAY STEVENS** Born Ray Ragsdale on 1/24/41 in Clarksdale, Georgia. Production work in the mid-60s. Own TV show in the summer of 1970. The #1 novelty recording artist of the rock era. | | |
| 7/14/62 | **9** | 8 | 1 **Ahab, The Arab**........................................ [N] | *5* | Mercury 71966 |
| 6/29/63 | **14** | 5 | 2 Harry The Hairy Ape ................................ [N] | *17* | Mercury 72125 |
| 10/26/63 | **29** | 1 | 3 Speed Ball ............................................... [N] | *59* | Mercury 72189 |
| | | | **KEVIN STEVENSON - see SUNDANCE** | | |
| | | | **STEVIE B** Singer/self-taught musician, Stevie B. Hill, born in Miami. In high school band with Howard Johnson. | | |
| 11/14/87 | **69** | 11 | 1 Party Your Body ....................................... | | LMR 74000 |
| | | | **AMII STEWART** Born in Washington, DC in 1956. Disco singer/dancer/actress. In the Broadway musical "Bubbling Brown Sugar". | | |
| 2/10/79 | **6** | 16 | 1▲**Knock On Wood** .......................................... | *1* | Ariola 7736 |
| 6/09/79 | **36** | 11 | 2 Light My Fire/137 Disco Heaven ...................... | *69* | Ariola 7753 |
| 10/04/80 | **76** | 3 | 3 My Guy/My Girl .......................................... AMII STEWART & JOHNNY BRISTOL | *63* | Handshake 5300 |
| 3/16/85 | **46** | 13 | 4 Friends .................................................... | | Emergency 4548 |

| DEBUT DATE | PEAK POS | WKS CHR | ARTIST — Record Title | POP POS | Label & Number |
|---|---|---|---|---|---|
| | | | **BILLY STEWART** Born on 3/24/37 in Washington, DC. Died in an auto accident on 1/17/70. Singer/keyboardist. Sang in family gospel group, the Stewart Singers. In the band of his uncle, Houn' Dog Ruffin (father of The Temptations' David Ruffin). Discovered by Bo Diddley in 1956. First recorded for Chess/Argo in 1956. Did not record from 1957-62. Nicknamed "Fat Boy". | | |
| 8/11/62 | 18 | 5 | 1 Reap What You Sow ............................................. | 79 | Chess 1820 |
| 10/12/63 | 25 | 1 | 2 Strange Feeling................................................... | 70 | Chess 1868 |
| 2/06/65 | 6 | 21 | 3 **I Do Love You**................................................... | 26 | Chess 1922 |
| 6/19/65 | 4 | 13 | 4 **Sitting In The Park** ........................................ | 24 | Chess 1932 |
| 5/14/66 | 38 | 2 | 5 Love Me ............................................................. | | Chess 1960 |
| 8/06/66 | 7 | 11 | 6 **Summertime**..................................................... from the musical "Porgy & Bess" | 10 | Chess 1966 |
| 10/22/66 | 11 | 9 | 7 Secret Love.......................................................... revival of Doris Day's 1954 pop hit (POS 1) | 29 | Chess 1978 |
| 2/18/67 | 41 | 2 | 8 Everyday I Have The Blues ............................. | 74 | Chess 1991 |
| 10/14/67 | 49 | 2 | 9 Why Do I Love You So/ | | |
| 1/27/68 | 34 | 8 | 10   Cross My Heart........................................ | 86 | Chess 2002 |
| 7/27/68 | 48 | 2 | 11 Tell Me The Truth ........................................... | | Chess 2053 |
| | | | **JERMAINE STEWART** Singer/dancer from Ohio. Appeared as dancer on Soul Train in Chicago while a teenager. Did back-up vocals with Shalamar and Boy George. | | |
| 10/06/84+ | 17 | 19 | 1 The Word Is Out............................................ | 41 | Arista 9256 |
| 2/15/86 | 64 | 15 | 2 We Don't Have To Take Our Clothes Off ........... | 5 | Arista 9424 |
| 9/06/86 | 18 | 12 | 3 Jody ................................................................. | 42 | Arista 9476 |
| 3/26/88 | 15 | 14 | 4 Say It Again .................................................... | 27 | Arista 9636 |
| 7/02/88 | 69 | 8 | 5 Get Lucky......................................................... | | Arista 9714 |
| | | | **MEL STEWART** | | |
| 8/27/83 | 76 | 7 | 1 No Work, No Pay............................................ | | Mercury 578 |
| | | | **ROD STEWART** Pop/rock singer born on 1/10/45 in London. Member of many rock groups including the Jeff Beck Group from 1967-69, and Faces from 1969-75. | | |
| 1/27/79 | 5 | 15 | 1▲**Da Ya Think I'm Sexy?**................................. | 1 | Warner 8724 |
| 1/10/81 | 65 | 6 | 2 Passion ............................................................ | 5 | Warner 49617 |
| | | | **ARBEE STIDHAM** Born on 2/9/17 in DeValls Bluff, Arkansas. Vocalist/alto saxophonist/guitarist/harmonica player. Own band in 1930. Moved to Chicago in 1954. Learned guitar after auto accident made it impossible to play saxes. Active into the 80s. | | |
| 6/12/48 | 1¹ | 24 | 1 **My Heart Belongs To You** ............................ Best Seller #1(1) / Juke Box #1(1) | | Victor 2572 |
| | | | **STING** Born Gordon Sumner on 10/2/51 in Wallsend, England. Lead singer/bass guitarist of the Police. In the films "Quadrophenia", "Dune", "The Bride", "Plenty" and others. Nicknamed Sting because of a yellow and black jersey he liked to wear. | | |
| 6/08/85 | 17 | 16 | 1 If You Love Somebody Set Them Free .............. | 3 | A&M 2738 |
| 10/31/87 | 39 | 11 | 2 We'll Be Together.............................................. | 7 | A&M 2983 |
| | | | **STIRLING SILVER** Born Donny Sterling, member of the Parliament/Funkadelic organization. Vocalist/drummer/bass guitarist. | | |
| 6/12/76 | 100 | 1 | 1 Sunshine (When I Got You) ............................. | | Columbia 10329 |
| | | | **STONE** | | |
| 2/06/82 | 55 | 10 | 1 Time................................................................. | | West End 1239 |
| | | | **STONE CITY BAND** Group consisting of Kenny Hawkins, Tom McDermott, Levi Ruffin, Jr., Daniel LeMelle, Jerry Livingston, Jerry Rainer and Nat Hughes. | | |
| 3/08/80 | 48 | 9 | 1 Strut Your Stuff.............................................. | | Gordy 7179 |
| 5/31/80 | 66 | 4 | 2 Little Runaway ................................................ | | Gordy 7182 |
| 7/02/83 | 76 | 4 | 3 Bad Lady.......................................................... | | Gordy 1681 |
| 9/17/83 | 53 | 8 | 4 Ladies Choice.................................................. all of above: arranged & produced by Rick James | | Gordy 1693 |

| DEBUT DATE | PEAK POS | WKS CHR | ARTIST — Record Title | POP POS | Label & Number |
|---|---|---|---|---|---|
| | | | **SLY STONE** Born Sylvester Stewart on 3/15/44 in Dallas. Vocalist/keyboardist/producer/leader/ founder of Sly & The Family Stone. | | |
| 8/23/75 | **3** | 15 | 1 I Get High On You ............................... | *52* | Epic 50135 |
| 12/20/75+ | **75** | 7 | 2 Le Lo Li ............................... | | Epic 50175 |
| 9/27/86 | **2**¹ | 18 | 3 **Crazay** ............................... JESSE JOHNSON featuring SLY STONE | *53* | A&M 2878 |
| | | | **STONEY & MEATLOAF** Female vocalist "Stoney" from Detroit with pop singer Marvin Lee Aday (Meatloaf). | | |
| 5/29/71 | **36** | 3 | 1 What You See Is What You Get........................ | *71* | Rare Earth 5027 |
| | | | **STORIES** New York rock quartet led by vocalist Ian Lloyd. Included Michael Brown (founding member of Left Banke). | | |
| 8/11/73 | **22** | 12 | 1●Brother Louie................................ | *1* | Kama Sutra 577 |
| | | | **STORM** | | |
| 2/16/74 | **88** | 4 | 1 I Don't Know Why (I Love You The Way I Do)..... | | Phi-Kappa 500 |
| | | | **GALE STORM** Born Josephine Cottle on 4/5/22 in Bloomington, Texas. Moved to Hollywood in 1939, leading lady in films during the 40s and early 50s. Own TV series "My Little Margie" from 1952-55, also "The Gale Storm Show", 1956-62. | | |
| 11/19/55 | **15** | 1 | 1 I Hear You Knockin' ................................ Jockey #15 | *2* | Dot 15412 |
| | | | **THE NICK STRAKER BAND** | | |
| 8/01/81 | **35** | 12 | 1 A Little Bit Of Jazz ................................ | | Prelude 8034 |
| | | | **STREET CHRISTIANS** | | |
| 2/19/72 | **50** | 2 | 1 Hey, Did You Give Some Love Today ................ | | Pip 8928 |
| | | | **STREET FARE** | | |
| 12/19/87+ | **47** | 15 | 1 Come And Get This Love ................................ | | Atlantic 89162 |
| | | | **STREET PEOPLE** Group led by singer/songwriter/producer Ray Dahrouge. | | |
| 10/18/75 | **98** | 2 | 1 Never Get Enough Of Your Love........................ | | Vigor 1722 |
| 1/31/76 | **13** | 12 | 2 You're My One Weakness Girl ........................ | | Vigor 1728 |
| 8/21/76 | **57** | 9 | 3 I Wanna Spend My Whole Life With You............ | *109* | Vigor 1732 |
| 11/06/76 | **66** | 6 | 4 Wanna Slow Dance With You Baby (At The Disco) ................................ | | Vigor 1734 |
| 6/18/77 | **93** | 4 | 5 Liberated Lady ................................ | | Vigor 1737 |
| | | | **STREET PLAYERS** | | |
| 11/03/79 | **87** | 3 | 1 Boogie Down ................................ | | Ariola 7770 |
| | | | **BARBRA STREISAND - see DONNA SUMMER** | | |
| | | | **STRIKERS** 7-man New York City funk band. | | |
| 4/18/81 | **23** | 19 | 1 Body Music ................................ | | Prelude 8025 |
| 8/22/81 | **58** | 8 | 2 Inch By Inch ................................ | | Prelude 8033 |
| | | | **THE STRING-A-LONGS** Instrumental quintet: Keith McCormack, Aubrey Lee de Cordova, Richard Stephens & Jimmy Torres (guitars), and Don Allen (drums). | | |
| 3/20/61 | **19** | 5 | 1 Wheels........................................ [I] | *3* | Warwick 603 |
| | | | **STROKE** | | |
| 10/19/85 | **86** | 4 | 1 You Are The One ................................ | | Omni 99583 |
| | | | **BARRETT STRONG** Born on 2/5/41 in Mississippi. Singer/songwriter. Wrote many of The Temptations' hits with Norman Whitfield, including "Just My Imagination", "Papa Was A Rollin' Stone", "Ball Of Confusion" and "Cloud Nine". Cousin of Nolan and Jimmy Strong of the Diablos. | | |
| 1/25/60 | **2**⁶ | 21 | 1 **Money (That's What I Want)**........................ originally released on Tamla 54027 | *23* | Anna 1111 |
| 8/25/73 | **78** | 6 | 2 Stand Up And Cheer For The Preacher.............. | | Epic 11011 |
| 5/03/75 | **41** | 11 | 3 Is It True ................................ | | Capitol 4052 |

| DEBUT DATE | PEAK POS | WKS CHR | ARTIST — Record Title | POP POS | Label & Number |
|---|---|---|---|---|---|
| | | | **STUDENTS** | | |
| | | | Group from Youngstown, Ohio. | | |
| 5/29/61 | **26** | 8 | 1 I'm So Young................................................. | | Argo 5386 |
| | | | originally released on Note 10012, recorded in 1958; also released on Checker 902 | | |
| | | | **STUFF 'N' RAMJETT** | | |
| 2/14/76 | **55** | 11 | 1 It's Been A Long Long Time ......................... | | Chelsea 3036 |
| | | | **THE STYLE COUNCIL** | | |
| | | | English duo: Paul Weller (ex-vocalist of The Jam) and Mick Talbot (keyboards). Expanded to a trio in 1988 with the addition of female vocalist Dee C. Lee. | | |
| 5/05/84 | **88** | 5 | 1 My Ever Changing Moods............................... | 29 | Geffen 29359 |
| | | | **THE STYLISTICS**  ★★65★★ | | |
| | | | Philadelphia group formed in 1908. Consisted of Russell Thompkins, Jr. (b: 3/21/51), lead; Airron Love, James Smith, James Dunn and Herbie Murrell. Thompkins, Love and Smith sang with the Percussions; Murrell and Dunn with the Monarchs from 1965-68. First recorded for Sebring in 1969. | | |
| 1/02/71 | **7** | 15 | 1 You're A Big Girl Now .................................. | 73 | Avco Embs. 4555 |
| 5/29/71 | **6** | 12 | 2 Stop, Look, Listen (To Your Heart) ............... | 39 | Avco Embs. 4572 |
| 10/30/71+ | **10** | 17 | 3●You Are Everything .................................... | 9 | Avco 4581 |
| 3/04/72 | **2**² | 13 | 4●Betcha By Golly, Wow ................................ | 3 | Avco 4591 |
| 6/10/72 | **6** | 10 | 5 People Make The World Go Round ................. | 25 | Avco 4595 |
| 10/14/72 | **4** | 15 | 6●I'm Stone In Love With You .......................... | 10 | Avco 4603 |
| 2/17/73 | **5** | 11 | 7●Break Up To Make Up ................................. | 5 | Avco 4611 |
| 5/26/73 | **8** | 9 | 8 You'll Never Get To Heaven (If You Break My Heart) .................................................. | 23 | Avco 4618 |
| 10/13/73 | **3** | 18 | 9 Rockin' Roll Baby ....................................... | 14 | Avco 4625 |
| 3/16/74 | **5** | 16 | 10●You Make Me Feel Brand New ...................... | 2 | Avco 4634 |
| | | | all of above: produced by Thom Bell | | |
| 7/27/74 | **8** | 14 | 11 Let's Put It All Together ............................ | 18 | Avco 4640 |
| 10/26/74 | **4** | 15 | 12 Heavy Fallin' Out ..................................... | 41 | Avco 4647 |
| 1/18/75 | **13** | 12 | 13 Star On A TV Show ................................... | 47 | Avco 4649 |
| 4/12/75 | **7** | 12 | 14 Thank You Baby......................................... | 70 | Avco 4652 |
| 7/12/75 | **18** | 12 | 15 Can't Give You Anything (But My Love)............ | 51 | Avco 4656 |
| 11/22/75 | **23** | 11 | 16 Funky Weekend......................................... | 76 | Avco 4661 |
| 2/21/76 | **17** | 10 | 17 You Are Beautiful ..................................... | 79 | Avco 4664 |
| 5/29/76 | **52** | 7 | 18 Can't Help Falling In Love .......................... | | H&L 4669 |
| | | | originally a #2 pop hit for Elvis Presley (1962) | | |
| 9/18/76 | **43** | 9 | 19 Because I Love You, Girl ............................. | | H&L 4674 |
| 4/02/77 | **87** | 2 | 20 Shame And Scandal In The Family ................... | | H&L 4681 |
| 7/23/77 | **90** | 3 | 21 I'm Coming Home...................................... | | H&L 4686 |
| | | | 11-21: produced by Hugo Peretti & Luigi Creatore | | |
| 7/08/78 | **22** | 14 | 22 First Impressions ..................................... | | Mercury 74006 |
| 2/17/79 | **93** | 4 | 23 Love At First Sight .................................... | | Mercury 74042 |
| 9/06/80 | **18** | 22 | 24 Hurry Up This Way Again ............................ | | TSOP 4789 |
| 2/28/81 | **70** | 4 | 25 And I'll See You No More ............................. | | TSOP 4798 |
| 8/15/81 | **79** | 4 | 26 What's Your Name?.................................... | | TSOP 02195 |
| 11/03/84 | **47** | 10 | 27 Give A Little ........................................... | | Streetwise 1136 |
| 2/16/85 | **86** | 2 | 28 Some Things Never Change ......................... | | Streetwise 1137 |
| 3/01/86 | **77** | 7 | 29 Special.................................................... | | Streetwise 1138 |
| 6/14/86 | **63** | 7 | 30 Let's Go Rocking (Tonight)........................... | | Streetwise 2241 |
| | | | **SUAVE'** | | |
| | | | Los Angeles native, born on 2/22/66. Son of Waymond Anderson, Sr. (member of GQ). | | |
| 3/12/88 | **3** | 15 | 1 My Girl.................................................. | 20 | Capitol 44124 |
| 6/18/88 | **22** | 12 | 2 Shake Your Body ....................................... | | Capitol 44178 |
| | | | **SUE ANN** | | |
| | | | Born Sue Ann Carwell in Minneapolis. Discovered by Andre Cymone at age 16. Brother Carl was in Free Life. | | |
| 7/11/81 | **72** | 7 | 1 Let Me Let You Rock Me............................... | | Warner 49750 |
| | | | **SUGAR BABES** | | |
| | | | Teenage female trio from Los Angeles: Kimiko Whittaker, Stacie Irvin and Patrice Lydia. | | |
| 4/11/87 | **58** | 8 | 1 We Rock The Beat...................................... | | MCA 52998 |

| DEBUT DATE | PEAK POS | WKS CHR | ARTIST — Record Title | POP POS | Label & Number |
|---|---|---|---|---|---|
| | | | **SUGAR BILLY** | | |
| 1/11/75 | 7 | 14 | 1 **Super Duper Love - Part 1 (Are You Diggin' On Me)** ................................................ | | Fast Track 2501 |
| 5/24/75 | 43 | 9 | 2 Sugar Pie ................................................ | | Fast Track 2503 |
| | | | **SUGAR DADDY** | | |
| 1/24/81 | 74 | 5 | 1 Another One Bites The Dust ............................ | | BC 4007 |
| | | | rap version of Queen's hit | | |
| | | | **SUGARHILL GANG** | | |
| | | | New York rap trio formed in Harlem. Consisted of Michael "Wonder Mike" Wright, Guy "Master Gee" O'Brien and Henry "Big Bank Hank" Jackson. One of the first commercially-successful rap acts. | | |
| 10/13/79 | 4 | 19 | 1 Rapper's Delight ...................................... | 36 | Sugar Hill 542 |
| | | | based on the rhythm track from Chic's "Good Times" | | |
| 12/13/80+ | 15 | 18 | 2 8th Wonder ............................................ | 82 | Sugar Hill 753 |
| 6/27/81 | 49 | 10 | 3 Showdown .............................................. | | Sugar Hill 558 |
| | | | FURIOUS FIVE MEETS THE SUGARHILL GANG | | |
| 12/05/81+ | 13 | 17 | 4 Apache ................................................ | 53 | Sugar Hill 567 |
| 7/17/82 | 55 | 9 | 5 The Lover In You ...................................... | | Sugar Hill 581 |
| 3/12/83 | 71 | 5 | 6 The Word Is Out ....................................... | | Sugar Hill 597 |
| 8/27/83 | 50 | 7 | 7 Kick It Live From 9 To 5 .............................. | | Sugar Hill 459 |
| 6/09/84 | 78 | 6 | 8 Livin' In The Fast Lane ............................... | | Sugar Hill 32021 |
| | | | **DONNA SUMMER** ★★52★★ | | |
| | | | Born Adrian Donna Gaines on 12/31/48 in Boston. With group Crow, played local clubs. In German production of "Hair", European productions of "Godspell", "The Me Nobody Knows" and "Porgy And Bess". Settled in Germany, where she recorded "Love To Love You Baby" in 1979. In the film "Thank God It's Friday" in 1979. Married Bruce Sudano of Brooklyn Dreams in 1980. The Queen of Disco. | | |
| 12/06/75+ | 3 | 13 | 1●Love To Love You Baby ................................ | 2 | Oasis 401 |
| 4/24/76 | 21 | 9 | 2 Could It Be Magic .................................... | 52 | Oasis 405 |
| 6/26/76 | 35 | 9 | 3 Try Me, I Know We Can Make It ........................ | 80 | Oasis 406 |
| 12/18/76+ | 24 | 9 | 4 Spring Affair ........................................ | 47 | Casablanca 872 |
| 2/05/77 | 21 | 12 | 5 Winter Melody ........................................ | 43 | Casablanca 874 |
| 6/04/77 | 20 | 11 | 6 Can't We Just Sit Down (And Talk It Over)/ | | |
| 8/06/77 | 9 | 19 | 7● I Feel Love ......................................... | 6 | Casablanca 884 |
| 12/17/77+ | 28 | 13 | 8 I Love You ........................................... | 37 | Casablanca 907 |
| 3/04/78 | 21 | 11 | 9 Rumour Has It ........................................ | 53 | Casablanca 916 |
| 5/27/78 | 5 | 16 | 10●Last Dance .......................................... | 3 | Casablanca 926 |
| | | | from the film "Thank God It's Friday" | | |
| 9/23/78 | 8 | 14 | 11●MacArthur Park ...................................... | 1 | Casablanca 939 |
| 1/20/79 | 10 | 14 | 12●Heaven Knows ........................................ | 4 | Casablanca 959 |
| | | | DONNA SUMMER with BROOKLYN DREAMS | | |
| | | | 1, 3-9 & 12: written by Summer, Giorgio Moroder & Pete Bellotte | | |
| 4/28/79 | 3 | 14 | 13▲Hot Stuff ........................................... | 1 | Casablanca 978 |
| 6/02/79 | 1[1] | 19 | 14▲Bad Girls ........................................... | 1 | Casablanca 988 |
| 9/01/79 | 13 | 14 | 15●Dim All The Lights .................................. | 2 | Casablanca 2201 |
| 11/03/79+ | 20 | 12 | 16●No More Tears (Enough Is Enough) .................... | 1 | Columbia 11125 |
| | | | BARBRA STREISAND/DONNA SUMMER | | |
| 1/26/80 | 9 | 13 | 17●On The Radio ........................................ | 5 | Casablanca 2236 |
| 9/20/80 | 35 | 10 | 18 Walk Away ........................................... | 36 | Casablanca 2300 |
| 9/27/80 | 13 | 16 | 19●The Wanderer ........................................ | 3 | Geffen 49563 |
| | | | 2-9, 11-15, 17-19: produced by Giorgio Moroder & Pete Bellotte | | |
| 7/03/82 | 4 | 17 | 20 Love Is In Control (Finger On The Trigger) ..... | 10 | Geffen 29982 |
| 10/02/82 | 31 | 10 | 21 State Of Independence ................................ | 41 | Geffen 29895 |
| | | | all-star choir includes: James Ingram, Michael Jackson, Kenny Loggins, Lionel Richie, Dionne Warwick and Stevie Wonder | | |
| 12/25/82+ | 30 | 17 | 22 The Woman In Me ...................................... | 33 | Geffen 29805 |
| 6/04/83 | 1[3] | 19 | 23 She Works Hard For The Money ................... | 3 | Mercury 812370 |
| 9/17/83 | 9 | 14 | 24 Unconditional Love .................................. | 43 | Mercury 814088 |
| | | | backing vocals by Musical Youth | | |
| 12/03/83+ | 35 | 13 | 25 Love Has A Mind Of It's Own ......................... | 70 | Mercury 814922 |
| | | | with Matthew Ward of the gospel group "2nd Chapter of Acts" | | |
| 8/18/84 | 20 | 13 | 26 There Goes My Baby .................................. | 21 | Geffen 29291 |
| 11/10/84 | 51 | 9 | 27 Supernatural Love ................................... | 75 | Geffen 29142 |
| 8/22/87 | 10 | 14 | 28 **Dinner With Gershwin** ............................ | 48 | Geffen 28418 |

**394**

| DEBUT DATE | PEAK POS | WKS CHR | ARTIST — Record Title | POP POS | Label & Number |
|---|---|---|---|---|---|
| | | | **BILL SUMMERS & SUMMERS HEAT** | | |
| | | | Percussionist; formerly with Herbie Hancock's Head Hunters. | | |
| 7/16/77 | 84 | 4 | 1 Come Into My Life ............................................ | | Prestige 765 |
| | | | vocal by Charles Meeks | | |
| 3/17/79 | 45 | 11 | 2 Straight To The Bank ...................................... | | Prestige 768 |
| | | | vocals by Leo Miller & Virginia Ayers | | |
| 1/05/80 | 57 | 6 | 3 Walking On Sunshine....................................... | | Prestige 770 |
| | | | written by Eddy Grant | | |
| 3/07/81 | 16 | 20 | 4 Call It What You Want ................................... | 103 | MCA 51073 |
| 8/01/81 | 50 | 9 | 5 Summer Fun ................................................... | | MCA 51138 |
| 12/19/81+ | 25 | 13 | 6 Jam The Box.................................................... | | MCA 51221 |
| 3/27/82 | 38 | 10 | 7 At The Concert ............................................... | | MCA 52027 |
| 7/17/82 | 53 | 9 | 8 Give Your Love To Me .................................... | | MCA 52077 |
| 10/23/82 | 34 | 9 | 9 Seventeen ...................................................... | | MCA 52115 |
| 12/17/83+ | 63 | 7 | 10 It's Over ......................................................... | | MCA 52325 |
| | | | **SUN** | | |
| | | | Group from Dayton, Ohio consisting of Nikki Buzz (vocals), Randy Fredrix (guitar), Cldye Isom (bass) and Timmy Hollans (drums). | | |
| 4/24/76 | 31 | 15 | 1 Wanna Make Love (Come Flick My Bic) ............ | 76 | Capitol 4254 |
| 2/19/77 | 50 | 9 | 2 Boogie Bopper ............................................... | | Capitol 4382 |
| 3/11/78 | 92 | 3 | 3 Dance (Do What You Wanna Do) ...................... | | Capitol 4538 |
| 6/03/78 | 18 | 16 | 4 Sun Is Here .................................................... | | Capitol 4587 |
| 5/26/79 | 25 | 19 | 5 Radiation Level .............................................. | | Capitol 4713 |
| 10/27/79 | 67 | 7 | 6 Pure Fire ....................................................... | | Capitol 4780 |
| 6/14/80 | 56 | 8 | 7 Space Ranger (Majic's In The Air)...................... | | Capitol 4873 |
| 4/04/81 | 57 | 9 | 8 Reaction Satisfaction (Jam Ya'll: Funk It Up) ..... | | Capitol 4981 |
| 3/20/82 | 81 | 4 | 9 Slamm Dunk The Ffunk ................................. | | Capitol 5092 |
| 7/28/84 | 89 | 3 | 10 Legs (Bring Out The Wolf In Me)...................... | | Air City 501 |
| | | | **SUNBEAR** | | |
| 7/02/77 | 96 | 3 | 1 I Heard The Voice Of Music Say ...................... | | Soul Train 11001 |
| | | | **SUNDANCE featuring KEVIN STEVENSON** | | |
| 1/30/88 | 80 | 8 | 1 I Do .............................................................. | | Fatima 1219 |
| | | | **SUNFIRE** | | |
| 10/30/82 | 75 | 6 | 1 Shake Your Body ........................................... | | Warner 29897 |
| | | | **SUNNY & THE SUNGLOWS** | | |
| | | | Group from San Antonio, Texas, formed in 1959. Group led by Sunny Ozuna, with Jesse, Oscar and Ray Villanueva, Tony Tostado, Gilbert Fernandez, and Alfred Luna. | | |
| 9/21/63 | 12 | 10 | 1 Talk To Me ........................................[I] | 11 | Tear Drop 3014 |
| 11/16/63 | 45 | 7 | 2 Rags To Riches ............................................. | Hot | Tear Drop 3022 |
| 2/22/64 | 71 | 5 | 3 Out Of Sight-Out Of Mind ............................. | Hot | Tear Drop 3027 |
| | | | shown as: **SUNNY & THE SUNLINERS** | | |
| | | | **SUNRIZE** | | |
| | | | Former backing band for the Isley Brothers. Consisted of leader Everett Collins (keyboards, drums), David Townsend (guitar), Tony Herbert (bass), Kevin Jones (percussion) and Ronnie Scruggs (vocals). Debut album produced by the Isleys. | | |
| 8/28/82 | 19 | 14 | 1 Who's Stickin' It?........................................... | | Boardwalk 151 |
| | | | **THE SUNSHINE BAND - see KC & THE SUNSHINE BAND** | | |
| | | | **SUPER MAX** | | |
| 2/24/79 | 96 | 2 | 1 Love Machine ................................................ | | Voyage 1003 |
| | | | **SUPER NATURE** | | |
| 10/26/85 | 46 | 13 | 1 The Show Stoppa ........................................... | | Pop Art 1413 |
| | | | **THE SUPERBS** | | |
| 10/03/64 | 83 | 5 | 1 Baby Baby All The Time.................................. | Hot | Dore 715 |
| | | | **SUPERIOR MOVEMENT** | | |
| | | | Chicago vocal group originally called Fourth Movement. Consisted of first tenors Calvin Ford, Stanley Ratliff and David Williams; second tenor Billy Avery; and baritone Tyrone Powell. | | |
| 10/17/81 | 77 | 5 | 1 For You ......................................................... | | CIM 02502 |
| 5/22/82 | 47 | 10 | 2 Wide Shot ..................................................... | | CIM 02906 |

| DEBUT<br>DATE | PEAK<br>POS | WKS<br>CHR | ARTIST — Record Title | POP<br>POS | Label & Number |
|---|---|---|---|---|---|
| | | | **SUPERLATIVES** | | |
| 3/01/69 | **39** | 3 | 1 I Don't Know How To Say I Love You (Don't Walk Away) .......................................... | | Westbound 114 |
| | | | **THE SUPREMES** ★★25★★ | | |
| | | | Vocal group from Detroit, formed as the Primettes in 1959. Group consisted of lead singer Diana Ross (b: 3/26/44), Mary Wilson (b: 3/6/44) and Florence Ballard (b: 6/30/43; d: 2/22/76 of cardiac arrest). Recorded for LuPine in 1960. Signed to Motown's Tamla label in 1960. Changed name to The Supremes in 1961. Ballard discharged from group in 1967, replaced by Cindy Birdsong, formerly with Patti LaBelle's Blue Belles. Ross left in 1969 for solo career, replaced by Jean Terrell. Birdsong left in 1972, replaced by Lynda Lawrence. Terrell and Lawrence left in 1973, Mary Wilson re-formed group with Scherrie Payne (sister of Freda Payne) and Cindy Birdsong. Birdsong left again in 1976, replaced by Susaye Greene. In 1978, Wilson toured England with Karen Ragland and Karen Jackson, but lost rights to the name "Supremes" thereafter. | | |
| 12/29/62 | **26** | 1 | 1 Let Me Go The Right Way ............................... | 90 | Motown 1034 |
| 11/30/63+ | **23** | 11 | 2 When The Lovelight Starts Shining Through His Eyes..................................................... | Hot | Motown 1051 |
| 3/14/64 | **93** | 2 | 3 Run, Run, Run................................................. | Hot | Motown 1054 |
| 7/11/64 | **1**² | 14 | 4 **Where Did Our Love Go** ............................. | Hot | Motown 1060 |
| 10/03/64 | **1**⁴ | 13 | 5 **Baby Love** ................................................... | Hot | Motown 1066 |
| 1/30/65 | **3** | 1 | 6 **Come See About Me** .................................... | 1 | Motown 1068 |
| 2/20/65 | **2**⁴ | 14 | 7 **Stop! In The Name Of Love** ....................... | 1 | Motown 1074 |
| 5/01/65 | **1**¹ | 11 | 8 **Back In My Arms Again**.............................. | 1 | Motown 1075 |
| 8/14/65 | **6** | 10 | 9 **Nothing But Heartaches** ............................ | 11 | Motown 1080 |
| 11/06/65 | **2**² | 13 | 10 **I Hear A Symphony**.................................... | 1 | Motown 1083 |
| 1/29/66 | **10** | 10 | 11 **My World Is Empty Without You** .................. | 5 | Motown 1089 |
| 5/07/66 | **7** | 10 | 12 **Love Is Like An Itching In My Heart**............. | 9 | Motown 1094 |
| 8/20/66 | **1**² | 13 | 13 **You Can't Hurry Love** ................................. | 1 | Motown 1097 |
| 11/12/66 | **1**⁴ | 13 | 14 **You Keep Me Hangin' On** ............................ | 1 | Motown 1101 |
| 2/11/67 | **1**² | 11 | 15 **Love Is Here And Now You're Gone**.............. | 1 | Motown 1103 |
| 4/22/67 | **12** | 8 | 16 The Happening .......................................... | 1 | Motown 1107 |
| | | | from the film of the same title | | |
| | | | **DIANA ROSS & THE SUPREMES:** | | |
| 8/19/67 | **4** | 10 | 17 **Reflections**.................................................. | 2 | Motown 1111 |
| 11/25/67 | **16** | 6 | 18 In And Out Of Love..................................... | 9 | Motown 1116 |
| 3/30/68 | **17** | 8 | 19 Forever Came Today..................................... | 28 | Motown 1122 |
| | | | 2-19: written by Eddie Holland, Lamont Dozier & Brian Holland | | |
| 6/29/68 | **43** | 3 | 20 Some Things You Never Get Used To ................ | 30 | Motown 1126 |
| 10/26/68 | **2**³ | 13 | 21 **Love Child** ................................................... | 1 | Motown 1135 |
| 12/14/68+ | **2**³ | 12 | 22 **I'm Gonna Make You Love Me**...................... | 2 | Motown 1137 |
| 2/08/69 | **8** | 6 | 23 **I'm Livin' In Shame** .................................... | 10 | Motown 1139 |
| 3/22/69 | **8** | 7 | 24 **I'll Try Something New**............................... | 25 | Motown 1142 |
| 5/10/69 | **21** | 4 | 25 The Composer ............................................ | 27 | Motown 1146 |
| 6/07/69 | **17** | 7 | 26 No Matter What Sign You Are...................... | 31 | Motown 1148 |
| 9/20/69 | **33** | 4 | 27 The Weight ............................................... | 46 | Motown 1153 |
| | | | 22, 24 & 27: DIANA ROSS & THE SUPREMES & THE TEMPTATIONS | | |
| 11/15/69 | **1**⁴ | 15 | 28 **Someday We'll Be Together**............................ | 1 | Motown 1156 |
| | | | **THE SUPREMES:** | | |
| 3/14/70 | **5** | 13 | 29 **Up The Ladder To The Roof** ....................... | 10 | Motown 1162 |
| 7/25/70 | **11** | 10 | 30 Everybody's Got The Right To Love.................. | 21 | Westbound 1167 |
| 11/14/70 | **1**¹ | 14 | 31 **Stoned Love**.................................................. | 7 | Motown 1172 |
| 12/12/70+ | **7** | 9 | 32 **River Deep-Mountain High**........................... | 14 | Motown 1173 |
| | | | **THE SUPREMES & FOUR TOPS** | | |
| 5/22/71 | **8** | 9 | 33 **Nathan Jones**.............................................. | 16 | Motown 1182 |
| 6/19/71 | **41** | 4 | 34 You Gotta Have Love In Your Heart.................. | 55 | Motown 1181 |
| | | | **THE SUPREMES & FOUR TOPS** | | |
| 1/15/72 | **5** | 12 | 35 **Floy Joy** ..................................................... | 16 | Motown 1195 |
| 5/13/72 | **21** | 8 | 36 Automatically Sunshine ............................... | 37 | Motown 1200 |
| 8/12/72 | **22** | 7 | 37 Your Wonderful, Sweet Sweet Love .................. | 59 | Motown 1206 |
| 7/14/73 | **74** | 2 | 38 Bad Weather ............................................... | 87 | Motown 1225 |
| 7/19/75 | **69** | 6 | 39 He's My Man ............................................... | | Motown 1358 |
| 10/25/75 | **93** | 1 | 40 Where Do I Go From Here ............................. | | Motown 1374 |
| 6/12/76 | **25** | 12 | 41 I'm Gonna Let My Heart Do The Walking........... | 40 | Motown 1391 |
| 11/06/76 | **50** | 11 | 42 You're My Driving Wheel ............................... | 85 | Motown 1407 |

| DEBUT DATE | PEAK POS | WKS CHR | ARTIST — Record Title | POP POS | Label & Number |
|---|---|---|---|---|---|
| | | | **THE SUPREMES — Continued** | | |
| 3/05/77 | **83** | 4 | 43 Let Yourself Go .......................................... | | Motown 1415 |
| | | | **SURF M.C.'s** | | |
| | | | "Beach rap" trio from northern California. Includes rappers Sidewalk (Paul Rodriguez) and M.C.I.V.E. (Ivan T. Mumm) with DJ Kool G (Tony Douglas Gilmore). | | |
| 8/22/87 | **90** | 3 | 1 Surf Or Die.............................................. | | Profile 5150 |
| | | | **SURFACE** | | |
| | | | New Jersey trio: Bernard Jackson (lead singer), David Townsend (son of producer Ed Townsend) and Dave Conley. | | |
| 7/30/83 | **84** | 4 | 1 Falling In Love ........................................... | | Salsoul 7056 |
| 10/18/86 | **80** | 5 | 2 Let's Try Again........................................... | | Columbia 06273 |
| 2/28/87 | **2**² | 22 | 3 **Happy** ...................................................... | *20* | Columbia 06611 |
| 8/08/87 | **8** | 14 | 4 Lately ....................................................... | | Columbia 07257 |
| 11/28/87+ | **22** | 12 | 5 Let's Try Again ..................................... [R] | | Columbia 7644 |
| | | | **THE SURFARIS** | | |
| | | | Teenage surf band from Glendora, California. Consisted of Ron Wilson (drummer), Jim Fuller (lead guitar), Bob Berryhill (rhythm guitar), Pat Connolly (bass) and Jim Pash (sax, clarinet). | | |
| 7/20/63 | **10** | 10 | 1 **Wipe Out** .................................................. [I] originally released on DFS 11/12 | *2* | Dot 16479 |
| | | | **ALFONZO SURRETT** | | |
| 6/28/80 | **44** | 12 | 1 Make It Feel Good ...................................... | | MCA 41249 |
| | | | **MIKE & BRENDA SUTTON** | | |
| | | | Husband/wife duo. | | |
| 12/19/81+ | **45** | 12 | 1 We'll Make It ............................................. | | Sam 5023 |
| 6/12/82 | **49** | 9 | 2 Don't Hold Back.......................................... | | Sam 5028 |
| 10/30/82 | **82** | 3 | 3 Don't Let Go Of Me ..................................... | | Sam 5030 |
| 5/26/84 | **46** | 10 | 4 Live It Up (Love It Up)/ | | |
| 7/28/84 | **67** | 5 | 5 Kraazy ............................................... above 2 shown as: **SUTTONS** | | Rocshire 95060 |
| | | | **SUZY Q** | | |
| 8/01/81 | **64** | 8 | 1 Get On Up Do It Again.................................. | | Atlantic 3837 |
| | | | **THE SWALLOWS** | | |
| | | | Baltimore-based group, formed in 1946 as the Oakaleers: Eddie Rich, Irving Turner, Earl Hurley, Herman "Junior" Denby, Frederick "Money" Johnson and Norris "Bunky" Mack. Bobby Hendricks was in the group in the mid-50s. Another group by this name was formed by Eddie Rich in 1957 and recorded for Federal. | | |
| 8/04/51 | **9** | 3 | 1 **Will You Be Mine** .................................... Best Seller #9 / Juke Box #10 | | King 4458 |
| 8/02/52 | **8** | 4 | 2 **Beside You** .............................................. Juke Box #8 / Best Seller #10 | | King 4525 |
| | | | **SWAMP DOGG** | | |
| | | | Born Jerry Williams, Jr. in July of 1942, in Portsmouth, Virginia. Singer/producer. First recorded as Little Jerry for Mechanic in 1954. Recorded for several labels, production for Atlantic, others, to 1971. Assumed name Swamp Dogg in 1971. | | |
| 1/29/66 | **32** | 4 | 1 Baby, You're My Everything........................... shown as: **LITTLE JERRY WILLIAMS** | *133* | Calla 105 |
| 4/25/70 | **33** | 6 | 2 Mama's Baby - Daddy's Maybe...................... | *113* | Canyon 30 |
| 7/09/77 | **71** | 5 | 3 My Heart Just Can't Stop Dancing.................. | | Mus./Prv. 6306 |
| | | | **T.J. SWAN - see M.C. SHAN** | | |
| | | | **BETTYE SWANN** | | |
| | | | Born Betty Jean Champion on 10/24/44 in Shreveport, Louisiana. Moved to Los Angeles in the late 50s. In vocal group the Fawns, recorded for Money in 1964. | | |
| 2/27/65 | **27** | 5 | 1 Don't Wait Too Long.................................... written by Carolyn Franklin | *131* | Money 108 |
| 5/06/67 | **1**² | 20 | 2 **Make Me Yours** ........................................ | *21* | Money 126 |
| 9/30/67 | **36** | 8 | 3 Fall In Love With Me.................................... | *67* | Money 129 |
| 3/22/69 | **14** | 10 | 4 Don't Touch Me .......................................... | *38* | Capitol 2382 |
| 5/13/72 | **16** | 10 | 5 Victim Of A Foolish Heart............................. | *63* | Atlantic 2869 |
| 12/16/72+ | **26** | 12 | 6 Today I Started Loving You Again................... | *46* | Atlantic 2921 |
| 8/18/73 | **88** | 3 | 7 'Til I Get It Right ........................................ | | Atlantic 2950 |
| 5/04/74 | **71** | 7 | 8 The Boy Next Door ...................................... | | Atlantic 3019 |

| DEBUT DATE | PEAK POS | WKS CHR | ARTIST — Record Title | POP POS | Label & Number |
|---|---|---|---|---|---|
| 5/31/75 | **83** | 7 | **BETTYE SWANN — Continued**<br>9 All The Way In Or All The Way Out ................. | | Atlantic 3262 |
| | | | **SWEAT BAND**<br>Offshoot of Bootsy's Rubber Band, including Maceo Parker (saxophone), Joel Johnson (keyboards) and Carl Smalls (drums). Parker had been with James Brown; Smalls had been in Undisputed Truth and The Dramatics. | | |
| 10/25/80+ | **25** | 17 | 1 Freak To Freak................................................<br>produced by George Clinton & "Bootsy" Collins | | Uncle Jam 9901 |
| | | | **KEITH SWEAT**<br>Singer/songwriter born and raised in Harlem. | | |
| 11/14/87+ | **1** ³ | 21 | 1 **I Want Her**...................................................... | 5 | Elektra 69431 |
| 3/19/88 | **3** | 16 | 2 **Something Just Ain't Right** ......................... | 79 | Vintertn. 69411 |
| 7/02/88 | **2** ² | 18 | 3 **Make It Last Forever** ...................................<br>KEITH SWEAT with JACCI McGHEE | 59 | Vintertn. 69386 |
| | | | **JIMMY SWEENEY**<br>Born Jimmy Bell in Nashville. First recorded for Tennessee in 1950. Also recorded as "Jimmy Destry" and "Bob Sweeney". | | |
| 7/21/62 | **24** | 2 | 1 She Wears My Ring............................................<br>originally released on Hickory 1136, recorded in 1960 | | Buckley 1101 |
| | | | **SWEET CREAM**<br>Detroit trio of sisters. | | |
| 7/01/78 | **41** | 12 | 1 I Don't Know What I'd Do (If You Ever Left Me)... | | Shady Brook 1044 |
| | | | **THE SWEETHEARTS - see GENE & WENDELL** | | |
| | | | **THE SWEET INSPIRATIONS**<br>Vocal quartet: Emily "Cissy" Houston, Estelle Brown, Sylvia Shemwell & Myrna Smith. Spent nearly six years as studio group, primarily for Atlantic. Work included backing Aretha Franklin and Elvis Presley. Houston went solo in 1970. | | |
| 6/17/67 | **36** | 5 | 1 Why (Am I Treated So Bad)............................. | 57 | Atlantic 2410 |
| 7/29/67 | **13** | 6 | 2 Let It Be Me ................................................... | 94 | Atlantic 2418 |
| 3/09/68 | **5** | 14 | 3 **Sweet Inspiration** ......................................... | 18 | Atlantic 2476 |
| 7/06/68 | **30** | 4 | 4 To Love Somebody .......................................... | 74 | Atlantic 2529 |
| 9/14/68 | **41** | 3 | 5 Unchained Melody ........................................... | 73 | Atlantic 2551 |
| 5/03/69 | **42** | 3 | 6 Crying In The Rain .......................................... | 112 | Atlantic 2620 |
| 12/27/69+ | **25** | 9 | 7 (Gotta Find) A Brand New Lover-Part 1 ............ | 117 | Atlantic 2686 |
| 10/03/70 | **45** | 4 | 8 This World ...................................................... | 123 | Atlantic 2750 |
| 4/17/71 | **44** | 2 | 9 Evidence ........................................................ | | Atlantic 2779 |
| | | | **SWEET MUSIC** | | |
| 4/17/76 | **69** | 9 | 1 I Get Lifted .....................................................<br>written by Harry W. Casey and Rick Finch (both of KC & The Sunshine Band) | | Wand 11295 |
| | | | **SWEET SENSATION**<br>8-member group from Manchester, England led by Marcel King (vocals), with additional vocals by St. Clair Palmer, Vincent James and Junior Daye. | | |
| 11/16/74 | **63** | 12 | 1 Sad Sweet Dreamer ........................................ | 14 | Pye 71002 |
| | | | **SWEET TEE**<br>Female rapper, Toi Jackson, from Queens, New York. Discovered by Salt 'N' Pepa's producer, Hurby Lovebug. | | |
| 1/16/88 | **48** | 9 | 1 I Got Da Feelin'............................................... | | Profile 5169 |
| | | | **SWEET THUNDER**<br>Group from Youngstown, Ohio. Consisted of Booker Newberry (vocals), David Thomas (keyboards), Charles Buie (lead vocals, guitar), Rudell Alexander (bass) and John Aaron (drums). | | |
| 6/24/78 | **21** | 12 | 1 Baby, I Need Your Love Today......................... | | Fant./WMOT 826 |
| 6/23/79 | **63** | 5 | 2 I Leave You Stronger ...................................... | | Fantasy 860 |
| | | | **JOE SWIFT**<br>Vocalist based in the Los Angeles area during the late 40s. | | |
| 11/20/48 | **10** | 4 | 1 **That's Your Last Boogie**...............................<br>Best Seller #10 / Juke Box #15<br>with the Johnny Otis Orchestra | | Exclusive 51X |
| | | | **SWISS MOVEMENT** | | |
| 11/02/74 | **72** | 6 | 1 Try Something.................................................. | | Casablanca 805 |

| DEBUT DATE | PEAK POS | WKS CHR | ARTIST — Record Title | POP POS | Label & Number |
|---|---|---|---|---|---|
| | | | **SWITCH** | | |
| | | | Sextet from Mansfield, Ohio. Formed in 1975 as First Class. Discovered by Jermaine Jackson. Consisted of Bobby DeBarge, Phillip Ingram (lead vocals), Greg Williams, Tommy DeBarge, Eddie Fluellen and Jody Sims. Williams, Sims and Bobby DeBarge were in White Heat. Brothers Bobby and Tommy DeBarge were later in family group, DeBarge. | | |
| 7/29/78 | 6 | 26 | 1 **There'll Never Be**............................................ | 36 | Gordy 7159 |
| 1/27/79 | 22 | 13 | 2 I Wanna Be Closer...................................... | | Gordy 7163 |
| 5/26/79 | 16 | 20 | 3 Best Beat In Town.................................... | 69 | Gordy 7168 |
| 10/06/79 | 10 | 19 | 4 I Call Your Name .................................... | 83 | Gordy 7175 |
| 5/24/80 | 41 | 9 | 5 Don't Take My Love Away ......................... | | Gordy 7181 |
| 11/08/80+ | 9 | 21 | 6 **Love Over And Over Again** ..................... | | Gordy 7193 |
| 4/18/81 | 57 | 8 | 7 You And I.............................................. | | Gordy 7199 |
| 11/14/81 | 73 | 5 | 8 I Do Love You......................................... | | Gordy 7214 |
| 2/27/82 | 70 | 6 | 9 Call On Me ........................................... | | Gordy 1603 |
| 5/12/84 | 55 | 15 | 10 Switch It Baby...................................... | | Total Exp. 2401 |
| | | | **SYBIL** | | |
| | | | Honored, at age 23, by the Black Fashion Achievers & Entertainers Awards as the outstanding performer of New Jersey in 1986. | | |
| 4/25/87 | 46 | 12 | 1 Let Yourself Go ...................................... | | Next Plat. 50057 |
| 9/05/87 | 54 | 14 | 2 My Love Is Guaranteed ........................... | | Next Plat. 50067 |
| | | | **ROOSEVELT SYKES** | | |
| | | | Born on 1/31/06 in Elmar, Arkansas. Died in July of 1983 in New Orleans (77). Vocalist/pianist/organist. Also known as Easy Papa Johnson and Willie Kelly. Moved to St. Louis in 1925. First recorded for Okeh in 1929. Toured with St. Louis Jimmy in the late 30s. Moved to Chicago in 1941. Nicknamed "Honeydripper" long before famous hit record of the same name. Active until death. | | |
| 2/17/45 | 1[7] | 13 | 1 **I Wonder**............................................. | | Bluebird 0721 |
| 11/24/45 | 3 | 4 | 2 **The Honeydripper** ................................. | | Bluebird 0737 |
| 9/07/46 | 2[1] | 5 | 3 **Sunny Road** ........................................ | | Victor 1906 |
| | | | **THE SYLVERS** | | |
| | | | Memphis family of 10 brothers and sisters: Olympia-Ann, Leon, Charmaine, James, Edmund, Ricky, Angelia, Pat, Foster and Jonathon Sylvers. | | |
| 9/02/72 | 14 | 12 | 1 Fool's Paradise ...................................... | 94 | Pride 1001 |
| 12/30/72+ | 10 | 13 | 2 **Wish That I Could Talk To You** .................... | 77 | Pride 1019 |
| 7/14/73 | 33 | 8 | 3 Stay Away From Me................................. | 89 | Pride 1029 |
| 1/26/74 | 50 | 9 | 4 Through The Love In My Heart ....................... | | MGM 14678 |
| 11/29/75+ | 1[1] | 25 | 5 ●**Boogie Fever**....................................... | 1 | Capitol 4179 |
| 6/26/76 | 19 | 15 | 6 Cotton Candy ........................................ | 59 | Capitol 4255 |
| 10/09/76 | 3 | 21 | 7 ●**Hot Line** ............................................ | 5 | Capitol 4336 |
| 4/23/77 | 6 | 11 | 8 **High School Dance**............................... | 17 | Capitol 4405 |
| 10/15/77 | 12 | 15 | 9 Any Way You Want Me ............................ | 72 | Capitol 4493 |
| 1/28/78 | 45 | 10 | 10 New Horizon ........................................ | | Capitol 4532 |
| 9/02/78 | 15 | 14 | 11 Don't Stop, Get Off ................................ | | Casablanca 938 |
| 11/03/84 | 42 | 10 | 12 In One Love And Out The Other.................... | | Geffen 29293 |
| 3/23/85 | 76 | 6 | 13 Falling For Your Love .............................. | | Geffen 29061 |
| | | | **EDMUND SYLVERS** | | |
| | | | Born on 1/25/57 in Memphis. Member of The Sylvers family group. | | |
| 8/02/80 | 38 | 11 | 1 That Burning Love ................................. | | Casablanca 2270 |
| | | | **FOSTER SYLVERS** | | |
| | | | Born on 2/25/62 in Memphis. Youngest member of The Sylvers family group. | | |
| 5/19/73 | 7 | 13 | 1 **Misdemeanor**............................................ also released on Pride 1031 | 22 | MGM 14580 |
| 10/06/73 | 63 | 7 | 2 Hey, Little Girl ..................................... | 92 | MGM 14630 |
| | | | **SYLVESTER** | | |
| | | | Born Sylvester James in Los Angeles. Moved to San Francisco in 1967. With vocal group, the Cockettes. In film "The Rose". Backing vocals by Martha Wash, Izora Rhodes (later known as Two Tons O' Fun and The Weather Girls), and Jeanie Tracy. | | |
| 7/22/78 | 4 | 20 | 1 **Dance (Disco Heat)**.................................... | 19 | Fantasy 827 |
| 12/23/78+ | 20 | 13 | 2 You Make Me Feel (Mighty Real)................... | 36 | Fantasy 846 |
| 4/07/79 | 27 | 11 | 3 I (Who Have Nothing) ............................ | 40 | Fantasy 855 |
| 12/01/79+ | 43 | 9 | 4 Can't Stop Dancing................................. | | Fantasy 879 |
| 2/23/80 | 30 | 14 | 5 You Are My Friend ................................. | | Fantasy 883 |
| 5/30/81 | 44 | 11 | 6 Here Is My Love .................................... | | Fant./Honey 912 |

| DEBUT DATE | PEAK POS | WKS CHR | ARTIST — Record Title | POP POS | Label & Number |
|---|---|---|---|---|---|
| | | | **SYLVESTER — Continued** | | |
| 1/22/83 | 67 | 7 | 7 All I Need ............................................... | | Megatone 1005 |
| 2/18/84 | 68 | 6 | 8 Too Late................................................ | | Megatone 1011 |
| 11/29/86+ | 19 | 17 | 9 Someone Like You ................................. | | Warner 28572 |
| | | | **TONY SYLVESTER & THE NEW INGREDIENT** | | |
| | | | Born Enrique Antonio Silvester on 10/7/41 in Colon, Panama. With the Poets and Main Ingredient. Re-formed Main Ingredient with Cuba Gooding and Luther Simmons in 1979. | | |
| 9/18/76 | 95 | 3 | 1 The Magic Touch..................................... | | Mercury 73831 |
| | | | **SYLVIA** | | |
| | | | Born Sylvia Vanderpool on 5/6/36 in New York City. Singer/songwriter/producer. First recorded with Hot Lips Page for Columbia in 1950, as Little Sylvia. Half of Mickey & Sylvia duo. Married Joe Robinson, owner of All-Platinum/Vibration Records. Their son Joe was leader of West Street Mob. Sylvia owns Sugar Hill Records. | | |
| 3/24/73 | 1 [2] | 13 | 1 ● Pillow Talk ............................................ | 3 | Vibration 521 |
| 7/14/73 | 21 | 7 | 2 Didn't I.................................................. | 70 | Vibration 524 |
| 8/18/73 | 39 | 7 | 3 Soul Je T'Aime ....................................... | 99 | Vibration 525 |
| | | | **SYLVIA & RALFI PAGAN** | | |
| 1/12/74 | 62 | 5 | 4 Alfredo/ | | Vibration 527 |
| | | 2 | 5    Private Performance ............................ | | Vibration 527 |
| 2/23/74 | 16 | 16 | 6 Sweet Stuff ........................................... | 103 | Vibration 529 |
| 4/27/74 | 45 | 11 | 7 Sho Nuff Boogie (Part I) ......................... | | All Platinum 2350 |
| | | | **SYLVIA & THE MOMENTS** | | |
| 7/27/74 | 68 | 6 | 8 Easy Evil .............................................. | | Vibration 530 |
| 5/15/76 | 54 | 7 | 9 L.A. Sunshine......................................... | | Vibration 567 |
| 10/08/77 | 65 | 9 | 10 Lay It On Me .......................................... | | Vibration 570 |
| 6/10/78 | 43 | 9 | 11 Automatic Lover...................................... | | Vibration 576 |
| 4/10/82 | 53 | 9 | 12 It's Good To Be The Queen....................... | | Sugar Hill 781 |
| | | | **SYMBA** | | |
| 8/16/80 | 70 | 5 | 1 Hold On ................................................ | | Venture 127 |
| 12/27/80+ | 55 | 11 | 2 Hey You ................................................ | | Venture 137 |
| | | | **SYMBOL 8** | | |
| 6/11/77 | 62 | 8 | 1 Party Life .............................................. | | Shock 5 |
| | | | **SYMBOLIC THREE featuring D.J. DR. SHOCK** | | |
| 12/28/85+ | 59 | 9 | 1 No Show ............................................... | | Reality 250 |
| | | | **SYREETA** | | |
| | | | Born Rita Wright in Pittsburgh. Singer/songwriter. Worked as secretary and back-up vocalist at Motown. First recorded under real name in 1968. Married to Stevie Wonder from 1972-74. | | |
| 7/05/75 | 75 | 9 | 1 Harbour Love ......................................... | | Motown 1353 |
| 1/19/80 | 86 | 3 | 2 With You I'm Born Again........................... | 4 | Motown 1477 |
| | | | **BILLY PRESTON & SYREETA** | | |
| 6/28/80 | 72 | 7 | 3 One More Time For Love .......................... | 52 | Tamla 54312 |
| | | | **BILLY PRESTON & SYREETA** | | |
| 11/14/81+ | 41 | 14 | 4 Quick Slick ............................................ | | Tamla 54333 |
| | | | **THE SYSTEM** | | |
| | | | New York City-based techno-funk duo: Mic Murphy (b: Raleigh, NC; vocals, guitar) and David Frank (b: Dayton, OH; synthesizer). | | |
| 1/29/83 | 10 | 19 | 1 You Are In My System............................. | 64 | Mirage 99937 |
| 5/21/83 | 55 | 8 | 2 Sweat................................................... | | Mirage 99891 |
| 3/03/84 | 48 | 11 | 3 I Wanna Make You Feel Good .................... | | Mirage 99786 |
| 6/29/85 | 21 | 15 | 4 The Pleasure Seekers.............................. | 108 | Mirage 99639 |
| 10/12/85 | 8 | 16 | 5 This Is For You ....................................... | | Mirage 99607 |
| 2/14/87 | 1 [1] | 21 | 6 Don't Disturb This Groove........................ | 4 | Atlantic 89320 |
| 6/27/87 | 7 | 16 | 7 Nighttime Lover ..................................... | | Atlantic 89222 |
| 6/04/88 | 23 | 12 | 8 Coming To America ................................. | 91 | Atco 99320 |
| | | | **GABOR SZABO** | | |
| | | | Born on 3/8/36 in Budapest, Hungary. Died on 2/26/82. Jazz guitarist/composer. First recorded as leader for Impulse in 1966. Wrote score for the film "Repulsion". | | |
| 9/18/71 | 43 | 6 | 1 Breezin'................................................. | | Blue Thumb 200 |
| | | | **GABOR SZABO & BOBBY WOMACK** | | |

| DEBUT DATE | PEAK POS | WKS CHR | ARTIST — Record Title | POP POS | Label & Number |
|---|---|---|---|---|---|
| 10/16/76 | 77 | 6 | **GABOR SZABO — Continued**<br>2  Keep Smilin' .............................................. [I] | | Mercury 73840 |

# T

**TAKANAKA**

| 4/19/86 | 87 | 2 | 1  Teaser..................................................... | | Amherst 306 |

**TA MARA & THE SEEN**
Minneapolis quintet led by Margaret Cox. Cox is a veteran Minneapolis night club singer. Group includes guitarist Oliver Leiber, son of songwriter Jerry Leiber.

| 9/21/85 | 3 | 19 | 1  **Everybody Dance**........................................ | 24 | A&M 2768 |
| 12/14/85+ | 19 | 15 | 2  Affecttion............................................... | | A&M 2797 |
| 3/29/86 | 85 | 5 | 3  Thinking About You ................................ | | A&M 2818 |
| 5/28/88 | 54 | 8 | 4  Blueberry Gossip ..................................... | | A&M 1204 |

**TAMPA RED**
Born Hudson Woodbridge on 12/15/03 in Smithville, Georgia. Died on 3/19/81 (77). Vocalist/guitarist/pianist. Later assumed mother's maiden name, Whittaker. Moved To Tampa, Florida in the early 20s, then to Chicago in 1925. First recorded for Paramount in 1928. With Georgia Tom Dorsey to early 30s. Fondly remembered for his open-house jam sessions for blues musicians in Chicago. Retired in the early 70s. Also see Big Maceo.

| 12/19/42+ | 4 | 4 | 1  **Let Me Play With Your Poodle**.......................<br>with Big Maceo on piano | | Bluebird 0700 |
| 9/01/45 | 5 | 1 | 2  **Detroit Blues**...........................................<br>with Blind John Davis on piano | | Bluebird 0731 |
| 9/17/49 | 9 | 3 | 3  **When Things Go Wrong With You** ..................<br>Juke Box #9 / Best Seller #11<br>also issued on 45 rpm (#50-0019) | | Victor 22-0035 |
| 10/27/51 | 7 | 1 | 4  **Pretty Baby Blues**......................................<br>Juke Box #7<br>above 2: featuring Little Johnnie Jones on piano | | RCA 0136 |

**THE TAMS**
Atlanta quintet: brothers Charles and Joseph (lead singer) Pope, with Robert Smith, Floyd Ashton and Horace Key. First recorded for Swan in 1960.

| 10/20/62 | 12 | 10 | 1  Untie Me............................................... | 60 | Arlen 11 |
| 12/14/63+ | 9 | 14 | 2  **What Kind Of Fool (Do You Think I Am)** ......... | Hot | ABC-Para. 10502 |
| 3/21/64 | 70 | 5 | 3  You Lied To Your Daddy ............................ | Hot | ABC-Para. 10533 |
| 4/04/64 | 79 | 3 | 4  It's All Right (You're Just In Love) ................... | Hot | ABC-Para. 10533 |
| 7/18/64 | 41 | 8 | 5  Hey Girl Don't Bother Me........................... | Hot | ABC-Para. 10573 |
| 11/28/64 | 87 | 1 | 6  Silly Little Girl ....................................... | Hot | ABC-Para. 10601 |
| 6/22/68 | 26 | 9 | 7  Be Young, Be Foolish, Be Happy ..................... | 61 | ABC 11066 |

**THE TARRIERS**
Folk trio: Erik Darling, Bob Carey and movie actor Alan Arkin. Darling became a member of The Rooftop Singers.

| 2/09/57 | 14 | 1 | 1  The Banana Boat Song................................<br>Best Seller #14 / Jockey #14 | 4 | Glory 249 |

**A TASTE OF HONEY**
Disco quartet, formed in Los Angeles in 1972. Consisted of Janice Marie Johnson (vocals, guitar), Hazel Payne (vocals, bass), Perry Kimble (keyboards) and Donald Johnson (drums). Group re-formed as a duo in 1980 with Janice Johnson and Hazel Payne.

| 5/13/78 | 1¹ | 25 | 1▲**Boogie Oogie Oogie** ..................................... | 1 | Capitol 4565 |
| 2/17/79 | 69 | 4 | 2  Disco Dancin'.......................................... | | Capitol 4668 |
| 7/14/79 | 13 | 14 | 3  Do It Good ............................................ | 79 | Capitol 4744 |
| 7/05/80 | 16 | 16 | 4  Rescue Me ............................................. | | Capitol 4888 |
| 11/01/80 | 64 | 7 | 5  I'm Talkin' 'Bout You................................. | | Capitol 4932 |
| 1/31/81 | 1¹ | 24 | 6●**Sukiyaki**............................................... | 3 | Capitol 4953 |
| 3/13/82 | 9 | 14 | 7  **I'll Try Something New**............................... | 41 | Capitol 5099 |
| 7/17/82 | 75 | 4 | 8  We've Got The Groove................................. | | Capitol 5132 |

**HOWARD TATE**
Vocalist from Macon, Georgia. Moved to Philadelphia at age 7. Worked in various gospel groups, sang with Gainors vocal group before going solo in 1962.

| 8/20/66 | 12 | 11 | 1  Ain't Nobody Home ................................. | 63 | Verve 10420 |

| DEBUT DATE | PEAK POS | WKS CHR | ARTIST — Record Title | POP POS | Label & Number |
|---|---|---|---|---|---|
| | | | **HOWARD TATE — Continued** | | |
| 12/31/66+ | 12 | 10 | 2 Look At Granny Run, Run .............................. | 67 | Verve 10464 |
| 7/01/67 | 40 | 6 | 3 Baby, I Love You.......................................... | | Verve 10525 |
| 2/03/68 | 15 | 8 | 4 Stop........................................................ | 76 | Verve 10573 |
| 7/12/69 | 28 | 12 | 5 These Are The Things That Make Me Know You're Gone.............................................. | 120 | Turntable 505 |
| 3/07/70 | 31 | 6 | 6 My Soul's Got A Hole In It .............................. | 100 | Turntable 1018 |
| | | | **TOMMY TATE** | | |
| | | | Born on 9/29/44 in Homestead, Florida. | | |
| 6/24/72 | 22 | 11 | 1 School Of Love ............................................. | | KoKo 2112 |
| 6/19/76 | 62 | 8 | 2 Hardtimes S.O.S. .......................................... | | KoKo 722 |
| 11/13/76 | 93 | 5 | 3 If You Ain't Man Enough ................................. | | KoKo 723 |
| | | | **TAVARES**   ★★60★★ | | |
| | | | Family group from New Bedford, Massachusetts. Consisted of brothers Ralph, Antone "Chubby", Feliciano "Butch", Arthur "Pooch" and Perry Lee "Tiny" Tavares. Worked as Chubby & The Turnpikes from 1964-69. | | |
| 8/11/73 | 5 | 20 | 1 **Check It Out** ............................................. | 35 | Capitol 3674 |
| 1/12/74 | 10 | 15 | 2 **That's The Sound That Lonely Makes**............ | 70 | Capitol 3794 |
| 5/11/74 | 10 | 13 | 3 **Too Late** ................................................... | 59 | Capitol 3882 |
| 9/21/74 | 1¹ | 18 | 4 **She's Gone** ................................................ | 50 | Capitol 3957 |
| 1/25/75 | 4 | 16 | 5 **Remember What I Told You To Forget** .......... | 25 | Capitol 4010 |
| 7/26/75 | 1¹ | 17 | 6 **It Only Takes A Minute**................................ | 10 | Capitol 4111 |
| 11/29/75+ | 8 | 12 | 7 **Free Ride** .................................................. | 52 | Capitol 4184 |
| 2/21/76 | 11 | 15 | 8 The Love I Never Had...................................... | | Capitol 4221 |
| 5/22/76 | 3 | 19 | 9●**Heaven Must Be Missing An Angel (Part 1)**..... | 15 | Capitol 4270 |
| 10/30/76 | 14 | 14 | 10 Don't Take Away The Music............................ | 34 | Capitol 4348 |
| 3/26/77 | 1¹ | 17 | 11 **Whodunit** ................................................ | 22 | Capitol 4398 |
| 7/23/77 | 14 | 11 | 12 Goodnight My Love........................................ | | Capitol 4453 |
| 11/12/77+ | 36 | 14 | 13 More Than A Woman ...................................... | 32 | Capitol 4500 |
| | | | from the film "Saturday Night Fever" | | |
| 2/18/78 | 48 | 11 | 14 The Ghost Of Love (Part 1)............................ | | Capitol 4544 |
| 7/08/78 | 94 | 2 | 15 Timber ...................................................... | | Capitol 4583 |
| 11/25/78+ | 5 | 22 | 16 **Never Had A Love Like This Before** .............. | | Capitol 4658 |
| 5/05/79 | 77 | 4 | 17 Straight From The Heart ............................... | | Capitol 4703 |
| 12/22/79+ | 10 | 17 | 18 **Bad Times**................................................ | 47 | Capitol 4811 |
| 4/19/80 | 42 | 9 | 19 I Can't Go On Living Without You .................... | | Capitol 4846 |
| 10/18/80 | 17 | 16 | 20 Love Uprising ............................................. | | Capitol 4933 |
| 2/14/81 | 64 | 5 | 21 Loneliness ................................................. | | Capitol 4969 |
| 7/11/81 | 45 | 10 | 22 Turn Out The Nightlight ................................ | | Capitol 5019 |
| 10/10/81 | 47 | 9 | 23 Loveline ................................................... | | Capitol 5043 |
| 8/21/82 | 16 | 17 | 24 A Penny For Your Thoughts............................ | 33 | RCA 13292 |
| 2/12/83 | 24 | 10 | 25 Got To Find My Way Back To You .................... | | RCA 13433 |
| 9/03/83 | 10 | 14 | 26 **Deeper In Love** ......................................... | | RCA 13611 |
| 11/26/83+ | 29 | 12 | 27 Words And Music ......................................... | | RCA 13684 |
| | | | **TAWATHA** | | |
| | | | Tawatha Agee from Philadelphia. Former backup singer with Mtume and Roxy Music. | | |
| 5/23/87 | 7 | 15 | 1 **Thigh Ride**................................................ | | Epic 07117 |
| 9/26/87 | 50 | 11 | 2 Did I Dream You ........................................... | | Epic 07407 |
| 12/19/87 | 46 | 11 | 3 Are You Serious ........................................... | | Epic 07662 |
| | | | **ALEX TAYLOR** | | |
| | | | James Taylor's older brother. | | |
| 12/09/78+ | 80 | 9 | 1 Don't Look At Me That Way.......................... | | Bang 739 |
| | | | **BOBBY TAYLOR & THE VANCOUVERS** | | |
| | | | Interracial sextet based in Vancouver, Canada. Included guitarist Tommy Chong, of Cheech & Chong fame, Wes Henderson, Robbie King, Ted Lewis and Eddie Patterson. Bobby Taylor discovered The Jackson 5. | | |
| 4/20/68 | 5 | 12 | 1 **Does Your Mama Know About Me** ................. | 29 | Gordy 7069 |
| 9/07/68 | 40 | 6 | 2 I Am Your Man ............................................ | 85 | Gordy 7073 |
| 11/16/68 | 16 | 9 | 3 Malinda .................................................... | 48 | Gordy 7079 |
| 8/30/75 | 83 | 2 | 4 Why Play Games.......................................... | | Playboy 6046 |
| | | | BOBBY TAYLOR | | |

| DEBUT DATE | PEAK POS | WKS CHR | ARTIST — Record Title | POP POS | Label & Number |
|---|---|---|---|---|---|
| | | | **DEBBIE TAYLOR** | | |
| 3/30/68 | **37** | 4 | 1 Check Yourself ............................................. | | Decca 32259 |
| 3/22/69 | **18** | 11 | 2 Never Gonna Let Him Know ............................ | 86 | GWP 501 |
| 11/29/75+ | **32** | 11 | 3 I Don't Wanna Leave You ............................... | 100 | Arista 0144 |
| | | | **FELICE TAYLOR** | | |
| | | | Born on 1/29/48 in Richmond, California. Recorded with sisters Darlene and Norma as the Sweets for Valiant in 1965. | | |
| 1/28/67 | **44** | 5 | 1 It May Be Winter Outside (But In My Heart It's Spring)................................................. | 42 | Mustang 3024 |
| | | | written and produced by Barry White | | |
| | | | **GARY TAYLOR** | | |
| 4/16/88 | **31** | 10 | 1 Compassion ................................................. | | Virgin 99351 |
| | | | **GLORIA TAYLOR** | | |
| 10/18/69 | **9** | 12 | 1 **You Got To Pay The Price**............................. | 49 | Silver Fox 14 |
| 2/28/70 | **43** | 4 | 2 Grounded ................................................... | | Silver Fox 19 |
| 2/16/74 | **96** | 3 | 3 Deep Inside You........................................... | | Columbia 45986 |
| | | | **JOHNNIE TAYLOR**      ★★37★★ | | |
| | | | Born on 5/5/38 in Crawfordsville, Arkansas. With gospel group, the Highway QC's in Chicago, early 50s. In vocal group the Five Echoes, recorded for Sabre in 1954. In The Soul Stirrers gospel group before going solo. First solo recording for Sar in 1961. | | |
| 11/30/63 | **98** | 1 | 1 Baby, We've Got Love ................................... | Hot | Derby 1006 |
| 3/26/66 | **19** | 9 | 2 I Had A Dream ............................................ | | Stax 186 |
| 8/06/66 | **15** | 11 | 3 I Got To Love Somebody's Baby...................... | | Stax 193 |
| 12/09/67+ | **33** | 8 | 4 Somebody's Sleeping In My Bed ..................... | 95 | Stax 235 |
| 4/13/68 | **34** | 6 | 5 Next Time ................................................. | | Stax 247 |
| 6/22/68 | **45** | 2 | 6 I Ain't Particular ........................................ | | Stax 253 |
| 10/19/68 | **1**³ | 16 | 7●**Who's Making Love** .................................... | 5 | Stax 0009 |
| 1/25/69 | **2**² | 9 | 8 **Take Care Of Your Homework** ..................... | 20 | Stax 0023 |
| 5/10/69 | **4** | 11 | 9 **Testify (I Wonna)** ..................................... | 36 | Stax 0033 |
| 8/16/69 | **10** | 8 | 10 **I Could Never Be President** ...................... | 48 | Stax 0046 |
| 12/13/69+ | **4** | 14 | 11 **Love Bones**............................................. | 43 | Stax 0055 |
| 6/06/70 | **3** | 14 | 12 **Steal Away** ............................................. | 37 | Stax 0068 |
| 10/17/70 | **4** | 11 | 13 **I Am Somebody, Part II** ........................... | 39 | Stax 0078 |
| 1/09/71 | **1**² | 13 | 14 **Jody's Got Your Girl And Gone** .................. | 28 | Stax 0085 |
| 5/22/71 | **13** | 11 | 15 I Don't Wanna Lose You.............................. | 86 | Stax 0089 |
| 8/28/71 | **10** | 10 | 16 **Hijackin' Love**......................................... | 64 | Stax 0096 |
| 1/15/72 | **12** | 9 | 17 Standing In For Jody .................................. | 74 | Stax 0114 |
| 4/15/72 | **16** | 9 | 18 Doing My Own Thing................................... | 109 | Stax 0122 |
| | | | shown as: **JOHNNIE TAYLOR** (The Soul Philosopher) | | |
| 9/23/72 | **13** | 12 | 19 Stop Doggin' Me ........................................ | 101 | Stax 0142 |
| 6/23/73 | **1**² | 13 | 20●**I Believe In You (You Believe In Me)** ............. | 11 | Stax 0161 |
| 10/06/73 | **2**² | 15 | 21 **Cheaper To Keep Her** ............................... | 15 | Stax 0176 |
| 1/12/74 | **5** | 17 | 22 **We're Getting Careless With Our Love** .......... | 34 | Stax 0193 |
| 5/18/74 | **13** | 13 | 23 I've Been Born Again .................................. | 78 | Stax 0208 |
| 10/05/74 | **26** | 11 | 24 It's September ........................................... | | Stax 0226 |
| 7/19/75 | **51** | 10 | 25 Try Me Tonight .......................................... | | Stax 0241 |
| 1/31/76 | **1**⁶ | 21 | 26▲**Disco Lady**............................................. | 1 | Columbia 10281 |
| | | | first single certified platinum by R.I.A.A. | | |
| 6/05/76 | **5** | 14 | 27 **Somebody's Gettin' It** ............................... | 33 | Columbia 10334 |
| 2/12/77 | **3** | 15 | 28 **Love Is Better In The A.M. (Part 1)**.............. | 77 | Columbia 10478 |
| 5/28/77 | **17** | 10 | 29 Your Love Is Rated X .................................. | | Columbia 10541 |
| 9/17/77 | **24** | 12 | 30 Disco 9000 ................................................ | 86 | Columbia 10610 |
| 4/01/78 | **32** | 13 | 31 Keep On Dancing ....................................... | 101 | Columbia 10709 |
| 7/15/78 | **84** | 4 | 32 Ever Ready ................................................ | | Columbia 10776 |
| 9/22/79 | **37** | 12 | 33 (Ooh-Wee) She's Killing Me/ | | |
| 12/15/79+ | **79** | 7 | 34     Play Something Pretty .............................. | | Columbia 11084 |
| 8/09/80 | **77** | 4 | 35 I Got This Thing For Your Love ..................... | | Columbia 11315 |
| 9/11/82 | **24** | 15 | 36 What About My Love ................................... | | Beverly Glen 2003 |
| 1/08/83 | **55** | 8 | 37 I'm So Proud ............................................. | | Beverly Glen 2004 |
| 12/22/84+ | **74** | 8 | 38 Lady, My Whole World Is You........................ | | Malaco 2107 |

**403**

| DEBUT DATE | PEAK POS | WKS CHR | ARTIST — Record Title | POP POS | Label & Number |
|---|---|---|---|---|---|
| | | | **JOHNNIE TAYLOR — Continued** | | |
| 6/06/87 | **74** | 9 | 39  Don't Make Me Late.................................... | | Malaco 2135 |
| | | | **KOKO TAYLOR** | | |
| | | | Born Cora Walton on 9/28/35 in Memphis. Chicago-based blues singer. Worked local clubs with Buddy Guy and Junior Wells. Recorded with J.B. Lenoir on the USA label in 1963. | | |
| 4/16/66 | **4** | 13 | 1  **Wang Dang Doodle**..................................... | *58* | Checker 1135 |
| | | | **LITTLE JOHNNY TAYLOR** | | |
| | | | Born Johnny Young on 2/11/43 in Memphis. Blues singer/harmonica player. Moved to Los Angeles in 1950. With Mighty Clouds Of Joy and Stars Of Bethel gospel groups. Duets with Ted Taylor (no relation) in the 70s. | | |
| 5/25/63 | **27** | 1 | 1  You'll Need Another Favor............................ | *125* | Galaxy 718 |
| 8/17/63 | **1**[1] | 15 | 2  **Part Time Love**........................................ | *19* | Galaxy 722 |
| 1/04/64 | **78** | 4 | 3  Since I Found A New Love ............................ | *Hot* | Galaxy 725 |
| 10/29/66 | **43** | 2 | 4  Zig Zag Lightning ....................................... | | Galaxy 748 |
| 11/20/71+ | **9** | 11 | 5  **Everybody Knows About My Good Thing** ........ | *60* | Ronn 55 |
| 3/18/72 | **41** | 4 | 6  It's My Fault Darling................................... | | Ronn 59 |
| 8/12/72 | **16** | 10 | 7  Open House At My House ............................. | | Ronn 64 |
| 4/14/73 | **37** | 4 | 8  I'll Make It Worth Your While ...................... | | Ronn 69 |
| 7/27/74 | **83** | 4 | 9  You're Savin' Your Best Lovin' For Me............. | | Ronn 78 |
| | | | **TED TAYLOR** | | |
| | | | Born Austin Taylor on 2/16/37 in Farm Town, Oklahoma. Died in an auto accident on 10/22/87. Formerly with the Glory Bound Travellers and Mighty Clouds Of Joy gospel groups. Joined the Santa Monica Soul Seekers, group became the Cadets/ Jacks in 1954. Went solo in 1955. First recorded for Ebb in 1957. | | |
| 11/27/65+ | **14** | 12 | 1  Stay Away From My Baby............................. | *99* | Okeh 7231 |
| 8/23/69 | **30** | 7 | 2  It's Too Late ............................................. | *118* | Ronn 34 |
| 7/11/70 | **26** | 11 | 3  Something Strange Is Goin' On In My House....... | | Ronn 44 |
| 8/14/71 | **44** | 2 | 4  How's Your Love Life Baby .......................... | | Ronn 52 |
| 8/18/73 | **93** | 2 | 5  What A Fool............................................. | | Ronn 72 |
| 6/05/76 | **64** | 9 | 6  Steal Away .............................................. | | Alarm 112 |
| | | | **T-CONNECTION** | | |
| | | | Group from Nassau, Bahamas. Consisted of Theophilus "T" Coakley (vocals, keyboards), David Mackey (guitar), Kirkwood Coakley (bass, drums) and Anthony Flowers (drums). | | |
| 3/26/77 | **15** | 16 | 1  Do What You Wanna Do ............................. | *46* | Dash 5032 |
| 11/26/77+ | **27** | 15 | 2  On Fire .................................................. | *103* | Dash 5041 |
| 1/27/79 | **32** | 9 | 3  At Midnight.............................................. | *56* | Dash 5048 |
| 3/24/79 | **28** | 13 | 4  Saturday Night ......................................... | | Dash 5051 |
| 1/31/81 | **10** | 16 | 5  **Everything Is Cool** .................................. | | Capitol 4968 |
| 5/16/81 | **47** | 11 | 6  Groove City............................................. | | Capitol 4995 |
| 12/26/81+ | **37** | 13 | 7  A Little More Love ..................................... | | Capitol 5076 |
| 4/07/84 | **73** | 7 | 8  Take It To The Limit.................................... | | Capitol 5337 |
| | | | **TEARS FOR FEARS** | | |
| | | | British duo of Roland Orzabal (vocals, guitar) and Curt Smith (vocals, bass). Assisted by Manny Elias (drums) and Ian Stanley (keyboards). | | |
| 8/24/85 | **56** | 8 | 1  Shout...................................................... | *1* | Mercury 880294 |
| | | | **TEASE** | | |
| | | | Group from Los Angeles: Kipper Jones (lead vocals), Thomas Organ, Jr. (guitar), Jay Shanklin (bass) and Derek Organ (drums). The father of Organ brothers, Thomas Sr., was guitarist for The O'Jays. | | |
| 3/22/86 | **11** | 19 | 1  Firestarter ................................................ | | Epic 05789 |
| 8/02/86 | **81** | 7 | 2  Better Wild (Than Mild) .............................. | | Epic 06212 |
| 11/22/86 | **87** | 4 | 3  I Wish You Were Here ................................ | | Epic 06317 |
| 4/02/88 | **34** | 11 | 4  I Can't Stand The Rain ............................... | | Epic 07740 |
| | | | **TECHNOFUNK - see REGGIE GRIFFIN** | | |
| | | | **THE TEDDY BEARS** | | |
| | | | Los Angeles trio: Phil Spector (b: 12/26/40 in the Bronx), Carol Connors (lead singer; real name: Annette Kleinbard) and Marshall Leib. Spector became a well-known writer and producer; owner of Philles Records. | | |
| 11/17/58 | **10** | 13 | 1  **To Know Him, Is To Love Him** ...................... | *1* | Dore 503 |

| DEBUT DATE | PEAK POS | WKS CHR | | ARTIST — Record Title | POP POS | Label & Number |
|---|---|---|---|---|---|---|
| | | | | **WILLIE TEE** Born Wilson Turbinton on 2/6/44 in New Orleans. Vocalist/pianist. Formed own band, the Seminoles, with brother Earl. First recorded for AFO in 1960. Produced Margie Joseph and Wild Magnolias. | | |
| 2/27/65 | **12** | 13 | 1 | Teasin' You.................................................... originally released on Nola 708 | *97* | Atlantic 2273 |
| | | | | **TEENAGERS - see FRANKIE LYMON** | | |
| | | | | **TEEN DREAM** | | |
| 5/02/87 | **41** | 10 | 1 | Let's Get Busy............................................ **TEEN DREAM with VALENTINO** | | Warner 28602 |
| 1/16/88 | **78** | 5 | 2 | Toy............................................................. | | Warner 28138 |
| | | | | **THE TEEN QUEENS** Los Angeles duo formed in 1955: Betty and Rosie Collins, the sisters of Aaron Collins of the Cadets/Jacks. | | |
| 2/18/56 | **2**¹ | 13 | 1 | Eddie My Love............................................... Jockey #2 / Best Seller #3 / Juke Box #4 | *14* | RPM 453 |
| | | | | **TEMPER** Includes producer/composer Anthony Malloy (of Anthony & The Camp). | | |
| 8/18/84 | **64** | 8 | 1 | No Favors .................................................... | | MCA 52412 |
| | | | | **NINO TEMPO & APRIL STEVENS** Session saxophonist Nino, from Niagara Falls, New York, was born on 1/6/35. His sister April Stevens was born on 4/29/36. | | |
| 10/05/63 | **4** | 8 | 1 | Deep Purple .................................................. **NINO TEMPO & APRIL STEVENS** #1 hit for Larry Clinton & His Orchestra in 1939; arranged & directed by Jimmy Haskell | *1* | Atco 6273 |
| 10/06/73 | **78** | 7 | 2 | Sister James ...........................................[I] **NINO TEMPO & 5th AVE. SAX** | *53* | A&M 1461 |
| | | | | **THE TEMPREES** Trio of Del Juan Calvin, Harold "Scottie" Scott and Jasper "Jabbo" Phillips. Calvin replaced by William Norvell Johnson in 1972. In the film "Wattstax" in 1972. | | |
| 5/06/72 | **47** | 3 | 1 | Explain It To Her Mama................................ | | We Produce 1807 |
| 9/23/72 | **17** | 10 | 2 | Dedicated To The One I Love........................... | *93* | We Produce 1808 |
| 9/01/73 | **75** | 9 | 3 | Love's Maze ................................................ | | We Produce 1811 |
| 2/28/76 | **78** | 6 | 4 | I Found Love On A Disco Floor ...................... | | Epic 50192 |
| | | | | **THE TEMPTATIONS**   ★★4★★ Group formed in Detroit in 1960. Consisted of Eddie Kendricks, Paul Williams (d: 8/17/73), Melvin Franklin, Otis Williams and Elbridge Bryant, who was replaced by David Ruffin in 1964. Originally called the Primes and Elgins, first recorded for Miracle in 1961. Ruffin (cousin of Billy Stewart) replaced by Dennis Edwards (ex-Contours) in 1968. Kendricks and Paul Williams left in 1971, replaced by Ricky Owens (ex-Vibrations) and Richard Street. Owens was replaced by Damon Harris. Harris left in 1975, replaced by Glenn Leonard. Edwards left group, 1977-79, replaced by Louis Price. Ali Ollie Woodson replaced Edwards from 1984-87. 1988 lineup: Williams, Franklin, Street, Edwards and Ron Tyson. Recognized as America's all-time favorite soul group. | | |
| 5/12/62 | **22** | 3 | 1 | Dream Come Home..................................... | | Gordy 7001 |
| 2/29/64 | **11** | 11 | 2 | The Way You Do The Things You Do .............. | *Hot* | Gordy 7028 |
| 5/30/64 | **33** | 9 | 3 | I'll Be In Trouble ........................................ | *Hot* | Gordy 7032 |
| 9/12/64 | **26** | 8 | 4 | Girl (Why You Wanna Make Me Blue)............. | *Hot* | Gordy 7035 |
| 1/30/65 | **1**⁶ | 13 | 5 | My Girl......................................................... | *1* | Gordy 7038 |
| 4/03/65 | **3** | 13 | 6 | It's Growing ................................................ | *18* | Gordy 7040 |
| 7/31/65 | **4** | 15 | 7 | Since I Lost My Baby/ | *17* | |
| 8/28/65 | **22** | 5 | 8 | You've Got To Earn It ................................. | *123* | Gordy 7043 |
| 10/30/65 | **4** | 13 | 9 | My Baby/ | *13* | |
| 11/06/65 | **15** | 15 | 10 | Don't Look Back ......................................... | *83* | Gordy 7047 |
| 3/19/66 | **1**¹ | 12 | 11 | Get Ready .................................................. | *29* | Gordy 7049 |
| 5/28/66 | **1**⁸ | 17 | 12 | Ain't Too Proud To Beg................................. | *13* | Gordy 7054 |
| 8/27/66 | **1**⁵ | 15 | 13 | Beauty Is Only Skin Deep ........................... | *3* | Gordy 7055 |
| 11/26/66 | **1**² | 14 | 14 | (I Know) I'm Losing You............................... | *8* | Gordy 7057 |
| 5/13/67 | **2**⁴ | 12 | 15 | All I Need ................................................... | *8* | Gordy 7061 |
| 8/12/67 | **3** | 12 | 16 | You're My Everything ................................. | *6* | Gordy 7063 |
| 10/21/67 | **3** | 13 | 17 | (Loneliness Made Me Realize) It's You That I Need ...................................................... | *14* | Gordy 7065 |

| DEBUT DATE | PEAK POS | WKS CHR | | ARTIST — Record Title | POP POS | Label & Number |
|---|---|---|---|---|---|---|
| | | | | **THE TEMPTATIONS — Continued** | | |
| 1/20/68 | **1**³ | 14 | 18 | **I Wish It Would Rain/** | **4** | |
| 3/09/68 | **41** | 6 | 19 | I Truly, Truly Believe................... | 116 | Gordy 7068 |
| 5/18/68 | **1**¹ | 11 | 20 | **I Could Never Love Another (After Loving You)**.................. | 13 | Gordy 7072 |
| 8/17/68 | **4** | 13 | 21 | **Please Return Your Love To Me**................... | 26 | Gordy 7074 |
| 11/23/68 | **2**³ | 13 | 22 | **Cloud Nine**.................. | 6 | Gordy 7081 |
| 12/14/68+ | **2**³ | 12 | 23 | **I'm Gonna Make You Love Me**................... | 2 | Motown 1137 |
| 3/01/69 | **1**² | 13 | 24 | **Run Away Child, Running Wild** .............. | 6 | Gordy 7084 |
| 3/22/69 | **8** | 7 | 25 | **I'll Try Something New**................... | 25 | Motown 1142 |
| 5/31/69 | **2**¹ | 10 | 26 | **Don't Let The Joneses Get You Down**............ | 20 | Gordy 7086 |
| 8/30/69 | **1**⁵ | 15 | 27 | **I Can't Get Next To You** .............. | 1 | Gordy 7093 |
| 9/20/69 | **33** | 4 | 28 | The Weight .................. | 46 | Motown 1153 |
| | | | | 23, 25 & 28: **DIANA ROSS & THE SUPREMES & THE TEMPTATIONS** | | |
| 1/24/70 | **2**³ | 13 | 29 | **Psychedelic Shack** .................. | 7 | Gordy 7096 |
| 5/30/70 | **2**⁵ | 13 | 30 | **Ball Of Confusion (That's What The World Is Today)**.................. | 3 | Gordy 7099 |
| 10/10/70 | **8** | 9 | 31 | **Ungena Za Ulimwengu (Unite The World)/** | 33 | |
| | | 4 | 32 | Hum And Dance Along.................. | | Gordy 7102 |
| 2/13/71 | **1**³ | 14 | 33 | **Just My Imagination (Running Away With Me)** | 1 | Gordy 7105 |
| 7/24/71 | **29** | 7 | 34 | It's Summer.................. | 51 | Gordy 7109 |
| 11/13/71 | **8** | 10 | 35 | **Superstar (Remember How You Got Where You Are)**.................. | 18 | Gordy 7111 |
| 3/04/72 | **10** | 10 | 36 | **Take A Look Around** .................. | 30 | Gordy 7115 |
| 7/15/72 | **27** | 5 | 37 | Funky Music Sho Nuff Turns Me On/ | | |
| | | 5 | 38 | Mother Nature.................. | 92 | Gordy 7119 |
| 10/14/72 | **5** | 18 | 39 | **Papa Was A Rollin' Stone** .............. | 1 | Gordy 7121 |
| 3/03/73 | **1**² | 13 | 40 | **Masterpiece** .................. | 7 | Gordy 7126 |
| 6/16/73 | **8** | 8 | 41 | **The Plastic Man** .................. | 40 | Gordy 7129 |
| 8/18/73 | **2**¹ | 17 | 42 | **Hey Girl (I Like Your Style)**.................. | 35 | Gordy 7131 |
| 12/15/73+ | **1**¹ | 16 | 43 | **Let Your Hair Down** .................. | 27 | Gordy 7133 |
| 3/09/74 | **8** | 15 | 44 | **Heavenly**.................. | 43 | Gordy 7135 |
| 6/08/74 | **8** | 11 | 45 | **You've Got My Soul On Fire**.................. | 74 | Gordy 7136 |
| 12/21/74+ | **1**¹ | 12 | 46 | **Happy People**.................. | 40 | Gordy 7138 |
| 3/08/75 | **1**¹ | 14 | 47 | **Shakey Ground**.................. | 26 | Gordy 7142 |
| 7/12/75 | **9** | 12 | 48 | **Glasshouse**.................. | 37 | Gordy 7144 |
| 1/24/76 | **3** | 13 | 49 | **Keep Holding On** .................. | 54 | Gordy 7146 |
| 5/29/76 | **21** | 11 | 50 | Up The Creek (Without A Paddle) .................. | 94 | Gordy 7150 |
| 10/30/76 | **22** | 12 | 51 | Who Are You.................. | | Gordy 7152 |
| 11/05/77+ | **21** | 13 | 52 | In A Lifetime.................. | | Atlantic 3436 |
| 3/04/78 | **58** | 6 | 53 | Think For Yourself.................. | | Atlantic 3461 |
| 10/07/78 | **42** | 8 | 54 | Bare Back.................. | | Atlantic 3517 |
| 11/25/78+ | **31** | 14 | 55 | Ever Ready Love.................. | | Atlantic 3538 |
| 4/26/80 | **11** | 13 | 56 | **Power**.................. | 43 | Gordy 7183 |
| 7/26/80 | **55** | 6 | 57 | Struck By Lightning Twice.................. | | Gordy 7188 |
| 11/29/80 | **69** | 8 | 58 | Take Me Away.................. | | Motown 1501 |
| 8/15/81 | **36** | 13 | 59 | Aiming At Your Heart.................. | 67 | Gordy 7208 |
| 4/24/82 | **6** | 17 | 60 | **Standing On The Top - Part 1** .................. | 66 | Gordy 1616 |
| | | | | **THE TEMPTATIONS featuring RICK JAMES** | | |
| 8/14/82 | **82** | 5 | 61 | More On The Inside .................. | | Gordy 1631 |
| 3/12/83 | **17** | 15 | 62 | Love On My Mind Tonight .................. | 88 | Gordy 1666 |
| 10/22/83 | **67** | 7 | 63 | Miss Busy Body (Get Your Body Busy).............. | | Gordy 1707 |
| 3/03/84 | **13** | 18 | 64 | Sail Away .................. | 54 | Gordy 1720 |
| 10/27/84+ | **2**¹ | 21 | 65 | **Treat Her Like A Lady** .................. | 48 | Gordy 1765 |
| 3/09/85 | **14** | 13 | 66 | My Love Is True (Truly For You) .................. | | Gordy 1781 |
| 6/15/85 | **81** | 5 | 67 | How Can You Say That It's Over .................. | | Gordy 1789 |
| 11/23/85+ | **14** | 15 | 68 | Do You Really Love Your Baby .................. | | Gordy 1818 |
| 3/08/86 | **63** | 7 | 69 | Touch Me .................. | | Gordy 1834 |
| 5/10/86 | **63** | 8 | 70 | A Fine Mess .................. | | Motown 1837 |
| | | | | from the film of the same title | | |
| 8/09/86 | **4** | 20 | 71 | **Lady Soul** .................. | 47 | Gordy 1856 |

| DEBUT DATE | PEAK POS | WKS CHR | ARTIST — Record Title | POP POS | Label & Number |
|---|---|---|---|---|---|
| | | | **THE TEMPTATIONS — Continued** | | |
| 12/06/86+ | 25 | 13 | 72 To Be Continued.............................................. | | Gordy 1871 |
| 4/18/87 | 45 | 8 | 73 Someone ..................................................... | | Gordy 1881 |
| 9/12/87 | 3 | 18 | 74 **I Wonder Who She's Seeing Now** ..................... | | Motown 1908 |
| 12/26/87+ | 8 | 15 | 75 **Look What You Started** .............................. | | Motown 1920 |
| 4/23/88 | 53 | 10 | 76 Do You Wanna Go With Me ............................ | | Motown 1933 |
| | | | **10 SPEED** Micki Denton, lead singer of Detroit sextet. | | |
| 2/04/84 | 84 | 4 | 1 Tour De France............................................. | | Quality 052 |
| | | | **JEAN TERRELL** Replaced Diana Ross, as lead singer, in The Supremes from 1970-73. Sister of boxer Ernie Terrell; no relation to singer Tammi Terrell. | | |
| 5/27/78 | 72 | 5 | 1 Don't Stop Reaching For The Top..................... | | A&M 2039 |
| | | | **TAMMI TERRELL** Born Tammy Montgomery in 1946 in Philadelphia; died of a brain tumor on 3/16/70. First recorded for Wand in 1961. Worked with James Brown Revue. Tumor diagnosed after collapsing on stage in 1967. Recorded a string of hits with Marvin Gaye from 1967-70. | | |
| 1/29/66 | 27 | 6 | 1 I Can't Believe You Love Me.......................... | 72 | Motown 1086 |
| 6/04/66 | 25 | 5 | 2 Come On And See Me................................... | 80 | Motown 1095 |
| 1/18/69 | 31 | 6 | 3 This Old Heart Of Mine (Is Weak For You) ......... | 67 | Motown 1138 |
| | | | **TONY TERRY** Singer raised in Washington, DC. Sang with the Freedom Gospel Singers from age 8. Attended the Ellington School of the Arts. Appeared in the Broadway musicals "Black Nativity" and "Mama, I Want To Sing". | | |
| 9/26/87 | 10 | 19 | 1 **She's Fly** ................................................. | 80 | Epic 07417 |
| 1/23/88 | 4 | 15 | 2 **Lovey Dovey** ............................................ | | Epic 07697 |
| 5/28/88 | 16 | 13 | 3 **Forever Yours** ......................................... | 80 | Epic 07900 |
| | | | **JOE TEX**  ★★45★★ Born Joseph Arrington, Jr. on 8/8/33 in Rogers, Texas; died of a heart attack on 8/13/82. Sang with local gospel groups. Won recording contract at Apollo Theater talent contest in 1954. First recorded for King in 1955. Became a convert to Muslim faith, changed name to Joseph Hazziez in July, 1972. Also see The Soul Clan. | | |
| 1/30/65 | 2¹ | 8 | 1 **Hold What You've Got** ............................... | 5 | Dial 4001 |
| 2/27/65 | 10 | 8 | 2 **You Got What It Takes/** | 51 | |
| 2/20/65 | 15 | 9 | 3     You Better Get It .................................. | 46 | Dial 4003 |
| 4/24/65 | 12 | 7 | 4 A Woman Can Change A Man ........................ | 56 | Dial 4006 |
| 7/03/65 | 20 | 7 | 5 One Monkey Don't Stop No Show ................... | 65 | Dial 4011 |
| 8/28/65 | 1³ | 15 | 6 **I Want To (Do Everything For You)**.............. | 23 | Dial 4016 |
| 12/11/65+ | 1¹ | 14 | 7 **A Sweet Woman Like You** .......................... | 29 | Dial 4022 |
| 3/19/66 | 2¹ | 12 | 8 **The Love You Save (May Be Your Own)**......... | 56 | Dial 4026 |
| 5/28/66 | 9 | 8 | 9 **S.Y.S.L.J.F.M. (The Letter Song)** ................. | 39 | Dial 4028 |
| 8/06/66 | 8 | 8 | 10 **I Believe I'm Gonna Make It** ...................... | 67 | Dial 4033 |
| 10/15/66 | 20 | 7 | 11 I've Got To Do A Little Bit Better ................... | 64 | Dial 4045 |
| 12/24/66+ | 15 | 8 | 12 Papa Was Too................................................ | 44 | Dial 4051 |
| 3/18/67 | 24 | 8 | 13 Show Me...................................................... | 35 | Dial 4055 |
| 6/24/67 | 24 | 6 | 14 Woman Like That, Yeah ................................ | 54 | Dial 4059 |
| 8/19/67 | 24 | 8 | 15 A Woman's Hands ........................................ | 63 | Dial 4061 |
| 11/11/67 | 2² | 15 | 16●**Skinny Legs And All** ............................... | 10 | Dial 4063 |
| 2/24/68 | 7 | 8 | 17 **Men Are Gettin' Scarce** ............................ | 33 | Dial 4069 |
| 6/01/68 | 26 | 5 | 18 I'll Never Do You Wrong .............................. | 59 | Dial 4076 |
| 8/24/68 | 13 | 6 | 19 Keep The One You Got ................................. | 52 | Dial 4083 |
| 10/26/68 | 29 | 6 | 20 You Need Me, Baby....................................... | 81 | Dial 4086 |
| 4/19/69 | 10 | 7 | 21 **Buying A Book** ....................................... [S] | 47 | Dial 4090 |
| 8/02/69 | 46 | 2 | 22 That's The Way ........................................... | 94 | Dial 4093 |
| 9/11/71 | 20 | 9 | 23 Give The Baby Anthing The Baby Wants ........... | 102 | Dial 1008 |
| 1/22/72 | 1¹ | 17 | 24●**I Gotcha/** | 2 | |
| | | 3 | 25     Mother's Prayer ................................... | | Dial 1010 |
| 5/27/72 | 12 | 9 | 26 You Said A Bad Word ................................... | 41 | Dial 1012 |
| 2/10/73 | 41 | 8 | 27 Woman Stealer ........................................... | 103 | Dial 1020 |
| 7/12/75 | 27 | 11 | 28 Under Your Powerful Love ............................ | | Dial 1154 |
| 2/14/76 | 74 | 5 | 29 Have You Ever.............................................. | | Dial 1156 |

| DEBUT DATE | PEAK POS | WKS CHR | ARTIST — Record Title | POP POS | Label & Number |
|---|---|---|---|---|---|
| | | | **JOE TEX — Continued** | | |
| 1/29/77 | 7 | 22 | 30●Ain't Gonna Bump No More (With No Big Fat Woman).......... | 12 | Epic 50313 |
| 9/24/77 | 84 | 4 | 31 Hungry For Your Love ..................................... | | Epic 50426 |
| 1/28/78 | 70 | 6 | 32 Rub Down.................................................... | | Epic 50494 |
| 12/16/78+ | 48 | 9 | 33 Loose Caboose.............................................. | | Dial 2800 |
| | | | **T.F.O.** | | |
| 5/31/80 | 82 | 6 | 1 I Come Here To Party...................................... | | Venture 126 |
| 7/11/81 | 87 | 6 | 2 Happy Family .............................................. | | Venture 142 |
| | | | **SISTER ROSETTA THARPE** | | |
| | | | Born Rosetta Nubin in 1915 in Cotton Plant, Arkansas. Died on 10/9/73 in Philadelphia (stroke). Vocalist/guitarist. First recorded for Decca in 1938. With Cab Calloway in 1940 and Lucky Millinder from 1941-42. Recorded as Sister Katy Marie on Downbeat/Swingtime in 1947. Teamed with Marie Knight from 1947-54. Toured England with Chris Barber in 1957; France in 1966. Active through the late 60s. Energetic guitar stylings influential to many R&B artists. | | |
| 4/28/45 | 2² | 11 | 1 **Strange Things Are Happening Every Day** ..... | | Decca 8669 |
| 7/17/48 | 13 | 1 | 2 Precious Memories ......................................... Jockey #13 | | Decca 48070 |
| 12/25/48+ | 6 | 9 | 3 **Up Above My Head, I Hear Music In The Air** ... Best Seller #6 / Juke Box #9 above 3: with the Sam Price Trio; above 2: vocals by Marie Knight | | Decca 48090 |
| 12/24/49+ | 6 | 3 | 4 **Silent Night** ................................................ [X] Best Seller #6 with the James Roots Quartet | | Decca 48119 |
| | | | **THERESA** | | |
| | | | Duo of Theresa King and Victor Porter. | | |
| 6/27/87 | 18 | 17 | 1 Last Time ................................................... | | RCA 5229 |
| 12/05/87+ | 51 | 13 | 2 Sweet Memories ............................................ | | RCA 5348 |
| 6/18/88 | 66 | 7 | 3 What Cha Gonna Do ....................................... | | RCA 8328 |
| | | | **THIRD WORLD** | | |
| | | | Reggae fusion band from Jamaica. William "Bunny Rugs" Clarke (lead singer), Stephen "Cat" Coore, Michael "Ibo" Cooper, Richard Daley, Willie Stewart and Irvin "Carrot" Jarrett. To England and the U.S. from 1975-76. Toured with Stevie Wonder in 1982. | | |
| 3/06/76 | 62 | 7 | 1 Disco Hop ................................................... | | Abraxas 1701 |
| 11/11/78+ | 9 | 21 | 2 **Now That We Found Love** ............................. | 47 | Island 8663 |
| 8/15/81 | 88 | 2 | 3 Dancing On The Floor (Hooked On Love) ........... | | Columbia 02170 |
| 3/20/82 | 23 | 12 | 4 Try Jah Love................................................. | 101 | Columbia 02744 |
| 2/23/85 | 51 | 14 | 5 Sense Of Purpose .......................................... | | Columbia 04733 |
| 7/27/85 | 76 | 5 | 6 One To One................................................. | | Columbia 05415 |
| | | | **CARLA THOMAS** ★★123★★ | | |
| | | | Born on 12/21/42 in Memphis. Daughter of Rufus Thomas; sister of Vaneese Thomas. Sang with the Teentown Singers at age 10. First recorded with Rufus for Satellite in 1960. Had several duets with Otis Redding. | | |
| 2/06/61 | 5 | 14 | 1 Gee Whiz (Look At His Eyes) ......................... originally released on Satellite 104 | 10 | Atlantic 2086 |
| 5/29/61 | 20 | 3 | 2 A Love Of My Own......................................... | 56 | Atlantic 2101 |
| 11/03/62 | 9 | 5 | 3 **I'll Bring It Home To You** .............................. | 41 | Atlantic 2163 |
| 7/27/63 | 28 | 2 | 4 What A Fool I've Been ................................... | 93 | Atlantic 2189 |
| 6/06/64 | 92 | 2 | 5 That's Really Some Good/ | Hot | |
| 6/20/64 | 94 | 1 | 6 Night Time Is The Right Time...................... above 2: **RUFUS** (Thomas) **& CARLA** | Hot | Stax 151 |
| 8/01/64 | 67 | 9 | 7 I've Got No Time To Lose............................... | Hot | Atlantic 2238 |
| 11/28/64 | 71 | 4 | 8 A Woman's Love ........................................... | Hot | Atlantic 2258 |
| 2/20/65 | 39 | 3 | 9 How Do You Quit (Someone You Love) .............. | | Atlantic 2272 |
| 6/26/65 | 30 | 7 | 10 Stop! Look What You're Doing........................ | 92 | Stax 172 |
| 5/07/66 | 11 | 16 | 11 Let Me Be Good To You................................. | 62 | Stax 188 |
| 9/03/66 | 3 | 15 | 12 **B-A-B-Y**................................................... | 14 | Stax 195 |
| 1/21/67 | 29 | 7 | 13 Something Good (Is Going To Happen To You) .... | 74 | Stax 207 |
| 5/13/67 | 2¹ | 13 | 14 **Tramp**.................................................... **OTIS** (Redding) **& CARLA** | 26 | Stax 216 |
| 7/08/67 | 11 | 6 | 15 I'll Always Have Faith In You ......................... | 85 | Stax 222 |
| 9/02/67 | 8 | 8 | 16 **Knock On Wood**.......................................... **OTIS & CARLA** | 30 | Stax 228 |

| DEBUT DATE | PEAK POS | WKS CHR | ARTIST — Record Title | POP POS | Label & Number |
|---|---|---|---|---|---|
| | | | **CARLA THOMAS** — Continued | | |
| 1/06/68 | 16 | 7 | 17 Pick Up The Pieces ........................... | 68 | Stax 239 |
| 3/02/68 | 21 | 7 | 18 Lovey Dovey ...................................... | 60 | Stax 244 |
| | | | OTIS & CARLA | | |
| 10/19/68 | 38 | 4 | 19 Where Do I Go/ | 86 | |
| | | | from the Broadway musical "Hair" | | |
| 8/02/69+ | 36 | 4 | 20 I've Fallen In Love ............................ | 117 | Stax 0011 |
| 2/22/69 | 9 | 11 | 21 I Like What You're Doing (To Me) ................. | 49 | Stax 0024 |
| 5/09/70 | 41 | 5 | 22 Guide Me Well .................................. | 107 | Stax 0056 |
| 1/29/72 | 49 | 2 | 23 You Got A Cushion To Fall On ....................... | | Stax 0113 |
| | | | **EVELYN THOMAS** | | |
| | | | Also see Fatback. | | |
| 4/27/85 | 84 | 4 | 1 Heartless ........................................ | | Vanguard 35259 |
| | | | **IRMA THOMAS** | | |
| | | | Born Irma Lee on 2/18/41 in Ponchatoula, Louisiana. The Soul Queen of New Orleans. Discovered by New Orleans' bandleader Tommy Ridgley. | | |
| 5/09/60 | 22 | 3 | 1 Don't Mess With My Man ....................... | | Ron 328 |
| 3/28/64 | 17 | 12 | 2 Wish Someone Would Care ........................... *Hot* | | Imperial 66013 |
| 7/04/64 | 52 | 6 | 3 Anyone Who Knows What Love Is (Will Understand) ............................... *Hot* | | Imperial 66041 |
| 11/07/64 | 98 | 2 | 4 Times Have Changed ........................... *Hot* | | Imperial 66069 |
| 12/19/64+ | 63 | 8 | 5 He's My Guy .................................... *Hot* | | Imperial 66080 |
| 2/24/68 | 42 | 2 | 6 Good To Me ..................................... | | Chess 2036 |
| | | | written by Otis Redding | | |
| | | | **JOE THOMAS** | | |
| | | | Born Joseph Vankert Thomas on 6/19/09 in Uniontown, Pennsylvania. Saxophonist/ clarinetist/vocalist/leader. With Jimmie Lunceford from 1933-47, led band after Lunceford's death. Own band in 1945, recorded for Melodisc. Left music to become an undertaker in Kansas City in the early 50s. Died on 8/3/86 (77) in Kansas City. | | |
| 9/24/49 | 7 | 3 | 1 **Page Boy Shuffle**/ | [I] | |
| | | | Jockey #7 | | |
| 10/22/49 | 11 | 1 | 2 Teardrops ....................................... [I] | | King 4299 |
| | | | JOE THOMAS ORCHESTRA | | |
| | | | Best Seller #11 / Juke Box #14 | | |
| | | | originally released on Sensation 16 | | |
| | | | **JOE THOMAS** | | |
| 2/14/76 | 81 | 6 | 1 Masada ......................................... [I] | | Groove M. 1035 |
| 6/10/78 | 70 | 8 | 2 Two Doors Down ................................ | | LRC 904 |
| | | | written by Dolly Parton - her version hit POS 19 on pop charts | | |
| 8/12/78 | 76 | 11 | 3 Plato's Retreat ................................. | | LRC 94 |
| 5/26/79 | 87 | 2 | 4 Make Your Move ............................... | | LRC 907 |
| | | | **JON THOMAS** | | |
| | | | Vocalist/keyboardist from Cincinnati. First recorded for Chess/Checker in 1954. Staff musician at King Records, played on Little Willie John's "Fever", and many others from 1956-60. | | |
| 7/04/60 | 3 | 11 | 1 **Heartbreak (It's Hurtin' Me)** ........................ | 48 | ABC-Para. 10122 |
| | | | **LEONE THOMAS** | | |
| 3/27/76 | 65 | 6 | 1 Thank You Baby, Part I & II ........................... | | Don 102 |
| | | | **LILLO THOMAS** | | |
| | | | Vocalist from Brooklyn. When 16 years old, set a world record for the 200 meter dash, qualified for the 1984 Olympic track team, but an auto accident in Brazil kept him from competing. Toured with Eddie Murphy in 1985. Also see Paul Laurence. | | |
| 7/23/83 | 22 | 17 | 1 (You're A) Good Girl ........................... | | Capitol 5245 |
| 11/19/83 | 68 | 10 | 2 Who Do You Think You Are? ..................... | | Capitol 5292 |
| 2/04/84 | 79 | 5 | 3 Just My Imagination (Running Away With Me).... | | Capitol 5313 |
| 7/07/84 | 11 | 17 | 4 Your Love's Got A Hold On Me ................... | 102 | Capitol 5357 |
| 10/27/84 | 28 | 14 | 5 (Can't Take Half) All Of You ...................... | | Capitol 5415 |
| | | | LILLO THOMAS & MELBA MOORE | | |
| 2/16/85 | 60 | 8 | 6 Settle Down .................................... | | Capitol 5440 |
| 2/21/87 | 9 | 14 | 7 **Sexy Girl** ...................................... | | Capitol 5656 |
| 5/23/87 | 2¹ | 15 | 8 I'm In Love .................................... | | Capitol 5698 |
| 9/05/87 | 11 | 12 | 9 Downtown ...................................... | | Capitol 44065 |
| 11/28/87+ | 7 | 16 | 10 **Wanna Make Love (All Night Long)** .............. | | Capitol 44035 |

| DEBUT DATE | PEAK POS | WKS CHR | | ARTIST — Record Title | POP POS | Label & Number |
|---|---|---|---|---|---|---|
| | | | | **NOLAN THOMAS**<br>18-year-old New Jersey native. | | |
| 11/24/84+ | 26 | 20 | 1 | Yo' Little Brother............................................ | 57 | Mirage 99697 |
| 6/15/85 | 48 | 8 | 2 | One Bad Apple................................................ | 105 | Mirage 99651 |
| 11/07/87 | 76 | 7 | 3 | Leave The Lights On....................................... | | Ligosa 51 |
| | | | | MONET with NOLAN THOMAS | | |
| | | | | **PHILIP-MICHAEL THOMAS**<br>Plays Ricardo Tubbs on the TV series "Miami Vice". | | |
| 12/28/85+ | 75 | 7 | 1 | Just The Way I Planned It ............................. | | Atlantic 99581 |
| | | | | **RUFUS THOMAS**   ★★199★★<br>Born on 3/26/17 in Cayce, Mississippi. Singer/songwriter/choreographer. Father of<br>singers Carla and Vaneese Thomas. First recorded for Talent in 1950. Disc jockey<br>at WDIA-Memphis from 1953-74. | | |
| 4/18/53 | 3 | 8 | 1 | **Bear Cat**.................................................... | | Sun 181 |
| | | | | Rufus HOUND DOG Thomas, Jr.<br>Best Seller #3 / Juke Box #3<br>answer song to Willie Mae Thornton's "Hound Dog" | | |
| 2/09/63 | 22 | 3 | 2 | The Dog ........................................................ | 87 | Stax 130 |
| 10/26/63 | 5 | 5 | 3 | **Walking The Dog** ....................................... | 10 | Stax 140 |
| 2/01/64 | 48 | 9 | 4 | Can Your Monkey Do The Dog ....................... | Hot | Stax 144 |
| 4/11/64 | 86 | 2 | 5 | Somebody Stole My Dog ................................. | Hot | Stax 149 |
| 6/06/64 | 92 | 2 | 6 | That's Really Some Good/ | Hot | |
| 6/20/64 | 94 | 1 | 7 | Night Time Is The Right Time..................... | Hot | Stax 151 |
| | | | | above 2: RUFUS & CARLA (Thomas) | | |
| 10/10/64 | 49 | 7 | 8 | Jump Back .................................................... | Hot | Stax 157 |
| 8/26/67 | 43 | 4 | 9 | Sophisticated Sissy ....................................... | | Stax 221 |
| 1/17/70 | 5 | 14 | 10 | **Do The Funky Chicken** ............................... | 28 | Stax 0059 |
| 8/01/70 | 42 | 4 | 11 | Sixty Minute Man - Part II/ | | Stax 0071 |
| | | 4 | 12 | The Preacher And The Man .......................... | | Stax 0071 |
| 12/12/70+ | 1² | 15 | 13 | **(Do The) Push And Pull, Part I** ..................... | 25 | Stax 0079 |
| 5/15/71 | 34 | 4 | 14 | The World Is Round ...................................... | | Stax 0090 |
| 8/14/71 | 2² | 12 | 15 | **The Breakdown (Part I)** ............................... | 31 | Stax 0098 |
| 12/25/71+ | 11 | 10 | 16 | Do The Funky Penguin (Part I)....................... | 44 | Stax 0112 |
| 3/30/74 | 93 | 2 | 17 | The Funky Bird ............................................ | | Stax 0192 |
| 8/17/74 | 63 | 7 | 18 | Boogie Ain't Nuttin' (But Gettin' Down) ............ | | Stax 0219 |
| 5/10/75 | 74 | 7 | 19 | Do The Double Bump ..................................... | | Stax 0236 |
| 9/04/76 | 92 | 7 | 20 | If There Were No Music ................................ | | Art. Of Am. 126 |
| | | | | **TASHA THOMAS**<br>Born in Jeutyn, Alaska. Moved to New York in 1970. Played Auntie Em in Broadway's<br>"The Wiz". Session singer for Kiss, Cat Stevens, Diana Ross and others. | | |
| 12/16/78+ | 25 | 14 | 1 | Shoot Me (With Your Love)............................. | 91 | Atlantic 3542 |
| | | | | **TIMMY THOMAS**<br>Born on 11/13/44 in Evansville, Indiana. Singer/songwriter/keyboardist. Played<br>with Donald Byrd and Cannonball Adderley. Studio musician at Gold Wax Records<br>in Memphis. Session work for Betty Wright and KC & The Sunshine Band. | | |
| 11/11/72+ | 1² | 18 | 1 | **Why Can't We Live Together**....................... | 3 | Glades 1703 |
| 4/07/73 | 23 | 7 | 2 | People Are Changin' ...................................... | 75 | Glades 1709 |
| 7/14/73 | 48 | 6 | 3 | Let Me Be Your Eyes ..................................... | 107 | Glades 1712 |
| 11/03/73+ | 19 | 14 | 4 | What Can I Tell Her ...................................... | 102 | Glades 1717 |
| 3/09/74 | 62 | 9 | 5 | One Brief Moment ......................................... | | Glades 1719 |
| 11/02/74 | 31 | 12 | 6 | I've Got To See You Tonight/ | | |
| 3/08/75 | 78 | 7 | 7 | You're The Song (I've Always Wanted To Sing) . | | Glades 1723 |
| 6/21/75 | 69 | 6 | 8 | Sexy Woman .................................................. | | Glades 1727 |
| 4/02/77 | 74 | 7 | 9 | Stone To The Bone ........................................ | | Glades 1740 |
| 10/07/78 | 92 | 3 | 10 | Freak In, Freak Out ...................................... | | TM 1749 |
| 4/04/81 | 73 | 6 | 11 | Are You Crazy??? (Pt. 1) ............................... | | Marlin 3348 |
| 4/28/84 | 29 | 11 | 12 | Gotta Give A Little Love (Ten Years After)......... | 80 | Gold Mt. 82004 |
| 8/18/84 | 90 | 2 | 13 | Love Is Never Too Late ................................. | | Gold Mt. 82008 |
| | | | | **VANEESE THOMAS**<br>Daughter of Rufus Thomas and sister of Carla Thomas. | | |
| 6/13/87 | 10 | 15 | 1 | **Let's Talk It Over**...................................... | | Geffen 28365 |
| | | | | sax solo by Najee | | |

| DEBUT DATE | PEAK POS | WKS CHR | ARTIST — Record Title | POP POS | Label & Number |
|---|---|---|---|---|---|
| | | | **VANEESE THOMAS — Continued** | | |
| 10/17/87+ | 12 | 16 | 2 (I Wanna Get) Close To You............................ | | Gcffen 28216 |
| 3/05/88 | 76 | 6 | 3 Heading In The Right Direction...................... | | Geffen 27984 |
| | | | **THOMPSON TWINS** | | |
| | | | British trio: Tom Bailey (vocals, keyboard), Alannah Currie (percussion) and Joe Leeway (synthesizer). Leeway left in 1986. | | |
| 5/15/82 | 69 | 6 | 1 In The Name Of Love .................................. | | Arista 0671 |
| | | | **ROY THOMPSON** | | |
| 1/14/67 | 43 | 3 | 1 Sookie Sookie............................................. | | Okeh 7267 |
| | | | **SONNY THOMPSON** | | |
| | | | Born Alfonso Thompson in Chicago on 8/22/23. Bandleader/pianist. First recorded for Sultan in 1946. Much session work for King, Federal and DeLuxe Records into the mid-50s. Backed vocalist Lula Reed from 1951-61. | | |
| 5/22/48 | 1³ | 31 | 1 **Long Gone, Pts. 1 & 2** ............................. [I] | 29 | Miracle 126 |
| | | | Best Seller #1(3) / Juke Box #1(2) | | |
| 8/28/48 | 1¹ | 13 | 2 **Late Freight** ...................................... [I] | | Miracle 128 |
| | | | Best Seller #1(1) / Juke Box #1(1) | | |
| 3/26/49 | 10 | 1 | 3 **Blue Dreams/** [I] | | |
| | | | Juke Box #10 | | |
| 4/09/49 | 14 | 1 | 4 Blues On Rhumba .................................. [I] | | Miracle 131 |
| | | | Best Seller #14 above 4: with His Three Sharps & Flats | | |
| 9/10/49 | 12 | 2 | 5 Still Gone - Parts I & II ............................. [I] | | Miracle 139 |
| | | | Best Seller #12 | | |
| 3/29/52 | 8 | 1 | 6 **Mellow Blues, I & II**........................... [I] | | King 4488 |
| | | | Best Seller #8 | | |
| 7/12/52 | 5 | 8 | 7 **I'll Drown In My Tears** ............................. | | King 4527 |
| | | | Best Seller #5 / Juke Box #6 | | |
| 8/16/52 | 7 | 6 | 8 **Let's Call It A Day**...................................... | | King 4541 |
| | | | Juke Box #7 / Best Seller #9 above 2: vocals by Lula Reed | | |
| | | | **FONZI THORNTON** | | |
| | | | Born Alfonzo Thornton in New York City. While in college, own vocal group, Fonzi, worked as back-up singers for Candi Staton and Melba Moore. Thornton sang background for Chic. | | |
| 4/09/83 | 43 | 12 | 1 Beverly ................................................ | | RCA 13454 |
| | | | **WILLIE MAE "BIG MAMA" THORNTON** | | |
| | | | Born on 12/11/26 in Montgomery, Alabama. Died of a heart attack on 7/25/84 (57). Vocalist/drummer/harmonica player. Nicknamed Big Mama. With Hot Harlem Revue from 1941-48. Moved to Houston in 1948. First recorded for E&W in 1951. Did soundtrack for the film "Vanishing Point", in 1971. Active until her death. | | |
| 3/28/53 | 1⁷ | 14 | 1 **Hound Dog** ...................................... | | Peacock 1612 |
| | | | Juke Box #1(7) / Best Seller #1(6) with "Kansas City Bill" (Johnny Otis) & Orchestra; Elvis Presley's 1956 version became one of the biggest hits of the rock era | | |
| | | | **THP ORCHESTRA** | | |
| | | | Canadian disco production. | | |
| 3/18/78 | 46 | 8 | 1 Two Hot For Love........................................ | 103 | Butterfly 1206 |
| | | | **THE THREE DEGREES** | | |
| | | | Philadelphia trio discovered by Richard Barrett. Originally consisted of Fayette Pinkney, Linda Turner and Shirley Porter. Turner and Porter replaced by Sheila Ferguson and Valerie Holiday in 1966. | | |
| 6/13/70 | 4 | 13 | 1 **Maybe** ............................................. | 29 | Roulette 7079 |
| | | | written by Richard Barrett | | |
| 9/12/70 | 7 | 11 | 2 **I Do Take You** ........................................ | 48 | Roulette 7088 |
| 1/16/71 | 19 | 7 | 3 You're The One............................................ | 77 | Roulette 7091 |
| 5/08/71 | 33 | 5 | 4 There's So Much Love All Around Me ............... | 98 | Roulette 7102 |
| 2/12/72 | 46 | 2 | 5 Tradewinds ................................................ | | Roulette 7117 |
| 10/06/73 | 58 | 9 | 6 Dirty Ol' Man ............................................. | | Phil. Int. 3534 |
| 3/02/74 | 1¹ | 17 | 7● **TSOP (The Sound Of Philadelphia)** ............ [I] | 1 | Phil. Int. 3540 |
| | | | **MFSB featuring THE THREE DEGREES** theme from the TV show "Soul Train" | | |
| 3/09/74 | 74 | 6 | 8 Year Of Decision ....................................... | | Phil. Int. 3539 |
| 7/13/74 | 42 | 7 | 9 Love Is The Message.................................... | 85 | Phil. Int. 3547 |
| | | | **MFSB featuring THE THREE DEGREES** | | |
| 9/28/74 | 4 | 20 | 10● **When Will I See You Again** ...................... | 2 | Phil. Int. 3550 |

**411**

| DEBUT DATE | PEAK POS | WKS CHR | ARTIST — Record Title | POP POS | Label & Number |
|---|---|---|---|---|---|
| | | | **THE THREE DEGREES — Continued** | | |
| 3/08/75 | 18 | 12 | 11  I Didn't Know .................................... | | Phil. Int. 3561 |
| 6/28/75 | 64 | 7 | 12  Take Good Care Of Yourself ........................ | | Phil. Int. 3568 |
| 11/25/78+ | 39 | 12 | 13  Giving Up, Giving In................................ | | Ariola 7721 |
| 3/03/79 | 27 | 10 | 14  Woman In Love..................................... | | Ariola 7742 |
| | | | **THREE DOG NIGHT** | | |
| | | | Los Angeles pop-rock group formed in 1968, featuring lead singers Danny Hutton, Cory Wells and Chuck Negron. | | |
| 4/24/71 | 46 | 2 | 1●Joy To The World ................................. | *1* | Dunhill 4272 |
| | | | written by Hoyt Axton | | |
| | | | **THREE FLAMES** | | |
| | | | Combo formed in New York City by Tiger George Haynes (guitar), Roy Testamark (piano) and Averill "Rill" Pollard (bass). First recorded for Gotham in 1946. Own NBC-TV show in 1949. Long stay at Bon Soir in New York to 1964. Haynes in Broadway musicals, films and TV since 1956, including show "The Wiz" from 1974-78, as the Tin Man. | | |
| 3/08/47 | 3 | 1 | 1  **Open The Door, Richard**........................[C] | *1* | Columbia 37268 |
| | | | Juke Box #13 | | |
| | | | vocal by Tiger Haynes | | |
| | | | **THREE MILLION** | | |
| 11/19/83 | 72 | 7 | 1  I've Been Robbed ............................... | | Cotillion 99812 |
| | | | **3 OUNCES OF LOVE** | | |
| 5/13/78 | 87 | 4 | 1  Star Love................................... | | Motown 1439 |
| | | | **JOHNNY THUNDER** | | |
| | | | Singer from Leesburg, Florida. Discovered by producer Teddy Vann. | | |
| 1/19/63 | 6 | 9 | 1  **Loop De Loop** ................................. | *4* | Diamond 129 |
| 3/18/67 | 13 | 8 | 2  Make Love To Me ............................... | *96* | Diamond 218 |
| | | | **JOHNNY THUNDER & RUBY WINTERS** | | |
| | | | revival of Jo Stafford's 1954 pop hit (POS 1) | | |
| | | | **MARGO THUNDER** | | |
| 8/10/74 | 72 | 7 | 1  The Soul Of A Woman ........................... | | Haven 7001 |
| 12/21/74+ | 25 | 12 | 2  Expressway To Your Heart...................... | | Haven 7008 |
| | | | **THUNDERFLASH** | | |
| 5/14/83 | 46 | 10 | 1  Not A Day Too Soon ........................... | | Jampower 005 |
| | | | **BOBBY THURSTON** | | |
| | | | Vocalist/percussionist. Own band, Spectrum Ltd. Worked for US State Department. | | |
| 3/08/80 | 78 | 10 | 1  You Got What It Takes......................... | | Prelude 8009 |
| | | | **ANDREW TIBBS** | | |
| | | | Chicago-based blues singer. Recorded with brother Kenneth as the Tibbs Brothers for Atco in 1956. | | |
| 1/22/49 | 13 | 1 | 1  I Feel Like Cryin' ............................ | | Aristocrat 1103 |
| | | | Juke Box #13 | | |
| | | | with Tom Archia's All-Stars | | |
| | | | **TIERRA** | | |
| | | | Formed in Los Angeles in 1972 by brothers Rudy (guitar) & Steve (trombone, timbales) Salas. Both had been in El Chicano. Included Bobby Navarrete (reeds), Joey Guerra (keyboards), Steve Falomir (bass), Philip Madayag (drums) and Andre Baeza (percussion). | | |
| 11/22/80+ | 9 | 24 | 1  **Together**................................. | *18* | Boardwalk 5702 |
| 8/01/81 | 51 | 8 | 2  Gonna Find Her ............................... | | Boardwalk 112 |
| 10/24/81 | 33 | 10 | 3  La La Means I Love You ....................... | *72* | Boardwalk 129 |
| 9/18/82 | 61 | 6 | 4  Hidden Tears................................. | | Boardwalk 152 |
| | | | **TIJUANA BRASS - see HERB ALPERT** | | |
| | | | **JOHNNY TILLOTSON** | | |
| | | | Born on 4/20/39 in Jacksonville, Florida; raised in Palatka, Florida. On local radio "Young Folks Revue" from age 9; own band in high school. Deejay on WWPF. Appeared on the "Toby Dowdy" TV show in Jacksonville, then own show. Signed by Cadence Records in 1958. In the film "Just For Fun". | | |
| 11/21/60 | 27 | 2 | 1  Poetry In Motion .............................. | *2* | Cadence 1384 |
| 5/26/62 | 6 | 12 | 2  **It Keeps Right On A-Hurtin'** ....................... | *3* | Cadence 1418 |

| DEBUT DATE | PEAK POS | WKS CHR | ARTIST — Record Title | POP POS | Label & Number |
|---|---|---|---|---|---|
| | | | **THE TIME** | | |
| | | | Funk group formed in Minneapolis by Prince in 1981. Original lineup: Morris Day (lead singer), Terry Lewis, Jimmy "Jam" Harris, Monte Moir, Jesse Johnson and Jellybean Johnson. Disbanded in 1984. Day and Jesse Johnson went solo; Lewis and Harris became a highly successful songwriting/producing team. | | |
| 8/15/81 | **6** | 19 | 1 **Get It Up** ........................................... | | Warner 49774 |
| 11/28/81+ | **7** | 18 | 2 **Cool (Part 1)**................................... | 90 | Warner 49864 |
| 4/17/82 | **49** | 9 | 3 Girl/ | | |
| | | 9 | 4 The Stick.......................................... | | Warner 50039 |
| 8/21/82 | **2³** | 19 | 5 **777-9311** ......................................... | 88 | Warner 29952 |
| 11/20/82 | **24** | 11 | 6 The Walk........................................... | 104 | Warner 29856 |
| 3/12/83 | **77** | 4 | 7 Gigolos Get Lonely Too ....................... | | Warner 29764 |
| 6/30/84 | **11** | 15 | 8 Ice Cream Castles ............................... | 106 | Warner 29247 |
| 9/22/84 | **6** | 17 | 9 **Jungle Love** .................................... | 20 | Warner 29181 |
| 1/19/85 | **33** | 11 | 10 The Bird............................................ | 36 | Warner 29094 |
| | | | above 2: from the film "Purple Rain" | | |
| | | | **TIMEX SOCIAL CLUB** | | |
| | | | Berkeley, California rap group led by vocalist Michael Marshall; produced by Jay King, who later formed and fronted Club Nouveau. | | |
| 4/26/86 | **1²** | 24 | 1 **Rumors**............................................ | 8 | Jay 7001 |
| 12/27/86+ | **15** | 18 | 2 Thinkin' About Ya............................... | | Danya 975 |
| 5/23/87 | **15** | 15 | 3 Mixed Up World ................................. | | Danya 980 |
| | | | **GEORGE TINDLEY** | | |
| | | | Vocalist/producer from Philadelphia. In group, the Dreams, recorded for Savoy in 1954. With Steve Gibson's Red Caps from 1959-60. Formed own Modern Red Caps in 1962. | | |
| 8/16/69 | **35** | 3 | 1 Ain't That Peculiar............................. | | Wand 11205 |
| 3/14/70 | **45** | 4 | 2 Wan-Tu-Wah-Zuree............................ | | Wand 11215 |
| | | | **TKA** | | |
| | | | New York Spanish Harlem quintet. TKA: Total Knowledge In Action. Reduced to a trio in 1987. Included: Anthony "Tony" Ortiz, Louis "Kayel" Sharpe and Ralph "Aby" Cruz. | | |
| 4/05/86 | **56** | 10 | 1 One Way Love .................................... | 75 | Tommy Boy 866 |
| 2/13/88 | **63** | 8 | 2 Tears May Fall.................................... | | Tommy Boy 907 |
| | | | **T-K-O'S** | | |
| 2/26/66 | **18** | 9 | 1 The Fat Man.................................... | | Ten Star 104 |
| | | | **TMP BAND** | | |
| 7/19/86 | **49** | 10 | 1 Ring Ring ........................................ | | Critique 8515 |
| | | | **TNT BAND** | | |
| 1/25/69 | **32** | 5 | 1 The Meditation ................................. | 117 | Cotique 136 |
| | | | **ART & DOTTY TODD** | | |
| | | | Pop duo consisting of Arthur W. Todd (b: 3/11/20) and Dotty Todd (b: 6/22/23), both from Elizabeth, New Jersey. Married in 1941. | | |
| 5/12/58 | **9** | 6 | 1 **Chanson d'Amour (Song Of Love)**.................. | 6 | Era 1064 |
| | | | Jockey #9 / Best Seller #16 | | |
| | | | **THE TOKENS** | | |
| | | | Vocal group originally formed as the Linc-Tones at Lincoln High School in Brooklyn in 1955. Consisted of Hank Medress, Neil Sedaka, Eddie Rabkin and Cynthia Zolitin. First recorded for Melba in 1956. Medress re-formed The Tokens with brothers Phil & Mitch Margo, and Jay Siegel; recorded for Warwick in 1960. Formed own label, B.T. Puppy in 1964. | | |
| 1/06/62 | **7** | 7 | 1●The Lion Sleeps Tonight.................... | 1 | RCA 7954 |
| | | | also known as "Wimoweh" - a South African Zulu song | | |
| | | | **ISRAEL "Popper Stopper" TOLBERT** | | |
| 10/24/70 | **13** | 11 | 1 Big Leg Woman (With A Short Short Mini Skirt).. | 61 | Warren 106 |
| | | | **TOM & JERRIO** | | |
| | | | Dance duo of Robert "Tommy Dark" Tharp and Jerry "Jerry-O" Murray. Tharp was a baritone in the Ideals vocal group from 1952-65. | | |
| 4/24/65 | **11** | 11 | 1 Boo-Ga-Loo ...................................... | 47 | ABC-Para. 10638 |
| | | | **TOM TOM CLUB** | | |
| | | | Studio project headed by Chris Frantz and wife Tina Weymouth of Talking Heads. | | |
| 1/23/82 | **2²** | 17 | 1 **Genius Of Love** ............................. | 31 | Sire 49882 |

| DEBUT DATE | PEAK POS | WKS CHR | ARTIST — Record Title | POP POS | Label & Number |
|---|---|---|---|---|---|
| | | | **TOMORROW'S EDITION** | | |
| 2/13/82 | 48 | 9 | 1 U Turn Me On .................................................. | | Atlantic 4010 |
| 9/11/82 | 70 | 6 | 2 In The Grooves ............................................... | | Atlantic 89995 |
| | | | **TOMORROW'S PROMISE** | | |
| 10/20/73 | 31 | 15 | 1 You're Sweet, You're Fine, You're Everything .... | | Capitol 3695 |
| 4/20/74 | 59 | 9 | 2 That's The Way It Will Stay ........................... | | Capitol 3855 |
| 10/18/75 | 83 | 5 | 3 You're Everything Good To Me ....................... | | Mercury 73700 |
| | | | **GARY TOMS EMPIRE** | | |
| | | | Group from New York City, formed in 1973. Consisted of Gary Toms (keyboards), Helen Jacobs (vocals), Rick Kenny (guitar), Eric Oliver (trumpet), Les Rose (sax), John Freeman (bass), Rick Murray (drums) and Warren Tesoro (percussion). | | |
| 5/31/75 | **5** | 16 | 1 **7-6-5-4-3-2-1 (Blow Your Whistle)** ............... | 46 | Pickwick I. 6504 |
| 11/08/75 | 32 | 10 | 2 Drive My Car ................................................. | 69 | Pickwick I. 6509 |
| 4/03/76 | 47 | 7 | 3 Love Me Right ............................................... | | Pickwick I. 6517 |
| 9/18/76 | 53 | 7 | 4 Stand Up And Shout ...................................... | 109 | Pickwick I. 6524 |
| 10/21/78 | 78 | 6 | 5 Welcome To Harlem ....................................... | | Mercury 74023 |
| | | | **TONES** | | |
| | | | Baltimore trio; made cameo appearance in the 1982 film "Diner". | | |
| 10/22/83 | 72 | 8 | 1 One More Time .............................................. | | Criminal 1702 |
| | | | **OSCAR TONEY, JR.** | | |
| | | | Born on 5/26/39 in Selma, Alabama; raised in Columbus, Georgia. Own gospel group, Sensational Melodies Of Joy, while in high school. Own group, the Searchers, first recorded for Max in 1957. Recorded solo for King in 1958. Oscar's three sisters sang as the Tonettes. | | |
| 5/27/67 | **4** | 13 | 1 **For Your Precious Love** ............................... | 23 | Bell 672 |
| 9/02/67 | 37 | 5 | 2 Turn On Your Love Light ................................ | 65 | Bell 681 |
| 2/17/68 | 47 | 2 | 3 Without Love (There Is Nothing) ..................... | 90 | Bell 699 |
| | | | **TONY & CAROL** | | |
| 4/29/72 | 43 | 5 | 1 You And I ..................................................... | | Roulette 7123 |
| | | | **TONY! TONI! TONE!** | | |
| | | | R&B/funk trio from Oakland, California: brothers Dwayne & Raphael Wiggins with cousin Timothy Christian. | | |
| 4/16/88 | **1**[1] | 15 | 1 **Little Walter** ............................................... | 47 | Wing 887385 |
| | | | **TOP SHELF** | | |
| 7/11/70 | 42 | 2 | 1 Give It Up .................................................... | | LoLo 2304 |
| 7/26/80 | 98 | 2 | 2 Love Is Gone ................................................. | | Sound Trek 10541 |
| | | | **TORNADER** | | |
| | | | Duo from the Caribbean, consisting of Larry Alexander and Sandy Torano. | | |
| 5/28/77 | 52 | 8 | 1 Back Up (Hit It Again) ................................... | | Polydor 14389 |
| | | | **THE TORNADOES** | | |
| | | | English surf-rock instrumental quintet organized by producer Joe Meek in 1962. Original lineup: Alan Caddy (lead guitar), George Bellamy, Roger LaVerne Jackson, Heinz Burt and Clem Cattini. Meek committed suicide on 2/3/67. | | |
| 12/22/62+ | **5** | 7 | 1 **Telstar** ............................................... [I] | 1 | London 9561 |
| | | | **MITCHELL TOROK** | | |
| | | | Born on 10/28/29 in Houston. Singer/songwriter/guitarist. | | |
| 9/07/59 | 26 | 2 | 1 Caribbean .................................................... | 27 | Guyden 2018 |
| | | | same version charted in 1953 (POS 26-Pop) on Abbott 140 | | |
| | | | **GEORGE TORRENCE & THE NATURALS** | | |
| 3/30/68 | 40 | 2 | 1 (Mama Come Quick, And Bring Your) Lickin' Stick ........................................................ | 91 | Shout 224 |
| | | | **PETER TOSH** | | |
| | | | Born Winston Hubert MacIntosh on 10/9/44 in Jamaica. Former member of Bob Marley's Wailers. Fatally shot on 9/11/87 (42), during a robbery of his home in Kingston. | | |
| 6/13/81 | 43 | 11 | 1 Nothing But Love ........................................... | | EMI America 8083 |
| | | | **TOTAL CONTRAST** | | |
| | | | British techno-soul group. | | |
| 11/30/85 | 80 | 4 | 1 Takes A Little Time........................................ | | London 882070 |
| 3/15/86 | 88 | 4 | 2 The River ..................................................... | | London 886032 |

| DEBUT DATE | PEAK POS | WKS CHR | ARTIST — Record Title | POP POS | Label & Number |
|---|---|---|---|---|---|
| | | | **TOTAL CONTRAST — Continued** | | |
| 5/24/86 | 64 | 9 | 3 What You Gonna Do About It ......................... | | London 886051 |
| 12/05/87+ | 55 | 9 | 4 Kiss............................................................. | | London 886215 |
| | | | **TOTO** | | |
| | | | Pop-rock group formed in Los Angeles in 1978. Consists of prominent session musicians. Lead vocals by Bobby Kimball. | | |
| 6/09/79 | 18 | 13 | 1 Georgy Porgy.............................................. | 48 | Columbia 10944 |
| | | | **TOUCH** | | |
| 7/02/77 | 99 | 2 | 1 Energizer.................................................... | | Brunswick 55538 |
| | | | **TOUCH** | | |
| 5/16/87 | 48 | 11 | 1 Without You................................................. | | Supertronics 017 |
| | | | **TOUCH OF CLASS** | | |
| | | | Group consisting of Peter and Gerald Jackson, Herbert Brevard and Michael Hailstock. | | |
| 11/08/75 | 65 | 10 | 1 I'm In Heaven - Part 1 ................................... | | Midland I. 10393 |
| 3/06/76 | 85 | 3 | 2 Don't Want No Other Lover ............................ | | Midland I. 10545 |
| 5/07/77 | 45 | 8 | 3 You Got To Know Better ............................... | | Midsong Int. 10754 |
| 8/11/79 | 62 | 6 | 4 I Need Action .............................................. | | Roadshow 11663 |
| | | | **TOWER OF POWER** | | |
| | | | Group from Oakland, California, formed in 1967 as the Motowns. Consisted of Greg Adams (trumpet), Mic Gillette (trombone), Steve "Funky Doctor" Kupka, Emilio "Mimi" Castillo and Lenny Pickett (saxophones), Chester Thompson (keyboards) and Francis "Rocco" Prestia (bass). Vocalists included Rufus Miller, Lenny Williams and Edward McGhee. | | |
| 8/26/72 | 24 | 8 | 1 You're Still A Young Man ............................... | 29 | Warner 7612 |
| 6/16/73 | 11 | 13 | 2 So Very Hard To Go..................................... | 17 | Warner 7687 |
| 9/08/73 | 27 | 11 | 3 This Time It's Real ...................................... | 65 | Warner 7733 |
| 12/08/73+ | 39 | 16 | 4 What Is Hip?............................................... | 91 | Warner 7748 |
| 4/27/74 | 27 | 13 | 5 Time Will Tell .............................................. | 69 | Warner 7796 |
| 7/20/74 | 22 | 12 | 6 Don't Change Horses (In The Middle Of A Stream)..................................................... | 26 | Warner 7828 |
| 1/18/75 | 85 | 6 | 7 Only So Much Oil In The Ground..................... | 102 | Warner 8055 |
| 4/19/75 | 77 | 6 | 8 Willing To Learn .......................................... | | Warner 8083 |
| 9/06/75 | 57 | 8 | 9 You're So Wonderful, So Marvelous ................. | | Warner 8121 |
| 10/09/76 | 62 | 9 | 10 You Ought To Be Havin' Fun ........................... | 68 | Columbia 10409 |
| 1/15/77 | 95 | 4 | 11 Ain't Nothin' Stoppin' Us Now ........................ | | Columbia 10461 |
| 5/13/78 | 98 | 2 | 12 Lovin' You Is Gonna See Me Thru ................... | 106 | Columbia 10718 |
| 8/18/79 | 61 | 9 | 13 Rock Baby ................................................. | | Columbia 11012 |
| | | | **CAROL LYNN TOWNES** | | |
| 7/21/84 | 22 | 12 | 1 99 1/2.......................................................<br>from the film "Breakin" | 77 | Polydor 881008 |
| 3/02/85 | 65 | 6 | 2 Believe In The Beat ..................................... <br>from the film "Breakin' 2 Electric Boogaloo" | 109 | Polydor 881413 |
| | | | **EDDIE TOWNS** | | |
| 2/15/86 | 18 | 15 | 1 Best Friends................................................ | | Total Exp. 2433 |
| 10/04/86 | 69 | 7 | 2 Magic In The Air (All Around You Everywhere)...<br>shown only as: **ET** | | Total Exp. 2442 |
| | | | **ED TOWNSEND** | | |
| | | | Born on 4/16/29 in Fayetteville, Tennessee. With Horace Heidt, and Far East tour in the early 50s. Own production and publishing company since the mid-50s. | | |
| 4/28/58 | 7 | 15 | 1 **For Your Love** .......................................... <br>Jockey #7 / Best Seller #10<br>with the Gerald Wilson Orchestra | 13 | Capitol 3926 |
| | | | **THE TOYS** | | |
| | | | Trio from Woodrow Wilson High School, Jamaica, New York: Barbara Harris, June Montiero and Barbara Parritt. Appearances on "Shindig" TV show in 1965. In film "The Girl In Daddy's Bikini". | | |
| 10/23/65 | 4 | 12 | 1 ● **A Lover's Concerto** ................................... <br>adapted from Bach: Minuet In G | 2 | DynoVoice 209 |
| 7/20/68 | 43 | 2 | 2 Sealed With A Kiss...................................... | 112 | Musicor 1319 |

| DEBUT DATE | PEAK POS | WKS CHR | ARTIST — Record Title | POP POS | Label & Number |
|---|---|---|---|---|---|
| | | | **TRAMAINE** Gospel singer Tramaine Hawkins. | | |
| 9/28/85 | **7** | 18 | 1 **Fall Down (Spirit Of Love)** ............................ | | A&M 2763 |
| 2/01/86 | **26** | 13 | 2 In The Morning Time ..................................... | | A&M 2805 |
| 8/01/87 | **56** | 8 | 3 The Rock.................................................... | | A&M 2956 |
| | | | **THE TRAMMPS** Philadelphia disco group. Recorded in 1965 as the Volcanos (led by Gene Faith, who later went solo). Also known as the Moods. Consisted of Earl Young (lead bass voice, drums), Jimmy Ellis (lead tenor), Dennis Harris (guitar), Ron Kersey (keyboards), John Hart (organ), Stanley Wade (bass) and Michael Thompson (drums). Own label, Golden Fleece, in 1973. Later vocal lineup: Ellis (lead), Harold and Stanley Wade (tenors), Robert Upchurch (baritone) and Young (bass). | | |
| 7/01/72 | **17** | 12 | 1 Zing Went The Strings Of My Heart ................... revival of Judy Garland's 1943 pop hit (POS 22) | 64 | Buddah 306 |
| 2/24/73 | **34** | 6 | 2 Pray All You Sinners ..................................... | | Buddah 339 |
| 12/29/73+ | **75** | 8 | 3 Love Epidemic............................................. | | Golden Fl. 3251 |
| 5/18/74 | **44** | 10 | 4 Where Do We Go From Here.............................. | | Golden Fl. 3253 |
| 11/23/74 | **72** | 7 | 5 Trusting Heart............................................. | 101 | Golden Fl. 3255 |
| 9/06/75 | **70** | 7 | 6 Hooked For Life............................................ | | Atlantic 3286 |
| 12/13/75+ | **10** | 14 | 7 **Hold Back The Night**.................................... | 35 | Buddah 507 |
| 4/10/76 | **12** | 16 | 8 That's Where The Happy People Go.................... | 27 | Atlantic 3306 |
| 8/28/76 | **67** | 7 | 9 Soul Searchin' Time ...................................... | | Atlantic 3345 |
| 11/27/76 | **76** | 7 | 10 Ninety-Nine And A Half ................................. | 105 | Atlantic 3365 |
| 3/05/77 | **9** | 15 | 11 **Disco Inferno**............................................. from the film "Saturday Night Fever" | 11 | Atlantic 3389 |
| 7/02/77 | **52** | 8 | 12 I Feel Like I've Been Livin' (On The Dark Side Of The Moon) ................................................ | 105 | Atlantic 3403 |
| 12/10/77+ | **80** | 9 | 13 The Night The Lights Went Out ....................... | 104 | Atlantic 3442 |
| 8/05/78 | **50** | 9 | 14 Seasons For Girls.......................................... | | Atlantic 3460 |
| 12/23/78+ | **91** | 4 | 15 Soul Bones................................................... | | Atlantic 3537 |
| | | | **TRAMPS** | | |
| 2/26/83 | **79** | 5 | 1 Up On The Hill............................................. | | Venture 5024 |
| | | | **TRAVIS & BOB** Travis Pritchett and Bob Weaver from Jackson, Alabama. | | |
| 4/27/59 | **21** | 4 | 1 Tell Him No.................................................. | 8 | Sandy 1017 |
| | | | **McKINLEY TRAVIS** | | |
| 6/27/70 | **31** | 6 | 1 Baby, Is There Something On Your Mind .......... | 91 | Pride 2 |
| | | | **TREASURES** | | |
| 12/04/76 | **99** | 2 | 1 You Ain't Playin' With No Toy........................ | | Mercury 73838 |
| | | | **TRENIERS** Family combo built around twins Claude and Clifford from Mobile, Alabama. With Jimmie Lunceford from 1944-45. As Trenier Twins, recorded for Mercury from 1947-50. Added brothers Buddy and Milt in 1951. Appeared in the films "Don't Knock The Rock", "The Girl Can't Help It" and "Calypso Heat Wave". Stunning, raucous stage show anticipated rock 'n' roll in the early 50s. | | |
| 9/01/51 | **10** | 1 | 1 Go Go Go ................................................... Juke Box #10 also released on Epic 9127 | | Okeh 6804 |
| | | | **TRIBE** Group formed in Los Angeles in 1974. Consisted of Edward Romias (guitar), Earl Foster (keyboards), Robert Apodaca (bass), Donald Eubank (percussion) and Benton Miles Little (drums). Produced by Difosco Ervin (Big Dee Irwin). | | |
| 7/28/73 | **56** | 10 | 1 Koke (Part 1)............................................... | | ABC 11366 |
| 3/23/74 | **50** | 8 | 2 Tribe......................................................... | | ABC 11409 |
| | | | **TRINERE** | | |
| 6/08/85 | **68** | 9 | 1 All Night..................................................... | | Jam Pack. 104 |
| 2/22/86 | **32** | 16 | 2 I'll Be All You Ever Need ............................... | | Jam Pack. 20001 |
| 8/02/86 | **69** | 8 | 3 How Can We Be Wrong.................................. | | Jam Pack. 20003 |
| 11/22/86 | **69** | 8 | 4 I Know You Love Me...................................... | | Jam Pack. 20004 |
| 2/28/87 | **67** | 10 | 5 They're Playing Our Song ............................... | | Jam Pack. 2007 |

| DEBUT DATE | PEAK POS | WKS CHR | ARTIST — Record Title | POP POS | Label & Number |
|---|---|---|---|---|---|
| | | | **TRIPLE "S" CONNECTION** Chicago trio, recorded as Livin' Proof in 1977. Included twin brothers Steven and Sterling Rice, with Stan Sheppard (formed the Skool Boyz in 1981). | | |
| 2/09/80 | **60** | 8 | 1 Singing A Song About You .............................. | | 20th Century 2440 |
| | | | **TROOP** | | |
| 5/28/88 | **2**¹ | 18 | 1 **Mamacita**.................................................. | | Atlantic 89078 |
| | | | **TROUBLE** | | |
| 5/17/80 | **72** | 4 | 1 E-Flat Boogie................................................ | | Al & K. 1001 |
| | | | **TROUBLE FUNK** | | |
| 5/08/82 | **63** | 6 | 1 Hey Fellas................................................... | | Sugar Hill 575 |
| 5/28/83 | **77** | 6 | 2 Trouble Funk Express.................................. | | D.E.T.T. 1001 |
| 10/19/85 | **80** | 5 | 3 Still Smokin' .............................................. | | Island 99613 |
| 7/26/86 | **66** | 9 | 4 Good To Go ................................................ above 2: from the film "Good To Go" | | Island 99538 |
| | | | **TONY TROUTMAN** From Hamilton, Ohio; member of the family group, Zapp. | | |
| 5/17/75 | **82** | 7 | 1 I Truly Love You.......................................... | | Gram-O. 457118 |
| 6/12/82 | **57** | 14 | 2 Your Man Is Home Tonight ........................... | | T. Main 200 |
| | | | **BENNY TROY** | | |
| 3/22/75 | **57** | 9 | 1 I've Always Had You...................................... | | De-Lite 1566 |
| | | | **DORIS TROY** Born Doris Payne on 1/6/37 in New York City. Vocalist/songwriter. Backing vocalist on Pink Floyd's album "Dark Side Of The Moon". | | |
| 6/22/63 | **3** | 14 | 1 **Just One Look**.............................................. featuring Horace Ott on piano | *10* | Atlantic 2188 |
| | | | **TRUCKIN' COMPANY - see GARNET MIMMS** | | |
| | | | **TRUE LOVE** Real name: Terrance Reed. Raised in Trenton, New Jersey. | | |
| 12/12/87+ | **63** | 10 | 1 Love Rap Ballad............................................ | | Critique 96731 |
| | | | **ANDREA TRUE CONNECTION** Disco act led by white Nashville-born vocalist Andrea True. Andrea moved to New York in 1968 and wrote commercials for radio and TV. Her break came while singing at the Riverboat in the Empire State Building, 1974. | | |
| 2/14/76 | **23** | 16 | 1 ●More, More, More (Pt. 1).............................. | *4* | Buddah 515 |
| 8/21/76 | **95** | 1 | 2 Party Line ................................................. | *80* | Buddah 538 |
| | | | **THE TRUMPETEERS** Gospel group formed in Baltimore in 1946. Consisted of Joseph Johnson (lead), Raleigh Tunrage (tenor), Joseph Armstrong (baritone) and James Keels (bass). Johnson had been in the Royal Lights Juniors, Willing Four, and Golden Gate Quartet. On CBS radio from 1947. Group remained active with personnel changes, until the death of Johnson in 1984. | | |
| 5/29/48 | **8** | 3 | 1 **Milky White Way** ...................................... Juke Box #8 / Best Seller #10 | | Score 5001 |
| | | | **TRUSSEL** Band from Petersburg, Virginia, named for a railroad trestle. Formed in 1972; first called the Snackshop Band. Consisted of Michael "Chicken" Gray, William "Maggie" McGhee, Hannon B. "Juicy" Lane, Lenwood Jones, Michael Spratley, Ronald "Bunky" Smith and Larry O. "Tiger" Tynes. Worked as back-up for Evelyn King in 1979. | | |
| 1/05/80 | **23** | 16 | 1 Love Injection.............................................. | | Elektra 46560 |
| 5/31/80 | **86** | 2 | 2 Big City Rocker ........................................... | | Elektra 46627 |
| 7/19/80 | **61** | 6 | 3 I Love It ..................................................... | | Elektra 46664 |
| | | | **THE TRUTH** Duo of Larry Hancock and Leo Green. Discovered by the O'Jays. | | |
| 8/16/80 | **47** | 9 | 1 Coming Home ............................................... | | Devaki 4001 |
| 12/27/80+ | **51** | 11 | 2 Understanding.............................................. | | Devaki 4002 |
| 9/05/81 | **80** | 5 | 3 It's Gonna Take A Miracle ............................. | | Devaki 4003 |
| | | | **THE TRUTH** | | |
| 12/07/74+ | **74** | 7 | 1 I Can't Go On .............................................. | | Roulette 7160 |

| DEBUT DATE | PEAK POS | WKS CHR | ARTIST — Record Title | POP POS | Label & Number |
|---|---|---|---|---|---|
| | | | **THE T.S.U. TORONADOES** | | |
| | | | Band from Texas State University; recorded in Houston. | | |
| 1/25/69 | 34 | 5 | 1 Getting The Corners ...................................... | 75 | Atlantic 2579 |
| | | | **TTF** | | |
| | | | Group from Homestead, Florida, formed by Willie Brown, Jr. (organ), Brett Brown (bass) and Alton Hudson (drums). Added Tony Gonzales (trumpet), Tony Izquierdo (saxophone), Andrew Most (guitar) and Deborah Peevy (vocals). Ages ranged from 15 to 19. Name means Today, Tomorrow, Forever. | | |
| 1/05/80 | 78 | 3 | 1 It's A Groove (Keep On Dancin')........................ | | RSO 1010 |
| 6/07/80 | 21 | 18 | 2 (Baby) I Can't Get Over Losing You................... | | RSO 1035 |
| 8/08/81 | 50 | 9 | 3 Mighty Fine............................................... | | Gold Coast 1100 |
| | | | **JUNIOR TUCKER** | | |
| | | | 16-year-old Jamaican. | | |
| 6/04/83 | 61 | 7 | 1 Bad Girls .................................................. | | Geffen 29627 |
| | | | written by Ray Parker, Jr. | | |
| | | | **TOMMY TUCKER** | | |
| | | | Born Robert Higginbotham on 3/5/39 in Springfield, Ohio. Vocalist/pianist. First recorded for Hi in 1959. Died of poisoning on 1/22/82. | | |
| 2/08/64 | 11 | 11 | 1 Hi-Heel Sneakers......................................... | *Hot* | Checker 1067 |
| 5/16/64 | 96 | 2 | 2 Long Tall Shorty......................................... | *Hot* | Checker 1075 |
| | | | above 2: produced by Herb Abramson | | |
| | | | **THE TUNE WEAVERS** | | |
| | | | Group from Woburn, Massachusetts, formed in 1956. Consisted of Margo Sylvia (lead), husband John Sylvia, Gilbert Lopez (Margo's brother) and Charlotte Davis (Margo's cousin). | | |
| 9/16/57 | 4 | 11 | 1 **Happy, Happy Birthday Baby**...................... | 5 | Checker 872 |
| | | | Best Seller #4 / Jockey #4 | | |
| | | | with Frank Paul's Orchestra; originally on Casa Grande 4037 | | |
| | | | **THE TURBANS** | | |
| | | | Philadelphia quartet: Al Banks (lead), Matthew Platt (tenor), Charles Williams (baritone) and Andrew "Chet" Jones (bass). Disbanded in 1961. | | |
| 11/26/55 | 3 | 8 | 1 **When You Dance**....................................... | 33 | Herald 458 |
| | | | Juke Box #3 / Jockey #10 / Best Seller #12 | | |
| | | | **IKE & TINA TURNER**     ★★105★★ | | |
| | | | Husband and wife duo: guitarist Ike Turner (b: 11/5/31 in Clarksdale, MS) and vocalist Tina (born Anna Mae Bullock on 11/26/38 in Brownsville, TN). Married from 1958-76. At age 11, Ike was backing pianist for bluesmen Sonny Boy Williamson (Aleck Ford) and Robert Nighthawk (of the Nighthawks). Formed own band, the Kings of Rhythm, while in high school. They backed Jackie Brenston's hit "Rocket '88'". Prolific session, production and guitar work during the 1950s. In 1960, developed a dynamic stage show around Tina; "The Ike & Tina Turner Revue" featured her backing vocalists, The Ikettes, and Ike's Kings Of Rhythm. Disbanded in 1974. In in the mid-80s, Tina emerged as a highly successful solo artist. Also see B.B. King. | | |
| 8/01/60 | 2$^1$ | 21 | 1 **A Fool In Love**........................................... | 27 | Sue 730 |
| 12/19/60+ | 5 | 9 | 2 **I Idolize You** ............................................ | 82 | Sue 735 |
| 7/24/61 | 2$^2$ | 21 | 3 **It's Gonna Work Out Fine**.......................... | 14 | Sue 749 |
| 12/25/61+ | 4 | 12 | 4 **Poor Fool** ................................................ | 38 | Sue 753 |
| 3/31/62 | 9 | 10 | 5 **Tra La La La La** ........................................ | 50 | Sue 757 |
| 10/03/64 | 95 | 3 | 6 I Can't Believe What You Say (For Seeing What You Do)............................................... | *Hot* | Kent 402 |
| 4/24/65 | 33 | 4 | 7 Tell Her I'm Not Home................................. | 108 | Loma 2011 |
| 6/05/65 | 32 | 4 | 8 Good Bye, So Long ..................................... | 107 | Modern 1007 |
| 5/04/68 | 50 | 2 | 9 So Fine................................................... | 117 | Innis 6667 |
| | | | **IKE & TINA & THE IKETTES** | | |
| 5/17/69 | 23 | 7 | 10 I've Been Loving You Too Long...................... | 68 | Blue Thumb 101 |
| 5/24/69 | 46 | 2 | 11 I'm Gonna Do All I Can (To Do Right By My Man) | 98 | Minit 32060 |
| 8/09/69 | 37 | 2 | 12 The Hunter ............................................. | 93 | Blue Thumb 102 |
| 12/27/69+ | 22 | 10 | 13 Bold Soul Sister........................................ | 59 | Blue Thumb 104 |
| 2/07/70 | 21 | 8 | 14 Come Together ......................................... | 57 | Minit 32087 |
| | | | **IKE & TINA TURNER & THE IKETTES** | | |
| 6/13/70 | 25 | 5 | 15 I Want To Take You Higher.......................... | 34 | Liberty 56177 |
| | | | **IKE & TINA TURNER & THE IKETTES** | | |
| 11/28/70 | 41 | 4 | 16 Workin' Together ....................................... | 105 | Liberty 56207 |
| 2/27/71 | 5 | 9 | 17●Proud Mary............................................ | 4 | Liberty 56216 |
| 5/29/71 | 31 | 6 | 18 Ooh Poo Pah Doo ...................................... | 60 | United Art. 50782 |
| 11/27/71 | 47 | 3 | 19 I'm Yours (Use Me Anyway You Wanna) ........... | 104 | United Art. 50873 |

| DEBUT DATE | PEAK POS | WKS CHR | ARTIST — Record Title | POP POS | Label & Number |
|---|---|---|---|---|---|
| | | | **IKE & TINA TURNER — Continued** | | |
| 4/01/72 | **47** | 2 | 20 Up In Heah............................................ | *83* | United Art. 50881 |
| 4/21/73 | **47** | 2 | 21 Early One Morning ................................ | | United Art. 174 |
| 8/25/73 | **11** | 15 | 22 Nutbush City Limits .............................. | *22* | United Art. 298 |
| 4/13/74 | **43** | 9 | 23 Sweet Rhode Island Red ....................... | *106* | United Art. 409 |
| | | | written by Tina | | |
| 8/17/74 | **29** | 21 | 24 Sexy Ida (Part 1) .................................. | *65* | United Art. 528 |
| 5/24/75 | **31** | 10 | 25 Baby-Get It On..................................... | *88* | United Art. 598 |
| | | | 1-2, 4-6, 13 & 25: written by Ike Turner | | |
| | | | **JOE TURNER** ★★**92**★★ | | |
| | | | Born on 5/18/11 in Kansas City, Missouri; died of a heart attack on 11/24/85. Vocalist known as "Big Joe". Early in career teamed with boogie-woogie pianist Pete Johnson. Big break came at the "Spirituals To Swing" concert, Carnegie Hall, in 1938. First recorded for Vocalion in 1938. Appeared in the film "Shake, Rattle And Rock" in 1957. Active until his death. Also see Pete Johnson. | | |
| 8/03/46 | **6** | 1 | 1 **My Gal's A Jockey** ............................... | | National 4002 |
| | | | with Bill Moore's Lucky Seven; also released on National 9106 | | |
| 3/11/50 | **9** | 1 | 2 **Still In The Dark** ................................ | | Freedom 1531 |
| | | | Juke Box #9 / Best Seller #12 | | |
| 6/30/51 | **2**⁴ | 25 | 3 **Chains Of Love**.................................... | *30* | Atlantic 939 |
| | | | Juke Box #2 / Best Seller #2 | | |
| | | | a reported million-seller | | |
| 12/15/51+ | **3** | 8 | 4 **Chill Is On** ......................................... | | Atlantic 949 |
| | | | Juke Box #3 | | |
| 4/12/52 | **3** | 8 | 5 **Sweet Sixteen**..................................... | | Atlantic 960 |
| | | | Juke Box #3 / Best Seller #4 | | |
| 8/02/52 | **5** | 6 | 6 **Don't You Cry** ..................................... | | Atlantic 970 |
| | | | Juke Box #5 | | |
| | | | above 4: with Van "Piano Man" Walls & His Orchestra | | |
| 9/19/53 | **1**⁸ | 25 | 7 **Honey Hush** ........................................ | *23* | Atlantic 1001 |
| | | | Juke Box #1 / Best Seller #2 | | |
| | | | a different version was released in 1959 on Atlantic 2044, hit POS 53 on the pop charts; a reported million-seller | | |
| 1/23/54 | **6** | 7 | 8 **TV Mama** ............................................ | | Atlantic 1016 |
| | | | Juke Box #6 / Best Seller #9 | | |
| | | | with Fats Domino (piano) & Pluma Davis' Orchestra | | |
| 5/08/54 | **1**³ | 32 | 9 **Shake, Rattle, And Roll**....................... | *22* | Atlantic 1026 |
| | | | Juke Box #1 / Best Seller #2 / Jockey #15 | | |
| 11/06/54 | **9** | 3 | 10 **Well All Right** ..................................... | | Atlantic 1040 |
| | | | Juke Box #9 | | |
| 3/19/55 | **2**¹ | 15 | 11 **Flip Flop And Fly** ............................... | | Atlantic 1053 |
| | | | Jockey #2 / Juke Box #2 / Best Seller #3 | | |
| 8/27/55 | **3** | 12 | 12 **Hide And Seek**.................................... | | Atlantic 1069 |
| | | | Jockey #3 / Juke Box #3 / Best Seller #11 | | |
| 1/07/56 | **8** | 5 | 13 **Morning, Noon And Night/** | | |
| | | | Jockey #8 | | |
| | | | above 7: with His Blues Kings | | |
| 1/14/56 | **7** | 4 | 14 **The Chicken And The Hawk (Up, Up And Away)**........................................ | | Atlantic 1080 |
| | | | Juke Box #7 / Jockey #13 / Best Seller #13 | | |
| 4/21/56 | **2**² | 12 | 15 **Corrine Corrina/** | *41* | |
| | | | Juke Box #2 / Best Seller #3 / Jockey #4 | | |
| | | 1 | 16 Boogie Woogie Country Girl ................. | | Atlantic 1088 |
| | | | Juke Box flip | | |
| 9/01/56 | **12** | 2 | 17 Rock A While/ | | |
| | | | Best Seller #12 | | |
| 9/22/56 | **8** | 2 | 18 **Lipstick Powder And Paint**................. | | Atlantic 1100 |
| | | | Juke Box #8 | | |
| | | | 15 & 18: with The Cookies (vocals) | | |
| 9/09/57 | **12** | 3 | 19 Love Roller Coaster .............................. | | Atlantic 1146 |
| | | | Jockey #12 | | |
| | | | with Choker Campbell & His Orchestra | | |
| 5/26/58 | **15** | 1 | 20 (I'm Gonna) Jump For Joy ..................... | | Atlantic 1184 |
| | | | Jockey #15 | | |
| | | | with Howard Biggs' Orchestra | | |
| | | | **RUBY TURNER - see JONATHAN BUTLER** | | |

| DEBUT DATE | PEAK POS | WKS CHR | ARTIST — Record Title | POP POS | Label & Number |
|---|---|---|---|---|---|
| | | | **SAMMY TURNER** Born Samuel Black on 6/2/32 in Paterson, New Jersey. Served in USAF Airborne during Korean War. Worked as an accountant in New Jersey. Joined the Twisters as lead tenor, recorded with them for Big Top, then went solo. Recorded for Motown, 20th Century Fox, and Verve in the mid-60s. | | |
| 7/27/59 | **14** | 10 | 1 Lavender-Blue ............................... old traditional folk song from England, 1750 | 3 | Big Top 3016 |
| 11/09/59 | **2**¹ | 14 | 2 **Always** ............................... 4 versions of this song hit the Top 10 in 1926 | 19 | Big Top 3029 |
| 3/21/60 | **13** | 3 | 3 Paradise ............................... all of above: produced by Jerry Leiber & Mike Stoller | 46 | Big Top 3032 |
| | | | **SPYDER TURNER** Born Dwight D. Turner in 1947 in Beckley, West Virginia. Moved to Detroit in the late 50s. Formed vocal group, the Nonchalants, in high school. Went solo in 1966. | | |
| 12/24/66+ | **3** | 15 | 1 **Stand By Me** ............................... [N] vocal impressions of Jackie Wilson, David Ruffin, Billy Stewart, Smokey Robinson and Chuck Jackson | 12 | MGM 13617 |
| | | | **TINA TURNER** Born Anna Mae Bullock on 11/26/38 in Brownsville, Tennessee. Vocalist/actress. In successful recording duo with husband Ike Turner, from 1958-74; divorced in 1976. The Ikettes were her female backing group. In the films "Tommy" (1975) and "Mad Max Beyond Thunderdome" (1985). | | |
| 11/08/75 | **61** | 7 | 1 Whole Lotta Love ............................... Led Zeppelin's version charted in 1969 (POS 4-Pop) | | United Art. 724 |
| 1/28/84 | **3** | 17 | 2 **Let's Stay Together** ............................... | 26 | Capitol 5322 |
| 6/02/84 | **2**⁵ | 24 | 3● **What's Love Got To Do With It** ............... | 1 | Capitol 5354 |
| 9/22/84 | **6** | 17 | 4 **Better Be Good To Me** ............................... | 5 | Capitol 5387 |
| 1/19/85 | **3** | 17 | 5 **Private Dancer** ............................... | 7 | Capitol 5433 |
| 5/04/85 | **50** | 9 | 6 Show Some Respect ............................... | 37 | Capitol 5461 |
| 7/13/85 | **3** | 15 | 7 **We Don't Need Another Hero (Thunderdome)** .. | 2 | Capitol 5491 |
| 10/19/85 | **41** | 8 | 8 One Of The Living ............................... above 2: from the film "Mad Max Beyond Thunderdome" | 15 | Capitol 5518 |
| 8/30/86 | **3** | 14 | 9 **Typical Male** ............................... | 2 | Capitol 5615 |
| 11/29/86+ | **18** | 13 | 10 Two People ............................... | 30 | Capitol 5644 |
| | | | **TITUS TURNER** Born on 5/11/33 in Atlanta. Singer/songwriter. Wrote "That'll Be The Day", "Hey, Doll Baby", "Stagger Lee" and "All Around The World". First recorded for Okeh in 1951. Now deceased. | | |
| 4/13/59 | **29** | 1 | 1 Return Of Stagolee ............................... with Hal Singer (sax) & Mickey Baker (guitar) | | King 5186 |
| | | | **STANLEY TURRENTINE** Born in 1934 in Pittsburgh. Tenor saxophonist. Married for a time to Shirley Scott. | | |
| 11/27/76+ | **68** | 8 | 1 You'll Never Find Another Love Like Mine...... [I] | | Fantasy 782 |
| 10/13/79 | **50** | 8 | 2 Concentrate On You ............................... [I] | | Elektra 46533 |
| 9/26/81 | **79** | 3 | 3 Havin' Fun With Mr. T. ............................... [I] | | Elektra 47156 |
| | | | **TWENNYNINE with LENNY WHITE** New York band led by Lenny White (former drummer of the jazz-rock band, Return To Forever). Included Donald Blackman, Denzil Miller, Eddie Martinez, Nick Moroch and Barry Johnson. Vocals by Carla Vaughan and Jocelyn Smith. White recorded solo in 1980. | | |
| 10/27/79+ | **3** | 22 | 1 **Peanut Butter** ............................... | 83 | Elektra 46552 |
| 9/27/80 | **19** | 18 | 2 Kid Stuff ............................... | 106 | Elektra 47043 |
| 1/10/81 | **25** | 14 | 3 Fancy Dancer ............................... | | Elektra 47087 |
| 10/10/81 | **62** | 9 | 4 All I Want ............................... | | Elektra 47208 |
| | | | **THE 21st CENTURY** Chicago group formed in 1970. Consisted of Fred Williams, Alphonso Smith, Tyrone Moores, Pierre Johnson and Alonzo Martin. First recorded for Golden Tone in 1974. Signed to Motown in 1976, changed name to 21st Creation. | | |
| 3/22/75 | **69** | 13 | 1 Remember The Rain? ............................... | 100 | RCA 10201 |
| 8/30/75 | **71** | 7 | 2 Child ............................... | | RCA 10364 |
| | | | **TWILIGHT 22** A dance-rap production led by New York synthesizer player Gordon Bahary (b: 1960). Worked with Harry Chapin in 1975, and with Stevie Wonder from 1976. | | |
| 11/05/83+ | **7** | 20 | 1 **Electric Kingdom** ............................... | 79 | Vanguard 35241 |
| 5/19/84 | **56** | 10 | 2 Siberian Nights ............................... | | Vanguard 35246 |
| 10/27/84 | **59** | 3 | 3 Street Love ............................... | | Vanguard 35250 |

| DEBUT DATE | PEAK POS | WKS CHR | ARTIST — Record Title | POP POS | Label & Number |
|---|---|---|---|---|---|
| | | | **TWIN IMAGE** | | |
| 4/13/85 | 84 | 4 | 1 My Baby Loves Me (Do Do) .............................. | | Capitol 5460 |
| | | | **CONWAY TWITTY** | | |
| | | | Pop-country singer/actor born Harold Jenkins on 9/1/33 in Friars Point, Mississippi; raised in Helena, Arkansas. First recorded for Mercury in 1957. Offered a professional career with the Philadelphia Phillies when drafted into the Army. Owns a tourist complex, Twitty City, in Hendersonville, Tennessee. | | |
| 10/13/58 | 12 | 9 | 1 It's Only Make Believe................................... | *1* | MGM 12677 |
| | | | Best Seller #12 | | |
| 11/09/59 | 18 | 8 | 2 Danny Boy .............................................. | *10* | MGM 12826 |
| | | | based on the traditional Irish song "Londonderry Air" of 1855 | | |
| 3/14/60 | 27 | 2 | 3 Lonely Blue Boy ........................................ | *6* | MGM 12857 |
| | | | **THE 2 LIVE CREW** | | |
| | | | Rap quartet: Fresh Kid-Ice, Brother Marquis, Treach DJ Mr. Mixx & Luke Skyywalker. | | |
| 5/21/88 | 53 | 10 | 1 Move Somethin' ........................................ | | Luke Sky. 112 |
| | | | **TWO TONS O' FUN** | | |
| | | | Duo of Martha Wash and Izora Rhodes. Did back-up for Sylvester. Later recorded as The Weather Girls. | | |
| 4/19/80 | 29 | 11 | 1 Just Us/ | | |
| | | 7 | 2 I Got The Feeling ...................................... | | Honey 888 |
| 8/16/80 | 53 | 7 | 3 Taking Away Your Space............................... | | Honey 896 |
| 1/31/81 | 55 | 8 | 4 Never Like This ........................................ | | Honey 906 |
| | | | shown only as: **TWO TONS** | | |
| | | | **THE TYMES** | | |
| | | | Group formed in Philadelphia in 1956. Consisted of George Williams (lead singer), George Hilliard, Donald Banks, Albert Berry and Norman Burnett. First called the Latineers. Berry and Hilliard were replaced by female singers Terri Gonzalez and Melanie Moore in the early 70s. | | |
| 6/29/63 | 4 | 10 | 1 **So Much In Love** ......................................... | *1* | Parkway 871 |
| 10/05/63 | 23 | 2 | 2 Wonderful! Wonderful! ................................. | *7* | Parkway 884 |
| 12/07/63+ | 19 | 11 | 3 Somewhere .............................................. | *Hot* | Parkway 891 |
| 11/23/68 | 33 | 6 | 4 People.................................................... | *39* | Columbia 44630 |
| | | | from the film "Funny Girl" | | |
| 8/17/74 | 20 | 14 | 5 You Little Trustmaker .................................. | *12* | RCA 10022 |
| 12/28/74+ | 75 | 6 | 6 Ms. Grace ............................................... | *91* | RCA 10128 |
| 2/21/76 | 3 | 18 | 7 **It's Cool**................................................ | *68* | RCA 10561 |
| | | | **TYZIK** | | |
| | | | Jazz trumpeter/flugelhornist, Jeff Tyzik. | | |
| 6/23/84 | 46 | 11 | 1 Jammin' In Manhattan..............................[I] | | Polydor 821795 |

# U

| DEBUT DATE | PEAK POS | WKS CHR | ARTIST — Record Title | POP POS | Label & Number |
|---|---|---|---|---|---|
| | | | **ULLANDA** | | |
| | | | Female disco singer Ullanda McCullough. | | |
| 7/14/79 | 65 | 7 | 1 Want Ads/ | | |
| 10/13/79 | 84 | 4 | 2 Around And Around ................................. | | Ocean 7500 |
| | | | **UNCLE LOUIE** | | |
| | | | Band led by brothers Eddie Dillard (guitar) and Frank Dillard (bass). | | |
| 6/30/79 | 19 | 17 | 1 Full Tilt Boogie (Pt. 1) ............................... | | Marlin 3335 |
| | | | **VERONICA UNDERWOOD** | | |
| 8/17/85 | 61 | 9 | 1 Victim Of Desire........................................ | | Philly W. 99632 |
| | | | **THE UNDISPUTED TRUTH** | | |
| | | | Group consisting of Joe Harris, Billie Calvin and Brenda Evans. Personnel changed in 1973 to Harris, Tyrone Berkeley, Tyrone Douglas, Calvin Stevens and Virginia McDonald. Drummer Carl Smalls later a member of Sweat Band. Taka Boom replaced Douglas and McDonald in 1976. | | |
| 3/20/71 | 43 | 2 | 1 Save My Love For A Rainy Day ...................... | | Gordy 7106 |
| 6/26/71 | 2³ | 17 | 2 **Smiling Faces Sometimes** ........................... | *3* | Gordy 7108 |
| 12/18/71+ | 24 | 6 | 3 You Make Your Own Heaven And Hell Right Here On Earth ..................................... | *72* | Gordy 7112 |
| 3/04/72 | 35 | 4 | 4 What It Is ............................................... | *71* | Gordy 7114 |

| DEBUT DATE | PEAK POS | WKS CHR | ARTIST — Record Title | POP POS | Label & Number |
|---|---|---|---|---|---|
| | | | **THE UNDISPUTED TRUTH — Continued** | | |
| 6/17/72 | **24** | 6 | 5 Papa Was A Rollin' Stone ............................... | 63 | Gordy 7117 |
| 11/25/72 | **43** | 5 | 6 Girl You're Alright ......................................... | 107 | Gordy 7122 |
| 4/21/73 | **46** | 2 | 7 Mama I Got A Brand New Thing (Don't Say No) ... | 109 | Gordy 7124 |
| 7/14/73 | **40** | 7 | 8 Law Of The Land ......................................... | | Gordy 7130 |
| 3/23/74 | **19** | 16 | 9 Help Yourself ............................................. | 63 | Gordy 7134 |
| 7/27/74 | **39** | 13 | 10 I'm A Fool For You...................................... | | Gordy 7139 |
| 5/10/75 | **62** | 8 | 11 UFO'S ...................................................... | | Gordy 7143 |
| 9/20/75 | **77** | 7 | 12 Higher Than High.......................................... | | Gordy 7145 |
| 8/07/76 | **37** | 13 | 13 You + Me = Love............................................ | 48 | Whitfield 8231 |
| 12/18/76+ | **68** | 9 | 14 Let's Go Down To The Disco ........................... | | Whitfield 8295 |
| | | | above 2: also released together on a 12″ single (#8306) of which #14 was shown as the "B" side on pop charts | | |
| 4/14/79 | **55** | 10 | 15 Show Time - Part 1 ..................................... | | Whitfield 8781 |
| | | | **THE UNIFICS** | | |
| | | | Group formed at Howard University in Washington, DC. Consisted of Al Johnson (b: 1948, Newport News, VA; lead), Michel Ward & Greg Cook (tenors) and Harold Worthington (baritone). Ward and Worthington left in early 1970, replaced by Marvin Brown and Tom Fauntleroy. | | |
| 9/21/68 | **3** | 13 | 1 **Court Of Love**.............................................. | 25 | Kapp 935 |
| 12/14/68+ | **9** | 13 | 2 **The Beginning Of My End** ............................ | 36 | Kapp 957 |
| 4/12/69 | **27** | 7 | 3 It's A Groovy World! ..................................... | 97 | Kapp 985 |
| 8/09/69 | **36** | 3 | 4 Toshisumasu.............................................. | | Kapp 2026 |
| | | | all of above: written & produced by Guy Draper | | |
| | | | **UNIQUE** | | |
| 9/10/83 | **78** | 5 | 1 What I Got Is What You Need .......................... | | Prelude 8077 |
| | | | **UNIVERSAL ROBOT BAND** | | |
| | | | New York-based integrated disco sextet. | | |
| 4/09/77 | **48** | 16 | 1 Dance And Shake Your Tambourine ................. | 93 | Red Greg 207 |
| | | | **UNLIMITED TOUCH** | | |
| | | | 6-piece group from Brooklyn, with 4 male musicians and 2 female vocalists. | | |
| 1/17/81 | **33** | 12 | 1 I Hear Music In The Streets............................. | | Prelude 8023 |
| 5/23/81 | **29** | 15 | 2 Searching To Find The One............................. | | Prelude 8029 |
| | | | **USA for AFRICA** | | |
| | | | USA: United Support of Artists - a collection of 46 major artists formed to help the suffering people of Africa and the U.S.A. | | |
| 3/30/85 | **1** ² | 14 | 1▲We Are The World........................... | 1 | Columbia 04839 |
| | | | soloists (in order): Lionel Richie, Stevie Wonder, Paul Simon, Kenny Rogers, James Ingram, Tina Turner, Michael Jackson, Diana Ross, Dionne Warwick, Willie Nelson, Al Jarreau, Bruce Springsteen, Kenny Loggins, Steve Perry, Daryl Hall, Huey Lewis, Cyndi Lauper, Kim Carnes, Bob Dylan, and Ray Charles - written by Michael Jackson & Lionel Richie | | |
| | | | **UTFO** | | |
| | | | Brooklyn rap-break trio: The Kangol Kid, Doctor Ice, and The Educated Rapper. Also see Roxanne. | | |
| 1/05/85 | **10** | 17 | 1 **Roxanne, Roxanne/** | 77 | |
| | | | also released on Select 62254 | | |
| 2/23/85 | **44** | 10 | 2 The Real Roxanne.................................... | | Select 1182 |
| | | | **ROXANNE with UTFO** | | |
| 6/15/85 | **32** | 13 | 3 Leader Of The Pack .................................... | | Select 62259 |
| 9/28/85 | **79** | 5 | 4 Bite It ...................................................... | | Select 62263 |
| 12/21/85+ | **36** | 13 | 5 Fairytale Lover ........................................... | | Select 1186 |
| 10/18/86 | **50** | 9 | 6 Split Personality ......................................... | | Select 1190 |
| 8/22/87 | **43** | 16 | 7 Ya Cold Wanna Be With Me............................ | | MCA 62293 |

| DEBUT DATE | PEAK POS | WKS CHR | ARTIST — Record Title | POP POS | Label & Number |
|---|---|---|---|---|---|

# V

### RITCHIE VALENS
Born Richard Valenzuela on 5/13/41 in Pacoima, California. Latin rock and roll singer/songwriter/guitarist. Killed in the plane crash that also took the lives of Buddy Holly and the Big Bopper on 2/3/59. In the film "Go Johnny Go". The 1987 film "La Bamba" was based on his life.

| | | | | | |
|---|---|---|---|---|---|
| 11/10/58 | 27 | 1 | 1 Come On, Let's Go | 42 | Del-Fi 4106 |
| 2/02/59 | 11 | 10 | 2 Donna | 2 | Del-Fi 4110 |

above 2: written by Valens

### JOHN VALENTI
Blue-eyed soul singer from Chicago.

| | | | | | |
|---|---|---|---|---|---|
| 8/14/76 | 10 | 14 | 1 Anything You Want | 37 | Ariola Am. 7625 |

### DAVE VALENTIN
Jazz/Latin flutist from the South Bronx. Professional debut at age 12. Attended the High School of Music and Art in New York City.

| | | | | | |
|---|---|---|---|---|---|
| 11/08/80 | 82 | 4 | 1 Sidra's Dream [I] | | Arista/GRP 2508 |

### THE VALENTINE BROTHERS
John and Billy Valentine from Columbus, Ohio. Billy had been with Young-Holt Unlimited. Worked in the chorus of the touring company of the musical "The Wiz".

| | | | | | |
|---|---|---|---|---|---|
| 4/24/82 | 41 | 14 | 1 Money's Too Tight | | Bridge 1982 |
| 11/06/82 | 43 | 12 | 2 Let Me Be Close To You | | Bridge 1984 |
| 6/30/84 | 28 | 13 | 3 Lonely Nights | | A&M 2647 |

### LEZLI VALENTINE
Female vocalist from New Jersey. First worked as a secretary-receptionist at All-Platinum Records.

| | | | | | |
|---|---|---|---|---|---|
| 8/31/68 | 42 | 5 | 1 I Won't Do Anything | | All Platinum 2305 |

## VALENTINO - see TEEN DREAM

### THE VALENTINOS
Cleveland family group. Originated as the Womack Brothers gospel group. Consisted of Bobby Womack, with his brothers Cecil, Curtis, Friendly Jr. and Harris. First recorded on Sam Cooke's label in 1962.

| | | | | | |
|---|---|---|---|---|---|
| 7/28/62 | 8 | 13 | 1 Lookin' For A Love | 72 | Sar 132 |
| 6/27/64 | 94 | 2 | 2 It's All Over Now | Hot | Sar 152 |

### FRANKIE VALLI
Born Francis Castelluccio on 5/3/37 in Newark, New Jersey. Recorded his first solo single in 1953 as Frank Valley on the Corona label. Formed own group, the Variatones in 1955, and changed their name to the Four Lovers in 1956, which evolved into The 4 Seasons by 1961. Began solo work in 1965.

| | | | | | |
|---|---|---|---|---|---|
| 5/31/75 | 31 | 14 | 1 Swearin' To God | 6 | Private S. 45021 |
| 8/12/78 | 40 | 7 | 2▲Grease | 1 | RSO 897 |

from the film of the same title

### VAN & TITUS

| | | | | | |
|---|---|---|---|---|---|
| 7/27/68 | 41 | 3 | 1 Cry Baby Cry | | Elf 90016 |

### THE VAN DYKES
Vocal trio formed in Fort Worth, Texas in 1964. Consisted of Rondalis Tandy (lead), Wenzon Mosley (tenor) and James May (baritone). First recorded for Hue in 1965. Group disbanded in 1968.

| | | | | | |
|---|---|---|---|---|---|
| 3/12/66 | 24 | 6 | 1 No Man Is An Island | 94 | Mala 520 |
| 7/16/66 | 28 | 6 | 2 I've Got To Go On Without You | 109 | Mala 530 |
| 10/22/66 | 25 | 6 | 3 Never Let Me Go | | Mala 539 |
| 1/07/67 | 24 | 5 | 4 You Need Confidence | | Mala 549 |

### VAN HALEN
Rock band formed in Pasadena in 1974: brothers Eddie & Alex Van Halen, with Michael Anthony and lead singer David Lee Roth (replaced by Sammy Hagar in 1985).

| | | | | | |
|---|---|---|---|---|---|
| 4/07/84 | 88 | 3 | 1●Jump | 1 | Warner 29384 |

| DEBUT DATE | PEAK POS | WKS CHR | ARTIST — Record Title | POP POS | Label & Number |
|---|---|---|---|---|---|
| | | | **LUTHER VANDROSS** ★★85★★ | | |
| | | | Born on 4/20/51 in New York City. Singer/producer/songwriter. Commercial jingle singer, then a top session vocalist/arranger. Member of the studio group Roundtree in 1978. | | |
| | | | **LUTHER:** | | |
| 5/08/76 | **28** | 10 | 1 It's Good For The Soul - Pt. I ........................... | *102* | Cotillion 44200 |
| 9/25/76 | **34** | 12 | 2 Funky Music (Is A Part Of Me)/ | | |
| | | 12 | 3 The 2nd Time Around ............................... | | Cotillion 44205 |
| 4/23/77 | **93** | 4 | 4 This Close To You ..................................... | | Cotillion 44216 |
| | | | **LUTHER VANDROSS:** | | |
| 8/08/81 | **1** ² | 21 | 5 **Never Too Much**.................................... | *33* | Epic 02409 |
| 12/19/81+ | **10** | 15 | 6 **Don't You Know That?** ......................... | *107* | Epic 02658 |
| 4/17/82 | **72** | 6 | 7 Sugar And Spice (I Found Me A Girl) ................ | | Epic 02842 |
| 9/04/82 | **4** | 16 | 8 **If This World Were Mine** ..................... | *101* | Columbia 03204 |
| | | | **CHERYL LYNN & LUTHER VANDROSS** | | |
| 9/18/82 | **3** | 20 | 9 **Bad Boy/Having A Party** ..................... | *55* | Epic 03205 |
| 1/08/83 | **17** | 15 | 10 Since I Lost My Baby ............................. | | Epic 03487 |
| 4/16/83 | **72** | 6 | 11 Promise Me ....................................... | | Epic 03804 |
| 10/08/83 | **7** | 16 | 12 **How Many Times Can We Say Goodbye**.......... | *27* | Arista 9073 |
| | | | **DIONNE WARWICK & LUTHER VANDROSS** | | |
| 11/26/83+ | **9** | 18 | 13 **I'll Let You Slide** .......................... | *102* | Epic 04231 |
| 3/03/84 | **5** | 18 | 14 **Superstar/Until You Come Back To Me (That's What I'm Gonna Do)**.................... | *87* | Epic 04969 |
| | | | available only as a 12″ single | | |
| 6/16/84 | **48** | 9 | 15 Make Me A Believer ............................. | | Epic 04494 |
| 2/16/85 | **4** | 18 | 16 **'Til My Baby Comes Home**.................... | *29* | Epic 04760 |
| 6/15/85 | **4** | 16 | 17 **It's Over Now** ............................... | *101* | Epic 04944 |
| 10/05/85 | **11** | 14 | 18 Wait For Love.................................... | | Epic 05610 |
| 1/25/86 | **59** | 8 | 19 If Only For One Night ......................... | | Epic 05751 |
| 6/28/86 | **3** | 21 | 20 **Give Me The Reason** ......................... | *57* | Epic 06129 |
| | | | from the film "Ruthless People" | | |
| 11/08/86+ | **1** ² | 19 | 21 **Stop To Love** ................................ | *15* | Epic 06523 |
| 3/07/87 | **1** ¹ | 17 | 22 **There's Nothing Better Than Love**.............. | *50* | Epic 06978 |
| | | | **LUTHER VANDROSS with GREGORY HINES** | | |
| 6/13/87 | **6** | 14 | 23 **I Really Didn't Mean It** ..................... | | Epic 07201 |
| 10/10/87 | **94** | 5 | 24 So Amazing........................................ | | Epic 07434 |
| | | | **THE VANGUARDS** | | |
| 11/29/69 | **49** | 3 | 1 Somebody Please ................................. | | Whiz 612 |
| 5/16/70 | **33** | 9 | 2 It's Too Late For Love........................... | | Lamp 652 |
| | | | **VANITY** | | |
| | | | Real name: Denise Matthews, from Toronto, Canada. Former model and actress. Lead singer of Vanity 6 (assembled by Prince). Starred in the films "52 Pick-Up" (1986) and "Action Jackson" (1987). | | |
| 9/08/84 | **15** | 14 | 1 Pretty Mess..................................... | *75* | Motown 1752 |
| 12/01/84+ | **23** | 13 | 2 Mechanical Emotion ............................ | *107* | Motown 1767 |
| 3/15/86 | **9** | 14 | 3 **Under The Influence** ........................ | *56* | Motown 1833 |
| | | | **VANITY 6** | | |
| | | | Trio formed as back-up for Prince. Consisted of Denise Matthews, Susan Moonsie and Brenda Bennett. Matthews recorded solo as Vanity. | | |
| 9/25/82 | **7** | 18 | 1 **Nasty Girl**.................................... | *101* | Warner 29908 |
| | | | **GINO VANNELLI** | | |
| | | | Born on 6/16/52 in Montreal, Canada. Pop/soul-styled singer/songwriter. | | |
| 9/16/78 | **21** | 17 | 1 I Just Wanna Stop.............................. | *4* | A&M 2072 |
| 2/17/79 | **91** | 4 | 2 Wheels Of Life ................................. | *78* | A&M 2114 |
| 4/11/81 | **45** | 9 | 3 Living Inside Myself............................ | *6* | Arista 0588 |
| | | | **SARAH VAUGHAN** | | |
| | | | Born on 3/27/24 in Newark, New Jersey. Jazz singer. Studied piano from 1931-39. Won amateur contest at the Apollo Theater in 1942, which led to her joining Earl Hines' band as vocalist and second pianist. First recorded solo for Continental in 1944. With Billy Eckstine from 1944-45. Married manager/trumpet player George Treadwell in 1947. Dubbed "The Divine One". Still active in the 80s. | | |
| 8/31/59 | **5** | 11 | 1 **Broken-Hearted Melody**............................. | *7* | Mercury 71477 |
| | | | with the Ray Ellis Orchestra | | |

| DEBUT DATE | PEAK POS | WKS CHR | ARTIST — Record Title | POP POS | Label & Number |
|---|---|---|---|---|---|
| | | | **SARAH VAUGHAN — Continued** | | |
| 11/16/59 | 8 | 9 | 2 **Smooth Operator** ....................................... | *44* | Mercury 71519 |
| | | | with the Belford Hendricks Orchestra | | |
| 3/09/74 | 80 | 4 | 3 I Need You More ....................................... | | Mainstream 5553 |
| | | | **BOBBY VEE** | | |
| | | | Pop singer/actor born Robert Velline on 4/30/43 in Fargo, North Dakota. In 1959, formed own band, The Shadows, which filled in for Buddy Holly's scheduled show after Holly's death in a plane crash. | | |
| 10/24/60 | 22 | 5 | 1 Devil Or Angel ....................................... | *6* | Liberty 55270 |
| 1/05/63 | 8 | 9 | 2 **The Night Has A Thousand Eyes** .................. | *3* | Liberty 55521 |
| | | | **TATA VEGA** | | |
| | | | Born Carmen Rosa Vega on 10/7/51 in Queens, New York. Also see Lou Rawls. | | |
| 10/09/76 | 90 | 5 | 1 Full Speed Ahead ....................................... | | Tamla 54271 |
| 5/26/79 | 58 | 7 | 2 I Just Keep Thinking About You Baby ............. | | Tamla 54299 |
| | | | **THE VELVELETTES** | | |
| | | | Female group formed at Western Michigan State University in the early 60s. Consisted of sisters Millie and Carol "Cal" Gill, cousins Bertha & Norma Barbee and Betty Kelly. First recorded for I.P.G. Records in 1963. Kelly left to join the Vandellas, 1964-67. | | |
| 10/17/64 | 45 | 8 | 1 Needle In A Haystack................................... | *Hot* | V.I.P. 25007 |
| 1/30/65 | 21 | 8 | 2 He Was Really Sayin' Somethin' ...................... | *64* | V.I.P. 25013 |
| 10/01/66 | 43 | 3 | 3 These Things Will Keep Me Loving You............ | *102* | Soul 32025 |
| | | | **CHARLIE VENTURA** | | |
| | | | Born Charles Venturo on 12/2/16 in Philadelphia. Saxophonist/leader. With Gene Krupa from 1942-46. Own band in 1946. Active into the 80s in New England. | | |
| 3/26/49 | 13 | 1 | 1 Lullaby In Rhythm ....................................... | | Victor 20-3346 |
| | | | Juke Box #13 | | |
| | | | vocals by Jackie Cain & Roy Kral; also issued on 45 rpm (#47-2891) | | |
| | | | **THE VENTURES** | | |
| | | | Guitar-based instrumental rock and roll band formed in the Seattle/Tacoma area. Original lineup: Nokie Edwards, Bob Bogle, Don Wilson and Howie Johnson. | | |
| 8/29/60 | 13 | 7 | 1 Walk--Don't Run ....................................... [I] | *2* | Dolton 25 |
| | | | **BILLY VERA** | | |
| | | | Born William McCord, Jr. on 5/28/44 in Riverside, California. Raised in Westchester County, New York. Wrote hit songs for many pop, R&B and country artists. Formed The Beaters in Los Angeles in 1979, an R&B-based, 10-piece band. | | |
| 12/09/67+ | 20 | 8 | 1 Storybook Children ................................... | *54* | Atlantic 2445 |
| | | | **BILLY VERA & JUDY CLAY** | | |
| 3/02/68 | 41 | 4 | 2 Country Girl-City Man................................... | *36* | Atlantic 2480 |
| | | | **BILLY VERA & JUDY CLAY** | | |
| | | | above 2: with The Sweet Inspirations | | |
| 1/24/87 | 70 | 8 | 3 At This Moment ....................................... | *1* | Rhino 74403 |
| | | | **BILLY VERA & THE BEATERS** | | |
| | | | popularized through play on TV's "Family Ties"; originally released in 1981 on Alfa 7005 | | |
| | | | **LARRY VERNE** | | |
| | | | Born on 2/8/36 in Minneapolis. | | |
| 10/03/60 | 9 | 5 | 1 **Mr. Custer** ....................................... [N] | *1* | Era 3024 |
| | | | **THE VIBRATIONS** | | |
| | | | Group from Los Angeles, originally recorded as The Jayhawks. Consisted of James Johnson, Carl Fisher, Richard Owens, Dave Govan and Don Bradley. Also recorded as The Marathons. Owens joined The Temptations for a short time in 1971. | | |
| 3/13/61 | 13 | 5 | 1 The Watusi ............................................... | *25* | Checker 969 |
| 6/05/61 | 25 | 3 | 2 Peanut Butter........................................... | *20* | Arvee 5027 |
| | | | **THE MARATHONS** | | |
| 3/28/64 | 26 | 9 | 3 My Girl Sloopy........................................... | *Hot* | Atlantic 2221 |
| 10/30/65 | 26 | 9 | 4 Misty ....................................................... | *63* | Okeh 7230 |
| 11/19/66 | 47 | 2 | 5 And I Love Her ........................................... | *118* | Okeh 7257 |
| 4/22/67 | 39 | 6 | 6 Pick Me ................................................... | | Okeh 7276 |
| 5/04/68 | 38 | 2 | 7 Love In Them There Hills ............................. | *93* | Okeh 7311 |
| | | | **VICKY "D"** | | |
| 2/06/82 | 64 | 8 | 1 This Beat Is Mine ....................................... | | Sam 5024 |

| DEBUT DATE | PEAK POS | WKS CHR | ARTIST — Record Title | POP POS | Label & Number |
|---|---|---|---|---|---|
| | | | **VIDEEO** <br> Memphis-based duo: Tom Jones III (lead singer) and David Weatherspoon, Jr. | | |
| 6/05/82 | **50** | 14 | 1 Thang (Gimme Some Of That Thang)................ | | H.C.R.C. 71474 |
| 11/13/82 | **91** | 3 | 2 Closet Freak.................................................. | | H.C.R.C. 03258 |
| | | | **VILLAGE PEOPLE** <br> New York campy disco group: Victor Willis, Randy Jones, David Hodo, Felipe Rose, Glenn Hughes and Alexander Briley. In the film "Can't Stop The Music", in 1980. | | |
| 11/04/78+ | **32** | 16 | 1▲Y.M.C.A.................................................. | *2* | Casablanca 945 |
| 3/24/79 | **30** | 12 | 2●In The Navy ............................................... | *3* | Casablanca 973 |
| | | | **THE VILLAGE SOUL CHOIR** | | |
| 1/31/70 | **27** | 14 | 1 The Cat Walk ........................................... | *55* | Abbott 2010 |
| | | | **THE VILLAGE STOMPERS** <br> Greenwich Village, New York dixieland-styled band. | | |
| 10/26/63 | **22** | 4 | 1 Washington Square .................................. [I] | *2* | Epic 9617 |
| | | | **VIN-ZEE** <br> Born Vincent "Vinzarelli" Brown in Manhattan. Star roller skater, appeared in the film "Get Rollin'". | | |
| 7/04/81 | **44** | 11 | 1 Funky Bcbop................................................. | | Emergency 4512 |
| | | | **GENE VINCENT & His Blue Caps** <br> Born Vincent Eugene Craddock on 2/11/35 in Norfolk, Virginia; died from an ulcer hemorrhage on 10/12/71. Innovative rock and roll singer/songwriter/guitarist. Formed own band, The Bluecaps, in 1956. Injured in car accident that killed Eddie Cochran in England in 1960. | | |
| 7/28/56 | **8** | 2 | 1 **Be-Bop-A-Lula**....................................... <br> Juke Box #8 / Jockey #11 | *7* | Capitol 3450 |
| 9/30/57 | **7** | 5 | 2 **Lotta Lovin'**......................................... <br> Best Seller #7 / Jockey #9 | *13* | Capitol 3763 |
| 12/23/57+ | **8** | 5 | 3 **Dance To The Bop**................................. <br> Jockey #8 | *23* | Capitol 3839 |
| | | | **EDDIE VINSON** <br> Blues-jazz bandleader/alto saxophonist/vocalist, born on 12/19/17 in Houston. Nicknamed "Cleanhead". With Lil Green and Bill Broonzy in 1941. Moved to New York in 1942. First recorded for Okeh in 1942, with Cootie Williams. With Williams until 1945, then own band. Several overseas tours from 1968-78. Died of a heart attack on 7/2/88 (70). Also see Cootie Williams. | | |
| 3/15/47 | **1**[2] | 23 | 1 **Ole Maid Boogie/** | | |
| 5/10/47 | **5** | 1 | 2 **Kidney Stew Blues**................................. | | Mercury 8028 |
| 11/19/49 | **6** | 2 | 3 **Somebody Done Stole My Cherry Red**............. <br> Juke Box #6 | | King 4313 |
| | | | **BOBBY VINTON** <br> Born Stanley Robert Vinton on 4/16/35 in Canonsburg, Pennsylvania. Father was a bandleader. Formed own band while in high school; toured as backing band for Dick Clark's "Caravan of Stars" in 1960. Left band for a singing career in 1962. Own TV series from 1975-78. | | |
| 6/30/62 | **5** | 13 | 1●**Roses Are Red (My Love)**............................ | *1* | Epic 9509 |
| | | | **THE VIRTUES** <br> Philadelphia rock instrumental trio led by Frank ("Virtue") Virtuoso, who later operated a successful recording studio in Philadelphia, from 1962. | | |
| 4/27/59 | **27** | 4 | 1 Guitar Boogie Shuffle................................ [I] | *5* | Hunt 324 |
| | | | **THE VISCOUNTS** <br> New Jersey instrumental quintet: Harry Haller (tenor saxophone), Bobby Spievak (guitar), Larry Vecchio (organ), Joe Spievak (bass) and Clark Smith (drums). | | |
| 3/14/60 | **17** | 4 | 1 Harlem Nocturne....................................... [I] | *52* | Madison 123 |
| | | | **VISUAL** | | |
| 3/26/83 | **76** | 6 | 1 The Music Got Me ..................................... [I] | | Prelude 8067 |
| | | | **VITAMIN "E"** | | |
| 7/09/77 | **68** | 6 | 1 Sharing ................................................... | | Buddah 574 |

| DEBUT DATE | PEAK POS | WKS CHR | ARTIST — Record Title | POP POS | Label & Number |
|---|---|---|---|---|---|
| | | | **VOCALEERS** | | |
| | | | Vocal group formed in Harlem, New York in 1952. Consisted of Joe Duncan (lead), Herman Dunham (first tenor), William Walker (second tenor), Melvin Walton (baritone) and Teddy Williams (bass). Won Apollo talent contest. Dunham later sang lead with the Solitaires. | | |
| 5/30/53 | 4 | 6 | 1 **Is It A Dream** ............................................... | | Red Robin 114 |
| | | | Juke Box #4 / Best Seller #8 | | |
| | | | **VOICE MASTERS** | | |
| | | | Detroit group, formed in 1959. Consisted of Ty Hunter, Lamont Dozier, David Ruffin, Walter Gaines and C.P. Spencer. First recorded for Anna in 1959. Hunter and Dozier had been in the Romeos; Spencer and Gaines had been in the Five Jets. Hunter, Spencer and Gaines were members of The Originals. | | |
| 6/27/70 | 44 | 2 | 1 Dance Right Into My Heart............................ | | Bamboo 113 |
| | | | **VOICES OF EAST HARLEM** | | |
| | | | Group consisting of twenty singers, aged 12-21. Appeared at the Moratorium Concert in Madison Square Garden with Blood, Sweat And Tears, and Harry Belafonte. | | |
| 6/30/73 | 57 | 10 | 1 Giving Love................................................ | | Just Sunsh. 504 |
| | | | **VOLCANOS** | | |
| | | | Group from Philadelphia, led by Gene Faith. After Faith left group for a solo career, group became known as the Moods. With the addition of Earl Young, group became The Trammps. | | |
| 7/17/65 | 33 | 5 | 1 Storm Warning ........................................... | | Arctic 106 |
| | | | **VOLTAGE BROTHERS** | | |
| | | | Group from Rochester, New York, formed as The Destinations. Expanded to 11 members, moved to Atlanta. Lead vocals by Rudi Meeks, Richard Freeman and Douglas Knight. | | |
| 6/14/86 | 89 | 3 | 1 Love's A Criminal ...................................... | | MTM 72067 |
| 10/25/86 | 96 | 3 | 2 Insecure ................................................... | | MTM 73052 |
| | | | **THE VONTASTICS** | | |
| | | | Chicago quartet: Bobby Newsome, Kenneth Golar, Jose Holmes and Raymond Penn. Group won talent contest sponsored by WVON, named for station call letters. First recorded for Satellite in 1965. | | |
| 9/03/66 | 7 | 12 | 1 **Day Tripper** ........................................... | 100 | St. Lawrence 1014 |
| | | | **THE VOXPOPPERS** | | |
| 4/14/58 | 10 | 4 | 1 **Wishing For Your Love**............................... | 18 | Mercury 71282 |
| | | | Jockey #10 | | |
| | | | originally released on Amp-3 1004 | | |
| | | | **VOYAGE** | | |
| | | | European disco group. Sylvia Mason, lead singer. | | |
| 7/15/78 | 85 | 2 | 1 From East To West ...................................... | | Marlin 3322 |
| 2/24/79 | 73 | 5 | 2 Souvenirs .................................................. | 41 | Marlin 3330 |
| | | | **VOYEUR** | | |
| 5/18/85 | 70 | 5 | 1 Paradise.................................................... | | MCA/Camel 52563 |

# W

| DEBUT DATE | PEAK POS | WKS CHR | ARTIST — Record Title | POP POS | Label & Number |
|---|---|---|---|---|---|
| | | | **W.A.G.B.** | | |
| 5/15/82 | 81 | 4 | 1 I Can Get You Over...................................... | | Street Sounds 1 |
| | | | **ADAM WADE** | | |
| | | | Born on 3/17/37 in Pittsburgh. TV actor/host of the 1976 game show "Musical Chairs". Worked in "Guys & Dolls" musical in Las Vegas, in 1978. TV talk show host in Los Angeles, in the 80s. | | |
| 5/08/61 | 20 | 3 | 1 Take Good Care Of Her............................... | 7 | Coed 546 |
| 6/12/61 | 21 | 3 | 2 The Writing On The Wall ............................. | 5 | Coed 550 |
| 8/28/61 | 16 | 4 | 3 As If I Didn't Know..................................... | 10 | Coed 553 |
| | | | all of above: with George Paxton & His Orchestra | | |
| | | | **J.W. WADE** | | |
| 8/20/83 | 49 | 9 | 1 (You Know) It's Natural ................................ | | Larc 81026 |
| | | | **THE WAILERS** | | |
| | | | Teenage rock and roll instrumental quintet from Tacoma, Washington; formed in 1958. Consisted of John Greek, Rick Dangel, Mark Marush, Kent Morrill (lead vocals) and Mike Burk. | | |
| 7/13/59 | 24 | 1 | 1 Tall Cool One ...................................... [I] | 36 | Golden Crest 518 |

| DEBUT DATE | PEAK POS | WKS CHR | ARTIST — Record Title | POP POS | Label & Number |
|---|---|---|---|---|---|
| | | | **NARADA MICHAEL WALDEN** | | |
| | | | Born Michael Walden on 4/23/52 in Kalamazoo, Michigan. Singer/songwriter/drummer/ producer. Toured with Soul Revival. With the Mahavishnu Orchestra from 1972-76, given name Narada by guru Sri Chinmoy. Solo and much session work since 1976. | | |
| 4/23/77 | 81 | 5 | 1 Delightful .............................................. | | Atlantic 3385 |
| 2/03/79 | 9 | 20 | 2 I Don't Want Nobody Else (To Dance With You) ...... | 47 | Atlantic 3541 |
| 6/30/79 | 80 | 5 | 3 Give Your Love A Chance ............................. | | Atlantic 3580 |
| 12/01/79+ | 4 | 21 | 4 I Shoulda Loved Ya ................................. | 66 | Atlantic 3631 |
| 4/05/80 | 35 | 10 | 5 Tonight I'm Alright ................................ | | Atlantic 3655 |
| 10/04/80 | 22 | 13 | 6 The Real Thang ..................................... | | Atlantic 3764 |
| 12/20/80+ | 46 | 11 | 7 I Want You ......................................... | | Atlantic 3783 |
| 5/01/82 | 19 | 12 | 8 You're #1 .......................................... | | Atlantic 4037 |
| 8/07/82 | 39 | 9 | 9 Summer Lady ....................................... | | Atlantic 89996 |
| 4/02/83 | 40 | 12 | 10 Reach Out........................................... | | Atlantic 89858 |
| | | | new version of The Temptations' hit "Reach Out I'll Be There" | | |
| 2/16/85 | 39 | 10 | 11 Gimme, Gimme, Gimme ............................. | 106 | Warner 29077 |
| | | | **NARADA MICHAEL WALDEN with PATTI AUSTIN** | | |
| 6/01/85 | 82 | 3 | 12 The Nature Of Things................................ | | Warner 29017 |
| 4/09/88 | 21 | 13 | 13 Divine Emotions ................................... | | Reprise 27967 |
| | | | shown only as: **NARADA** from the film "Bright Lights, Big City" | | |
| | | | **WALDO** | | |
| | | | Washington, D.C. quintet. | | |
| 3/06/82 | 63 | 9 | 1 You Bring Out The Freak In Me ...................... | | Columbia 02745 |
| | | | **BOBBI WALKER** | | |
| | | | Female vocalist. | | |
| 6/28/80 | 62 | 7 | 1 Something About You ................................ | | Casablanca 2274 |
| | | | **DAVID T. WALKER** | | |
| | | | Born in Los Angeles. Guitarist/composer. With The Olympics and Midnighters. To New York City from 1961-66. Band director at Motown in Detroit. Much session work on the West Coast. | | |
| 12/06/69 | 46 | 2 | 1 My Baby Loves Me.................................... | 128 | Revue 11060 |
| 12/19/70+ | 35 | 6 | 2 Love Vibrations ..................................... | 117 | Zea 50005 |
| 10/06/73 | 95 | 4 | 3 Press On............................................ | | Ode 66037 |
| 9/11/76 | 92 | 3 | 4 I Wish You Love..................................... | | Ode 66125 |
| | | | **GLORIA WALKER** | | |
| 11/09/68 | 7 | 9 | 1 Talking About My Baby............................... | 60 | Flaming Arrow 35 |
| | | | **JR. WALKER & THE ALL STARS**   ★★68★★ | | |
| | | | Group formed in South Bend, Indiana by Walker (born Autry DeWalt II in Blythesville, Arkansas, 1942). Included Walker, sax, vocals; Willie Woods, guitar; Vic Thomas, organ; and James Graves, drums. First recorded for Harvey in 1962. Most recent group included son Autry DeWalt, Jr. on drums. | | |
| 2/13/65 | 1⁴ | 17 | 1 Shotgun. ............................................ | 4 | Soul 35008 |
| 6/19/65 | 10 | 9 | 2 Do The Boomerang.................................... | 36 | Soul 35012 |
| 8/14/65 | 7 | 13 | 3 Shake And Fingerpop/ | 29 | |
| 9/25/65 | 7 | 14 | 4 Cleo's Back ....................................[I] | 43 | Soul 35013 |
| 1/29/66 | 14 | 7 | 5 Cleo's Mood ...................................[I] | 50 | Soul 35017 |
| | | | originally released on Harvey 117 | | |
| 5/07/66 | 4 | 14 | 6 (I'm A) Road Runner................................. | 20 | Soul 35015 |
| 8/13/66 | 3 | 14 | 7 How Sweet It Is (To Be Loved By You) ........... | 18 | Soul 35024 |
| 11/26/66 | 35 | 4 | 8 Money (That's What I Want) Part 1 .................. | 52 | Soul 35026 |
| 3/04/67 | 11 | 8 | 9 Pucker Up Buttercup ............................... | 31 | Soul 35030 |
| 8/12/67 | 33 | 3 | 10 Shoot Your Shot .................................... | 44 | Soul 35036 |
| 12/09/67+ | 8 | 12 | 11 Come See About Me.................................. | 24 | Soul 35041 |
| 8/31/68 | 7 | 12 | 12 Hip City - Pt. 2.................................... | 31 | Soul 35048 |
| 2/01/69 | 19 | 5 | 13 Home Cookin........................................ | 42 | Soul 35055 |
| 5/31/69 | 1² | 16 | 14 What Does It Take (To Win Your Love).......... | 4 | Soul 35062 |
| 11/08/69 | 3 | 12 | 15 These Eyes......................................... | 16 | Soul 35067 |
| 2/28/70 | 2² | 10 | 16 Gotta Hold On To This Feeling...................... | 21 | Soul 35070 |
| 7/18/70 | 3 | 12 | 17 Do You See My Love (For You Growing) ......... | 32 | Soul 35073 |
| 1/09/71 | 33 | 4 | 18 Holly Holy/ | 75 | |
| 2/27/71 | 50 | 1 | 19 Carry Your Own Load ............................... | 117 | Soul 35081 |

| DEBUT DATE | PEAK POS | WKS CHR | ARTIST — Record Title | POP POS | Label & Number |
|---|---|---|---|---|---|
| | | | **JR. WALKER & THE ALL STARS — Continued** | | |
| 8/14/71 | 18 | 9 | 20 Take Me Girl, I'm Ready | 50 | Soul 35084 |
| 12/04/71 | 24 | 10 | 21 Way Back Home | 52 | Soul 35090 |
| 4/08/72 | 10 | 10 | 22 **Walk In The Night** [I] | 46 | Soul 35095 |
| 8/05/72 | 46 | 3 | 23 Groove Thang [I] | | Soul 35097 |
| 2/17/73 | 50 | 2 | 24 Gimme That Beat (Part 1) | 101 | Soul 35104 |
| 2/14/76 | 43 | 8 | 25 I'm So Glad | | Soul 35116 |
| 9/29/79 | 89 | 2 | 26 Wishing On A Star | | Whitfield 49052 |

## MEL WALKER - see JOHNNY OTIS and ESTHER PHILLIPS

## T-BONE WALKER
Born Aaron Thibeaux Walker on 5/28/10 in Linden, Texas. Died of pneumonia on 3/16/75. Vocalist/guitarist/pianist/violinist. Also called Oak Cliff T-Bone. Self-taught; toured with medicine shows during the mid-20s. First recorded for Columbia in 1929. With Cab Calloway, Milt Larkins and Ma Rainey from 1930-34. Moved to Los Angeles in 1934. Own band in 1940. Stage antics with guitar closely followed by early Elvis Presley. Also see Freddie Slack.

| DEBUT DATE | PEAK POS | WKS CHR | ARTIST — Record Title | POP POS | Label & Number |
|---|---|---|---|---|---|
| 1/18/47 | 3 | 2 | 1 **Bobby Sox Blues** | | Blk. & Wht. 110 |
| | | | with Jack McVea's All-Stars | | |
| 1/24/48 | 5 | 6 | 2 **Call It Stormy Monday (But Tuesday Is Just As Bad)** | | Blk. & Wht. 122 |
| | | | also on Capitol 57-70014 | | |
| 2/14/48 | 10 | 1 | 3 **Long Skirt Baby Blues** | | Blk. & Wht. 123 |
| 7/17/48 | 8 | 1 | 4 **I'm Waiting For Your Call** | | Blk. & Wht. 126 |
| | | | Juke Box #8 | | |
| 8/21/48 | 11 | 2 | 5 Midnight Blues | | Blk. & Wht. 127 |
| | | | Juke Box #11 | | |
| 10/09/48 | 8 | 4 | 6 **West Side Baby** | | Comet T- 50 |
| | | | Best Seller #8 / Juke Box #13 | | |
| 3/05/49 | 13 | 1 | 7 Description Blues | | Comet T- 52 |
| | | | Juke Box #13 | | |
| 3/19/49 | 7 | 4 | 8 **T-Bone Shuffle** | | Comet T- 53 |
| | | | Juke Box #7 / Best Seller #11 | | |
| | | | also released on Capitol 57-70042 | | |
| 2/04/50 | 15 | 1 | 9 Go Back To The One You Love | | Capitol 799 |
| | | | Juke Box #15 | | |

## WALLACE BROTHERS
Member Johnny Simon later joined the Naturals.

| DEBUT DATE | PEAK POS | WKS CHR | ARTIST — Record Title | POP POS | Label & Number |
|---|---|---|---|---|---|
| 8/29/64 | 97 | 2 | 1 Lover's Prayer | Hot | Sims 189 |

## JERRY WALLACE
Born on 12/15/28 in Kansas City, Missouri; raised in Glendale, Arizona. Pop-country singer/guitarist. First recorded for Allied in 1951. Appeared on the TV shows "Night Gallery" and "Hec Ramsey".

| DEBUT DATE | PEAK POS | WKS CHR | ARTIST — Record Title | POP POS | Label & Number |
|---|---|---|---|---|---|
| 9/29/58 | 11 | 2 | 1 How The Time Flies | 11 | Challenge 59013 |
| | | | Jockey #11 / Best Seller #17 | | |
| | | | a Cole Porter tune | | |
| 10/19/59 | 12 | 6 | 2 Primrose Lane | 8 | Challenge 59047 |
| | | | JERRY WALLACE with The Jewels | | |

## FATS WALLER
Born Thomas Waller on 5/21/04 in New York City; died on 12/15/43. Extremely gifted keyboardist/composer; recording since 1922. Appeared in the film "Stormy Weather". Wrote "Ain't Misbehavin'", "Honeysuckle Rose", and many others. The late 70's hit musical "Ain't Misbehavin'" is based on his songs.

| DEBUT DATE | PEAK POS | WKS CHR | ARTIST — Record Title | POP POS | Label & Number |
|---|---|---|---|---|---|
| 11/07/42 | 6 | 1 | 1 **Jitterbug Waltz** [I] | | Bluebird 11518 |
| | | | Waller plays electric organ; also released on Victor 20-2639 | | |

## DEXTER WANSEL
Keyboardist/producer/arranger from Philadelphia.

| DEBUT DATE | PEAK POS | WKS CHR | ARTIST — Record Title | POP POS | Label & Number |
|---|---|---|---|---|---|
| 8/14/76 | 91 | 6 | 1 Life On Mars (Part I) | | Phil. Int. 3599 |
| 6/03/78 | 87 | 5 | 2 Solutions | | Phil. Int. 3647 |
| 9/15/79 | 91 | 3 | 3 It's Been Cool | | Phil. Int. 3702 |
| 11/24/79+ | 40 | 11 | 4 The Sweetest Pain | | Phil. Int. 3724 |

| DEBUT DATE | PEAK POS | WKS CHR | ARTIST — Record Title | POP POS | Label & Number |
|---|---|---|---|---|---|
| | | | **WAR** ★★**97**★★ | | |
| | | | Band formed in Long Beach, California in 1969. Consisted of Leroy "Lonnie" Jordan (keyboards), Howard Scott (guitar), Charles Miller (saxophone; murdered in 1980), Morris "B.B." Dickerson (bass), Harold Brown & Thomas "Papa Dee" Allen (percussion) and Lee Oskar (harmonica). Eric Burdon's backup band until 1971. Dickerson was replaced by Luther Rabb. Lee Oskar recorded solo, beginning in 1976. Alice Tweed Smyth (vocals) added in 1978. Pat Rizzo (horns) and Ron Hammond (former member of Aalon; percussion) added in 1979. Smyth left group in 1982. | | |
| 4/24/71 | 38 | 3 | 1 Lonely Feelin' .................... | 107 | United Art. 50746 |
| 8/21/71 | 18 | 11 | 2 All Day Music .................... | 35 | United Art. 50815 |
| 1/15/72 | 12 | 12 | 3●Slippin' Into Darkness.................... | 16 | United Art. 50867 |
| 12/02/72+ | 3 | 15 | 4●The World Is A Ghetto .................... | 7 | United Art. 50975 |
| 3/31/73 | 5 | 8 | 5●The Cisco Kid.................... | 2 | United Art. 163 |
| 7/21/73 | 6 | 14 | 6 Gypsy Man.................... | 8 | United Art. 281 |
| 11/03/73 | 18 | 12 | 7 Me And Baby Brother .................... | 15 | United Art. 350 |
| 6/08/74 | 17 | 11 | 8 Ballero.................... [I] | 33 | United Art. 432 |
| 5/03/75 | 9 | 16 | 9●Why Can't We Be Friends?.................... | 6 | United Art. 629 |
| 9/13/75 | 1¹ | 15 | 10 Low Rider .................... | 7 | United Art. 706 |
| 7/10/76 | 4 | 14 | 11●Summer.................... | 7 | United Art. 834 |
| 6/25/77 | 2¹ | 17 | 12 L.A. Sunshine .................... | 45 | Blue Note 1009 |
| 11/19/77+ | 5 | 18 | 13 Galaxy.................... | 39 | MCA 40820 |
| 4/15/78 | 70 | 6 | 14 Hey Senorita .................... | | MCA 40883 |
| 7/01/78 | 21 | 15 | 15 Youngblood (Livin' In The Streets).................... | | United Art. 1213 |
| 10/28/78 | 87 | 3 | 16 Sing A Happy Song .................... | | United Art. 1247 |
| 3/31/79 | 12 | 16 | 17 Good, Good Feelin' .................... | 101 | MCA 40995 |
| 12/15/79+ | 32 | 13 | 18 Don't Take It Away .................... | | MCA 41158 |
| 5/03/80 | 96 | 3 | 19 I'll Be Around.................... | | MCA 41209 |
| 6/13/81 | 90 | 5 | 20 Cinco De Mayo.................... | | LAX 02120 |
| 2/27/82 | 18 | 13 | 21 You Got The Power.................... | 66 | RCA 13061 |
| 6/05/82 | 13 | 16 | 22 Outlaw .................... | 94 | RCA 13238 |
| 6/25/83 | 50 | 7 | 23 Life (Is So Strange) .................... | | RCA 13544 |
| 3/02/85 | 79 | 4 | 24 Groovin.................... | | Coco Plum 2002 |
| 2/14/87 | 98 | 3 | 25 Livin' In The Red .................... | | Priority 9502 |
| 6/20/87 | 59 | 11 | 26 Low Rider.................... new version of #10 above | | Priority 9364 |
| | | | **ANITA WARD** | | |
| | | | Born on 12/20/57 in Memphis. Professional debut at age 9, first recorded in 1971. Toured in Rust College female quartet. | | |
| 5/12/79 | 1⁵ | 18 | 1 **Ring My Bell** .................... | 1 | Juana 3422 |
| 10/13/79 | 52 | 7 | 2 Don't Drop My Love.................... above 2: written & produced by Frederick Knight | 87 | Juana 3425 |
| | | | **BILLY WARD - see THE DOMINOES** | | |
| | | | **ROBIN WARD** | | |
| | | | Real name: Jackie Ward. Pop female singer originally from Nebraska. | | |
| 11/16/63 | 23 | 2 | 1 Wonderful Summer.................... | 14 | Dot 16530 |
| | | | **SINGIN' SAMMY WARD** | | |
| | | | Vocalist from Detroit. | | |
| 8/21/61 | 23 | 8 | 1 Who's The Fool.................... | | Tamla 54030 |
| | | | **LEON WARE** | | |
| | | | Singer/songwriter/producer from Detroit. Wrote "Got To Have You Back", hit for The Isley Brothers in 1967. First solo album in 1972. | | |
| 12/08/79+ | 42 | 10 | 1 What's Your Name .................... | | Fabulous 748 |
| 2/14/81 | 66 | 6 | 2 Baby Don't Stop Me .................... | | Elektra 47093 |
| 5/16/81 | 74 | 4 | 3 Rockin' You Eternally.................... | | Elektra 47139 |
| | | | **WARP 9** | | |
| 12/11/82+ | 50 | 10 | 1 Nunk (New Wave Funk) .................... | | Prism 350 |
| 4/30/83 | 52 | 10 | 2 Light Years Away.................... above 2: produced & mixed by Jellybean Benitez | | Prism 360 |
| | | | **DEE DEE WARWICK** | | |
| | | | Singer born in 1945. Younger sister of Dionne. Sang in gospel group, the Drinkard Singers. Backup work for many artists. | | |
| 8/07/65 | 28 | 7 | 1 We're Doing Fine.................... | 96 | Blue Rock 4027 |

| DEBUT DATE | PEAK POS | WKS CHR | ARTIST — Record Title | POP POS | Label & Number |
|---|---|---|---|---|---|
| | | | **DEE DEE WARWICK — Continued** | | |
| 8/06/66 | **9** | 16 | 2 **I Want To Be With You** | *41* | Mercury 72584 |
| | | | from the Broadway musical "Golden Boy" | | |
| 12/17/66+ | **13** | 12 | 3 I'm Gonna Make You Love Me | *88* | Mercury 72638 |
| 5/06/67 | **43** | 6 | 4 When Love Slips Away | *92* | Mercury 72667 |
| 2/15/69 | **14** | 11 | 5 Foolish Fool | *57* | Mercury 72880 |
| 6/21/69 | **42** | 3 | 6 That's Not Love | *106* | Mercury 72927 |
| 5/16/70 | **9** | 10 | 7 **She Didn't Know (She Kept On Talking)** | *70* | Atco 6754 |
| | | | backed by The Dixie Flyers | | |
| 2/20/71 | **44** | 4 | 8 Cold Night In Georgia | | Atco 6796 |
| 5/08/71 | **24** | 8 | 9 Suspicious Minds | *80* | Atco 6810 |
| 5/03/75 | **73** | 6 | 10 Get Out Of My Life | | Private S. 45011 |
| | | | **DIONNE WARWICK** ★★**22**★★ | | |
| | | | Born Marie Dionne Warwick on 12/12/40 in East Orange, New Jersey. In church choir from age 6. With the Drinkard Singers gospel group. Formed trio, the Gospelaires, with sister Dee Dee and their aunt Cissy Houston. Attended Hartt College of Music, Hartford, Connecticut. Much backup studio work in New York during the late 50s. Added an "e" to her last name for a time in the early 70s. She was Burt Bacharach and Hal David's main "voice" for the songs they composed. Also see Donna Summer. | | |
| 1/12/63 | **5** | 10 | 1 **Don't Make Me Over** | *21* | Scepter 1239 |
| 4/27/63 | **26** | 1 | 2 This Empty Place | *84* | Scepter 1247 |
| 12/07/63+ | **8** | 14 | 3 **Anyone Who Had A Heart** | *Hot* | Scepter 1262 |
| 4/25/64 | **6** | 13 | 4 **Walk On By** | *Hot* | Scepter 1274 |
| 8/15/64 | **34** | 9 | 5 You'll Never Get To Heaven (If You Break My Heart)/ | *Hot* | |
| 8/01/64 | **71** | 6 | 6 A House Is Not A Home | *Hot* | Scepter 1282 |
| | | | from the film of the same title | | |
| 10/24/64 | **20** | 8 | 7 Reach Out For Me | *Hot* | Scepter 1285 |
| 3/06/65 | **36** | 3 | 8 Who Can I Turn To | *62* | Scepter 1298 |
| | | | from the Broadway musical "The Roar of The Greasepaint" | | |
| 11/13/65 | **38** | 3 | 9 Looking With My Eyes | *64* | Scepter 12111 |
| 1/01/66 | **35** | 4 | 10 Are You There (With Another Girl) | *39* | Scepter 12122 |
| 4/23/66 | **5** | 9 | 11 **Message To Michael** | *8* | Scepter 12133 |
| 8/13/66 | **49** | 2 | 12 Trains And Boats And Planes | *22* | Scepter 12153 |
| 10/15/66 | **20** | 8 | 13 I Just Don't Know What To Do With Myself | *26* | Scepter 12167 |
| 1/14/67 | **47** | 3 | 14 Another Night | *49* | Scepter 12181 |
| 3/25/67 | **44** | 3 | 15 The Beginning Of Loneliness/ | *79* | |
| 5/13/67 | **5** | 12 | 16 **Alfie** | *15* | Scepter 12187 |
| | | | from the film of the same title | | |
| 9/02/67 | **27** | 5 | 17 The Windows Of The World | *32* | Scepter 12196 |
| 11/11/67 | **8** | 10 | 18● I Say A Little Prayer/ | *4* | |
| 2/17/68 | **13** | 10 | 19 (Theme From) Valley Of The Dolls | *2* | Scepter 12203 |
| | | | from the film of the same title | | |
| 5/11/68 | **23** | 7 | 20 Do You Know The Way To San Jose | *10* | Scepter 12216 |
| 9/21/68 | **43** | 4 | 21 Who Is Gonna Love Me? | *33* | Scepter 12226 |
| 12/07/68 | **47** | 3 | 22 Promises, Promises | *19* | Scepter 12231 |
| | | | from the Broadway musical of the same title | | |
| 3/01/69 | **7** | 9 | 23 **This Girl's In Love With You** | *7* | Scepter 12241 |
| 5/31/69 | **33** | 5 | 24 The April Fools | *37* | Scepter 12249 |
| 10/04/69 | **13** | 10 | 25 You've Lost That Lovin' Feeling | *16* | Scepter 12262 |
| 1/10/70 | **17** | 7 | 26 I'll Never Fall In Love Again | *6* | Scepter 12273 |
| | | | from the Broadway musical "Promises, Promises" | | |
| 5/09/70 | **45** | 4 | 27 Let Me Go To Him | *32* | Scepter 12276 |
| 10/17/70 | **26** | 8 | 28 Make It Easy On Yourself | *37* | Scepter 12294 |
| 4/10/71 | **41** | 2 | 29 Who Gets The Guy | *57* | Scepter 12309 |
| | | | all of above (except 8, 19 & 25): written by Burt Bacharach and Hal David; all of above (except 11 & 28): produced by Burt Bacharach and Hal David | | |
| 7/14/73 | **62** | 6 | 30 (I'm) Just Being Myself | | Warner 7693 |
| 7/20/74 | **2**² | 15 | 31● **Then Came You** | *1* | Atlantic 3022 |
| | | | **DIONNE WARWICKE & SPINNERS** | | |
| 11/09/74 | **66** | 7 | 32 Sure Thing | | Warner 8026 |
| 5/03/75 | **30** | 11 | 33 Take It From Me | | Warner 8088 |
| 11/15/75+ | **5** | 16 | 34 **Once You Hit The Road** | *79* | Warner 8154 |
| 4/10/76 | **75** | 5 | 35 His House And Me | | Warner 8183 |

| DEBUT DATE | PEAK POS | WKS CHR | ARTIST — Record Title | POP POS | Label & Number |
|---|---|---|---|---|---|
| | | | **DIONNE WARWICK — Continued** | | |
| 11/20/76 | 91 | 3 | 36 I Didn't Mean To Love You.................... | | Warner 8280 |
| 3/19/77 | 65 | 7 | 37 By The Time I Get To Phoenix/Say A Little Prayer ........................................ | | ABC 12253 |
| | | | ISAAC HAYES & DIONNE WARWICK | | |
| 6/02/79 | 18 | 23 | 38● I'll Never Love This Way Again...................... | 5 | Arista 0419 |
| 10/27/79 | 25 | 15 | 39 Deja Vu ............................................ | 15 | Arista 0459 |
| 3/29/80 | 33 | 10 | 40 After You ........................................ | 65 | Arista 0498 |
| | | | from the film of the same title; above 3: produced by Barry Manilow | | |
| 8/02/80 | 19 | 14 | 41 No Night So Long .............................. | 23 | Arista 0527 |
| 11/15/80 | 41 | 11 | 42 We Never Said Goodbye...................... | | Arista 0572 |
| 6/13/81 | 43 | 9 | 43 Some Changes Are For Good .............. | 65 | Arista 0602 |
| 4/17/82 | 22 | 13 | 44 Friends In Love................................. | 38 | Arista 0673 |
| | | | DIONNE WARWICK & JOHNNY MATHIS | | |
| 10/16/82 | 14 | 16 | 45 Heartbreaker.................................... | 10 | Arista 1015 |
| 2/26/83 | 43 | 11 | 46 Take The Short Way Home .............. | 41 | Arista 1040 |
| | | | above 2: backing vocals by Robin Gibb | | |
| 10/08/83 | 7 | 16 | 47 **How Many Times Can We Say Goodbye**........... | 27 | Arista 9073 |
| | | | DIONNE WARWICK & LUTHER VANDROSS | | |
| 1/28/84 | 45 | 8 | 48 Got A Date...................................... | | Arista 9146 |
| 2/09/85 | 47 | 10 | 49 Finder Of Lost Loves ........................ | | Arista 9281 |
| | | | DIONNE WARWICK & GLENN JONES from the TV series of the same title | | |
| 11/16/85+ | 1³ | 20 | 50● **That's What Friends Are For** ...................... | 1 | Arista 9422 |
| | | | **DIONNE & FRIENDS** with Friends: Elton John, Gladys Knight and Stevie Wonder; Dionne sings lead for over one minute, with each "friend" contributing about 30-40 seconds of solo vocals | | |
| 3/22/86 | 49 | 9 | 51 Whisper In The Dark........................ | 72 | Arista 9460 |
| 7/11/87 | 5 | 14 | 52 **Love Power** ...................................... | 12 | Arista 9567 |
| | | | DIONNE WARWICK & JEFFREY OSBORNE | | |
| 10/17/87 | 20 | 15 | 53 Reservations For Two ...................... | 62 | Arista 9638 |
| | | | DIONNE & KASHIF | | |
| 2/13/88 | 42 | 9 | 54 Another Chance To Love ................. | | Arista 9656 |
| | | | DIONNE WARWICK & HOWARD HEWETT | | |
| | | | **WAS (NOT WAS)** Detroit rock funk ensemble fronted by composer/bassist Don Fagenson and lyricist/flutist David Weiss. Includes vocalists Sweet Pea Atkinson and Sir Harry Bowens. | | |
| 3/20/82 | 68 | 7 | 1 Tell Me That I'm Dreaming............... | | ZE 1000 |
| | | | **BABY WASHINGTON** Born Justine Washington (aka: Jeanette Washington) on 11/13/40 in Bamberg, South Carolina; raised in Harlem. Vocalist/pianist. Member of the vocal group, The Hearts, in 1956. First recorded solo for J&S in 1957. | | |
| 1/05/59 | 22 | 5 | 1 The Time............................................ | | Neptune 101 |
| 6/22/59 | 20 | 5 | 2 The Bells .......................................... | | Neptune 104 |
| 6/05/61 | 17 | 4 | 3 Nobody Cares (about me) ................. | 60 | Neptune 122 |
| | | | JEANETTE (BABY) WASHINGTON | | |
| 9/15/62 | 16 | 3 | 4 Handful Of Memories ...................... | 116 | Sue 767 |
| 4/20/63 | 10 | 4 | 5 **That's How Heartaches Are Made**................ | 40 | Sue 783 |
| 8/03/63 | 21 | 3 | 6 Leave Me Alone ............................... | 62 | Sue 790 |
| 10/12/63 | 100 | 1 | 7 Hey Lonely One ............................... | Hot | Sue 794 |
| 3/21/64 | 93 | 3 | 8 I Can't Wait Until I See My Baby ...................... | Hot | Sue 797 |
| | | | JUSTINE WASHINGTON | | |
| 9/19/64 | 100 | 1 | 9 The Clock ........................................ | Hot | Sue 104 |
| 11/28/64 | 98 | 2 | 10 It'll Never Be Over For Me................ | Hot | Sue 114 |
| 7/10/65 | 10 | 9 | 11 **Only Those In Love** ........................ | 73 | Sue 129 |
| 9/27/69 | 35 | 3 | 12 I Don't Know ................................. | | Cotillion 44047 |
| 5/19/73 | 30 | 7 | 13 Forever ........................................... | 119 | Master 5 9103 |
| | | | BABY WASHINGTON & DON GARDNER | | |
| 8/04/73 | 76 | 8 | 14 Just Can't Get You Out Of My Mind ................. | | Master 5 9104 |
| 12/01/73+ | 32 | 12 | 15 I've Got To Break Away........................ | | Master 5 9107 |
| 1/11/75 | 88 | 4 | 16 Can't Get Over Losing You ........................ | | Master 5 3500 |
| 5/24/80 | 67 | 7 | 17 Wolf Tickets.................................... | | Casablanca 2260 |
| | | | PARLET featuring JEANETTE WASHINGTON | | |

| DEBUT DATE | PEAK POS | WKS CHR | | ARTIST — Record Title | POP POS | Label & Number |
|---|---|---|---|---|---|---|
| | | | | **DEBORAH WASHINGTON** | | |
| | | | | Born on 3/16/54 in Philadelphia. Studied drama at Penn State University. Appeared in "Baretta", "Maude" and "What's Happening" TV series. | | |
| 7/08/78 | 38 | 12 | 1 | Ready Or Not............................................ | | Ariola 7700 |
| 11/25/78 | 93 | 2 | 2 | Standing In The Shadow Of Love.................... | | Ariola 7719 |
| | | | | **DINAH WASHINGTON**   ★★16★★ | | |
| | | | | Born Ruth Lee Jones on 8/29/24 in Tuscaloosa, Alabama; died on 12/14/63 (overdose of alcohol and pills). Jazz-blues vocalist/pianist. Moved to Chicago in 1927. With Sallie Martin Gospel Singers, 1940-41, and local club work in Chicago, 1941-43. With Lionel Hampton, 1943-46. First recorded for Keynote in 1943. Solo touring from 1946. Married 7 times, once to singer Eddie Chamblee. Also see Lionel Hampton. | | |
| 3/20/48 | 6 | 1 | 1 | **Ain't Misbehavin'** ..................................... | | Mercury 8072 |
| 6/19/48 | 7 | 5 | 2 | **West Side Baby** ........................................ Juke Box #7 / Best Seller #10 | | Mercury 8079 |
| 6/19/48 | 15 | 1 | 3 | Resolution Blues............................... Juke Box #15 | | Mercury 8082 |
| 7/10/48 | 13 | 1 | 4 | Walkin' And Talkin' ..................................... Best Seller #13 / Juke Box #15 above 3: with Rudy Martin's Trio | | Mercury 8079 |
| 7/24/48 | 11 | 3 | 5 | I Want To Cry............................................ Best Seller #11 | | Mercury 8082 |
| 9/11/48 | 1[1] | 14 | 6 | **Am I Asking Too Much** .............................. Juke Box #1 / Best Seller #4 | | Mercury 8095 |
| 10/23/48 | 2[1] | 11 | 7 | **It's Too Soon To Know** .............................. Juke Box #2 / Best Seller #3 | | Mercury 8107 |
| 4/02/49 | 8 | 1 | 8 | **You Satisfy**............................................. Juke Box #8 6 & 8: with Dave Young's Orchestra | | Mercury 8102 |
| 7/30/49 | 1[2] | 15 | 9 | **Baby, Get Lost/** Best Seller #1(2) / Juke Box #1(1) | | |
| 8/20/49 | 3 | 8 | 10 | **Long John Blues**...................................... Juke Box #3 / Best Seller #12 3, 5 & 10: with Cootie Williams' Orchestra | | Mercury 8148 |
| 11/26/49 | 9 | 2 | 11 | **Good Daddy Blues**.................................... Best Seller #9 | | Mercury 8154 |
| 3/04/50 | 3 | 6 | 12 | I Only Know ............................................ Best Seller #3 / Juke Box #6 | | Mercury 8163 |
| 4/08/50 | 5 | 8 | 13 | It Isn't Fair ............................................ Best Seller #5 / Juke Box #6 | | Mercury 8169 |
| 6/17/50 | 5 | 11 | 14 | I Wanna Be Loved ...................................... Best Seller #5 / Juke Box #6 | 22 | Mercury 8181 |
| 10/07/50 | 3 | 4 | 15 | I'll Never Be Free........................................ Best Seller #3 / Juke Box #6 9, 19 & above 5: with Teddy Stewart's Orchestra | | Mercury 8187 |
| 12/23/50 | 8 | 2 | 16 | **Time Out For Tears** .................................. Juke Box #8 | | Mercury 5503 |
| 1/06/51 | 10 | 1 | 17 | **Harbor Lights** ......................................... Juke Box #10 | | Mercury 5488 |
| 3/03/51 | 7 | 1 | 18 | **My Heart Cries For You**............................. Juke Box #7 | | Mercury 8209 |
| 3/03/51 | 10 | 1 | 19 | I Only Know............................................. [R] Juke Box #10 | | Mercury 8163 |
| 5/26/51 | 6 | 2 | 20 | **I Won't Cry Anymore** ............................... Best Seller #6 / Juke Box #8 16-18 & 20: with Jimmy Carroll's Orchestra | | Mercury 8211 |
| 11/03/51 | 3 | 15 | 21 | **Cold, Cold Heart**...................................... Juke Box #3 / Best Seller #3 | | Mercury 5728 |
| 3/08/52 | 3 | 5 | 22 | **Wheel Of Fortune/** Best Seller #3 / Juke Box #5 | | |
| 3/15/52 | 7 | 3 | 23 | **Tell Me Why**............................................ Juke Box #7 | | Mercury 8267 |
| 3/29/52 | 4 | 2 | 24 | **Trouble In Mind/** Best Seller #4 / Juke Box #5 | | |
| 4/05/52 | 5 | 4 | 25 | **New Blowtop Blues**.................................... Juke Box #5 / Best Seller #7 above 5: with Jimmy Cobb's Orchestra | | Mercury 8269 |
| 10/24/53 | 3 | 8 | 26 | **TV Is The Thing (This Year)/** Juke Box #3 / Best Seller #5 | | |
| 11/14/53 | 10 | 2 | 27 | **Fat Daddy** ............................................. Best Seller #10 | | Mercury 70214 |

| DEBUT DATE | PEAK POS | WKS CHR | ARTIST — Record Title | POP POS | Label & Number |
|---|---|---|---|---|---|
| | | | **DINAH WASHINGTON — Continued** | | |
| 10/09/54 | **3** | 10 | 28 **I Don't Hurt Anymore/** Best Seller #3 / Juke Box #7 | | |
| 10/23/54 | **9** | 2 | 29 **Dream** .................. Best Seller #9 | | Mercury 70439 |
| 12/18/54 | **4** | 8 | 30 **Teach Me Tonight**........... Best Seller #4 / Juke Box #6 / Jockey #8 | 23 | Mercury 70497 |
| 2/19/55 | **8** | 5 | 31 **That's All I Want From You**............ Best Seller #8 / Jockey #14 | | Mercury 70537 |
| 5/28/55 | **13** | 4 | 32 **If It's The Last Thing I Do/** Best Seller #13 | | |
| | | 3 | 33 **I Diddie** ............. Best Seller flip | | Mercury 70600 |
| 10/29/55 | **11** | 3 | 34 **I Concentrate On You** ............ Best Seller #11 | | Mercury 70694 |
| 11/26/55+ | **13** | 2 | 35 **I'm Lost Without You Tonight/** Best Seller #13 | | |
| 11/26/55 | **14** | 1 | 36 **You Might Have Told Me**........... Best Seller #14 | | Mercury 70728 |
| 9/29/56 | **13** | 1 | 37 **Soft Winds** .................. Best Seller #13 recorded in 1954; 28-29, 32 & 37: with Hal Mooney's Orchestra | | Mercury 70906 |
| 12/15/58 | **27** | 1 | 38 Make Me A Present Of You.............. | | Mercury 71377 |
| 6/15/59 | **4** | 17 | 39 **What A Diff'rence A Day Makes** ............... revival of the Dorsey Brothers' 1934 hit (POS 5) | 8 | Mercury 71435 |
| 11/09/59 | **15** | 9 | 40 Unforgettable ............... revival of Nat King Cole's 1952 pop hit (POS 12) | 17 | Mercury 71508 |
| 1/25/60 | **1**[10] | 17 | 41 **Baby (You've Got What It Takes)** ............... DINAH WASHINGTON & BROOK BENTON | 5 | Mercury 71565 |
| 5/23/60 | **1**[4] | 13 | 42 **A Rockin' Good Way (To Mess Around And Fall In Love)** ............... DINAH WASHINGTON & BROOK BENTON | 7 | Mercury 71629 |
| 6/20/60 | **1**[1] | 16 | 43 **This Bitter Earth** ............... | 24 | Mercury 71635 |
| 11/07/60 | **16** | 5 | 44 Love Walked In............... 3 versions of this tune hit the Top 10 in 1938; above 3: with Belford Hendricks' Orchestra | 30 | Mercury 71696 |
| 11/20/61 | **5** | 10 | 45 **September In The Rain**............... revival of Guy Lombardo's #1 hit in 1937 | 23 | Mercury 71876 |
| | | | **DONNA WASHINGTON** Vocalist from Los Angeles, produced by Chuck Jackson. | | |
| 4/25/81 | **26** | 15 | 1 **'Scuse Me, While I Fall In Love** ............... | | Capitol 4991 |
| | | | **ELLA WASHINGTON** Vocalist from Miami. First recorded for Octavia in 1965. Turned to gospel singing in 1973. | | |
| 2/01/69 | **38** | 6 | 1 He Called Me Baby ............... | 77 | Sound Stage 2621 |
| | | | **GROVER WASHINGTON, JR.** Saxophonist, born on 12/12/43 in Buffalo, New York. Own band, the Four Clefs, at age 16. Session work in Philadelphia, where he now resides. Also see Rose Royce. | | |
| 3/04/72 | **42** | 3 | 1 Inner City Blues............... | 120 | Kudu 902 |
| 10/28/72 | **49** | 3 | 2 No Tears In The End ............... | | Kudu 909 |
| 4/12/75 | **16** | 17 | 3 Mister Magic ............... [I] | 54 | Kudu 924 |
| 4/22/78 | **57** | 6 | 4 Summer Song ............... | | Kudu 942 |
| 12/16/78+ | **75** | 7 | 5 Do Dat ............... [I] | | Motown 1454 |
| 7/14/79 | **57** | 7 | 6 Tell Me About It Now ............... [I] | | Elektra 46060 |
| 5/24/80 | **88** | 4 | 7 Snake Eyes ............... [I] | | Motown 1486 |
| 11/22/80 | **62** | 10 | 8 Let It Flow ("For Dr. J") ............... [I] | | Elektra 47071 |
| 2/07/81 | **3** | 21 | 9 **Just The Two Of Us** ............... GROVER WASHINGTON, JR. with BILL WITHERS | 2 | Elektra 47103 |
| 11/28/81+ | **13** | 16 | 10 Be Mine (Tonight)............... vocal by Grady Tate | 92 | Elektra 47246 |
| 3/20/82 | **65** | 6 | 11 Jamming ............... written by Bob Marley | 102 | Elektra 47425 |
| 12/11/82+ | **14** | 19 | 12 The Best Is Yet To Come ............... GROVER WASHINGTON, JR. with PATTI LaBELLE | 104 | Elektra 69887 |
| 8/18/84 | **79** | 4 | 13 Inside Moves ............... [I] | | Elektra 69708 |
| 7/25/87 | **35** | 10 | 14 Summer Nights............... [I] | | Columbia 07240 |

| DEBUT DATE | PEAK POS | WKS CHR | ARTIST — Record Title | POP POS | Label & Number |
|---|---|---|---|---|---|
| | | | **JEANETTE WASHINGTON - see BABY WASHINGTON** | | |
| | | | **JERRY WASHINGTON** | | |
| | | | Vocalist from South Carolina. | | |
| 3/10/73 | **48** | 3 | 1 Right Here Is Where You Belong ...................... | *120* | Excello 2327 |
| 9/01/73 | **75** | 8 | 2 Let Me Love Right Or Wrong/ | | |
| | | 1 | 3 I Won't Leave You Hanging........................... | | Excello 2333 |
| | | | **JUSTINE WASHINGTON - see BABY WASHINGTON** | | |
| | | | **SADAO WATANABE** | | |
| | | | Jazz clarinetist born in Utsunomiya, Japan, in 1933. | | |
| 9/29/84 | **79** | 3 | 1 If I'm Still Around Tomorrow........................... | | Elektra 69700 |
| | | | vocal by Roberta Flack | | |
| | | | **FREDDIE WATERS** | | |
| 7/30/77 | **62** | 15 | 1 I'm Afraid To Let You Into My Life ................... | | October 1011 |
| 1/24/81 | **88** | 5 | 2 You Can Make It If You Try............................. | | Kari 115 |
| | | | **MUDDY WATERS** ★★**133**★★ | | |
| | | | Born McKinley Morganfield on 4/4/15 in Rolling Fork, Mississippi. Died on 4/30/83 (68). Vocalist/guitarist/harmonica player. Self-taught harmonica in the early 20s, guitar in the early 30s. First recorded for Library of Congress in in 1941. Moved to Chicago in 1943. A pivotal figure in the development of the Chicago blues style. Frequent tours of Europe, film and TV appearances. Also see Sonny Boy Williamson (Aleck Ford). | | |
| 9/18/48 | **11** | 2 | 1 (I Feel Like) Going Home............................... | | Aristocrat 1305 |
| | | | Juke Box #11 / Best Seller #11 | | |
| 1/13/51 | **10** | 1 | 2 **Louisiana Blues**................................... | | Chess 1441 |
| | | | Best Seller #10 | | |
| 4/14/51 | **8** | 1 | 3 **Long Distance Call** ............................... | | Chess 1452 |
| | | | Best Seller #8 | | |
| | | | with Walter Horton on harmonica | | |
| 7/14/51 | **10** | 1 | 4 **Honey Bee**......................................... | | Chess 1468 |
| | | | Juke Box #10 | | |
| | | | with Jimmy Rogers on guitar | | |
| 11/24/51 | **9** | 3 | 5 **Still A Fool** ...................................... | | Chess 1480 |
| | | | Juke Box #9 | | |
| 2/23/52 | **10** | 1 | 6 **She Moves Me** ..................................... | | Chess 1490 |
| | | | Best Seller #10 | | |
| 11/21/53 | **6** | 2 | 7 **Mad Love** ......................................... | | Chess 1550 |
| | | | Juke Box #6 / Best Seller #9 | | |
| 3/13/54 | **3** | 13 | 8 **I'm Your Hoochie Cooche Man** ...................... | | Chess 1560 |
| | | | Juke Box #3 / Best Seller #8 | | |
| 6/05/54 | **4** | 13 | 9 **Just Make Love To Me**.............................. | | Chess 1571 |
| | | | Juke Box #4 / Best Seller #4 | | |
| 10/23/54 | **4** | 9 | 10 **I'm Ready** ........................................ | | Chess 1579 |
| | | | Juke Box #4 / Best Seller #5 | | |
| 7/30/55 | **5** | 6 | 11 **Manish Boy** ....................................... | | Chess 1602 |
| | | | Juke Box #5 / Jockey #6 / Best Seller #9 | | |
| | | | new version of Bo Diddley's "I'm A Man" | | |
| | | | 2, 9 & 11: with Little Walter on harmonica | | |
| 12/24/55 | **11** | 2 | 12 Sugar Sweet/ | | |
| | | | Best Seller #11 / Jockey #14 | | |
| 1/14/56 | **7** | 6 | 13 **Trouble, No More**................................. | | Chess 1612 |
| | | | Jockey #7 | | |
| 5/05/56 | **7** | 6 | 14 **Forty Days & Forty Nights** ........................ | | Chess 1620 |
| | | | Juke Box #7 / Best Seller #12 | | |
| 9/08/56 | **9** | 2 | 15 **Don't Go No Farther** ............................. | | Chess 1630 |
| | | | Juke Box #9 / Best Seller #12 | | |
| 10/20/58 | **9** | 13 | 16 **Close To You**..................................... | | Chess 1704 |
| | | | **TIP WATKINS** | | |
| 5/28/77 | **81** | 3 | 1 People Gonna Talk (Part 1) ......................... | | H&L 4683 |
| | | | **JODY WATLEY** | | |
| | | | Born on 1/30/59 in Chicago. Female vocalist of Shalamar (1977-84) and former dancer on TV's "Soul Train". Her godfather was Jackie Wilson. | | |
| 1/31/87 | **1**³ | 18 | 1 **Looking For A New Love**............................. | *2* | MCA 52956 |
| 5/02/87 | **3** | 14 | 2 **Still A Thrill** .................................... | *56* | MCA 53081 |
| 8/22/87 | **3** | 15 | 3 **Don't You Want Me** ................................ | *6* | MCA 53162 |
| 12/19/87+ | **3** | 16 | 4 **Some Kind Of Lover** ............................... | *10* | MCA 53235 |
| | | | production and instruments by Andre Cymone | | |

| DEBUT DATE | PEAK POS | WKS CHR | ARTIST — Record Title | POP POS | Label & Number |
|---|---|---|---|---|---|
| | | | **JODY WATLEY — Continued** | | |
| 4/30/88 | **11** | 12 | 5  Most Of All..................................................... | *60* | MCA 53258 |
| | | | **ANTHONY WATSON** | | |
| 4/06/85 | **85** | 6 | 1  Solid Love Affair.......................................... | | SRO 231 |
| | | | **JOHNNY "GUITAR" WATSON**   ★★**194**★★ | | |
| | | | Born on 2/3/35 in Houston. Vocalist/guitarist/pianist. First recorded (as Young John Watson) for Federal in 1952. Also see Larry Williams. | | |
| 10/15/55 | **10** | 3 | 1  **Those Lonely, Lonely Nights** ......................... | | RPM 436 |
| | | | Jockey #10 | | |
| 3/03/62 | **6** | 13 | 2  **Cuttin' In** .................................................. | | King 5579 |
| 3/04/67 | **23** | 10 | 3  Mercy, Mercy, Mercy.................................... | 96 | Okeh 7274 |
| | | | **LARRY WILLIAMS & JOHNNY WATSON** | | |
| 1/27/68 | **40** | 3 | 4  Nobody...................................................... | | Okeh 7300 |
| | | | **LARRY WILLIAMS & JOHNNY WATSON** | | |
| 5/04/74 | **67** | 10 | 5  Treat Me Like I'm Your Man.......................... | | Fantasy 721 |
| 6/14/75 | **28** | 17 | 6  I Don't Want To Be A Lone Ranger................. | 99 | Fantasy 739 |
| 11/08/75 | **76** | 11 | 7  It's Too Late ............................................. | | Fantasy 752 |
| 7/17/76 | **40** | 12 | 8  I Need It ................................................... | *101* | DJM 1013 |
| 10/30/76 | **19** | 13 | 9  Superman Lover ......................................... | *101* | DJM 1019 |
| 6/04/77 | **5** | 15 | 10  A Real Mother For Ya ................................ | *41* | DJM 1024 |
| 10/08/77 | **34** | 10 | 11  Lover Jones .............................................. | | DJM 1029 |
| 2/18/78 | **59** | 6 | 12  Love That Will Not Die ............................... | | DJM 1034 |
| 11/04/78 | **32** | 13 | 13  Gangster Of Love ...................................... | | DJM 1101 |
| 7/07/79 | **83** | 3 | 14  What The Hell Is This?................................ | | DJM 1106 |
| 5/24/80 | **28** | 16 | 15  Love Jones ............................................... | | DJM 1304 |
| 9/20/80 | **45** | 8 | 16  Telephone Bill .......................................... | | DJM 1305 |
| 1/09/82 | **62** | 7 | 17  The Planet Funk ........................................ | | A&M 2383 |
| 8/25/84 | **77** | 7 | 18  Strike On Computers ................................. | | Valley Vue 769 |
| | | | **PAULA WATSON** | | |
| | | | Singer/pianist. | | |
| 11/06/48 | **2**¹ | 14 | 1  **A Little Bird Told Me**................................ | *6* | Supreme 1507 |
| | | | Best Seller #2 / Juke Box #3 | | |
| 3/05/49 | **13** | 2 | 2  You Broke Your Promise ............................. | | Supreme 1512 |
| | | | Juke Box #13 | | |
| | | | also released on Monogram 114 | | |
| | | | **WATTS 103rd STREET RHYTHM BAND - see CHARLES WRIGHT** | | |
| | | | **WAX** | | |
| 12/19/81 | **79** | 5 | 1  Get Loose .................................................. | | RCA 12325 |
| | | | **THOMAS WAYNE** | | |
| | | | Born Thomas Wayne Perkins on 7/22/40 in Battsville, Mississippi. Killed in an auto accident on 8/15/71. Brother of guitarist Luther Perkins of Johnny Cash's band. First recorded for Mercury in 1957. Own record label, Chalet, in 1971. | | |
| 3/02/59 | **20** | 6 | 1  Tragedy..................................................... | *5* | Fernwood 109 |
| | | | produced by Scotty Moore (Elvis' former guitarist); backed by The DeLons | | |
| | | | **JAMES WAYNES** | | |
| | | | Blues vocalist based in New Orleans. | | |
| 4/21/51 | **2**¹ | 14 | 1  **Tend To Your Business** .............................. | | Sittin' in 588 |
| | | | Best Seller #2 / Juke Box #5 | | |
| | | | **WE THE PEOPLE** | | |
| | | | Group from New York City, which included Robert Taylor, Shabi Weems, Billy McKeechun and Terri Gonzalez. | | |
| 11/25/72 | **47** | 3 | 1  You Made A Brand New World ........................ | | Lion 122 |
| 4/21/73 | **49** | 2 | 2  Forgotten Man............................................ | | Lion 148 |
| 5/11/74 | **86** | 4 | 3  Making My Daydream Real............................ | | Lion 164 |
| | | | **WEAPONS OF PEACE** | | |
| | | | Group from Chicago, formed in 1970. Consisted of Finis Henderson III (lead vocals), Lonell Dantzler, Bill Leathers, Randy Hardy and David Johnson. Worked Black Esthetics Festival in Chicago, in 1970. Played at wedding reception for Sammy Davis, Jr. | | |
| 10/30/76 | **64** | 4 | 1  Just Can't Be That Way (Ruth's Song).............. | | Playboy 6082 |

| DEBUT DATE | PEAK POS | WKS CHR | ARTIST — Record Title | POP POS | Label & Number |
|---|---|---|---|---|---|
| | | | **WEAPONS OF PEACE — Continued** | | |
| 1/08/77 | 78 | 5 | 2  City .............................................................. | | Playboy 6093 |
| 4/09/77 | 90 | 2 | 3  Roots Mural Theme/Many Rains Ago (Oluwa) ..... | | Playboy 6101 |
| | | | **THE WEATHER GIRLS** | | |
| | | | San Francisco duo of Martha Wash and Izora Rhodes. Formerly known as Two Tons O' Fun. Backup singers for Sylvester in the late 70s. | | |
| 12/04/82+ | 34 | 18 | 1  It's Raining Men............................................ | 46 | Columbia 03354 |
| 10/29/83 | 89 | 3 | 2  Success ........................................................ | | Columbia 04159 |
| 8/17/85 | 76 | 4 | 3  Well-A-Wiggy ................................................ | 107 | Columbia 05428 |
| | | | **CARL WEATHERS** | | |
| | | | Film actor/singer. Attended San Diego State on a football scholarship. Played pro ball with the Oakland Raiders and the Canadian B.C. Lions. Appeared as "Apollo Creed" in the "Rocky" movie series. | | |
| 8/08/81 | 71 | 8 | 1  You Ought To Be With Me................................ | | Mirage 3834 |
| | | | **OSCAR WEATHERS** | | |
| 4/04/70 | 37 | 4 | 1  Your Fool Still Loves You ............................... | | Top & Bottom 402 |
| 2/27/71 | 35 | 6 | 2  You Wants To Play ........................................ | 125 | Top & Bottom 405 |
| 5/06/72 | 31 | 5 | 3  Pledging My Love .......................................... | | Top & Bottom 412 |
| 7/14/73 | 51 | 6 | 4  Tell It Like It Is ............................................ | 113 | Blue Cndl. 1498 |
| | | | **EBONEE WEBB - see EBONEE** | | |
| | | | **LANCE WEBB** | | |
| 2/04/84 | 83 | 4 | 1  Life's Charade .............................................. | | Beantown 710 |
| | | | **WEBS** | | |
| 12/02/67 | 37 | 7 | 1  This Thing Called Love ................................... | 102 | Pop-Side 4593 |
| 2/10/68 | 32 | 3 | 2  Give In ........................................................ | | Pop-Side 4595 |
| 11/02/68 | 44 | 2 | 3  We Belong Together ....................................... | | Verve 10610 |
| | | | **WEE GEE** | | |
| | | | Born William F. Howard II. | | |
| 4/15/78 | 86 | 6 | 1  You've Been A Part Of Me.............................. | | Juney 533 |
| 3/22/80 | 77 | 6 | 2  Hold On (To Your Dreams) ............................. | | Cotillion 45012 |
| | | | **WEEKS & CO.** | | |
| | | | Group from New York City, led by Richie Weeks. | | |
| 12/19/81+ | 75 | 7 | 1  Rock Your World ........................................... | | Chez Ro 2519 |
| 5/14/83 | 75 | 5 | 2  If You're Looking For Fun.............................. | | Salsoul 7053 |
| | | | **LENNY WELCH** | | |
| | | | Vocalist born on 5/15/38 in Asbury Park, New Jersey. | | |
| 4/11/60 | 28 | 1 | 1  You Don't Know Me........................................ | 45 | Cadence 1373 |
| 10/26/63 | 4 | 16 | 2  **Since I Fell For You** ................................... | Hot | Cadence 1439 |
| 3/21/64 | 25 | 9 | 3  Ebb Tide....................................................... | Hot | Cadence 1422 |
| | | | featured in the film "Sweet Bird Of Youth" | | |
| 7/04/64 | 92 | 2 | 4  If You See My Love ....................................... | Hot | Cadence 1446 |
| 1/17/70 | 27 | 8 | 5  Breaking Up Is Hard To Do ............................ | 34 | Commonw. 3004 |
| 9/15/73 | 92 | 3 | 6  Since I Don't Have You................................... | | Mainstream 5545 |
| 3/23/74 | 71 | 6 | 7  Eye Witness News ......................................... | | Mainstream 5554 |
| | | | **LAWRENCE WELK** | | |
| | | | Born on 3/11/03 in Strasburg, North Dakota. Accordionist and polka/sweet bandleader since the mid-20s. Band's style labeled "champagne music". Own national TV musical variety show began on 7/2/55 and ran into the 70s. | | |
| 1/30/61 | 10 | 9 | 1 ●Calcutta ................................................ [I] | 1 | Dot 16161 |
| | | | featuring Frank Scott on harpsichord | | |
| | | | **WELL RED** | | |
| 11/28/87+ | 26 | 14 | 1  Get Lucky...................................................... | | Virgin 99398 |
| | | | **BRANDI WELLS** | | |
| | | | Vocalist from Philadelphia, former lead singer of Breeze and Slick. | | |
| 8/22/81 | 76 | 4 | 1  When It's Love .............................................. | | WMOT 02244 |
| 1/09/82 | 27 | 15 | 2  Watch Out .................................................... | | WMOT 02654 |

| DEBUT DATE | PEAK POS | WKS CHR | ARTIST — Record Title | POP POS | Label & Number |
|---|---|---|---|---|---|
| | | | **JEAN WELLS** | | |
| | | | Born in West Palm Beach, Florida on 8/1/42; raised in Belgrade, Florida. Self-taught on piano, sang in gospel groups as a child. Worked clubs in Philadelphia. First recorded in 1959. | | |
| 5/20/67 | **31** | 5 | 1 After Loving You ........................................ | | Calla 128 |
| 10/28/67 | **33** | 4 | 2 I Feel Good ............................................. | | Calla 137 |
| 12/16/67+ | **25** | 8 | 3 Have A Little Mercy..................................... | | Calla 143 |
| 6/08/68 | **45** | 2 | 4 Try Me & See............................................ | | Calla 150 |
| | | | **JUNIOR WELLS** | | |
| | | | Born Amos Blackmore on 12/9/34 in Memphis. Singer/harmonica player. Moved to Chicago in 1946, worked local clubs with the Three Deuces, Three Aces and Four Aces bands to 1952. With Muddy Waters from 1952-55, recorded for States in 1953. Montreux Blues Festival, Switzerland, in 1974. | | |
| 6/06/60 | **23** | 3 | 1 Little By Little.......................................... | | Profile 4011 |
| 7/27/68 | **40** | 2 | 2 You're Tuff Enough ..................................... | | Blue Rock 4052 |
| | | | **MARY WELLS**    ★★**106**★★ | | |
| | | | Vocalist born on 5/13/43 in Detroit. At age 17, presented "Bye Bye Baby", a tune she had written for Jackie Wilson, to Wilson's songwriter, Berry Gordy, Jr. Gordy signed her to his new label and she became the first artist to record for Motown. Also was the first to have a Top 10 and #1 single for that label. Married for a time to Cecil Womack (of Womack & Womack). | | |
| 12/19/60+ | **8** | 15 | 1 **Bye Bye Baby** ........................................ | *45* | Motown 1003 |
| 7/24/61 | **9** | 8 | 2 **I Don't Want To Take A Chance** .................... | *33* | Motown 1011 |
| 4/28/62 | **2**¹ | 14 | 3 **The One Who Really Loves You** .................... | *8* | Motown 1024 |
| 9/01/62 | **1**¹ | 13 | 4 **You Beat Me To The Punch**......................... | *9* | Motown 1032 |
| 12/08/62+ | **1**⁴ | 14 | 5 **Two Lovers** ........................................... | *7* | Motown 1035 |
| 3/02/63 | **6** | 10 | 6 **Laughing Boy** ........................................ | *15* | Motown 1039 |
| 6/15/63 | **8** | 7 | 7 **Your Old Stand By**................................... | *40* | Motown 1042 |
| 10/26/63 | **8** | 5 | 8 **What's Easy For Two Is So Hard For One/** | *29* | |
| 10/26/63 | **10** | 5 | 9   **You Lost The Sweetest Boy**........................ | *22* | Motown 1048 |
| 4/04/64 | **1**² | 15 | 10 **My Guy**............................................... | *Hot* | Motown 1056 |
| | | | 3-8 & 10: written & produced by Smokey Robinson | | |
| 5/02/64 | **19** | 9 | 11 Once Upon A Time/ | *Hot* | |
| 5/16/64 | **17** | 10 | 12   What's The Matter With You Baby ................. | *Hot* | Motown 1057 |
| | | | above 2: **MARVIN GAYE & MARY WELLS** | | |
| 10/31/64 | **45** | 8 | 13 Ain't It The Truth/ | *Hot* | |
| 11/07/64 | **88** | 3 | 14   Stop Takin' Me For Granted ......................... | *Hot* | 20th Century 544 |
| 1/30/65 | **13** | 2 | 15 Use Your Head.......................................... | *34* | 20th Century 555 |
| 3/20/65 | **15** | 8 | 16 Never, Never Leave Me ................................ | *54* | 20th Century 570 |
| 2/19/66 | **6** | 11 | 17 **Dear Lover**........................................... | *51* | Atco 6392 |
| 5/25/68 | **22** | 9 | 18 The Doctor............................................... | *65* | Jubilee 5621 |
| 10/11/69 | **38** | 3 | 19 Never Give A Man The World.......................... | | Jubilee 5676 |
| 12/27/69+ | **35** | 6 | 20 Dig The Way I Feel ..................................... | *115* | Jubilee 5684 |
| 10/05/74 | **95** | 4 | 21 If You Can't Give Her Love (Give Her Up) .......... | | Reprise 1308 |
| 2/06/82 | **69** | 6 | 22 Gigolo .................................................... | | Epic 02664 |
| | | | **TERRI WELLS** | | |
| | | | Female singer formerly in City Limits. Worked as back-up vocalist for Lou Rawls, Jean Carn, MFSB and Leon Huff. | | |
| 7/07/84 | **81** | 3 | 1 I'll Be Around.......................................... | | Philly W. 99753 |
| 10/06/84 | **66** | 10 | 2 I'm Givin' All My Love.................................. | | Philly W. 96924 |
| | | | **FRED WESLEY & THE J.B.'s** | | |
| | | | James Brown's super-funk backup band led by trombonist/keyboardist Fred Wesley. He and other JB members were members of the Parliament/Funkadelic organization. Also see James Brown, Nat Kendrick, and Maceo & The Macks. | | |
| | | | **THE J.B.'s:** | | |
| 1/29/72 | **11** | 11 | 1 Gimme Some More ..................................... [I] | *67* | People 602 |
| 5/13/72 | **29** | 8 | 2 Pass The Peas ......................................... [I] | *95* | People 607 |
| | | | **FRED WESLEY & THE J.B.'s:** | | |
| 5/12/73 | **1**² | 15 | 3●**Doing It To Death**.................................... | *22* | People 621 |
| | | | above 3: written, produced & arranged by James Brown | | |
| 10/06/73 | **24** | 11 | 4 If You Don't Get It The First Time, Back Up And Try It Again................................................ | *104* | People 627 |
| 2/02/74 | **26** | 13 | 5 Same Beat .............................................. | | People 632 |
| 6/01/74 | **32** | 12 | 6 Damn Right I Am Somebody.......................... | | People 638 |

| DEBUT DATE | PEAK POS | WKS CHR | ARTIST — Record Title | POP POS | Label & Number |
|---|---|---|---|---|---|
| | | | **FRED WESLEY & THE J.B.'s — Continued** | | |
| 12/28/74+ | 80 | 6 | 7  Breakin' Bread ............................................ | | People 648 |
| | | | **FRED & THE NEW J.B.'s** | | |
| 3/22/75 | 64 | 8 | 8  Makin' Love ............................................... | | People 651 |
| 6/21/75 | 63 | 7 | 9  It's The J.B.'s Monaurail, Part 1 ................... | | People 655 |
| 8/06/77 | 93 | 5 | 10  Up For The Down Stroke ............................ | | Atlantic 3408 |
| | | | **FRED WESLEY & THE HORNY HORNS** | | |
| 6/21/80 | 40 | 15 | 11  House Party .............................................. | | RSO 1037 |
| | | | **FRED WESLEY** | | |
| | | | **WEST COAST CREW** | | |
| | | | Rap group. | | |
| 3/22/86 | 61 | 8 | 1  Jail Bait ..................................................... | | KMA 004 |
| | | | **WEST STREET MOB** | | |
| | | | New Jersey funk/dance quartet led by Joey Robinson (son of Joe & Sylvia Robinson - owners of Sugar Hill Records). | | |
| 8/08/81 | 18 | 16 | 1  Let's Dance (Make Your Body Move) ................ | 88 | Sugar Hill 763 |
| | | | hit pop charts on Sugar Hill 559 | | |
| 1/30/82 | 73 | 5 | 2  Got To Give It Up ....................................... | | Sugar Hill 773 |
| 4/03/82 | 44 | 9 | 3  Sing A Simple Song ..................................... | 89 | Sugar Hill 576 |
| 9/18/82 | 55 | 8 | 4  Ooh Baby.................................................... | | Sugar Hill 588 |
| 9/10/83 | 37 | 11 | 5  Break Dancin'-Electric Boogie ........................ | | Sugar Hill 460 |
| | | | **BELINDA WEST** | | |
| 10/25/80 | 92 | 2 | 1  Seabiscuit In The Fifth................................. | | Panorama 12094 |
| | | | **KIM WESTON** | | |
| | | | Born Agatha Natalie Weston in Detroit. Sang in gospel groups. Discovered by Eddie Holland. Worked as stage actress in New York City. Had youth theater workshop in Detroit. | | |
| 7/27/63 | 24 | 2 | 1  Love Me All The Way................................... | 88 | Tamla 54076 |
| 10/24/64 | 61 | 6 | 2  What Good Am I Without You ........................ | Hot | Tamla 54104 |
| | | | **MARVIN GAYE & KIM WESTON** | | |
| 10/09/65 | 4 | 10 | 3  **Take Me In Your Arms (Rock Me A Little While)** .................................................. | 50 | Gordy 7046 |
| 3/19/66 | 13 | 7 | 4  Helpless ..................................................... | 56 | Gordy 7050 |
| 1/21/67 | 4 | 12 | 5  **It Takes Two** ............................................ | 14 | Tamla 54141 |
| | | | **MARVIN GAYE & KIM WESTON** | | |
| 1/20/68 | 39 | 6 | 6  Nobody...................................................... | | MGM 13881 |
| 1/24/70 | 49 | 2 | 7  Danger-Heartbreak Ahead ............................. | | People 1001 |
| 6/13/70 | 50 | 2 | 8  Lift Ev'ry Voice And Sing ............................ | 120 | Pride 1 |
| | | | **WHAM!** | | |
| | | | Pop duo from Bushey, England: George Michael (b: Georgios Kyriacos Panayiotou on 6/26/63; lead singer) and Andrew Ridgeley (b: 1/26/63; guitarist). Disbanded in 1986. Michael recorded solo. | | |
| 1/19/85 | 8 | 15 | 1●**Careless Whisper**......................................... | 1 | Columbia 04691 |
| | | | released in England as a solo single by George Michael | | |
| 4/06/85 | 12 | 17 | 2  Everything She Wants.................................. | 1 | Columbia 04840 |
| 1/11/86 | 55 | 8 | 3  I'm Your Man ............................................. | 3 | Columbia 05721 |
| | | | all of above: written & produced by George Michael | | |
| | | | **WHATNAUTS** | | |
| | | | Baltimore vocal group: Billy Herndon (lead), Garrett Jones (tenor) and Gerald "Chunky" Pinkney (baritone). | | |
| 2/07/70 | 19 | 6 | 1  Message From A Black Man ........................... | 99 | A&I 001 |
| | | | **THE WHATNAUTS & THE WHATNAUTS BAND** | | |
| 6/06/70 | 47 | 3 | 2  Please Make The Love Go Away...................... | | Stang 5014 |
| 4/03/71 | 14 | 10 | 3  I'll Erase Away Your Pain............................. | 71 | Stang 5023 |
| 8/07/71 | 37 | 7 | 4  We're Friends By Day (And Lovers By Night)...... | 100 | Stang 5030 |
| 5/05/73 | 23 | 7 | 5  Instigating (Trouble Making) Fool .................... | | GSF 6897 |
| 12/07/74+ | 25 | 14 | 6  Girls (Part I) .............................................. | | Stang 5057 |
| | | | **MOMENTS & WHATNAUTS** | | |
| 1/30/82 | 46 | 11 | 7  Help Is On The Way ..................................... | | Harlem Int. 111 |
| | | | **AUDREY WHEELER - see JEFF LORBER** | | |
| | | | **WHIRLWIND** | | |
| | | | Disco trio consisting of Sandie Ancrum with her brothers Charles and Eddie. | | |
| 10/02/76 | 91 | 6 | 1  Full Time Thing (Between Dusk And Dawn)........ | 91 | Roulette 7195 |

| DEBUT DATE | PEAK POS | WKS CHR | ARTIST — Record Title | POP POS | Label & Number |
|---|---|---|---|---|---|
| | | | **THE WHISPERS** ★★39★★ | | |
| | | | Los Angeles group, formed in 1964. Consisted of Gordy Harmon, twin brothers Walter and Wallace "Scotty" Scott, Marcus Hutson and Nicholas Caldwell. First recorded for Dore in 1964. Harmon replaced by Leaveil Degree in 1973. Also see Carrie Lucas. | | |
| 8/02/69 | 17 | 7 | 1 Time Will Come ............................................ | | Soul Clock 107 |
| 8/29/70 | 6 | 11 | 2 **Seems Like I Gotta Do Wrong**...................... | 50 | Soul Clock 1004 |
| 12/26/70+ | 31 | 6 | 3 There's A Love For Everyone ...................... | 116 | Janus 140 |
| 5/01/71 | 19 | 6 | 4 Your Love Is So Doggone Good ...................... | 93 | Janus 150 |
| 1/08/72 | 35 | 8 | 5 Can't Help But Love You .............................. | 114 | Janus 174 |
| 7/22/72 | 27 | 8 | 6 I Only Meant To Wet My Feet ...................... | | Janus 184 |
| 12/30/72+ | 45 | 3 | 7 Somebody Loves You........................... | 94 | Janus 200 |
| 1/05/74 | 32 | 13 | 8 A Mother For My Children ......................... | 92 | Janus 231 |
| 6/15/74 | 40 | 9 | 9 Bingo ......................................................... | | Janus 238 |
| 10/05/74 | 60 | 10 | 10 What More Can A Girl Ask For ...................... | | Janus 244 |
| 12/13/75+ | 40 | 12 | 11 In Love Forever ......................................... | | Soul Train 10430 |
| 6/26/76 | 10 | 15 | 12 **One For The Money (Part 1)** ...................... | 88 | Soul Train 10700 |
| 10/09/76 | 21 | 15 | 13 Living Together (In Sin) .............................. | 101 | Soul Train 10773 |
| 2/26/77 | 91 | 4 | 14 You're Only As Good As You Are .................. | | Soul Train 10878 |
| 7/02/77 | 10 | 17 | 15 **Make It With You** ...................................... | 94 | Soul Train 10996 |
| 11/26/77+ | 54 | 9 | 16 I'm Gonna Make You My Wife ...................... | | Soul Train 11139 |
| 4/22/78 | 10 | 18 | 17 **(Let's Go) All The Way**............................ | 101 | Solar 11246 |
| 9/02/78 | 13 | 22 | 18 (Olivia) Lost And Turned Out........................ | | Solar 11353 |
| 6/02/79 | 43 | 11 | 19 Can't Do Without Love ............................... | | Solar 11590 |
| 8/25/79 | 66 | 6 | 20 Homemade Lovin' ...................................... | | Solar 11685 |
| 10/13/79 | 21 | 15 | 21 A Song For Donny ...................................... | | Solar 11739 |
| | | | tribute to Donny Hathaway; lyrics written by Carrie Lucas | | |
| 1/19/80 | 1⁵ | 20 | 22●**And The Beat Goes On** ............................. | 19 | Solar 11894 |
| 3/15/80 | 3 | 19 | 23 **Lady** ....................................................... | 28 | Solar 11928 |
| 1/10/81 | 2³ | 20 | 24 **It's A Love Thing**.................................... | 28 | Solar 12154 |
| 5/23/81 | 40 | 10 | 25 I Can Make It Better ................................... | 105 | Solar 12232 |
| 9/05/81 | 17 | 15 | 26 This Kind Of Lovin' .................................... | | Solar 12295 |
| 1/23/82 | 8 | 15 | 27 **In The Raw** ............................................. | 103 | Solar 47961 |
| 5/01/82 | 22 | 12 | 28 Emergency.................................................. | | Solar 48008 |
| 3/05/83 | 4 | 16 | 29 **Tonight** .................................................. | 84 | Solar 69842 |
| 5/14/83 | 4 | 18 | 30 **Keep On Lovin' Me**................................... | | Solar 69827 |
| 8/27/83 | 32 | 9 | 31 This Time .................................................. | 110 | Solar 69809 |
| 11/03/84 | 10 | 15 | 32 **Contagious**............................................. | 105 | Solar 69683 |
| 2/09/85 | 17 | 14 | 33 Some Kinda Lover ...................................... | 106 | Solar 69658 |
| 5/25/85 | 60 | 7 | 34 Don't Keep Me Waiting................................ | | Solar 69639 |
| 4/18/87 | 1¹ | 18 | 35 **Rock Steady**............................................ | 7 | Solar 70006 |
| | | | co-written by Babyface and L.A. Reid (of The Deele) | | |
| 8/22/87 | 12 | 15 | 36 Just Gets Better With Time........................... | | Solar 70012 |
| 11/28/87+ | 16 | 15 | 37 In The Mood .............................................. | | Solar 70017 |
| 4/09/88 | 74 | 6 | 38 No Pains, No Gains ..................................... | | Solar 70020 |
| | | | **WHISTLE** | | |
| | | | Rap trio consisting of K.D., Jazz, and Silver Spinner. | | |
| 2/22/86 | 17 | 16 | 1 (Nothing Serious) Just Buggin'........................ | | Select 62267 |
| 9/27/86 | 61 | 9 | 2 Just For Fun .............................................. | | Select 62274 |
| 12/27/86 | 92 | 3 | 3 Santa Is A B-Boy........................................ | | Select 62279 |
| 4/11/87 | 31 | 10 | 4 Barbara's Bedroom....................................... | | Select 62280 |
| 2/20/88 | 41 | 12 | 5 Falling In Love .......................................... | | Select 62302 |
| 7/02/88 | 95 | 4 | 6 Still My Girl ............................................. | | Select 62312 |
| | | | **ARTIE WHITE** | | |
| | | | Vocalist/guitarist from Chicago. | | |
| 5/28/77 | 99 | 1 | 1 Leaning Tree............................................... | | Altee 111 |

| DEBUT DATE | PEAK POS | WKS CHR | ARTIST — Record Title | POP POS | Label & Number |
|---|---|---|---|---|---|
| | | | **BARRY WHITE** ★★**46**★★ | | |
| | | | Born on 9/12/44 in Galveston, Texas; raised in Los Angeles. Singer/songwriter/ keyboardist/producer/arranger. At age 11, played piano on Jesse Belvin's hit "Goodnight My Love". With Upfronts vocal group, recorded for Lummtone in 1960. Recorded with Atlantic in 1964. Recorded as Barry Lee for Downey, Veep in 1965. A&R man for Mustang/Bronco from 1966-67. Formed female vocal trio Love Unlimited in 1969, which included future wife Glodean James. Leader of 40-piece Love Unlimited Orchestra. | | |
| 4/07/73 | **1** [2] | 15 | 1●I'm Gonna Love You Just A Little More Baby . | 3 | 20th Century 2018 |
| 7/28/73 | **5** | 14 | 2 I've Got So Much To Give | 32 | 20th Century 2042 |
| 10/20/73 | **2** [2] | 16 | 3●Never, Never Gonna Give Ya Up | 7 | 20th Century 2058 |
| 2/23/74 | **6** | 16 | 4 Honey Please, Can't Ya See | 44 | 20th Century 2077 |
| 7/27/74 | **1** [3] | 17 | 5●Can't Get Enough Of Your Love, Babe | 1 | 20th Century 2120 |
| 11/09/74+ | **1** [1] | 17 | 6●You're The First, The Last, My Everything .... | 2 | 20th Century 2133 |
| 3/08/75 | **1** [1] | 14 | 7 What Am I Gonna Do With You | 8 | 20th Century 2177 |
| 5/31/75 | **4** | 14 | 8 I'll Do For You Anything You Want Me To | 40 | 20th Century 2208 |
| 12/27/75+ | **4** | 14 | 9 Let The Music Play | 32 | 20th Century 2265 |
| 3/27/76 | **14** | 11 | 10 You See The Trouble With Me | | 20th Century 2277 |
| 7/04/76 | **29** | 11 | 11 Baby, We Better Try To Get It Together | 92 | 20th Century 2298 |
| 10/30/76+ | **20** | 14 | 12 Don't Make Me Wait Too Long | 105 | 20th Century 2309 |
| 2/19/77 | **25** | 12 | 13 I'm Qualified To Satisfy You | | 20th Century 2328 |
| 8/13/77 | **1** [5] | 20 | 14●It's Ecstasy When You Lay Down Next To Me . | 4 | 20th Century 2350 |
| 1/07/78 | **8** | 12 | 15 Playing Your Game, Baby | 101 | 20th Century 2361 |
| 3/25/78 | **13** | 16 | 16 Oh What A Night For Dancing | 24 | 20th Century 2365 |
| 9/16/78 | **2** [3] | 20 | 17 Your Sweetness Is My Weakness | 60 | 20th Century 2380 |
| 1/20/79 | **45** | 10 | 18 Just The Way You Are | 102 | 20th Century 2395 |
| 4/07/79 | **37** | 10 | 19 Any Fool Could See (You Were Meant For Me) .... | | Un. Gold 1401 |
| 7/07/79 | **58** | 7 | 20 It Ain't Love, Babe (Until You Give It) | | Un. Gold 1404 |
| 9/08/79 | **53** | 8 | 21 I Love To Sing The Songs I Sing | | 20th Century 2416 |
| 12/08/79 | **64** | 7 | 22 How Did You Know It Was Me? | | 20th Century 2433 |
| 2/02/80 | **75** | 5 | 23 Love Ain't Easy | | Un. Gold 1411 |
| 4/19/80 | **43** | 10 | 24 Sheet Music | | Un. Gold 1415 |
| 7/12/80 | **25** | 13 | 25 Love Makin' Music | | Un. Gold 1418 |
| 11/08/80 | **71** | 6 | 26 I Believe In Love | | Un. Gold 1420 |
| 3/21/81 | **78** | 5 | 27 Didn't We Make It Happen, Baby | | Un. Gold 70064 |
| | | | BARRY WHITE & GLODEAN WHITE | | |
| 5/30/81 | **79** | 5 | 28 I Want You | | Un. Gold 02087 |
| | | | BARRY WHITE & GLODEAN WHITE | | |
| 11/07/81+ | **49** | 13 | 29 Beware | | Un. Gold 02580 |
| 7/31/82 | **12** | 16 | 30 Change | | Un. Gold 02956 |
| 12/04/82 | **65** | 7 | 31 Passion | | Un. Gold 03379 |
| 10/03/87 | **17** | 12 | 32 Sho' You Right | | A&M 2943 |
| 12/26/87+ | **27** | 14 | 33 For Your Love (I'll Do Most Anything) | | A&M 3000 |
| | | | **BEVERLY WHITE** | | |
| | | | Vocalist with Claude Hopkins in 1937. | | |
| 5/15/43 | **9** | 1 | 1 **Don't Stop Now** | | Beacon 111 |
| | | | also released on Joe Davis 7112 | | |
| | | | **GLODEAN WHITE - see LOVE UNLIMITED and BARRY WHITE** | | |
| | | | **JOHN WHITE** | | |
| | | | Born in Harrisburg, Pennsylvania. Sang in family gospel group, toured with Reverend James Cleveland and Shirley Caesar. Self-taught on piano. Worked as a demo singer in New York City. | | |
| 7/25/87 | **27** | 13 | 1 (Can't) Get You Out Of My System | | Geffen 28332 |
| | | | **KARYN WHITE - see JEFF LORBER** | | |
| | | | **LENNY WHITE** | | |
| | | | Percussionist born on 12/19/49. Former drummer of the jazz-rock band Return To Forever; leader of the New York band Twennynine. | | |
| 3/01/80 | **47** | 9 | 1 Best Of Friends | | Elektra 46597 |
| 4/30/83 | **31** | 9 | 2 Didn't Know About Love (Till I Found You) | | Elektra 69832 |

| DEBUT DATE | PEAK POS | WKS CHR | ARTIST — Record Title | POP POS | Label & Number |
|---|---|---|---|---|---|
| | | | **MAURICE WHITE** | | |
| | | | Leader of Earth, Wind & Fire, born on 12/19/41 in Memphis. In band at age 11, with classmate Booker T. Jones (Booker T. & The MG's). To Chicago at age 16. Worked as a session drummer at Chess Records while in high school. Member of The Ramsey Lewis Trio from 1967-69. In 1969, formed own band, the Salty Peppers, with brother Verdine White. In 1971, they formed Earth, Wind & Fire of which Maurice was a producer/songwriter/percussionist/vocalist. | | |
| 8/24/85 | 6 | 16 | 1 **Stand By Me** ............................................. | 50 | Columbia 05571 |
| 11/30/85+ | 30 | 15 | 2 I Need You ................................................... | 95 | Columbia 05726 |
| 4/19/86 | 89 | 3 | 3 Lady Is Love ............................................... | | Columbia 05836 |
| | | | **CHARLIE WHITEHEAD** | | |
| | | | Born on 9/6/42 in Franklin, Virginia. Also recorded as Raw Spitt. | | |
| 5/17/75 | 24 | 14 | 1 Love Being Your Fool.................................. | 106 | Island 007 |
| | | | **JOHN WHITEHEAD** | | |
| | | | Native of North Philadelphia. Half of songwriting/recording duo Gene McFadden & Whitehead. They wrote and produced for many Philadelphia acts; co-creators of "The Sound Of Philadelphia". John served time in prison for tax evasion. | | |
| 3/19/88 | 50 | 10 | 1 I Need Money Bad ........................................ | | Mercury 870160 |
| | | | **KENNY & JOHNNY WHITEHEAD** | | |
| | | | Brothers. | | |
| 6/07/86 | 79 | 6 | 1 I Jumped Out Of My Skin............................. | | Phil. Int. 50030 |
| | | | shown only as: **KENNY & JOHNNY** | | |
| 9/20/86 | 79 | 7 | 2 Stylin'....................................................... | | Phil. Int. 50041 |
| | | | **PAUL WHITEMAN** | | |
| | | | The most popular bandleader of the pre-swing era. Born on 3/28/1890 in Denver. Formed own band in 1919. Band featured jazz greats Henry Busse (trumpet), Ferde Grofe (piano, arranger) and Bix Beiderbecke (cornet). Vocalist Bing Crosby made his professional debut with Whiteman's band in 1926. Paul died on 12/29/67 (77). | | |
| 10/24/42 | 1³ | 22 | 1 **Trav'lin' Light** ......................................... | 23 | Capitol 116 |
| | | | vocal by Billie Holiday (listed only as "Lady Day") | | |
| | | | **MARVA WHITNEY** | | |
| 5/24/69 | 19 | 7 | 1 It's My Thing (You Can't Tell Me Who To Sock It To)...................................................... | 82 | King 6229 |
| | | | written & produced by James Brown | | |
| 8/16/69 | 22 | 6 | 2 Things Got To Get Better (Get Together)............ | 110 | King 6249 |
| 10/25/69 | 32 | 3 | 3 I Made A Mistake Because It's Only You Pt. 2..... | | King 6268 |
| | | | **WHIZ KID** | | |
| 4/13/85 | 74 | 7 | 1 He's Got The Beat ....................................... | | Tommy Boy 854 |
| | | | **WHODINI** | | |
| | | | New York rap duo: Jalil "Whodini" Hutchins and John Fletcher. | | |
| 12/04/82+ | 45 | 10 | 1 Magic's Wand ............................................. | | Jive 2004 |
| 6/25/83 | 55 | 8 | 2 The Haunted House Of Rock........................... | | Jive 9031 |
| 9/08/84 | 4 | 23 | 3 **Friends/** | 87 | |
| | | 19 | 4 Five Minutes Of Funk ............................. | [I] | Jive 9276 |
| 1/05/85 | 43 | 12 | 5 Freaks Come Out At Night ........................... | 104 | Jive 9302 |
| 4/13/85 | 64 | 8 | 6 Big Mouth (Acapella Mix) ............................. | | Jive 9331 |
| 5/03/86 | 19 | 14 | 7 Funky Beat ............................................... | | Jive 9461 |
| 7/19/86 | 10 | 14 | 8 **One Love**.................................................. | | Jive 9507 |
| 11/08/86 | 58 | 6 | 9 Growing Up ............................................... | | Jive 9537 |
| 9/19/87 | 20 | 11 | 10 Be Yourself ............................................... | | Jive 9629 |
| | | | **WHODINI featuring MILLIE JACKSON** | | |
| | | | **WHOLE DARN FAMILY** | | |
| 11/20/76 | 95 | 4 | 1 Ain't Nothin' But Something To Do ................. | | Soul Int. 105 |
| | | | **SPENCER WIGGINS** | | |
| 9/19/70 | 44 | 5 | 1 Double Lovin'............................................. | | Fame 1470 |
| | | | **EDDIE WILCOX ORCHESTRA with SUNNY GALE** | | |
| | | | Born Edwin Felix Wilcox on 12/27/07 in Method, North Carolina. Died on 9/29/68. Pianist/arranger/leader. With Jimmie Lunceford from 1929-47. Led band after Lunceford's death, with Joe Thomas, from 1947-49. Arranger/leader for Derby Records in 1951. Own Raecox/Enrica labels with Teddy "Mr. Bear" McRae, in the late 50s. Philadelphia-born vocalist Sunny Gale was with Hal McIntyre's band. | | |
| 2/16/52 | 2² | 8 | 1 **Wheel Of Fortune**...................................... | 13 | Derby 787 |
| | | | Best Seller #2 / Juke Box #3 | | |

| DEBUT DATE | PEAK POS | WKS CHR | ARTIST — Record Title | POP POS | Label & Number |
|---|---|---|---|---|---|
| | | | **WILD CHERRY** | | |
| | | | White funk band formed in Steubenville, Ohio in the early 70s. Consisted of Bob Parissi (lead vocals, guitar), Bryan Bassett (guitar), Mark Avsec (keyboards), Allen Wentz (bass) and Ron Beitle (drums). | | |
| 7/04/76 | 1² | 20 | 1 ▲ **Play That Funky Music** ............................ | 1 | Epic 50225 |
| 1/22/77 | 41 | 7 | 2 Baby Don't You Know .................................. | 43 | Epic 50306 |
| 4/09/77 | 62 | 8 | 3 Hot To Trot ............................................ | 95 | Epic 50362 |
| 3/04/78 | 49 | 8 | 4 I Love My Music ...................................... | 69 | Epic 50500 |
| | | | all of above: written & produced by Parissi | | |
| | | | **WILD MAGNOLIAS** | | |
| | | | New Orleans Mardi Gras "Indian tribe". Consisted of "Big Chief" Bo Dollis, "Chief" Monk Boudreaux, "Gator" June Johnson, Jr., "Crip" Adams, "Quarter Moon" Tobias", "Gate" Johnson, "Bubba" Scott and James Smothers. Backed by Wilson "Willie Tee" Turbinton Band. Appeared at Carnegie Hall, New York and Capitol Center, Washington, DC, in 1974. | | |
| 11/02/74 | 74 | 6 | 1 Smoke My Peace Pipe (Smoke It Right) ............. | | Polydor 14242 |
| | | | **EUGENE WILDE** | | |
| | | | Real name is Ron Broomfield. Vocalist/songwriter. Member of the Miami-based family group Life. | | |
| 10/13/84+ | 1¹ | 23 | 1 **Gotta Get You Home Tonight** ....................... | 83 | Philly W. 99710 |
| 2/23/85 | 22 | 15 | 2 Rainbow ............................................... | | Philly W. 99675 |
| 6/22/85 | 69 | 7 | 3 Chey Chey Kule ...................................... | | Philly W. 99640 |
| 10/12/85 | 1³ | 22 | 4 **Don't Say No Tonight** .............................. | 76 | Philly W. 99608 |
| 2/01/86 | 10 | 15 | 5 **Diana** ............................................... | | Philly W. 99573 |
| 5/31/86 | 79 | 4 | 6 30 Mins. To Talk ..................................... | | MCA 52824 |
| | | | **MATTHEW WILDER** | | |
| | | | Born and raised in Manhattan; moved to Los Angeles in the late 70s. Singer/songwriter/keyboardist. Session singer for Rickie Lee Jones and Bette Midler. | | |
| 11/12/83 | 76 | 5 | 1 Break My Stride ...................................... | 5 | Private I 04113 |
| | | | **ED WILEY** | | |
| | | | Tenor saxophonist. | | |
| 3/25/50 | 3 | 14 | 1 **Cry, Cry Baby** ...................................... | | Sittin' In 545 |
| | | | Juke Box #3 / Best Seller #4 | | |
| | | | vocal by Teddy Reynolds | | |
| | | | **MICHELLE WILEY** | | |
| 5/21/77 | 52 | 7 | 1 I Feel So At Home Here .............................. | | 20th Century 2317 |
| | | | **WILL TO POWER** | | |
| | | | Florida-based trio formed and fronted by producer Bob Rosenberg. | | |
| 8/15/87 | 40 | 12 | 1 Dreamin' .............................................. | 53 | Epic 07199 |
| | | | **ALYSON WILLIAMS - see CHUCK STANLEY** | | |
| | | | **ANDRE WILLIAMS** | | |
| | | | Born in 1936 in Chicago. Sang in Cobbs Baptist Church Choir in the 40s. Moved to Detroit in the early 50s. Formed group the Five Dollars. First recorded for Fortune in 1955. Record production from the early 60s. | | |
| 2/09/57 | 9 | 4 | 1 **Bacon Fat** ........................................... | | Epic 9196 |
| | | | Best Seller #9 / Jockey #13 | | |
| | | | with the Five Dollars (vocal group); | | |
| | | | originally released on Fortune 831 | | |
| 10/12/68 | 46 | 2 | 2 Cadillac Jack ......................................... | | Checker 1205 |
| | | | **ANDY WILLIAMS** | | |
| | | | Born Howard Andrew Williams on 12/3/28 in Wall Lake, Iowa. One of America's greatest Pop/MOR singers. On Steve Allen's "Tonight Show" from 1952-55. Own NBC-TV variety series from 1962-67; 1969-71. Formerly married to singer/actress Claudine Longet. | | |
| 3/30/57 | 14 | 1 | 1 Butterfly .............................................. | 1 | Cadence 1308 |
| | | | Jockey #14 | | |
| 4/20/59 | 27 | 1 | 2 The Hawaiian Wedding Song ........................ | 11 | Cadence 1358 |
| | | | song written in 1926, with new lyrics added | | |
| 10/26/59 | 20 | 4 | 3 Lonely Street ......................................... | 5 | Cadence 1370 |
| 5/04/63 | 7 | 5 | 4 **Can't Get Used To Losing You** .................... | 2 | Columbia 42674 |
| | | | all of above: produced by Robert Mersey | | |
| | | | **BEAU WILLIAMS** | | |
| | | | Vocalist from Houston. | | |
| 9/22/84 | 64 | 9 | 1 You Are The One ...................................... | | Capitol 5395 |

| DEBUT DATE | PEAK POS | WKS CHR | ARTIST — Record Title | POP POS | Label & Number |
|---|---|---|---|---|---|
| | | | **BEAU WILLIAMS** — Continued | | |
| 9/06/86 | **38** | 12 | 2 There's Just Something About You ................. | | Capitol 5611 |
| 4/18/87 | **94** | 3 | 3 All Because Of You....................................... | | Capitol 5689 |
| | | | **BILLY WILLIAMS** | | |
| | | | Born on 12/28/10 in Waco, Texas; died on 10/17/72 in Chicago. Lead singer of The Charioteers from 1930-50. Formed own Billy Williams Quartet with Eugene Dixon, Claude Riddick and John Ball in 1950. Many appearances on TV, especially "Your Show Of Shows" with Sid Caesar. By early 60s, had lost voice due to diabetes. Moved to Chicago and worked as social worker until his death. | | |
| 7/29/57 | **9** | 1 | 1 I'm Gonna Sit Right Down & Write Myself A Letter ..................................................... <br> Jockey #9 | *3* | Coral 61830 |
| | | | **BOBBY WILLIAMS** | | |
| 6/19/76 | **87** | 8 | 1 You Need Love Like I Do ................................. | | R&R 15312 |
| | | | **BOBBY EARL WILLIAMS** | | |
| 2/09/74 | **74** | 5 | 1 That's The Way She Is .................................. | | 9 Chains 7000 |
| | | | **CAROL WILLIAMS** | | |
| | | | Vocalist from London. | | |
| 5/01/76 | **98** | 1 | 1 More............................................................. | *102* | Salsoul 2006 |
| | | | **COOTIE WILLIAMS** | | |
| | | | Born Charles Melvin Williams on 7/24/08 in Mobile, Alabama. Died on 9/15/85 (77). Trumpeter/leader. With Duke Ellington from 1929-40, Benny Goodman from 1940-41, then formed own band. Wrote "Concerto For Cootie" in 1940; became hit with lyrics added as "Do Nothing 'Til You Hear From Me", in 1943. Re-joined Ellington from 1962-74. Also see Benny Goodman and Dinah Washington. | | |
| 5/20/44 | **2²** | 39 | 1 Cherry Red Blues........................................... | *23* | Hit 7084 |
| 10/28/44 | **9** | 3 | 2 Is You Or Is You Ain't................................... | | Hit 7108 |
| 1/06/45 | **1¹** | 13 | 3 Somebody's Got To Go.................................... <br> features Bud Powell (piano), Eddie "Lockjaw" Davis (tenor sax) and Eddie Vinson (tenor sax); <br> all of above: vocals by Eddie "Cleanhead" Vinson | | Hit 7119 |
| | | | **D-TRAIN WILLIAMS - see JAMES WILLIAMS** | | |
| | | | **DANNY WILLIAMS** | | |
| | | | Born in Port Elizabeth, South Africa. Moved to England as a youngster. | | |
| 3/07/64 | **9** | 14 | 1 White On White ............................................ | *Hot* | United Art. 685 |
| 6/20/64 | **84** | 4 | 2 A Little Toy Balloon ...................................... | *Hot* | United Art. 729 |
| | | | **DARNELL WILLIAMS** | | |
| | | | Actor/singer born in London; raised in Brooklyn. Played "Jesse Hubbard" on the daytime TV series "All My Children". | | |
| 10/08/83 | **67** | 5 | 1 Pure Satisfaction ......................................... | | My Disc 04085 |
| | | | **DAVID WILLIAMS** | | |
| 1/07/84 | **73** | 5 | 1 Take The Ball And Run.................................. | | Ocean Fr. 2002 |
| | | | **DEE WILLIAMS SEXTET** | | |
| | | | Los Angeles band led by Devonia "Lady Dee" Williams (piano). Williams also worked with Big Jay McNeely and Johnny Otis. | | |
| 3/12/49 | **13** | 1 | 1 Bongo Blues................................................ [I] <br> Juke Box #13 | | Savoy 684 |
| | | | **DENIECE WILLIAMS** ★★99★★ | | |
| | | | Born Deniece Chandler on 6/3/51 in Gary, Indiana. Vocalist/songwriter. Recorded for Toddlin' Town, early 60s. Member of Wonderlove, Stevie Wonder's back-up group, from 1972-75. | | |
| 11/13/76+ | **2¹** | 20 | 1 Free/ | *25* | |
| 6/04/77 | **74** | 3 | 2  Cause You Love My Baby ............................. | | Columbia 10429 |
| 7/02/77 | **65** | 8 | 3 That's What Friends Are For........................... | *103* | Columbia 10556 |
| 12/10/77+ | **13** | 15 | 4 Baby, Baby My Love's All For You ................... | | Columbia 10648 |
| 3/04/78 | **1⁴** | 20 | 5●Too Much, Too Little, Too Late ..................... <br> JOHNNY MATHIS/DENIECE WILLIAMS | *1* | Columbia 10693 |
| 7/08/78 | **10** | 12 | 6 You're All I Need To Get By ......................... <br> JOHNNY MATHIS & DENIECE WILLIAMS | *47* | Columbia 10772 |
| 6/02/79 | **26** | 15 | 7 I've Got The Next Dance................................ | *73* | ARC 10971 |
| 10/06/79 | **32** | 14 | 8 I Found Love................................................ | *105* | ARC 11063 |
| 3/07/81 | **17** | 14 | 9 What Two Can Do ......................................... | | ARC 60504 |
| 5/30/81 | **45** | 10 | 10 It's Your Conscience..................................... | | ARC 02108 |

**444**

| DEBUT DATE | PEAK POS | WKS CHR | ARTIST — Record Title | POP POS | Label & Number |
|---|---|---|---|---|---|
| | | | **DENIECE WILLIAMS — Continued** | | |
| 8/08/81 | 11 | 15 | 11 Silly ..................................... | *53* | ARC 02406 |
| 3/27/82 | 1² | 17 | 12 **It's Gonna Take A Miracle** ............. | *10* | ARC 02812 |
| 7/17/82 | 29 | 12 | 13 Waiting By The Hotline .................... | *103* | ARC 03015 |
| 10/30/82 | 72 | 5 | 14 Waiting .................................. | | ARC 03261 |
| 4/23/83 | 9 | 18 | 15 **Do What You Feel** ....................... | *102* | Columbia 03807 |
| 8/13/83 | 28 | 10 | 16 I'm So Proud ............................. | | Columbia 04037 |
| 2/25/84 | 32 | 12 | 17 Love Won't Let Me Wait .................. | *106* | Columbia 04379 |
| | | | JOHNNY MATHIS & DENIECE WILLIAMS | | |
| 4/14/84 | 1³ | 19 | 18● **Let's Hear It For The Boy** ............... | *1* | Columbia 04417 |
| | | | from the film "Footloose" | | |
| 7/28/84 | 22 | 13 | 19 Next Love .............................. | *81* | Columbia 04537 |
| 10/13/84 | 22 | 14 | 20 Black Butterfly .......................... | | Columbia 04641 |
| 7/19/86 | 60 | 10 | 21 Wiser And Weaker ....................... | | Columbia 06157 |
| 10/04/86 | 76 | 5 | 22 Healing ................................. | | Columbia 06318 |
| 4/11/87 | 6 | 15 | 23 **Never Say Never** ........................ | | Columbia 07021 |
| 8/22/87 | 24 | 11 | 24 I Confess ............................... | | Columbia 07357 |
| | | | **EDDIE WILLIAMS** | | |
| | | | Bassist/leader. His band included Floyd Dixon (piano, vocals). | | |
| 9/17/49 | 2⁴ | 17 | 1 **Broken Hearted** ........................ | | Supreme 1535 |
| | | | Best Seller #2 / Juke Box #2 | | |
| | | | **ESTHER WILLIAMS** | | |
| 10/02/76 | 79 | 7 | 1 You Gotta Let Me Show You ............... | | Friends & Co 129 |
| 12/16/78+ | 90 | 5 | 2 Yours & Yours' Alone .................... | | Friends & Co 130 |
| | | | **JAMES (D-TRAIN) WILLIAMS** | | |
| | | | Singer from Brooklyn. Recorded in "D" Train duo with keyboardist Hubert Eaves III from 1981-85. | | |
| 8/23/86 | 53 | 8 | 1 You Are Everything ...................... | | Columbia 06256 |
| 11/08/86+ | 10 | 16 | 2 **Misunderstanding** ........................ | | Columbia 06410 |
| 3/14/87 | 22 | 12 | 3 Oh How I Love You (Girl) ............... | | Columbia 06672 |
| 7/02/88 | 11 | 14 | 4 In Your Eyes ............................ | | Columbia 07930 |
| | | | **JEANETTE WILLIAMS** | | |
| 4/26/69 | 39 | 5 | 1 Stuff ................................... | | Back Beat 601 |
| 1/31/70 | 50 | 2 | 2 I Can Feel A Heartbreak ................. | | Back Beat 609 |
| | | | **JOE WILLIAMS & The King Kolax Orchestra** | | |
| | | | Born Joseph Goreed on 12/12/18 in Cordele, Georgia. Moved to Chicago in 1922. Tuberculosis collapsed left lung at age 15. With gospel group, the Jubilee Boys in 1935. With Johnny Long, Jimmie Noone, Les Hite, Coleman Hawkins, and Lionel Hampton to 1943. First recorded for Okeh in 1946, with Red Saunders. With Count Basie from 1954-61. Numerous overseas tours, TV appearances, jazz festivals, etc. Frequently reunited with Count Basie. | | |
| 10/25/52 | 8 | 5 | 1 **Everyday I Have The Blues** ............. | | Checker 762 |
| | | | Juke Box #8 | | |
| | | | a new version by Count Basie with Williams, "Every Day", charted in 1955 | | |
| | | | **JOHNNY WILLIAMS** | | |
| | | | Born on 1/15/42 in Tyler, Alabama. To Chicago in 1956. With Royal Jubilees gospel group. First recorded in 1965. Died in December of 1986. | | |
| 9/09/72 | 12 | 14 | 1 Slow Motion (Part 1) .................... | *78* | Phil. Int. 3518 |
| | | | **LARRY WILLIAMS** | | |
| | | | Born on 5/10/35 in New Orleans; committed suicide on 1/7/80 in Los Angeles. R&B-rock and roll singer/songwriter/pianist. With Lloyd Price in the early 50s. Convicted of narcotics dealing in 1960, jail term interrupted his career. | | |
| 4/20/57 | 11 | 3 | 1 Just Because ............................ | | Specialty 597 |
| | | | Jockey #11 | | |
| 6/24/57 | 1¹ | 16 | 2 **Short Fat Fannie/** | *5* | |
| | | | Jockey #1 / Best Seller #2 | | |
| | | 1 | 3 High School Dance ....................... | | Specialty 608 |
| | | | Best Seller flip | | |
| 11/04/57 | 4 | 9 | 4 **Bony Moronie** .......................... | *14* | Specialty 615 |
| | | | Jockey #4 / Best Seller #9 | | |
| 3/04/67 | 23 | 10 | 5 Mercy, Mercy, Mercy ..................... | *96* | Okeh 7274 |
| | | | LARRY WILLIAMS & JOHNNY WATSON | | |

| DEBUT DATE | PEAK POS | WKS CHR | ARTIST — Record Title | POP POS | Label & Number |
|---|---|---|---|---|---|
| | | | **LARRY WILLIAMS — Continued** | | |
| 1/27/68 | **40** | 3 | 6 Nobody............................................ | | Okeh 7300 |
| | | | LARRY WILLIAMS & JOHNNY WATSON | | |
| | | | **L.C. WILLIAMS** | | |
| | | | Born on 3/12/30 in Crockett, Texas. Died of a lung disease on 10/18/60 in Houston. Vocalist/drummer. Moved to Houston in 1945. First recorded for Gold Star in 1947. Often teamed with Lightnin' Hopkins, to 1960. | | |
| 10/08/49 | **8** | 3 | 1 **Ethel Mae**.................................... | | Freedom 1517 |
| | | | Juke Box #8 / Best Seller #12 with J.C. Conney's Combo | | |
| | | | **LEE WILLIAMS & THE CYMBALS** | | |
| 4/29/67 | **41** | 3 | 1 I Love You More............................. | | Carnival 521 |
| | | | **LENNY WILLIAMS** | | |
| | | | Born in February of 1945, in Little Rock, Arkansas; raised in Oakland, California. First recorded for Fantasy in the early 60s. With Tower Of Power from 1973-76. Also see Kenny G. | | |
| 10/18/75 | **94** | 4 | 1 Since I Met You ............................ | | Motown 1369 |
| 9/03/77 | **31** | 15 | 2 Shoo Doo Fu Fu Ooh! ..................... | 105 | ABC 12300 |
| 12/03/77+ | **62** | 11 | 3 Choosing You .............................. | 108 | ABC 12289 |
| 4/01/78 | **74** | 7 | 4 Look Up With Your Mind ................. | | ABC 12345 |
| 7/29/78 | **40** | 14 | 5 You Got Me Running....................... | 104 | ABC 12387 |
| 10/28/78 | **20** | 14 | 6 Midnight Girl.............................. | 102 | ABC 12423 |
| 6/16/79 | **30** | 11 | 7 Doing The Loop De Loop ................. | | MCA 41034 |
| 10/06/79 | **43** | 8 | 8 Love Hurt Me, Love Healed Me ......... | | MCA 41118 |
| 9/27/80 | **34** | 10 | 9 Ooh Child .................................. | 109 | MCA 41306 |
| 1/17/81 | **58** | 8 | 10 Messing With My Mind ................... | | MCA 51033 |
| 10/03/81 | **57** | 8 | 11 Freefall (Into Love) ....................... | | MCA 51179 |
| 12/17/83+ | **51** | 10 | 12 Love Soldier................................ | | Rocshire 95044 |
| 4/07/84 | **44** | 12 | 13 Always...................................... | | Rocshire 95056 |
| 9/06/86 | **67** | 8 | 14 Ten Ways Of Loving You ................. | | Knobhill 970 |
| | | | **LINDA WILLIAMS** | | |
| | | | Vocalist/keyboardist from New York City. Studied music theory at the Manhattan School of Music. Taught vocal music at J.H.S. 263 in Brooklyn. Worked with Billy Taylor's Jazzmobile Workshop. Accompanist-conductor for Natalie Cole for 4 years. | | |
| 10/13/79 | **48** | 10 | 1 No Love, No Where, Without You ...................... | | Arista 0442 |
| | | | **LITTLE JERRY WILLIAMS - see SWAMP DOGG** | | |
| | | | **MAURICE WILLIAMS & THE ZODIACS** | | |
| | | | Vocal group from Lancaster, SC, led by pianist/songwriter Maurice Williams. Originally recorded as The Gladiolas, became The Zodiacs in 1960. Williams re-formed group with Wiley Bennett, Henry Gaston, Charles Thomas, Albert Hill, and Little Willie Morrow in 1960. Recorded with the Pips in 1967. A new group is still active in the Atlantic Seaboard area. Also see The Gladiolas. | | |
| 9/26/60 | **3** | 18 | 1 **Stay**....................................... | 1 | Herald 552 |
| | | | **MIKE WILLIAMS** | | |
| 7/30/66 | **38** | 4 | 1 Lonely Soldier ............................. | 69 | Atlantic 2339 |
| | | | arranged by Gene "Daddy G" Barge | | |
| | | | **OTIS WILLIAMS - see THE CHARMS** | | |
| | | | **PATRICK WILLIAMS** | | |
| 1/08/83 | **72** | 5 | 1 Lou's Blues................................. | | PCM 201 |
| | | | **PAUL WILLIAMS** | | |
| | | | Saxophonist/leader. With Clarence Dorsey in 1946. First recorded with King Porter, for Paradise in 1947. Formed own band in late 1947. Band had vocalists Joan Shaw, Connie Allen, Danny Cobb and Jimmy Brown. Included sidemen Phil Guilbeau (trumpet) and Noble "Thin Man" Watts (tenor sax). Recorded into the 60s as house musician at Atlantic. Director of Lloyd Price and James Brown bands to 1964. Left music and became a salesman in New York. Opened booking agency in 1968. Also see Bill Moore. | | |
| 2/14/48 | **8** | 7 | 1 **35-30**...................................... [I] | | Savoy 661 |
| | | | Juke Box #8 / Best Seller #9 also released on Savoy 798 | | |
| 8/14/48 | **15** | 1 | 2 The Twister Pts 1&2 ...................... [I] | | Savoy 665 |
| | | | Juke Box #15 | | |
| 9/18/48 | **11** | 3 | 3 Waxie Maxie................................ [I] | | Savoy 670 |
| | | | Best Seller #11 / Juke Box #12 | | |

| DEBUT DATE | PEAK POS | WKS CHR | ARTIST — Record Title | POP POS | Label & Number |
|---|---|---|---|---|---|
| | | | **PAUL WILLIAMS — Continued** | | |
| 1/08/49 | 6 | 2 | 4 Walkin' Around .................................... [I] | | Savoy 680 |
| | | | Juke Box #6 | | |
| | | | above 3: with Wild Bill Moore on tenor sax | | |
| 2/05/49 | 1 14 | 32 | 5 The Hucklebuck ................................... [I] | | Savoy 683 |
| | | | Juke Box #1(14) / Best Seller #1(12) | | |
| | | | also released on Savoy 799, 1143, 1557 | | |
| 7/16/49 | 12 | 1 | 6 House Rocker/ | [I] | |
| | | | Juke Box #12 | | |
| 7/23/49 | 13 | 1 | 7 He Knows How To Hucklebuck ..................... | | Savoy 702 |
| | | | Juke Box #13 / Best Seller #15 | | |
| | | | with Joan Shaw on vocals | | |
| 9/17/49 | 13 | 2 | 8 Pop Corn .................................. [I] | | Savoy 711 |
| | | | **SONNY BOY WILLIAMS** | | |
| | | | Singer/boogie pianist Enoch Williams from Indianapolis. Performed with the Cabin Kids on NBC in the late 30s. | | |
| 6/19/43 | 9 | 1 | 1 Rubber Bounce ............................... | | Decca 8651 |
| | | | **VANESSA WILLIAMS** | | |
| | | | Singer/actress, born in Tarrytown, New York. In 1983, became the first black woman to win the Miss America pageant; relinquished crown due to porn magazine scandal. | | |
| 5/21/88 | 4 | 15 | 1 The Right Stuff ........................................ | *44* | Wing 887386 |
| | | | **VESTA WILLIAMS** | | |
| 10/25/86 | 9 | 16 | 1 Once Bitten Twice Shy ............................. | | A&M 2880 |
| 2/07/87 | 46 | 10 | 2 Something About You ............................... | | A&M 2903 |
| 5/09/87 | 17 | 15 | 3 Don't Blow A Good Thing ............................ | | A&M 2926 |
| 10/03/87 | 90 | 3 | 4 You Make Me Want To (Love Again)................. | | A&M 2957 |
| | | | **WILSON WILLIAMS** | | |
| | | | Vocalist from Detroit. | | |
| 4/08/78 | 80 | 5 | 1 Up The Down Stairs.................................. | | ABC 12344 |
| 7/08/78 | 92 | 3 | 2 Sho You Rite ....................................... | | ABC 12377 |
| | | | **SONNY BOY WILLIAMSON** | | |
| | | | Born John Lee Williamson on 3/30/14 in Jackson, Tennessee. Murdered on 6/1/48 in Chicago. Harmonica player; moved to Chicago in 1934, worked with small bands until 1945. First recorded for Bluebird in 1937. | | |
| 2/01/47 | 4 | 1 | 1 Shake The Boogie ................................. | | Victor 2056 |
| 12/18/48 | 15 | 1 | 2 Better Cut That Out................................ | | Victor 3218 |
| | | | Best Seller #15 | | |
| | | | **SONNY BOY WILLIAMSON** | | |
| | | | Born Aleck Ford on 12/5/1899 in Glendora, Mississippi. Also known as Alex "Rice" Miller. Died on 5/25/65 in Helena, Arkansas. Guitarist/harmonica player since age 5. Appeared on the Grand Ole Opry in the mid-30s. Worked as "Sonny Boy Williamson" on KFFA-Helena from 1941-45. First recorded for United Artists in 1947. A major delineator of the blues harmonica style. | | |
| 10/15/55 | 3 | 11 | 1 Don't Start Me Talkin' ............................ | | Checker 824 |
| | | | Juke Box #3 / Jockey #5 / Best Seller #7 | | |
| | | | with Muddy Waters & Jimmy Rogers (guitar) | | |
| 11/17/56 | 14 | 1 | 2 Keep It To Yourself ............................... | | Checker 847 |
| | | | Best Seller #14 | | |
| 4/06/63 | 24 | 4 | 3 Help Me.............................................. | | Checker 1036 |
| | | | **BRUCE WILLIS** | | |
| | | | Plays "David Addison" on the TV series "Moonlighting". Married actress Demi Moore on 11/21/87. Appeared in the films "Blind Date" (1987) and "Die Hard" (1988). | | |
| 1/24/87 | 20 | 11 | 1 Respect Yourself.................................... | *5* | Motown 1876 |
| 6/13/87 | 72 | 6 | 2 Under The Boardwalk ............................. | *59* | Motown 1896 |
| | | | **CHUCK WILLIS** ★★151★★ | | |
| | | | Born on 1/31/28 in Atlanta; died on 4/10/58 (peritonitis). Singer/songwriter. First recorded for Columbia in 1951. Wrote "The Door Is Still Open", "Close Your Eyes", "Oh What A Dream", and many others. | | |
| 10/25/52 | 2 2 | 10 | 1 My Story.............................................. | | Okeh 6905 |
| | | | Juke Box #2 / Best Seller #3 | | |
| 5/02/53 | 4 | 6 | 2 Goin' To The River ................................ | | Okeh 6952 |
| | | | Juke Box #4 / Best Seller #10 | | |
| 7/25/53 | 6 | 12 | 3 Don't Deceive Me ................................. | | Okeh 6985 |
| | | | Best Seller #6 / Juke Box #6 | | |
| 2/06/54 | 4 | 9 | 4 You're Still My Baby.............................. | | Okeh 7015 |
| | | | Best Seller #4 / Juke Box #5 | | |

| DEBUT DATE | PEAK POS | WKS CHR | ARTIST — Record Title | POP POS | Label & Number |
|---|---|---|---|---|---|
| | | | **CHUCK WILLIS — Continued** | | |
| 7/10/54 | **8** | 4 | 5 **I Feel So Bad** ............................ <br> Best Seller #8 / Juke Box #9 | | Okeh 7029 |
| 7/07/56 | **3** | 14 | 6 **It's Too Late** ............................. <br> Jockey #3 / Best Seller #5 / Juke Box #8 | | Atlantic 1098 |
| 11/17/56 | **7** | 5 | 7 **Juanita/** <br> Juke Box #7 / Jockey #11 <br> above 2: with The Cookies (vocal group) | | |
| 12/01/56 | **11** | 2 | 8 Whatcha' Gonna Do When Your Baby Leaves You .................... <br> Best Seller #11 | | Atlantic 1112 |
| 4/20/57 | **1**² | 18 | 9 **C.C. Rider**.............................. <br> Jockey #1 / Juke Box #2 / Best Seller #3 <br> inspired the "Stroll" dance craze; <br> 6-9: with the Jesse Stone Orchestra & Chorus | *12* | Atlantic 1130 |
| 2/03/58 | **15** | 5 | 10 **Betty And Dupree** ...................... <br> Best Seller #15 <br> above 2: featuring Gene "Daddy G" Barge on saxophone | *33* | Atlantic 1168 |
| 5/05/58 | **1**¹ | 17 | 11 **What Am I Living For/** <br> Jockey #1 / Best Seller #3 | *9* | |
| 6/16/58 | **9** | 3 | 12 **Hang Up My Rock And Roll Shoes**.............. <br> Jockey #9 <br> above 2: with the Reggie Obrecht Orchestra & Chorus | *24* | Atlantic 1179 |
| 9/08/58 | **12** | 6 | 13 My Life.............................. | *46* | Atlantic 1192 |
| 12/15/58 | **19** | 5 | 14 Keep A-Driving ........................... | | Atlantic 2005 |
| | | | **M-D-L-T WILLIS** <br> Family group from Ashtabula, Ohio. Consisted of Maxine, Diane, LaVerne and Tina Willis. Moved to Los Angeles in 1965. Worked as the Willis Sisters. Toured the United States and Europe with Peggy Fleming's "Concert On Ice". | | |
| 11/23/74 | **89** | 5 | 1 What's Your Game ......................... | | Ivory Tower 101 |
| | | | **TIMMY WILLIS** | | |
| 2/24/68 | **39** | 2 | 1 Mr. Soul Satisfaction ...................... | *120* | Veep 1279 |
| 6/07/69 | **44** | 3 | 2 I Finally Found A Woman ................... | | Jubilee 5660 |
| 3/07/70 | **46** | 3 | 3 Easy As Saying 1-2-3 ...................... | | Jubilee 5690 |
| | | | **WILLOWS** <br> Vocal group from New York City, formed as the Five Willows in 1952. Consisted of Tony Middleton (lead), Richard Davis, Ralph Martin, Joseph Martin and Freddy Donovan. Middleton went solo in the late 50s. | | |
| 4/28/56 | **11** | 3 | 1 Church Bells May Ring.................. <br> Best Seller #11 / Jockey #14 <br> chimes played by Neil Sedaka | *62* | Melba 102 |
| | | | **AL WILSON** <br> Born on 6/19/39 in Meridian, Mississippi. Singer/drummer. Moved to San Bernadino, California in the late 50s. Member of The Rollers from 1960-62. With Johnny "Legs" Harris & The Statesmen in the mid-60s. | | |
| 2/03/68 | **39** | 6 | 1 Do What You Gotta Do .................... | *102* | Soul City 761 |
| 8/10/68 | **32** | 5 | 2 The Snake ............................. | *27* | Soul City 767 |
| 10/20/73+ | **10** | 18 | 3● Show And Tell................................ | *1* | Rocky Road 30073 |
| 3/02/74 | **23** | 15 | 4 Touch And Go .......................... | *57* | Rocky Road 30076 |
| 9/28/74 | **19** | 12 | 5 La La Peace Song......................... | *30* | Rocky Road 30200 |
| 12/28/74+ | **18** | 11 | 6 I Won't Last A Day Without You/Let Me Be The One ...................... | *70* | Rocky Road 30202 |
| 2/28/76 | **3** | 17 | 7 **I've Got A Feeling (We'll Be Seeing Each Other Again)**.................... | *29* | Playboy 6062 |
| 7/04/76 | **28** | 12 | 8 Baby I Want Your Body .................... | | Playboy 6076 |
| 6/23/79 | **84** | 4 | 9 Count The Days ......................... | | Roadshow 11583 |
| | | | **ART WILSON** | | |
| 5/14/83 | **56** | 7 | 1 Stay............................... | | Tabu 03850 |
| | | | **BOBBY WILSON** <br> Vocalist/pianist/guitarist. | | |
| 4/21/73 | **34** | 6 | 1 Here Is Where Love Is .................... | | Chain 2101 |
| 2/15/75 | **60** | 9 | 2 Deeper And Deeper....................... | | Buddah 449 |

| DEBUT DATE | PEAK POS | WKS CHR | | ARTIST — Record Title | POP POS | Label & Number |
|---|---|---|---|---|---|---|
| | | | | **JACKIE WILSON** ★★26★★ | | |
| | | | | Born on 6/9/34 in Detroit; died on 1/21/84. Sang with local gospel groups; became an amateur boxer. Worked as solo singer until 1953, then joined Billy Ward's Dominoes as Clyde McPhatter's replacement. Solo since 1957. His goddaughter is Jody Watley. Jackie collapsed from a stroke, on stage, at the Latin Casino in Camden, New Jersey, on 9/25/75; spent rest of his life in hospitals. | | |
| 4/21/58 | 7 | 10 | 1 | To Be Loved .............................................. | 22 | Brunswick 55052 |
| | | | | Jockey #7 / Best Seller #11 with the Milton Delugg Orchestra also released on Brunswick 55070 | | |
| 11/17/58 | 1 ⁷ | 22 | 2 | Lonely Teardrops ....................................... | 7 | Brunswick 55105 |
| 4/06/59 | 2 ⁴ | 12 | 3 | That's Why (I Love You So) ........................ | 13 | Brunswick 55121 |
| 6/22/59 | 6 | 11 | 4 | I'll Be Satisfied ........................................ | 20 | Brunswick 55136 |
| | | | | all of above: written by Berry Gordy, Jr. & Tyran Carlo | | |
| 9/14/59 | 1 ¹ | 9 | 5 | You Better Know It .................................... | 37 | Brunswick 55149 |
| | | | | from the film "Go Johnny Go" | | |
| 11/30/59 | 3 | 18 | 6 | Talk That Talk ......................................... | 34 | Brunswick 55165 |
| 4/04/60 | 1 ³ | 19 | 7 | Doggin' Around/ | 15 | |
| 4/11/60 | 3 | 13 | 8 | Night ........................................... | 4 | Brunswick 55166 |
| 7/11/60 | 1 ⁴ | 13 | 9 | A Woman, A Lover, A Friend ...................... | 15 | Brunswick 55167 |
| 11/21/60 | 10 | 8 | 10 | Am I The Man/ | 32 | |
| 11/28/60 | 20 | 6 | 11 | Alone At Last ............................... | 8 | Brunswick 55170 |
| | | | | based on Tchaikovsky's "Piano Concerto in B Flat" | | |
| 2/13/61 | 10 | 7 | 12 | The Tear Of The Year/ | 44 | |
| 2/20/61 | 25 | 1 | 13 | My Empty Arms.............................. | 9 | Brunswick 55201 |
| 4/17/61 | 11 | 6 | 14 | Please Tell Me Why ................................... | 20 | Brunswick 55208 |
| 6/26/61 | 9 | 5 | 15 | I'm Comin' On Back To You ........................ | 19 | Brunswick 55216 |
| 8/07/61 | 25 | 2 | 16 | Years From Now/ | 37 | |
| 8/21/61 | 19 | 5 | 17 | You Don't Know What It Means ................... | 79 | Brunswick 55219 |
| 8/04/62 | 17 | 6 | 18 | I Just Can't Help It ................................... | 70 | Brunswick 55229 |
| 3/23/63 | 1 ³ | 14 | 19 | Baby Workout ........................................... | 5 | Brunswick 55239 |
| 7/13/63 | 21 | 4 | 20 | Shake A Hand ........................................... | 42 | Brunswick 55243 |
| | | | | JACKIE WILSON & LINDA HOPKINS | | |
| 7/27/63 | 21 | 4 | 21 | Shake! Shake! Shake! ................................. | 33 | Brunswick 55246 |
| 9/21/63 | 61 | 5 | 22 | Baby Get It (And Don't Quit It)..................... | Hot | Brunswick 55250 |
| 5/23/64 | 94 | 1 | 23 | Big Boss Line ............................................ | Hot | Brunswick 55266 |
| 8/22/64 | 89 | 2 | 24 | Squeeze Her-Tease Her (But Love Her)............. | Hot | Brunswick 55269 |
| 3/13/65 | 25 | 7 | 25 | Danny Boy................................................. | 94 | Brunswick 55277 |
| | | | | traditional Irish song written in 1855 | | |
| 7/03/65 | 25 | 11 | 26 | No Pity (In The Naked City) ........................ | 59 | Brunswick 55280 |
| 11/06/65 | 34 | 4 | 27 | I Believe I'll Love On.................................. | 96 | Brunswick 55283 |
| 2/05/66 | 37 | 3 | 28 | Think Twice............................................... | 93 | Brunswick 55287 |
| | | | | JACKIE WILSON & LaVERN BAKER | | |
| 10/08/66 | 5 | 16 | 29 | Whispers (Gettin' Louder)............................ | 11 | Brunswick 55300 |
| 3/04/67 | 11 | 10 | 30 | I Don't Want To Lose You/ | 84 | |
| 2/18/67 | 43 | 2 | 31 | Just Be Sincere ....................................... | 91 | Brunswick 55309 |
| 6/03/67 | 35 | 4 | 32 | I've Lost You............................................. | 82 | Brunswick 55321 |
| 8/26/67 | 1 ¹ | 14 | 33 | (Your Love Keeps Lifting Me) Higher And Higher.............................................. | 6 | Brunswick 55336 |
| 12/16/67+ | 22 | 5 | 34 | Since You Showed Me How To Be Happy .......... | 32 | Brunswick 55354 |
| 3/09/68 | 26 | 6 | 35 | For Your Precious Love................................ | 49 | Brunswick 55365 |
| | | | | JACKIE WILSON & COUNT BASIE | | |
| 5/04/68 | 37 | 4 | 36 | Chain Gang .............................................. | 84 | Brunswick 55373 |
| | | | | JACKIE WILSON & COUNT BASIE | | |
| 7/20/68 | 12 | 10 | 37 | I Get The Sweetest Feeling............................ | 34 | Brunswick 55381 |
| 4/05/69 | 39 | 3 | 38 | I Still Love You.......................................... | 105 | Brunswick 55402 |
| 9/13/69 | 21 | 5 | 39 | Helpless ................................................... | 108 | Brunswick 55418 |
| 5/02/70 | 34 | 7 | 40 | Let This Be A Letter (To My Baby) ................. | 91 | Brunswick 55435 |
| 12/12/70+ | 9 | 12 | 41 | This Love Is Real ...................................... | | Brunswick 55443 |
| 11/13/71 | 18 | 9 | 42 | Love Is Funny That Way ............................. | 95 | Brunswick 55461 |
| 2/19/72 | 22 | 6 | 43 | You Got Me Walking ................................... | 93 | Brunswick 55467 |
| 5/13/72 | 44 | 3 | 44 | The Girl Turned Me On................................ | | Brunswick 55475 |
| 5/12/73 | 45 | 2 | 45 | Because Of You ......................................... | | Brunswick 55495 |
| 7/28/73 | 95 | 5 | 46 | Sing A Little Song ...................................... | | Brunswick 55499 |

| DEBUT DATE | PEAK POS | WKS CHR | ARTIST — Record Title | POP POS | Label & Number |
|---|---|---|---|---|---|
| | | | **JACKIE WILSON — Continued** | | |
| 11/15/75 | 91 | 4 | 47 Don't Burn No Bridges ................................... | | Brunswick 55522 |
| | | | JACKIE WILSON & THE CHI-LITES | | |
| | | | **JIMMY WILSON** | | |
| | | | Born in Houston; died in 1965 in Dallas. With Pilgrim Travelers gospel group. Moved to Los Angeles in 1947. First recorded for Rhythm in 1950. | | |
| 7/04/53 | 10 | 1 | 1 Tin Pan Alley .............................................. | | Big Town 101 |
| | | | Juke Box #10 | | |
| | | | **MARY WILSON** | | |
| | | | Born on 3/6/44 in Mississippi; raised in Detroit. Founding member of The Supremes. | | |
| 10/20/79 | 95 | 3 | 1 Red Hot.................................................... | | Motown 1467 |
| | | | **MERI WILSON** | | |
| | | | Dallas-based song stylist. | | |
| 8/20/77 | 91 | 3 | 1● Telephone Man ........................................ [N] | *18* | GRT 127 |
| | | | **NANCY WILSON** | | |
| | | | Born on 2/20/37 in Chillicothe, Ohio. Jazz stylist with Rusty Bryant's Carolyn Club Band in Columbus. First recorded for Dot in 1956. Also see Ramsey Lewis. | | |
| 4/07/62 | 11 | 5 | 1 Save Your Love For Me ................................. | | Capitol 4693 |
| | | | with Cannonball Adderly | | |
| 9/14/63 | 22 | 2 | 2 Tell Me The Truth ...................................... | 73 | Capitol 4991 |
| 6/27/64 | 11 | 11 | 3 (You Don't Know) How Glad I Am .................... | *Hot* | Capitol 5198 |
| 9/10/66 | 48 | 2 | 4 You've Got Your Troubles............................... | | Capitol 5673 |
| 6/01/68 | 15 | 7 | 5 Face It Girl, It's Over ................................. | 29 | Capitol 2136 |
| 10/05/68 | 24 | 8 | 6 Peace Of Mind ......................................... | 55 | Capitol 2283 |
| 3/29/69 | 44 | 2 | 7 You'd Better Go ......................................... | *111* | Capitol 2422 |
| 11/15/69 | 27 | 6 | 8 Can't Take My Eyes Off You.......................... | 52 | Capitol 2644 |
| 12/12/70+ | 41 | 4 | 9 Now I'm A Woman...................................... | 93 | Capitol 2934 |
| 10/05/74 | 46 | 10 | 10 Streetrunner ........................................... | | Capitol 3956 |
| 12/28/74+ | 10 | 14 | 11 **You're As Right As Rain** ............................ | | Capitol 3973 |
| 9/27/75 | 74 | 8 | 12 He Called Me Baby ................................... | | Capitol 4117 |
| 12/13/75+ | 54 | 9 | 13 Don't Let Me Be Lonely Tonight..................... | | Capitol 4189 |
| | | | written by James Taylor; pop hit for Taylor in 1972 (POS 14) | | |
| 7/24/76 | 91 | 3 | 14 Now..................................................... | | Capitol 4284 |
| 11/27/76 | 96 | 2 | 15 In My Loneliness (When We Were Young) ......... | | Capitol 4350 |
| 9/10/77 | 47 | 13 | 16 I've Never Been To Me................................ | | Capitol 4476 |
| | | | #3 pop hit for Charlene in 1982 | | |
| 6/10/78 | 94 | 5 | 17 I'm Gonna Let Ya ..................................... | | Capitol 4578 |
| 7/21/79 | 83 | 6 | 18 Life, Love And Harmony............................... | | Capitol 4741 |
| | | | **PRECIOUS WILSON** | | |
| | | | Male vocalist; former member of the Jamaican techno-funk quintet Eruption. | | |
| 4/19/86 | 40 | 12 | 1 I'll Be Your Friend.................................... | | Jive 9456 |
| | | | **SHANICE WILSON** | | |
| | | | Native of Pittsburgh. To Los Angeles at age 7. Began singing commercial jingles at age 8. First recorded for A&M, in 1987, at age 14. | | |
| 9/12/87 | 6 | 15 | 1 **(Baby Tell Me) Can You Dance**...................... | 50 | A&M 2939 |
| 12/26/87+ | 6 | 15 | 2 No 1/2 Steppin' ....................................... | | A&M 2990 |
| 4/09/88 | 53 | 12 | 3 The Way You Love Me................................ | | A&M 3018 |
| | | | **TIMOTHY WILSON** | | |
| 12/23/67+ | 45 | 4 | 1 Baby, Baby Please..................................... | | Buddah 19 |
| | | | **WILTON PLACE STREET BAND** | | |
| | | | Los Angeles studio project produced and arranged by Trevor Lawrence (resided on Wilton Place in Los Angeles). | | |
| 2/05/77 | 41 | 12 | 1 Disco Lucy (I Love Lucy Theme) ................... [I] | *24* | Island 078 |
| | | | discofied theme from the TV series "I Love Lucy" | | |
| 7/02/77 | 82 | 3 | 2 Baby Love, Sweet Sweet Love........................ | | Island 086 |
| | | | **THE WINANS** | | |
| | | | Family gospel quartet: brothers Michael, Ronald, Marvin and Carvin (twins) Winans. Born and raised in Detroit. Also see Michael Jackson. | | |
| 11/09/85 | 42 | 15 | 1 Let My People Go (Part I) ............................ | | Qwest 28874 |
| 8/15/87 | 15 | 15 | 2 Ain't No Need To Worry .............................. | | Qwest 28274 |
| | | | THE WINANS featuring ANITA BAKER | | |

| DEBUT DATE | PEAK POS | WKS CHR | ARTIST — Record Title | POP POS | Label & Number |
|---|---|---|---|---|---|
| | | | **BE BE & CE CE WINANS** Gospel singers from Detroit. Younger brother and sister of The Winans. | | |
| 7/04/87 | **77** | 7 | 1 I.O.U. Me ................................................ | | Capitol 44009 |
| | | | **ANGELA WINBUSH** Composer/producer/back-up vocalist. In duo, Rene & Angela, with Rene Moore from 1980-86. | | |
| 9/05/87 | **1**[2] | 19 | 1 **Angel** ........................................... | | Mercury 888831 |
| 12/19/87+ | **4** | 15 | 2 **Run To Me** ................................... | | Mercury 870033 |
| 4/30/88 | **47** | 9 | 3 C'Est Toi (It's You) ....................................... | | Mercury 870305 |
| | | | **WINDJAMMER** Formed in New Orleans in 1981. Consisted of Kevin McLin and Roy Paul Joseph (guitars), Fred McCray (keyboards), Chris Severin (bass) and Carl Dennis (lead vocals, percussion). First recorded for Hep Me in 1982. | | |
| 2/26/83 | **52** | 7 | 1 You've Got Me Dancing ................................. | | MCA 52163 |
| 4/21/84 | **34** | 12 | 2 Live Without Your Love ................................. | | MCA 52367 |
| 9/07/85 | **79** | 8 | 3 So Hard ...................................................... | | MCA 52622 |
| | | | **WINDSTORM** | | |
| 8/16/80 | **98** | 2 | 1 Rockin' ...................................................... | | Polydor 2095 |
| | | | **WINDY CITY** Vocal group from Chicago, consisting of Darryl Butler, Carl Winbush, Samuel Beasley, Morris Butler and Raymond Bennett. | | |
| 5/17/80 | **72** | 6 | 1 I Still Love You............................................. | | Kelli-Arts 4501 |
| | | | **THE WING & A PRAYER FIFE & DRUM CORPS.** Big band from New York City, with vocals by Linda November, Vivian Cherry, Arlene Martell and Helen Miles. | | |
| 12/13/75+ | **32** | 11 | 1 Baby Face....................................... *14* | | Wing & Prayer 103 |
| | | | 4 versions hit the Top 10 in 1926 | | |
| | | | **PETE WINGFIELD** Keyboardist from England. Worked with Freddie King, Jimmy Witherspoon and Van Morrison. In Olympic Runners band. | | |
| 7/26/75 | **15** | 18 | 1 Eighteen With A Bullet.................................. *15* | | Island 026 |
| | | | hit #18 with a bullet on the 11/22/75 "Hot 100" chart | | |
| | | | **WINNERS** 8-piece band from New York City, originally known as Wee Willie & The Winners. | | |
| 9/16/78 | **93** | 3 | 1 Get Ready For The Future ............................. | | Ariola 7715 |
| | | | **THE WINSTONS** Washington, DC group consisting of Richard Spencer (lead), Ray Maritano, Quincy Mattison, Phil Tolotta, Sonny Peckrol and G.C. Coleman. Toured as back-up band for The Impressions. Spencer, Mattison and Coleman had been in the Otis Redding band. | | |
| 6/07/69 | **2**[5] | 12 | 1●Color Him Father............................... *7* | | Metromedia 117 |
| | | | written by Spencer; won 1969 Grammy award for best R&B song | | |
| | | | **HUGO WINTERHALTER with EDDIE HEYWOOD** RCA conductor/arranger Winterhalter was born on 8/15/09 in Wilkes-Barre, Pennsylvania; died of cancer on 9/17/73. Heywood, jazz pianist/composer/ arranger, was born on 12/4/15 in Atlanta. | | |
| 9/08/56 | **7** | 9 | 1 **Canadian Sunset** ............................ [I] *2* | | Victor 6537 |
| | | | Best Seller #7 / Juke Box #10 written by Heywood | | |
| | | | **ROBERT WINTERS & FALL** Vocalist/keyboardist from Detroit. Stricken with polio at age 5; confined to a wheelchair. Moved to Los Angeles in 1973. Worked with Stevie Wonder, Larry Graham and Johnny Winter. Own group, Fall, features vocalist Walter Turner. | | |
| 12/27/80+ | **11** | 25 | 1 Magic Man ................................................ *101* | | Buddah 624 |
| 5/30/81 | **46** | 11 | 2 When Will My Love Be Right .......................... | | Buddah 627 |
| 11/20/82+ | **39** | 11 | 3 Do It Any Way You Want................................ | | Casablanca 2361 |
| | | | **RUBY WINTERS** Vocalist born in Louisville; raised in Cincinnati. | | |
| 3/18/67 | **13** | 8 | 1 Make Love To Me ...................................... *96* | | Diamond 218 |
| | | | **JOHNNY THUNDER & RUBY WINTERS** revival of Jo Stafford's 1954 pop hit (POS 1) | | |
| 11/11/67 | **47** | 3 | 2 I Want Action............................................. *109* | | Diamond 230 |
| 2/08/69 | **15** | 6 | 3 I Don't Want To Cry ................................... *97* | | Diamond 255 |
| 5/10/69 | **40** | 3 | 4 Just A Dream .......................................... | | Diamond 258 |

| DEBUT DATE | PEAK POS | WKS CHR | ARTIST — Record Title | POP POS | Label & Number |
|---|---|---|---|---|---|
| | | | **RUBY WINTERS — Continued** | | |
| 9/27/69 | **23** | 6 | 5 Always David ................................................ | *121* | Diamond 265 |
| 12/13/69+ | **19** | 9 | 6 Guess Who.................................................... | *99* | Diamond 269 |
| 12/15/73+ | **39** | 10 | 7 I Will ........................................................... | | Polydor 14202 |
| 11/22/75 | **95** | 6 | 8 Without You................................................. | | Playboy 6048 |
| 6/10/78 | **97** | 3 | 9 I Will ..................................................... [R] | | Millennium 612 |
| | | | **STEVE WINWOOD** | | |
| | | | Born on 5/12/48 in Birmingham, England. Rock singer/keyboardist/guitarist. Lead singer of the rock bands: The Spencer Davis Group, Blind Faith, and Traffic. | | |
| 6/25/88 | **30** | 12 | 1 Roll With It ................................................ | *1* | Virgin 99326 |
| | | | **WISH - see FONDA RAE** | | |
| | | | **BILL WITHERS**   ★★110★★ | | |
| | | | Born on 7/4/38 in Slab Fork, West Virginia. Vocalist/guitarist/composer. Moved to California in 1967 and made demo records of his songs. First recorded for Sussex in 1970, produced by Booker T. Jones. Made professional singing debut in 1971. Married to actress Denise Nicholas. | | |
| 7/10/71 | **6** | 16 | 1● **Ain't No Sunshine**..................................... | *3* | Sussex 219 |
| 11/06/71 | **18** | 8 | 2 Grandma's Hands.......................................... | *42* | Sussex 227 |
| | | | above 2: produced by Booker T. Jones | | |
| 4/29/72 | **1**¹ | 17 | 3● **Lean On Me**.............................................. | *1* | Sussex 235 |
| 9/02/72 | **2**² | 13 | 4● **Use Me**.................................................... | *2* | Sussex 241 |
| 12/30/72+ | **17** | 5 | 5 Let Us Love ................................................. | *47* | Sussex 247 |
| 2/10/73 | **12** | 9 | 6 Kissing My Love .......................................... | *31* | Sussex 250 |
| 7/07/73 | **25** | 6 | 7 Friend Of Mine............................................ | *80* | Sussex 257 |
| 3/23/74 | **10** | 15 | 8 **The Same Love That Made Me Laugh** ............ | *50* | Sussex 513 |
| 7/20/74 | **15** | 13 | 9 You ............................................................. | | Sussex 518 |
| 11/30/74+ | **13** | 12 | 10 Heartbreak Road......................................... | *89* | Sussex 629 |
| 7/26/75 | **68** | 8 | 11 It's All Over Now......................................... | | United Art. 674 |
| | | | BOBBY WOMACK & BILL WITHERS | | |
| 12/06/75+ | **10** | 13 | 12 **Make Love To Your Mind** ........................... | *76* | Columbia 10255 |
| 3/27/76 | **54** | 8 | 13 I Wish You Well .......................................... | | Columbia 10308 |
| 11/06/76 | **74** | 7 | 14 If I Didn't Mean You Well ............................ | | Columbia 10420 |
| 1/29/77 | **88** | 2 | 15 Close To Me ................................................ | | Columbia 10459 |
| 10/22/77+ | **6** | 22 | 16 **Lovely Day** ............................................... | *30* | Columbia 10627 |
| 4/15/78 | **75** | 3 | 17 Lovely Night For Dancing ............................ | | Columbia 10702 |
| 2/03/79 | **30** | 14 | 18 Don't It Make It Better ............................... | | Columbia 10892 |
| 5/26/79 | **85** | 3 | 19 You Got The Stuff (Part 1)............................ | | Columbia 10958 |
| 2/07/81 | **3** | 21 | 20 **Just The Two Of Us** ................................... | *2* | Elektra 47103 |
| | | | GROVER WASHINGTON, JR. with BILL WITHERS | | |
| 12/26/81+ | **83** | 6 | 21 U.S.A. ......................................................... | | Columbia 02651 |
| 8/25/84 | **13** | 15 | 22 In The Name Of Love ................................... | *58* | Polydor 881221 |
| | | | RALPH MacDONALD with BILL WITHERS | | |
| 4/06/85 | **22** | 14 | 23 Oh Yeah! .................................................... | *106* | Columbia 04841 |
| 7/13/85 | **46** | 12 | 24 Something That Turns You On ....................... | | Columbia 05424 |
| | | | **JIMMY WITHERSPOON** | | |
| | | | Born on 8/8/23 in Gurdon, Arkansas. Vocalist/bassist. Moved to Los Angeles in 1935. Merchant Marine from 1941-43; performed in Calcutta, India, 1943-44. With Jay McShann from 1944-47. First recorded for Philo/Aladdin in 1945. With Buddy Floyd, Roy Milton and Al Wichard from 1947-51. Toured with own band, 1948-52. | | |
| 3/05/49 | **1**¹ | 34 | 1 **Ain't Nobody's Business, Parts I & II**............. | | Supreme 1506 |
| | | | Best Seller #1 / Juke Box #3 | | |
| | | | also released on Swingtime 263 | | |
| 9/24/49 | **5** | 4 | 2 **In The Evening When The Sun Goes Down** ...... | | Supreme 1533 |
| | | | Juke Box #5 / Best Seller #7 | | |
| | | | above 2: with the Jay McShann Orchestra | | |
| 12/24/49 | **4** | 10 | 3 **No Rollin' Blues/** | | |
| | | | Juke Box #4 / Best Seller #5 | | |
| 12/31/49+ | **4** | 11 | 4 **Big Fine Girl**............................................. | | Modern 721 |
| | | | Best Seller #4 / Juke Box #10 | | |
| | | | above 2: with the Gene Gilbeaux Quartet | | |
| 4/12/52 | **7** | 2 | 5 **Wind Is Blowing** ........................................ | | Modern 857 |
| | | | Best Seller #7 | | |
| | | | live concert recording in Los Angeles, 1950 | | |
| 1/04/75 | **31** | 14 | 6 Love Is A Five Letter Word ............................ | | Capitol 3998 |
| | | | produced in England by Mike Vernon | | |

| DEBUT DATE | PEAK POS | WKS CHR | ARTIST — Record Title | POP POS | Label & Number |
|---|---|---|---|---|---|
| | | | **WOLF** | | |
| | | | Real name: Bill Wolfer. Keyboardist/synthesizer/vocorder player. | | |
| 12/25/82+ | **47** | 10 | 1 Papa Was A Rollin' Stone .................................. | 55 | Constell. 69849 |
| | | | **WOMACK & WOMACK** | | |
| | | | Songwriting duo of husband-and-wife Cecil Womack and Linda Cooke. Cecil (b: 1947, Cleveland) sang in family gospel group, the Womack Brothers. The brother of Bobby Womack, Cecil was previously married to Mary Wells. Linda (b: 1952) is the daughter of the late Sam Cooke, and a songwriter since 1964. Married in 1976. | | |
| 2/11/84 | **87** | 3 | 1 T.K.O. ....................................................... | | Elektra 69762 |
| 5/12/84 | **25** | 15 | 2 Baby I'm Scared Of You............................... | | Elektra 69733 |
| 6/15/85 | **44** | 10 | 3 Strange & Funny........................................ | | Elektra 69637 |
| | | | **BOBBY WOMACK** ★★**42**★★ | | |
| | | | Born on 3/4/44 in Cleveland. Vocalist/guitarist/songwriter. Brother of Cecil Womack (Womack & Womack). Sang in family gospel group, the Womack Brothers. Group recorded for Sar as The Valentinos and The Lovers, 1962-64. Toured as guitarist with Sam Cooke. Solo recording for Him label in 1965. Back-up guitarist on many sessions, including Wilson Pickett, Box Tops, Joe Tex, Aretha Franklin and Janis Joplin. Married for a time to Sam Cooke's widow. Also see Wilton Felder. | | |
| 3/23/68 | **33** | 10 | 1 What Is This................................................ | | Minit 32037 |
| 8/24/68 | **16** | 14 | 2 Fly Me To The Moon .................................. | 52 | Minit 32048 |
| 12/14/68+ | **20** | 9 | 3 California Dreamin'.................................... | 43 | Minit 32055 |
| 4/12/69 | **48** | 2 | 4 I Left My Heart In San Francisco..................... | 119 | Minit 32059 |
| 8/16/69 | **43** | 3 | 5 It's Gonna Rain.......................................... | | Minit 32071 |
| 11/08/69 | **14** | 8 | 6 How I Miss You Baby................................... | 93 | Minit 32081 |
| 4/04/70 | **23** | 8 | 7 More Than I Can Stand ............................... | 90 | Minit 32093 |
| 8/22/70 | **30** | 4 | 8 I'm Gonna Forget About You......................... | | Liberty 56186 |
| 5/15/71 | **30** | 5 | 9 The Preacher (Part 2)/More Than I Can Stand..... | 111 | United Art. 50773 |
| 9/18/71 | **43** | 6 | 10 Breezin'................................................... | | Blue Thumb 200 |
| | | | **GABOR SZABO & BOBBY WOMACK** | | |
| 9/25/71 | **40** | 3 | 11 Communication ......................................... | | United Art. 50816 |
| 12/04/71+ | **2**¹ | 17 | 12 **That's The Way I Feel About Cha**................. | 27 | United Art. 50847 |
| 4/29/72 | **1**¹ | 14 | 13 **Woman's Gotta Have It** ............................ | 60 | United Art. 50902 |
| 8/26/72 | **16** | 11 | 14 Sweet Caroline (Good Times Never Seemed So Good)/ | 51 | |
| | | | Neil Diamond's version charted in 1969 (POS 4-Pop) | | |
| 12/16/72+ | **8** | 13 | 15● Harry Hippie........................................... | 31 | United Art. 50946 |
| 3/31/73 | **19** | 6 | 16 Across 110th Street..................................... | 56 | United Art. 196 |
| | | | from the film of the same title; 12, 15 & 16: with the backing group, Peace | | |
| 6/16/73 | **2**¹ | 14 | 17 **Nobody Wants You When You're Down And Out**/ | 29 | |
| 11/03/73 | **80** | 7 | 18 I'm Through Trying To Prove My Love To You.. | 101 | United Art. 255 |
| 1/26/74 | **1**³ | 17 | 19● **Lookin' For A Love** ................................. | 10 | United Art. 375 |
| 6/08/74 | **5** | 15 | 20 You're Welcome, Stop On By ......................... | 59 | United Art. 439 |
| 10/26/74 | **18** | 9 | 21 I Don't Know ............................................ | | United Art. 561 |
| 3/29/75 | **6** | 13 | 22 **Check It Out** .......................................... | 91 | United Art. 021 |
| 7/26/75 | **68** | 8 | 23 It's All Over Now........................................ | | United Art. 674 |
| | | | **BOBBY WOMACK & BILL WITHERS** | | |
| 11/29/75+ | **13** | 12 | 24 Where There's A Will, There's A Way ............... | | United Art. 735 |
| 2/21/76 | **5** | 13 | 25 **Daylight** ................................................ | | United Art. 763 |
| 11/20/76+ | **43** | 10 | 26 Home Is Where The Heart Is......................... | | Columbia 10437 |
| | | | **BOBBY WOMACK & BROTHERHOOD** | | |
| 3/26/77 | **90** | 3 | 27 Standing In The Safety Zone ......................... | | Columbia 10493 |
| 2/18/78 | **47** | 12 | 28 Trust Your Heart ........................................ | | Columbia 10672 |
| 6/02/79 | **40** | 11 | 29 How Could You Break My Heart..................... | | Arista 0421 |
| 11/21/81+ | **3** | 20 | 30 **If You Think You're Lonely Now**/ | 101 | |
| 9/12/81 | **55** | 8 | 31 Secrets..................................................... | | Beverly Glen 2000 |
| 3/27/82 | **26** | 11 | 32 Where Do We Go From Here......................... | | Beverly Glen 2001 |
| 2/11/84 | **3** | 17 | 33 **Love Has Finally Come At Last** ..................... | 88 | Beverly Glen 2012 |
| | | | **BOBBY WOMACK & PATTI LaBELLE** | | |
| 6/09/84 | **54** | 8 | 34 Tell Me Why ............................................. | | Beverly Glen 2014 |
| 11/03/84 | **76** | 7 | 35 It Takes A Lot Of Strength To Say Goodbye ....... | | Beverly Glen 2018 |
| | | | **BOBBY WOMACK & PATTI LaBELLE** | | |

| DEBUT DATE | PEAK POS | WKS CHR | ARTIST — Record Title | POP POS | Label & Number |
|---|---|---|---|---|---|
| | | | **BOBBY WOMACK — Continued** | | |
| 5/11/85 | **74** | 6 | 36 Someday We'll All Be Free............................ | | Beverly Glen 2021 |
| 8/10/85 | **2**² | 17 | 37 **I Wish He Didn't Trust Me So Much**.............. | | MCA 52624 |
| 11/16/85 | **50** | 11 | 38 Let Me Kiss It Where It Hurts........................ | | MCA 52709 |
| 11/29/86 | **57** | 8 | 39 (I Wanna) Make Love To You ........................ | | MCA 52955 |
| | | | **STEVIE WONDER** ★★**6**★★ | | |
| | | | Born Steveland Morris on 5/13/50 in Saginaw, Michigan. Singer/songwriter/ multi-instrumentalist/producer. Blind since birth. Signed to Motown in 1960, did back-up work. First recorded in 1962, renamed "Little Stevie Wonder" by Berry Gordy, Jr. Married to Syreeta Wright from 1970-72. Near-fatal auto accident on 8/16/73. Winner of 16 Grammy Awards. In the films "Bikini Beach" and "Muscle Beach Party". Also see Bobbi Humphrey, Chaka Khan, Donna Summer and Dionne Warwick. | | |
| | | | LITTLE STEVIE WONDER: | | |
| 6/29/63 | **1**⁶ | 15 | 1 **Fingertips - Pt 2** ...................................... | 1 | Tamla 54080 |
| 10/05/63 | **33** | 6 | 2 Workout Stevie, Workout ............................ | Hot | Tamla 54086 |
| 2/29/64 | **52** | 9 | 3 Castles In The Sand.................................... | Hot | Tamla 54090 |
| | | | STEVIE WONDER: | | |
| 6/13/64 | **29** | 8 | 4 Hey Harmonica Man .................................. | Hot | Tamla 54096 |
| 9/18/65 | **30** | 4 | 5 High Heel Sneakers ................................... | 59 | Tamla 54119 |
| 1/01/66 | **1**⁵ | 15 | 6 **Uptight (Everything's Alright)** ................... | 3 | Tamla 54124 |
| 4/23/66 | **4** | 11 | 7 **Nothing's Too Good For My Baby/** | 20 | |
| 6/25/66 | **8** | 8 | 8 **With A Child's Heart** ............................... | 131 | Tamla 54130 |
| 7/30/66 | **1**¹ | 12 | 9 **Blowin' In The Wind** ................................ | 9 | Tamla 54136 |
| 11/19/66+ | **3** | 13 | 10 A Place In The Sun .................................... | 9 | Tamla 54139 |
| 3/11/67 | **31** | 6 | 11 Travlin' Man/ | 32 | |
| 5/06/67 | **9** | 9 | 12 **Hey Love** ............................................. | 90 | Tamla 54147 |
| 6/24/67 | **1**⁴ | 15 | 13 **I Was Made To Love Her** .......................... | 2 | Tamla 54151 |
| 10/21/67 | **4** | 11 | 14 **I'm Wondering**...................................... | 12 | Tamla 54157 |
| 4/20/68 | **1**¹ | 12 | 15 **Shoo-Be-Doo-Be-Doo-Da-Day** ................... | 9 | Tamla 54165 |
| 8/03/68 | **2**² | 10 | 16 **You Met Your Match** .............................. | 35 | Tamla 54168 |
| 11/16/68+ | **2**¹ | 13 | 17 **For Once In My Life** ............................... | 2 | Tamla 54174 |
| 3/08/69 | **16** | 6 | 18 I Don't Know Why/ | 39 | |
| 6/14/69 | **4** | 13 | 19 **My Cherie Amour**.................................. | 4 | Tamla 54180 |
| 11/01/69 | **5** | 11 | 20 **Yester-Me, Yester-You, Yesterday** ............. | 7 | Tamla 54188 |
| 2/14/70 | **11** | 9 | 21 Never Had A Dream Come True ..................... | 26 | Tamla 54191 |
| 7/04/70 | **1**⁶ | 15 | 22 **Signed, Sealed, Delivered I'm Yours** ........... | 3 | Tamla 54196 |
| 10/24/70 | **2**³ | 12 | 23 **Heaven Help Us All** ............................... | 9 | Tamla 54200 |
| 3/20/71 | **3** | 12 | 24 **We Can Work It Out** .............................. | 13 | Tamla 54202 |
| 8/21/71 | **4** | 12 | 25 **If You Really Love Me**.............................. | 8 | Tamla 54208 |
| | | | written by Wonder & Syreeta Wright | | |
| 5/27/72 | **13** | 9 | 26 Superwoman (Where Were You When I Needed You) ...................................... | 33 | Tamla 54216 |
| 9/30/72 | **36** | 5 | 27 Keep On Running ...................................... | 90 | Tamla 54223 |
| 11/25/72+ | **1**³ | 17 | 28 **Superstition**....................................... | 1 | Tamla 54226 |
| 3/24/73 | **3** | 11 | 29 **You Are The Sunshine Of My Life**................. | 1 | Tamla 54232 |
| 8/18/73 | **1**¹ | 15 | 30 **Higher Ground** .................................... | 4 | Tamla 54235 |
| 11/10/73 | **1**² | 16 | 31 **Living For The City** ............................... | 8 | Tamla 54242 |
| 4/06/74 | **2**¹ | 16 | 32 **Don't You Worry 'Bout A Thing** ................... | 16 | Tamla 54245 |
| 8/10/74 | **1**² | 16 | 33 **You Haven't Done Nothin'** ......................... | 1 | Tamla 54252 |
| | | | background vocals by The Jackson 5 | | |
| 11/16/74 | **1**² | 17 | 34 **Boogie On Reggae Woman**........................ | 3 | Tamla 54254 |
| 12/11/76+ | **1**⁵ | 18 | 35 **I Wish** ............................................... | 1 | Tamla 54274 |
| 4/16/77 | **1**¹ | 14 | 36 **Sir Duke** ............................................. | 1 | Tamla 54281 |
| | | | a tribute to Duke Ellington | | |
| 9/03/77 | **18** | 11 | 37 Another Star ............................................ | 32 | Tamla 54286 |
| 11/12/77 | **36** | 11 | 38 As.......................................................... | 36 | Tamla 54291 |
| 1/27/79 | **26** | 11 | 39 Pops, We Love You (A Tribute To Father) .......... | 59 | Motown 1455 |
| | | | **DIANA ROSS, MARVIN GAYE, SMOKEY ROBINSON & STEVIE WONDER** song written for Berry Gordy Sr.'s 90th birthday | | |
| 11/10/79+ | **5** | 15 | 40 **Send One Your Love** .............................. | 4 | Tamla 54303 |
| 3/08/80 | **56** | 7 | 41 Outside My Window................................... | 52 | Tamla 54308 |
| 9/20/80 | **1**⁷ | 24 | 42 **Master Blaster (Jammin')** ........................ | 5 | Tamla 54317 |
| 12/20/80+ | **4** | 18 | 43 **I Ain't Gonna Stand For It** ........................ | 11 | Tamla 54320 |

| DEBUT DATE | PEAK POS | WKS CHR | ARTIST — Record Title | POP POS | Label & Number |
|---|---|---|---|---|---|
| | | | **STEVIE WONDER — Continued** | | |
| 4/04/81 | **29** | 11 | 44  Lately........................................ | *64* | Tamla 54323 |
| 8/29/81 | **74** | 5 | 45  Did I Hear You Say You Love Me.............. | | Tamla 54328 |
| 1/23/82 | **1**⁹ | 21 | 46  **That Girl**.................................. | *4* | Tamla 1602 |
| 4/17/82 | **8** | 19 | 47●**Ebony And Ivory**........................... | *1* | Columbia 02860 |
| | | | **PAUL McCARTNEY with STEVIE WONDER** | | |
| 6/05/82 | **2**⁴ | 18 | 48  **Do I Do**.................................... | *13* | Tamla 1612 |
| 9/11/82 | **10** | 12 | 49  **Ribbon In The Sky**......................... | *54* | Tamla 1639 |
| 11/13/82 | **35** | 10 | 50  Used To Be................................... | *46* | Motown 1650 |
| | | | **CHARLENE & STEVIE WONDER** | | |
| 8/25/84 | **1**³ | 20 | 51●**I Just Called To Say I Love You**............ | *1* | Motown 1745 |
| 12/01/84+ | **4** | 16 | 52  **Love Light In Flight**...................... | *17* | Motown 1769 |
| | | | above 2: from the film "The Woman In Red" | | |
| 9/07/85 | **1**⁶ | 20 | 53  **Part-Time Lover**........................... | *1* | Tamla 1808 |
| 11/23/85+ | **2**² | 17 | 54  **Go Home**................................... | *10* | Tamla 1817 |
| 2/22/86 | **8** | 15 | 55  **Overjoyed**................................. | *24* | Tamla 1832 |
| 6/14/86 | **19** | 13 | 56  Land Of La La............................... | *86* | Tamla 1846 |
| 10/17/87 | **1**² | 16 | 57  **Skeletons**................................. | *19* | Motown 1907 |
| 1/16/88 | **1**¹ | 12 | 58  **You Will Know**............................. | *77* | Motown 1919 |
| 4/23/88 | **4** | 11 | 59  Get It...................................... | *80* | Motown 1930 |
| | | | **STEVIE WONDER & MICHAEL JACKSON** | | |
| 6/25/88 | **88** | 4 | 60  My Love.................................... | *80* | Columbia 07781 |
| | | | **JULIO IGLESIAS featuring STEVIE WONDER** | | |
| | | | **GERRY WOO** | | |
| | | | Singer/dancer from Detroit. Student at UCLA. | | |
| 5/02/87 | **27** | 13 | 1  Hey There Lonely Girl...................... | | Polydor 885720 |
| 1/30/88 | **23** | 12 | 2  How Long.................................. | | Polydor 887126 |
| | | | **BRENTON WOOD** | | |
| | | | Born Alfred Smith on 7/26/41 in Shreveport; raised in San Pedro, California. Singer/songwriter/pianist. First recorded with Little Freddy & The Rockets in 1958. Formed vocal group, The Quotations, at Compton College. | | |
| 5/20/67 | **19** | 8 | 1  The Oogum Boogum Song..................... | *34* | Double Shot 111 |
| 8/12/67 | **19** | 11 | 2  Gimme Little Sign.......................... | *9* | Double Shot 116 |
| 12/23/67+ | **30** | 7 | 3  Baby You Got It............................ | *34* | Double Shot 121 |
| 7/27/68 | **42** | 2 | 4  Some Got It, Some Don't.................... | | Double Shot 130 |
| 9/17/77 | **92** | 4 | 5  Come Softly To Me.......................... | | Cream 7718 |
| | | | **WOODS EMPIRE** | | |
| | | | Family quintet from Diamond Bar, California: Linda, Rhonda, Idris, Judy and Tommy Woods. | | |
| 7/04/81 | **68** | 7 | 1  Sweet Delight.............................. | | Tabu 02130 |
| | | | **REN WOODS** | | |
| | | | Female vocalist from Portland, Oregon. Own vocal group from age 9. Toured Vietnam with Bob Hope at age 14. Played Dorothy in the touring company of "The Wiz". Appeared in the films "Hair", "The Jerk" and "Car Wash". | | |
| 12/15/79+ | **45** | 9 | 1  I'm In Love With You....................... | | ARC 11146 |
| 2/20/82 | **38** | 9 | 2  Take Me To Heaven......................... | | Elektra 47403 |
| | | | **REV. MACEO WOODS & THE CHRISTIAN TABERNACLE BAPTIST CHURCH CHOIR** | | |
| 12/06/69 | **28** | 6 | 1  Hello Sunshine............................. | *121* | Volt 4025 |
| | | | **STEVIE WOODS** | | |
| | | | Vocalist, based in Los Angeles. Originally from Columbus, Ohio. | | |
| 10/17/81 | **36** | 15 | 1  Steal The Night............................ | *25* | Cotillion 46016 |
| 2/06/82 | **57** | 8 | 2  Just Can't Win 'Em All..................... | *38* | Cotillion 46030 |
| 9/18/82 | **42** | 10 | 3  Woman In My Life.......................... | | Cotillion 99980 |
| 11/19/83+ | **54** | 10 | 4  Ain't That Peculiar........................ | | Cotillion 99815 |
| | | | **SHEB WOOLEY** | | |
| | | | Born on 4/10/21 in Erick, Oklahoma. Singer/songwriter/actor. Played "Pete Nolan" in the TV series "Rawhide". Also made comical recordings under pseudonym, "Ben Colder". Appeared in the films "Rocky Mountain" and "Giant". | | |
| 8/11/58 | **18** | 1 | 1  The Purple People Eater........................ [N] | *1* | MGM 12651 |
| | | | Best Seller #18 | | |

| DEBUT DATE | PEAK POS | WKS CHR | ARTIST — Record Title | POP POS | Label & Number |
|---|---|---|---|---|---|
| | | | **WORD OF MOUTH featuring D.J. CHEESE** | | |
| | | | Rap group. | | |
| 8/10/85 | **62** | 9 | 1 King Kut ...................................................... | | Profile 5076 |
| 9/27/86 | **46** | 7 | 2 Coast To Coast ............................................. | | Profile 5106 |
| | | | **THE WORLD CLASS WRECKIN CRU** | | |
| 1/09/88 | **30** | 26 | 1 Turn Off The Lights...................................... | *84* | Kru'-Cut 006 |
| | | | **WORLD PREMIERE** | | |
| | | | Brooklyn-based foursome. | | |
| 2/18/84 | **54** | 9 | 1 Share The Night............................................. | | Easy St. 4506 |
| | | | **THE WORLD'S FAMOUS SUPREME TEAM** | | |
| | | | Rap/funk group with British entrepreneur, Malcolm McLaren, former manager of the New York Dolls; also formed the Sex Pistols in 1975 - the leaders of Britain's "punk" movement. | | |
| 2/04/84 | **56** | 9 | 1 World Famous ........................................... | | Island 99790 |
| | | | **MALCOLM McLAREN & The World's Famous Supreme Team** | | |
| 5/05/84 | **15** | 16 | 2 Hey D.J. ..................................................... | | Island 99772 |
| 11/17/84 | **69** | 7 | 3 Radio Man ................................................... | | Island 99683 |
| | | | **BERNIE WORRELL** | | |
| | | | Born on 4/19/44 in Long Beach, New Jersey. Keyboardist, one of the original members of Parliament. Played piano from age 3. Toured with the Talking Heads. | | |
| 4/14/79 | **92** | 2 | 1 Insurance Man For The Funk ......................... | | Arista 0407 |
| | | | **LINK WRAY & HIS RAY MEN** | | |
| | | | Link was born on 5/2/35 in Dunn, North Carolina. Rock and roll guitarist. Part American Indian. Joined family band, the Palomino Ranch Gang in the early 50s. First recorded as "Lucky" Wray for Starday in 1956. | | |
| 5/19/58 | **11** | 10 | 1 Rumble ...................................... [I] *16* | | Cadence 1347 |
| | | | Jockey #11 / Best Seller #14 | | |
| | | | **WRECKING CREW** | | |
| | | | Band from Chicago, formed in 1977 by the former rhythm section for the Staple Singers: Nicholas Toler Williams (lead guitar, vocals), Jack Chatman (bass) and Timothy Terrell Austin (drums). Other members were Bridget Paig (trumpet, trombone), Michael Jackson (saxophone), Mark Rogers (trombone, trumpet), Anthony Space (keyboards), Wilbert Anderson Crosby (guitar) and Michael Avery (lead vocalist). | | |
| 1/15/83 | **84** | 2 | 1 Chance To Dance ............................................. | | Erect 114 |
| 12/24/83+ | **87** | 5 | 2 Pixie Dust..................................................... | | Snd. Flor. 202 |
| | | | **BERNARD WRIGHT** | | |
| | | | Born in 1965 in New York City. Keyboardist since age 4. Toured with Lenny White at age 13; with Tom Browne in 1979. Solo debut in 1981. | | |
| 4/04/81 | **33** | 12 | 1 Just Chillin' Out ........................................... | | GRP 2511 |
| 7/18/81 | **78** | 4 | 2 Haboglabotribin' ........................................... | | GRP 2514 |
| 6/12/82 | **88** | 2 | 3 Won't You Let Me Love You............................ | | GRP 2520 |
| 9/17/83 | **39** | 13 | 4 Funky Beat .................................................. | | Arista 9070 |
| 10/05/85 | **6** | 19 | 5 **Who Do You Love** ...................................... | | Manhattan 50011 |
| 2/01/86 | **23** | 13 | 6 After You ..................................................... | | Manhattan 50024 |
| | | | **BETTY WRIGHT** ★★**91**★★ | | |
| | | | Singer, born on 12/21/53 in Miami. In family gospel group Echoes Of Joy, from 1956 with sister Jeanette Holloway and brothers Phillip "Leno Phillips" and Milton Wright. First recorded for Deep City in 1966. Hostess of TV talk shows in Miami. Also see Peter Brown. | | |
| 8/03/68 | **15** | 15 | 1 Girls Can't Do What The Guys Do .................... | *33* | Alston 4569 |
| 8/29/70 | **40** | 5 | 2 Pure Love .................................................... | | Alston 4587 |
| 7/31/71 | **44** | 6 | 3 I Love The Way You Love ................................ | *109* | Alston 4594 |
| 11/20/71 | **2**[8] | 16 | 4●**Clean Up Woman**.......................................... | *6* | Alston 4601 |
| 4/08/72 | **21** | 5 | 5 If You Love Me Like You Say/ | | |
| | | 3 | 6 I'm Gettin' Tired Baby ............................... | *121* | Alston 4609 |
| 6/24/72 | **18** | 8 | 7 Is It You Girl ................................................ | *101* | Alston 4611 |
| 9/23/72 | **6** | 15 | 8 **Baby Sitter** .................................................. | *46* | Alston 4614 |
| 4/07/73 | **11** | 9 | 9 It's Hard To Stop (Doing Something When It's Good To You) ..................................... | *72* | Alston 4617 |
| 9/08/73 | **10** | 16 | 10 **Let Me Be Your Lovemaker** .......................... | *55* | Alston 4619 |
| 3/02/74 | **66** | 6 | 11 It's Bad For Me To See You ............................ | | Alston 4620 |
| 6/01/74 | **12** | 16 | 12 Secretary...................................................... | *62* | Aiston 4622 |

| DEBUT DATE | PEAK POS | WKS CHR | ARTIST — Record Title | POP POS | Label & Number |
|---|---|---|---|---|---|
| | | | **BETTY WRIGHT — Continued** | | |
| 10/26/74+ | 28 | 21 | 13 Shoorah! Shoorah!/ | | |
| | | 7 | 14  Tonight Is The Night ................................... | | Alston 3711 |
| 3/29/75 | 15 | 12 | 15 Where Is The Love ..................................... | 96 | Alston 3713 |
| 8/02/75 | 28 | 11 | 16 Ooola La................................................ | | Alston 3715 |
| 12/06/75+ | 21 | 12 | 17 Slip And Do It ........................................ | | Alston 3718 |
| 8/07/76 | 23 | 13 | 18 If I Ever Do Wrong .................................. | | Alston 3722 |
| 12/18/76+ | 64 | 8 | 19 Life .................................................... | | Alston 3725 |
| 8/06/77 | 73 | 5 | 20 You Can't See For Lookin' ......................... | | Alston 3734 |
| 9/02/78 | 11 | 15 | 21 Tonight Is The Night Pt.I (Rap)..................... | | Alston 3740 |
| | | | new version of #14 above | | |
| 2/03/79 | 68 | 3 | 22 Lovin' Is Really My Game ........................... | | Alston 3745 |
| 7/14/79 | 48 | 10 | 23 My Love Is ............................................ | | Alston 3747 |
| 3/21/81 | 42 | 10 | 24 What Are You Going To Do With It.................. | | Epic 51009 |
| 10/03/81 | 65 | 7 | 25 Goodbye You Hello Him .............................. | | Epic 02521 |
| 2/12/83 | 22 | 16 | 26 She's Older Now....................................... | | Epic 03523 |
| 6/30/84 | 75 | 4 | 27 One Step Up, Two Steps Back ....................... | | Jamaica 3 |
| 1/11/86 | 44 | 16 | 28 Pain.................................................... | | First String 965 |
| 7/12/86 | 82 | 8 | 29 The Sun Don't Shine ................................. | | First String 968 |
| 3/26/88 | 14 | 20 | 30 No Pain, No Gain ..................................... | | MS. B. 4501 |

### BILLY WRIGHT

Born on 5/21/32 in Atlanta. Vocalist/dancer. Started as dancer in road show. Went solo in 1949. Mainly active as emcee in Atlanta clubs into the 70s.

| 10/15/49 | 3 | 5 | 1 **Blues For My Baby/** | | |
|---|---|---|---|---|---|
| | | | Juke Box #3 / Best Seller #5 | | |
| 10/22/49 | 9 | 2 | 2  **You Satisfy** ......................................... | | Savoy 710 |
| | | | Best Seller #9 / Juke Box #12 | | |
| | | | above 2: with the Neil James Orchestra | | |
| 7/14/51 | 9 | 1 | 3 **Stacked Deck** ..................................... | | Savoy 781 |
| | | | Juke Box #9 | | |
| 10/06/51 | 10 | 1 | 4 **Hey Little Girl**................................... | | Savoy 810 |
| | | | Juke Box #10 | | |
| | | | also released on Regent 1033 | | |

### CHARLES WRIGHT & THE WATTS 103rd ST. BAND

Charles was born in 1942 in Clarksdale, Mississippi. Vocalist/pianist/guitarist/producer/leader of an 8-man, soul-funk band from the Watts section of Los Angeles. Evolved from The Soul Runners. Big break came through assistance by comedian Bill Cosby.

#### THE WATTS 103RD STREET RHYTHM BAND:

| 10/07/67 | 44 | 3 | 1 Spreadin' Honey ...................................... [I] | 73 | Keymen 108 |
|---|---|---|---|---|---|
| 2/22/69 | 12 | 14 | 2 Do Your Thing ........................................ | 11 | Warner 7250 |
| 7/26/69 | 12 | 9 | 3 Till You Get Enough .................................. | 67 | Warner 7298 |

#### CHARLES WRIGHT & THE WATTS 103rd STREET RHYTHM BAND:

| 11/08/69 | 35 | 2 | 4 Must Be Your Thing.................................. | 103 | Warner 7338 |
|---|---|---|---|---|---|
| 3/07/70 | 23 | 20 | 5 Love Land ............................................. | 16 | Warner 7365 |
| 8/29/70 | 3 | 13 | 6 **Express Yourself** .................................. | 12 | Warner 7417 |
| 4/24/71 | 9 | 10 | 7 **Your Love (Means Everything To Me)** ............ | 73 | Warner 7475 |
| 9/29/73 | 27 | 11 | 8 Doin' What Comes Naturally ........................ | | Dunhill 4364 |

### GARY WRIGHT

Born on 4/26/43 in Creskill, New Jersey. Actor/rock singer/songwriter/keyboardist. Co-leader of the rock group Spooky Tooth.

| 8/14/76 | 98 | 1 | 1 Love Is Alive ......................................... | 2 | Warner 8143 |
|---|---|---|---|---|---|

### O.V. WRIGHT

Singer, born Overton Vertis Wright on 10/9/39 in Leno, Tennessee; died on 11/16/80. With Sunset Travellers, Spirit Of Memphis and Highway QC's, gospel groups. Had original recording of Otis Redding's hit "That's How Strong My Love Is", on Goldwax in 1964.

| 7/24/65 | 6 | 14 | 1 **You're Gonna Make Me Cry**.......................... | 86 | Back Beat 548 |
|---|---|---|---|---|---|
| 4/22/67 | 4 | 12 | 2 **Eight Men, Four Women** ............................. | 80 | Back Beat 580 |
| 8/12/67 | 25 | 5 | 3 Heartaches-Heartaches ............................... | | Back Beat 583 |
| | | | written by Willie Mitchell | | |
| 12/02/67 | 46 | 4 | 4 What About You ...................................... | | Back Beat 586 |
| 5/18/68 | 36 | 8 | 5 Oh Baby Mine ........................................ | | Back Beat 591 |
| 10/18/69 | 43 | 3 | 6 I'll Take Care Of You ................................ | | Back Beat 607 |

| DEBUT DATE | PEAK POS | WKS CHR | ARTIST — Record Title | POP POS | Label & Number |
|---|---|---|---|---|---|
| | | | **O.V. WRIGHT — Continued** | | |
| 4/18/70 | **48** | 2 | 7 Love The Way You Love ............................ | | Back Beat 611 |
| 10/10/70 | **11** | 13 | 8 Ace Of Spade ...................................... | *54* | Back Beat 615 |
| 3/06/71 | **21** | 9 | 9 When You Took Your Love From Me ............... | *118* | Back Beat 620 |
| 8/28/71 | **19** | 11 | 10 A Nickel And A Nail ............................. | *103* | Back Beat 622 |
| 12/08/73+ | **33** | 16 | 11 I'd Rather Be (Blind, Crippled & Crazy)............. | | Back Beat 628 |
| 6/01/74 | **62** | 7 | 12 I've Been Searching ............................. | | Back Beat 631 |
| 8/16/75 | **82** | 7 | 13 What More Can I Do (To Prove My Love For You) | | ABC 12119 |
| 9/04/76 | **87** | 6 | 14 Rhymes.......................................... | | Hi 2313 |
| 7/23/77 | **43** | 12 | 15 Into Something (Can't Shake Loose) ............... | | Hi 77501 |
| 1/14/78 | **50** | 10 | 16 Precious, Precious ............................... | | Hi 77506 |
| 7/01/78 | **91** | 2 | 17 I Don't Do Windows ............................. | | Hi 78514 |
| | | | **RUBEN WRIGHT** | | |
| 5/14/66 | **29** | 6 | 1 I'm Walking Out On You ........................... | | Capitol 5588 |

**WRITERS**
Jazz sextet consisting of Hugh McCracken and Jeff Mironov (guitars), Jerry Peters (keyboards), Anthony Jackson (bass), Harvey Mason (drums), Ralph MacDonald (percussion) and Frank Floyd (vocals).

| | | | | | |
|---|---|---|---|---|---|
| 9/01/79 | **95** | 3 | 1 What's Come Over Me ........................... | | Columbia 11051 |
| | | | **WUF TICKET** | | |
| 12/04/82+ | **21** | 14 | 1 Ya Mama ........................................ | | Prelude 644 |

**MICHAEL WYCOFF**
Vocalist from Torrance, California. Worked as backup singer/keyboardist for Natalie Cole and Phoebe Snow. Brother-in-law of D. J. Rogers.

| | | | | | |
|---|---|---|---|---|---|
| 11/15/80 | **43** | 11 | 1 Feel My Love ................................... | | RCA 12108 |
| 4/11/81 | **52** | 8 | 2 One Alone....................................... | | RCA 12179 |
| | | | MICHAEL WYCOFF featuring MERRY CLAYTON | | |
| 3/06/82 | **64** | 8 | 3 Still Got The Magic (Sweet Delight) ................. | | RCA 13055 |
| 5/29/82 | **47** | 7 | 4 Looking Up To You............................... | | RCA 13214 |
| 6/11/83 | **83** | 4 | 5 There's No Easy Way ............................ | | RCA 13516 |
| 9/10/83 | **23** | 12 | 6 Tell Me Love ................................... | | RCA 13585 |

**POPCORN WYLIE**
Born Richard Wylie on 6/6/39 in Detroit. Musician/songwriter/arranger/producer. First recorded for Motown in 1961, as Popcorn & The Mohawks.

| | | | | | |
|---|---|---|---|---|---|
| 9/18/71 | **40** | 6 | 1 Funky Rubber Band.............................. | *109* | Soul 35087 |

**WYND CHYMES**

| | | | | | |
|---|---|---|---|---|---|
| 7/09/83 | **82** | 4 | 1 Pretty Girls, Everywhere ........................ | | RCA 13517 |

**PHILIPPE WYNNE**
Born on 4/3/41 in Cincinnati. Died of a heart attack on 7/13/84. With the Afro-Kings while stationed in Germany. With "Bootsy" Collins' Pacesetters in 1968. Lead singer of the Spinners from 1971-77. Solo thereafter. Collapsed and died during performance at Ivey's Nightclub in Oakland, California. Affectionately called "The Rubberband Man". Also see Gene Dunlap.

| | | | | | |
|---|---|---|---|---|---|
| 4/30/77 | **17** | 9 | 1 Hats Off To Mama ........................ | | Cotillion 44217 |
| | | | shown as: **PHILIPPE WYNN** | | |
| 11/26/77 | **62** | 9 | 2 Take Me As I Am-Pt. I ......................... | | Cotillion 44227 |
| 11/08/80 | **81** | 4 | 3 Never Gonna Tell It (Part 1) ..................... | | Uncle Jam 9900 |
| 3/19/83 | **54** | 6 | 4 You Ain't Going Anywhere But Gone ............... | | Sugar Hill 795 |
| 12/17/83+ | **33** | 12 | 5 Wait 'Til Tomorrow/Bye Bye Love.................... | | Fantasy 944 |
| | | | medley featuring The Everly Brothers' 1957, #2 pop hit | | |

# X

**X-RAYS**
Band led by Milton "Tippy" Larkins (b: 10/10/10, Houston). Vocalist/trombonist/trumpeter. Own band in 1936; included Eddie Vinson and Arnett Cobb, later Illinois Jacquet and T-Bone Walker. Formed the X-Rays in the late 40s.

| | | | | | |
|---|---|---|---|---|---|
| 1/08/49 | **3** | 5 | 1 **I'll Always Be In Love With You** ................. | | Savoy 681 |
| | | | Juke Box #3 / Best Seller #9 | | |
| | | | vocals by the X-Rays and Milt Larkins; | | |
| | | | also released on Savoy 7007 | | |

| DEBUT DATE | PEAK POS | WKS CHR | ARTIST — Record Title | POP POS | Label & Number |
|---|---|---|---|---|---|
| | | | **X-25 BAND** | | |
| 9/25/82 | **65** | 7 | 1 Black Hole Bop...................................[I] | | H.C.R.C. 01396 |
| | | | **XAVIER** | | |
| | | | 8-member group; lead vocals by Xavier Smith and Ayanna Little. | | |
| 1/30/82 | **6** | 16 | 1 **Work That Sucker To Death** ........................ | 104 | Liberty 1445 |
| 5/08/82 | **59** | 9 | 2 Do It To The Max ......................................... | | Liberty 1464 |
| | | | **XAVION** | | |
| | | | Sextet from Memphis. | | |
| 1/05/85 | **72** | 7 | 1 Get Me Hot................................................ | | Asylum 69670 |

# Y

| | | | **YAMBU** | | |
|---|---|---|---|---|---|
| 12/13/75+ | **39** | 12 | 1 Sunny ......................................................... | | Montuno 8003 |
| | | | **"WEIRD AL" YANKOVIC** | | |
| | | | Los Angeles novelty singer/accordionist. Specializes in song parodies. | | |
| 4/07/84 | **84** | 4 | 1 Eat It ......................................................[N] | 12 | Rock 'n' R. 04374 |
| | | | parody of Michael Jackson's "Beat It"; features Rick Derringer as guitarist and producer | | |
| | | | **YARBROUGH & PEOPLES** | | |
| | | | Dallas duo of Cavin Yarbrough and Alisa Peoples. Discovered by The Gap Band. | | |
| 11/22/80+ | **1**⁵ | 27 | 1● **Don't Stop The Music**................................. | 19 | Mercury 76085 |
| 7/25/81 | **74** | 5 | 2 Third Degree ............................................ | | Mercury 76111 |
| 12/18/82+ | **10** | 17 | 3 **Heartbeats**............................................... | 101 | Total Exp. 8204 |
| 4/09/83 | **20** | 11 | 4 Feels So Good............................................ | | Total Exp. 8208 |
| 3/17/84 | **1**¹ | 21 | 5 **Don't Waste Your Time** .............................. | 48 | Total Exp. 2400 |
| 7/21/84 | **20** | 13 | 6 Be A Winner ............................................. | | Total Exp. 2403 |
| 11/30/85+ | **2**¹ | 21 | 7 Guilty...................................................... | | Total Exp. 2425 |
| 5/03/86 | **6** | 16 | 8 **I Wouldn't Lie** .......................................... | 93 | Total Exp. 2437 |
| 8/09/86 | **46** | 9 | 9 Wrapped Around Your Finger....................... | | Total Exp. 2441 |
| | | | **YAZ** | | |
| | | | British electronic pop duo: Vince Clarke (formerly of Depeche Mode; keyboards, synthesizers) and Genevieve Alison Moyet (vocals). Duo formerly named Yazoo. | | |
| 8/28/82 | **31** | 12 | 1 Situation ................................................... | 73 | Sire 29953 |
| | | | **YELLOW MAGIC ORCHESTRA** | | |
| | | | Japanese electronic trio: Ryuichi Sakamoto, Yukihiro Takahashi and Haruomi Hosono. | | |
| 1/19/80 | **18** | 17 | 1 Computer Game.........................................[I] | 60 | Horizon 127 |
| | | | theme from "The Circus" | | |
| | | | **YES** | | |
| | | | Progressive rock group formed in London in 1968, led by vocalist Jon Anderson. Many personnel changes. Group disbanded in 1980. Re-formed in 1983; lineup included: Anderson, Tony Kaye, Chris Squire, Alan White and Trevor Rabin. | | |
| 2/04/84 | **69** | 5 | 1 Owner Of A Lonely Heart.............................. | 1 | Atco 99817 |
| | | | **YOUNG HEARTS** | | |
| | | | Group from Los Angeles, formed in the late 60s. Consisted of Ronald Preyer, Charles Ingersoll, Earl Carter and James Moore. Re-formed as a trio with Preyer, Ingersoll and Bobbie Solomon. Solomon died of cancer on 5/30/75, at the age of 31. | | |
| 3/30/68 | **29** | 7 | 1 Oh, I'll Never Be The Same ........................... | 109 | Minit 32039 |
| 10/12/68 | **19** | 12 | 2 I've Got Love For My Baby ........................... | 94 | Minit 32049 |
| 6/15/74 | **70** | 5 | 3 Me & You............................................... | | 20th Century 2080 |
| 10/12/74 | **48** | 10 | 4 Wake Up And Start Standing/ | | |
| 2/22/75 | **81** | 2 | 5 Dedicate (My Life To You) .......................... | | 20th Century 2130 |
| | | | **YOUNG-HOLT UNLIMITED** | | |
| | | | Chicago instrumental group: Eldee Young (bass), Isaac "Red" Holt (drums; both of the Ramsey Lewis Trio) and Don Walker (piano). Walker left by 1968. | | |
| 12/24/66+ | **12** | 9 | 1 Wack Wack...............................................[I] | 40 | Brunswick 55305 |
| | | | shown as: **THE YOUNG HOLT TRIO** | | |
| 11/30/68+ | **3** | 13 | 2● Soulful Strut............................................[I] | 3 | Brunswick 55391 |
| | | | exact same recording as Barbara Acklin's "Am I The Same Girl", except vocal part replaced by piano | | |

| DEBUT DATE | PEAK POS | WKS CHR | ARTIST — Record Title | POP POS | Label & Number |
|---|---|---|---|---|---|
| | | | **YOUNG-HOLT UNLIMITED — Continued** | | |
| 6/14/69 | 49 | 3 | 3  Just A Melody ............................................ [I] | | Brunswick 55410 |
| | | | **YOUNG RASCALS - see THE RASCALS** | | |
| | | | **YOUNG VANDALS** | | |
| 3/28/70 | 41 | 2 | 1  I've Been Good To You/ | | |
| | | 5 | 2     Too Busy Thinking 'Bout My Baby ................ | | T-Neck 917 |
| 8/29/70 | 35 | 6 | 3  In My Opinion.................................................. | | T-Neck 923 |
| | | | **KAREN YOUNG** | | |
| 8/12/78 | 24 | 15 | 1  Hot Shot.................................................... | *67* | West End 1211 |
| | | | **KATHY YOUNG - see THE INNOCENTS** | | |
| | | | **LESTER YOUNG** | | |
| | | | Born on 8/27/09 in Woodville, Mississippi. Died on 3/15/59 in New York City. Tenor saxophonist/clarinetist. Moved to Minneapolis in 1920, worked in family touring band. First recorded for Vocalion in 1936, with Count Basie. Nickname "Prez" from "The President", given to him by Billie Holiday. With Jazz At The Philharmonic, own combos, from 1945-56. Frequent bouts with ill health. | | |
| 3/25/44 | 5 | 4 | 1  **Sometimes I'm Happy**................................ [I] | | Keynote 604 |
| 3/25/44 | 9 | 1 | 2  **Just You, Just Me** ..................................... [I] | | Keynote 603 |
| 5/20/44 | 10 | 2 | 3  **Lester Leaps Again**................................... [I] | | Keynote 1202 |
| | | | **PAUL YOUNG** | | |
| | | | Born on 1/17/56 in Bedfordshire, England. Pop-rock vocalist/guitarist. | | |
| 10/05/85 | 60 | 7 | 1  I'm Gonna Tear Your Playhouse Down .............. | *13* | Columbia 05577 |
| | | | **RETTA YOUNG** | | |
| | | | Born in 1949 in South Carolina. Sang with cousins Bertha Addison and Madge Quince as the Moderations. Recorded as the Devotions for Silver Dollar in 1971. Went solo in 1971. | | |
| 7/19/75 | 88 | 3 | 1  (Sending Out An) S.O.S. ............................... | | All Platinum 2355 |
| | | | **TOMMIE YOUNG** | | |
| 3/03/73 | 28 | 8 | 1  Do You Still Feel The Same Way? .................... | | Soul Power 112 |
| 7/14/73 | 69 | 4 | 2  She Don't Have To See You............................ | | Soul Power 114 |
| | | | **VAL YOUNG** | | |
| | | | Female singer from Detroit. With the Brides Of Funkenstein from 1978-79. Vocalist with The Gap Band. | | |
| 10/19/85 | 17 | 15 | 1  Seduction ............................................... | | Gordy 1812 |
| 2/08/86 | 21 | 14 | 2  If You Should Ever Be Lonely ......................... | | Gordy 1830 |
| 6/06/87 | 53 | 11 | 3  Private Conversations................................. | | Amherst 312 |
| | | | **LONNIE YOUNGBLOOD** | | |
| | | | Saxophonist, first recorded for Fairmount in 1965, with his band that included Jimi Hendrix. In house band at All-Platinum Records. | | |
| 7/22/72 | 32 | 6 | 1  Sweet Sweet Tootie ................................... | | Turbo 026 |
| 12/07/74+ | 39 | 10 | 2  Man To Woman........................................... | | Shakat 708 |
| | | | answer song to Shirley Brown's "Woman To Woman" | | |
| 7/25/81 | 82 | 4 | 3  The Best Way To Break A Habit ..................... | | Radio 3820 |
| | | | **TIMI YURO** | | |
| | | | Born Rosemarie Timothy Aurro Yuro on 8/4/40 in Chicago. Moved to Los Angeles in 1952. First recorded for Liberty in 1959. Lost voice in 1980 and underwent three throat operations. | | |
| 8/21/61 | 22 | 2 | 1  Hurt ...................................................... | *4* | Liberty 55343 |
| 9/01/62 | 16 | 6 | 2  What's A Matter Baby (Is It Hurting You)........... | *12* | Liberty 55469 |
| | | | above 2: produced by Clyde Otis | | |
| 10/12/63 | 64 | 7 | 3  Gotta Travel On ........................................... | *Hot* | Liberty 55634 |
| | | | **YUTAKA** | | |
| | | | Born Yutaka Yokokura in Tokyo, Japan. Male jazz-pop vocalist/keyboardist. | | |
| 7/04/81 | 61 | 7 | 1  Love Light .................................................. | *81* | Alfa 7004 |
| | | | vocals by Yutaka and Patti Austin | | |

| DEBUT DATE | PEAK POS | WKS CHR | ARTIST — Record Title | POP POS | Label & Number |
|---|---|---|---|---|---|

# Z

### JOHN ZACHERLE
Born on 9/26/18 in Philadelphia. "The Cool Ghoul" - hosted a horror movies TV show in Philadelphia.

| | | | | | |
|---|---|---|---|---|---|
| 3/31/58 | **19** | 1 | 1 Dinner With Drac - Part 1 .........................[N] Best Seller #19 | *6* | Cameo 130 |

### PIA ZADORA
Actress/singer born Pia Schipani in 1955, in New York City. In the films "Butterfly" (1982) and "The Lonely Lady" (1983).

| | | | | | |
|---|---|---|---|---|---|
| 2/05/83 | **88** | 5 | 1 The Clapping Song ........................................ | *36* | Elektra 69889 |
| 3/02/85 | **61** | 9 | 2 When The Rain Begins To Fall......................... JERMAINE JACKSON/PIA ZADORA from the film "Voyage of the Rock Aliens" | *54* | Curb 52521 |

### MICHAEL ZAGER'S MOON BAND featuring Peabo Bryson
Studio group led by writer/arranger Michael Zager (b: 1943, Jersey City, NJ). With band, Ten Wheel Drive, from 1968-73. TV/radio commercial production to 1975. Produced Love Child's Afro Cuban Blues Band, Street Corner Symphony, and Andrea True Connection.

| | | | | | |
|---|---|---|---|---|---|
| 1/17/76 | **25** | 13 | 1 Do It With Feeling ........................................ | *94* | Bang 720 |
| 1/07/78 | **6** | 21 | 2 **Reaching For The Sky**................................... | *102* | Capitol 4522 |
| 2/18/78 | **15** | 18 | 3 Let's All Chant ..............................[I] THE MICHAEL ZAGER BAND | *36* | Private S. 45184 |
| 6/17/78 | **76** | 10 | 4 Do It With Feeling ........................[R] | | Bang 737 |
| 11/25/78+ | **2²** | 18 | 5 **I'm So Into You** ........................................ | *109* | Capitol 4656 |

### ROBIN ZANDER - see REBBIE JACKSON

### ZAPP
Dayton, Ohio funk band formed by the Troutman brothers: Roger "Zapp", Lester, Tony and Larry. "Bootsy" Collins produced and played on first session. Shirley Murdock was backup singer.

| | | | | | |
|---|---|---|---|---|---|
| 8/23/80 | **2²** | 24 | 1 **More Bounce To The Ounce - Part I** .............. | *86* | Warner 49534 |
| 12/20/80+ | **26** | 15 | 2 Be Alright - Part I......................................... | | Warner 49623 |
| 7/10/82 | **1²** | 16 | 3 **Dance Floor (Part I)** ................................... | *101* | Warner 29961 |
| 10/23/82 | **10** | 14 | 4 **Doo Wa Ditty (Blow That Thing)**.................... | *103* | Warner 29891 |
| 7/30/83 | **4** | 15 | 5 **I Can Make You Dance (Part I)** ...................... | *102* | Warner 29553 |
| 10/15/83 | **15** | 15 | 6 Heartbreaker (Part I).................................... | *107* | Warner 29462 |
| 1/28/84 | **77** | 5 | 7 Spend My Whole Life .................................... | | Warner 29380 |
| 10/26/85 | **41** | 9 | 8 It Doesn't Really Matter ............................... | | Warner 28879 |
| 1/11/86 | **8** | 18 | 9 **Computer Love Part I**.................................. | | Warner 28805 |
| 5/10/86 | **81** | 3 | 10 Itchin' For Your Twitchin' ............................ | | Warner 28719 |

### ZINGARA
Quartet from Los Angeles. Vocals by Wali Ali.

| | | | | | |
|---|---|---|---|---|---|
| 12/27/80+ | **29** | 17 | 1 Love's Calling.............................................. | | Wheel 5001 |

### ZION BAPTIST CHURCH CHOIR

| | | | | | |
|---|---|---|---|---|---|
| 5/12/73 | **33** | 9 | 1 I'll Make It Alright....................................... | | Myrrh 115 |
| 10/20/73 | **87** | 7 | 2 Let's Ride To The Mt. Top.............................. | | Myrrh 121 |

### THE ZODIACS - see MAURICE WILLIAMS

### ZOOM
Band formed by drummer George Mitchell in Los Angeles, in 1977. Originally known as P.L.U.M. Group included: Darryl Williams, Henry Prejean, Floyd "Butch" Bonner, Marcus Robinson, S. Todd Duncan and John Haynes. Vocals by Nolan Semco.

| | | | | | |
|---|---|---|---|---|---|
| 11/07/81 | **54** | 8 | 1 Saturday, Saturday Night .............................. | | Polydor 2186 |
| 2/27/82 | **39** | 13 | 2 Love Seasons ............................................. | | Polydor 2197 |

### ZULEMA
Born Zulema Cusseaux on 1/3/47 in Tampa, Florida. Female singer/songwriter/multi-instrumentalist. Formed vocal group Faith, Hope & Charity. Went solo in 1971.

| | | | | | |
|---|---|---|---|---|---|
| 9/22/73 | **91** | 4 | 1 Telling The World Goodbye............................ | | Sussex 504 |
| 1/18/75 | **58** | 12 | 2 Wanna Be Where You Are .............................. | | RCA 10116 |
| 10/28/78 | **46** | 8 | 3 Change.................................................... | | Lejoint 34001 |
| 2/03/79 | **76** | 9 | 4 I'm Not Dreaming......................................... | | Lejoint 34002 |

# THE SONG TITLES

This section lists, alphabetically, all titles in the artist section. The artist's name is listed next to each title along with the highest position attained and year of peak popularity. Some titles show the letter F as a position, indicating the title was listed as a flip side and did not chart on its own.

**Songs with identical titles are listed together. The artists' names are listed below in chronological order, even though they may be different tunes.** Since 15% of the records were not available for play by our staff, it was impossible to determine if all of the same-named titles were also the same composition.

Cross references have been used throughout to aid in finding a title.

Please keep the following in mind when searching for titles:

A title which substitutes a letter with an apostrophe appears before a title using the complete spelling. (Lovin' is listed before Loving).

Titles beginning with a contraction follow titles that begin with a similar non-contracted word (Can't follows Can).

Titles such as I.O.U. and SOS will be found at the beginning of their respective letters.

| | |
|---|---|
| 9/83 | **Baby, Come To Me** |
| | *Patti Austin with James Ingram* |
| 20/66 | **Baby, Do The Philly Dog** *Olympics* |
| 9/53 | **Baby Doll** *Marvin & Johnny* |
| 16/69 | **Baby, Don't Be Looking In My Mind** |
| | *Joe Simon* |
| 6/84 | **Baby Don't Break Your Baby's Heart** |
| | *Kashif* |
| 10/77 | **Baby Don't Change Your Mind** |
| | *Gladys Knight & The Pips* |
| 1/53 | **Baby, Don't Do It** *'5' Royales* |
| 29/87 | **Baby Don't Go Too Far** *Luther Ingram* |
| 7/62 | **Baby Don't Leave Me** *Joe Henderson* |
| 65/75 | **(Baby) Don't Let It Mess Your Mind** |
| | *Donny Gerrard* |
| 66/81 | **Baby Don't Stop Me** *Leon Ware* |
| 36/70 | **Baby Don't Take Your Love** |
| | *Faith, Hope & Charity* |
| | **Baby Don't You Cry** |
| 3/43 | *Buddy Johnson* |
| 39/64 | *Ray Charles* |
| 27/64 | **Baby Don't You Do It** *Marvin Gaye* |
| 41/77 | **Baby Don't You Know** *Wild Cherry* |
| 30/63 | **Baby Don't You Weep** |
| | *Garnet Mimms & The Enchanters* |
| | **Baby Face** |
| 12/58 | *Little Richard* |
| 32/76 | *Wing & A Prayer Fife & Drum Corps.* |
| 76/85 | *Merc & Monk* |
| 61/63 | **Baby Get It (And Don't Quit It)** |
| | *Jackie Wilson* |
| 31/75 | **Baby-Get It On** *Ike & Tina Turner* |
| 1/49 | **Baby, Get Lost** *Dinah Washington* |
| 49/83 | **Baby Gets High** *Peter Brown* |
| 60/87 | **Baby Go-Go** *Nona Hendryx* |
| 18/75 | **Baby, Hang Up The Phone** *Carl Graves* |
| 44/67 | **Baby, Help Me** *Percy Sledge* |
| 59/76 | **Baby, Hold On To Me** *John Edwards* |
| 21/80 | **(Baby) I Can't Get Over Losing You** *TTF* |
| 72/81 | **Baby, I Do Love You** *Greg Phillinganes* |
| | **Baby I Don't Care** *..see: (You're So Square)* |
| 89/78 | **Baby I Just Wanna Love You** *Jonelle Allen* |
| | **Baby, I Love You** |
| 24/64 | *Ronettes* |
| 21/66 | *Jimmy Holiday* |
| 1/67 | *Aretha Franklin* |
| 40/67 | *Howard Tate* |
| 6/70 | *Little Milton* |
| 68/74 | *Benny Johnson* |
| 19/77 | **Baby, I Love Your Way** *Walter Jackson* |
| 22/66 | **Baby I Need You** *Manhattans* |
| 21/78 | **Baby, I Need Your Love Today** |
| | *Sweet Thunder* |
| | **Baby I Need Your Loving** |
| 11/64 | *Four Tops* |
| 30/70 | *O.C. Smith* |
| 47/72 | *Geraldine Hunt* |
| 17/82 | *Carl Carlton* |
| 72/83 | **Baby I Want You Back** *Junior* |
| 28/76 | **Baby I Want Your Body** *Al Wilson* |
| 80/83 | **Baby I Will** *Michael Lovesmith* |
| 8/53 | **Baby I'm Doin' It** *Annisteen Allen* |
| | **Baby I'm For Real** |
| 1/69 | *Originals* |
| 38/72 | *Esther Phillips* |
| 54/80 | *Hamilton Bohannon* |
| 53/87 | *Sherrick* |
| 76/76 | **Baby, I'm Gonna Love You** *Phyllis Hyman* |
| 5/84 | **Baby, I'm Hooked (Right Into Your Love)** |
| | *Con Funk Shun* |
| 28/67 | **Baby, I'm Lonely** *Intruders* |
| 25/84 | **Baby I'm Scared Of You** |
| | *Womack & Womack* |
| 25/85 | **Baby I'm Sorry** *R.J.'s Latest Arrival* |

| | |
|---|---|
| | **Baby I'm Through** |
| 82/74 | *Emotions* |
| 59/78 | *Emotions* |
| 5/65 | **Baby, I'm Yours** *Barbara Lewis* |
| 4/73 | **Baby I've Been Missing You** *Independents* |
| 31/70 | **Baby, Is There Something On Your Mind** |
| | *McKinley Travis* |
| 94/77 | **Baby It Ain't No Way** *Little Milton* |
| 6/49 | **Baby, It's Cold Outside** |
| | *Ella Fitzgerald & Louis Jordan* |
| 26/66 | **Baby, It's Over** *Bob & Earl* |
| | **Baby, It's You** |
| 10/53 | *Spaniels* |
| 3/62 | *Shirelles* |
| 76/76 | *Masqueraders* |
| 37/84 | *Stacy Lattisaw & Johnny Gill* |
| 69/85 | *Curtis Mayfield* |
| 50/73 | **Baby Lay Your Head Down** *Eddie Floyd* |
| 5/51 | **Baby Let Me Hold Your Hand** *Ray Charles* |
| 5/71 | **Baby Let Me Kiss You** *King Floyd* |
| 4/72 | **Baby Let Me Take You (In My Arms)** |
| | *Detroit Emeralds* |
| 23/87 | **Baby Let's Kiss** *Jesse Johnson* |
| 12/55 | **Baby Let's Play House** *Arthur Gunter* |
| 39/81 | **Baby Let's Rap Now** *Moments* |
| 68/75 | **Baby Let's Talk It Over** *Al Downing* |
| | **Baby Love** |
| 1/64 | *Supremes* |
| 79/77 | *Mother's Finest* |
| 78/83 | *Aurra* |
| 30/86 | *Regina* |
| 82/77 | **Baby Love, Sweet Sweet Love** |
| | *Wilton Place Street Band* |
| 12/69 | **Baby Make Me Feel So Good** |
| | *Five Stairsteps & Cubie* |
| 48/68 | **Baby Make Your Own Sweet Music** |
| | *Bandwagon* |
| 61/81 | **Baby Not Tonight** *Madagascar* |
| 33/68 | **Baby, Now That I've Found You** |
| | *Foundations* |
| 9/67 | **Baby Please Come Back Home** *J.J. Barnes* |
| 8/52 | **Baby, Please Don't Go** *Orioles* |
| 1/66 | **Baby Scratch My Back** *Slim Harpo* |
| 29/71 | **Baby Show It** *Festivals* |
| 74/78 | **Baby Sinister** *Slave* |
| 51/84 | **Baby Sister** *Koko-Pop* |
| 6/72 | **Baby Sitter** *Betty Wright* |
| 27/61 | **Baby Sittin' Boogie** *Buzz Clifford* |
| | **Baby Talk** |
| 28/59 | *Jan & Dean* |
| 75/85 | *Alisha* |
| 6/87 | **(Baby Tell Me) Can You Dance** |
| | *Shanice Wilson* |
| 1/75 | **Baby That's Backatcha** *Smokey Robinson* |
| 45/80 | **Baby (This Love That We've Found)** *Heat* |
| 57/88 | **Baby Tonight** *Marlon Jackson* |
| 6/70 | **(Baby) Turn On To Me** *Impressions* |
| 29/76 | **Baby, We Better Try To Get It Together** |
| | *Barry White* |
| 98/63 | **Baby, We've Got Love** *Johnnie Taylor* |
| 10/60 | **Baby What Do You Want Me To Do** |
| | *Jimmy Reed* |
| 37/66 | **Baby What I Mean** *Drifters* |
| 82/64 | **Baby What You Want Me To Do** |
| | *Etta James* |
| 60/80 | **Baby, When Love Is In Your Heart (It's In Your Eyes)** *Joe Simon* |
| 1/63 | **Baby Workout** *Jackie Wilson* |
| 82/73 | **Baby You Belong To Me** *Magic Touch* |
| 21/61 | **Baby You Don't Know** *Roy Milton* |
| 30/68 | **Baby You Got It** *Brenton Wood* |
| 36/78 | **Baby, You Got My Nose Open** |
| | *Harold Melvin & The Blue Notes* |
| 40/75 | **Baby You Know (I'm Gonna Miss You)** |
| | *Montclairs* |

| 52/79 | **Beyond The Clouds** *Quartz* |
|---|---|
| 15/60 | **Beyond The Sea** *Bobby Darin* |
| 5/43 | **Bicycle Bounce** *Erskine Hawkins* |
| 50/80 | **Big Bang Theory** *Parliament* |
| | **Big Beat** |
| 15/57 | *Fats Domino* |
| 69/84 | *Spoonie Gee* |
| 94/64 | **Big Boss Line** *Jackie Wilson* |
| | **Big Boss Man** |
| 13/61 | *Jimmy Reed* |
| 62/85 | *B.B. King* |
| 10/60 | **Big Boy Pete** *Olympics* |
| 86/80 | **Big City Rocker** *Trussel* |
| 63/82 | **Big Fat Bottom** *Redd Hot* |
| 4/50 | **Big Fine Girl** *Jimmy Witherspoon* |
| | **Big Fun** |
| 6/82 | *Kool & The Gang* |
| 8/87 | *Gap Band* |
| 1/62 | **Big Girls Don't Cry** *4 Seasons* |
| 10/59 | **Big Hunk O' Love** *Elvis Presley* |
| 16/60 | **Big Hurt** *Miss Toni Fisher* |
| 2/61 | **Big John** *Shirelles* |
| 13/70 | **Big Leg Woman** |
| | *Israel 'Popper Stopper' Tolbert* |
| 9/58 | **Big Man** *Four Preps* |
| 64/85 | **Big Mouth (Acapella Mix)** *Whodini* |
| 28/61 | **Big Mr. C.** *Link-Eddy Combo* |
| 97/64 | **Big Party** *Barbara & The Browns* |
| 6/52 | **Big Question** *Percy Mayfield* |
| 17/80 | **Big Time** *Rick James* |
| 88/74 | **Big Time Lover** |
| | *Cornelius Brothers & Sister Rose* |
| 25/60 | **Big Time Spender** *Cornbread & Biscuits* |
| 8/51 | **Big Town** *Roy Brown* |
| | **Biggest Joke In Town** *..see: (You're The)* |
| 29/67 | **Biggest Man** *Tommy Hunt* |
| 35/80 | **Biggest Part Of Me** *Ambrosia* |
| 84/64 | **Billie Baby** *Lloyd Price* |
| | **Billie Jean** |
| 1/83 | *Michael Jackson* |
| 25/83 | *Slingshot (medley)* |
| 61/83 | *Club House (medley)* |
| 52/75 | **Billy's Back Home** *Billy Paul* |
| 40/74 | **Bingo** *Whispers* |
| 7/54 | **Bip Bam** *Drifters/Clyde McPhatter* |
| 33/85 | **Bird, The** *Time* |
| 2/58 | **Bird Dog** *Everly Brothers* |
| 27/63 | **Bird's The Word** *Rivingtons* |
| 18/63 | **Birdland** *Chubby Checker* |
| 21/65 | **Birds And The Bees** *Jewel Akens* |
| | **Birth & Death Of A Gangster** |
| | *..see: (Alvin Stone)* |
| 36/81 | **Birthday Party** |
| | *Grandmaster Flash & The Furious Five* |
| 52/85 | **Bit By Bit** *Stephanie Mills* |
| 79/85 | **Bite It** *UTFO* |
| 84/85 | **Bite This** *Roxanne Shante* |
| 48/77 | **Bite Your Granny** *Morning, Noon, & Night* |
| 43/69 | **Black Berries** *Isley Brothers* |
| 22/84 | **Black Butterfly** *Deniece Williams* |
| 19/73 | **Black Byrd** *Donald Byrd* |
| 29/70 | **Black Fox** *Freddy Robinson* |
| 65/82 | **Black Hole Bop** *X-25 Band* |
| | **Black Night** |
| 1/51 | *Charles Brown* |
| 99/65 | *Bobby Bland* |
| 11/66 | **Black Nights** *Lowell Fulsom* |
| 8/69 | **Black Pearl** |
| | *Sonny Charles & The Checkmates, Ltd.* |
| 15/71 | **Black Seeds Keep On Growing** |
| | *Main Ingredient* |
| 11/57 | **Black Slacks** |
| | *Joe Bennett & The Sparkletones* |
| 86/76 | **Black Speck** *O.B. McClinton* |

| 75/78 | **Black Water Gold** *Sunshine Band* |
|---|---|
| 43/70 | **Black Women** *Don Covay* |
| 82/77 | **Blackberry Jam** *Leroy Hutson* |
| 8/55 | **Blackjack** *Ray Charles* |
| 35/83 | **Blame It On Love** |
| | *Smokey Robinson & Barbara Mitchell* |
| 3/78 | **Blame It On The Boogie** *Jacksons* |
| 16/63 | **Blame It On The Bossa Nova** *Eydie Gorme* |
| 40/76 | **Bless My Soul** *Skip Mahoney & The Casuals* |
| 39/64 | **Bless Our Love** *Gene Chandler* |
| 29/71 | **Bless You** *Martha Reeves & The Vandellas* |
| 29/69 | **Bless Your Heart** *Isley Brothers* |
| 14/77 | **Blessed Is The Woman (With A Man Like Mine)** *Shirley Brown* |
| | **Blind Man** |
| 78/65 | *Bobby Bland* |
| 86/65 | *Little Milton* |
| 67/75 | **Blind Over You** *Chicago Gangsters* |
| 56/77 | **Bloat On Featuring The Bloaters** |
| | *Cheech & Chong* |
| 12/50 | **Block Buster Boogie** *Cecil Payne Orchestra* |
| 63/84 | **Block Party** *Stacy Lattisaw & Johnny Gill* |
| 61/77 | **Blockbuster Boy** *Sister Sledge* |
| 80/74 | **Blood Brothers** *Gene Redding* |
| | **Blood Is Thicker Than Water** |
| 33/71 | *Eddie Floyd* |
| 10/74 | *William DeVaughn* |
| 6/51 | **Bloodshot Eyes** *Wynonie Harris* |
| 69/84 | **Bloodstone's Party** *Bloodstone* |
| 3/47 | **Blow Mr. Jackson** *Joe Liggins* |
| 5/47 | **Blow Top Blues** *Lionel Hampton* |
| | **Blow Your Whistle** |
| 27/73 | *KC & The Sunshine Band* |
| 31/74 | *Soul Searchers* |
| 1/66 | **Blowin' In The Wind** *Stevie Wonder* |
| 2/49 | **Blue And Lonesome** *Memphis Slim* |
| 23/60 | **Blue Angel** *Roy Orbison* |
| 26/63 | **Blue Bayou** *Roy Orbison* |
| 10/49 | **Blue Dreams** *Sonny Thompson* |
| 5/46 | **Blue Flame** *Lenny Lewis* |
| 15/81 | **Blue Jeans** *Chocolate Milk* |
| 1/50 | **Blue Light Boogie** *Louis Jordan* |
| 34/78 | **Blue Love** *Rufus & Chaka Khan* |
| 1/57 | **Blue Monday** *Fats Domino* |
| | **Blue Moon** |
| 12/49 | *Billy Eckstine* |
| 1/61 | *Marcels* |
| | **Blue Shadows** |
| 1/50 | *Lowell Fulson* |
| 25/65 | *B.B. King* |
| 2/56 | **Blue Suede Shoes** *Carl Perkins* |
| 14/55 | **Blue Velvet** *Clovers* |
| 54/88 | **Blueberry Gossip** *Ta Mara & The Seen* |
| 1/56 | **Blueberry Hill** *Fats Domino* |
| 45/81 | **Bluer Than Blue** *Peaches & Herb* |
| 1/48 | **Blues After Hours** *Pee Wee Crayton* |
| 12/49 | **Blues At Dawn** *Edgar Hayes* |
| 10/49 | **Blues At Midnight** *Ivory Joe Hunter* |
| 3/45 | **Blues At Sunrise** *Ivory Joe Hunter* |
| 3/49 | **Blues For My Baby** *Billy Wright* |
| 4/49 | **Blues For The Red Boy** *Todd Rhodes* |
| 14/49 | **Blues On Rhumba** *Sonny Thompson* |
| 2/53 | **Blues With A Feeling** *Little Walter* |
| 1/55 | **Bo Diddley** *Bo Diddley* |
| 5/56 | **Bo Weevil** *Fats Domino* |
| 3/47 | **Bobby Sox Blues** *T-Bone Walker* |
| 26/59 | **Bobby Sox To Stockings** *Frankie Avalon* |
| 14/62 | **Bobby's Girl** *Marcie Blane* |
| 39/84 | **Body** *Jacksons* |
| 4/44 | **Body And Soul** *Coleman Hawkins* |
| 71/87 | **Body & Soul (Take Me)** *Mtume* |
| 25/77 | **Body English** *King Floyd* |
| 42/81 | **Body Fever** *Bar-Kays* |
| 85/75 | **Body Heat** *Quincy Jones* |

## Body Language
| | |
|---|---|
| 87/77 | *GF & Friends* |
| 35/79 | *Spinners* |
| 45/80 | *Patti Austin* |
| 30/82 | *Queen* |
| 72/83 | **Body Mechanic** *Quadrant Six* |
| 75/82 | **Body Moves** *Rare Essence* |
| 23/81 | **Body Music** *Strikers* |
| 12/82 | **Body Slam!** *Bootsy's Rubber Band* |
| 72/81 | **Body Snatcher** *R.J.'s Latest Arrival* |
| 31/85 | **Body Snatchers** *Midnight Star* |
| 3/84 | **Body Talk** *Deele* |
| 19/77 | **Body Vibes** *Ohio Players* |
| 13/77 | **Bodyheat** *James Brown* |
| 41/80 | **Bodyshine** *Instant Funk* |
| 67/77 | **Bohannon Disco Symphony** |
| | *Hamilton Bohannon* |
| 65/76 | **Bohannon's Beat** *Hamilton Bohannon* |
| 22/70 | **Bold Soul Sister** *Ike & Tina Turner* |
| 2/61 | **Boll Weevil Song** *Brook Benton* |
| 97/76 | **Bom Bom** *Jimmy Castor* |
| 74/83 | **Bomb Body** *General Caine* |
| 11/81 | **Bon Bon Vie (Gimme The Good Life)** |
| | *T.S. Monk* |
| 55/64 | **Bon-Doo-Wah** *Orlons* |
| 7/50 | **Bon Ton Roula** *Clarence Garlow* |
| 13/49 | **Bongo Blues** *Dee Williams Sextet* |
| 42/73 | **Bongo Rock** *Incredible Bongo Band* |
| 4/57 | **Bony Moronie** *Larry Williams* |
| 11/65 | **Boo-Ga-Loo** *Tom & Jerrio* |
| 5/67 | **Boogaloo Down Broadway** |
| | *Fantastic Johnny C* |
| 22/66 | **Boogaloo Party** *Flamingos* |
| 63/74 | **Boogie Ain't Nuttin' (But Gettin' Down)** |
| | *Rufus Thomas* |
| 3/49 | **Boogie At Midnight** *Roy Brown* |
| 7/81 | **Boogie Body Land** *Bar-Kays* |
| 50/77 | **Boogie Bopper** *Sun* |
| 31/77 | **Boogie Child** *Bee Gees* |
| 1/49 | **Boogie Chillen'** *John Lee Hooker* |
| | **Boogie Down** |
| 1/74 | *Eddie Kendricks* |
| 67/75 | *Van McCoy* |
| 87/79 | *Street Players* |
| 9/83 | *Jarreau* |
| 76/85 | **Boogie Down Bronx** *Man Parrish* |
| 1/76 | **Boogie Fever** *Sylvers* |
| 56/82 | **Boogie In Your Butt** *Eddie Murphy* |
| 70/74 | **Boogie Joe, The Grinder** *Quincy Jones* |
| 81/74 | **Boogie Man** *Greg Perry* |
| 5/77 | **Boogie Nights** *Heatwave* |
| 1/74 | **Boogie On Reggae Woman** *Stevie Wonder* |
| 1/78 | **Boogie Oogie Oogie** *A Taste Of Honey* |
| 29/78 | **Boogie Shoes** *KC & The Sunshine Band* |
| 43/79 | **Boogie Town** *FLB* |
| 93/75 | **Boogie Up The Nation** *Soul Searchers* |
| 2/79 | **Boogie Wonderland** |
| | *Earth, Wind & Fire with The Emotions* |
| 6/43 | **Boogie Woogie** *Tommy Dorsey Orchestra* |
| 10/44 | **Boogie-Woogie Ball** *Five Red Caps* |
| 1/47 | **Boogie Woogie Blue Plate** *Louis Jordan* |
| F/56 | **Boogie Woogie Country Girl** *Joe Turner* |
| 37/79 | **Boogie Woogie Dancin' Shoes** |
| | *Claudja Barry* |
| 12/49 | **Boogie Woogie Santa Claus** *Mabel Scott* |
| 53/81 | **Boogie's Gonna Get Ya'** *Rafael Cameron* |
| | **Book Of Love** |
| 3/58 | *Monotones* |
| 62/64 | *Raindrops* |
| 37/66 | **Booker-Loo** *Booker T. & The MG's* |
| 16/62 | **Boom Boom** *John Lee Hooker* |
| 10/65 | **Boot-Leg** *Booker T. & The MG's* |
| 1/52 | **Booted** *Roscoe Gordon* |
| 38/79 | **Bootsy Get Live** *Bootsy* |
| 32/76 | **Booty, The** *Fatback Band* |

| | |
|---|---|
| 78/75 | **Booty Bumpin' (The Double Bump)** |
| | *Oliver Sain* |
| 13/71 | **Booty Butt** *Ray Charles Orchestra* |
| 1/78 | **Bootzilla** *Bootsy's Rubber Band* |
| 14/77 | **Bop Gun (Endangered Species)** *Parliament* |
| 3/55 | **Bop-Ting-A-Ling** |
| | *LaVern Baker & The Gliders* |
| | **Border Song (Holy Moses)** |
| 43/70 | *Dorothy Morrison* |
| 5/71 | *Aretha Franklin* |
| 7/85 | **Borderlines, The** *Jeffrey Osborne* |
| 27/69 | **Born Again** *Sam & Dave* |
| 4/68 | **Born Free** *Hesitations* |
| 52/85 | **Born In The U.S.A.** *Stanley Clarke Band* |
| 41/69 | **Born To Be Wild** *Wilson Pickett* |
| 8/76 | **Born To Get Down (Born To Mess** |
| | **Around)** *Muscle Shoals Horns* |
| 48/71 | **Born To Wander** *Rare Earth* |
| 11/58 | **Born Too Late** *Poni-Tails* |
| 49/67 | **Born Under A Bad Sign** *Albert King* |
| 14/86 | **Borrowed Love** *S.O.S. Band* |
| 12/79 | **Boss, The** *Diana Ross* |
| 28/63 | **Boss Guitar** *Duane Eddy* |
| 20/63 | **Bossa Nova Baby** *Elvis Presley* |
| 28/74 | **Both Ends Against The Middle** |
| | *Jackie Moore* |
| | **Bottle, The** |
| 59/75 | *Bataan* |
| 98/77 | *Gil Scott-Heron/Merry Clayton* |
| 7/83 | **Bottom's Up** *Chi-Lites* |
| 22/63 | **Bounce, The** *Olympics* |
| 5/80 | **Bounce, Rock, Skate, Roll** |
| | *Vaughan Mason & Crew* |
| 41/72 | **Bound** *Ponderosa Twins + One* |
| 45/80 | **Bourgie', Bourgie'** |
| | *Gladys Knight & The Pips* |
| 45/71 | **'Bout Love** *Clydie King* |
| 94/76 | **Bout To Make Me Leave Home** *Syl Johnson* |
| 6/65 | **Boy From New York City** *Ad Libs* |
| 71/74 | **Boy Next Door** *Bettye Swann* |
| 69/85 | **Boyfriend** *Shirley Brown* |
| 29/83 | **Boys** *Mary Jane Girls* |
| 37/66 | **Boys Are Made To Love** *Karen Small* |
| 51/73 | **Bra** *Cymande* |
| 84/85 | **Brand New Beat** *Koko-Pop* |
| | **Brand New Lover** *..see: (Gotta Find)* |
| F/71 | **Brand New Me** *Aretha Franklin* |
| 41/69 | **Branded Bad** *O'Jays* |
| 21/78 | **Brandy** *O'Jays* |
| 83/87 | **Brass Monkey** *Beastie Boys* |
| | **Brazil** |
| 8/43 | *Jimmy Dorsey* |
| 9/43 | *Xavier Cugat* |
| 13/75 | *Ritchie Family* |
| 88/76 | **Brazilica** *Ramsey Lewis* |
| 49/80 | **Brazos River Breakdown** *Stix Hooper* |
| 37/83 | **Break Dancin'-Electric Boogie** |
| | *West Street Mob* |
| 1/77 | **Break It To Me Gently** *Aretha Franklin* |
| 79/85 | **Break It Up** *Mary Jane Girls* |
| | **Break My Heart** |
| 9/79 | *David Ruffin* |
| 48/86 | *Jimmy G. & The Tackheads* |
| 76/83 | **Break My Stride** *Matthew Wilder* |
| 82/85 | **Break The Ice** *Michael Lovesmith* |
| 5/73 | **Break Up To Make Up** *Stylistics* |
| 12/68 | **Break Your Promise** *Delfonics* |
| 16/73 | **Breakaway** *Millie Jackson* |
| 23/84 | **Breakdance** *Irene Cara* |
| | **Breakdown, The** |
| 2/71 | *Rufus Thomas* |
| 30/71 | *Parliament* |
| 25/82 | **Breakin' Away** *Al Jarreau* |
| 80/75 | **Breakin' Bread** *Fred & The New J.B.'s* |
| 78/85 | **(Breakin') Super Turf** *Herb The 'K'* |

| | | |
|---|---|---|
| 63/79 | **Breakin' The Funk** *Faze-O* | |
| 32/84 | **Breakin' Together** *O'Bryan* | |
| | **Breakin' Up** *..see: (Best Part Of)* | |
| 3/84 | **Breakin'...There's No Stopping Us** | |
| | *Ollie & Jerry* | |
| | **Breaking Up Is Hard To Do** | |
| 12/62 | *Neil Sedaka* | |
| 27/70 | *Lenny Welch* | |
| 91/76 | *Jimmy Bee* | |
| | **Breaking Up Somebody's Home** | |
| 13/72 | *Ann Peebles* | |
| 35/73 | *Albert King* | |
| | **Breakout!** | |
| 46/82 | *Patrice Rushen* | |
| 73/84 | *Starpoint* | |
| 4/80 | **Breaks, The** *Kurtis Blow* | |
| | **Breathless** | |
| 3/58 | *Jerry Lee Lewis* | |
| 9/86 | *Mtume* | |
| | **Breezin'** | |
| 43/71 | *Gabor Szabo & Bobby Womack* | |
| 55/76 | *George Benson* | |
| 58/87 | **Brenda** *O.C. Smith* | |
| 4/77 | **Brick House** *Commodores* | |
| | **Bridge Over Troubled Water** | |
| 1/71 | *Aretha Franklin* | |
| 49/79 | *Linda Clifford* | |
| 3/61 | **Bright Lights Big City** *Jimmy Reed* | |
| 41/79 | **Brighter Days** *Vernon Burch* | |
| 18/85 | **Bring Back Your Love** *Glenn Jones* | |
| 35/72 | **Bring It Home (And Give It To Me)** | |
| | *Hot Sauce* | |
| 9/56 | **Bring It Home To Me** *Buddy Johnson* | |
| | **Bring It On Home** | |
| 45/70 | *Lou Rawls* | |
| 66/82 | *Ronnie Dyson* | |
| | **Bring It On Home To Me** | |
| 2/62 | *Sam Cooke* | |
| 4/68 | *Eddie Floyd* | |
| 73/83 | **Bring It On...Bring It On** *James Brown* | |
| 7/67 | **Bring It Up** *James Brown* | |
| 3/71 | **Bring The Boys Home** *Freda Payne* | |
| 90/79 | **Bring The Family Back** *Billy Paul* | |
| 56/88 | **Bring The Noise** *Public Enemy* | |
| 7/61 | **Bristol Stomp** *Dovells* | |
| 28/62 | **Bristol Twistin' Annie** *Dovells* | |
| 57/86 | **Broken Glass** *George Duke* | |
| 18/62 | **Broken Heart** *Fiestas* | |
| 62/85 | **Broken Heart Can Mend** *Alexander O'Neal* | |
| 2/49 | **Broken Hearted** *Eddie Williams* | |
| 5/59 | **Broken-Hearted Melody** *Sarah Vaughan* | |
| 22/73 | **Brother Louie** *Stories* | |
| 2/70 | **Brother Rapp** *James Brown* | |
| 18/73 | **Brother's Gonna Work It Out** *Willie Hutch* | |
| 5/56 | **Brown-Eyed Handsome Man** *Chuck Berry* | |
| 37/68 | **Brown Eyed Woman** *Bill Medley* | |
| 81/83 | **Buffalo Bill** *Indeep* | |
| | **Buffalo Soldier** | |
| 28/70 | *Flamingos* | |
| 71/83 | *Bob Marley & The Wailers* | |
| 91/77 | **Bull City Party** *N.C.C.U.* | |
| 69/85 | **Bullet Proof** *George Clinton* | |
| 52/84 | **Bullish** *Herb Alpert/Tijuana Brass* | |
| 33/87 | **Bullseye** *Lakeside* | |
| 63/76 | **Bump De Bump Yo Boodie** | |
| | *Muscle Shoals Horns* | |
| 20/75 | **Bump Me Baby** *Dooley Silverspoon* | |
| 61/75 | **Bumpin'** *Ground Hog* | |
| 72/75 | **Bumpin' And Stompin'** *Garland Green* | |
| 1/81 | **Burn Rubber (Why You Wanna Hurt Me)** | |
| | *Gap Band* | |
| 9/55 | **Burn That Candle** *Bill Haley & His Comets* | |
| | **Burnin' Love** | |
| 62/82 | *Plush* | |
| 8/86 | *Con Funk Shun* | |

| | | |
|---|---|---|
| 68/82 | **Burnin' Up** *Imagination* | |
| 5/60 | **Burning Bridges** *Jack Scott* | |
| 36/68 | **Burning Spear** *Soulful Strings* | |
| 83/86 | **Burning Up** *Michael Jonzun* | |
| 43/72 | **Bus, The** *Billy Preston* | |
| 76/79 | **Bussle** *Opus Seven* | |
| 70/86 | **Bust This Rhyme** *M.C. Chill* | |
| 3/63 | **Busted** *Ray Charles* | |
| 29/65 | **Buster Browne** *Willie Mitchell* | |
| 1/79 | **Bustin' Loose** | |
| | *Chuck Brown & The Soul Searchers* | |
| 8/79 | **Bustin' Out** *Rick James* | |
| 9/61 | **But I Do** *Clarence 'Frogman' Henry* | |
| 4/66 | **But It's Alright** *J.J. Jackson* | |
| 10/62 | **But On The Other Hand Baby** *Ray Charles* | |
| 82/83 | **Butter Up** *Elektrik Dred* | |
| | **Butterfly** | |
| 10/57 | *Charlie Gracie* | |
| 14/57 | *Andy Williams* | |
| 15/49 | **Buttermilk** *Jay McShann* | |
| 10/69 | **Buying A Book** *Joe Tex* | |
| 5/57 | **Buzz-Buzz-Buzz** *Hollywood Flames* | |
| | **Buzz Me** | |
| 1/46 | *Louis Jordan* | |
| 2/46 | *Ella Mae Morse* | |
| | **By The Time I Get To Phoenix** | |
| 28/69 | *Mad Lads* | |
| 37/69 | *Isaac Hayes* | |
| 65/77 | *Isaac Hayes & Dionne Warwick (medley)* | |
| 37/79 | **By The Way You Dance (I Knew It Was** | |
| | **You)** *Bunny Sigler* | |
| 35/78 | **By Way Of Love's Express** | |
| | *Ashford & Simpson* | |
| 27/80 | **By Your Side** *Con Funk Shun* | |
| 48/86 | **Bye-Bye** *Janice* | |
| 8/61 | **Bye Bye Baby** *Mary Wells* | |
| 8/48 | **Bye Bye Baby Blues** *Ravens* | |
| | **Bye Bye Love** | |
| 5/57 | *Everly Brothers* | |
| 33/84 | *Philippe Wynne (medley)* | |
| 13/55 | **Bye Bye Young Men** *Ruth Brown* | |
| 72/82 | **Bye Gones** *Tom Browne* | |

# C

| | | |
|---|---|---|
| 7/87 | **C'est La Vie** *Robbie Nevil* | |
| 47/88 | **C'est Toi (It's You)** *Angela Winbush* | |
| | **C'mon** *..see: Come On* | |
| | **C.C. Rider** | |
| 1/57 | *Chuck Willis* | |
| 9/63 | *LaVern Baker* | |
| 12/66 | *Bobby Powell* | |
| 20/84 | **C.O.D. (I'll Deliver)** *Mtume* | |
| 40/76 | **Cadillac Assembly Line** *Albert King* | |
| 6/50 | **Cadillac Baby** *Roy Brown* | |
| 46/68 | **Cadillac Jack** *Andre Williams* | |
| 94/76 | **Cajun Moon** *Herbie Mann* | |
| 10/61 | **Calcutta** *Lawrence Welk* | |
| | **Caldonia** | |
| 1/45 | *Louis Jordan* | |
| 2/45 | *Erskine Hawkins* | |
| 14/49 | *Sugar Chile Robinson* | |
| 95/64 | *James Brown* | |
| 22/61 | **Calendar Girl** *Neil Sedaka* | |
| 20/69 | **California Dreamin'** *Bobby Womack* | |
| 11/70 | **California Girl** *Eddie Floyd* | |
| 48/74 | **California My Way** *Main Ingredient* | |
| 49/69 | **California Soul** *5th Dimension* | |
| 5/48 | **Call It Stormy Monday** *T-Bone Walker* | |

| | | |
|---|---|---|
| | **Candy** | |
| 11/56 | *Big Maybelle* | |
| 12/65 | *Astors* | |
| 39/68 | *Frankie & The Spindles* | |
| 1/87 | *Cameo* | |
| | **Candy From Your Baby** | |
| | *..see: (Come And Take This)* | |
| | **Candy Girl** | |
| 13/63 | *4 Seasons* | |
| 1/83 | *New Edition* | |
| 23/83 | **Candy Man** *Mary Jane Girls* | |
| 15/48 | **Candy Store Blues** | |
| | *Toni Harper & Eddie Beale Sextet* | |
| 58/64 | **Candy To Me** *Eddie Holland* | |
| 22/58 | **Cannonball** *Duane Eddy* | |
| 33/79 | **Captain Boogie** *Wardell Piper* | |
| 1/76 | **Car Wash** *Rose Royce* | |
| 14/49 | **Caravan** *Billy Eckstine* | |
| 1/85 | **Caravan Of Love** *Isley, Jasper, Isley* | |
| 55/81 | **Career Girl** *Carrie Lucas* | |
| 15/49 | **Careful Love** *Jimmy Liggins* | |
| 8/74 | **Careful Man** *John Edwards* | |
| 8/85 | **Careless Whisper** *Wham!* | |
| 26/59 | **Caribbean** *Mitchell Torok* | |
| 6/75 | **Caribbean Festival** *Kool & The Gang* | |
| 1/84 | **Caribbean Queen (No More Love On The Run)** *Billy Ocean* | |
| 46/86 | **Carme** *Rockwell* | |
| 9/58 | **Carol** *Chuck Berry* | |
| 12/74 | **Carry Me** *Joe Simon* | |
| 44/72 | **Carry On** *Jean Knight* | |
| 50/71 | **Carry Your Own Load** | |
| | *Jr. Walker & The All Stars* | |
| 1/87 | **Casanova** *Levert* | |
| 9/67 | **Casanova (Your Playing Days Are Over)** *Ruby Andrews* | |
| 4/51 | **Castle Rock** *Johnny Hodges* | |
| 52/64 | **Castles In The Sand** *Little Stevie Wonder* | |
| 38/78 | **Castles Of Sand** *Jermaine Jackson* | |
| 7/56 | **Casual Look** *Six Teens* | |
| 67/64 | **Cat, The** *Jimmy Smith* | |
| 27/70 | **Cat Walk** *Village Soul Choir* | |
| 69/79 | **Catch Me** *Pockets* | |
| 13/87 | **Catch Me (I'm Falling)** *Pretty Poison* | |
| 92/79 | **Catch Me On The Rebound** *Loleatta Holloway* | |
| 92/87 | **Catch 22** *Peabo Bryson* | |
| 33/80 | **Catchin' Up On Love** *Kinsman Dazz* | |
| 7/76 | **Catfish** *Four Tops* | |
| 28/70 | **Cathy Called** *Eddie Holman* | |
| 1/60 | **Cathy's Clown** *Everly Brothers* | |
| 94/87 | **Caught In The Act** *Jocelyn Brown* | |
| 13/76 | **Caught In The Act (Of Gettin' It On)** *Facts Of Life* | |
| 6/86 | **Caught Up In The Rapture** *Anita Baker* | |
| 74/77 | **Cause You Love My Baby** *Deniece Williams* | |
| 47/78 | **Cause You're Mine Now** *R.B. Hudmon* | |
| 12/55 | **'Cause You're My Lover** *Five Keys* | |
| 5/45 | **Cecil's Boogie** *Cecil Gant* | |
| 10/48 | **Cecilia** *Rose Murphy* | |
| 77/78 | **Celebrate** *Brass Construction* | |
| | **Celebrate Our Love** | |
| 34/87 | *Ray, Goodman & Brown* | |
| 87/87 | *Oliver Cheatham* | |
| 1/80 | **Celebration** *Kool & The Gang* | |
| 5/46 | **Cement Mixer (Put-Ti, Put-Ti)** *Slim Gaillard Trio* | |
| 4/84 | **Centipede** *Rebbie Jackson* | |
| 82/86 | **Ceramic Girl** *Ready For The World* | |
| 9/87 | **Certified True** *Bar-Kays* | |
| | **Chain Gang** | |
| 2/60 | *Sam Cooke* | |
| 37/60 | *Jackie Wilson & Count Basie* | |
| 1/68 | **Chain Of Fools** *Aretha Franklin* | |
| 85/85 | **Chain Reaction** *Diana Ross* | |

| | | |
|---|---|---|
| 8/68 | **Chained** *Marvin Gaye* | |
| 70/64 | **Chained And Bound** *Otis Redding* | |
| 49/67 | **Chained To Your Heart** *Bobby Moore & The Rhythm Aces* | |
| 6/63 | **Chains** *Cookies* | |
| 6/70 | **Chains And Things** *B.B. King* | |
| | **Chains Of Love** | |
| 2/51 | *Joe Turner* | |
| 9/69 | *Bobby Bland* | |
| 10/71 | **Chairman Of The Board** *Chairmen Of The Board* | |
| 28/77 | **Chalk It Up** *Jerry Butler* | |
| 18/74 | **Chameleon** *Herbie Hancock* | |
| 91/75 | **Chance For Peace** *Lonnie Liston Smith* | |
| 84/83 | **Chance To Dance** *Wrecking Crew* | |
| 30/76 | **Chance With You** *Brother To Brother* | |
| 12/57 | **Chances Are** *Johnny Mathis* | |
| | **Change** | |
| 46/78 | *Zulema* | |
| 12/82 | *Barry White* | |
| 9/65 | **Change Is Gonna Come** *Sam Cooke* | |
| 43/75 | **Change (Makes You Want To Hustle)** *Donald Byrd* | |
| 7/84 | **Change Of Heart** *Change* | |
| 77/78 | **Change Of Pace** *Brotherhood* | |
| 34/82 | **Change The World** *Alfonzo* | |
| 6/75 | **Change With The Times** *Van McCoy* | |
| 86/85 | **Change Your Mind** *Dutch Robinson* | |
| 25/85 | **Change Your Wicked Ways** *Pennye Ford* | |
| 5/47 | **Changeable Woman Blues** *Johnny Moore's Three Blazers* | |
| 46/83 | **Changes** *Imagination* | |
| 15/75 | **Changes (Messin' With My Mind)** *Vernon Burch* | |
| 63/84 | **Changes (We Go Through)** *Divine Sounds* | |
| 24/76 | **Changin'** *Brass Construction* | |
| 9/58 | **Chanson d'Amour (Song Of Love)** *Art & Dotty Todd* | |
| 3/58 | **Chantilly Lace** *Big Bopper* | |
| 1/64 | **Chapel Of Love** *Dixie Cups* | |
| 34/86 | **Character, The** *Morris Day* | |
| 2/59 | **Charlie Brown** *Coasters* | |
| 4/79 | **Chase Me** *Con Funk Shun* | |
| 17/75 | **Chasing Rainbows** *Blue Magic* | |
| 30/83 | **Cheap Thrills** *Planet Patrol* | |
| 2/73 | **Cheaper To Keep Her** *Johnnie Taylor* | |
| 57/77 | **Cheaters Never Win** *Love Committee* | |
| 19/82 | **Cheating In The Next Room** *Z.Z. Hill* | |
| | **Check It Out** | |
| 5/73 | *Tavares* | |
| 6/75 | *Bobby Womack* | |
| 39/83 | *Dynasty* | |
| 78/77 | **Check It Out** *Sophisticated Ladies* | |
| F/73 | **Check Me Out** *Eddie Floyd* | |
| | **Check Out Your Mind** | |
| 3/70 | *Impressions* | |
| 35/73 | *Maxayn* | |
| 37/68 | **Check Yourself** *Debbie Taylor* | |
| 64/82 | **Checking You Out** *Aurra* | |
| | **Cheek To Cheek** | |
| 75/78 | *Kay-Gees* | |
| 76/83 | *Dazz Band* | |
| | **Cherchez La Femme** *..see: Whispering* | |
| 1/85 | **Cherish** *Kool & The Gang* | |
| 11/71 | **Cherish What Is Dear To You** *Freda Payne* | |
| | **Cherry** | |
| 5/44 | *Erskine Hawkins* | |
| 10/44 | *Harry James* | |
| 27/60 | **Cherry Pie** *Skip & Flip* | |
| 2/44 | **Cherry Red Blues** *Cootie Williams* | |
| 69/85 | **Chey Chey Kule** *Eugene Wilde* | |
| 1/51 | **Chica Boo** *Lloyd Glenn's Combo* | |
| 82/79 | **Chica Boom** *Staples* | |
| 49/74 | **Chicago, Damn** *Bobbi Humphrey* | |
| 35/87 | **Chicago Song** *David Sanborn* | |

# D

| | |
|---|---|
| 8/58 | **Dede Dinah** *Frankie Avalon* |
| 81/75 | **Dedicate (My Life To You)** *Young Hearts* |
| | **Dedicated To The One I Love** |
| 2/61 | *Shirelles* |
| 17/72 | *Temprees* |
| | **Deep In The Heart Of Harlem** |
| 90/64 | *Clyde McPhatter* |
| 43/67 | *Walter Jackson* |
| 96/74 | **Deep Inside You** *Gloria Taylor* |
| 6/85 | **Deep Inside Your Love** |
| | *Ready For The World* |
| 4/63 | **Deep Purple** *Nino Tempo & April Stevens* |
| 65/77 | **Deeper** *New Birth* |
| | **Deeper & Deeper** |
| 9/70 | *Freda Payne* |
| 60/75 | *Bobby Wilson* |
| 10/83 | **Deeper In Love** *Tavares* |
| 21/70 | **Deeper (In Love With You)** *O'Jays* |
| 74/87 | **Deeper Love** *Meli'sa Morgan* |
| 25/79 | **Deja Vu** *Dionne Warwick* |
| 44/87 | **Delancey Street** *Dana Dane* |
| 81/77 | **Delightful** *Narada Michael Walden* |
| 18/83 | **Delirious** *Prince* |
| 18/63 | **Denise** *Randy & The Rainbows* |
| 13/49 | **Description Blues** *T-Bone Walker* |
| | **Desire** |
| 38/80 | *Masqueraders* |
| 49/80 | *Andy Gibb* |
| 46/86 | *Gap Band* |
| 90/86 | *Randy Crawford* |
| 17/58 | **Desire Me** *Sam Cooke* |
| 59/82 | **Desires** *Rafael Cameron* |
| 61/80 | **Despair** *Millie Jackson* |
| 66/83 | **Desperate** *Michael Sterling* |
| 28/68 | **Destination: Anywhere** *Marvelettes* |
| 46/71 | **Determination** *Ebonys* |
| 50/70 | **Detour** *Persians* |
| 5/45 | **Detroit Blues** *Tampa Red* |
| 47/67 | **Detroit City** *Solomon Burke* |
| | **Devil In Disguise** *..see: (You're The)* |
| 55/78 | **Devil In Mrs. Jones** *Jerry Butler* |
| 32/76 | **Devil Is Doing His Work** *Chi-Lites* |
| | **Devil Or Angel** |
| 3/56 | *Clovers* |
| 22/60 | *Bobby Vee* |
| 29/66 | **Devil With Angel's Smile** *Intruders* |
| 2/77 | **Devil's Gun** *C.J. & Co.* |
| 2/58 | **Devoted To You** *Everly Brothers* |
| 23/74 | **Devotion** *Earth, Wind & Fire* |
| 26/86 | **Dial My Number** *Pauli Carman* |
| 36/65 | **Dial That Telephone** *Effie Smith* |
| 1/87 | **Diamonds** *Herb Alpert* |
| 27/60 | **Diamonds And Pearls** *Paradons* |
| | **Diana** |
| 1/57 | *Paul Anka* |
| 10/86 | *Eugcne Wilde* |
| 2/52 | **Diane** *Buddy Lucas* |
| 25/59 | **Diary, The** *Neil Sedaka* |
| 50/87 | **Did I Dream You** *Tawatha* |
| 74/81 | **Did I Hear You Say You Love Me** |
| | *Stevie Wonder* |
| 13/49 | **Did You See Jackie Robinson Hit The** |
| | **Ball?** *Buddy Johnson* |
| 11/55 | **Diddley Daddy** *Bo Diddley* |
| 21/73 | **Didn't I** *Sylvia* |
| 49/80 | **Didn't I Blow Your Mind** *Millie Jackson* |
| 3/70 | **Didn't I (Blow Your Mind This Time)** |
| | *Delfonics* |
| 32/71 | **Didn't It Look So Easy** *Stairsteps* |
| 31/83 | **Didn't Know About Love (Till I Found** |
| | **You)** *Lenny White* |
| 55/78 | **Didn't Take Your Man** *Ann Peebles* |
| 2/87 | **Didn't We Almost Have It All** |
| | *Whitney Houston* |
| 74/82 | **Didn't We Do It** *Billy Always* |

| | |
|---|---|
| 78/81 | **Didn't We Make It Happen, Baby** |
| | *Barry White & Glodean White* |
| 11/69 | **Didn't You Know (You'd Have To Cry** |
| | **Sometime)** *Gladys Knight & The Pips* |
| 81/80 | **Different Kinda Different** *Johnny Mathis* |
| 17/67 | **Different Strokes** *Syl Johnson* |
| 42/79 | **Dig A Little Deeper** *Latimore* |
| 35/70 | **Dig The Way I Feel** *Mary Wells* |
| 4/86 | **Digital Display** *Ready For The World* |
| 13/79 | **Dim All The Lights** *Donna Summer* |
| 10/55 | **Dim, Dim The Lights (I Want Some** |
| | **Atmosphere)** *Bill Haley & His Comets* |
| 24/88 | **Dinner For Two** *Michael Cooper* |
| 19/58 | **Dinner With Drac** *John Zacherle* |
| 10/87 | **Dinner With Gershwin** *Donna Summer* |
| 17/84 | **Dirty Dancer** *Bar-Kays* |
| 5/88 | **Dirty Diana** *Michael Jackson* |
| 12/87 | **Dirty Looks** *Diana Ross* |
| 13/67 | **Dirty Man** *Laura Lee* |
| 65/81 | **Dirty Mind** *Prince* |
| 58/73 | **Dirty Ol' Man** *Three Degrees* |
| 40/66 | **Dirty Work Going On** *Little Joe Blue* |
| 93/77 | **Dis-Gorilla** *Rick Dees & His Cast Of Idiots* |
| 24/77 | **Disco 9000** *Johnnie Taylor* |
| 36/76 | **Disco Body** *Jackie Moore* |
| 60/76 | **Disco Connection** *Isaac Hayes Movement* |
| 69/79 | **Disco Dancin'** *A Taste Of Honey* |
| 42/81 | **Disco Dream** *Mean Machine* |
| 15/76 | **Disco Duck** *Rick Dees & His Cast Of Idiots* |
| 80/76 | **Disco-Fied** *Rhythm Heritage* |
| 62/76 | **Disco Hop** *Third World* |
| 9/77 | **Disco Inferno** *Trammps* |
| 87/76 | **Disco Is The Thing Today** *Meters* |
| 1/76 | **Disco Lady** *Johnnie Taylor* |
| 41/77 | **Disco Lucy (I Love Lucy Theme)** |
| | *Wilton Place Street Band* |
| 1/79 | **Disco Nights (Rock-Freak)** *GQ* |
| 40/75 | **Disco Queen** *Hot Chocolate* |
| 92/77 | **Disco Reggae (Tony's Groove)** *Kalyan* |
| 30/76 | **Disco Sax** *Houston Person* |
| 62/75 | **Disco Stomp** *Hamilton Bohannon* |
| 7/78 | **Disco To Go** *Brides Of Funkenstein* |
| 92/77 | **Disco Train** *Jerry Rix* |
| 68/80 | **Discoed To Death** *Latimore* |
| 18/85 | **Disrespect** *Gap Band* |
| 61/74 | **Disrespect Can Wreck** *Escorts* |
| | **Distant Lover** |
| 12/74 | *Marvin Gaye* |
| 34/86 | *Controllers* |
| 61/80 | **Distracted** *Al Jarreau* |
| 14/87 | **Divas Need Love Too** *Klymaxx* |
| 21/88 | **Divine Emotions** *Narada* |
| 74/64 | **Do Anything You Wanna** *Harold Betters* |
| 75/79 | **Do Dat** *Grover Washington, Jr.* |
| 29/77 | **Do Do Wap Is Strong In Here** |
| | *Curtis Mayfield* |
| 13/86 | **Do Fries Go With That Shake** |
| | *George Clinton* |
| 2/82 | **Do I Do** *Stevie Wonder* |
| 34/64 | **Do I Love You?** *Ronettes* |
| 57/74 | **Do I Need You** *Ann Peebles* |
| 50/71 | **Do It** *Billy Sha-Rae* |
| | **Do It Again (medley)** |
| 25/83 | *Slingshot* |
| 61/83 | *Club House* |
| 56/79 | **Do It All** *Michael Henderson* |
| 96/78 | **Do It All Night** *Curtis Mayfield* |
| | **Do It Any Way You Wanna** |
| 1/75 | *People's Choice* |
| 35/83 | *Cashmere* |
| 39/83 | **Do It Any Way You Want** |
| | *Robert Winters & Fall* |
| 4/74 | **Do It Baby** *Miracles* |
| 100/75 | **Do It, Do It** *Peppers* |
| 23/74 | **Do It, Fluid** *Blackbyrds* |

| | | |
|---|---|---|
| 37/71 | **Do It For Me** *General Crook* | |
| 13/79 | **Do It Good** *A Taste Of Honey* | |

37/71 **Do It For Me** *General Crook*
13/79 **Do It Good** *A Taste Of Honey*
**Do It In The Name Of Love**
17/73    *Candi Staton*
4/75    *Ben E. King*
9/82 **Do It (Let Me See You Shake)** *Bar-Kays*
49/70 **Do It Like Mama** *Simtec & Wylie*
15/81 **Do It Now** *S.O.S. Band*
72/74 **Do It Over** *Olympic Runners*
67/65 **Do It Right** *Brook Benton*
40/67 **Do It Right Now** *Roscoe Robinson*
24/82 **Do It Roger** *Roger*
60/77 **Do It The French Way** *Crown Heights Affair*
1/74 **Do It ('Til You're Satisfied)** *B.T. Express*
18/82 **Do It To Me** *Vernon Burch*
17/86 **Do It To Me Good (Tonight)**
   *Michael Henderson*
5/76 **Do It To My Mind** *Johnny Bristol*
59/82 **Do It To The Max** *Xavier*
65/82 **Do It To The Music** *Raw Silk*
58/76 **Do It While You Can** *Billy Preston*
**Do It With Feeling**
25/76    *Michael Zager's Moon Band*
76/78    *Michael Zager's Moon Band*
49/79 **Do It With Your Body** *7th Wonder*
**Do It Yourself** *..see: (If You Want It)*
1/86 **Do Me Baby** *Meli'sa Morgan*
**Do Me Right**
7/71    *Detroit Emeralds*
34/80    *Dynasty*
75/86    *Main Ingredient*
**Do Nothin' Till You Hear From Me**
1/44    *Duke Ellington*
4/44    *Woody Herman*
8/44    *Stan Kenton*
22/62 **Do-Re-Mi** *Lee Dorsey*
37/67 **Do Right Woman-Do Right Man**
   *Aretha Franklin*
14/82 **Do Something** *Goodie*
**Do Something For Me**
6/51    *Dominoes*
15/56    *Little Willie John*
39/66 **Do Something For Yourself** *Bobby Powell*
22/77 **Do That Stuff** *Parliament*
**Do That To Me One More Time**
58/80    *Captain & Tennille*
55/88    *Rena Scott*
8/63 **Do The Bird** *Dee Dee Sharp*
10/65 **Do The Boomerang**
   *Jr. Walker & The All Stars*
**Do The Bus Stop** *..see: (Are You Ready)*
17/68 **Do The Choo Choo** *Archie Bell & The Drells*
74/75 **Do The Double Bump** *Rufus Thomas*
5/70 **Do The Funky Chicken** *Rufus Thomas*
11/72 **Do The Funky Penguin** *Rufus Thomas*
8/60 **(Do The) Mashed Potatoes**
   *Nat Kendrick & The Swans*
1/71 **(Do The) Push And Pull** *Rufus Tnomas*
17/67 **Do The Thing** *Lou Courtney*
38/68 **Do Unto Me** *James & Bobby Purify*
78/64 **Do-Wah-Diddy** *Exciters*
73/79 **Do What Comes So Natural** *Gene Chandler*
14/58 **Do What You Did** *Thurston Harris*
14/85 **Do What You Do** *Jermaine Jackson*
**Do What You Feel**
56/76    *Atlanta Disco Band*
93/76    *Rimshots*
63/78    *Creme D' Cocoa*
9/83    *Deniece Williams*
**Do What You Gotta Do**
39/68    *Al Wilson*
43/68    *Nina Simone*
6/72 **Do What You Set Out To Do** *Bobby Bland*

**Do What You Wanna Do**
15/77    *T-Connection*
56/82    *Starpoint*
F/77 **Do What You Want** *Billy Preston*
**Do What You Want, Be What You Are**
23/77    *Daryl Hall & John Oates*
94/77    *Lew Kirton*
56/78 **Do What You Want To Do** *Dramatics*
40/73 **Do You Ever** *Manhattans*
62/78 **Do You Feel All Right**
   *KC & The Sunshine Band*
54/88 **Do You Feel It** *Tyrone Davis*
1/86 **Do You Get Enough Love** *Shirley Jones*
37/87 **Do You Have To Go** *Garry Glenn*
23/68 **Do You Know The Way To San Jose**
   *Dionne Warwick*
83/84 **Do You Know What I Mean** *Gwen McCrae*
73/83 **Do You Like It...(Girl)** *Slave*
**Do You Love Me**
1/62    *Contours*
78/76    *Lowell Fulson*
24/81    *Patti Austin*
37/86    *Durell Coleman*
13/78 **Do You Love Somebody** *Luther Ingram*
1/79 **Do You Love What You Feel**
   *Rufus & Chaka Khan*
9/48 **Do You Or Don't You Love Me**
   *Nellie Lutcher*
**Do You Really Love Me**
84/73    *Four Mints*
43/80    *Rene & Angela*
68/84    *Bryan Loren*
61/87    *Janice Bullock*
14/86 **Do You Really Love Your Baby**
   *Temptations*
39/83 **Do You Really Want To Hurt Me**
   *Culture Club*
40/86 **Do You Remember Me?** *Jermaine Jackson*
3/70 **Do You See My Love (For You Growing)**
   *Jr. Walker & The All Stars*
28/73 **Do You Still Feel The Same Way?**
   *Tommie Young*
**Do You Still Love Me**
80/83    *Amuzement Park*
5/86    *Meli'sa Morgan*
92/75 **(Do You Wanna) Dance Dance Dance**
   *Calhoon*
19/76 **Do You Wanna Do A Thing** *Bloodstone*
13/85 **Do You Wanna Get Away** *Shannon*
3/77 **Do You Wanna Get Funky With Me**
   *Peter Brown*
8/79 **Do You Wanna Go Party**
   *KC & The Sunshine Band*
53/88 **Do You Wanna Go With Me** *Temptations*
60/84 **Do You Wanna Lover** *Hotbox*
30/80 **Do You Wanna Make Love**
   *Millie Jackson & Isaac Hayes*
68/86 **Do You Want It Bad Enuff** *Jenny Burton*
63/85 **Do You Want It Right Now** *Siedah Garrett*
2/58 **Do You Want To Dance** *Bobby Freeman*
4/77 **Do Your Dance** *Rose Royce*
38/70 **Do Your Duty** *Betty LaVette*
36/80 **Do Your Thang**
   *One Way featuring Al Hudson*
**Do Your Thing**
12/69    *Watts 103rd Street Rhythm Band*
3/72    *Isaac Hayes*
30/75    *James & Bobby Purify*
84/78 **Do Yourself A Favor** *Newcomers*
4/49 **Doby's Boogie** *Freddie Mitchell*
**Dock Of The Bay** *..see: (Sittin' On)*
22/68 **Doctor, The** *Mary Wells*
43/77 **Dr. Funkenstein** *Parliament*
23/77 **Doctor Love** *First Choice*
57/76 **Dr. Love Power** *Ann Peebles*

# F

| | |
|---|---|
| 7/85 | **Fall Down (Spirit Of Love)** *Tramaine* |
| | **Fall In Love With Me** |
| 36/67 | *Bettye Swann* |
| 4/83 | *Earth, Wind & Fire* |
| 7/57 | **Fallen Star** *Jimmy Newman* |
| | **Fallin' In Love** |
| 24/75 | *Hamilton, Joe Frank & Reynolds* |
| 51/76 | *New Birth* |
| 61/76 | **(Fallin' Like) Dominoes** *Donald Byrd* |
| 1/87 | **Falling** *Melba Moore* |
| 76/85 | **Falling For Your Love** *Sylvers* |
| | **Falling In Love** |
| 84/83 | *Surface* |
| 16/87 | *Fat Boys* |
| 41/88 | *Whistle* |
| 39/66 | **Falling In Love Again** *Kelly Brothers* |
| 21/75 | **Fame** *David Bowie* |
| 74/80 | **Family** *Hubert Laws* |
| 1/71 | **Family Affair** *Sly & The Family Stone* |
| 85/77 | **Family Again** *Sly & The Family Stone* |
| 81/83 | **Family Man** *Daryl Hall & John Oates* |
| 45/76 | **Family Reunion** *O'Jays* |
| 46/69 | **Family Tree** *Patti Austin* |
| 4/46 | **Fan It** *Woody Herman* |
| | **Fancy Dancer** |
| 9/77 | *Commodores* |
| 25/81 | *Twennynine with Lenny White* |
| 23/75 | **Fancy Lady** *Billy Preston* |
| 1/60 | **Fannie Mae** *Buster Brown* |
| 1/81 | **Fantastic Voyage** *Lakeside* |
| | **Fantasy** |
| 12/78 | *Earth, Wind & Fire* |
| 53/79 | *Bruni Pagan* |
| 54/77 | **Fantasy Is Reality** *Parliament* |
| 99/75 | **Far As We Felt Like Goin'** *LaBelle* |
| 26/76 | **Far East Mississippi** *Ohio Players* |
| 6/50 | **Faraway Blues** |
| | *Little Esther/Johnny Otis Orchestra* |
| | **Farewell** |
| 5/49 | *Little Willie Littlefield* |
| 32/69 | *Ethics* |
| 37/84 | **Farewell My Summer Love** |
| | *Michael Jackson* |
| 7/70 | **Farther On Down The Road** *Joe Simon* |
| 1/57 | **Farther Up The Road** *Bobby 'Blue' Bland* |
| 26/87 | **Fascination** *Levert* |
| | *(also see: Keep Feeling)* |
| 40/85 | **Fast Girls** *Janet Jackson* |
| 60/84 | **Fast Life** *Dr. Jeckyll & Mr. Hyde* |
| 65/84 | **Fat Boys** *Disco 3* |
| 27/85 | **Fat Boys Are Back** *Fat Boys* |
| 10/53 | **Fat Daddy** *Dinah Washington* |
| | **Fat Man** |
| 2/50 | *Fats Domino* |
| 18/66 | *T-K-O'S* |
| 11/49 | **Fat Meat And Greens** *Edgar Hayes* |
| 6/88 | **Father Figure** *George Michael* |
| 61/74 | **Fear No Evil** *Mission* |
| 83/82 | **Feel Alright** *Komiko* |
| 29/77 | **Feel Free** *Four Tops* |
| 45/74 | **Feel Good** *Rufus Featuring Chaka Khan* |
| | **Feel It** |
| 63/77 | *Crusaders* |
| 51/81 | *Revelation* |
| 79/82 | **Feel It, Don't Fight It** *Atkins* |
| 47/67 | **Feel Kind Of Bad** *Radiants* |
| 98/77 | **Feel Like Being Funky** *Avalanche '77'* |
| 100/77 | **Feel Like Dancing** *Oliver Sain* |
| | **Feel Like Making Love** |
| 1/74 | *Roberta Flack* |
| 71/76 | *Millie Jackson* |
| 27/81 | **Feel Me** *Cameo* |
| | **Feel My Love** |
| 43/80 | *Michael Wycoff* |
| 62/81 | *Slave* |

| | |
|---|---|
| 71/81 | **Feel My Love Tonight** *Stacy Lattisaw* |
| | **Feel So Bad** |
| 7/67 | *Little Milton* |
| 16/71 | *Ray Charles* |
| 2/55 | **Feel So Good** *Shirley & Lee* |
| 72/87 | **Feel So Good To Me** *Najee* |
| 17/85 | **Feel So Real** *Steve Arrington* |
| 7/79 | **Feel That You're Feelin'** |
| | *Maze Featuring Frankie Beverly* |
| 31/77 | **Feel The Beat (Everybody Disco)** |
| | *Ohio Players* |
| 13/78 | **Feel The Fire** *Peabo Bryson* |
| | **Feel The Need** |
| 42/72 | *Damon Shawn* |
| 18/75 | *Graham Central Station* |
| 73/77 | *Detroit Emeralds* |
| 67/84 | *Anita Baker* |
| 22/73 | **Feel The Need In Me** *Detroit Emeralds* |
| 25/76 | **Feel The Spirit (In '76)** *Leroy Hutson* |
| 67/81 | **Feelin'** *Cameron* |
| 5/53 | **Feelin' Good** *Little Junior's Blue Flames* |
| 89/79 | **Feelin' Happy** *Lee Oskar* |
| 32/82 | **Feelin' Lucky Lately** *High Fashion* |
| 25/75 | **Feelin' That Glow** *Roberta Flack* |
| 77/79 | **Feelin' The Love** *Gavin Christopher* |
| 91/64 | **Feeling Is Gone** *Bobby Bland* |
| 9/69 | **Feeling Is Right** *Clarence Carter* |
| 42/73 | **Feeling Of Loneliness** *Cliff Nobles & Co.* |
| 9/77 | **Feelings** *Walter Jackson* |
| 37/88 | **Feels Good To Feel Good** |
| | *Gary Glenn featuring Sheila Hutchinson* |
| 63/87 | **Feels Like The First Time** *Sinitta* |
| | **Feels So Good** |
| 20/67 | *Bunny Sigler (medley)* |
| 68/78 | *Chuck Mangione* |
| 20/83 | *Yarbrough & Peoples* |
| 3/84 | **Feels So Real (Won't Let Go)** |
| | *Patrice Rushen* |
| 36/70 | **Feet Start Walking** *Doris Duke* |
| 12/73 | **Fell For You** *Dramatics* |
| 49/86 | **Female Intuition** *Mai Tai* |
| 75/88 | **Females (Get On Up)** *Cookie Crew* |
| 43/82 | **Femmes Fatales** *Saint Tropez* |
| 19/73 | **Fencewalk** *Mandrill* |
| | **Fever** |
| 1/56 | *Little Willie John* |
| 5/58 | *Peggy Lee* |
| 89/80 | **Few More Kisses To Go** *Isaac Hayes* |
| 1/78 | **Ffun** *Con Funk Shun* |
| 33/83 | **Fickle** *Michael Henderson* |
| 25/85 | **Fidelity** *Cheryl Lynn* |
| 63/77 | **Fiesta** *Gato Barbieri* |
| 12/49 | **Fiesta In Old Mexico** *Camille Howard Trio* |
| 46/66 | **Fife Piper** *Dynatones* |
| 85/84 | **15 Rounds** *Steve Arrington's Hall Of Fame* |
| | **15 Years & I'm Still Serving Time** |
| 4/45 | *Erskine Hawkins* |
| 4/46 | *Pearl Bailey* |
| 10/76 | **Fifth Of Beethoven** *Walter Murphy* |
| 81/84 | **50/50 Love** *C.L. Blast* |
| 1/75 | **Fight The Power** *Isley Brothers* |
| 37/80 | **Figures Can't Calculate** *William DeVaughn* |
| 91/80 | **Fill Me Up** *Elaine & Ellen* |
| 96/77 | **Fill This World With Love** *Ann Peebles* |
| 85/77 | **Finally Found Someone** *Side Effect* |
| 1/74 | **Finally Got Myself Together (I'm A Changed Man)** *Impressions* |
| 71/76 | **Find 'Em, Fool 'Em & Forget 'Em** |
| | *Dobie Gray* |
| 10/61 | **Find Another Girl** *Jerry Butler* |
| 38/78 | **Find Me A Girl** *Jacksons* |
| 97/76 | **Find Yourself Somebody To Love** *Rhythm* |
| 47/85 | **Finder Of Lost Loves** |
| | *Dionne Warwick & Glenn Jones* |

## Finder's Keepers
| | |
|---|---|
| 7/73 | *Chairmen Of The Board* |
| 49/76 | *Soul Children* |
| 96/65 | **Finders Keepers, Losers Weepers** |
| | *Nella Dodds* |
| 84/78 | **Fine And Healthy Thing** *Leon Haywood* |
| 2/48 | **Fine Brown Frame** *Nellie Lutcher* |
| 63/86 | **Fine Mess** *Temptations* |
| 62/86 | **Fine Young Tender** |
| | *Aleem featuring Leroy Burgess* |
| 2/86 | **Finest, The** *S.O.S. Band* |
| 23/76 | **Finger Fever** *Dramatics* |
| 85/74 | **Finger Pointers** *Choice Four* |
| 2/60 | **Finger Poppin' Time** |
| | *Hank Ballard & The Midnighters* |
| 1/63 | **Fingertips** *Little Stevie Wonder* |
| | **Fire** |
| 1/75 | *Ohio Players* |
| 14/79 | *Pointer Sisters* |
| 2/72 | **Fire And Water** *Wilson Pickett* |
| 72/79 | **Fire Up** *ADC Band* |
| 4/79 | **Firecracker** *Mass Production* |
| 11/86 | **Firestarter** *Tease* |
| 65/79 | **First Come, First Serve** *Rose Royce* |
| 69/73 | **First Day** *Softones* |
| 12/65 | **First I Look At The Purse** *Contours* |
| | **First Impressions** |
| 22/78 | *Stylistics* |
| 50/82 | *High Inergy* |
| 27/60 | **First Name Initial** *Annette* |
| 79/74 | **First Round Knockout** *New Censation* |
| 20/79 | **First Time Around** *Skyy* |
| 4/72 | **First Time Ever I Saw Your Face** |
| | *Roberta Flack* |
| 20/74 | **First Time We Met** *Independents* |
| 50/81 | **First True Love Affair** *Jimmy Ross* |
| 4/74 | **Fish Ain't Bitin'** *Lamont Dozier* |
| 1/88 | **Fishnet** *Morris Day* |
| 3/43 | **Five Guys Named Moe** *Louis Jordan* |
| | **Five Long Years** |
| 1/52 | *Eddie Boyd* |
| 13/59 | *Little Junior Parker* |
| F/84 | **Five Minutes Of Funk** *Whodini* |
| 1/52 | **5-10-15 Hours** *Ruth Brown* |
| 5/70 | **5-10-15-20 (25-30 Years Of Love)** |
| | *Presidents* |
| 21/83 | **Fix It** *Teena Marie* |
| 63/84 | **Fix It In The Mix** *Pretty Tony* |
| 21/86 | **Flame Of Love** *Jean Carne* |
| 25/82 | **Flamethrower** *J. Geils Band* |
| 34/82 | **Flamethrower Rap** *Felix & Jarvis* |
| | **Flamingo** |
| 1/51 | *Earl Bostic* |
| 17/61 | *Little Willie John* |
| 25/63 | **Flapjacks** *Googie Rene Combo* |
| 10/43 | **Flash** *Harry James* |
| 1/78 | **Flash Light** *Parliament* |
| | **Flashback** |
| 75/74 | *5th Dimension* |
| 70/79 | *Ashford & Simpson* |
| 89/82 | *C.M. Lord* |
| 59/84 | *Klique* |
| 2/83 | **Flashdance...What A Feeling** *Irene Cara* |
| 2/55 | **Flip Flop And Fly** *Joe Turner* |
| | **Flirt** |
| 10/82 | *Cameo* |
| 3/88 | *Evelyn King* |
| 7/49 | **Flo And Joe** *Nat King Cole* |
| 10/61 | **Float, The** *Hank Ballard & The Midnighters* |
| 1/77 | **Float On** *Floaters* |
| 16/76 | **Flowers** *Emotions* |
| 5/72 | **Floy Joy** *Supremes* |
| 11/61 | **Fly, The** *Chubby Checker* |

## Fly Girl
| | |
|---|---|
| 6/85 | *Boogie Boys* |
| 80/85 | *Intrigues* |
| 20/77 | **Fly Like An Eagle** *Steve Miller* |
| | **Fly Me To The Moon** |
| 31/65 | *LaVern Baker* |
| 38/66 | *Sam & Bill* |
| 16/68 | *Bobby Womack* |
| 1/75 | **Fly, Robin, Fly** *Silver Convention* |
| | **Flyin' High** |
| 22/75 | *Blackbyrds* |
| 21/78 | *Commodores* |
| | **Flying Home** |
| 3/43 | *Lionel Hampton* |
| 9/43 | *Lionel Hampton* |
| 4/56 | **Flying Saucer** *Buchanan & Goodman* |
| 15/84 | **Fo-Fi-Fo** *Pieces Of A Dream* |
| 28/69 | **Follow The Leader** *Major Lance* |
| 20/65 | **Follow Your Heart** *Manhattans* |
| 5/56 | **Fool, The** *Sanford Clark* |
| 1/51 | **Fool, Fool, Fool** *Clovers* |
| | **Fool For You** |
| 1/55 | *Ray Charles* |
| 3/68 | *Impressions* |
| 2/60 | **Fool In Love** *Ike & Tina Turner* |
| 35/79 | **Fool On The Street** *Rick James* |
| | **Fool Such As I** *..see: (Now And Then There's)* |
| | **Fool That I Am** |
| 3/47 | *Gladys Palmer* |
| 14/61 | *Etta James* |
| 72/74 | **Fool's Hall Of Fame** *Ike Lovely* |
| | **Fool's Paradise** |
| 14/72 | *Sylvers* |
| 24/86 | *Meli'sa Morgan* |
| 82/76 | **Fooled Around And Fell In Love** |
| | *Elvin Bishop* |
| 14/69 | **Foolish Fool** *Dee Dee Warwick* |
| 9/63 | **Foolish Little Girl** *Shirelles* |
| 91/86 | **Foolish Pride** *Daryl Hall* |
| 10/57 | **Fools Fall In Love** *Drifters* |
| 11/58 | **Fools Like Me** *Jerry Lee Lewis* |
| | **Fools Rush In** |
| 6/49 | *Billy Eckstine* |
| 5/61 | *Brook Benton* |
| 24/63 | *Ricky Nelson* |
| 20/61 | **Foot Stompin'** *Flares* |
| 39/75 | **Foot Stompin Music** *Hamilton Bohannon* |
| 9/76 | **Fopp** *Ohio Players* |
| 98/76 | **For All We Know** *Esther Phillips* |
| 91/77 | **For Elise** *Philarmonics* |
| 4/71 | **(For God's Sake) Give More Power To The People** *Chi-Lites* |
| 52/79 | **For Goodness Sakes, Look At Those Cakes** *James Brown* |
| 2/61 | **For My Baby** *Brook Benton* |
| 53/76 | **For Old Time Sake** *Dorothy Moore* |
| 2/69 | **For Once In My Life** *Stevie Wonder* |
| | **For Sentimental Reasons** *..see: (I Love You)* |
| 51/74 | **For The Good Times** *7th Wonder* |
| 3/74 | **For The Love Of Money** *O'Jays* |
| | **For The Love Of You** |
| 10/75 | *Isley Brothers* |
| F/76 | *Houston Person* |
| 14/80 | **For Those Who Like To Groove** |
| | *Ray Parker Jr. & Raydio* |
| | **For You** |
| 23/66 | *Spellbinders* |
| 45/70 | *Presidents* |
| 77/81 | *Superior Movement* |
| 50/83 | *L.T.D.* |
| 73/79 | **For You (A Disco Concerto)** *Noel Pointer* |
| 60/80 | **For You, For Love** *Average White Band* |
| | **For You, My Love** |
| 1/49 | *Larry Darnell* |
| 8/50 | *Nat King Cole Trio with Nellie Lutcher* |

**For Your Love**

| | |
|---|---|
| 7/58 | *Ed Townsend* |
| 14/65 | *Sam & Bill* |
| 10/67 | *Peaches & Herb* |
| 17/73 | *Gwen McCrae* |
| 34/84 | *S.O.S. Band* |
| 27/88 | **For Your Love (I'll Do Most Anything)** |
| | *Barry White* |
| 27/78 | **For Your Love, Love, Love** *Joe Simon* |

**For Your Precious Love**

| | |
|---|---|
| 3/58 | *Jerry Butler & The Impressions* |
| 26/64 | *Garnet Mimms & The Enchanters* |
| 25/66 | *Jerry Butler* |
| 4/67 | *Oscar Toney, Jr.* |
| 26/68 | *Jackie Wilson & Count Basie* |
| 58/81 | *Impressions* |
| 6/49 | **'Fore Day In The Morning** *Roy Brown* |

**Forever**

| | |
|---|---|
| 24/63 | *Marvelettes* |
| 30/73 | *Baby Washington & Don Gardner* |
| 42/80 | *Mass Production* |
| 87/80 | *Chuck Cissel* |
| 79/74 | **Forever And A Day** *Mel & Tim* |
| 30/83 | **Forever By Your Side** *Manhattans* |

**Forever Came Today**

| | |
|---|---|
| 17/68 | *Supremes* |
| 6/75 | *Jackson 5* |
| 22/75 | **Forever In Love** *Love Unlimited Orchestra* |
| 4/80 | **Forever Mine** *O'Jays* |
| 52/81 | **Forever Yesterday (For The Children)** |
| | *Gladys Knight & The Pips* |
| 16/88 | **Forever Yours** *Tony Terry* |
| 25/66 | **Forget About Me** *Prince Harold* |
| 10/67 | **Forget It** *Sandpebbles* |
| 4/82 | **Forget Me Nots** *Patrice Rushen* |
| 99/76 | **Forgetting Someone** |
| | *Country Boys & City Girls* |
| 5/49 | **Forgive And Forget** *Orioles* |

**Forgive Me Girl**

| | |
|---|---|
| 6/79 | *Spinners (medley)* |
| 49/85 | *Force M.D.'s* |
| 10/55 | **Forgive This Fool** *Roy Hamilton* |
| 49/73 | **Forgotten Man** *We The People* |
| 40/85 | **Fork In The Road** *Rebbie Jackson* |
| 7/56 | **Forty Days & Forty Nights** *Muddy Waters* |
| 17/59 | **Forty Miles Of Bad Road** *Duane Eddy* |
| 19/68 | **46 Drums - 1 Guitar** *Little Carl Carlton* |
| 14/49 | **47th St. Jive** *Andy Kirk* |
| 2/79 | **Found A Cure** *Ashford & Simpson* |
| 16/60 | **Found Love** *Jimmy Reed* |
| 17/67 | **Four Walls (Three Windows and Two** |
| | **Doors)** *J.J. Jackson* |
| 87/85 | **14K** *Teena Marie* |
| 66/84 | **Fox Trappin** *Numonics* |

**Foxy Lady**

| | |
|---|---|
| 17/76 | *Crown Heights Affair* |
| 55/80 | *Slave* |
| | *(also see: You're A)* |
| 37/84 | **Fragile...Handle With Care** *Cherrelle* |
| 99/75 | **Frame Of Mind** *Vernon Burch* |

**Frankie**

| | |
|---|---|
| 17/59 | *Connie Francis* |
| 32/85 | *Sister Sledge* |

**Frankie And Johnny**

| | |
|---|---|
| 14/61 | *Brook Benton* |
| 4/63 | *Sam Cooke* |
| 9/51 | **Frankie Lee** *Joe Liggins* |
| 52/87 | **Freak-A-Holic** *Egyptian Lover* |
| 6/85 | **Freak-A-Ristic** *Atlantic Starr* |
| 2/83 | **Freak-A-Zoid** *Midnight Star* |
| 92/78 | **Freak In, Freak Out** *Timmy Thomas* |
| 73/76 | **Freak-N-Stein** *Blue Magic* |
| 36/79 | **Freak The Freak The Funk (Rock)** |
| | *Fatback* |
| 25/81 | **Freak To Freak** *Sweat Band* |

| | |
|---|---|
| 60/80 | **Freakin Time** *Asphalt Jungle* |
| 43/85 | **Freaks Come Out At Night** *Whodini* |
| 2/84 | **Freakshow On The Dance Floor** *Bar-Kays* |
| 27/82 | **Freaky Behavior** *Bar-Kays* |
| 3/81 | **Freaky Dancin'** *Cameo* |
| 29/78 | **Freaky Deaky** *Roy Ayers* |
| 71/79 | **Freaky People** *Crowd Pleasers* |
| 2/72 | **Freddie's Dead** *Curtis Mayfield* |

**Free**

| | |
|---|---|
| 71/76 | *Natural Four* |
| 2/77 | *Deniece Williams* |
| 48/88 | *Will Downing* |
| 95/76 | **Free & Red Hot** *Shelly Black* |
| 26/77 | **Free And Single** *Brothers Johnson* |
| 84/77 | **Free As The Wind** *Crusaders* |
| 62/82 | **Free Dancer** *Brick* |
| 23/77 | **Free Love** *Jean Carn* |
| 9/75 | **Free Man** *South Shore Commission* |
| 30/69 | **Free Me** *Otis Redding* |
| 10/79 | **Free Me From My Freedom/Tie Me To A Tree** |
| | **(Handcuff Me)** *Bonnie Pointer* |
| 8/76 | **Free Ride** *Tavares* |
| 33/72 | **Free Your Mind** *Politicians* |

**Freedom**

| | |
|---|---|
| 16/71 | *Isley Brothers* |
| 19/80 | *Grandmaster Flash & The Furious Five* |
| 25/86 | *Pointer Sisters* |
| 28/70 | **Freedom Blues** *Little Richard* |
| 100/77 | **Freedom To Express Yourself** |
| | *Denise LaSalle* |
| 39/69 | **Freedom Train** *James Carr* |
| 7/48 | **Freedom Train Blues** *Little Son Jackson* |
| 57/81 | **Freefall (Into Love)** *Lenny Williams* |
| 74/84 | **Freestyle** *Freestyle Express* |
| 37/81 | **Freeway** *Peaches & Herb* |
| 1/85 | **Freeway Of Love** *Aretha Franklin* |
| F/82 | **Freeze-Frame** *J. Geils Band* |

**Fresh**

| | |
|---|---|
| 22/84 | *Tyrone Brunson* |
| 76/84 | *Fresh 3 M.C.'s* |
| 1/85 | *Kool & The Gang* |
| 77/83 | **Fresh Idea** *Deco* |
| 89/86 | **Freshest Rhymes In The World** |
| | *Dr. Jeckyll & Mr. Hyde* |
| 25/69 | **Friend, Lover, Woman, Wife** *O.C. Smith* |

**Friend Of Mine**

| | |
|---|---|
| 25/73 | *Bill Withers* |
| 15/76 | *Little Milton* |
| 50/82 | *Gladys Knight & The Pips* |
| | **Friendly Neighborhood Freak** |
| | *..see: (I'm Your)* |

**Friends**

| | |
|---|---|
| 34/75 | *B.B. King* |
| 4/84 | *Whodini* |
| 46/85 | *Amii Stewart* |
| 54/86 | **Friends And Lovers** |
| | *Gloria Loring & Carl Anderson* |
| 22/82 | **Friends In Love** |
| | *Dionne Warwick & Johnny Mathis* |
| 22/73 | **Friends Or Lovers** *Act I* |
| 2/69 | **Friendship Train** *Gladys Knight & The Pips* |
| 4/46 | **Frim Fram Sauce** |
| | *Ella Fitzgerald & Louis Armstrong* |
| 11/49 | **Frisco Bay** *Memphis Slim* |
| 28/73 | **Frisky** *Sly & The Family Stone* |
| 48/70 | **From Atlanta To Goodbye** *Manhattans* |
| 85/78 | **From East To West** *Voyage* |
| 3/75 | **From His Woman To You** *Barbara Mason* |
| 72/76 | **From My Heart To Yours** *Charles Earland* |
| 44/80 | **From 9:00 Until** *Lakeside* |
| 94/78 | **From Now On** *Linda Clifford* |
| 43/72 | **From The Love Side** *Hank Ballard* |
| 16/68 | **From The Teacher To The Preacher** |
| | *Gene Chandler & Barbara Acklin* |
| 37/73 | **From Toys To Boys** *Emotions* |

| 4/43 | **From Twilight 'Til Dawn** *Ceele Burke* |
| 10/76 | **From Us To You** *Stairsteps* |
| 86/85 | **Fulfill Your Fantasy** *Keith Pole* |
| | **Full Of Fire** |
| 1/75 | *Al Green* |
| 24/81 | *Shalamar* |
| 90/76 | **Full Speed Ahead** *Tata Vega* |
| 19/79 | **Full Tilt Boogie** *Uncle Louie* |
| 91/76 | **Full Time Thing (Between Dusk And Dawn)** *Whirlwind* |
| 54/80 | **Fun City** *Vernon Burch* |
| 82/75 | **Fun House** *Bobbi Humphrey* |
| | **Function At The Junction** |
| 42/66 | *Shorty Long* |
| 66/74 | *Energy* |
| 23/82 | **Fungi Mama/Bebopafunkadiscolypso** *Tom Browne* |
| 100/77 | **Funk De Mambo** *Karma* |
| 11/72 | **Funk Factory** *Wilson Pickett* |
| 20/77 | **Funk Funk** *Cameo* |
| 87/80 | **Funk Is On** *Instant Funk* |
| 11/78 | **Funk 'n' Roll (Dancin' In The 'Funkshine')** *Quazar* |
| 27/78 | **Funk-O-Nots** *Ohio Players* |
| 15/80 | **Funk You Up** *Sequence* |
| 33/80 | **Funkdown** *Cameron* |
| 27/78 | **Funkentelechy** *Parliament* |
| 1/80 | **Funkin' For Jamaica (N.Y.)** *Tom Browne* |
| 21/81 | **Funktown USA** *Rafael Cameron* |
| 40/71 | **Funky** *Chambers Brothers* |
| | **Funky Beat** |
| 39/83 | *Bernard Wright* |
| 19/86 | *Whodini* |
| 44/81 | **Funky Bebop** *Vin-Zee* |
| 93/74 | **Funky Bird** *Rufus Thomas* |
| 40/68 | **Funky Boo-Ga-Loo** *Jerryo* |
| | **Funky Broadway** |
| 1/67 | *Wilson Pickett* |
| 17/67 | *Dyke & The Blazers* |
| 22/70 | **Funky Chicken** *Willie Henderson* |
| 48/67 | **Funky Donkey** *Pretty Purdie* |
| 20/70 | **Funky Drummer** *James Brown* |
| 49/68 | **Funky Fever** *Clarence Carter* |
| 9/68 | **Funky Judge** *Bull & The Matadors* |
| 49/73 | **Funky Key** *Dynamics* |
| 45/71 | **Funky L.A.** *Paul Humphrey* |
| 41/86 | **Funky Little Beat** *Connie* |
| 16/70 | **Funky Man** *Kool & The Gang* |
| 45/77 | **Funky Monkey** *Mandrill* |
| | **Funky Music** |
| 52/74 | *Thomas East & The Fabulous Playboys* |
| 32/77 | *Ju-Par Universal Orchestra* |
| 34/76 | **Funky Music (Is A Part Of Me)** *Luther Vandross* |
| 68/75 | **Funky Music Is The Thing** *Dynamic Corvettes* |
| | **Funky Music Sho Nuff Turns Me On** |
| 6/71 | *Edwin Starr* |
| 27/72 | *Temptations* |
| 32/74 | *Yvonne Fair* |
| 7/71 | **Funky Nassau** *Beginning Of The End* |
| 17/74 | **Funky Party** *Clarence Reid* |
| 4/75 | **Funky President (People It's Bad)** *James Brown* |
| 40/71 | **Funky Rubber Band** *Popcorn Wylie* |
| 22/81 | **Funky Sensation** *Gwen McCrae* |
| 41/74 | **Funky Song** *Ripple* |
| | *(also see: Hey Who's Gotta)* |
| 68/83 | **Funky Soul Makossa** *Nairobi & The Awesome Foursome* |
| 39/81 | **Funky Sound (Tear The Roof Off)** *Sequence* |
| 23/79 | **Funky Space Reincarnation** *Marvin Gaye* |
| 5/68 | **Funky Street** *Arthur Conley* |
| 5/73 | **Funky Stuff** *Kool & The Gang* |

| 22/68 | **Funky Walk (East)** *Dyke & The Blazers* |
| 22/68 | **Funky Way** *Calvin Arnold* |
| 23/75 | **Funky Weekend** *Stylistics* |
| 1/73 | **Funky Worm** *Ohio Players* |
| 2/80 | **Funkytown** *Lipps, Inc.* |
| | **Funny** |
| 25/59 | *Jesse Belvin* |
| 3/61 | *Maxine Brown* |
| 13/64 | *Joe Hinton* |
| 70/73 | *Priscilla Price* |
| 36/66 | **Funny Changes** *Chuck Bernard* |
| 48/69 | **Funny Feeling** *Delfonics* |
| | **Funny How Time Slips Away** |
| 7/76 | *Dorothy Moore* |
| 43/83 | *Spinners* |
| 37/80 | **Funtime** *Peaches & Herb* |
| 75/79 | **Future Now** *Pleasure* |
| 02/70 | **Future Past** *Danny Johnson* |
| 11/73 | **Future Shock** *Curtis Mayfield* |

# G

| | **G.I. Jive** |
| 1/44 | *Louis Jordan* |
| 1/44 | *Johnny Mercer* |
| 3/53 | **Gabbin' Blues** *Big Maybelle* |
| 5/78 | **Galaxy** *War* |
| 81/79 | **Game Seven** *Chuck Brown & The Soul Searchers* |
| 11/87 | **Games** *Shalamar* |
| 47/69 | **Games People Play** *Donald Height* |
| 46/69 | **Gang War (Don't Make Sense)** *Corner Boys* |
| 37/70 | **Gangs Back Again** *Kool & The Gang* |
| 50/74 | **Gangster Boogie Bump** *Willie Henderson* |
| 32/78 | **Gangster Of Love** *Johnny 'Guitar' Watson* |
| 21/80 | **Gangsters Of The Groove** *Heatwave* |
| 77/83 | **Garden Party** *Herb Alpert* |
| | **Gee** |
| 2/54 | *Crows* |
| 26/61 | *Hollywood Flames* |
| | **Gee Baby** |
| 2/51 | *Johnny Otis Orchestra* |
| 14/60 | *Joe & Ann* |
| 1/44 | **Gee, Baby, Ain't I Good To You?** *Nat King Cole* |
| 14/56 | **Gee Whittakers** *Five Keys* |
| | **Gee Whiz** |
| 15/61 | *Innocents* |
| 64/80 | *Interlude* |
| 5/61 | **Gee Whiz (Look At His Eyes)** *Carla Thomas* |
| | **Geek You Up** *..see: (We Are Here To)* |
| 43/75 | **Gemini** *Miracles* |
| 23/81 | **General Hospi-Tale** *Afternoon Delights* |
| 62/83 | **Generator Pop** *P.Funk All Stars* |
| 2/82 | **Genius Of Love** *Tom Tom Club* |
| 31/82 | **Genius Rap** *Dr. Jeckyll & Mr. Hyde* |
| 48/85 | **Gentle (Calling Your Name)** *Frederick* |
| 50/69 | **Gentle On My Mind** *Aretha Franklin* |
| 60/84 | **Gentleman** *Randy Hall* |
| F/71 | **Georgia Blues** *Joe Simon* |
| 3/60 | **Georgia On My Mind** *Ray Charles* |
| | **Georgy Porgy** |
| 18/79 | *Toto* |
| 77/80 | *Side Effect* |
| 75/84 | *Charme* |
| 1/58 | **Get A Job** *Silhouettes* |
| 85/84 | **Get A Little, Give A Little** *Z.Z. Hill* |
| 86/79 | **Get Another Love** *Chantal Curtis* |
| 32/75 | **Get Dancin'** *Disco Tex & The Sex-O-Lettes* |
| | *(also see: Everybody)* |

| | |
|---|---|
| **Get Down** | |
| 32/67 | *Harvey Scales* |
| 13/71 | *Curtis Mayfield* |
| 40/75 | *Kay-Gees* |
| 3/79 | *Gene Chandler* |
| 82/88 | *Derek B* |
| 59/75 | **Get Down Baby** |
| | *Joe Quarterman & Free Soul* |
| 1/75 | **Get Down, Get Down (Get On The Floor)** |
| | *Joe Simon* |
| 59/80 | **Get-Down Mellow Sound** |
| | *Players Association* |
| 4/82 | **Get Down On It** *Kool & The Gang* |
| 32/70 | **Get Down People** *Fabulous Counts* |
| 37/83 | **Get Down Saturday Night** *Oliver Cheatham* |
| 1/75 | **Get Down Tonight** |
| | *KC & The Sunshine Band* |
| 73/83 | **Get Dressed** *George Clinton* |
| 30/68 | **Get-E-Up (The Horse)** *Preparations* |
| | **Get Fresh At The Weekend** |
| | *..see: Showing Out* |
| 46/77 | **Get Happy** *Jimmy 'Bo' Horne* |
| 56/83 | **Get In Touch With Me** *Collage* |
| 25/70 | **Get Into Something** *Isley Brothers* |
| 69/77 | **Get Into Your Life** *Deloyd* |
| 35/73 | **Get Involved** *George Soule* |
| | **Get It** |
| 6/53 | *Royals* |
| 59/80 | *Dramatics* |
| 4/88 | *Stevie Wonder & Michael Jackson* |
| 37/72 | **Get It All** *Mandrill* |
| 46/69 | **Get It From The Bottom** *Steelers* |
| 1/83 | **Get It Right** *Aretha Franklin* |
| | **Get It Together** |
| 11/67 | *James Brown* |
| 2/73 | *Jackson 5* |
| | **Get It Up** |
| 21/77 | *Ben E. King & AWB* |
| 6/81 | *Time* |
| 24/76 | **Get It While It's Hot** *Eddie Kendricks* |
| | **Get Loose** |
| 79/81 | *Wax* |
| 61/83 | *Evelyn 'Champagne' King* |
| | **Get Lucky** |
| 26/88 | *Well Red* |
| 69/88 | *Jermaine Stewart* |
| 72/85 | **Get Me Hot** *Xavion* |
| 7/43 | **Get Me On Your Mind** *Jay McShann* |
| 1/78 | **Get Off** *Foxy* |
| 32/69 | **Get Off My Back Woman** *B.B. King* |
| 79/86 | **Get Off My Tip!** *Masterdon Committee* |
| 26/84 | **Get Off (You Fascinate Me)** *Patrice Rushen* |
| 39/76 | **Get Off Your Aahh! And Dance** *Foxy* |
| 82/84 | **Get On Freak** *Catch* |
| 41/69 | **Get On The Case** *Infinity* |
| 1/72 | **Get On The Good Foot** *James Brown* |
| | **Get On Up** |
| 3/67 | *Esquires* |
| 12/78 | *Tyrone Davis* |
| 64/81 | **Get On Up Do It Again** *Suzy Q* |
| | **Get On Up, Get On Down** |
| 56/78 | *Roy Ayers* |
| 76/78 | *Roundtree* |
| 38/65 | **Get Out** *Harold Melvin & The Blue Notes* |
| 73/75 | **Get Out Of My Life** *Dee Dee Warwick* |
| 5/66 | **Get Out Of My Life, Woman** *Lee Dorsey* |
| 65/81 | **Get Out Your Handkerchief** |
| | *Ashford & Simpson* |
| 1/88 | **Get Outta My Dreams, Get Into My Car** |
| | *Billy Ocean* |

| | |
|---|---|
| **Get Ready** | |
| 1/66 | *Temptations* |
| 20/70 | *Rare Earth* |
| 46/70 | *King Curtis & The Kingpins* |
| 34/71 | *Syl Johnson* |
| 82/79 | *Smokey Robinson* |
| 93/78 | **Get Ready For The Future** *Winners* |
| 24/75 | **Get Ready For The Get Down** *Willie Hutch* |
| 48/80 | **Get Ready, Get Set** *Chaka Khan* |
| 98/75 | **Get Sexy** *Paul Kelly* |
| 7/75 | **Get The Cream Off The Top** |
| | *Eddie Kendricks* |
| 4/76 | **Get The Funk Out Ma Face** |
| | *Brothers Johnson* |
| 41/78 | **Get To Me** *Luther Ingram* |
| 15/81 | **Get Tough** *Kleeer* |
| | **Get Up** |
| 56/79 | *Brass Construction* |
| 35/80 | *Vernon Burch* |
| 5/76 | **Get Up And Boogie (That's Right)** |
| | *Silver Convention* |
| | **Get Up And Dance** |
| 61/77 | *Memphis Horns* |
| 82/79 | *Freedom* |
| 49/72 | **Get Up And Do Something For Yourself** |
| | *Solomon Burke* |
| | **Get Up And Get Down** |
| 16/72 | *Dramatics* |
| 98/79 | *All Points Bulletin Band* |
| 4/71 | **Get Up, Get Into It, Get Involved** |
| | *James Brown* |
| 15/56 | **Get Up Get Up** *LaVern Baker* |
| 2/70 | **Get Up (I Feel Like Being Like A) Sex** |
| | **Machine** *James Brown* |
| 96/74 | **Get Up Off My Mind** *Denise LaSalle* |
| 4/76 | **Get Up Offa That Thing** *James Brown* |
| 62/76 | **Get Up '76** *Esquires* |
| 72/81 | **Get What You Want** *Spunk* |
| | **Get You Out Of My System** *..see: (Can't)* |
| 50/76 | **Get You Somebody New** *LaBelle* |
| 55/84 | **Get Your Body On The Job** |
| | *Southside Johnny & The Jukes* |
| 76/82 | **Get Your Body Up** *Starpoint* |
| 46/72 | **Get Your Business Straight** *Albert Collins* |
| 3/46 | **Get Your Kicks On Route 66** *Nat King Cole* |
| 14/71 | **Get Your Lie Straight** *Bill Coday* |
| 97/77 | **Get Your Stuff Off** *Ingram* |
| 44/74 | **Get Your Thing Together** *Annette Snell* |
| 4/49 | **Get Yourself Another Fool** |
| | *Charles Brown Trio* |
| 48/67 | **Get Yourself Together** *Caesars* |
| | **Getaway** |
| 1/76 | *Earth, Wind & Fire* |
| 33/77 | *Salsoul Orchestra* |
| 72/86 | **Gettin' Away With Murder** *Patti Austin* |
| 79/83 | **Gettin' Money** *Dr. Jeckyll & Mr. Hyde* |
| 16/77 | **Gettin' Ready For Love** *Diana Ross* |
| 47/82 | **Gettin' To The Good Part** *Herbie Hancock* |
| 39/74 | **Gettin' What You Want (Losin' What You** |
| | **Got)** *William Bell* |
| 75/75 | **Getting It On '75** *Dennis Coffey* |
| 65/65 | **Getting Mighty Crowded** *Betty Everett* |
| 34/69 | **Getting The Corners** *T.S.U. Toronadoes* |
| 61/74 | **Getting Together** |
| | *Brothers Guiding Light Featuring David* |
| 23/70 | **Ghetto, The** *Donny Hathaway* |
| 4/73 | **Ghetto Child** *Spinners* |
| 73/73 | **Ghetto Cowboy** *Clyde Brown* |
| 38/82 | **Ghetto Life** *Rick James* |
| 25/71 | **Ghetto Woman** *B.B. King* |
| 71/76 | **Ghettos Of The Mind** *Pleasure* |
| 48/78 | **Ghost Of Love** *Tavares* |
| 1/84 | **Ghostbusters** *Ray Parker Jr.* |
| 66/77 | **Gift Wrap My Love** *Reflections* |
| 73/82 | **Gigolette** *Ozone* |

**Gigolo, The**
5/82   *O'Bryan*
69/82   *Mary Wells*
77/83  **Gigolos Get Lonely Too**  *Time*
39/85  **Gimme, Gimme, Gimme**
    *Narada Michael Walden with Patti Austin*
19/67  **Gimme Little Sign**  *Brenton Wood*
**Gimme Some**
22/70   *General Crook*
47/75   *Jimmy 'Bo' Horne*
11/72  **Gimme Some More**  *JB's*
92/76  **Gimme Some (Of Your Love)**
    *Norma Jenkins*
8/80  **Gimme Some Time**
    *Natalie Cole & Peabo Bryson*
53/80  **Gimme Something Real**  *Wardell Piper*
50/73  **Gimme That Beat**
    *Jr. Walker & The All Stars*
**Gimme What You Got**
63/80   *Al Jarreau*
41/84   *Chi-Lites*
10/58  **Ginger Bread**  *Frankie Avalon*
**Girl**
44/77   *Billy Preston*
49/82   *Time*
51/73  **Girl Blue**  *Main Ingredient*
14/78  **Girl Callin'**  *Chocolate Milk*
7/57  **Girl Can't Help It**  *Little Richard*
79/85  **Girl, Cut It Out**  *Roger*
16/67  **Girl Don't Care**  *Gene Chandler*
3/80  **Girl, Don't Let It Get You Down**  *O'Jays*
26/67  **Girl I Need You**  *Artistics*
79/85  **Girl If You Take Me Home**  *Full Force*
28/83  **Girl Is Fine (So Fine)**  *Fatback*
1/83  **Girl Is Mine**
    *Michael Jackson/Paul McCartney*
**Girl Next Door**
31/87   *Bobby Brown*
59/87   *Chico DeBarge*
30/80  **Girl Of My Dream**  *Manhattans*
33/87  **Girl Pulled The Dog**  *General Kane*
62/86  **Girl Talk**  *Boogie Boys*
44/72  **Girl Turned Me On**  *Jackie Wilson*
6/68  **Girl Watcher**  *O'Kaysions*
26/64  **Girl (Why You Wanna Make Me Blue)**
    *Temptations*
22/82  **Girl, You Are The One**  *Alfonzo*
13/73  **Girl You Need A Change Of Mind**
    *Eddie Kendricks*
43/72  **Girl You're Alright**  *Undisputed Truth*
13/69  **Girl You're Too Young**
    *Archie Bell & The Drells*
81/80  **Girl's Alright With Me**  *Masterpiece*
70/83  **Girl's Night Out**  *Ladies' Choice*
**Girlfriend**
1/86   *Bobby Brown*
1/88   *Pebbles*
**Girls**
68/64   *Major Lance*
72/82   *General Caine*
81/86  **Girls Ain't Nothing But Trouble**
    *D.J. Jazzy Jeff & The Fresh Prince*
21/85  **Girls Are More Fun**  *Ray Parker Jr.*
13/67  **Girls Are Out To Get You**  *Fascinations*
15/68  **Girls Can't Do What The Guys Do**
    *Betty Wright*
33/64  **Girls Grow Up Faster Than Boys**  *Cookies*
31/65  **Girls Have Feelings Too**  *Barbara Mason*
18/71  **Girls In The City**  *Esquires*
8/69  **Girls It Ain't Easy**  *Honey Cone*
80/84  **Girls Just Want To Have Fun**
    *Cyndi Lauper*
54/85  **Girls Love The Way He Spins**
    *Grandmaster Flash*
79/85  **Girls On My Mind**  *Fatback*

25/75  **Girls**  *Moments & Whatnauts*
21/70  **Girls Will Be Girls, Boys Will Be Boys**
    *Isley Brothers*
36/76  **Give A Broken Heart A Break**  *Impact*
47/84  **Give A Little**  *Stylistics*
76/85  **Give And Take**  *Brass Construction*
40/68  **Give 'Em Love**  *Soul Children*
36/67  **Give Everybody Some**  *Bar-Kays*
23/69  **Give Her A Transplant**  *Intruders*
32/68  **Give In**  *Webs*
32/80  **Give It All You Got**  *Chuck Mangione*
10/69  **Give It Away**  *Chi-Lites*
**Give It Back**
    *..see: (If You Don't Want My Love)*
26/80  **Give It On Up (If You Want To)**  *Mtume*
**Give It To Me Baby**
1/81   *Rick James*
53/82   *Cheri*
89/80  **Give It To You**  *RCR*
**Give It Up**
42/70   *Top Shelf*
80/82   *Pleasure*
**Give It Up Or Turnit A Loose**
1/69   *James Brown*     \
77/74   *Lyn Collins*
2/76  **Give It Up (Turn It Loose)**  *Tyrone Davis*
5/75  **Give It What You Got**  *B.T. Express*
76/79  **Give Love A Chance**  *Cameo*
**Give Me** *..also see: Gimme*
80/80  **Give Me A Break**  *Ritchie Family*
75/76  **Give Me All Your Sweet Lovin'**
    *Chuck Armstrong*
6/52  **Give Me Central 209**  *Lightnin' Hopkins*
8/70  **Give Me Just A Little More Time**
    *Chairmen Of The Board*
47/74  **Give Me Just Another Day**  *Miracles*
45/69  **Give Me Some Credit**  *Ann Peebles*
41/80  **Give Me Some Emotion**  *Webster Lewis*
98/75  **Give Me Some Of Your Sweet Love**
    *Barbara Acklin*
20/77  **Give Me Some Skin**
    *James Brown & The J.B.'s*
67/84  **Give Me The Dance**  *Kym*
57/84  **Give Me The Lovin'**  *Chic*
1/80  **Give Me The Night**  *George Benson*
3/86  **Give Me The Reason**  *Luther Vandross*
75/81  **Give Me Time**  *Minnie Riperton*
6/84  **Give Me Tonight**  *Shannon*
78/75  **Give Me Your Best Shot Baby**  *Ebb Tide*
18/75  **Give Me Your Heart**  *Bloodstone*
**Give Me Your Love**
9/73   *Barbara Mason*
22/82   *Peabo Bryson*
**Give More Power To The People**
    *..see: (For God's Sake)*
34/68  **Give My Love A Try**  *Linda Jones*
20/71  **Give The Baby Anthing The Baby Wants**
    *Joe Tex*
51/75  **Give The Little Man A Great Big Hand**
    *William DeVaughn*
1/75  **Give The People What They Want**  *O'Jays*
24/80  **Give Up The Funk (Let's Dance)**
    *B.T. Express*
3/73  **Give Your Baby A Standing Ovation**  *Dells*
80/79  **Give Your Love A Chance**
    *Narada Michael Walden*
53/82  **Give Your Love To Me**
    *Bill Summers & Summers Heat*
73/79  **Given In To Love**  *Lakeside*
8/86  **Givin' It (To You)**  *Skyy*
47/80  **Givin' It Up Is Givin' Up**
    *Patrice Rushen & D.J. Rogers*
15/87  **Givin' You Back The Love**
    *Isley, Jasper, Isley*
57/73  **Giving Love**  *Voices Of East Harlem*

| | | | |
|---|---|---|---|

**Guess Who**

2/49   *Ivory Joe Hunter*
7/59   *Jesse Belvin*
19/70   *Ruby Winters*
21/72   *B.B. King*
69/81   *Larry Graham*
42/78 **Guess Who's Back In Town**
    *Heaven & Earth*
41/70 **Guide Me Well**  *Carla Thomas*
**Guilty**
29/72   *Al Green*
19/75   *First Choice*
2/86   *Yarbrough & Peoples*
27/59 **Guitar Boogie Shuffle**  *Virtues*
79/76 **Guitar Man**  *Albert King*
1/46 **Gypsy, The**  *Ink Spots*
6/73 **Gypsy Man**  *War*
2/61 **Gypsy Woman**  *Impressions*

**H**

8/77 **Ha Cha Cha (Funktion)**  *Brass Construction*
78/81 **Haboglabotribin'**  *Bernard Wright*
65/80 **Half A Love**  *Aretha Franklin*
26/85 **Half Crazy**  *Johnny Gill*
10/73 **Hallelujah Day**  *Jackson 5*
5/56 **Hallelujah I Love Her So**  *Ray Charles*
44/69 **Hallways Of My Mind**  *Dells*
1/44 **Hamp's Boogie Woogie**  *Lionel Hampton*
26/70 **Hand Clapping Song**  *Meters*
76/83 **Hand Dance**  *Reddings*
92/64 **Hand It Over**  *Chuck Jackson*
16/62 **Handful Of Memories**  *Baby Washington*
1/55 **Hands Off**  *Jay McShann*
3/60 **Handy Man**  *Jimmy Jones*
35/69 **Hang 'Em High**  *Booker T. & The MG's*
**Hang It Up**
48/69   *Laura Lee*
16/79   *Patrice Rushen*
25/73 **Hang Loose**  *Mandrill*
52/81 **Hang On In There**
    *Harold Melvin & The Blue Notes*
**Hang On In There Baby**
2/74   *Johnny Bristol*
73/80   *Alton & Johnny*
6/65 **Hang On Sloopy**  *Ramsey Lewis Trio*
14/85 **Hang On To Your Love**  *Sade*
70/80 **Hang Tough**  *Rockie Robbins*
9/58 **Hang Up My Rock And Roll Shoes**
    *Chuck Willis*
48/82 **Hangin'**  *Chic*
45/84 **Hangin' Downtown**  *Cameo*
1/85 **Hangin' On A String (Contemplating)**
    *Loose Ends*
**Hangin' Out**
36/80   *Kool & The Gang*
67/80   *ADC Band*
71/86   *Fizzy Qwick*
50/84 **Hangin' Out At The Mall**  *Bobby Nunn*
28/71 **Hanging On (To) A Memory**
    *Chairmen Of The Board*
39/66 **Hanky Panky**
    *Tommy James & The Shondells*
83/73 **Hanna-Mae**  *Deep Velvet*
12/67 **Happening, The**  *Supremes*
20/79 **Happiness**  *Pointer Sisters*
20/74 **Happiness Is**  *New York City*
27/74 **Happiness Is Being With You**  *Tyrone Davis*

**Happiness Is Just Around The Bend**

7/74   *Main Ingredient*
43/83   *Cuba Gooding*
**Happy**
8/75   *Eddie Kendricks*
90/84   *Dutch Robinson*
2/87   *Surface*
16/80 **Happy Anniversary**  *Ray, Goodman & Brown*
99/78 **Happy Beat**  *Mandrill*
30/76 **Happy Being Lonely**  *Chi-Lites*
7/61 **Happy Days**  *Marv Johnson*
35/80 **Happy Endings**  *Ashford & Simpson*
87/80 **Happy Face**  *Con Funk Shun*
87/81 **Happy Family**  *T.F.O.*
74/82 **Happy Feeling**  *Denroy Morgan*
51/79 **Happy For Love**  *Pockets*
4/57 **Happy, Happy Birthday Baby**
    *Tune Weavers*
70/82 **Happy Hour**  *Deodato*
42/76 **Happy Man**  *Impact*
**Happy Music**
3/76   *Blackbyrds*
69/82   *Sheree Brown*
5/59 **Happy Organ**  *Dave 'Baby' Cortez*
1/75 **Happy People**  *Temptations*
28/79 **H.A.P.P.Y. Radio**  *Edwin Starr*
10/68 **Happy Song (Dum-Dum)**  *Otis Redding*
**Harbor Lights**
10/51   *Dinah Washington*
15/60   *Platters*
75/75 **Harbour Love**  *Syreeta*
52/85 **Hard Core Reggae**  *Fat Boys*
21/87 **Hard Day**  *George Michael*
29/66 **Hard Day's Night**  *Ramsey Lewis Trio*
2/58 **Hard Headed Woman**  *Elvis Presley*
1/50 **Hard Luck Blues**  *Roy Brown*
**Hard Times**
7/52   *Charles Brown*
75/81   *Kurtis Blow*
11/84   *Run-D.M.C.*
53/85   *Lonnie Hill*
17/85 **Hard Times For Lovers**  *Jennifer Holliday*
71/82 **Hard Times (It's Gonna Be Alright)**
    *Change*
15/82 **Hard To Get**  *Rick James*
**Hard To Handle**
38/68   *Otis Redding*
40/68   *Patti Drew*
13/76 **Hard Work**  *John Handy*
49/72 **Harder I Try (The Bluer I Get)**
    *Free Movement*
41/84 **Hardrock**  *Herbie Hancock*
62/76 **Hardtimes S.O.S.**  *Tommy Tate*
87/74 **Harlem**  *5th Dimension*
17/60 **Harlem Nocturne**  *Viscounts*
86/74 **Harlem River Drive**  *Bobbi Humphrey*
44/64 **Harlem Shuffle**  *Bob & Earl*
48/84 **Harmony**  *R.J.'s Latest Arrival*
43/68 **Harper Valley P.T.A. Gossip**  *Effie Smith*
8/73 **Harry Hippie**  *Bobby Womack*
14/63 **Harry The Hairy Ape**  *Ray Stevens*
9/76 **Harvest For The World**  *Isley Brothers*
46/84 **H-A-T-E (Don't Live Here Anymore)**
    *Staple Singers*
17/77 **Hats Off To Mama**  *Philippe Wynn*
55/83 **Haunted House Of Rock**  *Whodini*
25/68 **Have A Little Mercy**  *Jean Wells*
11/58 **Have Faith**  *Gene Allison*
21/62 **Have Fun**  *Ann Cole*
57/83 **Have It Your Way**  *S.O.S. Band*
**Have Mercy Baby**
1/52   *Dominoes*
92/65   *James Brown*
74/76 **Have You Ever**  *Joe Tex*

| | |
|---|---|
| 1/87 | **Have You Ever Loved Somebody** |
| | *Freddie Jackson* |
| 77/74 | **Have You Ever Tried It** *Ashford & Simpson* |
| 92/87 | **Have You Seen Davy** *Davy D* |
| | **Have You Seen Her** |
| 1/71 | *Chi-Lites* |
| 48/81 | *Chi-Lites* |
| 61/85 | **Haven't I Heard That Line Before** |
| | *Gene Chandler* |
| 46/79 | **Haven't Stop Dancing Yet** *Gonzalez* |
| 7/80 | **Haven't You Heard** *Patrice Rushen* |
| 79/81 | **Havin' Fun With Mr. T.** *Stanley Turrentine* |
| | **Having A Party** |
| 4/62 | *Sam Cooke* |
| 7/73 | *Ovations* |
| 62/77 | *Pointer Sisters* |
| 83/78 | *Norma Jean* |
| 3/82 | *Luther Vandross (medley)* |
| 27/59 | **Hawaiian Wedding Song** *Andy Williams* |
| 2/47 | **Hawk's Boogie** *Erskine Hawkins* |
| 10/42 | **Hay-Foot, Straw Foot** *Duke Ellington* |
| 13/55 | **He** *Al Hibbler* |
| 24/67 | **He Ain't Give You None** *Freddie Scott* |
| | **He Called Me Baby** |
| 38/69 | *Ella Washington* |
| 9/71 | *Candi Staton* |
| 74/75 | *Nancy Wilson* |
| 67/74 | **He Didn't Know** *Garland Green* |
| 33/68 | **He Don't Really Love You** *Delfonics* |
| 13/49 | **He Knows How To Hucklebuck** |
| | *Paul Williams* |
| 38/69 | **He Knows The Key (Is Always In The Mailbox)** *Vivian Copeland* |
| 25/70 | **He Made A Woman Out Of Me** |
| | *Betty LaVette* |
| | **He Treats Your Daughter Mean** |
| | *..see: (Mama)* |
| 39/88 | **He Turned Me Out** *Pointer Sisters* |
| 9/87 | **He Wants My Body** *Starpoint* |
| 21/65 | **He Was Really Sayin' Somethin'** |
| | *Velvelettes* |
| 75/74 | **He Was The Man** *Leon Lee* |
| 98/76 | **He Who Laughs Last Laughs The Best** |
| | *Monday After* |
| 1/60 | **He Will Break Your Heart** *Jerry Butler* |
| 24/66 | **He'll Be Back** *Players* |
| | **He'll Have To Go (Stay)** |
| 11/60 | *Jeanne Black* |
| 13/60 | *Jim Reeves* |
| 51/64 | *Solomon Burke* |
| 8/86 | **He'll Never Love You (Like I Do)** |
| | *Freddie Jackson* |
| 65/85 | **He's A Cobra** *Rockwell* |
| 2/76 | **He's A Friend** *Eddie Kendricks* |
| 55/64 | **He's A Good Guy (Yes He Is)** *Marvelettes* |
| | **He's A Pretender** |
| 62/83 | *High Inergy* |
| 76/86 | *La Toya Jackson* |
| 2/47 | **He's A Real Gone Guy** *Nellie Lutcher* |
| 2/62 | **He's A Rebel** *Crystals* |
| 92/76 | **He's Always Somewhere Around** |
| | *Donny Gerrard* |
| 74/85 | **He's Got The Beat** *Whiz Kid* |
| 3/58 | **He's Got The Whole World (In His Hands)** *Laurie London* |
| 32/81 | **He's Just A Runaway** *Sister Sledge* |
| 5/57 | **He's Mine** *Platters* |
| 63/65 | **He's My Guy** *Irma Thomas* |
| 69/75 | **He's My Man** *Supremes* |
| 1/63 | **He's So Fine** *Chiffons* |
| 10/80 | **He's So Shy** *Pointer Sisters* |
| 18/63 | **He's Sure The Boy I Love** *Crystals* |
| 90/73 | **He's The Father Of My Children** *Pat Lundi* |
| 1/79 | **He's The Greatest Dancer** *Sister Sledge* |
| 1/87 | **Head To Toe** *Lisa Lisa & Cult Jam* |

| | |
|---|---|
| 76/88 | **Heading In The Right Direction** |
| | *Vaneese Thomas* |
| 65/86 | **Headline News** *William Bell* |
| 3/86 | **Headlines** *Midnight Star* |
| 76/86 | **Healing** *Deniece Williams* |
| 18/76 | **Hear The Words, Feel The Feeling** |
| | *Margie Joseph* |
| 5/72 | **Hearsay** *Soul Children* |
| | **Heart And Soul** |
| 10/61 | *Cleftones* |
| 45/67 | *Incredibles* |
| 29/70 | **Heart Association** *Emotions* |
| | **Heart Be Still** |
| 43/67 | *Lorraine Ellison* |
| 26/76 | *Carl Graves* |
| 29/84 | **Heart Don't Lie** *La Toya Jackson* |
| 31/65 | **Heart Full Of Love** *Invincibles* |
| 67/81 | **Heart Heart** *Geraldine Hunt* |
| 29/86 | **Heart Is Not So Smart** |
| | *El DeBarge with DeBarge* |
| 5/87 | **Heart Of Gold** *Bert Robinson* |
| 48/87 | **Heart On The Line** *Jennifer Holliday* |
| 76/83 | **Heart Stop Beating In Time** |
| | *Marilyn McCoo* |
| | **Heart To Heart** |
| 57/82 | *Ronnie Dyson* |
| 71/83 | *Kenny Loggins* |
| 66/80 | **Heartache No. 9** *Delegation* |
| 19/61 | **Heartaches** *Marcels* |
| 19/60 | **Heartaches By The Number** *Guy Mitchell* |
| 25/67 | **Heartaches-Heartaches** *O.V. Wright* |
| | **Heartbeat** |
| 10/81 | *Taana Gardner* |
| 12/85 | *Dazz Band* |
| 10/83 | **Heartbeats** *Yarbrough & Peoples* |
| 99/64 | **Heartbreak Hill** *Fats Domino* |
| | **Heartbreak Hotel** |
| 3/56 | *Elvis Presley* |
| 2/81 | *Jacksons* |
| | **Heartbreak (It's Hurtin' Me)** |
| 3/60 | *Jon Thomas* |
| 11/60 | *Little Willie John* |
| 13/75 | **Heartbreak Road** *Bill Withers* |
| | **Heartbreaker** |
| 14/82 | *Dionne Warwick* |
| 15/83 | *Zapp* |
| 68/83 | *Musical Youth* |
| 84/85 | **Heartless** *Evelyn Thomas* |
| | **Hearts Of Stone** |
| 1/54 | *Charms* |
| 22/61 | *Bill Black's Combo* |
| 13/86 | **Heat Of Heat** *Patti Austin* |
| 59/79 | **Heat Of The Beat** |
| | *Roy Ayers/Wayne Henderson* |
| 22/87 | **Heat Stroke** *Janice Christie* |
| 1/63 | **Heat Wave** *Martha & The Vandellas* |
| 2/70 | **Heaven Help Us All** *Stevie Wonder* |
| 12/86 | **Heaven In Your Arms** *R.J.'s Latest Arrival* |
| 37/78 | **Heaven Is Only One Step Away** *Controllers* |
| 76/81 | **Heaven Is Waiting** *Tom Grant* |
| 10/79 | **Heaven Knows** |
| | *Donna Summer with Brooklyn Dreams* |
| 3/76 | **Heaven Must Be Missing An Angel** |
| | *Tavares* |
| | **Heaven Must Have Sent You** |
| 9/66 | *Elgins* |
| 52/79 | *Bonnie Pointer* |
| 13/56 | **Heaven On Earth** *Platters* |
| 23/77 | **Heaven On Earth (So Fine)** *Spinners* |
| 93/77 | **Heaven On The Seventh Floor** *Mighty Pope* |
| 32/76 | **Heaven Only Knows** *Love Committee* |
| 68/75 | **Heaven Right Here On Earth** *Natural Four* |
| 21/84 | **Heaven Sent You** *Stanley Clarke* |
| 8/74 | **Heavenly** *Temptations* |
| 79/83 | **Heavenly Angel** *Hiroshima* |

| | | | | |
|---|---|---|---|
| 36/80 | **Heavenly Body** *Chi-Lites* | 65/87 | **Here Now** *Sandra Feva* |
| 4/52 | **Heavenly Father** | 14/80 | **Here We Go** *Minnie Riperton* |
| | *Edna McGriff with Buddy Lucas* | | **Here We Go Again** |
| 4/74 | **Heavy Fallin' Out** *Stylistics* | 5/67 | *Ray Charles* |
| 9/53 | **Heavy Juice** *Tiny Bradshaw* | 52/76 | *People's Choice* |
| 8/76 | **Heavy Love** *David Ruffin* | 11/80 | *Isley Brothers* |
| 61/81 | **Heavy Love Affair** *Marvin Gaye* | 89/64 | **Here's A Heart** *Diplomats* |
| 6/71 | **Heavy Makes You Happy (Sha-Na-Boom Boom)** *Staple Singers* | 26/61 | **Here's My Confession** |
| | | | *Wyatt (Earp) McPherson* |
| 42/88 | **Heavy On My Mind** *Club Nouveau* | 23/81 | **Here's To You** *Skyy* |
| 34/80 | **Heavy On Pride (Light On Love)** | 64/84 | **Hero** *Gladys Knight & The Pips* |
| | *Smokey Robinson* | | **Heroes** |
| 7/56 | **Heebie Jeebies** *Little Richard* | 27/80 | *Commodores* |
| 26/74 | **Hell Of A Fix** *Marion Jarvis* | 37/83 | *Stanley Clarke/George Duke* |
| 1/84 | **Hello** *Lionel Richie* | 1/46 | **Hey! Ba-Ba-Re-Bop** *Lionel Hampton* |
| 81/87 | **Hello Rochelle** *J.E. The P.C. From D.C.* | 18/74 | **Hey Babe** *Joneses* |
| | **Hello Stranger** | 2/62 | **Hey! Baby** *Bruce Channel* |
| 1/63 | *Barbara Lewis* | 68/82 | **Hey Baby (Give It All To Me)** |
| 57/77 | *Yvonne Elliman* | | *Curtis Mayfield* |
| 20/85 | *Carrie Lucas* | 40/72 | **Hey Big Brother** *Rare Earth* |
| 28/69 | **Hello Sunshine** *Rev. Maceo Woods* | 44/70 | **Hey Blackman** *Ed Robinson* |
| 38/79 | **H.E.L.P.** *Four Tops* | 23/64 | **Hey, Bobba Needle** *Chubby Checker* |
| 73/80 | **Help From My Friends** *Parlet* | 15/84 | **Hey D.J.** *World's Famous Supreme Team* |
| 46/82 | **Help Is On The Way** *Whatnauts* | 50/72 | **Hey, Did You Give Some Love Today** |
| 24/63 | **Help Me** *Sonny Boy Williamson* | | *Street Christians* |
| 32/71 | **Help Me Find A Way (To Say I Love You)** | 8/56 | **Hey, Doll Baby** *Clovers* |
| | *Little Anthony & The Imperials* | 63/82 | **Hey Fellas** *Trouble Funk* |
| | **Help Me Make It Through The Night** | | **Hey, Girl** |
| 13/71 | *Joe Simon* | 10/63 | *Freddie Scott* |
| 38/71 | *O.C. Smith* | F/86 | *Isaac Hayes* |
| 13/72 | *Gladys Knight & The Pips* | 41/64 | **Hey Girl Don't Bother Me** *Tams* |
| 83/85 | **Help Me Out** *Labyrinth featuring Julie Loco* | 2/73 | **Hey Girl (I Like Your Style)** *Temptations* |
| 9/49 | **Help Me Some** *Memphis Slim* | 41/86 | **Hey Good Lookin'** *George Clinton* |
| 1/53 | **Help Me Somebody** *'5' Royales* | 29/64 | **Hey Harmonica Man** *Stevie Wonder* |
| 95/75 | **Help Me Understand You** *Jimmy Lewis* | 29/69 | **Hey Joe** *Wilson Pickett* |
| 44/82 | **Help (...Save This Frantic Heart Of Mine)** *Fredi Grace & Rhinstone* | 43/67 | **Hey Joyce** *Lou Courtney* |
| | | 13/69 | **Hey Jude** *Wilson Pickett* |
| | **Help The Poor** | 4/43 | **Hey Lawdy Mama** *Andy Kirk* |
| 98/64 | *B.B. King* | 16/67 | **Hey, Leroy, Your Mama's Callin' You** |
| 36/71 | *B.B. King* | | *Jimmy Castor* |
| | **Help Yourself** | | **Hey, Little Girl** |
| 19/74 | *Undisputed Truth* | 6/51 | *John Godfrey Trio* |
| 58/78 | *Brass Construction* | 10/51 | *Billy Wright* |
| 31/68 | **Help Yourself (To All Of My Lovin')** | 2/59 | *Dee Clark* |
| | *James & Bobby Purify* | 12/63 | *Major Lance* |
| 28/83 | **Help Yourself To My Love** *Kashif* | 63/73 | *Foster Sylvers* |
| | **Helpless** | 100/63 | **Hey Lonely One** *Baby Washington* |
| 13/66 | *Kim Weston* | | **Hey Love** |
| 21/69 | *Jackie Wilson* | 9/67 | *Stevie Wonder* |
| 74/75 | **Helplessly** *Moment Of Truth* | F/71 | *Delfonics* |
| 20/87 | **Helplessly In Love** *New Edition* | 69/87 | *King Sun-D Moet* |
| 14/55 | **Henry's Got Flat Feet** *Midnighters* | 40/80 | **Hey Lover** *Chocolate Milk* |
| 72/83 | **Here Comes My Love** *Rocket* | 2/52 | **Hey, Miss Fannie** *Clovers* |
| 57/84 | **Here Comes That Beat!** | 47/72 | **Hey Mister** *Ray Charles* |
| | *Pumpkin & The Profile All-Stars* | 3/53 | **Hey Mrs. Jones** *Jimmy Forrest* |
| 29/79 | **Here Comes The Hurt Again** *Manhattans* | 68/81 | **Hey Nineteen** *Steely Dan* |
| | **Here Comes The Judge** | 1/63 | **Hey Paula** *Paul & Paula* |
| 4/68 | *Shorty Long* | 31/74 | **Hey, Pokey-A-Way** *Meters* |
| 4/68 | *Pigmeat Markham* | 34/70 | **Hey Romeo** *Sequins* |
| 17/88 | **Here Comes The Night** *Meli'sa Morgan* | 29/71 | **Hey Ruby (Shut Your Mouth)** |
| 44/80 | **Here Comes The Sun** *Fat Larry's Band* | | *Ruby & The Party Gang* |
| 93/75 | **Here For The Party** *Bottom & Company* | 70/78 | **Hey Senorita** *War* |
| | **Here I Am** | 57/75 | **Hey There Little Firefly** *Firefly* |
| F/75 | *Chi-Lites* | | **Hey There Lonely Girl (Boy)** |
| 26/81 | *Dynasty* | 4/70 | *Eddie Holman* |
| 35/75 | **Here I Am Again** *Candi Staton* | 66/80 | *Flakes* |
| 14/68 | **Here I Am Baby** *Marvelettes* | 71/83 | *Stacy Lattisaw* |
| 2/73 | **Here I Am (Come And Take Me)** *Al Green* | 27/87 | *Gerry Woo* |
| | **Here I Go Again** | 1/68 | **Hey, Western Union Man** *Jerry Butler* |
| 15/69 | *Smokey Robinson & The Miracles* | 57/76 | **Hey, What's That Dance You're Doing** |
| 18/86 | *Force M.D.'s* | | *Choice Four* |
| 45/87 | *Oran 'Juice' Jones* | 51/81 | **(Hey Who's Gotta) Funky Song** *Fantasy* |
| 19/59 | **Here I Stand** *Wade Flemons* | 55/81 | **Hey You** *Symba* |
| 44/81 | **Here Is My Love** *Sylvester* | 5/73 | **Hey You! Get Off My Mountain** *Dramatics* |
| 34/73 | **Here Is Where Love Is** *Bobby Wilson* | 98/63 | **Hi Diddle Diddle** *Inez Foxx* |

**498**

**Hi-Heel Sneakers**
11/64   *Tommy Tucker*
44/68   *Jose Feliciano*
23/84  **Hi, How Ya Doin'?**  *Kenny G*
61/82  **Hidden Tears**  *Tierra*
27/62  **Hide & Go Seek**  *Bunker Hill*
3/55   **Hide And Seek**  *Joe Turner*
5/61   **Hide Away**  *Freddy King*
7/62   **Hide 'Nor Hair**  *Ray Charles*
56/77  **Hideaway**  *Fantastic Four*
77/85  **Hiding Place**  *J. Blackfoot*
98/74  **Higga-Boom**  *Gene Harris*
13/80  **High**  *Skyy*
34/86  **High Fashion**  *Family*
30/65  **High Heel Sneakers**  *Stevie Wonder*
     **High Hopes**
20/59   *Frank Sinatra*
25/82   *S.O.S. Band*
19/86  **High Horse**  *Evelyn 'Champagne' King*
70/81  **High On The Boogie**  *Stargard*
12/79  **High On Your Love Suite**  *Rick James*
17/83  **High-Rise**  *Ashford & Simpson*
5/58   **High School Confidential**  *Jerry Lee Lewis*
     **High School Dance**
F/57   *Larry Williams*
6/77   *Sylvers*
30/59  **High School U.S.A.**  *Tommy Facenda*
19/80  **High Society**  *Norma Jean*
45/79  **High Steppin', Hip Dressin' Fella**
     *Love Unlimited*
     **Higher And Higher**
     *..see: (Your Love Keeps Lifting Me)*
1/73   **Higher Ground**  *Stevie Wonder*
1/74   **Higher Plane**  *Kool & The Gang*
77/75  **Higher Than High**  *Undisputed Truth*
24/75  **Hijack**  *Herbie Mann*
10/71  **Hijackin' Love**  *Johnnie Taylor*
7/68   **Hip City**  *Jr. Walker & The All Stars*
66/83  **Hip Hop, Be Bop (Don't Stop)**  *Man Parrish*
6/67   **Hip Hug-Her**  *Booker T. & The MG's*
8/49   **Hip Shakin' Mama**  *Chubby Newsom*
45/76  **Hipit**  *Hosanna*
75/76  **His House And Me**  *Dionne Warwick*
89/64  **His Kiss**  *Betty Harris*
44/72  **His Song Shall Be Sung**  *Lou Rawls*
37/85  **History**  *Mai Tai*
     **Hit And Run**
56/77   *Loleatta Holloway*
5/81   *Bar-Kays*
19/62  **Hit Record**  *Brook Benton*
1/61   **Hit The Road Jack**  *Ray Charles*
12/63  **Hitch Hike**  *Marvin Gaye*
25/68  **Hitch It To The Horse**  *Fantastic Johnny C*
6/53   **Hittin' On Me**  *Buddy Johnson*
5/49   **Hobo Blues**  *John Lee Hooker*
10/76  **Hold Back The Night**  *Trammps*
3/58   **Hold It**  *Bill Doggett*
55/86  **Hold It, Now Hit It**  *Beastie Boys*
     **Hold Me**
5/84   *Teddy Pendergrass*
61/85   *Menudo*
3/87   *Sheila E.*
2/49   **Hold Me, Baby**  *Amos Milburn*
70/81  **Hold Me Down**  *Lipps, Inc.*
21/68  **Hold Me Tight**  *Johnny Nash*
     **Hold On**
35/68   *Radiants*
88/76   *Sons Of Champlin*
38/80   *Natalie Cole*
70/80   *Symba*
9/87   *R.J.'s Latest Arrival*
10/65  **Hold On Baby**  *Sam Hawkins*
72/85  **Hold On (For Love's Sake)**  *Joyce Kennedy*

     **Hold On! I'm A Comin'**
1/66   *Sam & Dave*
20/67  **Chuck Jackson & Maxine Brown**
48/70  *Soul Children*
79/75  **Hold On (Just A Little Bit Longer)**
     *Anthony & The Imperials*
56/81  **Hold On To A Friend**  *Rufus*
70/79  **Hold On To Love**  *Seawind*
29/80  **Hold On To My Love**  *Jimmy Ruffin*
33/67  **Hold On (To This Old Fool)**  *Buddy Ace*
     **Hold On (To Your Dreams)**
77/80   *Wee Gee*
85/87   *Living Proof*
11/86  **Hold On To Your Love**  *Smokey Robinson*
     **Hold Tight**
91/77   *Vicki Sue Robinson*
40/81   *Change*
2/65   **Hold What You've Got**  *Joe Tex*
73/79  **Hold Your Horses**  *First Choice*
26/82  **Holdin' Out For Love**  *Angela Bofill*
92/78  **Holdin' Out (For Your Love)**
     *Rhythm Heritage*
73/83  **Holding Back**  *Jackie Moore*
29/86  **Holding Back The Years**  *Simply Red*
     **Holding On**
77/86   *Givens Family*
22/87   *Jonathan Butler*
1/78   **Holding On (When Love Is Gone)**  *L.T.D.*
5/65   **Hole In The Wall**  *Packers*
     **Holiday**
25/84   *Madonna*
9/87   *Kool & The Gang*
65/84  **Hollis Crew**  *Run-D.M.C.*
33/71  **Holly Holy**  *Jr. Walker & The All Stars*
3/77   **Hollywood**  *Rufus Featuring Chaka Khan*
45/75  **Hollywood Hot**  *Eleventh Hour*
17/78  **Hollywood Squares**  *Bootsy's Rubber Band*
1/74   **Hollywood Swinging**  *Kool & The Gang*
10/66  **Holy Cow**  *Lee Dorsey*
9/79   **Holy Ghost**  *Bar-Kays*
6/56   **Home At Last**  *Little Willie John*
19/69  **Home Cookin**  *Jr. Walker & The All Stars*
40/72  **Home Is Where The Hatred Is**
     *Esther Phillips*
43/77  **Home Is Where The Heart Is**
     *Bobby Womack & Brotherhood*
60/78  **Home-Made Jam**  *Bobbi Humphrey*
61/76  **Home To Myself**  *Brenda & The Tabulations*
28/86  **Homeboy**  *Steve Arrington*
3/74   **Homely Girl**  *Chi-Lites*
66/79  **Homemade Lovin'**  *Whispers*
5/49   **Homesick Blues**  *Charles Brown*
36/75  **Homewreckers**  *Tyrone Davis*
4/57   **Honest I Do**  *Jimmy Reed*
77/78  **Honest I Do Love You**  *Candi Staton*
58/75  **Honey Baby (Be Mine)**  *Innervision*
     **Honey Bee**
10/51   *Muddy Waters*
55/74   *Gloria Gaynor*
     **Honey Chile**
2/56   *Fats Domino*
5/68   *Martha Reeves & The Vandellas*
43/69  **Honey Come Back**  *Chuck Jackson*
24/85  **Honey For The Bees**  *Patti Austin*
     **Honey, Honey**
37/80   *David Hudson*
25/82   *Manhattans*
1/53   **Honey Hush**  *Joe Turner*
18/76  **Honey I**  *George McCrae*
44/69  **Honey (I Miss You)**  *O.C. Smith*
13/72  **Honey I Still Love You**  *Mark IV*
43/78  **Honey I'm Rich**  *Raydio*
1/54   **Honey Love**  *Drifters*
     *(also see: We've Got)*
6/74   **Honey Please, Can't Ya See**  *Barry White*

# I

| | |
|---|---|
| 60/84 | **I Can Dream About You** *Dan Hartman* |
| 50/70 | **I Can Feel A Heartbreak** *Jeanette Williams* |
| 47/71 | **I Can Feel It** *Carl Carlton* |
| 81/82 | **I Can Get You Over** *W.A.G.B.* |
| | **I Can Make It Better** |
| 23/77 | *Peabo Bryson* |
| 40/81 | *Whispers* |
| 21/73 | **I Can Make It Thru The Days (But Oh Those Lonely Nights)** *Ray Charles* |
| 4/83 | **I Can Make You Dance** *Zapp* |
| 33/82 | **I Can Make You Feel Good** *Shalamar* |
| 73/74 | **I Can Play (Just For You And Me)** |
| | *Maceo & The Macks* |
| 72/87 | **I Can Prove It** *Phil Fearon* |
| 42/68 | **I Can Remember** *James & Bobby Purify* |
| | **I Can See Clearly Now** |
| 38/72 | *Johnny Nash* |
| 35/78 | *Ray Charles* |
| 7/55 | **I Can See Everybody's Baby** *Ruth Brown* |
| 5/69 | **I Can Sing A Rainbow/Love Is Blue** *Dells* |
| 72/79 | **I Can Tell** *Chanson* |
| 4/73 | **I Can Understand It** *New Birth* |
| 45/69 | **I Can't Be All Bad** *Johnny Adams* |
| 33/70 | **I Can't Be You (You Can't Be Me)** |
| | *Glass House* |
| 29/85 | **I Can't Believe It (It's Over)** *Melba Moore* |
| 95/64 | **I Can't Believe What You Say** |
| | *Ike & Tina Turner* |
| 27/66 | **I Can't Believe You Love Me** *Tammi Terrell* |
| 90/81 | **I Can't Believe You're Going Away** |
| | *Mass Production* |
| 62/74 | **I Can't Break Away** *Chuck Jackson* |
| 12/88 | **I Can't Complain** |
| | *Melba Moore with Freddie Jackson* |
| 24/68 | **I Can't Dance To That Music You're Playin'** *Martha Reeves & The Vandellas* |
| 20/69 | **I Can't Do Enough** *Dells* |
| 84/87 | **I Can't Fight It** *Conway Brothers* |
| 65/74 | **I Can't Fight Your Love** *Modulations* |
| 41/84 | **I Can't Find** *Smokey Robinson* |
| 63/85 | **I Can't Forget You** *Patti LaBelle* |
| 44/70 | **I Can't Get Along Without You** |
| | *Maxine Brown* |
| | **I Can't Get Next To You** |
| 1/69 | *Temptations* |
| 11/70 | *Al Green* |
| 19/65 | **(I Can't Get No) Satisfaction** |
| | *Rolling Stones* |
| | **I Can't Get Over Losing You** *..see: (Baby)* |
| 9/77 | **I Can't Get Over You** *Dramatics* |
| 3/48 | **I Can't Give You Anything But Love** |
| | *Rose Murphy* |
| 1/82 | **I Can't Go For That (No Can Do)** |
| | *Daryl Hall & John Oates* |
| | **I Can't Go On** |
| 6/55 | *Fats Domino* |
| 74/75 | *Truth* |
| 42/80 | **I Can't Go On Living Without You** |
| | *Tavares* |
| 1/48 | **I Can't Go On Without You** |
| | *Bull Moose Jackson* |
| 66/64 | **I Can't Hear You** *Betty Everett* |
| | **I Can't Help It** |
| 27/71 | *Moments* |
| 27/77 | *Michael Henderson* |
| | **I Can't Help Myself** |
| 1/65 | *Four Tops* |
| 14/72 | *Donnie Elbert* |
| 42/80 | *Bonnie Pointer* |
| 83/84 | **I Can't Keep My Head** *Eramus Hall* |
| 10/74 | **I Can't Leave You Alone** *George McCrae* |
| 6/70 | **I Can't Leave Your Love Alone** |
| | *Clarence Carter* |
| 30/87 | **I Can't Let You Go** *Norwood* |
| 43/88 | **I Can't Live With Or Without You** *Dimples* |

| | |
|---|---|
| 15/86 | **I Can't Live Without My Radio** *L.L. Cool J* |
| 10/81 | **I Can't Live Without Your Love** |
| | *Teddy Pendergrass* |
| 7/56 | **I Can't Love You Enough** *LaVern Baker* |
| 33/69 | **I Can't Make It Alone** *Lou Rawls* |
| 38/75 | **I Can't Make It Without You** *Tyrone Davis* |
| 92/78 | **I Can't Move No Mountains** *Shirley Brown* |
| 21/67 | **I Can't Please You** *Jimmy Robins* |
| 48/67 | **I Can't Put My Finger On It** *Junior Parker* |
| 6/56 | **I Can't Quit You Baby** *Otis Rush* |
| 65/75 | **I Can't Quit Your Love** *Buck* |
| 31/66 | **I Can't Rest** *Fontella Bass* |
| 40/77 | **I Can't Say Goodbye** *Millie Jackson* |
| 29/69 | **I Can't Say No To You** *Betty Everett* |
| 2/44 | **I Can't See For Lookin'** *Nat King Cole* |
| 41/70 | **I Can't See Myself Doing Without You** |
| | *Detroit Emeralds* |
| 3/69 | **I Can't See Myself Leaving You** |
| | *Aretha Franklin* |
| 28/75 | **I Can't See What You See In Me** *Joneses* |
| 83/76 | **I Can't Seem To Forget You** |
| | *Heaven & Earth* |
| 47/82 | **I Can't Shake This Feeling** *Klique* |
| 41/72 | **I Can't Share You** *Naturals* |
| 46/64 | **I Can't Stand It** *Soul Sisters* |
| 1/43 | **I Can't Stand Losing You** *Ink Spots* |
| 4/68 | **I Can't Stand Myself (When You Touch Me)** *James Brown* |
| 35/83 | **I Can't Stand The Pain** *O'Jays* |
| | **I Can't Stand The Rain** |
| 6/73 | *Ann Peebles* |
| 30/78 | *Eruption* |
| 34/88 | *Tease* |
| 21/73 | **I Can't Stand To See You Cry** |
| | *Smokey Robinson & The Miracles* |
| | **I Can't Stay Away From You** |
| 34/67 | *Impressions* |
| 49/67 | *Fascinations* |
| 5/68 | **I Can't Stop Dancing** |
| | *Archie Bell & The Drells* |
| | **I Can't Stop Loving You** |
| 1/62 | *Ray Charles* |
| 62/81 | *Millie Jackson* |
| 87/80 | **I Can't Stop (Turning You On)** *Silk* |
| 45/70 | **I Can't Take It Like A Man** *Ben E. King* |
| 90/79 | **I Can't Turn The Boogie Loose** *Controllers* |
| 11/66 | **I Can't Turn You Lose** *Otis Redding* |
| 76/77 | **I Can't Understand** *Meadows Brothers* |
| 2/86 | **I Can't Wait** *Nu Shooz* |
| 65/86 | **I Can't Wait (To Rock The Mike)** *Spyder-D* |
| 93/64 | **I Can't Wait Until I See My Baby** |
| | *Justine Washington* |
| 32/82 | **I Can't Win For Losing** *Teddy Pendergrass* |
| 6/65 | **I Can't Work No Longer** |
| | *Billy Butler & The Chanters* |
| 61/77 | **I Caught Your Act** *Hues Corporation* |
| | **I Challenge Your Kiss** |
| 8/49 | *Four Jacks* |
| 11/49 | *Orioles* |
| 74/76 | **I Choose You** *Chicago Gangsters* |
| 22/66 | **I Chose To Sing The Blues** *Ray Charles* |
| 82/80 | **I Come Here To Party** *T.F.O.* |
| 12/87 | **I Commit To Love** *Howard Hewett* |
| 11/55 | **I Concentrate On You** *Dinah Washington* |
| 24/87 | **I Confess** *Deniece Williams* |
| 25/75 | **I Could Dance All Night** |
| | *Archie Bell & The Drells* |
| 72/63 | **I Could Have Danced All Night** |
| | *Ben E. King* |
| 20/78 | **I Could Have Loved You** *Moments* |
| 23/72 | **I Could Never Be Happy** *Emotions* |
| 10/69 | **I Could Never Be President** *Johnnie Taylor* |
| 1/68 | **I Could Never Love Another (After Loving You)** *Temptations* |
| 15/70 | **I Could Write A Book** *Jerry Butler* |

| 1/74 | I Feel A Song (In My Heart) |
| | Gladys Knight & The Pips |
| 1/84 | I Feel For You  Chaka Khan |
| | I Feel Good |
| 3/56 | Shirley & Lee |
| 33/67 | Jean Wells |
| 36/78 | Al Green |
| 1/87 | I Feel Good All Over  Stephanie Mills |
| 94/78 | I Feel His Love Getting Stronger |
| | Margie Joseph |
| 13/49 | I Feel Like Cryin'  Andrew Tibbs |
| 35/74 | I Feel Like Dynamite  King Floyd |
| 11/48 | (I Feel Like) Going Home  Muddy Waters |
| 52/77 | I Feel Like I've Been Livin' (On The Dark Side |
| | Of The Moon)  Trammps |
| 58/83 | I Feel Like Walking In The Rain |
| | Millie Jackson |
| 9/77 | I Feel Love  Donna Summer |
| 77/76 | I Feel Love In This Room Tonight |
| | Bo Kirkland & Ruth Davis |
| 12/75 | I Feel Sanctified  Commodores |
| 52/77 | I Feel So At Home Here  Michelle Wiley |
| | I Feel So Bad |
| 8/54 | Chuck Willis |
| 15/61 | Elvis Presley |
| 10/49 | I Feel That Old Age Coming On |
| | Wynonie Harris |
| 36/79 | I Feel You When You're Gone  Gangsters |
| 44/69 | I Finally Found A Woman  Timmy Willis |
| 3/67 | I Fooled You This Time  Gene Chandler |
| 10/69 | I Forgot To Be Your Lover  William Bell |
| | I Found A Love |
| 6/62 | Falcons |
| 6/67 | Wilson Pickett |
| 31/72 | Etta James |
| 32/65 | I Found A Love Oh What A Love |
| | Jo Ann & Troy |
| 11/68 | I Found A True Love  Wilson Pickett |
| 32/79 | I Found Love  Deniece Williams |
| 78/76 | I Found Love On A Disco Floor  Temprees |
| 8/85 | I Found My Baby  Gap Band |
| F/72 | I Found My Dad  Joe Simon |
| 38/83 | I Found Myself When I Lost You |
| | Tyrone Davis |
| 17/62 | I Found Out Too Late |
| | Jackie & The Starlites |
| 3/53 | I Found Out (What You Do When You Go |
| | 'Round There)  Du Droppers |
| 17/74 | I Found Sunshine  Chi-Lites |
| F/70 | I Found That Girl  Jackson 5 |
| 20/82 | (I Found) That Man Of Mine  Jones Girls |
| 46/69 | I Get A Groove |
| | Thomas East & The Fabulous Playboys |
| 66/87 | I Get A Rush  Rose Brothers |
| 79/79 | I Get Excited  David Ruffin |
| 3/75 | I Get High On You  Sly Stone |
| | I Get Lifted |
| 8/75 | George McCrae |
| 69/76 | Sweet Music |
| 30/77 | Latimore |
| 28/86 | I Get Off On You  Rose Brothers |
| 12/68 | I Get The Sweetest Feeling  Jackie Wilson |
| 37/80 | I Go Crazy  Lou Rawls |
| 88/85 | I Go Wild  Jak |
| 3/73 | I Got A Bag Of My Own  James Brown |
| 75/82 | I Got A Feeling  Khemistry |
| 64/77 | I Got A Notion  Al Hudson |
| 35/70 | I Got A Problem  Jesse Anderson |
| 16/68 | I Got A Sure Thing |
| | Ollie & The Nightingales |
| 30/70 | I Got A Thing, You Got A Thing, Everybody's |
| | Got A Thing  Funkadelic |
| 48/63 | I Got A Woman  Freddie Scott |
| 4/73 | I Got Ants In My Pants (and i want to |
| | dance)  James Brown |

| 49/75 | I Got Caught  Clarence Carter |
| 48/88 | I Got Da Feelin'  Sweet Tee |
| 1/51 | I Got Loaded  Peppermint Harris |
| 1/79 | I Got My Mind Made Up (You Can Get It |
| | Girl)  Instant Funk |
| 24/76 | I Got Over Love  Major Harris |
| 30/73 | (I Got) So Much Trouble In My Mind |
| | Joe Quarterman |
| 28/72 | I Got Some Help I Don't Need  B.B. King |
| 1/68 | I Got The Feelin'  James Brown |
| 5/87 | I Got The Feelin' (It's Over) |
| | Gregory Abbott |
| F/80 | I Got The Feeling  Two Tons O' Fun |
| 33/79 | I Got The Hots For Ya  Double Exposure |
| 77/80 | I Got This Thing For Your Love |
| | Johnnie Taylor |
| 31/73 | I Got To Be Myself  Rance Allen Group |
| 49/66 | I Got To Handle It  Capitols |
| 30/77 | I Got To Have Your Love  Fantastic Four |
| 15/66 | I Got To Love Somebody's Baby |
| | Johnnie Taylor |
| 22/71 | I Got To Tell Somebody  Betty Everett |
| 21/74 | I Got To Try It One Time  Millie Jackson |
| 4/63 | I Got What I Wanted  Brook Benton |
| 42/78 | I Got What You Need  Bunny Sigler |
| | I Got You Babe |
| 19/65 | Sonny & Cher |
| 32/68 | Etta James |
| 1/65 | I Got You (I Feel Good)  James Brown |
| 1/72 | I Gotcha  Joe Tex |
| 35/64 | I Gotta Dance To Keep From Crying |
| | Miracles |
| 40/70 | I Gotta Get Away (From My Own Self) |
| | Ray Godfrey |
| 11/56 | I Gotta Get Myself A Woman  Drifters |
| 44/77 | I Gotta Keep Dancin'  Carrie |
| 43/70 | I Gotta Let You Go |
| | Martha Reeves & The Vandellas |
| 31/66 | I Guess I'll Always Love You |
| | Isley Brothers |
| 15/68 | I Guess I'll Have To Cry, Cry, Cry |
| | James Brown |
| 59/85 | (I Guess) It Must Be Love  Thelma Houston |
| 32/68 | I Guess That Don't Make Me A Loser |
| | Brothers Of Soul |
| 19/66 | I Had A Dream  Johnnie Taylor |
| 23/76 | I Had A Love  Ben E. King |
| 3/53 | I Had A Notion  Joe Morris |
| | I Had A Talk With My Man |
| 41/64 | Mitty Collier |
| 74/74 | Inez Foxx |
| 53/81 | Linda Clifford |
| 5/72 | I Had It All The Time  Tyrone Davis |
| 4/43 | I Had The Craziest Dream  Harry James |
| 36/64 | I Have A Boyfriend  Chiffons |
| 13/70 | I Have Learned To Do Without You |
| | Mavis Staples |
| 1/86 | I Have Learned To Respect The Power Of |
| | Love  Stephanie Mills |
| 7/51 | I Have News For You  Roy Milton |
| 2/65 | I Hear A Symphony  Supremes |
| 33/81 | I Hear Music In The Streets |
| | Unlimited Touch |
| | I Hear You Knocking |
| 2/55 | Smiley Lewis |
| 15/55 | Gale Storm |
| 23/80 | I Heard It In A Love Song |
| | McFadden & Whitehead |
| | I Heard It Through The Grapevine |
| 1/67 | Gladys Knight & The Pips |
| 1/68 | Marvin Gaye |
| 1/81 | Roger |
| 96/77 | I Heard The Voice Of Music Say  Sunbear |
| 8/43 | I Heard You Cried Last Night |
| | Dick Haymes |

| | |
|---|---|
| 68/78 | **I Honestly Love You** *Staples* |
| 37/76 | **I Hope We Get To Love In Time** |
| | *Marilyn McCoo & Billy Davis, Jr.* |
| 5/61 | **I Idolize You** *Ike & Tina Turner* |
| 79/86 | **I Jumped Out Of My Skin** *Kenny & Johnny* |
| 1/84 | **I Just Called To Say I Love You** |
| | *Stevie Wonder* |
| 6/79 | **I Just Can't Control Myself** |
| | *Nature's Divine* |
| 18/74 | **I Just Can't Get Out Of My Mind** |
| | *Four Tops* |
| 17/62 | **I Just Can't Help It** *Jackie Wilson* |
| 90/78 | **I Just Can't Leave Your Love Alone** |
| | *B.B. King* |
| 81/75 | **I Just Can't Say Goodbye** *Philly Devotions* |
| 79/80 | **I Just Can't Shake The Feeling** |
| | *Ava Cherry* |
| | **I Just Can't Stop Loving You** |
| 79/73 | *Cornelius Brothers & Sister Rose* |
| 1/87 | *Michael Jackson* |
| 36/83 | **I Just Can't Walk Away** *Four Tops* |
| 20/66 | **I Just Don't Know What To Do With** |
| | **Myself** *Dionne Warwick* |
| 47/83 | **I Just Got To Have You** *Lanier & Co.* |
| 5/83 | **I Just Gotta Have You (Lover Turn Me** |
| | **On)** *Kashif* |
| 58/79 | **I Just Keep Thinking About You Baby** |
| | *Tata Vega* |
| 9/81 | **I Just Love The Man** *Jones Girls* |
| 81/79 | **I Just Wanna Be Your Girl** *Chapter 8* |
| | **I Just Wanna Dance With You** |
| 35/79 | *Dramatics* |
| 19/80 | *Starpoint* |
| 94/77 | **I Just Wanna Do My Thing** *Edwin Starr* |
| 24/85 | **I Just Wanna Hang Around You** |
| | *George Benson* |
| 64/82 | **I Just Wanna Hold You** *Black Ice* |
| 75/82 | **I Just Wanna (Spend Some Time With** |
| | **You)** *Alton Edwards* |
| 21/78 | **I Just Wanna Stop** *Gino Vannelli* |
| 36/79 | **I Just Wanna Wanna** *Linda Clifford* |
| 3/79 | **I Just Want To Be** *Cameo* |
| 65/73 | **I Just Want To Be Loved** *Lee Charles* |
| 87/80 | **I Just Want To Be The One In Your Life** |
| | *Eddie Kendricks* |
| 38/72 | **I Just Want To Be There** *Independents* |
| 36/78 | **I Just Want To Be With You** *Floaters* |
| 19/77 | **I Just Want To Be Your Everything** |
| | *Andy Gibb* |
| 30/71 | **I Just Want To Celebrate** *Rare Earth* |
| 75/80 | **I Just Want To Fall In Love** *Spinners* |
| 49/81 | **I Just Want To Love You** *Stanley Clarke* |
| 15/82 | **I Just Want To Satisfy** *O'Jays* |
| 7/82 | **I Keep Forgettin' (Every Time You're** |
| | **Near)** *Michael McDonald* |
| 39/74 | **I Keep On Lovin' You** *Z.Z. Hill* |
| 7/76 | **I Kinda Miss You** *Manhattans* |
| | **I Kissed You** *...see: ('Til)* |
| 5/87 | **I Knew You Were Waiting (For Me)** |
| | *Aretha Franklin & George Michael* |
| | **I Know** |
| 2/46 | *Jubilaires with Andy Kirk* |
| 7/51 | *Ruth Brown* |
| 23/60 | *Spaniels* |
| 10/83 | *Philip Bailey* |
| 14/56 | **I Know I Was Wrong** *Barons* |
| 12/71 | **I Know I'm In Love** *Chee-Chee & Peppy* |
| | **(I Know) I'm Losing You** |
| 1/66 | *Temptations* |
| 20/70 | *Rare Earth* |
| 3/47 | **I Know What You're Putting Down** |
| | *Louis Jordan* |
| 69/75 | **I Know Where You're Coming From** |
| | *Loleatta Holloway* |

| | |
|---|---|
| 4/46 | **I Know Who Threw The Whiskey In The** |
| | **Well** *Bull Moose Jackson* |
| 23/65 | **I Know Why** *Springers* |
| 1/62 | **I Know (You Don't Love Me No More)** |
| | *Barbara George* |
| 32/82 | **I Know You Got Another** *Reddings* |
| | **I Know You Got Soul** |
| 30/71 | *Bobby Byrd* |
| 64/87 | *Eric B. & Rakim* |
| 69/86 | **I Know You Love Me** *Trinere* |
| 80/81 | **I Know You Will** *Logg* |
| 45/82 | **I Know Your Hot Spot** *Enchantment* |
| 63/79 | **I Leave You Stronger** *Sweet Thunder* |
| 48/69 | **I Left My Heart In San Francisco** |
| | *Bobby Womack* |
| 75/77 | **(I Like Being) Close To You** *Ronnie Dyson* |
| 5/47 | **I Like 'Em Fat Like That** *Louis Jordan* |
| 21/68 | **I Like Everything About You** |
| | *Jimmy Hughes* |
| 9/78 | **I Like Girls** *Fatback* |
| | **I Like It** |
| 14/48 | *Ivory Joe Hunter* |
| 25/81 | *Cameo* |
| 2/83 | *DeBarge* |
| | **I Like It Like That** |
| 2/61 | *Chris Kenner* |
| 27/64 | *Miracles* |
| 5/50 | **I Like My Baby's Pudding** *Wynonie Harris* |
| 35/77 | **I Like The Feeling** *Luther Ingram* |
| 30/86 | **I Like The Way You Dance** *9.9* |
| 91/76 | **I Like To Dance** *Shirley & Company* |
| 4/77 | **I Like To Do It** *KC & The Sunshine Band* |
| 6/74 | **I Like To Live The Love** *B.B. King* |
| 80/74 | **I Like To Party** *Alpaca Phase III* |
| 40/71 | **I Like What You Give** *Nolan* |
| 9/69 | **I Like What You're Doing (To Me)** |
| | *Carla Thomas* |
| 65/86 | **I Like You** *Phyllis Nelson* |
| 11/70 | **I Like Your Lovin' (Do You Like Mine)** |
| | *Chi-Lites* |
| F/70 | **I Like Your Style** *Originals* |
| 9/71 | **I Likes To Do It** *People's Choice* |
| 93/78 | **I Live Across The Street** *Sho-Nuff* |
| 4/87 | **I Live For Your Love** *Natalie Cole* |
| 61/80 | **I Love It** *Trussel* |
| 46/68 | **(I Love) Lucy** *Albert King* |
| 1/75 | **I Love Music** *O'Jays* |
| | **I Love My Baby** |
| 4/50 | *Larry Darnell* |
| 40/69 | *Archie Bell & The Drells* |
| 49/78 | **I Love My Music** *Wild Cherry* |
| 31/78 | **I Love The Nightlife (Disco 'Round)** |
| | *Alicia Bridges* |
| | **I Love The Way You Love** |
| 2/60 | *Marv Johnson* |
| 44/71 | *Betty Wright* |
| 95/78 | *Ginie Lynn* |
| 39/80 | *Peabo Bryson* |
| 53/79 | **I Love To Sing The Songs I Sing** |
| | *Barry White* |
| | **I Love You** |
| 30/69 | *Eddie Holman* |
| 10/70 | *Otis Leaville* |
| 28/78 | *Donna Summer* |
| 28/79 | *New Birth* |
| 79/81 | **I Love You Anyway** *Dee Dee Sharp Gamble* |
| 8/87 | **I Love You Babe** *Babyface* |
| | **I Love You Baby** |
| 13/56 | *Jimmy Reed* |
| 35/65 | *Dottie & Ray* |
| 10/71 | **I Love You For All Seasons** *Fuzz* |
| | **(I Love You) For Sentimental Reasons** |
| 3/46 | *Nat King Cole* |
| 15/58 | *Sam Cooke* |
| 70/76 | *James Brown* |

| | |
|---|---|
| 29/58 | **I Love You Honey**  *John Lee Hooker* |
| 12/68 | **I Love You Madly**  *Fantastic Four* |
| | **I Love You More** |
| 41/67 | *Lee Williams & The Cymbals* |
| 14/81 | *Rene & Angela* |
| 30/67 | **I Love You More Than Words Can Say** |
| | *Otis Redding* |
| 20/72 | **I Love You More Than You'll Ever Know** |
| | *Donny Hathaway* |
| 6/50 | **I Love You, My Darlin'**  *Joe Fritz* |
| 6/66 | **I Love You 1000 Times**  *Platters* |
| | **I Love You So** |
| 6/49 | *Pee Wee Crayton* |
| 14/58 | *Chantels* |
| 8/49 | **I Love You So Much It Hurts** |
| | *Mills Brothers* |
| 40/72 | **I Love You - Stop**  *Stairsteps* |
| | **I Love You, Yes I Do** |
| 1/48 | *Bull Moose Jackson* |
| 10/61 | *Bull Moose Jackson* |
| 77/82 | **I Love Your Love**  *Donald Byrd* |
| 9/68 | **I Loved And I Lost**  *Impressions* |
| 2/59 | **I Loves You, Porgy**  *Nina Simone* |
| 59/76 | **I Luv Myself Better Than I Luv Myself** |
| | *Bill Cosby* |
| 32/69 | **I Made A Mistake Because It's Only You** |
| | *Marva Whitney* |
| 33/73 | **I May Not Be What You Want**  *Mel & Tim* |
| 46/79 | **I Might As Well Forget About Loving** |
| | **You**  *Kinsman Dazz* |
| | **I Miss You** |
| 7/72 | *Harold Melvin & The Blue Notes* |
| 8/74 | *Dells* |
| 11/85 | *Klymaxx* |
| 22/73 | **I Miss You Baby**  *Millie Jackson* |
| 39/66 | **I Miss You, Baby (How I Miss You)** |
| | *Marv Johnson* |
| 23/65 | **I Miss You So** |
| | *Little Anthony & The Imperials* |
| 62/79 | **I Need Action**  *Touch Of Class* |
| 14/70 | **I Need Help (I Can't Do It Alone)** |
| | *Bobby Byrd* |
| 40/76 | **I Need It**  *Johnny 'Guitar' Watson* |
| 55/74 | **I Need It Just As Bad As You**  *Laura Lee* |
| | **I Need Love** |
| 25/66 | *Barbara Mason* |
| 34/77 | *Persuaders* |
| 77/80 | *Shadow* |
| 68/86 | *Nona Hendryx* |
| 1/87 | *L.L. Cool J* |
| 50/88 | **I Need Money Bad**  *John Whitehead* |
| 55/88 | **I Need Somebody**  *Kechia Jenkins* |
| 50/77 | **I Need Somebody To Love Me** |
| | *Shirley Brown* |
| 54/74 | **I Need Someone**  *Linda Perry* |
| 30/71 | **I Need Someone (To Love Me)**  *Z.Z. Hill* |
| | **I Need You** |
| 22/65 | *Chuck Jackson* |
| 26/65 | *Impressions* |
| 28/71 | *Friends Of Distinction* |
| 13/83 | *Pointer Sisters* |
| 30/86 | *Maurice White* |
| 47/71 | **I Need You Baby**  *Jesse James* |
| 80/74 | **I Need You More**  *Sarah Vaughan* |
| 1/50 | **I Need You So**  *Ivory Joe Hunter* |
| 5/76 | **I Need You, You Need Me**  *Joe Simon* |
| | **I Need Your Lovin'** |
| 14/59 | *Roy Hamilton* |
| 4/62 | *Don Gardner & Dee Dee Ford* |
| 9/80 | *Teena Marie* |
| 52/87 | *Human League* |
| 84/87 | *Rue* |
| 34/83 | **I Never Forgot Your Eyes**  *Larry Graham* |
| 17/61 | **I Never Knew**  *Clyde McPhatter* |

| | |
|---|---|
| 1/67 | **I Never Loved A Man (The Way I Loved** |
| | **You)**  *Aretha Franklin* |
| 57/81 | **I Once Had Your Love (And I Can't Let** |
| | **Go)**  *Isley Brothers* |
| 86/75 | **I Only Feel This Way When I'm With** |
| | **You**  *Jimmy Briscoe & The Little Beavers* |
| 35/73 | **I Only Get This Feeling**  *Chuck Jackson* |
| | **I Only Have Eyes For You** |
| 3/59 | *Flamingos* |
| 20/72 | *Jerry Butler* |
| 63/79 | *Heaven & Earth* |
| 15/75 | **I Only Have Love**  *Syl Johnson* |
| | **I Only Know** |
| 3/50 | *Dinah Washington* |
| 10/51 | *Dinah Washington* |
| 27/72 | **I Only Meant To Wet My Feet**  *Whispers* |
| 88/77 | **I Only Wanted To Love You**  *Sass* |
| 63/83 | **I Owe It To Me**  *Dunn & Bruce Street* |
| 21/84 | **I Owe It To Myself**  *Prime Time* |
| 48/73 | **I Owe You Love**  *Brighter Side Of Darkness* |
| 60/80 | **I Owe You One**  *Shalamar* |
| | **I Pity The Fool** |
| 1/61 | *Bobby Bland* |
| 18/71 | *Ann Peebles* |
| 37/71 | **I Play Dirty**  *Little Milton* |
| 3/53 | **I Played The Fool**  *Clovers* |
| 37/80 | **I Pledge My Love**  *Peaches & Herb* |
| 42/67 | **I Prefer You**  *Etta James* |
| 45/84 | **I Promise (I Do Love You)**  *Dreamboy* |
| | **I Promise To Remember** |
| 10/56 | *Frankie Lymon & The Teenagers* |
| 80/87 | *Process & The Doo Rags* |
| 36/68 | **I Promise To Wait My Love** |
| | *Martha Reeves & The Vandellas* |
| 23/65 | **I Put A Spell On You**  *Nina Simone* |
| 68/88 | **I Put My Money Where My Mouth Is** |
| | *Rose Brothers* |
| 4/50 | **I Quit My Pretty Mama**  *Ivory Joe Hunter* |
| 9/44 | **I Realize Now**  *Nat King Cole* |
| 6/87 | **I Really Didn't Mean It**  *Luther Vandross* |
| 3/82 | **I Really Don't Need No Light** |
| | *Jeffrey Osborne* |
| 56/74 | **I Really Got It Bad For You**  *Persuasions* |
| | **I Really Love You** |
| 15/61 | *Stereos* |
| 37/66 | *Dee Dee Sharp* |
| 43/69 | *Ambassadors* |
| 47/81 | *Heaven & Earth* |
| 81/84 | *Harold Melvin & The Blue Notes* |
| 82/85 | **I Really Want You**  *Smoke City* |
| 47/76 | **I Refuse To Lose**  *James Brown* |
| 12/63 | **I Saw Linda Yesterday**  *Dickey Lee* |
| | **I Say A Little Prayer** |
| 8/67 | *Dionne Warwick* |
| 3/68 | *Aretha Franklin* |
| 65/77 | *Isaac Hayes & Dionne Warwick (medley)* |
| | **I Second That Emotion** |
| 1/68 | *Smokey Robinson & The Miracles* |
| 74/78 | *Thelma Jones* |
| 40/70 | **I Shall Be Released**  *Freddie Scott* |
| 47/77 | **I Sho Like Groovin' With Ya** |
| | *Johnny Bristol* |
| 33/74 | **I Shot The Sheriff**  *Eric Clapton* |
| 25/80 | **I Should Be Your Lover** |
| | *Harold Melvin & The Blue Notes* |
| 64/64 | **I Should Care**  *Gloria Lynne* |
| 4/80 | **I Shoulda Loved Ya**  *Narada Michael Walden* |
| 13/62 | **I Sold My Heart To The Junkman** |
| | *Blue-Belles* |
| 51/82 | **I Specialize In Love**  *Sharon Brown* |
| | **I Stand Accused** |
| 61/64 | *Jerry Butler* |
| 41/67 | *Inez & Charlie Foxx* |
| 48/67 | *Glories* |
| 23/70 | *Isaac Hayes* |

**I Want To Thank You**
47/68     *Raeletts*
37/82     *Alicia Myers*
1/59     **I Want To Walk You Home**   *Fats Domino*
**I Want You**
1/76     *Marvin Gaye*
41/79     *Wilson Pickett*
35/81     *Booker T.*
46/81     *Narada Michael Walden*
79/81     *Barry White & Glodean White*
81/86     *Tamiko Jones*
91/79     **I Want You Around Me**   *George McCrae*
1/70     **I Want You Back**   *Jackson 5*
67/81     **I Want You Closer**   *Starpoint*
23/80     **I Want You For Myself**   *George Duke*
49/79     **I Want You Here With Me**   *O'Jays*
3/56     **I Want You, I Need You, I Love You**
       *Elvis Presley*
**I Want You So Bad**
20/59     *James Brown*
34/69     *B.B. King*
50/70     **I Want You To Be My Baby**   *Jive Five*
98/65     **I Want You To Be My Boy**   *Exciters*
3/56     **I Want You To Be My Girl**
       *Frankie Lymon & The Teenagers*
17/65     **I Want You To Have Everything**
       *Lee Rogers*
56/88     **I Want Your Body**   *Madame X*
5/79     **I Want Your Love**   *Chic*
76/85     **I Want Your Lovin' (Just A Little Bit)**
       *Curtis Hairston*
43/87     **I Want Your Sex**   *George Michael*
7/75     **I Want'a Do Something Freaky To You**
       *Leon Haywood*
43/77     **I Wantcha Baby**   *Arthur Prysock*
41/66     **I Was A Born Loser**   *Bobby Lee*
6/73     **I Was Checkin' Out She Was Checkin' In**
       *Don Covay*
**I Was Made To Love Her**
1/67     *Stevie Wonder*
49/68     *King Curtis & The Kingpins*
79/82     **I Was Tired Of Being Alone (Glad I Got**
       **Cha)**   *Patrice Rushen*
46/74     **I Wash My Hands Of The Whole Damn**
       **Deal**   *New Birth*
**I (Who Have Nothing)**
16/63     *Ben E. King*
27/79     *Sylvester*
**I Will**
39/74     *Ruby Winters*
97/78     *Ruby Winters*
21/81     **I Will Fight**   *Gladys Knight & The Pips*
1/63     **I Will Follow Him**   *Little Peggy March*
29/63     **I Will Never Turn My Back On You**
       *Chuck Jackson*
4/79     **I Will Survive**   *Gloria Gaynor*
2/51     **I Will Wait**   *Four Buddies*
**I Wish**
4/45     *Mills Brothers*
1/77     *Stevie Wonder*
74/88     *Isley Brothers*
2/85     **I Wish He Didn't Trust Me So Much**
       *Bobby Womack*
32/68     **I Wish I Knew (How It Would Feel To Be**
       **Free)**   *Solomon Burke*
13/49     **I Wish I Was In Walla Walla**   *Nellie Lutcher*
11/74     **I Wish It Was Me**   *Tyrone Davis*
11/74     **I Wish It Was Me You Loved**   *Dells*
**I Wish It Would Rain**
1/68     *Temptations*
15/68     *Gladys Knight & The Pips*
28/88     **I Wish You Belonged To Me**   *Lou Rawls*
**I Wish You Love**
28/64     *Gloria Lynne*
92/76     *David T. Walker*

**I Wish You Well**
54/76     *Bill Withers*
61/78     *Maze Featuring Frankie Beverly*
87/86     **I Wish You Were Here**   *Tease*
49/84     **I Wish You Would**   *Jocelyn Brown*
41/70     **I Won't Cry**   *Johnny Adams*
6/51     **I Won't Cry Anymore**   *Dinah Washington*
42/68     **I Won't Do Anything**   *Lezli Valentine*
18/75     **I Won't Last A Day Without You (medley)**
       *Al Wilson*
F/73     **I Won't Leave You Hanging**
       *Jerry Washington*
42/73     **I Won't Let The Chump Break Your**
       **Heart**   *Carl Carlton*
**I Wonder**
1/45     *Private Cecil Gant*
1/45     *Roosevelt Sykes*
3/45     *Louis Armstrong*
6/45     *Warren Evans*
55/84     *Rodney Saulsberry*
6/85     **I Wonder If I Take You Home**
       *Lisa Lisa & Cult Jam*
23/63     **I Wonder What She's Doing Tonight**
       *Barry & The Tamerlanes*
3/87     **I Wonder Who She's Seeing Now**
       *Temptations*
**I Worship The Ground You Walk On**
25/66     *Jimmy Hughes*
34/68     *Jackie Montre-El*
11/85     **I Would Die 4 U**   *Prince*
17/74     **I Wouldn't Give You Up**
       *Ecstasy, Passion & Pain*
6/86     **I Wouldn't Lie**   *Yarbrough & Peoples*
3/75     **I Wouldn't Treat A Dog (The Way You Treated**
       **Me)**   *Bobby Bland*
79/79     **I (You) Can Dance All By My (Your) Self**
       *Dalton & Dubarri*
8/52     **I'd Be Satisfied**   *Billy Ward & His Dominoes*
37/74     **(I'd Know You) Anywhere**
       *Ashford & Simpson*
9/69     **I'd Rather Be An Old Man's Sweetheart**
       *Candi Staton*
33/74     **I'd Rather Be (Blind, Crippled & Crazy)**
       *O.V. Wright*
37/86     **I'd Rather Be Myself**   *Ebo*
25/76     **I'd Rather Be With You**
       *Bootsy's Rubber Band*
8/51     **I'd Rather Drink Muddy Water**
       *Grant Jones*
89/78     **I'd Rather Hurt Myself (Than To Hurt**
       **You)**   *Randy Brown*
48/71     **I'd Rather Stay A Child**
       *Richie's Room 222 Gang*
7/87     **I'd Still Say Yes**   *Klymaxx*
**I'll Always Be In Love With You**
3/49     *X-Rays*
8/49     *Ray-O-Vacs*
7/51     *Charles Brown*
11/67     **I'll Always Have Faith In You**
       *Carla Thomas*
6/73     **I'll Always Love My Mama**   *Intruders*
**I'll Always Love You**
60/64     *Brenda Holloway*
8/65     *Spinners*
21/88     *Taylor Dayne*
32/86     **I'll Be All You Ever Need**   *Trinere*
**I'll Be Around**
1/72     *Spinners*
96/80     *War*
81/84     *Terri Wells*
48/75     **I'll Be Comin Back**   *Greg Perry*
1/65     **I'll Be Doggone**   *Marvin Gaye*
8/56     **I'll Be Forever Loving You**   *El Dorados*
4/85     **I'll Be Good**   *Rene & Angela*
1/76     **I'll Be Good To You**   *Brothers Johnson*

3/62 **I'm Blue (The Gong-Gong Song)** *Ikettes*
22/80 **I'm Caught Up (In A One Night Love Affair)** *Inner Life*
20/86 **I'm Chillin'** *Kurtis Blow*
9/61 **I'm Comin' On Back To You** *Jackie Wilson*
**I'm Coming Home**
23/59    *Marv Johnson*
92/73    *Johnny Mathis*
3/74    *Spinners*
90/77    *Stylistics*
54/78 **I'm Coming Home Again** *Gladys Knight*
6/80 **I'm Coming Out** *Diana Ross*
43/80 **I'm Dancing For Your Love** *Rufus & Chaka Khan*
14/73 **I'm Doin' Fine Now** *New York City*
95/63 **I'm Down To My Last Heartbreak** *Wilson Pickett*
1/78 **I'm Every Woman** *Chaka Khan*
24/77 **I'm Falling In Love (medley)** *Hodges, James & Smith*
77/74 **I'm Falling In Love (I Feel Good All Over)** *Fantastic Four*
25/74 **I'm Falling In Love With You** *Little Anthony & The Imperials*
2/86 **I'm For Real** *Howard Hewett*
15/83 **I'm Freaky** *O'Bryan*
23/68 **I'm Gett'n Long Alright** *Raelettes*
F/72 **I'm Gettin' Tired Baby** *Betty Wright*
16/71 **I'm Girl Scoutin'** *Intruders*
66/84 **I'm Givin' All My Love** *Terri Wells*
75/83 **I'm Giving You All Of My Love** *Brothers Johnson*
9/53 **I'm Glad** *Mitzi Mars* *(also see: I'm Mad)*
32/66 **I'm Glad I Waited** *Players*
88/73 **I'm Glad To Do It** *Little Royal & The Swingmasters*
F/76 **I'm Glad You Walked Into My Life** *Four Tops*
18/62 **I'm Going Back To School** *Dee Clark*
22/75 **(I'm Going By) The Stars In Your Eyes** *Ron Banks & The Dramatics*
10/77 **I'm Going Down** *Rose Royce*
5/50 **I'm Going To Have Myself A Ball** *Tiny Bradshaw*
2/53 **I'm Gone** *Shirley & Lee*
22/59 **I'm Gonna Be A Wheel Some Day** *Fats Domino*
9/51 **I'm Gonna Dig Myself A Hole** *Arthur 'Big Boy' Crudup*
46/69 **I'm Gonna Do All I Can (To Do Right By My Man)** *Ike & Tina Turner*
26/68 **I'm Gonna Do What They Do To Me** *B.B. King*
30/70 **I'm Gonna Forget About You** *Bobby Womack*
1/59 **I'm Gonna Get Married** *Lloyd Price*
5/58 **I'm Gonna Get My Baby** *Jimmy Reed*
80/77 **I'm Gonna Have To Tell Her** *Banks & Hampton*
15/58 **(I'm Gonna) Jump For Joy** *Joe Turner*
3/42 **I'm Gonna Leave You At The Outskirts Of Town** *Louis Jordan*
25/76 **I'm Gonna Let My Heart Do The Walking** *Supremes*
94/78 **I'm Gonna Let Ya** *Nancy Wilson*
1/73 **I'm Gonna Love You Just A Little More Baby** *Barry White*
**I'm Gonna Make You Love Me**
13/67    *Dee Dee Warwick*
32/68    *Madeline Bell*
2/69    *Supremes/Temptations*
54/78 **I'm Gonna Make You My Wife** *Whispers*
9/66 **I'm Gonna Miss You** *Artistics*

25/61 **I'm Gonna Move To The Outskirts Of Town** *Ray Charles*
60/78 **I'm Gonna Need This Love** *N'cole*
3/52 **I'm Gonna Play The Honky Tonks** *Marie Adams*
44/73 **I'm Gonna Prove It** *Softones*
9/57 **I'm Gonna Sit Right Down & Write Myself A Letter** *Billy Williams*
**I'm Gonna Tear Your Playhouse Down**
31/73    *Ann Peebles*
60/85    *Paul Young*
15/62 **I'm Hanging Up My Heart For You** *Solomon Burke*
21/77 **I'm Here Again** *Thelma Houston*
79/77 **I'm His Wife (You're Just A Friend)** *Ann Sexton*
56/86 **I'm Hungry For Your Love** *Janice Christie*
23/68 **I'm In A Different World** *Four Tops*
65/75 **I'm In Heaven** *Touch Of Class*
**I'm In Love**
4/67    *Wilson Pickett*
1/74    *Aretha Franklin*
1/81    *Evelyn King*
2/87    *Lillo Thomas*
67/88    *Pointer Sisters*
**I'm In Love Again**
1/56    *Fats Domino*
84/87    *Tyrone Davis*
5/78 **I'm In Love (And I Love The Feeling)** *Rose Royce*
88/78 **I'm In Love With Love** *Kathy Barnes*
**I'm In Love With You**
45/80    *Ren Woods*
62/84    *Koko-Pop*
1/51 **I'm In The Mood** *John Lee Hooker*
72/79 **I'm In Too Deep** *James Bradley*
84/74 **I'm Into Something I Can't Shake** *Paul Kelly*
13/70 **I'm Just A Prisoner (Of Your Good Lovin')** *Candi Staton*
53/84 **(I'm Just A) Sucker For A Pretty Face** *Wes Phillips*
24/69 **I'm Just An Average Guy** *Masqueraders*
62/73 **(I'm) Just Being Myself** *Dionne Warwick*
14/78 **(I'm Just Thinking About) Cooling Out** *Jerry Butler*
29/81 **I'm Just Too Shy** *Jermaine Jackson*
6/54 **I'm Just Your Fool** *Buddy Johnson*
12/85 **I'm Leaving Baby** *Con Funk Shun*
6/63 **I'm Leaving It Up To You** *Dale & Grace*
8/69 **I'm Livin' In Shame** *Supremes*
**I'm Losing You** *..see: (I Know)*
**I'm Lost**
1/44    *Benny Carter*
4/44    *Nat King Cole*
13/56 **I'm Lost Without You Tonight** *Dinah Washington*
1/53 **I'm Mad** *Willie Mabon & his Combo* *(also see: I'm Glad)*
2/45 **I'm Making Believe** *Ella Fitzgerald & Ink Spots*
11/59 **I'm Movin' On** *Ray Charles*
30/76 **I'm Needing You, Wanting You** *Chuck Jackson*
43/73 **I'm Never Gonna Be Alone Anymore** *Cornelius Brothers & Sister Rose*
64/82 **I'm Never Gonna Say Goodbye** *Billy Preston*
13/59 **I'm Not Ashamed** *Bobby 'Blue' Bland*
76/79 **I'm Not Dreaming** *Zulema (and friend)*
7/86 **I'm Not Gonna Let** *Colonel Abrams*
26/87 **I'm Not Gonna Let You Go** *Melba Moore*
62/76 **I'm Not In Love** *Dee Dee Sharp Gamble*
12/70 **I'm Not My Brothers Keeper** *Flaming Ember*

| | |
|---|---|
| 9/87 | **I'm Not Perfect (But I'm Perfect For You)**  *Grace Jones* |
| 80/84 | **I'm Not That Bad A Man To Love**  *Bronner Brothers* |
| 78/84 | **I'm Not That Tough**  *Ashford & Simpson* |
| 52/85 | **I'm Not The Same Girl**  *Stacy Lattisaw* |
| | **I'm On Fire** |
| 20/75 | *Jim Gilstrap* |
| 73/81 | *Champaign* |
| 15/64 | **I'm On The Outside (Looking In)**  *Little Anthony & The Imperials* |
| 20/84 | **I'm On Your Side**  *Angela Bofill* |
| 27/83 | **I'm Out To Catch**  *Leon Haywood* |
| 24/65 | **I'm Over You**  *Jan Bradley* |
| 25/77 | **I'm Qualified To Satisfy You**  *Barry White* |
| | **I'm Ready** |
| 4/54 | *Muddy Waters* |
| 7/59 | *Fats Domino* |
| 21/81 | *Kano* |
| 2/66 | **I'm Ready For Love**  *Martha & The Vandellas* |
| 74/84 | **I'm Ready (If You're Ready)**  *Gap Band* |
| 2/88 | **I'm Real**  *James Brown* |
| 59/78 | **I'm Really Gonna Miss You**  *Billy Preston* |
| 72/87 | **I'm Searchin'**  *Debbie Deb* |
| 6/54 | **I'm Slippin' In**  *Spiders* |
| 46/82 | **I'm So Excited**  *Pointer Sisters* |
| | **I'm So Glad** |
| 35/71 | *Fuzz* |
| 43/76 | *Jr. Walker & The All Stars* |
| 18/70 | **I'm So Glad I Fell For You**  *David Ruffin* |
| 67/81 | **I'm So Glad I'm Standing Here Today**  *Crusaders/Joe Cocker* |
| 96/80 | **I'm So Glad That I'm A Woman**  *Love Unlimited* |
| 49/88 | **I'm So Happy**  *Walter Beasley* |
| 82/80 | **I'm So Hot**  *Denise LaSalle* |
| 2/79 | **I'm So Into You**  *Michael Zager's Moon Band* |
| 43/69 | **I'm So Lost**  *Moments* |
| | **I'm So Proud** |
| 14/64 | *Impressions* |
| 13/71 | *Main Ingredient* |
| 28/83 | *Deniece Williams* |
| 55/83 | *Johnnie Taylor* |
| 12/65 | **I'm So Thankful**  *Ikettes* |
| 36/72 | **I'm So Tired**  *Bobby Bland* |
| 26/61 | **I'm So Young**  *Students* |
| | **I'm Sorry** |
| 15/57 | *Platters* |
| 19/58 | *Kenny Martin* |
| 17/59 | *Bo Diddley* |
| 4/60 | *Brenda Lee* |
| 15/68 | *Delfonics* |
| 18/71 | *Bobby Bland* |
| 26/85 | *Will King* |
| 9/57 | **I'm Stickin' With You**  *Jimmy Bowen* |
| 70/85 | **I'm Still**  *Levert* |
| 27/69 | **I'm Still A Struggling Man**  *Edwin Starr* |
| 26/71 | **I'm Still Here**  *Notations* |
| 1/72 | **I'm Still In Love With You**  *Al Green* |
| | **I'm Still Waiting** |
| 36/66 | *Patti LaBelle & The Blue Belles* |
| 40/71 | *Diana Ross* |
| 73/87 | *Givens Family* |
| 4/72 | **I'm Stone In Love With You**  *Stylistics* |
| 64/80 | **I'm Talkin' 'Bout You**  *A Taste Of Honey* |
| 15/74 | **I'm The Midnight Special**  *Clarence Carter* |
| 24/82 | **I'm The One**  *Roberta Flack* |
| | **I'm The One You Need**  ..see: (Come 'Round Here) |
| | **I'm Through Trying To Prove My Love To You** |
| 80/73 | *Bobby Womack* |
| 58/75 | *Millie Jackson* |
| 4/45 | **I'm Tired**  *Cecil Gant* |

| | |
|---|---|
| 8/66 | **I'm Too Far Gone (To Turn Around)**  *Bobby Bland* |
| 5/61 | **I'm Tore Down**  *Freddy King* |
| 8/48 | **I'm Waiting For Your Call**  *T-Bone Walker* |
| 2/51 | **I'm Waiting Just For You**  *Lucky Millinder* |
| | **I'm Walkin'** |
| 1/57 | *Fats Domino* |
| 10/57 | *Ricky Nelson* |
| 29/66 | **I'm Walking Out On You**  *Ruben Wright* |
| F/74 | **I'm Weak For You**  *Harold Melvin & The Blue Notes* |
| 4/67 | **I'm Wondering**  *Stevie Wonder* |
| 3/77 | **I'm Your Boogie Man**  *KC & The Sunshine Band* |
| 37/84 | **I'm Your Candy Girl**  *Clockwork* |
| 79/76 | **(I'm Your) Friendly Neighborhood Freak**  *Calvin Arnold* |
| | **I'm Your Hoochie Cooche Man** |
| 3/54 | *Muddy Waters* |
| 49/66 | *Jimmy Smith* |
| 55/86 | **I'm Your Man**  *Wham!* |
| 20/63 | **I'm Your Part Time Love**  *Mitty Collier* |
| 5/66 | **I'm Your Puppet**  *James & Bobby Purify* |
| 83/85 | **I'm Your Superman**  *Jan Holmes* |
| 68/74 | **I'm Yours**  *Syl Johnson* |
| 4/50 | **I'm Yours To Keep**  *Herb Fisher Trio* |
| 47/71 | **I'm Yours (Use Me Anyway You Wanna)**  *Ike & Tina Turner* |
| 57/75 | **I've Always Had You**  *Benny Troy* |
| 7/50 | **I've Been A Fool**  *Shadows* |
| 10/88 | **I've Been A Fool For You**  *Miles Jaye* |
| 28/73 | **I've Been A Winner, I've Been A Loser**  *Smith Connection* |
| 19/59 | **I've Been Around**  *Fats Domino* |
| 13/74 | **I've Been Born Again**  *Johnnie Taylor* |
| 41/70 | **I've Been Good To You**  *Young Vandals* |
| 8/72 | **I've Been Lonely For So Long**  *Frederick Knight* |
| 33/67 | **I've Been Lonely Too Long**  *Young Rascals* |
| 10/51 | **I've Been Lost**  *Little Willie Littlefield* |
| | **I've Been Loving You Too Long (To Stop Now)** |
| 2/65 | *Otis Redding* |
| 23/69 | *Ike & Tina Turner* |
| | **I've Been Missing You** |
| 56/78 | *Archie Bell & The Drells* |
| 74/84 | *Kenny G* |
| 73/80 | **I've Been Pushed Aside**  *McFadden & Whitehead* |
| 72/83 | **I've Been Robbed**  *Three Million* |
| 62/74 | **I've Been Searching**  *O.V. Wright* |
| 35/65 | **I've Been Trying**  *Impressions* |
| 50/68 | **I've Been Turned On**  *Jo Armstead* |
| | **I've Been Watching You** |
| 36/81 | *Midnight Star* |
| 43/87 | *Chico DeBarge* |
| 18/84 | **I've Been Watching You (Jamie's Girl)**  *Randy Hall* |
| 46/68 | **I've Come A Long Way**  *Wilson Pickett* |
| 36/69 | **I've Fallen In Love**  *Carla Thomas* |
| 20/71 | **I've Found Someone Of My Own**  *Free Movement* |
| 45/69 | **I've Got A Feeling**  *Ollie & The Nightingales* |
| 3/76 | **I've Got A Feeling (We'll Be Seeing Each Other Again)**  *Al Wilson* |
| 2/46 | **I've Got A Right To Cry**  *Erskine Hawkins* |
| | **I've Got A Woman** |
| 1/55 | *Ray Charles* |
| 5/62 | *Jimmy McGriff* |
| 6/68 | **I've Got Dreams To Remember**  *Otis Redding* |
| 41/80 | **I've Got Faith In You**  *Cheryl Lynn* |
| 19/68 | **I've Got Love For My Baby**  *Young Hearts* |
| 1/77 | **I've Got Love On My Mind**  *Natalie Cole* |
| 7/54 | **I've Got My Eyes On You**  *Clovers* |
| 58/80 | **I've Got My Second Wind**  *Al Johnson* |

| | |
|---|---|
| 8/61 | **I've Got News For You**  *Ray Charles* |
| 67/64 | **I've Got No Time To Lose**  *Carla Thomas* |
| 33/64 | **I've Got Sand In My Shoes**  *Drifters* |
| 5/73 | **I've Got So Much To Give**  *Barry White* |
| 25/61 | **(I've Got) Spring Fever**  *Little Willie John* |
| 72/82 | **I've Got The Dance Fever**  *Bohannon* |
| 26/79 | **I've Got The Next Dance**  *Deniece Williams* |
| 89/64 | **I've Got The Skill**  *Jackie Ross* |
| 48/77 | **I've Got The Spirit**  *Billy Preston* |
| 32/74 | **I've Got To Break Away**  *Baby Washington* |
| 87/77 | **I've Got To Dance (To Keep From Crying)**  *Destination* |
| 20/66 | **I've Got To Do A Little Bit Better**  *Joe Tex* |
| | **I've Got To Go On Without You** |
| 28/66 | *Van Dykes* |
| 54/73 | *William Bell* |
| 23/68 | **I've Got To Have You**  *Fantastic Four* |
| 50/69 | **I've Got To Have Your Love**  *Eddie Floyd* |
| 42/81 | **I've Got To Learn To Say No!**  *Richard 'Dimples' Fields* |
| 31/74 | **I've Got To See You Tonight**  *Timmy Thomas* |
| 1/74 | **I've Got To Use My Imagination**  *Gladys Knight & The Pips* |
| 19/59 | **I've Had It**  *Bell Notes* |
| 1/43 | **I've Heard That Song Before**  *Harry James* |
| 6/80 | **I've Just Begun To Love You**  *Dynasty* |
| 3/44 | **I've Learned A Lesson I'll Never Forget**  *Five Red Caps* |
| 11/69 | **I've Lost Everything I've Ever Loved**  *David Ruffin* |
| 35/67 | **I've Lost You**  *Jackie Wilson* |
| 5/80 | **I've Loved You For A Long Time (medley)**  *Spinners* |
| 50/68 | **I've Made A Reservation (In My Life For You)**  *Neal Kimble* |
| 8/83 | **I've Made Love To You A Thousand Times**  *Smokey Robinson* |
| 47/77 | **I've Never Been To Me**  *Nancy Wilson* |
| | **I've Never Found A Girl (Man) (To Love Me Like You Do)** |
| 2/68 | *Eddie Floyd* |
| 17/72 | *Esther Phillips* |
| 10/67 | **I've Passed This Way Before**  *Jimmy Ruffin* |
| 22/61 | **I've Told Every Little Star**  *Linda Scott* |
| 11/84 | **Ice Cream Castles**  *Time* |
| 17/69 | **Ice Cream Song**  *Dynamics* |
| 37/78 | **If Ever I See You Again**  *Roberta Flack* |
| 6/84 | **If Ever You're In My Arms Again**  *Peabo Bryson* |
| 21/70 | **If He Can, You Can**  *Isley Brothers* |
| 60/76 | **If He Hadn't Slipped And Got Caught**  *Bobby Patterson* |
| | **If I Can't Have You** |
| 6/60 | *Etta & Harvey* |
| 30/72 | *Donnie Elbert* |
| 60/78 | *Yvonne Elliman* |
| 72/78 | **If I Can't Stop You**  *C.B. Overton* |
| 10/43 | **If I Cared A Little Bit Less**  *Ink Spots* |
| 2/68 | **If I Could Build My World Around You**  *Marvin Gaye & Tammi Terrell* |
| F/74 | **If I Could Love You Forever**  *Roy 'C'* |
| 29/73 | **If I Could Only Be Sure**  *Nolan Porter* |
| 73/73 | **If I Could Reach Out**  *Otis Clay* |
| 27/72 | **If I Could See The Light**  *8th Day* |
| | **If I Didn't Care** |
| 29/59 | *Connie Francis* |
| 7/70 | *Moments* |
| | **If I Didn't Love You** |
| 18/65 | *Chuck Jackson* |
| 30/68 | *Profiles* |
| 74/76 | **If I Didn't Mean You Well**  *Bill Withers* |
| 31/81 | **If I Don't Love You**  *Randy Brown* |
| 23/76 | **If I Ever Do Wrong**  *Betty Wright* |

| | |
|---|---|
| | **If I Ever Lose This Heaven** |
| 71/74 | *Quincy Jones* |
| 25/75 | *Average White Band* |
| 83/83 | **If I Had A Chance**  *Walter Jackson* |
| 87/77 | **If I Had A Girl**  *Chi-Lites* |
| 12/63 | **If I Had A Hammer**  *Trini Lopez* |
| 68/78 | **If I Had My Way**  *Walter Jackson* |
| 56/82 | **If I Had My Wish Tonight**  *David Lasley* |
| 43/82 | **If I Had The Chance**  *Chuck Cissel & Marva King* |
| 32/70 | **If I Lose Your Love**  *Detroit Emeralds* |
| 4/54 | **If I Loved You**  *Roy Hamilton* |
| 16/86 | **If I Ruled The World**  *Kurtis Blow* |
| 13/87 | **If I Say Yes**  *Five Star* |
| 12/87 | **If I Was Your Girlfriend**  *Prince* |
| 17/68 | **If I Were A Carpenter**  *Four Tops* |
| 22/73 | **If I Were Only A Child Again**  *Curtis Mayfield* |
| | **If I Were Your Woman** |
| 1/71 | *Gladys Knight & The Pips* |
| 19/88 | *Stephanie Mills* |
| 66/73 | **If I'm In Luck I Might Get Picked Up**  *Betty Davis* |
| 79/84 | **If I'm Still Around Tomorrow**  *Sadao Watanabe* |
| 74/74 | **If It Ain't Funky**  *Soul Searchers* |
| F/71 | **If It Ain't Love, It Don't Matter**  *Glass House* |
| 76/79 | **If It Ain't Love, It'll Go Away**  *Prince Phillip Mitchell* |
| 1/82 | **If It Ain't One Thing...It's Another**  *Richard 'Dimples' Fields* |
| 10/77 | **If It Don't Fit, Don't Force It**  *Kellee Patterson* |
| 2/88 | **If It Isn't Love**  *New Edition* |
| 21/69 | **If It Wasn't For Bad Luck**  *Ray Charles & Jimmy Lewis* |
| 57/74 | **If It Were Left Up To Me**  *Sly & The Family Stone* |
| 26/74 | **If It's In You To Do Wrong**  *Impressions* |
| 8/71 | **If It's Real What I Feel**  *Jerry Butler* |
| 10/50 | **If It's So, Baby**  *Robins* |
| | **If It's The Last Thing I Do** |
| 13/55 | *Dinah Washington* |
| 12/77 | *Thelma Houston* |
| 71/85 | **If Looks Could Kill (D.O.A.)**  *Nona Hendryx* |
| 16/70 | **If Love Ruled The World**  *Bobby Bland* |
| | **(If Loving You Is Wrong) I Don't Want To Be Right** |
| 1/72 | *Luther Ingram* |
| F/75 | *Millie Jackson* |
| 68/78 | **If My Friends Could See Me Now**  *Linda Clifford* |
| 30/70 | **If My Heart Could Speak**  *Manhattans* |
| 59/86 | **If Only For One Night**  *Luther Vandross* |
| 1/84 | **If Only You Knew**  *Patti LaBelle* |
| 65/79 | **If Somebody Cares**  *Controllers* |
| 67/64 | **If Somebody Told You**  *Anna King* |
| 41/71 | **If That Ain't A Reason (For Your Woman To Leave You)**  *Little Milton* |
| 37/81 | **If That'll Make You Happy**  *Gladys Knight & The Pips* |
| 55/74 | **If That's The Way You Want It**  *Skylark* |
| 92/76 | **If There Were No Music**  *Rufus Thomas* |
| | **If There's A Hell Below We're All Going To Go**  ..see: (Don't Worry) |
| 64/77 | **If This Is Heaven**  *Ann Peebles* |
| 26/67 | **If This Is Love (I'd Rather Be Lonely)**  *Precisions* |
| 27/72 | **If This Is What You Call Love (I Don't Want No Part Of It)**  *Persuaders* |
| 68/82 | **If This World**  *Coffee* |
| | **If This World Were Mine** |
| 27/68 | *Marvin Gaye & Tammi Terrell* |
| 4/82 | *Cheryl Lynn & Luther Vandross* |

**In The Evening When The Sun Goes Down**
4/49   *Charles Brown*
5/49   *Jimmy Witherspoon*
12/72  **In The Ghetto**  *Candi Staton*
31/83  **In The Groove**  *Ronnie Laws*
70/82  **In The Grooves**  *Tomorrow's Edition*
       **In The Heat Of The Night**
21/67  *Ray Charles*
64/84  *Ray Parker Jr.*
72/87  *Pauli Carman*
51/86  **In The House**  *Fat Boys*
       **In The Middle Of The Night**
3/49   *Amos Milburn*
71/73  *Little Richard*
       **In The Midnight Hour**
1/65   *Wilson Pickett*
37/66  *Little Mac & The Boss Sounds*
18/68  *Mirettes*
7/53   **In The Mission Of St. Augustine**  *Orioles*
       **In The Mix**
10/84  *Roger*
69/88  *Rose Brothers*
       **In The Mood**
7/59   *Ernie Fields*
56/78  *Leroy Hutson*
6/79   *Tyrone Davis*
16/88  *Whispers*
86/80  **In The Mood (To Groove)**  *Aurra*
75/80  **In The Moonlight**  *ADC Band*
       **In The Morning**
24/68  *Mighty Marvelows*
93/80  *Southroad Connection*
26/86  **In The Morning Time**  *Tramaine*
       **In The Name Of Love**
69/82  *Thompson Twins*
80/82  *Roberta Flack*
13/84  *Ralph MacDonald/Bill Withers*
30/79  **In The Navy**  *Village People*
79/81  **In The Night**  *Cheryl Lynn*
15/78  **In The Night-Time**  *Michael Henderson*
       **In The Rain**
1/72   *Dramatics*
36/73  *Arthur Prysock*
8/82   **In The Raw**  *Whispers*
3/56   **In The Still Of The Nite**  *Five Satins*
23/79  **In The Stone**  *Earth, Wind & Fire*
28/71  **In These Changing Times**  *Four Tops*
       **In Your Eyes**
82/87  *Jeffrey Osborne*
11/88  *James (D-Train) Williams*
58/81  **Inch By Inch**  *Strikers*
57/87  **Incredible**  *Scherrie Payne & Phillip Ingram*
86/84  **Indecisive**  *Catch*
41/88  **Indian Giver**  *Rainy Davis*
2/50   **Information Blues**  *Roy Milton*
35/80  **Inherit The Wind**  *Wilton Felder*
61/82  **Inner City**  *Mass Production*
42/72  **Inner City Blues**  *Grover Washington, Jr.*
1/71   **Inner City Blues (Make Me Wanna Holler)**  *Marvin Gaye*
11/85  **Innocent**  *Alexander O'Neal*
37/72  **Innocent Til Proven Guilty**  *Honey Cone*
17/79  **Insane**  *Cameo*
13/86  **Insatiable Woman**  *Isley, Jasper, Isley*
96/86  **Insecure**  *Voltage Brothers*
1/76   **Inseparable**  *Natalie Cole*
3/83   **Inside Love (So Personal)**  *George Benson*
79/84  **Inside Moves**  *Grover Washington, Jr.*
26/75  **Inside My Love**  *Minnie Riperton*
14/80  **Inside Of You**  *Ray, Goodman & Brown*
12/82  **Inside Out**  *Odyssey*
10/81  **Inside You**  *Isley Brothers*
53/86  **Inspector Gadget**  *Kartoon Krew*
56/75  **Inspiration Information**  *Shuggie Otis*
35/69  **Instant Groove**  *King Curtis & The Kingpins*

**Instant Love**
96/76  *Main Ingredient*
16/82  *Cheryl Lynn*
42/84  *Bloodstone*
       **Instant Replay**
44/78  *Dan Hartman*
15/88  *Mico Wave*
23/73  **Instigating (Trouble Making) Fool**
       *Whatnauts*
92/79  **Insurance Man For The Funk**
       *Bernie Worrell*
30/73  **International Playboy**  *Wilson Pickett*
48/84  **Intimate Connection**  *Kleeer*
24/78  **Intimate Friends**  *Eddie Kendricks*
1/44   **Into Each Life Some Rain Must Fall**
       *Ella Fitzgerald & Ink Spots*
43/77  **Into Something (Can't Shake Loose)**
       *O.V. Wright*
19/85  **Into The Groove**  *Madonna*
15/85  **Into The Night**  *B.B. King*
81/82  **Intro (Come To Blow Ya Mind)**  *Slave*
51/81  **Invitation To Love**  *Dazz Band*
91/77  **Invitation To The World**
       *Jimmy Briscoe & The Beavers*
15/60  **Irresistable You**  *Bobby Peterson Quintet*
F/84   **Irresistible Bitch**  *Prince*
55/86  **Is It A Crime**  *Sade*
4/53   **Is It A Dream**  *Vocaleers*
11/70  **Is It Because I'm Black**  *Syl Johnson*
       **Is It In**
67/74  *Eddie Harris*
77/80  *Jimmy 'Bo' Horne*
65/78  **Is It Love?**  *Larry Graham*
18/75  **Is It Love That We're Missin'**
       *Quincy Jones*
31/79  **Is It Love You're After**  *Rose Royce*
28/59  **Is It Real**  *Bobby 'Blue' Bland*
77/77  **Is It Really You**  *Mystique*
5/69   **Is It Something You've Got**  *Tyrone Davis*
12/79  **Is It Still Good To Ya**  *Ashford & Simpson*
41/75  **Is It True**  *Barrett Strong*
27/81  **Is It You**  *Lee Ritenour*
18/72  **Is It You Girl**  *Betty Wright*
2/78   **Is Seems To Hang On**  *Ashford & Simpson*
20/78  **Is This A Love Thing**  *Raydio*
28/80  **Is This The Best (Bop-Doo-Wah)**
       *L.A. Boppers*
8/83   **Is This The End**  *New Edition*
43/83  **Is This The Future**  *Fatback*
       **Is You Is Or Is You Ain't (Ma' Baby)**
3/44   *Louis Jordan*
9/44   *Cootie Williams*
40/69  **Isn't It Lonely Together**  *O.C. Smith*
11/73  **It Ain't Always What You Do**
       *Soul Children*
58/79  **It Ain't Love, Babe (Until You Give It)**
       *Barry White*
14/65  **It Ain't No Big Thing**  *Radiants*
32/75  **It Ain't No Fun**  *Shirley Brown*
       **It Ain't No Use**
68/64  *Major Lance*
34/72  *Z.Z. Hill*
12/76  **It Ain't The Real Thing**  *Bobby Bland*
43/68  **It Ain't What You Got**  *Jimmy Hughes*
61/84  **It Burns Me Up**  *Change*
       **It Can't Be Wrong**
2/43   *Dick Haymes*
3/43   *Four Vagabonds*
41/85  **It Doesn't Really Matter**  *Zapp*
91/73  **It Doesn't Take Much**  *Walter Jackson*
8/58   **It Don't Hurt No More**  *Nappy Brown*
6/77   **It Feels So Good To Be Loved So Bad**
       *Manhattans*
81/85  **It Gets To Me**  *Jimmy Castor*
9/42   **It Had To Be You**  *Jimmie Lunceford*

| | |
|---|---|
| 25/65 | **It Hurts Me Too** *Elmore James* |
| 3/57 | **It Hurts To Be In Love** *Annie Laurie* |
| 5/50 | **It Isn't Fair** *Dinah Washington* |
| 10/56 | **It Isn't Right** *Platters* |
| 18/61 | **It Keeps Rainin'** *Fats Domino* |
| 6/62 | **It Keeps Right On A-Hurtin'** |
| | *Johnny Tillotson* |
| | **It May Be Winter Outside (But In My Heart** |
| | **It's Spring)** |
| 44/67 | *Felice Taylor* |
| 35/74 | *Love Unlimited* |
| 14/55 | **It May Sound Silly** *Ivory Joe Hunter* |
| 2/44 | **It Must Be Jelly ('Cause Jam Don't Shake Like** |
| | **That)** *Glenn Miller* |
| | **It Must Be Love** |
| 10/79 | *Alton McClain & Destiny* |
| 54/83 | *Dayton* |
| | *(also see: I Guess)* |
| 30/81 | **It Must Be Magic** *Teena Marie* |
| 22/61 | **(It Never Happens) In Real Life** |
| | *Chuck Jackson* |
| 27/75 | **It Only Hurts For A Little While** *Notations* |
| 1/75 | **It Only Takes A Minute** *Tavares* |
| 9/68 | **It Should Have Been Me** |
| | *Gladys Knight & The Pips* |
| 27/82 | **It Should Have Been You** *Gwen Guthrie* |
| 5/54 | **It Should've Been Me** *Ray Charles* |
| 34/81 | **It Shows In The Eyes** *Ashford & Simpson* |
| 2/43 | **It Started All Over Again** |
| | *Tommy Dorsey Orchestra* |
| 76/84 | **It Takes A Lot Of Strength To Say** |
| | **Goodbye** *Bobby Womack & Patti LaBelle* |
| 53/82 | **It Takes Heart** *Greg Perry* |
| | **It Takes Two** |
| 4/67 | *Marvin Gaye & Kim Weston* |
| 72/85 | *Juicy* |
| 17/88 | *Rob Base & D.J. E-Z Rock* |
| 7/66 | **It Tears Me Up** *Percy Sledge* |
| 6/48 | **It Took A Long, Long Time** *Amos Milburn* |
| 71/77 | **It Took A Woman Like You** *Mystique* |
| 61/81 | **It Was So Easy** *Stacy Lattisaw* |
| 80/64 | **It Will Stand** *Showmen* |
| 13/63 | **It Won't Be This Way (Always)** *King Pins* |
| 96/76 | **It'll Come, It'll Come, It'll Come** |
| | *Ashford & Simpson* |
| 98/64 | **It'll Never Be Over For Me** |
| | *Baby Washington* |
| 16/78 | **It's A Better Than Good Time** |
| | *Gladys Knight & The Pips* |
| 34/88 | **It's A Cold, Cold World!** *Club Nouveau* |
| 27/79 | **It's A Disco Night (Rock Don't Stop)** |
| | *Isley Brothers* |
| 41/69 | **It's A Funky Thing-Right On** *Herbie Mann* |
| 78/80 | **It's A Groove (Keep On Dancin')** *TTF* |
| 27/69 | **It's A Groovy World!** *Unifics* |
| 84/77 | **It's A Lifetime Thing** *Thelma Houston* |
| 2/81 | **It's A Love Thing** *Whispers* |
| 92/63 | **It's A Mad, Mad, Mad, Mad World** |
| | *Shirelles* |
| 10/65 | **It's A Man Down There** *G.L. Crockett* |
| 1/66 | **It's A Man's Man's Man's World** |
| | *James Brown* |
| 49/67 | **It's A Mean World** *B.B. King* |
| | **It's A Miracle** |
| 33/69 | *Willie Hightower* |
| 75/84 | *Culture Club* |
| 81/81 | **It's A Monster Thing** *Clarence Carter* |
| 68/83 | **It's A Mystery To Me** *First Love* |
| 3/70 | **It's A New Day** *James Brown* |
| 23/71 | **It's A Sad Thing** *Ollie Nightingale* |
| 4/70 | **It's A Shame** *Spinners* |
| 10/50 | **It's A Sin** *Ivory Joe Hunter* |
| 79/87 | **It's A Thang** *Millie Jackson* |

| | |
|---|---|
| | **It's All In The Game** |
| 1/58 | *Tommy Edwards* |
| 6/70 | *Four Tops* |
| 86/80 | *Isaac Hayes* |
| | **It's All In Your Mind** |
| 13/70 | *Clarence Carter* |
| 18/78 | *Side Effect* |
| | **It's All Over** |
| 67/64 | *Walter Jackson* |
| 72/64 | *Ben E. King* |
| 12/73 | *Independents* |
| 75/77 | *Walter Jackson* |
| | **It's All Over Now** |
| 94/64 | *Valentinos* |
| 68/75 | *Bobby Womack & Bill Withers* |
| 1/63 | **It's All Right** *Impressions* |
| 79/64 | **It's All Right (You're Just In Love)** *Tams* |
| 4/70 | **It's All The Way Live** *Lakeside* |
| 23/72 | **It's All Up To You** *Dells* |
| 17/84 | **It's All Yours** *Starpoint* |
| | **It's Alright** |
| 19/75 | *Graham Central Station* |
| 60/82 | *Gino Soccio* |
| | **It's Alright (This Feeling)** |
| 42/75 | *Notations* |
| 74/78 | *Vivian Reed* |
| | **It's Alright With Me** |
| 34/79 | *Patti LaBelle* |
| 59/82 | *Isley Brothers* |
| 11/66 | **It's An Uphill Climb To The Bottom** |
| | *Walter Jackson* |
| 66/74 | **It's Bad For Me To See You** *Betty Wright* |
| | **It's Been A Long Long Time** |
| 35/67 | *Elgins* |
| 55/76 | *Stuff 'n' Ramjett* |
| | **It's Been A Long Time** |
| 17/69 | *Betty Everett* |
| 9/74 | *New Birth* |
| 14/58 | **(It's Been A Long Time) Pretty Baby** |
| | *Gino & Gina* |
| 91/79 | **It's Been Cool** *Dexter Wansel* |
| 6/87 | **It's Been So Long** *Melba Moore* |
| 74/76 | **It's Better Than Walkin' Out** |
| | *Marlena Shaw* |
| 21/74 | **It's Better To Have (And Don't Need)** |
| | *Don Covay* |
| 26/65 | **It's Better To Have It** *Barbara Lynn* |
| 3/76 | **It's Cool** *Tymes* |
| 89/87 | **It's Easy When You're On Fire** *Ella Brooks* |
| 1/77 | **It's Ecstasy When You Lay Down Next To** |
| | **Me** *Barry White* |
| 14/73 | **It's Forever** *Ebonys* |
| | **(It's Gonna Be A) Lonely Christmas** |
| 8/48 | *Orioles* |
| 5/49 | *Orioles* |
| 75/74 | **(It's Gonna Be) A Long Long Winter** |
| | *Linda Clifford* |
| 26/65 | **It's Gonna Be Alright** *Maxine Brown* |
| 15/84 | **It's Gonna Be Special** *Patti Austin* |
| 43/69 | **It's Gonna Rain** *Bobby Womack* |
| 36/70 | **It's Gonna Take A Lot To Bring Me** |
| | **Back** *Manhattans* |
| | **It's Gonna Take A Miracle** |
| 28/65 | *Royalettes* |
| 80/81 | *Truth* |
| 1/82 | *Deniece Williams* |
| 29/88 | **It's Gonna Take All Our Love** |
| | *Gladys Knight & The Pips* |
| 2/61 | **It's Gonna Work Out Fine** |
| | *Ike & Tina Turner* |
| 28/76 | **It's Good For The Soul** *Luther Vandross* |
| 69/82 | **It's Good To Be The King** *Mel Brooks* |
| 53/82 | **It's Good To Be The Queen** *Sylvia* |
| 15/65 | **It's Got The Whole World Shakin'** |
| | *Sam Cooke* |

| | |
|---|---|
| 91/76 | **It's Got To Be Magic** *Major Harris* |
| 21/67 | **It's Got To Be Mellow** *Leon Haywood* |
| 3/65 | **It's Growing** *Temptations* |
| 26/69 | **It's Hard To Get Along** *Joe Simon* |
| 11/73 | **It's Hard To Stop (Doing Something When It's Good To You)** *Betty Wright* |
| 74/76 | **It's Harder To Leave** *Jackie Moore* |
| 29/74 | **It's Her Turn To Live** *Smokey Robinson* |
| 12/71 | **It's Impossible** *New Birth* |
| | **It's In His Kiss** *..see: Shoop Shoop Song* |
| 50/70 | **It's Just A Game, Love** *Peaches & Herb* |
| | **It's Just A Matter Of Time** |
| 1/59 | *Brook Benton* |
| F/76 | *Peabo Bryson* |
| 30/59 | **It's Late** *Ricky Nelson* |
| 10/51 | **It's Later Than You Think** *Roy Milton* |
| 15/83 | **It's Like That** *Run-D.M.C.* |
| | **It's Love Baby (24 Hours A Day)** |
| 2/55 | *Louis Brooks* |
| 4/55 | *Ruth Brown* |
| 10/55 | *Midnighters* |
| 55/85 | **It's Madness** *Marvin Gaye* |
| 3/49 | **It's Midnight** *Little Willie Littlefield* |
| 45/83 | **It's Much Deeper** *Ashford & Simpson* |
| 96/79 | **It's Music** *Damon Harris* |
| 41/72 | **It's My Fault Darling** *Little Johnny Taylor* |
| 27/79 | **It's My House** *Diana Ross* |
| 91/73 | **It's My Life** *Mainstreeters* |
| 1/63 | **It's My Party** *Lesley Gore* |
| 19/69 | **It's My Thing** *Marva Whitney* |
| | **It's My Turn** |
| 14/80 | *Diana Ross* |
| 29/82 | *Aretha Franklin* |
| 22/82 | **It's Nasty (Genius Of Love)** *Grandmaster Flash & The Furious Five* |
| | **It's Natural** *..see: (You Know)* |
| 39/82 | **It's Not Me You Love** *Cliff Dawson* |
| 44/80 | **It's Not My Time** *L.V. Johnson* |
| 26/65 | **It's Not Unusual** *Tom Jones* |
| 74/80 | **It's Not What You Got (It's How You Use It)** *Carrie Lucas* |
| 13/49 | **It's Nothing** *Charles Brown Trio* |
| 7/60 | **It's Now Or Never** *Elvis Presley* |
| | **It's Only A Paper Moon** |
| 5/44 | *Nat King Cole* |
| 4/45 | *Ella Fitzgerald* |
| 12/58 | **It's Only Make Believe** *Conway Twitty* |
| 44/82 | **It's Our Own Affair** *Ray Parker Jr.* |
| | **It's Over** |
| 60/78 | *Cameo* |
| 63/84 | *Bill Summers & Summers Heat* |
| 4/85 | **It's Over Now** *Luther Vandross* |
| 34/83 | **It's Raining Men** *Weather Girls* |
| 26/74 | **It's September** *Johnnie Taylor* |
| 21/78 | **It's Serious** *Cameo* |
| 79/83 | **It's So Delicious** *Starpoint* |
| 24/58 | **It's So Fine** *LaVern Baker* |
| 35/67 | **It's So Hard Being A Loser** *Contours* |
| 37/71 | **It's So Hard For Me To Say Good-Bye** *Eddie Kendricks* |
| 38/75 | **It's So Hard To Say Goodbye To Yesterday** *G.C. Cameron* |
| 70/73 | **It's So Nice** *Sam Russell* |
| 29/71 | **It's Summer** *Temptations* |
| 100/76 | **It's Summertime** *Nazty* |
| 67/87 | **(It's That) Lovin' Feeling** *Jamaica Boys* |
| 37/66 | **It's The Beat** *Major Lance* |
| 63/75 | **It's The J.B.'s Monaurail** *Fred Wesley & The J.B.'s* |
| 82/76 | **It's The Music** *Natural Four* |
| 22/86 | **It's The New Style** *Beastie Boys* |
| 15/71 | **It's The Real Thing** *Electric Express* |
| | **It's The Same Old Song** |
| 2/65 | *Four Tops* |
| 30/78 | *KC & The Sunshine Band* |

| | |
|---|---|
| 8/72 | **(It's The Way) Nature Planned It** *Four Tops* |
| | **It's Time For Love** |
| 27/75 | *Chi-Lites* |
| 65/84 | *Pieces Of A Dream* |
| 13/60 | **It's Time To Cry** *Paul Anka* |
| 15/79 | **It's Too Funky In Here** *James Brown* |
| | **It's Too Late** |
| 3/56 | *Chuck Willis* |
| 20/59 | *Tarheel Slim & Little Ann* |
| 7/63 | *Wilson Pickett* |
| 30/69 | *Ted Taylor* |
| 38/72 | *Rueben Bell* |
| 39/73 | *Isley Brothers* |
| 76/75 | *Johnny 'Guitar' Watson* |
| 11/65 | **It's Too Late, Baby Too Late** *Arthur Prysock* |
| 33/70 | **It's Too Late For Love** *Vanguards* |
| | **It's Too Soon To Know** |
| 1/48 | *Orioles* |
| 2/48 | *Dinah Washington* |
| 6/48 | *Ella Fitzgerald* |
| 11/48 | *Ravens* |
| 21/87 | **It's Tricky** *Run-D.M.C.* |
| 23/69 | **It's True I'm Gonna Miss You** *Carolyn Franklin* |
| 24/63 | **It's Up To You** *Ricky Nelson* |
| 22/65 | **It's Wonderful To Be In Love** *Ovations* |
| 66/74 | **It's Worth The Hurt** *Gwen McCrae* |
| | **It's You** |
| 38/81 | *Afterbach* |
| 65/86 | *Troy Johnson* |
| | **It's You I Love** |
| F/57 | *Fats Domino* |
| 44/80 | *Teddy Pendergrass* |
| 58/83 | *Pamela Nivens* |
| 1/78 | **It's You That I Need** *Enchantment* |
| | **It's You That I Need** *..see: (Loneliness Made Me Realize)* |
| 45/81 | **It's Your Conscience** *Deniece Williams* |
| 73/81 | **It's Your Night** *Ray Parker Jr. & Raydio* |
| | **It's Your Thing** |
| 1/69 | *Isley Brothers* |
| 39/69 | *Senor Soul* |
| 81/75 | **It's Yours To Have** *Freda Payne* |
| 13/85 | **Itchin' For A Scratch** *Force M.D.'s* |
| 81/86 | **Itchin' For Your Twitchin'** *Zapp* |
| 67/83 | **Itching For Love** *Mikki* |
| 5/58 | **Itchy Twitchy Feeling** *Bobby Hendricks* |
| 10/60 | **Itsy Bitsy Teenie Weenie Yellow Polka Dot Bikini** *Brian Hyland* |
| 5/56 | **Ivory Tower** *Otis Williams & His Charms* |

# J

| | |
|---|---|
| 5/78 | **Jack And Jill** *Raydio* |
| 23/59 | **Jack O'Diamonds** *Ruth Brown* |
| 1/47 | **Jack, You're Dead** *Louis Jordan* |
| 14/49 | **Jackson's Blues** *Don Johnson Band* |
| 61/86 | **Jail Bait** *West Coast Crew* |
| 17/84 | **Jail House Rap** *Fat Boys* |
| 1/57 | **Jailhouse Rock** *Elvis Presley* |
| | **Jam, The** |
| 14/62 | *Bobby Gregg* |
| 15/76 | *Graham Central Station* |
| 13/79 | **Jam Fan (Hot)** *Bootsy's Rubber Band* |
| 29/80 | **Jam (Let's Take It To The Streets)** *Five Special* |
| 53/85 | **Jam-Master Jammin'** *Run-D.M.C.* |
| F/84 | **Jam-Master Jay** *Run-D.M.C.* |

| | | |
|---|---|---|
| 35/72 | **Just As Long As We're In Love** *Dells* | |
| | **Just As Long As We're Together** | |
| 14/75 | *Gloria Scott* | |
| 91/79 | *Prince* | |
| 8/72 | **Just As Long As You Need Me** | |
| | *Independents* | |
| 10/42 | **Just As Though You Were Here** *Ink Spots* | |
| 2/83 | **Just Be Good To Me** *S.O.S. Band* | |
| 4/81 | **Just Be My Lady** *Larry Graham* | |
| 43/67 | **Just Be Sincere** *Jackie Wilson* | |
| 19/64 | **Just Be True** *Gene Chandler* | |
| 12/82 | **Just Be Yourself** *Cameo* | |
| | **Just Because** | |
| 3/57 | *Lloyd Price* | |
| 11/57 | *Larry Williams* | |
| 69/79 | *Ray Charles* | |
| 25/72 | **Just Because He Wants To Make Love** | |
| | *Moments* | |
| 71/83 | **(Just Because) You'll Be Mine** | |
| | *Instant Funk* | |
| 75/87 | **Just Begun To Love You** *Renee Aldrich* | |
| | **Just Being Myself** *..see: (I'm)* | |
| | **Just Buggin'** *..see: (Nothing Serious)* | |
| 8/87 | **Just Call** *Sherrick* | |
| 64/76 | **Just Can't Be That Way (Ruth's Song)** | |
| | *Weapons Of Peace* | |
| 76/73 | **Just Can't Get You Out Of My Mind** | |
| | *Baby Washington* | |
| 57/82 | **Just Can't Win 'Em All** *Stevie Woods* | |
| 33/81 | **Just Chillin' Out** *Bernard Wright* | |
| | **Just Don't Want To Be Lonely** | |
| 29/73 | *Ronnie Dyson* | |
| 8/74 | *Main Ingredient* | |
| 95/78 | **Just Family** *Dee Dee Bridgewater* | |
| 16/60 | **Just For A Thrill** *Ray Charles* | |
| 61/86 | **Just For Fun** *Whistle* | |
| 16/84 | **Just For The Night** | |
| | *Evelyn 'Champagne' King* | |
| | **Just For You** | |
| 10/44 | *Five Red Caps* | |
| 33/65 | *Jerry Butler* | |
| 53/85 | *Gwen Guthrie* | |
| 85/85 | *Controllers* | |
| | **Just For Your Love** | |
| 26/59 | *Falcons* | |
| 17/77 | *Memphis Horns* | |
| 64/78 | **Just Freak** *Slave* | |
| 63/76 | **Just Friends** *Silver, Platinum & Gold* | |
| 93/78 | **Just Funnin'** *Mtume* | |
| | **Just Gets Better With Time** | |
| 71/86 | *Alfie* | |
| 12/87 | *Whispers* | |
| 1/88 | **Just Got Paid** *Johnny Kemp* | |
| 2/61 | **Just Got To Know** *Jimmy McCracklin* | |
| 22/88 | **Just Havin' Fun** *Fit* | |
| 92/80 | **Just How Sweet Is Your Love** *Rhyze* | |
| 97/74 | **Just In The Nick Of Time** *Chocolate Syrup* | |
| 9/59 | **Just Keep It Up** *Dee Clark* | |
| 8/42 | **Just Kiddin' Around** *Artie Shaw* | |
| | **Just Let Me Hold You For A Night** | |
| 76/76 | *Choice Four* | |
| 18/77 | *David Ruffin* | |
| 24/84 | **Just Let Me Wait** *Jennifer Holliday* | |
| 80/83 | **Just Like All The Rest** *Thelma Houston* | |
| 58/76 | **Just Like In The Movies** *Bloodstone* | |
| 57/80 | **Just Like You** *Heat* | |
| 21/67 | **Just Look What You've Done** | |
| | *Brenda Holloway* | |
| 4/54 | **Just Make Love To Me** *Muddy Waters* | |
| | **Just My Imagination (Running Away With Me)** | |
| 1/71 | *Temptations* | |
| 79/84 | *Lillo Thomas* | |
| | **Just My Luck** | |
| 62/81 | *Tyrone Davis* | |
| 25/84 | *Deele* | |

| | | |
|---|---|---|
| F/70 | **Just Now & Then** *Detroit Emeralds* | |
| 11/81 | **Just Once** *Quincy Jones/James Ingram* | |
| 41/67 | **Just Once In A Lifetime** | |
| | *Brenda & The Tabulations* | |
| 26/65 | **Just Once In My Life** *Righteous Brothers* | |
| 3/63 | **Just One Look** *Doris Troy* | |
| 19/81 | **Just One Moment Away** *Manhattans* | |
| 10/44 | **Just One More Chance** *Cozy Cole* | |
| 15/66 | **Just One More Day** *Otis Redding* | |
| 59/77 | **Just One Step** *Little Milton* | |
| 58/73 | **Just Out Of Reach** *Sam Dees* | |
| 7/61 | **Just Out Of Reach (Of My Two Open** | |
| | **Arms)** *Solomon Burke* | |
| 10/51 | **Just Right Bounce** *Piano Red* | |
| 9/71 | **Just Seven Numbers (Can Straighten Out My** | |
| | **Life)** *Four Tops* | |
| 4/87 | **Just That Type Of Girl** *Madame X* | |
| 33/87 | **Just The Facts** *Patti LaBelle* | |
| 3/81 | **Just The Two Of Us** | |
| | *Grover Washington, Jr./Bill Withers* | |
| 75/86 | **Just The Way I Planned It** | |
| | *Philip-Michael Thomas* | |
| 45/79 | **Just The Way You Are** *Barry White* | |
| 6/84 | **Just The Way You Like It** *S.O.S. Band* | |
| 1/76 | **Just To Be Close To You** *Commodores* | |
| 6/57 | **Just To Hold My Hand** *Clyde McPhatter* | |
| 81/80 | **Just To Make You Happy** *Perry & Sanlin* | |
| 2/87 | **Just To See Her** *Smokey Robinson* | |
| 29/80 | **Just Us** *Two Tons O' Fun* | |
| 46/78 | **Just Wanna Make A Dream Come True** | |
| | *Mass Production* | |
| 78/75 | **Just You And Me** *Tamiko Jones* | |
| 17/61 | **Just You And Me, Darling** *James Brown* | |
| 9/44 | **Just You, Just Me** *Lester Young* | |
| 26/76 | **Just Your Fool** *Leon Haywood* | |

# K

| | | |
|---|---|---|
| 17/71 | **K-Jee** *Nite-Liters* | |
| | **Ka-Ding-Dong** | |
| 8/56 | *Diamonds* | |
| 9/56 | *G-Clefs* | |
| 6/74 | **Kalimba Story** *Earth, Wind & Fire* | |
| 64/80 | **Kamali** *Herb Alpert* | |
| | **Kansas City** | |
| 1/59 | *Wilbert Harrison* | |
| 16/59 | *Hank Ballard & The Midnighters* | |
| 21/67 | *James Brown* | |
| 30/67 | **Karate** *Emperor's* | |
| 16/67 | **Karate-Boo-Ga-Loo** *Jerryo* | |
| 67/84 | **Karma Chameleon** *Culture Club* | |
| 86/77 | **Katrina** *Lifestyle* | |
| 10/49 | **Kee-Mo Ky-Mo (The Magic Song)** | |
| | *Nat King Cole* | |
| 60/79 | **Keeep Your Body Workin'** *Kleeer* | |
| 46/69 | **Keem-O-Sabe** *Electric Indian* | |
| 8/48 | **Keep A Dollar In Your Pocket** *Roy Milton* | |
| 19/58 | **Keep A-Driving** *Chuck Willis* | |
| 2/57 | **Keep A Knockin'** *Little Richard* | |
| 15/67 | **Keep A Light In The Window Till I Come** | |
| | **Home** *Solomon Burke* | |
| 66/74 | **Keep An Eye On Your Close Friends** | |
| | *Newcomers* | |
| 13/82 | **Keep Away Girls** *Stephanie Mills* | |
| | **Keep Dancin** *..see: (Aerobic Dancin)* | |
| 90/77 | **Keep Doing It** *Showdown* | |
| 56/83 | **(Keep Feeling) Fascination** *Human League* | |
| | **Keep Giving Me Love** | |
| 55/83 | *'D' Train* | |
| 31/85 | *Gladys Knight & The Pips* | |

| 3/76 | **Keep Holding On** _Temptations_ |
|---|---|
| 52/82 | **Keep In Touch** _Shades Of Love_ |
| 49/79 | **Keep It Comin'** _Atlantic Starr_ |
| 1/77 | **Keep It Comin' Love** |
| | _KC & The Sunshine Band_ |
| 22/83 | **Keep It Confidential** _Nona Hendryx_ |
| 4/80 | **Keep It Hot** _Cameo_ |
| 11/74 | **Keep It In The Family** _Leon Haywood_ |
| 20/82 | **Keep It Live (On The K.I.L.)** _Dazz Band_ |
| 14/56 | **Keep It To Yourself** _Sonny Boy Williamson_ |
| 16/79 | **Keep It Together (Declaration Of Love)** |
| | _Rufus_ |
| 38/66 | **Keep Looking** _Solomon Burke_ |
| 4/76 | **Keep Me Cryin'** _Al Green_ |
| | **Keep On** |
| 15/82 | _'D' Train_ |
| 85/86 | _Bobby Mardis_ |
| | **Keep On Dancing** |
| 13/68 | _Alvin Cash_ |
| 32/78 | _Johnnie Taylor_ |
| 15/79 | _Gary's Gang_ |
| | **Keep On Doin'** |
| 17/70 | _Isley Brothers_ |
| 51/83 | _Glenn Jones_ |
| 40/72 | **Keep On Doin' What You're Doin'** |
| | _Bobby Byrd_ |
| 28/81 | **Keep On It** _Starpoint_ |
| 81/79 | **Keep On Jumpin'** _Musique_ |
| 39/72 | **Keep On Keepin On** _Nolan Porter_ |
| 40/69 | **Keep On Living** _Gwen Owens_ |
| 4/83 | **Keep On Lovin' Me** _Whispers_ |
| 11/68 | **Keep On Lovin' Me Honey** |
| | _Marvin Gaye & Tammi Terrell_ |
| 20/70 | **Keep On Loving Me (You'll See The** |
| | **Change)** _Bobby Bland_ |
| 10/64 | **Keep On Pushing** _Impressions_ |
| 36/72 | **Keep On Running** _Stevie Wonder_ |
| 50/74 | **Keep On Searching** _Margie Alexander_ |
| 50/74 | **Keep On Steppin'** _Fatback Band_ |
| 1/73 | **Keep On Truckin'** _Eddie Kendricks_ |
| 17/88 | **Keep Risin' To The Top** _Doug E. Fresh_ |
| | **Keep Smilin'** |
| 46/74 | _Bunny Sigler_ |
| 77/76 | _Gabor Szabo_ |
| | **Keep That Same Old Feeling** |
| 21/76 | _Crusaders_ |
| 22/77 | _Side Effect_ |
| 60/83 | **Keep The Fire Burning** _Gwen McCrae_ |
| | **Keep The Home Fire Burnin'** |
| 5/75 | _Latimore_ |
| 83/79 | _Millie Jackson_ |
| 13/68 | **Keep The One You Got** _Joe Tex_ |
| 3/45 | **Keep Your Arms Around Me** |
| | _Arthur 'Big Boy' Crudup_ |
| 3/87 | **Keep Your Eye On Me** _Herb Alpert_ |
| | **Keep Your Eye On The Sparrow** |
| 42/75 | _Merry Clayton_ |
| 19/76 | _Rhythm Heritage_ |
| 6/62 | **Keep Your Hands Off My Baby** _Little Eva_ |
| 23/74 | **Keep Your Head To The Sky** |
| | _Earth, Wind & Fire_ |
| 13/57 | **Keeper Of My Heart** _Faye Adams_ |
| 7/72 | **Keeper Of The Castle** _Four Tops_ |
| 47/82 | **Keepin' Love New** _Howard Johnson_ |
| 14/83 | **Keepin' My Lover Satisfied** _Melba Moore_ |
| 72/82 | **Kelly's Eyes** _Andre Cymone_ |
| 69/81 | **Kemo-Kimo** _Webster Lewis_ |
| 6/58 | **Key To The Highway** _Little Walter_ |
| 69/81 | **Key To The World** _L.J. Reynolds_ |
| 96/74 | **Kiburi** _Incredible Bongo Band_ |
| 50/83 | **Kick It Live From 9 To 5** _Sugarhill Gang_ |
| 52/88 | **Kick It To The Curb** _Brothers Johnson_ |
| 10/82 | **Kickin' Back** _L.T.D._ |

| 19/80 | **Kid Stuff** _Twennynine with Lenny White_ |
|---|---|
| 1/60 | **Kiddio** _Brook Benton_ |
| 5/47 | **Kidney Stew Blues** _Eddie Vinson_ |
| 79/64 | **Kiko** _Jimmy McGriff_ |
| 42/76 | **Kill That Roach** _Miami_ |
| 47/70 | **Killer Joe** _Quincy Jones_ |
| 2/73 | **Killing Me Softly With His Song** |
| | _Roberta Flack_ |
| 27/63 | **Kind Of Boy You Can't Forget** _Raindrops_ |
| 87/85 | **Kind Of Girls We Like** _New Edition_ |
| 77/86 | **Kindness For Weakness** _Cut_ |
| 6/72 | **King Heroin** _James Brown_ |
| 30/86 | **King Holiday** |
| | _King Dream Chorus & Holiday Crew_ |
| 23/75 | **King Kong** _Jimmy Castor Bunch_ |
| 62/85 | **King Kut** |
| | _Word Of Mouth featuring D.J. Cheese_ |
| 14/85 | **King Of Rock** _Run-D.M.C._ |
| 1/48 | **King Size Papa** _Julia Lee_ |
| 26/79 | **King Tim III (Personality Jock)** _Fatback_ |
| 32/85 | **King Tut** _Paul Hardcastle_ |
| | **Kiss** |
| 1/86 | _Prince_ |
| 55/88 | _Total Contrast_ |
| | **Kiss And A Rose** |
| 8/49 | _Charioteers_ |
| 12/49 | _Orioles_ |
| 1/76 | **Kiss And Say Goodbye** _Manhattans_ |
| 52/85 | **Kiss And Tell** _Isley, Jasper, Isley_ |
| 13/86 | **Kiss Away The Pain** _Patti LaBelle_ |
| 12/56 | **Kiss From Your Lips** _Flamingos_ |
| 35/77 | **Kiss In 77** _James Brown_ |
| 8/52 | **Kiss Me Baby** _Ray Charles_ |
| 85/85 | **Kiss Me Now** _Klockwise_ |
| 57/77 | **Kiss Me (The Way I Like It)** _George McCrae_ |
| 8/52 | **Kiss Of Fire** _Billy Eckstine_ |
| 53/88 | **Kiss Serious** _Chico DeBarge_ |
| 92/78 | **Kiss You All Over** _Broadway_ |
| 13/86 | **Kisses In The Moonlight** _George Benson_ |
| 8/58 | **Kisses Sweeter Than Wine** _Jimmie Rodgers_ |
| 40/66 | **Kissin'** _Ideals_ |
| 83/74 | **Kissin' In The Back Row Of The Movies** |
| | _Drifters_ |
| 29/59 | **Kissin' Time** _Bobby Rydell_ |
| 16/88 | **K.I.S.S.I.N.G.** _Siedah Garrett_ |
| 12/73 | **Kissing My Love** _Bill Withers_ |
| | **Knee Deep** ..see: (not just) |
| 44/81 | **Knock! Knock!** _Dazz Band_ |
| 64/64 | **Knock! Knock! (Who's There?)** _Orlons_ |
| | **Knock On Wood** |
| 1/66 | _Eddie Floyd_ |
| 8/67 | _Otis & Carla_ |
| 6/79 | _Amii Stewart_ |
| 8/88 | **Knocked Out** _Paula Abdul_ |
| 39/66 | **Knockin' At Your Door** _Jimmy Reed_ |
| 12/83 | **Knockout** _Margie Joseph_ |
| 77/74 | **Know What You're Doing When You** |
| | **Leave** _Roshell Anderson_ |
| 28/67 | **Knucklehead** _Bar-Kays_ |
| 6/55 | **Ko Ko Mo** _Gene & Eunice_ |
| 56/73 | **Koke** _Tribe_ |
| 35/87 | **Koo Koo** _Sheila E._ |
| 30/59 | **Kookie, Kookie (Lend Me Your Comb)** |
| | _Edward Byrnes & Connie Stevens_ |
| 19/69 | **Kool And The Gang** _Kool & The Gang_ |
| 64/81 | **Kool Whip** _Fatback_ |
| F/70 | **Kool's Back Again** _Kool & The Gang_ |
| 67/84 | **Kraazy** _Suttons_ |
| 18/85 | **(Krush Groove) Can't Stop The Street** |
| | _Chaka Khan_ |
| 87/85 | **Krush Groovin'** _Krush Groove All Stars_ |
| 3/74 | **Kung Fu** _Curtis Mayfield_ |
| 1/75 | **Kung Fu Fighting** _Carl Douglas_ |

42/86 **L Is For Lover**  *Al Jarreau*
**L.A. Sunshine**
54/76   *Sylvia*
2/77   *War*
6/58 **La Dee Dah**  *Billy & Lillie*
92/75 **La-La-Love Chains**  *Silver, Platinum & Gold*
**La - La - Means I Love You**
2/68   *Delfonics*
33/81   *Tierra*
77/81   *L.A. Boppers*
**La La Peace Song**
19/74   *Al Wilson*
27/74   *O.C. Smith*
**Ladies Choice**
41/82   *Shotgun*
53/83   *Stone City Band*
1/79 **Ladies Night**  *Kool & The Gang*
33/79 **Ladies Only**  *Aretha Franklin*
**Lady**
3/80   *Whispers*
42/80   *Kenny Rogers*
88/73 **Lady Be Mine**  *Will King*
39/78 **Lady Blue**  *George Benson*
90/76 **Lady Bump**  *Penny McLean*
16/78 **Lady In Red**  *Alphonse Mouzon*
89/86 **Lady Is Love**  *Maurice White*
44/72 **Lady Lady Lady**  *Barbara Acklin*
         (also see: Theme From)
21/78 **Lady Love**  *Lou Rawls*
21/83 **Lady Love Me (One More Time)**
         *George Benson*
3/60 **Lady Luck**  *Lloyd Price*
1/75 **Lady Marmalade**  *LaBelle*
74/85 **Lady, My Whole World Is You**
         *Johnnie Taylor*
13/77 **Lady Of Magic**
         *Maze Featuring Frankie Beverly*
4/86 **Lady Soul**  *Temptations*
5/84 **Lady You Are**  *One Way*
5/81 **Lady (You Bring Me Up)**  *Commodores*
42/81 **Lady's Wild**  *Con Funk Shun*
57/76 **Laid Back Love**  *Major Harris*
13/48 **Lake Charles Boogie**  *Nellie Lutcher*
36/84 **Land Of Hunger**  *Earons*
19/86 **Land Of La La**  *Stevie Wonder*
77/81 **Land Of Make-Believe**  *Blue Magic*
1/66 **Land Of 1,000 Dances**  *Wilson Pickett*
3/80 **Landlord**  *Gladys Knight & The Pips*
6/49 **Landlord Blues**  *Ivory Joe Hunter*
21/71 **Language Of Love**  *Intrigues*
60/87 **Last Chance**  *Cyre'*
**Last Dance**
5/78   *Donna Summer*
26/84   *George Clinton*
68/80 **Last Dance At Danceland**  *Randy Crawford*
3/60 **Last Date**  *Floyd Cramer*
41/67 **Last Minute Miracle**  *Shirelles*
**Last Night**
6/54   *Little Walter*
2/61   *Mar-Keys*
14/82   *Stephanie Mills*
10/83 **Last Night A D.J. Saved My Life**  *Indeep*
3/45 **Last Night & Now Tonite Again**
         *Billy Eckstine*
28/72 **(Last Night) I Didn't Get To Sleep At All**
         *5th Dimension*
36/86 **Last Night I Needed Somebody**
         *Shirley Jones*

**Last Time**
18/87   *Theresa*
88/87   *Imagination*
2/84 **Last Time I Made Love**
         *Joyce Kennedy & Jeffrey Osborne*
15/74 **Last Time I Saw Him**  *Diana Ross*
48/67 **Lasting Love**  *Otis Clay*
6/49 **Late After Hours**  *'Great' Gates*
1/48 **Late Freight**  *Sonny Thompson*
40/87 **Late Night Hour**  *Kathy Mathis*
**Lately**
29/81   *Stevie Wonder*
8/87   *Surface*
37/67 **Later For Tomorrow**  *Ernie K-Doe*
18/70 **Laughin & Clownin**  *Ray Charles*
6/63 **Laughing Boy**  *Mary Wells*
69/74 **Laughter In The Rain**  *Lea Roberts*
29/66 **Laundromat Blues**  *Albert King*
14/59 **Lavender-Blue**  *Sammy Turner*
**Lavender Coffin**
9/49   *Fat Man Robinson*
13/49   *Lionel Hampton*
97/78 **Law And Order**  *Love Committee*
40/73 **Law Of The Land**  *Undisputed Truth*
1/52 **Lawdy Miss Clawdy**  *Lloyd Price*
6/72 **Lay-Away**  *Isley Brothers*
65/77 **Lay It On Me**  *Sylvia*
29/71 **Lay Lady Lay**  *Isley Brothers*
73/80 **Lay Me Gently**  *Gene Chandler*
46/75 **Lay Some Lovin' On Me**  *Jeannie Reynolds*
24/77 **Laying Beside You**  *Eugene Record*
8/51 **Laying The Boogie**  *Piano Red*
40/64 **Lazy Elsie Molly**  *Chubby Checker*
86/64 **Lazy Lady**  *Fats Domino*
14/58 **Lazy Mary**  *Lou Monte*
1/78 **Le Freak**  *Chic*
75/76 **Le Lo Li**  *Sly Stone*
13/78 **Le Spank**  *Le Pamplemousse*
**Lead Me On**
9/60   *Bobby Bland*
32/70   *Gwen McCrae*
37/79   *Maxine Nightingale*
**Leader Of The Pack**
1/64   *Shangri-Las*
32/85   *UTFO*
**Lean On Me**
50/68   *Tony Fax*
1/72   *Bill Withers*
17/76   *Melba Moore*
2/87   *Club Nouveau*
99/77 **Leaning Tree**  *Artie White*
13/58 **Leaps And Bounds**  *Bill Doggett*
71/86 **Learn From The Burn**  *Terri Dancer*
71/85 **Learn To Love Again**  *Lou Rawls*
18/74 **Learning To Love You Was Easy**  *Dells*
13/75 **Leave It Alone**  *Dynamic Superiors*
21/63 **Leave Me Alone**  *Baby Washington*
13/59 **Leave My Kitten Alone**  *Little Willie John*
23/75 **Leave My World**  *Johnny Bristol*
73/84 **Leave The Bridges Standing**
         *Shirley Brown*
96/74 **Leave The Kids Alone**  *Crown Heights Affair*
76/87 **Leave The Lights On**
         *Nonet with Nolan Thomas*
73/84 **Leave The Message Behind The Door**
         *Colonel Abrams*
76/74 **Leave Your Hat On**  *Etta James*
76/64 **Leaving Here**  *Eddie Holland*
1/73 **Leaving Me**  *Independents*
95/77 **Leaving You Is Killing Me**  *Vernon Burch*
79/73 **Lee**  *Detroit Emeralds*
31/67 **Lee Cross**  *Aretha Franklin*
2/45 **Left A Good Deal In Mobile**  *Joe Liggins*
71/87 **Left Me - Lonely**
         *M.C. Shan featuring T.J. Swan*

## Life And Death In G & A
| | |
|---|---|
| 25/69 | *Abaco Dream* |
| 48/75 | *Love Childs Afro Cuban Blues Band* |

65/77 **Life Goes On** *Faith, Hope & Charity*
69/74 **Life In The Country** *Ebonys*
40/79 **Life Is A Dance** *Chaka Khan*
65/74 **Life Is A Song Worth Singing**
    *Johnny Mathis*
27/61 **Life Is But A Dream, Sweetheart** *Classics*
74/77 **Life Is Music** *Ritchie Family*
50/83 **Life (Is So Strange)** *War*
74/83 **Life Is Something Special**
    *New York Citi Peech Boys*
83/79 **Life, Love And Harmony** *Nancy Wilson*
91/76 **Life On Mars** *Dexter Wansel*
83/84 **Life's Charade** *Lance Webb*
23/87 **Lifetime Love** *Joyce Sims*
50/70 **Lift Ev'ry Voice And Sing** *Kim Weston*

**Light My Fire**
| | |
|---|---|
| 29/68 | *Jose Feliciano* |
| 36/69 | *Rhetta Hughes* |
| 36/79 | *Amii Stewart (medley)* |

16/80 **Light Up The Night** *Brothers Johnson*
52/83 **Light Years Away** *Warp 9*
65/78 **Lighting A Fire (That You Can't Put Out)** *Patti Hendrix*
24/63 **Like A Baby** *James Brown*
88/88 **Like A Child** *Noel*
9/85 **Like A Virgin** *Madonna*
14/71 **Like An Open Door** *Fuzz*
62/81 **Like Sister And Brother** *Frank Hooker*
22/59 **Like Young** *Andre Previn & David Rose*
12/48 **Lillette** *Nat King Cole*
3/62 **Limbo Rock** *Chubby Checker*
11/59 **Linda Lu** *Ray Sharpe*

**Ling, Ting, Tong**
| | |
|---|---|
| 5/55 | *Charms* |
| 5/55 | *Five Keys* |

7/62 **Lion Sleeps Tonight** *Tokens*
28/86 **Lips To Find You** *Teena Marie*
79/84 **Lipservice** *Beatmaster*
63/85 **Lipstick Lover** *Andre Cymone*
10/59 **Lipstick On Your Collar** *Connie Francis*
8/56 **Lipstick Powder And Paint** *Joe Turner*

**Lipstick Traces (On A Cigarette)**
| | |
|---|---|
| 28/62 | *Benny Spellman* |
| 28/65 | *O'Jays* |

11/68 **Listen Here** *Eddie Harris*
90/77 **Listen To The Music** *Candi Staton*
44/83 **Listen To Your Heart** *Diane Richards*
52/82 **Lite Me Up** *Herbie Hancock*
**Little** *..also see: Li'l*
19/63 **Little Band Of Gold** *James Gilreath*
51/65 **Little Bell** *Dixie Cups*

**Little Bird Told Me**
| | |
|---|---|
| 2/48 | *Paula Watson* |
| 4/49 | *Blue Lu Barker* |

1/86 **Little Bit More**
    *Melba Moore with Freddie Jackson*
89/74 **Little Bit Of Good (Cures A Whole Lot Of Bad)** *Sam & Dave*
28/85 **Little Bit Of Heaven** *Natalie Cole*
35/81 **Little Bit Of Jazz** *Nick Straker Band*
95/77 **Little Bit Of Love** *Gap Band*
3/86 **Little Bit Of Love (Is All It Takes)**
    *New Edition*
49/83 **Little Bit Of Loving** *Tyrone Davis*

**Little Bit Of Soap**
| | |
|---|---|
| 7/61 | *Jarmels* |
| 95/65 | *Garnet Mimms* |

**Little Bitty Pretty One**
| | |
|---|---|
| 2/57 | *Thurston Harris* |
| 8/72 | *Jackson 5* |

## Little Boy
| | |
|---|---|
| 13/48 | *Rev. Kelsey's Congregation* |
| 92/64 | *Crystals* |

10/58 **Little Boy Blue** *Bobby Bland*
23/60 **Little By Little** *Junior Wells*

**Little Darlin'**
| | |
|---|---|
| 2/57 | *Diamonds* |
| 11/57 | *Gladiolas* |

10/66 **Little Darling, I Need You** *Marvin Gaye*
28/63 **Little Deuce Coupe** *Beach Boys*
16/61 **Little Egypt (Ying-Yang)** *Coasters*
25/72 **Little Ghetto Boy** *Donny Hathaway*
91/76 **Little Girl Blue** *Little Beaver*

**Little Girl, Don't Cry**
| | |
|---|---|
| 2/49 | *Bull Moose Jackson* |
| 15/49 | *Lucky Millinder* |

17/81 **Little Girl Don't You Worry**
    *Jermaine Jackson*
8/56 **Little Girl Of Mine** *Cleftones*
60/78 **Little Girls** *Patti LaBelle*
2/68 **Little Green Apples** *O.C. Smith*
5/51 **Little Joe's Boogie** *Joe Liggins*
46/64 **Little Latin Lupe Lu** *Kingsmen*
36/82 **Little Love** *Aurra*
4/54 **Little Mama** *Clovers*
54/64 **Little Marie** *Chuck Berry*
4/58 **Little Mary** *Fats Domino*
37/82 **Little More Love** *T-Connection*
18/67 **Little Ole Man (Uptight-Everything's Alright)** *Bill Cosby*
7/57 **Little Rain** *Jimmy Reed*
15/83 **Little Red Corvette** *Prince*
5/51 **Little Red Rooster**
    *Margie Day/Griffin Brothers*
7/63     *Sam Cooke*
66/80 **Little Runaway** *Stone City Band*
5/50 **Little School Girl** *Smokey Hogg*
10/51 **Little Side Car** *Larks*
1/58 **Little Star** *Elegants*
12/60 **Little Susie** *Ray Bryant Combo*
    *(also see: Li'l Suzy)*
84/64 **Little Toy Balloon** *Danny Williams*
1/88 **Little Walter** *Tony! Toni! Tone!*
6/52 **Little White Cloud That Cried**
    *Johnnie Ray*
11/48 **Little White Lies** *Martha Davis*

**Live It Up**
| | |
|---|---|
| 4/74 | *Isley Brothers* |
| 40/82 | *Dramatics* |

46/84 **Live It Up (Love It Up)** *Suttons*
21/88 **Live My Life** *Boy George*
42/64 **Live Wire** *Martha & The Vandellas*
60/84 **Live Wire (I Want A Girl That Sweats)**
    *Duke Bootee*
95/80 **Live With Me** *Wilson Pickett*
34/84 **Live Without Your Love** *Windjammer*
1/76 **Livin' For The Weekend** *O'Jays*
1/74 **Livin' For You** *Al Green*
6/84 **Livin' For Your Love** *Melba Moore*
78/84 **Livin' In The Fast Lane** *Sugarhill Gang*
4/77 **Livin' In The Life** *Isley Brothers*
79/82 **Livin' In The New Wave** *Andre Cymone*
98/87 **Livin' In The Red** *War*
7/79 **Livin' It Up (Friday Night)** *Bell & James*
7/75 **Living A Little, Laughing A Little**
    *Spinners*
12/87 **Living All Alone** *Phyllis Hyman*

**Living For The City**
| | |
|---|---|
| 1/73 | *Stevie Wonder* |
| 22/75 | *Ray Charles* |

74/87 **Living In A Box** *Living In A Box*
92/79 **Living In A World** *Beverly & Duane*
10/86 **Living In America** *James Brown*
34/88 **Living In The Limelight** *Glenn Jones*
45/81 **Living Inside Myself** *Gino Vannelli*

| | |
|---|---|
| 93/77 | **Living Inside Your Love** *Earl Klugh* |
| 21/76 | **Living Together (In Sin)** *Whispers* |
| 79/74 | **Living Together Is Keeping Us Apart** *Invitations* |
| 47/86 | **Lock And Key** *Klymaxx* |
| 25/63 | **Locking Up My Heart** *Marvelettes* |
| 1/62 | **Loco-Motion** *Little Eva* |
| 3/58 | **Lollipop** *Chordettes* |
| 22/69 | **Lollipop (I Like You)** *Intruders* |
| 23/84 | **Lollipop Luv** *Bryan Loren* |
| 8/48 | **Lolly Pop Mama** *Wynonie Harris* |
| 14/48 | **London Donnie** *Don Byas* |
| 27/74 | **Lone Ranger** *Oscar Brown Jr.* |
| 64/81 | **Loneliness** *Tavares* |
| 48/74 | **Loneliness Had Got A Hold On Me** *Roy 'C'* |
| 3/67 | **(Loneliness Made Me Realize) It's You That I Need** *Temptations* |
| 44/73 | **Loneliness (Will Bring Us Together Again)** *Brown Sugar* |
| 6/56 | **Lonely Avenue** *Ray Charles* |
| 22/62 | **Lonely Baby** *Ty Hunter* |
| 27/60 | **Lonely Blue Boy** *Conway Twitty* |
| 6/59 | **Lonely Boy** *Paul Anka* |
| | **Lonely Christmas** *..see: (It's Gonna Be A)* |
| 65/73 | **Lonely Days, Lonely Nights** *Don Downing* |
| 93/63 | **Lonely Drifter** *O'Jays* |
| 38/71 | **Lonely Feelin'** *War* |
| 10/58 | **Lonely Island** *Sam Cooke* |
| 25/72 | **Lonely Man** *Chi-Lites* |
| | **Lonely Nights** |
| 8/55 | *Hearts* |
| 28/84 | *Valentine Brothers* |
| 11/76 | **Lonely One** *Special Delivery featuring Terry Huff* |
| 45/87 | **Lonely Road** *Rose Royce* |
| | **Lonely Soldier** |
| 25/60 | *Jerry Butler* |
| 38/66 | *Mike Williams* |
| | **Lonely Street** |
| 20/59 | *Andy Williams* |
| 19/61 | *Clarence 'Frogman' Henry* |
| 1/58 | **Lonely Teardrops** *Jackie Wilson* |
| 9/60 | **Lonely Winds** *Drifters* |
| 15/48 | **Lonesome Blues** *Johnny Moore's Three Blazers* |
| 7/50 | **Lonesome Cabin Blues** *Mercy Dee* |
| 7/51 | **Lonesome Christmas** *Lowell Fulson* |
| 4/45 | **Lonesome Lover Blues** *Billy Eckstine* |
| 15/59 | **Lonesome Town** *Ricky Nelson* |
| 8/61 | **Lonesome Whistle Blues** *Freddy King* |
| 1/48 | **'Long About Midnight** *Roy Brown* |
| 8/50 | **Long About Sundown** *Roy Brown* |
| | **Long And Winding Road** |
| 91/76 | *New Birth* |
| 94/77 | *Melba Moore* |
| 63/74 | **Long As There's You (I Got Love)** *Leon Haywood* |
| 8/51 | **Long Distance Call** *Muddy Waters* |
| 75/79 | **Long Distance Love** *Latimore* |
| 1/48 | **Long Gone** *Sonny Thompson* |
| 3/49 | **Long John Blues** *Dinah Washington* |
| 64/81 | **Long Live Soul Music** *Spinners* |
| | **Long Lonely Nights** |
| 1/57 | *Clyde McPhatter* |
| 11/57 | *Lee Andrews & The Hearts* |
| 27/70 | *Dells* |
| 35/65 | **Long, Long Winter** *Impressions* *(also see: It's Gonna Be)* |
| 10/48 | **Long Skirt Baby Blues** *T-Bone Walker* |
| 6/78 | **Long Stroke** *ADC Band* |
| 9/48 | **Long Tall Mama** *Smokey Hogg* |
| 1/56 | **Long Tall Sally** *Little Richard* |
| 96/64 | **Long Tall Shorty** *Tommy Tucker* |
| 9/49 | **Long Time** *Charles Brown Trio* |
| 54/87 | **Long Time Coming** *Ready For The World* |

| | |
|---|---|
| 69/87 | **Look Around** *Freddie Jackson* |
| 12/67 | **Look At Granny Run, Run** *Howard Tate* |
| 42/69 | **Look At Mary Wonder (How I Got Over)** *Little Carl Carlton* |
| 1/75 | **Look At Me (I'm In Love)** *Moments* |
| 31/75 | **Look At You** *George McCrae* |
| 73/64 | **Look Away** *Garnet Mimms* |
| | **Look Before You Leap** |
| 77/83 | *Cheryl Lynn* |
| 82/83 | *Mikki* |
| 6/61 | **Look In My Eyes** *Chantels* |
| 29/81 | **Look In Your Eyes** *Maze Featuring Frankie Beverly* |
| 10/77 | **Look Into Your Heart** *Aretha Franklin* |
| 11/70 | **Look-Ka Py Py** *Meters* |
| 36/73 | **Look Me Up** *Blue Magic* |
| 43/74 | **Look On The Good Side** *Invitations* |
| 5/47 | **Look Out** *Louis Jordan* |
| | **Look Over Your Shoulder** |
| 27/68 | *O'Jays* |
| 45/73 | *Escorts* |
| 14/84 | **Look The Other Way** *Isley, Jasper, Isley* |
| 13/80 | **Look Up** *Patrice Rushen* |
| 74/78 | **Look Up With Your Mind** *Lenny Williams* |
| 25/72 | **Look What They've Done To My Song, Ma** *Ray Charles* |
| 31/71 | **Look What We've Done To Love** *Glass House* |
| 2/72 | **Look What You Done For Me** *Al Green* |
| 8/88 | **Look What You Started** *Temptations* |
| 27/77 | **Look What You've Done To My Heart** *Marilyn McCoo & Billy Davis, Jr.* |
| 59/86 | **Look What's Showing Through** *Rodney Franklin* |
| 68/85 | **Look Whatcha Done Now** *Rodney Saulsberry* |
| 68/82 | **Look Who's Lonely Now** *Randy Crawford* |
| | **Lookin' For A Love** |
| 8/62 | *Valentinos* |
| 1/74 | *Bobby Womack* |
| 47/79 | **Lookin' For Love** *Fat Larry's Band* |
| 5/72 | **Lookin' Through The Windows** *Jackson 5* |
| 64/83 | **Looking At Midnight** *Imagination* |
| | **Looking Back** |
| 2/58 | *Nat King Cole* |
| 42/69 | *Joe Simon* |
| 20/68 | **Looking For A Fox** *Clarence Carter* |
| 1/87 | **Looking For A New Love** *Jody Watley* |
| 42/80 | **Looking For Love** *Candi Staton* |
| 36/83 | **Looking For The Perfect Beat** *Afrika Bambaataa* |
| 47/82 | **Looking Up To You** *Michael Wycoff* |
| 38/65 | **Looking With My Eyes** *Dionne Warwick* |
| 17/70 | **Looky Looky (Look At Me Girl)** *O'Jays* |
| 6/63 | **Loop De Loop** *Johnny Thunder* |
| 19/82 | **Loopzilla** *George Clinton* |
| | **Loose Booty** |
| 49/73 | *Funkadelic* |
| 22/74 | *Sly & The Family Stone* |
| 48/79 | **Loose Caboose** *Joe Tex* |
| 1/88 | **Loosey's Rap** *Rick James featuring Roxanne Shante* |
| 48/73 | **Lord Don't Move The Mountains** *Inez Andrews* |
| 31/70 | **(Lord) Send Me Somebody** *Green Berets* |
| 34/65 | **Loser, The** *Skyliners* |
| | **Loser's Seat** *..see: (All Your Goodies Are Gone)* |
| 26/70 | **Losers Weepers** *Etta James* |
| 27/62 | **Losing Battle** *Johnny Adams* |
| 13/63 | **Losing You** *Brenda Lee* |
| | **Lost** |
| 17/59 | *Jerry Butler* |
| 15/68 | *Jerry Butler* |
| | **Lost And Turned Out** *..see: (Olivia)* |

| 7/56 | **Lost Dreams** *Ernie Freeman* |
| 98/78 | **Lost In A Love Zone** *Ruth Davis* |
| 1/87 | **Lost In Emotion** *Lisa Lisa & Cult Jam* |
| 6/85 | **Lost In Love** *New Edition* |
| 35/79 | **Lost In Loving You** *McCrarys* |
| 35/79 | **Lost In Music** *Sister Sledge* |
| 2/51 | **Lost Love** *Percy Mayfield* |
| 8/50 | **Lost My Baby** *Larry Darnell* |
| 2/62 | **Lost Someone** *James Brown* |
| 7/57 | **Lotta Lovin'** *Gene Vincent* |
| 72/83 | **Lou's Blues** *Patrick Williams* |
| 77/74 | **Louise** *Ray Charles* |
| 10/51 | **Louisiana Blues** *Muddy Waters* |
| 14/76 | **Love** *Graham Central Station* |
| 75/80 | **Love Ain't Easy** *Barry White* |
| 23/73 | **Love Ain't Gonna Run Me Away** |
| | *Luther Ingram* |
| 79/84 | **Love Ain't No Holiday** *Native* |
| 96/75 | **Love Ain't No Toy** *Yvonne Fair* |
| 49/70 | **Love Ain't Nothing But A Business** |
| | *Bobby Adams* |
| 6/81 | **Love Ail The Hurt Away** |
| | *Aretha Franklin & George Benson* |
| 7/86 | **Love Always** *El DeBarge* |
| 63/86 | **Love Always Finds A Way** *Peabo Bryson* |
| 44/79 | **Love And Desire** *Arpeggio* |
| | **Love And Happiness** |
| 22/73 | *Earnest Jackson* |
| 92/77 | *Al Green* |
| 66/85 | *David Sanborn* |
| 23/72 | **Love And Liberty** *Laura Lee* |
| 8/76 | **Love And Understanding (Come** |
| | **Together)** *Kool & The Gang* |
| 93/79 | **Love At First Sight** *Stylistics* |
| | **Love Attack** |
| 21/66 | *James Carr* |
| 40/78 | *Shotgun* |
| 60/81 | *Mighty Fire* |
| 73/85 | *Shantelle* |
| | **Love Ballad** |
| 1/76 | *L.T.D.* |
| 95/77 | *Gary Bartz* |
| 3/79 | *George Benson* |
| 24/75 | **Love Being Your Fool** *Charlie Whitehead* |
| 2/85 | **Love Bizarre** *Sheila E.* |
| 61/75 | **Love Blind** *Martha Reeves* |
| 4/70 | **Love Bones** *Johnnie Taylor* |
| 20/78 | **Love Brought Me Back** *D.J. Rogers* |
| 81/77 | **Love Bug** *Bumble Bee Unlimited* |
| 14/67 | **Love Bug Leave My Heart Alone** |
| | *Martha & The Vandellas* |
| 24/62 | **Love Came To Me** *Dion* |
| 31/73 | **Love Chain** *Candi Staton* |
| | **Love Changes** |
| 26/79 | *Mother's Finest* |
| 68/82 | *O.C. Smith* |
| 2/88 | *Kashif & Meli'sa Morgan* |
| 88/76 | **Love Chant** *Eli's Second Coming* |
| 2/68 | **Love Child** *Supremes* |
| 1/82 | **Love Come Down** *Evelyn King* |
| 68/82 | **Love Connection (Raise The Window** |
| | **Down)** *Spinners* |
| 15/75 | **Love Corporation** *Hues Corporation* |
| 44/80 | **Love Cycles** *D.J. Rogers* |
| 19/75 | **Love Don't Come No Stronger (Than Yours** |
| | **And Mine)** *Jeff Perry* |
| 31/88 | **Love Don't Give No Reason** |
| | *Smokey Robinson* |
| 5/78 | **Love Don't Live Here Anymore** *Rose Royce* |
| | **Love Don't Love Nobody** |
| 2/50 | *Roy Brown* |
| 4/74 | *Spinners* |
| 35/81 | *Jean Carn* |
| 6/80 | **Love Don't Make It Right** |
| | *Ashford & Simpson* |

| 52/81 | **Love Don't Strike Twice** *Blackbyrds* |
| 31/75 | **Love Don't You Go Through No Changes On** |
| | **Me** *Sister Sledge* |
| 59/84 | **Love Emergency** *Mikki* |
| 75/74 | **Love Epidemic** *Trammps* |
| | **Love Explosion** |
| 43/68 | *Troy Keyes* |
| 92/75 | *Bazuka* |
| 24/82 | **Love Fever** *Gayle Adams* |
| 3/75 | **Love Finds It's Own Way** |
| | *Gladys Knight & The Pips* |
| 9/49 | **Love For Christmas** *Felix Gross* |
| 6/86 | **Love 4/2** *Teddy Pendergrass* |
| 61/75 | **Love Freeze** *First Choice* |
| 75/84 | **Love Gone Bad** *Mavis Staples* |
| 8/72 | **Love Gonna Pack Up (And Walk Out)** |
| | *Persuaders* |
| 13/79 | **Love Gun** *Rick James* |
| | **Love Hangover** |
| 1/76 | *Diana Ross* |
| 39/76 | *5th Dimension* |
| 35/84 | **Love Has A Mind Of It's Own** |
| | *Donna Summer* |
| 15/81 | **Love Has Come Around** *Donald Byrd* |
| 3/84 | **Love Has Finally Come At Last** |
| | *Bobby Womack & Patti LaBelle* |
| 42/82 | **Love Has Found Its Way** *Dennis Brown* |
| 45/75 | **Love Has Found Its Way To Me** *Blue Magic* |
| 8/55 | **Love Has Joined Us Together** |
| | *Ruth Brown & Clyde McPhatter* |
| 68/77 | **Love Having You Around** *First Choice* |
| 43/79 | **Love Hurt Me, Love Healed Me** |
| | *Lenny Williams* |
| 1/73 | **Love I Lost** *Harold Melvin & The Blue Notes* |
| 48/68 | **Love I Need** *Ruby Andrews* |
| 11/76 | **Love I Never Had** *Tavares* |
| 60/78 | **Love, I Never Had It So Good** |
| | *Quincy Jones* |
| 10/67 | **Love I Saw In You Was Just A Mirage** |
| | *Smokey Robinson & The Miracles* |
| | **Love In 'C' Minor** |
| 29/77 | *Cerrone* |
| 85/77 | *Heart & Soul Orchestra* |
| 17/85 | **Love In Moderation** *Gwen Guthrie* |
| 59/80 | **Love In Perfect Harmony** *Fatback* |
| 31/81 | **Love In The Fast Lane** *Dynasty* |
| 38/68 | **Love In Them There Hills** *Vibrations* |
| 47/75 | **Love Inflation** *Joneses* |
| 23/80 | **Love Injection** *Trussel* |
| 16/75 | **Love Insurance** *Gwen McCrae* |
| | **Love Is** |
| 50/78 | *Brothers Johnson* |
| 32/79 | *Vernon Burch* |
| 6/87 | **Love Is A Dangerous Game** *Millie Jackson* |
| 30/67 | **Love Is A Doggone Good Thing** |
| | *Eddie Floyd* |
| | **Love Is A 5-Letter Word** |
| 12/65 | *James Phelps* |
| 31/75 | *Jimmy Witherspoon* |
| 1/87 | **Love Is A House** *Force M.D.'s* |
| | **Love Is A Hurtin' Thing** |
| 1/66 | *Lou Rawls* |
| 59/73 | *Soul Children* |
| 46/81 | **Love Is A Waiting Game** |
| | *Roberta Flack & Peabo Bryson* |
| 98/76 | **Love Is Alive** *Gary Wright* |
| 20/78 | **Love Is All You Need** *High Inergy* |
| 3/77 | **Love Is Better In The A.M.** *Johnnie Taylor* |
| | **Love Is Blue** *..see: I Can Sing A Rainbow* |
| 58/87 | **Love Is Contagious** *Taja Sevelle* |
| 11/87 | **Love Is For Suckers (Like Me And You)** |
| | *Full Force* |
| 10/86 | **Love Is Forever** *Billy Ocean* |
| 18/71 | **Love Is Funny That Way** *Jackie Wilson* |
| 98/80 | **Love Is Gone** *Top Shelf* |

| | | | | |
|---|---|---|---|---|
| 4/88 | **Love Struck** *Jesse Johnson* | | 17/59 | **Love's Burning Fire** *Beverly Ann Gibson* |
| | **Love T.K.O.** | | | **Love's Calling** |
| 2/80 | *Teddy Pendergrass* | | 29/81 | *Zingara* |
| 77/80 | *David Oliver* | | 48/85 | *Opus 10* |
| 9/86 | **Love Take Over** *Five Star* | | 5/82 | **Love's Comin' At Ya** *Melba Moore* |
| 72/75 | **Love Takes Tears** *Johnny Bristol* | | 24/81 | **Love's Dance** *Klique* |
| | **Love Talk** | | 41/66 | **Love's Gone Bad** *Chris Clark* |
| 70/76 | *Jim Gilstrap* | | 38/86 | **Love's Gonna Get You** *Jocelyn Brown* |
| 88/84 | *Prime Time* | | 61/76 | **Love's Got Me Tired (But I Ain't Tired Of** |
| 38/69 | **Love That A Woman Should Give To A** | | | **Love)** *Laura Lee* |
| | **Man** *Patti Drew* | | 28/71 | **Love's Lines, Angles And Rhymes** |
| 23/74 | **Love That Really Counts** *Natural Four* | | | *5th Dimension* |
| 59/78 | **Love That Will Not Die** | | 75/73 | **Love's Maze** *Temprees* |
| | *Johnny 'Guitar' Watson* | | 23/86 | **Love's On Fire** |
| 35/68 | **Love That's Real** *Intruders* | | | *Aleem featuring Leroy Burgess* |
| 31/72 | **Love The Life You Live** *Kool & The Gang* | | 87/75 | **Love's So Wonderful** *Natural Four* |
| 5/86 | **Love The One I'm With (A Lot Of Love)** | | 13/72 | **Love's Street And Fool's Road** |
| | *Melba & Kashif* | | | *Solomon Burke* |
| 3/71 | **Love The One You're With** *Isley Brothers* | | 34/80 | **Love's Sweet Sensation** |
| 92/79 | **Love The Way** *Jorge Santana* | | | *Curtis Mayfield & Linda Clifford* |
| 48/70 | **Love The Way You Love** *O.V. Wright* | | 10/74 | **Love's Theme** *Love Unlimited Orchestra* |
| 91/78 | **Love The Way You Love Me** *Eddie Horan* | | 47/81 | **Loveline** *Tavares* |
| 9/80 | **Love X Love** *George Benson* | | 1/84 | **Lovelite** *O'Bryan* |
| 34/78 | **Love To Burn** *O.C. Smith* | | 6/78 | **Lovely Day** *Bill Withers* |
| 92/75 | **Love To Dance This One With You** | | 70/65 | **Lovely, Lovely (Loverly, Loverly)** |
| | *Crystal Grass* | | | *Chubby Checker* |
| 3/76 | **Love To Love You Baby** *Donna Summer* | | 75/78 | **Lovely Night For Dancing** *Bill Withers* |
| 14/78 | **Love To See You Smile** *Bobby Bland* | | 2/80 | **Lovely One** *Jacksons* |
| 27/77 | **Love To The World** *L.T.D.* | | 14/70 | **Lovely Way She Loves** *Moments* |
| 48/80 | **Love Touch** *Jeff & Aleta* | | 50/87 | **Lover, The** *Egyptian Lover* |
| 46/83 | **Love Town** *Booker Newberry III* | | 20/79 | **Lover And Friend** *Minnie Riperton* |
| | **Love Train** | | 9/49 | **Lover Come Back To Me** *Al Hibbler* |
| 1/73 | *O'Jays* | | 64/88 | **Lover For Life** *Mission* |
| 28/74 | *Bunny Sigler* | | 55/82 | **Lover In You** *Sugarhill Gang* |
| 18/78 | **L-O-V-E-U** *Brass Construction* | | 34/77 | **Lover Jones** *Johnny 'Guitar' Watson* |
| | **Love Uprising** | | 5/45 | **Lover Man (Oh, Where Can You Be)** |
| 19/70 | *Otis Leaville* | | | *Billie Holiday* |
| 17/80 | *Tavares* | | F/70 | **Lover With A Reputation** *Bobby Bland* |
| 15/79 | **Love Vibration** *Joe Simon* | | 4/65 | **Lover's Concerto** *Toys* |
| 35/71 | **Love Vibrations** *David T. Walker* | | | **Lover's Holiday** |
| 16/60 | **Love Walked In** *Dinah Washington* | | 8/68 | *Peggy Scott & Jo Jo Benson* |
| | **Love We Had (Stays On My Mind)** | | 68/76 | *Leroy Hutson* |
| 8/71 | *Dells* | | 5/80 | *Change* |
| 64/73 | *Jerry Butler & Brenda Lee Eager* | | 26/87 | **Lover's Lane** *Georgio* |
| 90/79 | **Love When I'm In Your Arms** | | 97/64 | **Lover's Prayer** *Wallace Brothers* |
| | *Bobbi Humphrey* | | | **Lover's Question** |
| 41/79 | **Love Will Bring Us Back Together** | | 1/58 | *Clyde McPhatter* |
| | *Roy Ayers* | | 20/69 | *Otis Redding* |
| 2/86 | **Love Will Conquer All** *Lionel Richie* | | 20/85 | **Loverboy** *Billy Ocean* |
| 80/85 | **Love Will Find A Way** *George Howard* | | 9/85 | **Lovergirl** *Teena Marie* |
| 69/76 | **Love Will Keep Us Together** *Wilson Pickett* | | 34/85 | **Loveride** *Nuance featuring Vikki Love* |
| 88/81 | **Love Will Make It All Right** *Jerry Bell* | | | **Lovers** |
| 25/68 | **Love Will Rain On You** | | 42/87 | *Babyface* |
| | *Archie Bell & The Drells* | | 41/88 | *Alexander O'Neal* |
| 5/88 | **Love Will Save The Day** *Whitney Houston* | | 34/81 | **Lovers After All** |
| | **Love Won't Let Me Wait** | | | *Melissa Manchester & Peabo Bryson* |
| 1/75 | *Major Harris* | | 89/64 | **Lovers Always Forgive** |
| 78/80 | *Jackie Moore* | | | *Gladys Knight & The Pips* |
| 32/84 | *Johnny Mathis & Deniece Williams* | | 25/59 | **Lovers Never Say Goodbye** *Flamingos* |
| 49/68 | **Love Won't Wear Off** *J.R. Bailey* | | 16/62 | **Lovers Who Wander** *Dion* |
| | **Love You** *..also see: Love U* | | 72/73 | **Loves Me Like A Rock** *Dixie Hummingbirds* |
| 1/86 | **Love You Down** *Ready For The World* | | | **Lovey Dovey** |
| 57/79 | **Love You Inside Out** *Bee Gees* | | 2/54 | *Clovers* |
| 43/72 | **Love You Left Behind** *Syl Johnson* | | 12/59 | *Clyde McPhatter* |
| 47/82 | **Love You Madly** *Candela* | | 21/68 | *Otis & Carla* |
| 12/58 | **Love You Most Of All** *Sam Cooke* | | 4/88 | *Tony Terry* |
| 1/70 | **Love You Save** *Jackson 5* | | 40/85 | **Lovin'** *Jonzun Crew* |
| 2/66 | **Love You Save (May Be Your Own)** *Joe Tex* | | 38/87 | **Lovin' Ev'ry Minute Of It** *Doug E. Fresh* |
| 11/60 | **Love You So** | | | **Lovin' Feeling** *..see: (It's That)* |
| | *Ron Holden with The Thunderbirds* | | 51/78 | **Lovin' Fever** *High Inergy* |
| 1/86 | **Love Zone** *Billy Ocean* | | | **Lovin' Is Really My Game** |
| | **Love's** *..also see: Luv's* | | 14/77 | *Brainstorm* |
| 89/86 | **Love's A Criminal** *Voltage Brothers* | | 68/79 | *Betty Wright* |
| 7/57 | **Love's A Hurting Game** *Ivory Joe Hunter* | | 5/52 | **Lovin' Machine** *Wynonie Harris* |
| 75/83 | **Love's A Merry-Go-'Round** *Juicy* | | 22/73 | **Lovin' On Borrowed Time** *William Bell* |

# M

| | | | | |
|---|---|---|---|---|
| 19/85 | **Make Your Move On Me Baby** | | F/56 | **Mary Ann**  *Ray Charles* |
| | *Charlie Singleton* | | 23/87 | **Mary Goes 'Round**  *Ready For The World* |
| 13/76 | **Make Yours A Happy Home** | | 8/49 | **Mary Is Fine**  *Gatemouth Brown* |
| | *Gladys Knight & The Pips* | | 3/78 | **Mary Jane**  *Rick James* |
| 91/77 | **Makes You Blind**  *Glitter Band* | | 1/52 | **Mary Jo**  *Four Blazes* |
| | **Makin' Love** | | 7/59 | **Mary Lou**  *Ronnie Hawkins* |
| 27/59 | *Floyd Robinson* | | 29/88 | **Mary Mack**  *Babyface* |
| 64/75 | *Fred Wesley & The J.B.'s* | | 81/76 | **Masada**  *Joe Thomas* |
| 58/83 | **Makin' Love In The Fast Lane**  *Mellaa* | | 1/62 | **Mashed Potato Time**  *Dee Dee Sharp* |
| 49/78 | **Makin' Love Is Good For You** | | | **Mashed Potatoes**  *..see: (Do The)* |
| | *Brook Benton* | | 21/62 | **Mashed Potatoes U.S.A.**  *James Brown* |
| 14/65 | **Makin' Whoopee**  *Ray Charles* | | 1/80 | **Master Blaster (Jammin')**  *Stevie Wonder* |
| | **Making Love** | | 88/77 | **Master Booty**  *Fatback* |
| 73/80 | *Herbie Hancock* | | 8/73 | **Master Of Eyes (The Deepness Of Your** |
| 29/82 | *Roberta Flack* | | | **Eyes)**  *Aretha Franklin* |
| 83/76 | **Making Love Ain't No Fun (Without The One** | | 60/74 | **Master Plan**  *Kay-Gees* |
| | **You Love)**  *Ebonys* | | 1/73 | **Masterpiece**  *Temptations* |
| 7/87 | **Making Love In The Rain**  *Herb Alpert* | | 20/64 | **Matador, The**  *Major Lance* |
| 86/74 | **Making My Daydream Real**  *We The People* | | 49/85 | **Material Girl**  *Madonna* |
| 16/68 | **Malinda**  *Bobby Taylor & The Vancouvers* | | 14/85 | **Material Thangz**  *Deele* |
| 36/79 | **Mama Can't Buy You Love**  *Elton John* | | 82/78 | **Maximum Stimulation**  *Jimmy Castor* |
| 40/68 | **(Mama Come Quick, And Bring Your) Lickin'** | | 42/86 | **May I?**  *Isley Brothers* |
| | **Stick**  *George Torrence* | | 39/72 | **May The Best Man Win**  *Ollie Nightingale* |
| 8/63 | **Mama Didn't Lie**  *Jan Bradley* | | | **Maybe** |
| 37/73 | **Mama Feel Good**  *Lyn Collins* | | 2/58 | *Chantels* |
| 1/53 | **(Mama) He Treats Your Daughter Mean** | | 4/70 | *Three Degrees* |
| | *Ruth Brown* | | 68/83 | *Peabo Bryson/Roberta Flack* |
| 46/73 | **Mama I Got A Brand New Thing (Don't Say** | | 4/58 | **Maybe Baby**  *Crickets* |
| | **No)**  *Undisputed Truth* | | 3/71 | **Maybe Tomorrow**  *Jackson 5* |
| 10/57 | **Mama Look At Bubu**  *Harry Belafonte* | | 88/64 | **Maybe Tonight**  *Shirelles* |
| 2/61 | **Mama Said**  *Shirelles* | | 1/55 | **Maybellene**  *Chuck Berry* |
| 11/55 | **Mama, Talk To Your Daughter** | | 13/55 | **Maybelline**  *Jim Lowe* |
| | *J.B. Lenore* | | 70/74 | **Me & You**  *Young Hearts* |
| 16/72 | **Mama Told Me Not To Come**  *Wilson Pickett* | | 18/73 | **Me And Baby Brother**  *War* |
| 2/82 | **Mama Used To Say**  *Junior* | | | **Me And Mrs. Jones** |
| 72/76 | **Mama You're All Right With Me**  *Four Tops* | | 1/72 | *Billy Paul* |
| 33/70 | **Mama's Baby - Daddy's Maybe** | | 4/75 | *Ron Banks & The Dramatics* |
| | *Swamp Dogg* | | 54/76 | **Me And My Gemini**  *First Class* |
| 20/72 | **Mama's Little Baby**  *Brotherly Love* | | 40/67 | **Me And My Imagination**  *Ovations* |
| 2/71 | **Mama's Pearl**  *Jackson 5* | | 39/77 | **Me And My Music**  *Spinners* |
| 2/88 | **Mamacita**  *Troop* | | 82/79 | **Me And The Gang**  *Hamilton Bohannon* |
| 1/54 | **Mambo Baby** | | | **Me And You** |
| | *Ruth Brown & Her Rhythmakers* | | 38/69 | *O.C. Smith* |
| 4/51 | **Mambo Boogie**  *Johnny Otis Orchestra* | | 70/81 | *Chi-Lites* |
| 20/68 | **Man And A Half**  *Wilson Pickett* | | 41/69 | **Me Tarzan You Jane**  *Intruders* |
| 1/88 | **Man In The Mirror**  *Michael Jackson* | | 55/78 | **Mean Machine** |
| | **Man In You** | | | *Miracles featuring Billy Griffin* |
| | *..see: (You Can't Let The Boy Overpower)* | | 6/53 | **Mean Old World**  *Little Walter* |
| 45/66 | **Man Loves Two**  *Little Milton* | | | **Mean Woman Blues** |
| 16/68 | **Man Needs A Woman**  *James Carr* | | 11/57 | *Elvis Presley* |
| 85/79 | **Man Of Value**  *Tyrone Barkley* | | 8/63 | *Roy Orbison* |
| 27/67 | **Man Or Mouse**  *Junior Parker* | | 47/81 | **Meant For You**  *Debra Laws* |
| 43/86 | **Man Size Love**  *Klymaxx* | | 67/79 | **Meat The Beat**  *East Coast* |
| 4/72 | **Man Sized Job**  *Denise LaSalle* | | 23/85 | **Mechanical Emotion**  *Vanity* |
| 39/75 | **Man To Woman**  *Lonnie Youngblood* | | 8/84 | **Medicine Song**  *Stephanie Mills* |
| 88/76 | **Man's Got Too Much Dog In Him** | | 32/69 | **Meditation, The**  *TNT Band* |
| | *Shelbra Deane* | | 3/47 | **Meet Me At No Special Place**  *Nat King Cole* |
| 17/63 | **Man's Temptation**  *Gene Chandler* | | 18/62 | **Meet Me At The Twistin' Place** |
| 10/48 | **Manana**  *Mills Brothers* | | | *Johnnie Morisette* |
| 78/82 | **Maneater**  *Daryl Hall & John Oates* | | 4/85 | **Meeting In The Ladies Room**  *Klymaxx* |
| 40/74 | **Mango Meat**  *Mandrill* | | 12/65 | **Meeting Over Yonder**  *Impressions* |
| 74/81 | **Manhattan Melody**  *Herb Alpert* | | 36/84 | **Mega-Mix**  *Herbie Hancock* |
| 5/55 | **Manish Boy**  *Muddy Waters* | | 20/81 | **Melancholy Fire**  *Norman Connors* |
| | *(also see: I'm A Man)* | | 8/52 | **Mellow Blues**  *Sonny Thompson* |
| 13/48 | **Manteca**  *Dizzy Gillespie* | | 53/78 | **Mellow Lovin'**  *Judy Cheeks* |
| | **Many Rains Ago (Oluwa)** | | 82/76 | **Mellow Madness**  *Quincy Jones* |
| | *..see: Roots Mural Theme* | | 32/79 | **Mellow, Mellow Right On**  *Lowrell* |
| 33/88 | **Marc Anthony's Tune**  *Tyka Nelson* | | 35/68 | **Mellow Moonlight**  *Leon Haywood* |
| 93/76 | **Marching In The Street**  *Harvey Mason* | | 60/77 | **Melodies**  *Made In U.S.A.* |
| 13/49 | **Mardi Gras**  *Joe Lutcher* | | 21/71 | **Melting Pot**  *Booker T. & The MG's* |
| 2/53 | **Marie**  *Four Tunes* | | 54/85 | **Members Only**  *Bobby Bland* |
| 16/76 | **Married, But Not To Each Other** | | 16/79 | **Memory Lane**  *Minnie Riperton* |
| | *Denise LaSalle* | | 4/63 | **Memphis**  *Lonnie Mack* |
| 40/65 | **Marry Me**  *Johnny Daye* | | 6/67 | **Memphis Soul Stew**  *King Curtis* |
| 27/63 | **Martian Hop**  *Ran-Dells* | | 42/69 | **Memphis Underground**  *Herbie Mann* |

| | | | | |
|---|---|---|---|---|
| 5/85 | **Men All Pause**  *Klymaxx* | | 62/75 | **Migration**  *Creative Source* |
| | **Men Are Gettin' Scarce** | | 8/48 | **Milky White Way**  *Trumpeteers* |
| 7/68 | *Joe Tex* | | 52/83 | **Million Dollar Babe**  *Stacy Lattisaw* |
| 33/71 | *Chairmen Of The Board* | | 6/50 | **Million Dollar Secret**  *Helen Humes* |
| 7/53 | **Mend Your Ways**  *Ruth Brown* | | 45/73 | **Million Dollars**  *Soul Generation* |
| 1/88 | **Mercedes Boy**  *Pebbles* | | | **Million To One** |
| 49/87 | **Mercury Rising**  *Pointer Sisters* | | 8/60 | *Jimmy Charles* |
| 35/64 | **Mercy, Mercy**  *Don Covay & The Goodtimers* | | 28/68 | *Five Stairsteps & Cubie* |
| 1/71 | **Mercy Mercy Me (The Ecology)** | | 47/72 | *Manhattans* |
| | *Marvin Gaye* | | 4/46 | **Milton's Boogie**  *Roy Milton* |
| | **Mercy, Mercy, Mercy** | | 49/78 | **Mind Blowing Decisions**  *Heatwave* |
| 2/67 | *Cannonball Adderley* | | 91/78 | **Mind Pleaser**  *Cuba Gooding* |
| 23/67 | *Larry Williams & Johnny Watson* | | 25/83 | **Mind Up Tonight**  *Melba Moore* |
| 33/67 | *Marlena Shaw* | | 19/61 | **Mind Your Own Business**  *Eugene Church* |
| 6/53 | **Mercy, Mr. Percy**  *Varetta Dillard* | | 12/86 | **Mine All Mine**  *Ca$hflow* |
| | **Merry Christmas Baby** | | 25/66 | **Mine Exclusively**  *Olympics* |
| 3/48 | *Johnny Moore* | | 19/69 | **Mini-Skirt Minnie**  *Wilson Pickett* |
| 8/48 | *Johnny Moore* | | 91/78 | **Minnie The Moocher**  *Cab Calloway* |
| 9/50 | *Johnny Moore* | | 27/69 | **Minotaur, The**  *Dick Hyman* |
| | **Merry-Go-Round** | | | **Minute By Minute** |
| 26/61 | *Marv Johnson* | | 74/79 | *Doobie Brothers* |
| 20/76 | *Monday After* | | 12/80 | *Peabo Bryson* |
| 77/77 | *Ohio Players* | | 27/60 | **Mio Amore**  *Flamingos* |
| | **Message, The** | | 13/83 | **Miracles**  *Stacy Lattisaw* |
| 22/73 | *Cymandc* | | 66/83 | **Mirda Rock**  *Reggie Griffin & Technofunk* |
| 4/82 | *Grandmaster Flash & The Furious Five* | | 2/82 | **Mirror, Mirror**  *Diana Ross* |
| 19/70 | **Message From A Black Man**  *Whatnauts* | | 7/73 | **Misdemeanor**  *Foster Sylvers* |
| 31/68 | **Message From Maria**  *Joe Simon* | | | **Misery** |
| 21/70 | **Message From The Meters**  *Meters* | | 9/50 | *Little Esther/Johnny Otis Orchestra* |
| 32/83 | **Message II (Survival)** | | 44/63 | *Dynamics* |
| | *Melle Mel & Duke Bootee* | | 3/85 | **Misled**  *Kool & The Gang* |
| 1/76 | **Message In Our Music**  *O'Jays* | | | **Miss** ..also see: Ms. |
| 42/77 | **Message (Inspiration)**  *Brass Construction* | | 6/57 | **Miss Ann**  *Little Richard* |
| 5/66 | **Message To Michael**  *Dionne Warwick* | | 26/78 | **Miss Broadway**  *Belle Epoque* |
| 1/48 | **Messin' Around**  *Memphis Slim* | | 67/83 | **Miss Busy Body (Get Your Body Busy)** |
| 19/75 | **Messin' With My Mind**  *LaBelle* | | | *Temptations* |
| 54/74 | **Messing Up A Good Thing**  *John Edwards* | | 8/49 | **Miss Fanny Brown**  *Roy Brown* |
| 58/81 | **Messing With My Mind**  *Lenny Williams* | | 8/84 | **Miss Me Blind**  *Culture Club* |
| 21/85 | **Method Of Modern Love** | | 90/79 | **Miss Thing**  *Melba Moore* |
| | *Daryl Hall & John Oates* | | 33/78 | **Miss You**  *Rolling Stones* |
| 22/61 | **Mexico**  *Bob Moore* | | 8/57 | **Miss You So**  *Lillian Offitt* |
| 14/59 | **Miami**  *Eugene Church* | | 35/69 | **Mrs. Robinson**  *Booker T. & The MG's* |
| 10/85 | **Miami Vice Theme**  *Jan Hammer* | | | **Missing You** |
| 5/66 | **Michael**  *C.O.D.'s* | | F/72 | *Luther Ingram* |
| 3/63 | **Mickey's Monkey**  *Miracles* | | 1/85 | *Diana Ross* |
| 7/86 | **Midas Touch**  *Midnight Star* | | 14/49 | **Mississippi Blues**  *Floyd Dixon* |
| 45/81 | **Middle Of A Slow Dance**  *Klique* | | 61/85 | **Mistake No. 3**  *Culture Club* |
| | **Middle Of The Night** | | 20/71 | **Mr. And Mrs. Untrue**  *Candi Staton* |
| 3/52 | *Clovers* | | | **Mr. Big Stuff** |
| 63/85 | *Taka Boom* | | 1/71 | *Jean Knight* |
| 14/74 | **Midnight And You**  *Solomon Burke* | | 60/87 | *Heavy D. & The Boyz* |
| 11/48 | **Midnight Blues**  *T-Bone Walker* | | 3/59 | **Mr. Blue**  *Fleetwoods* |
| 5/74 | **Midnight Flower**  *Four Tops* | | 98/77 | **Mister Boogie Man**  *Avalanche '77'* |
| 12/59 | **Midnight Flyer**  *Nat King Cole* | | 9/60 | **Mr. Custer**  *Larry Verne* |
| 20/78 | **Midnight Girl**  *Lenny Williams* | | | **Mr. DJ** |
| 91/76 | **Midnight Groove**  *Love Unlimited Orchestra* | | 72/85 | *Concept* |
| 34/84 | **Midnight Hour**  *Roger* | | 90/87 | *Redd* |
| 72/76 | **Midnight Lady**  *David Morris Jr.* | | 13/75 | **Mr. D.J. (5 For The D.J.)**  *Aretha Franklin* |
| 36/84 | **Midnight Magnet**  *Teena Marie* | | 88/78 | **Mr. DJ You Know How To Make Me** |
| 8/75 | **Midnight Sky**  *Isley Brothers* | | | **Dance**  *Glass Family* |
| 47/76 | **Midnight Soul Patrol**  *Quincy Jones* | | 23/67 | **Mr. Dream Merchant**  *Jerry Butler* |
| | **Midnight Special** | | 1/42 | **Mr. Five By Five**  *Freddie Slack* |
| 12/48 | *Tiny Grimes* | | 53/78 | **Mr. Fix-It**  *Jeffree* |
| 13/62 | *Jimmy Smith* | | 8/84 | **Mr. Groove**  *One Way* |
| 20/59 | **Midnight Stroll**  *Revels* | | 1/57 | **Mr. Lee**  *Bobbettes* |
| 1/73 | **Midnight Train To Georgia** | | 16/75 | **Mister Magic**  *Grover Washington, Jr.* |
| | *Gladys Knight & The Pips* | | 16/73 | **Mr. Magic Man**  *Wilson Pickett* |
| 49/78 | **Mighty Army**  *New Birth* | | 38/79 | **Mr. Me, Mrs. You**  *Creme D' Cocoa* |
| 81/81 | **Mighty Body (Hotsy Totsy)**  *Leon Bryant* | | 10/76 | **Mr. Melody**  *Natalie Cole* |
| 47/75 | **Mighty Cloud Of Joy**  *Mighty Clouds Of Joy* | | 64/80 | **Mr. Miracle Man**  *Dee Edwards* |
| 50/81 | **Mighty Fine**  *TTF* | | 80/83 | **Mr. Nice Guy**  *Ronnie Laws* |
| 21/61 | **Mighty Good Lovin'**  *Miracles* | | 29/72 | **Mr. Penguin**  *Lunar Funk* |
| 22/76 | **Mighty High**  *Mighty Clouds Of Joy* | | 10/65 | **Mr. Pitiful**  *Otis Redding* |
| 1/74 | **Mighty Love**  *Spinners* | | | **Mr. Postman** ..see: Waitin' On A Letter |
| 4/74 | **Mighty Mighty**  *Earth, Wind & Fire* | | 39/68 | **Mr. Soul Satisfaction**  *Timmy Willis* |

| | |
|---|---|
| 76/83 | **Music Got Me** *Visual* |
| 7/75 | **Music In My Bones** *Joe Simon* |
| 81/79 | **Music Is My Way Of Life** *Patti LaBelle* |
| 97/77 | **Music Man** *Letta Mbulu* |
| 82/76 | **Music Matic** *Brick* |
| 12/61 | **Music, Music, Music** *Sensations* |
| 92/80 | **Music Speaks Louder Than Words** |
| | *Wilbert Longmire* |
| 29/80 | **Music Trance** *Ben E. King* |
| 31/71 | **Must Be Love Coming Down** *Major Lance* |
| 24/82 | **Must Be The Music** *Secret Weapon* |
| 35/69 | **Must Be Your Thing** |
| | *Charles Wright & The Watts 103rd Street* |
| | *Rhythm Band* |
| | **Mustang Sally** |
| 15/65 | *Sir Mack Rice* |
| 6/67 | *Wilson Pickett* |
| 67/77 | **Mutha Funk** *Shotgun* |
| 93/76 | **Mutha's Love** *Bobby Franklin* |
| 5/86 | **My Adidas** *Run-D.M.C.* |
| 11/66 | **My Answer** *Jimmy McCracklin* |
| | **My Babe** |
| 1/55 | *Little Walter* |
| 37/69 | *Willie Mitchell* |
| 4/65 | **My Baby** *Temptations* |
| 51/64 | **My Baby Don't Dig Me** *Ray Charles* |
| F/56 | **My Baby Left Me** *Elvis Presley* |
| | **My Baby Loves Me** |
| 3/66 | *Martha & The Vandellas* |
| 46/69 | *David T. Walker* |
| 84/85 | **My Baby Loves Me (Do Do)** *Twin Image* |
| 8/68 | **My Baby Must Be A Magician** *Marvelettes* |
| 45/69 | **My Baby Specializes** |
| | *William Bell & Judy Clay* |
| | **My Baby's Gone** |
| 6/50 | *Charles Brown* |
| 20/67 | *Donald Height* |
| 15/57 | **My Baby's Gone, On, On** *Johnnie & Joe* |
| 48/70 | **My Baby's Missing** *Gene Faith* |
| 43/66 | **My Back Scratcher** *Frank Frost* |
| 36/69 | **My Balloon's Going Up** |
| | *Archie Bell & The Drells* |
| 53/84 | **My Best Friend's Girlfriend** *Marcus Miller* |
| 5/56 | **My Blue Heaven** *Fats Domino* |
| 13/55 | **My Boy - Flat Top** *Boyd Bennett* |
| 2/64 | **My Boy Lollipop** *Millie Small* |
| 2/63 | **My Boyfriend's Back** *Angels* |
| 55/75 | **My Brand On You** *Denise LaSalle* |
| F/58 | **My Bucket's Got A Hole In It** *Ricky Nelson* |
| 4/69 | **My Cherie Amour** *Stevie Wonder* |
| 36/71 | **My Conscience** *Lovelites* |
| 5/53 | **My Country Man** *Big Maybelle* |
| 19/63 | **My Dad** *Paul Petersen* |
| 5/60 | **My Dearest Darling** *Etta James* |
| 23/69 | **My Deceiving Heart** *Impressions* |
| 81/81 | **My Destiny** *Alton McClain & Destiny* |
| 42/72 | **My Ding-A-Ling** *Chuck Berry* |
| 7/57 | **My Dream** *Platters* |
| 25/61 | **My Empty Arms** *Jackie Wilson* |
| 88/84 | **My Ever Changing Moods** *Style Council* |
| 33/73 | **My Everything You Are** *Mark IV* |
| 2/48 | **My Fault** *Brownie McGhee* |
| 76/78 | **My Favorite Fantasy** *Van McCoy* |
| 42/80 | **My Feet Keep Dancing** *Chic* |
| 77/81 | **My Feet Won't Move, But My Shoes Did The** |
| | **Boogie** *People's Choice* |
| 12/83 | **My First Love** *Rene & Angela* |
| 63/77 | **My First Mistake** *Chi-Lites* |
| 40/79 | **My Flame** *Bobby Caldwell* |
| 9/50 | **My Foolish Heart** *Gene Ammons* |
| 33/79 | **My Forbidden Lover** *Chic* |
| 2/87 | **My Forever Love** *Levert* |
| 6/46 | **My Gal's A Jockey** *Joe Turner* |

| | |
|---|---|
| | **My Girl** |
| 1/65 | *Temptations* |
| 43/70 | *Eddie Floyd* |
| 76/80 | *Amii Stewart (medley)* |
| 40/85 | *Hall & Oates/David Ruffin/Eddie Kendrick* |
| | *(medley)* |
| 3/88 | *Suave'* |
| 3/65 | **My Girl Has Gone** *Miracles* |
| 7/60 | **My Girl Josephine** *Fats Domino* |
| 22/85 | **My Girl Loves Me** *Shalamar* |
| 26/64 | **My Girl Sloopy** *Vibrations* |
| | **My Guy** |
| 1/64 | *Mary Wells* |
| 76/80 | *Amii Stewart & Johnny Bristol (medley)* |
| 14/82 | *Sister Sledge* |
| | **My Happiness** |
| 8/48 | *Ella Fitzgerald* |
| 11/59 | *Connie Francis* |
| 13/56 | **My Happiness Forever** *LaVern Baker* |
| 6/43 | **My Heart And I Decided** *Ella Fitzgerald* |
| 1/48 | **My Heart Belongs To You** *Arbee Stidham* |
| | **My Heart Cries For You** |
| 7/51 | *Dinah Washington* |
| 38/64 | *Ray Charles* |
| 48/87 | **My Heart Gets All The Breaks** *Monet* |
| 11/60 | **My Heart Has A Mind Of Its Own** |
| | *Connie Francis* |
| 11/59 | **My Heart Is An Open Book** |
| | *Carl Dobkins, Jr.* |
| 71/77 | **My Heart Just Can't Stop Dancing** |
| | *Swamp Dogg* |
| 46/73 | **My Heart Just Keeps On Breakin'** |
| | *Chi-Lites* |
| 50/68 | **My Heart Needs A Break** *Linda Jones* |
| 7/44 | **My Heart Tells Me** *Glen Gray* |
| 7/52 | **My Heart's Desire** *Jimmie Lee & Artis* |
| 48/84 | **My Heart's Divided** *Shannon* |
| 85/82 | **My Heart's Not In It** *Brenda Jones* |
| 19/60 | **My Hero** *Blue Notes* |
| | **My Honey And Me** |
| 19/69 | *Luther Ingram* |
| 18/72 | *Emotions* |
| 9/53 | **My Kind Of Woman** *Emitt Slay Trio* |
| 52/81 | **My Lady** *One Way* |
| 12/58 | **My Life** *Chuck Willis* |
| 4/44 | **My Little Brown Book** *Duke Ellington* |
| 4/75 | **My Little Lady** *Bloodstone* |
| | **My Love** |
| 12/60 | *Nat King Cole-Stan Kenton* |
| 10/74 | *Margie Joseph* |
| 6/83 | *Lionel Richie* |
| 51/78 | **My Love Ain't Never Been This Strong** |
| | *7th Wonder* |
| 43/80 | **My Love Don't Come Easy** *Jean Carn* |
| 44/83 | **My Love Grows Stronger** *Bloodstone* |
| 48/79 | **My Love Is** *Betty Wright* |
| 10/87 | **My Love Is Deep** *Lace* |
| 44/77 | **My Love Is Free** *Double Exposure* |
| 54/87 | **My Love Is Guaranteed** *Sybil* |
| 48/87 | **My Love Is On The Money** *La La* |
| 76/82 | **My Love Is Real** *Controllers* |
| 14/85 | **My Love Is True (Truly For You)** |
| | *Temptations* |
| 10/66 | **My Lover's Prayer** *Otis Redding* |
| 42/69 | **My Lucky Day** *Frankie Newsome* |
| 18/75 | **My Main Man** *Staple Singers* |
| 7/63 | **My Man - He's A Lovin' Man** *Betty LaVette* |
| 7/72 | **My Man, A Sweet Man** *Millie Jackson* |
| 27/59 | **My Melancholy Baby** *Tommy Edwards* |
| 41/87 | **My Mike Sounds Nice** *Salt-N-Pepa* |
| 20/72 | **My Mind Keeps Telling Me** *Eddie Holman* |
| 15/74 | **My Mistake (Was To Love You)** |
| | *Diana Ross & Marvin Gaye* |
| 6/50 | **My Mother Told Me** *Nat King Cole* |
| 98/76 | **My Music** *Bunny Sigler* |

| 49/67 | **Never Leave Me** *Thelma Jones* |
| 87/79 | **Never Let Go** *Eastbound Expressway* |
| | **Never Let Me Go** |
| 9/54 | *Johnny Ace* |
| 26/60 | *Lloyd Price* |
| 25/66 | *Van Dykes* |
| 26/83 | **Never Let You Down** |
| | *Maze Featuring Frankie Beverly* |
| 7/73 | **Never Let You Go** *Bloodstone* |
| 55/81 | **Never Like This** *Two Tons* |
| 29/66 | **Never Like This Before** *William Bell* |
| 96/77 | **Never Lose Never Win** *Chain Reaction* |
| 19/78 | **Never Make A Move Too Soon** *B.B. King* |
| | **Never My Love** |
| 45/71 | *5th Dimension* |
| 62/88 | *Chill Factor* |
| 2/73 | **Never, Never Gonna Give Ya Up** |
| | *Barry White* |
| 15/65 | **Never, Never Leave Me** *Mary Wells* |
| | **Never Never Never** |
| 46/71 | *Chee-Chee & Peppy* |
| 67/73 | *Shirley Bassey* |
| 16/83 | **Never Say I Do (If You Don't Mean It)** |
| | *Cliff Dawson & Renee Diggs* |
| 6/87 | **Never Say Never** *Deniece Williams* |
| 57/80 | **Never Seen A Girl Like You** *David Oliver* |
| 1/81 | **Never Too Much** *Luther Vandross* |
| 90/64 | **Never Trust A Woman** *B.B. King* |
| 74/81 | **Never Underestimate The Power Of A** |
| | **Woman** *Klymaxx* |
| 3/85 | **New Attitude** *Patti LaBelle* |
| 5/52 | **New Blowtop Blues** *Dinah Washington* |
| 87/85 | **New Day** *George Benson* |
| 44/69 | **New Day Begins** *Parliaments* |
| 34/87 | **New Dress** *Cheryl Lynn* |
| 59/88 | **New Girl On The Block** *Gerald Albright* |
| 45/78 | **New Horizon** *Sylvers* |
| 61/73 | **New Kind Of Woman** *Holland-Dozier* |
| 27/84 | **New Moves** *Crusaders* |
| | **New Orleans** |
| 5/60 | *Gary U.S. Bonds* |
| 4/76 | *Staple Singers* |
| 2/47 | **New Orleans Blues** |
| | *Johnny Moore's Three Blazers* |
| 74/79 | **New York** *Nuggets* |
| 17/83 | **New York New York** |
| | *Grandmaster Flash & The Furious Five* |
| 35/74 | **Newsy Neighbors** *First Choice* |
| 19/62 | **Next Door To An Angel** *Neil Sedaka* |
| 13/62 | **Next Door To The Blues** *Etta James* |
| 22/84 | **Next Love** *Deniece Williams* |
| | **Next Time** |
| 34/68 | *Johnnie Taylor* |
| 48/88 | *Brownmark* |
| 79/84 | **Next Time It's For Real** *Kleeer* |
| 7/57 | **Next Time You See Me** *Little Junior Parker* |
| 28/81 | **Next Time You'll Know** *Sister Sledge* |
| 66/76 | **Nice & Slow** *Santiago* |
| 20/76 | **Nice 'N' Naasty** *Salsoul Orchestra* |
| 21/74 | **Nice Girl Like You** *Intruders* |
| 19/71 | **Nickel And A Nail** *O.V. Wright* |
| 3/60 | **Night** *Jackie Wilson* |
| 100/76 | **Night And Day** *John Davis* |
| 5/52 | **Night And Day (I Miss You So)** *Roy Milton* |
| 20/79 | **Night Dancin'** *Taka Boom* |
| 7/81 | **Night (Feel Like Getting Down)** |
| | *Billy Ocean* |
| 8/78 | **Night Fever** *Bee Gees* |
| 42/68 | **Night Fo' Last** *Shorty Long* |
| 33/81 | **Night Games** *Stephanie Mills* |
| 8/63 | **Night Has A Thousand Eyes** *Bobby Vee* |
| 82/84 | **Night In New York** |
| | *Elbow Bones & The Racketeers* |
| 60/76 | **Night Life** *Miracles* |
| 93/78 | **Night People** *Lee Dorsey* |

| 80/78 | **Night The Lights Went Out** *Trammps* |
| | **(Night Time Is) The Right Time** |
| 5/59 | *Ray Charles* |
| 94/64 | *Rufus & Carla* |
| F/83 | *James Brown* |
| 59/80 | **Night Time Lover** *La Toya Jackson* |
| | **Night To Remember** |
| 8/82 | *Shalamar* |
| 61/86 | *Keith Patrick* |
| | **Night Train** |
| 1/52 | *Jimmy Forrest* |
| 5/62 | *James Brown* |
| 51/76 | **Night Walk** *Van McCoy* |
| 76/84 | **Night With The Boys** *Linda Clifford* |
| | **Nightime** |
| 82/84 | *Pretty Poison* |
| 83/88 | *Pretty Poison* |
| 64/81 | **Nightlife** *Kwick* |
| 29/83 | **Nightline** *Randy Crawford* |
| 21/86 | **Nightmares** *Dana Dane* |
| 58/87 | **Nights Of Pleasure** *Loose Ends* |
| 16/77 | **Nights On Broadway** *Candi Staton* |
| 23/82 | **Nights Over Egypt** *Jones Girls* |
| 1/85 | **Nightshift** *Commodores* |
| 7/87 | **Nighttime Lover** *System* |
| 56/73 | **Nija Walk (Street Walk)** *Fatback Band* |
| 19/67 | **Nine Pound Steel** *Joe Simon* |
| 44/76 | **Nine Times** *Moments* |
| F/82 | **Nine Times Out Of Ten** *Teddy Pendergrass* |
| 8/85 | **19** *Paul Hardcastle* |
| 32/66 | **19th Nervous Breakdown** *Rolling Stones* |
| 34/71 | **90 Day Freeze** *100 Proof Aged In Soul* |
| | **96 Tears** |
| 23/67 | *Big Maybelle* |
| 76/81 | *Thelma Houston* |
| 22/84 | **99 1/2** *Carol Lynn Townes* |
| | **Ninety-Nine And A Half (Won't Do)** |
| 13/66 | *Wilson Pickett* |
| 76/76 | *Trammps* |
| 13/72 | **992 Arguments** *O'Jays* |
| 51/83 | **1990** *Dr. America* |
| 4/82 | **1999** *Prince* |
| 10/55 | **Nip Sip** *Clovers* |
| 17/82 | **Nipple To The Bottle** *Grace Jones* |
| 1/88 | **Nite And Day** *Al B. Sure!* |
| F/83 | **Nite Life** *Shock* |
| | **Nitty Gritty** |
| 8/64 | *Shirley Ellis* |
| 2/69 | *Gladys Knight & The Pips* |
| 62/84 | **No** *Amuzement Park Band* |
| 72/80 | **No Better Love** *Shadow* |
| 40/75 | **No Charge** *Shirley Caesar* |
| 29/65 | **No Faith, No Love** *Mitty Collier* |
| 64/84 | **No Favors** *Temper* |
| 29/86 | **No Frills Love** *Jennifer Holliday* |
| 96/81 | **No George** *Leda Grace* |
| 6/88 | **No 1/2 Steppin'** *Shanice Wilson* |
| 29/86 | **No How-No Way** *Rene & Angela* |
| 16/60 | **No If's-No And's** *Lloyd Price* |
| 43/87 | **No Lies** *S.O.S. Band* |
| 48/79 | **No Love, No Where, Without You** |
| | *Linda Williams* |
| 83/82 | **No Love Without Changes** *Jerry Butler* |
| 24/66 | **No Man Is An Island** *Van Dykes* |
| 2/85 | **(No Matter How High I Get) I'll Still Be Lookin'** |
| | **Up To You** *Wilton Felder* |
| 17/69 | **No Matter What Sign You Are** *Supremes* |
| 76/73 | **No Matter Where** *G.C. Cameron* |
| 8/56 | **No Money Down** *Chuck Berry* |
| 24/86 | **No More** *Shirley Murdock* |
| 2/52 | **No More Doggin'** *Roscoe Gordon* |
| 49/83 | **No More Tears** *Anita Baker* |
| 20/80 | **No More Tears (Enough Is Enough)** |
| | *Barbra Streisand/Donna Summer* |
| 19/80 | **No Night So Long** *Dionne Warwick* |

F/58 **No, No** *Fats Domino*
34/76 **No, No, Joe** *Silver Convention*
9/61 **No, No, No** *Chanters*
9/63 **No One** *Ray Charles*
58/77 **No One Can Love You More** *Phyllis Hyman*
10/44 **No One Else Will Do** *Five Red Caps*
5/87 **No One In The World** *Anita Baker*
12/58 **No One Knows** *Dion & The Belmonts*
55/64 **No One To Cry To** *Ray Charles*
15/84 **No One's Gonna Love You** *S.O.S. Band*
14/88 **No Pain, No Gain** *Betty Wright*
74/88 **No Pains, No Gains** *Whispers*
43/84 **No Parking (On The Dance Floor)**
　　　　*Midnight Star*
10/64 **No Particular Place To Go** *Chuck Berry*
25/65 **No Pity (In The Naked City)** *Jackie Wilson*
26/75 **No Rebate On Love** *Dramatics*
14/59 **No Regrets** *Jimmy Barnes*
4/49 **No Rollin' Blues** *Jimmy Witherspoon*
22/68 **No Sad Songs** *Joe Simon*
75/84 **No Sell Out** *Malcolm X*
21/60 **No Shoes** *John Lee Hooker*
59/86 **No Show**
　　　　*Symbolic Three featuring D.J. Dr. Shock*
32/83 **No Stoppin' That Rockin'** *Instant Funk*
49/66 **No Stranger To Love** *Inez Foxx*
49/72 **No Tears In The End**
　　　　*Grover Washington, Jr.*
46/74 **No Time To Burn** *Black Heat*
93/84 **No Way** *Inner Life*
68/76 **No Way Back** *Dells*
76/83 **No Work, No Pay** *Mel Stewart*
　　　　**Nobody**
39/68 　　*Kim Weston*
40/68 　　*Larry Williams & Johnny Watson*
　　　　**Nobody But You**
3/58 　　*Dee Clark*
85/77 　　*John Edwards*
59/86 　　*Juicy*
7/69 **Nobody But You Babe** *Clarence Reid*
18/83 **Nobody Can Be You**
　　　　*Steve Arrington's Hall Of Fame*
89/86 **Nobody Can Make It On Their Own**
　　　　*Staple Singers*
17/61 **Nobody Cares (about me)**
　　　　*Jeanette (Baby) Washington*
19/79 **Nobody Knows** *Ashford & Simpson*
23/60 **Nobody Knows You When You're Down And**
　　　　**Out** *Nina Simone*
23/60 **Nobody Loves Me Like You** *Flamingos*
2/73 **Nobody Wants You When You're Down And**
　　　　**Out** *Bobby Womack*
51/75 **Nobody's Gonna Change Me**
　　　　*Dynamic Superiors*
87/84 **Nobody's Gonna Get This Lovin' But**
　　　　**You** *Krystol*
65/80 **Non Stop** *Forecast*
10/61 **North To Alaska** *Johnny Horton*
46/83 **Not A Day Too Soon** *Thunderflash*
77/84 **Not Guilty** *Gap Band*
1/79 **(not just) Knee Deep** *Funkadelic*
8/63 **Not Me** *Orlons*
　　　　**Not On The Outside**
13/69 　　*Moments*
32/72 　　*Linda Jones*
13/60 **Not One Minute More** *Della Reese*
76/86 **Not Tonight** *Junior*
69/85 **Not Too Young (To Fall In Love)**
　　　　*Alfonso Ribeiro*
34/81 **Nothin' But A Fool** *Natalie Cole*
9/61 **Nothing But Good**
　　　　*Hank Ballard & The Midnighters*
6/65 **Nothing But Heartaches** *Supremes*
43/81 **Nothing But Love** *Peter Tosh*
2/62 **Nothing Can Change This Love** *Sam Cooke*

3/65 **Nothing Can Stop Me** *Gene Chandler*
11/69 **Nothing Can Take The Place Of You**
　　　　*Brook Benton*
8/74 **Nothing From Nothing** *Billy Preston*
25/66 **Nothing In The World Can Hurt Me (Except**
　　　　**You)** *Buddy Ace*
　　　　**Nothing Remains The Same**
　　　　*..see: Yesterday Once More*
86/79 **Nothing Says I Love You Like I Love**
　　　　**You** *Jerry Butler*
17/86 **(Nothing Serious) Just Buggin'** *Whistle*
5/67 **Nothing Takes The Place Of You**
　　　　*Toussaint McCall*
22/87 **Nothing Ventured-Nothing Gained**
　　　　*Charlie Singleton*
4/66 **Nothing's Too Good For My Baby**
　　　　*Stevie Wonder*
　　　　**Now!**
92/63 　　*Lena Horne*
91/76 　　*Nancy Wilson*
16/59 **(Now And Then There's) A Fool Such As**
　　　　**I** *Elvis Presley*
10/77 **Now Do-U-Wanta Dance**
　　　　*Graham Central Station*
41/71 **Now I'm A Woman** *Nancy Wilson*
57/80 **Now I'm Fine** *Grey & Hanks*
3/72 **Now Run And Tell That** *Denise LaSalle*
44/67 **Now That I Got You Back** *J.J. Barnes*
68/81 **Now That I Know** *Emotions*
9/79 **Now That We Found Love** *Third World*
25/80 **Now That You're Mine Again** *Spinners*
56/80 **Now You Choose Me** *Pleasure*
　　　　**Nowhere To Run**
5/65 　　*Martha & The Vandellas*
53/77 　　*Dynamic Superiors*
15/84 **Nubian Nut** *George Clinton*
　　　　**Number One**
78/78 　　*Eloise Laws*
76/82 　　*Lady*
97/78 **#1 Dee Jay** *Goody Goody*
94/76 **Number Onederful** *Jay & The Techniques*
22/82 **Numbers** *Kraftwerk*
4/49 **Numbers Boogie** *Sugar Chile Robinson*
50/83 **Nunk (New Wave Funk)** *Warp 9*
　　　　**Nursery Rhymes**
22/76 　　*People's Choice*
50/86 　　*L.A. Dream Team*
11/73 **Nutbush City Limits** *Ike & Tina Turner*

# O

22/67 **O-O, I Love You** *Dells*
48/69 **O Wow** *Panic Button*
3/85 **Oak Tree** *Morris Day*
41/69 **Ob-La-Di, Ob-La-Da** *Arthur Conley*
8/85 **Object Of My Desire** *Starpoint*
9/84 **Obscene Phone Caller** *Rockwell*
90/85 **Obsession** *Howard Hewett*
17/78 **Ocean Of Thoughts And Dreams**
　　　　*Dramatics*
　　　　**Ode To Billie Joe**
6/67 　　*Kingpins*
8/67 　　*Bobbie Gentry*
46/68 　　*Mighty Flea*
78/79 **Off** *Kathy Barnes*
10/84 **Off And On Love** *Champaign*
1/88 **Off On Your Own (Girl)** *Al B. Sure!*
6/88 **Off The Hook (With Your Love)**
　　　　*R.J.'s Latest Arrival*

| | |
|---|---|
| | **Off The Wall** |
| 8/53 | *Little Walter* |
| 5/80 | *Michael Jackson* |
| | **Oh Babe** |
| 5/50 | *Larry Darnell* |
| 5/50 | *Roy Milton* |
| 5/50 | *Jimmy Preston* |
| 7/50 | *Wynonie Harris* |
| | **Oh, Baby** |
| 8/54 | *Little Walter* |
| 68/75 | *Wayne Miran & Rush Release* |
| 12/57 | **Oh Baby Doll** *Chuck Berry* |
| 23/64 | **Oh Baby Don't You Weep** *James Brown* |
| 36/68 | **Oh Baby Mine** *O.V. Wright* |
| 69/64 | **Oh! Baby (We Got A Good Thing Goin')** |
| | *Barbara Lynn* |
| 13/57 | **Oh, Boy!** *Crickets* |
| 27/59 | **Oh! Carol** *Neil Sedaka* |
| 39/80 | **Oh, Darlin** *Brothers By Choice* |
| | **Oh Girl** |
| 1/72 | *Chi-Lites* |
| 38/88 | *Glenn Jones* |
| | **Oh Happy Day** |
| 2/69 | *Edwin Hawkins' Singers* |
| 41/69 | *Dilly Mitchell Group* |
| 6/79 | **Oh Honey** *Delegation* |
| 16/66 | **Oh How Happy** *Shades Of Blue* |
| 22/87 | **Oh How I Love You (Girl)** |
| | *James (D-Train) Williams* |
| 11/68 | **Oh, How It Hurts** *Barbara Mason* |
| 41/81 | **(Oh I) Need Your Lovin'** *Eddie Kendricks* |
| 29/68 | **Oh, I'll Never Be The Same** *Young Hearts* |
| 4/58 | **Oh, Julie** *Crescendos* |
| 4/73 | **Oh La De Da** *Staple Singers* |
| 22/77 | **Oh Let Me Know It** |
| | *Special Delivery featuring Terry Huff* |
| 35/68 | **Oh Lord, Why Lord** *Los Pop Tops* |
| 14/86 | **Oh Louise** *Junior* |
| 7/75 | **Oh Me, Oh My (Dreams In My Arms)** |
| | *Al Green* |
| F/71 | **Oh Me Oh My (I'm A Fool For You Baby)** |
| | *Aretha Franklin* |
| 3/43 | **Oh! Miss Jaxon** *Charlie Barnet* |
| F/72 | **Oh, My Dear** *Dells* |
| 5/81 | **Oh No** *Commodores* |
| | **Oh No Not My Baby** |
| 24/65 | *Maxine Brown* |
| 30/73 | *Merry Clayton* |
| 70/76 | *Deblanc* |
| 19/58 | **Oh-Oh, I'm Falling In Love Again** |
| | *Jimmie Rodgers* |
| 7/86 | **Oh, People** *Patti LaBelle* |
| 1/85 | **Oh Sheila** *Ready For The World* |
| 10/70 | **Oh What A Day** *Dells* |
| 1/54 | **Oh What A Dream** |
| | *Ruth Brown & Her Rhythmakers* |
| 13/78 | **Oh What A Night For Dancing** |
| | *Barry White* |
| | **Oh What A Nite** |
| 4/56 | *Dells* |
| 1/69 | *Dells* |
| | **Oh Yeah!** |
| 45/67 | *Joe Cuba Sextet* |
| 22/85 | *Bill Withers* |
| 9/77 | **O-H-I-O** *Ohio Players* |
| 10/48 | **Ol' Man River** *Ravens* |
| 8/80 | **Old-Fashion Love** *Commodores* |
| 17/82 | **Old Fashioned Love** *Smokey Robinson* |
| 27/87 | **Old Flames Never Die** *Full Force* |
| 14/86 | **Old Friend** *Phyllis Hyman* |
| 17/60 | **Old Lamplighter** *Browns* |
| 35/69 | **Old Love** *Intruders* |
| 54/78 | **Old Man With Young Ideas** *Ann Peebles* |
| 74/81 | **Old Songs** *Frederick Knight* |
| 3/50 | **Old Time Shuffle Blues** *Lloyd Glenn* |

| | |
|---|---|
| 1/47 | **Ole Maid Boogie** *Eddie Vinson* |
| 13/78 | **(Olivia) Lost And Turned Out** *Whispers* |
| 56/83 | **On A Journey** *Peech Boys* |
| 22/67 | **On A Saturday Night** *Eddie Floyd* |
| | **On And Off** |
| 41/72 | *Anacostia* |
| 48/76 | *David Ruffin* |
| 2/74 | **On And On** *Gladys Knight & The Pips* |
| | **On Broadway** |
| 7/63 | *Drifters* |
| 2/78 | *George Benson* |
| 27/78 | **On Fire** *T-Connection* |
| 1/86 | **On My Own** |
| | *Patti LaBelle & Michael McDonald* |
| | **On My Word Of Honor** |
| 3/56 | *B.B. King* |
| 7/57 | *Platters* |
| 43/83 | **On Target** *Jones Girls* |
| 8/81 | **On The Beat** *B.B.&Q. Band* |
| 63/83 | **On The Dance Floor** |
| | *New Guys On The Block* |
| 13/69 | **On The Dock Of The Bay** *Dells* |
| 79/88 | **On The Edge** *Walter Beasley* |
| 36/82 | **On The Floor** *Fatback* |
| 33/83 | **On The Line** *G.T.* |
| 9/83 | **On The One For Fun** *Dazz Band* |
| 9/80 | **On The Radio** *Donna Summer* |
| 16/61 | **On The Rebound** *Floyd Cramer* |
| 72/86 | **On The Shelf** *B.B.&Q. Band* |
| 10/44 | **On The Sunnyside Of The Street** |
| | *Lionel Hampton* |
| 27/74 | **On The Verge Of Getting It On** *Funkadelic* |
| 13/82 | **On The Wings Of Love** *Jeffrey Osborne* |
| 26/77 | **On Your Face** *Earth, Wind & Fire* |
| 9/86 | **Once Bitten Twice Shy** *Vesta Williams* |
| 16/77 | **Once I've Been There** *Norman Connors* |
| 10/86 | **Once In A Lifetime Groove** *New Edition* |
| 44/80 | **Once Is Not Enough** *O'Jays* |
| 7/51 | **Once There Lived A Fool** |
| | *Jimmy Grissom with The Red Callender Sextet* |
| 15/88 | **Once, Twice, Three Time** *Howard Hewett* |
| | **Once Upon A Time** |
| 20/61 | *Rochell & The Candles* |
| 19/64 | *Marvin Gaye & Mary Wells* |
| 4/75 | **Once You Get Started** |
| | *Rufus Featuring Chaka Khan* |
| 5/76 | **Once You Hit The Road** *Dionne Warwick* |
| 52/81 | **One Alone** |
| | *Michael Wycoff featuring Merry Clayton* |
| 40/78 | **One And Only** *Gladys Knight & The Pips* |
| | **One Bad Apple** |
| 6/71 | *Osmonds* |
| 48/85 | *Nolan Thomas* |
| 14/75 | **One Beautiful Day** *Ecstasy, Passion & Pain* |
| 62/74 | **One Brief Moment** *Timmy Thomas* |
| 21/63 | **One Broken Heart For Sale** *Elvis Presley* |
| | **One Chain Don't Make No Prison** |
| 3/74 | *Four Tops* |
| 68/79 | *Santana* |
| 51/80 | **One Child Of Love** *Peaches & Herb* |
| 42/81 | **One Day In Your Life** *Michael Jackson* |
| 20/69 | **One Eye Open** *Maskman & The Agents* |
| 6/63 | **One Fine Day** *Chiffons* |
| 10/76 | **One For The Money** *Whispers* |
| 59/84 | **One For The Treble (Fresh)** *Davy DMX* |
| 67/64 | **One Girl** *Garnet Mimms* |
| 48/73 | **One Girl Too Late** |
| | *Brenda & The Tabulations* |
| 3/87 | **One Heartbeat** *Smokey Robinson* |
| 50/82 | **One Hello** *Randy Crawford* |
| 19/86 | **100 MPH** *Mazarati* |
| 73/86 | **100% Pure Pain** *O'Chi Brown* |
| 10/82 | **One Hundred Ways** |
| | *Quincy Jones featuring James Ingram* |
| 36/79 | **137 Disco Heaven (medley)** *Amii Stewart* |

| 14/71 | **Part Of You**  *Brenda & The Tabulations* |
| | **Part Time Love** |
| 1/63 | *Little Johnny Taylor* |
| 7/70 | *Ann Peebles* |
| 4/75 | *Gladys Knight & The Pips* |
| 1/85 | **Part-Time Lover**  *Stevie Wonder* |
| 8/60 | **Partin' Time**  *B.B. King* |
| | **Party** |
| 20/76 | *Van McCoy* |
| 81/77 | *Silk* |
| 24/78 | *Leon Haywood* |
| | (also see: Parrty) |
| 8/85 | **Party All The Time**  *Eddie Murphy* |
| 21/83 | **Party Animal**  *James Ingram* |
| 50/74 | **Party Bump**  *Gentlemen & Their Ladies* |
| | **Party Doll** |
| 3/57 | *Buddy Knox* |
| 13/57 | *Roy Brown* |
| | **Party Down** |
| 2/74 | *Little Beaver* |
| 19/76 | *Willie Hutch* |
| 8/86 | **Party Freak**  *Ca$hflow* |
| 51/74 | **Party Freaks**  *Miami featuring Robert Moore* |
| 77/85 | **Party Has Begun**  *Freestyle* |
| 16/76 | **Party Hearty**  *Oliver Sain* |
| 45/75 | **Party Is A Groovy Thing**  *People's Choice* |
| 30/77 | **Party Land**  *Blackbyrds* |
| 62/77 | **Party Life**  *Symbol 8* |
| | **Party Lights** |
| 3/62 | *Claudine Clark* |
| 9/77 | *Natalie Cole* |
| 36/80 | *Gap Band* |
| 95/76 | **Party Line**  *Andrea True Connection* |
| 65/75 | **Party Music**  *Pat Lundi* |
| 39/77 | **Party Night**  *Curtis Mayfield* |
| 93/80 | **Party On**  *Pure Energy* |
| 83/83 | **Party On The Corner** |
| | *Vaughan Mason featuring Butch Dayo* |
| | **Party People** |
| 39/79 | *Parliament* |
| 84/88 | *Royal House* |
| 66/88 | **Party Rebels**  *Centerfold* |
| 63/83 | **Party Right Here**  *Dazz Band* |
| 22/78 | **Party Song**  *Slave* |
| 77/84 | **Party Starts When I'm With You** |
| | *Rue Caldwell* |
| | **Party Time** |
| 84/76 | *Fatback Band* |
| 35/83 | *Kurtis Blow* |
| 97/76 | **Party Time Is Here To Stay** |
| | *Olympic Runners* |
| 94/79 | **Party Time Man**  *Futures* |
| | **Party Train** |
| 69/82 | *Bohannon* |
| 3/83 | *Gap Band* |
| 90/79 | **P.A.R.T.Y. (Where It Is)**  *Denise LaSalle* |
| 69/87 | **Party Your Body**  *Stevie B* |
| 53/84 | **Partyline**  *Brass Construction* |
| 65/78 | **Pasado**  *Pockets* |
| 8/83 | **Pass The Dutchie**  *Musical Youth* |
| 92/75 | **Pass The Feelin' On**  *Creative Source* |
| 29/72 | **Pass The Peas**  *JB's* |
| | **Passion** |
| 99/77 | *Ecstasy, Passion & Pain* |
| 65/81 | *Rod Stewart* |
| 65/82 | *Barry White* |
| 75/86 | **Passion And Pain**  *Janice McClain* |
| 18/86 | **Passion From A Woman**  *Krystol* |
| 76/80 | **Passionate Breezes**  *Dells* |
| 7/67 | **Pata Pata**  *Miriam Makeba* |
| 41/66 | **Patch My Heart**  *Mad Lads* |
| | **Patches** |
| 10/62 | *Dickey Lee* |
| 2/70 | *Clarence Carter* |
| 90/78 | **Path, The**  *Ralph MacDonald* |

| 1/58 | **Patricia**  *Perez Prado* |
| 34/87 | **Paul Revere**  *Beastie Boys* |
| 4/70 | **Pay To The Piper**  *Chairmen Of The Board* |
| 1/74 | **Payback, The**  *James Brown* |
| 10/68 | **Paying The Cost To Be Boss**  *B.B. King* |
| 65/74 | **Peace**  *O'Jays* |
| 21/72 | **Peace In The Valley Of Love**  *Persuaders* |
| | **Peace Of Mind** |
| 7/61 | *B.B. King* |
| 24/68 | *Nancy Wilson* |
| F/75 | **Peace Pipe**  *B.T. Express* |
| 94/78 | **Peaceful Journey**  *Fat Larry's Band* |
| 28/65 | **Peaches 'N' Cream**  *Ikettes* |
| 16/66 | **Peak Of Love**  *Bobby McClure* |
| | **Peanut Butter** |
| 25/61 | *Marathons* |
| 3/80 | *Twennynine with Lenny White* |
| 00/00 | *Gwen Guthrie* |
| 75/85 | *Gwen Guthrie* |
| 4/53 | **Pedal Pushin' Papa** |
| | *Billy Ward & His Dominoes* |
| 16/86 | **Pee-Wee's Dance**  *Joeski Love* |
| 20/59 | **Peek-A-Boo**  *Cadillacs* |
| 2/58 | **Peggy Sue**  *Buddy Holly* |
| 16/82 | **Penny For Your Thoughts**  *Tavares* |
| 8/84 | **Penny Lover**  *Lionel Richie* |
| | **People** |
| 100/64 | *Nat King Cole* |
| 33/68 | *Tymes* |
| 23/73 | **People Are Changin'**  *Timmy Thomas* |
| 3/65 | **People Get Ready**  *Impressions* |
| 81/77 | **People Gonna Talk**  *Tip Watkins* |
| 14/68 | **People Got To Be Free**  *Rascals* |
| 6/72 | **People Make The World Go Round** |
| | *Stylistics* |
| 60/83 | **People Next Door**  *Ray Parker Jr.* |
| 82/76 | **People Power**  *Billy Paul* |
| | **People Say** |
| 12/64 | *Dixie Cups* |
| 52/75 | *Meters* |
| 17/68 | **People Sure Act Funny**  *Arthur Conley* |
| 32/82 | **People Treat You Funky (When Ya Ain't Got** |
| | **No Money!)**  *Richard 'Dimples' Fields* |
| 99/77 | **People Users**  *Philadelphia Story* |
| 82/76 | **People Want Music**  *Controllers* |
| 34/72 | **Pepper Box**  *Peppers* |
| 8/62 | **Peppermint Twist** |
| | *Joey Dee & The Starliters* |
| 85/65 | **Percolatin'**  *Willie Mitchell* |
| 69/83 | **Perez Prado-Tito Puente Latin Medley** |
| | *Joe Cain & The Red Parrot Orchestra* |
| | **Perfect**  *..also see: (Closest Thing To)* |
| 10/84 | **Perfect Combination** |
| | *Stacy Lattisaw & Johnny Gill* |
| 16/81 | **Perfect Fit**  *Jerry Knight* |
| 32/82 | **Perfect Love**  *Atlantic Starr* |
| 66/87 | **(Perfect) 10**  *Madhouse* |
| 85/85 | **Perfect Way**  *Scritti Politti* |
| 5/53 | **Perfect Woman**  *Four Blazes* |
| 1/59 | **Personality**  *Lloyd Price* |
| 92/78 | **Personally**  *Jackie Moore* |
| | **Peter Gunn** |
| 12/59 | *Ray Anthony* |
| 96/77 | *Deodato* |
| 28/59 | **Petite Fleur (Little Flower)** |
| | *Chris Barber's Jazz Band* |
| 3/46 | **Petootie Pie**  *Ella Fitzgerald & Louis Jordan* |
| 5/48 | **Pettin' And Pokin'**  *Louis Jordan* |
| 19/74 | **Philadelphia**  *B.B. King* |
| 32/75 | **Philadelphia Freedom**  *Elton John Band* |
| | **Philly Dog** |
| 19/66 | *Mar-Keys* |
| 36/66 | *Herbie Mann* |
| 12/66 | **Philly Freeze**  *Alvin Cash & The Registers* |
| 83/77 | **Phoenix**  *Aquarian Dream* |

| | |
|---|---|
| 10/75 | **Phones Been Jumping All Day** |
| | *Jeannie Reynolds* |
| 61/84 | **Photogenic Memory** *Philip Bailey* |
| 28/82 | **Physical** *Olivia Newton-John* |
| 84/84 | **Physical Lover** *Detroyt* |
| 8/88 | **Piano In The Dark** *Brenda Russell* |
| 39/67 | **Pick Me** *Vibrations* |
| 85/79 | **Pick Me Up, I'll Dance** *Melba Moore* |
| | **Pick Up The Pieces** |
| 16/68 | *Carla Thomas* |
| 5/75 | *Average White Band* |
| 83/85 | **Pickin' Up Pieces** *Brenda K. Starr* |
| 8/68 | **Pickin' Wild Mountain Berries** |
| | *Peggy Scott & Jo Jo Benson* |
| | **Piece Of My Heart** |
| 10/67 | *Erma Franklin* |
| 93/78 | *Etta James* |
| 47/77 | **Piece Of The Action** *Mavis Staples* |
| 15/83 | **Pieces Of Ice** *Diana Ross* |
| 1/73 | **Pillow Talk** *Sylvia* |
| 12/83 | **Pilot Error** *Stephanie Mills* |
| 28/71 | **Pin The Tail On The Donkey** *Newcomers* |
| 14/48 | **Pinetop's Boogie Woogie** *Louis Jordan* |
| 9/88 | **Pink Cadillac** *Natalie Cole* |
| 1/50 | **Pink Champagne** *Joe Liggins* |
| 5/59 | **Pink Shoe Laces** *Dodie Stevens* |
| 6/77 | **Pinocchio Theory** *Bootsy's Rubber Band* |
| 11/63 | **Pipeline** *Chantay's* |
| | **Pistol Packin' Mama** |
| 3/43 | *Bing Crosby & Andrews Sisters* |
| 5/43 | *Al Dexter* |
| 10/55 | **Pitter Patter** *Nappy Brown* |
| 39/69 | **Pity For The Lonely** *Luther Ingram* |
| 87/84 | **Pixie Dust** *Wrecking Crew* |
| 50/68 | **Place** *Precisions* |
| 3/67 | **Place In The Sun** *Stevie Wonder* |
| 17/71 | **Plain And Simple Girl** *Garland Green* |
| 10/84 | **Plane Love** *Jeffrey Osborne* |
| 62/82 | **Planet Funk** *Johnny 'Guitar' Watson* |
| 4/82 | **Planet Rock** *Afrika Bambaataa* |
| 8/73 | **Plastic Man** *Temptations* |
| 76/78 | **Plato's Retreat** *Joe Thomas* |
| 21/82 | **Play At Your Own Risk** *Planet Patrol* |
| 2/55 | **Play It Fair** *LaVern Baker & The Gliders* |
| 99/76 | **Play Me A Love Song** *Paul Kelly* |
| 79/80 | **Play Something Pretty** *Johnnie Taylor* |
| 68/83 | **Play That Beat Mr. D.J.** |
| | *G.L.O.B.E. & Whiz Kid* |
| 1/76 | **Play That Funky Music** *Wild Cherry* |
| 56/87 | **Play This Only At Night** *Doug E. Fresh* |
| 69/88 | **Play Time** *Controllers* |
| 4/62 | **Playboy** *Marvelettes* |
| 7/74 | **Player, The** *First Choice* |
| 79/86 | **Player's Ball** *Mazarati* |
| 2/46 | **Playful Baby** *Wynonie Harris* |
| 46/82 | **Playing Hard To Get** *Vernon Burch* |
| 33/75 | **Playing On You** *Jerry Butler* |
| 8/78 | **Playing Your Game, Baby** *Barry White* |
| 8/88 | **Plaything** *Rebbie Jackson* |
| 11/56 | **Pleadin' For Love** *Larry Birdsong* |
| 9/58 | **Please Accept My Love** *B.B. King* |
| | **Please Be Careful (If You Can't Be Good)** |
| 4/43 | *Boone's Jumpin' Jacks* |
| 6/43 | *Bea Booze* |
| 21/60 | **Please Come Home For Christmas** |
| | *Charles Brown* |
| 21/65 | **Please Do Something** |
| | *Don Covay & The Goodtimers* |
| 9/49 | **Please Don't Go** *Roy Brown* |
| 55/88 | **Please Don't Go Girl** |
| | *New Kids On The Block* |
| 100/63 | **Please Don't Kiss Me Again** *Charmettes* |
| 3/53 | **Please Don't Leave Me** *Fats Domino* |
| 84/83 | **Please Don't Say No** *Motivation* |

| | |
|---|---|
| 91/78 | **Please Don't You Say Goodbye To Me** |
| | *Solomon Burke* |
| 6/54 | **Please Forgive Me** *Johnny Ace* |
| 4/53 | **Please Hurry Home** *B.B. King* |
| 9/56 | **Please Listen To Me** *Smiley Lewis* |
| 1/53 | **Please Love Me** *B.B. King* |
| 47/70 | **Please Make The Love Go Away** |
| | *Whatnauts* |
| 13/56 | **Please Mr. Disc Jockey** *Sensations* |
| 1/61 | **Please Mr. Postman** *Marvelettes* |
| | *(also see: Waitin' On A Letter)* |
| 18/59 | **Please Mr. Sun** *Tommy Edwards* |
| 6/75 | **Please Pardon Me (You Remind Me Of A** |
| | **Friend)** *Rufus Featuring Chaka Khan* |
| 83/87 | **Please, Please Me** *Soft Touch* |
| | **Please, Please, Please** |
| 5/56 | *James Brown* |
| 95/64 | *James Brown* |
| 4/68 | **Please Return Your Love To Me** |
| | *Temptations* |
| 13/57 | **Please Say You Want Me** *Schoolboys* |
| 7/52 | **Please Send Her Back To Me** *Four Blazes* |
| | **Please Send Me Someone To Love** |
| 1/50 | *Percy Mayfield* |
| 5/57 | *Moonglows* |
| 20/61 | *Wade Flemons* |
| 13/61 | **Please Stay** *Drifters* |
| 11/61 | **Please Tell Me Why** *Jackie Wilson* |
| 2/48 | **Pleasing You (As Long As I Live)** |
| | *Lonnie Johnson* |
| | **Pleasure Principle** |
| 66/78 | *Parlet* |
| 1/87 | *Janet Jackson* |
| 21/85 | **Pleasure Seekers** *System* |
| 15/57 | **Pledge Of Love** *Penguins* |
| | **Pledging My Love** |
| 1/55 | *Johnny Ace* |
| 49/69 | *Laura & Johnny* |
| 31/72 | *Oscar Weathers* |
| 27/60 | **Poetry In Motion** *Johnny Tillotson* |
| 8/44 | **Poinciana** *Benny Carter* |
| 4/70 | **Point It Out** |
| | *Smokey Robinson & The Miracles* |
| | **Point Of No Return** |
| 23/62 | *Gene McDaniels* |
| 36/86 | *Nu Shooz* |
| | **Poison Ivy** |
| 7/54 | *Willie Mabon* |
| 1/59 | *Coasters* |
| 1/61 | **Pony Time** *Chubby Checker* |
| 89/85 | **Poo Poo La La** *Roy Ayers* |
| 13/72 | **Pool Of Bad Luck** *Joe Simon* |
| 41/66 | **Poor Dog (Who Can't Wag His Own Tail)** |
| | *Little Richard* |
| 4/62 | **Poor Fool** *Ike & Tina Turner* |
| 3/58 | **Poor Little Fool** *Ricky Nelson* |
| 18/69 | **Poor Man** *Little Milton* |
| 1/55 | **Poor Me** *Fats Domino* |
| 10/52 | **Poor, Poor Me** *Fats Domino* |
| 13/49 | **Pop Corn** *Paul Williams* |
| 47/84 | **Pop Goes My Love** *Freeez* |
| 20/80 | **Pop It** *One Way featuring Al Hudson* |
| 8/85 | **Pop Life** *Prince* |
| 25/62 | **Pop Pop Pop-Pie** *Sherrys* |
| 1/86 | **(Pop, Pop, Pop, Pop) Goes My Mind** *Levert* |
| 3/72 | **Pop That Thang** *Isley Brothers* |
| 60/80 | **Pop Your Fingers** *Rose Royce* |
| 11/69 | **Popcorn, The** *James Brown* |
| | *(also see: Pop Corn)* |
| 25/83 | **Popcorn Love** *New Edition* |
| 13/62 | **Popeye (The Hitchhiker)** *Chubby Checker* |
| 26/79 | **Pops, We Love You (A Tribute To** |
| | **Father)** *Diana Ross, Marvin Gaye, Smokey* |
| | *Robinson & Stevie Wonder* |
| 68/76 | **Porcupine** *Nature Zone* |

21/76 **Queen Of My Soul** *Average White Band*
49/85 **Queen Of Rox (Shante Rox On)**
    *Roxanne Shante*
6/58 **Queen Of The Hop** *Bobby Darin*
5/60 **Question** *Lloyd Price*
19/74 **Quick, Fast, In A Hurry** *New York City*
41/82 **Quick Slick** *Syreeta*
72/84 **Quickie** *George Clinton*
8/64 **Quicksand** *Martha & The Vandellas*
88/85 **Quiet Guy** *Kiara*
78/64 **Quiet Place**
    *Garnet Mimms & The Enchanters*
25/76 **Quiet Storm** *Smokey Robinson*
**Quiet Village**
11/59     *Martin Denny*
68/77     *Ritchie Family*

# R

2/46 **R.M. Blucs** *Roy Milton*
78/88 **R U Tuff Enuff** *Rebbie Jackson*
25/79 **Radiation Level** *Sun*
35/83 **Radio Activity** *Royalcash*
69/84 **Radio Man** *World's Famous Supreme Team*
**Rag Mop**
4/50     *Doc Sausage & his Mad Lads*
4/50     *Lionel Hampton*
4/50     *Joe Liggins*
42/85 **Raging Waters** *Al Jarreau*
**Rags To Riches**
2/53     *Billy Ward & His Dominoes*
45/63     *Sunny & The Sunglows*
29/59 **Ragtime Cowboy Joe**
    *David Seville & The Chipmunks*
8/83 **Raid** *Lakeside*
1/86 **Rain, The** *Oran 'Juice' Jones*
5/85 **Rain Forest** *Paul Hardcastle*
**Rainbow**
10/57     *Russ Hamilton*
11/63     *Gene Chandler*
2/66     *Gene Chandler ('65)*
55/82     *Madagascar*
22/85     *Eugene Wilde*
92/76 **Rainbow In Your Eyes** *Al Jarreau*
15/59 **Rainbow Riot** *Bill Doggett*
**Raindrops**
3/61     *Dee Clark*
14/74     *Barbara Acklin*
38/70 **Raindrops Keep Fallin' On My Head**
    *Barbara Mason*
17/61 **Rainin' In My Heart** *Slim Harpo*
4/50 **Raining In My Heart** *Peppermint Harris*
81/75 **Rainy Days And Mondays** *Intruders*
90/77 **Rainy Days, Stormy Nights** *Impact*
18/88 **Rainy Night** *Chico DeBarge*
1/70 **Rainy Night In Georgia** *Brook Benton*
5/49 **Rainy Weather Blues** *Roy Brown*
81/86 **Raise The Roof** *Conway Brothers*
16/67 **Raise Your Hand** *Eddie Floyd*
34/79 **Raise Your Hands** *Brick*
10/57 **Ram-Bunk-Shush** *Bill Doggett*
7/62 **Ramblin' Rose** *Nat King Cole*
17/58 **Ramrod** *Duane Eddy*
42/75 **Rap, The** *Millie Jackson*
78/85 **Rap Is Here To Stay** *Spyder-D*
46/80 **Rapp Payback (Where iz Moses)**
    *James Brown*
65/81 **Rapper Dapper Snapper** *Edwin Birdsong*
4/79 **Rapper's Delight** *Sugarhill Gang*

68/85 **Rappin'** *Love Bug Starski*
74/81 **Rappin About Rappin (Uh-Uh-Uh)** *Junie*
73/85 **Rappin' Duke** *Shawn Brown*
33/81 **Rapture** *Blondie*
3/85 **Raspberry Beret** *Prince*
1/44 **Ration Blues** *Louis Jordan*
69/76 **Rattlesnake** *Ohio Players*
**Raunchy**
1/58     *Ernie Freeman*
1/58     *Bill Justis*
89/83 **Ray-Gun-Omics** *Project Future*
36/69 **Ray Of Hope** *Rascals*
17/81 **Razzamatazz** *Quincy Jones*
72/84 **Re-Ron** *Gil Scott-Heron*
2/78 **Reach For It** *George Duke*
32/75 **Reach For The Moon (Poor People)**
    *Angelo Bond*
**Reach Out**
40/83     *Narada Michael Walden*
59/83     *George Duke*
64/86     *CaShflow*
7/70 **Reach Out And Touch (Somebody's**
    **Hand)** *Diana Ross*
**Reach Out For Me**
71/63     *Lou Johnson*
20/64     *Dionne Warwick*
78/81     *Michael Henderson*
**Reach Out, I'll Be There**
1/66     *Four Tops*
17/71     *Diana Ross*
56/75     *Gloria Gaynor*
21/80 **Reach Your Peak** *Sister Sledge*
48/79 **Reachin' Out (For Your Love)** *Lee Moore*
6/78 **Reaching For The Sky**
    *Michael Zager's Moon Band featuring Peabo*
    *Bryson*
6/77 **Reaching For The World**
    *Harold Melvin & The Blue Notes*
16/86 **Reaction** *Rebbie Jackson*
57/81 **Reaction Satisfaction (Jam Ya'll: Funk It**
    **Up)** *Sun*
12/85 **Read My Lips** *Melba Moore*
28/83 **Ready For Some Action** *June Pointer*
69/84 **Ready For The Night** *Margie Joseph*
38/79 **Ready For Your Love** *Chapter 8*
**Ready Or Not**
38/78     *Deborah Washington*
25/79     *Herbie Hancock*
14/69 **Ready Or Not Here I Come (Can't Hide From**
    **Love)** *Delfonics*
8/56 **Ready Teddy** *Little Richard*
14/82 **Real Deal** *Isley Brothers*
18/66 **Real Humdinger** *J.J. Barnes*
**Real Love**
40/80     *Doobie Brothers*
17/83     *Lakeside*
92/87 **Real Lover** *Tony Deshawn*
5/77 **Real Mother For Ya**
    *Johnny 'Guitar' Watson*
51/80 **Real People** *Chic*
9/49 **Real Pretty Mama Blues** *Amos Milburn*
44/85 **Real Roxanne** *Roxanne with UTFO*
22/80 **Real Thang** *Narada Michael Walden*
**Real Thing**
20/65     *Tina Britt*
51/77     *Sergio Mendes*
65/80     *Pleasure*
11/81     *Brothers Johnson*
49/87     *Jellybean*
19/75 **Reality** *James Brown*
79/82 **Really Wanna See You** *Invisible Man's Band*
18/62 **Reap What You Sow** *Billy Stewart*
8/58 **Rebel-'Rouser** *Duane Eddy*
8/80 **Rebels Are We** *Chic*

| 25/63 | **River's Invitation** *Percy Mayfield* |
| 14/62 | **Roach, The** |
| | *Gene & Wendell with The Sweethearts* |
| 27/86 | **Roaches** *Bobby Jimmy & The Critters* |
| 59/87 | **Road Dog** *Blake & Hines* |
| 20/60 | **Road Runner** *Bo Diddley* |
| | (also see: I'm A) |
| 82/74 | **Road To Love** *Mandrill* |
| 10/49 | **Roamin' Blues** *Louis Jordan* |
| 10/45 | **Robin Hood** *Louis Prima* |
| | **R-O-C-K** |
| 15/56 | *Bill Haley & His Comets* |
| 64/79 | *East Coast* |
| 76/85 | *450SL* |
| 56/87 | *Tramaine* |
| | (also see: Rrrrrrock) |
| 25/87 | **Rock-A-Lott** *Aretha Franklin* |
| 12/56 | **Rock A While** *Joe Turner* |
| 89/79 | **Rock Along Slowly** *Duncan Sisters* |
| 16/58 | **Rock And Roll Is Here To Stay** |
| | *Danny & The Juniors* |
| 6/57 | **Rock And Roll Music** *Chuck Berry* |
| 3/55 | **Rock Around The Clock** |
| | *Bill Haley & His Comets* |
| 61/79 | **Rock Baby** *Tower Of Power* |
| 22/84 | **Rock Box** *Run-D.M.C.* |
| 37/76 | **Rock Creek Park** *Blackbyrds* |
| 67/79 | **Rock Don't Stop** *Chanson* |
| 85/80 | **Rock It** *Lipps, Inc.* |
| 82/79 | **Rock Me** *Frank Hooker & Positive People* |
| 53/74 | **Rock Me Again & Again & Again & Again &** |
| | **Again & Again** *Lyn Collins* |
| 4/52 | **Rock Me All Night Long** *Ravens* |
| 6/86 | **Rock Me Amadeus** *Falco* |
| 34/64 | **Rock Me Baby** *B.B. King* |
| 58/76 | **Rock Me Easy Baby** *Isaac Hayes* |
| 3/45 | **Rock Me, Mama** *Arthur 'Big Boy' Crudup* |
| 1/85 | **Rock Me Tonight (For Old Times Sake)** |
| | *Freddie Jackson* |
| | **Rock 'N' Roll** ..see: (Let's) |
| 13/57 | **Rock On** *Buddy Johnson* |
| 94/81 | **Rock Radio** *Gene Dunlap* |
| 82/82 | **Rock Shock** *B.B.C.S.& A.* |
| | **Rock Steady** |
| 2/71 | *Aretha Franklin* |
| 88/84 | *Jenny Burton* |
| 1/87 | *Whispers* |
| 17/86 | **Rock The Bells** *L.L. Cool J* |
| 2/74 | **Rock The Boat** *Hues Corporation* |
| 74/82 | **Rock The House (You'll Never Be)** |
| | *Pressure Drop* |
| 6/49 | **Rock The Joint** *Jimmy Preston* |
| 75/85 | **Rock The Nation** *Billy & Baby Gap* |
| 1/80 | **Rock With You** *Michael Jackson* |
| | **Rock You** ..see: (We Want To) |
| | **Rock Your Baby** |
| 1/74 | *George McCrae* |
| 70/76 | *Sunshine Band* |
| 75/82 | **Rock Your World** *Weeks & Co.* |
| 1/58 | **Rock-in Robin** *Bobby Day* |
| 1/51 | **Rocket '88'** *Jackie Brenston* |
| 5/88 | **Rocket 2 U** *Jets* |
| 14/58 | **Rockhouse** *Ray Charles* |
| 98/80 | **Rockin'** *Windstorm* |
| 33/75 | **Rockin' And Rollin' On The Streets Of** |
| | **Hollywood** *Buddy Miles* |
| 2/49 | **Rockin' At Midnight** *Roy Brown* |
| 2/51 | **Rockin' Blues** *Johnny Otis Orchestra* |
| 14/48 | **Rockin' Boogie** *Joe Lutcher* |
| | **Rockin' Chair** |
| 9/51 | *Fats Domino* |
| 1/75 | *Gwen McCrae* |
| 1/60 | **Rockin' Good Way (To Mess Around And Fall** |
| | **In Love)** *Dinah Washington & Brook Benton* |

| 12/69 | **Rockin' In The Same Old Boat** |
| | *Bobby Bland* |
| 11/83 | **Rockin' Radio** *Tom Browne* |
| 2/72 | **Rockin' Robin** *Michael Jackson* |
| 3/73 | **Rockin' Roll Baby** *Stylistics* |
| 6/74 | **Rockin' Soul** *Hues Corporation* |
| 50/82 | **Rockin' To The Beat** *Fatback* |
| 5/51 | **Rockin' With Red** *Piano Red* |
| 74/81 | **Rockin' You Eternally** *Leon Ware* |
| 5/57 | **Rocking Pneumonia And The Boogie Woogie** |
| | **Flu** *Huey 'Piano' Smith & The Clowns* |
| 6/83 | **Rockit** *Herbie Hancock* |
| 9/48 | **Roll 'Em** *Joe Liggins* |
| 2/56 | **Roll Over Beethoven** *Chuck Berry* |
| 30/88 | **Roll With It** *Steve Winwood* |
| 46/82 | **Roll With The Punches** *ADC Band* |
| 6/55 | **Roller Coaster** *Little Walter* |
| 52/80 | **Roller Skate** *Vaughan Mason & Crew* |
| 30/79 | **Roller-Skatin' Mate** *Peaches & Herb* |
| 8/55 | **Rollin' Stone** *Marigolds* |
| 7/75 | **Rolling Down A Mountainside** |
| | *Main Ingredient* |
| 68/84 | **Romancing The Stone** *Eddy Grant* |
| 64/85 | **Romeo** *Real Roxanne with Hitman Howie Tee* |
| 86/85 | **Romeo Where's Juliet?** *Collage* |
| 45/85 | **Roof Is On Fire (Scratchin')** |
| | *Rock Master Scott & The Dynamic Three* |
| 29/86 | **Room With A View** *Jeffrey Osborne* |
| 80/80 | **Roomful Of Mirrors** *Hiroshima* |
| 1/49 | **Roomin' House Boogie** *Amos Milburn* |
| 23/59 | **Rooster Blues** *Lightnin' Slim* |
| 13/57 | **Rooster Song** *Fats Domino* |
| 32/77 | **'Roots' Medley** *Quincy Jones* |
| 90/77 | **Roots Mural Theme/Many Rains Ago** |
| | **(Oluwa)** *Weapons Of Peace* |
| 37/76 | **Roots, Rock, Reggae** |
| | *Bob Marley & The Wailers* |
| 10/53 | **Rose Mary** *Fats Domino* |
| 1/88 | **Roses Are Red** |
| | *Mac Band Featuring The McCampbell Brothers* |
| 5/62 | **Roses Are Red (My Love)** *Bobby Vinton* |
| 20/80 | **Rotation** *Herb Alpert* |
| 85/85 | **Round And Round** *Jaki Graham* |
| 10/85 | **Roxanne, Roxanne** *UTFO* |
| 22/85 | **Roxanne's Revenge** *Roxanne Shante* |
| 22/79 | **Rrrrrrock** *Foxy* |
| 70/78 | **Rub Down** *Joe Tex* |
| 9/43 | **Rubber Bounce** *Sonny Boy Williams* |
| 1/76 | **Rubberband Man** *Spinners* |
| 10/61 | **Ruby** *Ray Charles* |
| | **Ruby Baby** |
| 10/56 | *Drifters* |
| 5/63 | *Dion* |
| 11/57 | **Rudolph The Red-Nosed Reindeer** |
| | *Cadillacs* |
| 66/64 | **Rules Of Love** *Orlons* |
| 3/45 | **Rum And Coca-Cola** *Andrews Sisters* |
| 11/58 | **Rumble** *Link Wray* |
| 83/75 | **Rumble In The Jungle** *Don Covay* |
| 1/86 | **Rumors** *Timex Social Club* |
| 21/78 | **Rumour Has It** *Donna Summer* |
| 63/79 | **Rumpofsteelskin** *Parliament* |
| 84/77 | **Run Away** *Salsoul Orchestra* |
| 1/69 | **Run Away Child, Running Wild** |
| | *Temptations* |
| 1/48 | **Run, Joe** *Louis Jordan* |
| 29/59 | **Run Red Run** *Coasters* |
| 93/64 | **Run, Run, Run** *Supremes* |
| | **Run To Me** |
| 26/76 | *Candi Staton* |
| 4/88 | *Angela Winbush* |
| 10/88 | **Run's House** *Run-D.M.C.* |
| 30/61 | **Runaround** *Regents* |
| 4/61 | **Runaround Sue** *Dion* |
| 3/61 | **Runaway** *Del Shannon* |

## She's Gone

| | |
|---|---|
| 1/74 | *Tavares* |
| 81/74 | *Lou Rawls* |
| 93/76 | *Daryl Hall & John Oates* |
| 86/82 | *Norman Connors* |
| 56/63 | **She's Got Everything** *Essex* |
| 9/56 | **She's Got It** *Little Richard* |
| 87/84 | **She's Got The Body** *Kiddo* |
| 29/81 | **She's Got The Papers (But I Got The Man)** *Barbara Mason* |
| 71/83 | **She's Got To Be (A Dancer)** *Jerry Knight* |
| 15/82 | **She's Just A Groupie** *Bobby Nunn* |
| | **She's Killing Me** *..see: (Ooh-Wee)* |
| | **She's Looking Good** |
| 44/67 | *Rodger Collins* |
| 7/68 | *Wilson Pickett* |
| 76/82 | **She's My Shining Star** *Fatback* |
| 50/85 | **She's Not A Sleaze** *Paul Laurence* |
| 3/71 | **She's Not Just Another Woman** *8th Day* |
| 13/62 | **She's Not You** *Elvis Presley* |
| 22/83 | **She's Older Now** *Betty Wright* |
| 43/80 | **She's Out Of My Life** *Michael Jackson* |
| 44/82 | **She's So Divine** *Limit* |
| 1/84 | **She's Strange** *Cameo* |
| 25/84 | **She's Trouble** *Musical Youth* |
| 13/65 | **She's With Her Other Love** *Leon Hayward* |
| 55/82 | **She's Wrapped Too Tight (She's A Button Buster)** *Edwin Birdsong* |
| 43/80 | **Sheet Music** *Barry White* |
| 6/62 | **Sheila** *Tommy Roe* |
| 17/64 | **Shelter Of Your Arms** *Sammy Davis, Jr.* |
| | **Sherry** |
| 1/62 | *4 Seasons* |
| 50/87 | *Blake & Hines* |
| 66/64 | **Shimmy Shimmy** *Orlons* |
| 14/60 | **Shimmy, Shimmy, Ko-Ko-Bop** *Little Anthony & The Imperials* |
| | **Shine** |
| 10/48 | *Mills Brothers* |
| 14/79 | *Bar-Kays* |
| 78/82 | **Shine-O-Myte (Rag Popping)** *William 'Bootsy' Collins* |
| | **Shine On** |
| 19/81 | *L.T.D.* |
| 15/82 | *George Duke* |
| 24/83 | **Shine On Me** *One Way* |
| 86/78 | **Shine On Silver Moon** *Marilyn McCoo & Billy Davis, Jr.* |
| 29/81 | **Shine Your Light** *Graingers* |
| 50/67 | **Shingaling '67** *Don Covay* |
| | **Shining Star** |
| 1/75 | *Earth, Wind & Fire* |
| 4/80 | *Manhattans* |
| | *(also see: You're My)* |
| 13/55 | **Ship Of Love** *Nutmegs* |
| 15/57 | **Shirley** *Schoolboys* |
| 16/87 | **Shiver** *George Benson* |
| 66/77 | **Sho Feels Good To Me** *Con Funk Shun* |
| 45/74 | **Sho Nuff Boogie** *Sylvia & The Moments* |
| | **Sho You Rite** |
| 92/78 | *Wilson Williams* |
| 17/87 | *Barry White* |
| 64/82 | **Shock The Monkey** *Peter Gabriel* |
| 16/74 | **Shoe Shoe Shine** *Dynamic Superiors* |
| 68/78 | **Shoe Soul** *Smokey Robinson* |
| 18/71 | **Shoes** *Brook Benton with The Dixie Flyers* |
| 1/75 | **Shoeshine Boy** *Eddie Kendricks* |
| 67/81 | **Shoestrings** *Ray, Goodman & Brown* |
| 1/68 | **Shoo-Be-Doo-Be-Doo-Da-Day** *Stevie Wonder* |
| 31/77 | **Shoo Doo Fu Fu Ooh!** *Lenny Williams* |
| 1/43 | **Shoo Shoo Baby** *Ella Mae Morse* |
| | **Shoop Shoop Song (It's In His Kiss)** |
| 6/64 | *Betty Everett* |
| 96/75 | *Linda Lewis* |

## Shoorah! Shoorah!

| | |
|---|---|
| 28/75 | *Betty Wright* |
| 75/76 | *Jenny Jackson* |
| 10/88 | **Shoot 'Em Up Movies** *Deele* |
| 25/79 | **Shoot Me (With Your Love)** *Tasha Thomas* |
| 49/84 | **Shoot The Moon** *Patti Austin* |
| 43/80 | **Shoot Your Best Shot** *Linda Clifford* |
| 33/67 | **Shoot Your Shot** *Jr. Walker & The All Stars* |
| 1/61 | **Shop Around** *Miracles* |
| 1/57 | **Short Fat Fannie** *Larry Williams* |
| 2/58 | **Short Shorts** *Royal Teens* |
| 34/73 | **Short Stopping** *Veda Brown* |
| 4/46 | **Shorty's Got To Go** *Lucky Millinder* |
| 1/65 | **Shotgun** *Jr. Walker & The All Stars* |
| 5/50 | **Shotgun Blues** *Lightnin' Hopkins* |
| 25/75 | **Shotgun Shuffle** *Sunshine Band* |
| 14/65 | **Shotgun Wedding** *Roy 'C'* |
| 15/57 | **Should I Ever Love Again** *Wynona Carr* |
| 91/83 | **Should I Love You** *Cee Farrow* |
| 17/88 | **Should I Say Yes?** *Nu Shooz* |
| 50/79 | **Shoulda Gone Dancin'** *High Inergy* |
| 7/51 | **Shouldn't I Know?** *Cardinals* |
| 56/85 | **Shout** *Tears For Fears* |
| | *(also see: Come On)* |
| 61/82 | **Shout About It** *Lamont Dozier* |
| 21/80 | **Shout And Scream** *Teddy Pendergrass* |
| 16/62 | **Shout And Shimmy** *James Brown* |
| 11/67 | **Shout Bamalama** *Mickey Murray* |
| 36/82 | **Shout For Joy** *Dunn & Bruce Street* |
| 12/78 | **Shout It Out** *B.T. Express* |
| 25/62 | **Shout! Shout! (Knock Yourself Out)** *Ernie Maresca* |
| 31/78 | **Shouting Out Love** *Emotions* |
| 4/85 | **Show, The** *Doug E. Fresh* |
| 33/87 | **Show A Little Love** *Mission* |
| 10/74 | **Show And Tell** *Al Wilson* |
| 83/79 | **Show Bizness** *Gil Scott-Heron* |
| 25/67 | **Show Business** *Lou Rawls* |
| | **Show Me** |
| 24/67 | *Joe Tex* |
| 3/84 | *Glenn Jones* |
| 34/87 | *Cover Girls* |
| 13/72 | **Show Me How** *Emotions* |
| 68/86 | **Show Me How It Works** *Mavis Staples* |
| 41/77 | **Show Me Love** *Curtis Mayfield* |
| | **Show Me The Way** |
| 35/83 | *Skyy* |
| 2/87 | *Regina Belle* |
| 30/68 | **Show Me The Way To Go** *Gene Chandler & Barbara Acklin* |
| 23/82 | **Show Me Where You're Coming From** *Carrie Lucas* |
| | **Show Must Go On** |
| 76/75 | *Sam Dees* |
| 84/77 | *Four Tops* |
| 50/85 | **Show Some Respect** *Tina Turner* |
| 46/85 | **Show Stoppa** *Super Nature* |
| | **Show Time** |
| 22/68 | *Detroit Emeralds* |
| 55/79 | *Undisputed Truth* |
| 68/82 | **Show You My Love** *Goldie Alexander* |
| 6/77 | **Show You The Way To Go** *Jacksons* |
| 49/81 | **Showdown** *Furious Five Meets The Sugarhill Gang* |
| 23/87 | **Showing Out (Get Fresh at the Weekend)** *Mel & Kim* |
| 79/77 | **Shuffle, The** *Van McCoy* |
| 10/48 | **Shuffle Woogie** *Joe Lutcher* |
| 97/75 | **Shut Off The Lights** *Betty Davis* |
| 68/80 | **Shut 'Um Down** *Gil Scott-Heron* |
| 56/84 | **Siberian Nights** *Twilight 22* |
| | **Sick And Tired** |
| 13/57 | *Chris Kenner* |
| 14/58 | *Fats Domino* |
| 15/83 | **Side By Side** *Earth, Wind & Fire* |

| | |
|---|---|
| 1/74 | **Sideshow** *Blue Magic* |
| 51/86 | **Sidewalk Talk** *Jellybean* |
| 81/65 | **Sidewinder, The** *Lee Morgan* |
| 82/80 | **Sidra's Dream** *Dave Valentin* |
| 83/84 | **Sight For Sore Eyes** *Ohio Players* |
| 1/87 | **Sign 'O' The Times** *Prince* |
| | **Sign Of The Times** |
| 78/79 | *Terry Callier* |
| 55/85 | *Grandmaster Flash* |
| 2/88 | **Sign Your Name** *Terence Trent D'Arby* |
| 77/63 | **Signed, Sealed, And Delivered** |
| | *James Brown* |
| 1/70 | **Signed, Sealed, Delivered I'm Yours** |
| | *Stevie Wonder* |
| | **Silent Night** |
| 8/48 | *Ravens* |
| 6/50 | *Sister Rosetta Tharpe* |
| | **Silhouettes** |
| 3/57 | *Rays* |
| 6/57 | *Diamonds* |
| 79/81 | *Futures* |
| 11/81 | **Silly** *Deniece Williams* |
| 87/64 | **Silly Little Girl** *Tams* |
| 94/76 | **Silly Putty** *Stanley Clarke* |
| 24/72 | **Silly Wasn't I** *Valerie Simpson* |
| 13/85 | **Silver Shadow** *Atlantic Starr* |
| 43/84 | **Simple** *Johnny Mathis* |
| 34/72 | **Simple Game** *Four Tops* |
| 70/75 | **Simple Things** *Minnie Riperton* |
| 29/70 | **Simply Call It Love** *Gene Chandler* |
| | **Since I Don't Have You** |
| 3/59 | *Skyliners* |
| 47/64 | *Chuck Jackson* |
| 92/73 | *Lenny Welch* |
| | **Since I Fell For You** |
| 3/47 | *Paul Gayten & His Trio* |
| 4/63 | *Lenny Welch* |
| 24/72 | *Laura Lee* |
| 24/77 | *Hodges, James & Smith (medley)* |
| 78/64 | **Since I Found A New Love** |
| | *Little Johnny Taylor* |
| 59/75 | **Since I Found My Baby** |
| | *Cornelius Brothers & Sister Rose* |
| | **Since I Lost My Baby** |
| 4/65 | *Temptations* |
| 17/83 | *Luther Vandross* |
| 94/75 | **Since I Met You** *Lenny Williams* |
| 1/57 | **Since I Met You Baby** *Ivory Joe Hunter* |
| 37/88 | **Since You Came Over Me** *Lace* |
| 22/68 | **Since You Showed Me How To Be Happy** |
| | *Jackie Wilson* |
| 14/59 | **Since You've Been Gone** *Clyde McPhatter* |
| | *(also see: Sweet Sweet Baby)* |
| | **Sincerely** |
| 1/55 | *Moonglows* |
| 43/72 | *Moonglows ('72)* |
| 75/76 | **Sing A Happy Funky Song** *Miz Davis* |
| | **Sing A Happy Song** |
| 87/78 | *War* |
| 7/79 | *O'Jays* |
| 95/73 | **Sing A Little Song** *Jackie Wilson* |
| 94/74 | **Sing A Sad Song** *Percy & Them* |
| | **Sing A Simple Song** |
| 28/69 | *Sly & The Family Stone* |
| 44/82 | *West Street Mob* |
| 1/76 | **Sing A Song** *Earth, Wind & Fire* |
| 60/80 | **Singing A Song About You** |
| | *Triple 'S' Connection* |
| 64/84 | **Singing Hey Yea** *Kids At Work* |
| 4/57 | **Singing The Blues** *Guy Mitchell* |
| 2/85 | **Single Life** *Cameo* |
| 70/79 | **Sinner Man** *Sarah Dash* |
| 1/77 | **Sir Duke** *Stevie Wonder* |
| 51/80 | **Sir Jam A Lot** *Captain Sky* |
| 36/85 | **Sister Fate** *Sheila E.* |

| | |
|---|---|
| 49/78 | **Sister Fine** *Impact* |
| 78/73 | **Sister James** *Nino Tempo & 5th Ave. Sax* |
| 66/85 | **Sisters Are Doin' It For Themselves** |
| | *Eurythmics & Aretha Franklin* |
| 26/80 | **Sit Down And Talk To Me** *Lou Rawls* |
| 78/81 | **Sit Up** *Sadane* |
| 7/57 | **Sittin' In The Balcony** *Eddie Cochran* |
| 82/78 | **Sittin' On A Poor Man's Throne** |
| | *Bobby Bland* |
| 33/72 | **Sittin' On A Time Bomb (Waitin' For The Hurt** |
| | **To Come)** *Honey Cone* |
| 3/50 | **Sittin' On It All The Time** *Wynonie Harris* |
| | **(Sittin' On) The Dock Of The Bay** |
| 1/68 | *Otis Redding* |
| 21/82 | *Reddings* |
| 58/88 | *Michael Bolton* |
| 6/50 | **Sitting By The Window** *Billy Eckstine* |
| | **Sitting In The Park** |
| 4/65 | *Billy Stewart* |
| 9/80 | *GQ* |
| 31/82 | **Situation** *Yaz* |
| 4/87 | **Situation #9** *Club Nouveau* |
| 5/87 | **6** *Madhouse* |
| 17/59 | **Six Nights A Week** *Crests* |
| 86/75 | **Six Nights And A Day** *Candi Staton* |
| 1/66 | **634-5789** *Wilson Pickett* |
| 4/59 | **16 Candles** *Crests* |
| 10/60 | **Sixteen Reasons** *Connie Stevens* |
| 58/82 | **Sixth Street (Turn It Up)** *Mighty Fire* |
| | **Sixty-Minute Man** |
| 1/51 | *Dominoes* |
| 42/70 | *Rufus Thomas* |
| 17/73 | *Clarence Carter* |
| 76/81 | **Sixty Thrills A Minute** *Mystic Merlin* |
| 57/80 | **Sizzlin' Hot** *Slave* |
| 13/67 | **Skate Now** *Lou Courtney* |
| 1/87 | **Skeletons** *Stevie Wonder* |
| 2/74 | **Skin Tight** *Ohio Players* |
| 46/81 | **Skinny** *Ohio Players* |
| 2/67 | **Skinny Legs And All** *Joe Tex* |
| 94/77 | **Skinnydippin** *Ramona Brooks* |
| 48/83 | **Skip To My Lou** *Finis Henderson* |
| 87/78 | **Skokiaan** *Herb Alpert/Hugh Masekela* |
| 72/85 | **Skool-Ology (Ain't No Strain)** *Rosie Gaines* |
| 85/78 | **Sky High** *Mass Production* |
| 15/60 | **Sky Is Crying** *Elmore James* |
| 32/80 | **Skyyzoo** *Skyy* |
| 50/88 | **Slam** *David Sanborn* |
| 81/82 | **Slamm Dunk The Ffunk** *Sun* |
| 17/72 | **Slaughter** *Billy Preston* |
| 20/86 | **Slave To The Rhythm** *Grace Jones* |
| 61/86 | **Sledgehammer** *Peter Gabriel* |
| | **Sleep** |
| 6/51 | *Earl Bostic* |
| 10/60 | *Little Willie John* |
| 4/59 | **Sleep Walk** *Santo & Johnny* |
| 50/74 | **Sleepin'** *Diana Ross* |
| 24/87 | **Sleeping Alone** *Controllers* |
| 51/86 | **Sleepless Nights** *Smokey Robinson* |
| 18/73 | **Slick** *Willie Hutch* |
| 19/78 | **Slick Superchick** *Kool & The Gang* |
| | **Slide, The** |
| 20/61 | *Googie Rene Combo* |
| 1/77 | *Slave* |
| 57/86 | **Slide Over** *Ready For The World* |
| 21/76 | **Slip And Do It** *Betty Wright* |
| 25/70 | **Slip Around** *Charles Hodges* |
| | **Slip Away** |
| 2/68 | *Clarence Carter* |
| 47/84 | *Skool Boyz* |
| 48/64 | **Slip-In Mules (No High Heel Sneakers)** |
| | *Sugar Pie DeSanto* |
| 1/43 | **Slip Of The Lip** *Duke Ellington* |
| 49/85 | **Slip n' Slide** *Roy Ayers* |

**Slipped, Tripped And Fell In Love**
25/71    *Clarence Carter*
42/71    *Ann Peebles*
88/86 **Slipped, Tripped (Fooled Around And Fell In Love)**   *Carl Carlton*
22/84 **Slippery People**   *Staple Singers*
1/75 **Slippery When Wet**   *Commodores*
2/56 **Slippin' And Slidin' (Peepin' And Hidin')**   *Little Richard*
12/72 **Slippin' Into Darkness**   *War*
46/73 **Slipping Away**   *Holland-Dozier*
44/72 **Slipping Into Darkness**   *Ramsey Lewis*
88/77 **Slow And Easy**   *B.B. King*
**Slow Dance**
76/78    *Stanley Clarke*
63/80    *David Ruffin*
35/84 **Slow Dancin'**   *Peabo Bryson*
**Slow Down**
100/77    *John Miles*
81/86    *Evelyn 'Champagne' King*
1/87    *Loose Ends*
12/68 **Slow Drag**   *Intruders*
7/81 **Slow Hand**   *Pointer Sisters*
**Slow Motion**
12/72    *Johnny Williams*
49/76    *Dells*
47/83 **Slow Movin'**   *Cameo*
36/88 **Slow Starter**   *Randy Hall*
3/62 **Slow Twistin'**   *Chubby Checker*
**Slow Walk**
3/56    *Sil Austin*
4/56    *Bill Doggett*
51/82 **Slow Your Body Down**   *Clifton Dyson*
46/69 **Slum Baby**   *Booker T. & The MG's*
14/70 **Sly, Slick, And The Wicked**   *Lost Generation*
**Smack Dab In The Middle**
52/64    *Ray Charles*
91/80    *Janice McClain*
56/83 **Small Town Lover**   *Cheri*
25/73 **Smarty Pants**   *First Choice*
**Smile**
42/65    *Betty Everett & Jerry Butler*
98/76    *David Sanborn*
6/78    *Emotions*
41/79    *Rance Allen Group*
21/72 **Smilin'**   *Sly & The Family Stone*
2/71 **Smiling Faces Sometimes**   *Undisputed Truth*
3/58 **Smoke Gets In Your Eyes**   *Platters*
74/74 **Smoke My Peace Pipe (Smoke It Right)**   *Wild Magnolias*
8/56 **Smoke Stack Lightning**   *Howlin' Wolf*
96/77 **Smokey**   *Funkadelic*
10/55 **Smokey Joe's Cafe**   *Robins*
35/66 **Smokey Joe's La La**   *Googie Rene Combo*
1/60 **Smokie**   *Bill Black's Combo*
13/75 **Smokin' Room**   *Carl Carlton*
10/62 **Smoky Places**   *Corsairs*
**Smooth Operator**
8/59    *Sarah Vaughan*
5/85    *Sade*
3/87 **Smooth Sailin' Tonight**   *Isley Brothers*
3/51 **Smooth Sailing**   *Ella Fitzgerald*
14/83 **Smurf, The**   *Tyrone Brunson*
32/68 **Snake, The**   *Al Wilson*
88/80 **Snake Eyes**   *Grover Washington, Jr.*
27/65 **Snake In The Grass**   *Paul Martin*
6/81 **Snap Shot**   *Slave*
**Snap Your Fingers**
2/62    *Joe Henderson*
71/64    *Barbara Lewis*
1/47 **Snatch And Grab It**   *Julia Lee*
4/69 **Snatching It Back**   *Clarence Carter*
91/79 **Sneakers (Fifty-Four)**   *Sea Level*

**Sneakin' Around**
2/49    *Rudy Render*
14/55    *B.B. King*
**Sneakin' Out**
5/46    *Erskine Hawkins*
62/85    *Linda Clifford*
16/75 **Sneakin' Up Behind You**   *Brecker Brothers*
10/48 **Sneaky Pete**   *Bull Moose Jackson*
**So Amazing**
94/87    *Luther Vandross*
12/88    *Gerald Albright*
**So Close**
5/59    *Brook Benton*
76/83    *Diana Ross*
34/80 **So Delicious**   *Pockets*
28/78 **So Easy**   *Con Funk Shun*
5/88 **So Emotional**   *Whitney Houston*
14/70 **So Excited**   *B.B. King*
91/64 **So Far Away**   *Hank Jacobs*
**So Fine**
3/59    *Fiestas*
50/68    *Ike & Tina Turner*
6/82    *Howard Johnson*
86/86    *Petite*
3/46 **So Glad You're Mine**   *Arthur 'Big Boy' Crudup*
15/79 **So Good, So Right**   *Brenda Russell*
9/76 **So Good (To Be Home With You)**   *Tyrone Davis*
79/85 **So Hard**   *Windjammer*
12/59 **So High So Low**   *LaVern Baker*
3/69 **So I Can Love You**   *Emotions*
9/75 **So In Love**   *Curtis Mayfield*
60/88 **So In Love With You**   *Reddings*
93/77 **So In To You**   *Atlanta Rhythm Section*
**So Long**
4/46    *Johnny Moore's Three Blazers*
4/49    *Ruth Brown*
5/56    *Fats Domino*
14/57    *Roy Hamilton*
11/87 **So Many Tears**   *Regina Belle*
1/59 **So Many Ways**   *Brook Benton*
14/62 **So Mean To Me**   *Little Milton*
24/59 **So Much**   *Little Anthony & The Imperials*
95/74 **So Much Confusion**   *King Floyd*
4/63 **So Much In Love**   *Tymes*
14/70 **So Much Love**   *Faith, Hope & Charity*
93/81 **So Much More**   *Ramsey Lewis*
**So Much Trouble In My Mind** *..see: (I Got)*
35/68 **So Nice**   *Mad Lads*
4/57 **So Rare**   *Jimmy Dorsey*
12/76 **So Sad The Song**   *Gladys Knight & The Pips*
16/60 **So Sad (To Watch Good Love Go Bad)**   *Everly Brothers*
41/67 **So Sharp**   *Dyke & The Blazers*
27/77 **So So Satisfied**   *Ashford & Simpson*
**So Strong** *..see: (Something Inside)*
59/74 **So Tied Up**   *Sam Dees*
**So Tired**
9/49    *Lonnie Johnson*
6/52    *Roy Milton*
6/58 **So Tough**   *Original Casuals*
11/73 **So Very Hard To Go**   *Tower Of Power*
77/83 **So Wrong**   *Patrick Simmons*
60/81 **So You Wanna Be A Star**   *Mtume*
82/77 **So You Win Again**   *Hot Chocolate*
49/69 **Sock It To 'Em Soul Brother**   *Bill Moss*
24/68 **Sock It To Me**   *Deacons*
19/68 **Sockin' 1-2-3-4**   *John Roberts*
3/53 **Soft**   *Tiny Bradshaw*
20/78 **Soft And Easy**   *Blackbyrds*
12/78 **Soft And Wet**   *Prince*
20/74 **Soft Soul Boogie Woogie**   *Wilson Pickett*
13/56 **Soft Winds**   *Dinah Washington*
87/77 **Solar Flight (Opus 1)**   *Mandre*

| | |
|---|---|
| 1/76 | **Sophisticated Lady (She's A Different Lady)** *Natalie Cole* |
| | **Sophisticated Sissy** |
| 43/67 | *Rufus Thomas* |
| 7/69 | *Meters* |
| 34/79 | **Sorry** *Natalie Cole* |
| 24/78 | **Sorry Doesn't Always Make It Right** *Gladys Knight & The Pips* |
| 14/59 | **Sorry (I Ran All The Way Home)** *Impalas* |
| | **Soul And Inspiration** *..see: (You're My)* |
| 91/79 | **Soul Bones** *Trammps* |
| 42/69 | **Soul Brother, Soul Sister** *Capitols* |
| 42/76 | **Soul City Walk** *Archie Bell & The Drells* |
| 10/67 | **Soul Dance Number Three** *Wilson Pickett* |
| 65/76 | **Soul Dog** *Soul Dog* |
| 95/64 | **Soul Dressing** *Booker T. & The MG's* |
| 3/67 | **Soul Finger** *Bar-Kays* |
| 8/65 | **Soul Heaven** *Dixie Drifter* |
| 92/64 | **Soul Hootenanny** *Gene Chandler* |
| 39/73 | **Soul Je T'Aime** *Sylvia & Ralfi Pagan* |
| 7/68 | **Soul-Limbo** *Booker T. & The MG's* |
| | **Soul Makossa** |
| 21/73 | *Manu Dibango* |
| 33/73 | *Afrique* |
| 1/67 | **Soul Man** *Sam & Dave* |
| 69/74 | **Soul March** *Fatback Band* |
| 34/68 | **Soul Meeting** *Soul Clan* |
| 18/77 | **Soul Of A Man** *Bobby Bland* |
| 72/74 | **Soul Of A Woman** *Margo Thunder* |
| 3/71 | **Soul Power** *James Brown* |
| 20/74 | **Soul Power 74** *Maceo & The Macks* |
| 78/73 | **Soul President Number One** *John & Ernest* |
| 33/69 | **Soul Pride** *James Brown* |
| 67/76 | **Soul Searchin' Time** *Trammps* |
| | **Soul Serenade** |
| 51/64 | *King Curtis* |
| 10/68 | *Willie Mitchell* |
| 72/73 | *Jimmy Castor Bunch* |
| 41/80 | **Soul Shadows** *Crusaders* |
| 13/69 | **Soul Shake** *Peggy Scott & Jo Jo Benson* |
| 18/69 | **Soul Sister, Brown Sugar** *Sam & Dave* |
| 65/74 | **Soul Street** *Eddie Floyd* |
| 42/67 | **Soul Superman** *Hesitations* |
| 31/67 | **Soul Time** *Shirley Ellis* |
| | **Soul Train** |
| 41/72 | *Ramrods* |
| 9/75 | *Soul Train Gang ('75')* |
| 1/62 | **Soul Twist** *King Curtis* |
| 3/69 | **Soulful Strut** *Young-Holt Unlimited* |
| 69/84 | **Sound Of Music** *Dayton* |
| 21/74 | **Sound Your Funky Horn** *KC & The Sunshine Band* |
| 14/82 | **Soup For One** *Chic* |
| 72/77 | **Sour And Sweet/Lemon In The Honey** *Dr. Buzzard's Original 'Savannah' Band* |
| 78/74 | **South African Man** *Hamilton Bohannon* |
| 4/63 | **South Street** *Orlons* |
| 95/79 | **Southern Comfort** *Mason Dixon Dance Band* |
| 21/65 | **Southern Country Boy** *Carter Brothers* |
| 9/80 | **Southern Girl** *Maze Featuring Frankie Beverly* |
| 73/79 | **Souvenirs** *Voyage* |
| 18/86 | **Soweto** *Jeffrey Osborne* |
| 28/77 | **Space Age** *Jimmy Castor* |
| 12/83 | **Space Cowboy** *Jonzun Crew* |
| 31/83 | **Space Is The Place** *Jonzun Crew* |
| 86/79 | **Space Princess** *Lonnie Liston Smith* |
| 1/73 | **Space Race** *Billy Preston* |
| 56/80 | **Space Ranger (Majic's In The Air)** *Sun* |
| 28/80 | **Spacer** *Sheila & B. Devotion* |
| | **Spanish Harlem** |
| 15/61 | *Ben E. King* |
| 1/71 | *Aretha Franklin* |
| 12/76 | **Spanish Hustle** *Fatback Band* |

| | |
|---|---|
| | **Spank, The** |
| 26/78 | *James Brown* |
| 55/79 | *Jimmy 'Bo' Horne* |
| 34/78 | **Spank Your Blank Blank** *Morris Jefferson* |
| 10/80 | **Sparkle** *Cameo* |
| 12/50 | **Sparrow's Flight** *Johnny Sparrow* |
| 22/67 | **Speak Her Name** *Walter Jackson* |
| 94/87 | **Speaking Japanese** *Kopper* |
| | **Special** |
| 76/82 | *Jimmy Cliff* |
| 77/86 | *Stylistics* |
| | **Special Delivery** |
| 11/48 | *Cecil Gant* |
| 94/75 | *Polly Brown* |
| 65/84 | *Angela Bofill* |
| 84/82 | **Special Effects** *L.J. Reynolds* |
| 1/80 | **Special Lady** *Ray, Goodman & Brown* |
| 73/75 | **Special Loving** *Barbara Acklin* |
| 36/70 | **Special Memory** *Jerry Butler* |
| | **Special Occasion** |
| 4/68 | *Smokey Robinson & The Miracles* |
| 30/78 | *Dorothy Moore* |
| 51/82 | *Millie Jackson* |
| 29/63 | **Speed Ball** *Ray Stevens* |
| 3/56 | **Speedoo** *Cadillacs* |
| 30/73 | **Spell** *Blue Magic* |
| 29/77 | **Spellbound** *Bar-Kays* |
| 77/84 | **Spend My Whole Life** *Zapp* |
| 76/88 | **Spend Some Time With Me** *Jamaica Boys* |
| | **Spend The Night With Me** |
| 80/78 | *Silver Convention* |
| 41/85 | *Rick James* |
| 32/83 | **Spice Of Life** *Manhattan Transfer* |
| 14/71 | **Spill The Wine** *Isley Brothers* |
| 45/73 | **Spinning Around** *Black Ivory* |
| 7/71 | **Spinning Around (I Must Be Falling In Love)** *Main Ingredient* |
| 45/69 | **Spinning Wheel** *Blood, Sweat & Tears* |
| 3/70 | **Spirit In The Dark** *Aretha Franklin* |
| 55/76 | **Spirit Of '76** *Booty People* |
| 1/75 | **Spirit Of The Boogie** *Kool & The Gang* |
| 51/82 | **Spirit Of The Dancer** *Evelyn King* |
| 59/80 | **Splashdown Time** *Breakwater* |
| 1/58 | **Splish Splash** *Bobby Darin* |
| 50/86 | **Split Personality** *UTFO* |
| 12/61 | **Spoonful** *Etta & Harvey* |
| | **Spread Love** |
| 75/78 | *Al Hudson & The Soul Partners* |
| 88/85 | *Fatback* |
| | **Spread Your Love** |
| 35/68 | *Jimmy Holiday* |
| 57/83 | *Earth, Wind & Fire* |
| 44/67 | **Spreadin' Honey** *Watts 103rd Street Rhythm Band* |
| 18/63 | **Spring** *Birdlegs* |
| 24/77 | **Spring Affair** *Donna Summer* |
| | **Spring Fever** *..see: (I've Got)* |
| 85/77 | **Spring High** *Ramsey Lewis* |
| 82/87 | **Spring Love** *Cover Girls* |
| 77/77 | **Spring Rain** *Silvetti* |
| 37/77 | **Spy For Brotherhood** *Miracles featuring Billy Griffin* |
| 3/81 | **Square Biz** *Teena Marie* |
| 89/64 | **Squeeze Her-Tease Her (But Love Her)** *Jackie Wilson* |
| | **Stack-A'Lee** *..see: Stagger Lee* |
| 9/51 | **Stacked Deck** *Billy Wright* |
| 34/82 | **Stage Fright** *Chic* |
| | **Stagger Lee** |
| 10/50 | *Archibald* |
| 1/59 | *Lloyd Price* |
| 13/67 | *Wilson Pickett* |
| | **Stairway To Heaven** |
| 16/60 | *Neil Sedaka* |
| F/76 | *O'Jays* |

**Sucker For A Pretty Face** ..see: (I'm Just A)

| | | |
|---|---|---|
| 41/68 | **Sudden Stop** | *Percy Sledge* |
| 5/85 | **Suddenly** | *Billy Ocean* |
| 13/65 | **Suddenly I'm All Alone** | *Walter Jackson* |
| 43/80 | **Sugar** | *Kenny Doss* |
| 72/82 | **Sugar And Spice (I Found Me A Girl)** | |
| | *Luther Vandross* | |
| 19/62 | **Sugar Babe** | *Buster Brown* |
| 50/84 | **Sugar Baby** | *Kids At Work* |
| 3/72 | **Sugar Daddy** | *Jackson 5* |
| 34/68 | **Sugar (Don't Take Away My Candy)** | |
| | *Jive Five featuring Eugene Pitt* | |
| 18/65 | **Sugar Dumpling** | *Sam Cooke* |
| 13/86 | **Sugar Free** | *Juicy* |
| 35/74 | **Sugar Lump** | *Leon Haywood* |
| 43/75 | **Sugar Pie** | *Sugar Billy* |
| 10/74 | **Sugar Pie Guy** | *Joneses* |
| 1/63 | **Sugar Shack** | *Jimmy Gilmer & The Fireballs* |
| 4/70 | **Sugar Sugar** | *Wilson Pickett* |
| 11/55 | **Sugar Sweet** | *Muddy Waters* |
| 3/85 | **Sugar Walls** | *Sheena Easton* |
| 67/73 | **Sugarcane** | *M.G.'s* |
| | **Sukiyaki** | |
| 18/63 | *Kyu Sakamoto* | |
| 1/81 | *A Taste Of Honey* | |
| 4/76 | **Summer** | *War* |
| 10/74 | **Summer Breeze** | *Isley Brothers* |
| 50/81 | **Summer Fun** | *Bill Summers & Summers Heat* |
| 84/84 | **Summer In The Street** | *Carrie Lucas* |
| 39/82 | **Summer Lady** | *Narada Michael Walden* |
| 56/79 | **Summer Love** | *David Oliver* |
| 36/75 | **Summer Madness** | *Kool & The Gang* |
| 35/87 | **Summer Nights** | *Grover Washington, Jr.* |
| 80/75 | **Summer Of '42** | *Biddu Orchestra* |
| 40/77 | **Summer Snow** | *Blue Magic* |
| 57/78 | **Summer Song** | *Grover Washington, Jr.* |
| 29/60 | **Summer's Gone** | *Paul Anka* |
| 29/59 | **Summer's Love** | |
| | *Richard Barrett with The Chantels* | |
| 7/66 | **Summertime** | *Billy Stewart* |
| 65/76 | **Summertime And I'm Feelin' Mellow** | |
| | *MFSB* | |
| 11/58 | **Summertime Blues** | *Eddie Cochran* |
| 45/74 | **Summertime In The City** | *Manhattans* |
| 47/86 | **Summertime, Summertime** | *Nocera* |
| 21/85 | **Sun City** | *Artists United Against Apartheid* |
| 82/86 | **Sun Don't Shine** | *Betty Wright* |
| 20/75 | **Sun Goddess** | |
| | *Ramsey Lewis and Earth, Wind & Fire* | |
| 18/78 | **Sun Is Here** | *Sun* |
| 12/57 | **Sun Is Shining** | *Jimmy Reed* |
| 13/69 | **Sunday** | *Moments* |
| 77/83 | **Sunday Afternoon** | *Invisible Man's Band* |
| 3/43 | **Sunday, Monday, or Always** | *Bing Crosby* |
| | **Sunny** | |
| 3/66 | *Bobby Hebb* | |
| 39/76 | *Yambu* | |
| 94/76 | *Bobby Hebb* | |
| | **Sunny Road** | |
| 2/46 | *Roosevelt Sykes* | |
| 4/46 | *Johnny Moore's Three Blazers* | |
| 46/80 | **Sunrise** | *Slick* |
| 10/52 | **Sunset To Dawn** | *Johnny Otis Orchestra* |
| | **Sunshine** | |
| 89/73 | *Percy Sledge* | |
| 17/75 | *O'Jays* | |
| 36/76 | *Impressions* | |
| 3/77 | *Enchantment* | |
| 61/76 | **Sunshine Day** | *Osibisa* |
| 85/76 | **Sunshine Keri** | *Lee Oskar* |
| | **Sunshine Lady** | |
| 72/73 | *Willie Hutch* | |
| 76/86 | *Latimore* | |
| 100/76 | **Sunshine (When I Got You)** | *Stirling Silver* |
| 1/70 | **Super Bad** | *James Brown* |

| | | |
|---|---|---|
| 17/77 | **Super Band** | *Kool & The Gang* |
| 49/76 | **Super Disco** | *Rimshots* |
| 7/75 | **Super Duper Love (Are You Diggin' On** | |
| | **Me)** *Sugar Billy* | |
| 17/73 | **Super Fly Meets Shaft** | *John & Ernest* |
| 3/81 | **Super Freak** | *Rick James* |
| 48/75 | **Super 'Jaws'** | *Seven Seas* |
| 29/83 | **Super Love** | *Johnny Gill* |
| 92/79 | **Super Lover** | *Rena Scott* |
| 54/77 | **Super Sexy** | *Leon Haywood* |
| 20/79 | **Super Sweet** | *Wardell Piper* |
| | **Super Turf** ..see: (Breakin') | |
| 24/78 | **Super Woman** | *Dells* |
| 3/88 | **Superbad** | *Chris Jasper* |
| 28/75 | **Superbad, Superslick** | *James Brown* |
| 75/86 | **Superbowl Shuffle** | |
| | *Chicago Bears Shufflin' Crew* | |
| 86/85 | **Superfine (From Behind)** | *Skool Boyz* |
| 5/73 | **Superfly** | *Curtis Mayfield* |
| 31/81 | **Superlove** | *Skyy* |
| | **Superman** | |
| 86/77 | *Celi Bee & The Buzzy Bunch* | |
| 63/79 | *Herbie Mann* | |
| 19/76 | **Superman Lover** | *Johnny 'Guitar' Watson* |
| 19/78 | **Supernatural Feeling** | *Blackbyrds* |
| 51/84 | **Supernatural Love** | *Donna Summer* |
| 1/75 | **Supernatural Thing** | *Ben E. King* |
| 72/78 | **Supernature** | *Cerrone* |
| 98/75 | **Supership** | *George 'Bad' Benson* |
| 22/88 | **Supersonic** | *J.J. Fad* |
| 42/76 | **Supersound** | *Jimmy Castor Bunch* |
| | **Superstar** | |
| 58/83 | *Lydia Murdock* | |
| 5/84 | *Luther Vandross (medley)* | |
| | *(also see: I'm A)* | |
| 8/71 | **Superstar (Remember How You Got Where You** | |
| | **Are)** *Temptations* | |
| 1/73 | **Superstition** | *Stevie Wonder* |
| 64/80 | **Superwoman** | *Side Effect* |
| 13/72 | **Superwoman (Where Were You When I Needed** | |
| | **You)** *Stevie Wonder* | |
| 72/80 | **Sure Shot** | *Crown Heights Affair* |
| 66/74 | **Sure Thing** | *Dionne Warwick* |
| 73/82 | **Sureyoureright** | *Steptoe* |
| 3/63 | **Surf City** | *Jan & Dean* |
| 90/87 | **Surf Or Die** | *Surf M.C.'s* |
| 18/63 | **Surfer Girl** | *Beach Boys* |
| 20/63 | **Surfin' U.S.A.** | *Beach Boys* |
| 87/84 | **Surprise Attack** | *Eddie Kendricks* |
| | **Surrender** | |
| 16/71 | *Diana Ross* | |
| 77/81 | *Peaches & Herb* | |
| 66/84 | *Deele* | |
| F/75 | **Survival** | *O'Jays* |
| 6/58 | **Susie Darlin'** | *Robin Luke* |
| 7/57 | **Susie-Q** | *Dale Hawkins* |
| 66/85 | **Suspicious** | *Deele* |
| 24/71 | **Suspicious Minds** | *Dee Dee Warwick* |
| 8/85 | **Sussudio** | *Phil Collins* |
| 5/47 | **Swanee River Boogie** | *Albert Ammons* |
| 14/57 | **Swanee River Rock (Talkin' 'Bout That** | |
| | **River)** *Ray Charles* | |
| 31/75 | **Swearin' To God** | *Frankie Valli* |
| | **Sweat** | |
| 55/83 | *System* | |
| 50/88 | *Ohio Players* | |
| 10/81 | **Sweat (Til You Get Wet)** | *Brick* |
| 14/48 | **Sweet And Lovely** | *Joe Liggins* |
| 6/86 | **Sweet And Sexy Thing** | *Rick James* |
| | **Sweet Baby** | |
| 30/72 | *Donnie Elbert* | |
| 6/81 | *Stanley Clarke/George Duke* | |
| 37/82 | *Harry Ray* | |
| 10/56 | **Sweet Baby Of Mine** | *Ruth Brown* |
| 45/68 | **Sweet Blindness** | *5th Dimension* |

| | |
|---|---|
| 16/72 | **Sweet Caroline (Good Times Never Seemed So Good)** *Bobby Womack* |
| 15/73 | **Sweet Charlie Babe** *Jackie Moore* |
| 38/74 | **Sweet Dan** *Betty Everett* |
| 45/68 | **Sweet Darlin'** *Martha Reeves & The Vandellas* |

16/72 **Sweet Caroline (Good Times Never Seemed So Good)** *Bobby Womack*
15/73 **Sweet Charlie Babe** *Jackie Moore*
38/74 **Sweet Dan** *Betty Everett*
45/68 **Sweet Darlin'**
　　　*Martha Reeves & The Vandellas*
68/81 **Sweet Delight** *Woods Empire*
32/74 **Sweet Exorcist** *Curtis Mayfield*
5/70 **Sweet Feeling** *Candi Staton*
91/75 **Sweet Fools** *Essence*
17/86 **Sweet Freedom** *Michael McDonald*
　　　**Sweet Georgia Brown**
7/48 　　*Joe Liggins*
9/49 　　*Brother Bones*
31/73 **Sweet Harmony** *Smokey Robinson*
13/59 **Sweet Home Chicago** *Little Junior Parker*
5/68 **Sweet Inspiration** *Sweet Inspirations*
8/56 **Sweet Little Angel** *B.B. King*
13/58 **Sweet Little Rock And Roll** *Chuck Berry*
1/58 **Sweet Little Sixteen** *Chuck Berry*
　　　**Sweet Love**
2/76 　　*Commodores*
2/86 　　*Anita Baker*
55/87 　　*Najee*
72/74 **Sweet Loving Woman** *Garland Green*
51/88 **Sweet Memories** *Theresa*
33/78 **Sweet Music Man** *Millie Jackson*
12/60 **Sweet Nothin's** *Brenda Lee*
43/74 **Sweet Rhode Island Red** *Ike & Tina Turner*
　　　**Sweet Sensation**
3/80 　　*Stephanie Mills*
4/88 　　*Levert*
　　　**Sweet Sixteen**
3/52 　　*Joe Turner*
2/60 　　*B.B. King*
37/72 　　*B.B. King*
9/62 **Sweet Sixteen Bars** *Earl Grant*
1/43 **Sweet Slumber** *Lucky Millinder*
55/87 **Sweet Somebody** *Donna Allen*
2/67 **Sweet Soul Music** *Arthur Conley*
1/75 **Sweet Sticky Thing** *Ohio Players*
16/74 **Sweet Stuff** *Sylvia*
43/76 **Sweet Summer Music** *Attitudes*
1/68 **(Sweet Sweet Baby) Since You've Been Gone** *Aretha Franklin*
29/74 **Sweet Sweet Lady** *Moments*
32/67 **Sweet, Sweet Lovin'** *Platters*
32/72 **Sweet Sweet Tootie** *Lonnie Youngblood*
47/82 **Sweet Tender Love** *Denroy Morgan*
1/76 **Sweet Thing** *Rufus Featuring Chaka Khan*
10/73 **Sweet Understanding Love** *Four Tops*
40/64 **Sweet William** *Millie Small*
1/66 **Sweet Woman Like You** *Joe Tex*
45/71 **Sweet Woman Love** *Geater Davis*
58/75 **Sweeter** *Major Lance*
19/81 **Sweeter As The Days Go By** *Shalamar*
7/69 **Sweeter He Is** *Soul Children*
40/87 **Sweeter Than Candy/Penitentiary III** *Gap Band*
52/77 **Sweeter Than The Sweet** *Staples*
44/67 **Sweetest One** *Metros*
40/80 **Sweetest Pain** *Dexter Wansel*
3/86 **Sweetest Taboo** *Sade*
　　　**Sweetest Thing This Side Of Heaven**
10/67 　　*Chris Bartley*
30/71 　　*Presidents*
24/86 **Sweetheart** *Rainy Davis*
10/61 **Sweets For My Sweet** *Drifters*
3/84 **Swept Away** *Diana Ross*
56/64 **S-W-I-M** *Bobby Freeman*
27/85 **Swing Low** *R.J.'s Latest Arrival*
54/83 **Swing That Sexy Thang** *Carl Carlton*
10/75 **Swing Your Daddy** *Jim Gilstrap*
17/58 **Swinging Shepherd Blues** *Johnny Pate Quintet*

3/61 **Switch-A-Roo** *Hank Ballard & The Midnighters*
55/84 **Switch It Baby** *Switch*
22/69 **Switch It On** *Cliff Nobles & Co.*
12/84 **Swoop (I'm Yours)** *Dazz Band*
11/88 **Symptons Of True Love** *Tracie Spencer*
1/87 **System Of Survival** *Earth, Wind & Fire*

# T

7/49 **T-Bone Shuffle** *T-Bone Walker*
8/49 **'T' Model Blues** *Lightnin' Hopkins*
1/51 **'T' 99 Blues** *Jimmy Nelson*
6/51 **T-Town Twist** *Roy Milton*
36/69 **T.C.B. Or T.Y.A.** *Bobby Patterson*
87/84 **T.K.O.** *Womack & Womack*
54/75 **T.L.C. (Tender Lovin' Care)** *MFSB*
1/74 **TSOP (The Sound Of Philadelphia)** *MFSB featuring The Three Degrees*
7/60 **Ta Ta** *Clyde McPhatter*
64/64 **T'ain't Nothin' To Me** *Coasters*
23/84 **Take A Chance** *Nuance featuring Vikki Love*
17/73 **Take A Closer Look At The Woman You're With** *Wilson Pickett*
10/69 **Take A Letter Maria** *R.B. Greaves*
29/82 **Take A Lickin' And Keep On Kickin'** *William 'Bootsy' Collins*
28/67 **Take A Look** *Aretha Franklin*
10/72 **Take A Look Around** *Temptations*
61/86 **Take A Piece Of Me** *Booker Newberry III*
2/69 **Take Care Of Your Homework** *Johnnie Taylor*
91/77 **Take Five** *Al Jarreau*
20/61 **Take Good Care Of Her** *Adam Wade*
10/88 **Take Good Care Of Me** *Jonathan Butler*
64/75 **Take Good Care Of Yourself** *Three Degrees*
94/84 **Take Him Back (Taxi)** *Anne Lesear*
1/42 **Take It And Git** *Andy Kirk*
19/81 **Take It Any Way You Want It** *Fatback*
33/75 **Take It Away From Him (Put It On Me)** *Paul Kelly*
　　　**Take It From Me**
30/75 　　*Dionne Warwick*
38/87 　　*Commodores*
39/83 **Take It Off** *Chocolate Milk*
23/70 **Take It Off Him And Put It On Me** *Clarence Carter*
24/78 **Take It On Up** *Pockets*
47/83 **Take It To The Hop** *Rufus*
　　　**Take It To The Limit**
28/80 　　*Norman Connors*
73/84 　　*T-Connection*
8/87 　　*Ray, Goodman & Brown*
　　　**Take It To The Top**
11/81 　　*Kool & The Gang*
67/82 　　*Merge*
　　　**Take Me As I Am**
35/73 　　*Lyn Collins*
62/77 　　*Philippe Wynne*
69/80 **Take Me Away** *Temptations*
　　　**Take Me Back**
10/54 　　*Linda Hayes*
15/65 　　*Little Anthony & The Imperials*
77/82 　　*Coffee*
36/67 **Take Me For A Little While** *Patti LaBelle & The Blue Belles*
18/71 **Take Me Girl, I'm Ready** *Jr. Walker & The All Stars*
21/79 **Take Me Home** *Cher*

| | |
|---|---|
| 76/78 | **There Will Be Love** *Lou Rawls* |
| 7/77 | **There Will Come A Day (I'm Gonna Happen To You)** *Smokey Robinson* |
| 8/74 | **There Will Never By Any Peace (Until God Is Seated At The Conference Table)** *Chi-Lites* |
| F/76 | **There You Are** *Millie Jackson* |
| 12/73 | **There You Go** *Edwin Starr* |
| 1/86 | **There'll Be Sad Songs (To Make You Cry)** *Billy Ocean* |
| 2/69 | **There'll Come A Time** *Betty Everett* |
| 6/78 | **There'll Never Be** *Switch* |
| 31/71 | **There's A Love For Everyone** *Whispers* |
| 91/75 | **There's A Man Out There Somewhere** *Lola Falana* |
| 11/61 | **There's A Moon Out Tonight** *Capris* |
| 36/75 | **There's A Red-Neck In The Soul Band** *Latimore* |
| 75/82 | **There's A Way** *Ronnie Laws* |
| | **(There's) Always Something There To Remind Me** |
| 49/64 | *Lou Johnson* |
| 50/70 | *R.B. Greaves* |
| 58/75 | **There's Another In My Life** *Prince Phillip Mitchell* |
| 59/74 | **There's Fever In The Funkhouse** *General Crook* |
| 6/69 | **There's Gonna Be A Showdown** *Archie Bell & The Drells* |
| 21/74 | **There's Got To Be Rain In Your Life (To Appreciate The Sunshine)** *Dorothy Norwood* |
| 38/86 | **There's Just Something About You** *Beau Williams* |
| 53/77 | **There's Love In The World (Tell The Lonely People)** *Mighty Clouds Of Joy* |
| | **There's No Easy Way** |
| 83/83 | *Michael Wycoff* |
| 14/84 | *James Ingram* |
| 36/82 | **There's No Guarantee** *Peabo Bryson* |
| 3/73 | **There's No Me Without You** *Manhattans* |
| 5/61 | **There's No Other (Like My Baby)** *Crystals* |
| 36/85 | **There's Nothin' Out There** *Peabo Bryson* |
| 1/87 | **There's Nothing Better Than Love** *Luther Vandross with Gregory Hines* |
| 33/71 | **There's So Much Love All Around Me** *Three Degrees* |
| 1/60 | **There's Something On Your Mind** *Bobby Marchan* |
| 82/74 | **(These Are) The Moments** *David Harris* |
| 28/69 | **These Are The Things That Make Me Know You're Gone** *Howard Tate* |
| 20/63 | **These Arms Of Mine** *Otis Redding* |
| 3/69 | **These Eyes** *Jr. Walker & The All Stars* |
| 25/63 | **These Foolish Things** *James Brown* |
| 5/53 | **These Foolish Things Remind Me Of You** *Billy Ward & His Dominoes* |
| 27/62 | **These Golden Rings** *Jive Five* |
| 4/65 | **These Hands (Small But Mighty)** *Bobby Bland* |
| 43/66 | **These Things Will Keep Me Loving You** *Velvelettes* |
| 5/46 | **They All Say I'm The Biggest Fool** *Buddy Johnson* |
| 1/75 | **They Just Can't Stop It the (Games People Play)** *Spinners* |
| | **(They Long To Be) Close To You** |
| 6/72 | *Jerry Butler featuring Brenda Lee Eager* |
| 69/87 | *Gwen Guthrie* |
| 50/84 | **They Only Come Out At Night** *Peter Brown* |
| 17/73 | **They Say The Girl's Crazy** *Invitations* |
| 67/87 | **They're Playing Our Song** *Trinere* |
| 37/85 | **Thief In The Night** *George Duke* |
| 7/87 | **Thigh Ride** *Tawatha* |
| 4/81 | **Thighs High (Grip Your Hips And Move)** *Tom Browne* |

| | |
|---|---|
| 1/71 | **Thin Line Between Love & Hate** *Persuaders* |
| 57/85 | **Thin Walls** *Thomas McClary* |
| 43/87 | **Thing For You** *Isaac Hayes* |
| 26/61 | **Thing Of The Past** *Shirelles* |
| 8/43 | **Things Ain't What They Used To Be** *Charlie Barnet* |
| 54/85 | **Things Can Only Get Better** *Howard Jones* |
| 22/69 | **Things Got To Get Better (Get Together)** *Marva Whitney* |
| 4/45 | **Things Have Changed** *Big Maceo* |
| | **Things That I Used To Do** |
| 1/54 | *Guitar Slim* |
| 99/64 | *James Brown* |
| 90/86 | **Things That Men Do** *Krystol* |
| | **Think** |
| 9/57 | *'5' Royales* |
| 7/60 | *James Brown* |
| 7/65 | *Jimmy McCracklin* |
| 1/68 | *Aretha Franklin* |
| 15/73 | *James Brown* |
| 37/73 | *Vicki Anderson & James Brown* |
| 43/73 | *Soul Searchers* |
| | **Think About It** |
| 9/72 | *Lyn Collins* |
| 49/73 | *King Floyd* |
| 93/75 | **Think Before You Stop** *Notations* |
| 58/78 | **Think For Yourself** *Temptations* |
| | **Think It Over** |
| 47/73 | *Delfonics* |
| 32/78 | *Cissy Houston* |
| 69/80 | **Think Positive** *Main Ingredient featuring Cuba Gooding* |
| | **Think Twice** |
| 6/61 | *Brook Benton* |
| 37/66 | *Jackie Wilson & LaVern Baker* |
| 36/66 | **Think Twice Before You Speak** *Al King* |
| 55/78 | **Thinkin' About It Too** *Al Jarreau* |
| 15/87 | **Thinkin' About Ya** *Timex Social Club* |
| | **Thinking About You** |
| 10/85 | *Whitney Houston* |
| 85/86 | *Ta Mara & The Seen* |
| 10/85 | **Thinking About Your Love** *Skipworth & Turner* |
| 8/52 | **Thinking And Drinking** *Amos Milburn* |
| | **Thinking Of You** |
| 14/55 | *Fats Domino* |
| 3/88 | *Earth, Wind & Fire* |
| | **Third Degree** |
| 3/53 | *Eddie Boyd* |
| 74/81 | *Yarbrough & Peoples* |
| 16/84 | **30 Days** *Run-D.M.C.* |
| 2/55 | **Thirty Days (To Come Back Home)** *Chuck Berry* |
| 79/86 | **30 Mins. To Talk** *Eugene Wilde* |
| 31/69 | **30-60-90** *Willie Mitchell* |
| 97/63 | **31 Flavors** *Shirelles* |
| 8/48 | **35-30** *Paul Williams* |
| 88/85 | **This Ain't No Fantasy** *Ramsey Lewis* |
| 81/75 | **This Ain't No Time To Be Giving Up** *Ripple* |
| 30/88 | **This Be The Def Beat** *Dana Dane* |
| 64/82 | **This Beat Is Mine** *Vicky 'D'* |
| | **This Bitter Earth** |
| 1/60 | *Dinah Washington* |
| 36/70 | *Satisfactions* |
| 17/66 | **This Can't Be True** *Eddie Holman* |
| 93/77 | **This Close To You** *Luther Vandross* |
| 42/77 | **This Could Be The Night** *R.B. Hudmon* |
| 26/63 | **This Empty Place** *Dionne Warwick* |
| 54/82 | **This Feeling Must Be Real** *Skool Boyz* |
| 77/73 | **This Feeling Of Losing You** *Donnie Elbert* |
| 57/80 | **This Feeling's Rated X-Tra** *Carl Carlton* |
| 83/79 | **This Funk Is Made For Dancing** *Broadway* |
| 31/82 | **This Gift Of Life** *Teddy Pendergrass* |

| | |
|---|---|
| 94/78 | **Timber** *Tavares* |
| | **Time, The** |
| 22/59 | *Baby Washington* |
| 39/70 | *Edwin Starr* |
| 39/72 | *Jackie Moore* |
| 32/74 | *Mighty Clouds Of Joy* |
| 55/82 | *Stone* |
| 78/84 | **Time After Time** *Cyndi Lauper* |
| 100/76 | **Time And Love** *Tom Scott* |
| 27/60 | **Time And The River** *Nat King Cole* |
| 34/83 | **Time (Clock Of The Heart)** *Culture Club* |
| 10/74 | **Time For Livin'** *Sly & The Family Stone* |
| 72/82 | **Time For Love** *B.B.&Q. Band* |
| 49/84 | **Time For Some Fun** *Central Line* |
| 37/73 | **Time Is Love** *Black Ivory* |
| 15/77 | **Time Is Movin'** *Blackbyrds* |
| | **Time Is Running Out** |
| 94/77 | *Brass Fever* |
| 66/84 | *Jonzun Crew* |
| 7/69 | **Time Is Tight** *Booker T. & The MG's* |
| | **Time Out For Tears** |
| 10/48 | *Savannah Churchill* |
| 8/50 | *Dinah Washington* |
| 88/87 | **Time Out For The Burglar** *Jacksons* |
| 53/78 | **Time Slips Away** *Ohio Players* |
| 2/73 | **Time To Get Down** *O'Jays* |
| 88/86 | **Time To Say Goodbye** *Kopper* |
| 32/81 | **Time To Think** *Rockie Robbins* |
| | **Time Waits For No One** |
| 34/65 | *Eddie & Ernie* |
| 37/70 | *Friends Of Distinction* |
| 17/69 | **Time Will Come** *Whispers* |
| 1/83 | **Time Will Reveal** *DeBarge* |
| | **Time Will Tell** |
| 11/56 | *Bobby Charles* |
| 27/74 | *Tower Of Power* |
| 98/64 | **Times Have Changed** *Irma Thomas* |
| 55/79 | **Timin'** *Maze Featuring Frankie Beverly* |
| | **Tin Pan Alley** |
| 10/53 | *Jimmy Wilson* |
| 51/74 | *Little Milton* |
| 86/86 | **Tin Soldier** *Michael Henderson* |
| 5/87 | **Tina Cherry** *Georgio* |
| 1/52 | **Ting-A-Ling** *Clovers* |
| 18/59 | **Tiny Tim** *LaVern Baker* |
| 37/67 | **Tip On In** *Slim Harpo* |
| 48/67 | **Tip Toe** *Robert Parker* |
| 1/45 | **Tippin' In** *Erskine Hawkins* |
| | **Tired Of Being Alone** |
| 7/71 | *Al Green* |
| 13/88 | *Right Choice* |
| 71/79 | **Tit For Tat** *Bobby Bland* |
| 72/74 | **Title Theme** *Isaac Hayes* |
| 9/67 | **To Be A Lover** *Gene Chandler* |
| 25/87 | **To Be Continued...** *Temptations* |
| | **To Be Loved** |
| 7/58 | *Jackie Wilson* |
| 62/79 | *Michael Henderson* |
| 8/70 | **To Be Young, Gifted And Black** |
| | *Nina Simone* |
| | **To Each His Own** |
| 3/46 | *Ink Spots* |
| 1/75 | *Faith, Hope & Charity* |
| 10/58 | **To Know Him, Is To Love Him** *Teddy Bears* |
| 12/73 | **To Know You Is To Love You** *B.B. King* |
| F/71 | **To Lay Down Beside You** *Joe Simon* |
| 41/70 | **To Live In The Past** *Percy Mayfield* |
| | **To Love Somebody** |
| 30/68 | *Sweet Inspirations* |
| 44/69 | *James Carr* |
| F/76 | **To Make You Love Me** |
| | *Bo Kirkland & Ruth Davis* |
| 3/88 | **To Prove My Love** *Michael Cooper* |

| | |
|---|---|
| 30/67 | **To Share Your Love** *Fantastic Four* |
| | **To Sir With Love** |
| 9/67 | *Lulu* |
| 71/79 | *Al Green* |
| 5/57 | **To The Aisle** *Five Satins* |
| 68/86 | **2 The Limit** *Octavia* |
| 45/68 | **To The One I Love** |
| | *Brenda & The Tabulations* |
| 22/70 | **To The Other Man** *Luther Ingram* |
| 7/70 | **To The Other Woman (I'm The Other** |
| | **Woman)** *Doris Duke* |
| 47/84 | **2 Win U Back** *Jones Girls* |
| 36/71 | **To You With Love** *Moments* |
| 18/72 | **Toast To The Fool** *Dramatics* |
| 27/68 | **Toast To You** *Louis Curry* |
| 7/75 | **Toby** *Chi-Lites* |
| 10/60 | **Today I Sing The Blues** *Aretha Franklin* |
| | **Today I Started Loving You Again** |
| 26/73 | *Bettye Swann* |
| 34/76 | *Bobby Bland* |
| 25/80 | **Today Is The Day** *Bar-Kays* |
| 81/84 | **Today's Your Lucky Day** |
| | *Harold Melvin & The Blue Notes* |
| | **Together** |
| 9/67 | *Intruders* |
| 62/77 | *O.C. Smith* |
| 9/81 | *Tierra* |
| 42/87 | *Genobia Jeter & Glenn Jones* |
| 10/66 | **Together Again** *Ray Charles* |
| 85/87 | **Together Forever** *Intrique* |
| 22/72 | **Together Let's Find Love** *5th Dimension* |
| 45/81 | **Together We Can Shine** *Linx* |
| | **Tom Cat** |
| 30/63 | *Rooftop Singers* |
| 93/75 | *Tom Scott & The L.A. Express* |
| 9/58 | **Tom Dooley** *Kingston Trio* |
| | **Tomorrow** |
| 74/77 | *Cissy Houston* |
| 81/85 | *L.J. Reynolds* |
| 51/78 | **Tomorrow I May Not Feel The Same** |
| | *Gene Chandler* |
| 1/48 | **Tomorrow Night** *Lonnie Johnson* |
| 82/73 | **Tomorrow's Train** *Ponderosa Twins + One* |
| | **Tonight** |
| 4/83 | *Whispers* |
| 7/84 | *Kool & The Gang* |
| 6/85 | *Ready For The World* |
| 59/87 | *Nu Romance Crew* |
| 5/83 | **Tonight, I Celebrate My Love** |
| | *Peabo Bryson/Roberta Flack* |
| 91/79 | **Tonight I Feel Like Dancing** *Mavis Staples* |
| 12/83 | **Tonight I Give In** *Angela Bofill* |
| 35/80 | **Tonight I'm Alright** |
| | *Narada Michael Walden* |
| 32/82 | **Tonight I'm Gonna Love You All Over** |
| | *Four Tops* |
| 70/78 | **Tonight I'm Gonna Make You A Star** |
| | *Brenda & Herb* |
| | **Tonight Is The Night** |
| F/75 | *Betty Wright* |
| 11/78 | *Betty Wright* |
| 18/81 | **Tonight We Love** *Rufus* |
| 22/81 | **Tonight You And Me** *Phyllis Hyman* |
| 57/64 | **Tonight You're Gonna Fall In Love With** |
| | **Me** *Shirelles* |
| | **Tonight's The Night** |
| 13/49 | *Julia Lee* |
| 14/60 | *Shirelles* |
| 2/65 | *Solomon Burke* |
| 59/75 | *S.S.O.* |
| 61/80 | *Sharon Paige and Harold Melvin & The Blue Notes* |
| 33/79 | **Tonight's The Night (Good Time)** *Kleeer* |

| | | | |
|---|---|---|---|
| 17/71 | **Warpath** *Isley Brothers* | 20/70 | **We Can Make It Baby** *Originals* |
| 79/81 | **Warriors** *Hiroshima* | 62/74 | **We Can Make It Last Forever** |
| 53/78 | **Was Dog A Doughnut** *Cat Stevens* | | *Ronnie Dyson* |
| 26/72 | **Was I Just A Fool** *Tyrone Davis* | 55/81 | **We Can Start Tonight** *Harvey Mason* |
| 33/69 | **Was It Good To You** *Isley Brothers* | | **We Can Work It Out** |
| 29/67 | **Washed Ashore (On A Lonely Island In The** | 3/71 | *Stevie Wonder* |
| | **Sea)** *Platters* | 34/81 | *Chaka Khan* |
| 22/63 | **Washington Square** *Village Stompers* | 14/48 | **We Can't Agree** *Louis Jordan* |
| 4/43 | **Washington Whirligig** *Charlie Barnet* | 38/65 | **We Can't Believe You're Gone** |
| 5/88 | **Wasn't I Good To Ya?** *da'Krash* | | *Bobby Harris* |
| 72/84 | **Watch My Body Talk** *Brenda Lee Eager* | 23/73 | **We Did It** *Syl Johnson* |
| | **Watch Out** | 43/80 | **We Don't** *Controllers* |
| 27/82 | *Brandi Wells* | 79/77 | **We Don't Cry Out Loud** *Moments* |
| 9/87 | *Patrice Rushen* | 64/86 | **We Don't Have To Take Our Clothes Off** |
| | **Watch Your Step** | | *Jermaine Stewart* |
| 58/64 | *Brooks O'Dell* | 16/83 | **We Don't Have To Talk (About Love)** |
| 23/86 | *Anita Baker* | | *Peabo Bryson* |
| | **Watching You** | 3/85 | **We Don't Need Another Hero** |
| 6/81 | *Slave* | | **(Thunderdome)** *Tina Turner* |
| 77/85 | *Joanna Gardner* | 51/84 | **We Don't Work For Free** |
| 2/88 | *Loose Ends* | | *Grandmaster Melle Mel & The Furious Five* |
| | **Waterbed** | 30/78 | **We Fell In Love While Dancing** |
| 79/74 | *LTG Exchange* | | *Bill Brandon* |
| 53/75 | *Herbie Mann* | 86/79 | **We Funk The Best** *B-H-Y* |
| 11/59 | **Waterloo** *Stonewall Jackson* | 5/82 | **We Go A Long Way Back** *Bloodstone* |
| | **Watermelon Man** | 9/56 | **We Go Together** *Moonglows* |
| 8/63 | *Mongo Santamaria* | 92/76 | **We Gonna Make It** *Roger Hatcher* |
| 8/65 | *Gloria Lynne* | 49/77 | **We Gonna Party Tonight** *Willie Hutch* |
| 13/61 | **Watusi, The** *Vibrations* | 26/66 | **We Got A Thing That's In The Groove** |
| 11/48 | **Waxie Maxie** *Paul Williams* | | *Capitols* |
| | **Way Back Home** | 35/75 | **We Got Each Other** *Barbara Mason* |
| 10/53 | *Big Maybelle* | 40/69 | **We Got Latin Soul** *Mongo Santamaria* |
| 24/71 | *Jr. Walker & The All Stars* | 7/69 | **We Got More Soul** *Dyke & The Blazers* |
| 42/80 | **Way Back When** *Brenda Russell* | 93/77 | **We Got Our Own Thing** *C.J. & Co.* |
| 14/60 | **Way Down Yonder In New Orleans** | 42/83 | **We Got The Juice** *Attitude* |
| | *Freddy Cannon* | F/76 | **We Got The Recipe** |
| 68/82 | **Way Out** *Steve Arrington's Hall Of Fame* | | *Bo Kirkland & Ruth Davis* |
| | **Way We Were** | 17/75 | **We Got To Get Our Thing Together** *Dells* |
| 6/75 | *Gladys Knight & The Pips (medley)* | 32/72 | **We Got To Have Peace** *Curtis Mayfield* |
| 33/79 | *Manhattans* | 56/79 | **We Got To Hit It Off** *Millie Jackson* |
| | **Way You Do The Things You Do** | 47/71 | **We Got To Live Together** *Buddy Miles* |
| 11/64 | *Temptations* | 17/69 | **We Must Be In Love** *Five Stairsteps & Cubie* |
| 40/85 | *Hall & Oates/David Ruffin/Eddie Kendrick* | 68/85 | **We Need Love** *Cashmere* |
| | *(medley)* | 29/82 | **We Need Love To Live** |
| 12/56 | **Way You Dog Me Around** *Diablos* | | *Maze Featuring Frankie Beverly* |
| 53/88 | **Way You Love Me** *Shanice Wilson* | 81/79 | **(We Need More) Loving Time** |
| | **Way You Make Me Feel** | | *Dorothy Moore* |
| 62/77 | *Melba Moore* | 13/73 | **We Need Order** *Chi-Lites* |
| 1/87 | *Michael Jackson* | 26/84 | **We Need Some Money (Bout Money)** |
| | **We All Are One** | | *Chuck Brown & The Soul Searchers* |
| 72/84 | *Curtis Hairston* | 10/77 | **We Never Danced To A Love Song** |
| 75/84 | *Jimmy Cliff* | | *Manhattans* |
| 17/75 | **We All Gotta Stick Together** *Four Tops* | 41/80 | **We Never Said Goodbye** *Dionne Warwick* |
| 1/79 | **We Are Family** *Sister Sledge* | 16/80 | **We Ought To Be Doin' It** *Randy Brown* |
| 51/81 | **(We Are Here To) Geek You Up** | 58/87 | **We Rock The Beat** *Sugar Babes* |
| | *Michael Henderson* | 74/77 | **We Should Really Be In Love** |
| 14/65 | **We Are In Love** *Bobby Byrd* | | *Dorothy Moore/Eddie Floyd* |
| 17/71 | **We Are Neighbors** *Chi-Lites* | 43/80 | **We Supply** *Stanley Clarke* |
| 47/83 | **We Are One** *Maze Featuring Frankie Beverly* | | **We The People** |
| 77/78 | **We Are The Future** *High Inergy* | 40/72 | *Soul Searchers* |
| 37/83 | **We Are The Jonzun Crew** *Jonzun Crew* | 36/76 | *General Johnson* |
| 1/85 | **We Are The World** *USA for Africa* | 64/73 | **We Want To Parrty, Parrty, Parrty** |
| 58/85 | **We Are The Young** *Dan Hartman* | | *Lyn Collins* |
| | **We Belong Together** | 76/82 | **(We Want To) Rock You** *Chaz* |
| 12/58 | *Robert & Johnny* | 44/81 | **We Want You (On The Floor)** *Lakeside* |
| 45/66 | *Dee Brown & Lola Grant* | 39/87 | **We'll Be Together** *Sting* |
| 44/68 | *Webs* | 14/66 | **(We'll Be) United** *Intruders* |
| 45/85 | *Rockie Robbins* | 15/69 | **We'll Cry Together** *Maxine Brown* |
| 19/78 | **We Both Deserve Each Other's Love** | 20/71 | **We'll Have It Made** *Spinners* |
| | *L.T.D.* | 45/82 | **We'll Make It** *Mike & Brenda Sutton* |
| 23/76 | **We Both Need Each Other** *Norman Connors* | 78/79 | **We're A Melody** *Jones Girls* |
| 79/80 | **We Came To Funk You Out** | 1/68 | **We're A Winner** *Impressions* |
| | *Southroad Connection* | 42/72 | **We're Almost Home** *Solomon Burke* |
| 76/75 | **We Can Love** *King Floyd* | 7/75 | **We're Almost There** *Michael Jackson* |
| 31/69 | **We Can Make It** *Ray Charles* | 84/83 | **We're At The Party** *Disco Four* |

| | |
|---|---|
| 58/87 | **We're Back** *Flos* |
| 28/65 | **We're Doing Fine** *Dee Dee Warwick* |
| 37/71 | **We're Friends By Day (And Lovers By Night)** *Whatnauts* |
| 5/74 | **We're Getting Careless With Our Love** *Johnnie Taylor* |
| 11/80 | **We're Goin' Out Tonight** *Cameo* |
| 16/84 | **We're Going All The Way** *Jeffrey Osborne* |
| 71/88 | **We're Going To Party** *Future* |
| | **We're Gonna Make It** |
| 1/65 | *Little Milton* |
| 67/75 | *Philly Devotions* |
| 14/48 | **We're Gonna Rock, We're Gonna Roll** *Bill Moore* |
| 90/78 | **We're In Love** *Patti Austin* |
| 6/81 | **We're In This Love Together** *Al Jarreau* |
| 84/78 | **We're On Our Way Home** *Brainstorm* |
| 30/75 | **We're On The Right Track** *South Shore Commission* |
| 17/68 | **We're Rolling On** *Impressions* |
| 98/77 | **We're Still Together** *Peaches & Herb* |
| 9/72 | **We've Come Too Far To End It Now** *Smokey Robinson & The Miracles* |
| 27/69 | **(We've Got) Honey Love** *Martha Reeves & The Vandellas* |
| 25/79 | **We've Got Love** *Peaches & Herb* |
| 75/82 | **We've Got The Groove** *A Taste Of Honey* |
| 99/76 | **We've Got To Get An Understanding** *Darrow Fletcher* |
| F/72 | **(We've Got To) Pull Together** *Nite-Liters* |
| 2/87 | **We've Only Just Begun (The Romance Is Not Over)** *Glenn Jones* |
| 33/83 | **Weak At The Knees** *Steve Arrington's Hall Of Fame* |
| 5/51 | **Weak Minded Blues** *Louis Jordan* |
| 27/68 | **Wear It On Our Face** *Dells* |
| 43/79 | **Wear It Out** *Stargard* |
| 1/58 | **Wear My Ring Around Your Neck** *Elvis Presley* |
| 18/71 | **Wear This Ring (With Love)** *Detroit Emeralds* |
| 23/69 | **Wedding Bell Blues** *5th Dimension* |
| 6/50 | **Wedding Boogie** *Little Esther/Johnny Otis Orchestra* |
| 37/71 | **Wedlock Is A Padlock** *Laura Lee* |
| 10/55 | **Wee Wee Hours** *Chuck Berry* |
| 40/85 | **Weekend Girl** *S.O.S. Band* |
| 37/78 | **Weekend Lover** *Odyssey* |
| 72/86 | **Weekend Special** *Brenda & The Big Dudes* |
| 1/52 | **Weepin' And Cryin'** *Griffin Brothers* |
| | **Weight, The** |
| 3/69 | *Aretha Franklin* |
| 33/69 | *Supremes/Temptations* |
| 9/80 | **Welcome Back Home** *Dramatics* |
| 15/65 | **Welcome Home** *Walter Jackson* |
| 20/62 | **Welcome Home Baby** *Shirelles* |
| 78/78 | **Welcome To Harlem** *Gary Toms Empire* |
| 45/82 | **Welcome To My Heart** *Isley Brothers* |
| 50/80 | **Welcome To My World** *Delegation* |
| 32/77 | **Welcome To Our World (Of Merry Music)** *Mass Production* |
| 13/82 | **Welcome To The Club** *Brothers Johnson* |
| 76/85 | **Well-A-Wiggy** *Weather Girls* |
| 9/54 | **Well All Right** *Joe Turner* |
| 2/50 | **Well, Oh Well** *Tiny Bradshaw* |
| 51/75 | **Wendy Is Gone** *Ronnie McNeir* |
| 36/86 | **West End Girls** *Pet Shop Boys* |
| | **West Side Baby** |
| 7/48 | *Dinah Washington* |
| 8/48 | *T-Bone Walker* |
| 68/78 | **West Side Encounter - West Side Story (Medley)** *Salsoul Orchestra* |
| 15/70 | **Westbound #9** *Flaming Ember* |
| 7/58 | **Western Movies** *Olympics* |
| 8/83 | **Wet My Whistle** *Midnight Star* |

| | |
|---|---|
| 25/87 | **Whammy** *One Way* |
| | **What A Diff'rence A Day Makes** |
| 4/59 | *Dinah Washington* |
| 10/75 | *Esther Phillips* |
| | **What A Feeling** *..see: Flashdance* |
| 93/73 | **What A Fool** *Ted Taylor* |
| | **What A Fool Believes** |
| 72/79 | *Doobie Brothers* |
| 17/81 | *Aretha Franklin* |
| 8/51 | **What A Fool I Was** *Percy Mayfield* |
| 28/63 | **What A Fool I've Been** *Carla Thomas* |
| 25/63 | **What A Guy** *Raindrops* |
| 50/68 | **What A Man** *Linda Lyndell* |
| 7/61 | **What A Price** *Fats Domino* |
| 40/73 | **What A Shame** *Dynamics* |
| 52/81 | **What A Surprise** *Pointer Sisters* |
| 84/84 | **What A Way To Put It** *Willie Clayton* |
| 38/86 | **What A Woman** *O'Jays* |
| 66/76 | **(What A) Wonderful World** *Johnny Nash* |
| 82/76 | **What About Love** *Brief Encounter* |
| | **What About Me** |
| 85/74 | *First Class* |
| 57/84 | *Kenny Rogers with Kim Carnes & James Ingram* |
| 52/86 | *Nicole* |
| 24/82 | **What About My Love** *Johnnie Taylor* |
| 17/60 | **What About Us** *Coasters* |
| 46/67 | **What About You** *O.V. Wright* |
| | **What Am I Gonna Do** |
| 74/74 | *Gloria Scott* |
| 82/81 | *Sho-Nuff* |
| 1/75 | **What Am I Gonna Do With You** *Barry White* |
| 1/58 | **What Am I Living For** *Chuck Willis* |
| 9/49 | **What Are You Doing New Year's Eve** *Orioles* |
| 42/81 | **What Are You Going To Do With It** *Betty Wright* |
| 6/66 | **What Becomes Of The Brokenhearted** *Jimmy Ruffin* |
| 12/57 | **What Can I Do** *Donnie Elbert* |
| 8/75 | **What Can I Do For You?** *LaBelle* |
| 68/77 | **What Can I Say** *Boz Scaggs* |
| | **What Can I Tell Her** |
| 39/70 | *J.P. Robinson* |
| 19/74 | *Timmy Thomas* |
| | **What Cha** *..also see: Whatcha* |
| 18/80 | **What Cha Doin'** *Seawind* |
| 66/88 | **What Cha Gonna Do** *Theresa* |
| 1/81 | **What Cha' Gonna Do For Me** *Chaka Khan* |
| 8/79 | **What Cha Gonna Do With My Lovin'** *Stephanie Mills* |
| 9/48 | **What Did You Do To Me** *Ivory Joe Hunter* |
| 99/76 | **What Did You Do With Your Love** *Lloyd Price* |
| 94/77 | **What Do You Do** *Donnie Elbert* |
| 94/73 | **What Do You See In Him?** *Darren Green* |
| 48/73 | **What Do You Want Me To Do** *Lou Courtney* |
| 53/63 | **What Does A Girl Do?** *Shirelles* |
| 69/86 | **What Does It Take** *Gloria D. Brown* |
| | **What Does It Take (To Win Your Love)** |
| 1/69 | *Jr. Walker & The All Stars* |
| 15/86 | *Kenny G* |
| 74/75 | **What Ever's Your Sign (You Got To Be Mine)** *Prophecy* |
| 44/74 | **What Goes Around (Comes Around)** *Black Ivory* |
| 11/74 | **What Goes Up (Must Come Down)** *Tyrone Davis* |
| 61/64 | **What Good Am I Without You** *Marvin Gaye & Kim Weston* |
| 3/48 | **What Have I Done?** *Hadda Brooks* |
| 1/86 | **What Have You Done For Me Lately** *Janet Jackson* |
| 59/77 | **What I Did For Love** *Inner City Jam Band* |

| 14/57 | **When I See You**  *Fats Domino* |
| 16/77 | **When I Think About You**  *Aretha Franklin* |
| 3/86 | **When I Think Of You**  *Janet Jackson* |
| 12/65 | **When I'm Gone**  *Brenda Holloway* |
| 15/56 | **When I'm With You**  *Moonglows* |
| 22/76 | **When I'm Wrong**  *B.B. King* |
| 76/81 | **When It's Love**  *Brandi Wells* |
| 82/78 | **When It's Over**  *Roberta Flack* |
| 5/81 | **When Love Calls**  *Atlantic Starr* |
| 56/88 | **When Love Comes Calling**  *Paul Johnson* |
| 10/77 | **When Love Is New**  *Arthur Prysock* |
| 43/67 | **When Love Slips Away**  *Dee Dee Warwick* |
| 2/56 | **When My Dreamboat Comes Home** |
| | *Fats Domino* |
| 8/54 | **When My Heart Beats Like A Hammer** |
| | *B.B. King* |
| 1/44 | **When My Man Comes Home** |
| | *Buddy Johnson* |
| 1/81 | **When She Was My Girl**  *Four Tops* |
| | **When Something Is Wrong With My Baby** |
| 2/67 | *Sam & Dave* |
| 57/83 | *Johnny Gill* |
| 95/63 | **When The Boy's Happy (The Girl's** |
| | **Happy)**  *Four Pennies* |
| 48/74 | **When The Fuel Runs Out**  *Executive Suite* |
| 6/86 | **When The Going Gets Tough, The Tough Get** |
| | **Going**  *Billy Ocean* |
| 1/42 | **When The Lights Go On Again (All Over The** |
| | **World)**  *Lucky Millinder* |
| 23/64 | **When The Lovelight Starts Shining Through** |
| | **His Eyes**  *Supremes* |
| 61/85 | **When The Rain Begins To Fall** |
| | *Jermaine Jackson/Pia Zadora* |
| 89/79 | **When The Whistle Blows (Anything Goes)** |
| | *La Flavour* |
| 10/44 | **When They Ask About You**  *Jimmy Dorsey* |
| 9/49 | **When Things Go Wrong With You** |
| | *Tampa Red* |
| F/70 | **When Tomorrow Comes**  *Emotions* |
| | **When We Get Married** |
| 8/70 | *Intruders* |
| 9/80 | *Larry Graham* |
| 31/67 | **When We're Made As One**  *Manhattans* |
| 4/74 | **When Will I See You Again**  *Three Degrees* |
| 46/81 | **When Will My Love Be Right** |
| | *Robert Winters & Fall* |
| 3/55 | **When You Dance**  *Turbans* |
| 48/71 | **When You Find A Fool, Bump His Head** |
| | *Bill Coday* |
| | **When You Get Right Down To It** |
| 12/70 | *Delfonics* |
| 37/71 | *Ronnie Dyson* |
| 14/85 | **When You Love Me Like This**  *Melba Moore* |
| 38/86 | **When You Love Someone** |
| | *Maze Featuring Frankie Beverly* |
| 81/73 | **When You Smile**  *Leroy Hutson* |
| 21/71 | **When You Took Your Love From Me** |
| | *O.V. Wright* |
| 43/82 | **When You Touch Me**  *Skyy* |
| 19/66 | **When You Wake Up**  *Cash McCall* |
| 13/79 | **When You Wake Up Tomorrow** |
| | *Candi Staton* |
| 31/79 | **When You're #1**  *Gene Chandler* |
| 42/84 | **When You're Far Away** |
| | *Gladys Knight & The Pips* |
| 27/68 | **When You're Gone** |
| | *Brenda & The Tabulations* |
| | **When You're Young And In Love** |
| 48/64 | *Ruby & The Romantics* |
| 9/67 | *Marvelettes* |
| 37/75 | *Ralph Carter* |
| 45/75 | *Choice Four* |
| 91/79 | *Stacy Lattisaw* |
| 88/86 | **Whenever You Need Somebody** |
| | *O'Chi Brown* |

| 39/87 | **Whenever You're Ready**  *Five Star* |
| 8/74 | **Where Are All My Friends** |
| | *Harold Melvin & The Blue Notes* |
| 42/70 | **Where Are You Going**  *Jerry Butler* |
| 7/52 | **Where Are You? (Now That I Need You)** |
| | *Mellow Moods* |
| 8/49 | **Where Can I Find My Baby** |
| | *Johnny Moore's Three Blazers* |
| | **Where Did I Go Wrong** |
| 82/64 | *Dee Dee Sharp* |
| 74/81 | *Heatwave* |
| 45/78 | **Where Did Love Go**  *Leroy Hutson* |
| | **Where Did Our Love Go** |
| 1/64 | *Supremes* |
| 6/71 | *Donnie Elbert* |
| 37/85 | *Reddings* |
| | **Where Did We Go Wrong** |
| 7/80 | *L.T.D.* |
| 42/86 | *Manhattans* |
| 2/88 | **Where Do Broken Hearts Go** |
| | *Whitney Houston* |
| 38/68 | **Where Do I Go**  *Carla Thomas* |
| 93/75 | **Where Do I Go From Here**  *Supremes* |
| 57/82 | **Where Do The Bop Go?**  *L.A. Boppers* |
| | **Where Do We Go From Here** |
| 44/74 | *Trammps* |
| 29/79 | *Enchantment* |
| 26/82 | *Bobby Womack* |
| 82/64 | **Where Does Love Go**  *Freddie Scott* |
| 60/76 | **Where Ever You Go** |
| | *Skip Mahoney & The Casuals* |
| | **Where Is The Love** |
| 1/72 | *Roberta Flack & Donny Hathaway* |
| 15/75 | *Betty Wright* |
| 76/77 | *Ralph MacDonald* |
| 27/67 | **Where Is The Party**  *Helena Ferguson* |
| 75/80 | **Where Is Your Love?**  *Emotions* |
| 96/77 | **Where Is Your Woman Tonight** |
| | *Soul Children* |
| 19/60 | **Where Or When**  *Dion & The Belmonts* |
| 6/73 | **Where Peaceful Waters Flow** |
| | *Gladys Knight & The Pips* |
| 65/74 | **Where The Lillies Grow**  *Sidney Joe Qualis* |
| 10/50 | **Where There Is No Love**  *Roy Milton* |
| 13/76 | **Where There's A Will, There's A Way** |
| | *Bobby Womack* |
| 4/59 | **Where Were You (On Our Wedding Day)?** |
| | *Lloyd Price* |
| 68/73 | **Where Were You (When I Needed You)** |
| | *Jimmy Briscoe & The Little Beavers* |
| 31/70 | **Wherever She Leadeth Me**  *Impressions* |
| 21/77 | **While I'm Alone** |
| | *Maze Featuring Frankie Beverly* |
| 41/79 | **While We Still Have Time**  *Cindy & Roy* |
| 26/69 | **While You're Out Looking For Sugar?** |
| | *Honey Cone* |
| 51/82 | **Whip Rap**  *Disco Four* |
| 49/86 | **Whisper In The Dark**  *Dionne Warwick* |
| 31/77 | **Whispering/Cherchez La Femme/Se Si** |
| | **Bon**  *Dr. Buzzard's Original 'Savannah' Band* |
| 5/57 | **Whispering Bells**  *Dell-Vikings* |
| 5/66 | **Whispers (Gettin' Louder)**  *Jackie Wilson* |
| 81/78 | **Whistle Bump**  *Eumir Deodato* |
| | **White Christmas** |
| 1/42 | *Bing Crosby* |
| 9/44 | *Bing Crosby* |
| 9/49 | *Ravens* |
| 2/55 | *Drifters* |
| 5/56 | *Drifters* |
| 12/56 | *Drifters* |
| 9/45 | **White Cliffs Of Dover**  *Louis Prima* |
| 5/84 | **White Horse**  *Laid Back* |
| 47/83 | **White Lines (Don't Do It)** |
| | *Grandmaster & Melle Mel* |
| 9/64 | **White On White**  *Danny Williams* |

| | |
|---|---|
| | **Wild One** |
| 10/60 | *Bobby Rydell* |
| 34/65 | *Martha & The Vandellas* |
| 28/63 | **Wild Weekend** *Rebels* |
| 12/49 | **Wild Wig** *Big Jay McNeely & Band* |
| 4/88 | **Wild, Wild West** *Kool Moe Dee* |
| 3/53 | **Wild Wild Young Men** *Ruth Brown* |
| 17/74 | **Wildflower** *New Birth* |
| 10/73 | **Will It Go Round In Circles** *Billy Preston* |
| 40/75 | **Will We Ever Come Together** *Black Ivory* |
| | **Will You Be Mine** |
| 9/51 | *Swallows* |
| F/83 | *Anita Baker* |
| 54/82 | **Will You Kiss Me One More Time** |
| | *Lou Rawls* |
| F/77 | **Will You Love Me Till Tomorrow** |
| | *Donnie Elbert* |
| 2/61 | **Will You Love Me Tomorrow** *Shirelles* |
| 38/72 | **Will You Still Love Me Tomorrow** |
| | *Roberta Flack* |
| 3/58 | **Willie And The Hand Jive** |
| | *Johnny Otis Show* |
| 27/74 | **Willie Pass The Water** *Ripple* |
| 77/75 | **Willing To Learn** *Tower Of Power* |
| 97/64 | **Willyam, Willyam** *Dee Dee Sharp* |
| 12/72 | **(Win, Place Or Show) She's A Winner** |
| | *Intruders* |
| 4/58 | **Win Your Love For Me** *Sam Cooke* |
| 60/83 | **Wind Beneath My Wings** *Lou Rawls* |
| | *(also see: Hero)* |
| 7/52 | **Wind Is Blowing** *Jimmy Witherspoon* |
| 59/81 | **Wind Me Up** *R.J.'s Latest Arrival* |
| 27/67 | **Windows Of The World** *Dionne Warwick* |
| 48/68 | **Windy** *Wes Montgomery* |
| 89/81 | **Windy City** *Rodney Franklin* |
| 65/77 | **Windy City Theme** |
| | *Carl Davis & The Chi-Sound Orchestra* |
| 38/79 | **Winner Takes All** *Isley Brothers* |
| 23/80 | **Winners** *Kleeer* |
| 44/76 | **Winners Together Or Losers Apart** |
| | *George & Gwen McCrae* |
| 21/77 | **Winter Melody** *Donna Summer* |
| | **Wipe Out** |
| 10/63 | *Surfaris* |
| 10/87 | *Fat Boys* |
| 60/86 | **Wiser And Weaker** *Deniece Williams* |
| 72/74 | **Wish I Had A Little Girl Like You** |
| | *Little Beaver* |
| 17/64 | **Wish Someone Would Care** *Irma Thomas* |
| 10/73 | **Wish That I Could Talk To You** *Sylvers* |
| 19/74 | **Wish That You Were Mine** *Manhattans* |
| 27/67 | **Wish You Didn't Have To Go** |
| | *James & Bobby Purify* |
| 81/79 | **Wish You Were Here** *Free Life* |
| 10/58 | **Wishing For Your Love** *Voxpoppers* |
| | **Wishing On A Star** |
| 52/78 | *Rose Royce* |
| 89/79 | *Jr. Walker & The All Stars* |
| 1/88 | **Wishing Well** *Terence Trent D'Arby* |
| | **Witch Doctor** |
| 1/58 | *David Seville* |
| 95/78 | *Paul Horn* |
| 35/79 | *Instant Funk* |
| 39/74 | **Witch Doctor Bump** *Chabukos* |
| 5/56 | **Witchcraft** *Spiders* |
| | **With A Child's Heart** |
| 8/66 | *Stevie Wonder* |
| 14/73 | *Michael Jackson* |
| 69/88 | **With Every Beat Of My Heart** |
| | *Leata Galloway* |
| 20/75 | **With Everything I Feel In Me** |
| | *Aretha Franklin* |
| 12/78 | **With Pen In Hand** *Dorothy Moore* |
| 12/67 | **With This Ring** *Platters* |
| 14/76 | **With You** *Moments* |

| | |
|---|---|
| 7/86 | **With You All The Way** *New Edition* |
| 86/80 | **With You I'm Born Again** |
| | *Billy Preston & Syreeta* |
| 49/68 | **Without A Doubt** *Major Lance* |
| 6/75 | **Without Love** *Aretha Franklin* |
| | **Without Love (There Is Nothing)** |
| 4/57 | *Clyde McPhatter* |
| 15/63 | *Ray Charles* |
| 47/68 | *Oscar Toney, Jr.* |
| 41/70 | *Tom Jones* |
| 43/64 | **Without The One You Love (Life's Not Worth** |
| | **While)** *Four Tops* |
| | **Without You** |
| 33/69 | *Vernon Garrett* |
| 95/75 | *Ruby Winters* |
| 78/80 | *Jimmy 'Bo' Horne* |
| 48/87 | *Touch* |
| 14/88 | *Peabo Bryson & Regina Belle* |
| 78/81 | **Without You I Cry** *Candi Staton* |
| 5/73 | **Without You In My Life** *Tyrone Davis* |
| 3/53 | **Woke Up This Morning** *B.B. King* |
| 67/80 | **Wolf Tickets** |
| | *Parlet featuring Jeanette Washington* |
| 77/82 | **Woman** *Ebonee Webb* |
| | **Woman, A Lover, A Friend** |
| 1/60 | *Jackie Wilson* |
| 15/85 | *Klique* |
| 12/65 | **Woman Can Change A Man** *Joe Tex* |
| 3/72 | **Woman Don't Go Astray** *King Floyd* |
| 31/68 | **Woman I Love** *B.B. King* |
| 27/79 | **Woman In Love** *Three Degrees* |
| 30/83 | **Woman In Me** *Donna Summer* |
| 42/82 | **Woman In My Life** *Stevie Woods* |
| 77/83 | **Woman In You** *Bee Gees* |
| 24/67 | **Woman Like That, Yeah** *Joe Tex* |
| | **Woman, Love And A Man** *..see: (Story Of)* |
| 1/81 | **Woman Needs Love (Just Like You Do)** |
| | *Ray Parker Jr. & Raydio* |
| 38/75 | **Woman Needs To Be Loved** *Tyrone Davis* |
| | **Woman Of The Future** *..see: (Almighty Fire)* |
| 71/84 | **Woman Out Of Control** *Ray Parker Jr.* |
| 41/73 | **Woman Stealer** *Joe Tex* |
| 1/74 | **Woman To Woman** *Shirley Brown* |
| 20/67 | **Woman Will Do Wrong** *Helene Smith* |
| 20/68 | **Woman With The Blues** *Lamp Sisters* |
| 9/65 | **Woman's Got Soul** *Impressions* |
| 1/72 | **Woman's Gotta Have It** *Bobby Womack* |
| 24/67 | **Woman's Hands** *Joe Tex* |
| 71/64 | **Woman's Love** *Carla Thomas* |
| 39/70 | **Woman's Way** *Rozetta Johnson* |
| 11/71 | **Women's Love Rights** *Laura Lee* |
| 7/61 | **Won't Be Long** *Aretha Franklin* |
| 82/77 | **Won't You Be Mine** *Michael Henderson* |
| 88/82 | **Won't You Let Me Love You** |
| | *Bernard Wright* |
| 7/52 | **Wonder Where My Baby's Gone** *Clovers* |
| 79/86 | **Wonder Where You Are** *Michael Sembello* |
| 33/79 | **Wonder Worm** *Captain Sky* |
| | **Wonderful** |
| 18/74 | *Isaac Hayes* |
| 76/77 | *Marilyn McCoo & Billy Davis, Jr.* |
| 23/62 | **Wonderful Dream** *Majors* |
| 23/63 | **Wonderful Summer** *Robin Ward* |
| 23/63 | **Wonderful! Wonderful!** *Tymes* |
| 2/60 | **Wonderful World** *Sam Cooke* |
| | *(also see: What A)* |
| 21/80 | **Wonderland** *Commodores* |
| 5/60 | **Wonderland By Night** *Bert Kaempfert* |
| 6/60 | **Wont'cha Come Home** *Lloyd Price* |
| 31/65 | **Wooly Bully** *Sam The Sham & The Pharoahs* |
| 77/80 | **Wop That Wandy** *Gangsters* |
| | **Word Is Out** |
| 71/83 | *Sugarhill Gang* |
| 17/85 | *Jermaine Stewart* |

**574**

**Your Good Thing (Is About To End)**
6/66   *Mable John*
3/69   *Lou Rawls*
64/73  **Your Heart Is Gold**  *Geater Davis*
45/82  **Your Imagination**  *Daryl Hall & John Oates*
59/79  **Your Lonely Heart**  *Natalie Cole*
**Your Love**
39/72  *Persians*
68/74  *Moment Of Truth*
1/75  *Larry Graham*
9/77  *Marilyn McCoo & Billy Davis, Jr.*
57/81  *Skool Boyz*
96/76  **(Your Love Has Got Me) Screamin'**
    *Blacksmoke*
33/78  **Your Love Is A Miracle**
    *Average White Band*
82/86  **Your Love Is Dynamite**  *Donnell Pitman*
75/80  **Your Love Is Good**  *Sheila & B. Devotion*
35/85  **Your Love Is King**  *Sade*
14/81  **Your Love Is On The One**  *Lakeside*
37/74  **Your Love Is Paradise**  *Executive Suite*
17/77  **Your Love Is Rated X**  *Johnnie Taylor*
24/88  **Your Love Is So Def**  *Full Force*
19/71  **Your Love Is So Doggone Good**  *Whispers*
16/78  **Your Love Is So Good For Me**  *Diana Ross*
1/67  **(Your Love Keeps Lifting Me) Higher And Higher**  *Jackie Wilson*
9/71  **Your Love (Means Everything To Me)**
    *Charles Wright & The Watts 103rd Street Rhythm Band*
11/84  **Your Love's Got A Hold On Me**
    *Lillo Thomas*
92/73  **Your Man And Your Best Friend**
    *Denise LaSalle*
57/82  **Your Man Is Home Tonight**
    *Tony Troutman*
65/74  **Your Mission (If You Decide To Accept It)**  *Lost Generation*
8/63  **Your Old Stand By**  *Mary Wells*
9/86  **Your Personal Touch**
    *Evelyn 'Champagne' King*
**Your Place Or Mine**
78/81  *Quinella*
12/85  *Bar-Kays*
**Your Precious Love**
2/67  *Marvin Gaye & Tammi Terrell*
15/72  *Linda Jones*
16/82  *Al Jarreau & Randy Crawford*

89/77  **Your Real Good Thing's About To Come To An End**  *Paulette Reaves*
86/84  **Your Red Hot Love**  *Chops*
1/86  **Your Smile**  *Rene & Angela*
46/70  **Your Sweet Loving**  *Margie Joseph*
2/78  **Your Sweetness Is My Weakness**
    *Barry White*
39/83  **Your Thing Is Your Thing**  *New Horizons*
3/71  **Your Time To Cry**  *Joe Simon*
35/84  **Your Touch**  *Bonnie Pointer*
7/67  **Your Unchanging Love**  *Marvin Gaye*
32/84  **Your Wife Is Cheatin' On Us**
    *Richard 'Dimples' Fields*
22/72  **Your Wonderful, Sweet Sweet Love**
    *Supremes*
90/79  **Yours & Yours' Alone**  *Esther Williams*
10/70  **Yours Love**  *Joe Simon*
44/68  **Yours Until Tomorrow**  *Vivian Reed*
21/77  **Yu-Ma (medley)**  *Marlena Shaw*
80/75  **Yum, Yum (Gimme Some)**  *Fatback Band*
49/72  **Yum Yum Yum (I Want Some)**  *Eddie Floyd*

# Z

19/79  **Zeke The Freak**  *Isaac Hayes*
42/87  **Zero In July**  *Focus*
15/87  **Zibble, Zibble (Get The Money) (AKA: Get Loose, Get Funky)**  *Gap Band*
43/66  **Zig Zag Lightning**  *Little Johnny Taylor*
17/72  **Zing Went The Strings Of My Heart**
    *Trammps*
72/75  **Zip, The**  *MFSB*
7/63  **Zip-A-Dee Doo-Dah**
    *Bob B. Soxx & The Blue Jeans*
12/57  **Zip Zip**  *Diamonds*
92/76  **Zone**  *Rhythm Makers*
89/86  **Zoom**  *Fat Larry's Band*
60/81  **Zulu**  *Quick*

# THE
# RECORD
# HOLDERS

# The **TOP 200** Artists

| Rank | Artist | Points |
|---|---|---|
| 1. | James Brown | 11872 |
| 2. | Aretha Franklin | 8731 |
| 3. | Ray Charles | 8462 |
| 4. | The Temptations | 8065 |
| 5. | Louis Jordan | 7361 |
| 6. | Stevie Wonder | 7122 |
| 7. | Marvin Gaye | 7029 |
| 8. | B.B. King | 6760 |
| 9. | Fats Domino | 6735 |
| 10. | Gladys Knight & The Pips | 6282 |

| Rank | Artist | Points |
|---|---|---|
| 11. | Bobby Bland | 6051 |
| 12. | The Isley Brothers | 5904 |
| 13. | Nat King Cole | 5353 |
| 14. | The Miracles | 5130 |
| 15. | Jerry Butler | 5127 |
| 16. | Dinah Washington | 5125 |
| 17. | Four Tops | 5023 |
| 18. | The Impressions | 4857 |
| 19. | Kool & The Gang | 4849 |
| 20. | The O'Jays | 4681 |

| Rank | Artist | Points |
|---|---|---|
| 21. | Wilson Pickett | 4678 |
| 22. | Dionne Warwick | 4637 |
| 23. | Diana Ross | 4541 |
| 24. | Joe Simon | 4520 |
| 25. | The Supremes | 4405 |
| 26. | Jackie Wilson | 4384 |
| 27. | Earth, Wind & Fire | 4206 |
| 28. | The Drifters | 4018 |
| 29. | Spinners | 3970 |
| 30. | Tyrone Davis | 3950 |

| Rank | Artist | Points |
|---|---|---|
| 31. | The Manhattans | 3943 |
| 32. | Elvis Presley | 3934 |
| 33. | Brook Benton | 3932 |
| 34. | Sam Cooke | 3883 |
| 35. | The Dells | 3873 |
| 36. | The Jacksons | 3805 |
| 37. | Johnnie Taylor | 3759 |
| 38. | Smokey Robinson | 3646 |
| 39. | The Whispers | 3623 |
| 40. | Michael Jackson | 3525 |

| Rank | Artist | Points |
|---|---|---|
| 41. | The Chi-Lites | 3511 |
| 42. | Bobby Womack | 3445 |
| 43. | Commodores | 3262 |
| 44. | Prince | 3207 |
| 45. | Joe Tex | 3153 |
| 46. | Barry White | 3138 |
| 47. | Al Green | 3070 |
| 48. | Gene Chandler | 3060 |
| 49. | Peabo Bryson | 3059 |
| 50. | Otis Redding | 3048 |

| Rank | Artist | Points |
|---|---|---|
| 51. | The Dramatics | 3044 |
| 52. | Donna Summer | 3024 |
| 53. | Cameo | 2974 |
| 54. | Natalie Cole | 2958 |
| 55. | Ruth Brown | 2931 |
| 56. | Bar-Kays | 2917 |
| 57. | Rick James | 2837 |
| 58. | Patti LaBelle | 2809 |
| 59. | Millie Jackson | 2777 |
| 60. | Tavares | 2735 |

| Rank | Artist | Points |
|---|---|---|
| 61. | The Moments | 2683 |
| 62. | Ashford & Simpson | 2673 |
| 63. | Etta James | 2671 |
| 64. | Rufus Featuring Chaka Khan | 2652 |
| 65. | The Stylistics | 2649 |
| 66. | Pointer Sisters | 2648 |
| 67. | The Gap Band | 2639 |
| 68. | Jr. Walker & The All Stars | 2623 |
| 69. | The Clovers | 2614 |
| 70. | Curtis Mayfield | 2591 |

| Rank | Artist | Points |
|---|---|---|
| 71. | Chuck Berry | 2557 |
| 72. | Solomon Burke | 2556 |
| 73. | Melba Moore | 2546 |
| 74. | Hank Ballard & The Midnighters | 2545 |
| 75. | Lloyd Price | 2535 |
| 76. | Ivory Joe Hunter | 2531 |
| 77. | Eddie Kendricks | 2519 |
| 78. | Ohio Players | 2495 |
| 79. | Teddy Pendergrass | 2461 |
| 80. | Roy Milton | 2439 |

| Rank | Artist | Points |
|---|---|---|
| 81. | Ray Parker Jr. | 2418 |
| 82. | Little Richard | 2415 |
| 83. | Little Milton | 2406 |
| 84. | Amos Milburn | 2374 |
| 85. | Luther Vandross | 2354 |
| 86. | Martha & The Vandellas | 2352 |
| 87. | The Platters | 2347 |
| 88. | The Staple Singers | 2342 |
| 89. | Roberta Flack | 2341 |
| 90. | The Intruders | 2335 |

| Rank | Artist | Points |
|---|---|---|
| 91. | Betty Wright | 2330 |
| 92. | Joe Turner | 2314 |
| 93. | The Emotions | 2305 |
| 94. | Stephanie Mills | 2305 |
| 95. | George Benson | 2291 |
| 96. | Lou Rawls | 2288 |
| 97. | War | 2279 |
| 98. | Con Funk Shun | 2274 |
| 99. | Deniece Williams | 2266 |
| 100. | Candi Staton | 2255 |

| Rank | Artist | Points |
|------|--------|--------|
| 101. | Isaac Hayes | 2246 |
| 102. | LaVern Baker | 2230 |
| 103. | The Marvelettes | 2196 |
| 104. | Harold Melvin & The Blue Notes | 2158 |
| 105. | Ike & Tina Turner | 2148 |
| 106. | Mary Wells | 2147 |
| 107. | Atlantic Starr | 2116 |
| 108. | Ben E. King | 2112 |
| 109. | Ink Spots | 2111 |
| 110. | Bill Withers | 2111 |

| Rank | Artist | Points |
|------|--------|--------|
| 111. | Maze Featuring Frankie Beverly | 2093 |
| 112. | Evelyn 'Champagne' King | 2079 |
| 113. | Jimmy Reed | 2077 |
| 114. | Johnny Otis Orchestra | 2071 |
| 115. | Shalamar | 2069 |
| 116. | Clarence Carter | 2068 |
| 117. | Larry Graham/ Graham Central Station | 2039 |
| 118. | Roy Brown | 2013 |
| 119. | Lionel Hampton | 1996 |
| 120. | Peaches & Herb | 1982 |

| Rank | Artist | Points |
|------|--------|--------|
| 121. | Fatback | 1958 |
| 122. | Billy Eckstine | 1937 |
| 123. | Carla Thomas | 1920 |
| 124. | Little Willie John | 1909 |
| 125. | KC & The Sunshine Band | 1900 |
| 126. | One Way | 1899 |
| 127. | Lionel Richie | 1892 |
| 128. | Esther Phillips | 1885 |
| 129. | Ella Fitzgerald | 1863 |
| 130. | New Edition | 1861 |

| Rank | Artist | Points |
|------|--------|--------|
| 131. | Jermaine Jackson | 1838 |
| 132. | Wynonie Harris | 1828 |
| 133. | Muddy Waters | 1824 |
| 134. | Johnny Moore's Three Blazers | 1823 |
| 135. | Parliament | 1814 |
| 136. | Little Walter | 1792 |
| 137. | Chubby Checker | 1790 |
| 138. | Clyde McPhatter | 1782 |
| 139. | The Delfonics | 1767 |
| 140. | Sly & The Family Stone | 1750 |

| Rank | Artist | Points |
|------|--------|--------|
| 141. | Archie Bell & The Drells | 1731 |
| 142. | Joe Liggins | 1718 |
| 143. | Chuck Jackson | 1716 |
| 144. | Stacy Lattisaw | 1716 |
| 145. | Buddy Johnson | 1713 |
| 146. | Chaka Khan | 1709 |
| 147. | Luther Ingram | 1700 |
| 148. | Jeffrey Osborne | 1696 |
| 149. | Leon Haywood | 1679 |
| 150. | Edwin Starr | 1666 |

| Rank | Artist | Points |
|------|--------|--------|
| 151. | Chuck Willis | 1661 |
| 152. | Duke Ellington | 1650 |
| 153. | The S.O.S. Band | 1642 |
| 154. | Teena Marie | 1624 |
| 155. | The Brothers Johnson | 1612 |
| 156. | Billy Ocean | 1580 |
| 157. | The Shirelles | 1576 |
| 158. | Major Lance | 1574 |
| 159. | Lakeside | 1569 |
| 160. | Charles Brown | 1568 |

| Rank | Artist | Points |
|------|--------|--------|
| 161. | Dazz Band | 1565 |
| 162. | Sister Sledge | 1537 |
| 163. | L.T.D. | 1532 |
| 164. | Erskine Hawkins | 1528 |
| 165. | The Five Stairsteps | 1526 |
| 166. | Billy Preston | 1523 |
| 167. | The Dominoes | 1516 |
| 168. | Starpoint | 1509 |
| 169. | Sam & Dave | 1505 |
| 170. | Lowell Fulson | 1502 |

| Rank | Artist | Points |
|------|--------|--------|
| 171. | Rose Royce | 1494 |
| 172. | The Main Ingredient | 1492 |
| 173. | David Ruffin | 1489 |
| 174. | Bull Moose Jackson | 1482 |
| 175. | Full Force | 1476 |
| 176. | Donny Hathaway | 1470 |
| 177. | Barbara Mason | 1461 |
| 178. | Run-D.M.C. | 1461 |
| 179. | The Coasters | 1459 |
| 180. | William Bell | 1452 |

| Rank | Artist | Points |
|------|--------|--------|
| 181. | Eddie Floyd | 1446 |
| 182. | Freddie Jackson | 1422 |
| 183. | Syl Johnson | 1419 |
| 184. | Brenda & The Tabulations | 1419 |
| 185. | Little Junior Parker | 1410 |
| 186. | Janet Jackson | 1407 |
| 187. | Slave | 1395 |
| 188. | Booker T. & The MG's | 1393 |
| 189. | Cheryl Lynn | 1381 |
| 190. | Carl Carlton | 1377 |

| Rank | Artist | Points |
|------|--------|--------|
| 191. | Skyy | 1372 |
| 192. | Mills Brothers | 1370 |
| 193. | Whitney Houston | 1365 |
| 194. | Johnny 'Guitar' Watson | 1344 |
| 195. | Al Jarreau | 1335 |
| 196. | The Orioles | 1329 |
| 197. | Funkadelic | 1326 |
| 198. | Kashif | 1313 |
| 199. | Rufus Thomas | 1311 |
| 200. | Chic | 1310 |

Artist's points are calculated using the following formula:

1. Each artist's charted records are awarded points based on their highest position (#1 = 100 points; #2 = 99, etc.).

2. Bonus points are awarded each record based on its highest charted position (#1 = 25 points; #2-5 = 20 points; #6-10 = 15 points; #11-20 = 10 points; #21-30 = 5 points; #31-40 = 2 points).

3. Total weeks charted are added in.

4. Total weeks an artist held the #1 position are also added in.

When two artists combine for a hit record (Ex: Stevie Wonder & Michael Jackson; Supremes/Temptations), their chart points are shared equally.

Artists such as "Ashford & Simpson" and "Ike & Tina Turner" are considered regular recording teams and their points are not split or shared by the artists individually.

# The TOP 200 Artists (A-Z)

| Artist | Rank | Artist | Rank | Artist | Rank |
|---|---|---|---|---|---|
| Ashford & Simpson | 62 | Carl Carlton | 190 | Duke Ellington | 152 |
| Atlantic Starr | 107 | Clarence Carter | 116 | The Emotions | 93 |
| LaVern Baker | 102 | Gene Chandler | 48 | Fatback | 121 |
| Hank Ballard & The Midnighters | 74 | Ray Charles | 3 | Ella Fitzgerald | 129 |
| Bar-Kays | 56 | Chubby Checker | 137 | The Five Stairsteps | 165 |
| Archie Bell & The Drells | 141 | The Chi-Lites | 41 | Roberta Flack | 89 |
| William Bell | 180 | Chic | 200 | Eddie Floyd | 181 |
| George Benson | 95 | The Clovers | 69 | Four Tops | 17 |
| Brook Benton | 33 | The Coasters | 179 | Aretha Franklin | 2 |
| Chuck Berry | 71 | Nat King Cole | 13 | Full Force | 175 |
| Bobby Bland | 11 | Natalie Cole | 54 | Lowell Fulson | 170 |
| Booker T. & The MG's | 188 | Commodores | 43 | Funkadelic | 197 |
| Brenda & The Tabulations | 184 | Con Funk Shun | 98 | The Gap Band | 67 |
| | | Sam Cooke | 34 | Marvin Gaye | 7 |
| The Brothers Johnson | 155 | Tyrone Davis | 30 | Larry Graham/Graham Central Station | 117 |
| Charles Brown | 160 | Dazz Band | 161 | Al Green | 47 |
| James Brown | 1 | The Delfonics | 139 | Lionel Hampton | 119 |
| Roy Brown | 118 | The Dells | 35 | Wynonie Harris | 132 |
| Ruth Brown | 55 | Fats Domino | 9 | Donny Hathaway | 176 |
| Peabo Bryson | 49 | The Dominoes | 167 | Erskine Hawkins | 164 |
| Solomon Burke | 72 | The Dramatics | 51 | Isaac Hayes | 101 |
| Jerry Butler | 15 | The Drifters | 28 | Leon Haywood | 149 |
| Cameo | 53 | Earth, Wind & Fire | 27 | Whitney Houston | 193 |
| | | Billy Eckstine | 122 | | |

# The **TOP 20** Artists By Decade

## THE FORTIES ('42-'49)

| | Points |
|---|---|
| 1. Louis Jordan | 6522 |
| 2. King Cole Trio | 2833 |
| 3. Ink Spots | 2111 |
| 4. Lionel Hampton | 1747 |
| 5. Duke Ellington | 1650 |
| 6. Billy Eckstine | 1565 |
| 7. Johnny Moore's Three Blazers | 1507 |
| 8. Ella Fitzgerald | 1506 |
| 9. Erskine Hawkins | 1417 |
| 10. Mills Brothers | 1370 |
| 11. Bull Moose Jackson | 1367 |
| 12. Dinah Washington | 1280 |
| 13. Julia Lee & Her Boyfriends | 1216 |
| 14. Joe Liggins | 1206 |
| 15. Ivory Joe Hunter | 1203 |
| 16. Nellie Lutcher | 1169 |
| 17. Amos Milburn | 1155 |
| 18. Wynonie Harris | 1116 |
| 19. Roy Brown | 1069 |
| 20. The Ravens | 999 |

## THE FIFTIES

| | Points |
|---|---|
| 1. Fats Domino | 5396 |
| 2. Dinah Washington | 3183 |
| 3. Elvis Presley | 2944 |
| 4. Ruth Brown | 2693 |
| 5. The Clovers | 2614 |
| 6. Ray Charles | 2408 |
| 7. B.B. King | 2261 |
| 8. Joe Turner | 2203 |
| 9. The Drifters | 2143 |
| 10. Little Richard | 2100 |
| 11. Johnny Otis Orchestra | 1988 |
| 12. Chuck Berry | 1959 |
| 13. Little Walter | 1792 |
| 14. LaVern Baker | 1768 |
| 15. The Platters | 1745 |
| 16. Muddy Waters | 1722 |
| 17. Lloyd Price | 1672 |
| 18. Nat King Cole | 1661 |
| 19. Chuck Willis | 1661 |
| 20. The Dominoes | 1516 |

## THE SIXTIES

| | Points |
|---|---|
| 1. James Brown | 5648 |
| 2. Ray Charles | 4833 |
| 3. Marvin Gaye | 3888 |
| 4. Bobby Bland | 3494 |
| 5. The Miracles | 3412 |
| 6. The Temptations | 3409 |
| 7. Aretha Franklin | 3182 |
| 8. The Supremes | 3162 |
| 9. Jackie Wilson | 3058 |
| 10. Otis Redding | 3048 |
| 11. The Impressions | 3017 |
| 12. Wilson Pickett | 2846 |
| 13. Brook Benton | 2677 |
| 14. Jerry Butler | 2656 |
| 15. Sam Cooke | 2620 |
| 16. Joe Tex | 2358 |
| 17. Stevie Wonder | 2326 |
| 18. B.B. King | 2219 |
| 19. Dionne Warwick | 2218 |
| 20. The Marvelettes | 2196 |

## THE SEVENTIES

| | Points |
|---|---|
| 1. James Brown | 5183 |
| 2. Aretha Franklin | 3405 |
| 3. The Isley Brothers | 3378 |
| 4. Gladys Knight & The Pips | 3164 |
| 5. Joe Simon | 3082 |
| 6. Tyrone Davis | 3068 |
| 7. Jackson 5 | 3052 |
| 8. The Temptations | 2864 |
| 9. Al Green | 2842 |
| 10. Spinners | 2746 |
| 11. Earth, Wind & Fire | 2625 |
| 12. The O'Jays | 2606 |
| 13. The Chi-Lites | 2575 |
| 14. Johnnie Taylor | 2543 |
| 15. Marvin Gaye | 2531 |
| 16. The Dramatics | 2516 |
| 17. Diana Ross | 2507 |
| 18. Barry White | 2432 |
| 19. Stevie Wonder | 2365 |
| 20. Four Tops | 2360 |

## THE EIGHTIES ('80-'88)

| | Points | | Points |
|---|---|---|---|
| 1. Prince | 2921 | 11. Peabo Bryson | 2096 |
| 2. Kool & The Gang | 2506 | 12. Melba Moore | 2063 |
| 3. Stevie Wonder | 2431 | 13. Diana Ross | 2034 |
| 4. Michael Jackson | 2319 | 14. One Way | 1899 |
| 5. Cameo | 2317 | 15. Smokey Robinson | 1898 |
| 6. The Gap Band | 2313 | 16. Lionel Richie | 1892 |
| 7. Luther Vandross | 2161 | 17. Atlantic Starr | 1882 |
| 8. Aretha Franklin | 2144 | 18. Ray Parker Jr. | 1876 |
| 9. Rick James | 2132 | 19. New Edition | 1861 |
| 10. Stephanie Mills | 2119 | 20. The Whispers | 1853 |

## Most Charted Records

1. 114 James Brown
2. 84 Aretha Franklin
3. 83 Ray Charles
4. 76 The Temptations
5. 74 B.B. King
6. 63 Fats Domino
7. 63 Bobby Bland
8. 62 Marvin Gaye
9. 60 Stevie Wonder
10. 58 Gladys Knight & The Pips
11. 58 Jerry Butler
12. 57 Louis Jordan
13. 57 The Isley Brothers
14. 54 Dionne Warwick
15. 50 Four Tops
16. 50 The Impressions
17. 49 Wilson Pickett
18. 49 Joe Simon
19. 48 The Miracles
20. 47 Nat King Cole
21. 47 The O'Jays
22. 47 Jackie Wilson
23. 45 Dinah Washington
24. 45 Diana Ross
25. 44 Kool & The Gang
26. 43 The Supremes
27. 43 The Dells
28. 41 Tyrone Davis
29. 41 The Manhattans
30. 41 The Chi-Lites

## Most Top 10 Hits

1. 57 James Brown
2. 54 Louis Jordan
3. 48 Aretha Franklin
4. 42 The Temptations
5. 42 Stevie Wonder
6. 40 Ray Charles
7. 39 Fats Domino
8. 35 Nat King Cole
9. 33 Marvin Gaye
10. 33 Dinah Washington
11. 30 Gladys Knight & The Pips
12. 25 Bobby Bland
13. 25 The Isley Brothers
14. 25 Kool & The Gang
15. 25 The Drifters
16. 25 The Jacksons
17. 24 B.B. King
18. 24 The Miracles
19. 24 Elvis Presley
20. 23 Four Tops
21. 23 The Supremes
22. 21 Michael Jackson
23. 21 Ruth Brown
24. 19 The O'Jays
25. 19 Earth, Wind & Fire
26. 19 Spinners
27. 19 Sam Cooke
28. 19 The Clovers
29. 19 Roy Milton
30. 19 Amos

## Most #1 Hits

1. 20 Aretha Franklin
2. 19 Stevie Wonder
3. 18 Louis Jordan
4. 17 James Brown
5. 14 The Temptations
6. 13 Marvin Gaye
7. 10 Ray Charles
8. 10 Gladys Knight & The Pips
9. 9 Fats Domino
10. 9 Kool & The Gang
11. 9 The O'Jays
12. 9 Michael Jackson
13. 8 The Supremes
14. 8 Earth, Wind & Fire
15. 7 Brook Benton
16. 7 Commodores
17. 6 The Isley Brothers
18. 6 Nat King Cole
19. 6 Jackie Wilson
20. 6 Spinners
21. 6 Elvis Presley
22. 6 The Jacksons
23. 6 Al Green
24. 6 Freddie Jackson

## Most Weeks At #1 Position

1. 113 Louis Jordan
2. 67 Stevie Wonder
3. 65 Aretha Franklin
4. 52 Marvin Gaye
5. 51 Fats Domino
6. 47 James Brown
7. 41 The Temptations
8. 40 Brook Benton
9. 33 Michael Jackson
10. 32 Ruth Brown
11. 31 Joe Liggins & His Honeydrippers
12. 29 Charles Brown
13. 27 Ray Charles
14. 24 Earth, Wind & Fire
15. 24 The Jacksons
16. 24 Ink Spots
17. 24 The Dominoes
18. 24 The Coasters
19. 24 Johnny Ace
20. 23 Gladys Knight & The Pips
21. 23 Nat King Cole
22. 23 The Platters
23. 22 The Drifters
24. 22 Lionel Hampton
25. 21 Julia Lee & Her Boyfriends
26. 20 The Supremes
27. 20 Elvis Presley
28. 20 Erskine Hawkins
29. 19 Jackie Wilson
30. 19 Chuck Berry
31. 19 Lionel Richie

# TOP 40 #1 HITS
## THE FORTIES ('42-'49)

| YR | WEEKS | | | | RANK | TITLE.............ARTIST |
|----|----|----|----|----|------|------|
| | CH | 40 | 10 | #1 | | |
| 45 | 27 | 27 | 27 | 18 | 1 | The Honeydripper . . . . . . . . . Joe Liggins & His Honeydrippers |
| 46 | 26 | 26 | 26 | 18 | 2 | Choo Choo Ch'Boogie . . . . . . . . . . . . . . . . . . . . . Louis Jordan |
| 47 | 27 | 27 | 27 | 17 | 3 | Ain't Nobody Here But Us Chickens . . . . . . . . . . Louis Jordan |
| 46 | 25 | 25 | 25 | 16 | 4 | Hey! Ba-Ba-Re-Bop . . . . . . . . . . . . . . . . . . . . Lionel Hampton |
| 49 | 27 | 27 | 24 | 15 | 5 | Trouble Blues . . . . . . . . . . . . . . . . . . . . . . . Charles Brown Trio |
| 49 | 32 | 32 | 31 | 14 | 6 | The Hucklebuck . . . . . . . . . . . . . . . . . . . . . . . . Paul Williams |
| 43 | 29 | 29 | 29 | 14 | 7 | Don't Cry, Baby . . . . . . . . . . . . . . . . . . . . . Erskine Hawkins |
| 47 | 24 | 24 | 24 | 14 | 8 | Boogie Woogie Blue Plate . . . . . . . . . . . . . . . . . Louis Jordan |
| 47 | 28 | 28 | 28 | 12 | 9 | Snatch And Grab It . . . . . . . . . . . . Julia Lee & Her Boyfriends |
| 49 | 23 | 23 | 22 | 12 | 10 | Saturday Night Fish Fry (Part I) . . . . . . . . . . . . Louis Jordan |
| 44 | 21 | 21 | 21 | 11 | 11 | Into Each Life Some Rain Must Fall . . Ella Fitzgerald & Ink Spots |
| 44 | 26 | 26 | 26 | 10 | 12 | Straighten Up And Fly Right . . . . . . . . . . . . . . . King Cole Trio |
| 48 | 28 | 28 | 23 | 9 | 13 | King Size Papa . . . . . . . . . . . . . . . . Julia Lee & Her Boyfriends |
| 46 | 13 | 13 | 13 | 9 | 14 | Buzz Me . . . . . . . . . . . . . . . . . . . . . . . . . . . . . . Louis Jordan |
| 47 | 25 | 25 | 25 | 8 | 15 | I Want To Be Loved (But Only By You) . . . . Savannah Churchill |
| 49 | 22 | 22 | 20 | 8 | 16 | For You, My Love . . . . . . . . . . . . . . . . . . . . . . . Larry Darnell |
| 45 | 20 | 20 | 20 | 8 | 17 | Who Threw The Whiskey In The Well? . . . . . . . Lucky Millinder |
| 44 | 18 | 18 | 18 | 8 | 18 | Do Nothin' Till You Hear From Me . . . . . . . . . . . Duke Ellington |
| 48 | 17 | 17 | 15 | 8 | 19 | I Can't Go On Without You . . . . . . . . . . . . Bull Moose Jackson |
| 48 | 33 | 33 | 29 | 7 | 20 | Tomorrow Night . . . . . . . . . . . . . . . . . . . . . . Lonnie Johnson |
| 45 | 26 | 26 | 26 | 7 | 21 | Caldonia . . . . . . . . . . . . . . . . . . . . . . . . . . . . . Louis Jordan |
| 47 | 20 | 20 | 20 | 7 | 22 | Jack, You're Dead . . . . . . . . . . . . . . . . . . . . . . . Louis Jordan |
| 43 | 16 | 16 | 16 | 7 | 23 | I Can't Stand Losing You . . . . . . . . . . . . . . . . . . . Ink Spots |
| 45 | 13 | 13 | 13 | 7 | 24 | I Wonder . . . . . . . . . . . . . . . . . . . . . . . . . . Roosevelt Sykes |
| 44 | 26 | 26 | 26 | 6 | 25 | G.I. Jive . . . . . . . . . . . . . . . . . . . . . . . . . . . . . Louis Jordan |
| 45 | 25 | 25 | 25 | 6 | 26 | Tippin' In . . . . . . . . . . . . . . . . . . . . . . . . . Erskine Hawkins |
| 44 | 13 | 13 | 13 | 6 | 27 | Hamp's Boogie Woogie . . . . . . . . . . . . . . . . . Lionel Hampton |
| 48 | 23 | 23 | 22 | 5 | 28 | Chicken Shack Boogie . . . . . . . . . . . . . . . . . . . Amos Milburn |
| 46 | 20 | 20 | 20 | 5 | 29 | Stone Cold Dead In The Market (He Had It Coming) |
| | | | | | | . . . . . . Ella Fitzgerald & Louis Jordan |
| 48 | 21 | 21 | 19 | 5 | 30 | Bewildered . . . . . . . . . . . . . . . . . . . . . . . . . . Red Miller Trio |
| 43 | 12 | 12 | 12 | 5 | 31 | Don't Stop Now . . . . . . . . . . . . . . . . . . . . . . Bunny Banks Trio |
| 43 | 22 | 22 | 22 | 4 | 32 | See See Rider Blues . . . . . . . . . . . . . . . . . . . . . . Bea Booze |
| 44 | 22 | 22 | 22 | 4 | 33 | Gee, Baby, Ain't I Good To You? . . . . . . . . . . . King Cole Trio |
| 48 | 22 | 22 | 19 | 4 | 34 | Corn Bread . . . . . . . . . . . . . . . . . . . . . . . . . . . . Hal Singer |
| 43 | 16 | 16 | 16 | 4 | 35 | You'll Never Know . . . . . . . . . . . . . . . . . . . . . . Dick Haymes |
| 44 | 14 | 14 | 14 | 4 | 36 | Main Stem . . . . . . . . . . . . . . . . . . . . . . . . . . Duke Ellington |
| 48 | 31 | 31 | 30 | 3 | 37 | Long Gone, Pts. 1 & 2 . . . . . . . . . . . . . . . . . . Sonny Thompson |
| 48 | 26 | 26 | 25 | 3 | 38 | I Love You, Yes I Do . . . . . . . . . . . . . . . . . Bull Moose Jackson |
| 43 | 25 | 25 | 25 | 3 | 39 | Don't Get Around Much Anymore . . . . . . . . . . Duke Ellington |
| 48 | 25 | 25 | 23 | 3 | 40 | Pretty Mama Blues . . . . . . . . . . . . . . . . . . . . . Ivory Joe Hunter |

All of the above were #1 hits. The ranking is based on weeks at #1.

YR:    Year record reached its peak position
WEEKS:    #1 — Total weeks record held #1 position
          10 — Total weeks charted in Top 10
          40 — Total weeks charted in Top 40
          CH — Total weeks charted

# THE FIFTIES

| YR | CH | 40 | 10 | #1 | RANK | TITLE............ARTIST |
|---|---|---|---|---|---|---|
| 51 | 30 | 30 | 30 | 14 | 1 | Sixty-Minute Man . . . . . . . . . . . . . . . . . . . . . . . The Dominoes |
| 51 | 24 | 24 | 24 | 14 | 2 | Black Night . . . . . . . . . . . . . . . . . . . . . . . . . . . . Charles Brown |
| 54 | 21 | 21 | 21 | 14 | 3 | Things That I Used To Do . . . . . . . . . . . . . . . . . . . Guitar Slim |
| 56 | 28 | 28 | 26 | 13 | 4 | Honky Tonk (Parts 1 & 2) . . . . . . . . . . . . . . . . . . Bill Doggett |
| 50 | 25 | 25 | 25 | 13 | 5 | Pink Champagne . . . . . . . . . . . Joe Liggins & His Honeydrippers |
| 57 | 21 | 21 | 19 | 13 | 6 | Searchin' . . . . . . . . . . . . . . . . . . . . . . . . . . . . . . The Coasters |
| 50 | 25 | 25 | 25 | 11 | 7 | Teardrops From My Eyes . . . . . . . . . . . . . . . . . . . Ruth Brown |
| 56 | 23 | 23 | 23 | 11 | 8 | Blueberry Hill . . . . . . . . . . . . . . . . . . . . . . . . . . Fats Domino |
| 55 | 26 | 26 | 22 | 11 | 9 | Ain't That A Shame . . . . . . . . . . . . . . . . . . . . . . Fats Domino |
| 53 | 21 | 21 | 21 | 11 | 10 | Money Honey . . . . . . . . . . . . . . Clyde McPhatter & The Drifters |
| 56 | 20 | 20 | 17 | 11 | 11 | The Great Pretender . . . . . . . . . . . . . . . . . . . . . . The Platters |
| 55 | 16 | 16 | 15 | 11 | 12 | Maybellene . . . . . . . . . . . . . . . . . . . . . . . . . . . . Chuck Berry |
| 53 | 21 | 21 | 21 | 10 | 13 | Shake A Hand . . . . . . . . . . . . . . . . . . . . . . . . . . . Faye Adams |
| 52 | 20 | 20 | 20 | 10 | 14 | Have Mercy Baby . . . . . . . . . . . . . . . . . . . . . . . The Dominoes |
| 55 | 19 | 19 | 19 | 10 | 15 | Pledging My Love . . . . . . . . . . . . . . . . . . . . . . . . . Johnny Ace |
| 50 | 22 | 22 | 22 | 9 | 16 | Double Crossing Blues <br> . . . . . . . Little Esther with The Johnny Otis Orchestra |
| 52 | 20 | 20 | 20 | 9 | 17 | My Song . . . . . . . . . . . . . Johnny Ace with The Beale Streeters |
| 56 | 20 | 20 | 19 | 9 | 18 | I'm In Love Again . . . . . . . . . . . . . . . . . . . . . . . Fats Domino |
| 54 | 19 | 19 | 19 | 9 | 19 | Hearts Of Stone . . . . . . . . . . . . . . . . . . . . . . . . The Charms |
| 59 | 15 | 15 | 13 | 9 | 20 | It's Just A Matter Of Time . . . . . . . . . . . . . . . . Brook Benton |
| 53 | 25 | 25 | 25 | 8 | 21 | Honey Hush . . . . . . . . . . . . . . . . . . . . . . . . . . . . Joe Turner |
| 54 | 23 | 23 | 23 | 8 | 22 | Honey Love . . . . . . . . . . . . . Drifters featuring Clyde McPhatter |
| 54 | 20 | 20 | 20 | 8 | 23 | You'll Never Walk Alone . . . . . . . . . . . . . . . . . . . Roy Hamilton |
| 52 | 20 | 20 | 20 | 8 | 24 | Juke . . . . . . . . . . . . . . . . . . . . Little Walter & His Night Cats |
| 52 | 19 | 19 | 19 | 8 | 25 | I Don't Know . . . . . . . . . . . . . . . . . . . . . . . . . . Willie Mabon |
| 54 | 17 | 17 | 17 | 8 | 26 | Oh What A Dream . . . . . . . . . . Ruth Brown & Her Rhythmakers |
| 57 | 16 | 16 | 16 | 8 | 27 | Blue Monday . . . . . . . . . . . . . . . . . . . . . . . . . . . Fats Domino |
| 56 | 16 | 16 | 15 | 8 | 28 | Long Tall Sally . . . . . . . . . . . . . . . . . . . . . . . . Little Richard |
| 55 | 30 | 30 | 26 | 7 | 29 | Only You (And You Alone) . . . . . . . . . . . . . . . . . . The Platters |
| 54 | 26 | 26 | 26 | 7 | 30 | Work With Me Annie . . . . . . . . Midnighters Formerly The Royals |
| 52 | 26 | 26 | 26 | 7 | 31 | Lawdy Miss Clawdy . . . . . . . . . . . . . . . . . . . . . . . . Lloyd Price |
| 52 | 20 | 20 | 20 | 7 | 32 | Night Train . . . . . . . . . . . . . . . . . . . . . . . . . . Jimmy Forrest |
| 58 | 22 | 22 | 19 | 7 | 33 | Lonely Teardrops . . . . . . . . . . . . . . . . . . . . . . . Jackie Wilson |
| 52 | 16 | 16 | 16 | 7 | 34 | 5-10-15 Hours . . . . . . . . . . . . . . . . . . . . . . . . . . Ruth Brown |
| 50 | 16 | 16 | 16 | 7 | 35 | Blue Light Boogie - Parts 1 & 2 . . . . . . . . . . . . . . Louis Jordan |
| 52 | 15 | 15 | 15 | 7 | 36 | Five Long Years . . . . . . . . . . . . . . . . . . . . . . . . . Eddie Boyd |
| 53 | 14 | 14 | 14 | 7 | 37 | Hound Dog . . . . . . . . . . . . . . Willie Mae "Big Mama" Thornton |
| 58 | 14 | 14 | 12 | 7 | 38 | Yakety Yak . . . . . . . . . . . . . . . . . . . . . . . . . . . . The Coasters |
| 59 | 15 | 15 | 11 | 7 | 39 | Kansas City . . . . . . . . . . . . . . . . . . . . . . . . . Wilbert Harrison |
| 51 | 22 | 22 | 22 | 6 | 40 | Fool, Fool, Fool . . . . . . . . . . . . . . . . . . . . . . . . . The Clovers |

# TOP 40 #1 HITS

# THE SIXTIES

| YR | WEEKS | | | | RANK | TITLE............ARTIST |
|---|---|---|---|---|---|---|
| | CH | 40 | 10 | #1 | | |
| 61 | 19 | 19 | 16 | 10 | 1 | Tossin' And Turnin' . . . . . . . . . . . . . . . . . . . . . . .Bobby Lewis |
| 60 | 17 | 17 | 15 | 10 | 2 | Baby (You've Got What It Takes) |
| | | | | | | . . . . . . .Dinah Washington & Brook Benton |
| 62 | 16 | 16 | 14 | 10 | 3 | I Can't Stop Loving You . . . . . . . . . . . . . . . . . . .Ray Charles |
| 65 | 18 | 18 | 15 | 9 | 4 | I Can't Help Myself . . . . . . . . . . . . . . . . . . . . . .Four Tops |
| 60 | 14 | 14 | 13 | 9 | 5 | Kiddio . . . . . . . . . . . . . . . . . . . . . . . . . . . . . .Brook Benton |
| 61 | 16 | 16 | 13 | 8 | 6 | Shop Around . . . . . . . . . . . . . . . . . . . . . . . . .The Miracles |
| 65 | 17 | 17 | 12 | 8 | 7 | Papa's Got A Brand New Bag (Part I) . . . . . . . . . .James Brown |
| 66 | 17 | 17 | 12 | 8 | 8 | Ain't Too Proud To Beg . . . . . . . . . . . . . . . . .The Temptations |
| 67 | 14 | 14 | 11 | 8 | 9 | Respect . . . . . . . . . . . . . . . . . . . . . . . . . . .Aretha Franklin |
| 61 | 23 | 23 | 16 | 7 | 10 | Please Mr. Postman . . . . . . . . . . . . . . . . . . . .The Marvelettes |
| | | | | | | |
| 60 | 16 | 16 | 14 | 7 | 11 | He Will Break Your Heart . . . . . . . . . . . . . . . . . .Jerry Butler |
| 67 | 14 | 14 | 13 | 7 | 12 | I Never Loved A Man (The Way I Loved You) . . . .Aretha Franklin |
| 67 | 18 | 17 | 11 | 7 | 13 | Soul Man . . . . . . . . . . . . . . . . . . . . . . . . . . . .Sam & Dave |
| 66 | 16 | 16 | 11 | 7 | 14 | 634-5789 (Soulsville, U.S.A.) . . . . . . . . . . . . . .Wilson Pickett |
| 68 | 14 | 14 | 10 | 7 | 15 | I Heard It Through The Grapevine . . . . . . . . . . . .Marvin Gaye |
| 65 | 16 | 16 | 13 | 6 | 16 | I Got You (I Feel Good) . . . . . . . . . . . . . . . . . .James Brown |
| 67 | 17 | 17 | 11 | 6 | 17 | I Heard It Through The Grapevine . . .Gladys Knight & The Pips |
| 69 | 15 | 15 | 11 | 6 | 18 | Too Busy Thinking About My Baby . . . . . . . . . . .Marvin Gaye |
| 63 | 15 | 15 | 10 | 6 | 19 | Fingertips - Pt 2 . . . . . . . . . . . . . . . . . . . . .Little Stevie Wonder |
| 65 | 13 | 13 | 10 | 6 | 20 | My Girl . . . . . . . . . . . . . . . . . . . . . . . . . . .The Temptations |
| | | | | | | |
| 68 | 12 | 12 | 9 | 6 | 21 | Say It Loud - I'm Black And I'm Proud (Part 1) . . . .James Brown |
| 69 | 15 | 15 | 12 | 5 | 22 | I Can't Get Next To You . . . . . . . . . . . . . . . . .The Temptations |
| 67 | 17 | 16 | 11 | 5 | 23 | Tell It Like It Is . . . . . . . . . . . . . . . . . . . . . . .Aaron Neville |
| 66 | 15 | 15 | 11 | 5 | 24 | Beauty Is Only Skin Deep . . . . . . . . . . . . . . .The Temptations |
| 66 | 15 | 15 | 11 | 5 | 25 | Uptight (Everything's Alright) . . . . . . . . . . . . . .Stevie Wonder |
| 61 | 16 | 16 | 10 | 5 | 26 | Mother-In-Law . . . . . . . . . . . . . . . . . . . . . . . . .Ernie K-Doe |
| 61 | 15 | 15 | 10 | 5 | 27 | Hit The Road Jack . . . . . . . . . . . . . . . . . . . . . . .Ray Charles |
| 69 | 13 | 13 | 10 | 5 | 28 | Share Your Love With Me . . . . . . . . . . . . . . .Aretha Franklin |
| 69 | 17 | 17 | 9 | 5 | 29 | Baby I'm For Real . . . . . . . . . . . . . . . . . . . . . . .The Originals |
| 62 | 13 | 13 | 9 | 5 | 30 | Duke Of Earl . . . . . . . . . . . . . . . . . . . . . . . . .Gene Chandler |
| | | | | | | |
| 68 | 13 | 12 | 8 | 5 | 31 | You're All I Need To Get By . . . . . .Marvin Gaye & Tammi Terrell |
| 65 | 19 | 19 | 13 | 4 | 32 | Rescue Me . . . . . . . . . . . . . . . . . . . . . . . . . . .Fontella Bass |
| 65 | 17 | 17 | 13 | 4 | 33 | Shotgun . . . . . . . . . . . . . . . . . . . . .Jr. Walker & The All Stars |
| 62 | 15 | 15 | 12 | 4 | 34 | Green Onions . . . . . . . . . . . . . . . . . .Booker T. & The MG's |
| 67 | 15 | 15 | 12 | 4 | 35 | I Was Made To Love Her . . . . . . . . . . . . . . . . . .Stevie Wonder |
| 62 | 19 | 19 | 11 | 4 | 36 | I Know (You Don't Love Me No More) . . . . . . . . .Barbara George |
| 60 | 17 | 17 | 11 | 4 | 37 | White Silver Sands . . . . . . . . . . . . . . . . . . .Bill Black's Combo |
| 63 | 16 | 16 | 11 | 4 | 38 | Heat Wave . . . . . . . . . . . . . . . . . . . . .Martha & The Vandellas |
| 62 | 16 | 16 | 11 | 4 | 39 | Mashed Potato Time . . . . . . . . . . . . . . . . . . . . .Dee Dee Sharp |
| 66 | 16 | 16 | 11 | 4 | 40 | When A Man Loves A Woman . . . . . . . . . . . . . . .Percy Sledge |

| YR | WEEKS | | | | RANK | TITLE............ARTIST |
|----|----|----|----|----|------|-------------------------|
| | CH | 40 | 10 | #1 | | |
| 72 | 16 | 16 | 13 | 9 | 1 | Let's Stay Together .........................Al Green |
| 77 | 20 | 16 | 12 | 7 | 2 | Serpentine Fire ......................Earth, Wind & Fire |
| 78 | 25 | 19 | 16 | 6 | 3 | One Nation Under A Groove (Part 1) .............Funkadelic |
| 77 | 20 | 17 | 13 | 6 | 4 | Float On.......................................The Floaters |
| 79 | 18 | 16 | 13 | 6 | 5 | Good Times ..................................Chic |
| 76 | 21 | 17 | 12 | 6 | 6 | Disco Lady ............................Johnnie Taylor |
| 70 | 14 | 14 | 12 | 6 | 7 | The Love You Save ......................Jackson 5 |
| 73 | 17 | 15 | 11 | 6 | 8 | Let's Get It On .........................Marvin Gaye |
| 70 | 15 | 15 | 11 | 6 | 9 | Signed, Sealed, Delivered I'm Yours ..........Stevie Wonder |
| 70 | 13 | 13 | 10 | 6 | 10 | I'll Be There.................................Jackson 5 |
| 78 | 21 | 18 | 13 | 5 | 11 | Use Ta Be My Girl.........................The O'Jays |
| 77 | 20 | 18 | 13 | 5 | 12 | It's Ecstasy When You Lay Down Next To Me .....Barry White |
| 77 | 20 | 18 | 12 | 5 | 13 | I've Got Love On My Mind...................Natalie Cole |
| 79 | 20 | 18 | 12 | 5 | 14 | Don't Stop 'Til You Get Enough ...........Michael Jackson |
| 78 | 20 | 17 | 12 | 5 | 15 | Le Freak ......................................Chic |
| 71 | 16 | 15 | 12 | 5 | 16 | Mr. Big Stuff...........................Jean Knight |
| 77 | 21 | 19 | 11 | 5 | 17 | Got To Give It Up (Pt. I) .....................Marvin Gaye |
| 71 | 15 | 15 | 11 | 5 | 18 | What's Going On .........................Marvin Gaye |
| 77 | 18 | 16 | 10 | 5 | 19 | I Wish ..................................Stevie Wonder |
| 70 | 17 | 16 | 10 | 5 | 20 | Love On A Two-Way Street ..................The Moments |
| 79 | 18 | 15 | 10 | 5 | 21 | Ring My Bell .............................Anita Ward |
| 74 | 17 | 14 | 10 | 5 | 22 | Feel Like Makin' Love ....................Roberta Flack |
| 71 | 13 | 13 | 10 | 5 | 23 | Family Affair ...................Sly & The Family Stone |
| 70 | 14 | 14 | 9 | 5 | 24 | Thank You (Falettinme Be Mice Elf Agin) ..Sly & The Family Stone |
| 72 | 14 | 14 | 9 | 5 | 25 | I'll Be Around ...............................Spinners |
| 76 | 23 | 20 | 14 | 4 | 26 | Dazz .......................................Brick |
| 77 | 22 | 21 | 13 | 4 | 27 | Best Of My Love ....................The Emotions |
| 78 | 20 | 17 | 12 | 4 | 28 | Too Much, Too Little, Too Late .Johnny Mathis/Deniece Williams |
| 76 | 18 | 16 | 12 | 4 | 29 | (Shake, Shake, Shake) Shake Your Booty <br> ......KC & The Sunshine Band |
| 76 | 19 | 15 | 12 | 4 | 30 | Something He Can Feel ..................Aretha Franklin |
| 70 | 18 | 18 | 11 | 4 | 31 | I Want You Back...........................Jackson 5 |
| 79 | 17 | 14 | 11 | 4 | 32 | Reunited .............................Peaches & Herb |
| 72 | 18 | 18 | 10 | 4 | 33 | Me And Mrs. Jones .........................Billy Paul |
| 71 | 22 | 17 | 10 | 4 | 34 | Groove Me ................................King Floyd |
| 79 | 18 | 16 | 10 | 4 | 35 | Aqua Boogie (A Psychoalphadiscobetabioaquadoloop) <br> .......Parliament |
| 73 | 18 | 15 | 10 | 4 | 36 | Midnight Train To Georgia .........Gladys Knight & The Pips |
| 72 | 16 | 15 | 10 | 4 | 37 | I'll Take You There ....................The Staple Singers |
| 72 | 15 | 15 | 10 | 4 | 38 | Get On The Good Foot (Part 1) ..............James Brown |
| 73 | 16 | 14 | 10 | 4 | 39 | Neither One Of Us (Wants To Be The First To Say Goodbye) <br> .......Gladys Knight & The Pips |
| 72 | 15 | 14 | 10 | 4 | 40 | (If Loving You Is Wrong) I Don't Want to Be Right .Luther Ingram |

# TOP 40 #1 HITS

## THE EIGHTIES ('80-'88)

| YR | WEEKS CH | 40 | 10 | #1 | RANK | TITLE............ARTIST |
|----|----|----|----|----|------|------------------------|
| 82 | 27 | 25 | 15 | 10 | 1 | **Sexual Healing** . . . . . . . . . . . . . . . . . . . . . . . . . . . . Marvin Gaye |
| 82 | 21 | 20 | 15 | 9 | 2 | **That Girl** . . . . . . . . . . . . . . . . . . . . . . . . . . . . Stevie Wonder |
| 83 | 23 | 19 | 14 | 9 | 3 | **Billie Jean** . . . . . . . . . . . . . . . . . . . . . . . . . . Michael Jackson |
| 83 | 25 | 19 | 13 | 8 | 4 | **Juicy Fruit** . . . . . . . . . . . . . . . . . . . . . . . . . . . . . . Mtume |
| 81 | 22 | 18 | 13 | 8 | 5 | **Let's Groove** . . . . . . . . . . . . . . . . . . . . . . . . Earth, Wind & Fire |
| 84 | 20 | 18 | 13 | 8 | 6 | **When Doves Cry** . . . . . . . . . . . . . . . . . . . . . . . . . . . . Prince |
| 81 | 24 | 21 | 15 | 7 | 7 | **Endless Love** . . . . . . . . . . . . . . . . . Diana Ross & Lionel Richie |
| 83 | 22 | 21 | 15 | 7 | 8 | **All Night Long (All Night)** . . . . . . . . . . . . . . . . . Lionel Richie |
| 80 | 24 | 20 | 13 | 7 | 9 | **Master Blaster (Jammin')** . . . . . . . . . . . . . . . . . Stevie Wonder |
| 80 | 25 | 21 | 15 | 6 | 10 | **Rock With You** . . . . . . . . . . . . . . . . . . . . . . Michael Jackson |
| 80 | 24 | 20 | 14 | 6 | 11 | **Celebration** . . . . . . . . . . . . . . . . . . . . . . . . Kool & The Gang |
| 80 | 22 | 18 | 13 | 6 | 12 | **Let's Get Serious** . . . . . . . . . . . . . . . . . . . Jermaine Jackson |
| 85 | 26 | 19 | 12 | 6 | 13 | **Rock Me Tonight (For Old Times Sake)** . . . . . . . Freddie Jackson |
| 85 | 20 | 15 | 11 | 6 | 14 | **Part-Time Lover** . . . . . . . . . . . . . . . . . . . . . . Stevie Wonder |
| 83 | 19 | 15 | 11 | 6 | 15 | **Cold Blooded** . . . . . . . . . . . . . . . . . . . . . . . . . . Rick James |
| 83 | 23 | 19 | 12 | 5 | 16 | **Time Will Reveal** . . . . . . . . . . . . . . . . . . . . . . . . . DeBarge |
| 82 | 26 | 20 | 11 | 5 | 17 | **Let It Whip** . . . . . . . . . . . . . . . . . . . . . . . . . . . Dazz Band |
| 81 | 25 | 19 | 11 | 5 | 18 | **Give It To Me Baby** . . . . . . . . . . . . . . . . . . . . . Rick James |
| 80 | 20 | 18 | 11 | 5 | 19 | **And The Beat Goes On** . . . . . . . . . . . . . . . . . The Whispers |
| 82 | 21 | 16 | 11 | 5 | 20 | **Love Come Down** . . . . . . . . . . . . . . . . . . . . . . . Evelyn King |
| 81 | 21 | 18 | 10 | 5 | 21 | **Being With You** . . . . . . . . . . . . . . . . . . . . Smokey Robinson |
| 81 | 27 | 17 | 10 | 5 | 22 | **Don't Stop The Music** . . . . . . . . . . . . . . Yarbrough & Peoples |
| 80 | 24 | 17 | 10 | 5 | 23 | **Take Your Time (Do It Right) Part 1** . . . . . . . . . The S.O.S. Band |
| 84 | 17 | 14 | 9 | 5 | 24 | **Somebody's Watching Me** . . . . . . . . . . . . . . . . . . . Rockwell |
| 85 | 17 | 14 | 8 | 5 | 25 | **Freeway Of Love** . . . . . . . . . . . . . . . . . . . Aretha Franklin |
| 84 | 17 | 14 | 8 | 5 | 26 | **Operator** . . . . . . . . . . . . . . . . . . . . . . . . . . Midnight Star |
| 84 | 26 | 21 | 14 | 4 | 27 | **If Only You Knew** . . . . . . . . . . . . . . . . . . . . . . Patti LaBelle |
| 83 | 26 | 21 | 13 | 4 | 28 | **Atomic Dog** . . . . . . . . . . . . . . . . . . . . . . . . . George Clinton |
| 84 | 20 | 17 | 12 | 4 | 29 | **She's Strange** . . . . . . . . . . . . . . . . . . . . . . . . . . . . Cameo |
| 81 | 31 | 21 | 11 | 4 | 30 | **Double Dutch Bus** . . . . . . . . . . . . . . . . . . . . Frankie Smith |
| 80 | 21 | 17 | 11 | 4 | 31 | **Funkin' For Jamaica (N.Y.)** . . . . . . . . . . . . . . . . . Tom Browne |
| 86 | 17 | 15 | 11 | 4 | 32 | **Kiss** . . . . . . . . . . . . . . . . . . . . . . . . . . . . . . . . . . Prince |
| 84 | 27 | 20 | 10 | 4 | 33 | **Caribbean Queen (No More Love On The Run)** . . . . . . Billy Ocean |
| 86 | 21 | 17 | 10 | 4 | 34 | **On My Own** . . . . . . . . . . . . Patti LaBelle & Michael McDonald |
| 82 | 20 | 16 | 10 | 4 | 35 | **Jump To It** . . . . . . . . . . . . . . . . . . . . . . . . Aretha Franklin |
| 80 | 19 | 15 | 10 | 4 | 36 | **Upside Down** . . . . . . . . . . . . . . . . . . . . . . . . . . Diana Ross |
| 85 | 22 | 16 | 9 | 4 | 37 | **Nightshift** . . . . . . . . . . . . . . . . . . . . . . . . . . Commodores |
| 86 | 20 | 15 | 9 | 4 | 38 | **Tasty Love** . . . . . . . . . . . . . . . . . . . . . . . . . Freddie Jackson |
| 80 | 17 | 15 | 9 | 4 | 39 | **Don't Say Goodnight (It's Time For Love) (Parts 1 & 2)** . . . . . . . The Isley Brothers |
| 82 | 20 | 15 | 8 | 4 | 40 | **And I Am Telling You I'm Not Going** . . . . . . . . Jennifer Holliday |

# RECORDS OF LONGEVITY

### Records with the most Total Weeks Charted

| RANK | PEAK YEAR | WKS. CHT. | TITLE....ARTIST |
|------|-----------|-----------|-----------------|
| 1. | 44 | 39 | **Cherry Red Blues** . . . . . . . . . . . . . . Cootie Williams |
| 2. | 83 | 38 | **Baby, Come To Me** . Patti Austin with James Ingram |
| 3. | 49 | 34 | **Ain't Nobody's Business, Parts I & II**  . . . . . . . Jimmy Witherspoon |
| 4. | 48 | 33 | **Tomorrow Night** . . . . . . . . . . . . . . Lonnie Johnson |
| 5. | 49 | 32 | **The Hucklebuck** . . . . . . . . . . . . . . . . . Paul Williams |
| 6. | 54 | 32 | **Shake, Rattle, And Roll** . . . . . . . . . . . . . . Joe Turner |
| 7. | 80 | 32 | **The Second Time Around** . . . . . . . . . . . . . Shalamar |
| 8. | 81 | 31 | **Double Dutch Bus** . . . . . . . . . . . . . . . Frankie Smith |
| 9. | 48 | 31 | **Long Gone, Pts. 1 & 2** . . . . . . . . . Sonny Thompson |
| 10. | 60 | 31 | **The Twist** . . . . . . . . . . . . . . . . . . . Chubby Checker |
| 11. | 51 | 30 | **Sixty-Minute Man** . . . . . . . . . . . . . . . The Dominoes |
| 12. | 55 | 30 | **Only You (And You Alone)** . . . . . . . . . . . The Platters |
| 13. | 43 | 29 | **Don't Cry, Baby**  . . . . . . . Erskine Hawkins & His Orchestra |
| 14. | 56 | 28 | **Honky Tonk (Parts 1 & 2)** . . . . . . . . . . . . Bill Doggett |
| 15. | 47 | 28 | **Snatch And Grab It** . . . . Julia Lee & Her Boyfriends |
| 16. | 48 | 28 | **King Size Papa** . . . . . . . Julia Lee & Her Boyfriends |
| 17. | 45 | 28 | **I Wonder** . . . . . . . . . . . . . . . . . . Private Cecil Gant |
| 18. | 85 | 28 | **You Give Good Love** . . . . . . . . . . . Whitney Houston |
| 19. | 43 | 28 | **Paper Doll** . . . . . . . . . . . . . . . . . . . Mills Brothers |
| 20. | 83 | 28 | **I Like It** . . . . . . . . . . . . . . . . . . . . . . . DeBarge |
| 21. | 79 | 28 | **Cruisin'** . . . . . . . . . . . . . . . . . . . Smokey Robinson |
| 22. | 87 | 28 | **As We Lay** . . . . . . . . . . . . . . . . . Shirley Murdock |
| 23. | 77 | 28 | **Good Thing Man** . . . . . . . . . . . . . . . . . Frank Lucas |
| 24. | 83 | 28 | **Electric Avenue** . . . . . . . . . . . . . . . . . Eddy Grant |
| 25. | 45 | 27 | **The Honeydripper**  . . . . . . . Joe Liggins & His Honeydrippers |
| 26. | 47 | 27 | **Ain't Nobody Here But Us Chickens** . Louis Jordan |
| 27. | 49 | 27 | **Trouble Blues** . . . . . . . . . . . . . . Charles Brown Trio |
| 28. | 82 | 27 | **Sexual Healing** . . . . . . . . . . . . . . . . . Marvin Gaye |
| 29. | 81 | 27 | **Don't Stop The Music** . . . . . . . Yarbrough & Peoples |
| 30. | 84 | 27 | **Caribbean Queen (No More Love On The Run)**  . . . . . . . Billy Ocean |
| 31. | 86 | 27 | **Shake You Down** . . . . . . . . . . . . . . . Gregory Abbott |
| 32. | 83 | 27 | **Ain't Nobody** . . . . . . . . . . . . . . Rufus & Chaka Khan |

"The Twist" is the only record listed above which charted more than once.

# TOP R&B LABELS

## Record Labels with the Most Charted R&B Hits

| RANK | CHART HITS | LABEL |
|---|---|---|
| 1. | 618 | **Atlantic** |
| 2. | 468 | **Columbia** |
| 3. | 438 | **Capitol** |
| 4. | 364 | **Mercury** |
| 5. | 350 | **Motown** |
| 6. | 346 | **Warner** |
| 7. | 328 | **RCA** |
| 8. | 259 | **MCA** |
| 9. | 236 | **Epic** |
| 10. | 229 | **Tamla** |
| 11. | 212 | **Arista** |
| 12. | 210 | **A&M** |
| 13. | 194 | **Gordy** |
| 14. | 168 | **Stax** |
| 15. | 162 | **Decca** |
| 16. | 156 | **King** |
| 17. | 149 | **ABC** |
| 18. | 146 | **Philadelphia International** |
| 19. | 136 | **Polydor** |
| 20. | 127 | **Elektra** |
| 21. | 120 | **Cotillion** |
| 22. | 113 | **Chess** |
| 23. | 104 | **Atco** |
| 24. | 103 | **Brunswick** |
| 25. | 98 | **Solar** |
| 26. | 96 | **United Artists** |
| 27. | 86 | **Spring** |
| 28. | 85 | **Imperial** |
| 29. | 83 | **Buddah** |
| 30. | 83 | **Casablanca** |
| 31. | 83 | **20th Century** |
| 32. | 75 | **Checker** |
| 33. | 75 | **Hi** |
| 34. | 73 | **Curtom** |
| 35. | 72 | **ABC-Paramount** |
| 36. | 72 | **Vee-Jay** |
| 37. | 70 | **Salsoul** |
| 38. | 66 | **Duke** |
| 39. | 65 | **Fantasy** |
| 40 | 65 | **MGM** |

# LABEL ABBREVIATIONS

ABC Impl. . . . . . . . . . . ABC Impulse
ABC-Para. . . . . . . . . ABC-Paramount
Abner/Fal. . . . . . . . . . Abner/Falcon
Alex St. . . . . . . . . . Alexander Street
Alpha Int. . . . . . . Alpha International
Ariola Am. . . . . . . . . . Ariola America
Art. Of Am. . . . . . . Artists Of America
Atl. Art. . . . . . . . . . . . Atlanta Artists
Audio Ar. . . . . . . . . . . . . Audio Arts
Aug. Snd. . . . . . . . . . Augusta Sound
Avco Embs. . . . . . . . . Avco Embassy
Bearsvil. . . . . . . . . . . . . . . Bearsville
Blk. & Wht. . . . . . . . . Black & White
Black F. . . . . . . . . . . . Black Fashion
Blue Cndl. . . . . . . . . . . Blue Candle
Cadet Con. . . . . . . . . Cadet Concept
Canadian A. . . . . Canadian American
Capitol A. . . . . . . . . Capitol America
Casabln. . . . . . . . . . . . . . Casablanca
CBS Assoc. . . . . . . . CBS Associated
Choc. City. . . . . . . . . Chocolate City
Cold Chill. . . . . . . . . . Cold Chillin'
Commod. . . . . . . . . . . . Commodore
Commonw. . . Commonwealth United
Constell. . . . . . . . . . . . Constellation
Creat. F. . . . . . . . . . . . Creative Funk
Cross Rds. . . . . . . . . . . Cross Roads
D.C. Int. . . . . . . . . D.C. International
Desert Mn. . . . . . . . . . . Desert Moon
Down To Ear. . . . . . . Down To Earth
Easy St. . . . . . . . . . . . . Easy Street
Ebony Snds. . . . . . . . Ebony Sounds
EMI Amer. . . . . . . . . . EMI America
EMI-Man. . . . . . . . . EMI-Manhattan
Egypt E. . . . . . . . . Egyptian Empire
Fant./Honey . . . . . . . Fantasy/Honey
Fant./WMOT . . . . . . . Fantasy/WMOT
1st American . . . . . . First American
1st String . . . . . . . . . . . First String
Fly. Dut. . . . . . . . . . Flying Dutchman
Fut. Stars . . . . . . . . . . . Future Stars
Gamble & H. . . . . . . Gamble & Huff
Golden Fl. . . . . . . . . . Golden Fleece
Gospel T. . . . . . . . . . . . Gospel Truth
Gram-O. . . . . . . . . . . . Gram-O-Phon
Grapevine . . . . . . . GWP's Grapevine
Green Mt. . . . . . . . . Green Mountain
Green St. . . . . . . . . . . . Green Street
Groove M. . . . . . . . . Groove Merchant
Heart & So. . . . . . . . . Heart & Soul
Hob/Scep. . . . . . . . . . . . Hob/Scepter
Hot Bt. So. . . . . . . . Hot Buttered Soul

House Of O. . . . . . . . House Of Orange
Int. Bros. . . . . . International Brothers
Jam Pack. . . . . . . . . . . . Jam Packed
Just Sunsh. . . . . . . . . Just Sunshine
Little C. . . . . . . . . . . . . . Little City
Long Dist. . . . . . . . . . . Long Distance
Luke Sky. . . . . . . . Luke Skyywalker
Master 5 . . . . . . . . . . . . Master Five
Midland . . . . . Midland International
Midsong . . . . Midsong International
Modern . . . . . . . . . . . . Modern Music
Move'n N G. . . . . . Move'n N Groov'n
Mr. Chand . . . . . . . . . Mister Chand
Muscle Sh. . . . . . . . . Muscle Shoals
Music Mac. . . . . . . . . Music Machine
Music Mer. . . . . . . . Music Merchant
Mus./Prv. . . . . . . . . Musicor/Privilege
National G. . . . . . . National General
Next Plat. . . . . . . . . . . Next Plateau
9 Chains . . . . . . . . . . . Nine Chains
Ocean Fr. . . . . . . . . . . Ocean Front
Orig. Sound . . . . . . . . Original Sound
Paisley P. . . . . . . . . . . . Paisley Park
Phil. Int. . . Philadelphia International
Philly W. . . . . . . . . . . . . Philly World
Pretty P. . . . . . . . . . . . . Pretty Pearl
Prom./MCA . . . . . . . . Promise/MCA
Rainy Wed. . . . . . . Rainy Wednesday
Rock 'n' R. . . . . . . . . . Rock 'n' Roll
Rolling S. . . . . . . . . . Rolling Stones
Scotti Br. . . . . . . . . . Scotti Brothers
Seventy 7 . . . . . . . . . Seventy Seven
Sittin' in . . . . . . . . . . Sittin' in with
Sleep B. . . . . . . . . . . . Sleeping Bag
Snd. Flor. . . . . . . . . Sounds of Florida
Snd. of NY . . . . . . . . . . Sound of NY
Snd. St. 7 . . . . . . . . . Sound Stage 7
Snds. of M. . . . . . Sounds of Memphis
SSS Int'l. . . . . . . . . SSS International
Sunshine S. . . . . . . . Sunshine Sound
Tetragamm. . . . . . . . Tetragrammaton
Total Exp. . . . . . . . . Total Experience
Tux. Music . . . . . . . . . Tuxedo Music
20th Cen. . . . . . . . . . . 20th Century
United Art. . . . . . . . . . United Artists
Unlim. G. . . . . . . . . . . Unlimited Gold
USA Car. . . . . . . . . . . . USA Carrere
Vintertn. . . . . . . . . . . Vintertainment
Warner/Spc. . . . . . . . Warner/Spector
Wondirect. . . . . . . . . . . Wondirection
World P.J. . . . . . . . World Pacific Jazz
World T. . . . . . . . . . . . . World Trade

From October 24, 1942 through July 2, 1988, 805 records have hit the #1 position on Billboard's R&B charts. Of those 805 records, 167 have crossed over and also hit #1 on Billboard's pop charts.

For the years 1948 through 1958, when Billboard published more than one weekly R&B chart, special columns are used to list the total weeks each record spent at #1 on each of these R&B charts.

The date shown is the earliest date that a record hit #1 on any of the R&B charts. The weeks column lists the total weeks at #1, from whichever chart it achieved its highest total. This total is not a combined total from the various R&B charts.

Because of the multiple charts used in this research, some dates are duplicated, as certain #1 hits may have peaked on the same week on different charts. Billboard also showed ties at #1 on some of these charts, therefore the total weeks for each year may calculate out to more than 52.

Beginning in 1976, Billboard ceased publishing a year-end issue. The year's last regular issue is considered frozen and all chart positions remain the same for the unpublished week. This frozen chart data is included in our tabulations.

See the introduction pages of this book for more details on researching the R&B charts.

DATE: Date record first peaked at the #1 position.

WKS: Total weeks record held the #1 position.

  ★: Hit #1 on Billboard's pop charts.

  *: Indicates record hit #1, dropped down, then returned to the #1 spot.

CHARTS COLUMN:
BS — Best Sellers
JB — Juke Box
JY — Jockeys

| DATE | WKS | RECORD TITLE......ARTIST |
|------|-----|-------------------------|
| | | **1942** |
| 10/24 | 1 | 1. Take It And Git .......................................... Andy Kirk |
| 10/31 | 2* | 2. Mr. Five By Five ............................ Freddie Slack/Ella Mae Morse |
| 11/07 | 3* | 3. Trav'lin' Light ........................... Paul Whiteman/Billie Holiday |
| 11/14 | 1 | 4. Stormy Monday Blues....................... Earl Hines/Billy Eckstine |
| 11/28 | 2* | 5. When The Lights Go On Again (All Over The World) .......... Lucky Millinder |
| 12/19 | 3 | ★ 6. White Christmas ...................................... Bing Crosby |
| | | **1943** |
| 1/16 | 4* | 1. See See Rider Blues....................................... Bea Booze |
| 1/23 | 1 | 2. What's The Use Of Getting Sober .......................... Louis Jordan |
| 1/30 | 1 | 3. That Ain't Right ....................................... King Cole Trio |
| 2/13 | 2 | 4. Apollo Jump ........................................ Lucky Millinder |
| 3/06 | 5* | 5. Don't Stop Now ...................................... Bunny Banks Trio |
| 3/27 | 2* | 6. Don't Get Around Much Anymore ........................... Ink Spots |
| 4/17 | 1 | 7. I've Heard That Song Before ................... Harry James/Helen Forrest |
| 4/24 | 7* | 8. I Can't Stand Losing You ,................................. Ink Spots |
| 5/29 | 3* | 9. Don't Get Around Much Anymore ....................... Duke Ellington |
| 7/17 | 4 | ★10. You'll Never Know .................................... Dick Haymes |
| 8/14 | 14* | 11. Don't Cry, Baby ..................................... Erskine Hawkins |
| 9/25 | 1 | 12. A Slip Of The Lip .................................... Duke Ellington |
| 10/02 | 1 | 13. Sentimental Lady .................................... Duke Ellington |
| 11/20 | 2* | 14. All For You...................................... King Cole Trio |
| 12/18 | 2* | 15. Shoo Shoo Baby ...................................... Ella Mae Morse |
| 12/25 | 1 | 16. Sweet Slumber ..................................... Lucky Millinder |
| | | **1944** |
| 1/01 | 1 | 1. Ration Blues....................................... Louis Jordan |
| 1/15 | 8* | 2. Do Nothin' Till You Hear From Me ...................... Duke Ellington |
| 1/22 | 1 | 3. G.I. Jive............................................ Johnny Mercer |
| 3/11 | 1 | 4. Solo Flight......................................... Benny Goodman |

| DATE | WKS | RECORD TITLE . . . . . . ARTIST | | |
|------|-----|---------------------------------|---|---|
| | | **1944** *(Continued)* | | |
| 3/25 | 1 | 5. Cow-Cow Boogie . . . . . . . . . . . . . . . . . . . . . . . Ella Fitzgerald & Ink Spots | | |
| 4/01 | 4* | 6. Main Stem . . . . . . . . . . . . . . . . . . . . . . . . . . . . . . . . . . Duke Ellington | | |
| 4/15 | 1 | 7. When My Man Comes Home . . . . . . . . . . . . . . . . . . . . . . Buddy Johnson | | |
| 4/29 | 10* | 8. Straighten Up And Fly Right . . . . . . . . . . . . . . . . King Cole Trio | | |
| 7/15 | 6* | ★ 9. G.I. Jive . . . . . . . . . . . . . . . . . . . . . . . . . . . . . . . . . . . . Louis Jordan | | |
| 8/19 | 1 | 10. Till Then . . . . . . . . . . . . . . . . . . . . . . . . . . . . . . . . . . Mills Brothers | | |
| 9/02 | 6* | 11. Hamp's Boogie Woogie . . . . . . . . . . . . . . . . . . . . . Lionel Hampton | | |
| 9/30 | 2* | 12. I'm Lost . . . . . . . . . . . . . . . . . . . . . . . . . . . . . . . . . . . . Benny Carter | | |
| 10/21 | 4 | 13. Gee, Baby, Ain't I Good To You? . . . . . . . . . . . . . . . King Cole Trio | | |
| 11/18 | 11* | ★14. Into Each Life Some Rain Must Fall . . . . . . . . . . Ella Fitzgerald & Ink Spots | | |
| | | **1945** | | |
| 2/10 | 1 | 1. Somebody's Got To Go . . . . . . . . . . . . . . . . . . . Cootie Williams/Eddie Vinson | | |
| 2/17 | 2 | 2. I Wonder . . . . . . . . . . . . . . . . . . . . . . . . . . . . . . . . . . Private Cecil Gant | | |
| 2/24 | 7 | 3. I Wonder . . . . . . . . . . . . . . . . . . . . . . . . . . . . . . . . . . Roosevelt Sykes | | |
| 4/14 | 6* | 4. Tippin' In . . . . . . . . . . . . . . . . . . . . . . . . . . . . . . . . . Erskine Hawkins | | |
| 4/21 | 1 | 5. Mop Mop . . . . . . . . . . . . . . . . . . . . . . . . . . . . . . . . . . . . Louis Jordan | | |
| 6/02 | 7 | 6. Caldonia . . . . . . . . . . . . . . . . . . . . . . . . . . . . . . . . . . . . Louis Jordan | | |
| 7/14 | 8 | 7. Who Threw The Whiskey In The Well? . . . . . Lucky Millinder/Wynonie Harris | | |
| 9/08 | 18 | 8. The Honeydripper . . . . . . . . . . . . . . . . . . . Joe Liggins & His Honeydrippers | | |
| | | **1946** | | |
| 1/12 | 9 | 1. Buzz Me . . . . . . . . . . . . . . . . . . . . . . . . . . . . . . . . . . . . . Louis Jordan | | |
| 3/16 | 16* | 2. Hey! Ba-Ba-Re-Bop . . . . . . . . . . . . . . . . . Lionel Hampton/Dinah Washington | | |
| 3/23 | 1 | 3. Don't Worry 'Bout That Mule . . . . . . . . . . . . . . . . . . Louis Jordan | | |
| 6/29 | 3* | ★ 4. The Gypsy . . . . . . . . . . . . . . . . . . . . . . . . . . . . . . . . . . . . . Ink Spots | | |
| 7/20 | 5 | 5. Stone Cold Dead In The Market (He Had It Coming) <br> . . . . . . . Ella Fitzgerald & Louis Jordan | | |
| 8/24 | 18* | 6. Choo Choo Ch'Boogie . . . . . . . . . . . . . . . . . . . . . . . . . Louis Jordan | | |
| 11/23 | 2* | 7. Ain't That Just Like A Woman . . . . . . . . . . . . . . . . . . . . . Louis Jordan | | |
| | | **1947** | | |
| 1/04 | 17* | 1. Ain't Nobody Here But Us Chickens . . . . . . . . . . . . . . . . . Louis Jordan | | |
| 4/26 | 2* | 2. Texas And Pacific . . . . . . . . . . . . . . . . . . . . . . . . . . . . . . Louis Jordan | | |
| 5/17 | 8* | 3. I Want To Be Loved (But Only By You) . . . . . . . . . . . . . Savannah Churchill | | |
| 5/24 | 2* | 4. Ole Maid Boogie . . . . . . . . . . . . . . . . . . . . . . . . . . . . . . . Eddie Vinson | | |
| 6/28 | 7* | 5. Jack, You're Dead . . . . . . . . . . . . . . . . . . . . . . . . . . . . . Louis Jordan | | |
| 8/30 | 14* | 6. Boogie Woogie Blue Plate . . . . . . . . . . . . . . . . . . . . . . Louis Jordan | | |
| 11/22 | 12* | 7. Snatch And Grab It . . . . . . . . . . . . . . . . . . . . Julia Lee & Her Boyfriends | | |

| | | **1948** | **CHARTS** | |
|------|-----|-----------|----|----|
| | | | BS | JB |
| 2/21 | 3 | 1. I Love You, Yes I Do . . . . . . . . . . . . . . . . . . Bull Moose Jackson | — | 3* |
| 3/20 | 9 | 2. King Size Papa . . . . . . . . . . . . . . . Julia Lee & Her Boyfriends | — | 9 |
| 5/22 | 7 | 3. Tomorrow Night . . . . . . . . . . . . . . . . . . . . . . Lonnie Johnson | 7* | 7* |
| | | *Billboard debuts R&B "Best Seller" chart on 5/22/48* | | |
| 6/19 | 1 | 4. Good Rockin' Tonight . . . . . . . . . . . . . . . . Wynonie Harris | 1 | 1 |
| 7/10 | 3 | 5. Long Gone, Pts. 1 & 2 . . . . . . . . . . . . . Sonny Thompson | 3* | 2* |
| 7/10 | 2 | 6. Run, Joe . . . . . . . . . . . . . . . . . . . . . . . . . . . . . . . Louis Jordan | — | 2* |
| 7/24 | 8 | 7. I Can't Go On Without You . . . . . . . . . Bull Moose Jackson | 8 | 4* |
| 9/04 | 2 | 8. Messin' Around . . . . . . . . . . . . . . . . . . . . . . . Memphis Slim | — | 2* |
| 9/11 | 1 | 9. My Heart Belongs To You . . . . . . . . . . . . . . . Arbee Stidham | 1 | 1 |

| DATE | WKS | RECORD TITLE . . . . . . . ARTIST | CHARTS | |
|---|---|---|---|---|
| | | **1948** *(Continued)* | **BS** | **JB** |
| 9/18 | 3 | 10. Pretty Mama Blues . . . . . . . . . . . . . . . . . . . . Ivory Joe Hunter | 3 | 3* |
| 10/02 | 4 | 11. Corn Bread . . . . . . . . . . . . . . . . . . . . . . . . . . . . . . . Hal Singer | 4* | 4* |
| 10/02 | 1 | 12. Late Freight . . . . . . . . . . . . . . . . . . . . . . . . Sonny Thompson | 1 | 1 |
| 10/09 | 1 | 13. Am I Asking Too Much . . . . . . . . . . . . . . . Dinah Washington | — | 1 |
| 11/06 | 3 | 14. Blues After Hours . . . . . . . . . . . . . . . . . . . . . Pee Wee Crayton | 1 | 3* |
| 11/27 | 1 | 15. It's Too Soon To Know . . . . . . . . . . . . . . . . . . . . . The Orioles | — | 1 |
| 12/04 | 5 | 16. Chicken Shack Boogie . . . . . . . . . . . . . . . . . . . Amos Milburn | 4* | 5* |
| 12/04 | 5 | 17. Bewildered . . . . . . . . . . . . . . . . . . . . . . . . . . . Red Miller Trio | 4* | 5* |
| 12/18 | 1 | 18. 'Long About Midnight . . . . . . . . . . . . . . . . . . . . . . Roy Brown | 1 | — |
| 12/25 | 3 | 19. Bewildered . . . . . . . . . . . . . . . . . . . . . . . . . . . . Amos Milburn | 3* | 2* |
| | | **1949** | | |
| 2/19 | 1 | 1. Boogie Chillen' . . . . . . . . . . . . . . . . . . . . . . John Lee Hooker | — | 1 |
| 2/19 | 1 | 2. Deacon's Hop . . . . . . . . . . . . . . . . . . . Big Jay McNeely & Band | 1 | 1 |
| 3/05 | 14 | 3. The Hucklebuck . . . . . . . . . . . . . . . . . . . . . . Paul Williams | 12* | 14* |
| 6/04 | 15 | 4. Trouble Blues . . . . . . . . . . . . . . . . . . . . . . Charles Brown Trio | 15 | 11* |
| 8/20 | 1 | 5. Ain't Nobody's Business, Parts I & II . . . . . Jimmy Witherspoon | 1 | — |
| 9/10 | 2 | 6. Roomin' House Boogie . . . . . . . . . . . . . . . . . . . Amos Milburn | — | 2 |
| 9/17 | 2 | 7. All She Wants To Do Is Rock . . . . . . . . . . . . . . Wynonie Harris | 1 | 2* |
| 9/17 | 1 | 8. Tell Me So . . . . . . . . . . . . . . . . . . . . . . . . . . . . . The Orioles | 1 | — |
| 9/24 | 2 | 9. Baby, Get Lost . . . . . . . . . . . . . . . . . . . . . . Dinah Washington | 2* | 1 |
| 10/08 | 1 | 10. Beans And Corn Bread . . . . . . . . . . . . . . . . . . . Louis Jordan | — | 1 |
| 10/15 | 12 | 11. Saturday Night Fish Fry . . . . . . . . . . . . . . . . Louis Jordan | 12* | 11* |
| 12/24 | 8 | 12. For You, My Love . . . . . . . . . . . . . . . . . . . . . . Larry Darnell | 6* | 8* |
| | | **1950** | | |
| 2/18 | 5 | 1. I Almost Lost My Mind . . . . . . . . . . . . . . . . . Ivory Joe Hunter | 2 | 5* |
| 3/04 | 9 | 2. Double Crossing Blues . . . . Little Esther/Johnny Otis Orchestra | 9 | 5* |
| 4/15 | 4 | 3. Mistrustin' Blues . . . . . . . . . . . . . . . . . Johnny Otis Orchestra | 4 | 4* |
| 5/13 | 2 | 4. I Need You So . . . . . . . . . . . . . . . . . . . . . . . . Ivory Joe Hunter | — | 2 |
| 5/27 | 13 | 5. Pink Champagne . . . . . . . . . . . . . . . . . . . . . . . . Joe Liggins | 11 | 13* |
| 7/08 | 1 | 6. Cupid's Boogie . . . . . . . . . Little Esther/Johnny Otis Orchestra | — | 1 |
| 8/19 | 3 | 7. Hard Luck Blues . . . . . . . . . . . . . . . . . . . . . . . . . . Roy Brown | 3 | — |
| 9/02 | 4 | ★ 8. Mona Lisa . . . . . . . . . . . . . . . . . . . . . . . . . . . Nat King Cole | — | 4 |
| 9/09 | 7 | 9. Blue Light Boogie - Parts 1 & 2 . . . . . . . . . . . . . . Louis Jordan | 7 | 4 |
| 10/28 | 4 | 10. Blue Shadows . . . . . . . . . . . . . . . . . . . . . . . Lowell Fulson | 1 | 4 |
| 11/04 | 4 | 11. Anytime, Any Place, Anywhere . . . . . . . . . . . . . . . Joe Morris | 4* | 3 |
| 11/25 | 2 | 12. Please Send Me Someone To Love . . . . . . . . . . . Percy Mayfield | 2* | 1 |
| 12/09 | 11 | 13. Teardrops From My Eyes . . . . . . . . . . . . . . . . . . . Ruth Brown | 11* | 7* |
| | | **1951** | | |
| 1/06 | 3 | 1. Bad, Bad Whiskey . . . . . . . . . . . . . . . . . . . . . . Amos Milburn | 1 | 3* |
| 3/03 | 14 | 2. Black Night . . . . . . . . . . . . . . . . . . . . . . . . . Charles Brown | 13 | 14 |
| 6/09 | 5 | 3. Rocket '88' . . . . . . . . . . . . . . . . . . . . . . . . . . . Jackie Brenston | 3 | 5 |
| 6/09 | 2 | 4. Chica Boo . . . . . . . . . . . . . . . . . . . . . . Lloyd Glenn's Combo | — | 2 |
| 6/30 | 14 | 5. Sixty-Minute Man . . . . . . . . . . . . . . . . . . . . The Dominoes | 14* | 12 |
| 9/01 | 2 | 6. Don't You Know I Love You . . . . . . . . . . . . . . . The Clovers | 2 | — |
| 9/22 | 4 | 7. The Glory Of Love . . . . . . . . . . . . . . . . . . . . . . The Five Keys | 4* | 2 |
| 11/03 | 1 | 8. "T" 99 Blues . . . . . . . . . . . . . . . . . . . . . . . . . Jimmy Nelson | — | 1 |

| DATE | WKS | RECORD TITLE . . . . . . ARTIST | CHARTS | |
|------|-----|--------------------------------|--------|---|
| | | **1951** *(Continued)* | BS | JB |
| 11/10 | 6 | 9. Fool, Fool, Fool . . . . . . . . . . . . . . . . . . . . . . The Clovers | 6* | 3 |
| 11/10 | 2 | 10. I Got Loaded . . . . . . . . . . . . . . . . . . Peppermint Harris | 1 | 2* |
| 11/17 | 4 | 11. I'm In The Mood . . . . . . . . . . . . . . . . . . . John Lee Hooker | — | 4* |
| 12/08 | 2 | 12. Because Of You . . . . . . . . . . . . . . . . . . . . . . Tab Smith | 2 | — |
| 12/29 | 4 | 13. Flamingo . . . . . . . . . . . . . . . . . . . . . . . . . . Earl Bostic | 4* | — |
| | | **1952** | | |
| 1/12 | 3 | 1. Weepin' And Cryin' . . . . . . . . . . . . . . . . . . . Griffin Brothers | — | 3 |
| 1/12 | 1 | ★ 2. Cry . . . . . . . . . . . . . . . . . . . . . . . . . . . . Johnnie Ray | 1 | 1 |
| 2/02 | 5 | 3. Three O'Clock Blues . . . . . . . . . . . . . . . . . . . B.B. King | 5 | 5* |
| 3/15 | 7 | 4. Night Train . . . . . . . . . . . . . . . . . . . . . Jimmy Forrest | 6 | 7 |
| 3/15 | 1 | 5. Booted . . . . . . . . . . . . . . . . . . . . . . . . . Roscoe Gordon | 1 | — |
| 5/03 | 7 | 6. 5-10-15 Hours . . . . . . . . . . . . . . . . . . . . . Ruth Brown | 7 | 6 |
| 6/14 | 10 | 7. Have Mercy Baby . . . . . . . . . . . . . . . . . . . The Dominoes | 7* | 10* |
| 6/21 | 1 | 8. Goin' Home . . . . . . . . . . . . . . . . . . . . . . . Fats Domino | 1 | — |
| 7/12 | 7 | 9. Lawdy Miss Clawdy . . . . . . . . . . . . . . . . . . Lloyd Price | 7* | 1 |
| 8/23 | 3 | 10. Mary Jo . . . . . . . . . . . . . . . . . . . . . . . . . Four Blazes | — | 3* |
| 9/06 | 1 | 11. Ting-A-Ling . . . . . . . . . . . . . . . . . . . . . . The Clovers | 1 | 1 |
| 9/27 | 9 | 12. My Song . . . . . . . . . . . . . . . . . . . . . . . . . Johnny Ace | 9 | — |
| 9/27 | 8 | 13. Juke . . . . . . . . . . . . . . . . . . . . . . . . . . Little Walter | 1 | 8* |
| 11/08 | 7 | 14. Five Long Years . . . . . . . . . . . . . . . . . . . . Eddie Boyd | 2 | 7* |
| 11/08 | 2 | 15. You Know I Love You . . . . . . . . . . . . . . . . . . . B.B. King | 2* | — |
| 12/27 | 8 | 16. I Don't Know . . . . . . . . . . . . . . . . . . . . . Willie Mabon | 8 | 7 |
| | | **1953** | | |
| 2/21 | 3 | 1. Baby, Don't Do It . . . . . . . . . . . . . . . . The "5" Royales | 3* | 3 |
| 3/07 | 5 | 2. (Mama) He Treats Your Daughter Mean . . . . . . . . . Ruth Brown | 5* | 5 |
| 4/18 | 7 | 3. Hound Dog . . . . . . . . . . . . . . Willie Mae 'Big Mama' Thornton | 6 | 7 |
| 5/30 | 2 | 4. I'm Mad . . . . . . . . . . . . . . . . . . . . . . . Willie Mabon | 2 | — |
| 6/13 | 5 | 5. Help Me Somebody . . . . . . . . . . . . . . . . . The "5" Royales | 5* | 5* |
| 7/04 | 3 | 6. Please Love Me . . . . . . . . . . . . . . . . . . . . . . B.B. King | — | 3* |
| 7/18 | 5 | 7. The Clock . . . . . . . . . . . . . . . . . . . . . . . . Johnny Ace | 5* | 4 |
| 8/22 | 5 | 8. Crying In The Chapel . . . . . . . . . . . . . . . . . . The Orioles | 4 | 5* |
| 9/19 | 10 | 9. Shake A Hand . . . . . . . . . . . . . . . . . . . . . . Faye Adams | 9 | 10* |
| 11/21 | 11 | 10. Money Honey . . . . . . . . . . . . Clyde McPhatter & The Drifters | 11 | 1 |
| 12/05 | 8 | 11. Honey Hush . . . . . . . . . . . . . . . . . . . . . . . Joe Turner | — | 8 |
| | | **1954** | BS | JB | JY |
| 1/30 | 14 | 1. Things That I Used To Do . . . . . . . . . . . . . . . Guitar Slim | 6 | 14 | — |
| 2/06 | 1 | 2. I'll Be True . . . . . . . . . . . . . . . . . . . . . . . Faye Adams | 1 | — | — |
| 3/27 | 8 | 3. You'll Never Walk Alone . . . . . . . . . . . . . Roy Hamilton | 8 | 5 | — |
| 5/22 | 7 | 4. Work With Me Annie . . . . . . . . . . . . . . . The Midnighters | 7 | 4 | — |
| 6/12 | 3 | 5. Shake, Rattle, And Roll . . . . . . . . . . . . . . . Joe Turner | — | 3 | — |
| 7/10 | 8 | 6. Honey Love . . . . . . . . Drifters featuring Clyde McPhatter | 8 | 8 | — |
| 9/04 | 8 | 7. Oh What A Dream . . . . . . . . . . . . . . . . . . . Ruth Brown | 4* | 8 | — |
| 9/25 | 2 | 8. Annie Had A Baby . . . . . . . . . . . . . . . . The Midnighters | 2 | — | — |
| 10/16 | 5 | 9. Hurts Me To My Heart . . . . . . . . . . . . . . . . Faye Adams | 5 | 5 | — |
| 11/20 | 1 | 10. Mambo Baby . . . . . . . . . . . . . . . . . . . . . Ruth Brown | 1 | 1 | — |
| 11/27 | 9 | 11. Hearts Of Stone . . . . . . . . . . . . . . . . . . . The Charms | 9 | 2 | 2 |
| 12/25 | 2 | 12. You Upset Me Baby . . . . . . . . . . . . . . . . . . . B.B. King | — | 2 | — |

| DATE | WKS | RECORD TITLE . . . . . . ARTIST | CHARTS | | |
|---|---|---|---|---|---|
| | | | BS | JB | JY |
| | | **1955** | | | |
| 1/15 | 3 | 1. Earth Angel (Will You Be Mine) . . . . . . . . The Penguins | 3 | 3* | 1 |
| 1/22 | 2 | 2. Sincerely . . . . . . . . . . . . . . . . . . . . The Moonglows | — | 2* | 1 |
| | | Billboard debuts R&B "Jockey" chart on 1/22/55 | | | |
| 2/12 | 10 | 3. Pledging My Love . . . . . . . . . . . . . . . . . . . . Johnny Ace | 9 | 9* | 10* |
| 4/09 | 4 | 4. The Wallflower . . . . . . . . . . . . . . . . . . . . . . Etta James | — | — | 4* |
| 4/23 | 5 | 5. My Babe . . . . . . . . . . . . . . . . . . . . . Little Walter | 4 | 5* | 2* |
| 5/07 | 1 | 6. I've Got A Woman . . . . . . . . . . . . . . . . Ray Charles | — | 1 | — |
| 5/21 | 3 | 7. Unchained Melody . . . . . . . . . . . . . . . Roy Hamilton | 3 | — | — |
| 6/11 | 11 | 8. Ain't That A Shame . . . . . . . . . . . . . Fats Domino | 11 | 8* | 10* |
| 6/18 | 1 | 9. Unchained Melody . . . . . . . . . . . . . . . . . Al Hibbler | — | 1 | — |
| 6/25 | 2 | 10. Bo Diddley . . . . . . . . . . . . . . . . . . . . . . Bo Diddley | — | 2* | — |
| 8/06 | 1 | 11. A Fool For You . . . . . . . . . . . . . . . . . . Ray Charles | — | — | 1 |
| 8/20 | 11 | 12. Maybellene . . . . . . . . . . . . . . . . . . . . Chuck Berry | 9 | 11 | 9 |
| 10/22 | 7 | 13. Only You (And You Alone) . . . . . . . . . The Platters | 7 | 6 | 5* |
| 10/29 | 3 | 14. All By Myself . . . . . . . . . . . . . . . . . . Fats Domino | — | — | 3 |
| 12/17 | 3 | 15. Hands Off . . . . . . . . . . . . . . . . . . . . . . Jay McShann | 3 | 2 | 2 |
| 12/31 | 1 | 16. Poor Me . . . . . . . . . . . . . . . . . . . . . . Fats Domino | — | — | 1 |
| 12/31 | 1 | 17. Adorable . . . . . . . . . . . . . . . . . . . . . . The Drifters | — | 1 | — |
| | | **1956** | | | |
| 1/07 | 11 | ★ 1. The Great Pretender . . . . . . . . . . . . . . . . . The Platters | 10 | 9 | 11 |
| 1/07 | 1 | 2. At My Front Door . . . . . . . . . . . . . . . . The El Dorados | — | 1 | — |
| 3/17 | 5 | 3. Why Do Fools Fall In Love | | | |
| | | . . . . . . The Teenagers featuring Frankie Lymon | 5 | — | 2 |
| 3/24 | 2 | 4. Drown In My Own Tears . . . . . . . . . . . . Ray Charles | — | 2 | 1 |
| 4/14 | 8 | 5. Long Tall Sally . . . . . . . . . . . . . . . . . Little Richard | 6 | 8 | 5 |
| 5/19 | 9 | 6. I'm In Love Again . . . . . . . . . . . . . . . . Fats Domino | 7 | 9* | 9 |
| 7/21 | 5 | 7. Fever . . . . . . . . . . . . . . . . . . . . Little Willie John | 3* | 1 | 5 |
| 7/28 | 1 | 8. Treasure Of Love . . . . . . . . . . . . . . . . . . Clyde McPhatter | — | 1 | — |
| 8/04 | 2 | 9. Rip It Up . . . . . . . . . . . . . . . . . . . . . . Little Richard | 2 | 1 | — |
| 8/18 | 2 | ★10. My Prayer . . . . . . . . . . . . . . . . . . . . . . The Platters | — | 2 | 2* |
| 8/25 | 13 | 11. Honky Tonk (Parts 1 & 2) . . . . . . . . . . . . . Bill Doggett | 13* | 1 | 5 |
| 9/01 | 3 | 13. Let The Good Times Roll . . . . . . . . . . . . Shirley & Lee | — | 3* | 3* |
| 9/15 | 6 | ★12. Hound Dog . . . . . . . . . . . . . . . . . . . . Elvis Presley | — | 6* | — |
| 10/27 | 1 | ★14. Don't Be Cruel . . . . . . . . . . . . . . . . . . . Elvis Presley | 1 | — | — |
| 11/03 | 11 | 15. Blueberry Hill . . . . . . . . . . . . . . . . . . . . Fats Domino | 8* | 8* | 11* |
| | | **1957** | | | |
| 1/05 | 3 | 1. Since I Met You Baby . . . . . . . . . . . . . Ivory Joe Hunter | — | 3 | 1 |
| 1/26 | 8 | 2. Blue Monday . . . . . . . . . . . . . . . . . . . . Fats Domino | 8 | 8* | 7 |
| 3/09 | 1 | 3. Jim Dandy . . . . . . . . . . . . . . LaVern Baker & The Gliders | — | — | 1 |
| 3/16 | 2 | 4. Love Is Strange . . . . . . . . . . . . . . . Mickey & Sylvia | — | — | 2 |
| 3/23 | 6 | 5. I'm Walkin' . . . . . . . . . . . . . . . . . . . . Fats Domino | 6 | 5 | 5 |
| 4/27 | 2 | 6. Lucille . . . . . . . . . . . . . . . . . . . . . . Little Richard | — | 2 | — |
| 4/29 | 5 | 7. School Day . . . . . . . . . . . . . . . . . . . . . Chuck Berry | 1 | 1 | 5* |
| 4/29 | 4 | ★ 8. All Shook Up . . . . . . . . . . . . . . . . . . . Elvis Presley | 4 | 4* | 2* |
| 6/03 | 13 | 9. Searchin' . . . . . . . . . . . . . . . . . . . . . The Coasters | 13 | 2 | 7* |
| 6/17 | 2 | 10. C.C. Rider . . . . . . . . . . . . . . . . . . . . Chuck Willis | — | — | 2* |
| | | Billboard terminates "Juke Box" chart on 6/24/57 | | | |
| 7/29 | 1 | 11. Short Fat Fannie . . . . . . . . . . . . . . . . Larry Williams | — | — | 1 |
| 8/19 | 2 | 12. Send For Me . . . . . . . . . . . . . . . . . Nat King Cole | — | — | 2 |
| 9/02 | 2 | 13. Farther Up The Road . . . . . . . . . . . . . Bobby Bland | — | — | 2* |

| DATE | WKS | RECORD TITLE......ARTIST | CHARTS | | |
|---|---|---|---|---|---|
| | | 1957 *(Continued)* | BS | JB | JY |
| 9/02 | 1 | ★14. (Let Me Be Your) Teddy Bear ............Elvis Presley | 1 | — | — |
| 9/09 | 2 | 15. Whole Lotta Shakin' Going On .......Jerry Lee Lewis | 2 | — | 1 |
| 9/16 | 1 | 16. Long Lonely Nights ................Clyde McPhatter | — | — | 1 |
| 9/23 | 2 | ★17. Diana ..........................Paul Anka | 2 | — | — |
| 9/30 | 4 | 18. Mr. Lee ........................The Bobbettes | — | — | 4* |
| 10/07 | 2 | ★19. Honeycomb ....................Jimmie Rodgers | 2 | — | 1 |
| 10/14 | 1 | ★20. Wake Up Little Susie ...........The Everly Brothers | — | — | 1 |
| 10/21 | 5 | ★21. Jailhouse Rock ..................Elvis Presley | 5 | — | 3 |
| 11/25 | 6 | ★22. You Send Me ......................Sam Cooke | 6 | — | 6 |
| | | 1958 | | | |
| 1/06 | 5 | ★ 1. At The Hop ..................Danny & The Juniors | 5 | — | — |
| 1/06 | 2 | 2. Raunchy ......................Ernie Freeman | — | — | 2 |
| 1/20 | 1 | 3. Raunchy ........................Bill Justis | — | — | 1 |
| 1/27 | 1 | 4. I'll Come Running Back To You............Sam Cookc | — | — | 1 |
| 2/03 | 6 | ★ 5. Get A Job ....................The Silhouettes | 4 | — | 6 |
| 3/10 | 3 | 6. Sweet Little Sixteen..................Chuck Berry | 3 | — | 3 |
| 3/31 | 4 | ★ 7. Tequila ........................The Champs | 4 | — | 4 |
| 4/28 | 3 | ★ 8. Twilight Time ....................The Platters | 3 | — | — |
| 5/05 | 3 | 9. Wear My Ring Around Your Neck ........Elvis Presley | — | — | 3 |
| 5/19 | 5 | ★10. All I Have To Do Is Dream ........The Everly Brothers | 5 | — | 3 |
| 5/26 | 1 | ★11. Witch Doctor ....................David Seville | — | — | 1 |
| 6/23 | 7 | ★12. Yakety Yak ......................The Coasters | 7 | — | 6* |
| 6/23 | 1 | 13. What Am I Living For ................Chuck Willis | — | — | 1 |
| 8/04 | 2 | 14. Splish Splash ....................Bobby Darin | — | — | 2 |
| 8/11 | 2 | ★15. Patricia........................Perez Prado | 2 | — | 1 |
| 8/25 | 1 | 16. Just A Dream ..................Jimmy Clanton | 1 | — | — |
| 9/01 | 4 | ★17. Little Star......................The Elegants | 4 | — | 4 |
| 9/01 | 1 | 18. When .........................Kalin Twins | — | — | 1 |
| 9/29 | 3 | ★19. It's All In The Game .............Tommy Edwards | 3 | — | — |
| 10/06 | 3 | 20. Rock-in Robin......................Bobby Day | — | — | 3 |
| | | Billboard terminates the "Best Seller" and "Jockey" charts and debuts one all-encompassing R&B chart on 10/20/58. | | | |
| 10/27 | 6 | 21. Topsy II ........................Cozy Cole | | | |
| 12/08 | 1 | 22. A Lover's Question ...............Clyde McPhatter | | | |
| 12/15 | 7 | 23. Lonely Teardrops ..................Jackie Wilson | | | |
| | | 1959 | | | |
| 2/02 | 1 | 1. Try Me .............................James Brown | | | |
| 2/09 | 4 | ★ 2. Stagger Lee ......................Lloyd Price | | | |
| 3/09 | 9 | 3. It's Just A Matter Of Time .................Brook Benton | | | |
| 5/11 | 7 | ★ 4. Kansas City .....................Wilbert Harrison | | | |
| 6/29 | 4 | 5. Personality........................Lloyd Price | | | |
| 7/27 | 1 | 6. There Goes My Baby ...................The Drifters | | | |
| 8/03 | 1 | 7. What'd I Say ........................Ray Charles | | | |
| 8/10 | 4 | 8. Thank You Pretty Baby ...............Brook Benton | | | |
| 9/07 | 3* | 9. I'm Gonna Get Married ..................Lloyd Price | | | |
| 9/21 | 1 | 10. I Want To Walk You Home .................Fats Domino | | | |
| 10/05 | 4* | 11. Poison Ivy .........................The Coasters | | | |
| 10/12 | 1 | 12. Sea Of Love ........................Phil Phillips | | | |
| 10/19 | 1 | 13. You Better Know It ...................Jackie Wilson | | | |

| DATE | WKS | RECORD TITLE . . . . . . ARTIST |
|------|-----|--------------------------------|

### 1959 (Continued)

| DATE | WKS | |
|------|-----|--|
| 11/16 | 3* | 14. So Many Ways . . . . . . . . . . . . . . . . . . . . . . . . . . . . . . . . . . . . . . . Brook Benton |
| 11/23 | 2 | 15. Don't You Know . . . . . . . . . . . . . . . . . . . . . . . . . . . . . . . . . . . . . . Della Reese |
| 12/07 | 3* | 16. The Clouds . . . . . . . . . . . . . . . . . . . . . . . . . . . . . . . . . . . . . The Spacemen |

### 1960

| DATE | WKS | |
|------|-----|--|
| 1/11 | 4 | 1. Smokie — Part 2 . . . . . . . . . . . . . . . . . . . . . . . . . . . . . . Bill Black's Combo |
| 2/08 | 10 | 2. Baby (You've Got What It Takes) . . . . . . . Dinah Washington & Brook Benton |
| 4/18 | 1 | 3. Fannie Mae . . . . . . . . . . . . . . . . . . . . . . . . . . . . . . . . . . . . . Buster Brown |
| 4/25 | 4 | 4. White Silver Sands . . . . . . . . . . . . . . . . . . . . . . . . . . . Bill Black's Combo |
| 5/23 | 3 | 5. Doggin' Around . . . . . . . . . . . . . . . . . . . . . . . . . . . . . . . . . Jackie Wilson |
| 6/13 | 1 | ★ 6. Cathy's Clown . . . . . . . . . . . . . . . . . . . . . . . . . . . The Everly Brothers |
| 6/20 | 4* | 7. A Rockin' Good Way (To Mess Around And Fall In Love) . . . . . . Dinah Washington & Brook Benton |
| 7/11 | 1 | 8. There's Something On Your Mind, Part 2 . . . . . . . . . . . . . Bobby Marchan |
| 7/25 | 1 | 9. This Bitter Earth . . . . . . . . . . . . . . . . . . . . . . . . . . . . Dinah Washington |
| 8/01 | 4 | 10. A Woman, A Lover, A Friend . . . . . . . . . . . . . . . . . . . . . . Jackie Wilson |
| 8/29 | 9 | 11. Kiddio . . . . . . . . . . . . . . . . . . . . . . . . . . . . . . . . . . . . . . . . Brook Benton |
| 10/31 | 1 | ★12. Save The Last Dance For Me . . . . . . . . . . . . . . . . . . . . . . The Drifters |
| 11/07 | 3* | 13. Let's Go, Let's Go, Let's Go . . . . . . . . . . . Hank Ballard & The Midnighters |
| 11/14 | 7* | 14. He Will Break Your Heart . . . . . . . . . . . . . . . . . . . . . . . . . Jerry Butler |

### 1961

| DATE | WKS | |
|------|-----|--|
| 1/16 | 8 | 1. Shop Around . . . . . . . . . . . . . . . . . . . . . . . . . . . . . . . . . . The Miracles |
| 3/13 | 2 | ★ 2. Pony Time . . . . . . . . . . . . . . . . . . . . . . . . . . . . . . . . . Chubby Checker |
| 3/27 | 1 | 3. I Pity The Fool . . . . . . . . . . . . . . . . . . . . . . . . . . . . . . . . Bobby Bland |
| 4/03 | 2 | ★ 4. Blue Moon . . . . . . . . . . . . . . . . . . . . . . . . . . . . . . . . . . . . The Marcels |
| 4/17 | 1 | 5. One Mint Julep . . . . . . . . . . . . . . . . . . . . . . . . . . . . . . . . Ray Charles |
| 4/24 | 5 | ★ 6. Mother-In-Law . . . . . . . . . . . . . . . . . . . . . . . . . . . . . . Ernie K-Doe |
| 5/29 | 4 | 7. Stand By Me . . . . . . . . . . . . . . . . . . . . . . . . . . . . . . . . Ben E. King |
| 6/26 | 1 | 8. Every Beat Of My Heart . . . . . . . . . . . . . . . . . . . . . . . . . . . . . . Pips |
| 7/03 | 10 | ★ 9. Tossin' And Turnin' . . . . . . . . . . . . . . . . . . . . . . . . . . . Bobby Lewis |
| 9/11 | 3 | 10. My True Story . . . . . . . . . . . . . . . . . . . . . . . . . . . . . . . The Jive Five |
| 10/02 | 5 | ★11. Hit The Road Jack . . . . . . . . . . . . . . . . . . . . . . . . . . . . . Ray Charles |
| 11/06 | 1 | 12. Ya Ya . . . . . . . . . . . . . . . . . . . . . . . . . . . . . . . . . . . . . . . Lee Dorsey |
| 11/13 | 7 | ★13. Please Mr. Postman . . . . . . . . . . . . . . . . . . . . . . . . . The Marvelettes |

### 1962

| DATE | WKS | |
|------|-----|--|
| 1/06 | 2 | 1. Unchain My Heart . . . . . . . . . . . . . . . . . . . . . . . . . . . . . Ray Charles |
| 1/20 | 4 | 2. I Know (You Don't Love Me No More) . . . . . . . . . . . . . . . . Barbara George |
| 2/17 | 5 | ★ 3. Duke Of Earl . . . . . . . . . . . . . . . . . . . . . . . . . . . . . . . Gene Chandler |
| 3/24 | 3 | 4. Twistin' The Nite Away . . . . . . . . . . . . . . . . . . . . . . . . . . Sam Cooke |
| 4/14 | 2 | 5. Soul Twist . . . . . . . . . . . . . . . . . . . . . . . . . . . . . . . . . . . King Curtis |
| 4/28 | 4 | 6. Mashed Potato Time . . . . . . . . . . . . . . . . . . . . . . . . . . Dee Dee Sharp |
| 5/26 | 10 | ★ 7. I Can't Stop Loving You . . . . . . . . . . . . . . . . . . . . . . . . . Ray Charles |
| 8/04 | 3 | 8. You'll Lose A Good Thing . . . . . . . . . . . . . . . . . . . . . . . Barbara Lynn |
| 8/25 | 3 | ★ 9. The Loco-Motion . . . . . . . . . . . . . . . . . . . . . . . . . . . . . . . Little Eva |
| 9/15 | 4* | 10. Green Onions . . . . . . . . . . . . . . . . . . . . . . . . . Booker T. & The MG's |
| 9/22 | 1 | 11. You Beat Me To The Punch . . . . . . . . . . . . . . . . . . . . . . . . Mary Wells |
| 10/06 | 1 | ★12. Sherry . . . . . . . . . . . . . . . . . . . . . . . . . . . . . . . . . . . . The 4 Seasons |

| DATE | WKS | RECORD TITLE . . . . . . ARTIST |
|---|---|---|
| | | **1962** *(Continued)* |
| 10/20 | 3* | 13. Do You Love Me . . . . . . . . . . . . . . . . . . . . . . . . . . . . . . . . . . . . . . . . The Contours |
| 11/17 | 3 | ★14. Big Girls Don't Cry . . . . . . . . . . . . . . . . . . . . . . . . . . . . . . . . . The 4 Seasons |
| 12/08 | 3* | 15. Release Me . . . . . . . . . . . . . . . . . . . . . . . . . . . . . . . . . . . . . . Esther Phillips |
| 12/15 | 3* | 16. You Are My Sunshine . . . . . . . . . . . . . . . . . . . . . . . . . . . . . . . . . . Ray Charles |
| | | **1963** |
| 1/19 | 4 | 1. Two Lovers . . . . . . . . . . . . . . . . . . . . . . . . . . . . . . . . . . . . . . . . . Mary Wells |
| 2/16 | 1 | 2. You've Really Got A Hold On Me . . . . . . . . . . . . . . . . . . . . . . . . The Miracles |
| 2/23 | 2 | ★ 3. Hey Paula . . . . . . . . . . . . . . . . . . . . . . . . . . . . . . . . . . . . . . . Paul & Paula |
| 3/09 | 2 | 4. That's The Way Love Is . . . . . . . . . . . . . . . . . . . . . . . . . . . . . Bobby Bland |
| 3/23 | 2 | ★ 5. Our Day Will Come . . . . . . . . . . . . . . . . . . . . Ruby & The Romantics |
| 4/06 | 4 | ★ 6. He's So Fine . . . . . . . . . . . . . . . . . . . . . . . . . . . . . . . . . . . . The Chiffons |
| 5/04 | 3 | 7. Baby Workout . . . . . . . . . . . . . . . . . . . . . . . . . . . . . . . . . . . Jackie Wilson |
| 5/25 | 1 | ★ 8. I Will Follow Him . . . . . . . . . . . . . . . . . . . . . . . . Little Peggy March |
| 6/01 | 1 | ★ 9. If You Wanna Be Happy . . . . . . . . . . . . . . . . . . . . . . . . . . . Jimmy Soul |
| 6/08 | 1 | 10. Another Saturday Night . . . . . . . . . . . . . . . . . . . . . . . . . . . . Sam Cooke |
| 6/15 | 3 | ★11. It's My Party . . . . . . . . . . . . . . . . . . . . . . . . . . . . . . . . . . . . Lesley Gore |
| 7/06 | 2 | 12. Hello Stranger . . . . . . . . . . . . . . . . . . . . . . . . . . . . . . . . Barbara Lewis |
| 7/20 | 2 | ★13. Easier Said Than Done . . . . . . . . . . . . . . . . . . . . . . . . . . . . . The Essex |
| 8/03 | 6 | ★14. Fingertips — Pt 2 . . . . . . . . . . . . . . . . . . . . . . . . . Little Stevie Wonder |
| 9/14 | 4 | 15. Heat Wave . . . . . . . . . . . . . . . . . . . . . . . . . . . . Martha & The Vandellas |
| 10/12 | 3* | 16. Cry Baby . . . . . . . . . . . . . . . . . . . . . . Garnet Mimms & The Enchanters |
| 10/19 | 1 | 17. Part Time Love . . . . . . . . . . . . . . . . . . . . . . . . . . . Little Johnny Taylor |
| 11/09 | 2 | 18. It's All Right . . . . . . . . . . . . . . . . . . . . . . . . . . . . . . . . . The Impressions |
| 11/23 | 1 | ★19. Sugar Shack . . . . . . . . . . . . . . . . . . . . . . . Jimmy Gilmer & The Fireballs |
| | | Billboard temporarily discontinues R&B chart on 11/30/63; R&B chart returns on 1/30/65 |
| | | **1964** |
| 5/16 | 2 | ★ 1. My Guy . . . . . . . . . . . . . . . . . . . . . . . . . . . . . . . . . . . . . . . . . . Mary Wells |
| 6/06 | 3 | ★ 2. Chapel Of Love . . . . . . . . . . . . . . . . . . . . . . . . . . . . . . . . The Dixie Cups |
| 8/22 | 2 | ★ 3. Where Did Our Love Go . . . . . . . . . . . . . . . . . . . . . . . . . . The Supremes |
| 10/31 | 4 | ★ 4. Baby Love . . . . . . . . . . . . . . . . . . . . . . . . . . . . . . . . . . . . The Supremes |
| 11/28 | 1 | ★ 5. Leader Of The Pack . . . . . . . . . . . . . . . . . . . . . . . . . . . The Shangri-Las |
| | | all 1964 titles are from Billboard's 'Hot 100' chart (no R&B charts published in 1964) |
| | | **1965** |
| 1/30 | 6 | ★ 1. My Girl . . . . . . . . . . . . . . . . . . . . . . . . . . . . . . . . . . . . . The Temptations |
| 3/13 | 4* | 2. Shotgun . . . . . . . . . . . . . . . . . . . . . . . . Jr. Walker & The All Stars |
| 4/03 | 3 | 3. Got To Get You Off My Mind . . . . . . . . . . . . . . . . . . . . . Solomon Burke |
| 5/01 | 3 | 4. We're Gonna Make It . . . . . . . . . . . . . . . . . . . . . . . . . . . . Little Milton |
| 5/22 | 1 | 5. I'll Be Doggone . . . . . . . . . . . . . . . . . . . . . . . . . . . . . . . . Marvin Gaye |
| 5/29 | 1 | ★ 6. Back In My Arms Again . . . . . . . . . . . . . . . . . . . . . . . . The Supremes |
| 6/05 | 9 | ★ 7. I Can't Help Myself . . . . . . . . . . . . . . . . . . . . . . . . . . . . . . . Four Tops |
| 8/07 | 1 | 8. In The Midnight Hour . . . . . . . . . . . . . . . . . . . . . . . . . Wilson Pickett |
| 8/14 | 8 | 9. Papa's Got A Brand New Bag . . . . . . . . . . . . . . . . . . . . . James Brown |
| 10/09 | 3 | 10. I Want To (Do Everything For You) . . . . . . . . . . . . . . . . . . . . . . Joe Tex |
| 10/30 | 4 | 11. Rescue Me . . . . . . . . . . . . . . . . . . . . . . . . . . . . . . . . . . Fontella Bass |
| 11/27 | 1 | 12. Ain't That Peculiar . . . . . . . . . . . . . . . . . . . . . . . . . . . . . . Marvin Gaye |
| 12/04 | 6* | 13. I Got You (I Feel Good) . . . . . . . . . . . . . . . . . . . . . . . . . James Brown |

| DATE | WKS | RECORD TITLE......ARTIST |
|---|---|---|
| | | **1966** |
| 1/08 | 1 | 1. A Sweet Woman Like You ........................... Joe Tex |
| 1/22 | 5 | 2. Uptight (Everything's Alright) .................. Stevie Wonder |
| 2/26 | 2 | 3. Baby Scratch My Back............................ Slim Harpo |
| 3/12 | 7 | 4. 634-5789 (Soulsville, U.S.A.) ............... Wilson Pickett |
| 4/30 | 1 | 5. Get Ready ................................ The Temptations |
| 5/07 | 4 | ★ 6. When A Man Loves A Woman .................... Percy Sledge |
| 6/04 | 2 | 7. It's A Man's Man's Man's World ................. James Brown |
| 6/18 | 1 | 8. Hold On! I'm A Comin' ......................... Sam & Dave |
| 6/25 | 8* | 9. Ain't Too Proud To Beg ................... The Temptations |
| 7/23 | 1 | 10. Let's Go Get Stoned ........................... Ray Charles |
| 8/27 | 1 | 11. Blowin' In The Wind ........................ Stevie Wonder |
| 9/03 | 2 | ★12. You Can't Hurry Love ....................... The Supremes |
| 9/17 | 1 | 13. Land Of 1,000 Dances ...................... Wilson Pickett |
| 9/24 | 5 | 14. Beauty Is Only Skin Deep .................. The Temptations |
| 10/29 | 2 | ★15. Reach Out, I'll Be There ...................... Four Tops |
| 11/12 | 1 | 16. Love Is A Hurtin' Thing........................ Lou Rawls |
| 11/19 | 1 | 17. Knock On Wood ............................. Eddie Floyd |
| 11/26 | 4 | ★18. You Keep Me Hangin' On ..................... The Supremes |
| 12/24 | 2 | 19. (I Know) I'm Losing You .................. The Temptations |
| | | **1967** |
| 1/07 | 5 | 1. Tell It Like It Is ........................... Aaron Neville |
| 2/11 | 4 | 2. Are You Lonely For Me ...................... Freddie Scott |
| 3/11 | 2 | ★ 3. Love Is Here And Now You're Gone ............ The Supremes |
| 3/25 | 7 | 4. I Never Loved A Man (The Way I Loved You) ..... Aretha Franklin |
| 5/13 | 1 | 5. Jimmy Mack............................ Martha & The Vandellas |
| 5/20 | 8 | ★ 6. Respect ............................... Aretha Franklin |
| 7/15 | 4* | 7. I Was Made To Love Her .................... Stevie Wonder |
| 7/22 | 2 | 8. Make Me Yours ............................. Bettye Swann |
| 8/26 | 2 | 9. Baby I Love You .......................... Aretha Franklin |
| 9/09 | 3 | 10. Cold Sweat ............................... James Brown |
| 9/30 | 1 | 11. Funky Broadway ......................... Wilson Pickett |
| 10/07 | 1 | 12. (Your Love Keeps Lifting Me) Higher And Higher .......... Jackie Wilson |
| 10/14 | 7 | 13. Soul Man ................................. Sam & Dave |
| 12/02 | 6 | 14. I Heard It Through The Grapevine ........... Gladys Knight & The Pips |
| | | **1968** |
| 1/13 | 1 | 1. I Second That Emotion ............... Smokey Robinson & The Miracles |
| 1/20 | 4 | 2. Chain Of Fools ........................... Aretha Franklin |
| 2/17 | 3 | 3. I Wish It Would Rain ...................... The Temptations |
| 3/09 | 1 | 4. We're A Winner............................ The Impressions |
| 3/16 | 3 | ★ 5. (Sittin' On) The Dock Of The Bay .............. Otis Redding |
| 4/06 | 3 | 6. (Sweet Sweet Baby) Since You've Been Gone ........... Aretha Franklin |
| 4/27 | 2 | 7. I Got The Feelin' ........................... James Brown |
| 5/11 | 1 | 8. Cowboys To Girls............................ The Intruders |
| 5/18 | 2 | ★ 9. Tighten Up ................... Archie Bell & The Drells |
| 6/01 | 1 | 10. Shoo-Be-Doo-Be-Doo-Da-Day ............... Stevie Wonder |
| 6/08 | 1 | 11. Ain't Nothing Like The Real Thing ......... Marvin Gaye & Tammi Terrell |
| 6/15 | 3 | 12. Think ................................ Aretha Franklin |

| DATE | WKS | RECORD TITLE........ARTIST |
|------|-----|---------------------------|
| | | **1968** *(Continued)* |
| 7/06 | 1 | 13. I Could Never Love Another (After Loving You) .........The Temptations |
| 7/13 | 4 | ★14. Grazing In The Grass .............................Hugh Masekela |
| 8/10 | 3 | 15. Stay In My Corner ...............................The Dells |
| 8/31 | 5 | 16. You're All I Need To Get By ............... Marvin Gaye & Tammi Terrell |
| 10/05 | 6 | 17. Say It Loud — I'm Black And I'm Proud .................James Brown |
| 11/16 | 1 | 18. Hey, Western Union Man ........................Jerry Butler |
| 11/23 | 3 | 19. Who's Making Love ............................Johnnie Taylor |
| 12/14 | 7 | ★20. I Heard It Through The Grapevine ...............Marvin Gaye |
| | | **1969** |
| 2/01 | 3 | 1. Can I Change My Mind ........................Tyrone Davis |
| 2/22 | 2 | ★ 2. Everyday People ....................Sly & The Family Stone |
| 3/08 | 2 | 3. Give It Up Or Turnit A Loose ....................James Brown |
| 3/22 | 2 | 4. Run Away Child, Running Wild ................The Temptations |
| 4/05 | 2 | 5. Only The Strong Survive .......................Jerry Butler |
| 4/19 | 4 | 6. It's Your Thing .........................The Isley Brothers |
| 5/17 | 3 | 7. The Chokin' Kind ............................Joe Simon |
| 6/07 | 6 | 8. Too Busy Thinking About My Baby ...................Marvin Gaye |
| 7/19 | 2 | 9. What Does It Take (To Win Your Love) .........Jr. Walker & The All Stars |
| 8/02 | 2 | 10. Mother Popcorn (You Got To Have A Mother For Me) .......James Brown |
| 8/16 | 1 | 11. Choice Of Colors ...........................The Impressions |
| 8/23 | 5 | 12. Share Your Love With Me ....................Aretha Franklin |
| 9/27 | 1 | 13. Oh, What A Night ............................The Dells |
| 10/04 | 5 | ★14. I Can't Get Next To You .......................The Temptations |
| 11/08 | 5 | 15. Baby I'm For Real .........................The Originals |
| 12/13 | 4 | ★16. Someday We'll Be Together ...............Diana Ross & The Supremes |
| | | **1970** |
| 1/10 | 4 | ★ 1. I Want You Back ...........................The Jackson 5 |
| 2/07 | 5 | ★ 2. Thank You (Falettinme Be Mice Elf Agin) .........Sly & The Family Stone |
| 3/14 | 1 | 3. Rainy Night In Georgia ........................Brook Benton |
| 3/21 | 2 | 4. Call Me ...............................Aretha Franklin |
| 4/04 | 4 | ★ 5. ABC ...............................The Jackson 5 |
| 5/02 | 2 | 6. Turn Back The Hands Of Time .....................Tyrone Davis |
| 5/16 | 5 | 7. Love On A Two-Way Street ......................The Moments |
| 6/20 | 6 | ★ 8. The Love You Save ..........................The Jackson 5 |
| 8/01 | 6 | 9. Signed, Sealed, Delivered I'm Yours ................Stevie Wonder |
| 9/12 | 3 | 10. Don't Play That Song .........................Aretha Franklin |
| 10/03 | 1 | ★11. Ain't No Mountain High Enough .....................Diana Ross |
| 10/10 | 6 | ★12. I'll Be There ..............................The Jackson 5 |
| 11/21 | 2 | 13. Super Bad (Part 1 & Part 2) .......................James Brown |
| 12/05 | 3 | ★14. The Tears Of A Clown ...............Smokey Robinson & The Miracles |
| 12/26 | 1 | 15. Stoned Love ..............................The Supremes |
| | | **1971** |
| 1/02 | 4* | 1. Groove Me ..............................King Floyd |
| 1/23 | 1 | 2. If I Were Your Woman ...................Gladys Knight & The Pips |
| 2/06 | 2 | 3. (Do The) Push And Pull ........................Rufus Thomas |
| 2/20 | 2 | 4. Jody's Got Your Girl And Gone .....................Johnnie Taylor |

| DATE | WKS | RECORD TITLE . . . . . . ARTIST |
|------|-----|-------------------------------|
| | | **1971** *(Continued)* |
| 3/06 | 3 | ★ 5. Just My Imagination (Running Away With Me) . . . . . . . . . .The Temptations |
| 3/27 | 5 | 6. What's Going On . . . . . . . . . . . . . . . . . . . . . . . . . . . . . . . . . . . . . . . .Marvin Gaye |
| 5/01 | 3 | 7. Never Can Say Goodbye . . . . . . . . . . . . . . . . . . . . . . . .The Jackson 5 |
| 5/22 | 2* | 8. Bridge Over Troubled Water . . . . . . . . . . . . . . . . . . . . . .Aretha Franklin |
| 5/29 | 3 | ★ 9. Want Ads. . . . . . . . . . . . . . . . . . . . . . . . . . . . . . . . . . . . .The Honey Cone |
| 6/26 | 1 | 10. Don't Knock My Love . . . . . . . . . . . . . . . . . . . . . . . . . . .Wilson Pickett |
| 7/03 | 5 | 11. Mr. Big Stuff . . . . . . . . . . . . . . . . . . . . . . . . . . . . . . . . . . . . .Jean Knight |
| 8/07 | 1 | 12. Hot Pants (She Got To Use What She Got, To Get What She Wants) |
| | | . . . . . .James Brown |
| 8/14 | 2 | 13. Mercy Mercy Me (The Ecology) . . . . . . . . . . . . . . . . . . . . . .Marvin Gaye |
| 8/28 | 3 | 14. Spanish Harlem . . . . . . . . . . . . . . . . . . . . . . . . . . . . . . . . .Aretha Franklin |
| 9/18 | 2 | 15. Stick-Up . . . . . . . . . . . . . . . . . . . . . . . . . . . . . . . . . . . . . .The Honey Cone |
| 10/02 | 2 | 16. Make It Funky . . . . . . . . . . . . . . . . . . . . . . . . . . . . . . . . . .James Brown |
| 10/16 | 2 | 17. Thin Line Between Love & Hate . . . . . . . . . . . . . . . . . . . .The Persuaders |
| 10/30 | 1 | 18. Trapped By A Thing Called Love . . . . . . . . . . . . . . . . . . . .Denise LaSalle |
| 11/06 | 2 | 19. Inner City Blues (Make Me Wanna Holler) . . . . . . . . . . . . . . .Marvin Gaye |
| 11/20 | 2 | 20. Have You Seen Her . . . . . . . . . . . . . . . . . . . . . . . . . . . . . . . . . .Chi-Lites |
| 12/04 | 5 | ★21. Family Affair . . . . . . . . . . . . . . . . . . . . . . . . . . . .Sly & The Family Stone |
| | | **1972** |
| 1/08 | 9 | ★ 1. Let's Stay Together . . . . . . . . . . . . . . . . . . . . . . . . . . . . . . . . . .Al Green |
| 3/11 | 1 | 2. Talking Loud And Saying Nothing . . . . . . . . . . . . . . . . . . . . .James Brown |
| 3/18 | 1 | 3. I Gotcha. . . . . . . . . . . . . . . . . . . . . . . . . . . . . . . . . . . . . . . . . . . . .Joe Tex |
| 3/25 | 4 | 4. In The Rain . . . . . . . . . . . . . . . . . . . . . . . . . . . . . . . . . . . . . . .Dramatics |
| 4/22 | 2 | 5. Day Dreaming . . . . . . . . . . . . . . . . . . . . . . . . . . . . . . . . .Aretha Franklin |
| 5/06 | 4 | ★ 6. I'll Take You There . . . . . . . . . . . . . . . . . . . . . . . . . . . .The Staple Singers |
| 6/03 | 2 | ★ 7. Oh Girl . . . . . . . . . . . . . . . . . . . . . . . . . . . . . . . . . . . . . . . . . . .Chi-Lites |
| 6/17 | 1 | 8. Woman's Gotta Have It . . . . . . . . . . . . . . . . . . . . . . . . . . .Bobby Womack |
| 6/24 | 1 | ★ 9. Lean On Me . . . . . . . . . . . . . . . . . . . . . . . . . . . . . . . . . . . . .Bill Withers |
| 7/01 | 1 | 10. Outa-Space . . . . . . . . . . . . . . . . . . . . . . . . . . . . . . . . . . . . .Billy Preston |
| 7/08 | 4 | 11. (If Loving You Is Wrong) I Don't Want To Be Right . . . . . . . . .Luther Ingram |
| 8/05 | 1 | 12. Where Is The Love . . . . . . . . . . . . . . . .Roberta Flack & Donny Hathaway |
| 8/12 | 2 | 13. I'm Still In Love With You . . . . . . . . . . . . . . . . . . . . . . . . . . . . .Al Green |
| 8/26 | 2 | 14. Power Of Love . . . . . . . . . . . . . . . . . . . . . . . . . . . . . . . . . . . . .Joe Simon |
| 9/09 | 1 | 15. Back Stabbers . . . . . . . . . . . . . . . . . . . . . . . . . . . . . . . . . . . . . . .O'Jays |
| 9/16 | 4 | 16. Get On The Good Foot . . . . . . . . . . . . . . . . . . . . . . . . . . . .James Brown |
| 10/14 | 5 | 17. I'll Be Around . . . . . . . . . . . . . . . . . . . . . . . . . . . . . . . . . . . . . .Spinners |
| 11/18 | 2 | 18. If You Don't Know Me By Now . . . . . . . . . . . .Harold Melvin & The Blue Notes |
| 12/02 | 1 | 19. You Ought To Be With Me . . . . . . . . . . . . . . . . . . . . . . . . . . . . .Al Green |
| 12/09 | 4 | ★20. Me And Mrs. Jones . . . . . . . . . . . . . . . . . . . . . . . . . . . . . . . . .Billy Paul |
| | | **1973** |
| 1/06 | 3 | ★ 1. Superstition. . . . . . . . . . . . . . . . . . . . . . . . . . . . . . . . . . . .Stevie Wonder |
| 1/27 | 2 | 2. Why Can't We Live Together . . . . . . . . . . . . . . . . . . . . . . . .Timmy Thomas |
| 2/10 | 1 | 3. Could It Be I'm Falling In Love . . . . . . . . . . . . . . . . . . . . . . . . . .Spinners |
| 2/17 | 4 | ★ 4. Love Train . . . . . . . . . . . . . . . . . . . . . . . . . . . . . . . . . . . . . . . . .O'Jays |
| 3/17 | 4 | 5. Neither One Of Us (Wants To Be The First To Say Goodbye) |
| | | . . . . . .Gladys Knight & The Pips |
| 4/14 | 2 | 6. Masterpiece . . . . . . . . . . . . . . . . . . . . . . . . . . . . . . . . . . .The Temptations |

| DATE | WKS | RECORD TITLE . . . . . . ARTIST |
|------|-----|-------------------------------|
| | | **1973** *(Continued)* |
| 4/28 | 2 | 7. Pillow Talk . . . . . . . . . . . . . . . . . . . . . . . . . . . . . . . . . . . . . . . . . . . . Sylvia |
| 5/12 | 1 | 8. Funky Worm . . . . . . . . . . . . . . . . . . . . . . . . . . . . . . . . . . . . . . Ohio Players |
| 5/19 | 1 | 9. Leaving Me . . . . . . . . . . . . . . . . . . . . . . . . . . . . . . . . . The Independents |
| 5/26 | 2 | 10. I'm Gonna Love You Just A Little More Baby . . . . . . . . . . . . . . Barry White |
| 6/09 | 4 | 11. One Of A Kind (Love Affair) . . . . . . . . . . . . . . . . . . . . . . . . . . . . . Spinners |
| 7/07 | 2 | 12. Doing It To Death . . . . . . . . . . . . . . . . . . . . Fred Wesley & The J.B.'s |
| 7/21 | 2 | 13. I Believe In You (You Believe In Me) . . . . . . . . . . . . . . . . . . Johnnie Taylor |
| 8/04 | 2 | 14. Angel . . . . . . . . . . . . . . . . . . . . . . . . . . . . . . . . . . . . . . Aretha Franklin |
| 8/18 | 6 | ★15. Let's Get It On . . . . . . . . . . . . . . . . . . . . . . . . . . . . . . . . . . Marvin Gaye |
| 9/29 | 1 | 16. Higher Ground . . . . . . . . . . . . . . . . . . . . . . . . . . . . . . . . . Stevie Wonder |
| 10/06 | 2 | ★17. Keep On Truckin' . . . . . . . . . . . . . . . . . . . . . . . . . . . . . Eddie Kendricks |
| 10/20 | 4 | ★18. Midnight Train To Georgia . . . . . . . . . . . . . . . Gladys Knight & The Pips |
| 11/17 | 1 | 19. Space Race . . . . . . . . . . . . . . . . . . . . . . . . . . . . . . . . . . . Billy Preston |
| 11/24 | 2 | 20. The Love I Lost . . . . . . . . . . . . . . . . . . . . Harold Mclvin & The Blue Notes |
| 12/08 | 3 | 21. If You're Ready (Come Go With Me) . . . . . . . . . . . . . . The Staple Singers |
| 12/29 | 2 | 22. Living For The City . . . . . . . . . . . . . . . . . . . . . . . . . . . . . . Stevie Wonder |
| | | **1974** |
| 1/12 | 1 | 1. Until You Come Back To Me (That's What I'm Gonna Do) . . . . Aretha Franklin |
| 1/19 | 1 | 2. I've Got To Use My Imagination . . . . . . . . . . . . . . Gladys Knight & The Pips |
| 1/26 | 1 | 3. Livin' For You . . . . . . . . . . . . . . . . . . . . . . . . . . . . . . . . . . . . . Al Green |
| 2/02 | 1 | 4. Let Your Hair Down . . . . . . . . . . . . . . . . . . . . . . . . . . . The Temptations |
| 2/09 | 3 | 5. Boogie Down . . . . . . . . . . . . . . . . . . . . . . . . . . . . . . . Eddie Kendricks |
| 3/02 | 2 | 6. Mighty Love . . . . . . . . . . . . . . . . . . . . . . . . . . . . . . . . . . . . . Spinners |
| 3/16 | 3 | 7. Lookin' For A Love . . . . . . . . . . . . . . . . . . . . . . . . . . . . . Bobby Womack |
| 4/06 | 2 | 8. Best Thing That Ever Happened To Me . . . . . . . . Gladys Knight & The Pips |
| 4/20 | 1 | ★ 9. TSOP (The Sound Of Philadelphia) . . . . . . MFSB featuring The Three Degrees |
| 4/27 | 2 | 10. The Payback . . . . . . . . . . . . . . . . . . . . . . . . . . . . . . . . . James Brown |
| 5/11 | 1 | 11. Dancing Machine . . . . . . . . . . . . . . . . . . . . . . . . . . . . . . . The Jackson 5 |
| 5/18 | 2 | 12. I'm In Love . . . . . . . . . . . . . . . . . . . . . . . . . . . . . . . . . . Aretha Franklin |
| 6/01 | 1 | 13. Be Thankful For What You Got . . . . . . . . . . . . . . . . . . . William DeVaughn |
| 6/08 | 1 | 14. Hollywood Swinging . . . . . . . . . . . . . . . . . . . . . . . . . . Kool & The Gang |
| 6/15 | 1 | 15. Sideshow . . . . . . . . . . . . . . . . . . . . . . . . . . . . . . . . . . . . . Blue Magic |
| 6/22 | 2 | 16. Finally Got Myself Together (I'm A Changed Man) . . . . . . . The Impressions |
| 7/06 | 2 | ★17. Rock Your Baby . . . . . . . . . . . . . . . . . . . . . . . . . . . . . George McCrae |
| 7/20 | 2 | 18. My Thang . . . . . . . . . . . . . . . . . . . . . . . . . . . . . . . . . . . James Brown |
| 8/03 | 5 | ★19. Feel Like Makin' Love . . . . . . . . . . . . . . . . . . . . . . . . . . . Roberta Flack |
| 9/07 | 3 | ★20. Can't Get Enough Of Your Love, Babe . . . . . . . . . . . . . . . . Barry White |
| 9/28 | 2 | ★21. You Haven't Done Nothin' . . . . . . . . . . . . . . . . . . . . . . . Stevie Wonder |
| 10/12 | 1 | 22. Papa Don't Take No Mess . . . . . . . . . . . . . . . . . . . . . . . . James Brown |
| 10/19 | 1 | 23. Do It ('Til You're Satisfied) . . . . . . . . . . . . . . . . . . . . . . . . B.T. Express |
| 10/26 | 1 | 24. Higher Plane . . . . . . . . . . . . . . . . . . . . . . . . . . . . . . . Kool & The Gang |
| 11/02 | 2 | 25. Let's Straighten It Out . . . . . . . . . . . . . . . . . . . . . . . . . . . . . Latimore |
| 11/16 | 2 | 26. Woman To Woman . . . . . . . . . . . . . . . . . . . . . . . . . . . . . Shirley Brown |
| 11/30 | 2 | 27. I Feel A Song (In My Heart) . . . . . . . . . . . . . . Gladys Knight & The Pips |
| 12/14 | 1 | 28. You Got The Love . . . . . . . . . . . . . . . . . Rufus Featuring Chaka Khan |
| 12/21 | 1 | 29. She's Gone . . . . . . . . . . . . . . . . . . . . . . . . . . . . . . . . . . . . Tavares |
| 12/28 | 2 | 30. Boogie On Reggae Woman . . . . . . . . . . . . . . . . . . . . . . Stevie Wonder |

| DATE | WKS | RECORD TITLE......ARTIST |
|------|-----|-------------------------|
| | | **1975** |
| 1/11 | 1 | ★ 1. Kung Fu Fighting ................................Carl Douglas |
| 1/18 | 1 | 2. You're The First, The Last, My Everything ..............Barry White |
| 1/25 | 2 | ★ 3. Fire ................................................Ohio Players |
| 2/08 | 1 | 4. Happy People ...............................The Temptations |
| 2/15 | 1 | 5. I Belong To You ..............................Love Unlimited |
| 2/22 | 1 | ★ 6. Lady Marmalade ........................................LaBelle |
| 3/01 | 1 | 7. Shame, Shame, Shame .....................Shirley & Company |
| 3/08 | 1 | 8. Express ......................................B.T. Express |
| 3/15 | 1 | 9. Supernatural Thing ..........................Ben E. King |
| 3/22 | 2 | ★10. Shining Star ..........................Earth, Wind & Fire |
| 4/05 | 1 | 11. Shoeshine Boy................................Eddie Kendricks |
| 4/12 | 2 | 12. L-O-V-E (Love)................................Al Green |
| 4/26 | 1 | 13. Shakey Ground ...............................The Temptations |
| 5/03 | 1 | 14. What Am I Gonna Do With You .....................Barry White |
| 5/10 | 2 | 15. Get Down, Get Down (Get On The Floor)................Joe Simon |
| 5/24 | 1 | 16. Baby That's Backatcha .......................Smokey Robinson |
| 5/31 | 1 | 17. Spirit Of The Boogie ...........................Kool & The Gang |
| 6/07 | 1 | 18. Love Won't Let Me Wait ...........................Major Harris |
| 6/14 | 1 | 19. Rockin' Chair ................................Gwen McCrae |
| 6/21 | 1 | 20. Give The People What They Want......................The O'Jays |
| 6/28 | 1 | 21. Look At Me (I'm In Love) .........................The Moments |
| 7/05 | 1 | 22. Slippery When Wet ................................Commodores |
| 7/12 | 1 | ★23. The Hustle....................Van McCoy & The Soul City Symphony |
| 7/19 | 3 | 24. Fight The Power................................The Isley Brothers |
| 8/09 | 1 | 25. Hope That We Can Be Together Soon |
| | | ......Sharon Paige and Harold Melvin & The Blue Notes |
| 8/16 | 1 | 26. Dream Merchant ...............................The New Birth |
| 8/23 | 1 | ★27. Get Down Tonight .....................K.C. & The Sunshine Band |
| 8/30 | 1 | 28. Your Love ..............................Graham Central Station |
| 9/06 | 2 | 29. How Long (Betcha' Got A Chick On The Side) .........The Pointer Sisters |
| 9/20 | 1 | 30. It Only Takes A Minute................................Tavares |
| 9/27 | 1 | 31. Do It Any Way You Wanna ......................People's Choice |
| 10/04 | 2 | 32. This Will Be................................Natalie Cole |
| 10/18 | 1 | 33. They Just Can't Stop It the (Games People Play) ..............Spinners |
| 10/25 | 1 | 34. To Each His Own ......................Faith, Hope & Charity |
| 11/01 | 1 | 35. Sweet Sticky Thing................................Ohio Players |
| 11/08 | 1 | 36. Low Rider ..........................................War |
| 11/15 | 1 | ★37. Fly, Robin, Fly................................Silver Convention |
| 11/22 | 2* | ★38. Let's Do It Again .......................The Staple Singers |
| 11/29 | 1 | ★39. That's The Way (I Like It) ..............KC & The Sunshine Band |
| 12/06 | 1 | 40. I Love Music ......................................O'Jays |
| 12/20 | 1 | 41. Full Of Fire ......................................Al Green |
| 12/27 | 1 | ★42. Love Rollercoaster .............................Ohio Players |
| | | **1976** |
| 1/03 | 1 | 1. Walk Away From Love ...............................David Ruffin |
| 1/10 | 2* | 2. Sing A Song .............................Earth, Wind & Fire |
| 1/17 | 2 | 3. Wake Up Everybody..................Harold Melvin & The Blue Notes |
| 2/07 | 1 | 4. Turning Point ....................................Tyrone Davis |

| DATE | WKS | RECORD TITLE . . . . . . ARTIST |
|---|---|---|
| | | **1976** *(Continued)* |
| 2/14 | 1 | 5. Inseparable . . . . . . . . . . . . . . . . . . . . . . . . . . . . . . . . . . . . . . . . . Natalie Cole |
| 2/21 | 2 | 6. Sweet Thing . . . . . . . . . . . . . . . . . . . . Rufus Featuring Chaka Khan |
| 3/06 | 1 | ★ 7. Boogie Fever . . . . . . . . . . . . . . . . . . . . . . . . . . . . . . . . . . . . . . . Sylvers |
| 3/13 | 6 | ★ 8. Disco Lady . . . . . . . . . . . . . . . . . . . . . . . . . . . . . . . . . . Johnnie Taylor |
| 4/24 | 2 | 9. Livin' For The Weekend . . . . . . . . . . . . . . . . . . . . . . . . . . . . The O'Jays |
| 5/08 | 1 | 10. Movin' . . . . . . . . . . . . . . . . . . . . . . . . . . . . . . . . . . . Brass Construction |
| 5/15 | 1 | ★11. Love Hangover . . . . . . . . . . . . . . . . . . . . . . . . . . . . . . . . . . Diana Ross |
| 5/22 | 1 | ★12. Kiss And Say Goodbye . . . . . . . . . . . . . . . . . . . . . . . . . . . Manhattans |
| 5/29 | 1 | 13. I Want You . . . . . . . . . . . . . . . . . . . . . . . . . . . . . . . . . . . . . Marvin Gaye |
| 6/05 | 1 | 14. Young Hearts Run Free . . . . . . . . . . . . . . . . . . . . . . . . . . . Candi Staton |
| 6/12 | 1 | 15. I'll Be Good To You . . . . . . . . . . . . . . . . . . . . . The Brothers Johnson |
| 6/19 | 1 | 16. Sophisticated Lady (She's A Different Lady) . . . . . . . . . . . . . . Natalie Cole |
| 6/26 | 4 | 17. Something He Can Feel . . . . . . . . . . . . . . . . . . . . . . . . . Aretha Franklin |
| 7/24 | 2 | 18. You'll Never Find Another Love Like Mine . . . . . . . . . . . . . . . . Lou Rawls |
| 8/07 | 2 | 19. Getaway . . . . . . . . . . . . . . . . . . . . . . . . . . . . . . . . . Earth, Wind & Fire |
| 8/21 | 1 | 20. Who'd She Coo? . . . . . . . . . . . . . . . . . . . . . . . . . . . . . . . . Ohio Players |
| 8/28 | 4* | ★21. (Shake, Shake, Shake) Shake Your Booty . . . . . . . . KC & The Sunshine Band |
| 9/04 | 2 | ★22. Play That Funky Music . . . . . . . . . . . . . . . . . . . . . . . . . . . Wild Cherry |
| 10/09 | 2 | 23. Just To Be Close To You . . . . . . . . . . . . . . . . . . . . . . . . . . Commodores |
| 10/23 | 1 | 24. The Rubberband Man . . . . . . . . . . . . . . . . . . . . . . . . . . . . . . Spinners |
| 10/30 | 1 | 25. Message In Our Music . . . . . . . . . . . . . . . . . . . . . . . . . . . The O'Jays |
| 11/06 | 2 | 26. Love Ballad . . . . . . . . . . . . . . . . . . . . . . . . . . . . . . . . . . . . . . . L.T.D. |
| 11/20 | 1 | ★27. You Don't Have To Be A Star (To Be In My Show) |
| | | . . . . . . . Marilyn McCoo & Billy Davis, Jr. |
| 11/27 | 4 | 28. Dazz . . . . . . . . . . . . . . . . . . . . . . . . . . . . . . . . . . . . . . . . . . . . . Brick |
| 12/25 | 2 | ★29. Car Wash . . . . . . . . . . . . . . . . . . . . . . . . . . . . . . . . . . . . . Rose Royce |
| | | **1977** |
| 1/08 | 1 | 1. Darlin' Darlin' Baby (Sweet, Tender, Love) . . . . . . . . . . . . . . . . . . O'Jays |
| 1/15 | 5 | ★ 2. I Wish . . . . . . . . . . . . . . . . . . . . . . . . . . . . . . . . . . . . Stevie Wonder |
| 2/19 | 1 | ★ 3. Don't Leave Me This Way . . . . . . . . . . . . . . . . . . . . . Thelma Houston |
| 2/26 | 5 | 4. I've Got Love On My Mind . . . . . . . . . . . . . . . . . . . . . . . Natalie Cole |
| 4/02 | 1 | 5. Tryin' To Love Two . . . . . . . . . . . . . . . . . . . . . . . . . . . . William Bell |
| 4/09 | 2 | 6. At Midnight (My Love Will Lift You Up) . . . . . . . Rufus Featuring Chaka Khan |
| 4/23 | 1 | 7. The Pride . . . . . . . . . . . . . . . . . . . . . . . . . . . . . . . The Isley Brothers |
| 4/30 | 5* | ★ 8. Got To Give It Up . . . . . . . . . . . . . . . . . . . . . . . . . . . . . Marvin Gaye |
| 5/21 | 1 | 9. Whodunit . . . . . . . . . . . . . . . . . . . . . . . . . . . . . . . . . . . . . . . Tavares |
| 5/28 | 1 | ★10. Sir Duke . . . . . . . . . . . . . . . . . . . . . . . . . . . . . . . . . . Stevie Wonder |
| 6/18 | 1 | 11. Break It To Me Gently . . . . . . . . . . . . . . . . . . . . . . . Aretha Franklin |
| 6/25 | 4* | ★12. Best Of My Love . . . . . . . . . . . . . . . . . . . . . . . . . . . . . . . . Emotions |
| 7/16 | 1 | 13. Easy . . . . . . . . . . . . . . . . . . . . . . . . . . . . . . . . . . . . . . Commodores |
| 7/30 | 1 | 14. Slide . . . . . . . . . . . . . . . . . . . . . . . . . . . . . . . . . . . . . . . . . . . Slave |
| 8/06 | 1 | 15. Strawberry Letter 23 . . . . . . . . . . . . . . . . . . . . . The Brothers Johnson |
| 8/13 | 6 | 16. Float On . . . . . . . . . . . . . . . . . . . . . . . . . . . . . . . . . . . The Floaters |
| 9/24 | 1 | 17. Keep It Comin' Love . . . . . . . . . . . . . . . . . . . . KC & The Sunshine Band |
| 10/01 | 5 | 18. It's Ecstasy When You Lay Down Next To Me . . . . . . . . . . . . . . Barry White |
| 11/05 | 2 | 19. (Every Time I Turn Around) Back In Love Again . . . . . . . . . . . . . . L.T.D. |
| 11/19 | 7 | 20. Serpentine Fire . . . . . . . . . . . . . . . . . . . . . . . . . . . Earth, Wind & Fire |

| DATE | WKS | RECORD TITLE . . . . . . ARTIST |
|------|-----|--------------------------------|
| | | **1978** |
| 1/07 | 2 | 1. Ffun . . . . . . . . . . . . . . . . . . . . . . . . . . . . . . . . . . . . . . . . . . . Con Funk Shun |
| 1/21 | 2 | 2. Our Love . . . . . . . . . . . . . . . . . . . . . . . . . . . . . . . . . . . . . . . . Natalie Cole |
| 2/04 | 2 | 3. Theme Song From "Which Way Is Up" . . . . . . . . . . . . . . . . . . . . . Stargard |
| 2/18 | 1 | 4. Too Hot Ta Trot . . . . . . . . . . . . . . . . . . . . . . . . . . . . . . . . . . . Commodores |
| 2/25 | 1 | 5. It's You That I Need . . . . . . . . . . . . . . . . . . . . . . . . . . . . . . . Enchantment |
| 3/04 | 3 | 6. Flash Light . . . . . . . . . . . . . . . . . . . . . . . . . . . . . . . . . . . . . . . Parliament |
| 3/25 | 1 | 7. Bootzilla . . . . . . . . . . . . . . . . . . . . . . . . . . . . . . . . . Bootsy's Rubber Band |
| 4/01 | 2 | 8. The Closer I Get To You . . . . . . . . . . . . Roberta Flack with Donny Hathaway |
| 4/15 | 4 | ★ 9. Too Much, Too Little, Too Late . . . . . . . . . Johnny Mathis/Deniece Williams |
| 5/13 | 2 | 10. Take Me To The Next Phase . . . . . . . . . . . . . . . . . . . . The Isley Brothers |
| 5/27 | 5 | 11. Use Ta Be My Girl . . . . . . . . . . . . . . . . . . . . . . . . . . . . . . . . The O'Jays |
| 7/01 | 1 | 12. Stuff Like That . . . . . . . . . . . . . . . . . . . . . . . . . . . . . . . . . Quincy Jones |
| 7/08 | 2 | 13. Close The Door . . . . . . . . . . . . . . . . . . . . . . . . . . . . . . Teddy Pendergrass |
| 7/22 | 2 | 14. You And I . . . . . . . . . . . . . . . . . . . . . . . . . . . . . . . . . . . . . . . Rick James |
| 8/05 | 1 | ★15. Boogie Oogie Oogie . . . . . . . . . . . . . . . . . . . . . . . . . . . . A Taste Of Honey |
| 8/12 | 2 | ★16. Three Times A Lady . . . . . . . . . . . . . . . . . . . . . . . . . . . . . Commodores |
| 8/26 | 2 | 17. Get Off . . . . . . . . . . . . . . . . . . . . . . . . . . . . . . . . . . . . . . . . . . . Foxy |
| 9/09 | 2 | 18. Holding On (When Love Is Gone) . . . . . . . . . . . . . . . . . . . . . . . . . L.T.D. |
| 9/23 | 1 | 19. Got To Get You Into My Life . . . . . . . . . . . . . . . . Earth, Wind & Fire |
| 9/30 | 6 | 20. One Nation Under A Groove . . . . . . . . . . . . . . . . . . . . . . . . Funkadelic |
| 11/11 | 3 | 21. I'm Every Woman . . . . . . . . . . . . . . . . . . . . . . . . . . . . . . Chaka Khan |
| 12/02 | 5 | ★22. Le Freak . . . . . . . . . . . . . . . . . . . . . . . . . . . . . . . . . . . . . . . . . Chic |
| | | **1979** |
| 1/06 | 1 | 1. Got To Be Real . . . . . . . . . . . . . . . . . . . . . . . . . . . . . . . . . . . Cheryl Lynn |
| 1/13 | 1 | 2. September . . . . . . . . . . . . . . . . . . . . . . . . . . . . . . . Earth, Wind & Fire |
| 1/20 | 4 | 3. Aqua Boogie . . . . . . . . . . . . . . . . . . . . . . . . . . . . . . . . . . . . Parliament |
| 2/17 | 4 | 4. Bustin' Loose . . . . . . . . . . . . . . . . . . . Chuck Brown & The Soul Searchers |
| 3/17 | 3* | 5. I Got My Mind Made Up (You Can Get It Girl) . . . . . . . . . . . . . Instant Funk |
| 3/31 | 1 | 6. He's The Greatest Dancer . . . . . . . . . . . . . . . . . . . . . . . . Sister Sledge |
| 4/14 | 2 | 7. Disco Nights (Rock-Freak) . . . . . . . . . . . . . . . . . . . . . . . . . . . . . G.Q. |
| 4/28 | 4 | ★ 8. Reunited . . . . . . . . . . . . . . . . . . . . . . . . . . . . . . . . . Peaches & Herb |
| 5/26 | 1 | 9. I Wanna Be With You . . . . . . . . . . . . . . . . . . . . . . . The Isley Brothers |
| 6/02 | 1 | 10. Ain't No Stoppin' Us Now . . . . . . . . . . . . . . . . . McFadden & Whitehead |
| 6/09 | 1 | 11. We Are Family . . . . . . . . . . . . . . . . . . . . . . . . . . . . . . . . Sister Sledge |
| 6/16 | 5 | ★12. Ring My Bell . . . . . . . . . . . . . . . . . . . . . . . . . . . . . . . . . . Anita Ward |
| 7/21 | 1 | ★13. Bad Girls . . . . . . . . . . . . . . . . . . . . . . . . . . . . . . . . . . Donna Summer |
| 7/28 | 6 | ★14. Good Times . . . . . . . . . . . . . . . . . . . . . . . . . . . . . . . . . . . . . . . Chic |
| 9/08 | 5 | ★15. Don't Stop 'Til You Get Enough . . . . . . . . . . . . . . . . Michael Jackson |
| 10/13 | 3 | 16. (not just) Knee Deep . . . . . . . . . . . . . . . . . . . . . . . . . . . . . Funkadelic |
| 11/03 | 3 | 17. Ladies Night . . . . . . . . . . . . . . . . . . . . . . . . . . . . . . Kool & The Gang |
| 11/24 | 1 | ★18. Still . . . . . . . . . . . . . . . . . . . . . . . . . . . . . . . . . . . . . . Commodores |
| 12/01 | 2 | 19. I Wanna Be Your Lover . . . . . . . . . . . . . . . . . . . . . . . . . . . . . Prince |
| 12/15 | 3 | 20. Do You Love What You Feel . . . . . . . . . . . . . . . . . . . . . . Rufus & Chaka |
| | | **1980** |
| 1/05 | 6 | ★ 1. Rock With You . . . . . . . . . . . . . . . . . . . . . . . . . . . . Michael Jackson |
| 2/16 | 1 | 2. The Second Time Around . . . . . . . . . . . . . . . . . . . . . . . . . . . Shalamar |
| 2/23 | 1 | 3. Special Lady . . . . . . . . . . . . . . . . . . . . . . . . . . Ray, Goodman & Brown |

| DATE | WKS | RECORD TITLE . . . . . . ARTIST |
|------|-----|--------------------------------|
| | | **1980** *(Continued)* |
| 3/01 | 5 | 4. And The Beat Goes On . . . . . . . . . . . . . . . . . . . . . . . . . . . . . . The Whispers |
| 4/05 | 2 | 5. Stomp! . . . . . . . . . . . . . . . . . . . . . . . . . . . . . . The Brothers Johnson |
| 4/19 | 4 | 6. Don't Say Goodnight (It's Time For Love) . . . . . . . . . . . . The Isley Brothers |
| 5/17 | 6 | 7. Let's Get Serious . . . . . . . . . . . . . . . . . . . . . . . . . . . . . Jermaine Jackson |
| 6/28 | 5 | 8. Take Your Time (Do It Right) . . . . . . . . . . . . . . . . . The S.O.S. Band |
| 8/02 | 2 | 9. One In A Million You . . . . . . . . . . . . . . . . . . . . . . . . . . . Larry Graham |
| 8/16 | 4 | ★10. Upside Down . . . . . . . . . . . . . . . . . . . . . . . . . . . . . . . Diana Ross |
| 9/13 | 3 | 11. Give Me The Night . . . . . . . . . . . . . . . . . . . . . . . . . . George Benson |
| 10/04 | 4 | 12. Funkin' For Jamaica (N.Y.) . . . . . . . . . . . . . . . . . . . . . . Tom Browne |
| 11/01 | 7 | 13. Master Blaster (Jammin') . . . . . . . . . . . . . . . . . . . . . Stevie Wonder |
| 12/20 | 6 | ★14. Celebration . . . . . . . . . . . . . . . . . . . . . . . . . . . Kool & The Gang |
| | | **1981** |
| 1/31 | 2 | 1. Fantastic Voyage . . . . . . . . . . . . . . . . . . . . . . . . . . . . . . . . Lakeside |
| 2/14 | 2 | 2. Burn Rubber (Why You Wanna Hurt Me) . . . . . . . . . . . . . . . Gap Band |
| 2/28 | 5 | 3. Don't Stop The Music . . . . . . . . . . . . . . . . . . . . Yarbrough & Peoples |
| 4/04 | 5 | 4. Being With You . . . . . . . . . . . . . . . . . . . . . . . . . . Smokey Robinson |
| 5/09 | 1 | 5. Sukiyaki . . . . . . . . . . . . . . . . . . . . . . . . . . . . . . . . A Taste Of Honey |
| 5/16 | 2 | 6. A Woman Needs Love (Just Like You Do) . . . . . . . . Ray Parker Jr. & Raydio |
| 5/30 | 2 | 7. What Cha' Gonna Do For Me . . . . . . . . . . . . . . . . . . . . . . Chaka Khan |
| 6/13 | 5 | 8. Give It To Me Baby . . . . . . . . . . . . . . . . . . . . . . . . . . . Rick James |
| 7/18 | 4 | 9. Double Dutch Bus . . . . . . . . . . . . . . . . . . . . . . . . . . Frankie Smith |
| 8/15 | 1 | 10. I'm In Love . . . . . . . . . . . . . . . . . . . . . . . . . . . . . . Evelyn King |
| 8/22 | 7 | ★11. Endless Love . . . . . . . . . . . . . . . . Diana Ross & Lionel Richie |
| 10/10 | 2 | 12. When She Was My Girl . . . . . . . . . . . . . . . . . . . . . . . . Four Tops |
| 10/24 | 2 | 13. Never Too Much . . . . . . . . . . . . . . . . . . . . . . . . Luther Vandross |
| 11/07 | 2 | 14. I Heard It Through The Grapevine . . . . . . . . . . . . . . . . . . . . . Roger |
| 11/21 | 1 | 15. Take My Heart (You Can Have It If You Want It) . . . . . . . . Kool & The Gang |
| 11/28 | 8 | 16. Let's Groove . . . . . . . . . . . . . . . . . . . . . . . . . . Earth, Wind & Fire |
| | | **1982** |
| 1/23 | 1 | 1. Turn Your Love Around . . . . . . . . . . . . . . . . . . . . . . George Benson |
| 1/30 | 1 | ★ 2. I Can't Go For That (No Can Do) . . . . . . . . . . . . . Daryl Hall & John Oates |
| 2/06 | 2 | 3. Call Me . . . . . . . . . . . . . . . . . . . . . . . . . . . . . . . . . . . . . . . Skyy |
| 2/20 | 9 | 4. That Girl . . . . . . . . . . . . . . . . . . . . . . . . . . . . . . . Stevie Wonder |
| 4/24 | 3 | 5. If It Ain't One Thing . . . It's Another . . . . . . . . . . Richard "Dimples" Fields |
| 5/15 | 2 | 6. It's Gonna Take A Miracle . . . . . . . . . . . . . . . . . . . Deniece Williams |
| 5/29 | 5* | 7. Let It Whip . . . . . . . . . . . . . . . . . . . . . . . . . . . . . . . . Dazz Band |
| 6/26 | 3* | 8. Early In The Morning . . . . . . . . . . . . . . . . . . . . . . . . The Gap Band |
| 7/24 | 4 | 9. And I Am Telling You I'm Not Going . . . . . . . . . . Jennifer Holliday |
| 8/21 | 2 | 10. Dance Floor . . . . . . . . . . . . . . . . . . . . . . . . . . . . . . . . . . Zapp |
| 9/04 | 4 | 11. Jump To It . . . . . . . . . . . . . . . . . . . . . . . . . . . . Aretha Franklin |
| 10/02 | 5 | 12. Love Come Down . . . . . . . . . . . . . . . . . . . . . . . . . . Evelyn King |
| 11/06 | 10 | 13. Sexual Healing . . . . . . . . . . . . . . . . . . . . . . . . . . . Marvin Gaye |
| | | **1983** |
| 1/15 | 3 | 1. The Girl Is Mine . . . . . . . . . . . . . . . . . . . Michael Jackson/Paul McCartney |
| 2/05 | 1 | 2. Outstanding . . . . . . . . . . . . . . . . . . . . . . . . . . . . . . The Gap Band |
| 2/12 | 9 | ★ 3. Billie Jean . . . . . . . . . . . . . . . . . . . . . . . . . . . . . Michael Jackson |

| DATE | WKS | RECORD TITLE......ARTIST |
|------|-----|-------------------------|
| | | **1983** *(Continued)* |
| 4/16 | 4 | 4. Atomic Dog ........................................George Clinton |
| 5/14 | 1 | 5. Candy Girl ...........................................New Edition |
| 5/21 | 1 | ★ 6. Beat It ..........................................Michael Jackson |
| 5/28 | 1 | 7. Save The Overtime (For Me)..................Gladys Knight & The Pips |
| 6/04 | 8 | 8. Juicy Fruit ...............................................Mtume |
| 7/30 | 3 | 9. She Works Hard For The Money .....................Donna Summer |
| 8/20 | 2 | 10. Get It Right .......................................Aretha Franklin |
| 9/03 | 6 | 11. Cold Blooded .........................................Rick James |
| 10/15 | 1 | 12. Ain't Nobody ...............................Rufus & Chaka Khan |
| 10/22 | 7 | ★13. All Night Long (All Night) ...........................Lionel Richie |
| 12/10 | 5 | 14. Time Will Reveal ........................................DeBarge |
| | | **1984** |
| 1/14 | 2 | 1. Joanna ....................................Kool & The Gang |
| 1/28 | 4 | 2. If Only You Knew .............................Patti LaBelle |
| 2/25 | 1 | 3. Encore ..........................................Cheryl Lynn |
| 3/03 | 5 | 4. Somebody's Watching Me ...........................Rockwell |
| 4/07 | 4 | 5. She's Strange ........................................Cameo |
| 5/05 | 3 | ★ 6. Hello ..........................................Lionel Richie |
| 5/26 | 1 | 7. Don't Waste Your Time....................Yarbrough & Peoples |
| 6/02 | 3 | ★ 8. Let's Hear It For The Boy ..................Deniece Williams |
| 6/23 | 1 | 9. Lovelite ...........................................O'Bryan |
| 6/30 | 8 | ★10. When Doves Cry ....................................Prince |
| 8/25 | 2 | ★11. Ghostbusters ...............................Ray Parker Jr. |
| 9/08 | 4 | ★12. Caribbean Queen (No More Love On The Run) ............Billy Ocean |
| 10/06 | 1 | ★13. Let's Go Crazy ...................Prince & The Revolution |
| 10/13 | 3 | ★14. I Just Called To Say I Love You .......................Stevie Wonder |
| 11/03 | 3 | 15. I Feel For You......................................Chaka Khan |
| 11/24 | 1 | 16. Cool It Now ......................................New Edition |
| 12/01 | 3 | 17. Solid.......................................Ashford & Simpson |
| 12/22 | 5 | 18. Operator......................................Midnight Star |
| | | **1985** |
| 1/26 | 1 | 1. Gotta Get You Home Tonight .....................Eugene Wilde |
| 2/02 | 3 | 2. Mr. Telephone Man ...............................New Edition |
| 2/23 | 3 | 3. Missing You .....................................Diana Ross |
| 3/16 | 4 | 4. Nightshift ....................................Commodores |
| 4/13 | 2 | 5. Back In Stride ...................Maze Featuring Frankie Beverly |
| 4/27 | 1 | 6. Rhythm Of The Night .................................DeBarge |
| 5/04 | 2 | ★ 7. We Are The World....................................USA for Africa |
| 5/18 | 1 | 8. Fresh .........................................Kool & The Gang |
| 5/25 | 1 | 9. You Give Good Love ..........................Whitney Houston |
| 6/01 | 6 | 10. Rock Me Tonight (For Old Times Sake) ...............Freddie Jackson |
| 7/13 | 1 | 11. Hangin' On A String (Contemplating) ...................Loose Ends |
| 7/20 | 2 | 12. Save Your Love (For #1) ........................Rene & Angela |
| 8/03 | 5 | 13. Freeway Of Love ...............................Aretha Franklin |
| 9/07 | 1 | ★14. Saving All My Love For You .....................Whitney Houston |
| 9/14 | 1 | 15. Cherish .....................................Kool & The Gang |
| 9/21 | 2 | ★16. Oh Sheila .................................Ready For The World |

| DATE | WKS | RECORD TITLE . . . . . . ARTIST |
|---|---|---|
| | | **1985** *(Continued)* |
| 10/05 | 2 | 17. You Are My Lady . . . . . . . . . . . . . . . . . . . . . . . . . . . . . . . . . . Freddie Jackson |
| 10/19 | 6 | ★18. Part-Time Lover . . . . . . . . . . . . . . . . . . . . . . . . . . . . . . . . . . . . Stevie Wonder |
| 11/30 | 3 | 19. Caravan Of Love . . . . . . . . . . . . . . . . . . . . . . . . . . . . . . Isley, Jasper, Isley |
| 12/21 | 3 | 20. Don't Say No Tonight . . . . . . . . . . . . . . . . . . . . . . . . . . . . . . Eugene Wilde |
| | | **1986** |
| 1/11 | 2 | ★ 1. Say You, Say Me . . . . . . . . . . . . . . . . . . . . . . . . . . . . . . . . . . . Lionel Richie |
| 1/25 | 3 | ★ 2. That's What Friends Are For . . . . . . . . . . . . . . . . . . . . . . Dionne & Friends |
| 2/15 | 3 | 3. Do Me Baby . . . . . . . . . . . . . . . . . . . . . . . . . . . . . . . . . . . . Meli'sa Morgan |
| 3/08 | 1 | ★ 4. How Will I Know . . . . . . . . . . . . . . . . . . . . . . . . . . . . . . . Whitney Houston |
| 3/15 | 1 | 5. Your Smile . . . . . . . . . . . . . . . . . . . . . . . . . . . . . . . . . . . . . Rene & Angela |
| 3/22 | 2 | 6. What Have You Done For Me Lately . . . . . . . . . . . . . . . . . . Janet Jackson |
| 4/05 | 4 | ★ 7. Kiss . . . . . . . . . . . . . . . . . . . . . . . . . . . . . . . . . . . Prince & The Revolution |
| 5/03 | 2 | 8. I Have Learned To Respect The Power Of Love . . . . . . . . . . . Stephanie Mills |
| 5/17 | 4 | ★ 9. On My Own . . . . . . . . . . . . . . . . . . . . . Patti LaBelle & Michael McDonald |
| 6/14 | 2 | 10. Nasty . . . . . . . . . . . . . . . . . . . . . . . . . . . . . . . . . . . . . . . . Janet Jackson |
| 6/28 | 2 | ★11. There'll Be Sad Songs (To Make You Cry) . . . . . . . . . . . . . . . . Billy Ocean |
| 7/12 | 1 | 12. Who's Johnny . . . . . . . . . . . . . . . . . . . . . . . . . . . . . . . . . . . . El DeBarge |
| 7/19 | 2 | 13. Rumors . . . . . . . . . . . . . . . . . . . . . . . . . . . . . . . . . . . Timex Social Club |
| 8/02 | 2 | 14. Closer Than Close . . . . . . . . . . . . . . . . . . . . . . . . . . . . . . . . . Jean Carne |
| 8/16 | 2 | 15. Do You Get Enough Love . . . . . . . . . . . . . . . . . . . . . . . . . . Shirley Jones |
| 8/30 | 1 | 16. Love Zone . . . . . . . . . . . . . . . . . . . . . . . . . . . . . . . . . . . . . . . Billy Ocean |
| 9/06 | 1 | 17. Ain't Nothin' Goin' On But The Rent . . . . . . . . . . . . . . . . . . Gwen Guthrie |
| 9/13 | 1 | 18. (Pop, Pop, Pop, Pop) Goes My Mind . . . . . . . . . . . . . . . . . . . . . . . . Levert |
| 9/20 | 2 | 19. The Rain . . . . . . . . . . . . . . . . . . . . . . . . . . . . . . . . . . Oran "Juice" Jones |
| 10/04 | 3 | 20. Word Up . . . . . . . . . . . . . . . . . . . . . . . . . . . . . . . . . . . . . . . . . . . Cameo |
| 10/25 | 2 | ★21. Shake You Down . . . . . . . . . . . . . . . . . . . . . . . . . . . . . . Gregory Abbott |
| 11/08 | 1 | 22. A Little Bit More . . . . . . . . . . . . . . . . . Melba Moore with Freddie Jackson |
| 11/15 | 4 | 23. Tasty Love . . . . . . . . . . . . . . . . . . . . . . . . . . . . . . . . . . . Freddie Jackson |
| 12/13 | 2 | 24. Love You Down . . . . . . . . . . . . . . . . . . . . . . . . . . . . Ready For The World |
| 12/27 | 2 | 25. Girlfriend . . . . . . . . . . . . . . . . . . . . . . . . . . . . . . . . . . . . . . . Bobby Brown |
| | | **1987** |
| 1/10 | 1 | 1. Control . . . . . . . . . . . . . . . . . . . . . . . . . . . . . . . . . . . . . . . Janet Jackson |
| 1/17 | 2 | 2. Stop To Love . . . . . . . . . . . . . . . . . . . . . . . . . . . . . . . . . Luther Vandross |
| 1/31 | 2 | 3. Candy . . . . . . . . . . . . . . . . . . . . . . . . . . . . . . . . . . . . . . . . . . . . Cameo |
| 2/14 | 1 | 4. Falling . . . . . . . . . . . . . . . . . . . . . . . . . . . . . . . . . . . . . . . Melba Moore |
| 2/21 | 2 | 5. Have You Ever Loved Somebody . . . . . . . . . . . . . . . . . . . . Freddie Jackson |
| 3/07 | 1 | 6. Slow Down . . . . . . . . . . . . . . . . . . . . . . . . . . . . . . . . . . . . . . Loose Ends |
| 3/14 | 1 | 7. Let's Wait Awhile . . . . . . . . . . . . . . . . . . . . . . . . . . . . . . . . Janet Jackson |
| 3/21 | 3 | 8. Looking For A New Love . . . . . . . . . . . . . . . . . . . . . . . . . . . . Jody Watley |
| 4/11 | 3 | 9. Sign 'O' The Times . . . . . . . . . . . . . . . . . . . . . . . . . . . . . . . . . . . . Prince |
| 5/02 | 1 | 10. Don't Disturb This Groove . . . . . . . . . . . . . . . . . . . . . . . . . . The System |
| 5/09 | 1 | 11. There's Nothing Better Than Love . . . . . Luther Vandross with Gregory Hines |
| 5/16 | 2 | ★12. Always . . . . . . . . . . . . . . . . . . . . . . . . . . . . . . . . . . . . . . . Atlantic Starr |
| 5/30 | 2 | ★13. Head To Toe . . . . . . . . . . . . . . . . . . . . . . . . . . . . . Lisa Lisa & Cult Jam |
| 6/13 | 1 | 14. Rock Steady . . . . . . . . . . . . . . . . . . . . . . . . . . . . . . . . . . . . . . Whispers |
| 6/20 | 2 | 15. Diamonds . . . . . . . . . . . . . . . . . . . . . . . . . . . . . . . . . . . . . Herb Alpert |
| 7/04 | 3 | 16. I Feel Good All Over . . . . . . . . . . . . . . . . . . . . . . . . . . . . . Stephanie Mills |

| DATE | WKS | RECORD TITLE......ARTIST |
|------|-----|--------------------------|
| | | **1987** *(Continued)* |
| 7/25 | 2 | 17. Fake ...........................................Alexander O'Neal |
| 8/08 | 1 | 18. The Pleasure Principle ...........................Janet Jackson |
| 8/15 | 1 | 19. Jam Tonight .....................................Freddie Jackson |
| 8/22 | 2 | 20. Casanova.................................................Levert |
| 9/05 | 2 | 21. Love Is A House .................................Force M.D.'s |
| 9/19 | 1 | ★22. I Just Can't Stop Loving You .....................Michael Jackson |
| 9/26 | 1 | 23. I Need Love ......................................L.L. Cool J |
| 10/03 | 1 | ★24. Lost In Emotion ..........................Lisa Lisa & Cult Jam |
| 10/10 | 1 | 25. (You're Puttin') A Rush On Me ....................Stephanie Mills |
| 10/17 | 3 | ★26. Bad ............................................Michael Jackson |
| 11/07 | 1 | 27. Lovin' You......................................The O'Jays |
| 11/14 | 2 | 28. Angel .........................................Angela Winbush |
| 11/28 | 2 | 29. Skeletons.......................................Stevie Wonder |
| 12/12 | 1 | 30. System Of Survival ..........................Earth, Wind & Fire |
| 12/19 | 1 | 31. I Want To Be Your Man ...............................Roger |
| 12/26 | 4 | ★32. The Way You Make Me Feel.......................Michael Jackson |
| | | **1988** |
| 1/23 | 1 | 1. Love Overboard ....................Gladys Knight & The Pips |
| 1/30 | 3 | 2. I Want Her......................................Keith Sweat |
| 2/20 | 2 | 3. Girlfriend ...........................................Pebbles |
| 3/05 | 1 | 4. You Will Know ....................................Stevie Wonder |
| 3/12 | 2 | 5. Fishnet ..........................................Morris Day |
| 3/26 | 1 | ★ 6. Man In The Mirror ..........................Michael Jackson |
| 4/02 | 1 | ★ 7. Wishing Well ........................Terence Trent D'Arby |
| 4/09 | 1 | 8. Ooo La La La .....................................Teena Marie |
| 4/16 | 1 | ★ 9. Get Outta My Dreams, Get Into My Car ...........Billy Ocean |
| 4/23 | 1 | 10. Da'Butt ...............................................E.U. |
| 4/30 | 3 | 11. Nite And Day .....................................Al B. Sure! |
| 5/21 | 1 | 12. Mercedes Boy .........................................Pebbles |
| 5/28 | 2 | 13. Just Got Paid .................................Johnny Kemp |
| 6/11 | 1 | 14. Little Walter ..............................Tony! Toni! Tone! |
| 6/18 | 1 | ★15. One More Try ...............................George Michael |
| 6/25 | 2 | 16. Joy ........................................Teddy Pendergrass |

# THE HITS

## If you're serious about Pop music,

## Joel Whitburn's
## TOP POP SINGLES
## 1955-1986

The complete history of *Billboard's* **Hot 100** and other early *Billboard* pop charts, plus thousands of new artist biographies. A complete up-to-date listing, by artist and by title, of each of the nearly 18,000 singles to appear on *Billboard's* pop charts. 756 pages. Hardcover $60 Softcover $50

## Joel Whitburn's
## POP ANNUAL
## 1955-1986

Every pop programmers dream - a book that lists all of *Billboard's* Pop and **Hot 100** charted singles in rank order, year by year. And now, for the first time, lists the playing time of each record, and features *Time Capsules* highlighting each year's major events! Includes a complete A-Z song title section. 684 pages. Hardcover $60 Softcover $50

## Billboard's
## TOP 10 CHARTS
## 1958-1988

The first complete listing of the Top 10 from every *Billboard* **Hot 100** ever published. A comprehensive week-by-week, chart-by-chart history of the Top 10, featuring the original **Hot 100** chart format and chart bullets. Records at their peak position are shown in boldface type. Also included is each week's *Highest Debut* and *Biggest Mover* from the entire **Hot 100**. 600 pages. Hardcover $60 Softcover $50

## Joel Whitburn's
## POP MEMORIES
## 1890-1954

From Edison to Elvis - the first book to document the history of America's recorded popular music from its very beginnings. Find out who had the hit versions of those popular standards you've heard for generations. Arranged by artist and by title, it lists over 12,000 songs and 1,500 artists. 660 pages. Hardcover $60 Softcover $50

# ARE HERE!

make sure you get the complete story.

## Joel Whitburn's
## TOP POP ALBUMS
## 1955-1985

The only book of its kind to list complete chart data for every album to ever appear on *Billboard's* weekly **Top Pop Albums** charts. Arranged by artist, it lists over 14,000 titles and 3,000 artists. 516 pages. Softcover $50

## Billboard's
## TOP 3000+ 1955-1987
## Compiled by Joel Whitburn

Every single that ever peaked in the Top 10 on *Billboard's* **Hot 100**, ranked in order of all-time popularity. Rank Section lists records according to chart performance from #1 to #3093, and includes complete chart data for each title. Indicates the currently available Top 10 records which can now be purchased directly from *Record Research*. Also includes a Title Section and Artist Section. 180 pages. Softcover $30

## Billboard's
## MUSIC & VIDEO YEARBOOK 1987

The complete story of 1987's charted music and videocassettes in one comprehensive volume. Covers 11 major *Billboard* charts. Updates all previous *Record Research* books and introduces a new section on *Billboard's* **Top Videocassettes Rentals and Sales** charts. Also features a special section listing 1987's #1 hits from 8 other important *Billboard* charts. 240 pages. Softcover $30

## Billboard's
## MUSIC YEARBOOK 1986
## MUSIC YEARBOOK 1985
## MUSIC YEARBOOK 1984
## MUSIC YEARBOOK 1983

Each yearbook is a complete listing of the singles and albums that debuted on *Billboard's* major charts throughout the year, with significant chart data. 1986 edition: 216 pages / 1985 edition: 240 pages / 1984 edition: 264 pages / 1983 edition: 276 pages. Softcover $30 each

## Joel Whitburn's
## BUBBLING UNDER THE HOT 100
## 1959-1981

Lists over 4,000 of the *hits that might have been*. Includes many regional hits that never made it nationally, and the near-hits by the superstars! The only reference book of its kind. 204 pages. Softcover $30

*Up And Coming on next page*

# UP AND COMING!

## TOP COUNTRY SINGLES 1944-1988

Here's the revision you've been waiting for — featuring thousands of artist biographies, title trivia and greatly expanded research. This book will begin with the first **Most Played Juke Box Folk Records** chart in 1944 and will list every single to ever hit *Billboard*'s **Best Selling, Disc Jockey, Juke Box,** and **Hot Country Singles** country charts.

# The **RECORD RESEARCH** *Collection*

| BOOK TITLE | Quantity | Price | Total |
|---|---|---|---|
| 1. Top Pop Singles 1955-1986 (Hardcover) | _____ | $60.00 | _____ |
| 2. Top Pop Singles 1955-1986 (Softcover) | _____ | $50.00 | _____ |
| 3. Pop Singles Annual 1955-1986 (Hardcover) | _____ | $60.00 | _____ |
| 4. Pop Singles Annual 1955-1986 (Softcover) | _____ | $50.00 | _____ |
| 5. Top 10 Charts 1958-1988 (Hardcover) | _____ | $60.00 | _____ |
| 6. Top 10 Charts 1958-1988 (Softcover) | _____ | $50.00 | _____ |
| 7. Pop Memories 1890-1954 (Hardcover) | _____ | $60.00 | _____ |
| 8. Pop Memories 1890-1954 (Softcover) | _____ | $50.00 | _____ |
| 9. Top R&B Singles 1942-1988 (Hardcover) | _____ | $60.00 | _____ |
| 10. Top R&B Singles 1942-1988 (Softcover) | _____ | $50.00 | _____ |
| 11. Top Pop Albums 1955-1985 | _____ | $50.00 | _____ |
| 12. Top 3000+ 1955-1987 | _____ | $30.00 | _____ |
| 13. Music & Video Yearbook 1987 | _____ | $30.00 | _____ |
| 14. Music Yearbook 1986 | _____ | $30.00 | _____ |
| 15. Music Yearbook 1985 | _____ | $30.00 | _____ |
| 16. Music Yearbook 1984 | _____ | $30.00 | _____ |
| 17. Music Yearbook 1983 | _____ | $30.00 | _____ |
| 18. Bubbling Under The Hot 100 1959-1981 | _____ | $30.00 | _____ |

All books are softcover except items 1, 3, 5, 7 & 9.

Shipping & Handling (see below) ............................................. _____

Total Payment $ _____

## Shipping & Handling

Please include a check or money order for full amount plus **$4.00** for postage and handling. All *Canadian* and *foreign* orders add **$4.00** for the first book ordered and **$2.00** for each additional book ordered. Canadian and foreign orders are shipped via surface mail. Call or write for air mail shipping rates.

For more information on the complete line of *Record Research* books, please write for a free catalog.

Payment Method     ☐ Check     ☐ Money Order
                            ☐ MasterCard   ☐ VISA

MasterCard or VISA #    _____ _____ _____ _____

Expiration Date ____ / ____
                      Mo.    Yr.

Signature _____

To Charge Your Order By Phone, Call 414-251-5408
(office hours: 8AM-5PM CST)

Name _____

Address _____

City _____

State _____ Zip _____

Record Research Inc.
P.O. Box 200
Menomonee Falls, Wisconsin 53051